eGrade Plus

www.wiley.com/college/horstmann
Based on the Activities You Do Every Day

W9-AZE-112

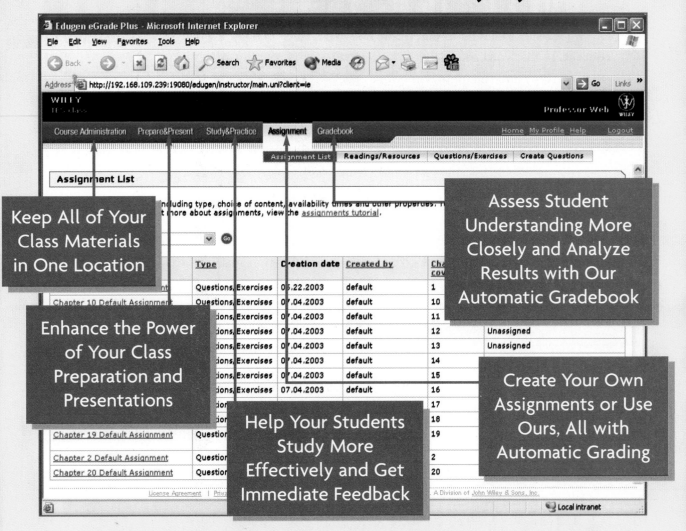

Keep All of Your Class Materials in One Location

Enhance the Power of Your Class Preparation and Presentations

Help Your Students Study More Effectively and Get Immediate Feedback

Assess Student Understanding More Closely and Analyze Results with Our Automatic Gradebook

Create Your Own Assignments or Use Ours, All with Automatic Grading

All the content and tools you need, all in one location, in an easy-to-use browser format.
Choose the resources you need, or rely on the arrangement supplied by us.

Now, many of Wiley's textbooks are available with eGrade Plus, a powerful online tool that provides a completely integrated suite of teaching and learning resources in one easy-to-use website. eGrade Plus integrates Wiley's world-renowned content with media, including a multimedia version of the text. Upon adoption of eGrade Plus, you can begin to customize your course with the resources shown here.

See for yourself!
Go to www.wiley.com/college/egradeplus for an online demonstration of this powerful new software.

Students, eGrade Plus Allows You to:

Study More Effectively

Get Immediate Feedback When You Practice on Your Own

Our website links directly to **electronic book content,** so that you can review the text while you study and complete homework online. Additional resources include **self-assessment quizzing with detailed feedback** as well as **lecture presentation slides.**

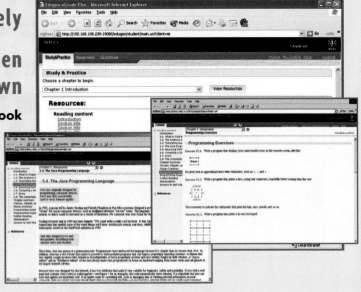

Complete Assignments / Get Help with Problem Solving

An "**Assignment**" area keeps all your assigned work in one location, making it easy for you to stay on task. In addition, many homework problems contain a **link** to the relevant section of the **electronic book,** providing you with a text explanation to help you conquer problem-solving obstacles as they arise.

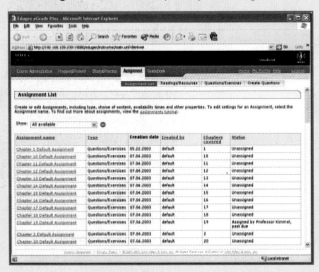

Keep Track of How You're Doing

A **Personal Gradebook** allows you to view your results from past assignments at any time.

Big Java

SECOND EDITION

Cay Horstmann

SAN JOSE STATE UNIVERSITY

WILEY

John Wiley & Sons, Inc.

EXECUTIVE EDITOR:	Bill Zobrist
EDITORIAL ASSISTANT:	Bridget Morrisey
MARKETING MANAGER:	Frank Lyman
SENIOR PRODUCTION EDITOR:	Ken Santor
SENIOR DESIGNER:	Karin Kincheloe
TEXT DESIGNER:	Nancy Field
COVER DESIGNER:	Howard Grossman
COVER ILLUSTRATOR:	Susan Cyr
PHOTO EDITOR:	Lisa Gee
PRODUCTION MANAGEMENT:	Cindy Johnson

This book was set in 10.5/12 Stempel Garamond by Publishing Services and printed and bound by Courier Kendallville. The cover was printed by Von Hoffmann, Inc.

This book is printed on acid-free paper ∞

Copyright © 2006 John Wiley & Sons, Inc. All rights reserved.

No part of this publication may be reproduced, stored in a retrieval system or transmitted in any form or by any means, electronic, mechanical, photocopying, recording, scanning or otherwise, except as permitted under Sections 107 or 108 of the 1976 United States Copyright Act, without either the prior written permission of the Publisher, or authorization through payment of the appropriate per-copy fee to the Copyright Clearance Center, 222 Rosewood Drive, Danvers, MA 01923, (978) 750-8400, fax (978) 646-8600. Requests to the Publisher for permission should be addressed to the Permissions Department, John Wiley and Sons, Inc., 111 River Street, Hoboken, NJ 07030-5774, (201) 748-6011, fax (201) 748-6008.
To order books, or for customer service, please call 1-800-CALL-Wiley (225-5945).

ISBN 0-471-69703-6

Printed in the United States of America

10 9 8 7 6 5 4 3 2

Preface

This book is an introductory text in computer science, focusing on programming principles and practices. Why should you choose this book for your first course in computer science? Here are the key reasons:

- The book's point of view goes beyond language syntax and focuses on computer science concepts.
- The object-oriented paradigm is emphasized from the outset, exposing you to classes from the first chapters so you won't have to un-learn procedural habits.
- The book will motivate you to master the practical aspects of programming, with lots of useful tips and a full chapter on testing and debugging.
- The book covers the concepts of the Java language, library (version 5.0), and tools at a depth that is sufficient to solve real-world programming problems.
- The book teaches the standard Java language—not a specialized "training wheels" environment.
- In the final chapters of the book, you will learn important techniques for server-side program development, such as database programming, XML, and JavaServer Faces.

The Use of Java

This book is based on the Java programming language. Java was chosen for four reasons:

- Object orientation
- Safety
- Simplicity
- Breadth of the standard library

At this point, the object-oriented point of view is the predominant paradigm for software design. Object orientation enables programmers to spend more time on the design of their programs and less time coding and debugging. This book starts out with objects and classes early so that readers do not have to un-learn procedural programming habits later.

Safety is an important feature of the Java language, and highly beneficial for beginning programmers. Common programming errors are reliably diagnosed when a Java program is compiled or executed. Using Java, you will be able to spend more time on completing substantial software projects instead of debugging programs with mysterious and irreproducible behavior.

Another major advantage of Java is its simplicity. It is possible to master the essential language constructs in a semester-long course.

Finally, the standard Java library has sufficient breadth that it can be used for most courses in a computer science curriculum. Graphics, user interface construction, database access, multithreading, and network programming are all part of the standard library. Thus, the skills learned in a beginning course based on Java will serve you well in subsequent courses.

New in This Edition

Use of Java 5.0

In this edition, all material has been reviewed and updated for the Java 5.0 release. When appropriate, the book takes advantage of the new features. In particular, generic collections and the enhanced for loop are used throughout. In addition, Java 5.0 finally provides convenient standard classes for console input and formatted output. These classes are used throughout the book.

This book also may be used with an older version of Java. Appendix D lists the modifications necessary to adapt programs for older compilers.

Object Orientation at a Student-Friendly Pace

Objects and classes are now introduced at a more student-friendly pace. Chapter 2 teaches how to use existing objects and methods, providing practice with and familiarizing students with the syntax and structure of an object-oriented language. Chapter 3 focuses on the steps involved in designing and implementing new classes.

Later in the book, the chapters on interfaces and inheritance have been reorganized and the examples simplified. The treatment of inner classes is now optional.

Additional Exercises

Longer programming projects have been added to most chapters. In addition, there are numerous self-check exercises that test the material of the preceding section.

Enhanced Coverage of Data Structures

Chapters 20 and 21 include additional algorithms and data structures, covering all topics of the Advanced Placement AB exam. A new chapter, Chapter 22, introduces Java generics.

Advanced Topics

The multithreading chapter (23) now makes use of the high-level synchronization mechanisms of Java 5.0. The database chapter (25) has been revised to focus on open-source solutions. The web programming chapter (27) has been completely rewritten to focus on JavaServer Faces, a new and robust technology that has been developed as the successor to servlets and JSP.

A Tour of the Book

The book can be naturally grouped into four parts, as illustrated by Figure 1. The organization of chapters offers the same flexibility as the previous edition; dependencies among the chapters are also shown in the figure.

Part A: Fundamentals (Chapters 1-10)

Chapters 1 through 9 cover the fundamentals of object-based programming: objects, methods, classes, variables, number types, strings, and control structures. Chapter 2 shows how to manipulate objects of predefined classes. In Chapter 3 you will build your own simple classes.

Chapter 5 introduces simple graphics programming. This is an optional chapter that can be skipped without loss of continuity. This material is provided because many students enjoy writing programs that create drawings, and because graphical shapes are splendid examples of objects.

Arrays and array lists are covered in Chapter 8. In previous editions of this book, arrays were covered after inheritance, and you can still do so without incurring any problems. However, many users of the book wanted to introduce arrays immediately after covering loops.

Chapter 9 takes up the subject of class design in a more systematic fashion, and it introduces a a very simple subset of the UML notation.

Chapter 10 covers testing and debugging, a subject that is unfortunately given short shrift in many textbooks.

Part B: Object-Oriented Design (Chapters 11-17)

Chapters 11 through 17 cover polymorphism, inheritance, exceptions, files and streams, object-oriented design, and, optionally, graphical user interface (GUI) programming.

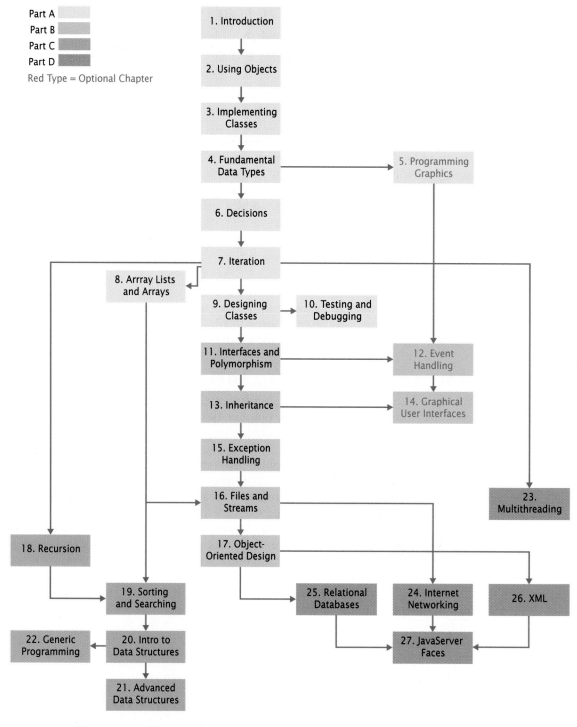

Figure 1 Chapter Dependencies

The discussion of polymorphism and inheritance is split into two chapters. Chapter 11 covers interfaces and polymorphism, whereas Chapter 13 covers inheritance. Introducing interfaces before inheritance pays off in an important way: Students immediately see polymorphism before getting bogged down with technical details such as superclass construction.

GUI programming is split into two chapters. Chapter 12 covers event-driven programming, relying simply on the notion of an interface introduced in Chapter 11. Chapter 14 covers GUI components and their layout. This chapter requires some knowledge of inheritance. It is possible to cover both of these chapters together, either before or after Chapter 13. Both of these chapters are entirely optional.

Exception handling, files, and streams are covered after inheritance, in Chapters 15 and 16. An understanding of inheritance is required for working with exceptions, and exceptions are needed whenever you use files and streams.

Chapter 17 contains an introduction to object-oriented design, including two significant case studies.

Part C: Data Structures and Algorithms (Chapters 18-22)

Chapters 18 through 22 contain an introduction to algorithms and data structures, covering recursion, sorting and searching, linked lists, binary trees, and hash tables. These topics may be outside the scope of a one-semester course, but can be covered as desired after Chapter 8 (see Figure 1).

Recursion is introduced from an object-oriented point of view: An object that solves a problem recursively constructs another object of the same class that solves a simpler problem. The idea of having the other object do the simpler job is more intuitive than having a function call itself.

Each data structure is presented in the context of the standard Java collections library. You will learn the essential abstractions of the standard library (such as iterators, sets, and maps) as well as the performance characteristics of the various collections. However, a detailed discussion of the implementation of advanced data structures is beyond the scope of this book.

Chapter 22 introduces Java generics. This chapter is suitable for advanced students who want to implement their own generic classes and methods.

Part D: Advanced Topics (Chapters 23-27)

Chapters 23 through 27 cover advanced Java programming techniques that definitely go beyond a first course in Java. Although, as already mentioned, a comprehensive coverage of the Java library would span many volumes, many instructors suggested that a textbook should give students additional reference material valuable beyond their first course. Some institutions also teach a second-semester course that covers more practical programming aspects such as database and network programming, rather than the more traditional in-depth material on data structures and algorithms. This book can be used in a two-semester course to give students an introduction to programming fundamentals and broad coverage of applications. Alternatively, the material in the final chapters can be useful for student projects.

The advanced topics introduce those technologies that are of particular interest to server-side programming: multithreading, networking, databases, XML, and web applications. The Internet has made it possible to deploy many useful applications on servers, often accessed by nothing more than a browser. This server-centric approach to application development was in part made possible by the Java language and libraries, and today, most of the industrial use of Java is in server-side programming.

Appendices

Appendix A contains a style guide for use with this book. Many instructors find it highly beneficial to require a consistent style for all assignments. If this style guide conflicts with instructor sentiment or local customs, however, it is available in electronic form so that it can be modified. Appendix B lists the Basic Latin and Latin-1 subsets of Unicode. Appendix C contains an overview of the classes and interfaces in the standard library covered in this book. Appendix D summarizes the adjustments that are necessary to use the example programs with an older version of the Java compiler. Additional appendices contain quick references on Java syntax, HTML, Java tools, binary numbers, UML, and more.

The Pedagogical Structure

This edition builds on the pedagogical elements in the last edition and offers additional aids for the reader. Each chapter begins with the customary overview of chapter objectives and motivational introduction. A listing of the chapter contents then provides a quick reference to the special features in the chapter.

Margin notes mark and reinforce new concepts and are summarized at chapter end.

Throughout each chapter, margin notes show where new concepts are introduced and provide an outline of key ideas. These notes are summarized at the end of the chapter as a chapter review.

Each section concludes with a set of self-check exercises. Use these exercises to check that you have understood the newly introduced topics. The self-check exercises are not trivial—they are purposefully designed to make you think through the new material. Answers to the self-check exercises are at the end of each chapter.

The program listings are carefully designed for easy reading, going well beyond simple color coding. Comments are typeset in a separate font that is easier to read than the monospaced "computer" font. Methods are set off by a subtle color outline. Keywords, strings, and numbers are color coded as they would be in a development environment such as BlueJ. (The code for all program listings in the book (plus any additional files needed for each example) is available on the Companion Web Site for the book at www.wiley.com/college/horstmann.)

Throughout the chapters, special features set off topics for added flexibility and easy reference. Syntax boxes highlight new syntactical constructs and their purpose. An alphabetical list of all of these constructs can be found on page xv.

Six additional features, entitled "Common Error", "How To", "Productivity Hint", "Quality Tip", "Advanced Topic", and "Random Fact", are identified with the icons below and set off so they don't interrupt the flow of the main material. Some of these are quite short; others extend over a page. Each topic is given the space that is needed for a full and convincing explanation—instead of being forced into a one-paragraph "tip". You can use the tables on pages xvi–xxiii to see the features in each chapter and the page numbers where they can be found.

- **Common Errors** describe the kinds of errors that students often make, with an explanation of why the errors occur, and what to do about them. Most students quickly discover the Common Error sections and read them on their own.

- **How To** sections are inspired by the Linux HOWTO guides. These sections are intended to answer the beginner's question, "Now what do I do?", by giving step-by-step instructions for common tasks.

- **Quality Tips** explain good programming practices. Because most of them require an initial investment of effort, these notes carefully motivate the reason behind the advice, and explain why the effort will be repaid later.

- **Productivity Hints** teach students how to use their tools more effectively. Many beginning students put little thought into their use of computers and software. They are often unfamiliar with tricks of the trade, such as keyboard shortcuts, global search and replace, or automation of common tasks with scripts.

- **Advanced Topics** cover nonessential or more difficult material. Some of these topics introduce alternative syntactical constructions that are not necessarily technically advanced. In many cases, the book uses one particular language construct but explains alternatives as Advanced Topics. You should feel free to use those constructs in your own programs if you prefer them. It has, however, been my experience that many students are grateful for the "keep it simple" approach, because it greatly reduces the number of gratuitous decisions they have to make.

- **Random Facts** provide historical and social information on computing—to fulfill the "historical and social context" requirements of the ACM curriculum guidelines—as well as capsule reviews of advanced computer science topics. Many students will read the Random Facts on their own while pretending to follow the lecture.

Web Resources and More

Companion Web Site

Additional resources are found on the book's Companion Web Site at `http://www.wiley.com/college/horstmann`. Navigate to the Instructor Companion Site or the Student Companion Site by selecting the appropriate button for this text.

Both the Student and Instructor Companion Sites include the following resources, with the exception of those marked "for instructors only".

- Solutions to the odd-numbered exercises
- Solutions to all exercises (for instructors only)
- A test bank (for instructors only)
- A laboratory manual
- A list of frequently asked questions
- Help with common compilers
- Lecture presentation slides that summarize each chapter and include code listings and figures from the book
- Source code for all examples in the book
- The programming style guide in electronic form, so you can modify it to suit local preferences
- A conversion guide for moving from the last edition to this one (for instructors only)

eGrade Plus

The first two pages of this book describe an innovative online tool for teachers and students: *eGrade Plus* can be adopted by instructors who wish to give students an alternative to the traditional printed text. *eGrade Plus* integrates many of the web resources listed above into an online version of this text, and is available for less than the cost of a printed book. For more information and a demo, please visit the web site listed on pages i–ii, or talk to your Wiley representative.

BlueJ Companion

Also available with this text is a BlueJ manual that has been customized specifically for use with this book. The manual comes with a CD-ROM that contains the BlueJ software as well as all the code examples from this book, formatted as BlueJ projects. For more information, please talk to your Wiley representative.

Acknowledgments

Many thanks to Paul Crockett, Bill Zobrist, Simon Durkin, Lisa Gee, Bridget Morrisey, Lisa Gee, Ken Santor, Martin Batey, and Phyllis Bregman at John Wiley & Sons, and the team at Publishing Services for their help with this book project. An especially deep acknowledgment and thanks goes to Cindy Johnson for her hard work, sound judgment, and amazing atttention to detail. Thanks also to Paul Nagin for his work on the slides, labs, homework solutions, and other supplements.

I am very grateful to the many individuals who reviewed the manuscript for this edition, made valuable suggestions, and brought an embarrassingly large number of errors and omissions to my attention. They include:

Tim Andresen, *Boise State University*
Ivan Bajic, *San Diego State University*
Ted Bangay, *Sheridan Community College*
Joseph Bowbeer
Tim Budd, *Oregon State University*
Robert Burton, *Brigham Young University*
Frank Butt, *IBM*
Jerry Cain, *Stanford University*
Deborah Coleman, *Rochester Institute of Technology*
Valentino Crespi, *California State University, Los Angeles*
Jim Cross, *Auburn University*
Russel Deaton, *University of Arkansas*
John Fendrich, *Bradley University*
David Geary, *Sabreware, Inc.*
Rick Giles, *Acadia University*
Jianchin Han, *California State University, Dominguez Hills*
Lisa Hansen, *Western New England College*
Elliotte Harold
Eileen Head, *SUNY Binghamton*
Norm Jacobson, *University of California, Irvine*
Aaron Keen, *California Polytechnic State University, San Lius Obispo*
Elliot Koffman, *Temple University*
Hunter Lloyd, *Montana State University*
John Martin, *North Dakota State University*
Scott McElresh, *Carnegie Mellon University*
Joan McGrory, *Christian Brothers University*
Carolyn Miller, *North Carolina State University*
Teng Moh, *San Jose State University*
Faye Navabi, *Arizona State University*
Kevin O'Gorman, *California Polytechnic State University, San Lius Obispo*
Kevin Parker, *Idaho State University*
Cornel Pokorny, *California Polytechnic State University, San Lius Obispo*

Robert Putnam, *California State University, Northridge*
Cyndi Rader, *Colorado School of Mines*
Neil Rankin, *Worcester Polytechnic Institute*
Brad Rippe, *Fullerton College*
Jeffrey Six, *University of Delaware*
Don Slater, *Carnegie Mellon University*
Ken Slonneger, *Iowa State University*
Peter Stanchev, *Kettering University*
Joseph Vybihal, *McGill University*
David Womack, *University of Texas, San Antonio*
A. Yanushka, *Christian Brothers University*

Alphabetical List of Syntax Boxes

Chapter	Common Errors	How Tos	Quality Tips
8 Arrays and Array Lists	Bounds Errors 283 Uninitialized Arrays 284 Length and Size 289 Underestimating the Size of a Data Set 307	Working with Array Lists and Arrays 301	Prefer Parameterized Array Lists 289 Make Parallel Arrays into Arrays of Objects 307
9 Designing Classes	Trying to Modify Primitive Type Parameters 331 Shadowing 349 Confusing Dots 356	Programming with Packages 356	Consistency 328 Minimize Side Effects 333 Don't Change the Contents of Parameter Variables 333
10 Testing and Debugging		Debugging 398	
11 Interfaces and Polymorphism	Forgetting to Define Implementing Methods as Public 415 Trying to Instantiate an Interface 418 Modifying the Signature in the Implementing Method 430		
12 Event Handling (Optional)	Forgetting to Attach a Listener 450 Forgetting to Repaint 459	Implementing a Graphical User Interface (GUI) 453	
13 Inheritance	Confusing Super- and Subclasses 472 Shadowing Instance Fields 479 Failing to Invoke the Superclass Method 480 Accidental Package Access 493 Making Inherited Methods Less Accessible 493 Defining the equals Method with the Wrong Parameter Type 500 Forgetting to Clone 502		Clone Mutable Instance Fields in Accessor Methods 502

Table of Special Features

Contents

Chapter 1

Introduction

- To understand the activity of programming
- To learn about the architecture of computers
- To learn about machine code and high-level programming languages
- To become familiar with your computing environment and your compiler
- To compile and run your first Java program
- To recognize syntax and logic errors

The purpose of this chapter is to familiarize you with the concept of programming. It reviews the architecture of a computer and discusses the difference between machine code and high-level programming languages. Finally, you will see how to compile and run your first Java program, and how to diagnose errors that may occur when a program is compiled or executed.

CHAPTER CONTENTS

1.1 What Is Programming?

You have probably used a computer for work or fun. Many people use computers for everyday tasks such as balancing a checkbook or writing a term paper. Computers are good for such tasks. They can handle repetitive chores, such as totaling up numbers or placing words on a page, without getting bored or exhausted. Computers also make good game machines because they can play sequences of sounds and pictures, involving the human user in the process.

The flexibility of a computer is quite an amazing phenomenon. The same machine can balance your checkbook, print your term paper, and play a game. In contrast, other machines carry out a much narrower range of tasks—a car drives and a toaster toasts.

> A computer must be programmed to perform tasks. Different tasks require different programs.

To achieve this flexibility, the computer must be *programmed* to perform each task. A computer itself is a machine that stores data (numbers, words, pictures), interacts with devices (the monitor screen, the sound system, the printer), and executes programs. Programs are sequences of instructions and decisions that the computer carries out to achieve a task. One program balances checkbooks; a different program, perhaps designed and constructed by a different company, processes words; and a third program, probably from yet another company, plays a game.

> A computer program executes a sequence of very basic operations in rapid succession.

Today's computer programs are so sophisticated that it is hard to believe that they are all composed of extremely primitive operations.

A typical operation may be one of the following:

- Put a red dot onto this screen position.
- Send the letter A to the printer.
- Get a number from this location in memory.
- Add up two numbers.
- If this value is negative, continue the program at that instruction.

> A computer program contains the instruction sequences for all tasks that it can execute.

A computer program tells a computer, in minute detail, the sequence of steps that are needed to complete a task. A program contains a huge number of simple operations, and the computer executes them at great speed. The computer has no intelligence—it simply executes instruction sequences that have been prepared in advance.

To use a computer, no knowledge of programming is required. When you write a term paper with a word processor, that software package has been programmed by the manufacturer and is ready for you to use. That is only to be expected—you can drive a car without being a mechanic and toast bread without being an electrician.

A primary purpose of this book is to teach you how to design and implement computer programs. You will learn how to formulate instructions for all tasks that your programs need to execute.

Keep in mind that programming a sophisticated computer game or word processor requires a team of many highly skilled programmers, graphic artists, and other professionals. Your first programming efforts will be more mundane. The concepts and skills you learn in this book form an important foundation, but you should not expect to immediately produce professional software. A typical college program in computer science or software engineering takes four years to complete; this book is intended as an introductory course in such a program.

Many students find that there is an immense thrill even in simple programming tasks. It is an amazing experience to see the computer carry out a task precisely and quickly that would take you hours of drudgery.

SELF CHECK

1. What is required to play a music CD on a computer?
2. Why is a CD player less flexible than a computer?
3. Can a computer program develop the initiative to execute tasks in a better way than its programmers envisioned?

1.2 The Anatomy of a Computer

To understand the programming process, you need to have a rudimentary understanding of the building blocks that make up a computer. This section will describe a personal computer. Larger computers have faster, larger, or more powerful components, but they have fundamentally the same design.

X 20468

Figure 1   Central Processing Unit

At the heart of the computer lies the *central processing unit* (CPU) (see Figure 1). It consists of a single *chip* (integrated circuit) or a small number of chips. A computer chip is a component with a plastic or metal housing, metal connectors, and inside wiring made principally from silicon. For a CPU chip, the inside wiring is enormously complicated. For example, the Pentium 4 chip (a popular CPU for personal computers at the time of this writing) contains over 50 million structural elements called *transistors*—the elements that enable electrical signals to control other electrical signals, making automatic computing possible. The CPU locates and executes the program instructions; it carries out arithmetic operations such as addition, subtraction, multiplication, and division; and it fetches data from storage and input/output devices and sends data back.

> At the heart of the computer lies the central processing unit (CPU).

The computer keeps data and programs in *storage*. There are two kinds of storage. *Primary storage,* also called *random-access memory* (RAM) or simply *memory,* is fast but expensive; it is made from memory chips (see Figure 2). Primary storage has two disadvantages. It is comparatively expensive, and it loses all its data when the power is turned off. *Secondary storage,* usually a *hard disk* (see Figure 3), provides less expensive storage that persists without electricity. A hard disk consists of rotating platters, which are coated with a magnetic material, and read/write heads, which can detect and change the patterns of varying magnetic flux on the platters. This is essentially the same recording and playback process that is used in audio or video tapes.

> Data and programs are stored in primary storage (memory) and secondary storage (such as a hard disk).

Some computers are self-contained units, whereas others are interconnected through *networks.* Home computers are usually intermittently connected to the Internet via a dialup or broadband connection. The computers in your computer lab are probably permanently connected to a local area network. Through the network cabling, the computer can read programs from central storage locations or

Figure 2
A Memory Module with Memory Chips

send data to other computers. For the user of a networked computer, it may not even be obvious which data reside on the computer itself and which are transmitted through the network.

Most computers have *removable storage* devices that can access data or programs on media such as floppy disks, tapes, or compact discs (CDs).

Figure 3   A Hard Disk

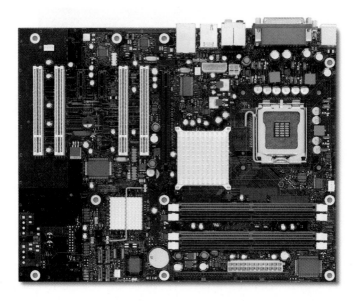

Figure 4   A Motherboard

To interact with a human user, a computer requires other peripheral devices. The computer transmits information to the user through a display screen, loudspeakers, and printers. The user can enter information and directions to the computer by using a keyboard or a pointing device such as a mouse.

The CPU, the RAM, and the electronics controlling the hard disk and other devices are interconnected through a set of electrical lines called a *bus.* Data travel along the bus from the system memory and peripheral devices to the CPU and back. Figure 4 shows a *motherboard,* which contains the CPU, the RAM, and connectors to peripheral devices.

Figure 5 gives a schematic overview of the architecture of a computer. Program instructions and data (such as text, numbers, audio, or video) are stored on the hard disk, on a CD, or on a network. When a program is started, it is brought into memory where it can be read by the CPU. The CPU reads the program one instruction at a time. As directed by these instructions, the CPU reads data, modifies it, and writes it back to RAM or to secondary storage. Some program instructions will cause the CPU to interact with the devices that control the display screen or the speaker. Because these actions happen many times over and at great speed, the human user will perceive images and sound. Similarly, the CPU can send instructions to a printer to mark the paper with patterns of closely spaced dots, which a human recognizes as text characters and pictures. Some program instructions read user input from the keyboard or mouse. The program analyzes the nature of these inputs and then executes the next appropriate instructions.

> The CPU reads machine instructions from memory. The instructions direct it to communicate with memory, secondary storage, and peripheral devices.

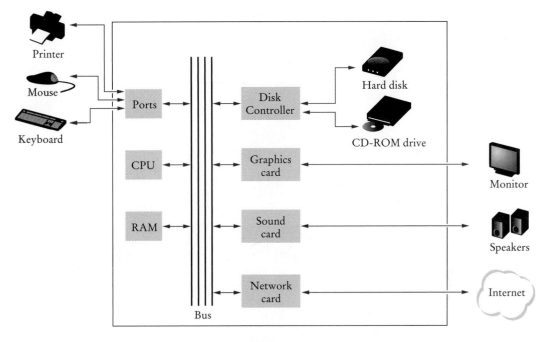

Figure 5   Schematic Diagram of a Computer

SELF CHECK

4. Where is a program stored when it is not currently running?
5. Which part of the computer carries out arithmetic operations, such as addition and multiplication?

RANDOM FACT 1.1

The ENIAC and the Dawn of Computing

The ENIAC (*e*lectronic *n*umerical *i*ntegrator *a*nd *c*omputer) was the first usable electronic computer. It was designed by J. Presper Eckert and John Mauchly at the University of Pennsylvania and was completed in 1946. Instead of transistors, which were not invented until two years after it was built, the ENIAC contained about 18,000 *vacuum tubes* in many cabinets housed in a large room (see Figure 6). Vacuum tubes burned out at the rate of several tubes per day. An attendant with a shopping cart full of tubes constantly made the rounds and replaced defective ones. The computer was programmed by connecting wires on panels. Each wiring configuration would set up the computer for a particular problem. To have the computer work on a different problem, the wires had to be replugged.

Work on the ENIAC was supported by the U.S. Navy, which was interested in computations of ballistic tables that would give the trajectory of a projectile, depending on the wind resistance, initial velocity, and atmospheric conditions. To compute the trajectories, one must

Figure 6   The ENIAC

find the numerical solutions of certain differential equations; hence the name "numerical integrator". Before machines like ENIAC were developed, humans did this kind of work, and until the 1950s the word "computer" referred to these people. The ENIAC was later used for peaceful purposes, such as the tabulation of U.S. census data.

1.3 Translating Human-Readable Programs to Machine Code

Generally, machine code depends on the CPU type. However, the instruction set of the Java virtual machine (JVM) can be executed on many CPUs.

On the most basic level, computer instructions are extremely primitive. The processor executes *machine instructions*. CPUs from different vendors, such as the Intel Pentium or the Sun SPARC, have different sets of machine instructions. To enable Java applications to run on multiple CPUs without modification, Java programs contain machine instructions for a so-called "Java virtual machine" (JVM), an idealized CPU that is simulated by a program run on the actual CPU. The difference between actual and virtual machine instructions is not important—all you need to know is that machine instructions are very simple, are encoded as numbers and stored in memory, and can be executed very quickly.

A typical sequence of machine instructions is

1. Load the contents of memory location 40.
2. Load the value 100.
3. If the first value is greater than the second value, continue with the instruction that is stored in memory location 240.

Actually, machine instructions are encoded as numbers so that they can be stored in memory. On the Java virtual machine, this sequence of instruction is encoded as the sequence of numbers

```
21 40
16 100
163 240
```

When the virtual machine fetches this sequence of numbers, it decodes them and executes the associated sequence of commands.

> Because machine instructions are encoded as numbers, it is difficult to write programs in machine code.

How can you communicate the command sequence to the computer? The most direct method is to place the actual numbers into the computer memory. This is, in fact, how the very earliest computers worked. However, a long program is composed of thousands of individual commands, and it is tedious and error-prone to look up the numeric codes for all commands and manually place the codes into memory. As we said before, computers are really good at automating tedious and error-prone activities, and it did not take long for computer programmers to realize that computers could be harnessed to help in the programming process.

> High-level languages allow you to describe tasks at a higher conceptual level than machine code.

In the mid-1950s, *high-level* programming languages began to appear. In these languages, the programmer expresses the idea behind the task that needs to be performed, and a special computer program, called a *compiler,* translates the high-level description into machine instructions for a particular processor.

For example, in Java, the high-level programming language that you will use in this book, you might give the following instruction:

```
if (intRate > 100)
    System.out.println("Interest rate error");
```

This means, "If the interest rate is over 100, display an error message". It is then the job of the compiler program to look at the sequence of characters if (intRate > 100) and translate that into

```
21 40 16 100 163 240 . . .
```

> A compiler translates programs written in a high-level language into machine code.

Compilers are quite sophisticated programs. They translate logical statements, such as the if statement, into sequences of computations, tests, and jumps. They assign memory locations for *variables*—items of information identified by symbolic names—like intRate. In this course, we will generally take the existence of a compiler for granted.

If you decide to become a professional computer scientist, you may well learn more about compiler-writing techniques later in your studies.

6. What is the code for the Java virtual machine instruction "Load the contents of memory location 100"?

7. Does a person who uses a computer for office work ever run a compiler?

1.4 The Java Programming Language

> Java was originally designed for programming consumer devices, but it was first successfully used to write Internet applets.

In 1991, a group led by James Gosling and Patrick Naughton at Sun Microsystems designed a programming language that they code-named "Green" for use in consumer devices, such as intelligent television "set-top" boxes. The language was designed to be simple and architecture neutral, so that it could be executed on a variety of hardware. No customer was ever found for this technology.

Gosling recounts that in 1994 the team realized, "We could write a really cool browser. It was one of the few things in the client/server mainstream that needed some of the weird things we'd done: architecture neutral, real-time, reliable, secure". Java was introduced to an enthusiastic crowd at the SunWorld exhibition in 1995.

> Java was designed to be safe and portable, benefiting both Internet users and students.

Since then, Java has grown at a phenomenal rate. Programmers have embraced the language because it is simpler than its closest rival, C++. In addition, Java has a rich *library* that makes it possible to write portable programs that can bypass proprietary operating systems—a feature that was eagerly sought by those who wanted to be independent of those proprietary systems and was bitterly fought by their vendors. A "micro edition" and an "enterprise edition" of the Java library make Java programmers at home on hardware ranging from smart cards and cell phones to the largest Internet servers.

Because Java was designed for the Internet, it has two attributes that make it very suitable for beginners: safety and portability. If you visit a web page that contains Java code (so-called *applets*—see Figure 7 for an example), the code automatically starts running. It is important that you can trust that applets are inherently safe. If an applet could do something evil, such as damaging data or reading personal information on your computer, then you would be in real danger every time you browsed the Web—an unscrupulous designer might put up a web page containing dangerous code that would execute on your machine as soon as you visited the page. The Java language has an assortment of security features that guarantees that no evil applets can run on your computer. As an added benefit, these features also help you to learn the language faster. The Java virtual machine can catch many kinds of beginners' mistakes and report them accurately. (In contrast, many beginners' mistakes in the C++ language merely produce programs that act in random and confusing ways.) The other benefit of Java is portability. The same Java program will run, without change, on Windows, UNIX, Linux, or the Macintosh. This too is a requirement for applets. When you visit a web page, the web server that serves up

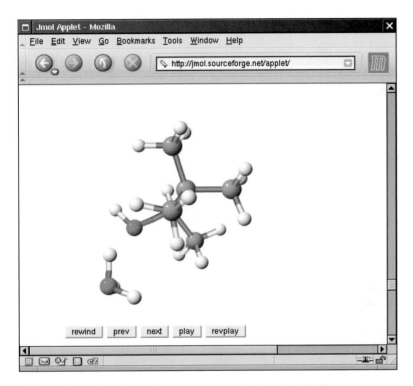

Figure 7   An Applet for Visualizing Molecules ([2])

the page contents has no idea what computer you are using to browse the Web. It simply returns you the portable code that was generated by the Java compiler. The virtual machine on your computer executes that portable code. Again, there is a benefit for the student. You do not have to learn how to write programs for different operating systems.

At this time, Java is firmly established as one of the most important languages for general-purpose programming as well as for computer science instruction. However, although Java is a good language for beginners, it is not perfect, for three reasons.

Because Java was not specifically designed for students, no thought was given to making it really simple to write basic programs. A certain amount of technical machinery is necessary in Java to write even the simplest programs. This is not a problem for professional programmers, but it is a drawback for beginning students. As you learn how to program in Java, there will be times when you will be asked to be satisfied with a preliminary explanation and wait for complete details in a later chapter.

Java was revised and extended many times during its life—see Table 1. You may need to configure your programming environment for the version of Java that this book uses (version 5.0 or above), or, if you use an older programming environment, you may need to change your programs slightly. (Appendix D contains the necessary instructions.)

Java has a very large library. Focus on learning those parts of the library that you need for your programming projects.

Finally, you cannot hope to learn all of Java in one semester. The Java language itself is relatively simple, but Java contains a vast set of *library packages* that are required to write useful programs. There are packages for graphics, user interface design, cryptography, networking, sound, database storage, and many other purposes. Even expert Java programmers cannot hope to know the contents of all of the packages—they just use those that they need for particular projects.

Using this book, you should expect to learn a good deal about the Java language and about the most important packages. Keep in mind that the central goal of this book is not to make you memorize Java minutiae, but to teach you how to think about programming.

Table 1 Java Versions		
Version	**Year**	**Important New Features**
1.0	1996	
1.1	1997	Inner classes
1.2	1998	Swing, Collections
1.3	2000	Performance enhancements
1.4	2002	Assertions, XML
5.0	2004	Generic classes, enhanced for loop, auto-boxing, enumerations

SELF CHECK

8. What are the two most important benefits of the Java language?
9. How long does it take to learn the entire Java library?

1.5 Becoming Familiar with Your Computer

Set aside some time to become familiar with the computer system and the Java compiler that you will use for your class work.

You may be taking your first programming course as you read this book, and you may well be doing your work on an unfamiliar computer system. Spend some time familiarizing yourself with the computer. Because computer systems vary widely, this book can only give an outline of the steps you need to follow. Using a new and unfamiliar computer system can be frustrating, especially if you are on your own. Look for training courses that your campus offers, or ask a friend to give you a brief tour.

Figure 8
A Shell Window

Step 1. Log In

If you use your home computer, you probably don't need to worry about this step. Computers in a lab, however, are usually not open to everyone. You may need an account name or number and a password to gain access to such a system.

Step 2. Locate the Java Compiler

Computer systems differ greatly in this regard. On some systems you must open a *shell window* (see Figure 8) and type commands to launch the compiler. Other systems have an *integrated development environment* in which you can write and test your programs (see Figure 9). Many university labs have information sheets and

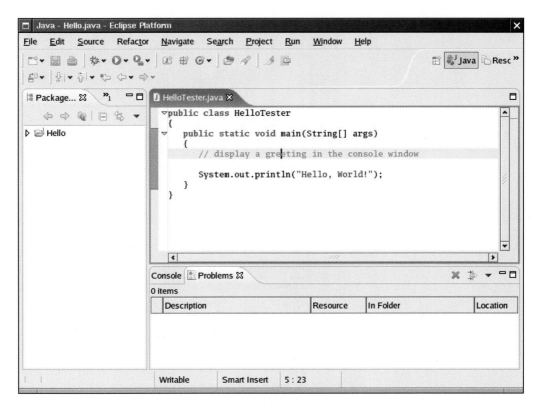

Figure 9 An Integrated Development Environment

tutorials that walk you through the tools that are installed in the lab. The companion web site for this book (reference [1] at the end of this chapter) contains instructions for several popular compilers.

Step 3. Understand Files and Folders

As a programmer, you will write Java programs, try them out, and improve them. Your programs are kept in *files*. A file is a collection of items of information that are kept together, such as the text of a word-processing document or the instructions of a Java program. Files have names, and the rules for legal names differ from one system to another. Some systems allow spaces in file names; others don't. Some distinguish between upper- and lowercase letters; others don't. Most Java compilers require that Java files end in an *extension*— .java; for example, Test.java. Java file names cannot contain spaces, and the distinction between upper- and lowercase letters is important.

Files are stored in *folders* or *directories*. These file containers can be *nested.* That is, a folder can contain not only files but also other folders, which themselves can contain more files and folders (see Figure 10). This hierarchy can be quite large, especially on networked computers, where some of the files may be on your local disk, others elsewhere on the network. While you need not be concerned with

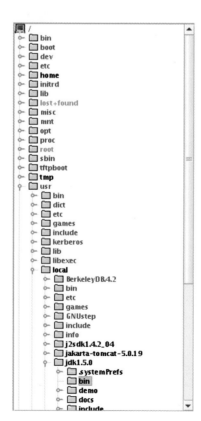

Figure 10
Nested Folders

every branch of the hierarchy, you should familiarize yourself with your local environment. Different systems have different ways of showing files and directories. Some use a graphical display and let you move around by clicking the mouse on folder icons. In other systems, you must enter commands to visit or inspect different locations.

Step 4. Write a Simple Program

In the next section, we will introduce a very simple program. You will need to learn how to type it in, how to run it, and how to fix mistakes.

Step 5. Save Your Work

Develop a strategy for keeping backup copies of your work before disaster strikes.

You will spend many hours typing Java program code and improving it. The resulting program files have some value, and you should treat them as you would other important property. A conscientious safety strategy is particularly important for computer files. They are more fragile than paper documents or other more tangible objects. It is easy to delete a file accidentally, and occasionally files are lost because of a computer malfunction. Unless you keep a copy, you must then retype the contents. Because you probably won't remember the entire file, you will likely find yourself spending almost as much time as you did to enter and improve it in the first place. This costs time, and it may cause you to miss deadlines. It is therefore crucial that you learn how to safeguard files and that you get in the habit of doing so *before* disaster strikes. You can make safety or *backup* copies of files by saving copies on a floppy or CD, into another folder, to your local area network, or on the Internet.

SELF CHECK

10. How are programming projects stored on a computer?
11. What do you do to protect yourself from data loss when you work on programming projects?

PRODUCTIVITY HINT 1.1

Understand the File System

In recent years, computers have become easier to use for home or office users. Many inessential details are now hidden from casual users. For example, many casual users simply place all their work inside a default folder (such as "Home" or "My Documents") and are blissfully ignorant about details of the file system.

But you need to know how to impose an organization on the data that you create. You also need to be able to locate and inspect files that are required for translating and running Java programs.

If you are not comfortable with files and folders, be sure to set aside some time to learn about these concepts. Enroll in a short course, or take a web tutorial. Many free tutorials are available on the Internet, but unfortunately their locations change frequently. Search the Web for "files and folders tutorial" and pick a tutorial that goes beyond the basics.

PRODUCTIVITY HINT 1.2

Have a Backup Strategy

Come up with a strategy for your backups *now*, before you lose any data. Here are a few pointers to keep in mind.

- *Select a backup medium.* Floppy disks are the traditional choice, but they can be unreliable. CD media are more reliable and hold far more information, but they are more expensive. An increasingly popular form of backup is Internet file storage. Many people use two levels of backup: a folder on the hard disk for quick and dirty backups, and a CD-ROM for higher security. (After all, a hard disk can crash—a particularly common problem with laptop computers.)

- *Back up often.* Backing up a file takes only a few seconds, and you will hate yourself if you have to spend many hours recreating work that you easily could have saved.

- *Rotate backups.* Use more than one set of disks or folders for backups, and rotate them. That is, first back up onto the first backup destination, then to the second and third, and then go back to the first. That way you always have three recent backups. Even if one of the floppy disks has a defect, or you messed up one of the backup directories, you can use one of the others.

- *Back up source files only.* The compiler translates the files that you write into files consisting of machine code. There is no need to back up the machine code files, because you can recreate them easily by running the compiler again. Focus your backup activity on those files that represent your effort. That way your backups won't fill up with files that you don't need.

- *Pay attention to the backup direction.* Backing up involves copying files from one place to another. It is important that you do this right—that is, copy from your work location to the backup location. If you do it the wrong way, you will overwrite a newer file with an older version.

- *Check your backups once in a while.* Double-check that your backups are where you think they are. There is nothing more frustrating than finding out that the backups are not there when you need them. This is particularly true if you use a backup program that stores files on an unfamiliar device (such as data tape) or in a compressed format.

- *Relax before restoring.* When you lose a file and need to restore it from backup, you are likely to be in an unhappy, nervous state. Take a deep breath and think through the recovery process before you start. It is not uncommon for an agitated computer user to wipe out the last backup when trying to restore a damaged file.

1.6 Compiling a Simple Program

You are now ready to write and run your first Java program. The traditional choice for the very first program in a new programming language is a program that displays a simple greeting: "Hello, World!". Let us follow that tradition. Here is the "Hello, World!" program in Java.

File HelloTester.java

```
 1  public class HelloTester
 2  {
 3     public static void main(String[] args)
 4     {
 5        // Display a greeting in the console window
 6
 7        System.out.println("Hello, World!");
 8     }
 9  }
```

Output

```
Hello, World!
```

We will examine this program in a minute. For now, you should make a new program file and call it HelloTester.java. Enter the program instructions and compile and run the program, following the procedure that is appropriate for your compiler.

> Java is case sensitive. You must be careful about distinguishing between upper- and lowercase letters.

Java is *case sensitive*. You must enter upper- and lowercase letters exactly as they appear in the program listing. You cannot type MAIN or PrintLn. If you are not careful, you will run into problems—see Common Error 1.2.

On the other hand, Java has *free-form layout*. You can use any number of spaces and line breaks to separate words. You can cram as many words as possible into each line,

```
public class HelloTester{public static void main(String[]
args){// Display a greeting in the console window
System.out.println("Hello, World!");}}
```

You can even write every word and symbol on a separate line,

```
public
class
HelloTester
{
public
static
void
main
(
. . .
```

> Lay out your programs so that they are easy to read.

However, good taste dictates that you lay out your programs in a readable fashion. We will give you recommendations for good layout throughout this book. Appendix A contains a summary of our recommendations.

When you run the test program, the message

```
Hello, World!
```

will appear somewhere on the screen (see Figures 11 and 12). The exact location depends on your programming environment.

Now that you have seen the program working, it is time to understand its makeup. The first line,

```
public class HelloTester
```

> Classes are the fundamental building blocks of Java programs.

starts a new *class*. Classes are a fundamental concept in Java, and you will begin to study them in Chapter 2. In Java, every program consists of one or more classes.

The keyword `public` denotes that the class is usable by the "public". You will later encounter `private` features. At this point, you should simply regard the

```
public class ClassName
{
   . . .
}
```

as a necessary part of the "plumbing" that is required to write any Java program. In Java, every source file can contain at most one public class, and the name of the public class must match the name of the file containing the class. For example, the class `HelloTester` *must* be contained in a file `HelloTester.java`. It is very important that the names *and the capitalization* match exactly. You can get strange error messages if you call the class `HELLOTester` or the file `hellotester.java`.

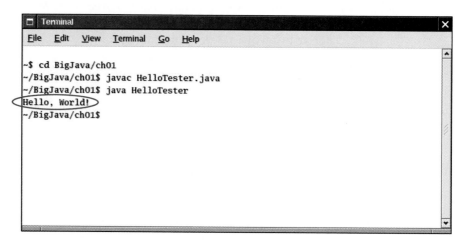

Figure 11   Running the `HelloTester` Program in a Console Window

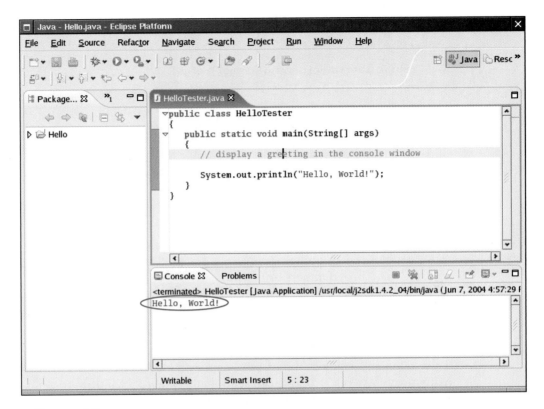

Figure 12
Running the HelloTester Program in an Integrated Development Environment

Every Java application contains a class with a main method. When the application starts, the instructions in the main method are executed.

Each class contains definitions of methods. Each method contains a sequence of instructions.

The construction

```
public static void main(String[] args)
{
}
```

defines a *method* called main. A method contains a collection of programming instructions that describe how to carry out a particular task. Every Java application must have a main method. Most Java programs contain other methods besides main, and you will see in Chapter 3 how to write other methods.

The *parameter* String[] args is a required part of the main method. (It contains *command line arguments*, which we will not discuss until Chapter 16.) The keyword static indicates that the main method does not operate on an *object*. (As you will see in Chapter 2, most methods in Java do operate on objects, and static methods are not common in large Java programs. Nevertheless, main must always be static, because it starts running before the program can create objects.)

At this time, simply consider

```
public class ClassName
{
    public static void main(String[] args)
    {
        . . .
    }
}
```

as yet another part of the "plumbing". Our first program has all instructions inside the main method of a class.

The first line inside the main method is a *comment*

```
// Display a greeting in the console window
```

> Use comments to help human readers understand your program.

This comment is purely for the benefit of the human reader, to explain in more detail what the next statement does. Any text enclosed between // and the end of the line is completely ignored by the compiler. Comments are used to explain the program to other programmers or to yourself.

The instructions or *statements* in the *body* of the main method—that is, the statements inside the curly braces ({})—are executed one by one. Each statement ends in a semicolon (;). Our method has a single statement:

```
System.out.println("Hello, World!");
```

This statement prints a line of text, namely "Hello, World!". However, there are many places where a program can send that string: to a window, to a file, or to a networked computer on the other side of the world. You need to specify that the destination for the string is the *system output*—that is, a console window. The console window is represented in Java by an object called out. Just as you needed to place the main method in a HelloTester class, the designers of the Java library needed to place the out object into a class. They placed it in the System class, which contains useful objects and methods to access system resources. To use the out object in the System class, you must refer to it as System.out.

To use an object, such as System.out, you specify what you want to do to it. In this case, you want to print a line of text. The println method carries out this task.

You do not have to implement this method—the programmers who wrote the Java library already did that for us—but you do need to *call* the method.

> A method is called by specifying an object, the method name, and the method parameters.

Whenever you call a method in Java, you need to specify three items (see Figure 13):

1. The object that you want to use (in this case, System.out)
2. The name of the method you want to use (in this case, println)
3. A pair of parentheses, containing any other information the method needs (in this case, "Hello, World!"). The technical term for this information is a *parameter* for the method. Note that the two periods in System.out.println have different meanings. The first period means "locate the out object in the System class". The second period means "apply the println method to that object".

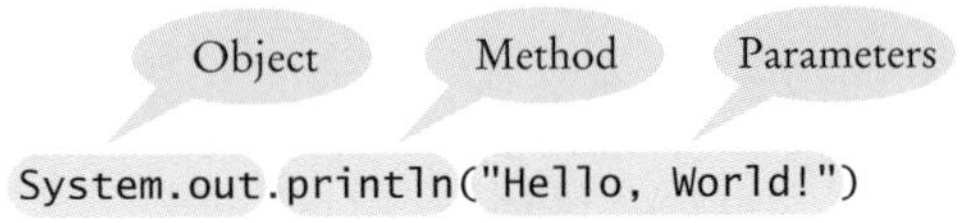

Object   Method   Parameters

Figure 13
Calling a Method   `System.out.println("Hello, World!")`

A sequence of characters enclosed in quotation marks

`"Hello, World!"`

> A string is a sequence of characters enclosed in quotation marks.

is called a *string.* You must enclose the contents of the string inside quotation marks so that the compiler knows you literally mean `"Hello, World!"`. There is a reason for this requirement. Suppose you need to print the word *main.* By enclosing it in quotation marks, `"main"`, the compiler knows you mean the sequence of characters m a i n, not the method named `main`. The rule is simply that you must enclose all text strings in quotation marks, so that the compiler considers them plain text and does not try to interpret them as program instructions.

You can also print numerical values. For example, the statement

`System.out.println(3 + 4);`

displays the number 7.

The `println` method prints a string or a number and then starts a new line. For example, the sequence of statements

```
System.out.println("Hello");
System.out.println("World!");
```

prints two lines of text:

```
Hello
World!
```

There is a second method, called `print`, that you can use to print an item without starting a new line. For example, the output of the two statements

```
System.out.print("00");
System.out.println(3 + 4);
```

is the single line

```
007
```

SYNTAX 1.1 **Method Call**

object.methodName(parameters)

Example:

`System.out.println("Hello, Dave!")`

Purpose:

To invoke a method on an object and supply any additional parameters

SELF CHECK

12. How would you modify the HelloTester program to print the words "Hello," and "World!" on two lines?

13. Would the program continue to work if you omitted the line starting with //?

14. What does the following set of statements print?

```
System.out.print("My lucky number is");
System.out.println(3 + 4 + 5);
```

COMMON ERROR 1.1

Omitting Semicolons

In Java every statement must end in a semicolon. Forgetting to type a semicolon is a common error. It confuses the compiler, because the compiler uses the semicolon to find where one statement ends and the next one starts. The compiler does not use line breaks or closing braces to recognize the end of statements. For example, the compiler considers

```
System.out.println("Hello")
System.out.println("World!");
```

a single statement, as if you had written

```
System.out.println("Hello") System.out.println("World!");
```

Then it doesn't understand that statement, because it does not expect the word System following the closing parenthesis after "Hello". The remedy is simple. Scan every statement for a terminating semicolon, just as you would check that every English sentence ends in a period.

ADVANCED TOPIC 1.1

Alternative Comment Syntax

In Java there are two methods for writing comments. You already learned that the compiler ignores anything that you type between // and the end of the current line. The compiler also ignores any text between a /* and */.

```
/* A simple Java program */
```

The // comment is easier to type if the comment is only a single line long. If you have a comment that is longer than a line, then the /* . . . */ comment is simpler:

```
/*
   This is a simple Java program that you can use to try out
   your compiler and virtual machine.
*/
```

It would be somewhat tedious to add the // at the beginning of each line and to move them around whenever the text of the comment changes.

In this book, we use // for comments that will never grow beyond a line, and /* . . . */ for longer comments. If you prefer, you can always use the // style. The readers of your code will be grateful for *any* comments, no matter which style you use.

1.7 Errors

Experiment a little with the HelloTester program. What happens if you make a typing error such as

```
System.ouch.println("Hello, World!");
System.out.println("Hello, World!");
System.out.println("Hello, Word!");
```

> A syntax error is a violation of the rules of the programming language. The compiler detects syntax errors.

In the first case, the compiler will complain. It will say that it has no clue what you mean by ouch. The exact wording of the error message is dependent on the compiler, but it might be something like "Undefined symbol ouch". This is a *compile-time error* or *syntax error.* Something is wrong according to the language rules and the compiler finds it. When the compiler finds one or more errors, it refuses to translate the program to Java virtual machine instructions, and as a consequence you have no program that you can run. You must fix the error and compile again. In fact, the compiler is quite picky, and it is common to go through several rounds of fixing compile-time errors before compilation succeeds for the first time.

If the compiler finds an error, it will not simply stop and give up. It will try to report as many errors as it can find, so you can fix them all at once. Sometimes, however, one error throws it off track. This is likely to happen with the error in the second line. Because the closing quotation mark is missing, the compiler will think that the); characters are still part of the string. In such cases, it is common for the compiler to emit bogus error reports for neighboring lines. You should fix only those error messages that make sense to you and then recompile.

The error in the third line is of a different kind. The program will compile and run, but its output will be wrong. It will print

```
Hello, Word!
```

> A logic error causes a program to take an action that the programmer did not intend. You must test your programs to find logic errors.

This is a *run-time error* or *logic error.* The program is syntactically correct and does something, but it doesn't do what it is supposed to do. The compiler cannot find the error. You, the programmer, must flush out this type of error. Run the program, and carefully look at its output.

During program development, errors are unavoidable. Once a program is longer than a few lines, it requires superhuman concentration to enter it correctly without slipping up once. You will find yourself omitting semicolons or quotes more often than you would like, but the compiler will track down these problems for you.

Logic errors are more troublesome. The compiler will not find them—in fact, the compiler will cheerfully translate any program as long as its syntax is correct—but the resulting program will do something wrong. It is the responsibility of the program author to test the program and find any logic errors. Testing programs is an important topic that you will encounter many times in this book. Another important aspect of good craftsmanship is *defensive programming:* structuring programs and development processes in such a way that an error in one part of a program does not trigger a disastrous response.

The error examples that you saw so far were not difficult to diagnose or fix, but as you learn more sophisticated programming techniques, there will also be much more room for error. It is an uncomfortable fact that locating all errors in a program is very difficult. Even if you can observe that a program exhibits faulty behavior, it may not at all be obvious what part of the program caused it and how you can fix it. Special software tools (so-called *debuggers*) let you trace through a program to find *bugs*—that is, logic errors. In Chapter 10 you will learn how to use a debugger effectively.

Note that these errors are different from the types of errors that you are likely to make in calculations. If you total up a column of numbers, you may miss a minus sign or accidentally drop a carry, perhaps because you are bored or tired. Computers do not make these kinds of errors.

This book uses a three-part error management strategy. First, you will learn about common errors and how to avoid them. Then you will learn defensive programming strategies to minimize the likelihood and impact of errors. Finally, you will learn debugging strategies to flush out those errors that remain.

SELF CHECK

15. Suppose you omit the `//` characters from the `HelloTester.java` program but not the remainder of the comment. Will you get a compile-time error or a run-time error?

16. How can you find logic errors in a program?

COMMON ERROR 1.2

Misspelling Words

If you accidentally misspell a word, then strange things may happen, and it may not always be completely obvious from the error messages what went wrong. Here is a good example of how simple spelling errors can cause trouble:

```java
public class HelloTester
{
    public static void Main(String[] args)
    {
        System.out.println("Hello, World!");
    }
}
```

This class defines a method called `Main`. The compiler will not consider this to be the same as the `main` method, because `Main` starts with an uppercase letter and the Java language is case sensitive. Upper- and lowercase letters are considered to be completely different from each other, and to the compiler `Main` is no better match for `main` than `rain`. The compiler will cheerfully compile your `Main` method, but when the Java virtual machine reads the compiled file, it will complain about the missing `main` method and refuse to run the program. Of course, the message "missing main method" should give you a clue where to look for the error.

If you get an error message that seems to indicate that the compiler is on the wrong track, it is a good idea to check for spelling and capitalization. All Java keywords use only lowercase letters. Names of classes usually start with an uppercase letter, names of methods and variables with a lowercase letter. If you misspell the name of a symbol (for example, `ouch` instead of `out`), the compiler will complain about an "undefined symbol". That error message is usually a good clue that you made a spelling error.

1.8 The Compilation Process

Some Java development environments are very convenient to use. Enter the code in one window, click on a button to compile, and click on another button to execute your program. Error messages show up in a second window, and the program runs in a third window. With such an environment you are completely shielded from the details of the compilation process. On other systems you must carry out every step manually, by typing commands into a shell window.

> An editor is a program for entering and modifying text, such as a Java program.

No matter which compilation environment you use, you begin your activity by typing in the program statements. The program that you use for entering and modifying the program text is called an *editor*. Remember to *save* your work to disk frequently, because otherwise the text editor stores the text only in the computer's memory. If something goes wrong with the computer and you need to restart it, the contents of the primary memory (including your program text) are lost, but anything stored on the hard disk is permanent even if you need to restart the computer.

> The Java compiler translates source code into class files that contain instructions for the Java virtual machine.

When you compile your program, the compiler translates the Java *source code* (that is, the statements that you wrote) into *class files*, which consist of virtual machine instructions and other information that is required for execution. The class files have the extension `.class`. For example, the virtual machine instructions for the `Hello-Tester` program are stored in a file `HelloTester.class`. As already mentioned, the compiler produces a class file only after you have corrected all syntax errors.

The class file contains the translation of only the instructions that you wrote. That is not enough to actually run the program. To display a string in a window, quite a bit of low-level activity is necessary. The authors of the `System` and `Print-Stream` classes (which define the `out` object and the `println` method) have implemented all necessary actions and placed the required class files into a *library*. A

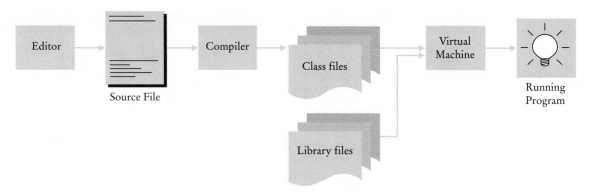

Figure 14   From Source Code to Running Program

library is a collection of code that has been programmed and translated by someone else, ready for you to use in your program.

The Java virtual machine loads the instructions for the program that you wrote, starts your program, and loads the necessary library files as they are required.

The steps of compiling and running your program are outlined in Figure 14.

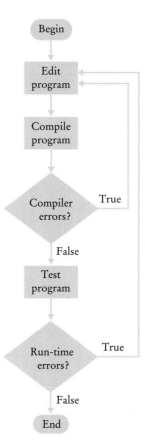

Figure 15
The Edit–Compile–Test Loop

The Java virtual machine loads program instructions from class files and library files.

Programming activity centers around these steps. Start in the editor, writing the source file. Compile the program and look at the error messages. Go back to the editor and fix the syntax errors. When the compiler succeeds, run the program. If you find a run-time error, you must look at the source code in the editor to try to determine the reason. Once you find the cause of the error, fix it in the editor. Compile and run again to see whether the error has gone away. If not, go back to the editor. This is called the *edit–compile–test loop* (see Figure 15). You will spend a substantial amount of time in this loop when working on programming assignments.

SELF CHECK

17. What do you expect to see when you load a class file into your text editor?
18. Why can't you test a program for run-time errors when it has compiler errors?

CHAPTER SUMMARY

1. A computer must be programmed to perform tasks. Different tasks require different programs.

2. A computer program executes a sequence of very basic operations in rapid succession.

3. A computer program contains the instruction sequences for all tasks that it can execute.

4. At the heart of the computer lies the central processing unit (CPU).

5. Data and programs are stored in primary storage (memory) and secondary storage (such as a hard disk).

6. The CPU reads machine instructions from memory. The instructions direct it to communicate with memory, secondary storage, and peripheral devices.

7. Generally, machine code depends on the CPU type. However, the instruction set of the Java virtual machine (JVM) can be executed on many CPUs.

8. Because machine instructions are encoded as numbers, it is difficult to write programs in machine code.

9. High-level languages allow you to describe tasks at a higher conceptual level than machine code.

10. A compiler translates programs written in a high-level language into machine code.

11. Java was originally designed for programming consumer devices, but it was first successfully used to write Internet applets.

12. Java was designed to be safe and portable, benefiting both Internet users and students.

13. Java has a very large library. Focus on learning those parts of the library that you need for your programming projects.

14. Set aside some time to become familiar with the computer system and the Java compiler that you will use for your class work.

15. Develop a strategy for keeping backup copies of your work before disaster strikes.

16. Java is case sensitive. You must be careful about distinguishing between upper- and lowercase letters.

17. Lay out your programs so that they are easy to read.

18. Classes are the fundamental building blocks of Java programs.

19. Every Java application contains a class with a `main` method. When the application starts, the instructions in the `main` method are executed.

20. Each class contains definitions of methods. Each method contains a sequence of instructions.

21. Use comments to help human readers understand your program.

22. A method is called by specifying an object, the method name, and the method parameters.

23. A string is a sequence of characters enclosed in quotation marks.

24. A syntax error is a violation of the rules of the programming language. The compiler detects syntax errors.

25. A logic error causes a program to take an action that the programmer did not intend. You must test your programs to find logic errors.

26. An editor is a program for entering and modifying text, such as a Java program.

27. The Java compiler translates source code into class files that contain instructions for the Java virtual machine.

28. The Java virtual machine loads program instructions from class files and library files.

FURTHER READING

1. `http://www.wiley.com/college/horstmann`   Instructions for using several popular Java compilers can be found by navigating to the companion site for this book.

2. `http://jmol.sourceforge.net/applet/`   The web site for the jmol applet for visualizing molecules.

CLASSES, OBJECTS, AND METHODS INTRODUCED IN THIS CHAPTER

Here is a list of all classes, methods, static variables, and constants introduced in this chapter. Turn to the documentation in Appendix C for more information.

```
java.io.PrintStream
    print
    println
java.lang.System
    out
```

REVIEW EXERCISES

Exercise R1.1. Explain the difference between using a computer program and programming a computer.

Exercise R1.2. What distinguishes a computer from a typical household appliance?

Exercise R1.3. Rank the storage devices that can be part of a computer system by
  a. Speed
  b. Cost
  c. Storage capacity

Exercise R1.4. What is the Java virtual machine?

Exercise R1.5. What is an applet?

Exercise R1.6. What is an integrated programming environment?

Exercise R1.7. What is a console window?

Exercise R1.8. Describe *exactly* what steps you would take to back up your work after you have typed in the HelloTester.java program.

Exercise R1.9. On your own computer or on a lab computer, find the exact location (folder or directory name) of
  a. The sample file HelloTester.java, which you wrote with the editor
  b. The Java program launcher java.exe
  c. The library file rt.jar that contains the run-time library

Exercise R1.10. How do you discover syntax errors? How do you discover logic errors?

Exercise R1.11. Write three versions of the HelloTester.java program that have different syntax errors. Write a version that has a logic error.

Exercise R1.12. What do the following statements print?

   a. `System.out.println("3 + 4");`

   b. `System.out.println(3 + 4);`

   c. `System.out.println(3 + "4");`

PROGRAMMING EXERCISES

Exercise P1.1. Write a program that displays your name inside a box on the console screen, like this:

Do your best to approximate lines with characters, such as |, -, and +.

Exercise P1.2. Write a program that prints a face, using text characters, hopefully better looking than this one:

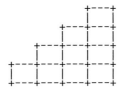

Use *comments* to indicate the statements that print the hair, ears, mouth, and so on.

Exercise P1.3. Write a program that prints a tic-tac-toe board:

```
+---+---+---+
|   |   |   |
+---+---+---+
|   |   |   |
+---+---+---+
|   |   |   |
+---+---+---+
```

Exercise P1.4. Write a program that prints a staircase:

```
                +---+
                |   |
            +---+---+
            |   |   |
        +---+---+---+
        |   |   |   |
    +---+---+---+---+
    |   |   |   |   |
    +---+---+---+---+
```

Exercise P1.5. Write a program that computes the sum of the first ten positive integers, $1 + 2 + \cdots + 10$. *Hint:* Write a program of the form

```
public class Sum10
{
   public static void main(String[] args)
   {
      System.out.println(          );
   }
}
```

Exercise P1.6. Write a program that computes the sum of the reciprocals $1/1 + 1/2 + \cdots + 1/10$. This is harder than it sounds. Try writing the program, and check the result. The program's result isn't likely to be correct. Then write the denominators as *floating-point numbers*, $1.0, 2.0, \ldots, 10.0$, and run the program again. Can you explain the difference in the results? We will explore this phenomenon in Chapter 4.

Exercise P1.7. Type in and run the following program:

```
import javax.swing.JOptionPane;

public class DialogTester
{
    public static void main(String[] args)
    {
        JOptionPane.showMessageDialog(null, "Hello, World!");
        System.exit(0);
    }
}
```

Then modify the program to show the message "Hello, *your name*!".

Exercise P1.8. Type in and run the following program:

```
import javax.swing.JOptionPane;

public class DialogTester
{
    public static void main(String[] args)
    {
        String name = JOptionPane.showInputDialog("What is your name?");
        System.out.println(name);
        System.exit(0);
    }
}
```

Then modify the program to print "Hello, *name*!", displaying the name that the user typed in.

PROGRAMMING PROJECTS

Project 1.1. This project builds on Exercises P1.7 and P1.8. Your program should show a sequence of two dialog boxes:

- First, an input dialog box that asks: "What would you like me to do?"
- Then a message dialog box that says: "I'm sorry, Dave. I'm afraid I can't do that."

This program ignores the user input. Extra credit if you read the user's name and customize the message.

ANSWERS TO SELF-CHECK QUESTIONS

1. A program that reads the data on the CD and sends output to the speakers and the screen.

2. A CD player can do one thing—play music CDs. It cannot execute programs.

3. No—the program simply executes the instruction sequences that the programmers have prepared in advance.

4. In secondary storage, typically a hard disk.

5. The central processing unit.

6. 21 100

7. No—a compiler is intended for programmers, to translate high-level programming instructions into machine code.

8. Safety and portability.

9. No one person can learn the entire library—it is too large.

10. Programs are stored in files, and files are stored in folders or directories.

11. You back up your files and folders.

12. `System.out.println("Hello,"); System.out.println("World!");`

13. Yes—the line starting with // is a comment, intended for human readers. The compiler ignores comments.

14. The printout is `My lucky number is12`. It would be a good idea to add a space after the `is`.

15. A compile-time error. The compiler will not know what to do with the word `display`.

16. You need to run the program and observe its behavior.

17. A sequence of random characters, some funny-looking. Class files contain virtual machine instructions that are encoded as binary numbers.

18. When a program has compiler errors, no class file is produced, and there is nothing to run.

Chapter 2

Using Objects

CHAPTER GOALS

- To learn about variables
- To understand the concepts of classes and objects
- To be able to call methods
- To learn about parameters and return values
- To be able to browse the API documentation
- To realize the difference between objects and object references

Most useful programs don't just manipulate numbers and strings. Instead, they deal with data items that are more complex and that more closely represent entities in the real world. Examples of these data items include bank accounts, employee records, and graphical shapes.

The Java language is ideally suited for designing and manipulating such data items, or *objects*. In Java, you define *classes* that describe the behavior of these objects. In this chapter, you will learn how to manipulate objects that belong to predefined classes. This knowledge will prepare you for the next chapter in which you will learn how to implement your own classes.

CHAPTER CONTENTS

2.1 Types and Variables

> In Java, every value
> has a type.

In Java, every value has a *type*. For example, `"Hello, World"` has the type `String`, the object `System.out` has the type `PrintStream`, and the number 13 has the type `int` (an abbreviation for "integer"). The type tells you what you can do with the values. You can call `println` on any object of type `PrintStream`. You can compute the sum or product of any two integers.

You often want to store values so that you can use them at a later time. To remember an object, you need to hold it in a *variable*. A variable is a storage location in the computer's memory that has a *type*, a *name*, and a *contents*. For example, here we declare three variables:

```
String greeting = "Hello, World!";
PrintStream printer = System.out;
int luckyNumber = 13;
```

> You use variables to store
> values that you want to
> use at a later time.

The first variable is called `greeting`. It can be used to store `String` values, and it is set to the value `"Hello, World!"`. The second variable stores a `PrintStream` value, and the third stores an integer.

Variables can be used in place of the objects that they store:

```
printer.println(greeting); // Same as System.out.println("Hello, World!")
printer.println(luckyNumber); // Same as System.out.println(13)
```

When you declare your own variables, you need to make two decisions.

- What type should you use use for the variable?
- What name should you give the variable?

SYNTAX 2.1 Variable Definition

typeName *variableName* = *value*;
or
typeName *variableName*;

Example:
```
String greeting = "Hello, Dave!";
```

Purpose:
To define a new variable of a particular type and optionally supply an initial value

---

The type depends on the intended use. If you need to store a string, use the String type for your variable.

It is an error to store a value whose class does not match the type of the variable. For example, the following is an error:

```
String greeting = 13; // ERROR: Types don't match
```

You cannot use a String variable to store an integer. The compiler checks type mismatches to protect you from errors.

When deciding on a name for a variable, you should make a choice that describes the purpose of the variable. For example, the variable name greeting is a better choice than the name g.

> Identifiers for variables, methods, and classes are composed of letters, digits, and underscore characters.

An *identifier* is the name of a variable, method, or class. Java imposes the following rules for identifiers:

- Identifiers can be made up of letters, digits, and the underscore (_) and dollar sign ($) characters. They cannot start with a digit, though. For example, greeting1 is legal but 1greeting is not.

- You cannot use other symbols such as ? or %. For example, hello! is not a legal identifier.

- Spaces are not permitted inside identifiers. Therefore, lucky number is not legal.

- Furthermore, you cannot use *reserved words*, such as public, as names; these words are reserved exclusively for their special Java meanings.

- Identifiers are also *case sensitive*; that is, greeting and Greeting are *different*.

> By convention, variable names should start with a lowercase letter.

These are firm rules of the Java language. If you violate one of them, the compiler will report an error. Moreover, there are a couple of *conventions* that you should follow so that other programmers will find your programs easy to read:

- Variable and method names should start with a lowercase letter. It is OK to use an occasional uppercase letter, such as luckyNumber. This mixture of lowercase and uppercase letters is sometimes called "camel case" because the uppercase letters stick out like the humps of a camel.

- Class names should start with an uppercase letter. For example, Greeting would be an appropriate name for a class, but not for a variable.

If you violate these conventions, the compiler won't complain, but you will confuse other programmers who read your code.

SELF CHECK

1. What is the type of the values 0 and "0"?
2. Which of the following are legal identifiers?

```
Greeting1
g
void
101dalmatians
Hello, World
<greeting>
```

3. Define a variable to hold your name. Use camel case in the variable name.

2.2 The Assignment Operator

> Use the assignment operator (=) to change the value of a variable.

You can change the value of an existing variable with the assignment operator (=). For example, consider the variable definition

```
int luckyNumber = 13;  ❶
```

If you want to change the value of the variable, simply assign the new value:

```
luckyNumber = 12;  ❷
```

The assignment replaces the original value of the variable (see Figure 1).

In the Java programming language, the = operator denotes an *action*, to replace the value of a variable. This usage differs from the traditional usage of the = symbol, as a statement about equality.

It is an error to use a variable that has never had a value assigned to it. For example, the sequence of statements

```
int luckyNumber;
System.out.println(luckyNumber);    // ERROR—uninitialized variable
```

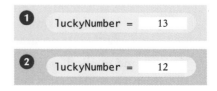

Figure 1
Assigning a New Value to a Variable

Figure 2
An Uninitialized Object Variable   luckyNumber =

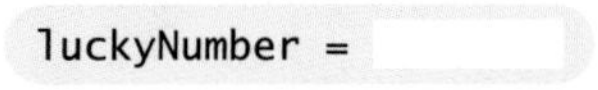

is an error. The compiler will complain about an "uninitialized variable" when you use a variable that has never been assigned a value. (See Figure 2.)

The remedy is to assign a value to the variable before you use it:

> All variables must be initialized before you access them.

```
int luckyNumber;
luckyNumber = 13;
System.out.println(luckyNumber); // OK
```

Or, even better, initialize the variable when you define it.

```
int luckyNumber = 13;
System.out.println(luckyNumber); // OK
```

SYNTAX 2.2 **Assignment**
---

variableName = *value*;

Example:

```
luckyNumber = 12;
```

Purpose:

To assign a new value to a previously defined variable

SELF CHECK

4. Is 12 = 12 a valid expression in the Java language?
5. How do you change the value of the greeting variable to "Hello, Nina!"?

2.3 Objects, Classes, and Methods

> Objects are entities in your program that you manipulate by calling methods.

An *object* is an entity that you can manipulate in your program. You don't usually know how the object is organized internally. However, the object has well-defined behavior, and that is what matters to us when we use it.

You manipulate an object by calling one or more of its *methods*. A method consists of a sequence of instructions that accesses the internal data. When you call the method, you do not know exactly what those instructions are, but you do know the purpose of the method.

> A method is a sequence of instructions that accesses the data of an object.

For example, you saw in Chapter 1 that System.out refers to an object. You manipulate it by calling the println method. When the

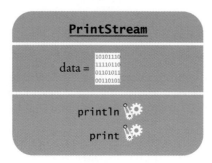

Figure 3   Representation of the System.out Object

println method is called, some activities occur inside the object, and the ultimate effect is that text appears in the console window. You don't know how that happens, and that's OK. What matters is that the method carries out the work that you requested.

Figure 3 shows a representation of the System.out object. The internal data is symbolized by a sequence of zeroes and ones. Think of each method (symbolized by the gears) as a piece of machinery that carries out its assigned task.

In Chapter 1, you encountered two objects:

- System.out
- "Hello, World!"

These objects belong to different *classes*. The System.out object belongs to the class PrintStream. The "Hello, World!" object belongs to the class String. A class specifies the methods that you can apply to its objects.

> A class defines the methods that you can apply to its objects.

You can use the println method with any object that belongs to the PrintStream class. System.out is one such object. It is possible to obtain other objects of the PrintStream class. For example, you can construct a PrintStream object to send output to a file. However, we won't discuss files until Chapter 16.

Just as the PrintStream class provides methods such as println and print for its objects, the String class provides methods that you can apply to String objects. One of them is the length method. The length method counts the number of characters in a string. You can apply that method to any object of type String. For example, the sequence of statements

```
String greeting = "Hello, World!";
int n = greeting.length();
```

sets n to the number of characters in the string object "Hello, World!". After the instructions in the length method are executed, n is set to 13. (The quotation marks are not part of the string, and the length method does not count them.)

The length method—unlike the println method—requires no input inside the parentheses. However, the length method yields an output, namely the character count.

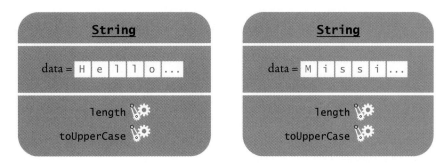

Figure 4 A Representation of Two String Objects

In the next section, you will see in greater detail how to supply method inputs and obtain method outputs.

Let us look at another method of the String class. When you apply the toUpperCase method to a String object, the method creates another String object that contains the characters of the original string, with lowercase letters converted to uppercase. For example, the sequence of statements

```
String river = "Mississippi";
String bigRiver = river.toUpperCase();
```

sets bigRiver to the String object "MISSISSIPPI".

When you apply a method to an object, you must make sure that the method is defined in the appropriate class. For example, it is an error to call

```
System.out.length(); // This method call is an error
```

The PrintStream class (to which System.out belongs) has no length method.

> The public interface of a class specifies what you can do with its objects. The hidden implementation describes how these actions are carried out.

Let us summarize. In Java, *every object belongs to a class. The class defines the methods for the objects.* For example, the String class defines the length and toUpperCase methods (as well as other methods—you will learn about most of them in Chapter 4). The methods form the *public interface* of the class, telling you what you can do with the objects of the class. A class also defines a *private implementation*, describing the data inside its objects and the instructions for its methods. Those details are hidden from the programmers who use objects and call methods.

Figure 4 shows two objects of the String class. Each object stores its own data (drawn as boxes that contain characters). Both objects support the same set of methods—the interface that is specified by the String class.

SELF CHECK

6. How can you compute the length of the string "Mississippi"?

7. How can you print out the uppercase version of "Hello, World!"?

8. Is it legal to call river.println()? Why or why not?

2.4 Method Parameters and Return Values

In this section, we will examine how to provide inputs into a method, and how to obtain the output of the method.

> A parameter is an input to a method.

Some methods require inputs that give details about the work that they need to do. For example, the println method has an input: the string that should be printed. Computer scientists use the technical term *parameter* for method inputs. We say that the string greeting is a parameter of the method call

```
System.out.println(greeting)
```

Figure 5 illustrates passing of the parameter to the method.

> The implicit parameter of a method call is the object on which the method is invoked.

Technically speaking, the greeting parameter is an *explicit parameter* of the println method. The object on which you invoke the method is also considered a parameter of the method call, called the *implicit parameter*. For example, System.out is the implicit parameter of the method call

```
System.out.println(greeting)
```

Some methods require multiple explicit parameters, others don't require any explicit parameters at all. An example of the latter is the length method of the String class (see Figure 6). All the information that the length method requires to do its job—namely, the character sequence of the string—is stored in the implicit parameter object.

> The return value of a method is a result that the method has computed for use by the code that called it.

The length method differs from the println method in another way: it has an output. We say that the method *returns a value*, namely the number of characters in the string. You can store the return value in a variable:

```
int n = greeting.length();
```

You can also use the return value as a parameter of another method:

```
System.out.println(greeting.length());
```

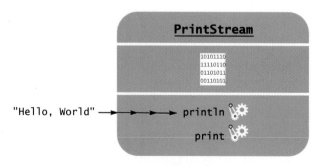

Figure 5   Passing a Parameter to the println Method

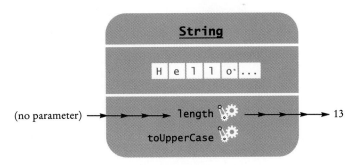

Figure 6 Invoking the `length` Method on a `String` Object

The method call `greeting.length()` returns a value—the integer 13. The return value becomes a parameter of the `println` method. Figure 7 shows the process.

Not all methods return values. One example is the `println` method. The `println` method interacts with the operating system, causing characters to appear in a window. But it does not return a value to the code that calls it.

Let us analyze a more complex method call. Here, we will call the `replace` method of the `String` class. The `replace` method carries out a search-and-replace operation, similar to that of a word processor. For example, the call

```
river.replace("issipp", "our")
```

constructs a new string that is obtained by replacing all occurrences of `"issipp"` in `"Mississippi"` with `"our"`. (In this situation, there was only one replacement.) The method returns the string object `"Missouri"` (which you can save in a variable or pass to another method).

As Figure 8 shows, this method call has

- one implicit parameter: the string `"Mississippi"`
- two explicit parameters: the strings `"issipp"` and `"our"`
- a return value: the string `"Missouri"`

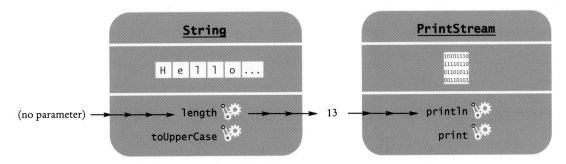

Figure 7 Passing the Result of a Method Call to Another Method

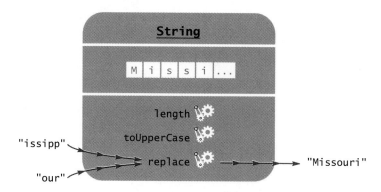

Figure 8   Calling the `replace` Method

When a method is defined in a class, the definition specifies the types of the explicit parameters and the return value. For example, the `String` class defines the `length` method as

```
public int length()
```

That is, there are no explicit parameters, and the return value has the type `int`. (For now, all the methods that we consider will be "public" methods—see Chapter 13 for more restricted methods.)

The type of the implicit parameter is the class that defines the method—`String` in our case. It is not mentioned in the method definition—hence the term "implicit".

The `replace` method is defined as

```
public String replace(String target, String replacement)
```

To call the `replace` method, you supply two explicit parameters, `target` and `replacement`, which both have type `String`. The returned value is another string.

When a method returns no value, the return type is declared with the reserved word `void`. For example, the `PrintStream` class defines the `println` method as

```
public void println(String output)
```

> A method name is overloaded if a class has more than one method with the same name (but different parameter types).

Occasionally, a class defines two methods with the same name and different explicit parameter types. For example, the `PrintStream` class defines a second method, also called `println`, as

```
public void println(int output)
```

That method is used to print an integer value. We say that the `println` name is *overloaded* because it refers to more than one method.

SELF CHECK

9. What are the implicit parameters, explicit parameters, and return values in the method call `river.length()`?

10. What is the result of the call `river.replace("p", "s")`?

11. What is the result of the call greeting.replace("World", "Dave").length()?
12. How is the toUpperCase method defined in the String class?

2.5 Number Types

> The double type denotes floating-point numbers that can have fractional parts.

Java has separate types for *integers* and *floating-point numbers*. Integers are whole numbers; floating-point numbers can have fractional parts. For example, 13 is an integer and 1.3 is a floating-point number.

The name "floating-point" describes the representation of the number in the computer as a sequence of the significant digits and an indication of the position of the decimal point. For example, the numbers 13000, 1.3, 0.00013 all have the same decimal digits: 13. When a floating-point number is multiplied or divided by 10, only the position of the decimal point changes; it "floats". This representation is related to the "scientific" notation 1.3×10^{-4}. (Actually, the computer represents numbers in base 2, not base 10, but the principle is the same.)

If you need to process numbers with a fractional part, you should use the type called double, which stands for "double precision floating-point number". Think of a number in double format as any number that can appear in the display panel of a calculator, such as 1.3 or –0.333333333.

Do not use commas when you write numbers in Java. For example, 13,000 must be written as 13000. To write numbers in exponential notation in Java, use the notation E*n* instead of "$\times 10^{n}$". For example, 1.3×10^{-4} is written as 1.3E-4.

You may wonder why Java has separate integer and floating-point number types. Pocket calculators don't need a separate integer type; they use floating-point numbers for all calculations. However, integers have several advantages over floating-point numbers. They take less storage space, are processed faster, and don't cause rounding errors. You will want to use the int type for quantities that can never have fractional parts, such as the length of a string. Use the double type for quantities that can have fractional parts, such as a grade point average.

There are several other number types in Java that are not as commonly used. We will discuss these types in Chapter 4. For most practical purposes, however, the int and double types are all you need for processing numbers.

> In Java, numbers are not objects and number types are not classes.

In Java, the number types (int, double, and the less commonly used types) are *primitive types*, not classes. Numbers are not objects. The number types have no methods.

However, you can combine numbers with operators such as + and -, as in 10 + n or n - 1. To multiply two numbers, use the * operator. For example, $10 \times n$ is written as 10 * n.

> Numbers can be combined by arithmetic operators such as +, -, and *.

As in mathematics, the * operator binds more strongly than the + operator. That is, x + y * 2 means the sum of x and y * 2. If you want to multiply the sum of x and y with 2, use parentheses:

```
(x + y) * 2
```

13. Which number type would you use for storing the area of a circle?

14. Why is the expression 13.println() an error?

15. Write an expression to compute the average of the values x and y.

2.6 Constructing Objects

Most Java programs will want to work on a variety of objects. In this section, you will see how to *construct* new objects. This allows you to go beyond string objects and the predefined System.out object.

To learn about object construction, let us turn to another class: the Rectangle class in the Java class library. Objects of type Rectangle describe rectangular shapes—see Figure 9. These objects are useful for a variety of purposes. You can assemble rectangles into bar charts, and you can program simple games by moving rectangles inside a window.

Note that a Rectangle object isn't a rectangular shape—it is an object that contains a set of numbers. The numbers *describe* the rectangle (see Figure 10). Each rectangle is described by the *x*- and *y*-coordinates of its top-left corner, its width, and its height.

Figure 9
Rectangular Shapes

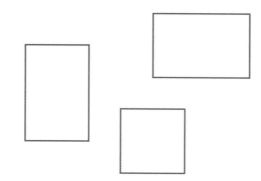

Rectangle	
x =	5
y =	10
width =	20
height =	30

Rectangle	
x =	35
y =	30
width =	20
height =	20

Rectangle	
x =	45
y =	0
width =	30
height =	20

Figure 10
Rectangle Objects

It is very important that you understand this distinction. In the computer, a Rectangle object is a block of memory that holds four numbers, for example $x = 5$, $y = 10$, *width* $= 20$, *height* $= 30$. In the imagination of the programmer who uses a Rectangle object, the object describes a geometric figure.

> Use the new operator, followed by a class name and parameters, to construct new objects.

To make a new rectangle, you need to specify the *x*, *y*, *width*, and *height* values. Then *invoke the* new *operator*, specifying the name of the class and the parameters that are required for constructing a new object. For example, you can make a new rectangle with its top-left corner at (5, 10), width 20, and height 30 as follows:

```
new Rectangle(5, 10, 20, 30)
```

Here is what happens in detail.

1. The new operator makes a Rectangle object.
2. It uses the parameters (in this case, 5, 10, 20, and 30) to initialize the data of the object.
3. It returns the object.

Usually the output of the new operator is stored in a variable. For example,

```
Rectangle box = new Rectangle(5, 10, 20, 30);
```

The process of creating a new object is called *construction*. The four values 5, 10, 20, and 30 are called the *construction parameters*. Note that the new expression is *not* a complete statement. You use the value of a new expression just like a method return value: Assign it to a variable or pass it to another method.

Some classes let you construct objects in multiple ways. For example, you can also obtain a Rectangle object by supplying no construction parameters at all (but you must still supply the parentheses):

```
new Rectangle()
```

This expression constructs a (rather useless) rectangle with its top-left corner at the origin (0, 0), width 0, and height 0.

SYNTAX 2.3 Object Construction

new *ClassName(parameters)*

Example:

```
new Rectangle(5, 10, 20, 30)
new Rectangle()
```

Purpose:

To construct a new object, initialize it with the construction parameters, and return a reference to the constructed object

SELF CHECK

16. How do you construct a square with center (100, 100) and side length 20?
17. What does the following statement print?

    ```
    System.out.println(new Rectangle().getWidth());
    ```

COMMON ERROR 2.1

Trying to Invoke a Constructor Like a Method

Constructors are not methods. You can only use a constructor with the `new` operator, not to reinitialize an existing object:

```
box.Rectangle(20, 35, 20, 30); // Error—can't reinitialize object
```

The remedy is simple: Make a new object and overwrite the current one.

```
box = new Rectangle(20, 35, 20, 30); // OK
```

2.7 Accessor and Mutator Methods

An accessor method does not change the state of its implicit parameter. A mutator method changes the state.

In this section we introduce a useful terminology for the methods of a class. A method that accesses an object and returns some information about it, without changing the object, is called an *accessor* method. In contrast, a method whose purpose is to modify the state of an object is called a *mutator* method.

For example, the `length` method of the `String` class is an accessor method. It returns information about a string, namely its length. But it doesn't modify the string at all when counting the characters.

The `Rectangle` class has a number of accessor methods. The `getX`, `getY`, `getWidth`, and `getHeight` methods return the *x*- and *y*-coordinates of the top-left corner, the width, and the height values. For example,

```
double width = box.getWidth();
```

Now let us consider a mutator method. Programs that manipulate rectangles frequently need to move them around, for example, to display animations. The `Rectangle` class has a method for that purpose, called `translate`. (Mathematicians use the term "translation" for a rigid motion of the plane.) This method moves a rectangle by a certain distance in the *x*- and *y*-directions. The method call,

```
box.translate(15, 25);
```

moves the rectangle by 15 units in the *x*-direction and 25 units in the *y*-direction (see Figure 11). Moving a rectangle doesn't change its width or height, but it changes the top-left corner. Afterwards, the top-left corner is at (20, 35).

This method is a mutator because it modifies the implicit parameter object.

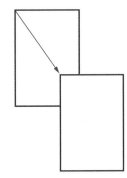

Figure 11
Using the `translate` Method to Move a Rectangle

SELF CHECK

18. Is the `toUpperCase` method of the `String` class an accessor or a mutator?

19. Which call to `translate` is needed to move the box rectangle so that its top-left corner is the origin (0, 0)?

2.8 Implementing a Test Program

In this section, we will implement a simple program that tests the behavior of objects. As with the `HelloTester` program of Chapter 1, the test program performs the following steps:

1. Provide a new class.

2. Supply a `main` method.

3. Inside the `main` method, construct one or more objects.

4. Apply methods to the objects.

5. Display the results of the method calls.

Whenever you write a program to test your own classes, you need to follow these steps as well.

> Java classes are grouped into packages. Use the `import` statement to use classes that are defined in other packages.

For this program, we need to carry out another step: We need to *import* the `Rectangle` class from a *package*. A package is a collection of classes with a related purpose. All classes in the standard library are contained in packages. The `Rectangle` class belongs to the package `java.awt` (where awt is an abbreviation for "Abstract Windowing Toolkit"), which contains many classes for drawing windows and graphical shapes.

To use the `Rectangle` class from the `java.awt` package, simply place the following line at the top of your program:

```
import java.awt.Rectangle;
```

Why didn't you have to import the `System` and `String` classes that were used in the `HelloTester` program? Because the `System` and `String` classes are in the `java.lang` package, and all classes from this package are automatically imported, so you never need to import them yourself.

SYNTAX 2.4 Importing a Class from a Package

---

import *packageName*.*ClassName*;

Example:

import java.awt.Rectangle;

Purpose:

To import a class from a package for use in a program

Here is a complete program that tests the moving of a rectangle.

File MoveTester.java

```
1   import java.awt.Rectangle;
2
3   public class MoveTester
4   {
5      public static void main(String[] args)
6      {
7         Rectangle box = new Rectangle(5, 10, 20, 30);
8
9         // Move the rectangle
10        box.translate(15, 25);
11
12        // Print information about the moved rectangle
13        System.out.println("After moving, the top-left corner is:");
14        System.out.println(box.getX());
15        System.out.println(box.getY());
16     }
17  }
```

Output

```
After moving, the top-left corner is:
20
35
```

SELF CHECK

20. The Random class is defined in the java.util package. What do you need to do in order to use that class in your program?

21. Why doesn't the MoveTester program print the width and height of the rectangle?

ADVANCED TOPIC 2.1

Testing Classes in an Interactive Environment

Some development environments are specifically designed to help students explore objects without having to provide tester classes. These environments can be very helpful for gaining insight into the behavior of objects, and for promoting object-oriented thinking. The BlueJ environment (shown in Figure 12) displays objects as blobs in a workbench. You can construct new objects, put them on the workbench, invoke methods, and see the return values, all without writing a line of code. You can download BlueJ at no charge from [2]. Another excellent environment for interactively exploring objects is Dr. Java [3].

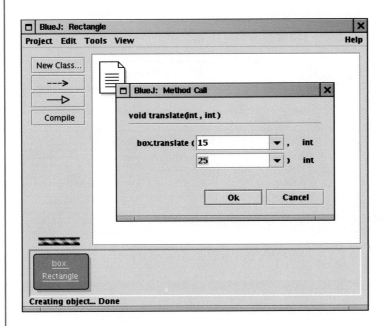

Figure 12   Testing a Method Call in BlueJ

2.9 The API Documentation

The classes and methods of the Java library are listed in the *API documentation*. The API is the "application programming interface". A programmer who uses the Java classes to put together a computer program (or *application*) is an *application programmer*. That's you. In contrast, the programmers who designed and implemented the library classes such as PrintStream and Rectangle are *system programmers*.

> The API (Application
> Programming Interface)
> documentation lists the
> classes and methods of
> the Java library.

You can find the API documentation on the Web [1]. Point your web browser to http://java.sun.com/j2se/1.5/docs/api/index.html. Alternatively, you can download and install the API documentation onto your own computer—see Productivity Hint 2.1.

The API documentation documents all classes in the Java library—there are thousands of them (see Figure 13). Most of the classes are rather specialized, and only a few are of interest to the beginning programmer.

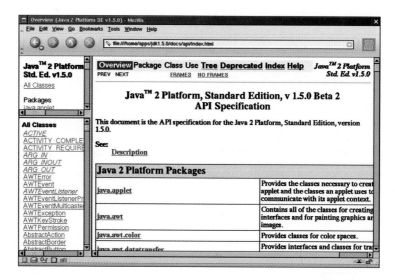

Figure 13   The API Documentation of the Standard Java Library

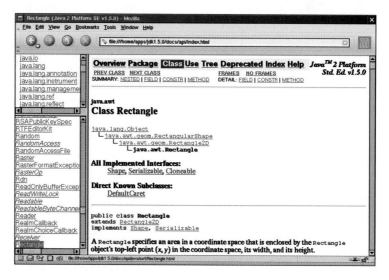

Figure 14   The API Documentation for the Rectangle Class

Locate the Rectangle link in the left pane, preferably by using the search function of your browser. Click on the link, and the right pane shows all the features of the Rectangle class (see Figure 14).

The API documentation for each class starts out with a section that describes the purpose of the class. Then come summary tables for the constructors and methods (see Figure 15). Click on the link of a method to get a detailed description (see Figure 16).

As you can see, the Rectangle class has quite a few methods. While occasionally intimidating for the beginning programmer, this is a strength of the standard library.

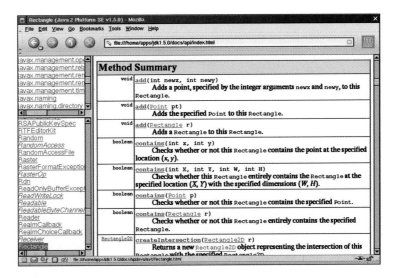

Figure 15 The Method Summary for the Rectangle Class

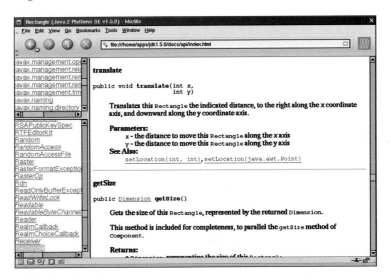

Figure 16 The API Documentation of the translate Method

If you ever need to do a computation involving rectangles, chances are that there is a method that does all the work for you.

Appendix C contains an abbreviated version of the API documentation. You may find the abbreviated documentation easier to use than the full documentation. It is fine if you rely on the abbreviated documentation for your first programs, but you should eventually move on to the real thing.

SELF CHECK

22. Look at the API documentation of the String class. Which method would you use to obtain the string "hello, world!" from the string "Hello, World!"?

23. In the API documentation of the String class, look at the description of the trim method. What is the result of applying trim to the string " Hello, Space ! "? (Note the spaces in the string.)

PRODUCTIVITY HINT 2.1

Don't Memorize—Use Online Help

The Java library has thousands of classes and methods. It is neither necessary nor useful trying to memorize them. Instead, you should become familiar with using the API documentation. Since you will need to use the API documentation all the time, it is best to download and install it onto your computer, particularly if your computer is not always connected to the Internet. You can download the documentation from http://java.sun.com/j2se/downloads/index.html.

2.10 Object References

In Java, a variable whose type is a class does not actually hold an object. It merely holds the memory *location* of an object. The object itself is stored elsewhere—see Figure 17.

> An object reference describes the location of an object.

We use the technical term *object reference* to denote the memory location of an object. When a variable contains the memory location of an object, we say that it *refers* to an object. For example, after the statement

```
Rectangle box = new Rectangle(5, 10, 20, 30);
```

the variable box refers to the Rectangle object that the new operator constructed. Technically speaking, the new operator returned a reference to the new object, and that reference is stored in the box variable.

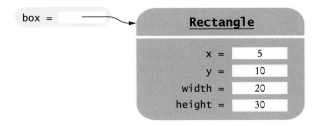

Figure 17 An Object Variable Containing an Object Reference

It is very important that you remember that the box variable *does not contain* the object. It *refers* to the object. You can have two object variables refer to the same object:

```
Rectangle box2 = box;
```

Now you can access the same Rectangle object both as box and as box2, as shown in Figure 18.

> Multiple object variables can contain references to the same object.

However, number variables actually store numbers. When you define

```
int luckyNumber = 13;
```

then the luckyNumber variable holds the number 13, not a reference to the number (see Figure 19).

You can see the difference between number variables and object variables when you make a copy of a variable. When you copy a primitive type value, the original and the copy of the number are independent values. But when you copy an object reference, both the original and the copy are references to the same object.

> Number variables store numbers. Object variables store references.

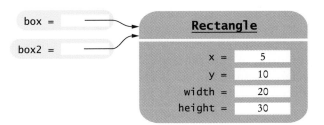

Figure 18 Two Object Variables Referring to the Same Object

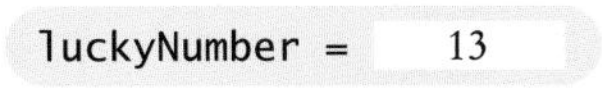

```
luckyNumber =    13
```

Figure 19 A Number Variable Stores a Number

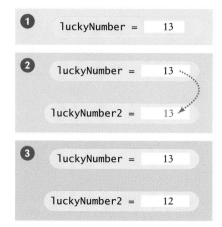

Figure 20
Copying Numbers

Consider the following code, which copies a number and then changes the copy (see Figure 20):

```
int luckyNumber = 13; ❶
int luckyNumber2 = luckyNumber; ❷
luckyNumber2 = 12; ❸
```

Now the variable `luckyNumber` contains the value 13, and `luckyNumber2` contains 12.

Now consider the seemingly analogous code with `Rectangle` objects.

```
Rectangle box = new Rectangle(5, 10, 20, 30); ❶
Rectangle box2 = box; // See Figure 21 ❷
box2.translate(15, 25); ❸
```

Since `box` and `box2` refer to the same rectangle after step ❷, both variables refer to the moved rectangle after the call to the `translate` method.

There is a reason for the difference between numbers and objects. In the computer, each number requires a small amount of memory. But objects can be very large. It is far more efficient to only manipulate the memory location.

Frankly speaking, most programmers don't worry too much about the difference between objects and object references. Much of the time, you will have the correct intuition when you think of "the object `box`" rather than the technically more accurate "the object reference stored in `box`". The difference between objects and object references only becomes apparent when you have multiple variables that refer to the same object.

SELF CHECK

24. What is the effect of the assignment `greeting2 = greeting`?
25. After calling `greeting2.toUpperCase()`, what are the contents of `greeting` and `greeting2`?

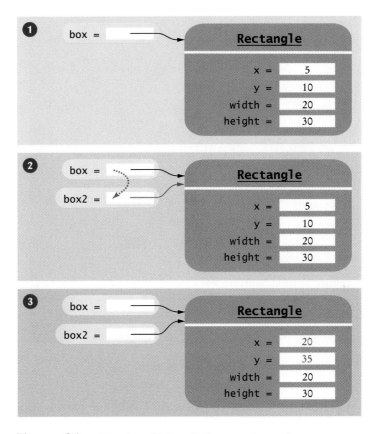

Figure 21 Copying Object References

RANDOM FACT 2.1

Mainframes—When Dinosaurs Ruled the Earth

When International Business Machines Corporation (IBM), a successful manufacturer of punched-card equipment for tabulating data, first turned its attention to designing computers in the early 1950s, its planners assumed that there was a market for perhaps 50 such devices, for installation by the government, the military, and a few of the country's largest corporations. Instead, they sold about 1,500 machines of their System 650 model and went on to build and sell more powerful computers.

The so-called mainframe computers of the 1950s, 1960s, and 1970s were huge. They filled rooms, which had to be climate-controlled to protect the delicate equipment (see Figure 22). Today, because of miniaturization technology, even mainframes are getting smaller, but they are still very expensive. (At the time of this writing, the cost for a midrange IBM 3090 is approximately 4 million dollars.)

These huge and expensive systems were an immediate success when they first appeared, because they replaced many roomfuls of even more expensive employees, who had previously performed the tasks by hand. Few of these computers do any exciting computations.

Figure 22   A Mainframe Computer

They keep mundane information, such as billing records or airline reservations; they just keep lots of them.

IBM was not the first company to build mainframe computers; that honor belongs to the Univac Corporation. However, IBM soon became the major player, partially because of technical excellence and attention to customer needs and partially because it exploited its strengths and structured its products and services in a way that made it difficult for customers to mix them with those of other vendors. In the 1960s, IBM's competitors, the so-called "Seven Dwarfs"—GE, RCA, Univac, Honeywell, Burroughs, Control Data, and NCR—fell on hard times. Some went out of the computer business altogether, while others tried unsuccessfully to combine their strengths by merging their computer operations. It was generally predicted that they would eventually all fail. It was in this atmosphere that the U.S. government brought an antitrust suit against IBM in 1969. The suit went to trial in 1975 and dragged on until 1982, when the Reagan Administration abandoned it, declaring it "without merit".

Of course, by then the computing landscape had changed completely. Just as the dinosaurs gave way to smaller, nimbler creatures, three new waves of computers had appeared: the minicomputers, workstations, and microcomputers, all engineered by new companies, not the Seven Dwarfs. Today, the importance of mainframes in the marketplace has diminished, and IBM, while still a large and resourceful company, no longer dominates the computer market.

Mainframes are still in use today for two reasons. They still excel at handling large data volumes. More importantly, the programs that control the business data have been refined over the last 20 or more years, fixing one problem at a time. Moving these programs to less expensive computers, with different languages and operating systems, is difficult and error-prone. In the 1990s, Sun Microsystems, a leading manufacturer of workstations and servers—and the inventor of Java—was eager to prove that its mainframe system could be "downsized" and replaced by its own equipment. Sun eventually succeeded, but it took over five years—far longer than it expected.

CHAPTER SUMMARY

1. In Java, every value has a type.

2. You use variables to store values that you want to use at a later time.

3. Identifiers for variables, methods, and classes are composed of letters, digits, and underscore characters.

4. By convention, variable names should start with a lowercase letter.

5. Use the assignment operator (=) to change the value of a variable.

6. All variables must be initialized before you access them.

7. Objects are entities in your program that you manipulate by calling methods.

8. A method is a sequence of instructions that accesses the data of an object.

9. A class defines the methods that you can apply to its objects.

10. The public interface of a class specifies what you can do with its objects. The hidden implementation describes how these actions are carried out.

11. A parameter is an input to a method.

12. The implicit parameter of a method call is the object on which the method is invoked.

13. The return value of a method is a result that the method has computed for use by the code that called it.

14. A method name is overloaded if a class has more than one method with the same name (but different parameter types).

15. The `double` type denotes floating-point numbers that can have fractional parts.

16. In Java, numbers are not objects and number types are not classes.

17. Numbers can be combined by arithmetic operators such as +, -, and *.

18. Use the `new` operator, followed by a class name and parameters, to construct new objects.

19. An accessor method does not change the state of its implicit parameter. A mutator method changes the state.

20. Java classes are grouped into packages. Use the `import` statement to use classes that are defined in other packages.

21. The API (Application Programming Interface) documentation lists the classes and methods of the Java library.

22. An object reference describes the location of an object.

23. Multiple object variables can contain references to the same object.

24. Number variables store numbers. Object variables store references.

FURTHER READING

1. `http://java.sun.com/j2se/1.5/docs/api/index.html`　The documentation of the Java API.

2. `http://www.bluej.org`　The BlueJ development environment.

3. `http://drjava.sourceforge.net`　The Dr. Java development environment.

CLASSES, OBJECTS, AND METHODS INTRODUCED IN THIS CHAPTER

```
java.lang.String
    length
    replace
    toLowerCase
    toUpperCase
java.awt.Rectangle
    translate
    getX
    getY
    getWidth
    getHeight
```

REVIEW EXERCISES

Exercise R2.1. Explain the difference between an object and an object reference.

Exercise R2.2. Explain the difference between an object and an object variable.

Exercise R2.3. Explain the difference between an object and a class.

Exercise R2.4. Give the Java code for an *object* of class Rectangle and for an *object variable* of class Rectangle.

Exercise R2.5. Explain the difference between the = symbol in Java and in mathematics.

Exercise R2.6. Give Java code to construct the following objects:

a. A rectangle with center (100, 100) and all side lengths equal to 50

b. A string "Hello, Dave!"

Create objects, not object variables.

Exercise R2.7. Repeat Exercise R2.6, but now define object variables that are initialized with the required objects.

Exercise R2.8. Find the errors in the following statements:

a. `Rectangle r = (5, 10, 15, 20);`

b. `double width = Rectangle(5, 10, 15, 20).getWidth();`

c. `Rectangle r;`
   `r.translate(15, 25);`

d. `r = new Rectangle();`
   `r.translate("far, far away!");`

Exercise R2.9. Name two accessor methods and two mutator methods of the Rectangle class.

Exercise R2.10. Look into the API documentation of the Rectangle class and locate the method

```
void add(int newx, int newy)
```

Read through the method documentation. Then determine the result of the following statements:

```
Rectangle box = new Rectangle(5, 10, 20, 30);
box.add(0, 0);
```

If you are not sure, write a small test program or use BlueJ.

Exercise R2.11. Find an overloaded method of the String class.

Exercise R2.12. Find an overloaded method of the Rectangle class.

PROGRAMMING EXERCISES

Exercise P2.1. Write a program that constructs a Rectangle object and then computes and prints its area. Use the getWidth and getHeight methods.

Exercise P2.2. Write a program that constructs a Rectangle object and then computes and prints its perimeter. Use the getWidth and getHeight methods.

Exercise P2.3. Write a program that constructs a `Rectangle` object, prints its location, and then translates and prints it three more times, so that, if the rectangles were drawn, they would form one large rectangle:

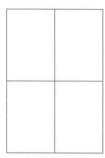

Exercise P2.4. The `intersection` method computes the *intersection* of two rectangles—that is, the rectangle that is formed by two overlapping rectangles:

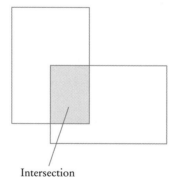

Intersection

You call this method as follows:

```
Rectangle r3 = r1.intersection(r2);
```

Write a program that constructs two rectangle objects, prints them, and then prints the rectangle object that describes the intersection. What happens when the rectangles do not overlap?

Exercise P2.5. In the Java library, a color is specified by its red, green, and blue components between 0 and 255. Write a program that constructs a `Color` object with red, green, and blue values of 50, 100, and 150. Then apply the `brighter` method and print the red, green, and blue values of the resulting color. (You won't actually see the color—see Programming Project 2.2 on how to display the color.)

Exercise P2.6. Repeat Exercise P2.5, but apply the `darker` method twice to the predefined object `Color.RED`.

Exercise P2.7. The `Random` class implements a *random number generator*, which produces sequences of numbers that appear to be random. To generate random integers, you construct an object of the `Random` class, and then apply the `nextInt` method. For example, the call `generator.nextInt(6)` gives you a random number between 0 and 5.

Write a program that uses the `Random` class to simulate the cast of a die, printing a random number between 1 and 6 every time that the program is run.

Exercise P2.8. Write a program that picks a combination in a lottery. In this lottery, players can choose 6 numbers (possibly repeated) between 1 and 49. (In a real lottery, repetitions aren't allowed, but we haven't yet discussed the programming constructs that would be required to deal with that problem.) Your program should print out a sentence such as "Play this combination—it'll make you rich!", followed by a lottery combination.

Exercise P2.9. Write a program that encodes a string by replacing all letters `"i"` with `"!"` and all letters `"s"` with `"$"`. Use the `replace` method. Demonstrate that you can correctly encode the string `"Mississippi"`.

Exercise P2.10. Write a program that switches the letters `"e"` and `"o"` in a string. Use the `replace` method repeatedly. Demonstrate that the string `"Hello, World!"` turns into `"Holle, Werld!"`

PROGRAMMING PROJECTS

Project 2.1. The `GregorianCalendar` class describes a point in time, as measured by the Gregorian calendar, the standard calendar that is commonly used throughout the world today. You construct a `GregorianCalendar` object from a year, month, and day of the month, like this:

```
GregorianCalendar cal = new GregorianCalendar(); // Today's date
GregorianCalendar eckertsBirthday = new GregorianCalendar(1919,
    Calendar.APRIL, 9);
```

Use constants `Calendar.JANUARY . . . Calendar.DECEMBER` to specify the month.

The add method can be used to add a number of days to a `GregorianCalendar` object:

```
cal.add(Calendar.DAY_OF_MONTH, 10); // Now cal is ten days from today
```

This is a mutator method—it changes the `cal` object.

The get method can be used to query a given `GregorianCalendar` object:

```
int dayOfMonth = cal.get(Calendar.DAY_OF_MONTH);
int month = cal.get(Calendar.MONTH);
int year = cal.get(Calendar.YEAR);
int weekday = cal.get(Calendar.DAY_OF_WEEK);
    // 1 is Sunday, 2 is Monday, ..., 7 is Saturday
```

Your task is to write a program that prints the following information:

- The date and weekday that is 100 days from today
- The weekday of your birthday
- The date that is 10,000 days from your birthday

Use the birthday of a computer scientist if you don't want to reveal your own birthday.

Project 2.2. Run the following program:

```java
import javax.swing.JFrame;
import javax.swing.JTextField;

public class FrameTester
{
   public static void main(String[] args)
   {
      JFrame frame = new JFrame();
      frame.setSize(200, 200);
      JTextField text = new JTextField("Hello, World!");
      text.setBackground(Color.PINK);
      frame.add(text);
      frame.setDefaultCloseOperation(JFrame.EXIT_ON_CLOSE);
      frame.setVisible(true);
   }
}
```

Modify the program as follows:

- Double the frame size
- Change the greeting to "Hello, *your name!*"
- Change the background color to pale green (see Exercise P2.5)

ANSWERS TO SELF-CHECK QUESTIONS

1. `int` and `String`
2. Only the first two are legal identifiers.
3. `String myName = "John Q. Public";`
4. No, the left-hand side of the = operator must be a variable.
5. `greeting = "Hello, Nina!";`
   Note that
   `String greeting = "Hello, Nina!";`
   is not the right answer—that statement defines a new variable.
6. `river.length()` or `"Mississippi".length()`
7. `System.out.println(greeting.toUpperCase());`
8. It is not legal. The variable `river` has type `String`. The `println` method is not a method of the `String` class.
9. The implicit parameter is `river`. There is no explicit parameter. The return value is 11.
10. `"Missississi"`

11. 12

12. As `public String toUpperCase()`, with no explicit parameter and return type `String`.

13. `double`

14. An `int` is not an object, and you cannot call a method on it.

15. `(x + y) * 0.5`

16. `new Rectangle(90, 90, 20, 20)`

17. 0

18. An accessor—it doesn't modify the original string but returns a new string with uppercase letters.

19. `box.translate(-5, -10)`, provided the method is called immediately after storing the new rectangle into `box`.

20. Add the statement `import java.util.Random;` at the top of your program.

21. Because the `translate` method doesn't modify the shape of the rectangle.

22. `toLowerCase`

23. `"Hello, Space !"`—only the leading and trailing spaces are trimmed.

24. Now `greeting` and `greeting2` both refer to the same `String` object.

25. Both variables still refer to the same string, and the string has not been modified. Recall that the `toUpperCase` method constructs a new string that contains uppercase characters, leaving the original string unchanged.

Chapter 3

Implementing Classes

CHAPTER GOALS

- To become familiar with the process of implementing classes
- To be able to implement simple methods
- To understand the purpose and use of constructors
- To understand how to access instance fields and local variables
- To appreciate the importance of documentation comments

In this chapter, you will learn how to design and implement your own classes. When designing a class, you need to decide upon the public interface of the class— that is, the methods through which you and programmers can manipulate the objects of the class. You then need to implement the methods. This step requires that you find a data representation for the objects, and supply the instructions for each method. Finally, you need to document your efforts so that other programmers can understand and use your creation.

CHAPTER CONTENTS

3.1 Black Boxes

When you lift the hood of a car, you will find a bewildering collection of mechanical components. You will probably recognize the motor and the tank for the windshield washer fluid. Your car mechanic will be able to identify many other components, such as the transmission and the electronic control module—the device that controls the timing of the spark plugs and the flow of gasoline into the motor. But ask your mechanic what is inside the electronic control module, and you will likely get a shrug.

It is a *black box*, something that magically does its thing. A car mechanic would never open the box—it contains electronic parts that can only be serviced at the factory. Of course, the device may have a color other than black, and it may not even be box-shaped. But engineers use the term "black box" to describe any device whose inner workings are hidden. Note that a black box is not totally mysterious. Its interaction with the outside world is well-defined. For example, the car mechanic can test that the engine control module sends the right firing signals to the spark plugs.

Why do car manufacturers put black boxes into cars? The black box greatly simplifies the work of the car mechanic, leading to lower repair costs. If the box fails, it is simply replaced with a new one. Before engine control modules were invented, gasoline flow into the engine was regulated by a mechanical device called a carburetor, a notoriously fussy mess of springs and latches that was expensive to adjust and repair.

Of course, for many drivers, the *entire car* is a "black box". Most drivers know nothing about its internal workings and never want to open the hood in the first place. The car has pedals, buttons, and a gas tank door. If you give it the right inputs, it does its thing, transporting you from here to there.

And for the engine control module manufacturer, the transistors and capacitors that go inside are black boxes, magically produced by an electronics component manufacturer.

In technical terms, a black box provides *encapsulation*, the hiding of unimportant details. Encapsulation is very important for human problem solving. A car mechanic is more efficient when the only decision is to test the electronic control module and to replace it when it fails, without having to think about the sensors and transistors inside. A driver is more efficient when the only worry is putting gas in the tank, not thinking about the motor or electronic control module inside.

However, there is another aspect to encapsulation. Somebody had to come up with the right *concept* for each particular black box. Why do the car parts manufacturers build electronic control modules and not another device? Why do the transportation device manufacturers build cars and not personal helicopters?

Concepts are discovered through the process of *abstraction*, taking away inessential features, until only the essence of the concept remains. For example, "car" is an abstraction, describing devices that transport small groups of people, traveling on the ground, and consuming gasoline. Is that the right abstraction? Or is a vehicle with an electric engine a "car"? We won't answer that question and instead move on to the significance of encapsulation and abstraction in computer science.

In old times, computer programs manipulated *primitive types* such as numbers and characters. As programs became more complex, they manipulated more and more of these primitive quantities, until programmers could no longer keep up. It was just too confusing to keep all that detail in one's head. As a result, programmers gave wrong instructions to their computers, and the computers faithfully executed them, yielding wrong answers.

Of course, the answer to this problem was obvious. Software developers soon learned to manage complexity. They encapsulated routine computations, forming software "black boxes" that can be put to work without worrying about the internals. They used the process of abstraction to invent data types that are at a higher level than numbers and characters.

At the time that this book is written, the most common approach for structuring computer programming is the *object-oriented* approach. The black boxes from which a program is manufactured are called objects. An object has an internal structure—perhaps just some numbers, perhaps other objects—and a well-defined behavior. Of course, the internal structure is hidden from the programmer who uses it. That programmer only learns about the object's behavior and then puts it to work in order to achieve a higher-level goal.

Who designs these objects? Other programmers! What do they contain? Other objects! This is where things get confusing for beginning students. In real life, the users of black boxes are quite different from their designers, and it is easy to understand the levels of abstraction (see Figure 1). With computer programs, there are also levels of abstraction (see Figure 2), but they are not as intuitive to the

Figure 1
Levels of Abstraction in Automotive Design

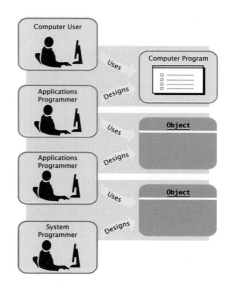

Figure 2
Levels of Abstraction in Software Design

uninitiated. To make matters potentially more confusing, you will often need to switch roles, being the designer of objects in the morning and the user of the same objects in the afternoon. In that regard, you will be like the builders of the first automobiles, who singlehandedly produced steering wheels and axles and then assembled their own creations into a car.

There is another challenging aspect of designing objects. Software is infinitely more flexible than hardware because it is unconstrained from physical limitations. Designers of electronic parts can exploit a limited number of physical effects to create transistors, capacitors, and the like. Transportation device manufacturers can't easily produce personal helicopters because of a whole host of physical limitations, such as fuel consumption and safety. But in software, anything goes. With few constraints from the outside world, you can design good and bad abstractions with equal facility. Understanding what makes good design is an important part of the education of a software engineer.

In Chapter 2, you learned to be an object user. You saw how to obtain objects, how to manipulate them, and how to assemble them into a program. In that chapter, your role was analogous to the automotive engineer who learns how to use an engine control module, and how to take advantage of its behavior in order to build a car.

In this chapter, you will move on to designing your own classes. You will see how to use the process of abstraction to define the behavior of previously unimagined objects. After the behavior has been defined, it needs to be *implemented*. You will learn additional Java programming techniques that enable your objects to carry out the desired behavior. In these sections, your role is analogous to the car parts engineer who designs the engine control module's behavior and then puts it together from transistors, capacitors, and other electronic parts.

1. In Chapters 1 and 2, you used System.out as a black box to cause output to appear on the screen. Who designed and implemented System.out?
2. Suppose you are working in a company that produces personal finance software. You are asked to design and implement a class for representing bank accounts. Who will be the users of your class?

3.2 Designing the Public Interface of a Class

In this section, we will discuss the process of designing a new class. Imagine that you are a member of a team that works on banking software. A fundamental concept in banking is a *bank account*. Your task is to design a BankAccount class that other programmers on the team can use.

> You use the process of abstraction to find the essential feature set for a class.

You use the process of abstraction to define exactly what a bank account is. Some features of bank accounts are essential (such as deposits), whereas others are not important (such as the gift that a customer may receive for opening a bank account).

Think about how an abstract painting strips away extraneous details and tries to represent only the essential features of an object. When you design a class, you also need to find the operations that are essential for manipulating objects in your program.

Here are what we consider the essential operations of a bank account:

- Deposit money
- Withdraw money
- Get the current balance

With a bank account, it is quite easy to discover the essential operations. With other classes, you may need to think more carefully. Keep in mind that the programmers who use your class will view its objects as black boxes. They do not know what values are stored inside them, or how the methods do their jobs.

In Java, operations are expressed as method calls. To figure out the exact specification of the method calls, imagine how a programmer would carry out the bank account operations. We'll assume that the variable harrysChecking contains a reference to an object of type BankAccount. We want to support method calls such as the following:

```
harrysChecking.deposit(2000);
harrysChecking.withdraw(500);
System.out.println(harrysChecking.getBalance());
```

Note that the first two methods are mutators. They modify the balance of the bank account and don't return a value. The third method is an accessor. It returns a value that you can print or store in a variable.

As you can see from the sample calls, the BankAccount class should define three methods:

- `public void deposit(double amount)`
- `public void withdraw(double amount)`
- `public double getBalance()`

Recall from Chapter 2 that `double` denotes the double-precision floating-point type, and `void` indicates that a method does not return a value.

When you define a method, you also need to provide the method *body*, consisting of statements that are executed when the method is called.

```
public void deposit(double amount)
{
    body—filled in later
}
```

You will see in Section 3.5 how to fill in the method body.

Every method definition contains the following parts:

- An *access specifier* (usually `public`)
- The *return type* (such as `void` or `double`)
- The name of the method (such as `deposit`)
- A list of the *parameters* of the method (if any), enclosed in parentheses (such as `double amount`)
- The *body* of the method: statements enclosed in braces

> A method definition contains an access specifier (usually `public`), a return type, a method name, parameters, and the method body.

The access specifier controls which other methods can call this method. Most methods should be declared as `public`. That way, all other methods in a program can call them. (Occasionally, it can be useful to have `private` methods. They can only be called from other methods of the same class.)

The return type is the type of the output value. The `deposit` method does not return a value, whereas the `getBalance` method returns a value of type `double`.

Each parameter (or input) to the method has both a type and a name. For example, the `deposit` method has a single parameter named `amount` of type `double`. For each parameter, choose a name that is both a legal variable name and a good description of the purpose of the input.

Next, you need to consider how users of your class want to construct objects. As you saw in Chapter 2, Java objects are created by calling constructors such as

```
new BankAccount()
```

What kind of bank account should result from this call? It seems reasonable to expect a new bank account with a zero balance. What if a programmer who uses our class wants to start out with another balance? A second constructor that sets the balance to an initial value would be useful:

```
BankAccount harrysChecking = new BankAccount(5000);
```

Syntax 3.1 Method Definition

accessSpecifier returnType methodName(parameterType parameterName, . . .)
{
    method body
}

Example:

```
public void deposit(double amount)
{
    . . .
}
```

Purpose:

To define the behavior of a method

Thus, we will provide two constructors:

- `public BankAccount()`
- `public BankAccount(double initialBalance)`

Note that a constructor is very similar to a method, with two important differences.

- The name of the constructor is always the same as the name of the class (e.g., `BankAccount`)
- Constructors have no return type (not even void)

> Constructors contain instructions to initialize objects. The constructor name is always the same as the class name.

Just like a method, a constructor also has a body—a sequence of statements that is executed when a new object is constructed.

```
public BankAccount()
{
    body—filled in later
}
```

The statements in the constructor body will set the internal data of the object that is being constructed—see Section 3.5.

Don't worry about the fact that there are two constructors with the same name—*all* constructors of a class have the same name, that is, the name of the class. The compiler can tell them apart because they take different parameters.

When defining a class, you place all constructor and method definitions inside, like this:

```
public class BankAccount
{
    // Constructors
    public BankAccount()
    {
        body—filled in later
```

```
    }

    public BankAccount(double initialBalance)
    {
        body—filled in later
    }

    // Methods
    public void deposit(double amount)
    {
        body—filled in later
    }

    public void withdraw(double amount)
    {
        body—filled in later
    }

    public double getBalance()
    {
        body—filled in later
    }

    private fields—filled in later
}
```

You will see how to supply the missing pieces in the following sections.

The public constructors and methods of a class form the *public interface* of the class. These are the operations that any programmer can use to create and manipulate BankAccount objects. Our BankAccount class is simple, but it allows programmers to carry out all of the important operations that commonly occur with bank accounts. For example, consider this program segment, authored by a programmer

SYNTAX 3.2 Constructor Definition

accessSpecifier ClassName(parameterType parameterName, . . .)
{
   constructor body
}

Example:

```
public BankAccount(double initialBalance)
{
    . . .
}
```

Purpose:

To define the behavior of a constructor

> ### SYNTAX 3.3 Class Definition
>
> *accessSpecifier* class *ClassName*
> {
>   *constructors*
>   *methods*
>   *fields*
> }
>
> **Example:**
>
> ```
> public class BankAccount
> {
>     public BankAccount(double initialBalance) { . . . }
>     public void deposit(double amount) { . . . }
>     . . .
> }
> ```
>
> **Purpose:**
>
> To define a class, its public interface, and its implementation details

who uses the BankAccount class. These statements transfer an amount of money from one bank account to another:

```
// Transfer from one account to another
double transferAmount = 500;
momsSavings.withdraw(transferAmount);
harrysChecking.deposit(transferAmount);
```

And here is a program segment that adds interest to a savings account:

```
double interestRate = 5; // 5% interest
double interestAmount
      = momsSavings.getBalance() * interestRate / 100;
momsSavings.deposit(interestAmount);
```

As you can see, programmers can use objects of the BankAccount class to carry out meaningful tasks, without knowing how the BankAccount objects store their data or how the BankAccount methods do their work.

Of course, as providers of the BankAccount class, we will need to supply the internal details. We will do so in Section 3.5. First, however, an important step remains: *documenting* the public interface. That is the topic of the next section.

SELF CHECK

3. How can you use the methods of the public interface to *empty* the harrys-Checking bank account?

4. Suppose you want a more powerful bank account abstraction that keeps track of an *account number* in addition to the balance. How would you change the public interface to accommodate this enhancement?

3.3 Commenting the Public Interface

When you define classes and methods, you should get into the habit of thoroughly *commenting* their behaviors. In Java there is a very useful standard form for *documentation comments*. If you use this form in your classes, a program called javadoc can automatically generate a neat set of HTML pages that describe them. (See Productivity Hint 3.1 for a description of this utility.)

> Use documentation comments to describe the classes and public methods of your programs.

A documentation comment is placed before the class or method definition that is being documented. It starts with a /**, a special comment delimiter used by the javadoc utility. Then you describe the method's *purpose*. Then, for each method parameter, you supply a line that starts with @param, followed by the parameter name and a short explanation. Finally, you supply a line that starts with @return, describing the return value. You omit the @param tag for methods that have no parameters, and you omit the @return tag for methods whose return type is void.

The javadoc utility copies the *first* sentence of each comment to a summary table in the HTML documentation. Therefore, it is best to write that first sentence with some care. It should start with an uppercase letter and end with a period. It does not have to be a grammatically complete sentence, but it should be meaningful when it is pulled out of the comment and displayed in a summary.

Here are two typical examples.

```
/**
    Withdraws money from the bank account.
    @param amount the amount to withdraw
*/
public void withdraw(double amount)
{
    implementation—filled in later
}

/**
    Gets the current balance of the bank account.
    @return the current balance
*/
public double getBalance()
{
    implementation—filled in later
}
```

The comments you have just seen explain individual *methods*. Supply a brief comment for each *class*, explaining its purpose. The comment syntax for class comments is very simple: Just place the documentation comment above the class.

```
/**
    A bank account has a balance that can be changed by
    deposits and withdrawals.
*/
public class BankAccount
{
    . . .
}
```

Your first reaction may well be "Whoa! Am I supposed to write all this stuff?" These comments do seem pretty repetitive. But you should take the time to write them, even if it feels silly.

It is always a good idea to write the method comment *first*, before writing the code in the method body. This is an excellent test to see that you firmly understand what you need to program. If you can't explain what a class or method does, you aren't ready to implement it.

> Provide documentation comments for every class, every method, every parameter, and every return value.

What about very simple methods? You can easily spend more time pondering whether a comment is too trivial to write than it takes to write it. In practical programming, very simple methods are rare. It is harmless to have a trivial method overcommented, whereas a complicated method without any comment can cause real grief to future maintenance programmers. According to the standard Java documentation style, *every* class, *every* method, *every* parameter, and *every* return value should have a comment.

The javadoc utility formats your comments into a neat set of documents that you can view in a web browser. It makes good use of the seemingly repetitive phrases. The first sentence of the comment is used for a *summary table* of all methods of your class (see Figure 3). The @param and @return comments are neatly formatted in the detail description of each method (see Figure 4). If you omit any of the comments, then javadoc generates documents that look strangely empty.

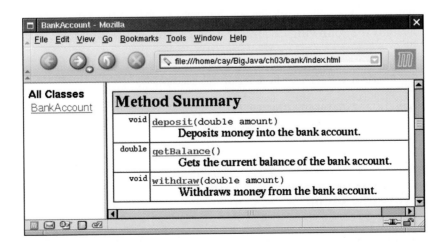

Figure 3   A Method Summary Generated by javadoc

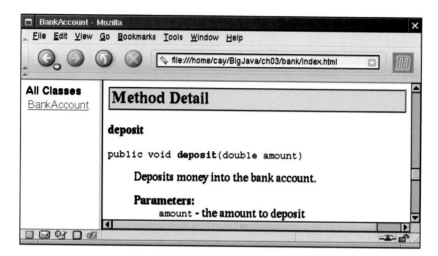

Figure 4   Method Detail Generated by javadoc

This documentation format should look familiar. The programmers who implement the Java library use javadoc themselves. They too document every class, every method, every parameter, and every return value, and then use javadoc to extract the documentation in HTML format.

SELF CHECK

5. Suppose we enhance the BankAccount class so that each account has an account number. Supply a documentation comment for the constructor

    ```
    public BankAccount(int accountNumber, double initialBalance)
    ```

6. Why is the following documentation comment questionable?

    ```
    /**
        Each account has an account number.
        @return  the account number of this account
    */
    public int getAccountNumber()
    ```

PRODUCTIVITY HINT 3.1

The javadoc Utility

Always insert documentation comments in your code, whether or not you use javadoc to produce HTML documentation. Most people find the HTML documentation convenient, so it is worth learning how to run javadoc. Some programming environments (such as BlueJ) can execute javadoc for you. Alternatively, you can invoke the javadoc utility from a command shell, by issuing the command

```
javadoc MyClass.java
```

or , if you want to document multiple Java files,

```
javadoc *.java
```

The javadoc utility produces files such as MyClass.html in HTML format, which you can inspect in a browser. If you know HTML (see Appendix I), you can embed HTML tags into the comments to specify fonts or add images. Perhaps most importantly, javadoc automatically provides *hyperlinks* to other classes and methods.

You can run javadoc before implementing any methods. Just leave all the method bodies empty. Don't run the compiler—it would complain about missing return values. Simply run javadoc on your file to generate the documentation for the public interface that you are about to implement.

The javadoc tool is wonderful because it does one thing right: It allows you to put the documentation *together with your code*. That way, when you update your programs, you can see right away which documentation needs to be updated. Hopefully, you will update it right then and there. Afterward, run javadoc again and get updated information that is timely and nicely formatted.

3.4 Instance Fields

Now that you understand the public interface of the BankAccount class, let's provide the implementation.

First, we need to determine the data that each bank account object contains. In the case of our simple bank account class, each object needs to store a single value, the current balance. (A more complex bank account class might store additional data—perhaps an account number, the interest rate paid, the date for mailing out the next statement, and so on.)

> An object uses instance fields to store its state— the data that it needs to execute its methods.

An object stores its data in *instance fields*. A *field* is a technical term for a storage location inside a block of memory. An *instance* of a class is an object of the class. Thus, an instance field is a storage location that is present in each object of the class.

The class declaration specifies the instance fields:

```
public class BankAccount
{
   . . .
   private double balance;
}
```

An instance field declaration consists of the following parts:

- An *access specifier* (usually private)
- The *type* of the instance field (such as double)
- The name of the instance field (such as balance)

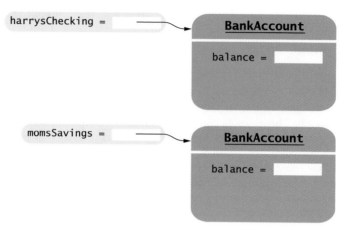

Figure 5   Instance Fields

Each object of a class has its own set of instance fields.

You should declare all instance fields as private.

Each object of a class has its own set of instance fields. For example, if harrysChecking and momsSavings are two objects of the BankAccount class, then each object has its own balance field, called harrys-Checking.balance and momsSavings.balance (see Figure 5).

Instance fields are generally declared with the access specifier private. That specifier means that they can be accessed only by the methods of the *same class*, not by any other method. For example, the balance variable can be accessed by the deposit method of the BankAccount class but not the main method of another class.

SYNTAX 3.4 **Instance Field Declaration**

```
accessSpecifier class ClassName
{
    . . .
    accessSpecifier fieldType fieldName;
    . . .
}
```

Example:

```
public class BankAccount
{
    . . .
    private double balance;
    . . .
}
```

Purpose:

To define a field that is present in every object of a class

```
public class BankRobber
{
    public static void main(String[] args)
    {
        BankAccount momsSavings = new BankAccount(1000);
        . . .
        momsSavings.balance = -1000; // Error
    }
}
```

Encapsulation is the process of hiding object data and providing methods for data access.

In other words, if the instance fields are declared as private, then all data access must occur through the public methods. Thus, the instance fields of an object are effectively hidden from the programmer who uses a class. They are of concern only to the programmer who implements the class. The process of hiding the data and providing methods for data access is called *encapsulation*. Although it is theoretically possible in Java to leave instance fields public, that is a very uncommon practice. We will always make instance fields private in this book.

SELF CHECK

7. Suppose we modify the BankAccount class so that each bank account has an account number. How does this change affect the instance fields?

8. What are the instance fields of the Rectangle class?

3.5 Implementing Constructors and Methods

Constructors contain instructions to initialize the instance fields of an object.

Now that we have determined the instance fields, let us complete the BankAccount class by supplying the bodies of the constructors and methods. Each body contains a sequence of statements. We'll start with the constructors because they are very straightforward. A constructor has a simple job: to initialize the instance fields of an object.

Recall that we designed the BankAccount class to have two constructors. The first constructor simply sets the balance to zero:

```
public BankAccount()
{
    balance = 0;
}
```

The second constructor sets the balance to the value supplied as the construction parameter:

```
public BankAccount(double initialBalance)
{
    balance = initialBalance;
}
```

To see how these constructors work, let us trace the statement

```
BankAccount harrysChecking = new BankAccount(1000);
```

one step at a time. Here are the steps that are carried out when the statement executes.

- Create a new object of type BankAccount.
- Call the second constructor (since a construction parameter is supplied).
- Set the parameter variable initialBalance to 1000.
- Set the balance instance field of the newly created object to initialBalance.
- Return an object reference, that is, the memory location of the object, as the value of the new expression.
- Store that object reference in the harrysChecking variable.

Let's move on to implementing the BankAccount methods. Here is the deposit method:

```
public void deposit(double amount)
{
   double newBalance = balance + amount;
   balance = newBalance;
}
```

To understand exactly what the method does, consider this statement:

```
harrysChecking.deposit(500);
```

This statement carries out the following steps:

- Set the parameter variable amount to 500.
- Fetch the balance field of the object whose location is stored in harrysChecking.
- Add the value of amount to balance and store the result in the variable newBalance.
- Store the value of newBalance in the balance instance field, overwriting the old value.

The withdraw method is very similar to the deposit method:

```
public void withdraw(double amount)
{
   double newBalance = balance - amount;
   balance = newBalance;
}
```

There is only one method left, getBalance. Unlike the deposit and withdraw methods, which modify the instance fields of the object on which they are invoked, the getBalance method returns an output value:

```
public double getBalance()
{
   return balance;
}
```

SYNTAX 3.5 **The return Statement**

return *expression*;
or
return;

Example:

return balance;

Purpose:

To specify the value that a method returns, and exit the method immediately. The return value becomes the value of the method call expression.

> Use the return statement to specify the value that a method returns to its caller.

The return statement is a special statement that instructs the method to terminate and return an output to the statement that called the method. In our case, we simply return the value of the balance instance field. You will later see other methods that compute and return more complex expressions.

We have now completed the implementation of the BankAccount class—see the code listing below. There is only one step remaining: testing that the class works correctly. That is the topic of the next section.

File BankAccount.java

```java
1   /**
2       A bank account has a balance that can be changed by
3       deposits and withdrawals.
4   */
5   public class BankAccount
6   {
7       /**
8           Constructs a bank account with a zero balance.
9       */
10      public BankAccount()
11      {
12          balance = 0;
13      }
14
15      /**
16          Constructs a bank account with a given balance.
17          @param initialBalance the initial balance
18      */
19      public BankAccount(double initialBalance)
20      {
21          balance = initialBalance;
22      }
```

```
23
24      /**
25          Deposits money into the bank account.
26          @param amount the amount to deposit
27      */
28      public void deposit(double amount)
29      {
30          double newBalance = balance + amount;
31          balance = newBalance;
32      }
33
34      /**
35          Withdraws money from the bank account.
36          @param amount the amount to withdraw
37      */
38      public void withdraw(double amount)
39      {
40          double newBalance = balance - amount;
41          balance = newBalance;
42      }
43
44      /**
45          Gets the current balance of the bank account.
46          @return the current balance
47      */
48      public double getBalance()
49      {
50          return balance;
51      }
52
53      private double balance;
54  }
```

SELF CHECK

9. How is the getWidth method of the Rectangle class implemented?
10. How is the translate method of the Rectangle class implemented?

3.6 Testing a Class

In the preceding section, we completed the implementation of the BankAccount class. What can you do with it? Of course, you can compile the file BankAccount.java. However, you can't *execute* the resulting BankAccount.class file. It doesn't contain a main method. That is normal—most classes don't contain a main method.

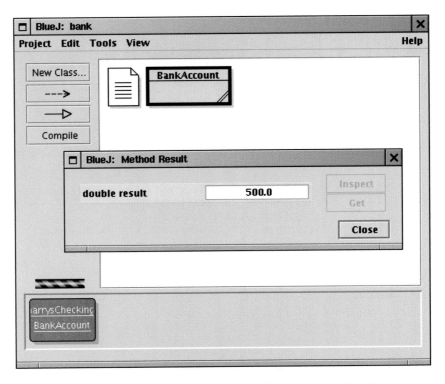

Figure 6 The Return Value of the getBalance Method in BlueJ

To do something with your class, you have two choices. Some interactive development environments have commands for constructing objects and invoking methods (see Advanced Topic 2.1). Then you can test a class simply by constructing an object, calling methods, and verifying that you get the expected return values. Figure 6 shows the result of calling the getBalance method on a BankAccount object in BlueJ.

> To test a class, use an environment for interactive testing, or write a second class to execute test instructions.

Alternatively, if you don't have a development environment that allows you to test a class interactively, you can write a *test class*. A test class is a class with a main method that contains statements to test another class. A test class typically carries out the following steps:

1. Construct one or more objects of the class that is being tested.
2. Invoke one or more methods.
3. Print out one or more results.

The MoveTester class in Section 2.8 is a good example of a test class. That class tests the Rectangle class—a class in the Java library.

Here is a class to test the BankAccount class. The main method constructs an object of type BankAccount, invokes the deposit and withdraw methods, and then displays the remaining balance on the console.

File BankAccountTester.java

```
 1  /**
 2      A class to test the BankAccount class.
 3  */
 4  public class BankAccountTester
 5  {
 6     /**
 7         Tests the methods of the BankAccount class.
 8         @param args not used
 9     */
10     public static void main(String[] args)
11     {
12        BankAccount harrysChecking = new BankAccount();
13        harrysChecking.deposit(2000);
14        harrysChecking.withdraw(500);
15        System.out.println(harrysChecking.getBalance());
16     }
17  }
```

Output

```
1500
```

To produce a program, you need to combine these two classes. The details for building the program depend on your compiler and development environment. In most environments, you need to carry out these steps:

1. Make a new subfolder for your program.

2. Make two files, one for each class.

3. Compile both files.

4. Run the test program.

Many students are surprised that such a simple program contains two classes. However, this is normal. The two classes have entirely different purposes. The BankAccount class describes objects that compute bank balances. The BankAccountTester class runs a test that puts a BankAccount object through its paces.

SELF CHECK

11. When you run the BankAccountTester program, how many objects of class BankAccount are constructed? How many objects of type BankAccountTester?

12. Why is the BankAccountTester class unnecessary in development environments that allow interactive testing, such as BlueJ?

How To 3.1

Designing and Implementing a Class

This is the first of several "How To" sections in this book. Users of the Linux operating system have how to guides that give answers to the common questions "How do I get started?" and "What do I do next?". Similarly, the How To sections in this book give you step-by-step procedures for carrying out specific tasks.

You will often be asked to design and implement a class. For example, a homework assignment might ask you to design a CashRegister class.

Step 1 Find out what you are asked to do with an object of the class.

For example, suppose you are asked to implement a CashRegister class. You won't have to model every feature of a real cash register—there are too many. The assignment should tell you *which aspects* of a cash register your class should simulate. Make a list, in plain English, of the operations that an object of your class should carry out, such as this one:

- Ring up the sales price for a purchased item.
- Enter the amount of payment.
- Calculate the amount of change due to the customer.

For simplicity, we are looking at a very simple cash register here. A more sophisticated model would be able to compute sales tax, daily sales totals, and so on.

Step 2 Specify the public interface.

Turn the list in Step 1 into a set of methods, with specific types for the parameters and the return values. Many programmers find this step simpler if they write out method calls that are applied to a sample object, like this:

```
CashRegister register = new CashRegister();
register.recordPurchase(29.95);
register.recordPurchase(9.95);
register.enterPayment(50);
double change = register.giveChange();
```

Now we have a specific list of methods.

- public void recordPurchase(double amount)
- public void enterPayment(double amount)
- public double giveChange()

To complete the public interface, you need to specify the constructors. Ask yourself what information you need in order to construct an object of your class. Sometimes you will want two constructors: one that sets all fields to a default and one that sets them to user-supplied values.

In the case of the cash register example, we can get by with a single constructor that creates an empty register. A more realistic cash register would start out with some coins and bills so that we can give exact change, but that is beyond the scope of our assignment.

Thus, we add a single constructor:

- public CashRegister()

Step 3 Document the public interface.

Here is the documentation, with comments, that describes the class and its methods:

```
/**
    A cash register totals up sales and computes change due.
*/
public class CashRegister
{
    /**
        Constructs a cash register with no money in it.
    */
    public CashRegister()
    {
    }

    /**
        Records the sale of an item.
        @param amount the price of the item
    */
    public void recordPurchase(double amount)
    {
    }

    /**
        Enters the payment received from the customer.
        @param amount the amount of the payment
    */
    public void enterPayment(double amount)
    {
    }

    /**
        Computes the change due and resets the machine for the next customer.
        @return the change due to the customer
    */
    public double giveChange()
    {
    }
}
```

Step 4 Determine instance fields.

Ask yourself what information an object needs to store to do its job. Remember, the methods can be called in any order! The object needs to have enough internal memory to be able to process every method using just its instance fields and the method parameters. Go through each method, perhaps starting with a simple one or an interesting one, and ask yourself what you need to carry out the method's task. Make instance fields to store the information that the method needs.

In the cash register example, you would want to keep track of the total purchase amount and the payment. You can compute the change due from these two amounts.

```
public class CashRegister
{
    . . .
    private double purchase;
    private double payment;
}
```

Step 5 Implement constructors and methods.

Implement the constructors and methods in your class, one at a time, starting with the easiest ones. For example, here is the implementation of the recordPurchase method:

```java
public void recordPurchase(double amount)
{
    double newTotal = purchase + amount;
    purchase = newTotal;
}
```

Here is the giveChange method. Note that this method is a bit more sophisticated—it computes the change due, and it also resets the cash register for the next sale.

```java
public double giveChange()
{
    double change = payment - purchase;
    purchase = 0;
    payment = 0;
    return change;
}
```

If you find that you have trouble with the implementation, you may need to go back to a previous step. Maybe your public interface wasn't good? Maybe you didn't have the right instance fields? It is common for a beginner to run into a couple of problems that require backtracking.

Once you have completed the implementation, compile your class and fix any compiler errors.

Step 6 Test your class.

Write a short test program and run it. The test program can carry out the method calls that you found in Step 2.

```java
public class CashRegisterTester
{
    public static void main(String[] args)
    {
        CashRegister register = new CashRegister();

        register.recordPurchase(29.50);
        register.recordPurchase(9.25);
        register.enterPayment(50);

        double change = register.giveChange();

        System.out.println(change);
    }
}
```

The output of this test program is:

```
11.25
```

Alternatively, if you use a program that lets you test objects interactively, such as BlueJ, construct an object and apply the method calls.

Using the Command Line Effectively

If your programming environment allows you to accomplish all routine tasks using menus and dialog boxes, you can skip this note. However, if you must invoke the editor, the compiler, the linker, and the program to test manually, then it is well worth learning about *command line editing*.

Most operating systems (including Linux, Mac OS X, UNIX, and Windows) have a *command line interface* to interact with the computer. (In Windows XP, you can get a command line window by selecting "Run . . ." from the Start menu and typing cmd.) You launch commands at a *prompt*. The command is executed, and on completion you get another prompt.

When you develop a program, you find yourself executing the same commands over and over. Wouldn't it be nice if you didn't have to type commands, such as

```
javac MyProg.java
```

more than once? Or if you could fix a mistake rather than having to retype the command in its entirety? Many command line interfaces have an option to do just that, by using the up and down arrow keys to recall old commands and the left and right arrow keys to edit lines. You can also perform *file completion*. For example, to select the file BankAccount.java, you only need to type the first couple of letters and then hit the "Tab" key.

The details depend on your operating system and its configuration—experiment on your own, or ask a "power user" for help.

3.7 Categories of Variables

We close this chapter with two sections of a more technical nature, examining variables and parameters in some detail.

You have seen three different categories of variables in this chapter:

1. *Instance fields* (sometimes called *instance variables*), such as the balance variable of the BankAccount class
2. *Local variables*, such as the newBalance variable of the deposit method
3. *Parameter variables*, such as the amount variable of the deposit method

> Instance fields belong to an object. Parameter variables and local variables belong to a method—they die when the method exits.

These variables are similar in one respect—they all hold values that belong to specific types. But they have a couple of important differences. The first difference is their *lifetime*.

An instance field belongs to an object. Each object has its own copy of each instance field. For example, if you have two BankAccount objects (say, harrysChecking and momsSavings), then each of them has its own balance field. When an object is constructed, its instance fields are created. The fields stay alive until no method uses the object any longer. (The Java virtual machine contains an agent called a *garbage collector* that periodically reclaims objects when they are no longer used.)

Local and parameter variables belong to a method. When the method runs, these variables come to life. When the method exits, they die immediately (see Figure 7). For example, if you call

```
harrysChecking.deposit(500); ❶
```

then a parameter variable called amount is created and initialized with the parameter value, 500. When the method returns, the amount variable dies. The same holds for the local variable newBalance. When the deposit method reaches the line

```
double newBalance = balance + amount; ❷
```

the variable comes to life and is initialized with the sum of the object's balance and the deposit amount. The lifetime of that variable extends to the end of the method.

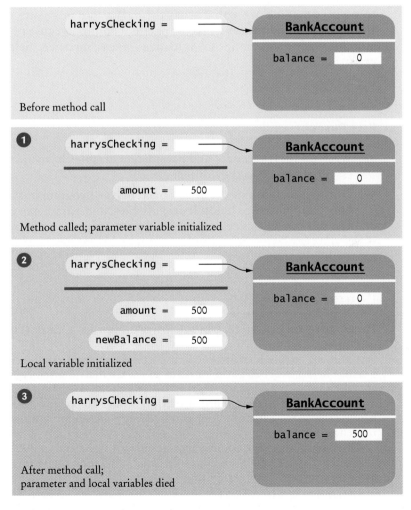

Figure 7 Lifetime of Variables

However, the deposit method has a lasting effect. Its next line,

```
balance = newBalance; ❸
```

sets the balance instance field, and that field lives beyond the end of the deposit method, as long as the BankAccount object is in use.

> Instance fields are initialized to a default value, but you must initialize local variables.

The second major difference between instance fields and local variables is *initialization*. You must initialize all local variables. If you don't initialize a local variable, the compiler complains when you try to use it.

Parameter variables are initialized with the values that are supplied in the method call.

Instance fields are initialized with a default value if you don't explicitly set them in a constructor. Instance fields that are numbers are initialized to 0. Object references are set to a special value called null. If an object reference is null, then it refers to no object at all. We will discuss the null value in greater detail in Section 6.2.5. Inadvertent initialization with 0 or null is a common cause of errors. Therefore, it is a matter of good style to initialize *every* instance field explicitly in every constructor.

SELF CHECK

13. What do local variables and parameter variables have in common? In which essential aspect do they differ?

14. During execution of the BankAccountTester program in the preceding section, how many instance fields, local variables, and parameter variables were created, and what were their names?

COMMON ERROR 3.1

Forgetting to Initialize Object References in a Constructor

Just as it is a common error to forget to initialize a local variable, it is easy to forget about instance fields. Every constructor needs to ensure that all instance fields are set to appropriate values.

If you do not initialize an instance field, the Java compiler will initialize it for you. Numbers are initialized with 0, but object references—such as string variables—are set to the null reference.

Of course, 0 is often a convenient default for numbers. However, null is hardly ever a convenient default for objects. Consider this "lazy" constructor for a modified version of the BankAccount class:

```java
public class BankAccount
{
```

```
    public BankAccount() {} // No statements
    . . .
    private double balance;
    private String owner;
}
```

The balance is set to 0, and the owner field is set to a null reference. This is a problem—it is illegal to call methods on the null reference.

If you forget to initialize a *local* variable in a *method*, the compiler flags this as an error, and you must fix it before the program runs. If you make the same mistake with an *instance* field in a class, the compiler provides a default initialization, and the error becomes apparent only when the program runs.

To avoid this problem, make it a habit to initialize every instance field in every constructor.

3.8 Implicit and Explicit Method Parameters

In Section 2.4, you learned that a method has an implicit parameter—the object on which the method is invoked—and explicit parameters, which are enclosed in parentheses. In this section, we will examine these parameters in greater detail.

Have a look at a particular invocation of the deposit method:

```
momsSavings.deposit(500);
```

Now look again at the code of the deposit method:

```
public void deposit(double amount)
{
    double newBalance = balance + amount;
    balance = newBalance;
}
```

The parameter variable amount is set to 500 when the deposit method starts. But what does balance mean exactly? After all, our program may have multiple Bank-Account objects, and *each of them* has its own balance.

Of course, since we deposit the money into momsSavings, balance must mean momsSavings.balance. In general, when you refer to an instance field inside a method, it means the instance field of the object on which the method was called.

> The implicit parameter of a method is the object on which the method is invoked. The this reference denotes the implicit parameter.

Thus, the call to the deposit method depends on two values: the object to which momsSavings refers, and the value 500. The amount parameter inside the parentheses is called an *explicit* parameter, because it is explicitly named in the method definition. However, the reference to the bank account object is not explicit in the method definition—it is called the *implicit parameter* of the method.

If you need to, you can access the implicit parameter—the object on which the method is called—with the keyword this. For example, in the preceding method invocation, this was set to momsSavings and amount was set to 500 (see Figure 8).

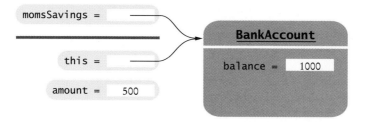

Figure 8   The Implicit Parameter of a Method Call

Every method has one implicit parameter. You don't give the implicit parameter a name. It is always called `this`. (There is one exception to the rule that every method has an implicit parameter: `static` methods do not. We will discuss them in Chapter 9.) In contrast, methods can have any number of explicit parameters—which you can name any way you like—or no explicit parameter at all.

Next, look closely at the implementation of the `deposit` method. The statement

```
double newBalance = balance + amount;
```

actually means

```
double newBalance = this.balance + amount;
```

> Use of an instance field name in a method denotes the instance field of the implicit parameter.

When you refer to an instance field in a method, the compiler automatically applies it to the `this` parameter. Some programmers actually prefer to manually insert the `this` parameter before every instance field because they find it makes the code clearer. Here is an example:

```
public void deposit(double amount)
{
    double newBalance = this.balance + amount;
    this.balance = newBalance;
}
```

You may want to try it out and see if you like that style.

You have now seen how to use objects and implement classes, and you have learned some important technical details about variables and method parameters. In the next chapter, you will learn more about the most fundamental data types of the Java language.

SELF CHECK

15. How many implicit and explicit parameters does the `withdraw` method of the `BankAccount` class have, and what are their names and types?

16. In the `deposit` method, what is the meaning of `this.amount`? Or, if the expression has no meaning, why not?

17. How many implicit and explicit parameters does the `main` method of the `BankAccountTester` class have, and what are they called?

COMMON ERROR 3.2

Trying to Call a Method Without an Implicit Parameter

Suppose your `main` method contains the instruction

```
withdraw(30); // Error
```

The compiler will not know which account to access to withdraw the money. You need to supply an object reference of type `BankAccount`:

```
BankAccount harrysChecking = new BankAccount();
harrysChecking.withdraw(30);
```

However, there is one situation in which it is legitimate to invoke a method without, seemingly, an implicit parameter. Consider the following modification to the `BankAccount` class. Add a method to apply the monthly account fee:

```
public class BankAccount
{  . . .
    public void monthlyFee()
    {
        withdraw(10); // Withdraw $10 from this account
    }
}
```

That means to withdraw from the same bank account object that is carrying out the `monthly-Fee` operation. In other words, the implicit parameter of the `withdraw` method is the (invisible) implicit parameter of the `monthlyFee` method.

If you find it confusing to have an invisible parameter, you can always use the `this` parameter to make the method easier to read:

```
public class BankAccount
{  . . .
    public void monthlyFee()
    {
        this.withdraw(10); // Withdraw $10 from this account
    }
}
```

ADVANCED TOPIC 3.1

Calling One Constructor from Another

Consider the `BankAccount` class. It has two constructors: a constructor without parameters to initialize the balance with zero, and another constructor to supply an initial balance. Rather than explicitly setting the balance to zero, one constructor can call another constructor of the same class instead. There is a shorthand notation to achieve this result:

```
public class BankAccount
{
    public BankAccount (double initialBalance)
    {
        balance = initialBalance;
```

```
      }

      public BankAccount()
      {
         this(0);
      }
      . . .
   }
```

The command `this(0);` means "Call another constructor of this class and supply the value 0". Such a constructor call can occur only as the *first line in another constructor.*

This syntax is a minor convenience. We will not use it in this book. Actually, the use of the keyword `this` is a little confusing. Normally, `this` denotes a reference to the implicit parameter, but if `this` is followed by parentheses, it denotes a call to another constructor of this class.

RANDOM FACT 3.1

Electronic Voting Machines

In the 2000 presidential elections in the United States, votes were tallied by a variety of machines. Some machines processed cardboard ballots into which voters punched holes to indicate their choices (see Figure 9). When voters were not careful, remains of paper—the now infamous "chads"—were partially stuck in the punch cards, causing votes to be miscounted. A manual recount was necessary, but it was not carried out everywhere due to time constraints and procedural wrangling. The election was very close, and there remain doubts in the minds of many people whether the election outcome would have been different if the voting machines had accurately counted the intent of the voters.

Figure 9   Punch Card Ballot

Subsequently, voting machine manufacturers have argued that electronic voting machines would avoid the problems caused by punch cards or optically scanned forms. In an electronic voting machine, voters indicate their preferences by pressing buttons or touching icons on a computer screen. Typically, each voter is presented with a summary screen for review before casting the ballot. The process is very similar to using an automatic bank teller machine (see Figure 10).

It seems plausible that these machines make it more likely that a vote is counted in the same way that the voter intends. However, there has been significant controversy surrounding some types of electronic voting machines. If a machine simply records the votes and prints out the totals after the election has been completed, then how do you know that the machine worked correctly? Inside the machine is a computer that executes a program, and, as you may know from your own experience, programs can have bugs.

In fact, some electronic voting machines do have bugs. There have been isolated cases where machines reported tallies that were impossible. When a machine reports far more or far fewer votes than voters, then it is clear that it malfunctioned. Unfortunately, it is then impossible to find out the actual votes. Over time, one would expect these bugs to be fixed in the software. More insidiously, if the results are plausible, nobody may ever investigate.

Many computer scientists have spoken out on this issue and confirmed that it is impossible, with today's technology, to tell that software is error free and has not been tampered with. Many of them recommend that electronic voting machines should be complemented by a *voter verifiable audit trail*. (A good source of information is [1].) Typically, a voter-verifiable machine prints out the choices that are being tallied. Each voter has a chance to review the printout, and then deposits it in an old-fashioned ballot box. If there is a problem with the electronic equipment, the printouts can be counted by hand.

As this book is written, this concept is strongly resisted both by manufacturers of electronic voting machines and by their customers, the cities and counties that run elections. Manufacturers are reluctant to increase the cost of the machines because they may not be able to pass the cost increase on to their customers, who tend to have tight budgets. Election

Figure 10
Touch Screen Voting Machine

officials fear problems with malfunctioning printers, and some of them have publicly stated that they actually prefer equipment that eliminates bothersome recounts.

What do you think? You probably use an automatic bank teller machine to get cash from your bank account. Do you review the paper record that the machine issues? Do you check your bank statement? Even if you don't, do you put your faith in other people who double-check their balances, so that the bank won't get away with widespread cheating?

At any rate, is the integrity of banking equipment more important or less important than that of voting machines? Won't every voting process have some room for error and fraud anyway? Is the added cost for equipment, paper, and staff time reasonable to combat a potentially slight risk of malfunction and fraud? Computer scientists cannot answer these questions—an informed society must make these tradeoffs. But, like all professionals, they have an obligation to speak out and give accurate testimony about the capabilities and limitations of computing equipment.

CHAPTER SUMMARY

1. You use the process of abstraction to find the essential feature set for a class.

2. A method definition contains an access specifier (usually `public`), a return type, a method name, parameters, and the method body.

3. Constructors contain instructions to initialize objects. The constructor name is always the same as the class name.

4. Use documentation comments to describe the classes and public methods of your programs.

5. Provide documentation comments for every class, every method, every parameter, and every return value.

6. An object uses instance fields to store its state—the data that it needs to execute its methods.

7. Each object of a class has its own set of instance fields.

8. You should declare all instance fields as private.

9. Encapsulation is the process of hiding object data and providing methods for data access.

10. Constructors contain instructions to initialize the instance fields of an object.

11. Use the `return` statement to specify the value that a method returns to its caller.

12. To test a class, use an environment for interactive testing, or write a second class to execute test instructions.

13. Instance fields belong to an object. Parameter variables and local variables belong to a method—they die when the method exits.

14. Instance fields are initialized to a default value, but you must initialize local variables.

15. The implicit parameter of a method is the object on which the method is invoked. The this reference denotes the implicit parameter.

16. Use of an instance field name in a method denotes the instance field of the implicit parameter.

FURTHER READING

1. http://verifiedvoting.org   A site with information on voter-verifiable voting machines, founded by Stanford computer science professor David Dill.

REVIEW EXERCISES

Exercise R3.1. Explain the difference between a local variable and a parameter variable.

Exercise R3.2. Explain the difference between an instance field and a local variable.

Exercise R3.3. Why is the BankAccount(double initialBalance) constructor not strictly necessary?

Exercise R3.4. Explain the difference between

```
BankAccount b;
```

and

```
BankAccount b = new BankAccount(5000);
```

Exercise R3.5. Explain the difference between

```
new BankAccount(5000);
```

and

```
BankAccount b = new BankAccount(5000);
```

Exercise R3.6. What happens in our implementation of the BankAccount class when more money is withdrawn from the account than the current balance? How could you implement an "overdraft penalty"?

Exercise R3.7. What is the value of b.balance after the following operations?

```
BankAccount b = new BankAccount(10);
b.deposit(5000);
b.withdraw(b.getBalance() / 2);
```

Exercise R3.8. If b1 and b2 store objects of class BankAccount, consider the following instructions.

```
b1.deposit(b2.getBalance());
b2.deposit(b1.getBalance());
```

Are the balances of b1 and b2 now identical? Explain.

Exercise R3.9. What is the this reference? Why would you use it?

Exercise R3.10. What does the following method do? Give an example of how you can call the method.

```
public class BankAccount
{
   public void mystery(BankAccount that, double amount)
   {
      this.balance = this.balance - amount;
      that.balance = that.balance + amount;
   }
   . . . // Other bank account methods
}
```

Exercise R3.11. Suppose you want to implement a class SavingsAccount. A savings account is similar to a bank account, but it has an interest rate and accumulates interest once a year. Design the public interface for this class.

Exercise R3.12. What are the accessors and mutators of the CashRegister class?

PROGRAMMING EXERCISES

Exercise P3.1. Write a program that constructs a bank account, deposits $1,000, withdraws $500, withdraws another $400, and then prints the remaining balance.

Exercise P3.2. Add a method

```
void addInterest(double rate)
```

to the BankAccount class that adds interest at the given rate. For example, after the statements

```
BankAccount momsSavings = new BankAccount(1000);
momsSavings.addInterest(10); // 10% interest
```

the balance in momsSavings is $1,100.

Exercise P3.3. Write a class SavingsAccount that is similar to the BankAccount class, except that it has an added instance field interest. Supply a constructor that sets both the initial balance and the interest rate. Supply a method addInterest (with no explicit parameter) that adds interest to the account. Write a program that constructs a savings account with an initial balance of $1,000 and an interest rate of 10%. Then apply the addInterest method five times and print the resulting balance.

Exercise P3.4. Implement a class `Employee`. An employee has a name (a string) and a salary (a `double`). Write a default constructor, a constructor with two parameters (`name` and `salary`), and methods to return the name and salary. Write a small program that tests your class.

Exercise P3.5. Enhance the class in Exercise P3.4 by adding a method `raiseSalary(double byPercent)` that raises the employee's salary by a certain percentage. Sample usage:

```
Employee harry = new Employee("Hacker, Harry", 55000);
harry.raiseSalary(10); // Harry gets a 10% raise
```

Exercise P3.6. Implement a class `Car` with the following properties. A car has a certain fuel efficiency (measured in miles/gallon or liters/km—pick one) and a certain amount of fuel in the gas tank. The efficiency is specified in the constructor, and the initial fuel level is 0. Supply a method `drive` that simulates driving the car for a certain distance, reducing the fuel level in the gas tank. Also supply methods `getGas`, returning the current fuel level, and `addGas`, to tank up. Sample usage:

```
Car myHybrid = new Car(49); // 49 miles per gallon
myHybrid.addGas(20); // Tank 20 gallons
myHybrid.drive(100); // Drive 100 miles
System.out.println(myHybrid.getGas()); // Print fuel remaining
```

Exercise P3.7. Implement a class `Student`. For the purpose of this exercise, a student has a name and a total quiz score. Supply an appropriate constructor and methods `getName()`, `addQuiz(int score)`, `getTotalScore()`, and `getAverageScore()`. To compute the latter, you also need to store the *number of quizzes* that the student took.

Exercise P3.8. Implement a class `Product`. A product has a name and a price, for example `new Product("Toaster", 29.95)`. Supply methods `getName`, `getPrice`, and `setPrice`. Write a program that makes two products, prints the name and price, reduces their prices by $5.00, and then prints them again.

Exercise P3.9. Implement a class `Circle` that has methods `getArea()` and `getPerimeter()`. In the constructor, supply the radius of the circle.

Exercise P3.10. Implement a class `Square` that has methods `getArea()` and `getPerimeter()`. In the constructor, supply the width of the square.

Exercise P3.11. Implement a class `SodaCan` with methods `getSurfaceArea()` and `getVolume()`. In the constructor, supply the height and radius of the can.

Exercise P3.12. Implement a class `RoachPopulation` that simulates the growth of a roach population. The constructor takes the size of the initial roach population. The `waitForDoubling` method simulates a period in which the population doubles. The `spray` method simulates spraying with insecticide, which reduces the population by 10%. The `getRoaches` method returns the current number of roaches. Implement the class and a test program that simulates a kitchen that starts out with 10 roaches. Wait, spray, print the roach count. Repeat three times.

Exercise P3.13. Implement a class RabbitPopulation that simulates the growth of a rabbit population. The rules are as follows: Start with one pair of rabbits. Rabbits are able to mate at the age of one month. A month later, each female produces another pair of rabbits. Assume that rabbits never die and that the female always produces one new pair (one male, one female) every month from the second month on. Implement a method waitAMonth that waits for one month, and a method getPairs that prints the current number of rabbit pairs. Write a test program that shows the growth of the rabbit population for ten months. *Hint:* Keep one instance field for the newborn rabbit pairs and another one for the rabbit pairs that are at least one month old.

Exercise P3.14. Implement a VotingMachine class that can be used for a simple election. Have methods to clear the machine state, to vote for a Democrat, to vote for a Republican, and to get the tallies for both parties. Extra credit if your program gives the nod to your favored party if the votes are tallied after 8 p.m. on the first Tuesday in November, but acts normally on all other dates. (*Hint:* Use the Gregorian-Calendar class—see Programming Project 2.1.)

PROGRAMMING PROJECTS

Project 3.1. In this project, you will enhance the BankAccount class and see how abstraction and encapsulation enable evolutionary changes to software.

Begin with a simple enhancement: charging a fee for every deposit and withdrawal. Supply a mechanism for setting the fee and modify the deposit and withdraw methods so that the fee is levied. Test your resulting class and check that the fee is computed correctly.

Now make a more complex change. The bank will allow a fixed number of free transactions (deposits or withdrawals) every month, and charge for transactions exceeding the free allotment. The charge is not levied immediately but at the end of the month.

Supply a new method deductMonthlyCharge to the BankAccount class that deducts the monthly charge and resets the transaction count. Produce a test program that verifies that the fees are calculated correctly over several months.

Project 3.2. In this project, you will explore an object-oriented alternative to the "Hello, World" program in Chapter 1.

Begin with a simple Greeter class that has a single method, sayHello. That method should *return* a string, not print it. Use BlueJ to create two objects of this class and invoke their sayHello methods.

That is boring—of course, both objects return the same answer.

Enhance the Greeter class so that each object produces a customized greeting. For example, the object constructed as new Greeter("Dave") should say "Hello, Dave". (Use the concat method to combine strings to form a longer string, or peek ahead at Section 4.6 to see how you can use the + operator for the same purpose.)

Add a method sayGoodbye to the Greeter class.

Finally, add a method refuseHelp to the Greeter class. It should return a string such as "I am sorry, Dave. I am afraid I can't do that."

Test your class in BlueJ. Make objects that greet the world and Dave, and invoke methods on them.

ANSWERS TO SELF-CHECK QUESTIONS

1. The programmers who designed and implemented the Java library.

2. Other programmers who work on the personal finance application.

3. `harrysChecking.withdraw(harrysChecking.getBalance())`

4. Add an accountNumber parameter to the constructors, and add a getAccountNumber method. There is no need for a setAccountNumber method—the account number never changes after construction.

5. ```
/**
    Constructs a new bank account with a given initial balance.
    @param accountNumber the account number for this account
    @param initialBalance the initial balance for this account
*/
```

6. The first sentence of the method description should describe the method—it is displayed in isolation in the summary table.

7. An instance field

   ```
   private int accountNumber;
   ```

   needs to be added to the class.

8. You can't tell from the public interface, but the source file (which is a part of the JDK) contains these definitions:

   ```
   private int x;
   private int y;
   private int width;
   private int height;
   ```

9. ```
public int getWidth()
{
    return width;
}
```

10. There is more than one correct answer. One possible implementation is as follows:

    ```
    public void translate(int dx, int dy)
    {
        int newx = x + dx;
        x = newx;
        int newy = y + dy;
        y = newy;
    }
    ```

11. One BankAccount object, no BankAccountTester object. The purpose of the BankAccountTester class is merely to hold the main method.

12. In those environments, you can issue interactive commands to construct BankAccount objects, invoke methods, and display their return values.

13. Variables of both categories belong to methods—they come alive when the method is called, and they die when the method exits. They differ in their initialization. Parameter variables are initialized with the call values; local variables must be explicitly initialized.

14. One instance field, named balance. Three local variables, one named harrysChecking and two named newBalance (in the deposit and withdraw methods); two parameter variables, both named amount (in the deposit and withdraw methods).

15. One implicit parameter, called this, of type BankAccount, and one explicit parameter, called amount, of type double.

16. It is not a legal expression. this is of type BankAccount and the BankAccount class has no field named amount.

17. No implicit parameter—the method is static—and one explicit parameter, called args.

Fundamental Data Types

CHAPTER GOALS

- To understand integer and floating-point numbers
- To recognize the limitations of the numeric types
- To become aware of causes for overflow and roundoff errors
- To understand the proper use of constants
- To write arithmetic expressions in Java
- To use the String type to define and manipulate character strings
- To learn how to read program input and produce formatted output

This chapter teaches how to manipulate numbers and character strings in Java. The goal of this chapter is to gain a firm understanding of the fundamental Java data types.

You will learn about the properties and limitations of the number types in Java. You will see how to manipulate numbers and strings in your programs. Finally, we cover the important topic of input and output, which enables you to implement interactive programs.

CHAPTER CONTENTS

4.1 Number Types

Java has eight primitive types, including four integer types and two floating-point types.

A numeric computation overflows if the result falls outside the range for the number type.

In Java, every value is either a reference to an object, or it belongs to one of the eight *primitive types* shown in Table 1.

Six of the primitive types are number types, four of them for integers and two for floating-point numbers.

Each of the integer types has a different range—Advanced Topic 4.2 explains why the range limits are related to powers of two. Generally, you will use the int type for integer quantities. However, occasionally, calculations involving integers can *overflow*. This happens if the result of a computation exceeds the range for the number type. For example:

```
int n = 1000000;
System.out.println(n * n);   // Prints -727379968
```

The product n * n is 10^{12}, which is larger than the largest integer (about $2 \cdot 10^9$). The result is truncated to fit into an int, yielding a value that is completely wrong. Unfortunately, there is no warning when an integer overflow occurs.

	Table 1 Primitive Types	
Type	**Description**	**Size**
int	The integer type, with range –2,147,483,648 . . . 2,147,483,647 (about 2 billion)	4 bytes
byte	The type describing a single byte, with range –128 . . . 127	1 byte
short	The short integer type, with range –32768 . . . 32767	2 bytes
long	The long integer type, with range –9,223,372,036,854,775,808 . . . 9,223,372,036,854,775,807	8 bytes
double	The double-precision floating-point type, with a range of about $\pm 10^{308}$ and about 15 significant decimal digits	8 bytes
float	The single-precision floating-point type, with a range of about $\pm 10^{38}$ and about 7 significant decimal digits	4 bytes
char	The character type, representing code units in the Unicode encoding scheme (see Advanced Topic 4.5)	2 bytes
boolean	The type with the two truth values false and true (see Chapter 6)	1 bit

If you run into this problem, the simplest remedy is to use the long type. Advanced Topic 4.1 shows you how to use the arbitary-precision BigInteger type in the unlikely event that even the long type overflows.

Overflow is not usually a problem for double-precision floating-point numbers. The double type has a range of about $\pm 10^{308}$ and about 15 significant digits. However, you want to avoid the float type—it has less than 7 significant digits. (Some programmers use float to save on memory if they need to store a huge set of numbers that do not require much precision.)

> Rounding errors occur when an exact conversion between numbers is not possible.

Rounding errors are a more serious issue with floating-point values. Rounding errors can occur when you convert between binary and decimal numbers, or between integers and floating-point numbers. When a value cannot be converted exactly, it is rounded to the nearest match. Consider this example:

```
double f = 4.35;
System.out.println(100 * f); // Prints 434.99999999999994
```

This problem is caused because computers represent numbers in the binary number system. In the binary number system, there is no exact representation of the fraction 1/10, just as there is no exact representation of the fraction 1/3 = 0.33333 in the decimal number system. (See Advanced Topic 4.2 for more information.)

For this reason, the double type is not appropriate for financial calculations. In this book, we will continue to use double values for bank balances and other financial quantities so that we keep our programs as simple as possible. However, professional programs need to use the `BigDecimal` type for this purpose—see Advanced Topic 4.1.

In Java, it is legal to assign an integer value to a floating-point variable:

```
int dollars = 100;
double balance = dollars; // OK
```

But the opposite assignment is an error: You cannot assign a floating-point expression to an integer variable.

```
double balance = 13.75;
int dollars = balance; // Error
```

To overcome this problem, you can convert the floating-point value to an integer with a cast:

```
int dollars = (int) balance;
```

> You use a cast (*typeName*) to convert a value to a different type.

The cast (`int`) converts the floating-point value `balance` to an integer by discarding the fractional part. For example, if `balance` is 13.75, then `dollars` is set to 13.

The cast tells the compiler that you agree to *information loss*, in this case, to the loss of the fractional part. You can also cast to other types, such as (`float`) or (`byte`).

> Use the `Math.round` method to round a floating-point number to the nearest integer.

If you want to round a floating-point number to the nearest whole number, use the `Math.round` method. This method returns a `long` integer, because large floating-point numbers cannot be stored in an `int`.

```
long rounded = Math.round(balance);
```

If `balance` is 13.75, then `rounded` is set to 14.

SYNTAX 4.1 Cast

(*typeName*) *expression*

Example:

(int) (balance * 100)

Purpose:

To convert an expression to a different type

SELF CHECK

1. Which are the most commonly used number types in Java?

2. When does the cast (`long`) x yield a different result from the call `Math.round(x)`?

3. How do you round the `double` value x to the nearest `int` value, assuming that you know that it is less than $2 \cdot 10^9$?

ADVANCED TOPIC 4.1

Big Numbers

If you want to compute with really large numbers, you can use big number objects. Big number objects are objects of the `BigInteger` and `BigDecimal` classes in the `java.math` package. Unlike the number types such as `int` or `double`, big number objects have essentially no limits on their size and precision. However, computations with big number objects are much slower than those that involve number types. Perhaps more importantly, you can't use the familiar arithmetic operators such as (+ - *) with them. Instead, you have to use methods called `add`, `subtract`, and `multiply`. Here is an example of how to create two big integers and how to multiply them.

```
BigInteger a = new BigInteger("1234567890");
BigInteger b = new BigInteger("9876543210");
BigInteger c = a.multiply(b);
System.out.println(c); // Prints 12193263111263526900
```

The `BigDecimal` type carries out floating-point computation without roundoff errors. For example,

```
BigDecimal d = new BigDecimal("4.35");
BigDecimal e = new BigDecimal("100");
BigDecimal f = d.multiply(e);
System.out.println(f); // Prints 435.00
```

ADVANCED TOPIC 4.2

Binary Numbers

You are familiar with decimal numbers, which use the digits 0, 1, 2, ..., 9. Each digit has a place value of 1, 10, 100 = 10^2, 1000 = 10^3, and so on. For example,

$$435 = 4 \cdot 10^2 + 3 \cdot 10^1 + 5 \cdot 10^0$$

Fractional digits have place values with negative powers of ten: 0.1 = 10^{-1}, 0.01 = 10^{-2}, and so on. For example,

$$4.35 = 4 \cdot 10^0 + 3 \cdot 10^{-1} + 5 \cdot 10^{-2}$$

Computers use binary numbers instead, which have just two digits (0 and 1) and place values that are powers of 2. Binary numbers are easier for computers to manipulate, because it is easier to build logic circuits that differentiate between "off" and "on" than it is to build circuits that can accurately tell ten different voltage levels apart.

It is easy to transform a binary number into a decimal number. Just compute the powers of two that correspond to ones in the binary number. For example,

$$1101 \text{ binary} = 1 \cdot 2^3 + 1 \cdot 2^2 + 0 \cdot 2^1 + 1 \cdot 2^0 = 8 + 4 + 1 = 13$$

Fractional binary numbers use negative powers of two. For example,

$$1.101 \text{ binary} = 1 \cdot 2^0 + 1 \cdot 2^{-1} + 0 \cdot 2^{-2} + 1 \cdot 2^{-3} = 1 + 0.5 + 0.125 = 1.625$$

Converting decimal numbers to binary numbers is a little trickier. Here is an algorithm that converts a decimal integer into its binary equivalent: Keep dividing the integer by 2, keeping track of the remainders. Stop when the number is 0. Then write the remainders as a binary number, starting with the last one. For example,

$$100 \div 2 = 50 \text{ remainder } 0$$

$$50 \div 2 = 25 \text{ remainder } 0$$

$$25 \div 2 = 12 \text{ remainder } 1$$

$$12 \div 2 = 6 \text{ remainder } 0$$

$$6 \div 2 = 3 \text{ remainder } 0$$

$$3 \div 2 = 1 \text{ remainder } 1$$

$$1 \div 2 = 0 \text{ remainder } 1$$

Therefore, 100 in decimal is 1100100 in binary.

To convert a fractional number <1 to its binary format, keep multiplying by 2. If the result is >1, subtract 1. Stop when the number is 0. Then use the digits before the decimal points as the binary digits of the fractional part, starting with the first one. For example,

$$0.35 \cdot 2 = 0.7$$

$$0.7 \cdot 2 = 1.4$$

$$0.4 \cdot 2 = 0.8$$

$$0.8 \cdot 2 = 1.6$$

$$0.6 \cdot 2 = 1.2$$

$$0.2 \cdot 2 = 0.4$$

Here the pattern repeats. That is, the binary representation of 0.35 is 0.01 0110 0110 0110 . . .

To convert any floating-point number into binary, convert the whole part and the fractional part separately. For example, 4.35 is 100.01 0110 0110 0110 . . . in binary.

You don't actually need to know about binary numbers to program in Java, but at times it can be helpful to understand a little about them. For example, knowing that an int is represented as a 32-bit binary number explains why the largest integer that you can represent in Java is 0111 1111 1111 1111 1111 1111 1111 1111 binary = 2,147,483,647 decimal. (The first bit is the sign bit. It is off for positive values.)

To convert an integer into its binary representation, you can use the static toString method of the Integer class. The call Integer.toString(n, 2) returns a string with the binary digits of the integer n. Conversely, you can convert a string containing binary digits into an integer with the call Integer.parseInt(digitString, 2). In both of these method calls, the second parameter denotes the base of the number system. It can be any number between 0 and 36. You can use these two methods to convert between decimal and binary integers. However, the Java library has no convenient method to do the same for floating-point numbers.

Now you can see why we had to fight with a roundoff error when computing 100 times 4.35. If you actually carry out the long multiplication, you get:

```
1 1 0 0 1 0 0 * 1 0 0.0 1|0 1 1 0|0 1 1 0|0 1 1 0 . . .

1 0 0.0 1|0 1 1 0|0 1 1 0|0 1 1 0 . . .
  1 0 0.0 1|0 1 1 0|0 1 1 0|0 1 1 . . .
    0
      0
        1 0 0.0 1|0 1 1 0|0 1 1 0 . . .
          0
            0
_____
1 1 0 1 1 0 0 1 0.1 1 1 1 1 1 1 1 . . .
```

That is, the result is 434, followed by an infinite number of 1s. The fractional part of the product is the binary equivalent of an infinite decimal fraction 0.999999 . . . , which is equal to 1. But the CPU can store only a finite number of 1s, and it discards some of them when converting the result to a decimal number.

RANDOM FACT 4.1

The Pentium Floating-Point Bug

In 1994, Intel Corporation released what was then its most powerful processor, the first of the Pentium series. Unlike previous generations of Intel's processors, the Pentium had a very fast floating-point unit. Intel's goal was to compete aggressively with the makers of higher-end processors for engineering workstations. The Pentium was an immediate success.

In the summer of 1994, Dr. Thomas Nicely of Lynchburg College in Virginia ran an extensive set of computations to analyze the sums of reciprocals of certain sequences of prime numbers. The results were not always what his theory predicted, even after he took into account the inevitable roundoff errors. Then Dr. Nicely noted that the same program did produce the correct results when run on the slower 486 processor, which preceded the Pentium in Intel's lineup. This should not have happened. The optimal roundoff behavior of floating-point calculations had been standardized by the Institute of Electrical and Electronics Engineers (IEEE), and Intel claimed to adhere to the IEEE standard in both the 486 and the Pentium processors. Upon further checking, Dr. Nicely discovered that indeed there was a very small set of numbers for which the product of two numbers was computed differently on the two processors. For example,

$$4,195,835 = ((4,195,835 / 3,145,727) \times 3,145,727)$$

is mathematically equal to 0, and it did compute as 0 on a 486 processor. On a Pentium processor, however, the result was 256.

As it turned out, Intel had independently discovered the bug in its testing and had started to produce chips that fixed it. (Subsequent versions of the Pentium, such as the Pentium III and IV, are free of the problem.) The bug was caused by an error in a table that was used to speed up the floating-point multiplication algorithm of the processor. Intel determined that the problem was exceedingly rare. They claimed that under normal use a typical consumer would only notice the problem once every 27,000 years. Unfortunately for Intel, Dr. Nicely had not been a normal user.

Now Intel had a real problem on its hands. It figured that replacing all the Pentium processors that it had already sold would cost it a great deal of money. Intel already had more orders for the chip than it could produce, and it would be particularly galling to have to give out the scarce chips as free replacements instead of selling them. Intel's management decided to punt on the issue and initially offered to replace the processors only for those customers who could prove that their work required absolute precision in mathematical calculations. Naturally, that did not go over well with the hundreds of thousands of customers who had paid retail prices of $700 and more for a Pentium chip and did not want to live with the nagging feeling that perhaps, one day, their income tax program would produce a faulty return.

Ultimately, Intel had to cave in to public demand and replaced all defective chips, at a cost of about 475 million dollars.

What do you think? Intel claims that the probability of the bug occurring in any calculation is extremely small—smaller than many chances you take every day, such as driving to work in an automobile. Indeed, many users had used their Pentium computers for many months without reporting any ill effects, and the computations that Professor Nicely was doing are hardly examples of typical user needs. As a result of its public relations blunder, Intel ended up paying a large amount of money. Undoubtedly, some of that money was added to chip prices and thus actually paid by Intel's customers. Also, a large number of processors, whose manufacture consumed energy and caused some environmental impact, were destroyed without benefiting anyone. Could Intel have been justified in wanting to replace only the processors of those users who could reasonably be expected to suffer an impact from the problem?

Suppose that, instead of stonewalling, Intel had offered you the choice of a free replacement processor or a $200 rebate. What would you have done? Would you have replaced your faulty chip, or would you have taken your chances and pocketed the money?

4.2 Constants

In many programs, you need to use numerical constants—values that do not change and that have a special significance for a computation.

A typical example for the use of constants is a computation that involves coin values, such as the following:

```
payment = dollars + quarters * 0.25 + dimes * 0.1
        + nickels * 0.05 + pennies * 0.01;
```

Most of the code is self-documenting. However, the four numeric quantities, 0.25, 0.1, 0.05, and 0.01 are included in the arithmetic expression without any explanation. Of course, in this case, you know that the value of a nickel is five cents, which explains the 0.05, and so on. However, the next person who needs to maintain this code may live in another country and may not know that a nickel is worth five cents.

Thus, it is a good idea to use symbolic names for all values, even those that appear obvious. Here is a clearer version of the computation of the total:

```
double quarterValue = 0.25;
double dimeValue = 0.1;
double nickelValue = 0.05;
double pennyValue = 0.01;
payment = dollars + quarters * quarterValue + dimes * dimeValue
       + nickels * nickelValue + pennies * pennyValue;
```

A final variable is a constant. Once its value has been set, it cannot be changed.

There is another improvement we can make. There is a difference between the nickels and nickelValue variables. The nickels variable can truly vary over the life of the program, as we calculate different payments. But nickelValue is always 0.05.

In Java, constants are identified with the keyword final. A variable tagged as final can never change after it has been set. If you try to change the value of a final variable, the compiler will report an error and your program will not compile.

Use named constants to make your programs easier to read and maintain.

Many programmers use all-uppercase names for constants (final variables), such as NICKEL_VALUE. That way, it is easy to distinguish between variables (with mostly lowercase letters) and constants. We will follow this convention in this book. However, this rule is a matter of good style, not a requirement of the Java language. The compiler will not complain if you give a final variable a name with lowercase letters.

Here is an improved version of the code that computes the value of a payment.

```
final double QUARTER_VALUE = 0.25;
final double DIME_VALUE = 0.1;
final double NICKEL_VALUE = 0.05;
final double PENNY_VALUE = 0.01;
payment = dollars + quarters * QUARTER_VALUE + dimes * DIME_VALUE
       + nickels * NICKEL_VALUE + pennies * PENNY_VALUE;
```

Frequently, constant values are needed in several methods. Then you should declare them together with the instance fields of a class and tag them as static and final. As before, final indicates that the value is a constant. The static keyword means that the constant belongs to the class—this is explained in greater detail in Chapter 9.)

```
public class CashRegister
{
    // Methods
    . . .

    // Constants
    public static final double QUARTER_VALUE = 0.25;
    public static final double DIME_VALUE = 0.1;
    public static final double NICKEL_VALUE = 0.05;
    public static final double PENNY_VALUE = 0.01;

    // Instance fields
    private double purchase;
    private double payment;
}
```

We declared the constants as public. There is no danger in doing this because constants cannot be modified. Methods of other classes can access a public constant by first specifying the name of the class in which it is defined, then a period, then the name of the constant, such as CashRegister.NICKEL_VALUE.

The Math class from the standard library defines a couple of useful constants:

```
public class Math
{
    . . .
    public static final double E = 2.7182818284590452354;
    public static final double PI = 3.14159265358979323846;
}
```

You can refer to these constants as Math.PI and Math.E in any of your methods. For example,

```
double circumference = Math.PI * diameter;
```

The sample program at the end of this section puts constants to work. The program shows a refinement of the CashRegister class of How To 3.1. The public interface of that class has been modified in order to solve a common business problem.

Busy cashiers sometimes make mistakes totaling up coin values. Our Cash-Register class features a method whose inputs are the *coin counts.* For example, the call

```
register.enterPayment(1, 2, 1, 1, 4);
```

enters a payment consisting of one dollar, two quarters, one dime, one nickel, and four pennies. The enterPayment method figures out the total value of the payment, $1.69. As you can see from the code listing, the method uses named constants for the coin values.

SYNTAX 4.2 **Constant Definition**

In a method:
final *typeName variableName* = *expression*;

In a class:
accessSpecifier static final *typeName variableName* = *expression*;

Example:

```
final double NICKEL_VALUE = 0.05;
public static final double LITERS_PER_GALLON = 3.785;
```

Purpose:

To define a constant in a method or a class

File CashRegister.java

```java
1   /**
2       A cash register totals up sales and computes change due.
3   */
4   public class CashRegister
5   {
6       /**
7           Constructs a cash register with no money in it.
8       */
9       public CashRegister()
10      {
11          purchase = 0;
12          payment = 0;
13      }
14
15      /**
16          Records the purchase price of an item.
17          @param amount the price of the purchased item
18      */
19      public void recordPurchase(double amount)
20      {
21          purchase = purchase + amount;
22      }
23
24      /**
25          Enters the payment received from the customer.
26          @param dollars the number of dollars in the payment
27          @param quarters the number of quarters in the payment
28          @param dimes the number of dimes in the payment
29          @param nickels the number of nickels in the payment
30          @param pennies the number of pennies in the payment
31      */
32      public void enterPayment(int dollars, int quarters,
33              int dimes, int nickels, int pennies)
34      {
35          payment = dollars + quarters * QUARTER_VALUE + dimes * DIME_VALUE
36              + nickels * NICKEL_VALUE + pennies * PENNY_VALUE;
37      }
38
39      /**
40          Computes the change due and resets the machine for the next customer.
41          @return the change due to the customer
42      */
43      public double giveChange()
44      {
45          double change = payment - purchase;
46          purchase = 0;
47          payment = 0;
48          return change;
49      }
50
51      public static final double QUARTER_VALUE = 0.25;
52      public static final double DIME_VALUE = 0.1;
```

```
53    public static final double NICKEL_VALUE = 0.05;
54    public static final double PENNY_VALUE = 0.01;
55
56    private double purchase;
57    private double payment;
58 }
```

File CashRegisterTester.java

```
1  /**
2     This class tests the CashRegister class.
3  */
4  public class CashRegisterTester
5  {
6     public static void main(String[] args)
7     {
8        CashRegister register = new CashRegister();
9
10       register.recordPurchase(0.75);
11       register.recordPurchase(1.50);
12       register.enterPayment(2, 0, 5, 0, 0);
13       System.out.print("Change=");
14       System.out.println(register.giveChange());
15
16       register.recordPurchase(2.25);
17       register.recordPurchase(19.25);
18       register.enterPayment(23, 2, 0, 0, 0);
19       System.out.print("Change=");
20       System.out.println(register.giveChange());
21    }
22 }
```

Output

```
Change=0.25
Change=2.0
```

SELF CHECK

4. What is the difference between the following two statements?

   ```
   final double CM_PER_INCH = 2.54;
   ```
   and
   ```
   public static final double CM_PER_INCH = 2.54;
   ```

5. What is wrong with the following statement?

   ```
   double circumference = 3.14 * diameter;
   ```

QUALITY TIP 4.1

Do Not Use Magic Numbers

A magic number is a numeric constant that appears in your code without explanation. For example, consider the following scary example that actually occurs in the Java library source:

```
h = 31 * h + ch;
```

Why 31? The number of days in January? One less than the number of bits in an integer? Actually, this code computes a "hash code" from a string—a number that is derived from the characters in such a way that different strings are likely to yield different hash codes. The value 31 turns out to scramble the character values nicely.

A better solution is to use a named constant:

```
final int HASH_MULTIPLIER = 31;
h = HASH_MULTIPLIER * h + ch;
```

You should never use magic numbers in your code. Any number that is not completely self-explanatory should be declared as a named constant. Even the most reasonable cosmic constant is going to change one day. You think there are 365 days in a year? Your customers on Mars are going to be pretty unhappy about your silly prejudice. Make a constant

```
final int DAYS_PER_YEAR = 365;
```

By the way, the device

```
final int THREE_HUNDRED_AND_SIXTY_FIVE = 365;
```

is counterproductive and frowned upon.

QUALITY TIP 4.2

Choose Descriptive Variable Names

In algebra, variable names are usually just one letter long, such as p or A, maybe with a subscript such as p_1. You might be tempted to save yourself a lot of typing by using short variable names in your Java programs:

```
payment = d + q * QV + di * DIV + n * NV + p * PV;
```

Compare this with the following statement:

```
payment = dollars + quarters * QUARTER_VALUE + dimes * DIME_VALUE
    + nickels * NICKEL_VALUE + pennies * PENNY_VALUE;
```

The advantage is obvious. Reading `dollars` is a lot less trouble than reading d and then figuring out that it must mean "dollars".

In practical programming, descriptive variable names are particularly important when programs are written by more than one person. It may be obvious to you that d stands for dollars, but is it obvious to the person who needs to update your code years later, long after you were promoted (or laid off)? For that matter, will you remember yourself what d means when you look at the code six months from now?

4.3 Assignment, Increment, and Decrement

The = operator is called the assignment operator. On the left, you need a variable name. The right-hand side can be a single value or an expression. The assignment operator sets the variable to the given value. So far, that's straightforward. But now let's look at a more interesting use of the assignment operator. Consider the statement

```
items = items + 1;
```

It means, "Compute the value of the expression items + 1, and place the result again into the variable items." (See Figure 1.) The net effect of executing this statement is to increment items by 1. For example, if items was 3 before execution of the statement, it is set to 4 afterwards. (This statement would be useful if the cash register kept track of the number of purchased items.)

The = sign does *not* mean that the left-hand side is equal to the right-hand side. Instead, it is an instruction to copy the right-hand-side value into the left-hand-side variable. You should not confuse this assignment operation with the = relation used in algebra to denote equality. The assignment operator is an instruction to do something, namely place a value into a variable. The mathematical equality states the fact that two values are equal. Of course, in mathematics it would make no sense to write that $i = i + 1$; no integer can equal itself plus 1.

> Assignment to a variable is not the same as mathematical equality.

The concepts of assignment and equality have no relationship with each other, and it is a bit unfortunate that the Java language (following C and C++) uses = to denote assignment. Other programming languages use a symbol such as <- or :=, which avoids the confusion.

> The ++ and -- operators increment and decrement a variable.

The increment operation is so common when writing programs that there is a special shorthand for it, namely

```
items++;
```

This statement also adds 1 to items. However, it is easier to type and read than the explicit assignment statement. As you might have guessed, there is also a decrement operator --. The statement

```
items--;
```

subtracts 1 from items.

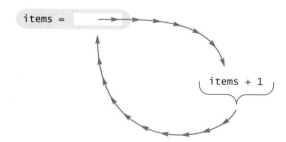

Figure 1
Incrementing a Variable

SELF CHECK

6. What is the meaning of the following statement?

   ```
   balance = balance + amount;
   ```

7. What is the value of n after the following sequence of statements?

   ```
   n--;
   n++;
   n--;
   ```

PRODUCTIVITY HINT 4.1

Avoid Unstable Layout

Arrange program code and comments so that the program is easy to read. For example, do not cram all statements on a single line, and make sure that braces { } line up.

However, be careful when you embark on beautification efforts. Some programmers like to line up the = signs in a series of assignments, like this:

```
nickels  = 0;
dimes    = 0;
quarters = 0;
```

This looks very neat, but the layout is not stable. Suppose you add a line like the one at the bottom of this:

```
nickels  = 0;
dimes    = 0;
quarters = 0;
halfDollars = 0;
```

Oops, now the = signs no longer line up, and you have the extra work of lining them up again.

Here is another example. Some programmers like to put a column of asterisks (*) in documentation comments, like this:

```
/**
 * Computes the change due and resets the cash register for the
 * next customer.
 * @return the change due to the customer
 */
```

It looks pretty, but it is tedious to rearrange the asterisks when editing comments.

You may not care about these issues. Perhaps you plan to beautify your program just before it is finished, when you are about to turn in your homework. That is not a particularly useful approach. In practice, programs are never finished. They are continuously improved and updated. It is better to develop the habit of laying out your programs well from the start and keeping them legible at all times. Therefore, it is a good idea to avoid layout schemes that are hard to maintain.

ADVANCED TOPIC 4.3

Combining Assignment and Arithmetic

In Java you can combine arithmetic and assignment. For example, the instruction

```
balance += amount;
```

is a shortcut for

```
balance = balance + amount;
```

Similarly,

```
items *= 2;
```

is another way of writing

```
items = items * 2;
```

Many programmers find this a convenient shortcut. If you like it, go ahead and use it in your own code. For simplicity, we won't use it in this book.

4.4 Arithmetic Operations and Mathematical Functions

You already saw how to add, subtract, and multiply values. Division is indicated with a /, not a fraction bar. For example,

$$\frac{a+b}{2}$$

becomes

```
(a + b) / 2
```

Parentheses are used just as in algebra: to indicate in which order the subexpressions should be computed. For example, in the expression (a + b) / 2, the sum a + b is computed first, and then the sum is divided by 2. In contrast, in the expression

```
a + b / 2
```

only b is divided by 2, and then the sum of a and b / 2 is formed. Just as in regular algebraic notation, multiplication and division bind more strongly than addition and subtraction. For example, in the expression a + b / 2, the / is carried out first, even though the + operation occurs farther to the left.

> If both arguments of the / operator are integers, the result is an integer and the remainder is discarded.

Division works as you would expect, as long as at least one of the numbers involved is a floating-point number. That is,

```
7.0 / 4.0
7 / 4.0
7.0 / 4
```

all yield 1.75. However, if both numbers are integers, then the result of the division is always an integer, with the remainder discarded. That is,

```
7 / 4
```

evaluates to 1, because 7 divided by 4 is 1 with a remainder of 3 (which is discarded). This can be a source of subtle programming errors—see Common Error 4.1.

If you are interested only in the remainder of an integer division, use the % operator:

> The % operator computes the remainder of a division.

```
7 % 4
```

is 3, the remainder of the integer division of 7 by 4. The % symbol has no analog in algebra. It was chosen because it looks similar to /, and the remainder operation is related to division.

Here is a typical use for the integer / and % operations. Suppose you want to know how much change a cash register should give, using separate values for dollars and cents. You can compute the value as an integer, denominated in cents, and then compute the whole dollar amount and the remaining change:

```
final int PENNIES_PER_NICKEL = 5;
final int PENNIES_PER_DIME = 10;
final int PENNIES_PER_QUARTER = 25;
final int PENNIES_PER_DOLLAR = 100;

// Compute total value in pennies
int total = dollars * PENNIES_PER_DOLLAR + quarters * PENNIES_PER_QUARTER
      + nickels * PENNIES_PER_NICKEL + dimes * PENNIES_PER_DIME + pennies;

// Use integer division to convert to dollars, cents
int dollars = total / PENNIES_PER_DOLLAR;
int cents = total % PENNIES_PER_DOLLAR;
```

For example, if total is 243, then dollars is set to 2 and cents to 43.

To compute x^n, you write Math.pow(x, n). However, to compute x^2 it is significantly more efficient simply to compute x * x.

> The Math class contains methods sqrt and pow to compute square roots and powers.

To take the square root of a number, you use the Math.sqrt method. For example, $\sqrt{x}$ is written as Math.sqrt(x).

In algebra, you use fractions, superscripts for exponents, and radical signs for roots to arrange expressions in a compact two-dimensional form. In Java, you have to write all expressions in a linear arrangement. For example, the subexpression

$$\frac{-b + \sqrt{b^2 - 4ac}}{2a}$$

of the quadratic formula becomes

```
(-b + Math.sqrt(b * b - 4 * a * c)) / (2 * a)
```

Figure 2 shows how to analyze such an expression. With complicated expressions like these, it is not always easy to keep the parentheses ( ) matched—see Common Error 4.2.

Table 2 shows additional methods of the Math class. Inputs and outputs are floating-point numbers.

Table 2	Mathematical Methods
Function	**Returns**
Math.sqrt(x)	Square root of x (≥ 0)
Math.pow(x, y)	x^y ($x > 0$, or $x = 0$ and $y > 0$, or $x < 0$ and y is an integer)
Math.sin(x)	Sine of x (x in radians)
Math.cos(x)	Cosine of x
Math.tan(x)	Tangent of x
Math.asin(x)	Arc sine ($\sin^{-1}x \in [-\pi/2, \pi/2]$, $x \in [-1, 1]$)
Math.acos(x)	Arc cosine ($\cos^{-1}x \in [0, \pi]$, $x \in [-1, 1]$)
Math.atan(x)	Arc tangent ($\tan^{-1}x \in [-\pi/2, \pi/2]$)
Math.atan2(y, x)	Arc tangent ($\tan^{-1}y/x \in [-\pi, \pi]$), x may be 0
Math.toRadians(x)	Convert x degrees to radians (i.e., returns $x \cdot \pi/180$)
Math.toDegrees(x)	Convert x radians to degrees (i.e., returns $x \cdot 180/\pi$)
Math.exp(x)	e^x
Math.log(x)	Natural log ($\ln(x)$, $x > 0$)
Math.round(x)	Closest integer to x (as a long)
Math.ceil(x)	Smallest integer $\geq x$ (as a double)
Math.floor(x)	Largest integer $\leq x$ (as a double)
Math.abs(x)	Absolute value $|x|$
Math.max(x, y)	The larger of x and y
Math.min(x, y)	The smaller of x and y

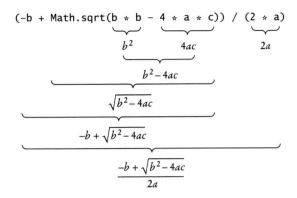

Figure 2 Analyzing an Expression

SELF CHECK

8. What is the value of 1729 / 100? Of 1729 % 100?
9. Why doesn't the following statement compute the average of s1, s2, and s3?

   ```
   double average = s1 + s2 + s3 / 3; // Error
   ```
10. What is the value of Math.sqrt(Math.pow(x, 2) + Math.pow(y, 2)) in mathematical notation?

COMMON ERROR 4.1

Integer Division

It is unfortunate that Java uses the same symbol, namely /, for both integer and floating-point division. These are really quite different operations. It is a common error to use integer division by accident. Consider this program segment that computes the average of three integers.

```
int s1 = 5; // Score of test 1
int s2 = 6; // Score of test 2
int s3 = 3; // Score of test 3
double average = (s1 + s2 + s3) / 3;   // Error
System.out.print("Your average score is ");
System.out.println(average);
```

What could be wrong with that? Of course, the average of s1, s2, and s3 is

$$\frac{s_1 + s_2 + s_3}{3}$$

Here, however, the / does not mean division in the mathematical sense. It denotes integer division, because the values s1 + s2 + s3 and 3 are both integers. For example, if the scores add up to 14, the average is computed to be 4, the result of the integer division of 14 by 3.

That integer 4 is then moved into the floating-point variable average. The remedy is to make either the numerator or denominator into a floating-point number:

```
double total = s1 + s2 + s3;
double average = total / 3;
```

or

```
double average = (s1 + s2 + s3) / 3.0;
```

COMMON ERROR 4.2

Unbalanced Parentheses

Consider the expression

```
1.5 * ((-(b - Math.sqrt(b * b - 4 * a * c)) / (2 * a))
```

What is wrong with it? Count the parentheses. There are five opening parentheses (and four closing parentheses). The parentheses are unbalanced. This kind of typing error is very common with complicated expressions. Now consider this expression.

```
1.5 * (Math.sqrt(b * b - 4 * a * c))) - ((b / (2 * a))
```

This expression has five opening parentheses (and five closing parentheses), but it is still not correct. In the middle of the expression,

```
1.5 * (Math.sqrt(b * b - 4 * a * c))) - ((b / (2 * a))
```

there are only two opening parentheses (but three closing parentheses), which is an error. In the middle of an expression, the count of opening parentheses must be greater than or equal to the count of closing parentheses, and at the end of the expression the two counts must be the same.

Here is a simple trick to make the counting easier without using pencil and paper. It is difficult for the brain to keep two counts simultaneously, so keep only one count when scanning the expression. Start with 1 at the first opening parenthesis; add 1 whenever you see an opening parenthesis; subtract 1 whenever you see a closing parenthesis. Say the numbers aloud as you scan the expression. If the count ever drops below zero, or if it is not zero at the end, the parentheses are unbalanced. For example, when scanning the previous expression, you would mutter

```
1.5 * (Math.sqrt(b * b - 4 * a * c) )   ) - ((b / (2 * a))
        1          2                 1 0  −1
```

and you would find the error.

QUALITY TIP 4.3

White Space

The compiler does not care whether you write your entire program onto a single line or place every symbol onto a separate line. The human reader, though, cares very much. You should use blank lines to group your code visually into sections. For example, you can signal to the reader that an output prompt and the corresponding input statement belong together by inserting a blank line before and after the group. You will find many examples in the source code listings in this book.

White space inside expressions is also important. It is easier to read

```
x1 = (-b + Math.sqrt(b * b - 4 * a * c)) / (2 * a);
```

than

```
x1=(-b+Math.sqrt(b*b-4*a*c))/(2*a);
```

Simply put spaces around all operators + - * / % =. However, don't put a space after a unary minus: a - used to negate a single quantity, as in -b. That way, it can be easily distinguished from a binary minus, as in a - b. Don't put spaces between a method name and the parentheses, but do put a space after every Java keyword. That makes it easy to see that the sqrt in Math.sqrt(x) is a method name, whereas the if in if (x > 0) . . . is a keyword.

QUALITY TIP 4.4

Factor Out Common Code

Suppose you want to find both solutions of the quadratic equation $ax^2 + bx + c = 0$. The quadratic formula tells us that the solutions are

$$x_{1,2} = \frac{-b \pm \sqrt{b^2 - 4ac}}{2a}$$

In Java, there is no analog to the ± operation, which indicates how to obtain two solutions simultaneously. Both solutions must be computed separately:

```
x1 = (-b + Math.sqrt(b * b - 4 * a * c)) / (2 * a);
x2 = (-b - Math.sqrt(b * b - 4 * a * c)) / (2 * a);
```

This approach has two problems. First, the computation of Math.sqrt(b * b - 4 * a * c) is carried out twice, which wastes time. Second, whenever the same code is replicated, the possibility of a typing error increases. The remedy is to factor out the common code:

```
double root = Math.sqrt(b * b - 4 * a * c);
x1 = (-b + root) / (2 * a);
x2 = (-b - root) / (2 * a);
```

You could go even further and factor out the computation of 2 * a, but the gain from factoring out very simple computations is too small to warrant the effort.

4.5 Calling Static Methods

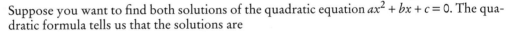

In the preceding section, you encountered the Math class, which contains a collection of helpful methods for carrying out mathematical computations. These methods have a special form: they are static methods that do not operate on an object.

That is, you don't call

```
double x = 4;
double root = x.sqrt(); // Error
```

because, in Java, numbers are not objects, so you can never invoke a method on a number. Instead, you pass a number as an explicit parameter to a method, enclosing the number in parentheses after the method name. For example, the number value x can be a parameter of the `Math.sqrt` method: `Math.sqrt(x)`.

> A static method does not operate on an object.

This call makes it appear as if the `sqrt` method is applied to an object called `Math`, because `Math` precedes `sqrt` just as `harrysChecking` precedes `getBalance` in a method call `harrysChecking.getBalance()`. However, `Math` is a class, not an object. A method such as `Math.round` that does not operate on any object is called a *static* method. (The term "static" is a historical holdover from the C and C++ programming languages. It has nothing to do with the usual meaning of the word.) Static methods do not operate on objects, but they are still defined inside classes. You must specify the class to which the `sqrt` method belongs—hence the call is `Math.sqrt(x)`.

How can you tell whether `Math` is a class or an object? All classes in the Java library start with an uppercase letter (such as `System`). Objects and methods start with a lowercase letter (such as `out` and `println`). (You can tell objects and methods apart because method calls are followed by parentheses.) Therefore, `System.out.println()` denotes a call of the `println` method on the `out` object inside the `System` class. On the other hand, `Math.sqrt(x)` denotes a call to the `sqrt` method inside the `Math` class. This use of upper- and lowercase letters is merely a convention, not a rule of the Java language. It is, however, a convention that the authors of the Java class libraries follow consistently. You should do the same in your programs. If you give names to objects or methods that start with uppercase letters, you will likely confuse your fellow programmers. Therefore, we strongly recommend that you follow the standard naming convention.

SYNTAX 4.3 Static Method Call

ClassName.*methodName*(*parameters*)

Example:

`Math.sqrt(4)`

Purpose:

To invoke a static method (a method that does not operate on an object) and supply its parameters

SELF CHECK

11. Why can't you call x.pow(y) to compute x^y?

12. Is the call `System.out.println(4)` a static method call?

COMMON ERROR 4.3

Roundoff Errors

Roundoff errors are a fact of life when calculating with floating-point numbers. You probably have encountered this phenomenon yourself with manual calculations. If you calculate 1/3 to two decimal places, you get 0.33. Multiplying again by 3, you obtain 0.99, not 1.00.

In the processor hardware, numbers are represented in the binary number system, not in decimal. You still get roundoff errors when binary digits are lost. They just may crop up at different places than you might expect. Here is an example:

```java
double f = 4.35;
int n = (int) (100 * f);
System.out.println(n); // Prints 434!
```

Of course, one hundred times 4.35 is 435, but the program prints 434.

Computers represent numbers in the binary system (see Advanced Topic 4.2). In the binary system, there is no exact representation for 4.35, just as there is no exact representation for 1/3 in the decimal system. The representation used by the computer is just a little less than 4.35, so 100 times that value is just a little less than 435. When a floating-point value is converted to an integer, the entire fractional part is discarded, even if it is almost 1. As a result, the integer 434 is stored in n. Remedy: Use `Math.round` to convert floating-point numbers to integers. The round method returns the *closest* integer.

```java
int n = (int) Math.round(100 * f);   // OK, n is 435
```

HOW TO 4.1

Carrying Out Computations

Many programming problems require that you use mathematical formulas to compute values. It is not always obvious how to turn a problem statement into a sequence of mathematical formulas and, ultimately, statements in the Java programming language.

Step 1 Understand the problem: What are the inputs? What are the desired outputs?

For example, suppose you are asked to simulate a postage stamp vending machine. A customer inserts money into the vending machine. Then the customer pushes a "First class stamps" button. The vending machine gives out as many first-class stamps as the customer paid for. (A first-class stamp cost 37 cents at the time this book was written.) Finally, the customer pushes a "Penny stamps" button. The machine gives the change in penny (1-cent) stamps.

In this problem, there is one input:

• The amount of money the customer inserts

There are two desired outputs:

• The number of first-class stamps the machine returns

• The number of penny stamps the machine returns

Step 2 Work out examples by hand.

This is a very important step. If you can't compute a couple of solutions by hand, it's unlikely that you'll be able to write a program that automates the computation.

Let's assume that a first-class stamp costs 37 cents and the customer inserts $1.00. That's enough for two stamps (74 cents) but not enough for three stamps ($1.11). Therefore, the machine returns two first-class stamps and 26 penny stamps.

Step 3 Find mathematical equations that compute the answers.

Given an amount of money and the price of a first-class stamp, how can you compute how many first-class stamps can be purchased with the money? Clearly, the answer is related to the quotient

$$\frac{\text{amount of money}}{\text{price of first-class stamp}}$$

For example, suppose the customer paid $1.00. Use a pocket calculator to compute the quotient: $1.00/$0.37 \approx 2.7027$.

How do you get "2 stamps" out of 2.7027? It's the integer part. By discarding the fractional part, you get the number of whole stamps the customer has purchased.

In mathematical notation,

$$\text{number of first-class stamps} = \left\lfloor \frac{\text{money}}{\text{price of first-class stamp}} \right\rfloor$$

where $\lfloor x \rfloor$ denotes the largest integer $\leq x$. That function is sometimes called the "floor function".

You now know how to compute the number of stamps that are given out when the customer pushes the "First-class stamps" button. When the customer gets the stamps, the amount of money is reduced by the value of the stamps purchased. For example, if the customer gets two stamps, the remaining money is $0.26—the difference between $1.00 and $2 \cdot \$0.37$. Here is the general formula:

remaining money = money – number of first-class stamps · price of first-class stamp

How many penny stamps does the remaining money buy? That's easy. If $0.26 is left, the customer gets 26 stamps. In general, the number of penny stamps is

number of penny stamps = 100 · remaining money

Step 4 Turn the mathematical equations into Java statements.

In Java, you can compute the integer part of a nonnegative floating-point value by applying an (int) cast. Therefore, you can compute the number of first-class stamps with the following statement:

```
firstClassStamps = (int) (money / FIRST_CLASS_STAMP_PRICE);
money = money - firstClassStamps * FIRST_CLASS_STAMP_PRICE;
```

Finally, the number of penny stamps is

```
pennyStamps = 100 * money;
```

That's not quite right, though. The value of pennyStamps should be an integer, but the right-hand side is a floating-point number. Therefore, the correct statement is

```
pennyStamps = (int) Math.round(100 * money);
```

Step 5 Build a class that carries out your computations.

How To 3.1 explains how to develop a class by finding methods and instance variables. In our case, we can find three methods:

- `void insert(double amount)`
- `int giveFirstClassStamps()`
- `int givePennyStamps()`

The state of a vending machine can be described by the amount of money that the customer has available for purchases. Therefore, we supply one instance variable, `money`.

Here is the implementation:

```java
public class StampMachine
{
    public StampMachine()
    {
        money = 0;
    }

    public void insert(double amount)
    {
        money = money + amount;
    }

    public int giveFirstClassStamps()
    {
        int firstClassStamps = (int) (money / FIRST_CLASS_STAMP_PRICE);
        money = money - firstClassStamps * FIRST_CLASS_STAMP_PRICE;
        return firstClassStamps;
    }

    public int givePennyStamps()
    {
        int pennyStamps = (int) Math.round(100 * money);
        money = 0;
        return pennyStamps;
    }

    public static final double FIRST_CLASS_STAMP_PRICE = 0.37;
    private double money;
}
```

Step 6 Test your class.

Run a test program (or use an integrated environment such as BlueJ) to verify that the values that your class computes are the same values that you computed by hand. In our example, try the statements

```java
StampMachine machine = new StampMachine();
machine.insert(1);
System.out.print("First class stamps: ");
System.out.println(machine.giveFirstClassStamps());
System.out.print("Penny stamps: ");
System.out.println(machine.givePennyStamps());
```

Check that the result is

```
First class stamps: 2
Penny stamps: 26
```

4.6 Strings

Next to numbers, strings are the most important data type that most programs use. A string is a sequence of characters, such as "Hello, World!". In Java, strings are enclosed in quotation marks, which are not themselves part of the string. Note that, unlike numbers, strings are objects. (You can tell that String is a class name because it starts with an uppercase letter. The primitive types int and double start with lowercase letters.)

> A string is a sequence of characters. Strings are objects of the String class.

The number of characters in a string is called the length of the string. For example, the length of "Hello, World!" is 13. You can compute the length of a string with the length method.

```
int n = message.length();
```

A string of length zero, containing no characters, is called the empty string and is written as "".

Use the + operator to put strings together to form a longer string.

```
String name = "Dave";
String message = "Hello, " + name;
```

> Strings can be concatenated, that is, put end to end to yield a new longer string. String concatenation is denoted by the + operator.

The + operator concatenates two strings, provided one of the expressions, either to the left or the right of a + operator, is a string. The other one is automatically forced to become a string as well, and both strings are concatenated.

For example, consider this code:

```
String a = "Agent";
int n = 7;
String bond = a + n;
```

> Whenever one of the arguments of the + operator is a string, the other argument is converted to a string.

Because a is a string, n is converted from the integer 7 to the string "7". Then the two strings "Agent" and "7" are concatenated to form the string "Agent7".

This concatenation is very useful to reduce the number of System.out.print instructions. For example, you can combine

```
System.out.print("The total is ");
System.out.println(total);
```

to the single call

```
System.out.println("The total is " + total);
```

The concatenation "The total is " + total computes a single string that consists of the string "The total is ", followed by the string equivalent of the number total.

Sometimes you have a string that contains a number, usually from user input. For example, suppose that the string variable input has the value "19". To get the integer value 19, you use the static parseInt method of the Integer class.

```
int count = Integer.parseInt(input);
    // count is the integer 19
```

H e l l o ,   W o r l d !
0 1 2 3 4 5 6 7 8 9 10 11 12

Figure 3   String Positions

If a string contains the digits of a number, you use the Integer.parseInt or Double.parseDouble method to obtain the number value.

To convert a string containing floating-point digits to its floating-point value, use the static parseDouble method of the Double class. For example, suppose input is the string "3.95".

```
double price = Double.parseDouble(input);
    // price is the floating-point number 3.95
```

However, if the string contains spaces or other characters that cannot occur inside numbers, an error occurs. For now, we will always assume that user input does not contain invalid characters.

The substring method computes substrings of a string. The call

Use the substring method to extract a part of a string.

```
s.substring(start, pastEnd)
```

returns a string that is made up of the characters in the string s, starting at position start, and containing all characters up to, but not including, the position pastEnd. Here is an example:

```
String greeting = "Hello, World!";
String sub = greeting.substring(0, 5); // sub is "Hello"
```

String positions are counted starting with 0.

The substring operation makes a string that consists of five characters taken from the string greeting. A curious aspect of the substring operation is the numbering of the starting and ending positions. The first string position is labeled 0, the second one 1, and so on. For example, Figure 3 shows the position numbers in the greeting string.

The position number of the last character (12 for the string "Hello, World!") is always 1 less than the length of the string.

Let us figure out how to extract the substring "World". Count characters starting at 0, not 1. You find that W, the eighth character, has position number 7. The first character that you don't want, !, is the character at position 12 (see Figure 4). Therefore, the appropriate substring command is

```
String sub2 = greeting.substring(7, 12);
```

It is curious that you must specify the position of the first character that you do want and then the first character that you don't want. There is one advantage to this

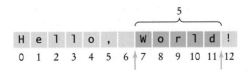

Figure 4   Extracting a Substring

setup. You can easily compute the length of the substring: It is pastEnd - start. For example, the string "World" has length 12 − 7 = 5.

If you omit the second parameter of the substring method, then all characters from the starting position to the end of the string are copied. For example,

```
String tail = greeting.substring(7); // Copies all characters from position 7 on
```

sets tail to the string "World!".

If you supply an illegal string position (a negative number, or a value that is larger than the length of the string), then your program terminates with an error message.

In this section, we have made the assumption that each character in a string occupies a single position. Unfortunately, that assumption is not quite correct. If you process strings that contain characters from international alphabets or special symbols, some characters may occupy two positions—see Advanced Topic 4.5.

SELF CHECK

13. Assuming the String variable s holds the value "Agent", what is the effect of the assignment s = s + s.length()?

14. Assuming the String variable river holds the value "Mississippi", what is the value of river.substring(1, 2)? Of river.substring(2, river.length() - 3)?

PRODUCTIVITY HINT 4.2

Reading Exception Reports

You will often have programs that terminate and display an error message, such as

```
Exception in thread "main" java.lang.StringIndexOutOfBoundsException:
    String index out of range: -4
  at java.lang.String.substring(String.java:1444)
  at Homework1.main(Homework1.java:16)
```

An amazing number of students simply give up at that point, saying "it didn't work", or "my program died", without ever reading the error message. Admittedly, the format of the exception report is not very friendly. But it is actually easy to decipher it.

When you have a close look at the error message, you will notice two pieces of useful information:

1. The name of the exception, such as StringIndexOutOfBoundsException

2. The line number of the code that contained the statement that caused the exception, such as Homework1.java:16

The name of the exception is always in the first line of the report, and it ends in Exception. If you get a StringIndexOutOfBoundsException, then there was a problem with accessing an invalid position in a string. That is useful information.

The line number of the offending code is a little harder to determine. The exception report contains the entire stack trace—that is, the names of all methods that were pending when the exception hit. The first line of the stack trace is the method that actually generated the exception. The last line of the stack trace is a line in main. Often, the exception was thrown by a method that is in the standard library. Look for the first line in your code that appears in the exception report. For example, skip the line that refers to

```
java.lang.String.substring(String.java:1444)
```

The next line in our example mentions a line number in your code, Homework1.java. Once you have the line number in your code, open up the file, go to that line, and look at it! In the great majority of cases, knowing the name of the exception and the line that caused it make it completely obvious what went wrong, and you can easily fix your error.

ADVANCED TOPIC 4.4

Escape Sequences

Suppose you want to display a string containing quotation marks, such as

```
Hello, "World"!
```

You can't use

```
System.out.println("Hello, "World"!");
```

As soon as the compiler reads "Hello, ", it thinks the string is finished, and then it gets all confused about World followed by two quotation marks. A human would probably realize that the second and third quotation marks were supposed to be part of the string, but a compiler has a one-track mind. If a simple analysis of the input doesn't make sense to it, it just refuses to go on, and reports an error. Well, how do you then display quotation marks on the screen? You precede the quotation marks inside the string with a *backslash* character. Inside a string, the sequence \" denotes a literal quote, not the end of a string. The correct display statement is, therefore

```
System.out.println("Hello, \"World\"!");
```

The backslash character is used as an *escape* character; the character sequence \" is called an escape sequence. The backslash does not denote itself; instead, it is used to encode other characters that would otherwise be difficult to include in a string.

Now, what do you do if you actually want to print a backslash (for example, to specify a Windows file name)? You must enter two \\ in a row, like this:

```
System.out.println("The secret message is in C:\\Temp\\Secret.txt");
```

This statement prints

```
The secret message is in C:\Temp\Secret.txt
```

Another escape sequence occasionally used is \n, which denotes a *newline* or line feed character. Printing a newline character causes the start of a new line on the display. For example, the statement

```
System.out.print("*\n**\n***\n");
```

prints the characters

```
*
**
***
```

on three separate lines. Of course, you could have achieved the same effect with three separate calls to println.

Finally, escape sequences are useful for including international characters in a string. For example, suppose you want to print "All the way to San José!", with an accented letter (é). If you use a U.S. keyboard, you may not have a key to generate that letter. Java uses the *Unicode* encoding scheme to denote international characters. For example, the é character has Unicode encoding 00E9. You can include that character inside a string by writing \u, followed by its Unicode encoding:

```
System.out.println("All the way to San Jos\u00E9!");
```

You can look up the codes for the U.S. English and Western European characters in Appendix B, and codes for thousands of characters in reference [1].

ADVANCED TOPIC 4.5

Strings and the char Type

Strings are sequences of Unicode characters (see Random Fact 4.2). Character constants look like string constants, except that character constants are delimited by single quotes: 'H' is a character, "H" is a string containing a single character. You can use escape sequences (see Advanced Topic 4.4) inside character constants. For example, '\n' is the newline character, and '\u00E9' is the character é. You can find the values of the character constants that are used in Western European languages in Appendix B.

Characters have numeric values. For example, if you look at Appendix B, you can see that the character 'H' is actually encoded as the number 72.

When Java was first designed, each Unicode character was encoded as a two-byte quantity. The char type was intended to hold the code of a Unicode character. However, as of 2003, Unicode had grown so large that some characters needed to be encoded as pairs of char values. Thus, you can no longer think of a char value as a character. Technically speaking, a char value is a *code unit* in the UTF-16 encoding of Unicode. That encoding represents the most common characters as a single char value, and less common or *supplementary* characters as a pair of char values.

The charAt method of the String class returns a code unit from a string. As with the substring method, the positions in the string are counted starting at 0. For example, the statement

```
String greeting = "Hello";
char ch = greeting.charAt(0);
```

sets ch to the value 'H'.

However, if you use char variables, your programs may fail with some strings that contain international or symbolic characters. For example, the single character ℤ (the mathematical symbol for the set of integers) is encoded by the two code units '\uD835' and '\uDD6B'.

If you call charAt(0) on the string containing the single character ℤ (that is, the string "\uD835\uDD6B"), you only get the first half of a supplementary character.

Therefore, you should only use char values if you are absolutely sure that you won't need to encode supplementary characters.

RANDOM FACT 4.2

International Alphabets

The English alphabet is pretty simple: upper- and lowercase a to z. Other European languages have accent marks and special characters. For example, German has three umlaut characters (ä, ö, ü) and a double-s character (ß). These are not optional frills; you couldn't write a page of German text without using these characters. German computer keyboards have keys for these characters (see Figure 5).

This poses a problem for computer users and designers. The American standard character encoding (called ASCII, for American Standard Code for Information Interchange) specifies 128 codes: 52 upper- and lowercase characters, 10 digits, 32 typographical symbols, and 34 control characters (such as space, newline, and 32 others for controlling printers and other devices). The umlaut and double-s are not among them. Some German data processing systems replace seldom-used ASCII characters with German letters: [\ ] { | } ~ are replaced with Ä Ö Ü ä ö ü ß. Most people can live without those ASCII characters, but programmers using Java definitely cannot. Other encoding schemes take advantage of the fact that one byte can encode 256 different characters, but only 128 are standardized by ASCII. Unfortunately, there are multiple incompatible standards for using the remaining 128 characters, resulting in a certain amount of aggravation among e-mail correspondents in different European countries.

Many countries don't use the Roman script at all. Russian, Greek, Hebrew, Arabic, and Thai letters, to name just a few, have completely different shapes (see Figure 6). To complicate matters, scripts like Hebrew and Arabic are written from right to left instead of from left to right, and many of these scripts have characters that stack above or below other characters, as those marked with a dotted circle in Figure 6 do in Thai. Each of these alphabets has between 30 and 100 letters, and the countries using them have established encoding standards for them.

The situation is much more dramatic in languages that use Chinese script: the Chinese dialects, Japanese, and Korean. The Chinese script is not alphabetic but ideographic—a character represents an idea or thing rather than a single sound. (See Figure 7; can you identify the characters for soup, chicken, and wonton?) Most words are made up of one, two, or three of these ideographic characters. Tens of thousands of ideographs are in active use, and China, Taiwan, Hong Kong, Japan, and Korea developed incompatible encoding standards for them.

Figure 5 A German Keyboard

Figure 6 The Thai Alphabet

The inconsistencies among character encodings have been a major nuisance for international electronic communication and for software manufacturers vying for a global market. Between 1988 and 1991 a consortium of hardware and software manufacturers developed a uniform encoding scheme called Unicode that is expressly designed to encode text in all written languages of the world (see reference [1]). In the first version of Unicode, about 39,000 characters were given codes, including 21,000 Chinese ideographs. A 2-byte code (which can encode over 65,000 characters) was chosen. It was thought to leave ample space for expansion for esoteric scripts, such as Egyptian hieroglyphs and the ancient script used on the island of Java.

Java was one of the first programming languages to embrace Unicode. The primitive type char denotes a 2-byte Unicode character. (All Unicode characters can be stored in Java strings, but which ones can actually be displayed depends on your computer system.)

CLASSIC SOUPS

		Sm.	Lg.
清燉雞湯 57.	House Chicken Soup (Chicken, Celery, Potato, Onion, Carrot)	1.50	2.75
雞飯湯 58.	Chicken Rice Soup	1.85	3.25
雞麵湯 59.	Chicken Noodle Soup	1.85	3.25
廣東雲吞 60.	Cantonese Wonton Soup	1.50	2.75
蕃茄蛋湯 61.	Tomato Clear Egg Drop Soup	1.65	2.95
雲吞湯 62.	Regular Wonton Soup	1.10	2.10
酸辣湯 63. 🖎	Hot & Sour Soup	1.10	2.10
蛋花湯 64.	Egg Drop Soup	1.10	2.10
雲蛋湯 65.	Egg Drop Wonton Mix	1.10	2.10
豆腐菜湯 66.	Tofu Vegetable Soup	NA	3.50
雞玉米湯 67.	Chicken Corn Cream Soup	NA	3.50
蟹肉玉米湯 68.	Crab Meat Corn Cream Soup	NA	3.50
海鮮湯 69.	Seafood Soup	NA	3.50

Figure 7 A Menu with Chinese Characters

Unfortunately, in 2003, the inevitable happened. Another large batch of Chinese ideographs had to be added to Unicode, pushing it beyond the 16-bit limit. Now, some characters need to be encoded with a pair of char values.

4.7 Reading Input

Use the Scanner class to read keyboard input in a console window.

The Java programs that you have made so far have constructed objects, called methods, printed results, and exited. They were not interactive and took no user input. In this section, you will learn one method for reading user input.

Because output is sent to System.out, you might think that you use System.in for input. Unfortunately, it isn't quite that simple. When Java was first designed, not much attention was given to reading keyboard input. It was assumed that all programmers would produce graphical user interfaces with text fields and menus. System.in was given a minimal set of features—it can only read one byte at a time. Finally, in Java version 5.0, a Scanner class was added that lets you read keyboard input in a convenient manner.

To construct a Scanner object, simply pass the System.in object to the Scanner constructor:

```java
Scanner in = new Scanner(System.in);
```

You can create a scanner out of any input stream (such as a file), but you will usually want to use a scanner to read keyboard input from System.in.

Once you have a scanner, you use the nextInt or nextDouble methods to read the next integer or floating-point number.

```java
System.out.print("Enter quantity: ");
int quantity = in.nextInt();

System.out.print("Enter price: ");
double price = in.nextDouble();
```

When the nextInt or nextDouble method is called, the program waits until the user types a number and hits the Enter key. You should always provide instructions for the user (such as "Enter quantity:") before calling a Scanner method. Such an instruction is called a *prompt*.

The nextLine method returns the next line of input (until the user hits the Enter key) as a String object. The next method returns the next *word*, terminated by any *white space*, that is, a space, the end of a line, or a tab.

```java
System.out.print("Enter city: ");
String city = in.nextLine();

System.out.print("Enter state code: ");
String state = in.next();
```

Here, we use the nextLine method to read a city name that may consist of multiple words, such as San Francisco. We use the next method to read the state code (such as CA), which consists of a single word.

Here is an example of a test class that takes user input. This class tests the CashRegister class and allows the user to supply a purchase price and coin counts.

File InputTester.java

```java
1  import java.util.Scanner;
2
3  /**
4     This class tests console input.
5  */
6  public class InputTester
7  {
8     public static void main(String[] args)
9     {
10        Scanner in = new Scanner(System.in);
11
12        CashRegister register = new CashRegister();
13
14        System.out.print("Enter price: ");
15        double price = in.nextDouble();
16        register.recordPurchase(price);
17
18        System.out.print("Enter dollars: ");
19        int dollars = in.nextInt();
20        System.out.print("Enter quarters: ");
21        int quarters = in.nextInt();
22        System.out.print("Enter dimes: ");
23        int dimes = in.nextInt();
24        System.out.print("Enter nickels: ");
25        int nickels = in.nextInt();
26        System.out.print("Enter pennies: ");
27        int pennies = in.nextInt();
28        register.enterPayment(dollars, quarters, dimes, nickels, pennies);
29
30        System.out.print("Your change is ");
31        System.out.println(register.giveChange());
32     }
33  }
```

Output

```
Enter price: 7.55
Enter dollars: 10
Enter quarters: 2
Enter dimes: 1
Enter nickels: 0
Enter pennies: 0
Your change is 3.05
```

15. Why can't input be read directly from System.in?

16. Suppose in is a Scanner object that reads from System.in, and your program calls

```
String name = in.next();
```

What is the value of name if the user enters John Q. Public?

ADVANCED TOPIC 4.6

Formatting Numbers

The default format for printing numbers is not always what you would like. For example, consider the following code segment:

```
double total = 3.50;
final double TAX_RATE = 8.5; // Tax rate in percent
double tax = total * TAX_RATE / 100; // tax is 0.2975
System.out.println("Total: " + total);
System.out.println("Tax:    " + tax);
```

The output is

```
Total: 3.5
Tax:   0.2975
```

You may prefer the numbers to be printed with two digits after the decimal point, like this:

```
Total: 3.50
Tax:   0.30
```

You can achieve this with the printf method of the PrintStream class. (Recall that System.out is an instance of PrintStream.) The first parameter of the printf method is a *format string* that shows how the output should be formatted. The format string contains characters that are simply printed, and *format specifiers:* codes that start with a % character and end with a letter that indicates the format type. There are quite a few formats—Table 3 shows the most important ones. The remaining parameters of printf are the values to be formatted. For example,

```
System.out.printf("Total:%5.2f", total);
```

prints the string Total:, followed by a floating-point number with a *width* of 5 and a *precision* of 2. The width is the total number of characters to be printed: in our case, a space, the digit 3, a period, and two digits. If you increase the width, more spaces are added. The precision is the number of digits after the decimal point.

This simple use of printf is sufficient for most formatting needs. Once in a while, you may see a more complex example, such as this one:

```
System.out.printf("%-6s%5.2f%n", "Tax:", total);
```

Here, we have three format specifiers. The first one is %-6s. The s indicates a string. The hyphen is a *flag,* modifying the format. (See Table 4 for the most common format flags. The flags immediately follow the % character.) The hyphen indicates left alignment. If the string

	Table 3 **Format Types**	
Code	**Type**	**Example**
d	Decimal integer	123
x	Hexadecimal integer	7B
o	Octal integer	173
f	Fixed floating-point	12.30
e	Exponential floating-point	1.23e+1
g	General floating-point (exponential notation used for very large or very small values)	12.3
s	String	Tax:
n	Platform-independent line end	

to be formatted is shorter than the width, it is placed to the left, and spaces are added to the right. (The default is right alignment, with spaces added to the left.) Thus, `%-6s` denotes a left-aligned string of width 6.

You have already seen `%5.2f`: a floating-point number of width 5 and precision 2. The final specifier is `%n`, indicating a platform-independent line end. In Windows, lines need to be terminated by *two* characters: a carriage return `'\r'` and a newline `'\n'`. In other operating systems, a `'\n'` suffices. The `%n` format emits the appropriate line terminators.

Moreover, this call to `printf` has two parameters. You can supply any number of parameter values to the `printf` method. Of course, they must match the format specifiers in the format string.

	Table 4 **Format Flags**	
Flag	**Meaning**	**Example**
-	Left justification	1.23 followed by spaces
0	Show leading zeroes	001.23
+	Show a plus sign for positive numbers	+1.23
(	Enclose negative numbers in parentheses	(1.23)
,	Show decimal separators	12,300
^	Convert letters to uppercase	1.23E+1

The format method of the String class is similar to the printf method. However, it returns a string instead of producing output. For example, the call

```
String message = String.format("Total:%5.2f", total);
```

sets the message variable to the string "Total: 3.50".

ADVANCED TOPIC 4.7

Reading Input from a Dialog Box

Prior to Java version 5.0, it was not an easy matter to read input in a console window. The easiest method was to create a separate pop-up window for each input (see Figure 8). This note tells you how to do that, in case you need to work with an older version of Java.

Call the static showInputDialog method of the JOptionPane class, and supply the string that prompts the input from the user. For example,

```
String input = JOptionPane.showInputDialog("Enter price:");
```

That method returns a String object. Of course, often you need the input as a number. Use the Integer.parseInt and Double.parseDouble methods to convert the string to a number:

```
double price = Double.parseDouble(input);
```

Finally, whenever you call JOptionPane.showInputDialog in your programs, you need to add a line

```
System.exit(0);
```

to the end of your main method. The showInputDialog method starts a user interface thread to handle user input. When the main method reaches the end, that thread is still running, and your program won't exit automatically. To force the program to exit, you need to call the exit method of the System class. The parameter of the exit method is the status code of the program. A code of 0 denotes successful completion; you can use nonzero status codes to denote various error conditions.

Figure 8   An Input Dialog Box

CHAPTER SUMMARY

1. Java has eight primitive types, including four integer types and two floating-point types.

2. A numeric computation overflows if the result falls outside the range for the number type.

3. Rounding errors occur when an exact conversion between numbers is not possible.

4. You use a cast (*typeName*) to convert a value to a different type.

5. Use the `Math.round` method to round a floating-point number to the nearest integer.

6. A `final` variable is a constant. Once its value has been set, it cannot be changed.

7. Use named constants to make your programs easier to read and maintain.

8. Assignment to a variable is not the same as mathematical equality.

9. The `++` and `--` operators increment and decrement a variable.

10. If both arguments of the `/` operator are integers, the result is an integer and the remainder is discarded.

11. The `%` operator computes the remainder of a division.

12. The `Math` class contains methods `sqrt` and `pow` to compute square roots and powers.

13. A static method does not operate on an object.

14. A string is a sequence of characters. Strings are objects of the `String` class.

15. Strings can be concatenated, that is, put end to end to yield a new longer string. String concatenation is denoted by the `+` operator.

16. Whenever one of the arguments of the `+` operator is a string, the other argument is converted to a string.

17. If a string contains the digits of a number, you use the `Integer.parseInt` or `Double.parseDouble` method to obtain the number value.

18. Use the `substring` method to extract a part of a string.

19. String positions are counted starting with 0.

20. Use the `Scanner` class to read keyboard input in a console window.

FURTHER READING

1. `http://www.unicode.org/` The web site of the Unicode consortium. It contains character tables that show the Unicode values of characters from many scripts.

CLASSES, OBJECTS, AND METHODS INTRODUCED IN THIS CHAPTER

```
java.io.PrintStream              java.lang.String
  printf                           format
java.lang.Double                   substring
  parseDouble                    java.lang.System
java.lang.Integer                  in
  parseInt                       java.math.BigDecimal
  toString                         add
  MAX_VALUE                        multiply
  MIN_VALUE                        subtract
java.lang.Math                   java.math.BigInteger
  E                                add
  PI                               multiply
  abs                              subtract
  acos                           java.util.Scanner
  asin                             next
  atan                             nextDouble
  atan2                            nextInt
  ceil                             nextLine
  cos
  exp
  floor
  log
  max
  min
  pow
  round
  sin
  sqrt
  tan
  toDegrees
  toRadians
```

REVIEW EXERCISES

Exercise R4.1. Write the following mathematical expressions in Java.

$$s = s_0 + v_0 t + \frac{1}{2} g t^2$$

$$G = 4\pi^2 \frac{a^3}{P^2 (m_1 + m_2)}$$

$$FV = PV \cdot \left(1 + \frac{INT}{100}\right)^{YRS}$$

$$c = \sqrt{a^2 + b^2 - 2ab\cos\gamma}$$

Exercise R4.2. Write the following Java expressions in mathematical notation.

> **a.** `dm = m * (Math.sqrt(1 + v / c) / (Math.sqrt(1 - v / c) - 1));`
>
> **b.** `volume = Math.PI * r * r * h;`
>
> **c.** `volume = 4 * Math.PI * Math.pow(r, 3) / 3;`
>
> **d.** `p = Math.atan2(z, Math.sqrt(x * x + y * y));`

Exercise R4.3. What is wrong with this version of the quadratic formula?

```
x1 = (-b - Math.sqrt(b * b - 4 * a * c)) / 2 * a;
x2 = (-b + Math.sqrt(b * b - 4 * a * c)) / 2 * a;
```

Exercise R4.4. Give an example of integer overflow. Would the same example work correctly if you used floating-point? Give an example of a floating-point roundoff error. Would the same example work correctly if you used integers? For this exercise, you should assume that the values are represented in a sufficiently small unit, such as cents instead of dollars, so that the values don't have a fractional part.

Exercise R4.5. Write a test program that executes the following code:

```
CashRegister register = new CashRegister();
register.recordPurchase(19.93);
register.enterPayment(20, 0, 0, 0, 0);
System.out.print("Your change is ");
System.out.println(register.giveChange());
```

The program prints the total as 0.07000000000000028. Explain why. Give a recommendation to improve the program so that users will not be confused.

Exercise R4.6. Let n be an integer and x a floating-point number. Explain the difference between

```
n = (int) x;
```

and

```
n = (int) Math.round(x);
```

Exercise R4.7. Let n be an integer and x a floating-point number. Explain the difference between

```
n = (int) (x + 0.5);
```

and

```
n = (int) Math.round(x);
```

For what values of x do they give the same result? For what values of x do they give different results?

Exercise R4.8. Explain the differences between 2, 2.0, '2', "2", and "2.0".

Exercise R4.9. Explain what each of the following two program segments computes:

```
x = 2;
y = x + x;
```

and

```
s = "2";
t = s + s;
```

Exercise R4.10. Uninitialized variables can be a serious problem. Should you always initialize every variable with zero? Explain the advantages and disadvantages of such a strategy.

Exercise R4.11. True or false? (x is an int and s is a String)

  a. `Integer.parseInt("" + x)` is the same as x

  b. `"" + Integer.parseInt(s)` is the same as s

  c. `s.substring(0, s.length())` is the same as s

Exercise R4.12. How do you get the first character of a string? The last character? How do you remove the first character? The last character?

Exercise R4.13. How do you get the last digit of an integer? The first digit? That is, if n is 23456, how do you find out that the first digit is 2 and the last digit is 6? Do not convert the number to a string. *Hint:* `%`, `Math.log`.

Exercise R4.14. This chapter contains several recommendations regarding variables and constants that make programs easier to read and maintain. Summarize these recommendations.

Exercise R4.15. What is a `final` variable? Can you define a `final` variable without supplying its value? (Try it out.)

Exercise R4.16. What are the values of the following expressions? In each line, assume that

```
double x = 2.5;
double y = -1.5;
int m = 18;
int n = 4;
String s = "Hello";
String t = "World";
```

  a. `x + n * y - (x + n) * y`

  b. `m / n + m % n`

  c. `5 * x - n / 5`

  d. `Math.sqrt(Math.sqrt(n))`

  e. `(int) Math.round(x)`

  f. `(int) Math.round(x) + (int) Math.round(y)`

  g. `s + t`

  h. `s + n`

  i. `1 - (1 - (1 - (1 - (1 - n))))`

  j. `s.substring(1, 3)`

  k. `s.length() + t.length()`

PROGRAMMING EXERCISES

Exercise P4.1. Enhance the CashRegister class by adding separate methods enter-Dollars, enterQuarters, enterDimes, enterNickels, and enterPennies. For example,

```
register.recordPurchase(20.37);
register.enterDollars(20);
register.enterQuarters(2);
System.out.println(register.giveChange()); // Prints 0.13
```

Exercise P4.2. Enhance the CashRegister class so that it keeps track of the total number of items in a sale. Count all recorded purchases and supply a method

```
int getItemCount()
```

that returns the number of items of the current purchase. Remember to reset the count at the end of the purchase.

Exercise P4.3. Write a program that prints the values

```
1
10
100
1000
10000
100000
1000000
10000000
100000000
1000000000
10000000000
100000000000
```

Implement a class

```
public class PowerGenerator
{
    /**
        Constructs a power generator.
        @param aFactor the number that will be multiplied by itself
    */
    public PowerGenerator(int aFactor) { . . . }

    /**
        Computes the next power.
    */
    public double nextPower() { . . . }
    . . .
}
```

Then supply a test class PowerGeneratorTest that calls System.out.println(myGenerator.nextPower()) twelve times.

Exercise P4.4. Write a program that prompts the user for two numbers, then prints

- The sum
- The difference
- The product
- The average
- The distance (absolute value of the difference)
- The maximum (the larger of the two)
- The minimum (the smaller of the two)

To do so, implement a class

```java
public class Pair
{
    /**
        Constructs a pair.
        @param aFirst the first value of the pair
        @param aSecond the second value of the pair
    */
    public Pair(double aFirst, double aSecond) { . . . }

    /**
        Computes the sum of the values of this pair.
        @return the sum of the first and second values
    */
    public double getSum() { . . . }
    . . .
}
```

Then implement a class `PairTest` that reads in two numbers, constructs a `Pair` object, invokes its methods, and prints the results.

Exercise P4.5. Write a program that reads in four integers and prints their sum and average. Define a class `DataSet` with methods

- `void addValue(int x)`
- `int getSum()`
- `double getAverage()`

Hint: Keep track of the sum and the count of the values. Then write a test program `DataSetTest` that reads four numbers and calls `addValue` four times.

Exercise P4.6. Write a program that reads in four integers and prints the largest and smallest value that the user entered. Use a class `DataSet` with methods

- `void addValue(int x)`
- `int getLargest()`
- `int getSmallest()`

Keep track of the smallest and largest value that you've seen so far. Then use the `Math.min` and `Math.max` methods to update it in the `addValue` method. What should you use as initial values? *Hint:* `Integer.MIN_VALUE`, `Integer.MAX_VALUE`.

Write a test program `DataSetTest` that reads four numbers and calls `addValue` four times.

Exercise P4.7. Write a program that prompts the user for a measurement in meters and then converts it into miles, feet, and inches. Use a class

```
public class Converter
{
    /**
        Constructs a converter that can convert between two units.
        @param aConversionFactor  the factor with which to multiply
        to convert to the target unit
    */
    public Converter(double aConversionFactor) { . . . }

    /**
        Converts from a source measurement to a target measurement.
        @param fromMeasurement  the measurement
        @return  the input value converted to the target unit
    */
    public double convertTo(double fromMeasurement) { . . . }
}
```

Then construct three instances, similar to this example:

```
final double MILE_TO_KM = 1.609;
Converter milesToMeters = new Converter(1000 * MILE_TO_KM);
```

Exercise P4.8. Write a program that prompts the user for a radius and then prints

- The area and circumference of the circle with that radius
- The volume and surface area of the sphere with that radius

Define classes Circle and Sphere.

Exercise P4.9. Implement a class SodaCan whose constructor receives the height and diameter of the soda can. Supply methods getVolume and getSurfaceArea. Supply a SodaCanTest class that tests your class.

Exercise P4.10. Write a program that asks the user for the length of the sides of a square. Then print

- The area and perimeter of the square
- The length of the diagonal (use the Pythagorean theorem)

Define a class Square.

Exercise P4.11. *Giving change.* Enhance the CashRegister class so that it directs a cashier how to give change. The cash register computes the amount to be returned to the customer, in pennies.

Add the following methods to the CashRegister class:

- int giveDollars()
- int giveQuarters()
- int giveDimes()
- int giveNickels()
- int givePennies()

Each method computes the number of dollar bills or coins to return to the customer, and reduces the change due by the returned amount. You may assume that the methods are called in this order. For example,

```
CashRegister register = new CashRegister();
register.recordPurchase(8.37);
register.enterPayment(10, 0, 0, 0, 0);
double dollars = register.returnDollars(); // Returns 1
double quarters = register.returnQuarters(); // Returns 2
double dimes = register.returnDimes(); // Returns 1
double nickels = register.returnNickels(); // Returns 0
double pennies = register.returnPennies(); // Returns 3
```

Exercise P4.12. Write a program that reads in an integer and breaks it into a sequence of individual digits in reverse order. For example, the input 16384 is displayed as

```
4
8
3
6
1
```

You may assume that the input has no more than five digits and is not negative.

Define a class DigitExtractor:

```
public class DigitExtractor
{
    /**
        Constructs a digit extractor that gets the digits
        of an integer in reverse order.
        @param anInteger the integer to break up into digits
    */
    public DigitExtractor(int anInteger) { . . . }

    /**
        Returns the next digit to be extracted.
        @return the next digit
    */
    public int nextDigit() { . . . }
}
```

Then call System.out.println(myExtractor.nextDigit()) five times.

Exercise P4.13. Implement a class QuadraticEquation whose constructor receives the coefficients a, b, c of the quadratic equation $ax^2 + bx + c = 0$. Supply methods getSolution1 and getSolution2 that get the solutions, using the quadratic formula. Write a test class QuadraticEquationTest that prompts the user for the values of a, b, and c, constructs a QuadraticEquation object, and prints the two solutions.

Exercise P4.14. Write a program that reads two times in military format (0900, 1730) and prints the number of hours and minutes between the two times. Here is a sample run. User input is in color.

```
Please enter the first time: 0900
Please enter the second time: 1730
8 hours 30 minutes
```

Extra credit if you can deal with the case where the first time is later than the second time:

```
Please enter the first time: 1730
Please enter the second time: 0900
15 hours 30 minutes
```

Implement a class TimeInterval whose constructor takes two military times. The class should have two methods getHours and getMinutes.

Exercise P4.15. *Writing large letters.* A large letter H can be produced like this:

```
*    *
*    *
*****
*    *
*    *
```

Define a class LetterH with a method

```
String getLetter()
{
    return "*   *\n*   *\n*****\n*   *\n*   *\n";
}
```

Do the same for the letters E, L, and O. Then write the message

```
H
E
L
L
O
```

in large letters.

Exercise P4.16. Write a program that prints a Christmas tree:

Remember to use escape sequences.

Exercise P4.17. Write a program that transforms numbers 1, 2, 3, . . ., 12 into the corresponding month names January, February, March, . . ., December. *Hint:* Make a very long string "January February March . . . ", in which you add spaces such that each month name has the same length. Then use substring to extract the month you want. Implement a class Month whose constructor parameter is the month number and whose getName method returns the month name.

Exercise P4.18. Write a program to compute the date of Easter Sunday. Easter Sunday is the first Sunday after the first full moon of spring. Use this algorithm, invented by the mathematician Carl Friedrich Gauss in 1800:

1. Let y be the year (such as 1800 or 2001).
2. Divide y by 19 and call the remainder a. Ignore the quotient.
3. Divide y by 100 to get a quotient b and a remainder c.
4. Divide b by 4 to get a quotient d and a remainder e.
5. Divide 8 * b + 13 by 25 to get a quotient g. Ignore the remainder.
6. Divide 19 * a + b - d - g + 15 by 30 to get a remainder h. Ignore the quotient.
7. Divide c by 4 to get a quotient j and a remainder k.
8. Divide a + 11 * h by 319 to get a quotient m. Ignore the remainder.
9. Divide 2 * e + 2 * j - k - h + m + 32 by 7 to get a remainder r. Ignore the quotient.
10. Divide h - m + r + 90 by 25 to get a quotient n. Ignore the remainder.
11. Divide h - m + r + n + 19 by 32 to get a remainder p. Ignore the quotient.

Then Easter falls on day p of month n. For example, if y is 2001:

```
a = 6
b = 20
c = 1
d = 5, e = 0
g = 6
h = 18
j = 0, k = 1
m = 0
r = 6
n = 4
p = 15
```

Therefore, in 2001, Easter Sunday fell on April 15. Write a class `Easter` with methods `getEasterSundayMonth` and `getEasterSundayDay`.

PROGRAMMING PROJECTS

Project 4.1. In this project, you will perform calculations with triangles. A triangle is defined by the *x*- and *y*-coordinates of its three corner points.

Your job is to compute the following properties of a given triangle:

- the lengths of all sides
- the angles at all corners
- the perimeter
- the area

Of course, you should implement a `Triangle` class with appropriate methods. Supply a program that prompts a user for the corner point coordinates and produces a nicely formatted table of the triangle properties.

This is a good team project for two students. Both students should agree on the Triangle interface. One student implements the Triangle class, the other simultaneously implements the user interaction and formatting.

Project 4.2. The CashRegister class has an unfortunate limitation: It is closely tied to the coin system in the United States and Canada. Research the system used in most of Europe. Your goal is to produce a cash register that works with euros and cents. Rather than designing another limited CashRegister implementation for the European market, you should design a separate Coin class and a cash register that can work with coins of all types.

ANSWERS TO SELF-CHECK QUESTIONS

1. int and double.
2. When the fractional part of x is ≥0.5.
3. By using a cast: (int) Math.round(x).
4. The first definition is used inside a method, the second inside a class.
5. (1) You should use a named constant, not the "magic number" 3.14.
   (2) 3.14 is not an accurate representation of π.
6. The statement adds the amount value to the balance variable.
7. One less than it was before.
8. 17 and 29.
9. Only s3 is divided by 3. To get the correct result, use parentheses. Moreover, if s1, s2, and s3 are integers, you must divide by 3.0 to avoid integer division:
   (s1 + s2 + s3) / 3.0
10. $\sqrt{x^2 + y^2}$
11. x is a number, not an object, and you cannot invoke methods on numbers.
12. No—the println method is called on the object System.out.
13. s is set to the string Agent5.
14. The strings "i" and "ssissi".
15. The class only has a method to read a single byte. It would be very tedious to form characters, strings, and numbers from those bytes.
16. The value is "John". The next method reads the next *word*.

5

Programming Graphics

CHAPTER GOALS

- To be able to write simple graphical applications
- To display graphical shapes, such as lines and ellipses
- To use colors
- To display drawings consisting of many shapes
- To read input from a dialog box
- To develop test cases that validate the correctness of your programs

In this chapter, you will learn how to write *graphical applications*: applications that display drawings inside a window. Graphical applications look more attractive than the console applications that we used in earlier chapters.

The material in this chapter is entirely optional. Feel free to skip it if you are not interested in drawing graphics. Sections 5.6 and 5.7 contain advanced material that is required only for sophisticated drawings.

CHAPTER CONTENTS

5.1 Frame Windows

> To show a frame, construct a JFrame object, set its size, and make it visible.

A graphical application shows information inside a frame window: a window with a title bar, as shown in Figure 1. In this section, you will learn how to display a frame window. In the next section, you will learn how to create a drawing inside the frame.

To show a frame, carry out the following steps:

1. Construct an object of the JFrame class:

   ```
   JFrame frame = new JFrame();
   ```

2. Set the size of the frame

   ```
   frame.setSize(300, 400);
   ```

   This frame will be 300 pixels wide and 400 pixels tall. If you omit this step the frame will be 0 by 0 pixels, and you won't be able to see it.

3. If you'd like, set the title of the frame.

   ```
   frame.setTitle("An Empty Frame");
   ```

   If you omit this step, the title bar is simply left blank.

4. Set the "default close operation":

   ```
   frame.setDefaultCloseOperation(JFrame.EXIT_ON_CLOSE);
   ```

   When the user closes the frame, the program automatically exits. Don't omit this step. If you do, the program continues running even after the frame is closed.

5. Make the frame visible.

   ```
   frame.setVisible(true);
   ```

The simple program below shows all of these steps. It produces the empty frame shown in Figure 1.

Figure 1 A Frame Window

In the program, we call the setSize method with constants FRAME_WIDTH and FRAME_HEIGHT—see Quality Tip 4.1.

The JFrame class is a part of the javax.swing package. Swing is the nickname for the graphical user interface library in Java. The "x" in javax denotes the fact that Swing started out as a Java *extension* before it was added to the standard library.

We will go into much greater detail about Swing programming in Chapters 12 and 14. For now, consider this program to be the essential plumbing that is required to show a frame.

EmptyFrameViewer.java

```
 1  import javax.swing.*;
 2
 3  public class EmptyFrameViewer
 4  {
 5     public static void main(String[] args)
 6     {
 7        JFrame frame = new JFrame();
 8
 9        final int FRAME_WIDTH = 300;
10        final int FRAME_HEIGHT = 400;
11
12        frame.setSize(FRAME_WIDTH, FRAME_HEIGHT);
13        frame.setTitle("An Empty Frame");
14        frame.setDefaultCloseOperation(JFrame.EXIT_ON_CLOSE);
15
16        frame.setVisible(true);
17     }
18  }
```

1. How do you display a square frame with a title bar that reads "Hello, World!"?
2. How can a program display two frames at once?

5.2 Drawing Shapes

In this section, you will learn how to make shapes appear inside a frame window. The first drawing will be exceedingly modest: just two rectangles (see Figure 2). You'll soon see how to produce more interesting drawings. The purpose of this example is to show you the basic outline of a program that creates a drawing. You cannot draw directly onto a frame. Whenever you want to show anything inside a frame, be it a button or a drawing, you have to construct a *component* object and add it to the frame. In the Swing toolkit, the JComponent class represents a blank component.

> In order to display a drawing in a frame, define a class that extends the JComponent class.

Since we don't want to add a blank component, we have to modify the JComponent class and specify how the component should be painted. The solution is to define a new class that extends the JComponent class. You will learn about the process of extending classes in Chapter 13. For now, simply use the following code as a template.

```
public class RectangleComponent extends JComponent
{
    public void paintComponent(Graphics g)
    {
        Drawing instructions go here
    }
}
```

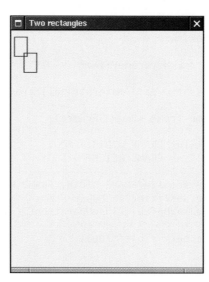

Figure 2
Drawing Rectangles

The extends keyword indicates that our component class, RectangleComponent, inherits the methods of JComponent. However, the RectangleComponent is different from the plain JComponent in one respect: The paintComponent method will contain instructions to draw the rectangles.

Place drawing instructions inside the paintComponent method. That method is called whenever the component needs to be repainted.

When the window is shown for the first time, the paintComponent method is called automatically. The method is also called when the window is resized, or when it is shown again after it was hidden.

The paintComponent method receives an object of type Graphics. The Graphics object stores the graphics state—the current color, font, and so on, that are used for drawing operations.

The Graphics class lets you manipulate the graphics state (such as the current color).

However, the Graphics class is primitive. When programmers clamored for a more object-oriented approach for drawing graphics, the designers of Java created the Graphics2D class, which extends the Graphics class. Whenever the Swing toolkit calls the paintComponent method, it actually passes a parameter of type Graphics2D. Programs with simple graphics do not need this feature. Because we want to use the more sophisticated methods to draw two-dimensional graphics objects, we need to recover the Graphics2D. This is accomplished by using a *cast*:

The Graphics2D class has methods to draw shape objects.

Use a cast to recover the Graphics2D object from the Graphics parameter of the paintComponent method.

```
public class RectangleComponent extends JComponent
{
    public void paintComponent(Graphics g)
    {
        // Recover Graphics2D
        Graphics2D g2 = (Graphics2D) g;
        . . .
    }
}
```

Now you are ready to draw shapes. The draw method of the Graphics2D class can draw shapes, such as rectangles, ellipses, line segments, polygons, and arcs. Here we draw a rectangle:

```
public class RectangleComponent extends JComponent
{
    public void paintComponent(Graphics g)
    {
        . . .
        Rectangle box = new Rectangle(5, 10, 20, 30);
        g2.draw(box);
        . . .
    }
}
```

The Graphics and Graphics2D classes are part of the java.awt package. (The acronym AWT stands for Abstract Windowing Toolkit.)

Here is the source code for the `RectangleComponent` class. Note that the `paintComponent` method of the `RectangleComponent` class draws two rectangles.

File RectangleComponent.java

```
1  import java.awt.Graphics;
2  import java.awt.Graphics2D;
3  import java.awt.Rectangle;
4  import javax.swing.JPanel;
5  import javax.swing.JComponent;
6
7  /**
8      A component that draws two rectangles.
9  */
10 public class RectangleComponent extends JComponent
11 {
12     public void paintComponent(Graphics g)
13     {
14        // Recover Graphics2D
15        Graphics2D g2 = (Graphics2D) g;
16
17        // Construct a rectangle and draw it
18        Rectangle box = new Rectangle(5, 10, 20, 30);
19        g2.draw(box);
20
21        // Move rectangle 15 units to the right and 25 units down
22        box.translate(15, 25);
23
24        // Draw moved rectangle
25        g2.draw(box);
26     }
27 }
```

In order to see the drawing, one task remains. You need to display the frame into which you added a component object. Follow these steps:

1. Construct a frame as described in the preceding section.

2. Construct an object of your component class:

```
RectangleComponent component = new RectangleComponent();
```

3. Add the component to the frame:

```
frame.add(component);
```

However, if you use an older version of Java (before version 5.0), you must make a slightly more complicated call:

```
frame.getContentPane().add(component);
```

4. Make the frame visible, as described in the preceding section.

The following listing shows the complete process.

File RectangleViewer.java

```
1   import javax.swing.JFrame;
2
3   public class RectangleViewer
4   {
5      public static void main(String[] args)
6      {
7         JFrame frame = new JFrame();
8
9         final int FRAME_WIDTH = 300;
10        final int FRAME_HEIGHT = 400;
11
12        frame.setSize(FRAME_WIDTH, FRAME_HEIGHT);
13        frame.setTitle("Two rectangles");
14        frame.setDefaultCloseOperation(JFrame.EXIT_ON_CLOSE);
15
16        RectangleComponent component = new RectangleComponent();
17        frame.add(component);
18
19        frame.setVisible(true);
20     }
21  }
```

Note that the rectangle drawing program consists of two classes:

- The RectangleComponent class, whose paintComponent method produces the drawing

- The RectangleViewer class, whose main method constructs a frame and a RectangleComponent, adds the component to the frame, and makes the frame visible

This division of labor is similar to that of the BankAccount/BankAccountTester classes in Chapter 3.

SELF CHECK

3. How do you modify the program to draw two squares?

4. How do you modify the program to draw one rectangle and one square?

5. What happens if you call g.draw(box) instead of g2.draw(box)?

ADVANCED TOPIC 5.1

Applets

> Applets are programs that run inside a web browser.

In the preceding section, you learned how to write a program that displays graphical shapes. Some people prefer to use applets for learning about graphics programming. Applets have two advantages. They don't need separate component and viewer classes; you only implement a single class. And, more importantly, applets run inside a web browser, allowing you to place your creations on a web page for all the world to admire.

To implement an applet, use this code outline:

```
public class MyApplet extends JApplet
{
    public void paint(Graphics g)
    {
        // Recover Graphics2D
        Graphics2D g2 = (Graphics2D) g;

        // Drawing instructions go here
        . . .
    }
}
```

This is almost the same outline as for a component, with two minor differences:

1. You extend `JApplet`, not `JComponent`.
2. You place the drawing code inside the `paint` method, not inside `paintComponent`.

The following applet draws two rectangles:

RectangleApplet.java

```
1  import java.awt.Graphics;
2  import java.awt.Graphics2D;
3  import java.awt.Rectangle;
4  import javax.swing.JApplet;
5
6  /**
7     An applet that draws two rectangles.
8  */
9  public class RectangleApplet extends JApplet
10 {
11     public void paint(Graphics g)
12     {
13         // Prepare for extended graphics
14         Graphics2D g2 = (Graphics2D) g;
15
16         // Construct a rectangle and draw it
17         Rectangle box = new Rectangle(5, 10, 20, 30);
18         g2.draw(box);
19
20         // Move rectangle 15 units to the right and 25 units down
21         box.translate(15, 25);
```

```
22
23        // Draw moved rectangle
24        g2.draw(box);
25    }
26 }
```

To run an applet, you need an HTML file with the applet tag.

To run this applet, you need an HTML file with an `applet` tag. HTML, the hypertext markup language, is the language used to describe web pages. (See Appendix I for more information on HTML.) Here is the simplest possible file to display the rectangle applet:

File RectangleApplet.html

```
1 <applet code="RectangleApplet.class" width="300" height="400">
2 </applet>
```

If you know HTML, you can proudly explain your creation, by adding text and more HTML tags:

File RectangleAppletExplained.html

```
 1 <html>
 2    <head>
 3       <title>Two rectangles</title>
 4    </head>
 5    <body>
 6       <p>Here is my <i>first applet</i>:</p>
 7       <applet code="RectangleApplet.class" width="300" height="400">
 8       </applet>
 9    </body>
10 </html>
```

An HTML file can have multiple applets. Simply add a separate `applet` tag for each applet.

You can give the HTML file any name you like. It is easiest to give the HTML file the same name as the applet. But some development environments already generate an HTML file with the same name as your project to hold your project notes; then you must give the HTML file containing your applet a different name.

To run the applet, you have two choices. You can use the applet viewer, a program that is included with the Java Software Development Kit from Sun Microsystems. You simply start the applet viewer, giving it the name of the HTML file that contains your applets:

```
appletviewer RectangleApplet.html
```

You view applets with the applet viewer or a Java-enabled browser.

The applet viewer only shows the applet, not the HTML text (see Figure 3).

You can also show the applet inside any Java 2–enabled web browser, such as Netscape or Mozilla. (If you use Internet Explorer, you probably need to configure it. By default,

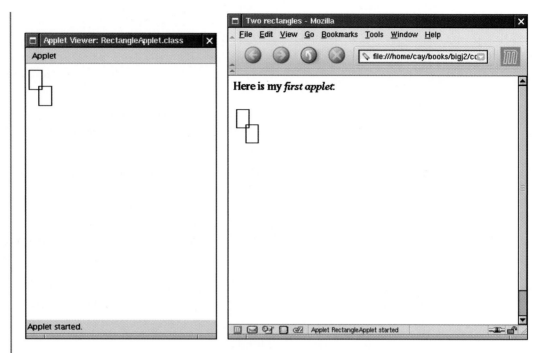

Figure 3
An Applet in the Applet Viewer

Figure 4
An Applet in a Web Browser

Microsoft supplies either an outdated version of Java or no Java at all. Go to the web site [1] and install the Java plugin.) Figure 4 shows the applet running in a browser. As you can see, both the text and the applet are displayed.

RANDOM FACT 5.1

The Evolution of the Internet

In 1962, J.C.R. Licklider was head of the first computer research program at DARPA, the Defense Advanced Research Projects Agency. He wrote a series of papers describing a "galactic network" through which computer users could access data and programs from other sites. This was well before computer networks were invented. By 1969, four computers—three in California and one in Utah—were connected to the ARPANET, the precursor of the Internet. The network grew quickly, linking computers at many universities and research organizations. It was originally thought that most network users wanted to run programs on remote computers. Using remote execution, a researcher at one institution would be able to access an underutilized computer at a different site. It quickly became apparent that remote execution was not what the network was actually used for. Instead, the "killer application" was electronic mail: the transfer of messages between computer users at different locations.

In 1972, Bob Kahn proposed to extend ARPANET into the *Internet*: a collection of interoperable networks. All networks on the Internet share common *protocols* for data transmission. Kahn and Vinton Cerf developed protocols, now called TCP/IP (Transmission Control Protocol/Internet Protocol). On January 1, 1983, all hosts on the Internet simultaneously switched to the TCP/IP protocol (which is used to this day).

Over time, researchers, computer scientists, and hobbyists published increasing amounts of information on the Internet. For example, the GNU (GNU's Not UNIX) project is producing a free set of high-quality operating system utilities and program development tools [2]. Project Gutenberg makes available the text of important classical books, whose copyright has expired, in computer-readable form [3]. In 1989, Tim Berners-Lee started work on hyperlinked documents, allowing users to browse by following links to related documents. This infrastructure is now known as the World Wide Web (WWW).

The first interfaces to retrieve this information were, by today's standards, unbelievably clumsy and hard to use. In March 1993, WWW traffic was 0.1% of all Internet traffic. All that changed when Marc Andreesen, then a graduate student working for NCSA (the National Center for Supercomputing Applications), released Mosaic. Mosaic displayed web pages in graphical form, using images, fonts, and colors (see Figure 5). Andreesen went on to fame and fortune at Netscape, and Microsoft licensed the Mosaic code to create Internet Explorer. By 1996, WWW traffic accounted for more than half of the data transported on the Internet.

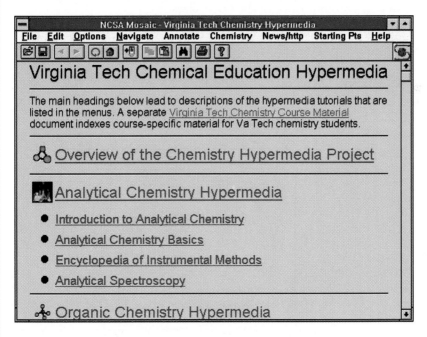

Figure 5   The NCSA Mosaic Browser

5.3 Graphical Shapes

In Section 5.2 you learned how to write a program that draws rectangles. In this section you will learn how to draw other shapes: ellipses and lines. With these graphical elements you can draw quite a few interesting pictures.

To draw an ellipse, you specify its bounding box (see Figure 6) in the same way that you would specify a rectangle, namely by the *x*- and *y*-coordinates of the top-left corner and the width and height of the box.

However, there is no simple `Ellipse` class that you can use. Instead, you must use one of the two classes `Ellipse2D.Float` and `Ellipse2D.Double`, depending on whether you want to store the ellipse coordinates as `float` or as `double` values. Because `double` values are more convenient to use than `float` values in Java, we will always use the `Ellipse2D.Double` class. Here is how you construct an ellipse:

```
Ellipse2D.Double ellipse = new Ellipse2D.Double(x, y, width, height);
```

> Ellipse2D.Double and Line2D.Double are classes that describe graphical shapes.

The class name `Ellipse2D.Double` looks different from the class names that you have encountered up to now. It consists of two class names `Ellipse2D` and `Double` separated by a period (.). This indicates that `Ellipse2D.Double` is a so-called inner class inside `Ellipse2D`. When constructing and using ellipses, you don't actually need to worry about the fact that `Ellipse2D.Double` is an inner class—just think of it as a class with a long name. However, in the `import` statement at the top of your program, you must be careful that you import only the outer class:

```
import java.awt.geom.Ellipse2D;
```

Drawing an ellipse is easy: Use exactly the same `draw` method of the `Graphics2D` class that you used for drawing rectangles.

```
g2.draw(ellipse);
```

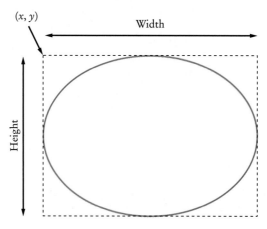

Figure 6 An Ellipse and Its Bounding Box

Figure 7 Basepoint and Baseline

To draw a circle, simply set the width and height to the same values:

```
Ellipse2D.Double circle = new Ellipse2D.Double(x, y, diameter, diameter);
g2.draw(circle);
```

Notice that (x, y) is the top-left corner of the bounding box, not the center of the circle.

To draw a line, use an object of the Line2D.Double class. A line is constructed by specifying its two end points. You can do this in two ways. Simply give the *x*- and *y*-coordinates of both end points:

```
Line2D.Double segment = new Line2D.Double(x1, y1, x2, y2);
```

Or specify each end point as an object of the Point2D.Double class:

```
Point2D.Double from = new Point2D.Double(x1, y1);
Point2D.Double to = new Point2D.Double(x2, y2);

Line2D.Double segment = new Line2D.Double(from, to);
```

The second option is more object-oriented and is often more useful, particularly if the point objects can be reused elsewhere in the same drawing.

> The drawString method draws a string, starting at its basepoint.

You often want to put text inside a drawing, for example, to label some of the parts. Use the drawString method of the Graphics2D class to draw a string anywhere in a window. You must specify the string and the *x*- and *y*-coordinates of the basepoint of the first character in the string (see Figure 7). For example,

```
g2.drawString("Message", 50, 100);
```

SELF CHECK

6. Give instructions to draw a circle with center (100, 100) and radius 25.
7. Give instructions to draw a letter "V" by drawing two line segments.
8. Give instructions to draw a string consisting of the letter "V".

5.4 Colors

When you first start drawing, all shapes are drawn with a black pen. To change the color, you need to supply an object of type Color. Java uses the RGB color model. That is, you specify a color by the amounts of the primary colors—red, green, and blue—that make up the color. The amounts are given as float values, which you must identify by a suffix F. They vary from 0.0F (primary color not present) to 1.0F (maximum amount present). For example,

```
Color magenta = new Color(1.0F, 0.0F, 1.0F);
```

constructs a Color object with maximum red, no green, and maximum blue, yielding a bright purple color called magenta.

> When you set a new color in the graphics context, it is used for subsequent drawing operations.

For your convenience, a variety of colors have been predefined in the Color class. Table 1 shows those predefined colors and their RGB values. For example, Color.PINK has been predefined to be the same color as new Color(1.0F, 0.7F, 0.7F).

Once you have an object of type Color, you can change the current color of the Graphics2D object with the setColor method. For

Table 1 Predefined Colors and Their RGB Values

Color	RGB Value
Color.BLACK	0.0F, 0.0F, 0.0F
Color.BLUE	0.0F, 0.0F, 1.0F
Color.CYAN	0.0F, 1.0F, 1.0F
Color.GRAY	0.5F, 0.5F, 0.5F
Color.DARKGRAY	0.25F, 0.25F, 0.25F
Color.LIGHTGRAY	0.75F, 0.75F, 0.75F
Color.GREEN	0.0F, 1.0F, 0.0F
Color.MAGENTA	1.0F, 0.0F, 1.0F
Color.ORANGE	1.0F, 0.8F, 0.0F
Color.PINK	1.0F, 0.7F, 0.7F
Color.RED	1.0F, 0.0F, 0.0F
Color.WHITE	1.0F, 1.0F, 1.0F
Color.YELLOW	1.0F, 1.0F, 0.0F

example, the following code draws a rectangle in black, then switches the color to red, and draws the next rectangle in red:

```
public void paintComponent(Graphics g)
{
    Graphics2D g2 = (Graphics2D) g;

    Rectangle box = new Rectangle(5, 10, 20, 30);
    g2.draw(box); // Draws in black

    box.translate(15, 25); // Moves rectangle

    g2.setColor(Color.RED); // Sets current color to red
    g2.draw(box); // Draws in red
}
```

If you want to color the inside of the shape, use the `fill` method instead of the `draw` method. For example,

```
g2.fill(box);
```

fills the inside of the rectangle with the current color.

SELF CHECK

9. What are the RGB color values of `Color.BLUE`?
10. How do you draw a yellow square on a red background?

5.5 Drawing Complex Shapes

It is a good idea to make a class for each complex graphical shape.

The next program shows how to put shapes together to draw a simple figure of a car (Figure 8). It is a good idea to make a separate class for each complex shape that you want to draw. For example, the program at the end of this section defines a `Car` class.

```
class Car
{
    . . .
    public void draw(Graphics2D g2)
    {
        // Drawing instructions
        . . .
    }
}
```

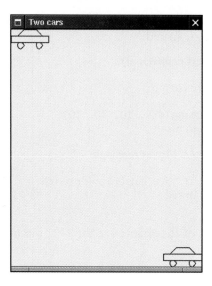

Figure 8   The Car Component Draws Two Car Shapes

To figure out how to draw a complex shape, make a sketch on graph paper.

The coordinates of the car parts seem a bit arbitrary. To come up with suitable values, draw the image on graph paper and read off the coordinates (Figure 9).

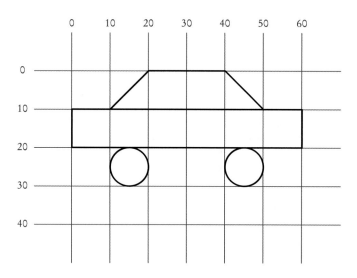

Figure 9   Using Graph Paper to Find Shape Coordinates

Our program draws two cars. We place one car in the top-left corner of the window, and the other car in the bottom right. To compute the bottom right position, we call the getWidth and getHeight methods of the JComponent class. These methods return the dimensions of the component. We subtract the dimensions of the car:

```
int x = getWidth() - 60;
int y = getHeight() - 30;
Car car2 = new Car(x, y);
```

Pay close attention to the call to getWidth inside the paintComponent method of CarComponent. The method call has no implicit parameter, which means that the method is applied to the same object that executes the paintComponent method. The component simply obtains *its own* width.

Run the program and resize the window. Note that the second car always ends up at the bottom-right corner of the window. Whenever the window is resized, the paintComponent method is called and the car position is recomputed, taking the current component dimensions into account.

Unfortunately, in programs such as these it is difficult to avoid the "magic numbers" for the coordinates of the various shapes.

File CarComponent.java

```
1  import java.awt.Graphics;
2  import java.awt.Graphics2D;
3  import javax.swing.JComponent;
4
5  /**
6      This component draws two car shapes.
7  */
8  public class CarComponent extends JComponent
9  {
10     public void paintComponent(Graphics g)
11     {
12        Graphics2D g2 = (Graphics2D) g;
13
14        Car car1 = new Car(0, 0);
15
16        int x = getWidth() - Car.WIDTH;
17        int y = getHeight() - Car.HEIGHT;
18
19        Car car2 = new Car(x, y);
20
21        car1.draw(g2);
22        car2.draw(g2);
23     }
24  }
```

File Car.java

```java
1  import java.awt.Graphics2D;
2  import java.awt.Rectangle;
3  import java.awt.geom.Ellipse2D;
4  import java.awt.geom.Line2D;
5  import java.awt.geom.Point2D;
6
7  /**
8     A car shape that can be positioned anywhere on the screen.
9  */
10 public class Car
11 {
12    /**
13       Constructs a car with a given top-left corner.
14       @param x the x-coordinate of the top-left corner
15       @param y the y-coordinate of the top-left corner
16    */
17    public Car(int x, int y)
18    {
19       xLeft = x;
20       yTop = y;
21    }
22
23    /**
24       Draws the car.
25       @param g2 the graphics context
26    */
27    public void draw(Graphics2D g2)
28    {
29       Rectangle body
30          = new Rectangle(xLeft, yTop + 10, 60, 10);
31       Ellipse2D.Double frontTire
32          = new Ellipse2D.Double(xLeft + 10, yTop + 20, 10, 10);
33       Ellipse2D.Double rearTire
34          = new Ellipse2D.Double(xLeft + 40, yTop + 20, 10, 10);
35
36       // The bottom of the front windshield
37       Point2D.Double r1
38          = new Point2D.Double(xLeft + 10, yTop + 10);
39       // The front of the roof
40       Point2D.Double r2
41          = new Point2D.Double(xLeft + 20, yTop);
42       // The rear of the roof
43       Point2D.Double r3
44          = new Point2D.Double(xLeft + 40, yTop);
45       // The bottom of the rear windshield
46       Point2D.Double r4
47          = new Point2D.Double(xLeft + 50, yTop + 10);
48
49       Line2D.Double frontWindshield
50          = new Line2D.Double(r1, r2);
51       Line2D.Double roofTop
52          = new Line2D.Double(r2, r3);
```

```
53          Line2D.Double rearWindshield
54              = new Line2D.Double(r3, r4);
55
56          g2.draw(body);
57          g2.draw(frontTire);
58          g2.draw(rearTire);
59          g2.draw(frontWindshield);
60          g2.draw(roofTop);
61          g2.draw(rearWindshield);
62      }
63
64      public static int WIDTH = 60;
65      public static int HEIGHT = 30;
66      private int xLeft;
67      private int yTop;
68  }
```

File CarViewer.java

```
1   import javax.swing.JFrame;
2
3   public class CarViewer
4   {
5      public static void main(String[] args)
6      {
7         JFrame frame = new JFrame();
8
9         final int FRAME_WIDTH = 300;
10        final int FRAME_HEIGHT = 400;
11
12        frame.setSize(FRAME_WIDTH, FRAME_HEIGHT);
13        frame.setTitle("Two cars");
14        frame.setDefaultCloseOperation(JFrame.EXIT_ON_CLOSE);
15
16        CarComponent component = new CarComponent();
17        frame.add(component);
18
19        frame.setVisible(true);
20     }
21  }
```

SELF CHECK

11. Which class needs to be modified to have the two cars positioned next to each other?
12. Which class needs to be modified to have the car tires painted in black, and what modification do you need to make?
13. How do you make the cars twice as big?

How To 5.1

Drawing Graphical Shapes

You can write programs that display a wide variety of graphical shapes. These instructions give you a step-by-step procedure for decomposing a drawing into parts and implementing a program that produces the drawing.

Step 1   Determine the shapes that you need for the drawing.

You can use the following shapes:

- Squares and rectangles
- Circles and ellipses
- Lines

The outlines of these shapes can be drawn in any color, and you can fill the insides of these shapes with any color. You can also use text to label parts of your drawing.

Some national flag designs consist of three equally wide sections of different colors, side by side:

You could draw such a flag using three rectangles. But if the middle rectangle is white, as it is, for example, in the flag of Italy (green, white, red), it is easier and looks better to draw a line on the top and bottom of the middle portion:

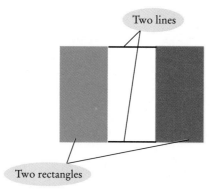

Step 2   Find the coordinates for the shapes.

You now need to find the exact positions for the geometric shapes.

- For rectangles, you need the *x*- and *y*-position of the top-left corner, the width, and the height.
- For ellipses, you need the top-left corner, width, and height of the bounding rectangle.
- For lines, you need the *x*- and *y*-positions of the starting point and the end point.
- For text, you need the *x*- and *y*-positions of the basepoint.

A commonly-used size for a window is 300 by 300 pixels. You may not want the flag crammed all the way to the top, so perhaps the upper-left corner of the flag should be at point (100, 100).

Many flags, such as the flag of Italy, have a width : height ratio of 3 : 2. (You can often find exact proportions for a particular flag by doing a bit of Internet research on one of several Flags of the World sites.) For example, if you make the flag 90 pixels wide, then it should be 60 pixels tall. (Why not make it 100 pixels wide? Then the height would be $100 \cdot 2 / 3 \approx 67$, which seems more awkward.)

Now you can compute the coordinates of all the important points of the shape:

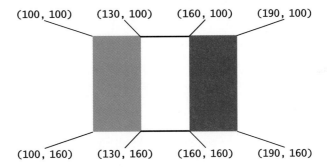

Step 3 Write Java statements to draw the shapes.

In our example, there are two rectangles and two lines:

```
Rectangle leftRectangle
    = new Rectangle(100, 100, 30, 60);
Rectangle rightRectangle
    = new Rectangle(160, 100, 30, 60);
Line2D.Double topLine
    = new Line2D.Double(130, 100, 160, 100);
Line2D.Double bottomLine
    = new Line2D.Double(130, 160, 160, 160);
```

If you are more ambitious, then you can express the coordinates in terms of a few variables. In the case of the flag, we have arbitrarily chosen the top-left corner and the width. All other coordinates follow from those choices. If you decide to follow the ambitious approach, then the rectangles and lines are determined as follows:

```
Rectangle leftRectangle = new Rectangle(
    xLeft, yTop,
    width / 3, width * 2 / 3);
Rectangle rightRectangle = new Rectangle(
    xLeft + 2 * width / 3, yTop,
    width / 3, width * 2 / 3);
Line2D.Double topLine = new Line2D.Double(
    xLeft + width / 3, yTop,
    xLeft + width * 2 / 3, yTop);
```

```
Line2D.Double bottomLine = new Line2D.Double(
    xLeft + width / 3, yTop + width * 2 / 3,
    xLeft + width * 2 / 3, yTop + width * 2 / 3);
```

Now you need to fill the rectangles and draw the lines. For the flag of Italy, the left rectangle is green and the right rectangle is red. Remember to switch colors before the filling and drawing operations:

```
g2.setColor(Color.GREEN);
g2.fill(leftRectangle);
g2.setColor(Color.RED);
g2.fill(rightRectangle);
g2.setColor(Color.BLACK);
g2.draw(topLine);
g2.draw(bottomLine);
```

Step 4   Combine the drawing statements with the component "plumbing".

```
public class MyComponent extends JComponent
{
    public void paintComponent(Graphics g)
    {
        Graphics2D g2 = (Graphics2D) g;
        // Your drawing code goes here
        . . .
    }
}
```

In our example, you can simply add all shapes and drawing instructions inside the paint-Component method:

```
public class ItalianFlagComponent extends JComponent
{
    public void paintComponent(Graphics g)
    {
        Graphics2D g2 = (Graphics2D) g;
        Rectangle leftRectangle
            = new Rectangle(100, 100, 30, 60);
        . . .
        g2.setColor(Color.GREEN);
        g2.fill(leftRectangle);
        . . .
    }
}
```

That approach is acceptable for simple drawings, but it is not very object-oriented. After all, a flag is an object. It is better to make a separate class for the flag. Then you can draw different flags at different positions and sizes. Specify the sizes in a constructor and supply a draw method:

```
public class ItalianFlag
{
    public ItalianFlag(double x, double y, double aWidth)
    {
        xLeft = x;
        yTop = y;
        width = aWidth;
```

```
    }

    public void draw(Graphics2D g2)
    {
        Rectangle leftRectangle = new Rectangle(
            xLeft, yTop,
            width / 3, width * 2 / 3);
        . . .
        2.setColor(Color.GREEN);
        2.fill(leftRectangle);
        . .


        te int xLeft;
        te int yTop;
        te double width;
```

d a separate class for the component, but it is very simple:

```
    ass ItalianFlagComponent extends JComponent

    void paintComponent(Graphics g)

    hics2D g2 = (Graphics2D) g;
    ianFlag flag = new ItalianFlag(100, 100, 90);
    .draw(g2);
```

the viewer class.

r class, with a main method in which you construct a frame, add your compo-
your frame visible. The viewer class is completely routine; you only need to
line to show a different component.

```
    .swing.*;

    ItalianFlagViewer

    tic void main(String[] args)

    frame = new JFrame();

    t FRAME_WIDTH = 300;
    t FRAME_HEIGHT = 300;

        frame.setSize(FRAME_WIDTH, FRAME_HEIGHT);
        frame.setDefaultCloseOperation(JFrame.EXIT_ON_CLOSE);

        ItalianFlagComponent component = new ItalianFlagComponent();
        frame.add(component);

        frame.setVisible(true);
    }
}
```

RANDOM FACT 5.2

Computer Graphics

Generating and manipulating visual images is one of the most exciting applications of the computer. We distinguish different kinds of graphics.

Diagrams, such as numeric charts or maps, are artifacts that convey information to the viewer (see Figure 10). They do not directly depict anything that occurs in the natural world, but are a tool for visualizing information.

Scenes are computer-generated images that attempt to depict images of the real or an imagined world (see Figure 11). It turns out to be quite challenging to render light and shadows accurately. Special effort must be taken so that the images do not look too neat and simple; clouds, rocks, leaves, and dust in the real world have a complex and somewhat random appearance. The degree of realism in these images is constantly improving.

Manipulated images are photographs or film footage of actual events that have been converted to digital form and edited by the computer (see Figure 12). For example, film sequences in the movie *Apollo 13* were produced by starting from actual images and changing the perspective, showing the launch of the rocket from a more dramatic viewpoint.

Computer graphics is one of the most challenging fields in computer science. It requires processing of massive amounts of information at very high speed. New algorithms are constantly invented for this purpose. Displaying an overlapping set of three-dimensional objects

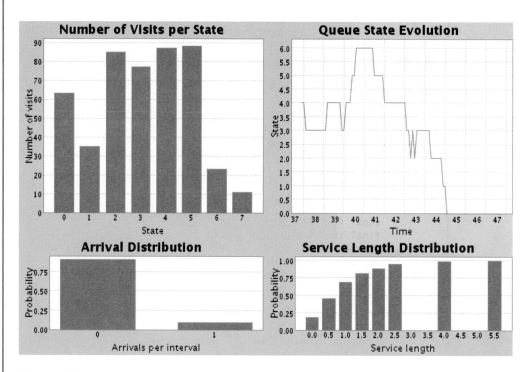

Figure 10   Diagrams

Figure 11   Scene

Figure 12
Manipulated Image

with curved boundaries requires advanced mathematical tools. Realistic modeling of textures and biological entities requires extensive knowledge of mathematics, physics, and biology.

5.6 Reading Text Input

The programs that you have seen so far are quite nice for drawing, but they aren't interactive—you can't change the positions of the shapes that are drawn on the screen. Interactive input in a graphical program turns out to be more complex than in a console program. In a console program, the programmer dictates the control flow and forces the user to enter input in a predetermined order. A graphical program, however, generally makes a large number of controls available to the program user (buttons, input fields, scroll bars, and so on), which users can manipulate in any order they please. Therefore, the program must be prepared to process input from multiple sources in random order. You will learn how to do that in Chapter 12.

> A graphical application can obtain input by displaying a JOptionPane.

In the meantime, we will simply read input with the showInputDialog method of the JOptionPane class that was described in Advanced Topic 4.7. The showInputDialog method displays a prompt and waits for user input (see Figure 13). It returns the string that the user typed.

If you ask the user for a number, you need to convert the string to a number. Use methods such as Integer.parseInt or Double.parseDouble.

For example, the following two statements allow the user to specify a value for the variable x:

```
String input = JOptionPane.showInputDialog("Enter x");
double x = Double.parseDouble(input);
```

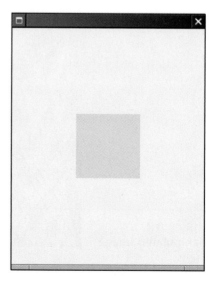

Figure 13
An Input Dialog Box

Figure 14
A Square Filled with a User-specified Color

The following program is an example. It prompts the user for red, green, and blue values, and then fills a square with the color that the user specified. For example, if you enter 1.0, 0.7, 0.7, then the square is pink (see Figure 14).

A sequence of input dialog boxes can be frustrating to the user, making it a poor choice for a user interface design. However, it is easy to program. In Chapter 12, you will learn how to gather input in a more professional way.

File ColorViewer.java

```
 1  import java.awt.Color;
 2  import javax.swing.JFrame;
 3  import javax.swing.JOptionPane;
 4
 5  public class ColorViewer
 6  {
 7     public static void main(String[] args)
 8     {
 9        JFrame frame = new JFrame();
10
11        final int FRAME_WIDTH = 300;
12        final int FRAME_HEIGHT = 400;
13
14        frame.setSize(FRAME_WIDTH, FRAME_HEIGHT);
15        frame.setDefaultCloseOperation(JFrame.EXIT_ON_CLOSE);
16
17        String input;
18
19        // Ask the user for red, green, blue values
20
21        input = JOptionPane.showInputDialog("red:");
22        double red = Double.parseDouble(input);
23
24        input = JOptionPane.showInputDialog("green:");
25        double green = Double.parseDouble(input);
26
27        input = JOptionPane.showInputDialog("blue:");
28        double blue = Double.parseDouble(input);
29
30        Color fillColor = new Color(
31              (float) red, (float) green, (float) blue);
32
33        ColoredSquareComponent component
34              = new ColoredSquareComponent(fillColor);
35        frame.add(component);
36
37        frame.setVisible(true);
38     }
39  }
```

File ColoredSquareComponent.java

```
 1  import java.awt.Color;
 2  import java.awt.Graphics;
 3  import java.awt.Graphics2D;
```

```
 4   import java.awt.Rectangle;
 5   import javax.swing.JComponent;
 6
 7   /**
 8       A component that shows a colored square.
 9   */
10   public class ColoredSquareComponent extends JComponent
11   {
12      /**
13          Constructs a component that shows a colored square.
14          @param aColor the fill color for the square
15      */
16      public ColoredSquareComponent(Color aColor)
17      {
18         fillColor = aColor;
19      }
20
21      public void paintComponent(Graphics g)
22      {
23         Graphics2D g2 = (Graphics2D) g;
24
25         // Select color in graphics context
26
27         g2.setColor(fillColor);
28
29         // Construct and fill a square whose center is
30         // the center of the window
31
32         final int SQUARE_LENGTH = 100;
33
34         Rectangle square = new Rectangle(
35             (getWidth() - SQUARE_LENGTH) / 2,
36             (getHeight() - SQUARE_LENGTH) / 2,
37             SQUARE_LENGTH,
38             SQUARE_LENGTH);
39
40         g2.fill(square);
41      }
42
43      private Color fillColor;
44   }
```

SELF CHECK

14. Why does this program produce three separate dialog boxes instead of inviting the user to type all three values in a single dialog box?

15. Why does this program place the showInputDialog call into the main method of the ColorViewer class and not into the paintComponent method of the ColorComponent class?

5.7 Comparing Visual and Numerical Information

The final example of this chapter shows how one can look at the same problem both visually and numerically. You want to figure out the intersection between a circle and a line. The circle has radius 100 and center (100, 100). Ask the user to specify the position of a vertical line. Then draw the circle, the line, and the intersection points (see Figure 15). Label them to display the exact locations.

Exactly where do the two shapes intersect? We need a bit of mathematics. The equation of a circle with radius r and center point (a, b) is

$$(x - a)^2 + (y - b)^2 = r^2$$

If you know x, then you can solve for y:

$$(y - b)^2 = r^2 - (x - a)^2$$

$$y - b = \pm\sqrt{r^2 - (x - a)^2}$$

$$y = b \pm\sqrt{r^2 - (x - a)^2}$$

That is easy to compute in Java:

```java
double root = Math.sqrt(r * r - (x - a) * (x - a));
double y1 = b + root;
double y2 = b - root;
```

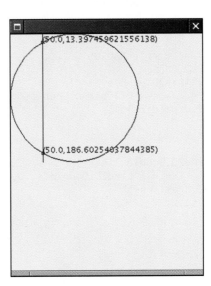

Figure 15
Intersection of a Line
and a Circle

But how do you know that you did both the math and the programming right?

If your program is correct, these two points will show up right on top of the actual intersections in the picture. If not, the two points will be at the wrong place.

If you look at Figure 15, you will see that the results match perfectly, which gives us confidence that everything is correct. See Quality Tip 5.1 for more information on verifying that this program works correctly.

Here is the complete program.

File IntersectionComponent.java

```java
 1  import java.awt.Graphics;
 2  import java.awt.Graphics2D;
 3  import java.awt.geom.Ellipse2D;
 4  import java.awt.geom.Line2D;
 5  import javax.swing.JComponent;
 6
 7  /**
 8      A component that computes and draws the intersection points
 9      of a circle and a line.
10  */
11  public class IntersectionComponent extends JComponent
12  {
13      /**
14          Constructs the component from a given x-value for the line.
15          @param anX the x-value for the line (between 0 and 200)
16      */
17      public IntersectionComponent(double anX)
18      {
19          x = anX;
20      }
21
22      public void paintComponent(Graphics g)
23      {
24          Graphics2D g2 = (Graphics2D) g;
25
26          // Draw the circle
27
28          final double RADIUS = 100;
29
30          Ellipse2D.Double circle
31              = new Ellipse2D.Double(0, 0, 2 * RADIUS, 2 * RADIUS);
32          g2.draw(circle);
33
34          // Draw the vertical line
35
36          Line2D.Double line
37              = new Line2D.Double(x, 0, x, 2 * RADIUS);
38          g2.draw(line);
39
```

```
40          // Compute the intersection points
41
42          double a = RADIUS;
43          double b = RADIUS;
44
45          double root = Math.sqrt(RADIUS * RADIUS - (x - a) * (x - a));
46          double y1 = b + root;
47          double y2 = b - root;
48
49          // Draw the intersection points
50
51          LabeledPoint p1 = new LabeledPoint(x, y1);
52          LabeledPoint p2 = new LabeledPoint(x, y2);
53
54          p1.draw(g2);
55          p2.draw(g2);
56       }
57
58       private double x;
59  }
```

File IntersectionViewer.java

```
1   import javax.swing.JFrame;
2   import javax.swing.JOptionPane;
3
4   public class IntersectionViewer
5   {
6      public static void main(String[] args)
7      {
8         JFrame frame = new JFrame();
9
10        final int FRAME_WIDTH = 300;
11        final int FRAME_HEIGHT = 400;
12
13        frame.setSize(FRAME_WIDTH, FRAME_HEIGHT);
14        frame.setDefaultCloseOperation(JFrame.EXIT_ON_CLOSE);
15
16        String input = JOptionPane.showInputDialog("Enter x");
17        double x = Double.parseDouble(input);
18        IntersectionComponent component
19              = new IntersectionComponent(x);
20        frame.add(component);
21
22        frame.setVisible(true);
23     }
24  }
```

File LabeledPoint.java

```java
1   import java.awt.Graphics2D;
2   import java.awt.geom.Ellipse2D;
3
4   /**
5       A point with a label showing the point's coordinates.
6   */
7   public class LabeledPoint
8   {
9      /**
10         Construct a labeled point.
11         @param anX the x-coordinate
12         @param aY the y-coordinate
13      */
14      public LabeledPoint(double anX, double aY)
15      {
16         x = anX;
17         y = aY;
18      }
19
20      /**
21         Draws the point as a small circle with a coordinate label.
22         @param g2 the graphics context
23      */
24      public void draw(Graphics2D g2)
25      {
26         // Draw a small circle centered around (x, y)
27
28         Ellipse2D.Double circle = new Ellipse2D.Double(
29               x - SMALL_CIRCLE_RADIUS,
30               y - SMALL_CIRCLE_RADIUS,
31               2 * SMALL_CIRCLE_RADIUS,
32               2 * SMALL_CIRCLE_RADIUS);
33
34         g2.draw(circle);
35
36         // Draw the label
37
38         String label = "(" + x + "," + y + ")";
39
40         g2.drawString(label, (float) x, (float) y);
41      }
42
43      private static final double SMALL_CIRCLE_RADIUS = 2;
44
45      private double x;
46      private double y;
47   }
```

At this point be careful to specify only lines that intersect the circle. If the line doesn't meet the circle, then the program will attempt to compute a square root of a negative number, and a math error will occur. We have not yet discussed how to implement a test to protect against this situation. That is the topic of the next chapter.

SELF CHECK

16. Suppose you make a mistake in the math, say, by using a + sign instead of a – sign in the formula for root. How can you tell that the program does not run correctly?

17. Which intersection points does the program draw when you provide an input of 0?

QUALITY TIP 5.1

Calculate Sample Data Manually

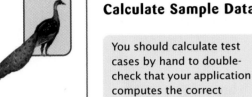

You should calculate test cases by hand to double-check that your application computes the correct answer.

It is usually difficult or impossible to prove that a given program functions correctly in all cases. For gaining confidence in the correctness of a program, or for understanding why it does not function as it should, manually calculated sample data are invaluable. If the program arrives at the same results as the manual calculation, our confidence in it is strengthened. If the manual results differ from the program results, we have a starting point for the debugging process.

Surprisingly, many programmers are reluctant to perform any manual calculations as soon as a program carries out the slightest bit of algebra. Their math phobia kicks in, and they irrationally hope that they can avoid the algebra and beat the program into submission by random tinkering, such as rearranging the + and – signs. Random tinkering is always a great time sink, but it rarely leads to useful results.

It is much smarter to look for test cases that are representative and easy to compute. In our example, let us look for three easy cases that we can compute by hand and then compare against program runs.

First, let the vertical line pass through the center of the circle. That is, x is 100. Then we expect the distance between the center and the intersection point to be the same as the radius of the circle. Now root = Math.sqrt(100 * 100 - 0 * 0), which is 100. Therefore, y1 is 0 and y2 is 200. Those are indeed the top and bottom points on the circle. Now, that wasn't so hard.

Next, let the line touch the circle on the right. Then x is 200 and root = Math.sqrt(100 * 100 - 100 * 100), which is 0. Therefore, y1 and y2 are both equal to 100, and indeed (200, 100) is the rightmost point of the circle. That also was pretty easy.

The first two cases were boundary cases of the problem. A program may work correctly for several special cases but still fail for more typical input values. Therefore we must come up with an intermediate test case, even if it means a bit more computation. Let us pick a simple value for x, say x = 50. Then

            root = Math.sqrt(100 * 100 - 50 * 50) = Math.sqrt(7500)

Using a calculator, you get approximately 86.6025. That yields y1 = 100 - 86.6025 = 13.3975 and y2 = 100 + 86.6025 = 186.6025. So what? Run the program and enter 50. You will find that the program also computes the same x- and y-values that you computed by hand. That is good—it confirms that you probably typed in the formulas correctly, and the intersection points really do fall in the right place.

CHAPTER SUMMARY

1. To show a frame, construct a JFrame object, set its size, and make it visible.

2. In order to display a drawing in a frame, define a class that extends the JComponent class.

3. Place drawing instructions inside the paintComponent method. That method is called whenever the component needs to be repainted.

4. The Graphics class lets you manipulate the graphics state (such as the current color).

5. The Graphics2D class has methods to draw shape objects.

6. Use a cast to recover the Graphics2D object from the Graphics parameter of the paintComponent method.

7. Applets are programs that run inside a web browser.

8. To run an applet, you need an HTML file with the applet tag.

9. You view applets with the applet viewer or a Java-enabled browser.

10. Ellipse2D.Double and Line2D.Double are classes that describe graphical shapes.

11. The drawString method draws a string, starting at its basepoint.

12. When you set a new color in the graphics context, it is used for subsequent drawing operations.

13. It is a good idea to make a class for each complex graphical shape.

14. To figure out how to draw a complex shape, make a sketch on graph paper.

15. A graphical application can obtain input by displaying a JOptionPane.

16. You should calculate test cases by hand to double-check that your application computes the correct answer.

FURTHER READING

1. http://java.com   The consumer-oriented web site for Java technology. Download the Java plugin from this site.

2. http://www.gnu.org   The web site of the GNU project.

3. http://www.gutenberg.org   The web site of Project Gutenberg, offering the text of classical books.

CLASSES, OBJECTS, AND METHODS INTRODUCED IN THIS CHAPTER

```
java.awt.Color              java.awt.Graphics2D          java.awt.geom.Point2D.Double
java.awt.Component            draw                        javax.swing.JComponent
   getHeight                  drawString                     paintComponent
   getWidth                   fill                        javax.swing.JFrame
   setSize                  java.awt.geom.Ellipse2D.Double   setDefaultCloseOperation
   setVisible               java.awt.Frame                javax.swing.JOptionPane
java.awt.Graphics             setTitle                     showInputDialog
   setColor                 java.awt.geom.Line2D.Double
```

REVIEW EXERCISES

Exercise R5.1. What is the difference between a console application and a graphical application?

Exercise R5.2. Who calls the paintComponent method of a component? When does the call to the paintComponent method occur?

Exercise R5.3. Why does the parameter of the paintComponent method have type Graphics and not Graphics2D?

Exercise R5.4. What is the purpose of a graphics context?

Exercise R5.5. Why are separate viewer and component classes used for graphical programs?

Exercise R5.6. Why does the car drawing program have a separate car class in addition to the viewer and component classes?

Exercise R5.7. How do you specify a text color?

Exercise R5.8. Which classes are used in this chapter for drawing graphical shapes?

Exercise R5.9. Write Java instructions to display the letters X and T in a graphics window, by plotting line segments.

Exercise R5.10. Let e be any ellipse. Write Java code to plot the ellipse e and another ellipse of the same size that touches e. *Hint:* You need to look up the accessors that tell you the dimensions of an ellipse.

Exercise R5.11. Introduce an error in the program IntersectionViewer.java, by computing double root = Math.sqrt(r * r + (x - a) * (x - a));. Run the program. What happens to the intersection points?

Exercise R5.12. Suppose you run the IntersectionViewer program and give a value of 30 for the x-position of the vertical line. Without actually running the program, determine what values you will obtain for the intersection points.

PROGRAMMING EXERCISES

Exercise P5.1. Write a graphics program that draws your name in red, contained inside a blue rectangle.

Exercise P5.2. Modify the program of Exercise P5.1 so that it asks the user for the name (or other message) to display.

Exercise P5.3. Write a graphics program that draws 12 strings, one each for the 12 standard colors, besides Color.WHITE, each in its own color.

Exercise P5.4. Write a graphics program that prompts the user to enter a radius. Draw a circle with that radius.

Exercise P5.5. Write a program that draws two solid circles: one in pink and one in purple. Use a standard color for one of them and a custom color for the other.

Exercise P5.6. Draw a "bull's eye"—a set of concentric rings in alternating black and white colors. *Hint:* Fill a black circle, then fill a smaller white circle on top, and so on.

Exercise P5.7. Write a program that fills the component with a large ellipse, filled with your favorite color, that touches the window boundaries. The ellipse should resize itself when you resize the window.

Exercise P5.8. Write a program that draws a picture of a house. It could be as simple as the accompanying figure, or if you like, make it more elaborate (3-D, skyscraper, marble columns in the entryway, whatever).

Implement a class House and supply a method draw(Graphics2D g2) that draws the house.

Exercise P5.9. Extend Exercise P5.8 by supplying a House constructor for specifying the position and size. Then populate your screen with a few houses of different sizes.

Exercise P5.10. Write a program to plot the following face.

Exercise P5.11. Write a program to plot the string "HELLO", using only lines and circles. Do not call drawString, and do not use System.out. Make classes LetterH, LetterE, LetterL, and LetterO.

Exercise P5.12. Make a bar chart to plot the following data set. Make the bars horizontal for easier labeling.

Bridge Name	Longest Span (ft)
Golden Gate	4,200
Brooklyn	1,595
Delaware Memorial	2,150
Mackinac	3,800

Exercise P5.13. Write a graphics program that displays the values of Exercise P5.12 as a pie chart. Draw only a circle and the edges of the pie slices. You don't have to color the slices. (If you want to color them, look at the online API documentation for the Arc2D class.)

Exercise P5.14. Write a program that displays the Olympic rings. Color the rings in the Olympic colors.

Exercise P5.15. Change the car drawing program to make the cars appear in different colors. Each Car object should store its own color.

Exercise P5.16. Change the Car class so that the size of a car can be specified in the constructor. Change the CarComponent class to make the cars appear twice the size of the original example.

PROGRAMMING PROJECTS

Project 5.1. Write a graphics program that draws a clock face with the current time. (Use the GregorianCalendar class.)

Hint: You need to find out the angles of the hour hand and the minute hand. The angle of the minute hand is easy: The minute hand travels 360 degrees in 60 minutes. The angle of the hour hand is harder; it travels 360 degrees in 12 × 60 minutes.

Design a class Clock and supply a method draw(Graphics2D g2) that draws the clock.

Project 5.2. Design a class Truck whose constructor takes the top-left corner point, the width, and the height of the truck. Supply a method draw(Graphics2D g2) that draws the truck. Then populate your screen with a couple of cars and trucks. Add a translate method to the Car and Truck classes, and make the cars and trucks move by a small amount at the beginning of every call to paintComponent.

ANSWERS TO SELF-CHECK QUESTIONS

1. Modify the EmptyFrameViewer program as follows:

    ```
    frame.setSize(300, 300);
    frame.setTitle("Hello, World!");
    ```

2. Construct two JFrame objects, set each of their sizes, and call setVisible(true) on each of them.

3. Rectangle box = new Rectangle(5, 10, 20, 20);

4. Replace the call to box.translate(15, 25) with

    ```
    box = new Rectangle(20, 35, 20, 20);
    ```

5. The compiler complains that g doesn't have a draw method.

6. g2.draw(new Ellipse2D.Double(75, 75, 50, 50));

7.  ```
    Line2D.Double segment1 = new Line2D.Double(0, 0, 10, 30);
    g2.draw(segment1);
    Line2D.Double segment2 = new Line2D.Double(10, 30, 20, 0);
    g2.draw(segment2);
    ```

8. g2.drawString("V", 0, 30);

9. 0.0F, 0.0F, and 1.0F

10. First fill a big red square, then fill a small yellow square inside:

    ```
    g2.setColor(Color.RED);
    g2.fill(new Rectangle(0, 0, 200, 200));
    g2.setColor(Color.YELLOW);
    g2.fill(new Rectangle(50, 50, 100, 100));
    ```

11. CarComponent

12. In the draw method of the Car class, call

    ```
    g2.fill(frontTire);
    g2.fill(rearTire);
    ```

13. Double all measurements in the draw method of the Car class.

14. If the user entered a string, such as "1.0 0.7 0.7", you would need to break it up into three separate strings. That can be done, but it is more tedious to program than three calls to showInputDialog.

15. You don't want the dialog boxes to appear every time the component is repainted.

16. The intersection points will be drawn at a location that is different from the true intersection of the line and the circle.

17. The point (0, 100) is drawn twice.
    ```

Decisions

CHAPTER GOALS

- To be able to implement decisions using `if` statements
- To understand how to group statements into blocks
- To learn how to compare integers, floating-point numbers, strings, and objects
- To recognize the correct ordering of decisions in multiple branches
- To program conditions using Boolean operators and variables

The programs we have seen so far were able to do fast computations and render graphs, but they were very inflexible. Except for variations in the input, they worked the same way with every program run. One of the essential features of nontrivial computer programs is their ability to make decisions and to carry out different actions, depending on the nature of the inputs. The goal of this chapter is to learn how to program simple and complex decisions.

CHAPTER CONTENTS

6.1 The if Statement

Computer programs often need to make *decisions*, taking different actions depending on a condition.

Consider the bank account class of Chapter 3. The withdraw method allows you to withdraw as much money from the account as you like. The balance just moves ever further into the negatives. That is not a realistic model for a bank account. Let's implement the withdraw method so that you cannot withdraw more money than you have in the account. That is, the withdraw method must make a *decision*: whether to allow the withdrawal or not.

> The if statement lets a program carry out different actions depending on a condition.

The if statement is used to implement a decision. The if statement has two parts: a condition and a body. If the *condition* is true, the *body* of the statement is executed. The body of the if statement consists of a statement:

```
if (amount <= balance)
    balance = balance - amount;
```

The assignment statement is carried out only when the amount to be withdrawn is less than or equal to the balance (see Figure 1).

Let us make the withdraw method of the BankAccount even more realistic. Most banks not only disallow withdrawals that exceed your account balance; they also charge you a penalty for every attempt to do so.

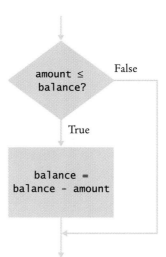

Figure 1
Flowchart for an if Statement

This operation can't be programmed simply by providing two complementary if statements, such as:

```
if (amount <= balance)
    balance = balance - amount;
if (amount > balance) // NO
    balance = balance - OVERDRAFT_PENALTY;
```

There are two problems with this approach. First, if you need to modify the condition amount <= balance for some reason, you must remember to update the condition amount > balance as well. If you do not, the logic of the program will no longer be correct. More importantly, if you modify the value of balance in the body of the first if statement (as in this example), then the second condition uses the new value.

To implement a choice between alternatives, use the if/else statement:

```
if (amount <= balance)
    balance = balance - amount;
else
    balance = balance - OVERDRAFT_PENALTY;
```

Now there is only one condition. If it is satisfied, the first statement is executed. Otherwise, the second is executed. The flowchart in Figure 2 gives a graphical representation of the branching behavior.

Quite often, however, the body of the if statement consists of multiple statements that must be executed in sequence whenever the condition is true. These statements must be grouped together to form a *block statement* by enclosing them in braces { }. Here is an example.

> A block statement groups several statements together.

```
if (amount <= balance)
{
    double newBalance = balance - amount;
    balance = newBalance;
}
```

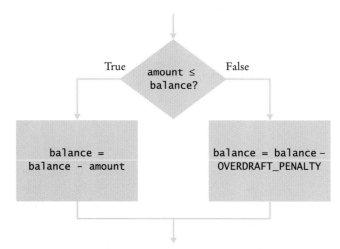

Figure 2
Flowchart for an `if/else` Statement

A statement such as

```
balance = balance - amount;
```

is called a *simple statement*. A conditional statement such as

```
if (x >= 0) y = x;
```

is called a *compound statement*. In Chapter 7, you will encounter loop statements; they too are compound statements.

SYNTAX 6.1 **The `if` Statement**

```
if (condition)
    statement

if (condition)
    statement₁
else
    statement₂
```

Example:

```
if (amount <= balance)
    balance = balance - amount;

if (amount <= balance)
    balance = balance - amount;
else
    balance = balance - OVERDRAFT_PENALTY;
```

Purpose:

To execute a statement when a condition is true or false

Syntax 6.2 Block Statement

```
{
    statement₁
    statement₂
    . . .
}
```

Example:

```
{
    double newBalance = balance - amount;
    balance = newBalance;
}
```

Purpose:

To group several statements together to form a single statement

The body of an `if` statement or the `else` alternative must be a statement—that is, a simple statement, a compound statement (such as another `if` statement), or a block statement.

SELF CHECK

1. Why did we use the condition `amount <= balance` and not `amount < balance` in the example for the `if`/`else` statement?

2. What is logically wrong with the statement

   ```
   if (amount <= balance)
       newBalance = balance - amount; balance = newBalance;
   ```

   and how do you fix it?

QUALITY TIP 6.1

Brace Layout

The compiler doesn't care where you place braces, but we strongly recommend that you follow a simple rule: *Line up { and }*.

```
if (amount <= balance)
{
    double newBalance = balance - amount;
    balance = newBalance;
}
```

This scheme makes it easy to spot matching braces.

Some programmers put the opening brace on the same line as the `if`:

```
if (amount <= balance) {
   double newBalance = balance - amount;
   balance = newBalance;
}
```

This saves a line of code, but it makes it harder to match the braces.

It is important that you pick a layout scheme and stick with it. Which scheme you choose may depend on your personal preference or a coding style guide that you must follow.

PRODUCTIVITY HINT 6.1

Indentation and Tabs

When writing Java programs, use indentation to indicate nesting levels:

```
public class BankAccount
{
|  . . .
|  public void withdraw(double amount)
|  {
|  |  if (amount <= balance)
|  |  {
|  |  |  double newBalance = balance - amount;
|  |  |  balance = newBalance;
|  |  }
|  }
|  . . .
}
0  1  2  3
Indentation level
```

How many spaces should you use per indentation level? Some programmers use eight spaces per level, but that isn't a good choice:

```
public class BankAccount
{
        . . .
        public void withdraw(double amount)
        {
                if (amount <= balance)
                {
                        double newBalance =
                                balance - amount;
                        balance = newBalance;
                }
        }
        . . .
}
```

It crowds the code too much to the right side of the screen. As a consequence, long expressions frequently must be broken into separate lines. More common values are two, three, or four spaces per indentation level.

How do you move the cursor from the leftmost column to the appropriate indentation level? A perfectly reasonable strategy is to hit the space bar a sufficient number of times. However, many programmers use the Tab key instead. A tab moves the cursor to the next tab stop. By default, there are tab stops every eight columns, but most editors let you change that value; you should find out how to set your editor's tab stops to, say, every three columns.

Some editors help you out with an *autoindent* feature. They automatically insert as many tabs or spaces as the preceding line because the new line is quite likely to belong to the same logical indentation level. If it isn't, you must add or remove a tab, but that is still faster than tabbing all the way from the left margin.

As nice as tabs are for data entry, they have one disadvantage: They can mess up printouts. If you send a file with tabs to a printer, the printer may either ignore the tabs altogether or set tab stops every eight columns. It is therefore best to save and print your files with spaces instead of tabs. Most editors have settings that convert tabs to spaces before you save or print a file.

ADVANCED TOPIC 6.1

The Selection Operator

Java has a selection operator of the form

condition ? *value*$_1$: *value*$_2$

The value of that expression is either *value*$_1$ if the condition is true or *value*$_2$ if it is false. For example, we can compute the absolute value as

```
y = x >= 0 ? x : -x;
```

which is a convenient shorthand for

```
if (x >= 0)
    y = x;
else
    y = -x;
```

The selection operator is similar to the if/else statement, but it works on a different syntactical level. The selection operator combines *values* and yields another value. The if/else statement combines *statements* and yields another statement.

For example, it would be an error to write

```
y = if (x > 0) x; else -x; // Error
```

The if/else construct is a statement, not a value, and you cannot assign it to a variable.

We don't use the selection operator in this book, but it is a convenient and legitimate construct that you will find in many Java programs.

6.2 Comparing Values

6.2.1 Relational Operators

Relational operators
compare values. The ==
operator tests for equality.

A relational operator tests the relationship between two values. An example is the <= operator that we used in the test

```
if (amount <= balance)
```

Java has six relational operators:

Java	Math Notation	Description
>	>	Greater than
>=	≥	Greater than or equal
<	<	Less than
<=	≤	Less than or equal
==	=	Equal
!=	≠	Not equal

As you can see, only two relational operators (> and <) look as you would expect from the mathematical notation. Computer keyboards do not have keys for ≥, ≤, or ≠, but the >=, <=, and != operators are easy to remember because they look similar.

The == operator is initially confusing to most newcomers to Java. In Java, the = symbol already has a meaning, namely assignment. The == operator denotes equality testing:

```
a = 5; // Assign 5 to a
if (a == 5) . . . // Test whether a equals 5
```

You will have to remember to use == for equality testing, and to use = for assignment.

6.2.2 Comparing Floating-Point Numbers

You have to be careful when comparing floating-point numbers, in order to cope with roundoff errors. For example, the following code multiplies the square root of 2 by itself and then subtracts 2.

```
double r = Math.sqrt(2);
double d = r * r - 2;
if (d == 0)
    System.out.println("sqrt(2) squared minus 2 is 0");
```

```
else
   System.out.println(
         "sqrt(2) squared minus 2 is not 0 but " + d);
```

Even though the laws of mathematics tell us that $r^2 - 2$ equals 0, this program fragment prints

```
sqrt(2) squared minus 2 is not 0 but 4.440892098500626E-16
```

Unfortunately, such roundoff errors are unavoidable. It plainly does not make sense in most circumstances to compare floating-point numbers exactly. Instead, test whether they are *close enough*.

> When comparing floating-point numbers, don't test for equality. Instead, check whether they are close enough.

To test whether a number x is close to zero, you can test whether the absolute value $|x|$ (that is, the number with its sign removed) is less than a very small threshold number. That threshold value is often called ε (the Greek letter epsilon). It is common to set ε to 10^{-14} when testing double numbers.

Similarly, you can test whether two numbers are approximately equal by checking whether their difference is close to 0.

$$|x - y| \le \varepsilon$$

In Java, we program the test as follows:

```
final double EPSILON = 1E-14;
if (Math.abs(x - y) <= EPSILON)
   // x is approximately equal to y
```

6.2.3 Comparing Strings

To test whether two strings are equal to each other, you must use the method called equals:

```
if (string1.equals(string2)) . . .
```

> Do not use the == operator to compare strings. Use the equals method instead.

Do not use the == operator to compare strings. The expression

```
if (string1 == string2) // Not useful
```

has an unrelated meaning. It tests whether the two string variables refer to the identical string object. You can have strings with identical contents stored in different objects, so this test never makes sense in actual programming; see Common Error 6.1.

In Java, letter case matters. For example, "Harry" and "HARRY" are not the same string. To ignore the letter case, use the equalsIgnoreCase method:

```
if (string1.equalsIgnoreCase(string2)) . . .
```

> The compareTo method compares strings in dictionary order.

If two strings are not identical to each other, you still may want to know the relationship between them. The compareTo method compares strings in dictionary order. If

```
string1.compareTo(string2) < 0
```

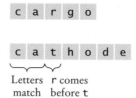

Figure 3
Lexicographic Comparison

Letters   r comes
match   before t

then the string `string1` comes before the string `string2` in the dictionary. For example, this is the case if `string1` is `"Harry"`, and `string2` is `"Hello"`. If

```
string1.compareTo(string2) > 0
```

then `string1` comes after `string2` in dictionary order. Finally, if

```
string1.compareTo(string2) == 0
```

then `string1` and `string2` are equal.

Actually, the "dictionary" ordering used by Java is slightly different from that of a normal dictionary. Java is case sensitive and sorts characters by putting numbers first, then uppercase characters, then lowercase characters. For example, 1 comes before B, which comes before a. The space character comes before all other characters.

Let us investigate the comparison process closely. When Java compares two strings, corresponding letters are compared until one of the strings ends or the first difference is encountered. If one of the strings ends, the longer string is considered the later one. If a character mismatch is found, the characters are compared to determine which string comes later in the dictionary sequence. This process is called lexicographic comparison. For example, let's compare `"car"` with `"cargo"`. The first three letters match, and we reach the end of the first string. Therefore `"car"` comes before `"cargo"` in the lexicographic ordering. Now compare `"cathode"` with `"cargo"`. The first two letters match. In the third character position, t comes after r, so the string `"cathode"` comes after `"cargo"` in lexicographic ordering. (See Figure 3.)

COMMON ERROR 6.1

Using == to Compare Strings

It is an extremely common error in Java to write == when `equals` is intended. This is particularly true for strings. If you write

```
if (nickname == "Rob")
```

then the test succeeds only if the variable `nickname` refers to the exact same string object as the string constant `"Rob"`. For efficiency, Java makes only one string object for every string constant. Therefore, the following test will pass:

```
String nickname = "Rob";
. . .
if (nickname == "Rob") // Test is true
```

However, if the string with the letters R o b has been assembled in some other way, then the test will fail:

```
String name = "Robert";
String nickname = name.substring(0, 3);
. . .
if (nickname == "Rob") // Test is false
```

This is a particularly distressing situation: The wrong code will sometimes do the right thing, sometimes the wrong thing. Because string objects are always constructed by the compiler, you never have an interest in whether two string objects are shared. You must remember never to use == to compare strings. Always use equals or compareTo to compare strings.

6.2.4 Comparing Objects

If you compare two object references with the == operator, you test whether the references refer to the same object. Here is an example:

```
Rectangle box1 = new Rectangle(5, 10, 20, 30);
Rectangle box2 = box1;
Rectangle box3 = new Rectangle(5, 10, 20, 30);
```

The comparison

```
box1 == box2
```

is true. Both object variables refer to the same object. But the comparison

```
box1 == box3
```

is false. The two object variables refer to different objects (see Figure 4). It does not matter that the objects have identical contents.

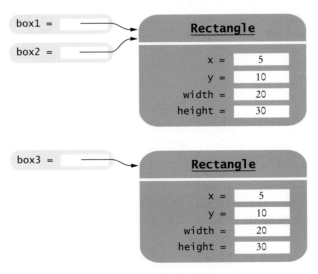

Figure 4 Comparing Object References

> The == operator tests whether two object references are identical. To compare the contents of objects, you need to use the equals method.

You can use the equals method to test whether two rectangles have the same contents, that is, whether they have the same upper-left corner and the same width and height. For example, the test

```
box1.equals(box3)
```

is true.

However, you must be careful when using the equals method. It works correctly only if the implementors of the class have defined it. The Rectangle class has an equals method that is suitable for comparing rectangles.

For your own classes, you need to supply an appropriate equals method. You will learn how to do that in Chapter 13. Until that point, you should not use the equals method to compare objects of your own classes.

6.2.5 Testing for null

> The null reference refers to no object.

An object reference can have the special value null if it refers to no object at all. It is common to use the null value to indicate that a value has never been set. For example,

```
String middleInitial = null; // Not set
if ( . . . )
   middleInitial = middleName.substring(0, 1);
```

You use the == operator (and not equals) to test whether an object reference is a null reference:

```
if (middleInitial == null)
   System.out.println(firstName + " " + lastName);
else
   System.out.println(firstName + " " + middleInitial + ". " + lastName);
```

Note that the null reference is not the same as the empty string "". The empty string is a valid string of length 0, whereas a null indicates that a string variable refers to no string at all.

SELF CHECK

3. What is the value of s.length() if s is
   a. the empty string ""?
   b. the string " " containing a space?
   c. null?

4. Which of the following comparisons are syntactically incorrect? Which of them are syntactically correct, but logically questionable?

```
String a = "1";
String b = "one";
double x = 1;
double y = 3 * (1.0 / 3);
```

a. `a == "1"`

b. `a == null`

c. `a.equals("")`

d. `a == b`

e. `a == x`

f. `x == y`

g. `x - y == null`

h. `x.equals(y)`

QUALITY TIP 6.2

Avoid Conditions with Side Effects

In Java, it is legal to nest assignments inside test conditions:

```
if ((d = b * b - 4 * a * c) >= 0) r = Math.sqrt(d);
```

It is legal to use the decrement operator inside other expressions:

```
if (n-- > 0) . . .
```

These are bad programming practices, because they mix a test with another activity. The other activity (setting the variable d, decrementing n) is called a *side effect* of the test.

As you will see in Advanced Topic 7.2, conditions with side effects can occasionally be helpful to simplify loops; for if statements they should always be avoided.

6.3 Multiple Alternatives

6.3.1 Sequences of Comparisons

Many computations require more than a single if/else decision. Sometimes, you need to make a series of related comparisons.

> Multiple conditions can be combined to evaluate complex decisions. The correct arrangement depends on the logic of the problem to be solved.

The following program asks for a value describing the magnitude of an earthquake on the Richter scale and prints a description of the likely impact of the quake. The Richter scale is a measurement for the strength of an earthquake. Every step in the scale, for example from 6.0 to 7.0, signifies a tenfold increase in the strength of the quake. The 1989 Loma Prieta earthquake that damaged the Bay Bridge in San Francisco and destroyed many buildings in several Bay area cities registered 7.1 on the Richter scale.

File Earthquake.java

```
1  /**
2      A class that describes the effects of an earthquake.
3  */
4  public class Earthquake
5  {
```

```
 6      /**
 7          Constructs an Earthquake object.
 8          @param magnitude the magnitude on the Richter scale
 9      */
10      public Earthquake(double magnitude)
11      {
12          richter = magnitude;
13      }
14
15      /**
16          Gets a description of the effect of the earthquake.
17          @return the description of the effect
18      */
19      public String getDescription()
20      {
21          String r;
22          if (richter >= 8.0)
23              r = "Most structures fall";
24          else if (richter >= 7.0)
25              r = "Many buildings destroyed";
26          else if (richter >= 6.0)
27              r = "Many buildings considerably damaged, some collapse";
28          else if (richter >= 4.5)
29              r = "Damage to poorly constructed buildings";
30          else if (richter >= 3.5)
31              r = "Felt by many people, no destruction";
32          else if (richter >= 0)
33              r = "Generally not felt by people";
34          else
35              r = "Negative numbers are not valid";
36          return r;
37      }
38
39      private double richter;
40  }
```

File EarthquakeTester.java

```
 1  import java.util.Scanner;
 2
 3  /**
 4      A class to test the Earthquake class.
 5  */
 6  public class EarthquakeTester
 7  {
 8      public static void main(String[] args)
 9      {
10          Scanner in = new Scanner(System.in);
11
12          System.out.print("Enter a magnitude on the Richter scale: ");
13          double magnitude = in.nextDouble();
14          Earthquake quake = new Earthquake(magnitude);
15          System.out.println(quake.getDescription());
16      }
17  }
```

Output

```
Enter a magnitude on the Richter scale: 7.1
Many buildings destroyed
```

Here we must sort the conditions and test against the largest cutoff first. Suppose we reverse the order of tests:

```
if (richter >= 0) // Tests in wrong order
    r = "Generally not felt by people";
else if (richter >= 3.5)
    r = "Felt by many people, no destruction";
else if (richter >= 4.5)
    r = "Damage to poorly constructed buildings";
else if (richter >= 6.0)
    r = "Many buildings considerably damaged, some collapse";
else if (richter >= 7.0)
    r = "Many buildings destroyed";
else if (richter >= 8.0)
    r = "Most structures fall";
```

This does not work. All nonnegative values of richter fall into the first case, and the other tests will never be attempted.

In this example, it is also important that we use an if/else/else test, not just multiple independent if statements. Consider this sequence of independent tests:

```
if (richter >= 8.0) // Didn't use else
    r = "Most structures fall";
if (richter >= 7.0)
    r = "Many buildings destroyed";
if (richter >= 6.0)
    r = "Many buildings considerably damaged, some collapse";
if (richter >= 4.5)
    r = "Damage to poorly constructed buildings";
if (richter >= 3.5)
    r = "Felt by many people, no destruction";
if (richter >= 0)
    r = "Generally not felt by people";
```

Now the alternatives are no longer exclusive. If richter is 6.0, then the last four tests all match, and r is set four times.

PRODUCTIVITY HINT 6.2

Keyboard Shortcuts for Mouse Operations

Programmers spend a lot of time with the keyboard. Programs and documentation are many pages long and require a lot of typing. This makes you different from the average computer user who uses the mouse more often than the keyboard.

Unfortunately for you, modern user interfaces are optimized for the mouse. The mouse is the most obvious tool for switching between windows, and for selecting commands. The constant switching between the keyboard and the mouse slows you down. You need to move a hand off the keyboard, locate the mouse, move the mouse, click the mouse, and move the hand back onto the keyboard. For that reason, most user interfaces have keyboard short-cuts: combinations of keystrokes that allow you to achieve the same tasks without having to switch to the mouse at all.

All Microsoft Windows applications use the following conventions:

- The Alt key plus the underlined letter in a menu name (such as the F in "File") pulls down that menu. Inside a menu, just type the underlined character in the name of a submenu to activate it. For example, Alt+F followed by O selects "File" "Open". Once your fingers know about this combination, you can open files faster than the fastest mouse artist.

- Inside dialog boxes, the Tab key is important; it moves from one option to the next. The arrow keys move within an option. The Enter key accepts the entire dialog box, and Esc cancels it.

- In a program with multiple windows, Ctrl+Tab usually toggles through the windows managed by that program, for example between the source and error windows.

- Alt+Tab toggles between applications, allowing you to toggle quickly between, for example, the text editor and a command shell window.

- Hold down the Shift key and press the arrow keys to highlight text. Then use Ctrl+X to cut the text, Ctrl+C to copy it, and Ctrl+V to paste it. These keys are easy to remember. The V looks like an insertion mark that an editor would use to insert text. The X should remind you of crossing out text. The C is just the first letter in "Copy". (OK, so it is also the first letter in "Cut"—no mnemonic rule is perfect.) You find these reminders in the Edit menu of most text editors.

Take a little bit of time to learn about the keyboard shortcuts that the program designers provided for you, and the time investment will be repaid many times during your program-ming career. When you blaze through your work in the computer lab with keyboard short-cuts, you may find yourself surrounded by amazed onlookers who whisper, "I didn't know you could do *that*."

PRODUCTIVITY HINT 6.3

Copy and Paste in the Editor

When you see code like

```
if (richter >= 8.0)
    r = "Most structures fall";
else if (richter >= 7.0)
    r = "Many buildings destroyed";
else if (richter >= 6.0)
    r = "Many buildings considerably damaged, some collapse";
else if (richter >= 4.5)
    r = "Damage to poorly constructed buildings";
else if (richter >= 3.5)
    r = "Felt by many people, no destruction";
```

you should think "copy and paste".

Make a template:

```
else if (richter >= )
    r = "";
```

and copy it. This is usually done by highlighting with the mouse and then selecting Edit and then Copy from the menu bar. If you follow Productivity Hint 6.2, you are smart and use the keyboard. Hit Shift+End to highlight the entire line, then Ctrl+C to copy it. Then paste it (Ctrl+V) multiple times and fill the text into the copies. Of course, your editor may use different commands, but the concept is the same.

The ability to copy and paste is always useful when you have code from an example or another project that is similar to your current needs. To copy, paste, and modify is faster than to type everything from scratch. You are also less likely to make typing errors.

ADVANCED TOPIC 6.2

The switch Statement

A sequence of if/else/else that compares a single integer value against several constant alternatives can be implemented as a switch statement. For example,

```
int digit;
. . .
switch (digit)
{
   case 1: System.out.print("one"); break;
   case 2: System.out.print("two"); break;
   case 3: System.out.print("three"); break;
   case 4: System.out.print("four"); break;
   case 5: System.out.print("five"); break;
   case 6: System.out.print("six"); break;
   case 7: System.out.print("seven"); break;
   case 8: System.out.print("eight"); break;
   case 9: System.out.print("nine"); break;
   default: System.out.print("error"); break;
}
```

This is a shortcut for

```
int digit;
. . .
if (digit == 1) System.out.print("one");
else if (digit == 2) System.out.print("two");
else if (digit == 3) System.out.print("three");
else if (digit == 4) System.out.print("four");
else if (digit == 5) System.out.print("five");
else if (digit == 6) System.out.print("six");
else if (digit == 7) System.out.print("seven");
else if (digit == 8) System.out.print("eight");
else if (digit == 9) System.out.print("nine");
else System.out.print("error");
```

Using the switch statement has one advantage. It is obvious that all branches test the same value, namely digit.

The switch statement can be applied only in narrow circumstances. The test cases must be constants, and they must be integers, characters, or enumerated constants. You cannot use a switch to branch on floating-point or string values. For example, the following is an error:

```
switch (name)
{
    case "one": . . . break; // Error
    . . .
}
```

Note how every branch of the switch was terminated by a break instruction. If the break is missing, execution falls through to the next branch, and so on, until finally a break or the end of the switch is reached. For example, consider the following switch statement:

```
switch (digit)
{
    case 1: System.out.print("one"); // Oops—no break
    case 2: System.out.print("two"); break;
    . . .
}
```

If digit has the value 1, then the statement after the case 1: label is executed. Because there is no break, the statement after the case 2: label is executed as well. The program prints "onetwo".

There are a few cases in which this fall-through behavior is actually useful, but they are very rare. Peter van der Linden [1, p. 38] describes an analysis of the switch statements in the Sun C compiler front end. Of the 244 switch statements, each of which had an average of 7 cases, only 3 percent used the fall-through behavior. That is, the default—falling through to the next case unless stopped by a break—was wrong 97 percent of the time. Forgetting to type the break is an exceedingly common error, yielding incorrect code.

We leave it to you to decide whether or not to use the switch statement. At any rate, you need to have a reading knowledge of switch in case you find it in the code of other programmers.

6.3.2 Nested Branches

Some computations have multiple *levels* of decision making. You first make one decision, and each of the outcomes leads to another decision. Here is a typical example.

In the United States, taxpayers pay federal income tax at different rates depending on their incomes and marital status. There are two main tax schedules: one for single taxpayers and one for married taxpayers "filing jointly", meaning that the married taxpayers add their incomes together and pay taxes on the total. (In fact, there are two other schedules, "head of household" and "married filing separately", which we will ignore for simplicity.) Table 1 gives the tax rate computations for each of the filing categories, using the values for the 1992 federal tax return. (We're using the 1992 tax rate schedule in this illustration because of its simplicity. Legislation in 1993 increased the number of rates in each status and added more complicated rules. By the time that you read this, the tax laws may well have become even more complex.)

Table 1 Federal Tax Rate Schedule (1992)			
If your filing status is Single:		**If your filing status is Married:**	
Tax Bracket	**Percentage**	**Tax Bracket**	**Percentage**
$0 . . . $21,450	15%	$0 . . . $35,800	15%
Amount over $21,450, up to $51,900	28%	Amount over $35,800, up to $86,500	28%
Amount over $51,900	31%	Amount over $86,500	31%

Now let us compute the taxes due, given a filing status and an income figure. First, we must branch on the filing status. Then, for each filing status, we must have another branch on income level.

The two-level decision process is reflected in two levels of if statements. We say that the income test is *nested* inside the test for filing status. (See Figure 5 for a flowchart.)

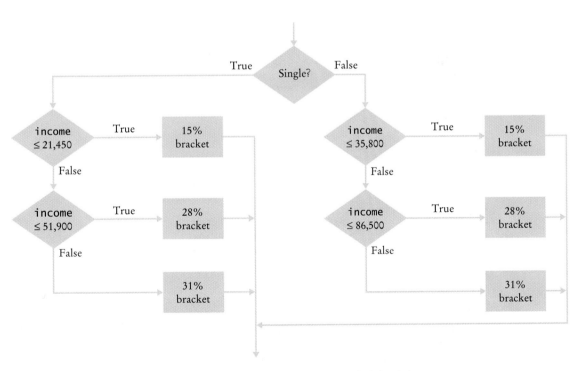

Figure 5   Income Tax Computation Using 1992 Schedule

File TaxReturn.java

```java
1   /**
2       A tax return of a taxpayer in 1992.
3   */
4   public class TaxReturn
5   {
6      /**
7          Constructs a TaxReturn object for a given income and
8          marital status.
9          @param anIncome the taxpayer income
10         @param aStatus either SINGLE or MARRIED
11     */
12     public TaxReturn(double anIncome, int aStatus)
13     {
14        income = anIncome;
15        status = aStatus;
16     }
17
18     public double getTax()
19     {
20        double tax = 0;
21
22        if (status == SINGLE)
23        {
24           if (income <= SINGLE_BRACKET1)
25              tax = RATE1 * income;
26           else if (income <= SINGLE_BRACKET2)
27              tax = RATE1 * SINGLE_BRACKET1
28                  + RATE2 * (income - SINGLE_BRACKET1);
29           else
30              tax = RATE1 * SINGLE_BRACKET1
31                  + RATE2 * (SINGLE_BRACKET2 - SINGLE_BRACKET1);
32                  + RATE3 * (income - SINGLE_BRACKET2);
33        }
34        else
35        {
36           if (income <= MARRIED_BRACKET1)
37              tax = RATE1 * income;
38           else if (income <= MARRIED_BRACKET2)
39              tax = RATE1 * MARRIED_BRACKET1
40                  + RATE2 * (income - MARRIED_BRACKET1);
41           else
42              tax = RATE1 * MARRIED_BRACKET1
43                  + RATE2 * (MARRIED_BRACKET2 - MARRIED_BRACKET1);
44                  + RATE3 * (income - MARRIED_BRACKET2);
45        }
46
47        return tax;
48     }
49
50     public static final int SINGLE = 1;
51     public static final int MARRIED = 2;
52
```

```
53      private static final double RATE1 = 0.15;
54      private static final double RATE2 = 0.28;
55      private static final double RATE3 = 0.31;
56
57      private static final double SINGLE_BRACKET1 = 21450;
58      private static final double SINGLE_BRACKET2 = 51900;
59
60      private static final double MARRIED_BRACKET1 = 35800;
61      private static final double MARRIED_BRACKET2 = 86500;
62
63      private double income;
64      private int status;
65   }
```

File TaxReturnTester.java

```
 1   import java.util.Scanner;
 2
 3   /**
 4      A class to test the TaxReturn class.
 5   */
 6   public class TaxReturnTester
 7   {
 8      public static void main(String[] args)
 9      {
10         Scanner in = new Scanner(System.in);
11
12         System.out.print("Please enter your income: ");
13         double income = in.nextDouble();
14
15         System.out.print("Please enter S (single) or M (married): ");
16         String input = in.next();
17         int status = 0;
18
19         if (input.equalsIgnoreCase("S"))
20            status = TaxReturn.SINGLE;
21         else if (input.equalsIgnoreCase("M"))
22            status = TaxReturn.MARRIED;
23         else
24         {
25            System.out.println("Bad input.");
26            return;
27         }
28
29         TaxReturn aTaxReturn = new TaxReturn(income, status);
30
31         System.out.println("The tax is "
32               + aTaxReturn.getTax());
33      }
34   }
```

Output

```
Please enter your income: 50000
Please enter S (single) or M (married): S
The tax is 11211.5
```

SELF CHECK

5. The if/else/else statement for the earthquake strength first tested for higher values, then descended to lower values. Can you reverse that order?

6. Some people object to higher tax rates for higher incomes, claiming that you might end up with *less* money after taxes when you get a raise for working hard. What is the flaw in this argument?

COMMON ERROR 6.2

The Dangling else Problem

When an if statement is nested inside another if statement, the following error may occur.

```
if (richter >= 0)
    if (richter <= 4)
        System.out.println("The earthquake is harmless");
else    // Pitfall!
    System.out.println("Negative value not allowed");
```

The indentation level seems to suggest that the else is grouped with the test richter >= 0. Unfortunately, that is not the case. The compiler ignores all indentation and follows the rule that an else always belongs to the closest if, like this:

```
if (richter >= 0)
    if (richter <= 4)
        System.out.println("The earthquake is harmless");
    else    // Pitfall!
        System.out.println("Negative value not allowed");
```

That isn't what we want. We want to group the else with the first if. For that, we must use braces.

```
if (richter >= 0)
{
    if (richter <= 4)
        System.out.println("The earthquake is harmless");
}
else
    System.out.println("Negative value not allowed");
```

To avoid having to think about the pairing of the else, we recommend that you *always* use a set of braces when the body of an if contains another if. In the following example, the braces are not strictly necessary, but they help clarify the code:

```
if (richter >= 0)
{
```

```
    if (richter <= 4)
        System.out.println("The earthquake is harmless");
    else
        System.out.println("Damage may occur");
}
```

The ambiguous else is called a *dangling* else, and it is enough of a syntactical blemish that some programming language designers developed an improved syntax that avoids it altogether. For example, Algol 68 uses the construction

if *condition* then *statement* else *statement* fi;

The else part is optional, but since the end of the if statement is clearly marked, the grouping is unambiguous if there are two ifs and only one else. Here are the two possible cases:

if c_1 then if c_2 then s_1 else s_2 fi fi;
if c_1 then if c_2 then s_1 fi else s_2 fi;

By the way, fi is just if backwards. Other languages use endif, which has the same purpose but is less fun.

QUALITY TIP 6.3

Prepare Test Cases Ahead of Time

Let us consider how we can test the tax computation program. Of course, we cannot try out all possible inputs of filing status and income level. Even if we could, there would be no point in trying them all. If the program correctly computes one or two tax amounts in a given bracket, then we have a good reason to believe that all amounts within that bracket will be correct. We want to aim for complete *coverage* of all cases.

There are two possibilities for the filing status and three tax brackets for each status. That makes six test cases. Then we want to test a handful of *error conditions*, such as a negative income. That makes seven test cases. For the first six, we need to compute manually what answer we expect. For the remaining one, we need to know what error reports we expect. We write down the test cases and then start coding.

Should you really test seven inputs for this simple program? You certainly should. Furthermore, if you find an error in the program that wasn't covered by one of the test cases, make another test case and add it to your collection. After you fix the known mistakes, *run all test cases again*. Experience has shown that the cases that you just tried to fix are probably working now, but that errors that you fixed two or three iterations ago have a good chance of coming back! If you find that an error keeps coming back, that is usually a reliable sign that you did not fully understand some subtle interaction between features of your program.

It is always a good idea to design test cases *before* starting to code. There are two reasons for this. Working through the test cases gives you a better understanding of the algorithm that you are about to program. Furthermore, it has been noted that programmers instinctively shy away from testing fragile parts of their code. That seems hard to believe, but you will often make that observation about your own work. Watch someone else test your program. There will be times when that person enters input that makes you very nervous because you are not sure that your program can handle it, and you never dared to test it yourself. This is a well-known phenomenon, and making the test plan before writing the code offers some protection.

PRODUCTIVITY HINT 6.4

Make a Schedule and Make Time for Unexpected Problems

Commercial software is notorious for being delivered later than promised. For example, Microsoft originally promised that the successor to its Windows XP operating system would be available in 2004, then early in 2005, then late in 2005. Some of the early promises might not have been realistic. It is in Microsoft's interest to let prospective customers expect the imminent availability of the product, so that they do not switch to a different product in the meantime. Undeniably, though, Microsoft had not anticipated the full complexity of the tasks it had set itself to solve.

Microsoft can delay the delivery of its product, but it is likely that you cannot. As a student or a programmer, you are expected to manage your time wisely and to finish your assignments on time. You can probably do simple programming exercises the night before the due date, but an assignment that looks twice as hard may well take four times as long, because more things can go wrong. You should therefore make a schedule whenever you start a programming project.

First, estimate realistically how much time it will take you to

- Design the program logic
- Develop test cases
- Type the program in and fix syntax errors
- Test and debug the program

For example, for the income tax program I might estimate 30 minutes for the design, because it is mostly done; 30 minutes for developing test cases; one hour for data entry and fixing syntax errors; and 2 hours for testing and debugging. That is a total of 4 hours. If I work 2 hours a day on this project, it will take me two days.

Then think of things that can go wrong. Your computer might break down. The lab might be crowded. You might be stumped by a problem with the computer system. (That is a particularly important concern for beginners. It is *very* common to lose a day over a trivial problem just because it takes time to track down a person who knows the "magic" command to overcome it.) As a rule of thumb, *double* the time of your estimate. That is, you should start four days, not two days, before the due date. If nothing goes wrong, great; you have the program done two days early. When the inevitable problem occurs, you have a cushion of time that protects you from embarrassment and failure.

ADVANCED TOPIC 6.3

Enumerated Types

In many programs, you use variables that can hold one of a finite number of values. For example, in the tax return class, the status field holds one of the values SINGLE or MARRIED. We arbitrarily defined SINGLE as the number 1 and MARRIED as 2. If, due to some programming error, the status field is set to another integer value (such as −1, 0, or 3), then the programming logic may produce invalid results.

In a simple program, this is not really a problem. But as programs grow over time, and more cases are added (such as the "married filing separately" and "head of household" categories), errors can slip in. Java version 5.0 introduces a remedy: *enumerated types*. An enumerated type has a finite set of values, for example

```
public enum FilingStatus { SINGLE, MARRIED }
```

You can have any number of values, but you must include them all in the enum declaration.
   You can declare variables of the enumerated type:

```
FilingStatus status = FilingStatus.SINGLE;
```

If you try to assign a value that isn't a FilingStatus, such as 2 or "S", then the compiler reports an error.
   Use the == operator to compare enumerated values, for example:

```
if (status == FilingStatus.SINGLE) . . .
```

It is common to nest an enum declaration inside a class, such as

```
public class TaxReturn
{
    public TaxReturn(double anIncome, FilingStatus aStatus) { . . . }
    . . .
    public enum FilingStatus { SINGLE, MARRIED }
    private FilingStatus status;
}
```

To access the enumeration outside the class in which it is defined, use the class name as a prefix:

```
TaxReturn return = new TaxReturn(income, TaxReturn.FilingStatus.SINGLE);
```

An enumerated type variable can be null. For example, the status field in the previous example can actually have three values: SINGLE, MARRIED, and null. This can be useful, for example to identify an uninitialized variable, or a potential pitfall.

SYNTAX 6.3 **Defining an Enumerated Type**

accessSpecifier enum *TypeName* { *value*$_1$, *value*$_2$, . . . }

Example:

```
public enum FilingStatus { SINGLE, MARRIED }
```

Purpose:

To define a type with a fixed number of values

6.4 Using Boolean Expressions

6.4.1 The boolean Type

In Java, an expression such as amount < 1000 has a value, just as the expression amount + 1000 has a value. The value of a relational expression is either true or false. For example, if amount is 500, then the value of amount < 1000 is true. Try it out: The program fragment

```
double amount = 0;
System.out.println(amount < 1000);
```

> The boolean type has two values: true and false.

prints true. The values true and false are not numbers, nor are they objects of a class. They belong to a separate type, called boolean. The Boolean type is named after the mathematician George Boole (1815–1864), a pioneer in the study of logic.

6.4.2 Predicate Methods

A *predicate method* is a method that returns a boolean value. Here is an example of a predicate method:

> A predicate method returns a boolean value.

```
public class BankAccount
{
    public boolean isOverdrawn()
    {
        return balance < 0;
    }
}
```

You can use the return value of the method as the condition of an if statement:

```
if (harrysChecking.isOverdrawn()) . . .
```

There are several useful static predicate methods in the Character class:

```
isDigit
isLetter
isUpperCase
isLowerCase
```

that let you test whether a character is a digit, a letter, an uppercase letter, or a lower-case letter:

```
if (Character.isUpperCase(ch)) . . .
```

It is a common convention to give the prefix "is" or "has" to the name of a predicate method.

The Scanner class has useful predicate methods for testing whether the next input will succeed. The hasNextInt method returns true if the next character sequence denotes an integer. It is a good idea to call that method before calling nextInt:

```
if (in.hasNext()) n = in.nextInt();
```

Similarly, the hasNextDouble method tests whether a call to nextDouble will succeed.

6.4.3 The Boolean Operators

Suppose you want to find whether amount is between 0 and 1000. Then two conditions have to be true: amount must be greater than 0, *and* it must be less than 1000. In Java you use the && operator to represent the *and* to combine test conditions. That is, you can write the test as follows:

> You can form complex tests with the Boolean operators && (and), || (or), and ! (not).

```
if (0 < amount && amount < 1000) . . .
```

The && operator combines several tests into a new test that passes only when all conditions are true. An operator that combines test conditions is called a *logical operator*.

The || (*or*) logical operator also combines two or more conditions. The resulting test succeeds if at least one of the conditions is true. For example, here is a test to check whether the string input is an "S" or "M":

```
if (input.equals("S") || input.equals("M")) . . .
```

Figure 6 shows flowcharts for these examples.

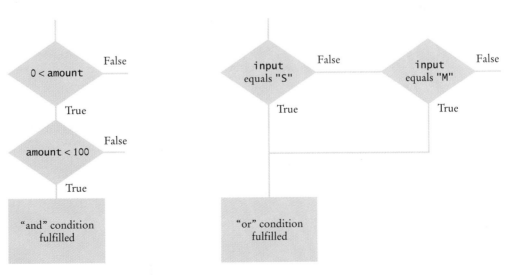

Figure 6 Flowcharts for && and || Combinations

Sometimes you need to *invert* a condition with the ! (*not*) logical operator. For example, we may want to carry out a certain action only if two strings are *not* equal:

```
if (!input.equals("S")) . . .
```

The ! operator takes a single condition and evaluates to true if that condition is false and to false if the condition is true.

Here is a summary of the three logical operations:

A	B	A && B
true	true	true
true	false	false
false	*Any*	false

A	B	A || B
true	*Any*	true
false	true	true
false	false	false

A	!A
true	false
false	true

COMMON ERROR 6.3

Multiple Relational Operators

Consider the expression

```
if (0 < amount < 1000) . . . // Error
```

This looks just like the mathematical notation for "amount is between 0 and 1000". But in Java, it is a syntax error.

Let us dissect the condition. The first half, 0 < amount, is a test with outcome true or false. The outcome of that test (true or false) is then compared against 1000. This seems to make no sense. Is true larger than 1000 or not? Can one compare truth values and numbers? In Java, you cannot. The Java compiler rejects this statement.

Instead, use && to combine two separate tests:

```
if (0 < amount && amount < 1000) . . .
```

Another common error, along the same lines, is to write

```
if (ch == 'S' || 'M') . . . // Error
```

to test whether ch is 'S' or 'M'. Again, the Java compiler flags this construct as an error. You cannot apply the || operator to characters. You need to write two Boolean expressions and join them with the || operator:

```
if (ch == 'S' || ch == 'M') . . .
```

COMMON ERROR 6.4

Confusing && and || Conditions

It is a surprisingly common error to confuse *and* and *or* conditions. A value lies between 0 and 100 if it is at least 0 *and* at most 100. It lies outside that range if it is less than 0 *or* greater than 100. There is no golden rule; you just have to think carefully.

Often the *and* or *or* is clearly stated, and then it isn't too hard to implement it. Sometimes, though, the wording isn't as explicit. It is quite common that the individual conditions are nicely set apart in a bulleted list, but with little indication of how they should be combined. The instructions for the 1992 tax return say that you can claim single filing status if any one of the following is true:

• You were never married.

• You were legally separated or divorced on December 31, 1992.

• You were widowed before January 1, 1992, and did not remarry in 1992.

Because the test passes if *any one* of the conditions is true, you must combine the conditions with *or*. Elsewhere, the same instructions state that you may use the more advantageous status of married filing jointly if all five of the following conditions are true:

• Your spouse died in 1990 or 1991 and you did not remarry in 1992.

• You have a child whom you can claim as dependent.

• That child lived in your home for all of 1992.

• You paid over half the cost of keeping up your home for this child.

• You filed (or could have filed) a joint return with your spouse the year he or she died.

Because *all* of the conditions must be true for the test to pass, you must combine them with an *and*.

ADVANCED TOPIC 6.4

Lazy Evaluation of Boolean Operators

The && and || operators in Java are computed using *lazy* (or *short circuit*) evaluation. In other words, logical expressions are evaluated from left to right, and evaluation stops as soon as the truth value is determined. When an *and* is evaluated and the first condition is false, then the second condition is skipped—no matter what it is, the combined condition must be false. When an *or* is evaluated and the first condition is true, the second condition is not evaluated, because it does not matter what the outcome of the second test is. Here is an example:

```
if (input != null && Integer.parseInt(input) > 0) . . .
```

If input is null, then the first condition is false, and thus the combined statement is false, no matter what the outcome of the second test. The second test is never evaluated if input is null, and there is no danger of parsing a null string (which would cause an exception).

If you do need to evaluate both conditions, then use the & and | operators (see Appendix F). When used with Boolean arguments, these operators always evaluate both arguments.

ADVANCED TOPIC 6.5

De Morgan's Law

> De Morgan's law shows how to simplify expressions in which the not operator (!) is applied to terms joined by the && or || operators.

In the preceding section, we programmed a test to see whether amount was between 0 and 1000. Let's find out whether the opposite is true:

```
if (!(0 < amount && amount < 1000)) . . .
```

This test is a little bit complicated, and you have to think carefully through the logic. "When it is *not* true that 0 < amount and amount < 1000 . . . " Huh? It is not true that some people won't be confused by this code.

The computer doesn't care, but humans generally have a hard time comprehending logical conditions with *not* operators applied to *and/or* expressions. De Morgan's law, named after the logician Augustus de Morgan (1806–1871), can be used to simplify these Boolean expressions. De Morgan's law has two forms: one for the negation of an *and* expression and one for the negation of an *or* expression:

!(A && B) is the same as !A || !B

!(A || B) is the same as !A && !B

Pay particular attention to the fact that the *and* and *or* operators are *reversed* by moving the *not* inwards. For example, the negation of "the input is S or the input is M",

```
!(input.equals("S") || input.equals("M"))
```

is "the input is not S *and* the input is not M"

```
!input.equals("S") && !input.equals("M")
```

Let us apply the law to the negation of "the amount is between 0 and 1000":

```
!(0 < amount && amount < 1000)
```

is equivalent to

```
!(0 < amount) || !(amount < 1000)
```

which can be further simplified to

```
0 >= amount || amount >= 1000
```

Note that the opposite of < is >=, not >!

6.4.4 Using Boolean Variables

You can use a Boolean variable if you know that there are only two possible values. Have another look at the tax program in Section 6.3.2. The marital status is either single or married. Instead of using an integer, you can use a variable of type boolean:

> You can store the outcome of a condition in a Boolean variable.

```
private boolean married;
```

The advantage is that you can't accidentally store a third value in the variable.

Then you can use the Boolean variable in a test:

```
if (married)
    . . .
else
    . . .
```

Sometimes Boolean variables are called *flags* because they can have only two states: "up" and "down".

It pays to think carefully about the naming of Boolean variables. In our example, it would not be a good idea to give the name maritalStatus to the Boolean variable. What does it mean that the marital status is true? With a name like married there is no ambiguity; if married is true, the taxpayer is married.

By the way, it is considered gauche to write a test such as

```
if (married == true) . . . // Don't
```

Just use the simpler test

```
if (married) . . .
```

In Chapter 7 we will use Boolean variables to control complex loops.

SELF CHECK

7. When does the statement
   ```
   System.out.println(x > 0 || x < 0);
   ```
   print false?

8. Rewrite the following expression, avoiding the comparison with false:
   ```
   if (Character.isDigit(ch) == false) . . .
   ```

RANDOM FACT 6.1

Artificial Intelligence

When one uses a sophisticated computer program, such as a tax preparation package, one is bound to attribute some intelligence to the computer. The computer asks sensible questions and makes computations that we find a mental challenge. After all, if doing our taxes were easy, we wouldn't need a computer to do it for us.

As programmers, however, we know that all this apparent intelligence is an illusion. Human programmers have carefully "coached" the software in all possible scenarios, and it simply replays the actions and decisions that were programmed into it.

Would it be possible to write computer programs that are genuinely intelligent in some sense? From the earliest days of computing, there was a sense that the human brain might be nothing but an immense computer, and that it might well be feasible to program computers to imitate some processes of human thought. Serious research into *artificial intelligence* (AI) began in the mid-1950s, and the first twenty years brought some impressive successes. Programs that play chess—surely an activity that appears to require remarkable intellectual powers—have become so good that they now routinely beat all but the best human players. In 1975 an *expert-system* program called Mycin gained fame for being better in diagnosing meningitis in patients than the average physician. *Theorem-proving* programs produced logically correct mathematical proofs. *Optical character recognition* software can read pages from a scanner, recognize the character shapes (including those that are blurred or smudged), and reconstruct the original document text, even restoring fonts and layout.

However, there were serious setbacks as well. From the very outset, one of the stated goals of the AI community was to produce software that could translate text from one language to another, for example from English to Russian. That undertaking proved to be enormously complicated. Human language appears to be much more subtle and interwoven with the human experience than had originally been thought. Even the grammar-checking programs that come with many word processors today are more a gimmick than a useful tool, and analyzing grammar is just the first step in translating sentences.

From 1982 to 1992, the Japanese government embarked on a massive research project, funded at over 50 billion Japanese yen. It was known as the *Fifth-Generation Project.* Its goal was to develop new hard- and software to greatly improve the performance of expert systems. At its outset, the project created great fear in other countries that the Japanese computer industry was about to become the undisputed leader in the field. However, the end results were disappointing and did little to bring artificial intelligence applications to market.

One reason that artificial intelligence programs have not performed as well as it was hoped seems to be that they simply don't know as much as humans do. In the early 1990s, Douglas Lenat and his colleagues decided to do something about it and initiated the CYC project (from enCYClopedia), an effort to codify the implicit assumptions that underlie human speech and writing. The team members started out analyzing news articles and asked themselves what unmentioned facts are necessary to actually understand the sentences. For example, consider the sentence "Last fall she enrolled in Michigan State." The reader automatically realizes that "fall" is not related to falling down in this context, but refers to the season. While there is a State of Michigan, here Michigan State denotes the university. A priori, a computer program has none of this knowledge. The goal of the CYC project was to extract and store the requisite facts—that is, (1) people enroll in universities; (2) Michigan is a state; (3) a state X is likely to have a university named X State University, often abbreviated as X State; (4) most people enroll in a university in the fall. In 1995, the project had codified about 100,000 common-sense concepts and about a million facts relating them. Even this massive amount of data has not proven sufficient for useful applications.

Successful artificial intelligence programs, such as chess-playing programs, do not actually imitate human thinking. They are just very fast in exploring many scenarios and have been tuned to recognize those cases that do not warrant further investigation. *Neural networks* are interesting exceptions: coarse simulations of the neuron cells in animal and human brains. Suitably interconnected cells appear to be able to "learn". For example, if a network of cells is presented with letter shapes, it can be trained to identify them. After a lengthy training period, the network can recognize letters, even if they are slanted, distorted, or smudged.

When artificial intelligence programs are successful, they can raise serious ethical issues. There are now programs that can scan résumés, select those that look promising, and show only those to a human for further analysis. How would you feel if you knew that your résumé had been rejected by a computer, perhaps on a technicality, and that you never had a chance to be interviewed? When computers are used for credit analysis, and the analysis software has been designed to deny credit systematically to certain groups of people (say, all applicants with certain ZIP codes), is that illegal discrimination? What if the software has not been designed in this fashion, but a neural network has "discovered" a pattern from historical data? These are troubling questions, especially because those that are harmed by such processes have little recourse.

CHAPTER SUMMARY

1. The `if` statement lets a program carry out different actions depending on a condition.

2. A block statement groups several statements together.

3. Relational operators compare values. The `==` operator tests for equality.

4. When comparing floating-point numbers, don't test for equality. Instead, check whether they are close enough.

5. Do not use the `==` operator to compare strings. Use the `equals` method instead.

6. The `compareTo` method compares strings in dictionary order.

7. The `==` operator tests whether two object references are identical. To compare the contents of objects, you need to use the `equals` method.

8. The `null` reference refers to no object.

9. Multiple conditions can be combined to evaluate complex decisions. The correct arrangement depends on the logic of the problem to be solved.

10. The `boolean` type has two values: `true` and `false`.

11. A predicate method returns a `boolean` value.

12. You can form complex tests with the Boolean operators `&&` (and), `||` (or), and `!` (not).

13. De Morgan's law shows how to simplify expressions in which the not operator (`!`) is applied to terms joined by the `&&` or `||` operators.

14. You can store the outcome of a condition in a Boolean variable.

FURTHER READING

1. Peter van der Linden, *Expert C Programming*, Prentice-Hall, 1994.

2. http://www.irs.ustreas.gov   The web site of the Internal Revenue Service.

CLASSES, OBJECTS, AND METHODS INTRODUCED IN THIS CHAPTER

```
java.lang.Character
   isDigit
   isLetter
   isUpperCase
   isLowerCase
java.lang.Object
   equals
java.lang.String
   equalsIgnoreCase
   compareTo
java.util.Scanner
   hasNextDouble
   hasNextInt
```

REVIEW EXERCISES

Exercise R6.1. Find the errors in the following `if` statements.

a. `if quarters > 0 then System.out.println(quarters + " quarters");`

b. `if (1 + x > Math.pow(x, Math.sqrt(2)) y = y + x;`

c. `if (x = 1) y++; else if (x = 2) y = y + 2;`

d. `if (x && y == 0) { x = 1; y = 1; }`

e. `if (1 <= x <= 10)`
`    System.out.println(x);`

f. `if (!s.equals("nickels") || !s.equals("pennies")`
`        || !s.equals("dimes") || !s.equals("quarters"))`
`    System.out.print("Input error!");`

g. `if (input.equalsIgnoreCase("N") || "NO")`
`    return;`

h. `int x = Integer.parseInt(input);`
`  if (x != null) y = y + x;`

i. `language = "English";`
`  if (country.equals("US"))`
`     if (state.equals("PR")) language = "Spanish";`
`  else if (country.equals("China"))`
`     language = "Chinese";`

Exercise R6.2. Explain the following terms, and give an example for each construct:

a. Expression

b. Condition

c. Statement

   d. Simple statement

   e. Compound statement

   f. Block

Exercise R6.3. Explain the difference between an `if/else/else` statement and nested `if` statements. Give an example for each.

Exercise R6.4. Give an example for an `if/else/else` statement where the order of the tests does not matter. Give an example where the order of the tests matters.

Exercise R6.5. Of the following pairs of strings, which comes first in lexicographic order?

   a. `"Tom"`, `"Dick"`

   b. `"Tom"`, `"Tomato"`

   c. `"church"`, `"Churchill"`

   d. `"car manufacturer"`, `"carburetor"`

   e. `"Harry"`, `"hairy"`

   f. `"C++"`, `" Car"`

   g. `"Tom"`, `"Tom"`

   h. `"Car"`, `"Carl"`

   i. `"car"`, `"bar"`

   j. `"101"`, `"11"`

   k. `"1.01"`, `"10.1"`

Exercise R6.6. Complete the following truth table by finding the truth values of the Boolean expressions for all combinations of the Boolean inputs p, q, and r.

p	q	r	(p && q) || !r	!(p && (q || !r))
false	false	false		
false	false	true		
false	true	false		
. . .				
5 more combinations				
. . .				

Exercise R6.7. Before you implement any complex algorithm, it is a good idea to understand and analyze it. The purpose of this exercise is to gain a better understanding of the tax computation algorithm of Section 6.3.2.

One feature of the tax code is the *marriage penalty.* Under certain circumstances, a married couple pays higher taxes than the sum of what the two partners would pay if they both were single. Find examples for such income levels.

Exercise R6.8. True or false? *A* && *B* is the same as *B* && *A* for any Boolean conditions *A* and *B*.

Exercise R6.9. Explain the difference between

```
s = 0;
if (x > 0) s++;
if (y > 0) s++;
```

and

```
s = 0;
if (x > 0) s++;
else if (y > 0) s++;
```

Exercise R6.10. Use de Morgan's law to simplify the following Boolean expressions.

   a. !(x > 0 && y > 0)

   b. !(x != 0 || y != 0)

   c. !(country.equals("US") && !state.equals("HI")
            && !state.equals("AK"))

   d. !(x % 4 != 0 || !(x % 100 == 0 && x % 400 == 0))

Exercise R6.11. Make up another Java code example that shows the dangling else problem, using the following statement: A student with a GPA of at least 1.5, but less than 2, is on probation; with less than 1.5, the student is failing.

Exercise R6.12. Explain the difference between the == operator and the equals method when comparing strings.

Exercise R6.13. Explain the difference between the tests

```
r == s
```

and

```
r.equals(s)
```

where both r and s are of type Rectangle.

Exercise R6.14. What is wrong with this test to see whether r is null? What happens when this code runs?

```
Rectangle r;
. . .
if (r.equals(null))
    r = new Rectangle(5, 10, 20, 30);
```

Exercise R6.15. Explain how the lexicographic ordering of strings differs from the ordering of words in a dictionary or telephone book. *Hint:* Consider strings, such as IBM, wiley.com, Century 21, While-U-Wait, and 7-11.

Exercise R6.16. Write Java code to test whether two objects of type Line2D.Double represent the same line when displayed on the graphics screen. *Do not* use a.equals(b).

```
Line2D.Double a;
Line2D.Double b;

if (your condition goes here)
   g2.drawString("They look the same!", x, y);
```

Hint: If p and q are points, then Line2D.Double(p, q) and Line2D.Double(q, p) look the same.

Exercise R6.17. Explain why it is more difficult to compare floating-point numbers than integers. Write Java code to test whether an integer n equals 10 and whether a floating-point number x equals 10.

Exercise R6.18. Consider the following test to see whether a point falls inside a rectangle.

```
Point2D.Double p = . . .
Rectangle r = . . .
boolean xInside = false;
if (r.getX() <= p.getX() && p.getX() <= r.getX() + r.getWidth())
   xInside = true;
boolean yInside = false;
if (r.getY() <= p.getY() && p.getY() <= r.getY() + r.getHeight())
   yInside = true;
if (xInside && yInside)
   g2.drawString("p is inside the rectangle.",
         p.getX(), p.getY());
```

Rewrite this code to eliminate the explicit true and false values, by setting xInside and yInside to the values of Boolean expressions.

Exercise R6.19. Give a set of test cases for the tax program in Section 6.3.2. Compute the expected results manually.

PROGRAMMING EXERCISES

Exercise P6.1. Write a program that prints all real solutions to the quadratic equation $ax^2 + bx + c = 0$. Read in a, b, c and use the quadratic formula. If the *discriminant* $b^2 - 4ac$ is negative, display a message stating that there are no real solutions.

Implement a class QuadraticEquation whose constructor receives the coefficients a, b, c of the quadratic equation. Supply methods getSolution1 and getSolution2 that get the solutions, using the quadratic formula.

Supply a method

```
boolean hasSolutions()
```

that returns false if the discriminant is negative.

Exercise P6.2. Write a program that takes user input describing a playing card in the following shorthand notation:

Notation	Meaning
A	Ace
2 . . . 10	Card values
J	Jack
Q	Queen
K	King
D	Diamonds
H	Hearts
S	Spades
C	Clubs

Your program should print the full description of the card. For example,

```
Enter the card notation:
QS
Queen of spades
```

Implement a class `Card` whose constructor takes the card letters and whose `get-Description` method returns a description of the card.

Exercise P6.3. As in the `IntersectionViewer` program of Chapter 5, compute and plot the intersection of a line and a circle. However, if the line and the circle do not intersect, do not plot the intersection points but display a message instead.

Exercise P6.4. Write a program that reads in three floating-point numbers and prints the three inputs in sorted order. For example:

```
Please enter three numbers:
4
9
2.5
The inputs in sorted order are
2.5
4
9
```

Exercise P6.5. Write a program that draws a circle with radius 100 and center (110, 120). Ask the user to specify the x- and y-coordinates of a point. If the point lies inside the circle, then show a message "Congratulations". Otherwise, show a message "You missed". In your exercise, define a class `Circle` and a method `boolean isInside(Point2D.Double p)`.

Exercise P6.6. Write a graphics program that asks the user to specify the radii of two circles. The first circle has center (100, 200), and the second circle has center (200, 100). Draw the circles. If they intersect, then display a message "Circles intersect". Otherwise, display "Circles don't intersect". *Hint:* Compute the distance between the centers and compare it to the radii. Your program should draw nothing if the user enters a negative radius. In your exercise, define a class Circle and a method boolean intersects(Circle other).

Exercise P6.7. Write a program that prints the question "Do you want to continue?" and reads a user input. If the user input is "Y", "Yes", "OK", "Sure", or "Why not?", print out "OK". If the user input is "N" or "No", then print out "Terminating". Otherwise, print "Bad input". The case of the user input should not matter. For example, "y" or "yes" are also valid inputs. Write a class InputChecker for this purpose.

Exercise P6.8. Write a program that translates a letter grade into a number grade. Letter grades are A B C D F, possibly followed by + or -. Their numeric values are 4, 3, 2, 1, and 0. There is no F+ or F-. A + increases the numeric value by 0.3, a - decreases it by 0.3. However, an A+ has the value 4.0.

```
Enter a letter grade:
B-
The numeric value is 2.7.
```

Use a class Grade with a method getNumericGrade.

Exercise P6.9. Write a program that translates a number between 0 and 4 into the closest letter grade. For example, the number 2.8 (which might have been the average of several grades) would be converted to B-. Break ties in favor of the better grade; for example, 2.85 should be a B.

Use a class Grade with a method getLetterGrade.

Exercise P6.10. Write a program that reads in four strings and prints the lexicographically smallest and largest one:

```
Enter four strings:
Charlie
Able
Delta
Baker
The lexicographic minimum is Able
The lexicographic maximum is Delta
```

Hint: Use a class that keeps track of the current maximum and minimum.

Exercise P6.11. Change the implementation of the getTax method in the TaxReturn class, by setting variables bracket1 and bracket2, depending on the marital status. Then have a single formula that computes the tax, depending on the income and the brackets. Verify that your results are identical to that of the TaxReturn class in this chapter.

Exercise P6.12. A year with 366 days is called a *leap year*. A year is a leap year if it is divisible by 4 (for example, 1980). However, since the introduction of the Gregorian calendar on October 15, 1582, a year is not a leap year if it is divisible by 100 (for example, 1900); however, it is a leap year if it is divisible by 400 (for example, 2000). Write a program that asks the user for a year and computes whether that year is a leap year. Implement a class Year with a predicate method boolean isLeapYear().

Exercise P6.13. Write a program that asks the user to enter a month (1 = January, 2 = February, and so on) and then prints the number of days of the month. For February, print "28 days".

```
Enter a month:
5
31 days
```

Implement a class Month with a method int getDays().

Exercise P6.14. Write a program that reads in two floating-point numbers and tests whether they are the same when rounded to two decimal places. Here are two sample runs.

```
Enter two floating-point numbers:
2.0
1.99998
They are the same when rounded to two decimal places.

Enter two floating-point numbers:
2.0
1.98999
They are different.
```

Exercise P6.15. Enhance the BankAccount class of Chapter 3 by

- Rejecting negative amounts in the deposit and withdraw methods
- Rejecting withdrawals that would result in a negative balance

Exercise P6.16. Write a program that reads in the name and hourly wage of an employee. Then ask how many hours the employee worked in the past week. Be sure to accept fractional hours. Compute the pay. Any overtime work (over 40 hours per week) is paid at 150 percent of the regular wage. Solve this problem by implementing a class Paycheck.

Exercise P6.17. Write a unit conversion program that asks users to identify the unit from which they want to convert and the unit to which they want to convert. Legal units are *in, ft, mi, mm, cm, m,* and *km. Hint:* Define objects of a class UnitConverter that convert to and from meters.

```
Convert from?
in
Convert to?
mm
Value?
10
10 in = 254 mm
```

Exercise P6.18. A line in the plane can be specified in various ways:

- by giving a point (x, y) and a slope m
- by giving two points (x_1, y_1), (x_2, y_2)
- as an equation in slope-intercept form $y = mx + b$
- as an equation $x = a$ if the line is vertical

Implement a class Line with four constructors, corresponding to the four cases above. Implement methods

```
boolean intersects(Line other)
boolean equals(Line other)
boolean isParallel(Line other)
```

PROGRAMMING PROJECTS

Project 6.1. Implement a *combination lock* class. A combination lock has a dial with 26 positions labeled A . . . Z. The dial needs to be set three times. If it is set to the correct combination, the lock can be opened. When the lock is closed again, the combination can be entered again. If a user sets the dial more than three times, the last three settings determine whether the lock can be opened. An important part of this exercise is to implement a suitable interface for the CombinationLock class.

Project 6.2. Get the instructions for last year's form 1040 from http://www.irs.ustreas.gov [2]. Find the tax brackets that were used last year for all categories of taxpayers (single, married filing jointly, married filing separately, and head of household). Write a program that computes taxes following that schedule. Ignore deductions, exemptions, and credits. Simply apply the tax rate to the income.

ANSWERS TO SELF-CHECK QUESTIONS

1. If the withdrawal amount equals the balance, the result should be a zero balance and no penalty.

2. Only the first assignment statement is part of the `if` statement. Use braces to group both assignment statements into a block statement.

3. (a) 0; (b) 1; (c) an exception is thrown

4. Syntactically incorrect: e, g, h. Logically questionable: a, d, f

5. Yes, if you also reverse the comparisons:

```
if (richter < 3.5)
   r = "Generally not felt by people";
else if (richter < 4.5)
   r = "Felt by many people, no destruction";
else if (richter < 6.0)
   r = "Damage to poorly constructed buildings";
. . .
```

6. The higher tax rate is only applied on the income in the higher bracket. Suppose you are single and make $51,800. Should you try to get a $200 raise? Absolutely—you get to keep 72% of the first $100 and 69% of the next $100.

7. When x is zero.

8. `if (!Character.isDigit(ch))` . . .

Iteration

CHAPTER GOALS

- To be able to program loops with the while, for, and do statements

- To avoid infinite loops and off-by-one errors

- To understand nested loops

- To learn how to process input

- To implement simulations

This chapter presents the various iteration constructs of the Java language. These constructs execute one or more statements repeatedly until a goal is reached. You will see how the techniques that you learn in this chapter can be applied to the processing of input data and the programming of simulations.

CHAPTER CONTENTS

7.1 while Loops

In this chapter you will learn how to write programs that repeatedly execute one or more statements. We will illustrate these concepts by looking at typical investment situations. Consider a bank account with an initial balance of $10,000 that earns 5% interest. The interest is computed at the end of every year on the current balance and then deposited into the bank account. For example, after the first year, the account has earned $500 (5% of $10,000) of interest. The interest gets added to the bank account. Next year, the interest is $525 (5% of $10,500), and the balance is $11,025. Table 1 shows how the balance grows in the first five years.

How many years does it take for the balance to reach $20,000? Of course, it won't take longer than 20 years, because at least $500 is added to the bank account each year. But it will take less than 20 years, because interest is computed on increasingly larger balances. To know the exact answer, we will write a program that repeatedly adds interest until the balance is reached.

> A while statement executes a block of code repeatedly. A condition controls how often the loop is executed.

In Java, the while statement implements such a repetition. The construct

```
while (condition)
    statement
```

keeps executing the statement while the condition is true. Most commonly, the statement is a block statement, that is, a set of statements delimited by { }.

Table 1 Growth of an Investment	
Year	**Balance**
0	$10,000.00
1	$10,500.00
2	$11,025.00
3	$11,576.25
4	$12,155.06
5	$12,762.82

In our case, we want to know when the bank account has reached a particular balance. While the balance is less, we keep adding interest and incrementing the year counter:

```
while (balance < targetBalance)
{
   years++;
   double interest = balance * rate / 100;
   balance = balance + interest;
}
```

Here is the program that solves our investment problem:

File Investment.java

```
1  /**
2     A class to monitor the growth of an investment that
3     accumulates interest at a fixed annual rate.
4  */
5  public class Investment
6  {
7     /**
8        Constructs an Investment object from a starting balance and
9        interest rate.
10       @param aBalance the starting balance
11       @param aRate the interest rate in percent
12    */
13    public Investment(double aBalance, double aRate)
14    {
15       balance = aBalance;
16       rate = aRate;
17       years = 0;
18    }
19
```

```
20    /**
21        Keeps accumulating interest until a target balance has
22        been reached.
23        @param targetBalance the desired balance
24    */
25    public void waitForBalance(double targetBalance)
26    {
27       while (balance < targetBalance)
28       {
29          years++;
30          double interest = balance * rate / 100;
31          balance = balance + interest;
32       }
33    }
34
35    /**
36        Gets the current investment balance.
37        @return the current balance
38    */
39    public double getBalance()
40    {
41       return balance;
42    }
43
44    /**
45        Gets the number of years this investment has accumulated
46        interest.
47        @return the number of years since the start of the investment
48    */
49    public int getYears()
50    {
51       return years;
52    }
53
54    private double balance;
55    private double rate;
56    private int years;
57 }
```

File InvestmentTester.java

```
1  /**
2      This program computes how long it takes for an investment
3      to double.
4  */
5  public class InvestmentTester
6  {
7     public static void main(String[] args)
8     {
9        final double INITIAL_BALANCE = 10000;
10       final double RATE = 5;
11       Investment invest = new Investment(INITIAL_BALANCE, RATE);
12       invest.waitForBalance(2 * INITIAL_BALANCE);
13       int years = invest.getYears();
```

```
14          System.out.println("The investment doubled after "
15              + years + " years");
16     }
17 }
```

Output

```
The investment doubled after 15 years
```

A while statement is often called a *loop*. If you draw a flowchart, you will see that the control loops backwards to the test after every iteration (see Figure 1).

The following loop,

```
while (true)
    statement
```

executes the statement over and over, without terminating. Whoa! Why would you want that? The program would never stop. There are two reasons. Some programs indeed never stop; the software controlling an automated teller machine, a telephone switch, or a microwave oven doesn't ever stop (at least not until the device is turned off). Our programs aren't usually of that kind, but even if you can't terminate the loop, you can exit from the method that contains it. This can be helpful when the termination test naturally falls in the middle of the loop (see Advanced Topic 7.3).

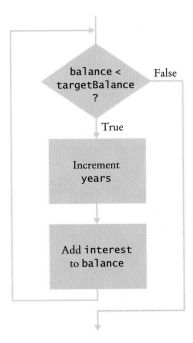

Figure 1 Flowchart of a while Loop

SYNTAX 7.1 The while Statement

```
while (condition)
   statement
```

Example:

```
while (balance < targetBalance)
{
   years++;
   double interest = balance * rate / 100;
   balance = balance + interest;
}
```

Purpose:

To repeatedly execute a statement as long as a condition is true

SELF CHECK

1. How often is the statement in the loop

   ```
   while (false) statement;
   ```

   executed?

2. What would happen if RATE was set to 0 in the main method of the Investment-Tester program?

COMMON ERROR 7.1

Infinite Loops

The most annoying loop error is an infinite loop: a loop that runs forever and can be stopped only by killing the program or restarting the computer. If there are output statements in the loop, then reams and reams of output flash by on the screen. Otherwise, the program just sits there and hangs, seeming to do nothing. On some systems you can kill a hanging program by hitting Ctrl+Break or Ctrl+C. On others, you can close the window in which the program runs.

A common reason for infinite loops is forgetting to advance the variable that controls the loop:

```
int years = 0;
while (years < 20)
{
   double interest = balance * rate / 100;
   balance = balance + interest;
}
```

Here the programmer forgot to add a statement for incrementing years in the loop. As a result, the value of years always stays 0, and the loop never comes to an end.

Another common reason for an infinite loop is accidentally incrementing a counter that should be decremented (or vice versa). Consider this example:

```
int years = 20;
while (years > 0)
{
    years++; // Oops, should have been years--
    double interest = balance * rate / 100;
    balance = balance + interest;
}
```

The years variable really should have been decremented, not incremented. This is a common error, because incrementing counters is so much more common than decrementing that your fingers may type the ++ on autopilot. As a consequence, years is always larger than 0, and the loop never terminates. (Actually, years eventually will exceed the largest representable positive integer and wrap around to a negative number. Then the loop exits—of course, that takes a long time, and the result is completely wrong.)

COMMON ERROR 7.2

Off-by-One Errors

Consider our computation of the number of years that are required to double an investment:

```
int years = 0;
while (balance < 2 * initialBalance)
{
    years++;
    double interest = balance * rate / 100;
    balance = balance + interest;
}
System.out.println(
        "The investment reached the target after "
        + years + " years.");
```

Should years start at 0 or at 1? Should you test for balance < 2 * initialBalance or for balance <= 2 * initialBalance? It is easy to be *off by one* in these expressions.

Some people try to solve off-by-one errors by randomly inserting +1 or -1 until the program seems to work. That is, of course, a terrible strategy. It can take a long time to compile and test all the various possibilities. Expending a small amount of mental effort is a real time saver.

> An off-by-one error is a common error when programming loops. Think through simple test cases to avoid this type of error.

Fortunately, off-by-one errors are easy to avoid, simply by thinking through a couple of test cases and using the information from the test cases to come up with a rationale for the correct loop condition.

Should years start at 0 or at 1? Look at a scenario with simple values: an initial balance of $100 and an interest rate of 50%. After year 1, the balance is $150, and after year 2 it is $225, or over $200. So the investment doubled after 2 years. The loop executed two times, incrementing years each time. Hence years must start at 0, not at 1.

In other words, the balance variable denotes the balance *after* the end of the year. At the outset, the balance variable contains the balance after year 0 and not after year 1.

Next, should you use a < or <= comparison in the test? That is harder to figure out, because it is rare for the balance to be exactly twice the initial balance. Of course, there is one case when this happens, namely when the interest is 100%. The loop executes once. Now years is 1, and balance is exactly equal to 2 * initialBalance. Has the investment doubled after one year? It has. Therefore, the loop should *not* execute again. If the test condition is balance < 2 * initialBalance, the loop stops, as it should. If the test condition had been balance <= 2 * initialBalance, the loop would have executed once more.

In other words, you keep adding interest while the balance *has not yet doubled.*

ADVANCED TOPIC 7.1

do Loops

Sometimes you want to execute the body of a loop at least once and perform the loop test after the body was executed. The do loop serves that purpose:

```
do
    statement
while (condition);
```

The *statement* is executed while the *condition* is true. The condition is tested after the statement is executed, so the statement is executed at least once.

For example, suppose you want to make sure that a user enters a positive number. As long as the user enters a negative number or zero, just keep prompting for a correct input. In this situation, a do loop makes sense, because you need to get a user input before you can test it.

```
double value;
do
{
    System.out.print("Please enter a positive number: ");
    value = in.nextDouble();
}
while (value <= 0);
```

Figure 2 is a flowchart of this loop.

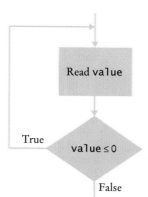

Figure 2
Flowchart of a do Loop

In practice, this situation is not very common. You can always replace a do loop with a while loop, by introducing a boolean control variable.

```java
boolean done = false;
while (!done)
{
   System.out.print("Please enter a positive number: ");
   value = in.nextDouble();
   if (value > 0) done = true;
}
```

RANDOM FACT 7.1

Spaghetti Code

In this chapter we are using flowcharts to illustrate the behavior of the loop statements. It used to be common to draw flowcharts for every method, on the theory that flowcharts were easier to read and write than the actual code (especially in the days of machine-language and assembler programming). Flowcharts are no longer routinely used for program development and documentation.

Flowcharts have one fatal flaw. Although it is possible to express the while and do loops with flowcharts, it is also possible to draw flowcharts that cannot be programmed with loops. Consider the chart in Figure 3. The top of the flowchart is simply a statement

```java
years = 1;
```

The lower part is a do loop:

```java
do
{
   years++;
   double interest = balance * rate / 100;
   balance = balance + interest;
}
while (balance < targetBalance);
```

But how can you join these two parts? According to the flowchart, you are supposed to jump from the first statement into the middle of the loop, skipping the first statement.

```java
years = 1;
goto a; // Not an actual Java statement
do
{
   years++;
   a:
   double interest = balance * rate / 100;
   balance = balance + interest;
}
while (balance < targetBalance);
```

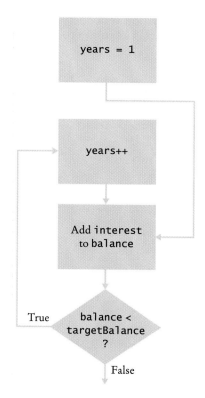

Figure 3   Spaghetti Code

In fact, why even bother with the do loop? Here is a faithful interpretation of the flowchart:

```
years = 1;
goto a; // Not an actual Java statement
b:
years++;
a:
double interest = balance * rate / 100;
balance = balance + interest;
if (balance < targetBalance) goto b;
```

This nonlinear control flow turns out to be extremely hard to read and understand if you have more than one or two goto statements. Because the lines denoting the goto statements weave back and forth in complex flowcharts, the resulting code is named *spaghetti code*.

In 1968 the influential computer scientist Edsger Dijkstra wrote a famous note, entitled "Goto Statements Considered Harmful" [1], in which he argued for the use of loops instead of unstructured jumps. Initially, many programmers who had been using goto for years were mortally insulted and promptly dug out examples in which the use of goto led to clearer or faster code. Some languages offer weaker forms of goto that are less harmful, such as the break statement in Java, discussed in Advanced Topic 7.4. Nowadays, most computer scientists accept Dijkstra's argument and fight bigger battles than optimal loop design.

7.2 for Loops

One of the most common loop types has the form

```
i = start;
while (i <= end)
{
   . . .
   i++;
}
```

Because this loop is so common, there is a special form for it that emphasizes the pattern:

```
for (i = start; i <= end; i++)
{
   . . .
}
```

You can also declare the loop counter variable inside the for loop header. That convenient shorthand restricts the use of the variable to the body of the loop (as will be discussed further in Advanced Topic 7.2).

```
for (int i = start; i <= end; i++)
{
   . . .
}
```

Let us use this loop to find out the size of our $10,000 investment if 5% interest is compounded for 20 years. Of course, the balance will be larger than $20,000, because at least $500 is added every year. You may be surprised to find out just how much larger the balance is.

SYNTAX 7.2 The for Statement

```
for (initialization; condition; update)
    statement
```

Example:

```
for (i = 1; i <= n; i++)
{
    double interest = balance * rate / 100;
    balance = balance + interest;
}
```

Purpose:

To execute an initialization, then keep executing a statement and updating an expression while a condition is true

In our loop, we let i go from 1 to n, the number of years for which we want to compound interest.

> You use a for loop when a variable runs from a starting to an ending value with a constant increment or decrement.

```
for (int i = 1; i <= n; i++)
{
    double interest = balance * rate / 100;
    balance = balance + interest;
}
```

Figure 4 shows the corresponding flowchart.

The three slots in the for header can contain any three expressions. You can count down instead of up:

```
for (years = n; years > 0; years--)
```

The increment or decrement need not be in steps of 1:

```
for (x = -10; x <= 10; x = x + 0.5) . . .
```

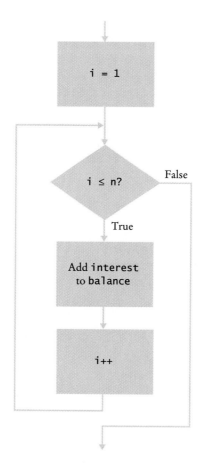

Figure 4   Flowchart of a for Loop

It is possible—but a sign of unbelievably bad taste—to put unrelated conditions into the loop header:

```
for (rate = 5; years-- > 0; System.out.println(balance))
   . . . // Bad taste
```

We won't even begin to decipher what that might mean. You should stick with for loops that initialize, test, and update a single variable.

File Investment.java

```java
 1  /**
 2      A class to monitor the growth of an investment that
 3      accumulates interest at a fixed annual rate.
 4  */
 5  public class Investment
 6  {
 7      /**
 8          Constructs an Investment object from a starting balance and
 9          interest rate.
10          @param aBalance the starting balance
11          @param aRate the interest rate in percent
12      */
13      public Investment(double aBalance, double aRate)
14      {
15          balance = aBalance;
16          rate = aRate;
17          years = 0;
18      }
19
20      /**
21          Keeps accumulating interest until a target balance has
22          been reached.
23          @param targetBalance the desired balance
24      */
25      public void waitForBalance(double targetBalance)
26      {
27          while (balance < targetBalance)
28          {
29              years++;
30              double interest = balance * rate / 100;
31              balance = balance + interest;
32          }
33      }
34
35      /**
36          Keeps accumulating interest for a given number of years.
37          @param n the number of years
38      */
39      public void waitYears(int n)
40      {
41          for (int i = 1; i <= n; i++)
42          {
43              double interest = balance * rate / 100;
44              balance = balance + interest;
```

```
45              }
46              years = years + n;
47          }
48
49      /**
50          Gets the current investment balance.
51          @return  the current balance
52      */
53      public double getBalance()
54      {
55          return balance;
56      }
57
58      /**
59          Gets the number of years this investment has accumulated
60          interest.
61          @return  the number of years since the start of the investment
62      */
63      public int getYears()
64      {
65          return years;
66      }
67
68      private double balance;
69      private double rate;
70      private int years;
71  }
```

File InvestmentTester.java

```
1   /**
2       This program computes how much an investment grows in
3       a given number of years.
4   */
5   public class InvestmentTester
6   {
7       public static void main(String[] args)
8       {
9           final double INITIAL_BALANCE = 10000;
10          final double RATE = 5;
11          final int YEARS = 20;
12          Investment invest = new Investment(INITIAL_BALANCE, RATE);
13          invest.waitYears(YEARS);
14          double balance = invest.getBalance();
15          System.out.printf("The balance after %d years is %.2f\n",
16                  YEARS, balance);
17      }
18  }
```

Output

```
The balance after 20 years is 26532.98
```

SELF CHECK

3. Rewrite the for loop in the waitYears method as a while loop.
4. How many times does the following for loop execute?

```
for (i = 0; i <= 10; i++)
    System.out.println(i * i);
```

QUALITY TIP 7.1

Use for Loops for Their Intended Purpose

A for loop is an *idiom* for a while loop of a particular form. A counter runs from the start to the end, with a constant increment:

```
for (set counter to start; test whether counter at end;
        update counter by increment)
{   . . .
    // counter, start, end, increment not changed here
}
```

If your loop doesn't match this pattern, don't use the for construction. The compiler won't prevent you from writing idiotic for loops:

```
// Bad style—unrelated header expressions
for (System.out.println("Inputs:");
     (x = in.nextDouble()) > 0;
     sum = sum + x)
   count++;

for (int i = 1; i <= years; i++)
{
    // Bad style—modifies counter
    if (balance >= targetBalance)
      i = years + 1;
    else
    {
        double interest = balance * rate / 100;
        balance = balance + interest;
    }
}
```

These loops will work, but they are plainly bad style. Use a while loop for iterations that do not fit the for pattern.

COMMON ERROR 7.3

Forgetting a Semicolon

Occasionally all the work of a loop is already done in the loop header. Suppose you ignored Quality Tip 7.1; then you could write an investment doubling loop as follows:

```
for (years = 1;
      (balance = balance + balance * rate / 100) < targetBalance;
      years++)
   ;
System.out.println(years);
```

The body of the `for` loop is completely empty, containing just one empty statement terminated by a semicolon.

If you do run into a loop without a body, it is important that you make sure the semicolon is not forgotten. If the semicolon is accidentally omitted, then the next line becomes part of the loop statement!

```
for (years = 1;
      (balance = balance + balance * rate / 100) < targetBalance;
      years++)
System.out.println(years);
```

You can avoid this error by using an empty block { } instead of an empty statement.

COMMON ERROR 7.4

A Semicolon Too Many

What does the following loop print?

```
sum = 0;
for (i = 1; i <= 10; i++);
   sum = sum + i;
System.out.println(sum);
```

Of course, this loop is supposed to compute $1 + 2 + \cdots + 10 = 55$. But actually, the print statement prints 11!

Why 11? Have another look. Did you spot the semicolon at the end of the `for` loop header? This loop is actually a loop with an empty body.

```
for (i = 1; i <= 10; i++)
   ;
```

The loop does nothing 10 times, and when it is finished, `sum` is still 0 and `i` is 11. Then the statement

```
sum = sum + i;
```

is executed, and `sum` is 11. The statement was indented, which fools the human reader. But the compiler pays no attention to indentation.

Of course, the semicolon at the end of the statement was a typing error. Someone's fingers were so used to typing a semicolon at the end of every line that a semicolon was added to the `for` loop by accident. The result was a loop with an empty body.

QUALITY TIP 7.2

Don't Use != to Test the End of a Range

Here is a loop with a hidden danger:

```
for (i = 1; i != n; i++)
```

The test i != n is a poor idea. How does the loop behave if n happens to be zero or negative? The test i != n is never false, because i starts at 1 and increases with every step.

The remedy is simple. Use <= rather than != in the condition:

```
for (i = 1; i <= n; i++)
```

ADVANCED TOPIC 7.2

Scope of Variables Defined in a for Loop Header

As mentioned, it is legal in Java to declare a variable in the header of a for loop. Here is the most common form of this syntax:

```
for (int i = 1; i <= n; i++)
{
   . . .
}

// i no longer defined here
```

The scope of the variable extends to the end of the for loop. Therefore, i is no longer defined after the loop ends. If you need to use the value of the variable beyond the end of the loop, then you need to define it outside the loop. In this loop, you don't need the value of i—you know it is n + 1 when the loop is finished. (Actually, that is not quite true—it is possible to break out of a loop before its end; see Advanced Topic 7.4). When you have two or more exit conditions, though, you may still need the variable. For example, consider the loop

```
for (i = 1; balance < targetBalance && i <= n; i++)
{
   . . .
}
```

You want the balance to reach the target, but you are willing to wait only a certain number of years. If the balance doubles sooner, you may want to know the value of i. Therefore, in this case, it is not appropriate to define the variable in the loop header.

Note that the variables named i in the following pair of for loops are independent:

```
for (int i = 1; i <= 10; i++)
   System.out.println(i * i);
for (int i = 1; i <= 10; i++) // Declares a new variable i
   System.out.println(i * i * i);
```

In the loop header, you can declare multiple variables, as long as they are of the same type, and you can include multiple update expressions, separated by commas:

```
for (int i = 0, j = 10; i <= 10; i++, j--)
{
    . . .
}
```

However, many people find it confusing if a for loop controls more than one variable. I recommend that you not use this form of the for statement (see Quality Tip 7.1). Instead, make the for loop control a single counter, and update the other variable explicitly:

```
int j = 10;
for (int i = 0; i <= 10; i++)
{
    . . .
    j--;
}
```

7.3 Nested Loops

Loops can be nested. A typical example of nested loops is printing a table with rows and columns.

Sometimes, the body of a loop is again a loop. We say that the inner loop is *nested* inside an outer loop. This happens often when you process two-dimensional structures, such as tables.

Let's look at an example that looks a bit more interesting than a table of numbers. We want to generate the following triangular shape:

```
[]
[][]
[][][]
[][][][]
[][][][][]
[][][][][][]
[][][][][][][]
```

The basic idea is simple. We generate a sequence of rows:

```
for (int i = 1; i <= width; i++)
{
    // Make triangle row
    . . .
}
```

How do you make a triangle row? Use another loop to concatenate the squares [] for that row. Then add a newline character at the end of the row. The ith row has i symbols, so the loop counter goes from 1 to i.

```
for (int j = 1; j <= i; j++)
    r = r + "[]";
r = r + "\n";
```

Putting both loops together yields two *nested loops:*

```
String r = "";
for (int i = 1; i <= width; i++)
{
   // Make triangle row
   for (int j = 1; j <= i; j++)
      r = r + "[]";
   r = r + "\n";
}
return r;
```

Here is the complete program:

File Triangle.java

```
1  /**
2     This class describes triangle objects that can be displayed
3     as shapes like this:
4     []
5     [][]
6     [][][].
7  */
8  public class Triangle
9  {
10    /**
11       Constructs a triangle.
12       @param aWidth the number of [] in the last row of the triangle
13    */
14    public Triangle(int aWidth)
15    {
16       width = aWidth;
17    }
18
19    /**
20       Computes a string representing the triangle.
21       @return a string consisting of [] and newline characters
22    */
23    public String toString()
24    {
25       String r = "";
26       for (int i = 1; i <= width; i++)
27       {
28          // Make triangle row
29          for (int j = 1; j <= i; j++)
30             r = r + "[]";
31          r = r + "\n";
32       }
33       return r;
34    }
35
36    private int width;
37 }
```

File TriangleTester.java

```
1  /**
2     This program tests the Triangle class.
3  */
4  public class TriangleTester
5  {
6     public static void main(String[] args)
7     {
8        Triangle small = new Triangle(3);
9        System.out.println(small.toString());
10
11       Triangle large = new Triangle(15);
12       System.out.println(large.toString());
13    }
14 }
```

Output

```
[]
[][]
[][][]

[]
[][]
[][][]
[][][][]
[][][][][]
[][][][][][]
[][][][][][][]
[][][][][][][][]
[][][][][][][][][]
[][][][][][][][][][]
[][][][][][][][][][][]
[][][][][][][][][][][][]
[][][][][][][][][][][][][]
[][][][][][][][][][][][][][]
[][][][][][][][][][][][][][][]
```

SELF CHECK

5. How would you modify the nested loops so that you print a square instead of a triangle?

6. What is the value of n after the following nested loops?

```
int n = 0;
for (int i = 1; i <= 5; i++)
   for (int j = 0; j < i; j++)
      n = n + j;
```

7.4 Processing Sentinel Values

Suppose you want to process a set of values, for example a set of measurements. Your goal is to analyze the data and display properties of the data set, such as the average or the maximum value. You prompt the user for the first value, then the second value, then the third, and so on. When does the input end?

One common method for indicating the end of a data set is a *sentinel value*, a value that is not part of the data. Instead, the sentinel value indicates that the data has come to an end.

Some programmers choose numbers such as 0 or –1 as sentinel values. But that is not a good idea. These values may well be valid inputs. A better idea is to use an input that is not a number, such as the letter Q. Here is a typical program run:

```
Enter value, Q to quit: 1
Enter value, Q to quit: 2
Enter value, Q to quit: 3
Enter value, Q to quit: 4
Enter value, Q to quit: Q
Average = 2.5
Maximum = 4.0
```

Of course, we need to read each input as a string, not a number. Once we have tested that the input is not the letter Q, we convert the string into a number.

```
System.out.print("Enter value, Q to quit: ");
String input = in.next();
if (input.equalsIgnoreCase("Q"))
    We are done
else
{
    double x = Double.parseDouble(input);
    . . .
}
```

Sometimes, the termination condition of a loop can only be evaluated in the middle of a loop. You can introduce a Boolean variable to control such a loop.

Now we have another problem. The test for loop termination occurs in the *middle* of the loop, not at the top or the bottom. You must first try to read input before you can test whether you have reached the end of input. In Java, there isn't a ready-made control structure for the pattern "do work, then test, then do more work". Therefore, we use a combination of a while loop and a boolean variable.

```
boolean done = false;
while (!done)
{
    Print prompt
    String input = read input;
    if (end of input indicated)
        done = true;
    else
    {
        Process input
    }
}
```

This pattern is sometimes called "loop and a half". Some programmers find it clumsy to introduce a control variable for such a loop. Advanced Topic 7.3 shows several alternatives.

Let's put together the data analysis program. To decouple the input handling from the computation of the average and the maximum, we'll introduce a class DataSet. You add values to a DataSet object with the add method. The getAverage method returns the average of all added data and the getMaximum method returns the largest.

File InputTester.java

```java
import java.util.Scanner;

/**
    This program computes the average and maximum of a set
    of input values.
*/
public class InputTester
{
    public static void main(String[] args)
    {
        Scanner in = new Scanner(System.in);
        DataSet data = new DataSet();

        boolean done = false;
        while (!done)
        {
            System.out.print("Enter value, Q to quit: ");
            String input = in.next();
            if (input.equalsIgnoreCase("Q"))
                done = true;
            else
            {
                double x = Double.parseDouble(input);
                data.add(x);
            }
        }

        System.out.println("Average = " + data.getAverage());
        System.out.println("Maximum = " + data.getMaximum());
    }
}
```

File DataSet.java

```java
/**
    Computes the average of a set of data values.
*/
public class DataSet
{
    /**
        Constructs an empty data set.
    */
```

```
 9        public DataSet()
10        {
11           sum = 0;
12           count = 0;
13           maximum = 0;
14        }
15
16        /**
17           Adds a data value to the data set.
18           @param x a data value
19        */
20        public void add(double x)
21        {
22           sum = sum + x;
23           if (count == 0 || maximum < x) maximum = x;
24           count++;
25        }
26
27        /**
28           Gets the average of the added data.
29           @return the average or 0 if no data has been added
30        */
31        public double getAverage()
32        {
33           if (count == 0) return 0;
34           else return sum / count;
35        }
36
37        /**
38           Gets the largest of the added data.
39           @return the maximum or 0 if no data has been added
40        */
41        public double getMaximum()
42        {
43           return maximum;
44        }
45
46        private double sum;
47        private double maximum;
48        private int count;
49     }
```

Output

```
Enter value, Q to quit: 10
Enter value, Q to quit: 0
Enter value, Q to quit: -1
Enter value, Q to quit: Q
Average = 3.0
Maximum = 10.0
```

7. Why does the InputTester class call in.next and not in.nextDouble?
8. Would the DataSet class still compute the correct maximum if you simplified the update of the maximum field in the add method to the following statement?

    if (maximum < x) maximum = x;

HOW TO 7.1

Implementing Loops

You write a loop because your program needs to repeat an action multiple times. As you have seen in this chapter, there are several loop types, and it isn't always obvious how to structure loop statements. This How To walks you through the thought process that is involved when programming a loop.

Step 1 List the work that needs to be done in every step of the loop body.

For example, suppose you need to read in input values in gallons and convert them to liters until the end of input is reached. Then the operations are:

- Read input.
- Convert the input to liters.
- Print out the response.

Suppose you need to scan through the characters of a string and count the vowels. Then the operations are:

- Get the next character.
- If it's a vowel, increase a counter.

Step 2 Find out how often the loop is repeated.

Typical answers might be:

- Ten times
- Once for each character in the string
- Until the end of input is reached
- While the balance is less than the target balance

If a loop is executed for a definite number of times, a for loop is usually appropriate. The first two answers above lead to for loops, such as

```
for (int i = 1; i <= 10; i++) . . .
for (int i = 0; i < str.length(); i++) . . .
```

The next two need to be implemented as while loops—you don't know how many times the loop body is going to be repeated.

Step 3 With a `while` loop, find out where you can determine that the loop is finished.

There are three possibilities:

- Before entering the loop
- In the middle of the loop
- At the end of the loop

For example, if you execute a loop while the balance is less than the target balance, you can check for that condition at the beginning of the loop. If the balance is less than the target balance, you enter the loop. If not, you are done. In such a case, your loop has the form

```
while (condition)
{
    Do work
}
```

However, checking for input requires that you first *read* the input. That means, you'll need to enter the loop, read the input, and then decide whether you want to go any further. Then your loop has the form

```
boolean done = false;
while (!done)
{
    Do the work needed to check the condition
    if (condition)
        done = true;
    else
    {
        Do more work
    }
}
```

This loop structure is sometimes called a "loop and a half".

Finally, if you know whether you need to go on after you have gone through the loop once, then you use a `do/while` loop:

```
do
{
    Do work
}
while (condition)
```

However, these loops are very rare in practice.

Step 4 Implement the loop by putting the operations from Step 1 into the loop body.

When you write a `for` loop, you usually use the loop index inside the loop body. For example, "get the next character" is implemented as the statement

```
char ch = str.charAt(i);
```

Step 5 Double-check your variable initializations.

If you use a Boolean variable `done`, make sure it is initialized to `false`. If you accumulate a result in a `sum` or `count` variable, make sure that you set it to 0 before entering the loop for the first time.

Step 6 Check for off-by-one errors.

Consider the simplest possible scenarios:

- If you read input, what happens if there is no input at all? Exactly one input?
- If you look through the characters of a string, what happens if the string is empty? If it has one character in it?
- If you accumulate values until some target has been reached, what happens if the target is 0? A negative value?

Manually walk through every instruction in the loop, including all initializations. Carefully check all conditions, paying attention to the difference between comparisons such as < and <=. Check that the loop is not traversed at all, or only once, and that the final result is what you expect.

If you write a for loop, check to see whether your bounds should be symmetric or asymmetric (see Quality Tip 7.3), and count the number of iterations (see Quality Tip 7.4).

QUALITY TIP 7.3

Symmetric and Asymmetric Bounds

It is easy to write a loop with i going from 1 to n:

```
for (i = 1; i <= n; i++) . . .
```

The values for i are bounded by the relation $1 \leq i \leq n$. Because there are $\leq$ comparisons on both bounds, the bounds are called *symmetric*.

When traversing the characters in a string, the bounds are *asymmetric*.

```
for (i = 0; i < str.length(); i++) . . .
```

> Make a choice between symmetric and asymmetric loop bounds.

The values for i are bounded by $0 \leq i <$ str.length(), with a $\leq$ comparison to the left and a < comparison to the right. That is appropriate, because str.length() is not a valid position.

It is not a good idea to force symmetry artificially:

```
for (i = 0; i <= str.length() - 1; i++) . . .
```

That is more difficult to read and understand.

For every loop, consider which form is most natural for the problem, and use that.

QUALITY TIP 7.4

Count Iterations

Finding the correct lower and upper bounds for an iteration can be confusing. Should I start at 0? Should I use <= b or < b as a termination condition?

> Count the number of iterations to check that your for loop is correct.

Counting the number of iterations is a very useful device for better understanding a loop. Counting is easier for loops with asymmetric bounds. The loop

```
for (i = a; i < b; i++) . . .
```

is executed b - a times. For example, the loop traversing the characters in a string,

```
for (i = 0; i < str.length(); i++) . . .
```

runs str.length() times. That makes perfect sense, because there are str.length() characters in a string.

The loop with symmetric bounds,

```
for (i = a; i <= b; i++)
```

is executed b - a + 1 times. That "+ 1" is the source of many programming errors. For example,

```
for (n = 0; n <= 10; n++)
```

runs 11 times. Maybe that is what you want; if not, start at 1 or use < 10.

One way to visualize this "+ 1" error is to think of the posts and sections of a fence. Suppose the fence has ten sections (=). How many posts (|) does it have?

```
|=|=|=|=|=|=|=|=|=|=|
```

A fence with ten sections has *eleven* posts. Each section has one post to the left, *and* there is one more post after the last section. Forgetting to count the last iteration of a "<=" loop is often called a "fence post error".

If the increment is a value c other than 1, and c divides b - a, then the counts are

$$(b - a) / c \qquad \text{for the asymmetric loop}$$

$$(b - a) / c + 1 \quad \text{for the symmetric loop}$$

For example, the loop for (i = 10; i <= 40; i += 5) executes $(40 - 10)/5 + 1 = 7$ times.

ADVANCED TOPIC 7.3

The "Loop and a Half" Problem

Reading input data sometimes requires a loop such as the following, which is somewhat unsightly:

```
boolean done = false;
while (!done)
{
    String input = in.next();
    if (input.equalsIgnoreCase("Q"))
        done = true;
    else
    {
        Process data
    }
}
```

The true test for loop termination is in the middle of the loop, not at the top. This is called a "loop and a half", because one must go halfway into the loop before knowing whether one needs to terminate.

Some programmers dislike the introduction of an additional Boolean variable for loop control. Two Java language features can be used to alleviate the "loop and a half" problem. I don't think either is a superior solution, but both approaches are fairly common, so it is worth knowing about them when reading other people's code.

You can combine an assignment and a test in the loop condition:

```java
while (!(input = in.next()).equalsIgnoreCase("Q"))
{
    Process data
}
```

The expression

```java
(input = in.next()).equalsIgnoreCase("Q")
```

means, "First call `in.next()`, then assign the result to `input`, then test whether it equals `"Q"`". This is an expression with a side effect. The primary purpose of the expression is to serve as a test for the `while` loop, but it also does some work—namely, reading the input and storing it in the variable `input`. In general, it is a bad idea to use side effects, because they make a program hard to read and maintain. In this case, however, that practice is somewhat seductive, because it eliminates the control variable `done`, which also makes the code hard to read and maintain.

The other solution is to exit the loop from the middle, either by a `return` statement or by a `break` statement (see Advanced Topic 7.4).

```java
public void processInput(Scanner in)
{
    while (true)
    {
        String input = in.next();
        if (input.equalsIgnoreCase("Q"))
            return;
        Process data
    }
}
```

ADVANCED TOPIC 7.4

The break and continue Statements

You already encountered the break statement in Advanced Topic 6.2, where it was used to exit a `switch` statement. In addition to breaking out of a `switch` statement, a break statement can also be used to exit a `while`, `for`, or `do` loop. For example, the break statement in the following loop terminates the loop when the end of input is reached.

```java
while (true)
{
    String input = in.next();
    if (input.equalsIgnoreCase("Q"))
        break;
    double x = Double.parseDouble(input);
    data.add(x);
}
```

In general, a break is a very poor way of exiting a loop. In 1990, a misused break caused an AT&T 4ESS telephone switch to fail, and the failure propagated through the entire U.S. network, rendering it nearly unusable for about nine hours. A programmer had used a break to terminate an if statement. Unfortunately, break cannot be used with if, so the program execution broke out of the enclosing switch statement, skipping some variable initializations and running into chaos [2, p. 38]. Using break statements also makes it difficult to use *correctness proof* techniques (see Advanced Topic 7.5).

However, when faced with the bother of introducing a separate loop control variable, some programmers find that break statements are beneficial in the "loop and a half" case. This issue is often the topic of heated (and quite unproductive) debate. In this book, we won't use the break statement, and we leave it to you to decide whether you like to use it in your own programs.

In Java, there is a second form of the break statement that is used to break out of a nested statement. The statement break *label*; immediately jumps to the *end* of the statement that is tagged with a label. Any statement (including if and block statements) can be tagged with a label—the syntax is

label: *statement*

The labeled break statement was invented to break out of a set of nested loops.

```
outerloop:
while (outer loop condition)
{  . . .
    while (inner loop condition)
    {  . . .
        if (something really bad happened)
            break outerloop;
    }
}
Jumps here if something really bad happened
```

Naturally, this situation is quite rare. We recommend that you try to introduce additional methods instead of using complicated nested loops.

Finally, there is another goto-like statement, the continue statement, which jumps to the end of the *current iteration* of the loop. Here is a possible use for this statement:

```
while (!done)
{
    String input = in.next();
    if (input.equalsIgnoreCase("Q"))
    {
        done = true;
        continue; // Jump to the end of the loop body
    }
    double x = Double.parseDouble(input);
    data.add(x);
    // continue statement jumps here
}
```

By using the continue statement, you don't need to place the remainder of the loop code inside an else clause. This is a minor benefit. Few programmers use this statement.

7.5 Random Numbers and Simulations

> In a simulation, you repeatedly generate random numbers and use them to simulate an activity.

In a simulation you generate random events and evaluate their outcomes. Here is a typical problem that can be decided by running a simulation: the *Buffon needle experiment*, devised by Comte Georges-Louis Leclerc de Buffon (1707–1788), a French naturalist. On each *try*, a one-inch long needle is dropped onto paper that is ruled with lines 2 inches apart. If the needle drops onto a line, count it as a hit. (See Figure 5.) Buffon conjectured that the quotient *tries/hits* approximates π.

Now, how can you run this experiment in the computer? You don't actually want to build a robot that drops needles on paper. The Random class of the Java library implements a *random number generator*, which produces numbers that appear to be completely random. To generate random numbers, you construct an object of the Random class, and then apply one of the following methods:

Method	Returns
nextInt(n)	A random integer between the integers 0 (inclusive) and n (exclusive)
nextDouble()	A random floating-point number between 0 (inclusive) and 1 (exclusive)

For example, you can simulate the cast of a die as follows:

```
Random generator = new Random();
int d = 1 + generator.nextInt(6);
```

The call generator.nextInt(6) gives you a random number between 0 and 5 (inclusive). Add 1 to obtain a number between 1 and 6.

To give you a feeling for the random numbers, run the following program a few times.

Figure 5 The Buffon Needle Experiment

File Die.java

```
1   import java.util.Random;
2
3   /**
4       This class models a die that, when cast, lands on a random
5       face.
6   */
7   public class Die
8   {
9       /**
10          Constructs a die with a given number of sides.
11          @param s the number of sides, e.g., 6 for a normal die
12      */
13      public Die(int s)
14      {
15          sides = s;
16          generator = new Random();
17      }
18
19      /**
20          Simulates a throw of the die.
21          @return the face of the die
22      */
23      public int cast()
24      {
25          return 1 + generator.nextInt(sides);
26      }
27
28      private Random generator;
29      private int sides;
30  }
```

File DieTester.java

```
1   /**
2       This program simulates casting a die ten times.
3   */
4   public class DieTester
5   {
6       public static void main(String[] args)
7       {
8           Die d = new Die(6);
9           final int TRIES = 10;
10          for (int i = 1; i <= TRIES; i++)
11          {
12              int n = d.cast();
13              System.out.print(n + " ");
14          }
15          System.out.println();
16      }
17  }
```

Output

```
6 5 6 3 2 6 3 4 4 1
```

Output (Second Run)

```
3 2 2 1 6 5 3 4 1 2
```

As you can see, this program produces a different stream of simulated die casts every time it is run. Actually, the numbers are not completely random. They are drawn from very long sequences of numbers that don't repeat for a long time. These sequences are computed from fairly simple formulas; they just behave like random numbers. For that reason, they are often called *pseudorandom* numbers. Generating good sequences of numbers that behave like truly random sequences is an important and well-studied problem in computer science. We won't investigate this issue further, though; we'll just use the random numbers produced by the Random class.

To run the Buffon needle experiment, we have to work a little harder. When you throw a die, it has to come up with one of six faces. When throwing a needle, however, there are many possible outcomes. You must generate *two* random numbers: one to describe the starting position and one to describe the angle of the needle with the x-axis. Then you need to test whether the needle touches a grid line. Stop after 10,000 tries.

Let us agree to generate the *lower* point of the needle. Its x-coordinate is irrelevant, and you may assume its y-coordinate y_{low} to be any random number between 0 and 2. However, because it can be a random *floating-point* number, we use the nextDouble method of the Random class. It returns a random floating-point number between 0 and 1. Multiply by 2 to get a random number between 0 and 2.

The angle α between the needle and the x-axis can be any value between 0 degrees and 180 degrees. The upper end of the needle has y-coordinate

$$y_{high} = y_{low} + \sin(\alpha)$$

The needle is a hit if y_{high} is at least 2. See Figure 6.

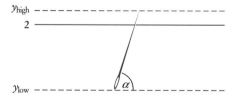

Figure 6
When Does the Needle Fall on a Line?

Here is the program to carry out the simulation of the needle experiment.

File Needle.java

```java
1  import java.util.Random;
2
3  /**
4     This class simulates a needle in the Buffon needle experiment.
5  */
6  public class Needle
7  {
8     /**
9        Constructs a needle.
10    */
11    public Needle()
12    {
13       hits = 0;
14       tries = 0;
15       generator = new Random();
16    }
17
18    /**
19       Drops the needle on the grid of lines and
20       remembers whether the needle hit a line.
21    */
22    public void drop()
23    {
24       double ylow = 2 * generator.nextDouble();
25       double angle = 180 * generator.nextDouble();
26
27       // Computes high point of needle
28
29       double yhigh = ylow + Math.sin(Math.toRadians(angle));
30       if (yhigh >= 2) hits++;
31       tries++;
32    }
33
34    /**
35       Gets the number of times the needle hit a line.
36       @return  the hit count
37    */
38    public int getHits()
39    {
40       return hits;
41    }
42
43    /**
44       Gets the total number of times the needle was dropped.
45       @return  the try count
46    */
47    public int getTries()
48    {
49       return tries;
50    }
51
```

```
52      private Random generator;
53      private int hits;
54      private int tries;
55   }
```

File NeedleTester.java

```
1   /**
2       This program simulates the Buffon needle experiment
3       and prints the resulting approximations of pi.
4   */
5   public class NeedleTester
6   {
7      public static void main(String[] args)
8      {
9         Needle n = new Needle();
10        final int TRIES1 = 10000;
11        final int TRIES2 = 1000000;
12
13        for (int i = 1; i <= TRIES1; i++)
14           n.drop();
15        System.out.printf("Tries = %d, Tries / Hits = %8.5f\n",
16              TRIES1, (double) n.getTries() / n.getHits());
17
18        for (int i = TRIES1 + 1; i <= TRIES2; i++)
19           n.drop();
20        System.out.printf("Tries = %d, Tries / Hits = %8.5f\n",
21              TRIES2, (double) n.getTries() / n.getHits());
22     }
23  }
```

Output

```
Tries = 10000, Tries / Hits =  3.08928
Tries = 1000000, Tries / Hits =  3.14204
```

The point of this program is not to compute π—there are far more efficient ways to do that. Rather, the point is to show how a physical experiment can be simulated on the computer. Buffon had to physically drop the needle thousands of times and record the results, which must have been a rather dull activity. The computer can execute the experiment quickly and accurately.

Simulations are very common computer applications. Many simulations use essentially the same pattern as the code of this example: In a loop, a large number of sample values are generated, and the values of certain observations are recorded for each sample. When the simulation is completed, the averages, or other statistics of interest from the observed values are printed out.

A typical example of a simulation is the modeling of customer queues at a bank or a supermarket. Rather than observing real customers, one simulates their arrival and their transactions at the teller window or checkout stand in the computer. One can try different staffing or building layout patterns in the computer simply by making changes in the program. In the real world, making many such changes and measuring their effects would be impossible, or at least, very expensive.

SELF CHECK

9. How do you use a random number generator to simulate the toss of a coin?
10. Why is the `NeedleTester` program not an efficient method for computing π?

ADVANCED TOPIC 7.5

Loop Invariants

Consider the task of computing a^n, where a is a floating-point number and n is a positive integer. Of course, you can multiply $a \cdot a \cdot \ldots \cdot a$, n times, but if n is large, you'll end up doing a lot of multiplication. The following loop computes a^n in far fewer steps:

```
double a = . . .;
int n = . . .;
double r = 1;
double b = a;
int i = n;
while (i > 0)
{
   if (i % 2 == 0) // n is even
   {
      b = b * b;
      i = i / 2;
   }
   else
   {
      r = r * b;
      i--;
   }
}
// Now r equals a to the nth power
```

Consider the case n = 100. The method performs the steps shown in Table 2.

Amazingly enough, the algorithm yields exactly a^{100}. Do you understand why? Are you convinced it will work for all values of n? Here is a clever argument to show that the method always computes the correct result. It demonstrates that whenever the program reaches the top of the `while` loop, it is true that

$$r \cdot b^i = a^n \qquad \text{(I)}$$

Certainly, it is true the first time around, because b = a and i = n. Suppose that (I) holds at the beginning of the loop. Label the values of r, b, and i as "old" when entering the loop, and as "new" when exiting the loop. Assume that upon entry

$$r_{old} \cdot b_{old}^{\,i_{old}} = a^n$$

Table 2	Computing a^{100}	
b	**i**	**r**
a	100	1
a^2	50	
a^4	25	
	24	a^4
a^8	12	
a^{16}	6	
a^{32}	3	
	2	a^{36}
a^{64}	1	
	0	a^{100}

In the loop you must distinguish two cases: i_{old} even and i_{old} odd. If i_{old} is even, the loop performs the following transformations:

$$r_{new} = r_{old}$$
$$b_{new} = b_{old}^2$$
$$i_{new} = i_{old}/2$$

Therefore,

$$r_{new} \cdot b_{new}{}^{i_{new}} = r_{old} \cdot \left(b_{old}\right)^{2 \cdot i_{old}/2}$$
$$= r_{old} \cdot b_{old}{}^{i_{old}}$$
$$= a^n$$

On the other hand, if i_{old} is odd, then

$$r_{new} = r_{old} \cdot b_{old}$$
$$b_{new} = b_{old}$$
$$i_{new} = i_{old} - 1$$

Therefore,

$$r_{new} \cdot b_{new}{}^{i_{new}} = r_{old} \cdot b_{old} \cdot b_{old}{}^{i_{old}-1}$$
$$= r_{old} \cdot b_{old}{}^{i_{old}}$$
$$= a^n$$

In either case, the new values for r, b, and i fulfill the *loop invariant* (I). So what? When the loop finally exits, (I) holds again:

$$r \cdot b^i = a^n$$

Furthermore, we know that i = 0, because the loop is terminating. But because i = 0, $r \cdot b^i = r \cdot b^0 = r$. Hence $r = a^n$, and the method really does compute the nth power of a.

This technique is quite useful, because it can explain an algorithm that is not at all obvious. The condition (I) is called a loop invariant because it is true when the loop is entered, at the top of each pass, and when the loop is exited. If a loop invariant is chosen skillfully, you may be able to deduce correctness of a computation. See [3] for another nice example.

RANDOM FACT 7.2

Correctness Proofs

In Advanced Topic 7.5 we introduced the technique of loop invariants. If you skipped that topic, have a glance at it now. That technique can be used to rigorously prove that a loop computes exactly the value that it is supposed to compute. Such a proof is far more valuable than any testing. No matter how many test cases you try, you always worry whether another case that you haven't tried yet might show a bug. A proof settles the correctness for *all possible inputs*.

For some time, programmers were very hopeful that proof techniques such as loop invariants would greatly reduce the need of testing. You would prove that each simple method is correct, and then put the proven components together and prove that they work together as they should. Once it is proved that main works correctly, no testing is required. Some researchers were so excited about these techniques that they tried to omit the programming step altogether. The designer would write down the program requirements, using the notation of formal logic. An automatic prover would prove that such a program could be written and generate the program as part of its proof.

Unfortunately, in practice these methods never worked very well. The logical notation to describe program behavior is complex. Even simple scenarios require many formulas. It is easy enough to express the idea that a method is supposed to compute a^n, but the logical formulas describing all methods in a program that controls an airplane, for instance, would fill many pages. These formulas are created by humans, and humans make errors when they deal with difficult and tedious tasks. Experiments showed that instead of buggy programs, programmers wrote buggy logic specifications and buggy program proofs.

Van der Linden [2, p. 287], gives some examples of complicated proofs that are much harder to verify than the programs they are trying to prove.

Program proof techniques are valuable for proving the correctness of individual methods that make computations in nonobvious ways. At this time, though, there is no hope to prove any but the most trivial programs correct in such a way that the specification and the proof can be trusted more than the program. There is hope that correctness proofs will become more applicable to real-life programming situations in the future. However, engineering and management are at least as important as mathematics and logic for the successful completion of large software projects.

CHAPTER SUMMARY

1. A `while` statement executes a block of code repeatedly. A condition controls how often the loop is executed.

2. An off-by-one error is a common error when programming loops. Think through simple test cases to avoid this type of error.

3. You use a `for` loop when a variable runs from a starting to an ending value with a constant increment or decrement.

4. Loops can be nested. A typical example of nested loops is printing a table with rows and columns.

5. Sometimes, the termination condition of a loop can only be evaluated in the middle of a loop. You can introduce a Boolean variable to control such a loop.

6. Make a choice between symmetric and asymmetric loop bounds.

7. Count the number of iterations to check that your `for` loop is correct.

8. In a simulation, you repeatedly generate random numbers and use them to simulate an activity.

FURTHER READING

1. E. W. Dijkstra, "Goto Statements Considered Harmful", *Communications of the ACM*, vol. 11, no. 3 (March 1968), pp. 147–148.

2. Peter van der Linden, *Expert C Programming*, Prentice-Hall, 1994.

3. Jon Bentley, *Programming Pearls*, Chapter 4, "Writing Correct Programs", Addison-Wesley, 1986.

4. Kai Lai Chung, *Elementary Probability Theory with Stochastic Processes*, Undergraduate Texts in Mathematics, Springer-Verlag, 1974.

5. Rudolf Flesch, *How to Write Plain English*, Barnes & Noble Books, 1979.

CLASSES, OBJECTS, AND METHODS INTRODUCED IN THIS CHAPTER

```
java.util.Random
   nextDouble
   nextInt
```

REVIEW EXERCISES

Exercise R7.1. Which loop statements does Java support? Give simple rules when to use each loop type.

Exercise R7.2. What does the following code print?

```
for (int i = 0; i < 10; i++)
{
    for (int j = 0; j < 10; j++)
        System.out.print(i * j % 10);
    System.out.println();
}
```

Exercise R7.3. How often do the following loops execute? Assume that i is an integer variable that is not changed in the loop body.

   a. `for (i = 1; i <= 10; i++)` . . .

   b. `for (i = 0; i < 10; i++)` . . .

   c. `for (i = 10; i > 0; i--)` . . .

   d. `for (i = -10; i <= 10; i++)` . . .

   e. `for (i = 10; i >= 0; i++)` . . .

   f. `for (i = -10; i <= 10; i = i + 2)` . . .

   g. `for (i = -10; i <= 10; i = i + 3)` . . .

Exercise R7.4. Rewrite the following for loop into a while loop.

```
int s = 0;
for (int i = 1; i <= 10; i++) s = s + i;
```

Exercise R7.5. Rewrite the following do loop into a while loop.

```
int n = 1;
double x = 0;
double s;
do
{
    s = 1.0 / (n * n);
    x = x + s;
    n++;
}
while (s > 0.01);
```

Exercise R7.6. What is an infinite loop? On your computer, how can you terminate a program that executes an infinite loop?

Exercise R7.7. What is a "loop and a half"? Give three strategies to implement the following "loop and a half":

```
loop
{
```

> *Read name of bridge*
> *If not OK, exit loop*
> *Read length of bridge in feet*
> *If not OK, exit loop*
> *Convert length to meters*
> *Print bridge data*
>   }

Use a Boolean variable, a `break` statement, and a method with multiple `return` statements. Which of these three approaches do you find clearest?

Exercise R7.8. How would you implement a loop that prompts a user to enter a number between 1 and 10, giving three tries to get it right?

Exercise R7.9. Sometimes students write programs with instructions such as "Enter data, 0 to quit" and that exit the data entry loop when the user enters the number 0. Explain why that is usually a poor idea.

Exercise R7.10. How would you use a random number generator to simulate the drawing of a playing card?

Exercise R7.11. What is an "off-by-one error"? Give an example from your own programming experience.

Exercise R7.12. Give an example of a `for` loop in which symmetric bounds are more natural. Give an example of a `for` loop in which asymmetric bounds are more natural.

Exercise R7.13. What are nested loops? Give an example where a nested loop is typically used.

PROGRAMMING EXERCISES

Exercise P7.1. *Currency conversion.* Write a program that asks the user to enter today's exchange rate between U.S. dollars and the euro. Then the program reads U.S. dollar values and converts each to euro values. Stop when the user enters Q.

Exercise P7.2. *Random walk.* Simulate the wandering of an intoxicated person in a square street grid. Draw a grid of 10 streets horizontally and 10 streets vertically. Represent the simulated drunkard by a dot, placed in the middle of the grid to start. For 100 times, have the simulated drunkard randomly pick a direction (east, west, north, south), move one block in the chosen direction, and draw the dot. After the iterations, display the distance that the drunkard has covered. (One might expect that on average the person might not get anywhere because the moves to different directions cancel one another out in the long run, but in fact it can be shown with probability 1 that the person eventually moves outside any finite region. See, for example, [4, Chapter 8] for more details.) Use classes for the grid and the drunkard.

Exercise P7.3. *Projectile flight.* Suppose a cannonball is propelled vertically into the air with a starting velocity v_0. Any calculus book will tell us that the position of the ball after t seconds is $s(t) = -0.5 \cdot g \cdot t^2 + v_0 \cdot t$, where $g = 9.81$ m/sec^2 is the gravitational force of the earth. No calculus book ever mentions why someone would want to carry out such an obviously dangerous experiment, so we will do it in the safety of the computer.

In fact, we will confirm the theorem from calculus by a simulation. In our simulation, we will consider how the ball moves in very short time intervals Δt. In a short time interval the velocity v is nearly constant, and we can compute the distance the ball moves as $\Delta s = v \cdot \Delta t$. In our program, we will simply set

```
double deltaT = 0.01;
```

and update the position by

```
s = s + v * deltaT;
```

The velocity changes constantly—in fact, it is reduced by the gravitational force of the earth. In a short time interval, v decreases by $g \cdot \Delta t$, and we must keep the velocity updated as

```
v = v - g * deltaT;
```

In the next iteration the new velocity is used to update the distance.

Now run the simulation until the cannonball falls back to the earth. Get the initial velocity as an input (100 m/sec is a good value). Update the position and velocity 100 times per second, but only print out the position every full second. Also print out the values from the exact formula $s(t) = -0.5 \cdot g \cdot t^2 + v_0 \cdot t$ for comparison. Use a class Cannonball.

What is the benefit of this kind of simulation when an exact formula is available? Well, the formula from the calculus book is *not* exact. Actually, the gravitational force diminishes the farther the cannonball is away from the surface of the earth. This complicates the algebra sufficiently that it is not possible to give an exact formula for the actual motion, but the computer simulation can simply be extended to apply a variable gravitational force. For cannonballs, the calculus-book formula is actually good enough, but computers are necessary to compute accurate trajectories for higher-flying objects such as ballistic missiles.

Exercise P7.4. Most cannonballs are not shot upright but at an angle. If the starting velocity has magnitude v and the starting angle is α, then the velocity is a vector with components $v_x = v \cdot \cos(\alpha)$, $v_y = v \cdot \sin(\alpha)$. In the x-direction the velocity does not change. In the y-direction the gravitational force takes its toll. Repeat the simulation from the previous exercise, but update the x and y components of the location and the velocity separately. Every full second, plot the location of the cannonball on the graphics display. Repeat until the cannonball has reached the earth again. Again, use a class Cannonball.

This kind of problem is of historical interest. The first computers were designed to carry out just such ballistic calculations, taking into account the diminishing gravity for high-flying projectiles and wind speeds.

Exercise P7.5. The *Fibonacci sequence* is defined by the following rule. The first two values in the sequence are 1 and 1. Every subsequent value is the sum of the two values preceding it. For example, the third value is $1 + 1 = 2$, the fourth value is $1 + 2 = 3$, and the fifth is $2 + 3 = 5$. If f_n denotes the nth value in the Fibonacci sequence, then

$$f_1 = 1$$
$$f_2 = 1$$
$$f_n = f_{n-1} + f_{n-2} \quad \text{if } n > 2$$

Write a program that prompts the user for n and prints the nth value in the Fibonacci sequence. Use a class `FibonacciGenerator` with a method `nextNumber`.

Hint: There is no need to store all values for f_n. You only need the last two values to compute the next one in the series:

```
fold1 = 1;
fold2 = 1;
fnew = fold1 + fold2;
```

After that, discard `fold2`, which is no longer needed, and set `fold2` to `fold1` and `fold1` to `fnew`.

Exercise P7.6. *Mean and standard deviation.* Write a program that reads a set of floating-point data values from the input. When the end of file is reached, print out the count of the values, the average, and the standard deviation. The average of a data set $x_1, \ldots, x_n$ is

$$\bar{x} = \frac{\sum x_i}{n}$$

where $\sum x_i = x_1 + \cdots + x_n$ is the sum of the input values. The standard deviation is

$$s = \sqrt{\frac{\sum (x_i - \bar{x})^2}{n - 1}}$$

However, that formula is not suitable for our task. By the time you have computed the mean, the individual x_i are long gone. Until you know how to save these values, use the numerically less stable formula

$$s = \sqrt{\frac{\sum x_i^2 - \frac{1}{n}\left(\sum x_i\right)^2}{n - 1}}$$

You can compute this quantity by keeping track of the count, the sum, and the sum of squares in the `DataSet` class as you process the input values.

Exercise P7.7. Write a graphical application that displays a checkerboard with 64 squares, alternating white and black.

Exercise P7.8. Write a graphical application that prompts a user to enter a number n and that draws n circles with random diameter and random location. The circles should be contained inside the window.

Exercise P7.9. Write a graphical application that draws a spiral, such as the following:

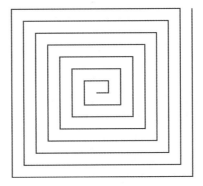

Exercise P7.10. *Factoring of integers.* Write a program that asks the user for an integer and then prints out all its factors. For example, when the user enters 150, the program should print

    2
    3
    5
    5

Use a class `FactorGenerator` with methods `nextFactor` and `hasMoreFactors`.

Exercise P7.11. *Prime numbers.* Write a program that prompts the user for an integer and then prints out all prime numbers up to that integer. For example, when the user enters 20, the program should print

    2
    3
    5
    7
    11
    13
    17
    19

Recall that a number is a prime number if it is not divisible by any number except 1 and itself.

Use a class `PrimeGenerator` with a method `nextPrime`.

Exercise P7.12. The *Heron method* is a method for computing square roots that was known to the ancient Greeks. If x is a guess for the value $\sqrt{a}$, then the average of x and a/x is a better guess.

Implement a class `RootApproximator` that starts with an initial guess of 1 and whose `nextGuess` method produces a sequence of increasingly better guesses. Supply a method `hasMoreGuesses` that returns `false` if two successive guesses are sufficiently close to each other. Then test your class like this:

```
RootApproximator r = new RootApproximator(n);
while (r.hasMoreGuesses())
    System.out.println(r.nextGuess());
```

Exercise P7.13. The best known iterative method for computing the roots of a function f (that is, the x-values for which $f(x)$ is 0) is Newton–Raphson approximation. To find the zero of a function whose derivative is also known, compute

$$x_{new} = x_{old} - f(x_{old})/f'(x_{old}).$$

For this exercise, write a program to compute nth roots of floating-point numbers. Prompt the user for a and n, then obtain $\sqrt[n]{a}$ by computing a zero of the function $f(x) = x^n - a$. Follow the approach of Exercise P7.12.

Exercise P7.14. The value of e^x can be computed as the power series

$$e^x = \sum_{n=0}^{\infty} \frac{x^n}{n!}$$

where $n! = 1 \cdot 2 \cdot 3 \cdot \ldots \cdot n$.

Write a program that computes e^x using this formula. Of course, you can't compute an infinite sum. Just keep adding values until an individual summand (term) is less than a certain threshold. At each step, you need to compute the new term and add it to the total. Update these terms as follows:

```
term = term * x / n;
```

Follow the approach of the preceding two exercises, by implementing a class `ExpApproximator`.

Exercise P7.15. Generate 100 random numbers between 0 and 1000 and add them to a `DataSet`. Print out the average and the maximum.

Exercise P7.16. Program the following simulation: Darts are thrown at random points onto the square with corners (1,1) and (–1,–1). If the dart lands inside the unit circle (that is, the circle with center (0,0) and radius 1), it is a hit. Otherwise it is a miss. Run this simulation and use it to determine an approximate value for π. Extra credit if you explain why this is a better method for estimating π than the Buffon needle program.

Exercise P7.17. It is easy and fun to draw graphs of curves with the Java graphics library. Simply draw 100 line segments joining the points $(x, f(x))$ and $(x + d, f(x + d))$, where x ranges from x_{min} to x_{max} and $d = (x_{max} - x_{min})/100$. Draw the curve $f(x) = x^3/100 - x + 10$, where x ranges from –10 to 10 in this fashion.

Exercise P7.18. Draw a picture of the "four-leaved rose" whose equation in polar coordinates is $r = \cos(2\theta)$. Let θ go from 0 to 2π in 100 steps. Each time, compute r and then compute the (x,y) coordinates from the polar coordinates by using the formula

$$x = r\cos\theta, y = r\sin\theta$$

You will get extra credit if you can vary the number of petals.

PROGRAMMING PROJECTS

Project 7.1. *Flesch Readability Index.* The following index [5] was invented by Flesch as a simple tool to gauge the legibility of a document without linguistic analysis.

- Count all words in the file. A *word* is any sequence of characters delimited by white space, whether or not it is an actual English word.
- Count all syllables in each word. To make this simple, use the following rules: Each *group* of adjacent vowels (a, e, i, o, u, y) counts as one syllable (for example, the "ea" in "real" contributes one syllable, but the "e . . . a" in "regal" count as two syllables). However, an "e" at the end of a word doesn't count as a syllable. Also, each word has at least one syllable, even if the previous rules give a count of 0.
- Count all sentences. A sentence is ended by a period, colon, semicolon, question mark, or exclamation mark.
- The index is computed by

$$\text{Index} = 206.835$$
$$- 84.6 \times \left(\text{Number of syllables/Number of words}\right)$$
$$- 1.015 \times \left(\text{Number of words/Number of sentences}\right)$$

rounded to the nearest integer.

This index is a number, usually between 0 and 100, indicating how difficult the text is to read. Some example indices for random material from various publications are:

Comics	95
Consumer ads	82
Sports Illustrated	65
Time	57
New York Times	39
Auto insurance policy	10
Internal Revenue Code	−6

Translated into educational levels, the indices are:

91–100	5th grader
81–90	6th grader
71–80	7th grader
66–70	8th grader
61–65	9th grader
51–60	High school student
31–50	College student
0–30	College graduate
Less than 0	Law school graduate

The purpose of the index is to force authors to rewrite their text until the index is high enough. This is achieved by reducing the length of sentences and by removing long words. For example, the sentence

> The following index was invented by Flesch as a simple tool to estimate the legibility of a document without linguistic analysis.

can be rewritten as

> Flesch invented an index to check whether a text is easy to read. To compute the index, you need not look at the meaning of the words.

Flesch's book [5] contains delightful examples of translating government regulations into "plain English".

Your program should read a text file in, compute the legibility index, and print out the equivalent educational level. Use classes Word and Document.

Project 7.2. *The game of Nim.* This is a well-known game with a number of variants. We will consider the following variant, which has an interesting winning strategy. Two players alternately take marbles from a pile. In each move, a player chooses how many marbles to take. The player must take at least one but at most half of the marbles. Then the other player takes a turn. The player who takes the last marble loses.

Write a program in which the computer plays against a human opponent. Generate a random integer between 10 and 100 to denote the initial size of the pile. Generate a random integer between 0 and 1 to decide whether the computer or the human takes the first turn. Generate a random integer between 0 and 1 to decide whether the computer plays *smart* or *stupid*. In stupid mode, the computer simply takes a random legal value (between 1 and $n/2$) from the pile whenever it has a turn. In smart mode the computer takes off enough marbles to make the size of the pile a power of two minus 1—that is, 3, 7, 15, 31, or 63. That is always a legal move, except if the size of the pile is currently one less than a power of 2. In that case, the computer makes a random legal move.

Note that the computer cannot be beaten in smart mode when it has the first move, unless the pile size happens to be 15, 31, or 63. Of course, a human player who has the first turn and knows the winning strategy can win against the computer.

When you implement this program, be sure to use classes Pile, Player, and Game. A player can be either stupid, smart, or human. (Human Player objects prompt for input.)

ANSWERS TO SELF-CHECK QUESTIONS

1. Never.
2. The waitForBalance method would never return due to an infinite loop.
3. ```
   int i = 1;
   while (i <= n)
   {
      double interest = balance * rate / 100;
      balance = balance + interest;
      i++;
   }
   ```
4. 11 times.
5. Change the inner loop to for (int j = 1; j <= width; j++).
6. 20.
7. Because we don't know whether the next input is a number or the letter Q.
8. No. If *all* input values are negative, the maximum is also negative. However, the maximum field is initialized with 0. With this simplification, the maximum would be falsely computed as 0.
9. int n = generator.nextInt(2); // 0 = heads, 1 = tails
10. The program repeatedly calls Math.toRadians(angle). You could simply call Math.toRadians(180) to compute π.
   ```

Chapter 8

Arrays and Array Lists

CHAPTER GOALS

- To become familiar with using arrays and array lists
- To learn about wrapper classes, auto-boxing, and the enhanced for loop
- To study common array algorithms
- To learn how to use two-dimensional arrays
- To understand when to choose array lists and arrays in your programs
- To implement partially filled arrays

In order to process large quantities of data, you need to collect values in a data structure. The most commonly used data structures in Java are arrays and array lists. In this chapter, you will learn how to construct arrays and array lists, fill them with values, and access the stored values. We introduce the enhanced for loop, a convenient statement for processing all elements of a collection. You will see how to use the enhanced for loop, as well as ordinary loops, to implement common array algorithms. The chapter concludes with a technical section on copying array values.

CHAPTER CONTENTS

8.1 Arrays

In many programs, you need to manipulate collections of related values. It would be impractical to use a sequence of variables such as data1, data2, data3, . . . , and so on. The array construct provides a better way of storing a collection of values.

An array is a sequence of values of the same type. For example, here is how you construct an array of 10 floating-point numbers:

> An array is a sequence of values of the same type.

```
new double[10]
```

The number of elements (here, 10) is called the length of the array.

The new operator merely constructs the array. You will want to store a reference to the array in a variable so that you can access it later.

The type of an array variable is the element type, followed by []. In this example, the type is double[], because the element type is double. Here is the declaration of an array variable:

```
double[] data = new double[10];
```

That is, data is a reference to an array of floating-point numbers. It is initialized with an array of 10 numbers (see Figure 1).

You can also form arrays of objects, for example

```
BankAccount[] accounts = new BankAccount[10];
```

When an array is first created, all values are initialized with 0 (for an array of numbers such as int[] or double[]), false (for a boolean[] array), or null (for an array of object references).

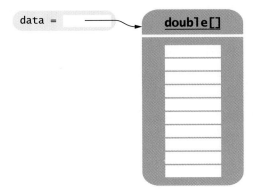

Figure 1 An Array Reference and an Array

Each element in the array is specified by an integer index that is placed inside square brackets ([]). For example, the expression

    data[4]

denotes the element of the data array with index 4.

You can store a value at that location with an assignment statement, such as the following.

    data[2] = 29.95;

> You access array elements with an integer index, using the notation a[i].

Now the position with index 2 of data is filled with the value 29.95 (see Figure 2).

To read out the data value at index 2, simply use the expression data[2] as you would any variable of type double:

    System.out.println("The value of this data item is "
        + data[2]);

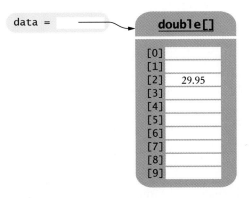

Figure 2 Storing a Value in an Array

If you look closely at Figure 2, you will notice that the index values start at 0. That is,

data[0] is the first element

data[1] is the second element

data[2] is the third element

and so on. This convention can be a source of grief for the newcomer, so you should pay close attention to the index values. In particular, the *last* element in the array has an index *one less than* the array length. For example, data refers to an array with length 10. The last element is data[9].

> Index values of an array range from 0 to length - 1. Accessing a nonexistent element results in a bounds error.

If you try to access an element that does not exist, then an exception is thrown. For example, the statement

data[10] = 29.95; // ERROR

is a bounds error.

To avoid bounds errors, you will want to know how many elements are in an array. The length field returns the number of elements: data.length is the length of the data array. Note that there are no parentheses following length—it is an instance variable of the array object, not a method. However, you cannot assign a new value to this instance variable. In other words, length is a final public instance variable. This is quite an anomaly. Normally, Java programmers use a method to inquire about the properties of an object. You just have to remember to omit the parentheses in this case.

> Use the length field to find the number of elements in an array.

The following code ensures that you only access the array when the index variable i is within the legal bounds:

if (0 <= i && i < data.length) data[i] = value;

Arrays suffer from a significant limitation: *their length is fixed*. If you start out with an array of 10 elements and later decide that you need to add additional elements, then you need to make a new array and copy all values of the existing array into the new array. We will discuss this process in detail in Section 8.7.

SYNTAX 8.1 Array Construction

new *typeName*[*length*]

Example:

new double[10]

Purpose:

To construct an array with a given number of elements

SYNTAX 8.2 Array Element Access

arrayReference[index]

Example:

data[2]

Purpose:

To access an element in an array

SELF CHECK

1. What elements does the data array contain after the following statements?
   ```
   double[] data = new double[10];
   for (int i = 0; i < data.length; i++) data[i] = i * i;
   ```

2. What do the following program segments print? Or, if there is an error, describe the error and specify whether it is detected at compile-time or at run-time.

   a.
   ```
   double[] a = new double[10];
   System.out.println(a[0]);
   ```

   b.
   ```
   double[] b = new double[10];
   System.out.println(b[10]);
   ```

   c.
   ```
   double[] c;
   System.out.println(c[0]);
   ```

COMMON ERROR 8.1

Bounds Errors

The most common array error is attempting to access a nonexistent position.

```
double[] data = new double[10];
data[10] = 29.95;
// Error—only have elements with index values 0 . . . 9
```

When the program runs, an out-of-bounds index generates an exception and terminates the program.

This is a great improvement over languages such as C and C++. With those languages there is no error message; instead, the program will quietly (or not so quietly) corrupt the memory location that is 10 elements away from the start of the array. Sometimes that corruption goes unnoticed, but at other times, the program will act flaky or die a horrible death many instructions later. These are serious problems that make C and C++ programs difficult to debug.

COMMON ERROR 8.2

Uninitialized Arrays

A common error is to allocate an array reference, but not an actual array.

```
double[] data;
data[0] = 29.95; // Error—data not initialized
```

Array variables work exactly like object variables—they are only references to the actual array. To construct the actual array, you must use the new operator:

```
double[] data = new double[10];
```

ADVANCED TOPIC 8.1

Array Initialization

You can initialize an array by allocating it and then filling each entry:

```
int[] primes = new int[5];
primes[0] = 2;
primes[1] = 3;
primes[2] = 5;
primes[3] = 7;
primes[4] = 11;
```

However, if you already know all the elements that you want to place in the array, there is an easier way. List all elements that you want to include in the array, enclosed in braces and separated by commas:

```
int[] primes = { 2, 3, 5, 7, 11 };
```

The Java compiler counts how many elements you want to place in the array, allocates an array of the correct size, and fills it with the elements that you specify.

If you want to construct an array and pass it on to a method that expects an array parameter, you can initialize an anonymous array as follows:

```
new int[] { 2, 3, 5, 7, 11 }
```

8.2 Array Lists

> The ArrayList class manages a sequence of objects.

Arrays are a rather primitive construct. In this section, we introduce the ArrayList class that lets you collect objects, just like an array does. Array lists offer two significant conveniences:

- Array lists can grow and shrink as needed
- The `ArrayList` class supplies methods for many common tasks, such as inserting and removing elements

Let us define an array list of bank accounts and fill it with objects. (The `BankAccount` class has been enhanced from the version in Chapter 3. Each bank account has an account number.)

```
ArrayList<BankAccount> accounts = new ArrayList<BankAccount>();
accounts.add(new BankAccount(1001));
accounts.add(new BankAccount(1015));
accounts.add(new BankAccount(1022));
```

> The `ArrayList` class is a generic class: `ArrayList<T>` collects objects of type T.

The type `ArrayList<BankAccount>` denotes an array list of bank accounts. The angle brackets around the `BankAccount` type tell you that `BankAccount` is a *type parameter*. You can replace `BankAccount` with any other class and get a different array list type. For that reason, `ArrayList` is called a *generic class*. You will learn more about generic classes in Chapter 22. For now, simply use an `ArrayList<T>` whenever you want to collect objects of type T. However, keep in mind that you cannot use primitive types as type parameters—there is no `ArrayList<int>` or `ArrayList<double>`.

When you construct an `ArrayList` object, it has size 0. You use the `add` method to add an object to the end of the array list. The size increases after each call to `add`. The `size` method yields the current size of the array list.

To get objects out of the array list, use the `get` method, not the [ ] operator. As with arrays, index values start at 0. For example, `accounts.get(2)` retrieves the account with index 2, the third element in the array list:

```
BankAccount anAccount = accounts.get(2);
```

As with arrays, it is an error to access a nonexistent element. The most common bounds error is to use the following:

```
int i = accounts.size();
anAccount = accounts.get(i);   // Error
```

The last valid index is `accounts.size() - 1`.

To set an array list element to a new value, use the set method.

```
BankAccount anAccount = new BankAccount(1729);
accounts.set(2, anAccount);
```

This call sets position 2 of the accounts array list to `anAccount`, overwriting whatever value was there before.

The set method can only overwrite existing values. It is different from the add method, which adds a new object to the end of the array list.

You can also insert an object in the middle of an array list. The call `accounts.add(i, a)` adds the object a at position i and moves all elements by one position, from the current element at position i to the last element in the array list.

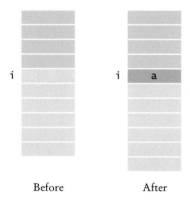

Before   After

Figure 3   Adding an Element in the Middle of an Array List

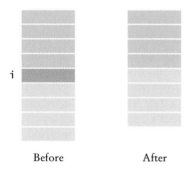

Before   After

Figure 4   Removing an Element from the Middle of an Array List

After each call to the add method, the size of the array list increases by 1 (see Figure 3).

Conversely, the call accounts.remove(i) removes the element at position i, moves all elements after the removed element down by one position, and reduces the size of the array list by 1 (see Figure 4).

The following program demonstrates the methods of the ArrayList class. Note that you import the generic class java.util.ArrayList, without the type parameter.

ArrayListTester.java

```
1   import java.util.ArrayList;
2
3   /**
4       This program tests the ArrayList class.
5   */
6   public class ArrayListTester
7   {
```

```
8     public static void main(String[] args)
9     {
10       ArrayList<BankAccount> accounts
11             = new ArrayList<BankAccount>();
12       accounts.add(new BankAccount(1001));
13       accounts.add(new BankAccount(1015));
14       accounts.add(new BankAccount(1729));
15       accounts.add(1, new BankAccount(1008));
16       accounts.remove(0);
17
18       System.out.println("size=" + accounts.size());
19       BankAccount first = accounts.get(0);
20       System.out.println("first account number="
21             + first.getAccountNumber());
22       BankAccount last = accounts.get(accounts.size() - 1);
23       System.out.println("last account number="
24             + last.getAccountNumber());
25     }
26 }
```

BankAccount.java

```
1  /**
2      A bank account has a balance that can be changed by
3      deposits and withdrawals.
4  */
5  public class BankAccount
6  {
7      /**
8          Constructs a bank account with a zero balance.
9          @param anAccountNumber  the account number for this account
10     */
11     public BankAccount(int anAccountNumber)
12     {
13        accountNumber = anAccountNumber;
14        balance = 0;
15     }
16
17     /**
18         Constructs a bank account with a given balance.
19         @param anAccountNumber  the account number for this account
20         @param initialBalance  the initial balance
21     */
22     public BankAccount(int anAccountNumber, double initialBalance)
23     {
24        accountNumber = anAccountNumber;
25        balance = initialBalance;
26     }
27
```

```
28    /**
29          Gets the account number of this bank account.
30          @return  the account number
31    */
32    public int getAccountNumber()
33    {
34          return accountNumber;
35    }
36
37    /**
38          Deposits money into the bank account.
39          @param amount  the amount to deposit
40    */
41    public void deposit(double amount)
42    {
43          double newBalance = balance + amount;
44          balance = newBalance;
45    }
46
47    /**
48          Withdraws money from the bank account.
49          @param amount  the amount to withdraw
50    */
51    public void withdraw(double amount)
52    {
53          double newBalance = balance - amount;
54          balance = newBalance;
55    }
56
57    /**
58          Gets the current balance of the bank account.
59          @return  the current balance
60    */
61    public double getBalance()
62    {
63          return balance;
64    }
65
66    private int accountNumber;
67    private double balance;
68 }
```

Output

```
size=3
first account number=1008
last account number=1729
```

SELF CHECK

3. How do you construct an array of 10 strings? An array list of strings?

4. What is the content of names after the following statements?

```
ArrayList<String> names = new ArrayList<String>();
names.add("A");
names.add(0, "B");
names.add("C");
names.remove(1);
```

COMMON ERROR 8.3

Length and Size

Unfortunately, the Java syntax for determining the number of elements in an array, an array list, and a string is not at all consistent.

Data Type	Number of Elements
Array	`a.length`
Array list	`a.size()`
String	`a.length()`

It is a common error to confuse these. You just have to remember the correct syntax for every data type.

QUALITY TIP 8.1

Prefer Parameterized Array Lists

Parameterized array lists, such as `ArrayList<BankAccount>`, were introduced to the Java language in 2004. Versions of Java prior to version 5.0 had only an untyped class `ArrayList`. The untyped array list can hold elements of any class. (Technically, it holds elements of type `Object`, the "lowest common denominator" of all Java classes.) Whenever you retrieve an element from an untyped array list, the compiler requires you to use a cast:

```
ArrayList accounts = new ArrayList();    // Untyped ArrayList
accounts.add(new BankAccount(1729));     // OK—can add any object
BankAccount a = (BankAccount) a.get(0); // Need cast
```

The cast is needed because the compiler does not keep track of the objects that were inserted into the array list, and the array list `get` method has return type `Object`.

Untyped array lists are still a part of the Java language—after all, we want to continue to use programs that were written before 2004. But you should not use them for new code. The casts are tedious and also a bit error-prone. If you apply the wrong cast, the compiler cannot detect your mistake. Instead, your program will throw an exception.

8.3 Wrappers and Auto-boxing

> To treat primitive type values as objects, you must use wrapper classes.

Because numbers are not objects in Java, you cannot directly insert them into array lists. For example, you cannot form an ArrayList<double>. To store sequences of numbers in an array list, you must turn them into objects by using wrapper classes.

There are wrapper classes for all eight primitive types:

Primitive Type	Wrapper Class
byte	Byte
boolean	Boolean
char	Character
double	Double
float	Float
int	Integer
long	Long
short	Short

Note that the wrapper class names start with uppercase letters, and that two of them differ from the names of the corresponding primitive type: Integer and Character.

Each wrapper class object contains a value of the corresponding primitive type. For example, an object of the class Double contains a value of type double (see Figure 5).

Wrapper objects can be used anywhere that objects are required instead of primitive type values. For example, you can collect a sequence of floating-point numbers in an ArrayList<Double>.

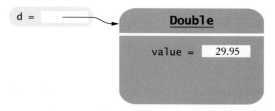

Figure 5   An Object of a Wrapper Class

Starting with Java version 5.0, conversion between primitive types and the corresponding wrapper classes is automatic. This process is called *auto-boxing* (even though *auto-wrapping* would have been more consistent).

For example, if you assign a number to a `Double` object, the number is automatically "put into a box", namely a wrapper object.

```
Double d = 29.95; // auto-boxing; same as Double d = new Double(29.95);
```

If you use an older version of Java, you need to provide the constructor yourself.

Conversely, starting with Java version 5.0, wrapper objects are automatically "unboxed" to primitive types.

```
double x = d; // auto-unboxing; same as double x = d.doubleValue();
```

With older versions, you need to call a method such as `doubleValue`, `intValue` or `booleanValue` for unboxing.

Auto-boxing even works inside arithmetic expressions. For example, the statement

```
Double e = d + 1;
```

is perfectly legal. It means:

- Auto-unbox `d` into a `double`
- Add 1
- Auto-box the result into a new `Double`
- Store a reference to the newly created wrapper object in `e`

If you use Java version 5.0 or higher, array lists of numbers are straightforward. Simply remember to use the wrapper type when you declare the array list, and then rely on auto-boxing.

```
ArrayList<Double> data = new ArrayList<Double>();
data.add(29.95);
double x = data.get(0);
```

With older versions of Java, using wrapper classes to store numbers in an array list is a considerable hassle because you must manually box and unbox the numbers.

No matter which Java version you use, you should know that storing wrapped numbers is quite inefficient. The use of wrappers is acceptable for short array lists, but you should use arrays for long sequences of numbers or characters.

SELF CHECK

5. What is the difference between the types `double` and `Double`?
6. Suppose `data` is an `ArrayList<Double>` of size > 0. How do you increment the element with index 0?

8.4 The Enhanced for Loop

Java version 5.0 introduces a very convenient shortcut for a common loop type. Often, you need to iterate through a sequence of elements—such as the elements of an array or array list. The enhanced for loop makes this process particularly easy to program.

> The enhanced for loop traverses all elements of a collection.

Suppose you want to total up all data values in an array data. Here is how you use the enhanced for loop to carry out that task.

```java
double[] data = . . .;
double sum = 0;
for (double e : data)
{
    sum = sum + e;
}
```

The loop body is executed for each element in the array data. At the beginning of each loop iteration, the next element is assigned to the variable e. Then the loop body is executed. You should read this loop as "for each e in data".

You may wonder why Java doesn't let you write "for each (e in data)". Unquestionably, this would have been neater, and the Java language designers seriously considered this. However, the "for each" construct was added to Java several years after its initial release. Had new keywords each and in been added to the language, then older programs that happened to use those identifiers as variable or method names (such as System.in) would no longer have compiled correctly.

You don't have to use the "for each" construct to loop through all elements in an array. You can implement the same loop with a straightforward for loop and an explicit index variable:

```java
double[] data = . . .;
double sum = 0;
for (int i = 0; i < data.length; i++)
{
    double e = data[i];
    sum = sum + e;
}
```

Note an important difference between the "for each" loop and the ordinary for loop. In the "for each" loop, the *element variable* e is assigned values data[0], data[1], and so on. In the ordinary for loop, the *index variable* i is assigned values 0, 1, and so on.

You can also use the enhanced for loop to visit all elements of an array list. For example, the following loop computes the total value of all accounts:

```java
ArrayList<BankAccount> accounts = . . . ;
double sum = 0;
for (BankAccount a : accounts)
{
    sum = sum + a.getBalance();
}
```

This loop is equivalent to the following ordinary for loop:

```
double sum = 0;
for (int i = 0; i < accounts.size(); i++)
{
    BankAccount a = accounts.get(i);
    sum = sum + a.getBalance();
}
```

The "for each" loop has a very specific purpose: traversing the elements of a collection, from the beginning to the end. Sometimes you don't want to start at the beginning, or you may need to traverse the collection backwards. In those situations, do not hesitate to use an ordinary for loop.

SYNTAX 8.3 **The "for each" Loop**

for (*Type variable* : *collection*)
   statement

Example:

for (double e : data)
   sum = sum + e;

Purpose:

To execute a loop for each element in the collection. In each iteration, the variable is assigned the next element of the collection. Then the statement is executed.

SELF CHECK

7. Write a "for each" loop that prints all elements in the array data.
8. Why is the "for each" loop not an appropriate shortcut for the following ordinary for loop?

```
for (int i = 0; i < data.length; i++) data[i] = i * i;
```

8.5 Simple Array Algorithms

8.5.1 Counting Matches

To count values in an array list, check all elements and count the matches until you reach the end of the array list.

Suppose you want to find how many accounts of a certain type you have. Then you must go through the entire collection and increment a counter each time you find a match. Here we count the number of accounts whose balance is at least as much as a given threshold:

```
public class Bank
{
```

```
      public int count(double atLeast)
      {
         int matches = 0;
         for (BankAccount a : accounts)
         {
            if (a.getBalance() >= atLeast) matches++;
               // Found a match
         }
         return matches;
      }
      . . .
      private ArrayList<BankAccount> accounts;
   }
```

8.5.2 Finding a Value

> To find a value in an array list, check all elements until you have found a match.

Suppose you want to know whether there is a bank account with a particular account number in your bank. Simply inspect each element until you find a match or reach the end of the array list. Note that the loop might fail to find an answer, namely if none of the accounts match. This search process is called a linear search through the array list.

```
public class Bank
{
   public BankAccount find(int accountNumber)
   {
      for (BankAccount a : accounts)
      {
         if (a.getAccountNumber() == accountNumber) // Found a match
            return a;
      }
      return null; // No match in the entire array list
   }
   . . .
}
```

Note that the method returns null if no match is found.

8.5.3 Finding the Maximum or Minimum

> To compute the maximum or minimum value of an array list, initialize a candidate with the starting element. Then compare the candidate with the remaining elements and update it if you find a larger or smaller value.

Suppose you want to find the account with the largest balance in the bank. Keep a candidate for the maximum. If you find an element with a larger value, then replace the candidate with that value. When you have reached the end of the array list, you have found the maximum.

There is just one problem. When you visit the beginning of the array, you don't yet have a candidate for the maximum. One way to overcome that is to set the candidate to the starting element of the array and start the comparison with the next element.

```
BankAccount largestYet = accounts.get(0);
for (int i = 1; i < accounts.size(); i++)
{
   BankAccount a = accounts.get(i);
   if (a.getBalance() > largestYet.getBalance())
      largestYet = a;
}
return largestYet;
```

Now we use an explicit for loop because the loop no longer visits all elements—it skips the starting element.

Of course, this approach works only if there is at least one element in the array list. It doesn't make a lot of sense to ask for the largest element of an empty collection. We can return null in that case:

```
if (accounts.size() == 0) return null;
BankAccount largestYet = accounts.get(0);
. . .
```

See Exercises R8.5 and R8.6 for slight modifications to this algorithm.

To compute the minimum of a data set, keep a candidate for the minimum and replace it whenever you encounter a *smaller* value. At the end of the array list, you have found the minimum.

The following sample program implements a Bank class that stores an array list of bank accounts. The methods of the Bank class use the algorithms that we have discussed in this section.

File Bank.java

```
 1  import java.util.ArrayList;
 2
 3  /**
 4      This bank contains a collection of bank accounts.
 5  */
 6  public class Bank
 7  {
 8     /**
 9         Constructs a bank with no bank accounts.
10     */
11     public Bank()
12     {
13        accounts = new ArrayList<BankAccount>();
14     }
15
16     /**
17         Adds an account to this bank.
18         @param a the account to add
19     */
20     public void addAccount(BankAccount a)
21     {
22        accounts.add(a);
23     }
24
```

```
25    /**
26        Gets the sum of the balances of all accounts in this bank.
27        @return the sum of the balances
28    */
29    public double getTotalBalance()
30    {
31        double total = 0;
32        for (BankAccount a : accounts)
33        {
34            total = total + a.getBalance();
35        }
36        return total;
37    }
38
39    /**
40        Counts the number of bank accounts whose balance is at
41        least a given value.
42        @param atLeast the balance required to count an account
43        @return the number of accounts having at least the given balance
44    */
45    public int count(double atLeast)
46    {
47        int matches = 0;
48        for (BankAccount a : accounts)
49        {
50            if (a.getBalance() >= atLeast) matches++; // Found a match
51        }
52        return matches;
53    }
54
55    /**
56        Finds a bank account with a given number.
57        @param accountNumber the number to find
58        @return the account with the given number, or null if there
59        is no such account
60    */
61    public BankAccount find(int accountNumber)
62    {
63        for (BankAccount a : accounts)
64        {
65            if (a.getAccountNumber() == accountNumber) // Found a match
66                return a;
67        }
68        return null; // No match in the entire array list
69    }
70
71    /**
72        Gets the bank account with the largest balance.
73        @return the account with the largest balance, or null if the
74        bank has no accounts
75    */
76    public BankAccount getMaximum()
77    {
```

```
78          if (accounts.size() == 0) return null;
79          BankAccount largestYet = accounts.get(0);
80          for (int i = 1; i < accounts.size(); i++)
81          {
82             BankAccount a = accounts.get(i);
83             if (a.getBalance() > largestYet.getBalance())
84                largestYet = a;
85          }
86          return largestYet;
87       }
88
89       private ArrayList<BankAccount> accounts;
90    }
```

File BankTester.java

```
1    /**
2        This program tests the Bank class.
3    */
4    public class BankTester
5    {
6       public static void main(String[] args)
7       {
8          Bank firstBankOfJava = new Bank();
9          firstBankOfJava.addAccount(new BankAccount(1001, 20000));
10         firstBankOfJava.addAccount(new BankAccount(1015, 10000));
11         firstBankOfJava.addAccount(new BankAccount(1729, 15000));
12
13         double threshold = 15000;
14         int c = firstBankOfJava.count(threshold);
15         System.out.println(c + " accounts with balance >= " + threshold);
16
17         int accountNumber = 1015;
18         BankAccount a = firstBankOfJava.find(accountNumber);
19         if (a == null)
20            System.out.println("No account with number " + accountNumber);
21         else
22            System.out.println("Account with number " + accountNumber
23                   + " has balance " + a.getBalance());
24
25         BankAccount max = firstBankOfJava.getMaximum();
26         System.out.println("Account with number "
27                + max.getAccountNumber()
28                + " has the largest balance.");
29       }
30    }
```

Output

```
2 accounts with balance >= 15000.0
Account with number 1015 has balance 10000.0
Account with number 1001 has the largest balance.
```

9. What does the find method do if there are two bank accounts with a matching account number?

10. Would it be possible to use a "for each" loop in the getMaximum method?

8.6 Two-Dimensional Arrays

Arrays and array lists can store linear sequences. Occasionally you want to store collections that have a two-dimensional layout. The traditional example is the tic-tac-toe board (see Figure 6).

> Two-dimensional arrays form a tabular, two-dimensional arrangement. You access elements with an index pair a[i][j].

Such an arrangement, consisting of rows and columns of values, is called a two-dimensional array or matrix. When constructing a two-dimensional array, you specify how many rows and columns you need. In this case, ask for 3 rows and 3 columns:

```
final int ROWS = 3;
final int COLUMNS = 3;
String[][] board = new String[ROWS][COLUMNS];
```

This yields a two-dimensional array with 9 elements

```
board[0][0]   board[0][1]   board[0][2]
board[1][0]   board[1][1]   board[1][2]
board[2][0]   board[2][1]   board[2][2]
```

To access a particular element, specify two subscripts in separate brackets:

```
board[i][j] = "x";
```

When filling or searching a two-dimensional array, it is common to use two nested loops. For example, this pair of loops sets all elements in the array to spaces.

```
for (int i = 0; i < ROWS; i++)
   for (int j = 0; j < COLUMNS; j++)
      board[i][j] = " ";
```

Here is a class and a test program for playing tic-tac-toe. This class does not check whether a player has won the game. That is left as the proverbial "exercise for the reader"—see Exercise P8.16.

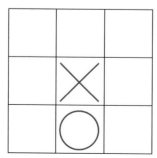

Figure 6
A Tic-Tac-Toe Board

File TicTacToe.java

```java
1   /**
2      A 3 x 3 tic-tac-toe board.
3   */
4   public class TicTacToe
5   {
6      /**
7         Constructs an empty board.
8      */
9      public TicTacToe()
10     {
11        board = new String[ROWS][COLUMNS];
12        // Fill with spaces
13        for (int i = 0; i < ROWS; i++)
14           for (int j = 0; j < COLUMNS; j++)
15              board[i][j] = " ";
16     }
17
18     /**
19        Sets a field in the board. The field must be unoccupied.
20        @param i  the row index
21        @param j  the column index
22        @param player  the player ("x" or "o")
23     */
24     public void set(int i, int j, String player)
25     {
26        if (board[i][j].equals(" "))
27           board[i][j] = player;
28     }
29
30     /**
31        Creates a string representation of the board, such as
32        |x o|
33        | x |
34        | o|.
35        @return  the string representation
36     */
37     public String toString()
38     {
39        String r = "";
40        for (int i = 0; i < ROWS; i++)
41        {
42           r = r + "|";
43           for (int j = 0; j < COLUMNS; j++)
44              r = r + board[i][j];
45           r = r + "|\n";
46        }
47        return r;
48     }
49
50     private String[][] board;
51     private static final int ROWS = 3;
52     private static final int COLUMNS = 3;
53  }
```

File TicTacToeTester.java

```java
1   import java.util.Scanner;
2
3   /**
4       This program tests the TicTacToe class by prompting the
5       user to set positions on the board and printing out the
6       result.
7   */
8   public class TicTacToeTester
9   {
10     public static void main(String[] args)
11     {
12        Scanner in = new Scanner(System.in);
13        String player = "x";
14        TicTacToe game = new TicTacToe();
15        boolean done = false;
16        while (!done)
17        {
18           System.out.print(game.toString());
19           System.out.print(
20              "Row for " + player + " (-1 to exit): ");
21           int row = in.nextInt();
22           if (row < 0) done = true;
23           else
24           {
25              System.out.print("Column for " + player + ": ");
26              int column = in.nextInt();
27              game.set(row, column, player);
28              if (player.equals("x"))
29                 player = "o";
30              else
31                 player = "x";
32           }
33        }
34     }
35  }
```

Output

```
|  |  |
|  |  |
|  |  |
Row for x (-1 to exit): 1
Column for x: 2
|  |  |
|  | x|
|  |  |
Row for o (-1 to exit): 0
Column for o: 0
|o |  |
|  | x|
|  |  |
Row for x (-1 to exit): -1
```

11. How do you declare and initialize a 4-by-4 array of integers?
12. How do you count the number of spaces in the tic-tac-toe board?

HOW TO 8.1

Working with Array Lists and Arrays

Step 1 Pick the appropriate data structure.

As a rule of thumb, your first choice should be an array list. Use an array if you collect numbers (or other primitive type values) and efficiency is an issue, or if you need a two-dimensional array.

Step 2 Construct the array list or array and save a reference in a variable.

For both array lists and arrays, you need to specify the element type. For an array, you also need to specify the length.

```
ArrayList<BankAccount> accounts = new ArrayList<BankAccount>();
double[] balances = new double[n];
```

Step 3 Add elements.

For an array list, simply call the add method. Each call adds an element at the end.

```
accounts.add(new BankAccount(1008));
accounts.add(new BankAccount(1729));
```

For an array, you use index values to access the elements.

```
balance[0] = 29.95;
balance[1] = 1000;
```

Step 4 Process elements.

The most common processing pattern involves visiting all elements in the collection. Use the "for each" loop for this purpose:

```
for (BankAccount a : accounts)
    Do something with a
```

If you don't need to look at all of the elements, use an ordinary loop instead. For example, to skip the initial element, you can use this loop.

```
for (int i = 1; i < accounts.size(); i++)
{
    BankAccount a = accounts.get(i);
        Do something with a
}
```

For arrays, you use .length instead of .size() and [i] instead of .get(i).

Two-Dimensional Arrays with Variable Row Lengths

When you declare a two-dimensional array with the command

```
int[][] a = new int[5][5];
```

then you get a 5-by-5 matrix that can store 25 elements:

```
a[0][0] a[0][1] a[0][2] a[0][3] a[0][4]
a[1][0] a[1][1] a[1][2] a[1][3] a[1][4]
a[2][0] a[2][1] a[2][2] a[2][3] a[2][4]
a[3][0] a[3][1] a[3][2] a[3][3] a[3][4]
a[4][0] a[4][1] a[4][2] a[4][3] a[4][4]
```

In this matrix, all rows have the same length. In Java it is possible to declare arrays in which the row length varies. For example, you can store an array that has a triangular shape, such as this one:

```
b[0][0]
b[1][0] b[1][1]
b[2][0] b[2][1] b[2][2]
b[3][0] b[3][1] b[3][2] b[3][3]
b[4][0] b[4][1] b[4][2] b[4][3] b[4][4]
```

To allocate such an array, you must work harder. First, you allocate space to hold five rows. Indicate that you will manually set each row by leaving the second array index empty:

```
int[][] b = new int[5][];
```

Then allocate each row separately.

```
for (int i = 0; i < b.length; i++)
    b[i] = new int[i + 1];
```

You can access each array element as b[i][j], but be careful that j is less than b[i].length. Naturally, such "ragged" arrays are not very common.

Multidimensional Arrays

You can declare arrays with more than two dimensions. For example, here is a three-dimensional array:

```
int[][][] rubiksCube = new int[3][3][3];
```

Each array element is specified by three index values,

```
rubiksCube[i][j][k]
```

However, these arrays are quite rare, particularly in object-oriented programs, and we will not consider them further.

8.7 Copying Arrays

> An array variable stores a reference to the array. Copying the variable yields a second reference to the same array.

Array variables work just like object variables—they hold a reference to the actual array. If you copy the reference, you get another reference to the same array (see Figure 7):

```java
double[] data = new double[10];
. . . // Fill array
double[] prices = data;
```

> Use the clone method to copy the elements of an array.

If you want to make a true copy of an array, call the clone method (see Figure 8).

```java
double[] prices = (double[]) data.clone();
```

Note that you need to cast the return value of the clone method from the type Object to the type double[].

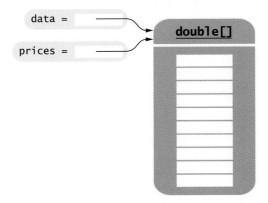

Figure 7   Two References to the Same Array

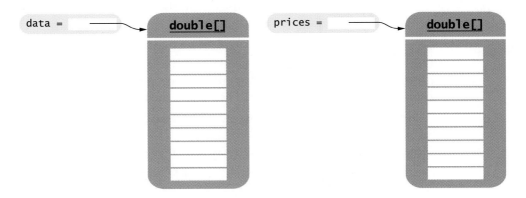

Figure 8   Cloning an Array

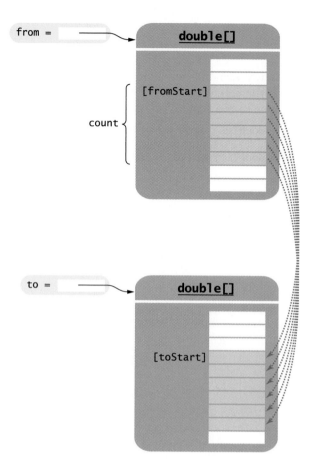

Figure 9 The System.arraycopy Method

Use the System.arraycopy method to copy elements from one array to another.

Occasionally, you need to copy elements from one array into another array. You can use the static System.arraycopy method for that purpose (see Figure 9):

```
System.arraycopy(from, fromStart, to, toStart, count);
```

One use for the System.arraycopy method is to add or remove elements in the middle of an array. To add a new element at position i into data, first move all elements from i onward one position up. Then insert the new value.

```
System.arraycopy(data, i, data, i + 1, data.length - i - 1);
data[i] = x;
```

Note that the last element in the array is lost (see Figure 10).

To remove the element at position i, copy the elements above the position downward (see Figure 11).

```
System.arraycopy(data, i + 1, data, i, data.length - i - 1);
```

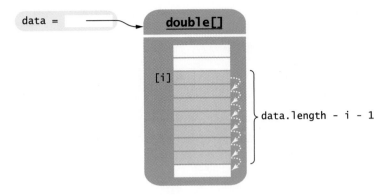

Figure 10   Inserting a New Element into an Array

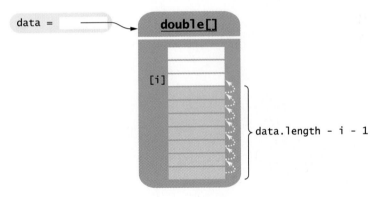

Figure 11   Removing an Element from an Array

Another use for System.arraycopy is to grow an array that has run out of space. Follow these steps:

- Create a new, larger array.
    ```
    double[] newData = new double[2 * data.length]; ❶
    ```
- Copy all elements into the new array
    ```
    System.arraycopy(data, 0, newData, 0, data.length); ❷
    ```
- Store the reference to the new array in the array variable.
    ```
    data = newData; ❸
    ```

Figure 12 shows the process.

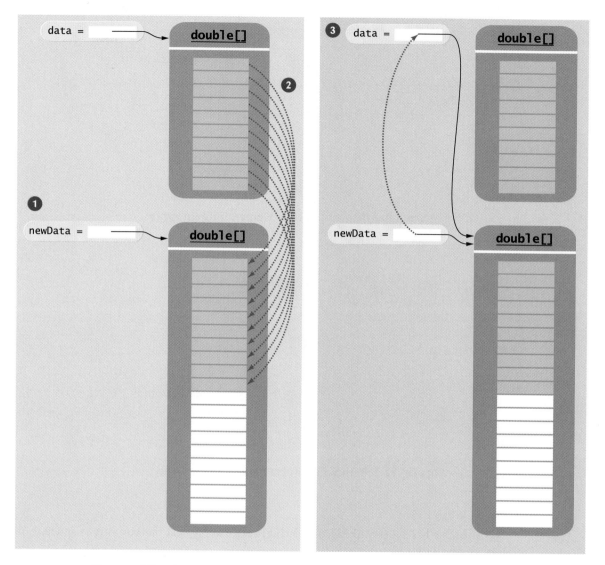

Figure 12   Growing an Array

13. How do you add or remove elements in the middle of an array list?

14. Why do we double the length of the array when it has run out of space rather than increasing it by one element?

COMMON ERROR 8.4

Underestimating the Size of a Data Set

Programmers commonly underestimate the amount of input data that a user will pour into an unsuspecting program. The most common problem caused by underestimating the amount of input data results from the use of fixed-sized arrays. Suppose you write a program to search for text in a file. You store each line in a string, and keep an array of strings. How big do you make the array? Surely nobody is going to challenge your program with an input that is more than 100 lines. Really? A smart grader can easily feed in the entire text of *Alice in Wonderland* or *War and Peace* (which are available on the Internet). All of a sudden, your program has to deal with tens or hundreds of thousands of lines. What will it do? Will it handle the input? Will it politely reject the excess input? Will it crash and burn?

A famous article [1] analyzed how several UNIX programs reacted when they were fed large or random data sets. Sadly, about a quarter didn't do well at all, crashing or hanging without a reasonable error message. For example, in some versions of UNIX the tape backup program tar cannot handle file names that are longer than 100 characters, which is a pretty unreasonable limitation. Many of these shortcomings are caused by features of the C language that, unlike Java, make it difficult to store strings of arbitrary size.

QUALITY TIP 8.2

Make Parallel Arrays into Arrays of Objects

Programmers who are familiar with arrays, but unfamiliar with object-oriented programming, sometimes distribute information across separate arrays. Here is a typical example. A program needs to manage bank data, consisting of account numbers and balances. Don't store the account numbers and balances in separate arrays.

```
// Don't do this
int[] accountNumbers;
double[] balances;
```

Arrays such as these are called parallel arrays (Figure 13). The ith slice (accountNumbers[i] and balances[i]) contains data that need to be processed together.

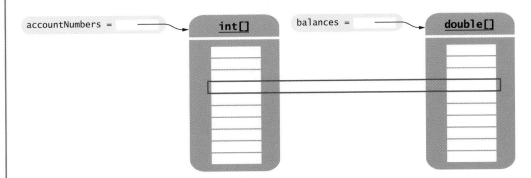

Figure 13   Avoid Parallel Arrays

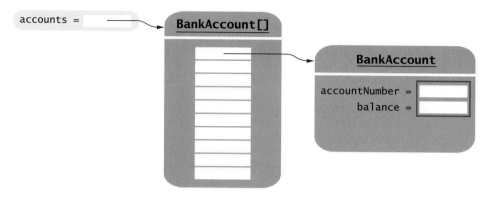

Figure 14   Reorganizing Parallel Arrays into an Array of Objects

> Avoid parallel arrays by changing them into arrays of objects.

If you find yourself using two arrays that have the same length, ask yourself whether you couldn't replace them with a single array of a class type. Look at a slice and find the concept that it represents. Then make the concept into a class. In our example each slice contains an account number and a balance, describing a bank account. Therefore, it is an easy matter to use a single array of objects

```
BankAccount[] accounts;
```

(See Figure 14.) Or, even better, use an `ArrayList<BankAccount>`.

Why is this beneficial? Think ahead. Maybe your program will change and you will need to store the owner of the bank account as well. It is a simple matter to update the `BankAccount` class. It may well be quite complicated to add a new array and make sure that all methods that accessed the original two arrays now also correctly access the third one.

ADVANCED TOPIC 8.4

Partially Filled Arrays

Suppose you write a program that reads a sequence of numbers into an array. How many numbers will the user enter? You can't very well ask the user to count the items before entering them—that is just the kind of work that the user expects the computer to do. Unfortunately, you now run into a problem. You need to set the size of the array before you know how many elements you need. Once the array size is set, it cannot be changed.

To solve this problem, make an array that is guaranteed to be larger than the largest possible number of entries, and partially fill it. For example, you can decide that the user will never enter more than 100 data values. Then allocate an array of size 100:

```
final int DATA_LENGTH = 100;
double[] data = new double[DATA_LENGTH];
```

Then keep a companion variable that tells how many elements in the array are actually used. It is an excellent idea always to name this companion variable by adding the suffix `Size` to the name of the array.

```
int dataSize = 0;
```

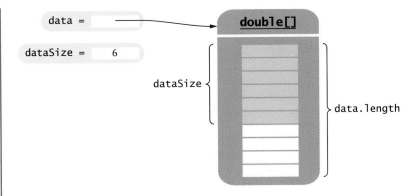

Figure 15 A Partially Filled Array

Now `data.length` is the capacity of the array `data`, and `dataSize` is the current size of the array (see Figure 15). Keep adding elements into the array, incrementing the `dataSize` variable each time.

```
data[dataSize] = x;
dataSize++;
```

This way, `dataSize` always contains the correct element count. When you run out of space, make a new array and copy the elements into it, as described in the preceding section.

Arrays lists use this technique behind the scenes. An array list contains an array of objects. When the array runs out of space, the array list allocates a larger array and copies the data. However, all of this happens inside the array list methods, so you never need to think about it.

ADVANCED TOPIC 8.5

Methods with a Variable Number of Parameters

Starting with Java version 5.0, it is possible to declare methods that receive a variable number of parameters. For example, we can modify the `add` method of the `DataSet` class of Chapter 7 so that one can add any number of values:

```
data.add(1, 3, 7);
data.add(4);
data.add(); // OK but useless
```

The modified `add` method must be declared as

```
public void add(double... xs)
```

The `...` symbol indicates that the method can receive any number of `double` values. The `xs` parameter is actually a `double[]` array that contains all values that were passed to the method. The method implementation traverses the parameter array and processes the values:

```
for (x : xs)
{
    sum = sum + x;
}
```

RANDOM FACT 8.1

An Early Internet Worm

In November 1988, a graduate student at Cornell University launched a virus program that infected about 6,000 computers connected to the Internet across the United States. Tens of thousands of computer users were unable to read their e-mail or otherwise use their computers. All major universities and many high-tech companies were affected. (The Internet was much smaller then than it is now.)

The particular kind of virus used in this attack is called a worm. The virus program crawled from one computer on the Internet to the next. The entire program is quite complex; its major parts are explained in [2]. However, one of the methods used in the attack is of interest here. The worm would attempt to connect to finger, a program in the UNIX operating system for finding information on a user who has an account on a particular computer on the network. Like many programs in UNIX, finger was written in the C language. C does not have array lists, only arrays, and when you construct an array in C, as in Java, you have to make up your mind how many elements you need. To store the user name to be looked up (say, walters@cs.sjsu.edu), the finger program allocated an array of 512 characters, under the assumption that nobody would ever provide such a long input. Unfortunately, C, unlike Java, does not check that an array index is less than the length of the array. If you write into an array, using an index that is too large, you simply overwrite memory locations that belong to some other objects. In some versions of the finger program, the programmer had been lazy and had not checked whether the array holding the input characters was large enough to hold the input. So the worm program purposefully filled the 512-character array with 536 bytes. The excess 24 bytes would overwrite a return address, which the attacker knew was stored just after the line buffer. When that function was finished, it didn't return to its caller but to code supplied by the worm (see Figure 16). That code ran under the same super-user privileges as finger, allowing the worm to gain entry into the remote system.

Had the programmer who wrote finger been more conscientious, this particular attack would not be possible. In C++ and C, all programmers must be especially careful not to overrun array boundaries.

One may well wonder what would possess a skilled programmer to spend many weeks or months to plan the antisocial act of breaking into thousands of computers and disabling them. It appears that the break-in was fully intended by the author, but the disabling of the computers was a side effect of continuous reinfection and efforts by the worm to avoid being

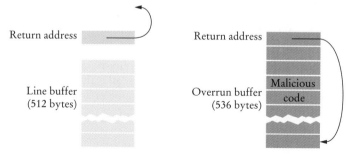

Return address

Line buffer
(512 bytes)

Return address

Overrun buffer
(536 bytes)

Malicious code

Figure 16 A "Buffer Overrun" Attack

killed. It is not clear whether the author was aware that these moves would cripple the attacked machines.

In recent years, the novelty of vandalizing other people's computers has worn off somewhat, and there are fewer jerks with programming skills who write new viruses. Other attacks by individuals with more criminal energy, whose intent has been to steal information or money, have surfaced. See [3] for a very readable account of the discovery and apprehension of one such person.

CHAPTER SUMMARY

1. An array is a sequence of values of the same type.

2. You access array elements with an integer index, using the notation a[i].

3. Index values of an array range from 0 to length - 1. Accessing a nonexistent element results in a bounds error.

4. Use the length field to find the number of elements in an array.

5. The ArrayList class manages a sequence of objects.

6. The ArrayList class is a generic class: ArrayList<T> collects objects of type T.

7. To treat primitive type values as objects, you must use wrapper classes.

8. The enhanced for loop traverses all elements of a collection.

9. To count values in an array list, check all elements and count the matches until you reach the end of the array list.

10. To find a value in an array list, check all elements until you have found a match.

11. To compute the maximum or minimum value of an array list, initialize a candidate with the starting element. Then compare the candidate with the remaining elements and update it if you find a larger or smaller value.

12. Two-dimensional arrays form a tabular, two-dimensional arrangement. You access elements with an index pair a[i][j].

13. An array variable stores a reference to the array. Copying the variable yields a second reference to the same array.

14. Use the clone method to copy the elements of an array.

15. Use the System.arraycopy method to copy elements from one array to another.

16. Avoid parallel arrays by changing them into arrays of objects.

FURTHER READING

1. Barton P. Miller, Louis Fericksen, and Bryan So, "An Empirical Study of the Reliability of Unix Utilities", *Communications of the ACM*, vol. 33, no. 12 (December 1990), pp. 32–44.

2. Peter J. Denning, *Computers under Attack*, Addison-Wesley, 1990.

3. Cliff Stoll, *The Cuckoo's Egg*, Doubleday, 1989.

CLASSES, OBJECTS, AND METHODS INTRODUCED IN THIS CHAPTER

```
java.lang.Boolean
   booleanValue
java.lang.Double
   doubleValue
java.lang.Integer
   intValue
java.lang.System
   arraycopy
java.util.ArrayList<E>
   add
   get
   remove
   set
   size
```

REVIEW EXERCISES

Exercise R8.1. What is an index? What are the bounds of an array list? What is a bounds error?

Exercise R8.2. Write a program that contains a bounds error. Run the program. What happens on your computer? How does the error message help you locate the error?

Exercise R8.3. Write Java code for a loop that simultaneously computes the maximum and minimum values of an array list. Use an array list of accounts as an example.

Exercise R8.4. Write a loop that reads 10 strings and inserts them into an array list. Write a second loop that prints out the strings in the opposite order from which they were entered.

Exercise R8.5. Consider the algorithm that we used for determining the maximum value in an array list. We set largestYet to the starting element, which meant that we were no longer able to use the "for each" loop. An alternate approach is to initialize largestYet with null, then loop through all elements. Of course, inside the loop you need to test whether largestYet is still null. Modify the loop that finds the bank account with the largest balance, using this technique. Is this approach more or less efficient than the one used in the text?

Exercise R8.6. Consider another variation of the algorithm for determining the maximum value. Here, we compute the maximum value of an array of numbers.

```
double max = 0; // Contains an error!
for (x : values)
{
    if (x > max) max = x;
}
```

However, this approach contains a subtle error. What is the error, and how can you fix it?

Exercise R8.7. For each of the following sets of values, write code that fills an array a with the values.

a. 1 2 3 4 5 6 7 8 9 10

b. 0 2 4 6 8 10 12 14 16 18 20

c. 1 4 9 16 25 36 49 64 81 100

d. 0 0 0 0 0 0 0 0 0 0

e. 1 4 9 16 9 7 4 9 11

Use a loop when appropriate.

Exercise R8.8. Write a loop that fills an array a with 10 random numbers between 1 and 100. Write code (using one or more loops) to fill a with 10 different random numbers between 1 and 100.

Exercise R8.9. What is wrong with the following loop?

```
double[] data = new double[10];
for (int i = 1; i <= 10; i++) data[i] = i * i;
```

Explain two ways of fixing the error.

Exercise R8.10. Write a program that constructs an array of 20 integers and fills the first ten elements with the numbers 1, 4, 9, . . . , 100. Compile it and launch the debugger. After the array has been filled with three numbers, inspect it. What are the contents of the elements in the array beyond those that you filled?

Exercise R8.11. Rewrite the following loops without using the "for each" construct. Here, data is an array of double values.

a. `for (x : data) sum = sum + x;`

b. `for (x : data) if (x == target) return true;`

c. `int i = 0;`
   `for (x : data) { data [i] = 2 * x; i++; }`

Exercise R8.12. Rewrite the following loops, using the "for each" construct. Here, data is an array of double values.

   a. `for (int i = 0; i < data.length; i++) sum = sum + data[i];`

   b. `for (int i = 1; i < data.length; i++) sum = sum + data[i];`

   c. `for (int i = 0; i < data.length; i++)`
        `if (data[i] == target) return i;`

Exercise R8.13. Give an example of

   a. A useful method that has an array of integers as a parameter that is not modified.

   b. A useful method that has an array of integers as a parameter that is modified.

   c. A useful method that has an array of integers as a return value.

Describe each method; don't implement the methods.

Exercise R8.14. A method that has an array list as a parameter can change the contents in two ways. It can change the contents of individual array elements, or it can rearrange the elements. Describe two useful methods with `ArrayList<BankAccount>` parameters that change an array list of `BankAccount` objects in each of the two ways just described.

Exercise R8.15. What are parallel arrays? Why are parallel arrays indications of poor programming? How can they be avoided?

Exercise R8.16. How do you perform the following tasks with arrays in Java?

   a. Test that two arrays contain the same elements in the same order

   b. Copy one array to another

   c. Fill an array with zeroes, overwriting all elements in it

   d. Remove all elements from an array list

Exercise R8.17. True or false?

   a. All elements of an array are of the same type.

   b. Array subscripts must be integers.

   c. Arrays cannot contain string references as elements.

   d. Arrays cannot use strings as subscripts.

   e. Parallel arrays must have equal length.

   f. Two-dimensional arrays always have the same numbers of rows and columns.

   g. Two parallel arrays can be replaced by a two-dimensional array.

   h. Elements of different columns in a two-dimensional array can have different types.

   i. Elements in an array list can have different types.

Exercise R8.18. True or false?

   a. A method cannot return a two-dimensional array.

   b. A method can change the length of an array parameter.

   c. A method can change the length of an array list that is passed as a parameter.

   d. An array list can hold values of any type.

PROGRAMMING EXERCISES

Exercise P8.1. Add the following methods to the Bank class:

```
public void addAccount(int accountNumber, double initialBalance)
public void deposit(int accountNumber, double amount)
public void withdraw(int accountNumber, double amount)
public double getBalance(int accountNumber)
```

Exercise P8.2. Implement a class Purse. A purse contains a collection of coins. For simplicity, we will only store the coin names in an ArrayList<String>. (We will discuss a better representation in Chapter 9.) Supply a method

```
void addCoin(String coinName)
```

Add a method toString to the Purse class that prints the coins in the purse in the format

```
Purse[Quarter,Dime,Nickel,Dime]
```

Exercise P8.3. Write a method reverse that reverses the sequence of coins in a purse. Use the toString method of the preceding assignment to test your code. For example, if reverse is called with a purse

```
Purse[Quarter,Dime,Nickel,Dime]
```

then the purse is changed to

```
Purse[Dime,Nickel,Dime,Quarter]
```

Exercise P8.4. Add a method

```
public void transfer(Purse other)
```

that transfers the contents of one purse to another. For example, if a is

```
Purse[Quarter,Dime,Nickel,Dime]
```

and b is

```
Purse[Dime,Nickel]
```

then after the call a.transfer(b), a is

```
Purse[Quarter,Dime,Nickel,Dime,Dime,Nickel]
```

and b is empty.

Exercise P8.5. Write a method for the Purse class

```
public boolean sameContents(Purse other)
```

that checks whether the other purse has the same coins in the same order.

Exercise P8.6. Write a method for the Purse class

```
public boolean sameCoins(Purse other)
```

that checks whether the other purse has the same coins, perhaps in a different order. For example, the purses

```
Purse[Quarter,Dime,Nickel,Dime]
```

and

```
Purse[Nickel,Dime,Dime,Quarter]
```

should be considered equal.

You will probably need one or more helper methods.

Exercise P8.7. Implement a class `Cloud` that contains an array list of `Point2D.Double` objects. Support methods

```
public void add(Point2D.Double aPoint)
public void draw(Graphics2D g2)
```

Draw each point as a tiny circle.

Write a graphical application that draws a cloud of 20 random points.

Exercise P8.8. Implement a class `Polygon` that contains an array list of `Point2D.Double` objects. Support methods

```
public void add(Point2D.Double aPoint)
public void draw(Graphics2D g2)
```

Draw the polygon by joining adjacent points with a line, and then closing it up by joining the end and start points.

Write a graphical application that draws a square and a pentagon using two `Polygon` objects.

Exercise P8.9. Write methods of the `Polygon` class of Exercise P8.8

```
public double perimeter()
```

and

```
public double area()
```

that compute the circumference and area of a polygon. To compute the perimeter, compute the distance between adjacent points, and total up the distances. The area of a polygon with corners $(x_0, y_0), \ldots, (x_{n-1}, y_{n-1})$ is

$$\frac{1}{2}\left(x_0 y_1 + x_1 y_2 + \cdots + x_{n-1} y_0 - y_0 x_1 - y_1 x_2 - \cdots - y_{n-1} x_0\right)$$

As test cases, compute the perimeter and area of a rectangle and of a regular hexagon.

Exercise P8.10. Write a program that reads a sequence of integers into an array and that computes the alternating sum of all elements in the array. For example, if the program is executed with the input data

$$1 \quad 4 \quad 9 \quad 16 \quad 9 \quad 7 \quad 4 \quad 9 \quad 11$$

then it computes

$$1 - 4 + 9 - 16 + 9 - 7 + 4 - 9 + 11 = -2$$

Exercise P8.11. Write a program that produces random permutations of the numbers 1 to 10. To generate a random permutation, you need to fill an array with the numbers 1 to 10 so that no two entries of the array have the same contents. You could do it by brute force, by calling `Random.nextInt` until it produces a value that is not yet in the array. Instead, you should implement a smart method. Make a second array and fill it with the numbers 1 to 10. Then pick one of those at random, remove it, and append it to the permutation array. Repeat 10 times. Implement a class `PermutationGenerator` with a method

```
int[] nextPermutation
```

Exercise P8.12. Write a class `Chart` with methods

```
public void add(int value)
public void draw(Graphics2D g2)
```

that displays a stick chart of the added values, like this:

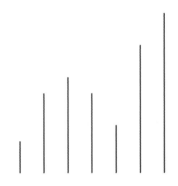

You may assume that the values are pixel positions.

Exercise P8.13. Write a class `BarChart` with methods

```
public void add(double value)
public void draw(Graphics2D g2)
```

that displays a chart of the added values. You may assume that all values in `data` are positive. Stretch the bars so that they fill the entire area of the screen. You must figure out the maximum of the values, and then scale each bar.

Exercise P8.14. Improve the `BarChart` class of Exercise P8.13 to work correctly when the data contains negative values.

Exercise P8.15. Write a class `PieChart` with methods

```
public void add(double value)
public void draw(Graphics2D g2)
```

that displays a pie chart of the values in `data`. You may assume that all data values are positive.

Exercise P8.16. Add a method `getWinner` to the `TicTacToe` class of Section 8.6. It should return "x" or "o" to indicate a winner, or " " if there is no winner yet. Recall that a winning position has three matching marks in a row, column, or diagonal.

Exercise P8.17. Write a graphical application that plays tic-tac-toe. Your program should draw the game board, change players after every successful move, and pronounce the winner.

Exercise P8.18. *Magic squares.* An $n \times n$ matrix that is filled with the numbers 1, 2, 3, . . . , n^2 is a magic square if the sum of the elements in each row, in each column, and in the two diagonals is the same value. For example,

16	3	2	13
5	10	11	8
9	6	7	12
4	15	14	1

Write a program that reads in n^2 values from the keyboard and tests whether they form a magic square when arranged as a square matrix. You need to test three features:

- Did the user enter n^2 numbers for some n?
- Do each of the numbers 1, 2, . . . , n^2 occur exactly once in the user input?
- When the numbers are put into a square, are the sums of the rows, columns, and diagonals equal to each other?

If the size of the input is a square, test whether all numbers between 1 and n^2 are present. Then compute the row, column, and diagonal sums. Implement a class Square with methods

```
public void add(int i)
public boolean isMagic()
```

Exercise P8.19. Implement the following algorithm to construct magic n-by-n^2 squares; it works only if n is odd. Place a 1 in the middle of the bottom row. After k has been placed in the (i, j) square, place $k + 1$ into the square to the right and down, wrapping around the borders. However, if the square to the right and down has already been filled, or if you are in the lower-right corner, then you must move to the square straight up instead. Here is the 5×5 square that you get if you follow this method:

11	18	25	2	9
10	12	19	21	3
4	6	13	20	22
23	5	7	14	16
17	24	1	8	15

Write a program whose input is the number n and whose output is the magic square of order n if n is odd. Implement a class `MagicSquare` with a constructor that constructs the square and a `toString` method that returns a representation of the square.

PROGRAMMING PROJECTS

Project 8.1. *Poker Simulator.* In this assignment, you will implement a simulation of a popular casino game usually called video poker. The card deck contains 52 cards, 13 of each suit. At the beginning of the game, the deck is shuffled. You need to devise a fair method for shuffling. (It does not have to be efficient.) Then the top five cards of the deck are presented to the player. The player can reject none, some, or all of the cards. The rejected cards are replaced from the top of the deck. Now the hand is scored. Your program should pronounce it to be one of the following:

- No pair—The lowest hand, containing five separate cards that do not match up to create any of the hands below.
- One pair—Two cards of the same value, for example two queens.
- Two pairs—Two pairs, for example two queens and two 5's.
- Three of a kind—Three cards of the same value, for example three queens.
- Straight—Five cards with consecutive values, not necessarily of the same suit, such as 4, 5, 6, 7, and 8. The ace can either precede a 2 or follow a king.
- Flush—Five cards, not necessarily in order, of the same suit.
- Full House—Three of a kind and a pair, for example three queens and two 5's
- Four of a Kind—Four cards of the same value, such as four queens.
- Straight Flush—A straight and a flush: Five cards with consecutive values of the same suit.
- Royal Flush—The best possible hand in poker. A 10, jack, queen, king, and ace, all of the same suit.

If you are so inclined, you can implement a wager. The player pays a JavaDollar for each game, and wins according to the following payout chart:

Hand	Payout	Hand	Payout
Royal Flush	250	Straight	4
Straight Flush	50	Three of a Kind	3
Four of a Kind	25	Two Pair	2
Full House	6	Pair of Jacks or Better	1
Flush	5		

Project 8.2. *The Game of Life* is a well-known mathematical game that gives rise to amazingly complex behavior, although it can be specified by a few simple rules. (It is not actually a game in the traditional sense, with players competing for a win.) Here are the rules. The game is played on a rectangular board. Each square can be either empty or occupied. At the beginning, you can specify empty and occupied cells in some way; then the game runs automatically. In each *generation*, the next generation is computed. A new cell is born on an empty square if it is surrounded by exactly three occupied neighbor cells. A cell dies of overcrowding if it is surrounded by four or more neighbors, and it dies of loneliness if it is surrounded by zero or one neighbor. A neighbor is an occupant of an adjacent square to the left, right, top, or bottom or in a diagonal direction. Figure 17 shows a cell and its neighbor cells.

Many configurations show interesting behavior when subjected to these rules. Figure 18 shows a *glider*, observed over five generations. Note how it moves. After four generations, it is transformed into the identical shape, but located one square to the right and below.

One of the more amazing configurations is the glider gun: a complex collection of cells that, after 30 moves, turns back into itself and a glider (see Figure 19).

Program the game to eliminate the drudgery of computing successive generations by hand. Use a two-dimensional array to store the rectangular configuration. Write a program that shows successive generations of the game. You may get extra credit if you implement a graphical application that allows the user to add or remove cells by clicking with the mouse.

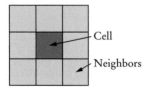

Figure 17   Neighborhood of a Cell in the Game of Life

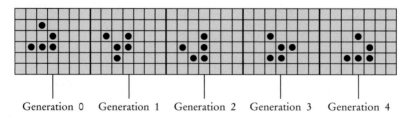

Generation 0   Generation 1   Generation 2   Generation 3   Generation 4

Figure 18   Glider

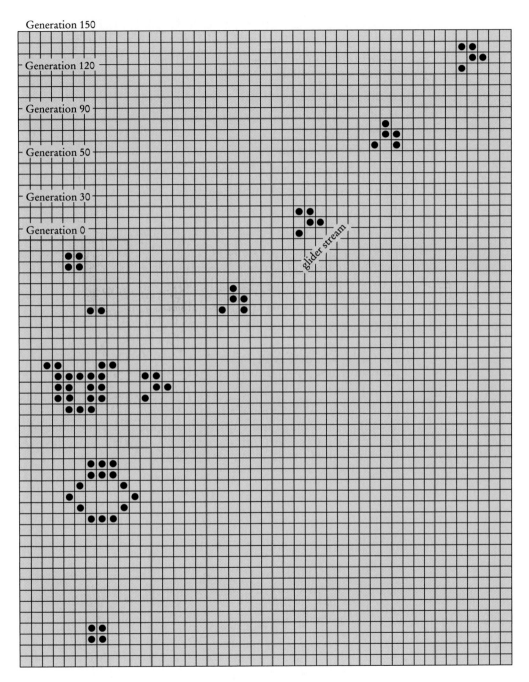

Figure 19   Glider Gun

ANSWERS TO SELF-CHECK QUESTIONS

1. 0, 1, 4, 9, 16, 25, 36, 49, 64, 81, but *not* 100.

2. **a.** 0

   b. a run-time error: array index out of bounds

   c. a compile-time error: c is not initialized

3. `new String[10];`
   `new ArrayList<String>();`

4. names contains the strings "B" and "C" at positions 0 and 1.

5. double is one of the eight primitive types. Double is a class type.

6. `data.set(0, data.get(0) + 1);`

7. `for (double x : data) System.out.println(x);`

8. The loop writes a value into data[i]. The "for each" loop does not have the index variable i.

9. It returns the first match that it finds.

10. Yes, but the first comparison would always fail.

11. `int[][] array = new int[4][4];`

12. ```
    int count = 0;
    for (int i = 0; i < ROWS; i++)
       for (int j = 0; j < COLUMNS; j++)
          if (board[i][j].equals(" ")) count++;
    ```

13. Use the add and remove methods.

14. Allocating a new array and copying the elements is time-consuming. You wouldn't want to go through the process every time you add an element.
    ```

Designing Classes

CHAPTER GOALS

- To learn how to choose appropriate classes to implement
- To understand the concepts of cohesion and coupling
- To minimize the use of side effects
- To document the responsibilities of methods and their callers with preconditions and postconditions
- To understand the difference between instance methods and static methods
- To introduce the concept of static fields
- To understand the scope rules for local variables and instance fields
- To learn about packages

In this chapter you will learn more about designing classes. First, we will discuss the process of discovering classes and defining methods. Next, we will discuss how the concepts of pre- and postconditions enable you to specify, implement, and invoke methods correctly. You will also learn about several more technical issues, such as static methods and variables. Finally, you will see how to use packages to organize your classes.

CHAPTER CONTENTS

9.1 Choosing Classes

You have used a good number of classes in the preceding chapters and probably designed a few classes yourself as part of your programming assignments. Designing a class can be a challenge—it is not always easy to tell how to start or whether the result is of good quality.

Students who have prior experience with programming in another programming language are used to programming *functions*. A function carries out an action. In object-oriented programming, the actions appear as methods. Each method, however, belongs to a class. Classes are collections of objects, and objects are not actions—they are entities. So you have to start the programming activity by identifying objects and the classes to which they belong.

Remember the rule of thumb from Chapter 2: Class names should be nouns, and method names should be verbs.

> A class should represent a single concept from the problem domain, such as business, science, or mathematics.

What makes a good class? Most importantly, a class should *represent a single concept*. Some of the classes that you have seen represent concepts from mathematics:

- `Point`
- `Rectangle`
- `Ellipse`

Other classes are abstractions of real-life entities.

- BankAccount
- CashRegister

For these classes, the properties of a typical object are easy to understand. A Rectangle object has a width and height. Given a BankAccount object, you can deposit and withdraw money. Generally, concepts from the part of the universe that a program concerns, such as science, business, or a game, make good classes. The name for such a class should be a noun that describes the concept. Some of the standard Java class names are a bit strange, such as Ellipse2D.Double, but you can choose better names for your own classes.

Another useful category of classes can be described as *actors*. Objects of an actor class do some kinds of work for you. Examples of actors are the Scanner class of Chapter 4 and the Random class in Chapter 7. A Scanner object scans a stream for numbers and strings. A Random object generates random numbers. It is a good idea to choose class names for actors that end in "-er" or "-or". (A better name for the Random class might be RandomNumberGenerator.)

Very occasionally, a class has no objects, but it contains a collection of related static methods and constants. The Math class is a typical example. Such a class is called a *utility class*.

Finally, you have seen classes with only a main method. Their sole purpose is to start a program. From a design perspective, these are somewhat degenerate examples of classes.

What might not be a good class? If you can't tell from the class name what an object of the class is supposed to do, then you are probably not on the right track. For example, your homework assignment might ask you to write a program that prints paychecks. Suppose you start by trying to design a class PaycheckProgram. What would an object of this class do? An object of this class would have to do everything that the homework needs to do. That doesn't simplify anything. A better class would be Paycheck. Then your program can manipulate one or more Paycheck objects.

Another common mistake, particularly by students who are used to writing programs that consist of functions, is to turn an action into a class. For example, if your homework assignment is to compute a paycheck, you may consider writing a class ComputePaycheck. But can you visualize a "ComputePaycheck" object? The fact that "ComputePaycheck" isn't a noun tips you off that you are on the wrong track. On the other hand, a Paycheck class makes intuitive sense. The word "paycheck" is a noun. You can visualize a paycheck object. You can then think about useful methods of the Paycheck class, such as computeTaxes, that help you solve the assignment.

SELF CHECK

1. What is the rule of thumb for finding classes?
2. Your job is to write a program that plays chess. Might ChessBoard be an appropriate class? How about MovePiece?

9.2 Cohesion and Coupling

In this section you will learn two useful criteria for analyzing the quality of the public interface of a class.

> The public interface of a class is cohesive if all of its features are related to the concept that the class represents.

A class should represent a single concept. The public methods and constants that the public interface exposes should be *cohesive*. That is, all interface features should be closely related to the single concept that the class represents.

If you find that the public interface of a class refers to multiple concepts, then that is a good sign that it may be time to use separate classes instead. Consider, for example, the public interface of the CashRegister class in Chapter 4:

```java
public class CashRegister
{
    public void enterPayment(int dollars, int quarters,
            int dimes, int nickels, int pennies)
    . . .
    public static final double NICKEL_VALUE = 0.05;
    public static final double DIME_VALUE = 0.1;
    public static final double QUARTER_VALUE = 0.25;
    . . .
}
```

There are really two concepts here: a cash register that holds coins and computes their total, and the values of individual coins. (For simplicity, we assume that the cash register only holds coins, not bills. Exercise P9.1 discusses a more general solution.)

It makes sense to have a separate Coin class and have coins responsible for knowing their values.

```java
public class Coin
{
    public Coin(double aValue, String aName) { . . . }
    public double getValue() { . . . }
    . . .
}
```

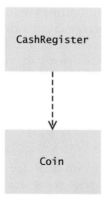

Figure 1
Dependency Relationship Between
the CashRegister and Coin Classes

Then the CashRegister class can be simplified:

```
public class CashRegister
{
    public void enterPayment(int coinCount, Coin coinType) { . . . }
    . . .
}
```

Now the CashRegister class no longer needs to know anything about coin values. The same class can equally well handle euros or zorkmids!

This is clearly a better solution, because it separates the responsibilities of the cash register and the coins. The only reason we didn't follow this approach in Chapter 4 was to keep the CashRegister example simple.

> A class depends on another class if it uses objects of that class.

Many classes need other classes in order to do their jobs. For example, the restructured CashRegister class now depends on the Coin class to determine the value of the payment.

To visualize relationships, such as dependence between classes, programmers draw class diagrams. In this book, we use the UML ("Unified Modeling Language") notation for objects and classes. UML is a notation for object-oriented analysis and design invented by Grady Booch, Ivar Jacobson, and James Rumbaugh, three leading researchers in object-oriented software development. The UML notation distinguishes between *object diagrams* and class diagrams. In an object diagram the class names are underlined; in a class diagram the class names are not underlined. In a class diagram, you denote dependency by a dashed line with a >-shaped open arrow tip that points to the dependent class. Figure 1 shows a class diagram indicating that the CashRegister class depends on the Coin class.

Note that the Coin class does *not* depend on the CashRegister class. Coins have no idea that they are being collected in cash registers, and they can carry out their work without ever calling any method in the CashRegister class.

If many classes of a program depend on each other, then we say that the *coupling* between classes is high. Conversely, if there are few dependencies between classes, then we say that the coupling is low (see Figure 2).

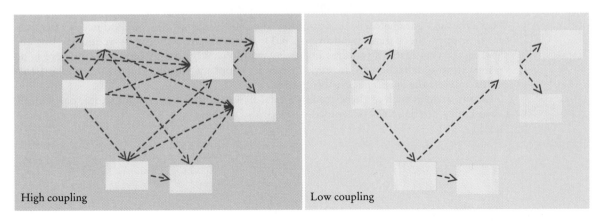

High coupling | Low coupling

Figure 2   High and Low Coupling Between Classes

> It is a good practice to minimize the coupling (i.e., dependency) between classes.

Why does coupling matter? If the Coin class changes in the next release of the program, all the classes that depend on it may be affected. If the change is drastic, the coupled classes must all be updated. Furthermore, if we would like to use a class in another program, we have to take with it all the classes on which it depends. Thus, we want to remove unnecessary coupling between classes.

SELF CHECK

3. Why is the CashRegister class from Chapter 4 not cohesive?
4. Why does the Coin class not depend on the CashRegister class?
5. Why should coupling be minimized between classes?

QUALITY TIP 9.1

Consistency

In this section you learned of two criteria to analyze the quality of the public interface of a class. You should maximize cohesion and remove unnecessary coupling. There is another criterion that we would like you to pay attention to—*consistency*. When you have a set of methods, follow a consistent scheme for their names and parameters. This is simply a sign of good craftsmanship.

Sadly, you can find any number of inconsistencies in the standard library. Here is an example. To show an input dialog box, you call

```
JOptionPane.showInputDialog(promptString)
```

To show a message dialog box, you call

```
JOptionPane.showMessageDialog(null, messageString)
```

What's the null parameter? It turns out that the showMessageDialog method needs a parameter to specify the parent window, or null if no parent window is required. But the showInputDialog method requires no parent window. Why the inconsistency? There is no reason. It would have been an easy matter to supply a showMessageDialog method that exactly mirrors the showInputDialog method.

Inconsistencies such as these are not a fatal flaw, but they are an annoyance, particularly because they can be so easily avoided.

9.3 Accessors, Mutators, and Immutable Classes

Recall that a *mutator* method modifies the object on which it is invoked, whereas an *accessor* method merely accesses information without making any modifications. For example, in the BankAccount class, the deposit and withdraw methods are mutator methods. Calling

```
account.deposit(1000);
```

modifies the state of the account object, but calling

```
double balance = account.getBalance();
```

does not modify the state of account.

> An immutable class has no mutator methods.

You can call an accessor method as many times as you like—you always get the same answer, and it does not change the state of your object. That is clearly a desirable property, because it makes the behavior of such a method very predictable. Some classes have been designed to have only accessor methods and no mutator methods at all. Such classes are called *immutable*. An example is the String class. Once a string has been constructed, its contents never change. No method in the String class can modify the contents of a string. For example, the toUpperCase method does not change characters from the original string. Instead, it constructs a *new* string that contains the uppercase characters:

```
String name = "John Q. Public";
String uppercased = name.toUpperCase(); // name is not changed
```

An immutable class has a major advantage: It is safe to give out references to its objects freely. If no method can change the object's value, then no code can modify the object at an unexpected time. In contrast, if you give out a BankAccount reference to any other method, you have to be aware that the state of your object may change—the other method can call the deposit and withdraw methods on the reference that you gave it.

SELF CHECK

6. Is the substring method of the String class an accessor or a mutator?
7. Is the Rectangle class immutable?

9.4 Side Effects

A mutator method modifies the object on which it is invoked, whereas an accessor method leaves it unchanged. This classification relates only to the object on which the method is invoked.

> A side effect of a method is any externally observable data modification.

A *side effect* of a method is any kind of modification of data that is observable outside the method. Mutator methods have a side effect, namely the modification of the implicit parameter.

Here is an example of a method with another kind of side effect, the updating of an explicit parameter:

```
public class BankAccount
{
   /**
      Transfers money from this account to another account.
      @param amount the amount of money to transfer
      @param other the account into which to transfer the money
   */
   public void transfer(double amount, BankAccount other)
   {
      balance = balance - amount;
      other.balance = other.balance + amount;
   }
   . . .
}
```

> You should minimize side effects that go beyond modification of the implicit parameter.

As a rule of thumb, updating an explicit parameter can be surprising to programmers, and it is best to avoid it whenever possible.

Another example of a side effect is output. Consider how we have always printed a bank balance:

```
System.out.println("The balance is now $"
   + momsSavings.getBalance());
```

Why don't we simply have a printBalance method?

```
public void printBalance() // Not recommended
{
   System.out.println("The balance is now $" + balance);
}
```

That would be more convenient when you actually want to print the value. But, of course, there are cases when you want the value for some other purpose. Thus, you can't simply drop the getBalance method in favor of printBalance.

More importantly, the printBalance method forces strong assumptions on the BankAccount class.

- The message is in English—you assume that the user of your software reads English. The majority of people on the planet don't.

- You rely on System.out. A method that relies on System.out won't work in an embedded system, such as the computer inside an automatic teller machine.

In other words, this design violates the rule of minimizing the coupling of the classes. The printBalance method couples the BankAccount class with the System and PrintStream classes. It is best to decouple input/output from the actual work of your classes.

8. If a refers to a bank account, then the call a.deposit(100) modifies the bank account object. Is that a side effect?

9. Consider the DataSet class of Chapter 7. Suppose we add a method

```
void read(Scanner in)
{
   while (in.hasNextDouble())
      add(in.nextDouble());
}
```

Does this method have a side effect?

COMMON ERROR 9.1

Trying to Modify Primitive Type Parameters

Methods can't update parameters of primitive type (numbers, char, and boolean). To illustrate this point, let us try to write a method that updates a number parameter:

```
public class BankAccount
{
   /**
      Transfers money from this account and tries to add it to a balance.
      @param amount the amount of money to transfer
      @param otherBalance balance to add the amount to
   */
   void transfer(double amount, double otherBalance)     ❷
   {
      balance = balance - amount;
      otherBalance = otherBalance + amount;
         // Won't work
   }  ❸
   . . .
}
```

This doesn't work. Let's consider a method call.

```
double savingsBalance = 1000;
harrysChecking.transfer(500, savingsBalance);     ❶
System.out.println(savingsBalance);     ❹
```

> In Java, a method can never change parameters of primitive type.

As the method starts, the parameter variable otherBalance is set to the same value as savingsBalance. Then the value of the otherBalance value is modified, but that modification has no effect on savingsBalance, because otherBalance is a separate variable (see Figure 3). When the method terminates, the otherBalance variable dies, and savingsBalance isn't increased.

Why did the example at the beginning of Section 9.4 work, where the second explicit parameter was a BankAccount reference? Then the parameter variable contained a copy of the object reference. Through that reference, the method is able to modify the object.

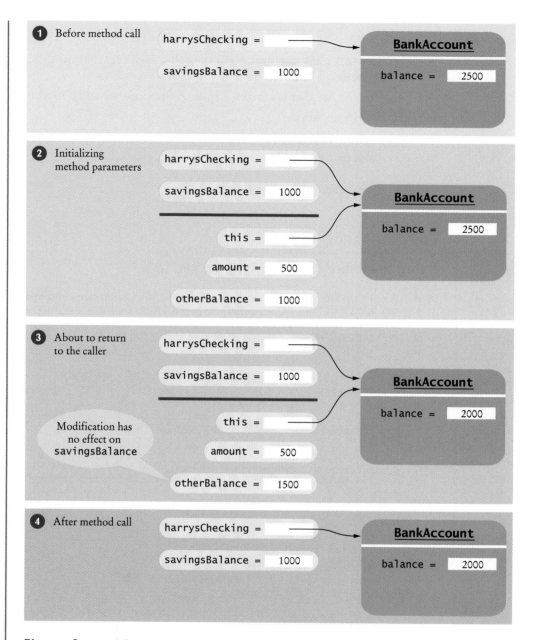

Figure 3   Modifying a Numeric Parameter Has No Effect on Caller

You already saw this difference between objects and primitive types in Chapter 2. As a consequence, a Java method can *never* modify numbers that are passed to it.

Quality Tip 9.2

Minimize Side Effects

In an ideal world, all methods would be accessors that simply return an answer without changing any value at all. (In fact, programs that are written in so-called *functional* programming languages, such as Scheme and ML, come close to this ideal.) Of course, in an object-oriented programming language, we use objects to remember state changes. Therefore, a method that just changes the state of its implicit parameter is certainly acceptable. Although side effects cannot be completely eliminated, they can be the cause of surprises and problems and should be minimized. Here is a classification of method behavior.

- Accessor methods with no changes to any explicit parameters—no side effects. Example: `getBalance`.
- Mutator methods with no changes to any explicit parameters—an acceptable side effect. Example: `withdraw`.
- Methods that change an explicit parameter—a side effect that should be avoided when possible. Example: `transfer`.
- Methods that change another object (such as `System.out`)—a side effect that should be avoided. Example: `printBalance`.

Quality Tip 9.3

Don't Change the Contents of Parameter Variables

As explained in Common Error 9.1 and Advanced Topic 9.1, a method can treat its parameter variables like any other local variables and change their contents. However, that change affects only the parameter variable within the method itself—not any values supplied in the method call. Some programmers take "advantage" of the temporary nature of the parameter variables and use them as "convenient" holders for intermediate results, as in this example:

```java
public void deposit(double amount)
{
    // Using the parameter variable to hold an intermediate value
    amount = balance + amount;   // Poor style
    . . .
}
```

That code would produce errors if another statement in the method referred to `amount` expecting it to be the value of the parameter, and it will confuse later programmers maintaining this method. You should always treat the parameter variables as if they were constants. Don't assign new values to them. Instead, introduce a new local variable.

```java
public void deposit(double amount)
{
    double newBalance = balance + amount;
    . . .
}
```

ADVANCED TOPIC 9.1

Call by Value and Call by Reference

In Java, method parameters are *copied* into the parameter variables when a method starts. Computer scientists call this call mechanism "call by value". There are some limitations to the "call by value" mechanism. As you saw in Common Error 9.1, it is not possible to implement methods that modify the contents of number variables. Other programming languages such as C++ support an alternate mechanism, called "call by reference". For example, in C++ it would be an easy matter to write a method that modifies a number, by using a so-called *reference parameter*. Here is the C++ code, for those of you who know C++:

```cpp
// This is C++
class BankAccount
{
public:
    void transfer(double amount, double& otherBalance)
        // otherBalance is a double&, a reference to a double
    {
        balance = balance - amount;
        otherBalance = otherBalance + amount; // Works in C++
    }
    . . .
};
```

You will sometimes read in Java books that "numbers are passed by value, objects are passed by reference". That is technically not quite correct. In Java, objects themselves are never passed as parameters; instead, both numbers and *object references* are copied by value. To see this clearly, let us consider another scenario. This method tries to set the otherAccount parameter to a new object:

```java
public class BankAccount
{
    public void transfer(double amount, BankAccount otherAccount)
    {
        balance = balance - amount;
        double newBalance = otherAccount.balance + amount;
        otherAccount = new BankAccount(newBalance); // Won't work
    }
}
```

> In Java, a method can change the state of an object reference parameter, but it cannot replace the object reference with another.

In this situation, we are not trying to change the state of the object to which the parameter variable otherAccount refers; instead, we are trying to replace the object with a different one (see Figure 4). Now the parameter variable otherAccount is replaced with a reference to a new account. But if you call the method with

```java
harrysChecking.transfer(500, savingsAccount);
```

then that change does not affect the savingsAccount variable that is supplied in the call.

As you can see, a Java method can update an object's state, but it cannot *replace* the contents of an object reference. This shows that object references are passed by value in Java.

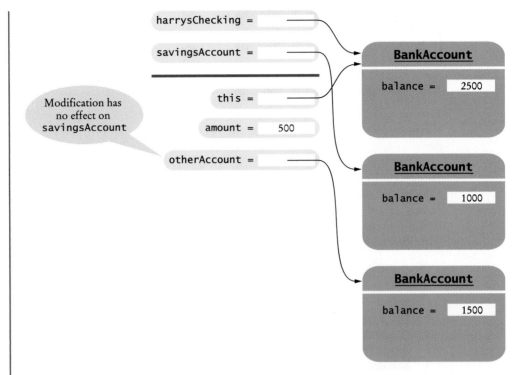

Figure 4 Modifying an Object Reference Parameter Has No Effect on the Caller

9.5 Preconditions and Postconditions

> A precondition is a requirement that the caller of a method must meet. If a method is called in violation of a precondition, the method is not responsible for computing the correct result.

A *precondition* is a requirement that the caller of a method must obey. For example, the deposit method of the BankAccount class has a precondition that the amount to be deposited should not be negative. It is the responsibility of the caller never to call a method if one of its preconditions is violated. If the method is called anyway, it is not responsible for producing a correct result.

Therefore, a precondition is an important part of the method, and you must document it. Here we document the precondition that the amount parameter must not be negative.

```
/**
   Deposits money into this account.
   @param amount the amount of money to deposit
   (Precondition: amount >= 0)
*/
```

Some javadoc extensions support a @precondition or @requires tag, but it is not a part of the standard javadoc program. Because the standard javadoc tool skips all unknown tags, we simply add the precondition to the method explanation or the appropriate @param tag.

Preconditions are typically provided for one of two reasons:

1. To restrict the parameters of a method
2. To require that a method is only called when it is in the appropriate *state*

For example, once a Scanner has run out of input, it is no longer legal to call the next method. Thus, a precondition for the next method is that the hasNext method returns true.

A method is responsible for operating correctly only when its caller has fulfilled all preconditions. The method is free to do *anything* if a precondition is not fulfilled. It would be perfectly legal if the method reformatted the hard disk every time it was called with a wrong input. Naturally, that isn't reasonable. What should a method actually do when it is called with inappropriate inputs? For example, what should account.deposit(-1000) do? There are two choices.

1. A method can check for the violation and *throw an exception*. Then the method does not return to its caller; instead, control is transferred to an exception handler. If no handler is present, then the program terminates. We will discuss exceptions in Chapter 15.
2. A method can skip the check and work under the assumption that the preconditions are fulfilled. If they aren't, then any data corruption (such as a negative balance) or other failures are the caller's fault.

The first approach can be inefficient, particularly if the same check is carried out many times by several methods. The second approach can be dangerous. The *assertion* mechanism was invented to give you the best of both approaches.

> An assertion is a logical condition in a program that you believe to be true.

An *assertion* is a condition that you believe to be true at all times in a particular program location. An assertion check tests whether an assertion is true. Here is a typical assertion check that tests a precondition:

```java
public double deposit (double amount)
{
    assert amount >= 0;
    balance = balance + amount;
}
```

In this method, the programmer expects that the quantity amount can never be negative. When the assertion is correct, no harm is done, and the program works in the normal way. If, for some reason, the assertion fails, *and assertion checking is enabled*, then the program terminates with an AssertionError.

However, if assertion checking is disabled, then the assertion is never checked, and the program runs at full speed. By default, assertion checking is disabled when you execute a program. To execute a program with assertion checking turned on, use this command:

```
java -enableassertions MyProg
```

SYNTAX 9.1 Assertion

```
assert condition;
```

Example:

```
assert amount >= 0;
```

Purpose:

To assert that a condition is fulfilled. If assertion checking is enabled and the condition is false, an assertion error is thrown.

You can also use the shortcut -ea instead of -enableassertions. You definitely want to turn assertion checking on during program development and testing.

You don't have to use assertions for checking preconditions—throwing an exception is another reasonable option. But assertions have one advantage: You can turn them off after you have tested your program, so that it runs at maximum speed. That way, you never have to feel bad about putting lots of assertions into your code. You can also use assertions for checking conditions other than preconditions.

Many beginning programmers think that it isn't "nice" to abort the program when a precondition is violated. Why not simply return to the caller instead?

```
public void deposit(double amount)
{
    if (amount < 0)
        return; // Not recommended
    balance = balance + amount;
}
```

That is legal—after all, a method can do anything if its preconditions are violated. But it is not as good as an assertion check. If the program calling the deposit method has a few bugs that cause it to pass a negative amount as an input value, then the version that throws the exception will make the bugs very obvious during testing—it is hard to ignore when the program aborts. The quiet version, on the other hand, will not alert you, and you may not notice that it performs some wrong calculations as a consequence. Think of assertions as the "tough love" approach to precondition checking.

> If a method has been called in accordance with its preconditions, then it must ensure that its postconditions are valid.

When a method is called in accordance with its preconditions, then the method promises to do its job correctly. A different kind of promise that the method makes is called a *postcondition*. There are two kinds of postconditions:

1. The return value is computed correctly.
2. The object is in a certain state after the method call is completed.

Here is a postcondition that makes a statement about the object state after the `deposit` method is called.

```
/**
    Deposits money into this account.
    (Postcondition: getBalance() >= 0)
    @param amount  the amount of money to deposit
    (Precondition: amount >= 0)
*/
```

As long as the precondition is fulfilled, this method guarantees that the balance after the deposit is not negative.

Some `javadoc` extensions support a `@postcondition` or `@ensures` tag. However, just as with preconditions, we simply add postconditions to the method explanation or the `@return` tag, because the standard `javadoc` program skips all tags that it doesn't know.

Some programmers feel that they must specify a postcondition for every method. When you use `javadoc`, however, you already specify a part of the postcondition in the `@return` tag, and you shouldn't repeat it in a postcondition.

```
// This postcondition statement is overly repetitive.
/**
    Returns the current balance of this account.
    @return  the account balance
    (Postcondition: The return value equals the account balance.)
*/
```

Note that we formulate pre- and postconditions only in terms of the *interface* of the class. Thus, we state the precondition of the `withdraw` method as `amount <= getBalance()`, not `amount <= balance`. After all, the caller, which needs to check the precondition, has access only to the public interface, not the private implementation.

Bertrand Meyer [2] compares preconditions and postconditions to contracts. In real life, contracts spell out the obligations of the contracting parties. For example, your mechanic may promise to fix the brakes of your car, and you promise in turn to pay a certain amount of money. If either party breaks the promise, then the other is not bound by the terms of the contract. In the same fashion, pre- and postconditions are contractual terms between a method and its caller. The method promises to fulfill the postcondition for all inputs that fulfill the precondition. The caller promises never to call the method with illegal inputs. If the caller fulfills its promise and gets a wrong answer, it can take the method to "programmer's court". If the caller doesn't fulfill its promise and something terrible happens as a consequence, it has no recourse.

SELF CHECK

10. Why might you want to add a precondition to a method that you provide for other programmers?

11. When you implement a method with a precondition and you notice that the caller did not fulfill the precondition, do you have to notify the caller?

ADVANCED TOPIC 9.2

Class Invariants

Advanced Topic 7.5 introduced the concept of loop invariants. A loop invariant is established when the loop is first entered, and it is preserved by all loop iterations. We then know that the loop invariant must be true when the loop exits, and we can use that information to reason about the correctness of a loop.

Class invariants fulfill a similar purpose. A class invariant is a statement about an object that is true after every constructor and that is preserved by every mutator (provided that the caller respects all preconditions). We then know that the class invariant must always be true, and we can use that information to reason about the correctness of our program.

Here is a simple example. Consider a `BankAccount` class with the following preconditions for the constructor and the mutators:

```
public class BankAccount
{
    /**
        Constructs a bank account with a given balance.
        @param initialBalance the initial balance
        (Precondition: initialBalance >= 0)
    */
    public BankAccount(double initialBalance) { . . . }
    {
        balance = initialBalance;
    }

    /**
        Deposits money into the bank account.
        @param amount the amount to deposit
        (Precondition: amount >= 0)
    */
    public void deposit(double amount) { . . . }

    /**
        Withdraws money from the bank account.
        @param amount the amount to withdraw
        (Precondition: amount <= getBalance())
    */
    public void withdraw(double amount) { . . . }

    . . .

}
```

Now we can formulate the following invariant:

```
getBalance() >= 0
```

To see why this invariant is true, first check the constructor; because the precondition of the constructor is

```
initialBalance >= 0
```

we can prove that the invariant is true after the constructor has set `balance` to `initialBalance`.

Next, check the mutators. The precondition of the deposit method is

```
amount >= 0
```

We can assume that the invariant condition holds before calling the method. Thus, we know that balance >= 0 before the method executes. The laws of mathematics tell us that the sum of two nonnegative numbers is again nonnegative, so we can conclude that balance >= 0 after the completion of the deposit. Thus, the deposit method preserves the invariant.

A similar argument shows that the withdraw method preserves the invariant.

Because the invariant is a property of the class, you document it with the class description:

```
/**
    A bank account has a balance that can be changed by
    deposits and withdrawals.
    (Invariant: getBalance() >= 0)
*/
public class BankAccount
{
    . . .
}
```

9.6 Static Methods

A static method is not invoked on an object.

Sometimes you need a method that is not invoked on an object. Such a method is called a *static method* or a *class method.* In contrast, the methods that you wrote up to now are often called *instance methods* because they operate on a particular instance of an object.

A typical example of a static method is the sqrt method in the Math class. When you call Math.sqrt(x), you don't supply any implicit parameter. (Recall that Math is the name of a class, not an object.)

Why would you want to write a method that does not operate on an object? The most common reason is that you want to encapsulate some computation that involves only numbers. Because numbers aren't objects, you can't invoke methods on them. For example, the call x.sqrt() can never be legal in Java.

Here is a typical example of a static method that carries out some simple algebra: to compute p percent of the amount a. Because the parameters are numbers, the method doesn't operate on any objects at all, so we make it into a static method:

```
/**
    Computes a percentage of an amount.
    @param p  the percentage to apply
    @param a  the amount to which the percentage is applied
    @return p percent of a
*/
public static double percentOf(double p, double a)
{
    return (p / 100) * a;
}
```

You need to find a home for this method. Let us come up with a new class (similar to the Math class of the standard Java library). Because the percentOf method has to do with financial calculations, we'll design a class Financial to hold it. Here is the class:

```
public class Financial
{
    public static double percentOf(double p, double a)
    {
        return (p / 100) * a;
    }
    // More financial methods can be added here.
}
```

When calling a static method, you supply the name of the class containing the method so that the compiler can find it. For example,

```
double tax = Financial.percentOf(taxRate, total);
```

Note that you do not supply an object of type Financial when you call the method.

Now we can tell you why the main method is static. When the program starts, there aren't any objects. Therefore, the *first* method in the program must be a static method.

You may well wonder why these methods are called static. The normal meaning of the word *static* ("staying fixed at one place") does not seem to have anything to do with what static methods do. Indeed, it's used by accident. Java uses the static keyword because C++ uses it in the same context. C++ uses static to denote class methods because the inventors of C++ did not want to invent another keyword. Someone noted that there was a relatively rarely used keyword, static, that denotes certain variables that stay in a fixed location for multiple method calls. (Java does not have this feature, nor does it need it.) It turned out that the keyword could be reused to denote class methods without confusing the compiler. The fact that it can confuse humans was apparently not a big concern. You'll just have to live with the fact that "static method" means "class method": a method that does not operate on an object and that has only explicit parameters.

SELF CHECK

12. Suppose Java had no static methods. Then all methods of the Math class would be instance methods. How would you compute the square root of *x*?

13. Harry turns in his homework assignment, a program that plays tic-tac-toe. His solution consists of a single class with many static methods. Why is this not an object-oriented solution?

9.7 Static Fields

Sometimes, you need to store values outside any particular object. You use *static fields* for this purpose. Here is a typical example. We will use a version of our BankAccount class in which each bank account object has both a balance and an account number:

```
public class BankAccount
{
   . . .
   private double balance;
   private int accountNumber;
}
```

We want to assign account numbers sequentially. That is, we want the bank account constructor to construct the first account with number 1001, the next with number 1002, and so on. Therefore, we must store the last assigned account number somewhere.

It makes no sense, though, to make this value into an instance field:

```
public class BankAccount
{
   . . .
   private double balance;
   private int accountNumber;
   private int lastAssignedNumber = 1000; // NO—won't work
}
```

In that case each *instance* of the BankAccount class would have its own value of lastAssignedNumber.

A static field belongs to the class, not to any object of the class.

Instead, we need to have a single value of lastAssignedNumber that is the same for the entire *class*. Such a field is called a static field, because you declare it using the static keyword.

```
public class BankAccount
{
   . . .
   private double balance;
   private int accountNumber;
   private static int lastAssignedNumber = 1000;
}
```

Every BankAccount object has its own balance and accountNumber instance fields, but there is only a single copy of the lastAssignedNumber variable (see Figure 5). That field is stored in a separate location, outside any BankAccount objects.

A static field is sometimes called a *class field* because there is a single field for the entire class.

Every method of a class can access its static fields. Here is the constructor of the BankAccount class, which increments the last assigned number and then uses it to initialize the account number of the object to be constructed:

```
public class BankAccount
{
```

```
public BankAccount()
{
    // Generates next account number to be assigned
    lastAssignedNumber++; // Updates the static field

    // Assigns field to account number of this bank account
    accountNumber = lastAssignedNumber; // Sets the instance field
}
    . . .
}
```

How do you initialize a static field? You can't set it in the class constructor:

```
public BankAccount()
{
    lastAssignedNumber = 1000; // NO—would reset to 1000 for each new object
    . . .
}
```

Then the initialization would occur each time a new instance is constructed.

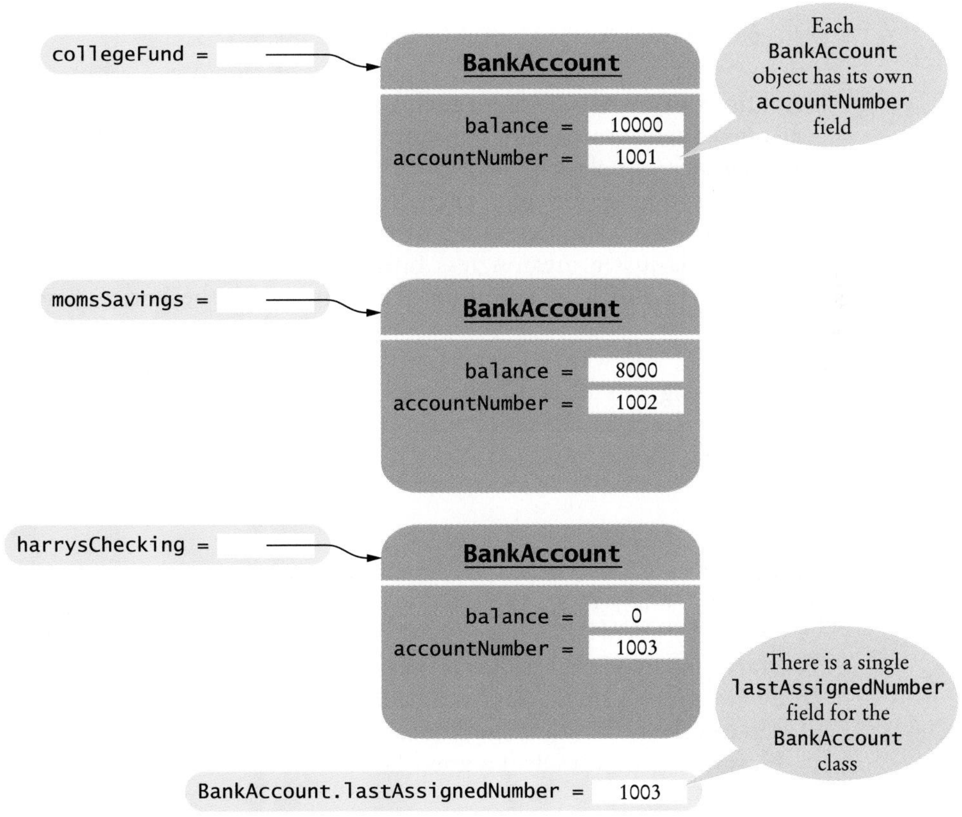

Figure 5 A Static Field and Instance Fields

There are three ways to initialize a static field:

1. Do nothing. The static field is then initialized with 0 (for numbers), false (for boolean values), or null (for objects).

2. Use an explicit initializer, such as

```
public class BankAccount
{
   . . .
   private static int lastAssignedNumber = 1000;
}
```

The initialization is executed once when the class is loaded.

3. Use a static initialization block (see Advanced Topic 9.3).

Like instance fields, static fields should always be declared as private to ensure that methods of other classes do not change their values. The exception to this rule are static *constants*, which may be either private or public. For example, the BankAccount class may want to define a public constant value, such as

```
public class BankAccount
{
   . . .
   public static final double OVERDRAFT_FEE = 5;
}
```

Methods from any class refer to such a constant as BankAccount.OVERDRAFT_FEE.

It makes sense to declare constants as static—you wouldn't want every object of the BankAccount class to have its own set of variables with these constant values. It is sufficient to have one set of them for the class.

Why are class variables called static? As with static methods, the static keyword itself is just a meaningless holdover from C++. But static fields and static methods have much in common: They apply to the entire *class*, not to specific instances of the class.

In general, you want to minimize the use of static methods and fields. If you find yourself using lots of static methods, then that's an indication that you may not have found the right classes to solve your problem in an object-oriented way.

SELF CHECK

14. Name two static fields of the System class.

15. Harry tells you that he has found a great way to avoid those pesky objects: Put all code into a single class and declare all methods and fields static. Then main can call the other static methods, and all of them can access the static fields. Will Harry's plan work? Is it a good idea?

ADVANCED TOPIC 9.3

Alternative Forms of Field Initialization

As you have seen, instance fields are initialized with a default value (0, false, or null, depending on their type). You can then set them to any desired value in a constructor, and that is the style that we prefer in this book.

However, there are two other mechanisms to specify an initial value for a field. Just as with local variables, you can specify initialization values for fields. For example,

```java
public class Coin
{
   . . .
   private double value = 1;
   private String name = "Dollar";
}
```

These default values are used for *every* object that is being constructed.

There is also another, much less common, syntax. You can place one or more *initialization blocks* inside the class definition. All statements in that block are executed whenever an object is being constructed. Here is an example:

```java
public class Coin
{
   . . .
   {
      value = 1;
      name = "Dollar";
   }
   private double value;
   private String name;
}
```

For static fields, you use a static initialization block:

```java
public class BankAccount
{
   . . .
   private static int lastAssignedNumber;

   static
   {
      lastAssignedNumber = 1000;
   }
}
```

All statements in the static initialization block are executed once when the class is loaded. Initialization blocks are rarely used in practice.

When an object is constructed, the initializers and initialization blocks are executed in the order in which they appear. Then the code in the constructor is executed. Because the rules for the alternative initialization mechanisms are somewhat complex, we recommend that you simply use constructors to do the job of construction.

9.8 Scope

9.8.1 Scope of Local Variables

> The scope of a variable is the region of a program in which the variable can be accessed.

When you have multiple variables or fields with the same name, there is the possibility of conflict. In order to understand the potential problems, you need to know about the *scope* of each variable: the part of the program in which the variable can be accessed.

The scope of a local variable extends from the point of its declaration to the end of the block that encloses it.

It sometimes happens that the same variable name is used in two methods. Consider the variables r in the following example:

```java
public class RectangleTester
{
    public static double area(Rectangle rect)
    {
        double r = rect.getWidth() * rect.getHeight();
        return r;
    }

    public static void main(String[] args)
    {
        Rectangle r = new Rectangle(5, 10, 20, 30);
        double a = area(r);
        System.out.println(r);
    }
}
```

These variables are independent from each other, or, in other words, their scopes are disjoint. You can have local variables with the same name r in different methods, just as you can have different motels with the same name "Bates Motel" in different cities.

> The scope of a local variable cannot contain the definition of another variable with the same name.

In Java, the scope of a local variable can never contain the definition of another local variable with the same name. For example, the following is an error:

```java
Rectangle r = new Rectangle(5, 10, 20, 30);
if (x >= 0)
{
    double r = Math.sqrt(x);
    // Error—can't declare another variable called r here
    . . .
}
```

However, you can have local variables with identical names if their scopes do not overlap, such as

```java
if (x >= 0)
{
    double r = Math.sqrt(x);
    . . .
```

```
    } // Scope of r ends here
    else
    {
        Rectangle r = new Rectangle(5, 10, 20, 30);
        // OK—it is legal to declare another r here
        . . .
    }
```

9.8.2 Scope of Class Members

A qualified name is prefixed by its class name or by an object reference, such as Math.sqrt or other.balance.

In this section, we consider the scope of fields and methods of a class. (These are collectively called the *members* of the class.) Private members have *class scope*: You can access all members in any of the methods of the class.

If you want to use a public field or method outside its class, you must *qualify* the name. You qualify a static field or method by specifying the class name, such as Math.sqrt or Math.PI. You qualify an instance field or method by specifying the object to which the field or method should be applied, such as harrysChecking.getBalance().

An unqualified instance field or method name refers to the this parameter.

Inside a method, you don't need to qualify fields or methods that belong to the same class. Instance fields automatically refer to the implicit parameter of the method, that is, the object on which the method is invoked. For example, consider the transfer method:

```
public class BankAccount
{
    public void transfer(double amount, BankAccount other)
    {
        balance = balance - amount; // i.e., this.balance
        other.balance = other.balance + amount;
    }
    . . .
}
```

Here, the unqualified name balance means this.balance. (Recall from Chapter 3 that this is a reference to the implicit parameter of any method.)

The same rule applies to methods. Thus, another implementation of the transfer method is

```
public class BankAccount
{
    public void transfer(double amount, BankAccount other)
    {
        withdraw(amount); // i.e., this.withdraw(amount);
        other.deposit(amount);
    }
    . . .
}
```

Whenever you see an instance method call without an implicit parameter, then the method is called on the this parameter. Such a method call is called a "self-call".

Similarly, you can use a static field or method of the same class without a qualifier. For example, consider the following version of the `withdraw` method:

```
public class BankAccount
{
    public void withdraw(double amount)
    {
        if (balance < amount) balance = balance - OVERDRAFT_FEE;
        else . . .
    }
    . . .
    private static double OVERDRAFT_FEE = 5;
}
```

Here, the unqualified name `OVERDRAFT_FEE` refers to `BankAccount.OVERDRAFT_FEE`.

9.8.3 Overlapping Scope

Problems arise if you have two identical variable names with overlapping scope. This can never occur with local variables, but the scopes of identically named local variables and instance fields can overlap. Here is a purposefully bad example.

```
public class Coin
{
    . . .
    public double getExchangeValue(double exchangeRate)
    {
        double value; // Local variable
        . . .
        return value;
    }

    private String name;
    private double value; // Field with the same name
}
```

> A local variable can shadow a field with the same name. You can access the shadowed field name by qualifying it with the `this` reference.

Inside the `getExchangeValue` method, the variable name `value` could potentially have two meanings: the local variable or the instance field. The Java language specifies that in this situation the *local* variable wins out. It *shadows* the instance field. This sounds pretty arbitrary, but there is actually a good reason: You can still refer to the instance field as `this.value`.

```
value = this.value * exchangeRate;
```

It isn't necessary to write code like this. You can easily change the name of the local variable to something else, such as `result`.

However, you should be aware of one common use of the `this` reference. When implementing constructors, many programmers find it tiresome to come up with different names for instance fields and parameters. Using the `this` reference solves that problem. Here is a typical example.

```
public Coin(double value, String name)
{
```

```
    this.value = value;
    this.name = name;
}
```

The expression this.value refers to the instance field, but value is the parameter. Of course, you can always rename the construction parameters to aValue and aName, as we have done in this book.

SELF CHECK

16. Consider the deposit method of the BankAccount class. What is the scope of the variables amount and newBalance?

17. What is the scope of the balance field of the BankAccount class?

COMMON ERROR 9.2

Shadowing

Accidentally using the same name for a local variable and an instance field is a surprisingly common error. As you saw in the preceding section, the local variable then *shadows* the instance field. Even though you may have meant to access the instance field, the local variable is quietly accessed. For some reason, this problem is most common in constructors. Look at this example of an incorrect constructor:

```
public class Coin
{
    public Coin(double aValue, String aName)
    {
        value = aValue;
        String name = aName; // Oops . . .
    }

    . . .

    private double value;
    private String name;
}
```

The programmer declared a local variable name in the constructor. In all likelihood, that was just a typo—the programmer's fingers were on autopilot and typed the keyword String, even though the programmer all the time intended to access the instance field. Unfortunately, the compiler gives no warning in this situation and quietly sets the local variable to the value of aName. The instance field of the object that is being constructed is never touched, and remains null. Some programmers give all instance field names a special prefix to distinguish them from other variables. A common convention is to prefix all instance field names with the prefix my, such as myValue or myName.

PRODUCTIVITY HINT 9.1

Global Search and Replace

Suppose you chose an unfortunate name for a method—say perc instead of percentOf—and you regret your choice. Of course, you can locate all occurrences of perc in your code and replace them manually. However, most programming editors have a command to search for the perc's automatically and replace them with percentOf.

You need to specify some details about the search:

- Do you want it to ignore case? That is, should Perc be a match? In Java you usually don't want that.

- Do you want it to match whole words only? If not, the perc in superconductor is also a match. In Java you usually want to match whole words.

- Is this a regular-expression search? No, but regular expressions can make searches even more powerful—see Productivity Hint 9.2.

- Do you want to confirm each replace, or simply go ahead and replace all matches? I usually confirm the first three or four, and when I see that it works as expected, I give the go-ahead to replace the rest. (By the way, a *global* replace means to replace all occurrences in the document.) Good text editors can undo a global replace that has gone awry. Find out whether yours will.

- Do you want the search to go from the point where the cursor is in the file through to the rest of the file, or should it search the currently selected text? Restricting replacement to a portion of the file can be very useful, but in this example you would want to move the cursor to the top of the file and then replace until the end of the file.

Not every editor has all these options. You should investigate what your editor offers.

PRODUCTIVITY HINT 9.2

Regular Expressions

Regular expressions describe character patterns. For example, numbers have a simple form. They contain one or more digits. The regular expression describing numbers is [0-9]+. The set [0-9] denotes any digit between 0 and 9, and the + means "one or more".

What good is it? Several utility programs use regular expressions to locate matching text. Also, the search commands of some programming editors understand regular expressions. The most popular program that uses regular expressions is *grep* (which stands for "global regular expression print"). You can run grep from a command prompt or from inside some compilation environments. Grep is part of the UNIX operating system, but versions are available for Windows and MacOS. It needs a regular expression and one or more files to search. When grep runs, it displays a set of lines that match the regular expression.

Suppose you want to look for all magic numbers (see Quality Tip 4.1) in a file. The command

```
grep [0-9]+ Homework.java
```

lists all lines in the file Homework.java that contain sequences of digits. That isn't terribly useful; lines with variable names x1 will be listed. OK, you want sequences of digits that do *not* immediately follow letters:

```
grep [^A-Za-z][0-9]+ Homework.java
```

The set [^A-Za-z] denotes any characters that are *not* in the ranges A to Z and a to z. This works much better, and it shows only lines that contain actual numbers.

For more information on regular expressions, consult one of the many tutorials on the Internet (such as [3]).

ADVANCED TOPIC 9.4

Static Imports

Starting with Java version 5.0, there is a variant of the import directive that lets you use static methods and fields without class prefixes. For example,

```
import static java.lang.System.*;
import static java.lang.Math.*;

public class RootTester
{
   public static void main(String[] args)
   {
      double r = sqrt(PI)  // Instead of Math.sqrt(Math.PI)
      out.println(r);      // Instead of System.out
   }
}
```

Static imports can make programs easier to read, particularly if they use many mathematical functions.

9.9 Packages

9.9.1 Organizing Related Classes into Packages

A package is a set of related classes.

A Java program consists of a collection of classes. So far, most of your programs have consisted of a small number of classes. As programs get larger, however, simply distributing the classes over multiple files isn't enough. An additional structuring mechanism is needed.

In Java, packages provide this structuring mechanism. A Java *package* is a set of related classes. For example, the Java library consists of dozens of packages, some of which are listed in Table 1.

Table 1   Important Packages in the Java Library

Package	Purpose	Sample Class
java.lang	Language support	Math
java.util	Utilities	Random
java.io	Input and output	PrintStream
java.awt	Abstract Windowing Toolkit	Color
java.applet	Applets	Applet
java.net	Networking	Socket
java.sql	Database access through Structured Query Language	ResultSet
javax.swing	Swing user interface	JButton
omg.org.CORBA	Common Object Request Broker Architecture for distributed objects	IntHolder

To put classes in a package, you must place a line

package *packageName*;

as the first instruction in the source file containing the classes. A package name consists of one or more identifiers separated by periods. (See Section 9.9.3 for tips on constructing package names.)

For example, let's put the Financial class introduced in this chapter into a package named com.horstmann.bigjava. The Financial.java file must start as follows:

```
package com.horstmann.bigjava;

public class Financial
{
   . . .
}
```

SYNTAX 9.2 Package Specification

package *packageName*;

Example:

package com.horstmann.bigjava;

Purpose:

To declare that all classes in this file belong to a particular package

In addition to the named packages (such as java.util or com.horstmann.bigjava), there is a special package, called the *default package*, which has no name. If you did not include any package statement at the top of your source file, its classes are placed in the default package.

9.9.2 Importing Packages

If you want to use a class from a package, you can refer to it by its full name (package name plus class name). For example, java.util.Scanner refers to the Scanner class in the java.util package:

```
java.util.Scanner in = new java.util.Scanner(System.in);
```

> The import directive lets you refer to a class of a package by its class name, without the package prefix.

Naturally, that is somewhat inconvenient. You can instead *import* a name with an import statement:

```
import java.util.Scanner;
```

Then you can refer to the class as Scanner without the package prefix.

You can import *all classes* of a package with an import statement that ends in .*. For example, you can use the statement

```
import java.util.*;
```

to import all classes from the java.util package. That statement lets you refer to classes like Scanner or Random without a java.util prefix.

However, you never need to import the classes in the java.lang package explicitly. That is the package containing the most basic Java classes, such as Math and Object. These classes are always available to you. In effect, an automatic import java.lang.*; statement has been placed into every source file.

Finally, you don't need to import other classes in the same package. For example, when you implement the class homework1.Tester, you don't need to import the class homework1.Bank. The compiler will find the Bank class without an import statement because it is located in the same package.

9.9.3 Package Names

Placing related classes into a package is clearly a convenient mechanism to organize classes. However, there is a more important reason for packages: to avoid *name clashes*. In a large project, it is inevitable that two people will come up with the same name for the same concept. This even happens in the standard Java class library (which has now grown to thousands of classes). There is a class Timer in the java.util package and another class called Timer in the javax.swing package. You can still tell the Java compiler exactly which Timer class you need, simply by referring to them as java.util.Timer and javax.swing.Timer.

Of course, for the package-naming convention to work, there must be some way to ensure that package names are unique. It wouldn't be good if the car maker BMW placed all its Java code into the package bmw, and some other programmer (perhaps Bertha M. Walters) had the same bright idea. To avoid this problem, the inventors of Java recommend that you use a package-naming scheme that takes advantage of the uniqueness of Internet domain names.

> Use a domain name in reverse to construct unambiguous package names.

For example, I have a domain name horstmann.com, and there is nobody else on the planet with the same domain name. (I was lucky that the domain name horstmann.com had not been taken by anyone else when I applied. If your name is Walters, you will sadly find that someone else beat you to walters.com.) To get a package name, turn the domain name around to produce a package name prefix, such as com.horstmann.

If you don't have your own domain name, you can still create a package name that has a high probability of being unique by writing your e-mail address backwards. For example, if Bertha Walters has an e-mail address walters@cs.sjsu.edu, then she can use a package name edu.sjsu.cs.walters for her own classes.

Some instructors will want you to place each of your assignments into a separate package, such as homework1, homework2, and so on. The reason is again to avoid name collision. You can have two classes, homework1.Bank and homework2.Bank, with slightly different properties.

9.9.4 How Classes Are Located

If the Java compiler is properly set up on your system, and you use only the standard classes, you ordinarily need not worry about the location of class files and can safely skip this section. If you want to add your own packages, however, or if the compiler cannot locate a particular class or package, you need to understand the mechanism.

> The path of a class file must match its package name.

A package is located in a subdirectory that matches the package name. The parts of the name between periods represent successively nested directories. For example, the package com.horstmann.bigjava would be placed in a subdirectory com/horstmann/bigjava. If the package is to be used only in conjunction with a single program, then you can place the subdirectory inside the directory holding that program's files. For example, if you do your homework assignments in a *base directory* /home/walters, then you can place the class files for the com.horstmann.bigjava package into the directory /home/walters/com/horstmann/bigjava, as shown in Figure 6. (Here, we are using UNIX-style file names. Under Windows, you might use c:\home\walters\com\horstmann\bigjava.)

However, if you want to place your programs into many different directories, such as /home/walters/hw1, /home/walters/hw2, . . . , then you probably don't want to have lots of identical subdirectories /home/walters/hw1/com/horstmann/bigjava, /home/walters/hw2/com/horstmann/bigjava, and so on. In that case, you want to make a single directory with a name such as /home/walters/lib/com/horstmann/bigjava, place all class files for the package in that directory, and tell the Java compiler once and for all how to locate the class files.

You need to add the directories that might contain packages to the *class path*. In the preceding example, you add the /home/walters/lib directory to that class path. The details for doing this depend on your compilation environment; consult the

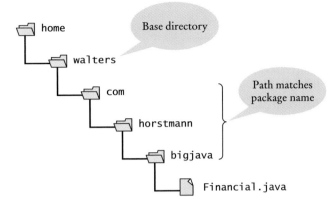

Figure 6
Base Directories and
Subdirectories for Packages

documentation for your compiler, or your instructor. If you use the Sun Java SDK, you need to set the class path. The exact command depends on the operating system. In UNIX, the command might be

    export CLASSPATH=/home/walters/lib:.

This setting places both the /home/walters/lib directory and the current directory onto the class path. (The period denotes the current directory.)

A typical example for Windows would be

    set CLASSPATH=c:\home\walters\lib;.

Note that the class path contains the *base directories* that may contain package directories. It is a common error to place the complete package address in the class path. If the class path mistakenly contains /home/walters/lib/com/horstmann /bigjava, then the compiler will attempt to locate the com.horstmann.bigjava package in /home/walters/lib/com/horstmann/bigjava/com/horstmann/bigjava and won't find the files.

SELF CHECK

18. Which of the following are packages?

    a. java

    b. java.lang

    c. java.util

    d. java.lang.Math

19. Can you write a Java program without ever using import statements?

20. Suppose your homework assignments are located in the directory /home/me/ cs101 (c:\me\cs101 on Windows). Your instructor tells you to place your homework into packages. In which directory do you place the class hw1.problem1.TicTacToeTester?

COMMON ERROR 9.3

Confusing Dots

In Java, the dot symbol (.) is used as a separator in the following situations:

- Between package names (`java.util`)
- Between package and class names (`homework1.Bank`)
- Between class and inner class names (`Ellipse2D.Double`)
- Between class and instance variable names (`Math.PI`)
- Between objects and methods (`account.getBalance()`)

When you see a long chain of dot-separated names, it can be a challenge to find out which part is the package name, which part is the class name, which part is an instance variable name, and which part is a method name. Consider

```
java.lang.System.out.println(x);
```

Because `println` is followed by an opening parenthesis, it must be a method name. Therefore, `out` must be either an object or a class with a static `println` method. (Of course, we know that `out` is an object reference of type `PrintStream`.) Again, it is not at all clear, without context, whether `System` is another object, with a public variable `out`, or a class with a `static` variable. Judging from the number of pages that the Java language specification [1] devotes to this issue, even the compiler has trouble interpreting these dot-separated sequences of strings.

To avoid problems, it is helpful to adopt a strict coding style. If class names always start with an uppercase letter, and variable, method, and package names always start with a lowercase letter, then confusion can be avoided.

HOW TO 9.1

Programming with Packages

This How To explains in detail how to place your programs into packages. For example, your instructor may ask you to place each homework assignment into a separate package. That way, you can have classes with the same name but different implementations in separate packages (such as `homework1.Bank` and `homework2.Bank`).

Step 1   Come up with a package name.

Your instructor may give you a package name to use, such as `homework1`. Or, perhaps you want to use a package name that is unique to you. Start with your e-mail address, written backwards. For example, `walters@cs.sjsu.edu` becomes `edu.sjsu.cs.walters`. Then add a sub-package that describes your project or homework, such as `edu.sjsu.cs.walters.homework1`.

Step 2   Pick a *base directory*.

The base directory is the directory that contains the directories for your various packages, for example, `/home/walters` or `c:\cs1`.

Step 3 Make a subdirectory from the base directory that matches your package name.

The subdirectory must be contained in your base directory. Each segment must match a segment of the package name. For example,

```
mkdir /home/walters/homework1
```

If you have multiple segments, build them up one by one:

```
mkdir c:\cs1\edu
mkdir c:\cs1\edu\sjsu
mkdir c:\cs1\edu\sjsu\cs
mkdir c:\cs1\edu\sjsu\cs\walters
mkdir c:\cs1\edu\sjsu\cs\walters\homework1
```

Step 4 Place your source files into the package subdirectory.

For example, if your homework consists of the files Test.java and Bank.java, then you place them into

```
/home/walters/homework1/Test.java
/home/walters/homework1/Bank.java
```

or

```
c:\cs1\edu\sjsu\cs\walters\homework1\Test.java
c:\cs1\edu\sjsu\cs\walters\homework1\Bank.java
```

Step 5 Use the package statement in each source file.

The first noncomment line of each file must be a package statement that lists the name of the package, such as

```
package homework1;
```

or

```
package edu.sjsu.cs.walters.homework1;
```

Step 6 Compile your source files from the *base directory*.

Change to the base directory (from Step 2) to compile your files. For example,

```
cd /home/walters
javac homework1/Test.java
```

or

```
cd \cs1
javac edu\sjsu\cs\walters\homework1\Test.java
```

Note that the Java compiler needs the *source file name and not the class name. That is, you need to supply file separators* (/ on UNIX, \ on Windows) and a file extension (.java).

Step 7 Run your program from the *base directory*.

Unlike the Java compiler, the Java interpreter needs the *class name (and not a file name) of the class containing the* main *method.* That is, use periods as package separators, and don't use a file extension. For example,

```
cd /home/walters
java homework1.Test
```

or

```
cd \cs1
java edu.sjsu.cs.walters.homework1.Test
```

RANDOM FACT 9.1

The Explosive Growth of Personal Computers

In 1971, Marcian E. "Ted" Hoff, an engineer at Intel Corporation, was working on a chip for a manufacturer of electronic calculators. He realized that it would be a better idea to develop a *general-purpose* chip that could be *programmed* to interface with the keys and display of a calculator, rather than to do yet another custom design. Thus, the *microprocessor* was born. At the time, its primary application was as a controller for calculators, washing machines, and the like. It took years for the computer industry to notice that a genuine central processing unit was now available as a single chip.

Hobbyists were the first to catch on. In 1974 the first computer *kit,* the Altair 8800, was available from MITS Electronics for about $350. The kit consisted of the microprocessor, a circuit board, a very small amount of memory, toggle switches, and a row of display lights. Purchasers had to solder and assemble it, then program it in machine language through the toggle switches. It was not a big hit.

The first big hit was the Apple II. It was a real computer with a keyboard, a monitor, and a floppy disk drive. When it was first released, users had a $3000 machine that could play Space Invaders, run a primitive bookkeeping program, or let users program it in BASIC. The original Apple II did not even support lowercase letters, making it worthless for word processing. The breakthrough came in 1979 with a new spreadsheet program, VisiCalc. In a spreadsheet, you enter financial data and their relationships into a grid of rows and columns (see Figure 7). Then you modify some of the data and watch in real time how the others change. For example, you can see how changing the mix of widgets in a manufacturing plant might affect estimated costs and profits. Middle managers in companies, who understood computers and were fed up with having to wait for hours or days to get their data runs back from the computing center, snapped up VisiCalc and the computer that was needed to run it. For them, the computer was a spreadsheet machine.

The next big hit was the IBM Personal Computer, ever after known as the PC. It was the first widely available personal computer that used Intel's 16-bit processor, the 8086, whose successors are still being used in personal computers today. The success of the PC was based not on any engineering breakthroughs but on the fact that it was easy to *clone.* IBM published specifications for plug-in cards, and it went one step further. It published the exact source code of the so-called BIOS (Basic Input/Output System), which controls the keyboard, monitor, ports, and disk drives and must be installed in ROM form in every PC. This allowed third-party vendors of plug-in cards to ensure that the BIOS code, and third-party extensions of it, interacted correctly with the equipment. Of course, the code itself was the property of IBM and could not be copied legally. Perhaps IBM did not foresee that functionally equivalent versions of the BIOS nevertheless could be recreated by others. Compaq, one of the first clone vendors, had fifteen engineers, who certified that they had never seen the original IBM code, write a new version that conformed precisely to the IBM specifications. Other companies did the same, and soon a variety of vendors were selling computers that ran the same software as IBM's PC but distinguished themselves by a lower price, increased portability, or better performance. In time, IBM lost its dominant position in the PC market. It is now one of many companies producing IBM PC-compatible computers.

IBM never produced an *operating system* for its PCs—that is, the software that organizes the interaction between the user and the computer, starts application programs, and manages disk storage and other resources. Instead, IBM offered customers the option of three separate operating systems. Most customers couldn't care less about the operating system. They chose the system that was able to launch most of the few applications that existed at the time.

A **VISICALC**™ Screen:

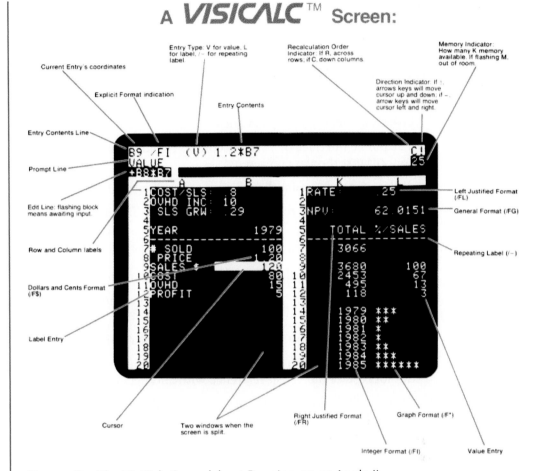

Figure 7 The VisiCalc Spreadsheet Running on an Apple II

It happened to be DOS (Disk Operating System) by Microsoft. Microsoft cheerfully licensed the same operating system to other hardware vendors and encouraged software companies to write DOS applications. A huge number of useful application programs for PC-compatible machines was the result.

PC applications were certainly useful, but they were not easy to learn. Every vendor developed a different *user interface:* the collection of keystrokes, menu options, and settings that a user needed to master to use a software package effectively. Data exchange between applications was difficult, because each program used a different data format. The Apple Macintosh changed all that in 1984. The designers of the Macintosh had the vision to supply an intuitive user interface with the computer and to force software developers to adhere to it. It took Microsoft and PC-compatible manufacturers years to catch up.

Accidental Empires [4] is highly recommended for an amusing and irreverent account of the emergence of personal computers.

At the time of this writing, it is estimated that two in three U.S. households own a personal computer. Most personal computers are used for accessing information from online sources, entertainment, word processing, and home finance (banking, budgeting, taxes).

> Some analysts predict that the personal computer will merge with the television set and cable network into an entertainment and information appliance.

CHAPTER SUMMARY

1. A class should represent a single concept from the problem domain, such as business, science, or mathematics.

2. The public interface of a class is cohesive if all of its features are related to the concept that the class represents.

3. A class depends on another class if it uses objects of that class.

4. It is a good practice to minimize the coupling (i.e., dependency) between classes.

5. An immutable class has no mutator methods.

6. A side effect of a method is any externally observable data modification.

7. You should minimize side effects that go beyond modification of the implicit parameter.

8. In Java, a method can never change parameters of primitive type.

9. In Java, a method can change the state of an object reference parameter, but it cannot replace the object reference with another.

10. A precondition is a requirement that the caller of a method must meet. If a method is called in violation of a precondition, the method is not responsible for computing the correct result.

11. An assertion is a logical condition in a program that you believe to be true.

12. If a method has been called in accordance with its preconditions, then it must ensure that its postconditions are valid.

13. A static method is not invoked on an object.

14. A static field belongs to the class, not to any object of the class.

15. The scope of a variable is the region of a program in which the variable can be accessed.

16. The scope of a local variable cannot contain the definition of another variable with the same name.

17. A qualified name is prefixed by its class name or by an object reference, such as `Math.sqrt` or `other.balance`.

18. An unqualified instance field or method name refers to the `this` parameter.

19. A local variable can shadow a field with the same name. You can access the shadowed field name by qualifying it with the `this` reference.

20. A package is a set of related classes.

21. The `import` directive lets you refer to a class of a package by its class name, without the package prefix.

22. Use a domain name in reverse to construct unambiguous package names.

23. The path of a class file must match its package name.

FURTHER READING

1. http://java.sun.com/docs/books/jls   The Java language specification.

2. Bertrand Meyer, *Object-Oriented Software Construction*, Prentice-Hall, 1989, Chapter 7.

3. http://www.zvon.org/other/PerlTutorial/Output   A dynamic tutorial for regular expressions.

4. Robert X. Cringely, *Accidental Empires*, Addison-Wesley, 1992.

REVIEW EXERCISES

Exercise R9.1. Consider the following problem description:

> Users place coins in a vending machine and select a product by pushing a button.
> If the inserted coins are sufficient to cover the purchase price of the product, the product is dispensed and change is given. Otherwise, the inserted coins are returned to the user.

What classes should you use to implement it?

Exercise R9.2. Consider the following problem description:

> Employees receive their biweekly paychecks. They are paid their hourly rates for each hour worked; however, if they worked more than 40 hours per week, they are paid overtime at 150% of their regular wage.

What classes should you use to implement it?

Exercise R9.3. Consider the following problem description:

> Customers order products from a store. Invoices are generated to list the items and quantities ordered, payments received, and amounts still due. Products are shipped to the shipping address of the customer, and invoices are sent to the billing address.

What classes should you use to implement it?

Exercise R9.4. Look at the public interface of the `java.lang.System` class and discuss whether or not it is cohesive.

Exercise R9.5. Suppose an `Invoice` object contains descriptions of the products ordered, and the billing and shipping address of the customer. Draw a UML diagram showing the dependencies between the classes Invoice, Address, Customer, and Product.

Exercise R9.6. Suppose a vending machine contains products, and users insert coins into the vending machine to purchase products. Draw a UML diagram showing the dependencies between the classes VendingMachine, Coin, and Product.

Exercise R9.7. On which classes does the class Integer in the standard library depend?

Exercise R9.8. On which classes does the class Rectangle in the standard library depend?

Exercise R9.9. Classify the methods of the class Scanner that are used in this book as accessors and mutators.

Exercise R9.10. Classify the methods of the class Rectangle as accessors and mutators.

Exercise R9.11. Which of the following classes are immutable?

  a. Rectangle

  b. String

  c. Random

Exercise R9.12. Which of the following classes are immutable?

  a. PrintStream

  b. Date

  c. Integer

Exercise R9.13. What side effect, if any, do the following three methods have:

```java
public class Coin
{
    public void print()
    {
        System.out.println(name + " " + value);
    }

    public void print(PrintStream stream)
    {
        stream.println(name + " " + value);
    }

    public String toString()
    {
        return name + " " + value;
    }
    . . .
}
```

Exercise R9.14. Ideally, a method should have no side effects. Can you write a program in which no method has a side effect? Would such a program be useful?

Exercise R9.15. Write preconditions for the following methods. Do not implement the methods.

    a. `public static double sqrt(double x)`

    b. `public static String romanNumeral(int n)`

    c. `public static double slope(Line2D.Double a)`

    d. `public static String weekday(int day)`

Exercise R9.16. What preconditions do the following methods from the standard Java library have?

    a. `Math.sqrt`   **d.** `Math.exp`

    b. `Math.tan`   **e.** `Math.pow`

    c. `Math.log`   **f.** `Math.abs`

Exercise R9.17. What preconditions do the following methods from the standard Java library have?

    a. `Integer.parseInt(String s)`

    b. `StringTokenizer.nextToken()`

    c. `Random.nextInt(int n)`

    d. `String.substring(int m, int n)`

Exercise R9.18. When a method is called with parameters that violate its precondition(s), it can terminate (by throwing an exception or an assertion error), or it can return to its caller. Give two examples of library methods (standard or the library methods used in this book) that return some result to their callers when called with invalid parameters, and give two examples of library methods that terminate.

Exercise R9.19. Consider a `CashRegister` class with methods

    • `public void enterPayment(int coinCount, Coin coinType)`

    • `public double getTotalPayment()`

Give a reasonable postcondition of the `enterPayment` method. What preconditions would you need so that the `CashRegister` class can ensure that postcondition?

Exercise R9.20. Consider the following method that is intended to swap the values of two floating-point numbers:

```
public static void falseSwap(double a, double b)
{
   double temp = a;
   a = b;
   b = temp;
}

public static void main(String[] args)
{
   double x = 3;
   double y = 4;
   falseSwap(x, y);
   System.out.println(x + " " + y);
}
```

Why doesn't the method swap the contents of x and y?

Exercise R9.21. How *can* you write a method that swaps two floating-point numbers? *Hint:* Point2D.Double.

Exercise R9.22. Draw a memory diagram that shows why the following method can't swap two BankAccount objects:

```
public static void falseSwap(BankAccount a, BankAccount b)
{
   BankAccount temp = a;
   a = b;
   b = temp;
}
```

Exercise R9.23. Consider an enhancement of the Die class of Chapter 7 with a static field

```
public class Die
{
   public Die(int s) { . . . }
   public int cast() { . . . }
   private int sides;
   private static Random generator = new Random();
}
```

Draw a memory diagram that shows three dice:

```
Die d4 = new Die(4);
Die d6 = new Die(6);
Die d8 = new Die(8);
```

Be sure to indicate the values of the sides and generator fields.

Exercise R9.24. Try compiling the following program. Explain the error message that you get.

```
public class PrintTester
{
   public void print(int x)
   {
      System.out.println(x);
   }

   public static void main(String[] args)
   {
      int n = 13;
      print(n);
   }
}
```

Exercise R9.25. Look at the methods in the Integer class. Which are static? Why?

Exercise R9.26. Look at the methods in the String class (but ignore the ones that take a parameter of type char[]). Which are static? Why?

Exercise R9.27. The in and out fields of the System class are public static fields of the System class. Is that good design? If not, how could you improve on it?

Exercise R9.28. In the following class, the variable n occurs in multiple scopes. Which declarations of n are legal and which are illegal?

```
public class X
{
   public int f()
   {
      int n = 1;
      return n;
   }

   public int g(int k)
   {
      int a;
      for (int n = 1; n <= k; n++)
         a = a + n;
      return a;
   }

   public int h(int n)
   {
      int b;
      for (int n = 1; n <= 10; n++)
         b = b + n;
      return b + n;
   }

   public int k(int n)
   {
      if (n < 0)
      {
         int k = -n;
         int n = (int) (Math.sqrt(k));
         return n;
      }
      else return n;
   }

   public int m(int k)
   {
      int a;
      for (int n = 1; n <= k; n++)
         a = a + n;
      for (int n = k; n >= 1; n++)
         a = a + n;
      return a;
   }

   private int n;
}
```

Exercise R9.29. What is a qualified name? What is an unqualified name?

Exercise R9.30. When you access an unqualified name in a method, what does that access mean? Discuss both instance and static features.

Exercise R9.31. Every Java program can be rewritten to avoid `import` statements. Explain how, and rewrite `IntersectionComponent.java` from Chapter 5 to avoid `import` statements.

Exercise R9.32. What is the default package? Have you used it before this chapter in your programming?

PROGRAMMING EXERCISES

Exercise P9.1. Implement the `Coin` classes described in Section 9.2. Modify the `CashRegister` class so that coins can be added to the cash register, by supplying a method

```
void enterPayment(int coinCount, Coin coinType)
```

The caller needs to invoke this method multiple times, once for each type of coin that is present in the payment.

Exercise P9.2. Modify the `giveChange` method of the `CashRegister` class so that it returns the number of coins of a particular type to return:

```
int giveChange(Coin coinType)
```

The caller needs to invoke this method for each coin type, in decreasing value.

Exercise P9.3. Real cash registers can handle both bills and coins. Design a single class that expresses the commonality of these concepts. Redesign the `CashRegister` class and provide a method for entering payments that are described by your class. Your primary challenge is to come up with a good name for this class.

Exercise P9.4. Enhance the `BankAccount` class by adding preconditions for the constructor and the `deposit` method that require the `amount` parameter to be at least zero, and a precondition for the `withdraw` method that requires `amount` to be at most the current balance. Use assertions to test the preconditions.

Exercise P9.5. Write static methods
- `public static double sphereVolume(double r)`
- `public static double sphereSurface(double r)`
- `public static double cylinderVolume(double r, double h)`
- `public static double cylinderSurface(double r, double h)`
- `public static double coneVolume(double r, double h)`
- `public static double coneSurface(double r, double h)`

that compute the volume and surface area of a sphere with radius r, a cylinder with circular base with radius r and height h, and a cone with circular base with radius r and height h. Place them into an appropriate class. Then write a program that prompts the user for the values of r and h, calls the six methods, and prints the results.

Exercise P9.6. Solve Exercise P9.5 by implementing classes Sphere, Cylinder, and Cone. Which approach is more object-oriented?

Exercise P9.7. Write methods

```
public static double perimeter(Ellipse2D.Double e);
public static double area(Ellipse2D.Double e);
```

that compute the area and the perimeter of the ellipse e. Use these methods in an applet that prompts the user to specify an ellipse. Then display messages with the perimeter and area of the ellipse. Why does it make sense to use a static method in this case?

Exercise P9.8. Write a method

```
public static double angle(Point2D.Double p, Point2D.Double q)
```

that computes the angle between the *x*-axis and the line joining two points. Add the method to a suitable class. Write a test program that asks the user to enter two points. Then display the angle. Why does it make sense to use a static method in this case?

Exercise P9.9. Write a method

```
public static boolean isInside(Point2D.Double p, Ellipse2D.Double e)
```

that tests whether a point is inside an ellipse. Add the method to a suitable class. Write a test program that asks the user to enter a point and an ellipse. Then print whether the point is contained inside the ellipse.

Exercise P9.10. Write a method

```
public static int readInt(Scanner in, String prompt, int min, int max)
```

that displays the prompt string, reads an integer, and tests whether it is between the minimum and maximum. If not, print an error message and repeat reading the input. Add the method to an appropriate class and provide a test program.

Exercise P9.11. Write methods

- `public static void drawH(Graphics2D g2, Point2D.Double p);`
- `public static void drawE(Graphics2D g2, Point2D.Double p);`
- `public static void drawL(Graphics2D g2, Point2D.Double p);`
- `public static void drawO(Graphics2D g2, Point2D.Double p);`

that show the letters H, E, L, O on the graphics window, where the point p is the top-left corner of the letter. Then call the methods to draw the words "HELLO" and "HOLE" on the graphics display. Draw lines and ellipses. Do not use the drawString method. Do not use System.out.

Exercise P9.12. Repeat Exercise P9.11 by designing classes LetterH, LetterE, LetterL, and LetterO, each with a constructor that takes a Point2D.Double (the top-left corner) and a method draw(Graphics2D g2).Which solution is more object-oriented?

Exercise P9.13. Consider the following algorithm for computing x^n for an integer n. If $n < 0$, x^n is $1/x^{-n}$. If n is positive and even, then $x^n = (x^{n/2})^2$. If n is positive and odd, then $x^n = x^{n-1} \cdot x$. Implement a static method intPower(double x, int n) that uses this algorithm. Add it to a class called Numeric.

Exercise P9.14. Improve the Needle class of Chapter 7. Turn the generator field into a static field so that all needles share a single random number generator.

Exercise P9.15. Implement a Coin and CashRegister class as described in Exercise P9.1. Place the Coin class into a package called money. Keep the CashRegister class in the default package.

Exercise P9.16. Write BankAccount and BankAccountTester classes in a package whose name is derived from your e-mail address, as described in Section 9.9.

PROGRAMMING PROJECTS

Project 9.1. Implement a program that prints paychecks for a group of student assistants. Deduct federal and Social Security taxes. (You may want to use the tax computation used in Chapter 6. Find out about Social Security taxes on the Internet.) Your program should prompt for the names, hourly wages, and hours worked of each student.

Project 9.2. For faster sorting of letters, the United States Postal Service encourages companies that send large volumes of mail to use a bar code denoting the ZIP code (see Figure 8).

The encoding scheme for a five-digit ZIP code is shown in Figure 9. There are full-height frame bars on each side. The five encoded digits are followed by a check digit, which is computed as follows: Add up all digits, and choose the check digit to make the sum a multiple of 10. For example, the sum of the digits in the ZIP code 95014 is 19, so the check digit is 1 to make the sum equal to 20.

★★★★★★★★★★★★★★★★ ECRLOT ★★ CO57

CODE C671RTS2
JOHN DOE   CO57
1009 FRANKLIN BLVD
SUNNYVALE   CA 95014 – 5143

‖‖‖‖‖‖‖‖‖‖‖‖‖‖‖‖‖‖‖‖‖‖‖‖‖‖‖‖‖‖‖

Figure 8   A Postal Bar Code

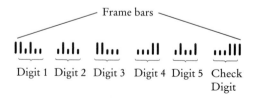

Digit 1 Digit 2 Digit 3 Digit 4 Digit 5 Check
                                              Digit

Figure 9   Encoding for Five-Digit Bar Codes

Each digit of the ZIP code, and the check digit, is encoded according to the following table:

	7	4	2	1	0
1	0	0	0	1	1
2	0	0	1	0	1
3	0	0	1	1	0
4	0	1	0	0	1
5	0	1	0	1	0
6	0	1	1	0	0
7	1	0	0	0	1
8	1	0	0	1	0
9	1	0	1	0	0
0	1	1	0	0	0

where 0 denotes a half bar and 1 a full bar. Note that they represent all combinations of two full and three half bars. The digit can be computed easily from the bar code using the column weights 7, 4, 2, 1, 0. For example, 01100 is

$$0 \cdot 7 + 1 \cdot 4 + 1 \cdot 2 + 0 \cdot 1 + 0 \cdot 0 = 6$$

The only exception is 0, which would yield 11 according to the weight formula.

Write a program that asks the user for a ZIP code and prints the bar code. Use : for half bars, | for full bars. For example, 95014 becomes

||:|:::|:|:||::::::||:|::|:::|||

(Alternatively, write a graphical application that draws real bars.)

Your program should also be able to carry out the opposite conversion: Translate bars into their ZIP code, reporting any errors in the input format or a mismatch of the digits.

ANSWERS TO SELF-CHECK QUESTIONS

1. Look for nouns in the problem description.
2. Yes (ChessBoard) and no (MovePiece).
3. Some of its features deal with payments, others with coin values.
4. None of the coin operations require the CashRegister class.
5. If a class doesn't depend on another, it is not affected by interface changes in the other class.
6. It is an accessor—calling substring doesn't modify the string on which the method is invoked. In fact, all methods of the String class are accessors.
7. No—translate is a mutator.
8. It is a side effect; this kind of side effect is common in object-oriented programming.
9. Yes—the method affects the state of the Scanner parameter.
10. Then you don't have to worry about checking for invalid values—it becomes the caller's responsibility.
11. No—you can take any action that is convenient for you.
12. Math m = new Math(); y = m.sqrt(x);
13. In an object-oriented solution, the main method would construct objects of classes Game, Player, and the like. Most methods would be instance methods that depend on the state of these objects.
14. System.in and System.out.
15. Yes, it works. Static methods can access static fields of the same class. But it is a terrible idea. As your programming tasks get more complex, you will want to use objects and classes to organize your programs.
16. The scope of amount is the entire deposit method. The scope of newBalance starts at the point at which the variable is defined and extends to the end of the method.
17. It starts at the beginning of the class and ends at the end of the class.
18. (a) No; (b) Yes; (c) Yes; (d) No
19. Yes—if you use fully qualified names for all classes, such as java.util.Random and java.awt.Rectangle.
20. /home/me/cs101/hw1/problem1 or, on Windows, c:\me\cs101\hw1\problem1.

Testing and Debugging

CHAPTER GOALS

- To learn how to carry out unit tests
- To understand the principles of test case selection and evaluation
- To learn how to use logging
- To become familiar with using a debugger
- To learn strategies for effective debugging

A **complex program** never works right the first time; it will contain errors, commonly called *bugs,* and will need to be tested. It is easier to test a program if it has been designed with testing in mind. This is a common engineering practice: On television circuit boards or in the wiring of an automobile, you will find lights and wire connectors that serve no direct purpose for the TV or car, but are put in place for the repair person in case something goes wrong. In the first part of this chapter you will learn how to instrument your programs in a similar way. It is a little more work upfront, but that work is amply repaid by shortened debugging times.

In the second part of this chapter you will learn how to run a debugger to cope with programs that don't do the right thing.

CHAPTER CONTENTS

10.1 Unit Tests

> Use unit tests to test classes in isolation.

The single most important testing tool is the *unit test*. A unit test checks a single method or a set of cooperating methods. In a unit test, you don't test the complete program that you are developing. Instead, you test the classes *in isolation*. That way, you will not be confused by the interactions between the classes in a larger program. After you have tested individual methods and classes thoroughly, it makes sense to put them into your program.

If you have ever put together a computer or fixed a car, you probably followed a similar process. Rather than simply throwing all the parts together and hoping for the best, you probably first tested each part in isolation. It takes a little longer at the beginning, but it greatly reduces the possibility of complete and mysterious failure once the parts are put together.

> Write a test harness to run a test.

For each test, you provide a simple class called a *test harness* that feeds parameters to the methods that are being tested. To learn about the mechanics of setting up test harnesses, we will use a simple example—a class that implements an approximation algorithm to compute square roots.

The algorithm, which was known to the ancient Greeks, starts by guessing a value x that might be somewhat close to the desired square root $\sqrt{a}$. The initial value doesn't have to be very close; $x = a$ is a perfectly good choice. Now consider the quantities x and a/x. If $x < \sqrt{a}$, then $a/x > a/\sqrt{a} = \sqrt{a}$. Similarly, if $x > \sqrt{a}$, then $a/x < a/\sqrt{a} = \sqrt{a}$. That is, $\sqrt{a}$ lies between x and a/x. Make the midpoint of that interval our improved guess of the square root (see Figure 1). Therefore set $x_{new} = (x + a/x)/2$ and repeat the procedure—that is, compute the midpoint between x_{new} and a/x_{new}. Stop when two successive approximations differ from each other by a very small amount.

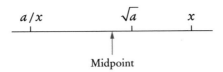

Figure 1 Approximating a Square Root

This method converges very rapidly. To compute $\sqrt{100}$, only eight steps are required:

```
Guess #1: 50.5
Guess #2: 26.24009900990099
Guess #3: 15.025530119986813
Guess #4: 10.840434673026925
Guess #5: 10.032578510960604
Guess #6: 10.000052895642693
Guess #7: 10.000000000139897
Guess #8: 10.0
```

The RootApproximator class implements the root approximation algorithm. Construct a RootApproximator to extract a square root of a given number. The nextGuess method computes the next guess, and the getRoot method keeps calling nextGuess until two guesses are sufficiently close.

File RootApproximator.java

```
1   /**
2       Computes approximations to the square root of
3       a number, using Heron's algorithm.
4   */
5   public class RootApproximator
6   {
7       /**
8           Constructs a root approximator for a given number.
9           @param aNumber  the number from which to extract the square root
10          (Precondition: aNumber >= 0)
11      */
12      public RootApproximator(double aNumber)
13      {
14          a = aNumber;
15          xold = 1;
16          xnew = a;
17      }
18
19      /**
20          Computes a better guess from the current guess.
21          @return  the next guess
22      */
23      public double nextGuess()
24      {
```

```
25        xold = xnew;
26        if (xold != 0)
27            xnew = (xold + a / xold) / 2;
28        return xnew;
29    }
30
31    /**
32        Computes the root by repeatedly improving the current
33        guess until two successive guesses are approximately equal.
34        @return the computed value for the square root
35    */
36    public double getRoot()
37    {
38        assert a >= 0;
39        while (!Numeric.approxEqual(xnew, xold))
40            nextGuess();
41        return xnew;
42    }
43
44    private double a; // The number whose square root is computed
45    private double xnew; // The current guess
46    private double xold; // The old guess
47 }
```

The Numeric class is a helper class. The approxEqual method tests whether two float-ing-point values are approximately equal, allowing for a small roundoff error. The Java library does not have any method to carry out this test. Therefore, we supply our own class. (See Exercise P10.13 for more information on comparing floating-point numbers.)

File Numeric.java

```
1  /**
2      A class for useful numeric methods.
3  */
4
5  public class Numeric
6  {
7      /**
8          Tests whether two floating-point numbers are
9          equal, except for a roundoff error.
10         @param x a floating-point number
11         @param y a floating-point number
12         @return true if x and y are approximately equal
13     */
14     public static boolean approxEqual(double x, double y)
15     {
16         final double EPSILON = 1E-12;
17         return Math.abs(x - y) <= EPSILON;
18     }
19 }
```

The guesses for $\sqrt{100}$ were computed by the following test program.

File RootApproximatorTester.java

```
1  import java.util.Scanner;
2
3  /**
4     This program prints ten approximations for a square root.
5  */
6  public class RootApproximatorTester
7  {
8     public static void main(String[] args)
9     {
10        System.out.print("Enter a number: ");
11        Scanner in = new Scanner(System.in);
12        double x = in.nextDouble();
13        RootApproximator r = new RootApproximator(x);
14        final int MAX_TRIES = 10;
15        for (int tries = 1; tries <= MAX_TRIES; tries++)
16        {
17           double y = r.nextGuess();
18           System.out.println("Guess #" + tries + ": " + y);
19        }
20        System.out.println("Square root: " + r.getRoot());
21     }
22  }
```

Output

```
Enter a number: 100
Guess #1: 50.5
Guess #2: 26.24009900990099
Guess #3: 15.025530119986813
Guess #4: 10.840434673026925
Guess #5: 10.032578510960604
Guess #6: 10.000052895642693
Guess #7: 10.000000000139897
Guess #8: 10.0
Guess #9: 10.0
Guess #10: 10.0
Square root: 10.0
```

Does the RootApproximator class work correctly for all inputs? Clearly, it needs to be tested with more values.

Of course, you can run the program again to test another value, and keep doing that until you are satisfied or bored. However, that approach has a serious limitation—the test is not repeatable. Suppose you detect and fix an error in your code. Of course, you will want to test the class again. You would need to remember which inputs you tried and type them in again. That is a disincentive to repeating the test. In the next section, you will see how to write test harnesses that make it easy to repeat unit tests.

1. What is the advantage of unit testing?
2. Why should a test harness be repeatable?

10.2 Providing Test Input

In this section, we discuss various mechanisms for providing test cases. One mechanism is to hardwire test inputs into the test harness, as shown in the following program. Then you can simply execute the test harness whenever you fix a bug in the class that is being tested. Advanced Topic 10.1 shows an alternate approach, in which test inputs are placed in a file instead.

File RootApproximatorHarness1.java

```
1  /**
2      This program computes square roots of selected input values.
3  */
4  public class RootApproximatorHarness1
5  {
6     public static void main(String[] args)
7     {
8        double[] testInputs = { 100, 4, 2, 1, 0.25, 0.01 };
9        for (double x : testInputs)
10       {
11          RootApproximator r = new RootApproximator(x);
12          double y = r.getRoot();
13          System.out.println("square root of " + x
14                 + " = " + y);
15       }
16    }
17 }
```

Output

```
square root of 100.0 = 10.0
square root of 4.0 = 2.0
square root of 2.0 = 1.414213562373095
square root of 1.0 = 1.0
square root of 0.25 = 0.5
square root of 0.01 = 0.1
```

You can also generate test cases automatically. If there are few possible inputs, it is feasible to run through a representative number of them with a loop.

File RootApproximatorHarness2.java

```
1   /**
2       This program computes square roots of input values
3       supplied by a loop.
4   */
5   public class RootApproximatorHarness2
6   {
7       public static void main(String[] args)
8       {
9           final double MIN = 1;
10          final double MAX = 10;
11          final double INCREMENT = 0.5;
12          for (double x = MIN; x <= MAX; x = x + INCREMENT)
13          {
14              RootApproximator r = new RootApproximator(x);
15              double y = r.getRoot();
16              System.out.println("square root of " + x
17                      + " = " + y);
18          }
19      }
20  }
```

Output

```
square root of 1.0 = 1.0
square root of 1.5 = 1.224744871391589
square root of 2.0 = 1.414213562373095
. . .
square root of 9.0 = 3.0
square root of 9.5 = 3.0822070014844885
square root of 10.0 = 3.162277660168379
```

Unfortunately, this test is restricted to only a small subset of values. To overcome that limitation, random generation of test cases can be useful:

File RootApproximatorHarness3.java

```
1   import java.util.Random;
2
3   /**
4       This program computes square roots of random inputs.
5   */
6   public class RootApproximatorHarness3
7   {
8       public static void main(String[] args)
9       {
10          final double SAMPLES = 100;
11          Random generator = new Random();
12          for (int i = 1; i <= SAMPLES; i++)
13          {
```

```
14              // Generate random test value
15
16              double x = 1000 * generator.nextDouble();
17              RootApproximator r = new RootApproximator(x);
18              double y = r.getRoot();
19              System.out.println("square root of " + x
20                  + " = " + y);
21          }
22      }
23  }
```

Output

```
square root of 810.4079626570873 = 28.467665212607223
square root of 480.50291114306344 = 21.9203766195534
square root of 643.5463246844379 = 25.36821485017103
square root of 506.5708496713842 = 22.507128863348704
square root of 539.6401504334708 = 23.230156057019308
square root of 795.0220214851004 = 28.196134867834285
. . .
```

Selecting good test cases is an important skill for debugging programs. You should test all features of the methods that you are testing. In the square root computation program, you should check typical test cases such as 100, 1/4, 0.01, 2, 10E12, and so on. These tests are positive tests. They consist of legitimate inputs, and you expect the program to handle them correctly.

Next, you should include *boundary test cases*: values that lie at the boundary of the set of acceptable inputs. For the root approximator, test what happens if the input is 0. Boundary cases are still legitimate inputs, and you expect that the program will handle them correctly—often in some trivial way or through special cases. Testing boundary cases is important, because programmers often make mistakes dealing with boundary conditions. Division by zero, extracting characters from empty strings, and accessing null pointers are common sources of errors.

> Boundary test cases are test cases that are at the boundary of acceptable inputs.

Finally, gather negative test cases. These are inputs that you expect the program to reject. A typical example is the square root of −2. If the getRoot method tried to compute the answer, it would never terminate. You can see why, by calling getNext a few times—the guesses oscillate and never get close enough to another.

```
Guess #1: -0.5
Guess #2: 1.75
Guess #3: 0.3035714285714286
Guess #4: -3.142331932773109
Guess #5: -1.2529309672222557
Guess #6: 0.1716630854488237
Guess #7: -5.739532701343778
Guess #8: -2.6955361385562107
Guess #9: -0.976784358209916
Guess #10: 0.5353752385394334
```

The getRoot method protects itself against this problem with an assert statement. An appropriate test case is to compute the square root of –2 with assertion checking enabled. The test passes if the test harness terminates with an assertion failure.

SELF CHECK

3. How can you repeat a unit test without having to retype input values?

4. Why is it important to test boundary cases?

ADVANCED TOPIC 10.1

Reading Test Inputs from a File

Hardwiring test cases into a test harness seems rather clumsy. It is more elegant to place the test values in a file.

The command line interfaces of most operating systems provide a way to link a file to the input of a program, as if all the characters in the file had actually been typed by a user. Type the following command:

```
java Program < data.txt
```

The program is executed, but it no longer reads input from the keyboard. Instead, the System.in object (and the Scanner that reads from System.in) gets the input from the file data.txt. This process is called *input redirection*.

If you have always launched your program from an integrated development environment, you need to find out whether your environment supports input redirection. If it does not, you need to open a command window (often called a shell) and launch the program in the command window by typing its name and redirection instructions.

You can also redirect output. To capture the output of a program in a file, use the command

```
java Program > output.txt
```

This is useful for archiving test cases.

The following program processes test inputs and stops when no additional inputs are available. The program is not meant for interactive use—there are no prompts.

File RootApproximatorHarness4.java

```
1   import java.util.Scanner;
2
3   /**
4       This program computes square roots of inputs supplied
5       through System.in.
6   */
7   public class RootApproximatorHarness4
8   {
9       public static void main(String[] args)
10      {
11          Scanner in = new Scanner(System.in);
12          boolean done = false;
```

```
13        while (in.hasNextDouble())
14        {
15            double x = in.nextDouble();
16            RootApproximator r = new RootApproximator(x);
17            double y = r.getRoot();
18
19            System.out.println("square root of " + x
20                + " = " + y);
21        }
22    }
23 }
```

Compile the program and prepare a file with test inputs, such as this one:

File test.in

```
1  100
2  4
3  2
4  1
5  0.25
6  0.01
```

Run the program like this

```
java RootApproximatorHarness4 < test.in > test.out
```

The output is captured in a file

File test.out

```
1  square root of 100.0 = 10.0
2  square root of 4.0 = 2.0
3  square root of 2.0 = 1.414213562373095
4  square root of 1.0 = 1.0
5  square root of 0.25 = 0.5
6  square root of 0.01 = 0.1
```

10.3 Test Case Evaluation

In the last section we worried about how to get test inputs. Now let us consider what to do with the outputs. How do you know whether the output is correct?

Sometimes you can verify the output by calculating the correct values by hand. For example, for a payroll program you can compute taxes manually.

Sometimes a computation does a lot of work, and it is not practical to do the computation manually. That is the case with many approximation algorithms, which may run through dozens or hundreds of iterations before they arrive at the final answer. The square root method of Section 10.1 is an example of such an approximation.

How can you test that the square root method works correctly? You can supply test inputs for which you know the answer, such as 4 and 100, and also 1/4 and 0.01, so that you don't restrict the inputs to integers.

Alternatively, you can write a test harness that verifies that the output values fulfill certain properties. For the square root program you can compute the square root, compute the square of the result, and verify that you obtained the original input:

File RootApproximatorHarness5.java

```java
import java.util.Random;

/**
   This program verifies the computation of square root values
   by checking a mathematical property of square roots.
*/
public class RootApproximatorHarness5
{
   public static void main(String[] args)
   {
      final double SAMPLES = 100;
      int passcount = 0;
      int failcount = 0;
      Random generator = new Random();
      for (int i = 1; i <= SAMPLES; i++)
      {
         // Generate random test value

         double x = 1000 * generator.nextDouble();
         RootApproximator r = new RootApproximator(x);
         double y = r.getRoot();

         // Check that test value fulfills square property

         if (Numeric.approxEqual(y * y, x))
         {
            System.out.print("Test passed: ");
            passcount++;
         }
         else
         {
            System.out.print("Test failed: ");
            failcount++;
         }

         System.out.println("x = " + x
               + ", root squared = " + y * y);
      }
      System.out.println("Pass: " + passcount);
      System.out.println("Fail: " + failcount);
   }
}
```

Output

```
Test passed: x = 913.6505141736327, root squared = 913.6505141736328
Test passed: x = 810.4959723987972, root squared = 810.4959723987972
Test passed: x = 503.84630929985883, root squared = 503.8463092998589
Test passed: x = 115.4885096006315, root squared = 115.48850960063153
Test passed: x = 384.973238438713, root squared = 384.973238438713
. . .
Pass: 100
Fail: 0
```

> An oracle is a slow but reliable method to compute a result for testing purposes.

Finally, there may be a less efficient way of computing the same value that a method produces. You can then run a test harness that computes the method to be tested, together with the slower process, and compares the answers. For example, $\sqrt{x} = x^{1/2}$, so you can use the slower Math.pow method to generate the same value. Such a slower but reliable method is called an *oracle*. The following example program shows how to compare the result of the method to be tested with the outcome of an oracle. Alternatively, you can write a separate program that writes the oracle values to a file, and then compare the results of your method against the precomputed oracle values.

File RootApproximatorHarness6.java

```java
1   import java.util.Random;
2
3   /**
4       This program verifies the computation of square root values
5       by using an oracle.
6   */
7   public class RootApproximatorHarness6
8   {
9       public static void main(String[] args)
10      {
11          final double SAMPLES = 100;
12          int passcount = 0;
13          int failcount = 0;
14          Random generator = new Random();
15          for (int i = 1; i <= SAMPLES; i++)
16          {
17              // Generate random test value
18
19              double x = 1000 * generator.nextDouble();
20              RootApproximator r = new RootApproximator(x);
21              double y = r.getRoot();
22
23              double oracleValue = Math.pow(x, 0.5);
24
25              // Check that test value approximately equals oracle value
26
27              if (Numeric.approxEqual(y, oracleValue))
28              {
```

```
29              System.out.print("Test passed: ");
30              passcount++;
31          }
32          else
33          {
34              System.out.print("Test failed: ");
35              failcount++;
36          }
37          System.out.println("square root = " + y
38                  + ", oracle = " + oracleValue);
39      }
40      System.out.println("Pass: " + passcount);
41      System.out.println("Fail: " + failcount);
42   }
43 }
```

Output

```
Test passed: square root = 718.3849112194539, oracle = 718.3849112194538
Test passed: square root = 641.2739466673618, oracle = 641.2739466673619
Test passed: square root = 896.3559528159169, oracle = 896.3559528159169
Test passed: square root = 591.4264541724909, oracle = 591.4264541724909
Test passed: square root = 721.029957736384, oracle = 721.029957736384
  . . .
Pass: 100
Fail: 0
```

SELF CHECK

5. Your task is to test a class that computes sales taxes for an Internet shopping site. Can you use an oracle?

6. Your task is to test a method that computes the area of an arbitrary polygon. Which polygons with known areas can you use as test inputs?

10.4 Regression Testing and Test Coverage

A test suite is a set of tests for repeated testing.

It is a common and useful practice to make a new test whenever you find a program bug. You can use that test to verify that your bug fix really works. Don't throw it away; feed it to the next version after that and all subsequent versions. Such a collection of test cases is called a *test suite*.

Regression testing involves repeating previously run tests to ensure that known failures of prior versions do not appear in new versions of the software.

You will be surprised how often a bug that you fixed will reappear in a future version. This is a phenomenon known as *cycling*. Sometimes you don't quite understand the reason for a bug and apply a quick fix that appears to work. Later, you apply a different quick fix that solves a second problem but makes the first problem appear again. Of course, it is always best to think through what really causes a bug and fix the root cause instead of doing a sequence of "Band-Aid" solutions. If you don't succeed in doing that, however, you at least want to have an honest appraisal of how well the program works. By keeping all old test cases around and testing them against every new version, you get that feedback. The process of testing against a set of past failures is called *regression testing*.

Testing the functionality of the program without consideration of its internal structure is called *black-box testing*. This is an important part of testing, because, after all, the users of a program do not know its internal structure. If a program works perfectly on all positive inputs and fails gracefully on all negative ones, then it does its job.

> Black-box testing describes a testing method that does not take the structure of the implementation into account.

However, it is impossible to ensure absolutely that a program will work correctly on all inputs just by supplying a finite number of test cases. As the famous computer scientist Edsger Dijkstra pointed out, testing can show only the presence of bugs—not their absence. To gain more confidence in the correctness of a program, it is useful to consider its internal structure. Testing strategies that look inside a program are called *white-box testing*. Performing unit tests of each method is a part of white-box testing.

> White-box testing uses information about the structure of a program.

You want to make sure that each part of your program is exercised at least once by one of your test cases. This is called *test coverage*. If some code is never executed by any of your test cases, you have no way of knowing whether that code would perform correctly if it ever were executed by user input. That means that you need to look at every if/else branch to see that each of them is reached by some test case. Many conditional branches are in the code only to take care of strange and abnormal inputs, but they still do something. It is a common phenomenon that they end up doing something incorrectly, but those faults are never discovered during testing, because nobody supplied the strange and abnormal inputs. Of course, these flaws become immediately apparent when the program is released and the first user types in a bad input and is incensed when the program crashes. A test suite should ensure that each part of the code is covered by some input.

> Test coverage is a measure of how many parts of a program have been tested.

For example, in testing the getTax method of the tax program in Chapter 6, you want to make sure that every if statement is entered for at least one test case. You should test both single and married taxpayers, with incomes in each of the three tax brackets.

It is a good idea to write the first test cases before the program is written completely. Designing a few test cases can give you insight into what the program should do, which is valuable for implementing it. You will also have something to throw at the program when it compiles for the first time. Of course, the initial set of test cases will be augmented as the debugging process progresses.

Modern programs can be quite challenging to test. In a program with a graphical user interface, the user can click random buttons with a mouse and supply input in random order. Programs that receive their data through a network connection need to be tested by simulating occasional network delays and failures. All this is much harder, because you cannot simply place keystrokes in a file. You need not worry about these complexities as you study this book, and there are tools to automate testing in these scenarios. The basic principles of regression testing (never throwing a test case away) and complete coverage (executing all code at least once) still hold.

SELF CHECK

7. Suppose you modified the code for a method. Why do you want to repeat tests that already passed with the previous version of the code?
8. Suppose a customer of your program finds an error. What action should you take beyond fixing the error?

PRODUCTIVITY HINT 10.1

Batch Files and Shell Scripts

If you need to perform the same tasks repeatedly on the command line, then it is worth learning about the automation features offered by your operating system.

Under Windows, you use batch files to execute a number of commands automatically. For example, suppose you need to test a program by running three test harnesses:

```
java RootApproximatorHarness1
java RootApproximatorHarness2
java RootApproximatorHarness3
```

Then you find a bug, fix it, and run the tests again. Now you need to type the three commands once more. There has to be a better way. Under DOS, put the commands in a text file and call it test.bat:

File test.bat

```
1  java RootApproximatorHarness1
2  java RootApproximatorHarness2
3  java RootApproximatorHarness3
```

Then you just type

```
test
```

and the three commands in the batch file execute automatically.

There are many uses for batch files, and it is well worth it to learn more about advanced features such as parameters and loops.

Batch files are a feature of the operating system, not of Java. On a UNIX system, shell scripts are used for the same purpose.

ADVANCED TOPIC 10.2

Unit Testing with JUnit

Designing and organizing test cases requires a certain amount of discipline. A popular tool for making this task more palatable is JUnit. The JUnit tool is freely available at http://junit.org, and it is also built into a number of development environments, including BlueJ and Eclipse.

When you use JUnit, you design a companion class for each class that you develop. By convention, the name of the companion class ends in Test, such as RootApproximatorTest. The test class must extend the class TestCase from the junit.framework package. For each test case, you define a method whose name starts with test, such as testSimpleCase. In each test case, you make some computations and then compute some condition that you believe to be true. You then pass the result to the assertTrue method. For example,

```java
import junit.framework.TestCase;

public class RootApproximatorTest extends TestCase
{
   public void testSimpleCase()
   {
      double x = 4;
      RootApproximator a = new RootApproximator(x);
      double r = a.getRoot();
      assertTrue(Numeric.approxEqual(r, 2));
   }

   public void testBoundaryCase()
   {
      double x = 0;
      RootApproximator a = new RootApproximator(x);
      double r = a.getRoot();
      assertTrue(Numeric.approxEqual(r, 0));
   }

   // More test cases
   . . .
}
```

Each test case method corresponds to one of the test harness classes that we discussed in the preceding sections. If any of the test cases fails, the JUnit tool catches the failure and shows an error message (see Figure 2).

The JUnit philosophy is simple. Whenever you implement a class, also make a companion test class. You design the tests as you design the program, one test method at a time. The test cases just keep accumulating in the test class. Whenever you have detected an actual failure, add a test case that flushes it out, so that you can be sure that you won't introduce that particular bug again. Whenever you modify your class, simply run the tests again.

If all tests pass, the user interface shows a green bar and you can relax. Otherwise, there is a red bar, but that's also good. It is much easier to fix a bug in isolation than inside a complex program.

Figure 2 Unit Testing with JUnit

10.5 Logging

A program trace consists of messages that show the path of execution.

Sometimes you run a program and you are not sure where it spends its time. To get a printout of the program flow, you can insert trace messages into the program, such as this one:

```java
public double getTax()
{
   . . .
   if (status == SINGLE)
   {
      System.out.println("status is SINGLE");
      . . .
   }
   . . .
}
```

However, there is a problem with using System.out.println for trace messages. When you are done testing the program, you need to remove all print statements that produce trace messages. If you find another error, however, you need to stick the print statements back in.

To overcome this problem, you should use the Logger class, which allows you to turn off the trace messages without removing them from the program.

Instead of printing directly to System.out, use the global logger object Logger.global and call

```
Logger.global.info("status is SINGLE");
```

By default, the message is printed. But if you call

```
Logger.global.setLevel(Level.OFF);
```

Logging messages can be deactivated when testing is complete.

at the beginning of the main method of your program, all log message printing is suppressed. Thus, you can turn off the log messages when your program works fine, and you can turn them back on if you find another error. In other words, using Logger.global.info is just like System.out.println, except that you can easily activate and deactivate the logging.

When you are tracing execution flow, the most important events are entering and exiting a method. At the beginning of a method, print out the parameters:

```
public TaxReturn(double anIncome, int aStatus)
{
   Logger.global.info("Parameters: anIncome = " + anIncome
         + " aStatus = " + aStatus);
   . . .
}
```

At the end of a method, print out the return value:

```
public double getTax()
{
   . . .
   Logger.global.info("Return value = " + tax);
   return tax;
}
```

Of course, you aren't restricted to "enter/exit" messages. You can report on progress inside a method. The Logger class has many other options for industrial-strength logging. You may want to check out the API documentation if you want to have more control over logging.

Logging messages can be useful to analyze the behavior of a program, but they have some definite disadvantages. It can be quite time-consuming to find out which logging messages to insert. If you insert too many messages, you produce a flurry of output that is hard to analyze; if you insert too few, you may not have enough information to spot the cause of the error. If you find that a hassle, you are not alone. Most professional programmers use a debugger, not logging messages, to locate complex errors in their code. Using a debugger is covered in the next section.

SELF CHECK

9. Should logging be activated during testing or when a program is used by its customers?

10. Why is it better to send trace messages to Logger.global than to System.out?

10.6 Using a Debugger

As you have undoubtedly realized by now, computer programs rarely run perfectly the first time. At times, it can be quite frustrating to find the bugs. Of course, you can insert logging messages to show the program flow as well as the values of key variables, run the program, and try to analyze the printout. If the printout does not clearly point to the problem, you may need to add and remove print commands and run the program again. That can be a time-consuming process.

> A debugger is a program that you can use to execute another program and analyze its run-time behavior.

Modern development environments contain special programs, called debuggers, that help you locate bugs by letting you follow the execution of a program. You can stop and restart your program and see the contents of variables whenever your program is temporarily stopped. At each stop, you have the choice of what variables to inspect and how many program steps to run until the next stop.

Some people feel that debuggers are just a tool to make programmers lazy. Admittedly some people write sloppy programs and then fix them up with a debugger, but the majority of programmers make an honest effort to write the best program they can before trying to run it through a debugger. These programmers realize that a debugger, while more convenient than logging statements, is not cost-free. It does take time to set up and carry out an effective debugging session.

In actual practice, you cannot avoid using a debugger. The larger your programs get, the harder it is to debug them simply by inserting logging statements. You will find that the time investment to learn about a debugger is amply repaid in your programming career.

Like compilers, debuggers vary widely from one system to another. On some systems they are quite primitive and require you to memorize a small set of arcane commands; on others they have an intuitive window interface. The screen shots in this chapter show the debugger in the Eclipse development environment, downloadable for free from the Eclipse Foundation web site [2]. Other integrated environments, such as BlueJ, also include debuggers. A free standalone debugger called JSwat is available from the JSwat Graphical Java Debugger web page [3].

You will have to find out how to prepare a program for debugging and how to start a debugger on your system. If you use an integrated development environment, which contains an editor, compiler, and debugger, this step is usually very easy. You just build the program in the usual way and pick a menu command to start debugging. On some systems, you must manually build a debug version of your program and invoke the debugger.

> You can make effective use of a debugger by mastering just three concepts: breakpoints, single-stepping, and inspecting variables.

Once you have started the debugger, you can go a long way with just three debugging commands: "set breakpoint", "single step", and "inspect variable". The names and keystrokes or mouse clicks for these commands differ widely between debuggers, but all debuggers support these basic commands. You can find out how, either from the documentation or a lab manual, or by asking someone who has used the debugger before.

When a debugger executes a program, the execution is suspended whenever a breakpoint is reached.

When you start the debugger, it runs at full speed until it reaches a breakpoint. Then execution stops, and the breakpoint that causes the stop is displayed (see Figure 3). You can now inspect variables and step through the program a line at a time, or continue running the program at full speed until it reaches the next breakpoint. When the program terminates, the debugger stops as well.

Breakpoints stay active until you remove them, so you should periodically clear the breakpoints that you no longer need.

Once the program has stopped, you can look at the current values of variables. Again, the method for selecting the variables differs among debuggers. Some debuggers always show you a window with the current local variables. On other debuggers you issue a command such as "inspect variable" and type in or click on the variable. The debugger then displays the contents of the variable. If all variables

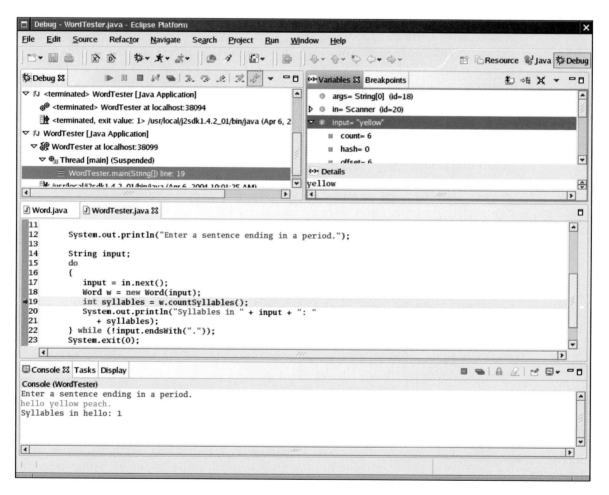

Figure 3   Stopping at a Breakpoint

contain what you expected, you can run the program until the next point where you want to stop.

When inspecting objects, you often need to give a command to "open up" the object, for example by clicking on a tree node. Once the object is opened up, you see its instance variables (see Figure 4).

> The single-step command executes the program one line at a time.

Running to a breakpoint gets you there speedily, but you don't know how the program got there. You can also step through the program a line at a time. Then you know how the program flows, but it can take a long time to step through it. The *single-step command* executes the current line and stops at the next program line. Most debuggers have two single-step commands, one called *step into*, which steps inside method calls, and one called *step over*, which skips over method calls.

For example, suppose the current line is

```
String input = in.next();
Word w = new Word(input);
int syllables = w.countSyllables();
System.out.println("Syllables in " + input + ": " + syllables);
```

When you step over method calls, you get to the next line:

```
String input = in.next();
Word w = new Word(input);
int syllables = w.countSyllables();
System.out.println("Syllables in " + input + ": " + syllables);
```

However, if you step into method calls, you enter the first line of the countSyllables method.

```
public int countSyllables()
{
    int count = 0;
    int end = text.length() - 1;
    . . .
}
```

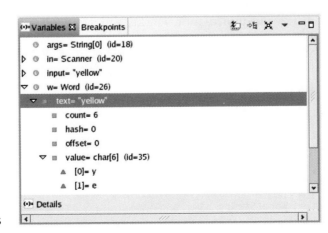

Figure 4
Inspecting Variables

You should step *into* a method to check whether it carries out its job correctly. You should step *over* a method if you know it works correctly.

Finally, when the program has finished running, the debug session is also finished. To run the program again, you may be able to reset the debugger, or you may need to exit the debugging program and start over. Details depend on the particular debugger.

SELF CHECK

11. In the debugger, you are reaching a call to System.out.println. Should you step into the method or step over it?
12. In the debugger, you are reaching the beginning of a method with a couple of loops inside. You want to find out the return value that is computed at the end of the method. Should you set a breakpoint, or should you step through the method?

10.7 A Sample Debugging Session

To have a realistic example for running a debugger, we will study a Word class whose primary purpose is to count the number of syllables in a word. The class uses this rule for counting syllables:

Each group of adjacent vowels (a, e, i, o, u, y) counts as one syllable (for example, the "ea" in "peach" contributes one syllable, but the "e ... o" in "yellow" counts as two syllables). However, an "e" at the end of a word doesn't count as a syllable. Each word has at least one syllable, even if the previous rules give a count of 0.

Also, when you construct a word from a string, any characters at the beginning or end of the string that aren't letters are stripped off. That is useful when you read the input using the next method of the Scanner class. Input strings can still contain quotation marks and punctuation marks, and we don't want them as part of the word.

Here is the source code. There are a couple of bugs in this class.

File Word.java

```
1  public class Word
2  {
3     /**
4        Constructs a word by removing leading and trailing non-
5        letter characters, such as punctuation marks.
6        @param s the input string
7     */
8     public Word(String s)
```

```
 9      {
10         int i = 0;
11         while (i < s.length() && !Character.isLetter(s.charAt(i)))
12            i++;
13         int j = s.length() - 1;
14         while (j > i && !Character.isLetter(s.charAt(j)))
15            j--;
16         text = s.substring(i, j);
17      }
18
19      /**
20         Returns the text of the word, after removal of the
21         leading and trailing nonletter characters.
22         @return the text of the word
23      */
24      public String getText()
25      {
26         return text;
27      }
28
29      /**
30         Counts the syllables in the word.
31         @return the syllable count
32      */
33      public int countSyllables()
34      {
35         int count = 0;
36         int end = text.length() - 1;
37         if (end < 0) return 0; // The empty string has no syllables
38
39         // An e at the end of the word doesn't count as a vowel
40         char ch = Character.toLowerCase(text.charAt(end));
41         if (ch == 'e') end--;
42
43         boolean insideVowelGroup = false;
44         for (int i = 0; i <= end; i++)
45         {
46            ch = Character.toLowerCase(text.charAt(i));
47            if ("aeiouy".indexOf(ch) >= 0)
48            {
49               // ch is a vowel
50               if (!insideVowelGroup)
51               {
52                  // Start of new vowel group
53                  count++;
54                  insideVowelGroup = true;
55               }
56            }
57         }
58
59         // Every word has at least one syllable
60         if (count == 0)
61            count = 1;
62
```

```
63           return count;
64       }
65
66       private String text;
67   }
```

Here is a simple test class. Type in a sentence, and the syllable counts of all words are displayed.

File WordTester.java

```
 1   import java.util.Scanner;
 2
 3   /**
 4       This program tests the countSyllables method of the Word class.
 5   */
 6   public class WordTester
 7   {
 8       public static void main(String[] args)
 9       {
10           Scanner in = new Scanner(System.in);
11
12           System.out.println("Enter a sentence ending in a period.");
13
14           String input;
15           do
16           {
17               input = in.next();
18               Word w = new Word(input);
19               int syllables = w.countSyllables();
20               System.out.println("Syllables in " + input + ": "
21                       + syllables);
22           }
23           while (!input.endsWith("."));
24       }
25   }
```

Supply this input:

```
hello yellow peach.
```

Then the output is

```
Syllables in hello: 1
Syllables in yellow: 1
Syllables in peach.: 1
```

That is not very promising.

First, set a breakpoint in the first line of the countSyllables method of the Word class, in line 38 of Word.java. Then start the program. The program will prompt you for the input. The program will stop at the breakpoint you just set.

```
  Scanner.java    J Word.java 
34        @return the syllable count
35     */
36     public int countSyllables()
37     {
38        int count = 0;
39        int end = text.length() - 1;
40        if (end < 0) return 0; // the empty string has no syllables
41
42        // an e at the end of the word doesn't count as a vowel
43        char ch = Character.toLowerCase(text.charAt(end));
44        if (ch == 'e') end--;
45
46        boolean insideVowelGroup = false;
```

Figure 5   Debugging the `countSyllables` Method

First, the `countSyllables` method checks the last character of the word to see if it is a letter `'e'`. Let's just verify that this works correctly. Run the program to line 41 (see Figure 5).

Now inspect the variable `ch`. This particular debugger has a handy display of all current local and instance variables—see Figure 6. If yours doesn't, you may need to inspect `ch` manually. You can see that `ch` contains the value `'l'`. That is strange. Look at the source code. The `end` variable was set to `text.length() - 1`, the last position in the `text` string, and `ch` is the character at that position.

Looking further, you will find that `end` is set to 3, not 4, as you would expect. And `text` contains the string `"hell"`, not `"hello"`. Thus, it is no wonder that `count-Syllables` returns the answer 1. We'll need to look elsewhere for the culprit. Apparently, the `Word` constructor contains an error.

Unfortunately, a debugger cannot go back in time. Thus, you must stop the debugger, set a breakpoint in the `Word` constructor, and restart the debugger. Supply the input once again. The debugger will stop at the beginning of the `Word` constructor. The constructor sets two variables `i` and `j`, skipping past any nonletters at the beginning and the end of the input string. Set a breakpoint past the end of the second loop (see Figure 7) so that you can inspect the values of `i` and `j`.

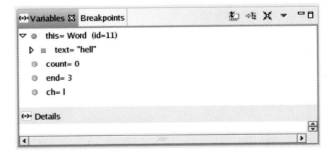

Figure 6   The Current Values of the Local and Instance Variables

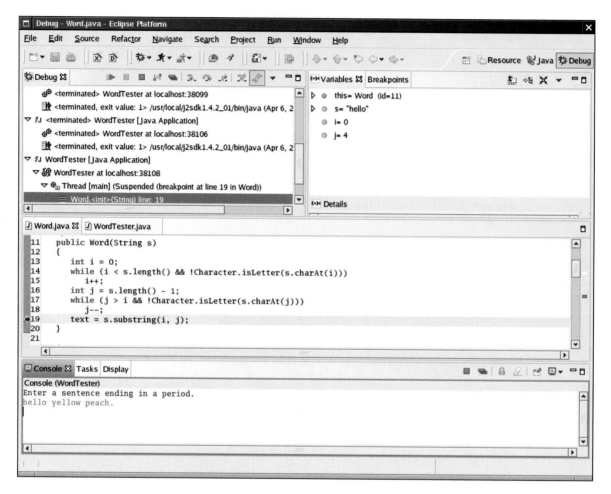

Figure 7 Debugging the Word Constructor

At this point, inspecting i and j shows that i is 0 and j is 4. That makes sense—there were no punctuation marks to skip. So why is text being set to "hell"? Recall that the substring method counts positions up to, but not including, the second parameter. Thus, the correct call should be

```
text = s.substring(i, j + 1);
```

This is a very typical off-by-one error.

Fix this error, recompile the program, and try the three test cases again. You will now get the output

```
Syllables in hello: 1
Syllables in yellow: 1
Syllables in peach.: 1
```

As you can see, there still is a problem. Erase all breakpoints and set a breakpoint in the countSyllables method. Start the debugger and supply the input "hello.".

When the debugger stops at the breakpoint, start single stepping through the lines of the method. Here is the code of the loop that counts the syllables:

```java
boolean insideVowelGroup = false;
for (int i = 0; i <= end; i++)
{
   ch = Character.toLowerCase(text.charAt(i));
   if ("aeiouy".indexOf(ch) >= 0)
   {
      // ch is a vowel
      if (!insideVowelGroup)
      {
         // Start of new vowel group
         count++;
         insideVowelGroup = true;
      }
   }
}
```

In the first iteration through the loop, the debugger skips the if statement. That makes sense, because the first letter, 'h', isn't a vowel. In the second iteration, the debugger enters the if statement, as it should, because the second letter, 'e', is a vowel. The insideVowelGroup variable is set to true, and the vowel counter is incremented. In the third iteration, the if statement is again skipped, because the letter 'l' is not a vowel. But in the fifth iteration, something weird happens. The letter 'o' is a vowel, and the if statement is entered. But the second if statement is skipped, and count is not incremented again.

Why? The insideVowelGroup variable is still true, even though the first vowel group was finished when the consonant 'l' was encountered. Reading a consonant should set insideVowelGroup back to false. This is a more subtle logic error, but not an uncommon one when designing a loop that keeps track of the processing state. To fix it, stop the debugger and add the following clause:

```java
if ("aeiouy".indexOf(ch) >= 0)
{
   . . .
}
else insideVowelGroup = false;
```

A debugger can be used only to analyze the presence of bugs, not to show that a program is bug-free.

Now recompile and run the test once again. The output is:

```
Syllables in hello: 2
Syllables in yellow: 2
Syllables in peach.: 1
```

Is the program now free from bugs? That is not a question the debugger can answer. Remember: Testing can show only the presence of bugs, not their absence.

SELF CHECK

13. What caused the first error that was found in this debugging session?

14. What caused the second error? How was it detected?

How To 10.1

Debugging

Now you know about the mechanics of debugging, but all that knowledge may still leave you helpless when you fire up a debugger to look at a sick program. There are a number of strategies that you can use to recognize bugs and their causes.

Step 1   Reproduce the error.

As you test your program, you notice that your program sometimes does something wrong. It gives the wrong output, it seems to print something completely random, it goes in an infinite loop, or it crashes. Find out exactly how to reproduce that behavior. What numbers did you enter? Where did you click with the mouse?

Run the program again; type in exactly the same answers, and click with the mouse on the same spots (or as close as you can get). Does the program exhibit the same behavior? If so, then it makes sense to fire up a debugger to study this particular problem. Debuggers are good for analyzing particular failures. They aren't terribly useful for studying a program in general.

Step 2   Simplify the error.

Before you fire up a debugger, it makes sense to spend a few minutes trying to come up with a simpler input that also produces an error. Can you use shorter words or simpler numbers and still have the program misbehave? If so, use those values during your debugging session.

Step 3   Divide and conquer.

> Use the divide-and-conquer technique to locate the point of failure of a program.

Now that you have a particular failure, you want to get as close to the failure as possible. The key point of debugging is to locate the code that produces the failure. Just as with real insect pests, finding the bug can be hard, but once you find it, squashing it is usually the easy part. Suppose your program dies with a division by 0. Because there are many division operations in a typical program, it is often not feasible to set breakpoints to all of them. Instead, use a technique of divide and conquer. Step over the methods in main, but don't step inside them. Eventually, the failure will happen again. Now you know which method contains the bug: It is the last method that was called from main before the program died. Restart the debugger and go back to that line in main, then step inside that method. Repeat the process.

Eventually, you will have pinpointed the line that contains the bad division. Maybe it is completely obvious from the code why the denominator is not correct. If not, you need to find the location where it is computed. Unfortunately, you can't go back in the debugger. You need to restart the program and move to the point where the denominator computation happens.

Step 4   Know what your program should do.

> During debugging, compare the actual contents of variables against the values you know they should have.

A debugger shows you what the program does. You must know what the program *should* do, or you will not be able to find bugs. Before you trace through a loop, ask yourself how many iterations you expect the program to make. Before you inspect a variable, ask yourself what you expect to see. If you have no clue, set aside some time and think first. Have a calculator handy to make independent computations. When you know what the value should be, inspect the variable. This is the moment of truth. If the program is still on the right track, then that value is what you expected, and you must look further for the bug. If the value is different, you may be on to something. Double-check your computation. If you are sure your value is correct, find out why your program comes up with a different value.

In many cases, program bugs are the result of simple errors such as loop termination conditions that are off by one. Quite often, however, programs make computational errors. Maybe they are supposed to add two numbers, but by accident the code was written to subtract them. Unlike your calculus instructor, programs don't make a special effort to ensure that everything is a simple integer (and neither do real-world problems). You will need to make some calculations with large integers or nasty floating-point numbers. Sometimes these calculations can be avoided if you just ask yourself, "Should this quantity be positive? Should it be larger than that value?" Then inspect variables to verify those theories.

Step 5 Look at all details.

When you debug a program, you often have a theory about what the problem is. Nevertheless, keep an open mind and look around at all details. What strange messages are displayed? Why does the program take another unexpected action? These details count. When you run a debugging session, you really are a detective who needs to look at every clue available.

If you notice another failure on the way to the problem that you are about to pin down, don't just say, "I'll come back to it later". That very failure may be the original cause for your current problem. It is better to make a note of the current problem, fix what you just found, and then return to the original mission.

Step 6 Make sure you understand each bug before you fix it.

Once you find that a loop makes too many iterations, it is very tempting to apply a "Band-Aid" solution and subtract 1 from a variable so that the particular problem doesn't appear again. Such a quick fix has an overwhelming probability of creating trouble elsewhere. You really need to have a thorough understanding of how the program should be written before you apply a fix.

It does occasionally happen that you find bug after bug and apply fix after fix, and the problem just moves around. That usually is a symptom of a larger problem with the program logic. There is little you can do with the debugger. You must rethink the program design and reorganize it.

RANDOM FACT 10.1

The First Bug

According to legend, the first bug was one found in 1947 in the Mark II, a huge electro-mechanical computer at Harvard University. It really was caused by a bug—a moth was trapped in a relay switch. Actually, from the note that the operator left in the log book next to the moth (see Figure 8), it appears as if the term "bug" had already been in active use at the time.

The pioneering computer scientist Maurice Wilkes wrote: "Somehow, at the Moore School and afterwards, one had always assumed there would be no particular difficulty in

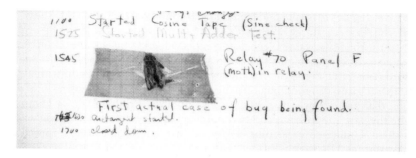

Figure 8   The First Bug

getting programs right. I can remember the exact instant in time at which it dawned on me that a great part of my future life would be spent finding mistakes in my own programs."

RANDOM FACT 10.2

The Therac-25 Incidents

The Therac-25 is a computerized device to deliver radiation treatment to cancer patients (see Figure 9). Between June 1985 and January 1987, several of these machines delivered serious overdoses to at least six patients, killing some of them and seriously maiming the others.

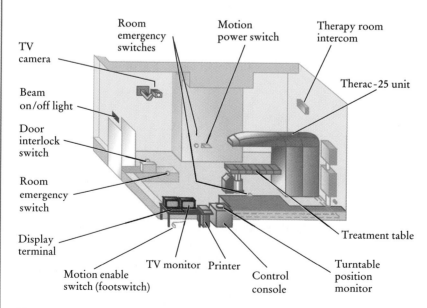

Figure 9   Typical Therac-25 Facility

The machines were controlled by a computer program. Bugs in the program were directly responsible for the overdoses. According to Leveson and Turner [1], the program was written by a single programmer, who had since left the manufacturing company producing the device and could not be located. None of the company employees interviewed could say anything about the educational level or qualifications of the programmer.

The investigation by the federal Food and Drug Administration (FDA) found that the program was poorly documented and that there was neither a specification document nor a formal test plan. (This should make you think. Do you have a formal test plan for your programs?)

The overdoses were caused by an amateurish design of the software that had to control different devices concurrently, namely the keyboard, the display, the printer, and of course the radiation device itself. Synchronization and data sharing between the tasks were done in an ad hoc way, even though safe multitasking techniques were known at the time. Had the programmer enjoyed a formal education that involved these techniques, or taken the effort to study the literature, a safer machine could have been built. Such a machine would have probably involved a commercial multitasking system, which might have required a more expensive computer.

The same flaws were present in the software controlling the predecessor model, the Therac-20, but that machine had hardware interlocks that mechanically prevented overdoses. The hardware safety devices were removed in the Therac-25 and replaced by checks in the software, presumably to save cost.

Frank Houston of the FDA wrote in 1985: "A significant amount of software for life-critical systems comes from small firms, especially in the medical device industry; firms that fit the profile of those resistant to or uninformed of the principles of either system safety or software engineering" [1].

Who is to blame? The programmer? The manager who not only failed to ensure that the programmer was up to the task but also didn't insist on comprehensive testing? The hospitals that installed the device, or the FDA, for not reviewing the design process? Unfortunately, even today there are no firm standards of what constitutes a safe software design process.

CHAPTER SUMMARY

1. Use unit tests to test classes in isolation.

2. Write a test harness to run a test.

3. Boundary test cases are test cases that are at the boundary of acceptable inputs.

4. An oracle is a slow but reliable method to compute a result for testing purposes.

5. A test suite is a set of tests for repeated testing.

6. Regression testing involves repeating previously run tests to ensure that known failures of prior versions do not appear in new versions of the software.

7. Black-box testing describes a testing method that does not take the structure of the implementation into account.

8. White-box testing uses information about the structure of a program.

9. Test coverage is a measure of how many parts of a program have been tested.

10. A program trace consists of messages that show the path of execution.

11. Logging messages can be deactivated when testing is complete.

12. A debugger is a program that you can use to execute another program and analyze its run-time behavior.

13. You can make effective use of a debugger by mastering just three concepts: breakpoints, single-stepping, and inspecting variables.

14. When a debugger executes a program, the execution is suspended whenever a breakpoint is reached.

15. The single-step command executes the program one line at a time.

16. A debugger can be used only to analyze the presence of bugs, not to show that a program is bug-free.

17. Use the divide-and-conquer technique to locate the point of failure of a program.

18. During debugging, compare the actual contents of variables against the values you know they should have.

FURTHER READING

1. Nancy G. Leveson and Clark S. Turner, "An Investigation of the Therac-25 Accidents," *IEEE Computer*, July 1993, pp. 18–41.

2. http://eclipse.org   The Eclipse Foundation web site.

3. http://www.bluemarsh.com/java/jswat   The JSwat Graphical Java Debugger web page.

CLASSES, OBJECTS, AND METHODS INTRODUCED IN THIS CHAPTER

```
java.util.logging.Level
     ALL
     INFO
     NONE
java.util.logging.Logger
     getLogger
     info
     setLevel
```

REVIEW EXERCISES

Exercise R10.1. Define the terms *unit test* and *test harness*.

Exercise R10.2. What is an *oracle*?

Exercise R10.3. Define the terms *regression testing* and *test suite*.

Exercise R10.4. What is the debugging phenomenon known as *cycling*? What can you do to avoid it?

Exercise R10.5. The arc sine function is the inverse of the sine function. That is, $y = \arcsin(x)$ if $x = \sin(y)$. It is defined only if $-1 \leq x \leq 1$. Suppose you need to write a Java method to compute the arc sine. List three positive test cases and one boundary test case with their expected return values, and two negative test cases.

Exercise R10.6. What is a program trace? When does it make sense to use a program trace, and when does it make more sense to use a debugger?

Exercise R10.7. Explain the differences between these debugger operations:
- Stepping into a method
- Stepping over a method

Exercise R10.8. Explain in detail how to inspect the information stored in a `Point2D.Double` object in your debugger.

Exercise R10.9. Explain in detail how to inspect the string stored in a `String` object in your debugger.

Exercise R10.10. Explain in detail how to use your debugger to inspect the balance stored in a `BankAccount` object.

Exercise R10.11. Explain the divide-and-conquer strategy to get close to a bug in a debugger.

Exercise R10.12. True or false:
- If a program has passed all tests in the test suite, it has no more bugs.
- If a program has a bug, that bug always shows up when running the program through a debugger.
- If all methods in a program were proven correct, then the program has no bugs.

PROGRAMMING EXERCISES

Exercise P10.1. The arc sine function is the inverse of the sine function. That is,

$$y = \arcsin(x) \text{ if } x = \sin(y)$$

where y is in radians. For example,

$$\arcsin(0) = 0$$
$$\arcsin(0.5) = \pi/6$$
$$\arcsin\left(\sqrt{2}/2\right) = \pi/4$$
$$\arcsin\left(\sqrt{3}/2\right) = \pi/3$$
$$\arcsin(1) = \pi/2$$
$$\arcsin(-1) = -\pi/2$$

The arc sine is defined only for values between −1 and 1. There is a Java standard library method to compute the arc sine, but you should not use it for this exercise. Write a Java class ArcSinApproximator that computes the arc sine from its Taylor series expansion

$$\arcsin(x) = x + \frac{x^3}{3!} + \frac{3^2 \cdot x^5}{5!} + \frac{3^2 \cdot 5^2 \cdot x^7}{7!} + \frac{3^2 \cdot 5^2 \cdot 7^2 \cdot x^9}{9!} + \cdots$$

Hint: Don't compute the powers and factorials explicitly. Instead, compute each term from the value of the preceding term.

You should compute the sum until a new term is $<10^{-6}$. This method will be used in subsequent exercises.

Exercise P10.2. Write a simple test harness for the ArcSinApproximator class that reads floating-point numbers from standard input and computes their arc sines, until the end of the input is reached. Then run that program and verify its outputs against the arc sine function of a scientific calculator.

Exercise P10.3. Write a test harness that automatically generates test cases for the ArcSinApproximator class, namely numbers between −1 and 1 in a step size of 0.1.

Exercise P10.4. Write a test harness that generates 10 random floating-point numbers between −1 and 1 and feeds them to ArcSinApproximator.

Exercise P10.5. Write a test harness that automatically tests the validity of the ArcSinApproximator class by verifying that

```
Math.sin(new ArcSinApproximator(x).getArcSin())
```

is approximately equal to x. Test it with 100 random inputs.

Exercise P10.6. The arc sine function can be computed from the arc tangent function, according to the formula

$$\arcsin(x) = \arctan\left(x / \sqrt{1 - x^2}\right)$$

Use that expression as an oracle to test that your arc sine method works correctly. Test your method with 100 random inputs and verify against the oracle.

Exercise P10.7. The domain of the arc sine function is $-1 \le x \le 1$. Test your class by computing arcsin(1.1). What happens?

Exercise P10.8. Place logging messages into the loop of the arc sine method that computes the power series. Print the value of the exponent of the current term, the value of the current term, and the current approximation to the result. What trace output do you get when you compute arcsin(0.5)?

Exercise P10.9. Add logging messages to the buggy Word class. Log relevant values, such as instance variable values, return values, and loop counters. Run your program with the same sample inputs used for the debugging session. Are the messages informative enough to spot the bug?

Exercise P10.10. Run a test harness of the ArcSinApproximator class through a debugger. Step inside the computation of arcsin(0.5). Step through the computation until the x^7 term has been computed and added to the sum. What is the value of the current term and of the sum at this point?

Exercise P10.11. Run a test harness of the arcsin method through a debugger. Step inside the computation of arcsin(0.5). Step through the computation until the x^n term has become smaller than 10^{-6}. Then inspect n. How large is it?

Exercise P10.12. The following class has two bugs:

```
public class RootApproximator
{
    public RootApproximator(double aNumber)
    {
        a = aNumber;
        x1 = aNumber;
    }

    public double nextGuess()
    {
        x1 = x0;
        x0 = (x1 + a / x1) / 2;
        return x1;
    }

    public double getRoot()
    {
        while (!Numeric.approxEqual(x0, x1))
            nextGuess();
        return x1;
```

```
        }
          private double a; // The number whose square root is computed
          private double x0;
          private double x1;
      }
```

Create a series of test cases to flush out the bugs. Then run a debugging session to find them. What changes did you make to the class to fix the bugs?

Exercise P10.13. We have cheated a bit in the algorithm that computes square roots. To see why, run the RootApproximatorHarness5 program after changing 1000 to 1000000. You will find that the test harness reports an alarming number of failures. The reason is that we were sloppy when comparing floating-point numbers. We tested whether two numbers are close to each other by checking whether their difference is close to 0.

$$|x - y| \le \varepsilon$$

However, this is not always good enough. Suppose x and y are rather large. Then they could be the same, except for a roundoff error, even if their difference was quite a bit larger than 10^{-14}. To overcome this problem, you need to divide by the magnitude of the numbers before comparing how close they are. Here is the formula: x and y are close enough if

$$\frac{|x - y|}{\max(|x|, |y|)} \le \varepsilon$$

For this test to work, both x and y must be nonzero. If one of the values is zero, you lose the magnitude information. Then all you can do is test whether the absolute value of the other number is at most ε.

Modify the Numeric.approxEqual method to carry out this test, and enhance the test harness to check much larger and much smaller values.

PROGRAMMING PROJECTS

Project 10.1. In this project, you will design and test a class for handling physical units. For example,

```
Unit length1 = new Unit(10, "cm");
Unit length2 = new Unit(5, "in");
Unit length3 = length1.add(length2);
Unit length4 = length3.convert("in");
```

You should support the following units:

- mm, cm, m, km
- mg, g, kg
- ml, l

If you live in a country that uses nonmetric units (i.e., Liberia, Myanmar, or the United States of America), also support your local units, such as

- inch, foot, mile
- ounce, pound
- fluid ounce, cup, pint, gallon

The add method yields a new Unit object whose unit is that of the implicit parameter, converting the explicit parameter if necessary. Thus, in the preceding example, length3 is measured in cm.

Neither the add nor the convert methods change their implicit parameters. They construct new Unit objects.

If the parameters are not compatible, then return a new Unit(0, "???"). That happens, for example, when trying to add meters and grams, or when converting meters to liters.

Write your test harness as you develop this solution. Whenever you work on a tricky situation, immediately design a test case for it.

Project 10.2. Your task is to implement a program that finds all *magic numbers* in a Java program. Recall from Quality Tip 4.1 that a magic number is a numerical value in a program that is not given a symbolic name. Your program will read input from System.in, using the Scanner class. A user of your program will use input redirection, such as

```
java MagicNumberFinder < MyProgram.java
```

You should break up the input into *tokens*:

- numbers
- identifiers
- quoted strings and characters
- operators and other syntactical marks, such as braces
- comments

Print out all numbers that you can find, except for

- numbers that initialize final variables
- numbers inside quoted strings, characters, and comments

Before you start programming, gather a series of test inputs that show both normal cases and tricky situations, such as numbers inside comments, comment delimiters inside quoted strings, and so on.

When you encounter your first bug, fire up a debugger. Take a screen capture that demonstrates the bug (for example, with the free Gimp program, or by using Alt + PrtScr on Windows, or Cmd + Shift + 4 on the Mac). Your screen capture should show the offending line of code and the invalid variable settings. Fix the bug and go back to the same spot. Take another screen capture to demonstrate your fix.

ANSWERS TO SELF-CHECK QUESTIONS

1. It is easier to test methods and classes in isolation than it is to understand failures in a complex program.
2. It should be easy and painless to repeat a test after fixing a bug.
3. By putting the values in a file, or by generating them programmatically.
4. Programmers commonly make mistakes when dealing with boundary conditions.
5. Probably not—there is no easily accessible but slow mechanism to compute sales taxes. You will probably need to verify the calculations by hand.
6. There are well-known formulas for the areas of triangles, rectangles, and regular n-gons.
7. It is possible to introduce errors when modifying code.
8. Add a test case to the test suite that verifies that the error is fixed.
9. Logging messages report on the internal workings of your program—your customers would not want to see them. They are intended for testing only.
10. It is easy to deactivate `Logger.global` when you no longer want to see the trace messages, and to reactivate it when you need to see them again.
11. You should step over it because you are not interested in debugging the internals of the `println` method.
12. You should set a breakpoint. Stepping through loops can be tedious.
13. The programmer misunderstood the second parameter of the substring method—it is the index of the first character not to be included in the substring.
14. The second error was caused by failing to reset `insideVowelGroup` to false at the end of a vowel group. It was detected by tracing through the loop and noticing that the loop didn't enter the conditional statement that increments the vowel count.

Interfaces and Polymorphism

Interface types are an important tool for developing *reusable* software components. The reuse is ultimately made possible by *polymorphism*, a key mechanism of object-oriented programming. By studying the invocation of methods of classes that implement a common interface, you will observe polymorphism in its purest form.

Often, it is beneficial to limit the scope of simple classes, by defining them as *inner* classes inside another class or method. This is particularly useful for classes that implement event-handler interfaces. However, if you are not interested in user-interface programming, you can safely omit the sections covering inner classes and timer events.

CHAPTER CONTENTS

11.1 Using Interfaces for Code Reuse

Use interface types to
make code more reusable.

It is often possible to make code more general and more reusable by
focusing on the essential operations that are carried out. *Interface
types* are used to express these common operations.

Consider the DataSet class of Chapter 7. We used that class to
compute the average and maximum of a set of input values. However, the class was
suitable only for computing the average of a set of *numbers*. If we wanted to process
bank accounts to find the bank account with the highest balance, we would have to
modify the class, like this:

```java
public class DataSet // Modified for BankAccount objects
{
   . . .
   public void add(BankAccount x)
   {
      sum = sum + x.getBalance();
      if (count == 0 || maximum.getBalance() < x.getBalance())
         maximum = x;
      count++;
   }

   public BankAccount getMaximum()
   {
      return maximum;
   }

   private double sum;
   private BankAccount maximum;
   private int count;
}
```

Or suppose we wanted to find the coin with the highest value among a set of coins. We would need to modify the DataSet class again.

```
public class DataSet // Modified for Coin objects
{
    . . .
    public void add(Coin x)
    {
        sum = sum + x.getValue();
        if (count == 0  || maximum.getValue() < x.getValue())
            maximum = x;
        count++;
    }

    public Coin getMaximum()
    {
        return maximum;
    }

    private double sum;
    private Coin maximum;
    private int count;
}
```

Clearly, the fundamental mechanics of analyzing the data is the same in all cases, but the details of measurement differ.

Suppose that the various classes agree on a single method getMeasure that obtains the measure to be used in the data analysis. For bank accounts, getMeasure returns the balance. For coins, getMeasure returns the coin value, and so on. Then we can implement a single reusable DataSet class whose add method looks like this:

```
sum = sum + x.getMeasure();
if (count == 0 || maximum.getMeasure() < x.getMeasure())
    maximum = x;
count++;
```

What is the type of the variable x? Ideally, x should refer to any class that has a getMeasure method.

In Java, an *interface type* is used to specify required operations. We will define an interface type that we call Measurable:

> A Java interface type declares a set of methods and their signatures.

```
public interface Measurable
{
    double getMeasure();
}
```

The interface declaration lists all methods that the interface type requires. The Measurable interface type requires a single method, but in general, an interface type can require multiple methods.

Note that the Measurable type is not a type in the standard library—it is a type that was created specifically for this book, in order to make the DataSet class more reusable.

> Unlike a class, an interface type provides no implementation.

An interface type is similar to a class, but there are several important differences:

- All methods in an interface type are *abstract;* that is, they have a name, parameters, and a return type, but they don't have an implementation.
- All methods in an interface type are automatically public.
- An interface type does not have instance fields.

Now we can use the interface type Measurable to declare the variables x and maximum.

```
public class DataSet
{
   . . .
   public void add(Measurable x)
   {
      sum = sum + x.getMeasure();
      if (count == 0  || maximum.getMeasure() < x.getMeasure())
         maximum = x;
      count++;
   }

   public Measurable getMaximum()
   {
      return maximum;
   }

   private double sum;
   private Measurable maximum;
   private int count;
}
```

> Use the implements keyword to indicate that a class implements an interface type.

This DataSet class is usable for analyzing objects of any class that *implements* the Measurable interface. A class implements an interface type if it declares the interface in an implements clause. It should then implement the method or methods that the interface requires.

```
class ClassName implements Measurable
{
   public double getMeasure()
   {
      Implementation
   }

   Additional methods and fields
}
```

A class can implement more than one interface type. Of course, the class must then define all the methods that are required by all the interfaces it implements.

Let us modify the BankAccount class to implement the Measurable interface.

```
public class BankAccount implements Measurable
{
   public double getMeasure()
   {
```

```
        return balance;
    }
      . . .
}
```

Note that the class must declare the method as `public`, whereas the interface need not—all methods in an interface are public.

Similarly, it is an easy matter to modify the `Coin` class to implement the `Measurable` interface.

```
public class Coin implements Measurable
{
    public double getMeasure()
    {
        return value;
    }
      . . .
}
```

In summary, the `Measurable` interface expresses what all measurable objects have in common. This commonality makes the `DataSet` class reusable. Objects of the `DataSet` class can be used to analyze collections of objects of *any* class that implements the `Measurable` interface. Following is a test program that illustrates that fact.

Figure 1 shows the relationships between the classes and interfaces. In the UML notation, interfaces are tagged with a "stereotype" indicator «interface». A dotted arrow with a triangular tip denotes the "*is-a*" relationship between a class and an interface. You have to look carefully at the arrow tips—a dotted line with an open arrow tip (⥰) denotes the "*uses*" relationship or dependency.

> Interfaces can reduce the coupling between classes.

This diagram shows that the `DataSet` class depends only on the `Measurable` interface. It is decoupled from the `BankAccount` and `Coin` classes.

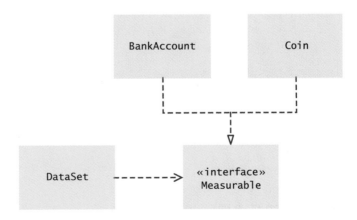

Figure 1   UML Diagram of the DataSet Class and the Classes That Implement the Measurable Interface

SYNTAX 11.1 Defining an Interface

```
public interface InterfaceName
{
    method signatures
}
```

Example:

```
public interface Measurable
{
    double getMeasure();
}
```

Purpose:

To define an interface and its method signatures. The methods are automatically public.

SYNTAX 11.2 Implementing an Interface

```
public class ClassName
        implements InterfaceName, InterfaceName, . . .
{
    methods
    fields
}
```

Example:

```
public class BankAccount implements Measurable
{
    // Other BankAccount methods
    public double getMeasure()
    {
        // Method implementation
    }
}
```

Purpose:

To define a new class that implements the methods of an interface

File DataSetTester.java

```
1  /**
2      This program tests the DataSet class.
3  */
4  public class DataSetTester
5  {
```

```
 6      public static void main(String[] args)
 7      {
 8          DataSet bankData = new DataSet();
 9
10          bankData.add(new BankAccount(0));
11          bankData.add(new BankAccount(10000));
12          bankData.add(new BankAccount(2000));
13
14          System.out.println("Average balance = "
15                  + bankData.getAverage());
16          Measurable max = bankData.getMaximum();
17          System.out.println("Highest balance = "
18                  + max.getMeasure());
19
20          DataSet coinData = new DataSet();
21
22          coinData.add(new Coin(0.25, "quarter"));
23          coinData.add(new Coin(0.1, "dime"));
24          coinData.add(new Coin(0.05, "nickel"));
25
26          System.out.println("Average coin value = "
27                  + coinData.getAverage());
28          max = coinData.getMaximum();
29          System.out.println("Highest coin value = "
30                  + max.getMeasure());
31      }
32  }
```

Output

```
Average balance = 4000.0
Highest balance = 10000.0
Average coin value = 0.13333333333333333
Highest coin value = 0.25
```

SELF CHECK

1. Suppose you want to use the DataSet class to find the Country object with the largest population. What condition must the Country class fulfill?
2. Why can't the add method of the DataSet class have a parameter of type Object?

COMMON ERROR 11.1

Forgetting to Define Implementing Methods as Public

The methods in an interface are not declared as public, because they are public by default. However, the methods in a class are not public by default—their default access level is "package" access, which we discuss in Chapter 13. It is a common error to forget the public keyword when defining a method from an interface:

```
public class BankAccount implements Measurable
{
    double getMeasure() // Oops—should be public
    {
        return balance;
    }
    . . .
}
```

Then the compiler complains that the method has a weaker access level, namely package access instead of public access. The remedy is to declare the method as public.

ADVANCED TOPIC 11.1

Constants in Interfaces

Interfaces cannot have instance fields, but it is legal to specify *constants*. For example, the SwingConstants interface defines various constants, such as SwingConstants.NORTH, SwingConstants.EAST, and so on.

When defining a constant in an interface, you can (and should) omit the keywords public static final, because all fields in an interface are automatically public static final. For example,

```
public interface SwingConstants
{
    int NORTH = 1;
    int NORTHEAST = 2;
    int EAST = 3;
    . . .
}
```

11.2 Converting Between Class and Interface Types

Interfaces are used to express the commonality between classes. In this section, we discuss when it is legal to convert between class and interface types.

Have a close look at the call

```
bankData.add(new BankAccount(10000));
```

from the test program of the preceding section. Here we pass an object of type BankAccount to the add method of the DataSet class. However, that method has a parameter of type Measurable:

```
public void add(Measurable x)
```

Is it legal to convert from the BankAccount type to the Measurable type?

You can convert from a class type to an interface type, provided the class implements the interface.

In Java, such a type conversion is legal. You can convert from a class type to the type of any interface that the class implements. For example,

```
BankAccount account = new BankAccount(10000);
Measurable x = account; // OK
```

Alternatively, x can refer to a Coin object, provided the Coin class has been modified to implement the Measurable interface.

```
Coin dime = new Coin(0.1, "dime");
Measurable x = dime; // Also OK
```

Thus, when you have an object variable of type Measurable, you don't actually know the exact type of the object to which x refers. All you know is that the object has a getMeasure method.

However, you cannot convert between unrelated types:

```
Measurable x = new Rectangle(5, 10, 20, 30); // Error
```

That assignment is an error, because the Rectangle class doesn't implement the Measurable interface.

Occasionally, it happens that you convert an object to an interface reference and you need to convert it back. This happens in the getMaximum method of the DataSet class. The DataSet stores the object with the largest measure, *as a* Measurable *reference*.

```
DataSet coinData = new DataSet();
coinData.add(new Coin(0.25, "quarter"));
coinData.add(new Coin(0.1, "dime"));
coinData.add(new Coin(0.05, "nickel"));
Measurable max = coinData.getMaximum();
```

Now what can you do with the max reference? *You* know it refers to a Coin object, but the compiler doesn't. For example, you cannot call the getName method:

```
String coinName = max.getName(); // Error
```

That call is an error, because the Measurable type has no getName method.

You need a cast to convert from an interface type to a class type.

However, as long as you are absolutely sure that max refers to a Coin object, you can use the *cast* notation to convert it back:

```
Coin maxCoin = (Coin) max;
String name = maxCoin.getName();
```

If you are wrong, and the object doesn't actually refer to a coin, your program will throw an exception and terminate.

This cast notation is the same notation that you saw in Chapter 4 to convert between number types. For example, if x is a floating-point number, then (int) x is the integer part of the number. The intent is similar—to convert from one type to another. However, there is one big difference between casting of number types and casting of class types. When casting number types, you *lose information*, and you use the cast to tell the compiler that you agree to the information loss. When casting object types, on the other hand, you *take a risk* of causing an exception, and you tell the compiler that you agree to that risk.

3. Can you use a cast `(BankAccount)` x to convert a `Measurable` variable x to a `BankAccount` reference?

4. If both `BankAccount` and `Coin` implement the `Measurable` interface, can a `Coin` reference be converted to a `BankAccount` reference?

COMMON ERROR 11.2

Trying to Instantiate an Interface

You can define variables whose type is an interface, for example:

```
Measurable x;
```

However, you can *never* construct an interface:

```
Measurable x = new Measurable(); // Error
```

Interfaces aren't classes. There are no objects whose types are interfaces. If an interface variable refers to an object, then the object must belong to some class—a class that implements the interface:

```
Measurable x = new BankAccount(); // OK
```

11.3 Polymorphism

When multiple classes implement the same interface, each class implements the methods of the interface in different ways. How is the correct method executed when the interface method is invoked? We will answer that question in this section.

It is worth emphasizing once again that it is perfectly legal—and in fact very common—to have variables whose type is an interface, such as

```
Measurable x;
```

Just remember that the object to which x refers doesn't have type `Measurable`. In fact, *no object* has type `Measurable`. Instead, the type of the object is some class that implements the `Measurable` interface, such as `BankAccount` or `Coin`.

Note that x can refer to objects of *different* types during its lifetime. Here the variable x first contains a reference to a bank account, then a reference to a coin.

```
x = new BankAccount(10000); // OK
x = new Coin(0.1, "dime"); // OK
```

What can you do with an interface variable, given that you don't know the class of the object that it references? You can invoke the methods of the interface:

```
double m = x.getMeasure();
```

The `DataSet` class took advantage of this capability by computing the measure of the added object, without worrying exactly what kind of object was added.

Now let's think through the call to the getMeasure method more carefully. *Which* getMeasure method? The BankAccount and Coin classes provide two *different* implementations of that method. How did the correct method get called if the caller didn't even know the exact class to which x belongs?

The Java virtual machine makes a special effort to locate the correct method that belongs to the class of the actual object. That is, if x refers to a BankAccount object, then the BankAccount.getMeasure method is called. If x refers to a Coin object, then the Coin.getMeasure method is called. This means that one method call

```
double m = x.getMeasure();
```

can call different methods depending on the momentary contents of x.

> Polymorphism denotes the principle that behavior can vary depending on the actual type of an object.

The principle that the actual type of the object determines the method to be called is called *polymorphism*. The term "polymorphism" comes from the Greek words for "many shapes". The same computation works for objects of many shapes, and adapts itself to the nature of the objects. In Java, all instance methods are polymorphic.

When you see a polymorphic method call, such as x.getMeasure(), there are several possible getMeasure methods that can be called. You have already seen another case in which the same method name can refer to different methods, namely when a method name is *overloaded:* that is, when a single class has several methods with the same name but different parameter types. For example, you can have two constructors BankAccount() and BankAccount(double). The compiler selects the appropriate method when compiling the program, simply by looking at the types of the parameters:

```
account = new BankAccount();
    // Compiler selects BankAccount()
account = new BankAccount(10000);
    // Compiler selects BankAccount(double)
```

> Early binding of methods occurs if the compiler selects a method from several possible candidates. Late binding occurs if the method selection takes place when the program runs.

There is an important difference between polymorphism and overloading. The compiler picks an overloaded method when translating the program, before the program ever runs. This method selection is called *early binding*. However, when selecting the appropriate getMeasure method in a call x.getMeasure(), the compiler does not make any decision when translating the method. The program has to run before anyone can know what is stored in x. Therefore, the virtual machine, and not the compiler, selects the appropriate method. This method selection is called *late binding*.

SELF CHECK

5. Why is it impossible to construct a Measurable object?
6. Why can you nevertheless declare a variable whose type is Measurable?
7. What do overloading and polymorphism have in common? Where do they differ?

11.4 Using Interfaces for Callbacks

In this section, we discuss how the DataSet class can be made even more reusable by supplying a different interface type. This type of interface provides a "callback" mechanism, allowing the DataSet class to call back a specific method when it needs more information.

To understand why a further improvement to the DataSet class is desirable, consider these limitations of the Measurable interface:

- You can add the Measurable interface only to classes under your control. If you want to process a set of Rectangle objects, you cannot make the Rectangle class implement another interface—it is a system class, which you cannot change.

- You can measure an object in only one way. If you want to analyze a set of savings accounts both by bank balance and by interest rate, you are stuck.

Therefore, let us rethink the DataSet class. The data set needs to measure the objects that are added. When the objects are required to be of type Measurable, the responsibility of measuring lies with the added objects themselves, which is the cause of the limitations that we noted. It would be better if another object could carry out the measurement. Let's move the measurement method into a different interface:

```
public interface Measurer
{
    double measure(Object anObject);
}
```

The measure method measures an object and returns its measurement. Here we use the fact that all objects can be converted to the type Object, the "lowest common denominator" of all classes in Java. We will discuss the Object type in greater detail in Chapter 13.

The improved DataSet class is constructed with a Measurer object (that is, an object of some class that implements the Measurer interface). That object is saved in a measurer instance field and used to carry out the measurements, like this:

```
public void add(Object x)
{
    sum = sum + measurer.measure(x);
    if (count == 0 || measurer.measure(maximum) < measurer.measure(x))
        maximum = x;
    count++;
}
```

The DataSet class simply makes a callback to the measure method whenever it needs to measure any object.

Now you can define measurers to take on any kind of measurement. For example, here is how you can measure rectangles by area. Define a class

```
public class RectangleMeasurer implements Measurer
{
    public double measure(Object anObject)
    {
```

```
        Rectangle aRectangle = (Rectangle) anObject;
        double area = aRectangle.getWidth() * aRectangle.getHeight();
        return area;
    }
}
```

Note that the measure method must accept a parameter of type Object, even though this particular measurer just wants to measure rectangles. The method signature must match the signature of the measure method in the Measurer interface. Therefore, the Object parameter is cast to the Rectangle type:

```
Rectangle aRectangle = (Rectangle) anObject;
```

What can you do with a RectangleMeasurer? You need it for a DataSet that compares rectangles by area. Construct an object of the RectangleMeasurer class and pass it to the DataSet constructor.

```
Measurer m = new RectangleMeasurer();
DataSet data = new DataSet(m);
```

Next, add rectangles to the data set.

```
data.add(new Rectangle(5, 10, 20, 30));
data.add(new Rectangle(10, 20, 30, 40));
. . .
```

The data set will ask the RectangleMeasurer object to measure the rectangles. In other words, the data set uses the RectangleMeasurer object to carry out callbacks.

Figure 2 shows the UML diagram of the classes and interfaces of this solution. As in Figure 1, the DataSet class is decoupled from the Rectangle class whose objects it processes. However, unlike in Figure 1, the Rectangle class is no longer coupled with another class. Instead, to process rectangles, you have to come up with a small "helper" class RectangleMeasurer. This helper class has only one purpose: to tell the DataSet how to measure its objects.

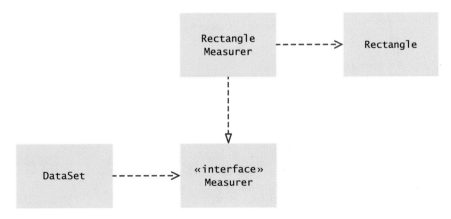

Figure 2 UML Diagram of the DataSet Class and the Measurer Interface

File DataSet.java

```java
1  /**
2      Computes the average of a set of data values.
3  */
4  public class DataSet
5  {
6      /**
7          Constructs an empty data set with a given measurer.
8          @param aMeasurer the measurer that is used to measure data values
9      */
10     public DataSet(Measurer aMeasurer)
11     {
12         sum = 0;
13         count = 0;
14         maximum = null;
15         measurer = aMeasurer;
16     }
17
18     /**
19         Adds a data value to the data set.
20         @param x a data value
21     */
22     public void add(Object x)
23     {
24         sum = sum + measurer.measure(x);
25         if (count == 0
26             || measurer.measure(maximum) < measurer.measure(x))
27             maximum = x;
28         count++;
29     }
30
31     /**
32         Gets the average of the added data.
33         @return the average or 0 if no data has been added
34     */
35     public double getAverage()
36     {
37         if (count == 0) return 0;
38         else return sum / count;
39     }
40
41     /**
42         Gets the largest of the added data.
43         @return the maximum or 0 if no data has been added
44     */
45     public Object getMaximum()
46     {
47         return maximum;
48     }
49
50     private double sum;
51     private Object maximum;
52     private int count;
53     private Measurer measurer;
54 }
```

File DataSetTester2.java

```
1   import java.awt.Rectangle;
2
3   /**
4       This program demonstrates the use of a Measurer.
5   */
6   public class DataSetTester2
7   {
8      public static void main(String[] args)
9      {
10        Measurer m = new RectangleMeasurer();
11
12        DataSet data = new DataSet(m);
13
14        data.add(new Rectangle(5, 10, 20, 30));
15        data.add(new Rectangle(10, 20, 30, 40));
16        data.add(new Rectangle(20, 30, 5, 10));
17
18        System.out.println("Average area = " + data.getAverage());
19        Rectangle max = (Rectangle) data.getMaximum();
20        System.out.println("Maximum area rectangle = " + max);
21     }
22  }
```

File Measurer.java

```
1   /**
2       Describes any class whose objects can measure other objects.
3   */
4   public interface Measurer
5   {
6      /**
7          Computes the measure of an object.
8          @param anObject the object to be measured
9          @return the measure
10     */
11     double measure(Object anObject);
12  }
```

File RectangleMeasurer.java

```
1   import java.awt.Rectangle;
2
3   /**
4       Objects of this class measure rectangles by area.
5   */
6   public class RectangleMeasurer implements Measurer
7   {
8      public double measure(Object anObject)
9      {
10        Rectangle aRectangle = (Rectangle) anObject;
11        double area = aRectangle.getWidth() * aRectangle.getHeight();
12        return area;
13     }
14  }
```

Output

```
Average area = 616.6666666666666
Maximum area rectangle = java.awt.Rectangle[x=10,y=20,width=30,height=40]
```

SELF CHECK

8. Suppose you want to use the `DataSet` class of Section 11.1 to find the longest `String` from a set of inputs. Why can't this work?

9. How can you use the `DataSet` class of this section to find the longest `String` from a set of inputs?

10. Why does the `measure` method of the `Measurer` interface have one more parameter than the `getMeasure` method of the `Measurable` interface?

11.5 Inner Classes

The `RectangleMeasurer` class is a very trivial class. We need this class only because the `DataSet` class needs an object of some class that implements the `Measurer` interface. When you have a class that serves a very limited purpose, such as this one, you can declare the class inside the method that needs it:

```
public class DataSetTester3
{
    public static void main(String[] args)
    {
        class RectangleMeasurer implements Measurer
        {
            . . .
        }

        Measurer m = new RectangleMeasurer();
        DataSet data = new DataSet(m);
        . . .
    }
}
```

> An inner class is declared inside another class. Inner classes are commonly used for tactical classes that should not be visible elsewhere in a program.

Such a class is called an *inner class*. An inner class is any class that is defined inside another class. This arrangement signals to the reader of your program that the `RectangleMeasurer` class is not interesting beyond the scope of this method. Since an inner class inside a method is not a publicly accessible feature, you don't need to document it as thoroughly.

You can also define an inner class inside an enclosing class, but outside of its methods. Then the inner class is available to all methods of the enclosing class.

When you compile the source files for a program that uses inner classes, have a look at the class files in your program directory—you will find that the inner classes are stored in files with curious names, such as `DataSetTester$1$Rectangle-`

Measurer.class. The exact names aren't important. The point is that the compiler turns an inner class into a regular class file.

SYNTAX 11.3 Inner Classes

Declared inside a method:
```
class OuterClassName
{
    method signature
    {
        . . .
        class InnerClassName
        {
            methods
            fields
        }
        . . .
    }
    . . .
}
```

Declared inside the class:
```
class OuterClassName
{
    methods
    fields
    accessSpecifier class InnerClassName
    {
        methods
        fields
    }
    . . .
}
```

Example:
```
public class Tester
{
    public static void main(String[] args)
    {
        class RectangleMeasurer implements Measurer
        {
            . . .
        }
        . . .
    }
}
```

Purpose:
To define an inner class whose scope is restricted to a single method or the methods of a single class

File DataSetTester3.java

```
1  import java.awt.Rectangle;
2
3  /**
4      This program demonstrates the use of a Measurer.
5  */
6  public class DataSetTester3
7  {
```

```
 8    public static void main(String[] args)
 9    {
10       class RectangleMeasurer implements Measurer
11       {
12          public double measure(Object anObject)
13          {
14             Rectangle aRectangle = (Rectangle) anObject;
15             double area
16                = aRectangle.getWidth() * aRectangle.getHeight();
17             return area;
18          }
19       }
20
21       Measurer m = new RectangleMeasurer();
22
23       DataSet data = new DataSet(m);
24
25       data.add(new Rectangle(5, 10, 20, 30));
26       data.add(new Rectangle(10, 20, 30, 40));
27       data.add(new Rectangle(20, 30, 5, 10));
28
29       System.out.println("Average area = " + data.getAverage());
30       Rectangle max = (Rectangle) data.getMaximum();
31       System.out.println("Maximum area rectangle = " + max);
32    }
33 }
```

SELF CHECK

11. Why would you use an inner class instead of a regular class?

12. How many class files are produced when you compile the DataSetTester3 program?

ADVANCED TOPIC 11.2

Anonymous Classes

An entity is *anonymous* if it does not have a name. In a program, something that is only used once doesn't usually need a name. For example, you can replace

```
Coin aCoin = new Coin(0.1, "dime");
data.add(aCoin);
```

with

```
data.add(new Coin(0.1, "dime"));
```

if the coin is not used elsewhere in the same method. The object new Coin(0.1, "dime") is an *anonymous object*. Programmers like anonymous objects, because they don't have to go through the trouble of coming up with a name. If you have struggled with the decision whether to call a coin c, dime, or aCoin, you'll understand this sentiment.

Inner classes often give rise to a similar situation. After a single object of the Rectangle-Measurer has been constructed, the class is never used again. In Java, it is possible to define *anonymous classes* if all you ever need is a single object of the class.

```
public static void main(String[] args)
{
    // Construct an object of an anonymous class
    Measurer m = new Measurer()
        // Class definition starts here
        {
            public double measure(Object anObject)
            {
                Rectangle aRectangle = (Rectangle) anObject;
                double area = aRectangle.getWidth() * aRectangle.getHeight();
                return area;
            }
        };

    DataSet data = new DataSet(m);
    . . .
}
```

This means: Construct an object of a class that implements the Measurer interface by defining the measure method as specified. Many programmers like this style, but we will not use it in this book.

11.6 Processing Timer Events

In this section we will study timer events, because timer event handling uses interfaces in the same way that events triggered by buttons and menus in a graphical program do. However, because timers are simpler than graphical programs, we can focus on the essential mechanism without being distracted by the code for placing buttons or building menus.

Timers are also useful for programming animations (see the next section and Exercises P11.13 and P11.14).

The Timer class in the javax.swing package generates a sequence of *events*, spaced apart at even time intervals. This is useful whenever you want to have an object updated in regular intervals. For example, in an animation, you may want to update a scene 10 times per second and redisplay the image, to give the illusion of movement.

> A timer generates timer events at fixed intervals.

When a timer event occurs, the timer must call some method. The designers of the Timer class had no idea how you would want to use the Timer. Therefore, they simply chose an interface, called Action-Listener, with a method that the timer can call:

> An event listener is notified when a particular event occurs.

```
public interface ActionListener
{
    void actionPerformed(ActionEvent event);
}
```

When you use a timer, you need to define a class that implements the Action-Listener interface. Place whatever action you want to occur inside the action-Performed method. Construct an object of that class. Pass it to the Timer constructor. Finally, start the timer.

```
class MyListener implements ActionListener
{
    public void actionPerformed(ActionEvent event)
    {
        // This action will be executed at each timer event
        Place listener action here
    }
}

MyListener listener = new MyListener();
Timer t = new Timer(interval, listener);
t.start();
```

Then the timer calls the actionPerformed method of the listener object every interval milliseconds.

You can think of the actionPerformed method as another example of a callback, similar to the measure method of the Measurer class. The timer calls the actionPerformed method whenever the time interval has elapsed, whereas the DataSet calls the measure method whenever it needs to measure an object.

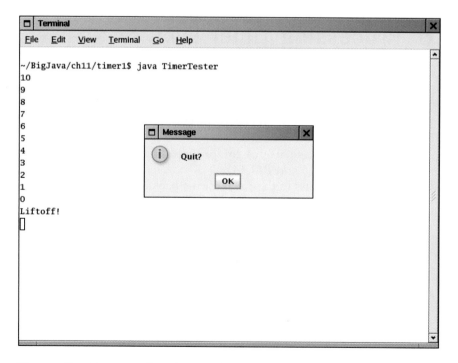

Figure 3   Running the TimerTester Program

The event parameter of the actionPerformed method contains more detailed information about the timer event. However, in practice, many listeners ignore this parameter.

Here is a somewhat silly example program—a timer that counts down to zero.

```
10
9
. . .
2
1
0
Liftoff!
```

However, unlike a for loop, which would print all lines immediately, there is a one-second delay between decrements.

To keep the program alive after setting up the timer, the program displays a message dialog box (see Figure 3). Click the "OK" button to quit the program.

File TimerTester.java

```java
1  import java.awt.event.ActionEvent;
2  import java.awt.event.ActionListener;
3  import javax.swing.JOptionPane;
4  import javax.swing.Timer;
5
6  /**
7     This program tests the Timer class.
8  */
9  public class TimerTester
10 {
11    public static void main(String[] args)
12    {
13       class CountDown implements ActionListener
14       {
15          public CountDown(int initialCount)
16          {
17             count = initialCount;
18          }
19
20          public void actionPerformed(ActionEvent event)
21          {
22             if (count >= 0)
23                System.out.println(count);
24             if (count == 0)
25                System.out.println("Liftoff!");
26             count--;
27          }
28
29          private int count;
30       }
31
32       CountDown listener = new CountDown(10);
33
```

```
34          final int DELAY = 1000; // Milliseconds between timer ticks
35          Timer t = new Timer(DELAY, listener);
36          t.start();
37
38          JOptionPane.showMessageDialog(null, "Quit?");
39          System.exit(0);
40       }
41 }
```

SELF CHECK

13. Why does a timer require a listener object?

14. How many times is the actionPerformed method called in the preceding program?

COMMON ERROR 11.3

Modifying the Signature in the Implementing Method

When you implement an interface, you must define each method *exactly* as it is specified in the interface. Accidentally making small changes to the parameter or return types is a common error. Here is the classic example,

```
class MyAction implements ActionListener
{
   public void actionPerformed()
   // Oops . . . forgot ActionEvent parameter
   {
      . . .
   }
}
```

As far as the compiler is concerned, this class has two methods:

```
public void actionPerformed(ActionEvent event)
public void actionPerformed()
```

The first method is undefined. The compiler will complain that the method is missing. You have to read the error message carefully and pay attention to the parameter and return types to find your error.

11.7 Accessing Surrounding Variables

An attractive feature of inner classes is that their methods can access variables that are defined in surrounding blocks. In this regard, method definitions of inner classes behave similarly to nested blocks.

Recall that a *block* is a statement group enclosed by braces. If a block is nested inside another, the inner block has access to all variables from the surrounding block:

```
{   // Outer block
    int count = 0;
    if (. . .)
    {   // Inner block
        count++;   // OK to access variable from outer block
    }   // End of inner block
}   // End of outer block
```

The same nesting works for inner classes. Except for some technical restrictions, which we will examine later in this section, the methods of an inner class can access the variables from the enclosing scope. This feature is very useful when implementing event handlers. It allows the inner class to access variables without having to pass them as constructor or method parameters.

> Methods of an inner class can access variables from the surrounding scope.

Let's look at an example. Suppose we want to use a timer for an animation. Ten times per second, we will move a shape to a different position. For simplicity, we will move a single rectangle and print the rectangle position, not draw the rectangle. (Exercise P11.15 asks you to add the drawing.)

The basic outline of the program is the following:

```
class Mover implements ActionListener
{
    public void actionPerformed(ActionEvent event)
    {
        Move the rectangle
    }
}

ActionListener listener = new Mover();
final int DELAY = 100; // Milliseconds between timer ticks
Timer t = new Timer(DELAY, listener);
t.start();
```

In the preceding section, we defined a `counter` variable inside the listener class. However, we do not want to bury the rectangle inside the listener class. In a real animation program, the animated objects are located outside the event listeners. Fortunately, this is not a problem. The `actionPerformed` method can access variables from the surrounding scope, like this:

```
public static void main(String[] args)
{
```

```
       . . .
       final Rectangle box = new Rectangle(5, 10, 20, 30);

       class Mover implements ActionListener
       {
          public void actionPerformed(ActionEvent event)
          {
             // Move the rectangle
             box.translate(1, 1);
          }
       }
       . . .
    }
```

Local variables that are accessed by an inner-class method must be declared as final.

There is a technical wrinkle. An inner class can access surrounding *local* variables only if they are declared as final. That sounds like a restriction, but it is usually not an issue in practice. Keep in mind that an object variable is final when the variable always refers to the same object. The state of the object can change, but the variable can't refer to a different object. For example, in our program, we never intended to have the box variable refer to multiple rectangles, so there was no harm in declaring it as final.

An inner class can also access *fields* of the surrounding class, again with a restriction. The field must belong to the object that constructed the inner class object. If the inner class object was created inside a static method, it can only access static surrounding fields.

Here is the source code for the program.

File TimerTester2.java

```
 1  import java.awt.Rectangle;
 2  import java.awt.event.ActionEvent;
 3  import java.awt.event.ActionListener;
 4  import javax.swing.JOptionPane;
 5  import javax.swing.Timer;
 6
 7  /**
 8     This program uses a timer to move a rectangle once per second.
 9  */
10  public class TimerTester2
11  {
12     public static void main(String[] args)
13     {
14        final Rectangle box = new Rectangle(5, 10, 20, 30);
15
16        class Mover implements ActionListener
17        {
18           public void actionPerformed(ActionEvent event)
19           {
20              box.translate(1, 1);
21              System.out.println(box);
22           }
23        }
```

```
24
25          ActionListener listener = new Mover();
26
27          final int DELAY = 100; // Milliseconds between timer ticks
28          Timer t = new Timer(DELAY, listener);
29          t.start();
30
31          JOptionPane.showMessageDialog(null, "Quit?");
32          System.out.println("Last box position: " + box);
33          System.exit(0);
34      }
35  }
```

Output

```
java.awt.Rectangle[x=6,y=11,width=20,height=30]
java.awt.Rectangle[x=7,y=12,width=20,height=30]
java.awt.Rectangle[x=8,y=13,width=20,height=30]
. . .
java.awt.Rectangle[x=28,y=33,width=20,height=30]
java.awt.Rectangle[x=29,y=34,width=20,height=30]
Last box position: java.awt.Rectangle[x=29,y=34,width=20,height=30]
```

Now you have seen how to build an event listener. This is a very common task when programming graphical user interfaces. Buttons, sliders, checkboxes, the mouse, timers, and other sources generate events. You need to attach an event listener to every event source that you want to track. For example, if your program should do something when a button is clicked, attach an event listener to the button. You will learn more about this process in the next chapter.

SELF CHECK

15. Why would an inner class method want to access a variable from a surrounding scope?
16. If an inner class accesses a local variable from a surrounding scope, what special rule applies?

RANDOM FACT 11.1

Operating Systems

Without an operating system, a computer would not be useful. Minimally, you need an operating system to locate files and to start programs. The programs that you run need services from the operating system to access devices and to interact with other programs. Operating systems on large computers need to provide more services than those on personal computers do.

Here are some typical services:

- *Program loading.* Every operating system provides some way of launching application programs. The user indicates what program should be run, usually by typing the name of the program or by clicking on an icon. The operating system locates the program code, loads it into memory, and starts it.

- *Managing files.* A storage device, such as a hard disk is, electronically, simply a device capable of storing a huge sequence of zeroes and ones. It is up to the operating system to bring some structure to the storage layout and organize it into files, folders, and so on. The operating system also needs to impose some amount of security and redundancy into the file system so that a power outage does not jeopardize the contents of an entire hard disk. Some operating systems do a better job in this regard than others.

- *Virtual memory.* RAM is expensive, and few computers have enough RAM to hold all programs and their data that a user would like to run simultaneously. Most operating systems extend the available memory by storing some data on the hard disk. The application programs do not realize whether a particular data item is in memory or in the virtual memory disk storage. When a program accesses a data item that is currently not in RAM, the processor senses this and notifies the operating system. The operating system swaps the needed data from the hard disk into RAM, simultaneously swapping out a memory block of equal size that had not been accessed for some time.

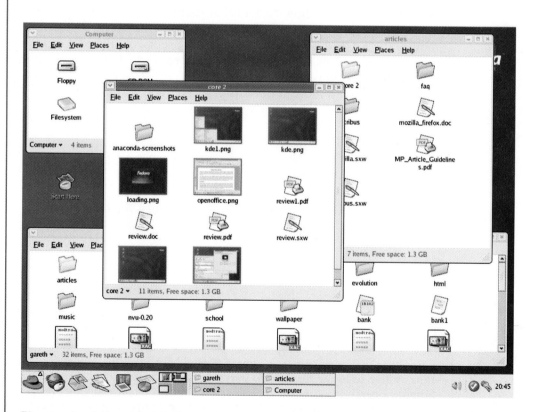

Figure 4   A Graphical Software Environment for the Linux Operating System

- *Handling multiple users.* The operating systems of large and powerful computers allow simultaneous access by multiple users. Each user is connected to the computer through a separate terminal. The operating system authenticates users by checking that each one has a valid account and password. It gives each user a small slice of processor time, then serves the next user.

- *Multitasking.* Even if you are the sole user of a computer, you may want to run multiple applications—for example, to read your e-mail in one window and run the Java compiler in another. The operating system is responsible for dividing processor time between the applications you are running, so that each can make progress.

- *Printing.* The operating system queues up the print requests that are sent by multiple applications. This is necessary to make sure that the printed pages do not contain a mixture of words sent simultaneously from separate programs.

- *Windows.* Many operating systems present their users with a desktop made up of multiple windows. The operating system manages the location and appearance of the window frames; the applications are responsible for the interiors.

- *Fonts.* To render text on the screen and the printer, the shapes of characters must be defined. This is especially important for programs that can display multiple type styles and sizes. Modern operating systems contain a central font repository.

- *Communicating between programs.* The operating system can facilitate the transfer of information between programs. That transfer can happen through *cut and paste* or *interprocess communication.* Cut and paste is a user-initiated data transfer in which the user copies data from one application into a transfer buffer (often called a "clipboard") managed by the operating system and inserts the buffer's contents into another application. Interprocess communication is initiated by applications that transfer data without direct user involvement.

- *Networking.* The operating system provides protocols and services for enabling applications to reach information on other computers attached to the network.

Today, the most popular operating systems for personal computers are Linux (see Figure 4), the Macintosh OS, and Microsoft Windows.

CHAPTER SUMMARY

1. Use interface types to make code more reusable.

2. A Java interface type declares a set of methods and their signatures.

3. Unlike a class, an interface type provides no implementation.

4. Use the `implements` keyword to indicate that a class implements an interface type.

5. Interfaces can reduce the coupling between classes.

6. You can convert from a class type to an interface type, provided the class implements the interface.

7. You need a cast to convert from an interface type to a class type.

8. Polymorphism denotes the principle that behavior can vary depending on the actual type of an object.

9. Early binding of methods occurs if the compiler selects a method from several possible candidates. Late binding occurs if the method selection takes place when the program runs.

10. An inner class is declared inside another class. Inner classes are commonly used for tactical classes that should not be visible elsewhere in a program.

11. A timer generates timer events at fixed intervals.

12. An event listener is notified when a particular event occurs.

13. Methods of an inner class can access variables from the surrounding scope.

14. Local variables that are accessed by an inner-class method must be declared as `final`.

CLASSES, OBJECTS, AND METHODS INTRODUCED IN THIS CHAPTER

```
java.awt.event.ActionListener
   actionPerformed
javax.swing.JOptionPane
   showMessageDialog
javax.swing.Timer
   start
   stop
```

REVIEW EXERCISES

Exercise R11.1. Suppose C is a class that implements the interfaces I and J. Which of the following assignments require a cast?

```
C c = . . .;
I i = . . .;
J j = . . .;
```

a. c = i;

b. j = c;

c. i = j;

Exercise R11.2. Suppose C is a class that implements the interfaces I and J. Which of the following assignments will throw an exception?

```
C c = new C();
```

a. I i = c;

b. J j = (J) i;

c. C d = (C) i;

Exercise R11.3. Suppose the class Sandwich implements the Edible interface. Which of the following assignments are legal?

a. Sandwich sub = new Sandwich();

b. Edible e = sub;

c. Rectangle cerealBox = new Rectangle(5, 10, 20, 30);

d. Edible f = cerealBox;

e. f = (Edible) cerealBox;

f. sub = e;

g. sub = (Sandwich) e;

h. sub = (Sandwich) cerealBox;

Exercise R11.4. How does a cast such as (BankAccount) x differ from a cast of number values such as (int) x?

Exercise R11.5. The classes Rectangle2D.Double, Ellipse2D.Double, and Line2D.Double implement the Shape interface. The Graphics2D class depends on the Shape interface but not on the rectangle, ellipse, and line classes. Draw a UML diagram denoting these facts.

Exercise R11.6. Suppose r contains a reference to a new Rectangle(5, 10, 20, 30). Which of the following assignments is legal? (Look inside the API documentation to check which interfaces the Rectangle class implements.)

a. Rectangle a = r;

b. Shape b = r;

c. String c = r;

d. ActionListener d = r;

e. Measurable e = r;

f. Serializable f = r;

g. Object g = r;

Exercise R11.7. Classes such as Rectangle2D.Double, Ellipse2D.Double and Line2D.Double implement the Shape interface. The Shape interface has a method

```
Rectangle getBounds()
```

that returns a rectangle completely enclosing the shape. Consider the method call:

```
Shape s = . . .;
Rectangle r = s.getBounds();
```

Explain why this is an example of polymorphism.

Exercise R11.8. In Java, a method call such as x.f() uses late binding—the exact method to be called depends on the type of the object to which x refers. Give two kinds of method calls that use early binding in Java.

Exercise R11.9. Suppose you need to process an array of employees to find the average and the highest salaries. Discuss what you need to do to use the first implementation of the `DataSet` class (which processes `Measurable` objects). What do you need to do to use the second implementation? Which is easier?

Exercise R11.10. What happens if you add a `String` object to the first implementation of the `DataSet`? What happens if you add a `String` object to a `DataSet` object of the second implementation that uses a `RectangleMeasurer` class?

Exercise R11.11. How would you reorganize the `TimerTester` program if you needed to make `CountDown` into a top-level class (that is, not an inner class)?

Exercise R11.12. How would you reorganize the `TimerTester2` program if you needed to make `Mover` into a top-level class (that is, not an inner class)?

Exercise R11.13. What is a callback? Can you think of another use for a callback for the `DataSet` class? (*Hint:* Exercise P11.8.)

Exercise R11.14. What is the difference between an event and an event listener?

Exercise R11.15. Can a `Timer` object notify multiple event listeners? If so, how? (Check the API documentation.)

Exercise R11.16. Consider this top-level and inner class. Which variables can the `f` method access?

```
public class T
{
   public void m(final int x, int y)
   {
      int a;
      final int b;

      class C implements I
      {
         public void f()
         {
            . . .
         }
      }

      final int c;
      . . .
   }

   private int t;
}
```

Exercise R11.17. What happens when an inner class tries to access a non-final local variable? Try it out and explain your findings.

PROGRAMMING EXERCISES

Exercise P11.1. Have the Die class of Chapter 7 implement the Measurable interface. Generate dice, cast them, and add them to the first implementation of the DataSet class. Display the average.

Exercise P11.2. Define a class Quiz that implements the Measurable interface. A quiz has a score and a letter grade (such as B+). Use the first implementation of the DataSet class to process a collection of quizzes. Display the average score and the quiz with the highest score (both letter grade and score).

Exercise P11.3. Define a class Person. A person has a name and a height in centimeters. Use the second implementation of the DataSet class to process a collection of Person objects. Display the average height and the name of the tallest person.

Exercise P11.4. Modify the first implementation of the DataSet class (the one processing Measurable objects) to also compute the minimum data element.

Exercise P11.5. Modify the second implementation of the DataSet class (the one using a Measurer object) to also compute the minimum data element.

Exercise P11.6. Using a different Measurer object, process a set of Rectangle objects to find the rectangle with the largest perimeter.

Exercise P11.7. Enhance the DataSet class so that it can either be used with a Measurer object or for processing Measurable objects. *Hint:* Supply a default constructor that implements a Measurer that processes Measurable objects.

Exercise P11.8. Define an interface Filter as follows:

```
public interface Filter
{
    boolean accept(Object x);
}
```

Modify the second implementation of the DataSet class to use both a Measurer and a Filter object. Only objects that the filter accepts should be processed. Demonstrate your modification by having a data set process a collection of bank accounts, filtering out all accounts with balances less than $1,000.

Exercise P11.9. Look up the definition of the standard Comparable interface in the API documentation. Modify the DataSet class to accept Comparable objects. With this interface, it is no longer meaningful to compute the average. The DataSet class should record the minimum and maximum data values. Test your modified DataSet class by adding a number of String objects. (The String class implements the Comparable interface.)

Exercise P11.10. Modify the Coin class to have it implement the Comparable interface.

Exercise P11.11. Use the interface

```
public interface Drawable
{
    void draw(Graphics2D g2);
}
```

and implement classes Car and House that implement this interface. The Car and House constructors should receive the position of the car or house, just as in Section 5.5.

Then write a method randomDrawable that randomly generates Drawable references. Randomly choose between a car and a house, then pick random positions. Call the method 10 times and draw all of the shapes.

Exercise P11.12. Write a method randomShape that randomly generates objects implementing the Shape interface: some mixture of rectangles, ellipses, and lines, with random positions. Call it 10 times and draw all of them.

Exercise P11.13. Write a program that uses a timer to print the current time once a second. *Hint:* The following code prints the current time:

```
Date now = new Date();
System.out.println(now);
```

The Date class is in the java.util package.

Exercise P11.14. Enhance the program that uses a timer to move a rectangle by adding a second rectangle and a second timer that moves it twice as often.

Exercise P11.15. Write a graphical application that uses a timer to display an animation of a rectangle in a panel. Ten times a second, have the actionPerformed method of a timer listener

- Move the rectangle to the right and down by one pixel.
- Call the repaint method of the panel.

Construct the timer in the constructor of the panel.

Exercise P11.16. Repeat Exercise P11.15, but animate a car, not a rectangle.

Exercise P11.17. The System.out.printf method has predefined formats for printing integers, floating-point numbers, and other data types. But it is also extensible. If you use the S format, you can print any class that implements the Formattable interface. That interface has a single method:

```
void formatTo(Formatter formatter, int flags, int width, int precision)
```

In this exercise, you should make the BankAccount class implement the Formattable interface. Ignore the flags and precision and simply format the bank balance, using the given width. In order to achieve this task, you need to get an Appendable reference like this:

```
Appendable a = formatter.out();
```

Appendable is another interface with a method

```
void append(CharSequence sequence)
```

CharSequence is yet another interface that is implemented by (among others) the String class. Construct a string by first converting the bank balance into a string and then padding it with spaces so that it has the desired width. Pass that string to the append method.

Exercise P11.18. Enhance the formatTo method of Exercise P11.17 by taking into account the precision.

PROGRAMMING PROJECTS

Project 11.1. Design an interface MoveableShape that can be used as a generic mechanism for animating a shape. A moveable shape must have two methods: move and draw. Write a generic AnimationPanel that paints and moves any MoveableShape (or array list of MoveableShape objects if you covered Chapter 8). Supply moveable rectangle and car shapes.

Project 11.2. Your task is to design a general program for managing board games with two players. Your program should be flexible enough to handle games such as tic-tac-toe, chess, or the Game of Nim of Project 7.2.

Design an interface Game that describes a board game. Think about what your program needs to do. It asks the first player to input a move—a string in a game-specific format, such as Be3 in chess. Your program knows nothing about specific games, so the Game interface must have a method such as

```
boolean isValidMove(String move)
```

Once the move is found to be valid, it needs to be executed—the interface needs another method executeMove. Next, your program needs to check whether the game is over. If not, the other player's move is processed. You should also provide some mechanism for displaying the current state of the board.

Design the Game interface and provide two implementations of your choice—such as Nim and Chess (or TicTacToe if you are less ambitious). Your GamePlayer class should manage a Game reference without knowing which game is played, and process the moves from both players. Supply two programs that differ only in the initialization of the Game reference.

ANSWERS TO SELF-CHECK QUESTIONS

1. It must implement the Measurable interface, and its getMeasure method must return the population.

2. The Object class doesn't have a getMeasure method, and the add method invokes the getMeasure method.

3. Only if x actually refers to a BankAccount object.

4. No—a Coin reference can be converted to a Measurable reference, but if you attempt to cast that reference to a BankAccount, an exception occurs.

5. Measurable is an interface. Interfaces have no fields and no method implementations.

6. That variable never refers to a Measurable object. It refers to an object of some class—a class that implements the Measurable interface.

7. Both describe a situation where one method name can denote multiple methods. However, overloading is resolved early by the compiler, by looking at the types of the parameter variables. Polymorphism is resolved late, by looking at the type of the implicit parameter object just before making the call.

8. The String class doesn't implement the Measurable interface.

9. Implement a class StringMeasurer that implements the Measurer interface.

10. A measurer measures an object, whereas getMeasure measures "itself", that is, the implicit parameter.

11. Inner classes are convenient for insignificant classes. Also, their methods can access variables and fields from the surrounding scope.

12. Four: one for the outer class, one for the inner class, and two for the DataSet and Measurer classes.

13. The timer needs to call some method whenever the time interval expires. It calls the actionPerformed method of the listener object.

14. It depends. The method is called once per second. The first eleven times, it prints a message. The remaining times, it exits silently. The timer is only terminated when the user quits the program.

15. Direct access is simpler than the alternative—passing the variable as a parameter to a constructor or method.

16. The local variable must be declared as final.

Event Handling

CHAPTER GOALS

- To understand the Java event model
- To install action and mouse event listeners
- To accept input from buttons, text fields, and the mouse

In the applications that you have written so far, user input was under control of the *program*. The program asked the user for input in a specific order. For example, a program might ask the user to supply first a name, then a dollar amount. But the programs that you use every day on your computer don't work like that. In a program with a modern graphical user interface, the *user* is in control. The user can use both the mouse and the keyboard and can manipulate many parts of the user interface in any desired order. For example, the user can enter information into text fields, pull down menus, click buttons, and drag scroll bars in any order. The program must react to the user commands, in whatever order they arrive. Having to deal with many possible inputs in random order is quite a bit harder than simply forcing the user to supply input in a fixed order.

In this chapter you will learn how to write Java programs that can react to user interface events, such as button pushes and mouse clicks. The Java window toolkit has a very sophisticated mechanism that allows a program to specify the events in which it is interested and which objects to notify when one of these events occurs.

CHAPTER CONTENTS

12.1 Events, Event Sources, and Event Listeners

User interface events include key presses, mouse moves, button clicks, menu selections, and so on.

Whenever the user of a graphical program types characters or uses the mouse anywhere inside one of the windows of the program, the Java window manager sends a notification to the program that an *event* has occurred. The window manager generates huge numbers of events. For example, whenever the mouse moves a tiny interval over a window, a "mouse move" event is generated. Events are also generated when the user presses a key, clicks a button, or selects a menu item.

An event listener belongs to a class that is provided by the application programmer. Its methods describe the actions to be taken when an event occurs.

Most programs don't want to be flooded by boring events. For example, when a button is clicked with the mouse, the mouse moves over the button, then the mouse button is pressed, and finally the button is released. Rather than receiving lots of irrelevant mouse events, a program can indicate that it only cares about button clicks, not about the underlying mouse events. However, if the mouse input is used for drawing shapes on a virtual canvas, it is necessary to closely track mouse events.

Every program must indicate which events it needs to receive. It does that by installing *event listener* objects. An event listener object belongs to a class that you define. The methods of your event listener classes contain the instructions that you want to have executed when the events occur.

> Event sources report on events. When an event occurs, the event source notifies all event listeners.

To install a listener, you need to know the *event source*. The event source is the user interface component that generates a particular event. You add an event listener object to the appropriate event sources. Whenever the event occurs, the event source calls the appropriate methods of all attached event listeners.

> Use JButton components for buttons. Attach an ActionListener to each button.

This sounds somewhat abstract, so let's run through an extremely simple program that prints a message whenever a button is clicked. Button listeners must belong to a class that implements the Action-Listener interface:

```
public interface ActionListener
{
    void actionPerformed(ActionEvent event);
}
```

This particular interface has a single method, actionPerformed. It is your job to supply a class whose actionPerformed method contains the instructions that you want executed whenever the button is clicked. Here is a very simple example of such a listener class:

File ClickListener.java

```
 1  import java.awt.event.ActionEvent;
 2  import java.awt.event.ActionListener;
 3
 4  /**
 5      An action listener that prints a message.
 6  */
 7  public class ClickListener implements ActionListener
 8  {
 9      public void actionPerformed(ActionEvent event)
10      {
11          System.out.println("I was clicked.");
12      }
13  }
```

We ignore the event parameter of the actionPerformed method—it contains additional details about the event, such as the time at which it occurred.

Once the listener class has been defined, we need to construct an object of the class and add it to the button:

```
ActionListener listener = new ClickListener();
button.addActionListener(listener);
```

Whenever the button is clicked, it calls

```
listener.actionPerformed(event);
```

As a result, the message is printed.

You can test this program out by opening a console window, starting the Button-Tester program from that console window, clicking the button, and watching the messages in the console window (see Figure 1).

Figure 1   Implementing an Action Listener

File ButtonTester.java

```
1   import java.awt.event.ActionListener;
2   import javax.swing.JButton;
3   import javax.swing.JFrame;
4
5   /**
6       This program demonstrates how to install an action listener.
7   */
8   public class ButtonTester
9   {
10     public static void main(String[] args)
11     {
12        JFrame frame = new JFrame();
13        JButton button = new JButton("Click me!");
14        frame.add(button);
15
16        ActionListener listener = new ClickListener();
17        button.addActionListener(listener);
18
19        frame.setSize(FRAME_WIDTH, FRAME_HEIGHT);
20        frame.setDefaultCloseOperation(JFrame.EXIT_ON_CLOSE);
21        frame.setVisible(true);
22     }
23
24     private static final int FRAME_WIDTH = 100;
25     private static final int FRAME_HEIGHT = 60;
26  }
```

SELF CHECK

1. Which objects are the event source and the event listener in the ButtonTester program?

2. Why is it legal to assign a ClickListener object to a variable of type ActionListener?

12.2 Building Applications with Buttons

In this section, you will learn how to structure a graphical application that contains buttons. We will study a simple investment viewer program that puts a button to work. Whenever the button is clicked, interest is added to a bank account, and the new balance is displayed (see Figure 2).

First, we construct an object of the JButton class. Pass the button label to the constructor:

```
JButton button = new JButton("Add Interest");
```

We also need a user interface component that displays a message, namely the current bank balance. Such a component is called a *label*. You pass the initial message string to the JLabel constructor, like this:

```
JLabel label = new JLabel("balance=" + account.getBalance());
```

> Use a JPanel container to group multiple user-interface components together.

The frame of our application contains both the button and the label. However, we cannot simply add both components directly to the frame—they would be placed on top of each other. The solution is to put them into a *panel*, a container for other user-interface components, and then add the panel to the frame:

```
JPanel panel = new JPanel();
panel.add(button);
panel.add(label);
frame.add(panel);
```

Now we are ready for the hard part—the event listener that handles button clicks. As in the preceding section, it is necessary to define a class that implements the ActionListener interface, and to place the button action into the actionPerformed method. Our listener class adds interest and displays the new balance:

```
class AddInterestListener implements ActionListener
{
   public void actionPerformed(ActionEvent event)
   {
      double interest = account.getBalance() * INTEREST_RATE / 100;
      account.deposit(interest);
      label.setText("balance=" + account.getBalance());
   }
}
```

Figure 2 An Application with a Button

> You often install event listeners as inner classes so that they can have access to the surrounding fields, methods, and final variables.

There is just a minor technicality. The `actionPerformed` method manipulates the `account` and `label` variables. These are local variables of the `main` method of the investment viewer program, not instance fields of the `AddInterestListener` class. To overcome this problem, we will make the `AddInterestListener` class into an inner class of the `main` method. Recall from Chapter 11 that inner class methods can access local variables from the surrounding scope, provided they have been declared as `final`.

We therefore need to declare the `account` and `label` variables as `final` so that the `actionPerformed` method can access them.

Let's put the pieces together.

```java
public static void main(String[] args)
{
    . . .
    JButton button = new JButton("Add Interest");
    final BankAccount account = new BankAccount(INITIAL_BALANCE);
    final JLabel label = new JLabel("balance=" + account.getBalance());

    class AddInterestListener implements ActionListener
    {
        public void actionPerformed(ActionEvent event)
        {
            double interest = account.getBalance()
                * INTEREST_RATE / 100;
            account.deposit(interest);
            label.setText("balance=" + account.getBalance());
        }
    }

    ActionListener listener = new AddInterestListener();
    button.addActionListener(listener);
    . . .
}
```

With a bit of practice, you will learn to glance at this code and translate it into plain English: "When the button is clicked, add interest and set the label text."

Here is the complete program. It demonstrates how to add multiple components to a frame, by using a panel, and how to implement listeners as inner classes.

File InvestmentViewer1.java

```java
1  import java.awt.event.ActionEvent;
2  import java.awt.event.ActionListener;
3  import javax.swing.JButton;
4  import javax.swing.JFrame;
5  import javax.swing.JLabel;
6  import javax.swing.JPanel;
7  import javax.swing.JTextField;
8
9  /**
10     This program displays the growth of an investment.
11  */
```

```
12  public class InvestmentViewer1
13  {
14     public static void main(String[] args)
15     {
16        JFrame frame = new JFrame();
17
18        // The button to trigger the calculation
19        JButton button = new JButton("Add Interest");
20
21        // The application adds interest to this bank account
22        final BankAccount account = new BankAccount(INITIAL_BALANCE);
23
24        // The label for displaying the results
25        final JLabel label = new JLabel(
26              "balance = " + account.getBalance());
27
28        // The panel that holds the user interface components
29        JPanel panel = new JPanel();
30        panel.add(button);
31        panel.add(label);
32        frame.add(panel);
33
34        class AddInterestListener implements ActionListener
35        {
36           public void actionPerformed(ActionEvent event)
37           {
38              double interest = account.getBalance()
39                    * INTEREST_RATE / 100;
40              account.deposit(interest);
41              label.setText(
42                    "balance = " + account.getBalance());
43           }
44        }
45
46        ActionListener listener = new AddInterestListener();
47        button.addActionListener(listener);
48
49        frame.setSize(FRAME_WIDTH, FRAME_HEIGHT);
50        frame.setDefaultCloseOperation(JFrame.EXIT_ON_CLOSE);
51        frame.setVisible(true);
52     }
53
54     private static final double INTEREST_RATE = 10;
55     private static final double INITIAL_BALANCE = 1000;
56
57     private static final int FRAME_WIDTH = 400;
58     private static final int FRAME_HEIGHT = 100;
59  }
```

SELF CHECK

3. How do you place the "balance = ..." message to the left of the "Add Interest" button?

4. Why was it not necessary to declare the button variable as final?

COMMON ERROR 12.1

Forgetting to Attach a Listener

If you run your program and find that your buttons seem to be dead, double-check that you attached the button listener. The same holds for other user interface components. It is a surprisingly common error to program the listener class and the event handler action without actually attaching the listener to the event source.

PRODUCTIVITY HINT 12.1

Don't Use a Container as a Listener

In this book, we use inner classes for event listeners. That approach works for many different event types. Once you master the technique, you don't have to think about it anymore. Many development environments automatically generate code with inner classes, so it is a good idea to be familiar with them.

However, some programmers bypass the event listener classes and instead turn a container (such as a panel or frame) into a listener. Here is a typical example. The actionPerformed method is added to the viewer class. That is, the viewer implements the ActionListener interface.

```
public class InvestmentViewer
      implements ActionListener // This approach is not recommended
{
   public InvestmentViewer()
   {
      JButton button = new JButton("Add Interest");
      button.addActionListener(this);
      . . .
   }

   public void actionPerformed(ActionEvent event)
   {
   }
   . . .
}
```

Now the actionPerformed method is a part of the InvestmentViewer class rather than part of a separate listener class. The listener is installed as this.

This technique has two major flaws. First, it separates the button definition from the button action. Also, it doesn't *scale* well. If the viewer class contains two buttons that each generate action events, then the actionPerformed method must investigate the event source, which leads to code that is tedious and error-prone.

12.3 Processing Text Input

So far, your graphical applications received text input by calling the `showInputDialog` method of the `JOptionPane` class, but that's not a natural user interface. Most graphical programs collect text input through *text fields* (see Figure 3). In this section, you will learn how to add text fields to a graphical application, and how to read what the user types into them.

> Use `JTextField` components to provide space for user input. Place a `JLabel` next to each text field.

The `JTextField` class provides a text field. When you construct a text field, you need to supply the width—the approximate number of characters that you expect the user to type.

```
final int FIELD_WIDTH = 10;
final JTextField rateField = new JTextField(FIELD_WIDTH);
```

Users can type additional characters, but then a part of the contents of the field becomes invisible.

You will want to label each text field so that the user knows what to type into it. Construct a `JLabel` object for each label:

```
JLabel rateLabel = new JLabel("Interest Rate: ");
```

You want to give the user an opportunity to enter all information into the text fields before processing it. Therefore, you should supply a button that the user can press to indicate that the input is ready for processing.

When that button is clicked, its `actionPerformed` method reads the user input from the text fields, using the `getText` method of the `JTextField` class. The `getText` method returns a `String` object. In our sample program, we turn the string into a number, using the `Double.parseDouble` method:

```
class AddInterestListener implements ActionListener
{
   public void actionPerformed(ActionEvent event)
   {
      double rate = Double.parseDouble(rateField.getText());
      . . .
   }
}
```

The following application is a useful prototype for a graphical user-interface front end for arbitrary calculations. You can easily modify it for your own needs. Place other input components into the frame. Change the contents of the `actionPerformed` method to carry out other calculations. Display the result in a label.

Figure 3   An Application with a Text Field

File InvestmentViewer2.java

```
1  import java.awt.event.ActionEvent;
2  import java.awt.event.ActionListener;
3  import javax.swing.JButton;
4  import javax.swing.JFrame;
5  import javax.swing.JLabel;
6  import javax.swing.JPanel;
7  import javax.swing.JTextField;
8
9  /**
10     This program displays the growth of an investment.
11  */
12 public class InvestmentViewer2
13 {
14    public static void main(String[] args)
15    {
16       JFrame frame = new JFrame();
17
18       // The label and text field for entering the interest rate
19       JLabel rateLabel = new JLabel("Interest Rate: ");
20
21       final int FIELD_WIDTH = 10;
22       final JTextField rateField = new JTextField(FIELD_WIDTH);
23       rateField.setText("" + DEFAULT_RATE);
24
25       // The button to trigger the calculation
26       JButton button = new JButton("Add Interest");
27
28       // The application adds interest to this bank account
29       final BankAccount account = new BankAccount(INITIAL_BALANCE);
30
31       // The label for displaying the results
32       final JLabel resultLabel = new JLabel(
33             "balance=" + account.getBalance());
34
35       // The panel that holds the user-interface components
36       JPanel panel = new JPanel();
37       panel.add(rateLabel);
38       panel.add(rateField);
39       panel.add(button);
40       panel.add(resultLabel);
41       frame.add(panel);
42
43       class AddInterestListener implements ActionListener
44       {
45          public void actionPerformed(ActionEvent event)
46          {
47             double rate = Double.parseDouble(
48                   rateField.getText());
49             double interest = account.getBalance()
50                   * rate / 100;
51             account.deposit(interest);
52             resultLabel.setText(
53                   "balance=" + account.getBalance());
```

```
54          }
55      }
56
57      ActionListener listener = new AddInterestListener();
58      button.addActionListener(listener);
59
60      frame.setSize(FRAME_WIDTH, FRAME_HEIGHT);
61      frame.setDefaultCloseOperation(JFrame.EXIT_ON_CLOSE);
62      frame.setVisible(true);
63   }
64
65   private static final double DEFAULT_RATE = 10;
66   private static final double INITIAL_BALANCE = 1000;
67
68   private static final int FRAME_WIDTH = 500;
69   private static final int FRAME_HEIGHT = 200;
70 }
```

SELF CHECK

5. What happens if you omit the first JLabel object?
6. If a text field holds an integer, what expression do you use to read its contents?

How To 12.1

Implementing a Graphical User Interface (GUI)

A GUI program allows users to supply inputs and specify actions. The InvestmentViewer2 program has only one input and one action. More sophisticated programs have more interesting user interactions, but the basic principles are the same.

Step 1   Enumerate the actions that your program needs to carry out.

For example, the investment viewer has a single action, to add interest. Other programs may have different actions, perhaps for making deposits, inserting coins, and so on.

Step 2   For each action, enumerate the inputs that you need.

For example, the investment viewer has a single input: the interest rate. Other programs may have different inputs, such as amounts of money, product quantities, and so on.

Step 3   For each action, enumerate the outputs that you need to show.

The investment viewer has a single output: the current balance. Other programs may show different quantities, messages, and so on.

Step 4   Supply the user interface components.

Right now, you need to use buttons for actions, text fields for inputs, and labels for outputs. In Chapter 14, you will see many more user-interface components that can be used for actions and inputs. In Chapter 5, you learned how to implement your own components to produce graphical output, such as charts or drawings.

Add the required buttons, text fields, and other components to a frame. In this chapter, you have seen how to lay out very simple user interfaces, by adding all components to a single panel and adding the panel to the frame. Chapter 14 shows you how you can achieve more complex layouts.

Step 5   Supply event handler classes.

For each button, you need to add an object of a listener class. The listener classes must implement the `ActionListener` interface. Supply a class for each action (or group of related actions), and put the instructions for the action in the `actionPerformed` method.

```
class Button1Listener implements ActionListener
{
    public void actionPerformed(ActionEvent event)
    {
        // button1 action goes here
        . . .
    }
}
```

Remember to declare any local variables accessed by the listener methods as `final`.

Step 6   Make listener objects and attach them to the event sources.

For action events, the event source is a button or other user-interface component, or a timer. You need to add a listener object to each event source, like this:

```
ActionListener listener1 = new Button1Listener();
button1.addActionListener(listener1);
```

Productivity Hint 12.2

Code Reuse

Suppose you are given the task of writing another graphical user-interface program that reads input from a couple of text fields and displays the result of some calculations in a label. You don't have to start from scratch. Instead, you can—and often should—*reuse* the outline of an existing program, such as the foregoing `InvestmentViewer2` program.

To reuse program code, simply make a copy of a program file and give the copy a new name. For example, you may want to copy `InvestmentViewer.java` to a file `TaxReturnViewer.java`. Then remove the code that is clearly specific to the old problem, but leave the outline in place. That is, keep the panel, text field, event listener, and so on. Fill in the code for your new calculations. Finally, rename classes, buttons, frame titles, and so on.

Once you understand the principles behind event listeners, frames, and panels, there is no need to rethink them every time. Reusing the structure of a working program makes your work more efficient.

However, reuse by "copy and rename" is still a mechanical and somewhat error-prone approach. It is even better to package reusable program structures into a set of common classes. The inheritance mechanism lets you design classes for reuse without copy and paste. We will cover inheritance in the next chapter.

12.4 Mouse Events

You use a mouse listener to capture mouse events.

If you write programs that show drawings, and you want users to manipulate the drawings with a mouse, then you need to process mouse events. Mouse events are more complex than button clicks. You can safely skip this section if you are not interested in interactive graphics programs.

A mouse listener must implement the MouseListener interface, which contains the following five methods:

```
public interface MouseListener
{
    void mousePressed(MouseEvent event);
        // Called when a mouse button has been pressed on a component
    void mouseReleased(MouseEvent event);
        // Called when a mouse button has been released on a component
    void mouseClicked(MouseEvent event);
        // Called when the mouse has been clicked on a component
    void mouseEntered(MouseEvent event);
        // Called when the mouse enters a component
    void mouseExited(MouseEvent event);
        // Called when the mouse exits a component
}
```

The mousePressed and mouseReleased methods are called whenever a mouse button is pressed or released. If a button is pressed and released in quick succession, and the mouse has not moved, then the mouseClicked method is called as well. The mouseEntered and mouseExited methods can be used to paint a user-interface component in a special way whenever the mouse is pointing inside it.

The most commonly used method is mousePressed. Users generally expect that their actions are processed as soon as the mouse button is pressed.

You add a mouse listener to a component by calling the addMouseListener method:

```
public class MyMouseListener implements MouseListener
{
    // Implements five methods
}

MouseListener listener = new MyMouseListener();
component.addMouseListener(listener);
```

Our sample program will enhance the RectangleComponentViewer program of Chapter 5. When the user clicks on the rectangle component with the mouse, then we want to move the rectangle. We first enhance the RectangleComponent class and add a moveTo method to move the rectangle to a new position.

File RectangleComponent.java

```java
 1  import java.awt.Graphics;
 2  import java.awt.Graphics2D;
 3  import java.awt.Rectangle;
 4  import javax.swing.JComponent;
 5
 6  /**
 7     This component allows the to user move a rectangle by clicking
 8     the mouse.
 9  */
10  public class RectangleComponent extends JComponent
11  {
12     public RectangleComponent()
13     {
14        // The rectangle that the paint method draws
15        box = new Rectangle(BOX_X, BOX_Y,
16              BOX_WIDTH, BOX_HEIGHT);
17     }
18
19     public void paintComponent(Graphics g)
20     {
21        super.paintComponent(g);
22        Graphics2D g2 = (Graphics2D) g;
23
24        g2.draw(box);
25     }
26
27     /**
28        Moves the rectangle to the given location.
29        @param x the x-position of the new location
30        @param y the y-position of the new location
31     */
32     public void moveTo(int x, int y)
33     {
34        box.setLocation(x, y);
35        repaint();
36     }
37
38     private Rectangle box;
39
40     private static final int BOX_X = 100;
41     private static final int BOX_Y = 100;
42     private static final int BOX_WIDTH = 20;
43     private static final int BOX_HEIGHT = 30;
44  }
```

Note the call to repaint in the moveTo method. This call is necessary to ensure that the component is repainted after the state of the rectangle object has been changed. Keep in mind that the component object does not contain the pixels that show the drawing. The component merely contains a Rectangle object, which itself contains four coordinate values. Calling setLocation updates the rectangle coordinate values. The call to repaint forces a call to the paintComponent method. The paintComponent method redraws the component, causing the rectangle to appear at the updated location.

Now, add a mouse listener to the component. Whenever the mouse is pressed, the listener moves the rectangle to the mouse location.

> The repaint method causes a component to repaint itself. Call this method whenever you modify the shapes that the paintComponent method draws.

```
class MousePressListener implements MouseListener
{
    public void mousePressed(MouseEvent event)
    {
        int x = event.getX();
        int y = event.getY();
        component.moveTo(x, y);
    }

    // Do-nothing methods
    public void mouseReleased(MouseEvent event) {}
    public void mouseClicked(MouseEvent event) {}
    public void mouseEntered(MouseEvent event) {}
    public void mouseExited(MouseEvent event) {}
}
```

It often happens that a particular listener specifies actions only for one or two of the listener methods. Nevertheless, all five methods of the interface must be implemented. The unused methods are simply implemented as do-nothing methods.

Go ahead and run the RectangleComponentViewer program. Whenever you click the mouse inside the frame, the top left corner of the rectangle moves to the mouse pointer (see Figure 4).

Figure 4   Clicking the Mouse Moves the Rectangle

File RectangleComponentViewer.java

```java
1   import java.awt.event.MouseListener;
2   import java.awt.event.MouseEvent;
3   import javax.swing.JFrame;
4
5   /**
6       This program displays a RectangleComponent.
7   */
8   public class RectangleComponentViewer
9   {
10      public static void main(String[] args)
11      {
12          final RectangleComponent component = new RectangleComponent();
13
14          // Add mouse press listener
15
16          class MousePressListener implements MouseListener
17          {
18              public void mousePressed(MouseEvent event)
19              {
20                  int x = event.getX();
21                  int y = event.getY();
22                  component.moveTo(x, y);
23              }
24
25              // Do-nothing methods
26              public void mouseReleased(MouseEvent event) {}
27              public void mouseClicked(MouseEvent event) {}
28              public void mouseEntered(MouseEvent event) {}
29              public void mouseExited(MouseEvent event) {}
30          }
31
32          MouseListener listener = new MousePressListener();
33          component.addMouseListener(listener);
34
35          JFrame frame = new JFrame();
36          frame.add(component);
37
38          frame.setSize(FRAME_WIDTH, FRAME_HEIGHT);
39          frame.setDefaultCloseOperation(JFrame.EXIT_ON_CLOSE);
40          frame.setVisible(true);
41      }
42
43      private static final int FRAME_WIDTH = 300;
44      private static final int FRAME_HEIGHT = 400;
45  }
```

SELF CHECK

7. What would happen if you omitted the call to repaint in the moveTo method?

8. Why must the MousePressListener class supply five methods?

COMMON ERROR 12.2

Forgetting to Repaint

A drawing program stores the data that are necessary to repaint the window. The paint-Component method retrieves the data; generates geometric shapes, such as lines, ellipses, and rectangles; and draws them. When you make a change to the data, your drawing is *not* automatically updated. You must tell the window manager that the data have changed, by calling the repaint method.

You may wonder why we don't just call the paintComponent method instead of calling repaint. However, to call paintComponent, we would need a Graphics object, which we don't have. It is possible to get such an object, but that is actually not a good idea. You should never call paintComponent directly—it can interfere with the window manager. Instead, use the repaint method to tell the component to repaint itself at the next convenient moment. Then the Swing framework calls the paintComponent method at an opportune moment, with an appropriate Graphics object.

ADVANCED TOPIC 12.1

Event Adapters

In the preceding section you saw how to install a mouse listener into a mouse event source and how the listener methods are called when an event occurs. Usually, a program is not interested in all listener notifications. For example, a program may only be interested in mouse clicks and may not care that these mouse clicks are composed of "mouse pressed" and "mouse released" events. Of course, the program could supply a listener that defines all those methods in which it has no interest as "do-nothing" methods, for example:

```
class MouseClickListener implements MouseListener
{
    public void mouseClicked(MouseEvent event)
    {
        // Mouse click action here
    }

    // Four do-nothing methods
    public void mouseEntered(MouseEvent event) {}
    public void mouseExited(MouseEvent event) {}
    public void mousePressed(MouseEvent event) {}
    public void mouseReleased(MouseEvent event) {}
}
```

This is boring. For that reason, some friendly soul has created a MouseAdapter class that implements the MouseListener interface such that all methods do nothing. You can *extend* that class, inheriting the do-nothing methods and overriding the methods that you care about, like this:

```
class MouseClickListener extends MouseAdapter
{
    public void mouseClicked(MouseEvent event)
    {
        // Mouse click action here
```

```
        }
    }
```

See Chapter 13 for more information on the process of extending classes.

RANDOM FACT 12.1

Programming Languages

Many hundreds of programming languages exist today, which is actually quite surprising. The idea behind a high-level programming language is to provide a medium for programming that is independent from the instruction set of a particular processor, so that one can move programs from one computer to another without rewriting them. Moving a program from one programming language to another is a difficult process, however, and it is rarely done. Thus, it seems that there would be little use for so many programming languages.

Unlike human languages, programming languages are created with specific purposes. Some programming languages make it particularly easy to express tasks from a particular problem domain. Some languages specialize in database processing; others in "artificial intelligence" programs that try to infer new facts from a given base of knowledge; others in multimedia programming. The Pascal language was purposefully kept simple because it was designed as a teaching language. The C language was developed to be translated efficiently into fast machine code, with a minimum of housekeeping overhead. The C++ language builds on C by adding features for object-oriented programming. The Java language was designed for securely deploying programs across the Internet.

In the early 1970s the U.S. Department of Defense (DoD) was seriously concerned about the high cost of the software components of its weapons equipment. It was estimated that more than half of the total DoD budget was spent on the development of this *embedded-systems* software—that is, software that is embedded in some machinery, such as an airplane or missile, to control it. One of the perceived problems was the great diversity of programming languages that were used to produce that software. Many of these languages, such as TACPOL, CMS-2, SPL/1, and JOVIAL, were virtually unknown outside the defense sector.

In 1976 a committee of computer scientists and defense industry representatives was asked to evaluate existing programming languages. The committee was to determine whether any of them could be made the DoD standard for all future military programming. To nobody's surprise, the committee decided that a new language would need to be created. Contractors were then invited to submit designs for such a new language. Of 17 initial proposals, four were chosen to develop their languages. To ensure an unbiased evaluation, the languages received code names: Red (by Intermetrics), Green (by CII Honeywell Bull), Blue (by Softech), and Yellow (by SRI International). All four languages were based on Pascal. The Green language emerged as the winner in 1979. It was named Ada in honor of the world's first programmer, Ada Lovelace (see Random Fact 19.1).

The Ada language was roundly derided by academics as a typical bloated Defense Department product. Military contractors routinely sought, and obtained, exemptions from the requirement that they had to use Ada on their projects. Outside the defense industry, few companies used Ada. Perhaps that is unfair. Ada had been *designed* to be complex enough to be useful for many applications, whereas other, more popular languages, notably C++, have *grown* to be just as complex and ended up being unmanageable.

The initial version of the C language was designed around 1972. Unlike Ada, C is a simple language that lets you program "close to the machine". It is also quite unsafe. Because different compiler writers added different features, the language actually sprouted various dialects. Some programming instructions were understood by one compiler but rejected by another. Such divergence is an immense pain to a programmer who wants to move code from one computer to another, and an effort got underway to iron out the differences and come up with a standard version of C. The design process ended in 1989 with the completion of the ANSI (American National Standards Institute) Standard. In the meantime, Bjarne Stroustrup of AT&T added features of the language Simula (an object-oriented language designed for carrying out simulations) to C. The resulting language was called C++. From 1985 until today, C++ has grown by the addition of many features, and a standardization process was completed in 1998. C++ has been enormously popular because programmers can take their existing C code and move it to C++ with only minimal changes. In order to keep compatibility with existing code, every innovation in C++ had to work around the existing language constructs, yielding a language that is powerful but somewhat cumbersome to use.

In 1995, Java was designed to be conceptually simpler and more internally consistent than C++, while retaining the syntax that is familiar to millions of C and C++ programmers. The Java *language* was a great design success. It is indeed clean and simple. As for the Java *library*, you know from your own experience that it is neither.

Keep in mind that a programming language is only part of the technology for writing programs. To be successful, a programming language needs feature-rich libraries, powerful tools, and a community of knowledgeable and enthusiastic users. Several very well-designed programming languages have withered on the vine, whereas other programming languages whose design was merely "good enough" have thrived in the marketplace.

CHAPTER SUMMARY

1. User interface events include key presses, mouse moves, button clicks, menu selections, and so on.

2. An event listener belongs to a class that is provided by the application programmer. Its methods describe the actions to be taken when an event occurs.

3. Event sources report on events. When an event occurs, the event source notifies all event listeners.

4. Use `JButton` components for buttons. Attach an `ActionListener` to each button.

5. Use a `JPanel` container to group multiple user-interface components together.

6. You often install event listeners as inner classes so that they can have access to the surrounding fields, methods, and final variables.

7. Use `JTextField` components to provide space for user input. Place a `JLabel` next to each text field.

8. You use a mouse listener to capture mouse events.

9. The `repaint` method causes a component to repaint itself. Call this method whenever you modify the shapes that the `paintComponent` method draws.

CLASSES, OBJECTS, AND METHODS INTRODUCED IN THIS CHAPTER

```
java.awt.Component
    addMouseListener
    repaint
java.awt.Container
    add
java.awt.Rectangle
    setLocation
java.awt.event.MouseEvent
    getX
    getY
java.awt.event.MouseListener
    mouseClicked
    mouseEntered
    mouseExited
    mousePressed
    mouseReleased
javax.swing.AbstractButton
    addActionListener
javax.swing.JButton
javax.swing.JLabel
javax.swing.JPanel
javax.swing.JTextField
javax.swing.text.JTextComponent
    getText
```

REVIEW EXERCISES

Exercise R12.1. What is an event object? An event source? An event listener?

Exercise R12.2. From a programmer's perspective, what is the most important difference between the user interfaces of a console application and a graphical application?

Exercise R12.3. What is the difference between an ActionEvent and a MouseEvent?

Exercise R12.4. Why does the ActionListener interface have only one method, whereas the MouseListener has five methods?

Exercise R12.5. Can a class be an event source for multiple event types?

Exercise R12.6. What information does an action event object carry? What additional information does a mouse event object carry?

Exercise R12.7. Why are we using inner classes for event listeners? If Java did not have inner classes, could we still implement event listeners? How?

Exercise R12.8. What is the difference between the paintComponent and repaint methods?

Exercise R12.9. What is the difference between a label and a text field?

Exercise R12.10. What is the difference between a frame and a panel?

PROGRAMMING EXERCISES

Exercise P12.1. Enhance the ButtonTester program so that it prints a message "I was clicked *n* times!" whenever the button is clicked. The value *n* should be incremented with each click.

Exercise P12.2. Enhance the ButtonTester program so that it has two buttons, each of which prints a message "I was clicked *n* times!" whenever the button is clicked. Each button should have a separate click count.

Exercise P12.3. Enhance the ButtonTester program so that it has two buttons labeled A and B, each of which prints a message "Button *x* was clicked!", where *x* is A or B.

Exercise P12.4. Implement a ButtonTester program as in Exercise P12.3, using only a single listener class.

Exercise P12.5. Enhance the ButtonTester program so that it prints the time at which the button was clicked.

Exercise P12.6. Implement the AddInterestListener in the InvestmentViewer1 program as a regular class (that is, not an inner class). *Hint:* Store references to the bank account and the label in the listener. Add a constructor to the listener class that sets the references.

Exercise P12.7. Write a program that demonstrates the growth of a roach population. Start with two roaches and double the number of roaches with each button click.

Exercise P12.8. Write a graphical front end for a bank account class. Supply text fields and buttons for depositing and withdrawing money, and for displaying the current balance in a label.

Exercise P12.9. Write a graphical application front end for an Earthquake class. Supply a text field and button for entering the strength of the earthquake. Display the earthquake description in a label.

Exercise P12.10. Write a graphical application front end for a DataSet class. Supply text fields and buttons for adding values, and display the current minimum, maximum, and average in a label.

Exercise P12.11. Write a program that prompts the user for an integer and then draws as many rectangles at random positions in a component as the user requested.

Exercise P12.12. Write a program that prompts the user to enter the *x*- and *y*-positions of the center and a radius. When the user clicks a "Draw" button, draw a circle with that center and radius in a component.

Exercise P12.13. Write a program that allows the user to specify a circle by typing the radius in a text field and then clicking on the center. Note that you don't need a "Draw" button.

Exercise P12.14. Write a program that allows the user to specify a circle with two mouse presses, the first one on the center and the second on a point on the periphery. *Hint:* In the mouse press handler, you must keep track of whether you already received the center point in a previous mouse press.

Exercise P12.15. Write a program that allows the user to specify a triangle with three mouse clicks. *Hint:* In the mouse press handler, you must keep track of how many corners you already received. When the user clicks for the first time, draw a small circle to mark the position. When the user clicks for the second time, draw a line joining the two points. Finally, after the third click, draw the entire triangle.

Exercise P12.16. Write a program that prompts the user to click on three points. Then draw a circle passing through the three points.

Exercise P12.17. Write a program that prompts the user to click on two points. Then draw a line joining the points and write a message displaying the *slope* of the line; that is, the "rise over run" ratio. The message should be displayed at the *midpoint* of the line.

Exercise P12.18. Write a program that draws a clock face with a time that the user enters in two text fields (one for the hours, one for the minutes).

Hint: You need to determine the angles of the hour hand and the minute hand. The angle of the minute hand is easy: The minute hand travels 360 degrees in 60 minutes. The angle of the hour hand is harder; it travels 360 degrees in 12×60 *minutes.*

Exercise P12.19. Write a program that asks the user to enter an integer n, and then draws an n-by-n grid.

Exercise P12.20. Write a program that draws a 10-by-10 grid. Whenever the user clicks inside one of the grid squares, color that grid square black.

PROGRAMMING PROJECTS

Project 12.1. Write a graphical application that simulates a cash register. Supply a text field to enter the price of a purchased item, buttons for adding an item and computing change, buttons for adding various coins, and a label with instructions detailing the coins to be returned to the user. Make sure to use a single method for the event listeners for the various coin buttons.

Project 12.2. Write a program that plots a *regression line;* that is, the line with the best fit through a collection of points. The regression line is the line with equation

$$y = \bar{y} + m(x - \bar{x}) ,$$

where

$$m = \frac{\sum x_i y_i - n \overline{x}\,\overline{y}}{\sum x_i^2 - n \overline{x}^2}$$

$\overline{x}$ is the mean of the x-values, and $\overline{y}$ is the mean of the y-values.

The user keeps clicking on points. You don't need to store the individual points, but you need to keep track of

- The count of input values
- The sum of x, y, x^2, and xy values

To draw the regression line, compute its end points at the left and right edges of the screen and draw a segment. Each time the user clicks on another point, repaint the graph.

ANSWERS TO SELF-CHECK QUESTIONS

1. The `button` object is the event source. The `listener` object is the event listener.
2. The `ClickListener` class implements the `ActionListener` interface.
3. First add `label` to the `panel`, then add `button`.
4. The `actionPerformed` method does not access that variable.
5. Then the text field is not labeled, and the user will not know its purpose.
6. `Integer.parseInt(textField.getText())`
7. The rectangle would only be painted at the new location when the component is repainted for some other reason, for example, when the frame is resized.
8. It implements the `MouseListener` interface, which has five methods.

Inheritance

CHAPTER GOALS

- To learn about inheritance
- To understand how to inherit and override superclass methods
- To be able to invoke superclass constructors
- To learn about protected and package access control
- To understand the common superclass Object and how to override its toString and equals methods

In this chapter, we discuss the important concept of inheritance. Specialized classes can be created that inherit behavior from more general classes. You will learn how to implement inheritance in Java, and how to make use of the Object class—the most general class in the inheritance hierachy.

CHAPTER CONTENTS

13.1 An Introduction to Inheritance

> Inheritance is a mechanism for extending existing classes by adding methods and fields.

Inheritance is a mechanism for enhancing existing classes. If you need to implement a new class and a class representing a more general concept is already available, then the new class can inherit from the existing class. For example, suppose you need to define a class SavingsAccount to model an account that pays a fixed interest rate on deposits. You already have a class BankAccount, and a savings account is a special case of a bank account. In this case, it makes sense to use the language construct of inheritance. Here is the syntax for the class definition:

```
class SavingsAccount extends BankAccount
{
    new methods
    new instance fields
}
```

In the SavingsAccount class definition you specify only new methods and instance fields. The SavingsAccount class *automatically inherits* all methods and instance fields of the BankAccount class. For example, the deposit method automatically applies to savings accounts:

```
SavingsAccount collegeFund = new SavingsAccount(10);
    // Savings account with 10% interest
collegeFund.deposit(500);
    // OK to use BankAccount method with SavingsAccount object
```

> The more general class is called a superclass. The more specialized class that inherits from the superclass is called the subclass.

We must introduce some more terminology here. The more general class that forms the basis for inheritance is called the *superclass.* The more specialized class that inherits from the superclass is called the *subclass.* In our example, BankAccount is the superclass and Savings-Account is the subclass.

In Java, every class that does not specifically extend another class is a subclass of the class Object. For example, the BankAccount class extends the class Object. The Object class has a small number of methods that make sense for all objects, such as the toString method, which you can use to obtain a string that describes the state of an object.

> Every class extends the Object class either directly or indirectly.

Figure 1 is a class diagram showing the relationship between the three classes Object, BankAccount, and SavingsAccount. In a class diagram, you denote inheritance by a solid arrow with a "hollow triangle" tip that points to the superclass.

> Inheriting from a class differs from implementing an interface: The subclass inherits behavior and state from the superclass.

You may wonder at this point in what way inheritance differs from implementing an interface. An interface is not a class. It has *no state and no behavior.* It merely tells you which methods you should implement. A superclass has state and behavior, and the subclasses inherit them.

Figure 1
An Inheritance Diagram

One advantage of inheritance is code reuse.

One important reason for inheritance is *code reuse*. By inheriting an existing class, you do not have to replicate the effort that went into designing and perfecting that class. For example, when implementing the SavingsAccount class, you can rely on the withdraw, deposit, and getBalance methods of the BankAccount class without touching them.

When defining a subclass, you specify added instance fields, added methods, and changed or overridden methods.

Let's see how savings account objects are different from BankAccount objects. We will set an interest rate in the constructor, and we need a method to apply that interest periodically. That is, in addition to the three methods that can be applied to every account, there is an additional method addInterest. The new method and instance field must be defined in the subclass.

```
public class SavingsAccount extends BankAccount
{
    public SavingsAccount(double rate)
    {
        Constructor implementation
    }

    public void addInterest()
    {
        Method implementation
    }

    private double interestRate;
}
```

Figure 2 shows the layout of a SavingsAccount object. It inherits the balance instance field from the BankAccount superclass, and it gains one additional instance field: interestRate.

Next, you need to implement the new addInterest method. The method computes the interest due on the current balance and deposits that interest to the account.

```
public class SavingsAccount extends BankAccount
{
    public SavingsAccount(double rate)
    {
        interestRate = rate;
    }
    public void addInterest()
    {
        double interest = getBalance() * interestRate / 100;
        deposit(interest);
    }
    private double interestRate;
}
```

You may wonder why the addInterest method calls the getBalance and deposit methods rather than directly updating the balance field of the superclass. This is a consequence of encapsulation. The balance field was defined as private in the BankAccount class. The addInterest method is defined in the SavingsAccount class. It does not have the right to access a private field of another class.

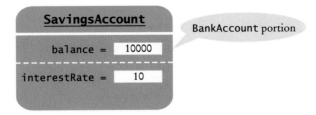

Figure 2 Layout of a Subclass Object

Note how the addInterest method calls the getBalance and deposit methods of the superclass without specifying an implicit parameter. This means that the calls apply to the same object, that is, the implicit parameter of the addInterest method.

SYNTAX 13.1 **Inheritance**

```
class SubclassName extends SuperclassName
{
    methods
    instance fields
}
```

Example:

```
public class SavingsAccount extends BankAccount
{
    public SavingsAccount(double rate)
    {
        interestRate = rate;
    }

    public void addInterest()
    {
        double interest = getBalance() * interestRate / 100;
        deposit(interest);
    }

    private double interestRate;
}
```

Purpose:

To define a new class that inherits from an existing class, and define the methods and instance fields that are added in the new class

For example, if you call

```
collegeFund.addInterest();
```

then the following instructions are executed:

```
double interest = collegeFund.getBalance()
      * collegeFund.interestRate / 100;
collegeFund.deposit(interest);
```

In other words, the statements in the addInterest method are a shorthand for the following statements:

```
double interest = this.getBalance()
      * this.interestRate / 100;
this.deposit(interest);
```

(Recall that the this variable holds a reference to the implicit parameter.)

SELF CHECK

1. Which instance fields does an object of class SavingsAccount have?
2. Name four methods that you can apply to SavingsAccount objects.
3. If the class Manager extends the class Employee, which class is the superclass and which is the subclass?

COMMON ERROR 13.1

Confusing Super- and Subclasses

If you compare an object of type SavingsAccount with an object of type BankAccount, then you find that

- The keyword extends suggests that the SavingsAccount object is an extended version of a BankAccount.

- The SavingsAccount object is larger; it has an added instance field interestRate.

- The SavingsAccount object is more capable; it has an addInterest method.

It seems a superior object in every way. So why is SavingsAccount called the *subclass* and BankAccount the *superclass*?

The *super/sub* terminology comes from set theory. Look at the set of all bank accounts. Not all of them are SavingsAccount objects; some of them are other kinds of bank accounts. Therefore, the set of SavingsAccount objects is a *subset* of the set of all BankAccount objects, and the set of BankAccount objects is a *superset* of the set of SavingsAccount objects. The more specialized objects in the subset have a richer state and more capabilities.

13.2 Inheritance Hierarchies

In the real world, you often categorize concepts into *hierarchies*. Hierarchies are frequently represented as trees, with the most general concepts at the root of the hierarchy and more specialized ones towards the branches. Figure 3 shows a typical example.

> Sets of classes can form complex inheritance hierarchies.

In Java it is equally common to group classes in complex *inheritance hierarchies*. The classes representing the most general concepts are near the root, more specialized classes towards the branches. For example, Figure 4 shows part of the hierarchy of Swing user interface components in Java.

When designing a hierarchy of classes, you ask yourself which features and behaviors are common to all the classes that you are designing. Those common properties are collected in a superclass. For example, all user interface components have a width and height, and the getWidth and getHeight methods of the JComponent class return the component's dimensions. More specialized properties can be found in subclasses. For example, buttons can have text and icon labels. The class AbstractButton, but not the superclass JComponent, has methods to set and get the button text and icon, and instance fields to store them. The individual button classes (such as JButton, JRadioButton, and JCheckBox) inherit these properties. In fact, the AbstractButton class was created to express the commonality between these buttons.

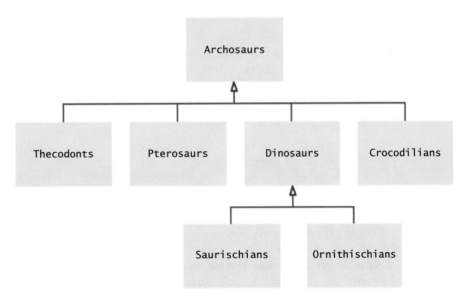

Figure 3 A Part of the Hierarchy of Ancient Reptiles

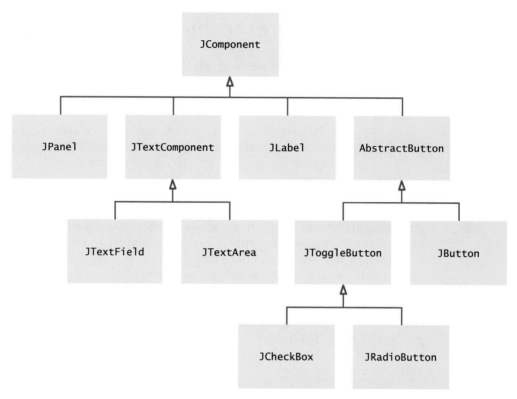

Figure 4   A Part of the Hierarchy of Swing User Interface Components

We will use a simpler example of a hierarchy in our study of inheritance concepts. Consider a bank that offers its customers the following account types:

1. The checking account has no interest, gives you a small number of free transactions per month, and charges a transaction fee for each additional transaction.

2. The savings account earns interest that compounds monthly. (In our implementation, the interest is compounded using the balance of the last day of the month, which is somewhat unrealistic. Typically, banks use either the average or the minimum daily balance. Exercise P13.1 asks you to implement this enhancement.)

Figure 5 shows the inheritance hierarchy. Exercise P13.2 asks you to add another class to this hierarchy.

Next, let us determine the behavior of these classes. All bank accounts support the getBalance method, which simply reports the current balance. They also support the deposit and withdraw methods, although the details of the implementation differ. For example, a checking account must keep track of the number of transactions to account for the transaction fees.

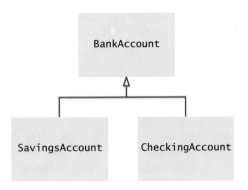

Figure 5   Inheritance Hierarchy for Bank Account Classes

The checking account needs a method deductFees to deduct the monthly fees and to reset the transaction counter. The deposit and withdraw methods must be redefined to count the transactions.

The savings account needs a method addInterest to add interest.

To summarize: The subclasses support all methods from the superclass, but their implementations may be modified to match the specialized purposes of the subclasses. In addition, subclasses are free to introduce additional methods.

SELF CHECK

4. What is the purpose of the JTextComponent class in Figure 4?

5. Which instance field will we need to add to the CheckingAccount class?

13.3 Inheriting Instance Fields and Methods

When you form a subclass of a given class, you can specify additional instance fields and methods. In this section we will discuss this process in detail.

When defining the methods for a subclass, there are three possibilities.

1. You can *override* methods from the superclass. If you specify a method with the same *signature* (that is, the same name and the same parameter types), it overrides the method of the same name in the superclass. Whenever the method is applied to an object of the subclass type, the overriding method, and not the original method, is executed. For example, Checking-Account.deposit overrides BankAccount.deposit.

2. You can *inherit* methods from the superclass. If you do not explicitly override a superclass method, you automatically inherit it. The superclass method can be applied to the subclass objects. For example, the SavingsAccount class inherits the BankAccount.getBalance method.

3. You can define new methods. If you define a method that did not exist in the superclass, then the new method can be applied only to subclass objects. For example, `SavingsAccount.addInterest` is a new method that does not exist in the superclass `BankAccount`.

The situation for instance fields is quite different. You can never override instance fields. For fields in a subclass, there are only two cases:

1. The subclass inherits all fields from the superclass. All instance fields from the superclass are automatically inherited. For example, all subclasses of the `BankAccount` class inherit the instance field `balance`.

2. Any new instance fields that you define in the subclass are present only in subclass objects. For example, the subclass `SavingsAccount` defines a new instance field `interestRate`.

What happens if you define a new field with the same name as a superclass field? For example, can you define another field named `balance` in the `SavingsAccount` class? This is legal but extremely undesirable. Each `SavingsAccount` object would have *two* instance fields of the same name. The two fields can hold different values, which is likely to lead to confusion—see Common Error 13.2.

We already implemented the `BankAccount` and `SavingsAccount` classes. Now we will implement the subclass `CheckingAccount` so that you can see in detail how methods and instance fields are inherited. Recall that the `BankAccount` class has three methods and one instance field:

```
public class BankAccount
{
    public double getBalance() { . . . }
    public void deposit(double amount) { . . . }
    public void withdraw(double amount) { . . . }

    private double balance;
}
```

The `CheckingAccount` class has an added method `deductFees` and an added instance field `transactionCount`, and it overrides the `deposit` and `withdraw` methods to increment the transaction count:

```
public class CheckingAccount extends BankAccount
{
    public void deposit(double amount) { . . . }
    public void withdraw(double amount) { . . . }
    public void deductFees() { . . . }

    private int transactionCount;
}
```

Each object of class `CheckingAccount` has two instance fields:

- `balance` (inherited from `BankAccount`)
- `transactionCount` (new to `CheckingAccount`)

You can apply four methods to CheckingAccount objects:

- getBalance() (inherited from BankAccount)
- deposit(double amount) (overrides BankAccount method)
- withdraw(double amount) (overrides BankAccount method)
- deductFees() (new to CheckingAccount)

Next, let us implement these methods. The deposit method increments the transaction count and deposits the money:

```
public class CheckingAccount extends BankAccount
{
   public void deposit(double amount)
   {
      transactionCount++;
      // Now add amount to balance
      . . .
   }
   . . .
}
```

Now we have a problem. We can't simply add amount to balance:

```
public class CheckingAccount extends BankAccount
{
   public void deposit(double amount)
   {
      transactionCount++;
      // Now add amount to balance
      balance = balance + amount; // Error
   }
   . . .
}
```

> A subclass has no access to private fields of its superclass.

Although every CheckingAccount object has a balance instance field, that instance field is *private* to the superclass BankAccount. Subclass methods have no more access rights to the private data of the superclass than any other methods. If you want to modify a private superclass field, you must use a public method of the superclass.

How can we add the deposit amount to the balance, using the public interface of the BankAccount class? There is a perfectly good method for that purpose—namely, the deposit method of the BankAccount class. So we must invoke the deposit method on some object. On which object? The checking account into which the money is deposited—that is, the implicit parameter of the deposit method of the CheckingAccount class. To invoke another method on the implicit parameter, you don't specify the parameter but simply write the method name, like this:

```
public class CheckingAccount extends BankAccount
{
   public void deposit(double amount)
   {
      transactionCount++;
      // Now add amount to balance
      deposit(amount); // Not complete
```

```
      }
         . . .
   }
```

But this won't quite work. The compiler interprets

```
   deposit(amount);
```

as

```
   this.deposit(amount);
```

The this parameter is of type CheckingAccount. There is a method called deposit in the CheckingAccount class. Therefore, that method will be called—but that is just the method we are currently writing! The method will call itself over and over, and the program will die in an infinite recursion (discussed in Chapter 18).

Use the super keyword to call a method of the superclass.

Instead, we must be specific that we want to invoke only the *superclass's* deposit method. There is a special keyword super for this purpose:

```
   public class CheckingAccount extends BankAccount
   {
      public void deposit(double amount)
      {
         transactionCount++;
         // Now add amount to balance
         super.deposit(amount);
      }
         . . .
   }
```

This version of the deposit method is correct. To deposit money into a checking account, update the transaction count and call the deposit method of the superclass.

The remaining methods are now straightforward.

```
   public class CheckingAccount extends BankAccount
   {
      . . .
      public void withdraw(double amount)
      {
         transactionCount++;
         // Now subtract amount from balance
         super.withdraw(amount);
      }
      public void deductFees()
      {
         if (transactionCount > FREE_TRANSACTIONS)
         {
            double fees = TRANSACTION_FEE
                  * (transactionCount - FREE_TRANSACTIONS);
            super.withdraw(fees);
         }
         transactionCount = 0;
      }
      . . .
      private static final int FREE_TRANSACTIONS = 3;
      private static final double TRANSACTION_FEE = 2.0;
   }
```

> ### Syntax 13.2 Calling a Superclass Method
>
> super.*methodName*(*parameters*);
>
> **Example:**
> ```
> public void deposit(double amount)
> {
>    transactionCount++;
>    super.deposit(amount);
> }
> ```
>
> **Purpose:**
> To call a method of the superclass instead of the method of the current class

SELF CHECK

6. Why does the withdraw method of the CheckingAccount class call super.withdraw?
7. Why does the deductFees method set the transaction count to zero?

COMMON ERROR 13.2

Shadowing Instance Fields

A subclass has no access to the private instance fields of the superclass. For example, the methods of the CheckingAccount class cannot access the balance field:

```
public class CheckingAccount extends BankAccount
{
   public void deposit(double amount)
   {
      transactionCount++;
      balance = balance + amount; // Error
   }
   . . .
}
```

It is a common beginner's error to "solve" this problem by adding *another* instance field with the same name.

```
public class CheckingAccount extends BankAccount
{
   public void deposit(double amount)
   {
```

```
            transactionCount++;
            balance = balance + amount;
        }
        . . .
        private double balance; // Don't
    }
```

Sure, now the `deposit` method compiles, but it doesn't update the correct balance! Such a `CheckingAccount` object has two instance fields, both named `balance` (see Figure 6). The `getBalance` method of the superclass retrieves one of them, and the `deposit` method of the subclass updates the other.

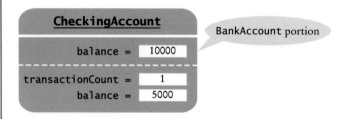

Figure 6 Shadowing Instance Fields

COMMON ERROR 13.3

Failing to Invoke the Superclass Method

A common error in extending the functionality of a superclass method is to forget the `super.` qualifier. For example, to withdraw money from a checking account, update the transaction count and then withdraw the amount:

```
public void withdraw(double amount)
{
    transactionCount++;
    withdraw(amount);
    // Error—should be super.withdraw(amount)
}
```

Here `withdraw(amount)` refers to the `withdraw` method applied to the implicit parameter of the method. The implicit parameter is of type `CheckingAccount`, and the `CheckingAccount` class has a `withdraw` method, so that method is called. Of course, that calls the current method all over again, which will call itself yet again, over and over, until the program runs out of memory. Instead, you must precisely identify which `withdraw` method you want to call.

Another common error is to forget to call the superclass method altogether. Then the functionality of the superclass mysteriously vanishes.

13.4 Subclass Construction

In this section, we discuss the implementation of constructors in subclasses. As an example, let us define a constructor to set the initial balance of a checking account.

We want to invoke the BankAccount constructor to set the balance to the initial balance. There is a special instruction to call the superclass constructor from a subclass constructor. You use the keyword super, followed by the construction parameters in parentheses:

```java
public class CheckingAccount extends BankAccount
{
    public CheckingAccount(double initialBalance)
    {
        // Construct superclass
        super(initialBalance);
        // Initialize transaction count
        transactionCount = 0;
    }
    . . .
}
```

> To call the superclass constructor, you use the super keyword in the first statement of the subclass constructor.

When the keyword super is followed by a parenthesis, it indicates a call to the superclass constructor. When used in this way, the constructor call must be *the first statement of the subclass constructor.* If super is followed by a period and a method name, on the other hand, it indicates a call to a superclass method, as you saw in the preceding section. Such a call can be made anywhere in any subclass method.

SYNTAX 13.3 Calling a Superclass Constructor

ClassName(parameters)
```
{
    super(parameters);
    . . .
}
```

Example:

```java
public CheckingAccount(double initialBalance)
{
    super(initialBalance);
    transactionCount = 0;
}
```

Purpose:

To invoke the constructor of the superclass. Note that this statement must be the first statement of the subclass constructor.

The dual use of the super keyword is analogous to the dual use of the this keyword (see Advanced Topic 3.1).

If a subclass constructor does not call the superclass constructor, the superclass is constructed with its default constructor (that is, the constructor that has no parameters). However, if all constructors of the superclass require parameters, then the compiler reports an error.

For example, you can implement the CheckingAccount constructor without calling the superclass constructor. Then the BankAccount class is constructed with its default constructor, which sets the balance to zero. Of course, then the CheckingAccount constructor must explicitly deposit the initial balance.

Most commonly, however, subclass constructors have some parameters that they pass on to the superclass and others that they use to initialize subclass fields.

SELF CHECK

8. Why didn't the SavingsAccount constructor in Section 13.1 call its superclass constructor?

9. When you invoke a superclass method with the super keyword, does the call have to be the first statement of the subclass method?

13.5 Converting Between Subclass and Superclass Types

It is often necessary to convert a subclass type to a superclass type. Occasionally, you need to carry out the conversion in the opposite direction. This section discusses the conversion rules.

> Subclass references can be converted to superclass references.

The class SavingsAccount extends the class BankAccount. In other words, a SavingsAccount object is a special case of a BankAccount object. Therefore, a reference to a SavingsAccount object can be converted to a BankAccount reference.

```
SavingsAccount collegeFund = new SavingsAccount(10);
BankAccount anAccount = collegeFund;
```

Furthermore, all references can be converted to the type Object.

```
Object anObject = collegeFund;
```

Now the three object references stored in collegeFund, anAccount, and anObject all refer to the same object of type SavingsAccount (see Figure 7).

However, the object reference anAccount knows less than the full story about the object to which it refers. Because anAccount is an object of type BankAccount, you can use the deposit and withdraw methods to change the balance of the savings account. You cannot use the addInterest method, though—it is not a method of the BankAccount superclass:

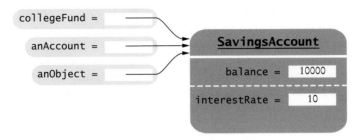

Figure 7   Variables of Different Types Refer to the Same Object

```
anAccount.deposit(1000); // OK
anAccount.addInterest();
    // No—not a method of the class to which anAccount belongs
```

And, of course, the variable anObject knows even less. You can't even apply the deposit method to it—deposit is not a method of the Object class.

Conversion of references is different from a numerical conversion, such as a conversion from an integer to a floating-point number. If you convert an integer, say 4, into the double value 4.0, then the representation changes: the double value 4.0 uses a different sequence of bits than the int value 4. However, when you convert a SavingsAccount reference to a BankAccount reference, then the value of the reference stays the same—it is the memory location of the object. However, after conversion, less information is known about the object. We only know that it is a bank account. It might be a plain bank account, a savings account, or another kind of bank account.

Why would anyone *want* to know less about an object and store a reference in an object field of a superclass? This can happen if you want to *reuse code* that knows about the superclass but not the subclass. Here is a typical example. Consider a transfer method that transfers money from one account to another:

```
public void transfer(double amount, BankAccount other)
{
   withdraw(amount);
   other.deposit(amount);
}
```

You can use this method to transfer money from one bank account to another:

```
BankAccount momsAccount = . . . ;
BankAccount harrysAccount = . . . ;
momsAccount.transfer(1000, harrysAccount);
```

You can *also* use the method to transfer money into a CheckingAccount:

```
CheckingAccount harrysChecking = . . . ;
momsAccount.transfer(1000, harrysChecking);
    // OK to pass a CheckingAccount reference to a method expecting a BankAccount
```

The transfer method expects a reference to a BankAccount, and it gets a reference to the subclass CheckingAccount. Fortunately, rather than complaining about a type mismatch, the compiler simply copies the subclass reference harrysChecking to the superclass reference other. The transfer method doesn't actually know that, in this case, other refers to a CheckingAccount reference. It knows only that other is a BankAccount, and it doesn't need to know anything else. All it cares about is that the other object can carry out the deposit method.

Very occasionally, you need to carry out the opposite conversion, from a super-class reference to a subclass reference. For example, you may have a variable of type Object, and you know that it actually holds a BankAccount reference. In that case, you can use a cast to convert the type:

```
BankAccount anAccount = (BankAccount) anObject;
```

However, this cast is somewhat dangerous. If you are wrong, and anObject actually refers to an object of an unrelated type, then an exception is thrown.

> The instanceof operator tests whether an object belongs to a particular type.

To protect against bad casts, you can use the instanceof operator. It tests whether an object belongs to a particular type. For example,

```
anObject instanceof BankAccount
```

returns true if the type of anObject is convertible to BankAccount. This happens if anObject refers to an actual BankAccount or a subclass such as Savings-Account. Using the instanceof operator, a safe cast can be programmed as follows:

```
if (anObject instanceof BankAccount)
{
    BankAccount anAccount = (BankAccount) anObject;
    . . .
}
```

SYNTAX 13.4 The instanceof Operator

object instanceof *TypeName*

Example:

```
if (anObject instanceof BankAccount)
{
    BankAccount anAccount = (BankAccount) anObject;
    . . .
}
```

Purpose:

To return true if the *object* is an instance of *TypeName* (or one of its subtypes), and false otherwise

---

SELF CHECK

10. Why did the second parameter of the transfer method have to be of type BankAccount and not, for example, SavingsAccount?

11. Why can't we change the second parameter of the transfer method to the type Object?

13.6 Polymorphism

In Java, the type of a variable does not completely determine the type of the object to which it refers. For example, a variable of type BankAccount can hold a reference to an actual BankAccount object or a subclass object such as SavingsAccount. You already encountered this phenomenon in Chapter 11 with variables whose type was an interface. A variable whose type is Measurable holds a reference to an object of a class that implements the Measurable interface, perhaps a Coin object or an object of an entirely different class.

What happens when you invoke a method? For example,

```
BankAccount anAccount = new CheckingAccount();
anAccount.deposit(1000);
```

Which deposit method is called? The anAccount parameter has type BankAccount, so it would appear as if BankAccount.deposit is called. On the other hand, the CheckingAccount class provides its own deposit method that updates the transaction count. The anAccount field actually refers to an object of the subclass Checking-Account, so it would be appropriate if the CheckingAccount.deposit method were called instead.

In Java, method calls *are always determined by the type of the actual object*, not the type of the object reference. That is, if the actual object has the type Checking-Account, then the CheckingAccount.deposit method is called. It does not matter that the object reference is stored in a field of type BankAccount. As we discussed in Chapter 11, the ability to refer to objects of multiple types with varying behavior is called *polymorphism*.

If polymorphism is so powerful, why not store all account references in variables of type Object? This does not work because the compiler needs to check that only legal methods are invoked. The Object type does not define a deposit method—the BankAccount type (at least) is required to make a call to the deposit method.

Have another look at the transfer method to see polymorphism at work. Here is the implementation of the method:

```
public void transfer(double amount, BankAccount other)
{
   withdraw(amount);
   other.deposit(amount);
}
```

Suppose you call

```
anAccount.transfer(1000, anotherAccount);
```

Two method calls are the result:

```
anAccount.withdraw(1000);
anotherAccount.deposit(1000);
```

Depending on the actual types of anAccount and anotherAccount, different versions of the withdraw and deposit methods are called.

If you look into the implementation of the transfer method, it may not be immediately obvious that the first method call

```
withdraw(amount);
```

depends on the type of an object. However, that call is a shortcut for

```
this.withdraw(amount);
```

The this parameter holds a reference to the implicit parameter, which can refer to a BankAccount or a subclass object.

The following program calls the polymorphic withdraw and deposit methods. You should manually calculate what the program should print for each account balance, and confirm that the correct methods have in fact been called.

File AccountTester.java

```java
1  /**
2       This program tests the BankAccount class and
3       its subclasses.
4  */
5  public class AccountTester
6  {
7      public static void main(String[] args)
8      {
9          SavingsAccount momsSavings
10              = new SavingsAccount(0.5);
11
12          CheckingAccount harrysChecking
13              = new CheckingAccount(100);
14
15          momsSavings.deposit(10000);
16
17          momsSavings.transfer(2000, harrysChecking);
18          harrysChecking.withdraw(1500);
19          harrysChecking.withdraw(80);
20
21          momsSavings.transfer(1000, harrysChecking);
22          harrysChecking.withdraw(400);
23
24          // Simulate end of month
25          momsSavings.addInterest();
26          harrysChecking.deductFees();
27
28          System.out.println("Mom's savings balance = $"
29              + momsSavings.getBalance());
30
31          System.out.println("Harry's checking balance = $"
32              + harrysChecking.getBalance());
33      }
34  }
```

File BankAccount.java

```java
 1  /**
 2      A bank account has a balance that can be changed by
 3      deposits and withdrawals.
 4  */
 5  public class BankAccount
 6  {
 7      /**
 8          Constructs a bank account with a zero balance.
 9      */
10      public BankAccount()
11      {
12          balance = 0;
13      }
14
15      /**
16          Constructs a bank account with a given balance.
17          @param initialBalance the initial balance
18      */
19      public BankAccount(double initialBalance)
20      {
21          balance = initialBalance;
22      }
23
24      /**
25          Deposits money into the bank account.
26          @param amount the amount to deposit
27      */
28      public void deposit(double amount)
29      {
30          balance = balance + amount;
31      }
32
33      /**
34          Withdraws money from the bank account.
35          @param amount the amount to withdraw
36      */
37      public void withdraw(double amount)
38      {
39          balance = balance - amount;
40      }
41
42      /**
43          Gets the current balance of the bank account.
44          @return the current balance
45      */
46      public double getBalance()
47      {
48          return balance;
49      }
50
```

```
51    /**
52         Transfers money from the bank account to another account.
53         @param amount  the amount to transfer
54         @param other  the other account
55    */
56    public void transfer(double amount, BankAccount other)
57    {
58         withdraw(amount);
59         other.deposit(amount);
60    }
61
62    private double balance;
63  }
```

File CheckingAccount.java

```
1   /**
2        A checking account that charges transaction fees.
3   */
4   public class CheckingAccount extends BankAccount
5   {
6        /**
7             Constructs a checking account with a given balance.
8             @param initialBalance  the initial balance
9        */
10       public CheckingAccount(double initialBalance)
11       {
12            // Construct superclass
13            super(initialBalance);
14
15            // Initialize transaction count
16            transactionCount = 0;
17       }
18
19       public void deposit(double amount)
20       {
21            transactionCount++;
22            // Now add amount to balance
23            super.deposit(amount);
24       }
25
26       public void withdraw(double amount)
27       {
28            transactionCount++;
29            // Now subtract amount from balance
30            super.withdraw(amount);
31       }
32
33       /**
34            Deducts the accumulated fees and resets the
35            transaction count.
36       */
```

```
37      public void deductFees()
38      {
39         if (transactionCount > FREE_TRANSACTIONS)
40         {
41            double fees = TRANSACTION_FEE *
42                  (transactionCount - FREE_TRANSACTIONS);
43            super.withdraw(fees);
44         }
45         transactionCount = 0;
46      }
47
48      private int transactionCount;
49
50      private static final int FREE_TRANSACTIONS = 3;
51      private static final double TRANSACTION_FEE = 2.0;
52   }
```

File SavingsAccount.java

```
1    /**
2        An account that earns interest at a fixed rate.
3    */
4    public class SavingsAccount extends BankAccount
5    {
6       /**
7           Constructs a bank account with a given interest rate.
8           @param rate  the interest rate
9       */
10      public SavingsAccount(double rate)
11      {
12         interestRate = rate;
13      }
14
15      /**
16          Adds the earned interest to the account balance.
17      */
18      public void addInterest()
19      {
20         double interest = getBalance() * interestRate / 100;
21         deposit(interest);
22      }
23
24      private double interestRate;
25   }
```

Output

```
Mom's savings balance = $7035.0
Harry's checking balance = $1116.0
```

SELF CHECK

12. If a is a variable of type BankAccount that holds a non-null reference, what do you know about the object to which a refers?

13. If a refers to a checking account, what is the effect of calling a.transfer(1000, a)?

ADVANCED TOPIC 13.1

Abstract Classes

When you extend an existing class, you have the choice whether or not to redefine the methods of the superclass. Sometimes, it is desirable to *force* programmers to redefine a method. That happens when there is no good default for the superclass, and only the subclass programmer can know how to implement the method properly.

Here is an example. Suppose the First National Bank of Java decides that every account type must have some monthly fees. Therefore, a deductFees method should be added to the BankAccount class:

```
public class BankAccount
{
   public void deductFees() { . . . }
   . . .
}
```

But what should this method do? Of course, we could have the method do nothing. But then a programmer implementing a new subclass might simply forget to implement the deductFees method, and the new account would inherit the do-nothing method of the superclass. There is a better way—declare the deductFees method as an *abstract method:*

```
public abstract void deductFees();
```

> An abstract method is a method whose implementation is not specified.

An abstract method has no implementation. This forces the implementors of subclasses to specify concrete implementations of this method. (Of course, some subclasses might decide to implement a do-nothing method, but then that is their choice—not a silently inherited default.)

You cannot construct objects of classes with abstract methods. For example, once the BankAccount class has an abstract method, the compiler will flag an attempt to create a new BankAccount() as an error. Of course, if the CheckingAccount subclass overrides the deductFees method and supplies an implementation, then you can create CheckingAccount objects.

> An abstract class is a class that cannot be instantiated.

A class for which you cannot create objects is called an *abstract class*. A class for which you can create objects is sometimes called a *concrete class*. In Java, you must declare all abstract classes with the keyword abstract:

```
public abstract class BankAccount
{
   public abstract void deductFees();
   . . .
}
```

A class that defines an abstract method, or that inherits an abstract method without overriding it, *must* be declared as abstract. You can also declare classes with no abstract methods as abstract. Doing so prevents programmers from creating instances of that class but allows them to create their own subclasses.

Note that you cannot construct an *object* of an abstract class, but you can still have an *object reference* whose type is an abstract class. Of course, the actual object to which it refers must be an instance of a concrete subclass:

```
BankAccount anAccount; // OK
anAccount = new BankAccount(); // Error—BankAccount is abstract
anAccount = new SavingsAccount(); // OK
anAccount = null; // OK
```

The reason for using abstract classes is to force programmers to create subclasses. By specifying certain methods as abstract, you avoid the trouble of coming up with useless default methods that others might inherit by accident.

Abstract classes differ from interfaces in an important way—they can have instance fields, and they can have concrete methods and constructors.

ADVANCED TOPIC 13.2

Final Methods and Classes

In Advanced Topic 13.1 you saw how you can force other programmers to create subclasses of abstract classes and override abstract methods. Occasionally, you may want to do the opposite and *prevent* other programmers from creating subclasses or from overriding certain methods. In these situations, you use the `final` keyword. For example, the `String` class in the standard Java library has been declared as

```
public final class String { . . . }
```

That means that nobody can extend the `String` class.

The `String` class is meant to be *immutable*—string objects can't be modified by any of their methods. Since the Java language does not enforce this, the class designers did. Nobody can create subclasses of `String`; therefore, you know that all `String` references can be copied without the risk of mutation.

You can also declare individual methods as final:

```
public class SecureAccount extends BankAccount
{
    . . .
    public final boolean checkPassword(String password)
    {
        . . .
    }
}
```

This way, nobody can override the `checkPassword` method with another method that simply returns `true`.

13.7 Access Control

Java has four levels of controlling access to fields, methods, and classes:

- `public` access
- `private` access
- `protected` access (see Advanced Topic 13.3)
- package access (the default, when no access modifier is given)

You have already used the `private` and `public` modifiers extensively. Private features can be accessed only by the methods of their own class. Public features can be accessed by methods of all classes. We will discuss protected access in Advanced Topic 13.3—we will not need it in this book.

> A field or method that is not declared as public, private, or protected can be accessed by all classes in the same package, which is usually not desirable.

If you do not supply an access control modifier, then the default is *package access.* That is, all methods of classes in the same package can access the feature. For example, if a class is declared as `public`, then all other classes in all packages can use it. But if a class is declared without an access modifier, then only the other classes in the same package can use it. Package access is a good default for classes, but it is extremely unfortunate for fields. Instance and static fields of classes should always be `private`. There are a few exceptions:

- Public constants (`public static final` fields) are useful and safe.
- Some objects, such as `System.out`, need to be accessible to all programs and therefore should be public.
- Very occasionally, several classes in a package must collaborate very closely. In that case, it may make sense to give some fields package access. But inner classes are usually a better solution—you have seen examples in Chapter 11.

It is a common error to *forget* the keyword `private`, thereby opening up a potential security hole. For example, at the time of this writing, the `Window` class in the `java.awt` package contained the following declaration:

```
public class Window extends Container
{
    String warningString;
    . . .
}
```

The programmer was careless and didn't make the field private. There actually was no good reason to grant package access to the `warningString` field—no other class accesses it. It is a security risk. Packages are not closed entities—any programmer can make a new class, add it to the `java.awt` package, and gain access to the warning-String fields of all `Window` objects! (Actually, this possibility bothered the Java implementors so much that recent versions of the virtual machine refuse to load unknown classes whose package name starts with "`java.`". Your own packages, however, do not enjoy this protection.)

Package access for fields is rarely useful, and most fields are given package access by accident because the programmer simply forgot the `private` keyword.

Methods should generally be `public` or `private`. We recommend avoiding the use of package-visible methods.

Classes and interfaces can have public or package access. Classes that are generally useful should have public access. Classes that are used for implementation reasons should have package access. You can hide them even better by turning them into inner classes; you saw examples of inner classes in Chapter 11. There are a few examples of public inner classes, such as the `Ellipse2D.Double` class that you saw in Chapter 5. However, in general, inner classes should not be public.

SELF CHECK

14. What is a common reason for defining package-visible instance fields?

15. If a class with a public constructor has package access, who can construct objects of it?

COMMON ERROR 13.4

Accidental Package Access

It is very easy to forget the `private` modifier for instance fields.

```
public class BankAccount
{
    . . .
    double balance; // Package access really intended?
}
```

Most likely, this was just an oversight. The programmer probably never intended to grant access to this field to other classes in the same package. The compiler won't complain, of course. Much later, some other programmer may take advantage of the access privilege, either out of convenience or out of evil intent. This is a serious problem, and you must get into the habit of scanning your field declarations for missing `private` modifiers.

COMMON ERROR 13.5

Making Inherited Methods Less Accessible

If a superclass declares a method to be publicly accessible, you cannot override it to be more private. For example,

```
public class BankAccount
{
    public void withdraw(double amount) { . . . }
    . . .
```

```
    }

    public class CheckingAccount extends BankAccount
    {
        private void withdraw(double amount) { . . . }
            // Error—subclass method cannot be more private
        . . .
    }
```

The compiler does not allow this, because the increased privacy would be an illusion. Anyone can still call the method through a superclass reference:

```
    BankAccount account = new CheckingAccount();
    account.withdraw(100000); // Calls CheckingAccount.withdraw
```

Because of polymorphism, the subclass method is called.

These errors are usually an oversight. If you forget the `public` modifier, your subclass method has package access, which is more restrictive. Simply restore the `public` modifier, and the error will go away.

ADVANCED TOPIC 13.3

Protected Access

We ran into a hurdle when trying to implement the `deposit` method of the `CheckingAccount` class. That method needed access to the `balance` instance field of the superclass. Our remedy was to use the appropriate method of the superclass to set the balance.

Java offers another solution to this problem. The superclass can declare an instance field as *protected*:

```
    public class BankAccount
    {
        . . .
        protected double balance;
    }
```

> Protected features can be accessed by all subclasses and all classes in the same package.

Protected data in an object can be accessed by the methods of the object's class and all its subclasses. For example, `CheckingAccount` inherits from `BankAccount`, so its methods can access the protected instance fields of the `BankAccount` class. Furthermore, protected data can be accessed by all methods of classes in the same package.

Some programmers like the `protected` access feature because it seems to strike a balance between absolute protection (making all fields private) and no protection at all (making all fields public). However, experience has shown that protected fields are subject to the same kinds of problems as public fields. The designer of the superclass has no control over the authors of subclasses. Any of the subclass methods can corrupt the superclass data. Furthermore, classes with protected fields are hard to modify. Even if the author of the superclass would like to change the data implementation, the protected fields cannot be changed, because someone somewhere out there might have written a subclass whose code depends on them.

In Java, protected fields have another drawback—they are accessible not just by sub-classes, but also by other classes in the same package.

It is best to leave all data private. If you want to grant access to the data to subclass meth-ods only, consider making the *accessor* method protected.

13.8 Object: The Cosmic Superclass

In Java, every class that is defined without an explicit extends clause automatically extends the class Object. That is, the class Object is the direct or indirect superclass of *every* class in Java (see Figure 8).

Of course, the methods of the Object class are very general. Here are the most useful ones:

Method	Purpose
String toString()	Returns a string representation of the object
boolean equals(Object otherObject)	Tests whether the object equals another object
Object clone()	Makes a full copy of an object

It is a good idea for you to override these methods in your classes.

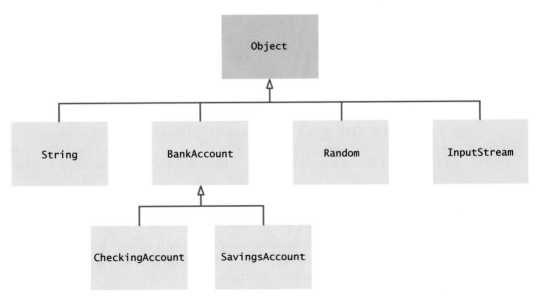

Figure 8 The Object Class Is the Superclass of Every Java Class

13.8.1 Overriding the toString Method

Define the toString
method to yield a string
that describes the object
state.

The toString method returns a string representation for each object.
It is used for debugging. For example,

```
Rectangle box = new Rectangle(5, 10, 20, 30);
String s = box.toString();
    // Sets s to "java.awt.Rectangle[x=5,y=10,width=20,height=30]"
```

In fact, this toString method is called whenever you concatenate a string with an
object. Consider the concatenation

```
"box=" + box;
```

On one side of the + concatenation operator is a string, but on the other side is an
object reference. The Java compiler automatically invokes the toString method to
turn the object into a string. Then both strings are concatenated. In this case, the
result is the string

```
"box=java.awt.Rectangle[x=5,y=10,width=20,height=30]"
```

The compiler can invoke the toString method, because it knows that *every* object
has a toString method: Every class extends the Object class, and that class defines
toString.

As you know, numbers are also converted to strings when they are concatenated
with other strings. For example,

```
int age = 18;
String s = "Harry's age is " + age;
    // Sets s to "Harry's age is 18"
```

In this case, the toString method is not involved. Numbers are not objects, and
there is no toString method for them. There is only a small set of primitive types,
however, and the compiler knows how to convert them to strings.

Let's try the toString method for the BankAccount class:

```
BankAccount momsSavings = new BankAccount(5000);
String s = momsSavings.toString();
    // Sets s to something like "BankAccount@d24606bf"
```

That's disappointing—all that's printed is the name of the class, followed by the
hash code, a seemingly random code. The hash code can be used to tell objects
apart—different objects are likely to have different hash codes. (See Chapter 21 for
the details.)

We don't care about the hash code. We want to know what is inside the object.
But, of course, the toString method of the Object class does not know what is
inside the BankAccount class. Therefore, we have to override the method and supply
our own version in the BankAccount class. We'll follow the same format that the
toString method of the Rectangle class uses: first print the name of the class, and
then the values of the instance fields inside brackets.

```
public class BankAccount
{
```

```
    . . .
    public String toString()
    {
        return "BankAccount[balance=" + balance + "]";
    }
}
```

This works better:

```
BankAccount momsSavings = new BankAccount(5000);
String s = momsSavings.toString();
    // Sets s to "BankAccount[balance=5000]"
```

PRODUCTIVITY HINT 13.1

Supply toString in All Classes

If you have a class whose toString() method returns a string that describes the object state, then you can simply call System.out.println(x) whenever you need to inspect the current state of an object x. This works because the println method of the PrintStream class invokes x.toString() when it needs to print an object, which is extremely helpful if there is an error in your program and the objects don't behave the way you think they should. You can simply insert a few print statements and peek inside the object state during the program run. Some debuggers can even invoke the toString method on objects that you inspect.

Sure, it is a bit more trouble to write a toString method when you aren't sure your program ever needs one—after all, it might work correctly on the first try. Then again, many programs don't work on the first try. As soon as you find out that yours doesn't, consider adding those toString methods to help you debug the program.

ADVANCED TOPIC 13.4

Inheritance and the toString Method

You just saw how to write a toString method: Form a string consisting of the class name and the names and values of the instance fields. However, if you want your toString method to be usable by subclasses of your class, you need to work a bit harder. Instead of hardcoding the class name, you should call the getClass method to obtain a *class* object, an object of the Class class that describes classes and their properties. Then invoke the getName method to get the name of the class:

```
public String toString()
{
    return getClass().getName() + "[balance="
        + balance + "]";
}
```

Then the toString method prints the correct class name when you apply it to a subclass, say a SavingsAccount.

```
SavingsAccount momsSavings = . . . ;
System.out.println(momsSavings);
// Prints "SavingsAccount[balance=10000]"
```

Of course, in the subclass, you should override toString and add the values of the subclass instance fields. Note that you must call super.toString to get the superclass field values—the subclass can't access them directly.

```
public class SavingsAccount extends BankAccount
{
    public String toString()
    {
        return super.toString() +
            "[interestRate=" + interestRate + "]";
    }
}
```

Now a savings account is converted to a string such as SavingsAccount[balance=10000][interestRate=10]. The brackets show which fields belong to the superclass.

13.8.2 Overriding the equals Method

Define the equals method to test whether two objects have equal state.

The equals method is called whenever you want to compare whether two objects have the same contents:

```
if (coin1.equals(coin2)) . . .
    // Contents are the same—see Figure 9
```

This is different from the test with the == operator, which tests whether the two references are to the *same object*:

```
if (coin1 == coin2) . . .
    // Objects are the same—see Figure 10
```

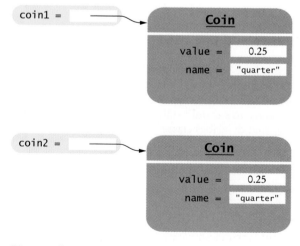

Figure 9 Two References to Equal Objects

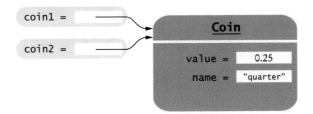

Figure 10   Two References to the Same Object

Let us implement the `equals` method for the `Coin` class. You need to override the `equals` method of the `Object` class:

```
public class Coin
{
    . . .
    public boolean equals(Object otherObject)
    {
        . . .
    }
    . . .
}
```

Now you have a slight problem. The `Object` class knows nothing about coins, so it defines the `otherObject` parameter of the `equals` method to have the type `Object`. When redefining the method, you are not allowed to change the object signature. Cast the parameter to the class `Coin`:

```
Coin other = (Coin) otherObject;
```

Then you can compare the two coins.

```
public boolean equals(Object otherObject)
{
    Coin other = (Coin) otherObject;
    return name.equals(other.name)
        && value == other.value;
}
```

Note that you must use `equals` to compare object fields, but use `==` to compare number fields.

When you override the `equals` method, you should also override the `hashCode` method so that equal objects have the same hash code—see Chapter 21 for details.

SELF CHECK

16. Should the call `x.equals(x)` always return `true`?

17. Can you implement `equals` in terms of `toString`? Should you?

COMMON ERROR 13.6

Defining the equals Method with the Wrong Parameter Type

Consider the following, seemingly simpler, version of the equals method for the Coin class:

```
public boolean equals(Coin other) // Don't do this!
{
    return name.equals(other.name) && value == other.value;
}
```

Here, the parameter of the equals method has the type Coin, not Object.

Unfortunately, this method *does not override* the equals method in the Object class. Instead, the Coin class now has two different equals methods:

```
boolean equals(Coin other) // Defined in the Coin class
boolean equals(Object otherObject) // Inherited from the Object class
```

This is error-prone because the wrong equals method can be called. For example, consider these variable definitions:

```
Coin aCoin = new Coin(0.25, "quarter");
Object anObject = new Coin(0.25, "quarter");
```

The call aCoin.equals(anObject) calls the second equals method, which returns false.

The remedy is to ensure that you use the Object type for the explicit parameter of the equals method.

ADVANCED TOPIC 13.5

Inheritance and the equals Method

You just saw how to write an equals method: Cast the otherObject parameter to the type of your class, and then compare the fields of the implicit parameter and the other parameter.

But what if someone called coin1.equals(x) where x wasn't a Coin object? Then the bad cast would generate an exception, and the program would die. Therefore, you first want to test whether otherObject really is an instance of the Coin class. The easiest test would be with the instanceof operator. However, that test is not specific enough. It would be possible for otherObject to belong to some subclass of Coin. To rule out that possibility, you should test whether the two objects belong to the *same class*. If not, return false.

```
if (getClass() != otherObject.getClass()) return false;
```

Moreover, the Java language specification [1] demands that the equals method return false when otherObject is null.

Here is an improved version of the equals method that takes these two points into account:

```
public boolean equals(Object otherObject)
{
    if (otherObject == null) return false;
    if (getClass() != otherObject.getClass())
        return false;

    Coin other = (Coin) otherObject;
    return name.equals(other.name) && value == other.value;
```

```
   }
```
When you define equals in a subclass, you should first call equals in the superclass, like this:
```
public CollectibleCoin extends Coin
{
   . . .
   public boolean equals(Object otherObject)
   {
      if (!super.equals(otherObject)) return false;

      CollectibleCoin other = (CollectibleCoin) otherObject;
      return year == other.year;
   }
   private int year;
}
```

13.8.3 The clone Method

You know that copying an object reference simply gives you two references to the same object:
```
BankAccount account = new BankAccount(1000);
BankAccount account2 = account;
account2.deposit(500);
   // Now both account and account2 refer to a bank account with a balance of 1500
```

> The clone method makes a new object with the same state as an existing object.

What can you do if you actually want to make a copy of an object? That is the purpose of the clone method. The clone method must return a *new* object that has an identical state to the existing object (see Figure 11).

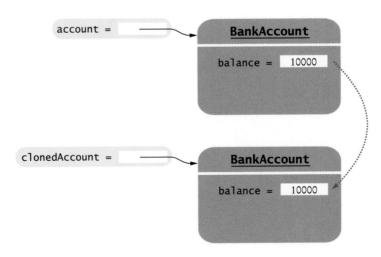

Figure 11
Cloning Objects

Implementing the clone method is quite a bit more difficult than implementing the toString or equals methods—see Advanced Topic 13.6 for details.

Let us suppose that someone has implemented the clone method for the Bank-Account class. Here is how to call it:

```
BankAccount clonedAccount = (BankAccount) account.clone();
```

The return type of the clone method is the class Object. When you call the method, you must use a cast to convince the compiler that account.clone() really has the same type as clonedAccount.

COMMON ERROR 13.7

Forgetting to Clone

In Java, object fields contain references to objects, not actual objects. This can be convenient for giving *two names to the same object:*

```
BankAccount harrysChecking = new BankAccount();
BankAccount slushFund = harrysChecking;
    // Use Harry's checking account for the slush fund
slushFund.deposit(80000)
    // A lot of money ends up in Harry's checking account
```

However, if you don't intend two references to refer to the same object, then this is a problem. In that case, you should use the clone method:

```
BankAccount slushFund = (BankAccount) harrysChecking.clone();
```

QUALITY TIP 13.1

Clone Mutable Instance Fields in Accessor Methods

Consider the following class:

```
public class Customer
{
    public Customer(String aName)
    {
        name = aName;
        account = new BankAccount();
    }

    public String getName()
    {
        return name;
    }

    public BankAccount getAccount();
    {
        return account;
```

```
        }

        private String name;
        private BankAccount account;
    }
```

This class looks very boring and normal, but the getAccount method has a curious property. It *breaks encapsulation,* because anyone can modify the object state without going through the public interface:

```
    Customer harry = new Customer("Harry Handsome");
    BankAccount account = harry.getAccount();
        // Anyone can withdraw money!
    account.withdraw(100000);
```

Maybe that wasn't what the designers of the class had in mind? Maybe they wanted class users only to inspect the account? In such a situation, you should *clone* the object reference:

```
    public BankAccount getAccount();
    {
        return (BankAccount) account.clone();
    }
```

Do you also need to clone the getName method? No—that method returns a string, and strings are immutable. It is safe to give out a reference to an immutable object.

ADVANCED TOPIC 13.6

Implementing the clone Method

The Object.clone method is the starting point for the clone methods in your own classes. It creates a new object of the same type as the original object. It also automatically copies the instance fields from the original object to the cloned object. Here is a first attempt to implement the clone method for the BankAccount class:

```
    public class BankAccount
    {
        . . .
        public Object clone()
        {
            // Not complete
            Object clonedAccount = super.clone();
            return clonedAccount;
        }
    }
```

However, this Object.clone method must be used with care. It only shifts the problem of cloning by one level; it does not completely solve it. Specifically, if an object contains a reference to another object, then the Object.clone method makes a copy of that object reference, not a clone of that object. Figure 12 shows how the Object.clone method works with a Customer object that has references to a String object and a BankAccount object. As you can see, the Object.clone method copies the references to the cloned Customer object and does not clone the objects to which they refer. Such a copy is called a *shallow copy.*

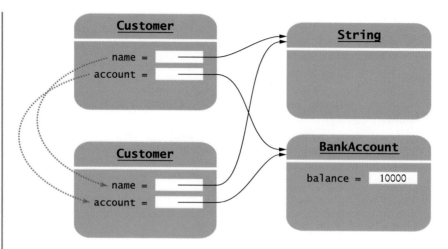

Figure 12   The `Object.clone` Method Makes a Shallow Copy

There is a reason why the `Object.clone` method does not systematically clone all sub-objects. In some situations, it is unnecessary. For example, if an object contains a reference to a string, there is no harm in copying the string reference, because Java string objects can never change their contents. The `Object.clone` method does the right thing if an object contains only numbers, Boolean values, and strings. But it must be used with caution when an object contains references to other objects.

For that reason, there are two safeguards built into the `Object.clone` method to ensure that it is not used accidentally. First, the method is declared `protected` (see Advanced Topic 13.3). This prevents you from accidentally calling `x.clone()` if the class to which `x` belongs hasn't redefined `clone` to be public.

As a second precaution, `Object.clone` checks that the object being cloned implements the `Cloneable` interface. If not, it throws an exception. The `Object.clone` method looks like this:

```java
public class Object
{
   protected Object clone()
       throws CloneNotSupportedException
   {
      if (this instanceof Cloneable)
      {
         // Copy the instance fields
         . . .
      }
      else
         throw new CloneNotSupportedException();
   }
}
```

Unfortunately, all that safeguarding means that the legitimate callers of `Object.clone()` pay a price—they must catch that exception *even if their class implements* `Cloneable`.

```java
public class BankAccount implements Cloneable
{
```

```
      . . .
   public Object clone()
   {
      try
      {
         return super.clone();
      }
      catch (CloneNotSupportedException e)
      {
         // Can't happen because we implement Cloneable but we still must catch it.
         return null;
      }
   }
}
```

If an object contains a reference to another mutable object, then you must call clone for that reference. For example, suppose the Customer class has an instance field of class Bank-Account. You can implement Customer.clone as follows:

```
public class Customer implements Cloneable
{
   . . .
   public Object clone()
   {
      try
      {
         Customer cloned = (Customer) super.clone();
         cloned.account = (BankAccount) account.clone();
         return cloned;
      }
      catch(CloneNotSupportedException e)
      {
         // Can't happen because we implement Cloneable
         return null;
      }
   }

   private String name;
   private BankAccount account;
}
```

ADVANCED TOPIC 13.7

Enumerated Types Revisited

In Advanced Topic 6.3, we introduced the concept of an enumerated type: a type with a finite number of values. An example is

```
public enum FilingStatus { SINGLE, MARRIED }
```

In Java, enumerated types are classes with special properties. They have a finite number of instances, namely the objects defined inside the braces. For example, there are exactly two objects of the FilingStatus class: FilingStatus.SINGLE and FilingStatus.MARRIED. Since FilingStatus has no public constructor, it is impossible to construct additional objects.

Enumeration classes extend the Enum class, from which they inherit toString and clone methods. The toString method returns a string that equals the object's name. For example, FilingStatus.SINGLE.toString() returns "SINGLE". The clone method returns the given object *without making a copy*. After all, it should not be possible to generate new objects of an enumeration class.

The Enum class inherits the equals method from its superclass, Object. Thus, two enumeration constants are only considered equal when they are identical.

You can add your own methods and constructors to an enumeration class, for example

```
public enum CoinType
{
    PENNY(0.01), NICKEL(0.05), DIME(0.1), QUARTER(0.25);
    CoinType(double aValue) { value = aValue; }
    public double getValue() { return value; }
    private double value;
}
```

This CoinType class has exactly four instances: CoinType.PENNY, CoinType.NICKEL, CoinType.DIME, and CoinType.QUARTER. If you have one of these four CoinType objects, you can apply the getValue method to obtain the coin's value.

Note that there is a major philosophical difference between this CoinType class and the Coin class that we have discussed elsewhere in this chapter. A Coin object represents a particular coin. You can construct as many Coin objects as you like. Different Coin objects can be equal to another. We consider two Coin objects equal when their names and values match. However, CoinType describes a type of coins, not an individual coin. The four CoinType objects are distinct from each other.

RANDOM FACT 13.1

Scripting Languages

Suppose you work for an office where you must help with the bookkeeping. Suppose that every sales person sends in a weekly spreadsheet with sales figures. One of your jobs is to copy and paste the individual figures into a master spreadsheet and then copy and paste the totals into a word processor document that gets e-mailed to several managers. This kind of repetitive work can be intensely boring. Can you automate it?

It would be a real challenge to write a Java program that can help you—you'd have to know how to read a spreadsheet file, how to format a word processor document, and how to send e-mail.

Fortunately, many office software packages include *scripting languages*. These are programming languages that are integrated with the software for the purpose of automating repetitive tasks. The best-known of these scripting languages is Visual Basic Script, which is a part of the Microsoft Office suite. The Macintosh operating system has a language called AppleScript for the same purpose.

In addition, scripting languages are available for many other purposes. JavaScript is used for web pages. (There is no relationship between Java and JavaScript—the name JavaScript was chosen for marketing reasons.) Tcl (short for "tool control language" and pronounced

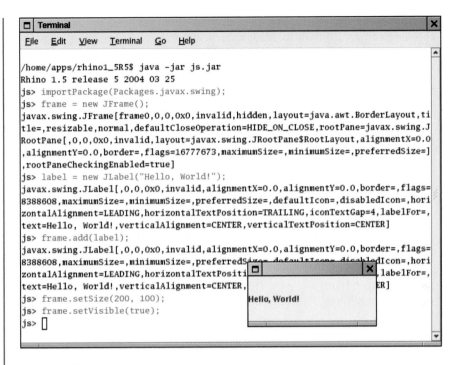

Figure 13 Writing a Rhino Script

"tickle") is an open source scripting language that has been ported to many platforms and is often used for scripting software test procedures. Shell scripts are used for automating software configuration, backup procedures, and other system administration tasks.

Scripting languages have two features that makes them easier to use than full-fledged programming languages such as Java. First, they are *interpreted*. The interpreter program reads each line of program code and executes it immediately without compiling it first. That makes experimenting much more fun—you get immediate feedback. Also, scripting languages are usually *loosely typed*, meaning you don't have to declare the types of variables. Every variable can hold values of any type. For example, Figure 13 shows a scripting session with Rhino, a JavaScript implementation that allows you to manipulate Java objects. The script stores frame and label objects in variables that are declared without types. It then calls methods that are executed immediately, without compilation. The frame pops up as soon as the line with the setVisible command is entered. (You can download Rhino from the Mozilla web site [2]). In recent years, authors of computer viruses have discovered how scripting languages simplify their lives. The famous "love bug" is a Visual Basic Script program that is sent as an attachment to an e-mail. The e-mail has an enticing subject line "I love you" and asks the recipient to click on an attachment masquerading as a love letter. In fact, the attachment is a script file that is executed when the user clicks on it. The script creates some damage on the recipient's computer and then, through the power of the scripting language, uses the Outlook e-mail client to mail itself to all addresses found in the address book. Try programming that in Java! By the way, the person suspected of authoring that virus was a student who had submitted a proposal to write a thesis researching how to write such programs. Perhaps not surprisingly, the proposal was rejected by the faculty.

Why do we still need Java if scripting is easy and fun? Scripts often have poor error checking and are difficult to adapt to new circumstances. Scripting languages lack many of the structuring and safety mechanisms (such as classes and type checking by the compiler) that are important for building robust and scalable programs.

CHAPTER SUMMARY

1. Inheritance is a mechanism for extending existing classes by adding methods and fields.

2. The more general class is called a superclass. The more specialized class that inherits from the superclass is called the subclass.

3. Every class extends the `Object` class either directly or indirectly.

4. Inheriting from a class differs from implementing an interface: The subclass inherits behavior and state from the superclass.

5. One advantage of inheritance is code reuse.

6. When defining a subclass, you specify added instance fields, added methods, and changed or overridden methods.

7. Sets of classes can form complex inheritance hierarchies.

8. A subclass has no access to private fields of its superclass.

9. Use the `super` keyword to call a method of the superclass.

10. To call the superclass constructor, you use the `super` keyword in the first statement of the subclass constructor.

11. Subclass references can be converted to superclass references.

12. The `instanceof` operator tests whether an object belongs to a particular type.

13. An abstract method is a method whose implementation is not specified.

14. An abstract class is a class that cannot be instantiated.

15. A field or method that is not declared as `public`, `private`, or `protected` can be accessed by all classes in the same package, which is usually not desirable.

16. Protected features can be accessed by all subclasses and all classes in the same package.

17. Define the `toString` method to yield a string that describes the object state.

18. Define the `equals` method to test whether two objects have equal state.

19. The `clone` method makes a new object with the same state as an existing object.

FURTHER READING

1. James Gosling, Bill Joy, and Guy Steele, *The Java Language Specification*, 3rd edition, Addison-Wesley, 2005.

2. http://www.mozilla.org/rhino   The Rhino interpreter for the JavaScript language.

CLASSES, OBJECTS, AND METHODS INTRODUCED IN THIS CHAPTER

```
java.lang.Cloneable
java.lang.CloneNotSupportedException
java.lang.Object
    clone
    toString
```


REVIEW EXERCISES

Exercise R13.1. What is the balance of b after the following operations?

```
SavingsAccount b = new SavingsAccount(10);
b.deposit(5000);
b.withdraw(b.getBalance() / 2);
b.addInterest();
```

Exercise R13.2. Describe all constructors of the SavingsAccount class. List all methods that are inherited from the BankAccount class. List all methods that are added to the SavingsAccount class.

Exercise R13.3. Can you convert a superclass reference into a subclass reference? A subclass reference into a superclass reference? If so, give examples. If not, explain why not.

Exercise R13.4. Identify the superclass and the subclass in each of the following pairs of classes.

- **a.** Employee, Manager
- **b.** Polygon, Triangle
- **c.** GraduateStudent, Student
- **d.** Person, Student
- **e.** Employee, GraduateStudent
- **f.** BankAccount, CheckingAccount
- **g.** Vehicle, Car
- **h.** Vehicle, Minivan
- **i.** Car, Minivan
- **j.** Truck, Vehicle

Exercise R13.5. Suppose the class Sub extends the class Sandwich. Which of the following assignments are legal?

```
Sandwich x = new Sandwich();
Sub y = new Sub();
```

a. x = y;   **c.** y = new Sandwich();

b. y = x;   **d.** x = new Sub();

Exercise R13.6. Draw an inheritance diagram that shows the inheritance relationships between the classes:

- Person
- Employee
- Student
- Instructor
- Classroom
- Object

Exercise R13.7. In an object-oriented traffic simulation system, we have the following classes:

- Vehicle
- Car
- Truck
- Sedan
- Coupe
- PickupTruck
- SportUtilityVehicle
- Minivan
- Bicycle
- Motorcycle

Draw an inheritance diagram that shows the relationships between these classes.

Exercise R13.8. What inheritance relationships would you establish among the following classes?

- Student
- Professor
- TeachingAssistant
- Employee
- Secretary
- DepartmentChair
- Janitor
- SeminarSpeaker
- Person
- Course
- Seminar
- Lecture
- ComputerLab

Exercise R13.9. Which of these conditions returns true? Check the Java documentation for the inheritance patterns.

a. Rectangle r = new Rectangle(5, 10, 20, 30);

b. if (r instanceof Rectangle) . . .

c. if (r instanceof Point) . . .

d. if (r instanceof Rectangle2D.Double) . . .

e. if (r instanceof RectangularShape) . . .

f. if (r instanceof Object) . . .

g. if (r instanceof Shape) . . .

Exercise R13.10. Explain the two meanings of the super keyword. Explain the two meanings of the this keyword. How are they related?

Exercise R13.11. (Tricky.) Consider the two calls

```java
public class D extends B
{
   public void f()
   {
      this.g(); // 1
   }
   public void g()
   {
      super.g(); // 2
   }
   . . .
}
```

Which of them is an example of polymorphism?

Exercise R13.12. Consider this program:

```java
public class AccountTest
{
   public static void main(String[] args)
   {
      SavingsAccount momsSavings
            = new SavingsAccount(0.5);

      CheckingAccount harrysChecking
            = new CheckingAccount(0);

      . . .
      endOfMonth(momsSavings);
      endOfMonth(harrysChecking);
      printBalance(momsSavings);
      printBalance(harrysChecking);
   }

   public static void endOfMonth(SavingsAccount savings)
   {
      savings.addInterest();
   }

   public static void endOfMonth(CheckingAccount checking)
   {
      checking.deductFees();
   }

   public static void printBalance(BankAccount account)
   {
      System.out.println("The balance is $"
            + account.getBalance());
   }
}
```

Are the calls to the endOfMonth methods resolved by early binding or late binding? Inside the printBalance method, is the call to getBalance resolved by early binding or late binding?

Exercise R13.13. Explain the terms *shallow copy* and *deep copy*.

Exercise R13.14. What access attribute should instance fields have? What access attribute should static fields have? How about static final fields?

Exercise R13.15. What access attribute should instance methods have? Does the same hold for static methods?

Exercise R13.16. The fields System.in and System.out are static public fields. Is it possible to overwrite them? If so, how?

Exercise R13.17. Why are public fields dangerous? Are public static fields more dangerous than public instance fields?

PROGRAMMING EXERCISES

Exercise P13.1. Enhance the addInterest method of the SavingsAccount class to compute the interest on the *minimum* balance since the last call to addInterest. *Hint:* You need to modify the withdraw method as well, and you need to add an instance field to remember the minimum balance.

Exercise P13.2. Add a TimeDepositAccount class to the bank account hierarchy. The time deposit account is just like a savings account, but you promise to leave the money in the account for a particular number of months, and there is a penalty for early withdrawal. Construct the account with the interest rate and the number of months to maturity. In the addInterest method, decrement the count of months. If the count is positive during a withdrawal, charge the withdrawal penalty.

Exercise P13.3. Implement a subclass Square that extends the Rectangle class. In the constructor, accept the *x*- and *y*-positions of the *center* and the side length of the square. Call the setLocation and setSize methods of the Rectangle class. Look up these methods in the documentation for the Rectangle class. Also supply a method getArea that computes and returns the area of the square. Write a sample program that asks for the center and side length, then prints out the square (using the toString method that you inherit from Rectangle) and the area of the square.

Exercise P13.4. Implement a superclass Person. Make two classes, Student and Instructor, that inherit from Person. A person has a name and a year of birth. A student has a major, and an instructor has a salary. Write the class definitions, the constructors, and the methods toString for all classes. Supply a test program that tests these classes and methods.

Exercise P13.5. Make a class Employee with a name and salary. Make a class Manager inherit from Employee. Add an instance field, named department, of type String. Supply a method toString that prints the manager's name, department, and salary.

Make a class Executive inherit from Manager. Supply appropriate toString methods for all classes. Supply a test program that tests these classes and methods.

Exercise P13.6. Write a superclass Worker and subclasses HourlyWorker and Salaried-Worker. Every worker has a name and a salary rate. Write a method computePay(int hours) that computes the weekly pay for every worker. An hourly worker gets paid the hourly wage for the actual number of hours worked, if hours is at most 40. If the hourly worker worked more than 40 hours, the excess is paid at time and a half. The salaried worker gets paid the hourly wage for 40 hours, no matter what the actual number of hours is. Supply a test program that uses polymorphism to test these classes and methods.

Exercise P13.7. Implement a superclass Vehicle and subclasses Car and Truck. A vehicle has a position on the screen. Write methods draw that draw cars and trucks as follows:

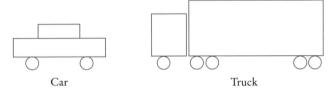

Car   Truck

Then write a method randomVehicle that randomly generates Vehicle references, with an equal probability for constructing cars and trucks, with random positions. Call it 10 times and draw all of them.

Exercise P13.8. Reorganize the bank account classes as follows. In the BankAccount class, introduce an abstract method endOfMonth with no implementation. Rename the addInterest and deductFees methods into endOfMonth in the subclasses. Which classes are now abstract and which are concrete? Write a static method void test(BankAccount account) that makes five random transactions, prints out the balance after each of them, and then calls endOfMonth and prints the balance once again. Test it with instances of all concrete account classes.

PROGRAMMING PROJECTS

Project 13.1. Your task is to program robots with varying behaviors. The robots try to escape a maze, such as the following:

```
*  *******
*     *   *
*  ***** *
*  *  *   *
*  *  *** *
*     *   *
*** *  * *
*     *  *
******* *
```

A robot has a position and a method void move(Maze m) that modifies the position. Provide a common superclass Robot whose move method does nothing. Provide subclasses RandomRobot, RightHandRuleRobot, and MemoryRobot. Each of these robots has a different strategy for escaping. The RandomRobot simply makes random moves. The RightHandRuleRobot moves around the maze so that it's right hand always touches a wall. The MemoryRobot remembers all positions that it has previously occupied and never goes back to a position that it knows to be a dead end.

Project 13.2. Implement the toString, equals, and clone methods for all subclasses of the BankAccount class, as well as the Bank class of Chapter 8. Write unit tests that verify that your methods work correctly. Be sure to test a Bank that holds objects from a mixture of account classes.

ANSWERS TO SELF-CHECK QUESTIONS

1. Two instance fields: balance and interestRate.
2. deposit, withdraw, getBalance, and addInterest.
3. Manager is the subclass; Employee is the superclass.
4. To express the common behavior of text fields and text components.
5. We need a counter that counts the number of withdrawals and deposits.
6. It needs to reduce the balance, and it cannot access the balance field directly.
7. So that the count can reflect the number of transactions for the following month.
8. It was content to use the default constructor of the superclass, which sets the balance to zero.
9. No—this is a requirement only for constructors. For example, the Checking-Account.deposit method first increments the transaction count, then calls the superclass method.
10. We want to use the method for all kinds of bank accounts. Had we used a parameter of type SavingsAccount, we couldn't have called the method with a CheckingAccount object.
11. We cannot invoke the deposit method on a variable of type Object.
12. The object is an instance of BankAccount or one of its sublcasses.
13. The balance of a is unchanged, and the transaction count is incremented twice.
14. Accidentally forgetting the private modifer.
15. Any methods of classes in the same package.
16. It certainly should—unless, of course, x is null.
17. If toString returns a string that describes all instance fields, you can simply call toString on the implicit and explicit parameters, and compare the results. However, comparing the fields is more efficient than converting them into strings.

Graphical User Interfaces

CHAPTER GOALS

- To use inheritance to customize frames

- To understand how user-interface components are added to a container

- To understand the use of layout managers to arrange user-interface components in a container

- To become familiar with common user-interface components, such as buttons, combo boxes, text areas, and menus

- To build programs that handle events from user-interface components

- To learn how to browse the Java documentation

Up to now, your graphical programs received user input from an option dialog box or a mouse. The graphical applications with which you are familiar, however, have many visual gadgets for information entry: buttons, scroll bars, menus, etc. In this chapter, you will learn how to use the most common user-interface components in the Java Swing user-interface toolkit. Swing has many more components than can be mastered in a first course, and even the basic components have advanced options that can't be covered here. In fact, few programmers try to learn everything about a particular user-interface component. It is more important to understand the concepts and to search the Java documentation for the details. This chapter walks you through one example to show you how the Java documentation is organized and how you can rely on it for your programming.

CHAPTER CONTENTS

14.1 Using Inheritance to Customize Frames

Define a JFrame subclass for a complex frame.

As you add more user interface components to a frame, the frame can get quite complex. Your programs will become easier to understand when you use inheritance for complex frames.

Design a subclass of JFrame. Store the components as instance fields. Initialize them in the constructor of your subclass. If the initialization code gets complex, simply add some helper methods.

Here, we carry out this process for the investment viewer program in Chapter 12.

```java
public class InvestmentFrame extends JFrame
{
    public InvestmentFrame()
    {
        account = new BankAccount(INITIAL_BALANCE);

        // Use instance fields for components
        resultLabel = new JLabel("balance=" + account.getBalance());

        // Use helper methods
        createRateField();
        createButton();
        createPanel();

        setSize(FRAME_WIDTH, FRAME_HEIGHT);
    }

    private void createRateField()
    {
```

```
        rateLabel = new JLabel("Interest Rate: ");
        final int FIELD_WIDTH = 10;
        rateField = new JTextField(FIELD_WIDTH);
        rateField.setText("" + DEFAULT_RATE);
    }

    // More helper methods
    . . .
    private JLabel rateLabel;
    private JTextField rateField;
    private JButton button;
    private JLabel resultLabel;
    private BankAccount account;
}
```

This approach differs from the programs in Chapter 12. In those programs, we simply configured the frame in the main method of a viewer class.

It is a bit more work to provide a separate class for the frame. However, the frame class makes it easier to organize the code that constructs the user-interface elements. We will use this approach for all examples in this chapter.

Of course, we still need a class with a main method:

```
public class InvestmentFrameViewer
{
    public static void main(String[] args)
    {
        JFrame frame = new InvestmentFrame();
        frame.setDefaultCloseOperation(JFrame.EXIT_ON_CLOSE);
        frame.setVisible(true);
    }
}
```

SELF CHECK

1. How many Java source files are required by the investment viewer application when we use inheritance to define the frame class?
2. Why does the InvestmentFrame constructor call setSize(FRAME_WIDTH, FRAME_HEIGHT), whereas the main method of the investment viewer class in Chapter 12 called frame.setSize(FRAME_WIDTH, FRAME_HEIGHT)?

ADVANCED TOPIC 14.1

Adding the main Method to the Frame Class

Have another look at the InvestmentFrame and InvestmentFrameViewer classes. Some programmers prefer to combine these two classes, by adding the main method to the frame class:

```
public class InvestmentFrame extends JFrame
{
    public static void main(String[] args)
    {
```

```
        JFrame frame = new InvestmentFrame();
        frame.setDefaultCloseOperation(JFrame.EXIT_ON_CLOSE);
        frame.setVisible(true);
    }

    public InvestmentFrame()
    {
        account = new BankAccount(INITIAL_BALANCE);

        // Use instance fields for components
        resultLabel = new JLabel("balance=" + account.getBalance());

        // Use helper methods
        createRateField();
        createButton();
        createPanel();

        setSize(FRAME_WIDTH, FRAME_HEIGHT);
    }
    . . .
}
```

This is a convenient shortcut that you will find in many programs, but it does muddle the responsibilities between the frame class and the program. Therefore, we do not use this approach in this book.

14.2 Layout Management

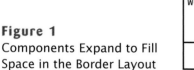

User-interface components are arranged by placing them inside containers.

Each container has a layout manager that directs the arrangement of its components.

Up to now, we have had limited control over the layout of user-interface components. In Chapter 12, we added buttons to a panel. The panel arranged the components from the left to the right. However, in many applications, you need more sophisticated arrangements.

In Java, you build up user interfaces by adding components into containers such as panels. Each container has its own *layout manager,* which determines how the components are laid out.

By default, a JPanel uses a *flow layout*. A flow layout simply arranges its components from left to right and starts a new row when there is no more room in the current row.

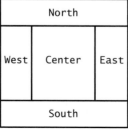

Figure 1

Components Expand to Fill Space in the Border Layout

Three useful layout managers are the border layout, flow layout, and grid layout.

Another commonly used layout manager is the *border layout*. The border layout groups the container into five areas: center, north, west, south, and east (see Figure 1). Not all of the areas need to be occupied.

The border layout is the default layout manager for a frame (or, more technically, the frame's content pane). But you can also use the border layout in a panel:

```
panel.setLayout(new BorderLayout());
```

When adding a component to a container with the border layout, specify the NORTH, EAST, SOUTH, WEST, or CENTER position.

Now the panel is controlled by a border layout, not the flow layout. When adding a component, you specify the position, like this:

```
panel.add(component, BorderLayout.NORTH);
```

The *grid layout* is a third layout that is sometimes useful. The grid layout arranges components in a grid with a fixed number of rows and columns, resizing each of the components so that they all have the same size. Like the border layout, it also expands each component to fill the entire allotted area. (If that is not desirable, you need to place each component inside a panel.) Figure 2 shows a number pad

The content pane of a frame has a border layout by default. A panel has a flow layout by default.

panel that uses a grid layout. To create a grid layout, you supply the number of rows and columns in the constructor, then add the components, row by row, left to right:

```
JPanel numberPanel = new JPanel();
numberPanel.setLayout(new GridLayout(4, 3));
numberPanel.add(button7);
numberPanel.add(button8);
numberPanel.add(button9);
numberPanel.add(button4);
  . . .
```

Sometimes you want to have a tabular arrangement of the components where columns have different sizes or one component spans multiple columns. A more complex layout manager called the *grid bag layout* can handle these situations. The grid bag layout is quite complex to use, however, and we do not cover it in this book; see, for example, [1] for more information.

Fortunately, you can create acceptable-looking layouts in nearly all situations by nesting panels. You give each panel an appropriate layout manager. Panels don't have visible borders, so you can use as many panels as you need to organize your components.

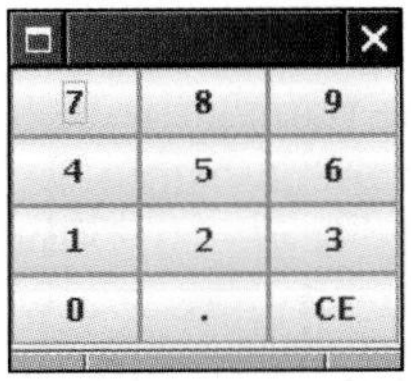

Figure 2
The Grid Layout

3. How do you add two buttons to the north area of a frame?

4. How can you stack three buttons on top of each other?

14.3 Choices

14.3.1 Radio Buttons

> For a small set of mutually exclusive choices, use a group of radio buttons or a combo box.

In this section you will see how to present a finite set of choices to the user. If the choices are mutually exclusive, use a set of *radio buttons*. In a radio button set, only one button can be selected at a time. When the user selects another button in the same set, the previously selected button is automatically turned off. (These buttons are called radio buttons because they work like the station selector buttons on a car radio: If you select a new station, the old station is automatically deselected.) For example, in Figure 3, the font sizes are mutually exclusive. You can select small, medium, or large, but not a combination of them.

> Add radio buttons into a ButtonGroup so that only one button in the group is on at any time.

To create a set of radio buttons, first create each button individually, and then add all buttons of the set to a ButtonGroup object:

```
JRadioButton smallButton = new JRadioButton("Small");
JRadioButton mediumButton = new JRadioButton("Medium");
JRadioButton largeButton = new JRadioButton("Large");

ButtonGroup group = new ButtonGroup();
group.add(smallButton);
group.add(mediumButton);
group.add(largeButton);
```

Note that the button group does *not* place the buttons close to each other on the container. The purpose of the button group is simply to find out which buttons to turn off when one of them is turned on. It is still your job to arrange the buttons on the screen.

The isSelected method is called to find out whether a button is currently selected or not. For example,

```
if (largeButton.isSelected()) size = LARGE_SIZE;
```

Call setSelected(true) on one of the radio buttons in a radio button group before making the enclosing frame visible.

> You can place a border around a panel to group its contents visually.

If you have multiple button groups, it is a good idea to group them together visually. You probably use panels to build up your user interface, but the panels themselves are invisible. You can add a *border* to a panel to make it visible. In Figure 3, for example; the panels containing the Size radio buttons and Style check boxes have borders.

There are a large number of border types. We will show only a couple of variations and leave it to the border enthusiasts to look up the others in the Swing

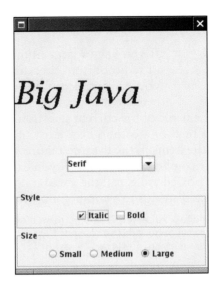

Figure 3
A Combo Box, Check Boxes,
and Radio Buttons

documentation. The `EtchedBorder` class yields a border with a three-dimensional, etched effect. You can add a border to any component, but most commonly you apply it to a panel:

```
JPanel panel = new JPanel();
panel.setBorder(new EtchedBorder());
```

If you want to add a title to the border (as in Figure 3), you need to construct a `TitledBorder`. You make a titled border by supplying a basic border and then the title you want. Here is a typical example:

```
panel.setBorder(new TitledBorder(new EtchedBorder(), "Size"));
```

14.3.2 Check Boxes

> For a binary choice, use a check box.

A check box is a user-interface component with two states: checked and unchecked. You use a group of check boxes when one selection does not exclude another. For example, the choices for "Bold" and "Italic" in Figure 3 are not exclusive. You can choose either, both, or neither. Therefore, they are implemented as a set of separate check boxes. Radio buttons and check boxes have different visual appearances. Radio buttons are round and have a black dot when selected. Check boxes are square and have a check mark when selected. (Strictly speaking, the appearance depends on the chosen look and feel. It is possible to create a different look and feel in which check boxes have a different shape or in which they give off a particular sound when selected.)

You construct a check box by giving the name in the constructor:

```
JCheckBox italicCheckBox = new JCheckBox("Italic");
```

Do not place check boxes inside a button group.

14.3.3 Combo Boxes

> For a large set of choices, use a combo box.

If you have a large number of choices, you don't want to make a set of radio buttons, because that would take up a lot of space. Instead, you can use a *combo box*. This component is called a combo box because it is a combination of a list and a text field. The text field displays the name of the current selection. When you click on the arrow to the right of the text field of a combo box, a list of selections drops down, and you can choose one of the items in the list (see Figure 4).

If the combo box is *editable*, you can also type in your own selection. To make a combo box editable, call the `setEditable` method.

You add strings to a combo box with the `addItem` method.

```
JComboBox facenameCombo = new JComboBox();
facenameCombo.addItem("Serif");
facenameCombo.addItem("SansSerif");
. . .
```

You get the item that the user has selected by calling the `getSelectedItem` method. However, because combo boxes can store other objects in addition to strings, the `getSelectedItem` method has return type `Object`. Hence you must cast the returned value back to `String`.

```
String selectedString
    = (String) facenameCombo.getSelectedItem();
```

You can select an item for the user with the `setSelectedItem` method.

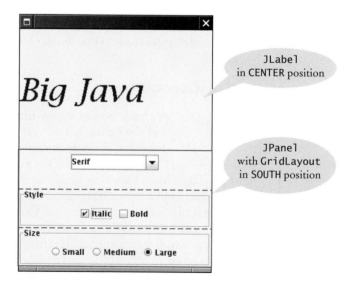

Figure 4
An Open Combo Box

Figure 5
The Components of the `ChoiceFrame`

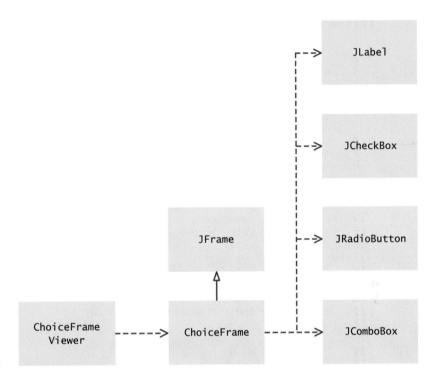

Figure 6
Classes of the
Font Choice Program

Radio buttons, check boxes, and combo boxes generate action events, just as buttons do.

Radio buttons, check boxes, and combo boxes generate an Action-Event whenever the user selects an item. In the following program, we don't care which component was clicked—all components notify the same listener object. Whenever the user clicks on any one of them, we simply ask each component for its current content, using the isSelected and getSelectedItem methods. We then redraw the text sample with the new font.

Figure 5 shows how the components are arranged in the frame. Figure 6 shows the UML diagram.

File ChoiceFrameViewer.java

```java
import javax.swing.JFrame;

/**
   This program tests the ChoiceFrame.
*/
public class ChoiceFrameViewer
{
   public static void main(String[] args)
   {
      JFrame frame = new ChoiceFrame();
      frame.setDefaultCloseOperation(JFrame.EXIT_ON_CLOSE);
      frame.setVisible(true);
   }
}
```

File ChoiceFrame.java

```java
1   import java.awt.BorderLayout;
2   import java.awt.Font;
3   import java.awt.GridLayout;
4   import java.awt.event.ActionEvent;
5   import java.awt.event.ActionListener;
6   import javax.swing.ButtonGroup;
7   import javax.swing.JButton;
8   import javax.swing.JCheckBox;
9   import javax.swing.JComboBox;
10  import javax.swing.JFrame;
11  import javax.swing.JLabel;
12  import javax.swing.JPanel;
13  import javax.swing.JRadioButton;
14  import javax.swing.border.EtchedBorder;
15  import javax.swing.border.TitledBorder;
16
17  /**
18     This frame contains a text field and a control panel
19     to change the font of the text.
20  */
21  public class ChoiceFrame extends JFrame
22  {
23     /**
24        Constructs the frame.
25     */
26     public ChoiceFrame()
27     {
28        // Construct text sample
29        sampleField = new JLabel("Big Java");
30        add(sampleField, BorderLayout.CENTER);
31
32        // This listener is shared among all components
33        class ChoiceListener implements ActionListener
34        {
35           public void actionPerformed(ActionEvent event)
36           {
37              setSampleFont();
38           }
39        }
40
41        listener = new ChoiceListener();
42
43        createControlPanel();
44        setSampleFont();
45        setSize(FRAME_WIDTH, FRAME_HEIGHT);
46     }
47
48     /**
49        Creates the control panel to change the font.
50     */
51     public void createControlPanel()
52     {
```

```
53          JPanel facenamePanel = createComboBox();
54          JPanel sizeGroupPanel = createCheckBoxes();
55          JPanel styleGroupPanel = createRadioButtons();
56
57          // Line up component panels
58
59          JPanel controlPanel = new JPanel();
60          controlPanel.setLayout(new GridLayout(3, 1));
61          controlPanel.add(facenamePanel);
62          controlPanel.add(sizeGroupPanel);
63          controlPanel.add(styleGroupPanel);
64
65          // Add panels to content pane
66
67          add(controlPanel, BorderLayout.SOUTH);
68       }
69
70       /**
71          Creates the combo box with the font style choices.
72          @return the panel containing the combo box
73       */
74       public JPanel createComboBox()
75       {
76          facenameCombo = new JComboBox();
77          facenameCombo.addItem("Serif");
78          facenameCombo.addItem("SansSerif");
79          facenameCombo.addItem("Monospaced");
80          facenameCombo.setEditable(true);
81          facenameCombo.addActionListener(listener);
82
83          JPanel panel = new JPanel();
84          panel.add(facenameCombo);
85          return panel;
86       }
87
88       /**
89          Creates the check boxes for selecting bold and italic styles.
90          @return the panel containing the check boxes
91       */
92       public JPanel createCheckBoxes()
93       {
94          italicCheckBox = new JCheckBox("Italic");
95          italicCheckBox.addActionListener(listener);
96
97          boldCheckBox = new JCheckBox("Bold");
98          boldCheckBox.addActionListener(listener);
99
100         JPanel panel = new JPanel();
101         panel.add(italicCheckBox);
102         panel.add(boldCheckBox);
103         panel.setBorder(
104             new TitledBorder(new EtchedBorder(), "Style"));
105
106         return panel;
```

```
107      }
108
109      /**
110          Creates the radio buttons to select the font size.
111          @return the panel containing the radio buttons
112      */
113      public JPanel createRadioButtons()
114      {
115          smallButton = new JRadioButton("Small");
116          smallButton.addActionListener(listener);
117
118          mediumButton = new JRadioButton("Medium");
119          mediumButton.addActionListener(listener);
120
121          largeButton = new JRadioButton("Large");
122          largeButton.addActionListener(listener);
123          largeButton.setSelected(true);
124
125          // Add radio buttons to button group
126
127          ButtonGroup group = new ButtonGroup();
128          group.add(smallButton);
129          group.add(mediumButton);
130          group.add(largeButton);
131
132          JPanel panel = new JPanel();
133          panel.add(smallButton);
134          panel.add(mediumButton);
135          panel.add(largeButton);
136          panel.setBorder(
137                new TitledBorder(new EtchedBorder(), "Size"));
138
139          return panel;
140      }
141
142      /**
143          Gets user choice for font name, style, and size
144          and sets the font of the text sample.
145      */
146      public void setSampleFont()
147      {
148          // Get font name
149          String facename
150                = (String) facenameCombo.getSelectedItem();
151
152          // Get font style
153
154          int style = 0;
155          if (italicCheckBox.isSelected())
156              style = style + Font.ITALIC;
157          if (boldCheckBox.isSelected())
158              style = style + Font.BOLD;
```

```
159
160        // Get font size
161
162        int size = 0;
163
164        final int SMALL_SIZE = 24;
165        final int MEDIUM_SIZE = 36;
166        final int LARGE_SIZE = 48;
167
168        if (smallButton.isSelected())
169           size = SMALL_SIZE;
170        else if (mediumButton.isSelected())
171           size = MEDIUM_SIZE;
172        else if (largeButton.isSelected())
173           size = LARGE_SIZE;
174
175        // Set font of text field
176
177        sampleField.setFont(new Font(facename, style, size));
178        sampleField.repaint();
179     }
180
181     private JLabel sampleField;
182     private JCheckBox italicCheckBox;
183     private JCheckBox boldCheckBox;
184     private JRadioButton smallButton;
185     private JRadioButton mediumButton;
186     private JRadioButton largeButton;
187     private JComboBox facenameCombo;
188     private ActionListener listener;
189
190     private static final int FRAME_WIDTH = 300;
191     private static final int FRAME_HEIGHT = 400;
192  }
```

SELF CHECK

5. What is the advantage of a JComboBox over a set of radio buttons? What is the disadvantage?

6. Why do all user interface components in the ChoiceFrame class share the same listener?

7. Why was the combo box placed inside a panel? What would have happened if it had been added directly to the control panel?

How To 14.1

Layout Management

A graphical user interface is made up of components such as buttons and text fields. The Swing library uses containers and layout managers to arrange these components. This How To explains how to group components into containers and how to pick the right layout managers.

Step 1   Make a sketch of your desired component layout.

Draw all the buttons, labels, text fields, and borders on a sheet of paper. Graph paper works best.

Here is an example—a user interface for ordering pizza. The user interface contains

- Three radio buttons
- Two check boxes
- A label: "Your Price:"
- A text field
- A border

┌─ Size ────────┐
│ ⦿ Small   │   ☒ Pepperoni
│ ○ Medium   │
│ ○ Large   │   ☒ Anchovies
└───────────────┘

Your Price: [   ]

Step 2   Find groupings of adjacent components with the same layout.

Usually, the component arrangement is complex enough that you need to use several panels, each with its own layout manager. Start by looking at adjacent components that are arranged top to bottom or left to right. If several components are surrounded by a border, they should be grouped together.

Here are the groupings from the pizza user interface:

┌─ Size ────────┐   ┌──────────────┐
│ ⦿ Small   │   │ ☒ Pepperoni │
│ ○ Medium   │   │   │
│ ○ Large   │   │ ☒ Anchovies │
└───────────────┘   └──────────────┘

┌──────────────────────────┐
│ Your Price: [   ] │
└──────────────────────────┘

Step 3 Identify layouts for each group.

When components are arranged horizontally, choose a flow layout. When components are arranged vertically, use a grid layout. The grid in this layout has as many rows as there are components, and it has one column.

In the pizza user interface example, you would choose

- A (3, 1) grid layout for the radio buttons
- A (2, 1) grid layout for the check boxes
- A flow layout for the label and text field

Step 4 Group the groups together.

Look at each group as one blob, and group the blobs together into larger groups, just as you grouped the components in the preceding step. If you note one large blob surrounded by smaller blobs, you can group them together in a border layout.

You may have to repeat the grouping again if you have a very complex user interface. You are done if you have arranged all groups in a single container.

For example, the three component groups of the pizza user interface can be arranged as follows:

- A group containing the first two component groups, placed in the center of a container with a border layout
- The third component group, in the southern area of that container

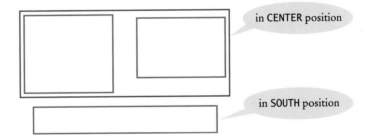

In this step, you may run into a couple of complications. The group "blobs" tend to vary in size more than the individual components. If you place them inside a grid layout, the grid layout forces them all to be the same size. Also, you occasionally would like a component from one group to line up with a component from another group, but there is no way for you to communicate that intent to the layout managers.

These problems can be overcome by using more sophisticated layout managers or implementing a custom layout manager. However, those techniques are beyond the scope of this book. Sometimes, you may want to start over with Step 1, using a component layout that is easier to manage. Or you can decide to live with minor imperfections of the layout. Don't worry about achieving the perfect layout—after all, you are learning programming, not user-interface design.

Step 5 Write the code to generate the layout.

This step is straightforward but potentially tedious, especially if you have a large number of components.

Start by constructing the components. Then construct a panel for each component group and set its layout manager if it is not a flow layout (the default for panels). Add a border to the panel if required. Finally, add the components to the panel. Continue in this fashion until you reach the outermost containers, which you add to the frame.

Of course, you also need to add event handlers to the components. That is the topic of How To 12.1.

Here is an outline of the code required for the pizza user interface.

```
JPanel radioButtonPanel = new JPanel();
radioButtonPanel.setLayout(new GridLayout(3, 1));
radioButton.setBorder(
      new TitledBorder(new EtchedBorder(), "Size"));
radioButtonPanel.add(smallButton);
radioButtonPanel.add(mediumButton);
radioButtonPanel.add(largeButton);

JPanel checkBoxPanel = new JPanel();
checkBoxPanel.setLayout(new GridLayout(2, 1));
checkBoxPanel.add(pepperoniButton());
checkBoxPanel.add(anchoviesButton());

JPanel pricePanel = new JPanel(); // Uses FlowLayout
pricePanel.add(new JLabel("Your Price:"));
pricePanel.add(priceTextField);

JPanel centerPanel = new JPanel(); // Uses FlowLayout
centerPanel.add(radioButtonPanel);
centerPanel.add(checkBoxPanel);

// Frame uses BorderLayout by default
add(centerPanel, BorderLayout.CENTER);
add(pricePanel, BorderLayout.SOUTH);
```

14.4 Menus

A frame contains a menu bar. The menu bar contains menus. A menu contains submenus and menu items.

Anyone who has ever used a graphical user interface is familiar with pull-down menus (see Figure 7). In Java it is easy to create these menus.

The container for the top-level menu items is called a *menu bar*. A *menu* is a collection of *menu items* and more menus (submenus). You add menu items and submenus with the add method:

```
JMenuItem fileExitItem = new JMenuItem("Exit");
fileMenu.add(fileExitItem);
```

Menu items generate action events.

A menu item has no further submenus. When the user selects a menu item, the menu item sends an action event. Therefore, you want to add a listener to each menu item:

```
fileExitItem.addActionListener(listener);
```

You add action listeners only to menu items, not to menus or the menu bar. When the user clicks on a menu name and a submenu opens, no action event is sent.

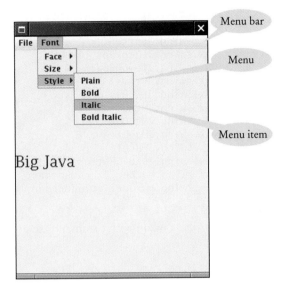

Figure 7
Pull-Down Menus

The following program builds up a small but typical menu and traps the action events from the menu items. To keep the program readable, it is a good idea to use a separate method for each menu or set of related menus. Have a look at the create-FaceItem method, which creates a menu item to change the font face. The same listener class takes care of three cases, with the name parameters varying for each menu item. The same strategy is used for the createSizeItem and createStyleItem methods.

File MenuFrameViewer.java

```
1   import javax.swing.JFrame;
2
3   /**
4       This program tests the MenuFrame.
5   */
6   public class MenuFrameViewer
7   {
8       public static void main(String[] args)
9       {
10          JFrame frame = new MenuFrame();
11          frame.setDefaultCloseOperation(JFrame.EXIT_ON_CLOSE);
12          frame.setVisible(true);
13      }
14  }
```

File MenuFrame.java

```
1   import java.awt.BorderLayout;
2   import java.awt.Font;
3   import java.awt.GridLayout;
4   import java.awt.event.ActionEvent;
```

```java
 5   import java.awt.event.ActionListener;
 6   import javax.swing.ButtonGroup;
 7   import javax.swing.JButton;
 8   import javax.swing.JCheckBox;
 9   import javax.swing.JComboBox;
10   import javax.swing.JFrame;
11   import javax.swing.JLabel;
12   import javax.swing.JMenu;
13   import javax.swing.JMenuBar;
14   import javax.swing.JMenuItem;
15   import javax.swing.JPanel;
16   import javax.swing.JRadioButton;
17   import javax.swing.border.EtchedBorder;
18   import javax.swing.border.TitledBorder;
19
20   /**
21       This frame has a menu with commands to change the font
22       of a text sample.
23   */
24   public class MenuFrame extends JFrame
25   {
26      /**
27          Constructs the frame.
28      */
29      public MenuFrame()
30      {
31         // Construct text sample
32         sampleField = new JLabel("Big Java");
33         add(sampleField, BorderLayout.CENTER);
34
35         // Construct menu
36         JMenuBar menuBar = new JMenuBar();
37         setJMenuBar(menuBar);
38         menuBar.add(createFileMenu());
39         menuBar.add(createFontMenu());
40
41         facename = "Serif";
42         fontsize = 24;
43         fontstyle = Font.PLAIN;
44
45         setSampleFont();
46         setSize(FRAME_WIDTH, FRAME_HEIGHT);
47      }
48
49      /**
50          Creates the File menu.
51          @return the menu
52      */
53      public JMenu createFileMenu()
54      {
55         JMenu menu = new JMenu("File");
56         menu.add(createFileExitItem());
57         return menu;
58      }
```

```
59
60      /**
61         Creates the File->Exit menu item and sets its action listener.
62         @return the menu item
63      */
64      public JMenuItem createFileExitItem()
65      {
66         JMenuItem item = new JMenuItem("Exit");
67         class MenuItemListener implements ActionListener
68         {
69            public void actionPerformed(ActionEvent event)
70            {
71               System.exit(0);
72            }
73         }
74         ActionListener listener = new MenuItemListener();
75         item.addActionListener(listener);
76         return item;
77      }
78
79      /**
80         Creates the Font submenu.
81         @return the menu
82      */
83      public JMenu createFontMenu()
84      {
85         JMenu menu = new JMenu("Font");
86         menu.add(createFaceMenu());
87         menu.add(createSizeMenu());
88         menu.add(createStyleMenu());
89         return menu;
90      }
91
92      /**
93         Creates the Face submenu.
94         @return the menu
95      */
96      public JMenu createFaceMenu()
97      {
98         JMenu menu = new JMenu("Face");
99         menu.add(createFaceItem("Serif"));
100        menu.add(createFaceItem("SansSerif"));
101        menu.add(createFaceItem("Monospaced"));
102        return menu;
103     }
104
105     /**
106        Creates the Size submenu.
107        @return the menu
108     */
109     public JMenu createSizeMenu()
110     {
111        JMenu menu = new JMenu("Size");
```

```
112        menu.add(createSizeItem("Smaller", -1));
113        menu.add(createSizeItem("Larger", 1));
114        return menu;
115     }
116
117     /**
118        Creates the Style submenu.
119        @return the menu
120     */
121     public JMenu createStyleMenu()
122     {
123        JMenu menu = new JMenu("Style");
124        menu.add(createStyleItem("Plain", Font.PLAIN));
125        menu.add(createStyleItem("Bold", Font.BOLD));
126        menu.add(createStyleItem("Italic", Font.ITALIC));
127        menu.add(createStyleItem("Bold Italic", Font.BOLD
128              + Font.ITALIC));
129        return menu;
130     }
131
132     /**
133        Creates a menu item to change the font face and set its action listener.
134        @param name the name of the font face
135        @return the menu item
136     */
137     public JMenuItem createFaceItem(final String name)
138     {
139        JMenuItem item = new JMenuItem(name);
140        class MenuItemListener implements ActionListener
141        {
142           public void actionPerformed(ActionEvent event)
143           {
144              facename = name;
145              setSampleFont();
146           }
147        }
148        ActionListener listener = new MenuItemListener();
149        item.addActionListener(listener);
150        return item;
151     }
152
153     /**
154        Creates a menu item to change the font size
155        and set its action listener.
156        @param name the name of the menu item
157        @param ds the amount by which to change the size
158        @return the menu item
159     */
160     public JMenuItem createSizeItem(String name, final int ds)
161     {
162        JMenuItem item = new JMenuItem(name);
163        class MenuItemListener implements ActionListener
164        {
```

```
165          public void actionPerformed(ActionEvent event)
166          {
167             fontsize = fontsize + ds;
168             setSampleFont();
169          }
170       }
171       ActionListener listener = new MenuItemListener();
172       item.addActionListener(listener);
173       return item;
174    }
175
176    /**
177       Creates a menu item to change the font style
178       and set its action listener.
179       @param name the name of the menu item
180       @param style the new font style
181       @return the menu item
182    */
183    public JMenuItem createStyleItem(String name, final int style)
184    {
185       JMenuItem item = new JMenuItem(name);
186       class MenuItemListener implements ActionListener
187       {
188          public void actionPerformed(ActionEvent event)
189          {
190             fontstyle = style;
191             setSampleFont();
192          }
193       }
194       ActionListener listener = new MenuItemListener();
195       item.addActionListener(listener);
196       return item;
197    }
198
199    /**
200       Sets the font of the text sample.
201    */
202    public void setSampleFont()
203    {
204       Font f = new Font(facename, fontstyle, fontsize);
205       sampleField.setFont(f);
206       sampleField.repaint();
207    }
208
209    private JLabel sampleField;
210    private String facename;
211    private int fontstyle;
212    private int fontsize;
213
214    private static final int FRAME_WIDTH = 300;
215    private static final int FRAME_HEIGHT = 400;
216 }
```

8. Why do JMenu objects not generate action events?
9. Why is the name parameter in the createFaceItem method declared as final?

14.5 Text Areas

> Use a JTextArea to show multiple lines of text.

In Chapter 12, you saw how to construct text fields. A text field holds a single line of text. To display multiple lines of text, use the JTextArea class.

When constructing a text area, you can specify the number of rows and columns:

```
final int ROWS = 10;
final int COLUMNS = 30;
JTextArea textArea = new JTextArea(ROWS, COLUMNS);
```

Use the setText method to set the text of a text field or text area. The append method adds text to the end of a text area. Use newline characters to separate lines, like this:

```
textArea.append(account.getBalance() + "\n");
```

If you want to use a text field or text area for display purposes only, call the set-Editable method like this

```
textArea.setEditable(false);
```

Now the user can no longer edit the contents of the field, but your program can still call setText and append to change it.

> You can add scroll bars to any component with a JScrollPane.

To add scroll bars to a text area, use a JScrollPane, like this:

```
JTextArea textArea = new JTextArea(ROWS, COLUMNS);
JScrollPane scrollPane = new JScrollPane(textArea);
```

Then add the scroll pane to the frame. Figure 8 shows the result.

The following sample program puts these concepts together. A user can enter numbers into the interest rate text field and then click on the "Add Interest" button). The interest rate is applied, and the updated balance is appended to the text area. The text area has scroll bars and is not editable.

Figure 8 The TextAreaViewer Application

This program is similar to the investment viewer program of Chapter 12, but it keeps track of all the bank balances, not just the last one.

File TextAreaViewer.java

```
1  import java.awt.BorderLayout;
2  import java.awt.event.ActionEvent;
3  import java.awt.event.ActionListener;
4  import javax.swing.JButton;
5  import javax.swing.JFrame;
6  import javax.swing.JLabel;
7  import javax.swing.JPanel;
8  import javax.swing.JScrollPane;
9  import javax.swing.JTextArea;
10 import javax.swing.JTextField;
11
12 /**
13     This program shows a frame with a text area that displays
14     the growth of an investment.
15 */
16 public class TextAreaViewer
17 {
18    public static void main(String[] args)
19    {
20       JFrame frame = new JFrame();
21
22       // The application adds interest to this bank account
23       final BankAccount account = new BankAccount(INITIAL_BALANCE);
24       // The text area for displaying the results
25       final int AREA_ROWS = 10;
26       final int AREA_COLUMNS = 30;
27
28       final JTextArea textArea = new JTextArea(
29             AREA_ROWS, AREA_COLUMNS);
30       textArea.setEditable(false);
31       JScrollPane scrollPane = new JScrollPane(textArea);
32
33       // The label and text field for entering the interest rate
34       JLabel rateLabel = new JLabel("Interest Rate: ");
35
36       final int FIELD_WIDTH = 10;
37       final JTextField rateField = new JTextField(FIELD_WIDTH);
38       rateField.setText("" + DEFAULT_RATE);
39
40       // The button to trigger the calculation
41       JButton calculateButton = new JButton("Add Interest");
42
43       // The panel that holds the input components
44       JPanel northPanel = new JPanel();
45       northPanel.add(rateLabel);
46       northPanel.add(rateField);
47       northPanel.add(calculateButton);
48
49       frame.add(northPanel, BorderLayout.NORTH);
50       frame.add(scrollPane);
```

```
51
52         class CalculateListener implements ActionListener
53         {
54            public void actionPerformed(ActionEvent event)
55            {
56               double rate = Double.parseDouble(
57                     rateField.getText());
58               double interest = account.getBalance()
59                     * rate / 100;
60               account.deposit(interest);
61               textArea.append(account.getBalance() + "\n");
62            }
63         }
64
65         ActionListener listener = new CalculateListener();
66         calculateButton.addActionListener(listener);
67
68         frame.setSize(FRAME_WIDTH, FRAME_HEIGHT);
69         frame.setDefaultCloseOperation(JFrame.EXIT_ON_CLOSE);
70         frame.setVisible(true);
71      }
72
73      private static final double DEFAULT_RATE = 10;
74      private static final double INITIAL_BALANCE = 1000;
75
76      private static final int FRAME_WIDTH = 400;
77      private static final int FRAME_HEIGHT = 200;
78   }
```

SELF CHECK

10. What is the difference between a text field and a text area?

11. Why did the TextAreaViewer program call textArea.setEditable(false)?

12. How would you modify the TextAreaViewer program if you didn't want to use scroll bars?

14.6 Exploring the Swing Documentation

> You should learn to navigate the API documentation to find out more about user-interface components.

In the preceding sections, you saw the basic properties of the most common user-interface components. We purposefully omitted many options and variations to simplify the discussion. You can go a long way by using only the simplest properties of these components. If you want to implement a more sophisticated effect, you can look inside the Swing documentation. You will probably find the documentation quite intimidating at first glance, though. The purpose of this section is to show you how you can use the documentation to your advantage without becoming overwhelmed.

Figure 9
A Color Mixer

Recall the Color class that was introduced in Chapter 5. Every combination of red, green, and blue values represents a different color. It should be fun to mix your own colors, with a slider for the red, green, and blue values (see Figure 9).

The Swing user interface toolkit has a large set of user-interface components. How do you know if there is a slider? You can buy a book that illustrates all Swing components, such as [2]. Or you can run the sample application included in the Java Development Kit that shows off all Swing components (see Figure 10). Or you can look at the names of all of the classes that start with J and decide that JSlider may be a good candidate.

Next, you need to ask yourself a few questions:

- How do I construct a JSlider?
- How can I get notified when the user has moved it?
- How can I tell to which value the user has set it?

If you can answer these questions, then you can put a slider to good use. Once you have mastered sliders, you can fritter away more time and find out how to set tick marks or otherwise enhance the visual beauty of your creation.

When you look at the documentation of the JSlider class, you will probably not be happy. There are over 50 methods in the JSlider class and over 250 inherited methods, and some of the method descriptions look downright scary, such as the one in Figure 11. Apparently some folks out there are concerned about the valueIsAdjusting property, whatever that may be, and the designers of this class felt it necessary to supply a method to tweak that property. Until you too feel that need, your best bet is to ignore this method. As the author of an introductory book, it pains me to tell you to ignore certain facts. But the truth of the matter is that the Java library is so large and complex that nobody understands it in its entirety, not even the designers of Java themselves. You need to develop the ability

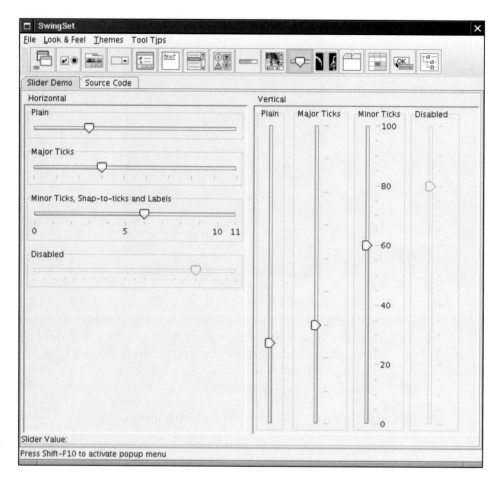

Figure 10
The SwingSet
Demo

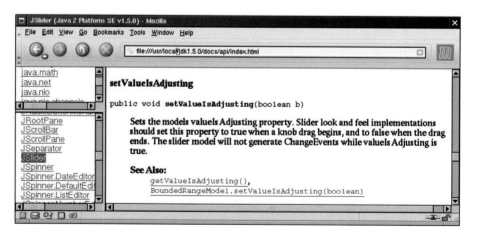

Figure 11   A Mysterious Method Description from the API Documentation

to separate fundamental concepts from ephemeral minutiae. For example, it is important that you understand the concept of event handling. Once you understand the concept, you can ask the question, "What event does the slider send when the user moves it?" But it is not important that you memorize how to set tick marks or that you know how to implement a slider with a custom look and feel.

Let us go back to our fundamental questions. In Java version 5.0, there are six constructors for the JSlider class. You want to learn about one or two of them. You must strike a balance somewhere between the trivial and the bizarre. Consider

```
public JSlider()
```
Creates a horizontal slider with the range 0 to 100 and an initial value of 50.

Maybe that is good enough for now, but what if you want another range or initial value? It seems too limited.

On the other side of the spectrum, there is

```
public JSlider(BoundedRangeModel brm)
```
Creates a horizontal slider using the specified BoundedRangeModel.

Whoa! What is that? You can click on the BoundedRangeModel link to get a long explanation of this class. This appears to be some internal mechanism for the Swing implementors. Let's try to avoid this constructor if we can. Looking further, we find

```
public JSlider(int min, int max, int value)
```
Creates a horizontal slider using the specified min, max, and value.

This sounds general enough to be useful and simple enough to be usable. You might want to stash away the fact that you can have vertical sliders as well.

Next, you want to know what events a slider generates. There is no addActionListener method. That makes sense. Adjusting a slider seems different from clicking a button, and Swing uses a different event type for these events. There is a method

```
public void addChangeListener(ChangeListener l)
```

Click on the ChangeListener link to find out more about this interface. It has a single method

```
void stateChanged(ChangeEvent e)
```

Apparently, that method is called whenever the user moves the slider. What is a ChangeEvent? Once again, click on the link, to find out that this event class has *no* methods of its own, but it inherits the getSource method from its superclass EventObject. The getSource method tells us which component generated this event, but we don't need that information—we know that the event came from the slider.

Now we have a plan: Add a change event listener to each slider. When the slider is changed, the stateChanged method is called. Find out the new value of the slider. Recompute the color value and repaint the color panel. That way, the color panel is continually repainted as the user moves one of the sliders.

To compute the color value, you will still need to get the current value of the slider. Look at all the methods that start with get. Sure enough, you find

```
public int getValue()
```
Returns the slider's value.

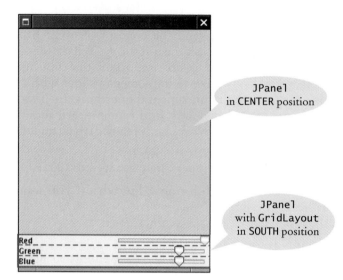

Figure 12
The Components of
the SliderFrame

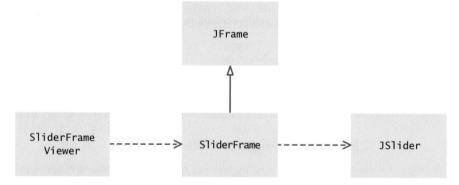

Figure 13
Classes of the
SliderFrameViewer
Program

Now you know everything you need to write the program. The program uses one new Swing component and one event listener of a new type. Of course, now that you have "tasted blood", you may want to add those tick marks—see Exercise P14.13.

Figure 12 shows how the components are arranged in the frame. Figure 13 shows the UML diagram.

File SliderFrameViewer.java

```
1   import javax.swing.JFrame;
2
3   public class SliderFrameViewer
4   {
5      public static void main(String[] args)
6      {
7         SliderFrame frame = new SliderFrame();
8         frame.setDefaultCloseOperation(JFrame.EXIT_ON_CLOSE);
9         frame.setVisible(true);
10     }
11  }
```

File SliderFrame.java

```java
1   import java.awt.BorderLayout;
2   import java.awt.Color;
3   import java.awt.GridLayout;
4   import javax.swing.JFrame;
5   import javax.swing.JLabel;
6   import javax.swing.JPanel;
7   import javax.swing.JSlider;
8   import javax.swing.event.ChangeListener;
9   import javax.swing.event.ChangeEvent;
10
11  public class SliderFrame extends JFrame
12  {
13     public SliderFrame()
14     {
15        colorPanel = new JPanel();
16
17        add(colorPanel, BorderLayout.CENTER);
18        createControlPanel();
19        setSampleColor();
20        setSize(FRAME_WIDTH, FRAME_HEIGHT);
21     }
22
23     public void createControlPanel()
24     {
25        class ColorListener implements ChangeListener
26        {
27           public void stateChanged(ChangeEvent event)
28           {
29              setSampleColor();
30           }
31        }
32
33        ChangeListener listener = new ColorListener();
34
35        redSlider = new JSlider(0, 100, 100);
36        redSlider.addChangeListener(listener);
37
38        greenSlider = new JSlider(0, 100, 70);
39        greenSlider.addChangeListener(listener);
40
41        blueSlider = new JSlider(0, 100, 70);
42        blueSlider.addChangeListener(listener);
43
44        JPanel controlPanel = new JPanel();
45        controlPanel.setLayout(new GridLayout(3, 2));
46
47        controlPanel.add(new JLabel("Red"));
48        controlPanel.add(redSlider);
49
50        controlPanel.add(new JLabel("Green"));
51        controlPanel.add(greenSlider);
52
```

```
53          controlPanel.add(new JLabel("Blue"));
54          controlPanel.add(blueSlider);
55
56          add(controlPanel, BorderLayout.SOUTH);
57      }
58
59      /**
60          Reads the slider values and sets the panel to
61          the selected color.
62      */
63      public void setSampleColor()
64      {
65          // Read slider values
66
67          float red = 0.01F * redSlider.getValue();
68          float green = 0.01F * greenSlider.getValue();
69          float blue = 0.01F * blueSlider.getValue();
70
71          // Set panel background to selected color
72
73          colorPanel.setBackground(new Color(red, green, blue));
74          colorPanel.repaint();
75      }
76
77      private JPanel colorPanel;
78      private JSlider redSlider;
79      private JSlider greenSlider;
80      private JSlider blueSlider;
81
82      private static final int FRAME_WIDTH = 300;
83      private static final int FRAME_HEIGHT = 400;
84  }
```

SELF CHECK

13. Suppose you want to allow users to pick a color from a color dialog box. Which class would you use? Look in the API documentation.

14. Why does a slider emit change events and not action events?

RANDOM FACT 14.1

Visual Programming

Programming as you know it involves typing code into a text editor and then running it. A programmer must be familiar with the programming language to write even the simplest of programs. When programming graphics, one must compute every screen position.

A new *visual* style of programming makes this much easier. When you use a visual programming environment, such as Visual Studio or NetBeans, you use your mouse to specify where text, buttons, and other fields should appear on the screen (see Figure 14). You still need to do some programming. You need to write code for every event. For example, you can drag a button to its desired location, but you still need to specify what should happen when the user clicks on it.

Visual programming offers two benefits. It is much easier to lay out a screen by dragging buttons and images with the mouse than it is to compute the coordinates in a program. The visual programming environment also makes it easy to place objects with sophisticated behavior onto the screen. For example, a calendar object can show the current month's calendar, with buttons to move to the next or previous month; all of that has been preprogrammed by someone (usually the hard way, using a traditional programming language), but you can add a fully working calendar to your program simply by dragging it off a toolbar and dropping it into your program.

A prebuilt component, such as a calendar chooser, usually has a large number of *properties* that you can simply choose from a table. For example, you can simply check whether you want the calendar to be weekly or monthly. The provider of the calendar component had to work hard to include both cases in the code, but the programmer using the component does not have to care. When written in Java, these prepackaged components are called *Java Beans*.

Figure 14 A Visual Programming Environment

User-interface design in a visual environment is *much* easier than writing the equivalent code in Java. In days a programmer can design an attractive user interface that would take weeks to complete by writing code. These systems are highly recommended for user interface programming.

CHAPTER SUMMARY

1. Define a JFrame subclass for a complex frame.

2. User-interface components are arranged by placing them inside containers. Containers can be placed inside larger containers.

3. Each container has a layout manager that directs the arrangement of its components.

4. Three useful layout managers are the border layout, flow layout, and grid layout.

5. When adding a component to a container with the border layout, specify the NORTH, EAST, SOUTH, WEST, or CENTER position.

6. The content pane of a frame has a border layout by default. A panel has a flow layout by default.

7. For a small set of mutually exclusive choices, use a group of radio buttons or a combo box.

8. Add radio buttons into a ButtonGroup so that only one button in the group is on at any time.

9. You can place a border around a panel to group its contents visually.

10. For a binary choice, use a check box.

11. For a large set of choices, use a combo box.

12. Radio buttons, check boxes, and combo boxes generate action events, just as buttons do.

13. A frame contains a menu bar. The menu bar contains menus. A menu contains submenus and menu items.

14. Menu items generate action events.

15. Use a JTextArea to show multiple lines of text.

16. You can add scroll bars to any component with a JScrollPane.

17. You should learn to navigate the API documentation to find out more about user-interface components.

FURTHER READING

1. Cay S. Horstmann and Gary Cornell, *Core Java 2 Volume 1: Fundamentals,* 7th edition, Prentice Hall, 2004.

2. Kim Topley, *Core Java Foundation Classes,* 2nd edition, Prentice Hall, 2002.

CLASSES, OBJECTS, AND METHODS INTRODUCED IN THIS CHAPTER

```
java.awt.BorderLayout
   CENTER
   EAST
   NORTH
   SOUTH
   WEST
java.awt.Container
   setLayout
java.awt.FlowLayout
java.awt.Font
java.awt.GridLayout
javax.swing.AbstractButton
   isSelected
   setSelected
javax.swing.ButtonGroup
   add
javax.swing.ImageIcon
javax.swing.JCheckBox
javax.swing.JComboBox
   addItem
   getSelectedItem
   isEditable
   setEditable
javax.swing.JComponent
   setBorder
   setFont
```

```
javax.swing.JFrame
   setJMenuBar
javax.swing.JMenu
   add
javax.swing.JMenuBar
   add
javax.swing.JMenuItem
javax.swing.JRadioButton
javax.swing.JScrollPane
javax.swing.JSlider
   addChangeListener
   getValue
javax.swing.JTextArea
   append
javax.swing.border.EtchedBorder
javax.swing.border.TitledBorder
javax.swing.event.ChangeEvent
javax.swing.event.ChangeListener
   stateChanged
javax.swing.text.JTextComponent
   isEditable
   setEditable
   setText
```

REVIEW EXERCISES

Exercise R14.1. Can you use a flow layout for the components in a frame? If yes, how?

Exercise R14.2. What is a layout manager? What is the advantage of a layout manager over telling the container "place this component at position (x, y)"?

Exercise R14.3. What happens when you place a single button into the CENTER area of a container that uses a border layout? Try it out, by writing a small sample program, if you aren't sure of the answer.

Exercise R14.4. What happens if you place multiple buttons into the SOUTH area? Try it out, by writing a small sample program, if you aren't sure of the answer.

Exercise R14.5. What happens when you add a button to a container that uses a border layout and omit the position? Try it out and explain.

Exercise R14.6. What happens when you try to add a button to another button? Try it out and explain.

Exercise R14.7. The SliderFrameViewer program uses a grid layout manager. Explain a drawback of the grid that is apparent from Figure 12. What could you do to overcome this drawback?

Exercise R14.8. What is the difference between the grid layout and the grid bag layout?

Exercise R14.9. Can you add icons to check boxes, radio buttons, and combo boxes? Browse the Java documentation to find out. Then write a small test program to verify your findings.

Exercise R14.10. What is the difference between radio buttons and check boxes?

Exercise R14.11. Why do you need a button group for radio buttons but not for check boxes?

Exercise R14.12. What is the difference between a menu bar, a menu, and a menu item?

Exercise R14.13. When browsing through the Java documentation for more information about sliders, we ignored the JSlider default constructor. Why? Would it have worked in our sample program?

Exercise R14.14. How do you construct a vertical slider? Consult the Swing documentation for an answer.

Exercise R14.15. Why doesn't a JComboBox send out change events?

Exercise R14.16. What component would you use to show a set of choices, just as in a combo box, but so that several items are visible at the same time? Run the Swing demo app or look at a book with Swing example programs to find the answer.

Exercise R14.17. How many Swing user interface components are there? Look at the Java documentation to get an approximate answer.

Exercise R14.18. How many methods does the JProgressBar component have? Be sure to count inherited methods. Look at the Java documentation.

PROGRAMMING EXERCISES

Exercise P14.1. Write an application with three buttons labeled "Red", "Green", and "Blue" that changes the background color of a panel in the center of the frame to red, green, or blue.

Exercise P14.2. Add icons to the buttons of Exercise P14.1.

Exercise P14.3. Write a calculator application. Use a grid layout to arrange buttons for the digits and for the + − × ÷ operations. Add a text field to display the result.

Exercise P14.4. Write an application with three radio buttons labeled "Red", "Green", and "Blue" that changes the background color of a panel in the center of the frame to red, green, or blue.

Exercise P14.5. Write an application with three check boxes labeled "Red", "Green", and "Blue" that adds a red, green, or blue component to the the background color of a panel in the center of the frame. This application can display a total of eight color combinations.

Exercise P14.6. Write an application with a combo box containing three items labeled "Red", "Green", and "Blue" that changes the background color of a panel in the center of the frame to red, green, or blue.

Exercise P14.7. Write an application with a Color menu and menu items labeled "Red", "Green", and "Blue" that changes the background color of a panel in the center of the frame to red, green, or blue.

Exercise P14.8. Write a program that displays a number of rectangles at random positions. Supply buttons "Fewer" and "More" that generate fewer or more random rectangles. Each time the user clicks on "Fewer", the count should be halved. Each time the user clicks on "More", the count should be doubled.

Exercise P14.9. Modify the program of Exercise P14.8 to replace the buttons with a slider to generate fewer or more random rectangles.

Exercise P14.10. Write an application with three labeled text fields, one each for the initial amount of a savings account, the annual interest rate, and the number of years. Add a button "Calculate" and a read-only text area to display the result, namely, the balance of the savings account after the end of each year.

Exercise P14.11. In the application from Exercise P14.10, replace the text area with a bar chart that shows the balance after the end of each year.

Exercise P14.12. Write a program that contains a text area, a button "Draw Graph", and a panel that draws a bar chart of the numbers that a user typed into the text area. Use a string tokenizer to break up the text in the text area.

Exercise P14.13. In the slider test program, add a set of tick marks to each slider that show the exact slider position.

PROGRAMMING PROJECTS

Project 14.1. Write a program that lets users design charts such as the following:

```
Golden Gate
Brooklyn
Delaware Memorial
Mackinac
```

Use appropriate components to ask for the length, label, and color, then apply them when the user clicks an "Add Item" button. Allow the user to switch between bar charts and pie charts.

Project 14.2. Write a program that displays a scrolling message in a panel. Use a timer for the scrolling effect. In the timer's action listener, move the starting position of the message and repaint. When the message has left the window, reset the starting position to the other corner. Provide a user interface to customize the message text, font, foreground and background colors, and the scrolling speed and direction.

ANSWERS TO SELF-CHECK QUESTIONS

1. Three: `InvestmentFrameViewer`, `InvestmentFrame`, and `BankAccount`.
2. The `InvestmentFrame` constructor adds the panel to *itself*.
3. First add them to a panel, then add the panel to the north end of a frame.
4. Place them inside a panel with a `GridLayout` that has three rows and one column.
5. If you have many options, a set of radio buttons takes up a large area. A combo box can show many options without using up much space. But the user cannot see the options as easily.
6. When any of the component settings is changed, the program simply queries all of them and updates the label.
7. To keep it from growing too large. It would have grown to the same width and height as the two panels below it.
8. When you open a menu, you have not yet made a selection. Only `JMenuItem` objects correspond to selections.
9. The parameter variable is accessed in a method of an inner class.
10. A text field holds a single line of text; a text area holds multiple lines.
11. The text area is intended to display the program output. It does not collect user input.
12. Don't construct a `JScrollPane` and add the `textArea` object directly to the frame.
13. `JColorChooser`.
14. Action events describe one-time changes, such as button clicks. Change events describe continuous changes.

Exception Handling

CHAPTER GOALS

- To learn how to throw exceptions
- To be able to design your own exception classes
- To understand the difference between checked and unchecked exceptions
- To learn how to catch exceptions
- To know when and where to catch an exception

Programs can fail for a variety of reasons; bad input and programmer error are just two of many possible causes. A program should deal with failure in a predictable manner.

There are two main aspects to handling failure: *detection* and *recovery*. A major challenge of error handling is that the point of detection is usually decoupled from the point of recovery. For example, the get method of the ArrayList class may detect that a nonexistent element is being accessed, and the parseInt method of the Integer class may detect that the string that it is processing can't be an integer, but neither of these methods has enough information to decide what to do about this failure. Should the user be asked to try a different operation? Should the program be aborted after saving the user's work? The logic for these actions is completely independent from the normal processing that these methods do. In Java, *exception handling* provides a flexible mechanism for passing control from the point of error detection to a competent recovery handler. This short chapter discusses the exception handling mechanism in detail and shows you how to use it appropriately in your programs.

CHAPTER CONTENTS

15.1 Throwing Exceptions

The exception handling mechanism solves a classic dilemma: What should a method do when it detects an error condition? The traditional—but problematic—solution is that the method returns a value that indicates whether it succeeded or failed. For example, the `Math.sqrt` method returns a special "not a number" value if you try to compute the square root of a negative number. However, this approach has two problems.

1. The calling method may forget to check the return value.
2. The calling method may not be able to do anything about the failure.

If the calling method forgets to check the return value, a failure notification may go completely undetected. Then the program keeps going, processing faulty information and mysteriously failing later.

If the caller knows about the failure but cannot do anything about it, it must fail too and let its caller worry about it. That turns out to be a real hassle for programmers, because many method calls would need to be checked for failure. Instead of programming for success:

```
x.doStuff();
```

you would always be programming for failure:

```
if (!x.doStuff()) return false;
```

That is fine when done occasionally, but if you have to check every method call, then your programs become very hard to read.

The exception handling mechanism has been designed to solve these two problems:

1. Exceptions can't be overlooked.

2. Exceptions are sent directly to an exception handler—not just the caller of the failed method.

> To signal an exceptional condition, use the throw statement to throw an exception object.

Let us look into the details of this mechanism. When you detect an error condition, your job is really easy. You just throw an appropriate exception object, and you are done. For example, suppose someone tries to withdraw too much money from a bank account.

```
public class BankAccount
{
    public void withdraw(double amount)
    {
        if (amount > balance)
            // Now what?
            . . .
    }
    . . .
}
```

First look for an appropriate exception class. The Java library provides many classes to signal all sorts of exceptional conditions. Figure 1 shows the most useful ones.

Look around for an exception type that might describe your situation. How about the IllegalStateException? Is the bank account in an illegal state for the withdraw operation? Not really—some withdraw operations could succeed. Is the parameter value illegal? Indeed it is. It is just too large. Therefore, let's throw an IllegalArgumentException. (The term *argument* is an alternative term for a parameter value.)

```
public class BankAccount
{
    public void withdraw(double amount)
    {
        if (amount > balance)
        {
            IllegalArgumentException exception
                = new IllegalArgumentException("Amount exceeds balance");
            throw exception;
        }
        balance = balance - amount;
    }
    . . .
}
```

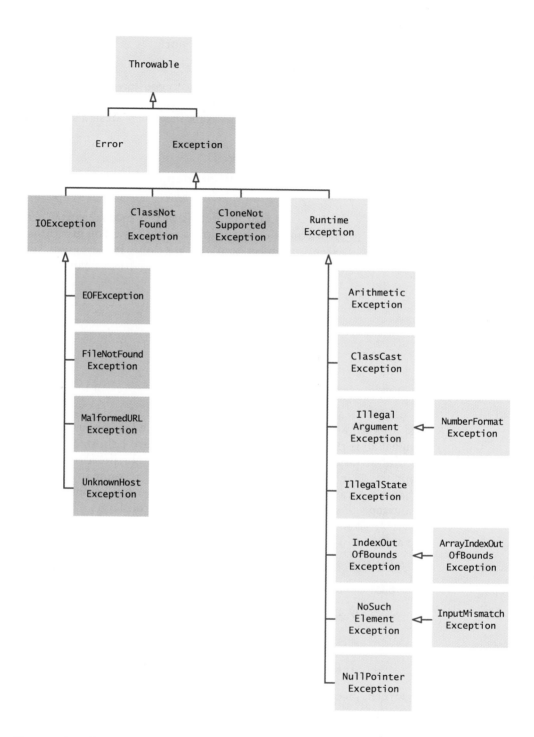

Figure 1   The Hierarchy of Exception Classes

Actually, you don't have to store the exception object in a variable. You can just throw the object that the new operator returns:

```
throw new IllegalArgumentException("Amount exceeds balance");
```

> When you throw an exception, the current method terminates immediately.

When you throw an exception, execution does not continue with the next statement but with an *exception handler*. For now, we won't worry about the handling of the exception. That is the topic of Section 15.3.

SYNTAX 15.1 **Throwing an Exception**

throw *exceptionObject*;

Example:

```
throw new IllegalArgumentException();
```

Purpose:

To throw an exception and transfer control to a handler for this exception type

---

SELF CHECK

1. How should you modify the deposit method to ensure that the balance is never negative?
2. Suppose you construct a new bank account object with a zero balance and then call withdraw(10). What is the value of balance afterwards?

15.2 Checked and Unchecked Exceptions

> There are two kinds of exceptions: checked and unchecked. Unchecked exceptions extend the class RuntimeException or Error.

Java exceptions fall into two categories, called *checked* and *unchecked* exceptions. When you call a method that throws a checked exception, the compiler checks that you don't ignore it. You must tell the compiler what you are going to do about the exception if it is ever thrown. For example, all subclasses of IOException are checked exceptions. On the other hand, the compiler does not require you to keep track of unchecked exceptions. Exceptions, such as NumberFormatException, IllegalArgumentException, and NullPointerException, are unchecked exceptions. More generally, all exceptions that belong to subclasses of RuntimeException are unchecked, and all other subclasses of the class Exception are checked. (In Figure 1, the checked exceptions are shaded in a darker color.) There is a second category of internal errors that are reported by throwing objects of type

Error. One example is the OutOfMemoryError, which is thrown when all available memory has been used up. These are fatal errors that happen rarely and are beyond your control. They too are unchecked.

> Checked exceptions are due to external circumstances that the programmer cannot prevent. The compiler checks that your program handles these exceptions.

Why have two kinds of exceptions? A checked exception describes a problem that is likely to occur at times, no matter how careful you are. The unchecked exceptions, on the other hand, are your fault. For example, an unexpected end of file can be caused by forces beyond your control, such as a disk error or a broken network connection. But you are to blame for a NullPointerException, because your code was wrong when it tried to use a null reference.

The compiler doesn't check whether you handle a NullPointer-Exception, because you should test your references for null before using them rather than install a handler for that exception. The compiler does insist that your program be able to handle error conditions that you cannot prevent.

Actually, those categories aren't perfect. For example, the Scanner.nextInt method throws an unchecked InputMismatchException if a user enters an input that is not an integer. A checked exception would have been more appropriate because the programmer cannot prevent users from entering incorrect input. (The designers of the Scanner class made this choice to make the class easy to use for beginning programmers.)

As you can see from Figure 1, the majority of checked exceptions occur when you deal with input and output. That is a fertile ground for external failures beyond your control—a file might have been corrupted or removed, a network connection might be overloaded, a server might have crashed, and so on. Therefore, you will need to deal with checked exceptions principally when programming with files and streams.

You can use the Scanner class to read data from a file, by passing a FileReader object to the Scanner constructor:

```
String filename = . . .;
FileReader reader = new FileReader(filename);
Scanner in = new Scanner(reader);
```

However, the FileReader constructor can throw a FileNotFoundException. The FileNotFoundException is a checked exception, so you need to tell the compiler what you are going to do about it. You have two choices. You can handle the exception, using the techniques that you will see in Section 15.3. Or you can simply tell the compiler that you are aware of this exception and that you want your method to be terminated when it occurs. The method that reads input rarely knows what to do about an unexpected error, so that is usually the better option.

To declare that a method should be terminated when a checked exception occurs within it, tag the method with a throws specifier.

```
public class DataSet
{
    public void read(String filename) throws FileNotFoundException
    {
        FileReader reader = new FileReader(filename);
        Scanner in = new Scanner(reader);
        . . .
```

```
      }
         . . .
   }
```

Add a throws specifier to a method that can throw a checked exception.

The throws clause in turn signals the caller of your method that it may encounter a FileNotFoundException. Then the caller needs to make the same decision—handle the exception, or tell its caller that the exception may be thrown.

If your method can throw checked exceptions of different types, you separate the class names by commas:

```
public void read(String filename)
      throws IOException, ClassNotFoundException
```

Always keep in mind that exception classes form an inheritance hierarchy. For example, FileNotFoundException is a subclass of IOException. Thus, if a method can throw both an IOException and a FileNotFoundException, you only tag it as throws IOException.

It sounds somehow irresponsible not to handle an exception when you know that it happened. Actually, though, it is usually best not to catch an exception if you don't know how to remedy the situation. After all, what can you do in a low-level read method? Can you tell the user? How? By sending a message to System.out? You don't know whether this method is called in an applet or maybe an embedded system (such as a vending machine), where the user may never see System.out. And even if your users can see your error message, how do you know that they can understand English? Your class may be used to build an application for users in another country. Or can you perhaps fix up the object and keep going? How? If you set a variable to null or an empty string, that may just cause the program to break later, with much greater mystery.

Of course, some methods in the program know how to communicate with the user or take other remedial action. By allowing the exception to reach those methods, you make it possible for the exception to be processed by a competent handler.

SYNTAX 15.2 Exception Specification

accessSpecifier returnType methodName(parameterType parameterName, . . .)
      throws *ExceptionClass*, *ExceptionClass*, . . .

Example:

```
public void read(BufferedReader in)
      throws IOException
```

Purpose:

To indicate the checked exceptions that this method can throw

3. Suppose a method calls the `FileReader` constructor and the read method of the `FileReader` class, which can throw an `IOException`. Which `throws` specification should you use?

4. Why is a `NullPointerException` not a checked exception?

15.3 Catching Exceptions

In a method that is ready to handle a particular exception type, place the statements that can cause the exception inside a try block, and the handler inside a catch clause.

Every exception should be handled somewhere in your program. If an exception has no handler, an error message is printed, and your program terminates. That may be fine for a student program. But you would not want a professionally written program to die just because some method detected an unexpected error. Therefore, you should install exception handlers for all exceptions that your program might throw.

You install an exception handler with the `try/catch` statement. Each `try` block contains one or more statements that may cause an exception. Each `catch` clause contains the handler for an exception type. Here is an example:

```
try
{
    String filename = . . .;
    FileReader reader = new FileReader(filename);
    Scanner in = new Scanner(reader);
    String input = in.next();
    int value = Integer.parseInt(input);
    . . .
}
catch (IOException exception)
{
    exception.printStackTrace();
}
catch (NumberFormatException exception)
{
    System.out.println("Input was not a number");
}
```

Three exceptions may be thrown in this try block: The `FileReader` constructor can throw a `FileNotFoundException`, `Scanner.next` can throw a `NoSuchElementException`, and `Integer.parseInt` can throw a `NumberFormatException`.

If any of these exceptions is actually thrown, then the rest of the instructions in the try block are skipped. Here is what happens for the various exception types:

- If a `FileNotFoundException` is thrown, then the catch clause for the `IOException` is executed. (Recall that `FileNotFoundException` is a subclass of `IOException`.)

- If a `NumberFormatException` occurs, then the second catch clause is executed.

- A `NoSuchElementException` is *not caught* by any of the catch clauses. The exception remains thrown until it is caught by another try block.

SYNTAX 15.3 General try Block

```
try
{
    statement
    statement
    . . .
}
catch (ExceptionClass exceptionObject)
{
    statement
    statement
    . . .
}
catch (ExceptionClass exceptionObject)
{
    statement
    statement
    . . .
}
. . .
```

Example:

```
try
{
    System.out.println("How old are you?");
    int age = in.nextInt();
    System.out.println("Next year, you'll be " + (age + 1));
}
catch (InputMismatchException exception)
{
    exception.printStackTrace();
}
```

Purpose:

To execute one or more statements that may generate exceptions. If an exception occurs and it matches one of the catch clauses, execute the first one that matches. If no exception occurs, or an exception is thrown that doesn't match any catch clause, then skip the catch clauses.

When the catch (IOException exception) block is executed, then some method in the try block has failed with an IOException. The variable exception contains a reference to the exception object that was thrown. The catch clause can analyze that object to find out more details about the failure. For example, you can get a printout of the chain of method calls that lead to the exception, by calling

```
exception.printStackTrace()
```

In these sample catch clauses, we merely inform the user of the source of the problem. A better way of dealing with the exception would be to give the user another chance to provide a correct input—see Section 15.6 for a solution.

It is important to remember that you should place catch clauses only in methods in which you can competently handle the particular exception type.

SELF CHECK

5. Suppose the file with the given file name exists and has no contents. Trace the flow of execution in the try block in this section.

6. Is there a difference between catching checked and unchecked exceptions?

QUALITY TIP 15.1

Throw Early, Catch Late

> It is better to declare that a method throws a checked exception than to handle the exception poorly.

When a method notices a problem that it cannot solve, it is generally better to throw an exception rather than try to come up with an imperfect fix (such as doing nothing or returning a default value).

Conversely, a method should only catch an exception if it can really remedy the situation. Otherwise, the best remedy is simply to have the exception propagate to its caller, allowing it to be caught by a competent handler.

These principles can be summarized with the slogan "throw early, catch late".

QUALITY TIP 15.2

Do Not Squelch Exceptions

When you call a method that throws a checked exception and you haven't specified a handler, the compiler complains. In your eagerness to continue your work, it is an understandable impulse to shut the compiler up by squelching the exception:

```
try
{
    FileReader reader = new FileReader(filename);
    // Compiler complained about FileNotFoundException
    . . .
}
catch (Exception e) {} // So there!
```

The do-nothing exception handler fools the compiler into thinking that the exception has been handled. In the long run, this is clearly a bad idea. Exceptions were designed to transmit problem reports to a competent handler. Installing an incompetent handler simply hides an error condition that could be serious.

15.4 The finally Clause

Occasionally, you need to take some action whether or not an exception is thrown. The finally construct is used to handle this situation. Here is a typical situation. A program can only open a finite number of files at one time. Therefore, you need to close all file readers after you are done with them.

In the following code segment, we open a file, call one or more methods, and then close the file:

```
FileReader reader = new FileReader(filename);
Scanner in = new Scanner(reader);
readData(in);
reader.close(); // May never get here
```

Now suppose that one of the methods before the last line throws an exception. Then the call to close is never executed! Solve this problem by placing the call to close inside a finally clause:

```
FileReader reader = new FileReader(filename);
try
{
    Scanner in = new Scanner(reader);
    readData(in);
}
finally
{
    reader.close();
}
```

> Once a try block is entered, the statements in a finally clause are guaranteed to be executed, whether or not an exception is thrown.

In a normal case, there will be no problem. When the try block is completed, the finally clause is executed, and the file is closed. However, if an exception occurs, the finally clause is also executed before the exception is passed to its handler.

Use the finally clause whenever you need to do some clean up, such as closing a file, to ensure that the clean up happens no matter how the method exits.

It is also possible to have a finally clause following one or more catch clauses. Then the code in the finally clause is executed whenever the try block is exited in any of three ways:

1. After completing the last statement of the try block

2. After completing the last statement of a catch clause, if this try block caught an exception

3. When an exception was thrown in the try block and not caught

However, we recommend that you don't mix catch and finally clauses in the same try block—see Quality Tip 15.3.

SYNTAX 15.4 finally Clause

```
try
{
    statement
    statement
    . . .
}
finally
{
    statement
    statement
    . . .
}
```

Example:

```
FileReader reader = new FileReader(filename);
try
{
    readData(reader);
}
finally
{
    reader.close();
}
```

Purpose:

To ensure that the statements in the finally clause are executed whether or not the statements in the try block throw an exception.

SELF CHECK

7. Why was the reader variable declared outside the try block?
8. Suppose the file with the given name does not exist. Trace the flow of execution of the code segment in this section.

QUALITY TIP 15.3

Do Not Use catch and finally in the Same try Statement

It is tempting to combine catch and finally clauses, but the resulting code can be hard to understand. Instead, you should use a try/finally statement to close resources and a separate try/catch statement to handle errors. For example,

```
try
{
    FileReader reader = new FileReader(filename);
    try
    {
        // Read input
    }
    finally
    {
        reader.close();
    }
}
catch (IOException exception)
{
    // Handle exception
}
```

Note that the nested statements work correctly if the call `reader.close()` throws an exception—see Exercise R15.12.

15.5 Designing Your Own Exception Types

Sometimes none of the standard exception types describe your particular error condition well enough. In that case, you can design your own exception class. Consider a bank account. Let's report an `InsufficientFundsException` when an attempt is made to withdraw an amount from a bank account that exceeds the current balance.

```
if (amount > balance)
{
    throw new InsufficientFundsException(
        "withdrawal of " + amount + " exceeds balance of " + balance);
}
```

> You can design your own exception types—subclasses of Exception or RuntimeException.

Now you need to define the `InsufficientFundsException` class. Should it be a checked or an unchecked exception? Is it the fault of some external event, or is it the fault of the programmer? We take the position that the programmer could have prevented the exceptional condition—after all, it would have been an easy matter to check whether `amount <= account.getBalance()` before calling the `withdraw` method. Therefore, the exception should be an unchecked exception and extend the `RuntimeException` class or one of its subclasses.

It is customary to provide two constructors for an exception class: a default constructor and a constructor that accepts a message string describing the reason for the exception. Here is the definition of the exception class.

```
public class InsufficientFundsException
        extends RuntimeException
{
```

```
      public InsufficientFundsException() {}

      public InsufficientFundsException(String message)
      {
          super(message);
      }
  }
```

When the exception is caught, its message string can be retrieved using the getMessage method.

SELF CHECK

9. What is the purpose of the call super(message) in the second Insufficient-FundsException constructor?

10. Suppose you read bank account data from a file. Contrary to your expectation, the next input value is not of type double. You decide to implement a BadData-Exception. Which exception class should you extend?

QUALITY TIP 15.4

Do Throw Specific Exceptions

When throwing an exception, you should choose an exception class that describes the situation as closely as possible. For example, it would be a bad idea to simply throw a Runtime-Exception object when a bank account has insufficient funds. This would make it far too difficult to catch the exception. After all, if you caught all exceptions of type Runtime-Exception, your catch clause would also be activated by exceptions of the type NullPointer-Exception, ArrayIndexOutOfBoundsException, and so on. You would then need to carefully examine the exception object and attempt to deduce whether the exception was caused by insufficient funds.

If the standard library does not have an exception class that describes your particular error situation, simply define a new exception class.

15.6 Case Study: A Complete Example

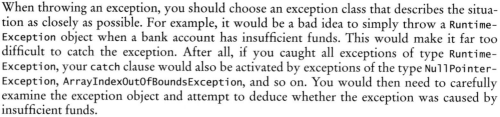

This section walks through a complete example of a program with exception handling. The program asks a user for the name of a file. The file is expected to contain data values. The first line of the file contains the total number of values, and the remaining lines contain the data. A typical input file looks like this:

```
3
1.45
-2.1
0.05
```

What can go wrong? There are two principal risks.

- The file might not exist.
- The file might have data in the wrong format.

Who can detect these faults? The FileReader constructor will throw an exception when the file does not exist. The methods that process the input values need to throw an exception when they find an error in the data format.

What exceptions can be thrown? The FileReader constructor throws a FileNot-FoundException when the file does not exist, which is very appropriate in our situation. The close method of the FileReader class can throw an IOException. Finally, when the file data is in the wrong format, we will throw a BadDataException, a custom checked exception class. We use a checked exception because corruption of a data file is beyond the control of the programmer.

Who can remedy the faults that the exceptions report? Only the main method of the DataSetTester program interacts with the user. It catches the exceptions, prints appropriate error messages, and gives the user another chance to enter a correct file.

File DataSetTester.java

```
 1  import java.io.FileNotFoundException;
 2  import java.io.IOException;
 3  import java.util.Scanner;
 4
 5  public class DataSetTester
 6  {
 7     public static void main(String[] args)
 8     {
 9        Scanner in = new Scanner(System.in);
10        DataSetReader reader = new DataSetReader();
11
12        boolean done = false;
13        while (!done)
14        {
15           try
16           {
17              System.out.println("Please enter the file name: ");
18              String filename = in.next();
19
20              double[] data = reader.readFile(filename);
21              double sum = 0;
22              for (double d : data) sum = sum + d;
23              System.out.println("The sum is " + sum);
24              done = true;
25           }
26           catch (FileNotFoundException exception)
27           {
28              System.out.println("File not found.");
29           }
30           catch (BadDataException exception)
31           {
32              System.out.println("Bad data: " + exception.getMessage());
33           }
```

```
34              catch (IOException exception)
35              {
36                  exception.printStackTrace();
37              }
38          }
39      }
40  }
```

The catch clauses in the main method give a human-readable error report if the file was not found or bad data was encountered. However, if another IOException occurs, then we print the stack trace so that a programmer can diagnose the problem.

The following readFile method of the DataSetReader class constructs the Scanner object and calls the readData method. It is completely unconcerned with any exceptions. If there is a problem with the input file, it simply passes the exception to its caller.

```
public double[] readFile(String filename)
        throws IOException, BadDataException
{
    FileReader reader = new FileReader(filename);
    try
    {
        Scanner in = new Scanner(reader);
        readData(in);
    }
    finally
    {
        reader.close();
    }
    return data;
}
```

Note how the finally clause ensures that the file is closed even when an exception occurs.

Also note that the throws specifier of the readFile method need not include the FileNotFoundException class because it is a subclass of IOException.

Next, here is the readData method. It reads the number of values, constructs an array, and calls readValue for each data value.

```
private void readData(Scanner in) throws BadDataException
{
    if (!in.hasNextInt())
        throw new BadDataException("Length expected");
    int numberOfValues = in.nextInt();
    data = new double[numberOfValues];

    for (int i = 0; i < numberOfValues; i++)
        readValue(in, i);

    if (in.hasNext())
        throw new BadDataException("End of file expected");
}
```

This method checks for two potential errors. The file might not start with an integer, or it might have additional data after reading all values.

However, this method makes no attempt to catch any exceptions. If the read-Value method throws an exception—which it will if there aren't enough values in the file—the exception is simply passed on to the caller.

Here is the readValue method:

```
private void readValue(Scanner in, int i) throws BadDataException
{
    if (!in.hasNextDouble())
        throw new BadDataException("Data value expected");
    data[i] = in.nextDouble();
}
```

To see the exception handling at work, look at a specific error scenario.

1. DataSetTester.main calls DataSetReader.readFile.

2. readFile calls readData.

3. readData calls readValue.

4. readValue doesn't find the expected value and throws a BadDataException.

5. readValue has no handler for the exception and terminates immediately.

6. readData has no handler for the exception and terminates immediately.

7. readFile has no handler for the exception and terminates immediately after executing the finally clause and closing the file.

8. DataSetTester.main has a handler for a BadDataException. That handler prints a message to the user. Afterwards, the user is given another chance to enter a file name. Note that the statements computing the sum of the values have been skipped.

This example shows the separation between error detection (in the DataSetReader. readValue method) and error handling (in the DataSetTester.main method). In between the two are the readData and readFile methods, which just pass exceptions along.

File DataSetReader.java

```
 1  import java.io.FileReader;
 2  import java.io.IOException;
 3  import java.util.Scanner;
 4
 5  /**
 6      Reads a data set from a file. The file must have the format
 7      numberOfValues
 8      value1
 9      value2
10      . . .
11  */
12  public class DataSetReader
13  {
```

```
14      /**
15          Reads a data set.
16          @param filename the name of the file holding the data
17          @return the data in the file
18      */
19      public double[] readFile(String filename)
20              throws IOException, BadDataException
21      {
22          FileReader reader = new FileReader(filename);
23          try
24          {
25              Scanner in = new Scanner(reader);
26              readData(in);
27          }
28          finally
29          {
30              reader.close();
31          }
32          return data;
33      }
34
35      /**
36          Reads all data.
37          @param in the scanner that scans the data
38      */
39      private void readData(Scanner in) throws BadDataException
40      {
41          if (!in.hasNextInt())
42              throw new BadDataException("Length expected");
43          int numberOfValues = in.nextInt();
44          data = new double[numberOfValues];
45
46          for (int i = 0; i < numberOfValues; i++)
47              readValue(in, i);
48
49          if (in.hasNext())
50              throw new BadDataException("End of file expected");
51      }
52
53      /**
54          Reads one data value.
55          @param in the scanner that scans the data
56          @param i the position of the value to read
57      */
58      private void readValue(Scanner in, int i) throws BadDataException
59      {
60          if (!in.hasNextDouble())
61              throw new BadDataException("Data value expected");
62          data[i] = in.nextDouble();
63      }
64
65      private double[] data;
66  }
```

File BadDataException.java

```
1   /**
2       This class reports bad input data.
3   */
4   public class BadDataException extends Exception
5   {
6       public BadDataException() {}
7       public BadDataException(String message)
8       {
9           super(message);
10      }
11  }
```

SELF CHECK

11. Why doesn't the `DataSetReader.readFile` method catch any exceptions?

12. Suppose the user specifies a file that exists and is empty. Trace the flow of execution.

RANDOM FACT 15.1

The Ariane Rocket Incident

The European Space Agency (ESA), Europe's counterpart to NASA, had developed a rocket model called Ariane that it had successfully used several times to launch satellites and scientific experiments into space. However, when a new version, the Ariane 5, was launched on June 4, 1996, from ESA's launch site in Kourou, French Guiana, the rocket veered off course about 40 seconds after liftoff. Flying at an angle of more than 20 degrees, rather than straight up, exerted such an aerodynamic force that the boosters separated, which triggered the automatic self-destruction mechanism. The rocket blew itself up.

The ultimate cause of this accident was an unhandled exception! The rocket contained two identical devices (called inertial reference systems) that processed flight data from measuring devices and turned the data into information about the rocket position. The onboard computer used the position information for controlling the boosters. The same inertial reference systems and computer software had worked fine on the Ariane 4.

Figure 2   The Explosion of the Ariane Rocket

However, due to design changes to the rocket, one of the sensors measured a larger acceleration force than had been encountered in the Ariane 4. That value, expressed as a floating-point value, was stored in a 16-bit integer (like a short variable in Java). Unlike Java, the Ada language, used for the device software, generates an exception if a floating-point number is too large to be converted to an integer. Unfortunately, the programmers of the device had decided that this situation would never happen and didn't provide an exception handler.

When the overflow did happen, the exception was triggered and, because there was no handler, the device shut itself off. The onboard computer sensed the failure and switched over to the backup device. However, that device had shut itself off for exactly the same reason, something that the designers of the rocket had not expected. They figured that the devices might fail for mechanical reasons, and the chances of two devices having the same mechanical failure was considered remote. At that point, the rocket was without reliable position information and went off course.

Perhaps it would have been better if the software hadn't been so thorough? If it had ignored the overflow, the device wouldn't have been shut off. It would have computed bad data. But then the device would have reported wrong position data, which could have been just as fatal. Instead, a correct implementation should have caught overflow exceptions and come up with some strategy to recompute the flight data. Clearly, giving up was not a reasonable option in this context.

The advantage of the exception-handling mechanism is that it makes these issues explicit to programmers—something to think about when you curse the Java compiler for complaining about uncaught exceptions.

CHAPTER SUMMARY

1. To signal an exceptional condition, use the throw statement to throw an exception object.

2. When you throw an exception, the current method terminates immediately.

3. There are two kinds of exceptions: checked and unchecked. Unchecked exceptions extend the class RuntimeException or Error.

4. Checked exceptions are due to external circumstances that the programmer cannot prevent. The compiler checks that your program handles these exceptions.

5. Add a throws specifier to a method that can throw a checked exception.

6. In a method that is ready to handle a particular exception type, place the statements that can cause the exception inside a try block, and the handler inside a catch clause.

7. It is better to declare that a method throws a checked exception than to handle the exception poorly.

8. Once a try block is entered, the statements in a finally clause are guaranteed to be executed, whether or not an exception is thrown.

9. You can design your own exception types—subclasses of Exception or Runtime-Exception.

CLASSES, OBJECTS, AND METHODS INTRODUCED IN THIS CHAPTER

```
java.io.EOFException                      java.lang.NumberFormatException
java.io.FileNotFoundException             java.lang.RuntimeException
java.io.IOException                       java.lang.Throwable
java.lang.Error                              getMessage
java.lang.IllegalArgumentException           printStackTrace
java.lang.IllegalStateException           java.util.InputMismatchException
java.lang.NullPointerException            java.util.NoSuchElementException
```

REVIEW EXERCISES

Exercise R15.1. What is the difference between throwing an exception and catching an exception?

Exercise R15.2. What is a checked exception? What is an unchecked exception? Is a NullPointerException checked or unchecked? Which exceptions do you need to declare with the throws keyword?

Exercise R15.3. Why don't you need to declare that your method might throw a NullPointerException?

Exercise R15.4. When your program executes a throw statement, which statement is executed next?

Exercise R15.5. What happens if an exception does not have a matching catch clause?

Exercise R15.6. What can your program do with the exception object that a catch clause receives?

Exercise R15.7. Is the type of the exception object always the same as the type declared in the catch clause that catches it?

Exercise R15.8. What kind of objects can you throw? Can you throw a string? An integer?

Exercise R15.9. What is the purpose of the finally clause? Give an example of how it can be used.

Exercise R15.10. What happens when an exception is thrown, the code of a finally clause executes, and that code throws an exception of a different kind than the original one? Which one is caught by a surrounding catch clause? Write a sample program to try it out.

Exercise R15.11. Which exceptions can the next and nextInt methods of the Scanner class throw? Are they checked exceptions or unchecked exceptions?

Exercise R15.12. Suppose the catch clause in the example of Quality Tip 15.3 had been moved to the inner try block, eliminating the outer try block. Does the modified code work correctly if (a) the FileReader constructor throws an exception and (b) the close method throws an exception?

Exercise R15.13. Suppose the program in Section 15.6 reads a file containing the following values:

```
0
1
2
3
```

What is the outcome? How could the program be improved to give a more accurate error report?

Exercise R15.14. Can the readFile method in Section 15.6 throw a NullPointer-Exception? If so, how?

PROGRAMMING EXERCISES

Exercise P15.1. Modify the BankAccount class to throw an IllegalArgumentException when the account is constructed with a negative balance, when a negative amount is deposited, or when an amount that is not between 0 and the current balance is withdrawn. Write a test program that causes all three exceptions to occur and that catches them all.

Exercise P15.2. Repeat Exercise P15.1, but throw exceptions of three exception types that you define.

Exercise P15.3. Write a program that asks the user to input a set of coin values and names. When the user enters a coin value that is not a number, give the user a second chance to enter the value. After two chances, quit the program. Add all correctly specified coins to a purse, and print its total value when the user is done entering data. Use exception handling to detect improper inputs.

Exercise P15.4. Repeat Exercise P15.3, but give the user as many chances as necessary to enter a correct coin value. Quit the program only when the user requests to exit.

Exercise P15.5. Modify the BankAccount class so that the withdraw method throws an InsufficientFundsException when the balance is less than the withdrawal amount. You need to define the exception class.

Exercise P15.6. Modify the DataSetReader class so that you do not call hasNextInt or hasNextDouble. Simply have nextInt and nextDouble throw an InputMismatchException or NoSuchElementException and catch it in the main method.

Exercise P15.7. Write a program that reads in a set of coin descriptions from a file. The input file has the format

```
coinName1 coinValue1
coinName2 coinValue2
. . .
```

Add a method

```
void read(Scanner in) throws IOException
```

to the Coin class. Throw an exception if the current line is not properly formatted. Then implement a method

```
static ArrayList<Coin> readFile(String filename) throws IOException
```

In the main method, call readFile. If an exception is thrown, give the user a chance to select another file. If you read all coins successfully, print the total value.

Exercise P15.8. Design a class Bank that contains a number of bank accounts. Each account has an account number and a current balance. Add an accountNumber field to the BankAccount class. Store the bank accounts in an array list. Write a readFile method of the Bank class for reading a file with the format

```
accountNumber1  balance1
accountNumber2  balance2
. . .
```

Implement read methods for the Bank and BankAccount classes. Write a sample program to read in a file with bank accounts, then print the account with the highest balance. If the file is not properly formatted, give the user a chance to select another file.

PROGRAMMING PROJECTS

Project 15.1. You can read the contents of a web page with this sequence of commands.

```
String address = "http://java.sun.com/index.html";
URL u = new URL(address);
URLConnection connection = u.openConnection();
InputStream stream = connection.getInputStream();
Scanner in = new Scanner(stream);
. . .
```

Some of these methods may throw exceptions—check out the API documentation. Design a class LinkFinder that finds all hyperlinks of the form

```
<a href="link">link text</a>
```

Throw an exception if you find a malformed hyperlink. Extra credit if your program can follow the links that it finds and find links in those web pages as well. (This is the method that search engines such as Google use to find web sites.)

ANSWERS TO SELF-CHECK QUESTIONS

1. Throw an exception if the amount being deposited is less than zero.

2. The balance is still zero because the last statement of the withdraw method was never executed.

3. The specification throws IOException is sufficient because FileNotFound-Exception is a subclass of IOException.

4. Because programmers should simply check for null pointers instead of trying to handle a NullPointerException.

5. The FileReader constructor succeeds, and in is constructed. Then the call in.next() throws a NoSuchElementException, and the try block is aborted. None of the catch clauses match, so none are executed. If none of the enclosing method calls catch the exception, the program terminates.

6. No—you catch both exception types in the same way, as you can see from the code example on page 558. Recall that IOException is a checked exception and NumberFormatException is an unchecked exception.

7. If it had been declared inside the try block, its scope would only have extended to the end of the try block, and the finally clause could not have closed it.

8. The FileReader constructor throws an exception. The finally clause is executed. Since reader is null, the call to close is not executed. Next, a catch clause that matches the FileNotFoundException is located. If none exists, the program terminates.

9. To pass the exception message string to the RuntimeException superclass.

10. Exception or IOException are both good choices. Because file corruption is beyond the control of the programmer, this should be a checked exception, so it would be wrong to extend RuntimeException.

11. It would not be able to do much with them. The DataSetReader class is a reusable class that may be used for systems with different languages and different user interfaces. Thus, it cannot engage in a dialog with the program user.

12. DataSetTester.main calls DataSetReader.readFile, which calls readData. The call in.hasNextInt() returns false, and readData throws a BadDataException. The readFile method doesn't catch it, so it propagates back to main, where it is caught.

Files and Streams

- To be able to read and write text files
- To become familiar with the concepts of text and binary formats
- To learn about encryption
- To understand when to use sequential and random file access
- To be able to read and write objects using serialization

In this chapter you will learn how to write Java programs that interact with disk files and other sources of bytes and characters. You will learn about text and binary formats, and about sequential and random access to the data in a file. We will discuss how you can use object serialization to save and load complex objects with very little effort. As an application of file access, you will study a program for encrypting and decrypting sensitive data.

16.1 Reading and Writing Text Files

We begin this chapter by discussing the common task of reading and writing files that contain text. Examples are files that are created with a simple text editor, such as Windows Notepad, as well as Java source code and HTML files.

The simplest mechanism for reading text is to use the Scanner class. You already know how to use a Scanner for reading console input. To read input from a disk file, first construct a FileReader object with the name of the input file, then use the FileReader to construct a Scanner object:

```
FileReader reader = new FileReader("input.txt");
Scanner in = new Scanner(reader);
```

> When reading text files, use the Scanner class.

This Scanner object reads text from the file input.txt. You can use the Scanner methods (such as next, nextLine, nextInt, and nextDouble) to read data from the input file.

To write output to a file, you construct a PrintWriter object with the given file name, for example

> When writing text files, use the PrintWriter class and the print/println methods.

```
PrintWriter out = new PrintWriter("output.txt");
```

If the output file already exists, it is emptied before the new data are written into it. If the file doesn't exist, an empty file is created.

Use the familiar print and println methods to send numbers, objects, and strings to a PrintWriter:

```
out.println(29.95);
out.println(new Rectangle(5, 10, 15, 25));
out.println("Hello, World!");
```

The print and println methods convert numbers to their decimal string representations and use the toString method to convert objects to strings.

When you are done writing to a PrintWriter, be sure to *close* it:

> You must close all files when you are done processing them.

```
out.close();
```

If your program exits without closing the PrintWriter, not all of the output may be written to the disk file.

The following program puts these concepts to work. It reads all lines of an input file and sends them to the output file, preceded by *line numbers*. If the input file is

```
Mary had a little lamb
Whose fleece was white as snow.
And everywhere that Mary went,
The lamb was sure to go!
```

then the program produces the output file

```
/* 1 */ Mary had a little lamb
/* 2 */ Whose fleece was white as snow.
/* 3 */ And everywhere that Mary went,
/* 4 */ The lamb was sure to go!
```

The line numbers are enclosed in /* */ delimiters so that the program can be used for numbering Java source files.

File LineNumberer.java

```java
1  import java.io.FileReader;
2  import java.io.IOException;
3  import java.io.PrintWriter;
4  import java.util.Scanner;
5
6  public class LineNumberer
7  {
8     public static void main(String[] args)
9     {
10        Scanner console = new Scanner(System.in);
11        System.out.print("Input file: ");
12        String inputFileName = console.next();
13        System.out.print("Output file: ");
14        String outputFileName = console.next();
15
16        try
17        {
18           FileReader reader = new FileReader(inputFileName);
19           Scanner in = new Scanner(reader);
20           PrintWriter out = new PrintWriter(outputFileName);
21           int lineNumber = 1;
22
23           while (in.hasNextLine())
24           {
25              String line = in.nextLine();
26              out.println("/* " + lineNumber + " */ " + line);
27              lineNumber++;
28           }
29
30           out.close();
31        }
32        catch (IOException exception)
33        {
34           System.out.println("Error processing file: " + exception);
35        }
36     }
37  }
```

SELF CHECK

1. What happens when you supply the same name for the input and output files to the LineNumberer program?
2. What happens when you supply the name of a nonexistent input file to the LineNumberer program?

COMMON ERROR 16.1

Backslashes in File Names

When you specify a file name as a constant string, and the name contains backslash characters (as in a Windows file name), you must supply each backslash twice:

```
in = new FileReader("c:\\homework\\input.dat");
```

Recall that a single backslash inside quoted strings is an *escape character* that is combined with another character to form a special meaning, such as \n for a newline character. The \\ combination denotes a single backslash.

When a user supplies a file name to a program, however, the user should not type the backslash twice.

ADVANCED TOPIC 16.1

File Dialog Boxes

The JFileChooser dialog box allows users to select a file by navigating through directories.

In a program with a graphical user interface, you will want to use a file dialog box (such as the one shown in Figure 1) whenever the users of your program need to pick a file. The JFileChooser class implements a file dialog box for the Swing user interface toolkit.

The JFileChooser class relies on another class, File, which describes disk files and directories. For example,

A File object describes a file or directory.

```
File inputFile = new File("input.txt");
```

describes the file input.txt in the current directory. The File class has methods to delete or rename the file. The file does not actually have to exist—you may want to pass the File object to an output stream or writer so that the file can be created. The exists method returns true if the file already exists.

You can pass a File object to the constructor of a file reader, writer, or

You cannot directly use a File object for reading or writing. You still need to construct a file reader, writer, or stream from the File object. Simply pass the File object in the constructor.

```
FileReader in = new FileReader(inputFile);
```

The JFileChooser class has many options to fine-tune the display of the dialog box, but in its most basic form it is quite simple: Construct a file chooser object; then call the showOpenDialog or showSaveDialog method. Both methods show the same dialog box, but the button for selecting a file is labeled "Open" or "Save", depending on which method you call.

For better placement of the dialog box on the screen, you can specify the user interface component over which to pop up the dialog box. If you don't care where the dialog box pops up, you can simply pass null. These methods return either JFileChooser.APPROVE_OPTION, if the user has chosen a file, or JFileChooser.CANCEL_OPTION, if the user canceled the selection. If a file was chosen, then you call the getSelectedFile method to obtain a File object that describes the file. Here is a complete example:

```
JFileChooser chooser = new JFileChooser();
FileReader in = null;
if (chooser.showOpenDialog(null) == JFileChooser.APPROVE_OPTION)
{
   File selectedFile = chooser.getSelectedFile();
   reader = new FileReader(selectedFile);
   . . .
}
```

Figure 1   A JFileChooser Dialog Box

ADVANCED TOPIC 16.2

Command Line Arguments

Depending on the operating system and Java development system used, there are different methods of starting a program—for example, by selecting "Run" in the compilation environment, by clicking on an icon, or by typing the name of the program at a prompt in a terminal or shell window. The latter method is called "invoking the program from the command line". When you use this method, you must type the name of the program, but you can also type in additional information that the program can use. These additional strings are called *command line arguments.*

For example, it is convenient to specify the input and output file names for the Line-Numberer program on the command line:

```
java LineNumberer input.txt numbered.txt
```

> When you launch a program from the command line, you can specify arguments after the program name. The program can access these strings by processing the args parameter of the main method.

The strings that are typed after the Java program name are placed into the args parameter of the main method. (Now you finally know the use of the args parameter that you have seen in so many programs!)

For example, with the given program invocation, the args parameter of the LineNumberer.main method has the following contents:

- args[0] is "input.txt"
- args[1] is "output.txt"

The main method can then process these parameters, for example:

```
if (args.length >= 1)
   inputFileName = args[0];
```

It is entirely up to the program what to do with the command line argument strings. It is customary to interpret strings starting with a hyphen (-) as options and other strings as file names. For example, we may want to enhance the LineNumberer program so that a -c option places line numbers inside comment delimiters; for example

```
java LineNumberer -c HelloWorld.java HelloWorld.txt
```

If the -c option is missing, the delimiters should not be included. Here is how the main method can analyze the command line arguments:

```
for (String a : args)
{
   if (a.startsWith("-")) // It's an option
   {
      if (a.equals("-c")) useCommentDelimiters = true;
   }
   else if (inputFileName == null) inputFileName = a;
   else if (outputFileName == null) outputFileName = a;
}
```

Should you support command line interfaces for your programs, or should you instead supply a graphical user interface with file chooser dialog boxes? For a casual and infrequent user, the graphical user interface is much better. The user interface guides the user along and makes it possible to navigate the application without much knowledge. But for a frequent user, graphical user interfaces have a major drawback—they are hard to automate. If you need to process hundreds of files every day, you could spend all your time typing file names into file chooser dialog boxes. But it is not difficult to call a program multiple times automatically with different command line arguments. Productivity Hint 10.1 discusses how to use shell scripts (also called batch files) for this purpose.

16.2 Text and Binary Formats

There are two fundamentally different ways to store data: in *text* format or *binary* format. In text format, data items are represented in human-readable form, as a sequence of *characters*. For example, the integer 12,345 is stored as the sequence of five characters:

```
'1' '2' '3' '4' '5'
```

In binary form, data items are represented in *bytes*. A byte is composed of 8 bits and can denote one of 256 values. For example, in binary format, the integer 12,345 is stored as a sequence of four bytes:

```
0 0 48 57
```

(because $12,345 = 48 \cdot 256 + 57$).

Streams access sequences of bytes. Readers and writers access sequences of characters.

If you store information in text form, as a sequence of characters, you need to use the Reader and Writer classes and their subclasses to process input and output. If you store information in binary form, as a sequence of bytes, you use the InputStream and OutputStream classes and their subclasses.

Text input and output are more convenient for humans, because it is easier to produce input (just use a text editor) and it is easier to check that output is correct (just look at the output file in an editor). However, binary storage is more compact and more efficient.

Use FileReader, FileWriter, FileInputStream, and FileOutputStream classes to read and write disk files.

To read text data from a disk file, you create a FileReader object:

```
FileReader reader = new FileReader("input.txt");
```

To read binary data from a disk file, you create a FileInputStream object instead:

```
FileInputStream inputStream =
        new FileInputStream("input.bin");
```

Similarly, you use FileWriter and FileOutputStream objects to write data to a disk file in text or binary form respectively:

```
FileWriter writer = new FileWriter("output.txt");
FileOutputStream outputStream = new FileOutputStream("output.bin");
```

The read method returns an integer, either –1, at the end of the file, or another value, which you need to cast to a char or byte.

The Reader class has a method, read, to read a single character at a time. (The FileReader class overrides this method to obtain the characters from a disk file.) However, the read method actually returns an int so that it can signal either that a character has been read or that the end of input has been reached. At the end of input, read returns -1. Otherwise it returns the character (as an integer between 0 and 65,535). You should test the return value and, if it is not -1, cast it to a char:

```
Reader reader = . . .;
int next = reader.read();
char c;
if (next != -1)
   c = (char) next;
```

The InputStream class also has a method, read, to read a single byte. The method also returns an int, namely either the byte that was input (as an integer between 0 and 255) or the integer -1 if the end of the input stream has been reached. You should test the return value and, if it is not -1, cast it to a byte:

```
InputStream in = . . .;
int next = in.read();
byte b;
if (next != -1)
    b = (byte) next;
```

Similarly, the Writer and FileOutputStream classes have a write method to write a single character or byte.

These basic methods are the only input and output methods that the file input and output classes provide. The Java stream package is built on the principle that each class should have a very focused responsibility. The job of a FileInputStream is to interact with files. Its job is to get bytes, not to analyze them. If you want to read numbers, strings, or other objects, you have to combine the class with other classes whose responsibility is to group individual bytes or characters together into numbers, strings, and objects. You will see an example of those classes in Section 16.5.

SELF CHECK

3. Suppose you need to read an image file that contains color values for each pixel in the image. Will you use a Reader or an InputStream?

4. Why do the read methods of the Reader and InputStream classes return an int and not a char or byte?

COMMON ERROR 16.2

Negative byte Values

In Java, the byte type is a *signed* type. There are 256 values of the byte type, from −128 to 127. The starting bit of the byte is the *sign bit*. If it is on, the number is negative. In converting an integer into a byte, only the least significant byte of the integer is taken, and the remaining bytes are ignored. The result can be negative even if the integer is positive. For example,

```
int n = 233; // Binary 00000000 00000000 00000000 11101001
byte b = (byte) n; // Binary 11101001, sign bit is on
if (b == n) . . . // Not true! b is negative, n is positive
```

When the byte is converted back to an integer, then the result is still negative. In particular, it is different from the original.

Here is an even trickier case. Consider this test:

```
int next = in.read();
byte b = (byte) next;
if (b == 'é') . . .
```

This test is *never* true, even if next was equal to the Unicode value for the 'é' character. That Unicode value happens to be 233, but a single byte is always a value between –128 and 127. American readers won't be too concerned, because all characters and symbols used in American English have Unicode values in the "safe" range between 1 and 127, but international programmers who use characters with Unicode values between 128 and 255 find this a source of continual frustration.

16.3 An Encryption Program

In this section, you will see a program that demonstrates typical file access techniques. The program *encrypts* a file—that is, scrambles it so that it is unreadable except to those who know the decryption method and the secret keyword. Ignoring over 2000 years of progress in the field of encryption, we will use a method familiar to Julius Caesar. The person performing any encryption chooses an *encryption key*; here the key is a number between 1 and 25 that indicates the shift to be used in encrypting each letter. For example, if the key is 3, replace A with D, B with E, and so on (see Figure 2).

To decrypt, simply use the negative of the encryption key. For example, to decrypt the message of Figure 2, use a key of –3.

In this program we process binary data—we read each byte separately, encrypt it, and write the encrypted byte.

```
int next = in.read();
if (next == -1)
   done = true;
else
{
   byte b = (byte) next;
   byte c = encrypt(b);
   out.write(c);
}
```

In a more complex encryption program, you would read a block of bytes, encrypt the block, and write it out.

Because the program reads binary data, it uses streams, not readers and writers.

Try out the program on a file of your choice. You will find that the encrypted file is unreadable. In fact, because the newline characters are transformed, you may not be able to read the encrypted file in a text editor. To decrypt, simply run the program again and supply the negative of the encryption key.

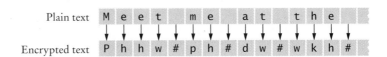

Figure 2   The Caesar Cipher

File Encryptor.java

```java
1  import java.io.File;
2  import java.io.FileInputStream;
3  import java.io.FileOutputStream;
4  import java.io.InputStream;
5  import java.io.OutputStream;
6  import java.io.IOException;
7
8  /**
9     An encryptor encrypts files using the Caesar cipher.
10    For decryption, use an encryptor whose key is the
11    negative of the encryption key.
12 */
13 public class Encryptor
14 {
15    /**
16       Constructs an encryptor.
17       @param aKey the encryption key
18    */
19    public Encryptor(int aKey)
20    {
21       key = aKey;
22    }
23
24    /**
25       Encrypts the contents of a file.
26       @param inFile the input file
27       @param outFile the output file
28    */
29    public void encryptFile(String inFile, String outFile)
30          throws IOException
31    {
32       InputStream in = null;
33       OutputStream out = null;
34
35       try
36       {
37          in = new FileInputStream(inFile);
38          out = new FileOutputStream(outFile);
39          encryptStream(in, out);
40       }
41       finally
42       {
43          if (in != null) in.close();
44          if (out != null) out.close();
45       }
46    }
47
48    /**
49       Encrypts the contents of a stream.
50       @param in the input stream
51       @param out the output stream
52    */
```

```
53     public void encryptStream(InputStream in, OutputStream out)
54           throws IOException
55     {
56        boolean done = false;
57        while (!done)
58        {
59           int next = in.read();
60           if (next == -1) done = true;
61           else
62           {
63              byte b = (byte) next;
64              byte c = encrypt(b);
65              out.write(c);
66           }
67        }
68     }
69
70     /**
71        Encrypts a byte.
72        @param b  the byte to encrypt
73        @return  the encrypted byte
74     */
75     public byte encrypt(byte b)
76     {
77        return (byte) (b + key);
78     }
79
80     private int key;
81  }
```

File EncryptorTester.java

```
1  import java.io.IOException;
2  import java.util.Scanner;
3
4  /**
5     A program to test the Caesar cipher encryptor.
6  */
7  public class EncryptorTester
8  {
9     public static void main(String[] args)
10    {
11       Scanner in = new Scanner(System.in);
12       try
13       {
14          System.out.print("Input file: ");
15          String inFile = in.next();
16          System.out.print("Output file: ");
17          String outFile = in.next();
18          System.out.print("Encryption key: ");
19          int key = in.nextInt();
20          Encryptor crypt = new Encryptor(key);
21          crypt.encryptFile(inFile, outFile);
```

```
22          }
23          catch (IOException exception)
24          {
25              System.out.println("Error processing file: " + exception);
26          }
27      }
28 }
```

SELF CHECK

5. Decrypt the following message: Khoor/#Zruog$.
6. Can you use this program to encrypt a binary file, for example, an image file?

RANDOM FACT 16.1

Encryption Algorithms

The exercises at the end of this chapter give a few algorithms to encrypt text. Don't actually use any of those methods to send secret messages to your lover. Any skilled cryptographer can break those schemes in a very short time—that is, reconstruct the original text without knowing the secret keyword.

In 1978 Ron Rivest, Adi Shamir, and Leonard Adleman introduced an encryption method that is much more powerful. The method is called RSA encryption, after the last names of its inventors. The exact scheme is too complicated to present here, but it is not difficult to follow. You can find the details in [1].

RSA is a remarkable encryption method. There are two keys: a public key and a private key. (See Figure 3.) You can print the public key on your business card (or in your e-mail signature block) and give it to anyone. Then anyone can send you messages that only you can decrypt. Even though everyone else knows the public key, and even if they intercept all the messages coming to you, they cannot break the scheme and actually read the messages. In 1994, hundreds of researchers, collaborating over the Internet, cracked an RSA message encrypted with a 129-digit key. Messages encrypted with a key of 230 digits or more are expected to be secure.

The inventors of the algorithm obtained a patent for it. That means that for a period of 20 years, anyone using it had to seek a license from the inventors. They have given permission for most noncommercial usage, but companies that implemented RSA in a product that they sold had to get the patent holder's permission and pay substantial royalties. The RSA patent expired on September 20, 2000, so you are now free to use the algorithm without restriction.

A patent is a deal that society makes with an inventor. For a period of 20 years after the filing date, the inventor has an exclusive right for its commercialization, may collect royalties from others wishing to manufacture the invention, and may even stop competitors from marketing it altogether. In return, the inventor must publish the invention, so that others may learn from it, and must relinquish all claims to it after the protection period ends. The presumption is that, in the absence of patent law, inventors would be reluctant to go through the trouble of inventing, or they would try to cloak their techniques to prevent others from copying their devices.

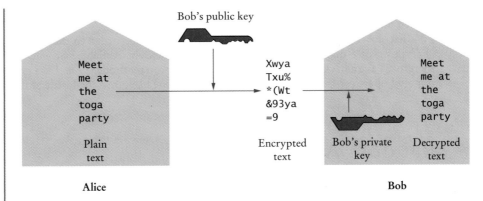

Bob's public key

| Meet me at the toga party | | Xwya Txu% *(Wt &93ya =9 | | Meet me at the toga party |

Plain text

Encrypted text

Bob's private key

Decrypted text

Alice

Bob

Figure 3 Public Key Encryption

What do you think? Are patents a fair deal? Unquestionably, some companies have chosen not to implement RSA, and instead chose a less capable method, because they could not or would not pay the royalties. Thus, it seems that the patent may have hindered, rather than advanced, commerce. Had there not been patent protection, would the inventors have published the method anyway, thereby giving the benefit for society without the cost of the 20-year monopoly? In this case, the answer is probably yes; the inventors were academic researchers, who live on salaries rather than sales receipts and are usually rewarded for their discoveries by a boost in their reputation and careers. Would their followers have been as active in discovering (and patenting) improvements? There is no way of knowing.

Further, is an algorithm even patentable in the first place? Or is it a mathematical fact that belongs to nobody? The patent office did take the latter attitude for a long time. The RSA inventors and many others described their inventions in terms of imaginary electronic devices, rather than algorithms, to circumvent that restriction. Nowadays, the patent office will award software patents.

There is another fascinating aspect to the RSA story. A programmer named Phil Zimmermann developed a program called PGP (for *Pretty Good Privacy*) [2]. PGP implements RSA. That is, you can have it generate a pair of public and private keys, publish the public key, receive encrypted messages from others who use their copy of PGP and your public key, and decrypt them with your private key. Even though the encryption can be performed on any personal computer, decryption is not feasible even with the most powerful computers. You can get a copy of PGP from the MIT distribution site for PGP [3]. As long as it is for personal use, there is no charge, courtesy of Zimmermann and the folks at MIT and RSA.

The existence of PGP bothers the government to no end. They worry that criminals use the package to correspond by e-mail and that the police cannot tap those "conversations". Foreign governments can send communications that the National Security Agency (the premier electronic spy organization of the United States) cannot decipher. In the 1990s, the U.S. government unsuccessfully attempted to standardize on a different encryption scheme, called Skipjack, to which government organizations hold a decryption key that—of course— they promise not to use without a court order. There have been serious proposals to make it illegal to use any other encryption method in the United States. At one time, the government considered charging Zimmermann with breaching another law that forbids the unauthorized export of munitions as a crime and defines cryptographic technology as "munitions". They made the argument that, even though Zimmermann never exported the program, he should have known that it would immediately spread through the Internet when he released it in the United States.

What do you think? Will criminals and terrorists be harder to detect and convict once encryption of e-mail and phone conversations is widely available? Should the government therefore have a backdoor key to any legal encryption method? Or is this a gross violation of our civil liberties? Is it even possible to put the genie back into the bottle at this time?

16.4 Random Access

Reading a file sequentially from the beginning to the end can be inefficient. In this section, you will learn how to directly access arbitrary locations in a file. Consider a file that contains a set of bank accounts. We want to change the balances of some of the accounts. Of course, we can read all account data into an array list, update the information that has changed, and save the data out again. If the data set in the file is very large, we may end up doing a lot of reading and writing just to update a handful of records. It would be better if we could locate the changed information in the file and just replace it.

> In sequential file access, a file is processed one byte at a time. Random access allows access at arbitrary locations in the file, without first reading the bytes preceding the access location.

This is quite different from the file access you have programmed up to now, where you read from a file, starting at the beginning and reading the entire contents until you reached the end. That access pattern is called *sequential access*. Now we would like to access specific locations in a file and change only those locations. This access pattern is called *random access* (see Figure 4). There is nothing "random" about random access—the term just means that you can read and modify any byte stored at any location in the file.

Only disk files support random access; the System.in and System.out streams, which are attached to the keyboard and the terminal window, do not. Each disk file has a special *file pointer* position. Normally, the file pointer is at the end of the file, and any output is appended to the end. However, if you move the file pointer to the middle of the file and write to the file, the output overwrites what is already there. The next read command starts reading input at the file pointer location. You can move the file pointer just beyond the last byte currently in the file but no further.

In Java, you use a RandomAccessFile object to access a file and move a file pointer. To open a random access file, you supply a file name and a string to specify the *open mode*. You can open a file either for reading only ("r") or for reading and writing

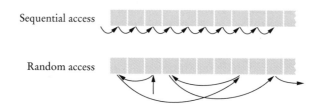

Figure 4
Sequential and Random Access

("rw"). For example, the following command opens the file bank.dat for both reading and writing:

```
RandomAccessFile f = new RandomAccessFile("bank.dat", "rw");
```

The method call

```
f.seek(n);
```

moves the file pointer to byte n counted from the beginning of the file. To find out the current position of the file pointer (counted from the beginning of the file), use

```
n = f.getFilePointer();
```

> A file pointer is a position in a random access file. Because files can be very large, the file pointer is of type long.

Because files can be very large, the file pointer values are long integers. To determine the number of bytes in a file, use the length method:

```
long fileLength = f.length();
```

In the example program at the end of this section, we use a random access file to store a set of bank accounts, each of which has an account number and a current balance. The test program lets you pick an account and deposit money into it.

If you want to manipulate a data set in a file, you have to pay special attention to the formatting of the data. Suppose you just store the data as text. Say account 1001 has a balance of $900, and account 1015 has a balance of 0.

We want to deposit $100 into account 1001. Suppose we place the file pointer to the first character of the old value.

If we now simply write out the new value, the result is

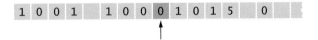

That is not working too well. The update is overwriting the space that separates the fields.

In order to be able to update values in a file, you must give each value a *fixed* size that is sufficiently large. As a result, every record in the file has the same size. This has another advantage: It is then easy to skip quickly to, say, the 50th record, without having to read the first 49 records in. Just set the file pointer to 49 × the record size.

When storing numbers in a file with fixed record sizes, it is easier to store them in binary format, rather than text format. For that reason, the RandomAccessFile class stores binary data. The readInt and writeInt methods read and write integers as four-byte quantities. The `readDouble` and `writeDouble` methods process double-precision floating-point numbers as eight-byte quantities.

```
double x = f.readDouble();
f.writeDouble(x);
```

If we save the account number as an integer and the balance as a `double` value, then each bank account record consists of 12 bytes: 4 bytes for the integer and 8 bytes for the double-precision floating-point value.

Now that we have determined the file layout, we can implement our random access file methods. In the program at the end of this section, we use a `BankData` class to translate between the random access file format and bank account objects. The `size` method determines the total number of accounts by dividing the file length by the size of a record.

```
public int size() throws IOException
{
   return (int) (file.length() / RECORD_SIZE);
}
```

To read the nth account in the file, the read method positions the file pointer to the offset n * RECORD_SIZE, then reads the data, and constructs a bank account object:

```
public BankAccount read(int n)
      throws IOException
{
   file.seek(n * RECORD_SIZE);
   int accountNumber = file.readInt();
   double balance = file.readDouble();
   return new BankAccount(accountNumber, balance);
}
```

Writing an account works the same way:

```
public void write(int n, BankAccount account)
      throws IOException
{
   file.seek(n * RECORD_SIZE);
   file.writeInt(account.getAccountNumber());
   file.writeDouble(account.getBalance());
}
```

The test program asks the user to enter an account number and an amount to deposit. If the account does not currently exist, it is created. The money is deposited, and then the user can choose to continue or quit. The bank data are saved and reloaded when the program is run again.

File BankDataTester.java

```
1  import java.io.IOException;
2  import java.io.RandomAccessFile;
3  import java.util.Scanner;
4
```

```
 5  /**
 6      This program tests random access. You can access existing
 7      accounts and deposit money, or create new accounts. The
 8      accounts are saved in a random access file.
 9  */
10  public class BankDataTester
11  {
12     public static void main(String[] args)
13           throws IOException
14     {
15        Scanner in = new Scanner(System.in);
16        BankData data = new BankData();
17        try
18        {
19           data.open("bank.dat");
20
21           boolean done = false;
22           while (!done)
23           {
24              System.out.print("Account number: ");
25              int accountNumber = in.nextInt();
26              System.out.print("Amount to deposit: ");
27              double amount = in.nextDouble();
28
29              int position = data.find(accountNumber);
30              BankAccount account;
31              if (position >= 0)
32              {
33                 account = data.read(position);
34                 account.deposit(amount);
35                 System.out.println("new balance="
36                       + account.getBalance());
37              }
38              else // Add account
39              {
40                 account = new BankAccount(accountNumber,
41                       amount);
42                 position = data.size();
43                 System.out.println("adding new account");
44              }
45              data.write(position, account);
46
47              System.out.print("Done? (Y/N) ");
48              String input = in.next();
49              if (input.equalsIgnoreCase("Y")) done = true;
50           }
51        }
52        finally
53        {
54           data.close();
55        }
56     }
57  }
```

File BankData.java

```java
1   import java.io.IOException;
2   import java.io.RandomAccessFile;
3
4   /**
5       This class is a conduit to a random access file
6       containing savings account data.
7   */
8   public class BankData
9   {
10      /**
11          Constructs a BankData object that is not associated
12          with a file.
13      */
14      public BankData()
15      {
16          file = null;
17      }
18
19      /**
20          Opens the data file.
21          @param filename the name of the file containing savings
22          account information
23      */
24      public void open(String filename)
25              throws IOException
26      {
27          if (file != null) file.close();
28          file = new RandomAccessFile(filename, "rw");
29      }
30
31      /**
32          Gets the number of accounts in the file.
33          @return the number of accounts
34      */
35      public int size()
36              throws IOException
37      {
38          return (int) (file.length() / RECORD_SIZE);
39      }
40
41      /**
42          Closes the data file.
43      */
44      public void close()
45              throws IOException
46      {
47          if (file != null) file.close();
48          file = null;
49      }
50
```

```
51      /**
52          Reads a savings account record.
53          @param n the index of the account in the data file
54          @return a savings account object initialized with the file data
55      */
56      public BankAccount read(int n)
57              throws IOException
58      {
59          file.seek(n * RECORD_SIZE);
60          int accountNumber = file.readInt();
61          double balance = file.readDouble();
62          return new BankAccount(accountNumber, balance);
63      }
64
65      /**
66          Finds the position of a bank account with a given number.
67          @param accountNumber the number to find
68          @return the position of the account with the given number,
69          or -1 if there is no such account
70      */
71      public int find(int accountNumber)
72              throws IOException
73      {
74          for (int i = 0; i < size(); i++)
75          {
76              file.seek(i * RECORD_SIZE);
77              int a = file.readInt();
78              if (a == accountNumber) // Found a match
79                  return i;
80          }
81          return -1; // No match in the entire file
82      }
83
84      /**
85          Writes a savings account record to the data file.
86          @param n the index of the account in the data file
87          @param account the account to write
88      */
89      public void write(int n, BankAccount account)
90              throws IOException
91      {
92          file.seek(n * RECORD_SIZE);
93          file.writeInt(account.getAccountNumber());
94          file.writeDouble(account.getBalance());
95      }
96
97      private RandomAccessFile file;
98
99      public static final int INT_SIZE = 4;
100     public static final int DOUBLE_SIZE = 8;
101     public static final int RECORD_SIZE
102             = INT_SIZE + DOUBLE_SIZE;
103 }
```

Output

```
Account number: 1001
Amount to deposit: 100
adding new account
Done? (Y/N) N
Account number: 1018
Amount to deposit: 200
adding new account
Done? (Y/N) N
Account number: 1001
Amount to deposit: 1000
new balance=1100.0
Done? (Y/N) Y
```

SELF CHECK

7. Why doesn't `System.out` support random access?
8. What is the advantage of the binary format for storing numbers? What is the disadvantage?

16.5 Object Streams

In the program of Section 16.4, you read `BankAccount` objects by reading each field value separately. Actually, there is an easier way. The `ObjectOutputStream` class can save entire objects out to disk, and the `ObjectInputStream` class can read them back in. Objects are saved in binary format; hence, you use streams and not writers.

For example, you can write a `BankAccount` object to a file as follows:

```
BankAccount b = . . .;
ObjectOutputStream out = new ObjectOutputStream(
      new FileOutputStream("bank.dat"));
out.writeObject(b);
```

> Use object streams to save and restore all instance fields of an object automatically.

The object output stream automatically saves all instance variables of the object to the stream. When reading the object back in, you use the `readObject` method of the `ObjectInputStream` class. That method returns an `Object` reference, so you need to remember the types of the objects that you saved and use a cast:

```
ObjectInputStream in = new ObjectInputStream(
      new FileInputStream("bank.dat"));
BankAccount b = (BankAccount) in.readObject();
```

The `readObject` method can throw a `ClassNotFoundException`—it is a checked exception, so you need to catch or declare it.

You can do even better than that, though. You can store a whole bunch of objects in an array list or array, or inside another object, and then save that object:

```
ArrayList<BankAccount> a = new ArrayList<BankAccount>();
// Now add many BankAccount objects into a
out.writeObject(a);
```

With one instruction, you can save the array list and *all the objects that it references*. You can read all of them back with one instruction:

```
ArrayList<BankAccount> a = (ArrayList<BankAccount>) in.readObject();
```

Of course, if the Bank class contains an ArrayList of bank accounts, then you can simply save and restore a Bank object. Then its array list, and all the BankAccount objects that it contains, are automatically saved and restored as well. The sample program at the end of this section uses this approach.

This is a truly amazing capability that is highly recommended (see Productivity Hint 16.1).

> Objects saved to an object stream must belong to classes that implement the Serializable interface.

To place objects of a particular class into an object stream, the class must implement the Serializable interface. That interface has no methods, so there is no effort involved in implementing it:

```
class BankAccount implements Serializable
{
    . . .
}
```

The process of saving objects to a stream is called *serialization* because each object is assigned a serial number on the stream. If the same object is saved twice, only the serial number is written out the second time. When the objects are read back in, duplicate serial numbers are restored as references to the same object.

Why don't all classes implement Serializable? For security reasons, some programmers may not want to serialize classes with confidential contents. Once a class is serializable, anyone can write its objects to disk and analyze the disk file. There are also some classes that contain values that are meaningless once a program exits, such as operating-system-specific font descriptors. These values should not be serialized.

Here is a sample program that puts serialization to work. The BankAccount and Bank classes are identical to those of Chapter 7, except that they both implement the Serializable interface. Run the program several times. Whenever the program exits, it saves the Bank object (and all bank account objects that the bank contains) into a file bank.dat. When the program starts again, the file is loaded, and the changes from the preceding program run are automatically reflected. However, if the file is missing (either because the program is running for the first time, or because the file was erased), then the program starts with a new bank.

File SerialTester.java

```
1  import java.io.File;
2  import java.io.IOException;
3  import java.io.FileInputStream;
4  import java.io.FileOutputStream;
5  import java.io.ObjectInputStream;
```

```
 6   import java.io.ObjectOutputStream;
 7
 8   /**
 9       This program tests serialization of a Bank object.
10       If a file with serialized data exists, then it is
11       loaded. Otherwise the program starts with a new bank.
12       Bank accounts are added to the bank. Then the bank
13       object is saved.
14   */
15   public class SerialTester
16   {
17       public static void main(String[] args)
18             throws IOException, ClassNotFoundException
19       {
20          Bank firstBankOfJava;
21
22          File f = new File("bank.dat");
23          if (f.exists())
24          {
25             ObjectInputStream in = new ObjectInputStream(
26                   new FileInputStream(f));
27             firstBankOfJava = (Bank) in.readObject();
28             in.close();
29          }
30          else
31          {
32             firstBankOfJava = new Bank();
33             firstBankOfJava.addAccount(new BankAccount(1001, 20000));
34             firstBankOfJava.addAccount(new BankAccount(1015, 10000));
35          }
36
37          // Deposit some money
38          BankAccount a = firstBankOfJava.find(1001);
39          a.deposit(100);
40          System.out.println(a.getAccountNumber() + ":" + a.getBalance());
41          a = firstBankOfJava.find(1015);
42          System.out.println(a.getAccountNumber() + ":" + a.getBalance());
43
44          ObjectOutputStream out = new ObjectOutputStream(
45                new FileOutputStream(f));
46          out.writeObject(firstBankOfJava);
47          out.close();
48       }
49   }
```

Output

```
1001:20100.0
1015:10000.0
```

Output (Second Program Run)

```
1001:20200.0
1015:10000.0
```

9. Why is it easier to save an object with an `ObjectOutputStream` than a `RandomAccessFile`?
10. What do you have to do to the `Coin` class so that its objects can be saved in an `ObjectOutputStream`?

How To 16.1

Using Files and Streams

Suppose your program needs to process data in files. This How To walks you through the steps that are involved.

Step 1 Select a data format.

The most important question you need to ask yourself concerns the format to use for saving your data.

- Does your program need to save and restore objects? Then use object streams.
- Does your program manipulate text, such as a plain text files? Then use readers and writers.
- Does your program manipulate binary data, such as image files or encrypted data? Then use binary streams.

We don't discuss random access files here because they are not commonly needed for student projects. If you need to have fast access to data, use a database.

Step 2 If you use object streams, make your classes implement the `Serializable` interface.

Simply go through your classes and tag them with `implements Serializable`. You don't need to add any additional methods.

Also go to the online API documentation to check that the library classes that you are using implement the `Serializable` interface. Fortunately, many of them do. In particular, `String` and `ArrayList` are serializable.

If your classes use geometric objects (such as `Point2D.Double`, `Ellipse2D.Double`, and so on), then you have to work harder, because those classes are unfortunately not serializable—see Advanced Topic 16.3.

Step 3 Use object streams if you are processing objects.

Now simply put all the objects you want to save into a class (or an array or array list—but why not make another class containing that?).

Saving all program data is a trivial operation:

```
ProgramData data = . . .;
ObjectOutputStream out = new ObjectOutputStream(
        new FileOutputStream("program.dat"));
out.writeObject(data);
out.close();
```

Similarly, to restore the program data, you use an `ObjectInputStream` and call

```
ProgramData data = (ProgramData) in.readObject();
```

The `readObject` method can throw a `ClassNotFoundException`. You must catch or declare that exception.

Step 4 Use readers and writers if you are processing text.

Use a scanner to read the input.

```
Scanner in = new Scanner(new FileReader("input.txt"));
```

Then use the familiar methods `next`, `nextInt`, and so on.
To write output, turn the file output stream into a `PrintWriter`:

```
PrintWriter out = new PrintWriter("output.txt");
```

Then use the familiar `print` and `println` methods:

```
out.println(text);
```

Step 5 Use streams if you are processing bytes.

Use this loop to process input one byte at a time:

```
InputStream in = new FileInputStream("input.bin");
boolean done = false;
while (!done)
{
    int next = in.read();
    if (next = -1)
        done = true;
    else
    {
        byte b = (byte) next;
        Process input
    }
}
in.close();
```

Similarly, write the output one byte at a time:

```
OutputStream out = new FileOutputStream("output.bin");
. . .
while (. . .)
{
    byte b = . . .;
    out.write(b);
}
out.close();
```

Use binary streams only if you are ready to process the input one byte at a time. This makes sense for encryption/decryption or processing the pixels in an image. In other situations, binary streams are not appropriate.

PRODUCTIVITY HINT 16.1

Use Object Streams

Object streams have a huge advantage over other data file formats. You don't have to come up with a way of breaking objects up into numbers and strings when writing a file. You don't have to come up with a way of combining numbers and strings back into objects when reading a file. The serialization mechanism takes care of this automatically. You simply write and read objects. For this to work, you need to have each of your classes implement the Serializable interface, which is trivial to do.

To save your data to disk, it is best to put them all into one large object (such as an array list or an object that describes your entire program state) and save that object. When you need to read the data back, read that object back in. It is easier for you to retrieve data from an object than it is to search for them in a file.

ADVANCED TOPIC 16.3

Serializing Geometric Objects

Many classes in the standard library are serializable—after all, it is a simple matter for class designers to add implements Serializable to their classes. Unfortunately, the geometry classes Point2D.Double, Rectangle2D.Double, Ellipse2D.Double, and Line2D.Double are not. There is no good reason for this. It was just an oversight.

The Point and Rectangle classes are serializable. If you can get by with integer coordinates, then you may want to use them instead of Point2D.Double and Rectangle2D.Double.

If you have classes with instance fields that are not serializable, you have to work a bit harder to make serialization work. Follow these steps.

First, mark the nonserializable instance fields with the keyword transient:

```
public class Car implements Serializable
{
   . . .
   private Rectangle body; // OK, Rectangle is serializable.
   private transient Ellipse2D.Double frontTire;
   private transient Ellipse2D.Double rearTire;
}
```

Then add two methods to save and restore the transient fields explicitly, like this:

```
private void writeObject(ObjectOutputStream out)
      throws IOException
{
   out.defaultWriteObject();

   out.writeDouble(frontTire.getX());
   out.writeDouble(frontTire.getY());
   out.writeDouble(frontTire.getWidth());
   out.writeDouble(frontTire.getHeight());

   out.writeDouble(rearTire.getX());
   out.writeDouble(rearTire.getY());
```

```
            out.writeDouble(rearTire.getWidth());
            out.writeDouble(rearTire.getHeight());
      }

      private void readObject(ObjectInputStream in)
            throws IOException, ClassNotFoundException
      {
         in.defaultReadObject();

         double x = in.readDouble();
         double y = in.readDouble();
         double width = in.readDouble();
         double height = in.readDouble();
         frontTire = new Ellipse2D.Double(x, y, width, height);

         x = in.readDouble();
         y = in.readDouble();
         width = in.readDouble();
         height = in.readDouble();
         rearTire = new Ellipse2D.Double(x, y, width, height);
      }
```

These special methods must be private, and they must call `defaultWriteObject/defaultReadObject` before saving and restoring the additional information.

CHAPTER SUMMARY

1. When reading text files, use the `Scanner` class.

2. When writing text files, use the `PrintWriter` class and the `print/println` methods.

3. You must close all files when you are done processing them.

4. The `JFileChooser` dialog box allows users to select a file by navigating through directories.

5. A `File` object describes a file or directory.

6. You can pass a `File` object to the constructor of a file reader, writer, or stream.

7. When you launch a program from the command line, you can specify arguments after the program name. The program can access these strings by processing the `args` parameter of the `main` method.

8. Streams access sequences of bytes. Readers and writers access sequences of characters.

9. Use `FileReader`, `FileWriter`, `FileInputStream`, and `FileOutputStream` classes to read and write disk files.

10. The read method returns an integer, either –1, at the end of the file, or another value, which you need to cast to a `char` or `byte`.

11. In sequential file access, a file is processed one byte at a time. Random access allows access at arbitrary locations in the file, without first reading the bytes preceding the access location.

12. A file pointer is a position in a random access file. Because files can be very large, the file pointer is of type `long`.

13. Use object streams to save and restore all instance fields of an object automatically.

14. Objects saved to an object stream must belong to classes that implement the `Serializable` interface.

FURTHER READING

1. Bruce Schneier, *Applied Cryptography*, John Wiley & Sons, 1994.

2. Phillip R. Zimmermann, *The Official PGP User's Guide*, MIT Press, 1995.

3. `http://web.mit.edu/network/pgp.html`   MIT Distribution Center for Pretty Good Privacy.

4. Abraham Sinkov, *Elementary Cryptanalysis*, Mathematical Association of America, 1966.

CLASSES, OBJECTS, AND METHODS INTRODUCED IN THIS CHAPTER

```
java.io.File                    java.io.RandomAccessFile
   exists                          getFilePointer
java.io.FileInputStream            length
java.io.FileOutputStream           readChar
java.io.FileReader                 readDouble
java.io.FileWriter                 readInt
java.io.InputStream                seek
   close                           writeChar
   read                            writeChars
java.io.ObjectInputStream          writeDouble
   readObject                      writeInt
java.io.ObjectOutputStream      java.io.Reader
   writeObject                     close
java.io.OutputStream               read
   close                        java.io.Serializable
   write                        java.io.Writer
java.io.PrintWriter                close
   print                           write
   println                      javax.swing.JFileChooser
                                   getSelectedFile
                                   showOpenDialog
                                   showSaveDialog
```

REVIEW EXERCISES

Exercise R16.1. What is the difference between a stream and a reader?

Exercise R16.2. How can you open a file for both reading and writing in Java?

Exercise R16.3. What happens if you try to write to a file reader? What happens if you try to write to a random access file that you opened only for reading? Try it out if you don't know.

Exercise R16.4. What happens if you try to open a file for reading that doesn't exist? What happens if you try to open a file for writing that doesn't exist?

Exercise R16.5. What happens if you try to open a file for writing, but the file or device is write-protected (sometimes called read-only)? Try it out with a short test program.

Exercise R16.6. How do you open a file whose name contains a backslash, like c:\temp\output.dat?

Exercise R16.7. How can you break the Caesar cipher? That is, how can you read a document that was encrypted with the Caesar cipher, even though you don't know the key?

Exercise R16.8. What is a command line? How can a program read its command line arguments?

Exercise R16.9. Give two examples of programs on your computer that read arguments from the command line.

Exercise R16.10. If a program Woozle is started with the command

```
java Woozle -Dname=piglet -I\eeyore -v heff.txt a.txt lump.txt
```

what are the values of args[0], args[1], and so on?

Exercise R16.11. What happens if you try to save in an object stream an object that is not serializable? Try it out and report your results.

Exercise R16.12. Of the classes that you encountered in this book, which implement the Serializable interface?

Exercise R16.13. Why is it better to save an entire ArrayList to an object stream instead of programming a loop that writes each element?

Exercise R16.14. What is the difference between sequential access and random access?

Exercise R16.15. What is the file pointer in a file? How do you move it? How do you tell the current position? Why is it a long integer?

Exercise R16.16. How do you move the file pointer to the first byte of a file? To the last byte? To the exact middle of the file?

Exercise R16.17. What happens if you try to move the file pointer past the end of a file? Can you move the file pointer of System.in? Try it out and report your results.

PROGRAMMING EXERCISES

Exercise P16.1. Write a program that asks the user for a file name and prints the number of characters, words, and lines in that file. Then the program asks for the name of the next file. When the user enters a file that doesn't exist (such as the empty string), the program exits.

Exercise P16.2. *Random monoalphabet cipher.* The Caesar cipher, which shifts all letters by a fixed amount, is ridiculously easy to crack—just try out all 25 possible keys. Here is a better idea. For the key, don't use numbers but words. Suppose the key word is FEATHER. Then first remove duplicate letters, yielding FEATHR, and append the other letters of the alphabet in reverse order. Now encrypt the letters as follows:

Write a program that encrypts or decrypts a file using this cipher. For example,

```
java Crypt -d -kFEATHER encrypt.txt output.txt
```

decrypts a file using the keyword FEATHER. It is an error not to supply a keyword.

Exercise P16.3. *Letter frequencies.* If you encrypt a file using the cipher of Exercise P16.2, it will have all of its letters jumbled up, and will look as if there is no hope of decrypting it without knowing the keyword. Guessing the keyword seems hopeless, too. There are just too many possible keywords. However, someone who is trained in decryption will be able to break this cipher in no time at all. The average letter frequencies of English letters are well known. The most common letter is E, which occurs about 13% of the time. Here are the average frequencies of the letters (see [4]).

A	8%	H	4%	O	7%	V	1%
B	<1%	I	7%	P	3%	W	2%
C	3%	J	<1%	Q	<1%	X	<1%
D	4%	K	<1%	R	8%	Y	2%
E	13%	L	4%	S	6%	Z	<1%
F	3%	M	3%	T	9%		
G	2%	N	8%	U	3%		

Write a program that reads an input file and prints the letter frequencies in that file. Such a tool will help a code breaker. If the most frequent letters in an encrypted file are H and K, then there is an excellent chance that they are the encryptions of E and T.

Exercise P16.4. *Vigenère cipher.* The trouble with a monoalphabetic cipher is that it can be easily broken by frequency analysis. The so-called Vigenère cipher overcomes this problem by encoding a letter into one of several cipher letters, depending on its position in the input document. Choose a keyword, for example TIGER. Then encode the first letter of the input text like this:

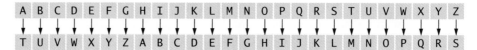

That is, the encoded alphabet is just the regular alphabet shifted to start at T, the first letter of the keyword TIGER. The second letter is encrypted according to the map

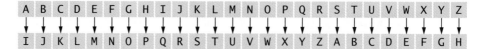

The third, fourth, and fifth letters in the input text are encrypted using the alphabet sequences beginning with characters G, E, and R. Because the key is only five letters long, the sixth letter of the input text is encrypted in the same way as the first.

Write a program that encrypts or decrypts an input text according to this cipher.

Exercise P16.5. *Playfair cipher.* Another way of thwarting a simple letter frequency analysis of an encrypted text is to encrypt pairs of letters together. A simple scheme to do this is the Playfair cipher. You pick a keyword and remove duplicate letters from it. Then you fill the keyword, and the remaining letters of the alphabet, into a 5 × 5 square. (Because there are only 25 squares, I and J are considered the same letter.) Here is such an arrangement with the keyword PLAYFAIR:

```
P L A Y F
I R B C D
E G H K M
N O Q S T
U V W X Z
```

To encrypt a letter pair, say AT, look at the rectangle with corners A and T:

```
P L A Y F
I R B C D
E G H K M
N O Q S T
U V W X Z
```

The encoding of this pair is formed by looking at the other two corners of the rectangle—in this case, FQ. If both letters happen to be in the same row or column, such as GO, simply swap the two letters. Decryption is done in the same way.

Write a program that encrypts or decrypts an input text according to this cipher.

Exercise P16.6. Write a program CopyFile that copies one file to another. The file names are specified on the command line. For example,

```
java CopyFile report.txt report.sav
```

Exercise P16.7. Write a program that *concatenates* the contents of several files into one file. For example,

```
java CatFiles chapter1.txt chapter2.txt chapter3.txt book.txt
```

makes a long file, book.txt, that contains the contents of the files chapter1.txt, chapter2.txt, and chapter3.txt. The output file is always the last file specified on the command line.

Exercise P16.8. Write a program Find that searches all files specified on the command line and prints out all lines containing a keyword. For example, if you call

```
java Find Buff report.txt address.txt Homework.java
```

then the program might print

```
report.txt: Buffet style lunch will be available at the
address.txt: Buffet, Warren|11801 Trenton Court|Dallas|TX
address.txt: Walters, Winnie|59 Timothy Circle|Buffalo|MI
Homework.java: BufferedReader in;
```

The keyword is always the first command line argument.

Exercise P16.9. Write a program that checks the spelling of all words in a file. It should read each word of a file and check whether it is contained in a word list. A word list is available on most UNIX systems in the file /usr/dict/words. (If you don't have access to a UNIX system, your instructor should be able to get you a copy.) The program should print out all words that it cannot find in the word list.

Exercise P16.10. Write a program that opens a file for reading and writing, and replaces each line with its reverse. For example, if you run

```
java Reverse Hello.java
```

then the contents of Hello.java are changed to

```
olleH ssalc cilbup
)sgra ][gnirtS(niam diov citats cilbup  {
;"n\!dlroW, olleH" = gniteerg gnirtS  {
;)gniteerg(tnirp.tuo.metsyS
}
}
```

Of course, if you run Reverse twice on the same file, you get back the original file.

Exercise P16.11. Write a program that reads a file from standard input and rewrites the file to standard output, replacing all tab characters '\t' with the *appropriate* number of spaces. Make the distance between tab columns a constant and set it to 3, the value we use in this book for Java programs. Then expand tabs to the number of spaces necessary to move to the next tab column. That may be *less* than three spaces. For example, consider the line containing "\t|\t||\t|". The first tab is changed to three spaces, the second to two spaces, and the third to one space.

Exercise P16.12. Implement a graphical user interface for the program in Section 16.5.

PROGRAMMING PROJECTS

Project 16.1. Write a graphical application in which the user clicks on a panel to add shapes (rectangles, ellipses, cars, etc.) at the mouse click location. The shapes are stored in an array list. When the user selects File->Save from the menu, save the selection of shapes in a file. When the user selects File->Open, load in a file. Use serialization.

Project 16.2. Write a toolkit that helps a cryptographer decrypt a file that was encrypted using a monoalphabet cipher. A monoalphabet cipher encrypts each character separately. Examples are the Caesar cipher and the cipher in Exercise P16.2. Analyze the letter frequencies as in Exercise P16.3. Use brute force to try all Caesar cipher keys, and check the output against a dictionary file. Allow the cryptographer to enter some substitutions and show the resulting text, with the unknown characters represented as ?. Try out your toolkit by decrypting files that you get from your classmates.

ANSWERS TO SELF-CHECK QUESTIONS

1. When the `PrintWriter` object is created, the output file is emptied. Sadly, that is the same file as the input file. The input file is now empty and the `while` loop exits immediately.

2. The program catches a `FileNotFoundException`, prints an error message, and terminates.

3. Image data is stored in a binary format—try loading an image file into a text editor, and you won't see much text. Therefore, you should use an `InputStream`.

4. They return a special value of -1 to indicate that no more input is available. If the return type had been `char` or `byte`, no special value would have been available that is distinguished from a legal data value.

5. It is `"Hello, World!"`, encrypted with a key of 3.

6. Yes—the program uses streams and encrypts each byte.

7. Suppose you print something, and then you call `seek(0)`, and print again to the same location. It would be difficult to reflect that behavior in the console window.

8. Advantage: The numbers use a fixed amount of storage space, making it possible to change their values without affecting surrounding data. Disadvantage: You cannot read a binary file with a text editor.

9. You can save the entire object with a single `writeObject` call. With a `RandomAccessFile`, you have to save each field separately.

10. Add `implements Serializable` to the class definition.

Object-Oriented Design

CHAPTER GOALS

- To learn about the software life cycle
- To learn how to discover new classes and methods
- To understand the use of CRC cards for class discovery
- To be able to identify inheritance, aggregation, and dependency relationships between classes
- To master the use of UML class diagrams to describe class relationships
- To learn how to use object-oriented design to build complex programs

To implement a software system successfully, be it as simple as your next homework project or as complex as the next air traffic monitoring system, some amount of planning, design, and testing is required. In fact, for larger projects, the amount of time spent on planning is much higher than the amount of time spent on programming and testing.

If you find that most of your homework time is spent in front of the computer, keying code in and fixing bugs, you are probably spending more time on your homework than you should. You could cut down your total time by spending more on the planning and design phase. This chapter tells you how to approach these tasks in a systematic manner, using the object-oriented design methodology.

CHAPTER CONTENTS

17.1 The Software Life Cycle

> The life cycle of software encompasses all activities from initial analysis until obsolescence.

> A formal process for software development describes phases of the development process and gives guidelines for how to carry out the phases.

In this section we will discuss the *software life cycle*: the activities that take place between the time a software program is first conceived and the time it is finally retired.

A software project usually starts because a customer has a problem and is willing to pay money to have it solved. The Department of Defense, the customer of many programming projects, was an early proponent of a *formal process* for software development. A formal process identifies and describes different phases and gives guidelines for carrying out the phases and when to move from one phase to the next.

Many software engineers break the development process down into the following five phases:

- Analysis
- Design
- Implementation
- Testing
- Deployment

In the *analysis* phase, you decide *what* the project is supposed to accomplish; you do not think about *how* the program will accomplish its tasks. The output of the analysis phase is a *requirements document*, which describes in complete detail what the program will be able to do once it is completed. Part of this requirements document can be a user manual that tells how the user will operate the program to derive the promised benefits. Another part sets performance criteria—how many inputs the program must be able to handle in what time, or what its maximum memory and disk storage requirements are.

In the *design* phase, you develop a plan for how you will implement the system. You discover the structures that underlie the problem to be solved. When you use object-oriented design, you decide what classes you need and what their most important methods are. The output of this phase is a description of the classes and methods, with diagrams that show the relationships among the classes.

In the *implementation* phase, you write and compile program code to implement the classes and methods that were discovered in the design phase. The output of this phase is the completed program.

In the *testing* phase, you run tests to verify that the program works correctly. The output of this phase is a report describing the tests that you carried out and their results.

In the *deployment* phase, the users of the program install it and use it for its intended purpose.

> The waterfall model of software development describes a sequential process of analysis, design, implementation, testing, and deployment.

When formal development processes were first established in the early 1970s, software engineers had a very simple visual model of these phases. They postulated that one phase would run to completion, its output would spill over to the next phase, and the next phase would begin. This model is called the *waterfall model* of software development (see Figure 1).

In an ideal world the waterfall model has a lot of appeal: You figure out what to do; then you figure out how to do it; then you do it; then you verify that you did it right; then you hand the product to the customer. When rigidly applied, though, the waterfall model simply did not work. It was very difficult to come up with a perfect requirement specification. It was quite common

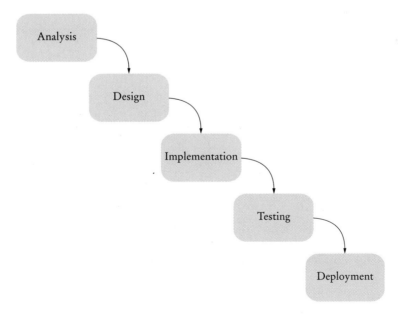

Figure 1 The Waterfall Model

to discover in the design phase that the requirements were inconsistent or that a small change in the requirements would lead to a system that was both easier to design and more useful for the customer, but the analysis phase was over, so the designers had no choice—they had to take the existing requirements, errors and all. This problem would repeat itself during implementation. The designers may have thought they knew how to solve the problem as efficiently as possible, but when the design was actually implemented, it turned out that the resulting program was not as fast as the designers had thought. The next transition is one with which you are surely familiar. When the program was handed to the quality assurance department for testing, many bugs were found that would best be fixed by reimplementing, or maybe even redesigning, the program, but the waterfall model did not allow for this. Finally, when the customers received the finished product, they were often not at all happy with it. Even though the customers typically were very involved in the analysis phase, often they themselves were not sure exactly what they needed. After all, it can be very difficult to describe how you want to use a product that you have never seen before. But when the customers started using the program, they began to realize what they would have liked. Of course, then it was too late, and they had to live with what they got.

> The spiral model of software development describes an iterative process in which design and implementation are repeated.

Having some level of iteration is clearly necessary. There simply must be a mechanism to deal with errors from the preceding phase. A *spiral model*, originally proposed by Barry Boehm in 1988, breaks the development process down into multiple phases (see Figure 2). Early phases focus on the construction of *prototypes*. A prototype is a small system that shows some aspects of the final system. Because prototypes model only a part of a system and do not need to withstand

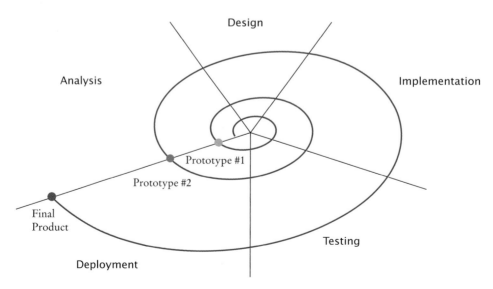

Figure 2 A Spiral Model

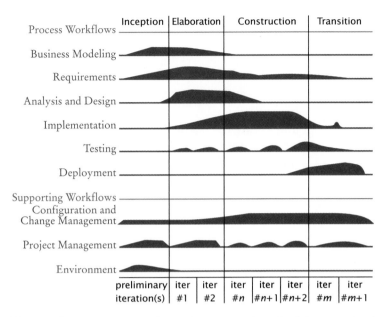

Figure 3   Activity Levels in the Rational Unified Process Methodology [1]

customer abuse, they can be implemented quickly. It is common to build a *user interface prototype* that shows the user interface in action. This gives customers an early chance to become more familiar with the system and to suggest improvements before the analysis is complete. Other prototypes can be built to validate interfaces with external systems, to test performance, and so on. Lessons learned from the development of one prototype can be applied to the next iteration of the spiral.

By building in repeated trials and feedback, a development process that follows the spiral model has a greater chance of delivering a satisfactory system. However, there is also a danger. If engineers believe that they don't have to do a good job because they can always do another iteration, then there will be many iterations, and the process will take a very long time to complete.

> Extreme Programming is a development methodology that strives for simplicity by removing formal structure and focusing on best practices.

Figure 3 shows activity levels in the "Rational Unified Process", a development process methodology by the inventors of UML. The details are not important, but as you can see, this is a complex process involving multiple iterations.

Even complex development processes with many iterations have not always met with success. In 1999, Kent Beck published an influential book [2] on *Extreme Programming*, a development methodology that strives for simplicity by cutting out most of the formal trappings of a traditional development methodolgy and instead focusing on a set of *practices:*

- *Realistic planning:* Customers are to make business decisions, programmers are to make technical decisions. Update the plan when it conflicts with reality.
- *Small releases:* Release a useful system quickly, then release updates on a very short cycle.

- *Metaphor:* All programmers should have a simple shared story that explains the system under development.
- *Simplicity:* Design everything to be as simple as possible instead of preparing for future complexity.
- *Testing:* Both programmers and customers are to write test cases. The system is continuously tested.
- *Refactoring:* Programmers are to restructure the system continuously to improve the code and eliminate duplication.
- *Pair programming:* Put programmers together in pairs, and require each pair to write code on a single computer.
- *Collective ownership:* All programmers have permission to change all code as it becomes necessary.
- *Continuous integration:* Whenever a task is completed, build the entire system and test it.
- *40-hour week:* Don't cover up unrealistic schedules with bursts of heroic effort.
- *On-site customer:* An actual customer of the system is to be accessible to team members at all times.
- *Coding standards:* Programmers are to follow standards that emphasize self-documenting code.

Many of these practices are common sense. Others, such as the pair programming requirement, are surprising. Beck claims that the value of the Extreme Programming approach lies in the synergy of these practices—the sum is bigger than the parts.

In your first programming course, you will not develop systems that are so complex that you need a full-fledged methodology to solve your homework problems. This introduction to the development process should, however, show you that successful software development involves more than just coding. In the remainder of this chapter we will have a closer look at the *design phase* of the software development process.

SELF CHECK

1. Suppose you sign a contract, promising that you will, for an agreed-upon price, design, implement, and test a software package exactly as it has been specified in a requirements document. What is the primary risk you and your customer are facing with this business arrangement?
2. Does Extreme Programming follow a waterfall or a spiral model?
3. What is the purpose of the "on-site customer" in Extreme Programming?

RANDOM FACT 17.1

Programmer Productivity

If you talk to your friends in this programming class, you will find that some of them consistently complete their assignments much more quickly than others. Perhaps they have more experience. However, even when programmers with the same education and experience are compared, wide variations in competence are routinely observed and measured. It is not uncommon to have the best programmer in a team be five to ten times as productive as the worst, using any of a number of reasonable measures of productivity [3].

That is a staggering range of performance among trained professionals. In a marathon race, the best runner will not run five to ten times faster than the slowest one. Software product managers are acutely aware of these disparities. The obvious solution is, of course, to hire only the best programmers, but even in recent periods of economic slowdown the demand for good programmers has greatly outstripped the supply.

Fortunately for all of us, joining the rank of the best is not necessarily a question of raw intellectual power. Good judgment, experience, broad knowledge, attention to detail, and superior planning are at least as important as mental brilliance. These skills can be acquired by individuals who are genuinely interested in improving themselves.

Even the most gifted programmer can deal with only a finite number of details in a given time period. Suppose a programmer can implement and debug one method every two hours, or one hundred methods per month. (This is a generous estimate. Few programmers are this productive.) If a task requires 10,000 methods (which is typical for a medium-sized program), then a single programmer would need 100 months to complete the job. Such a project is sometimes expressed as a "100-man-month" project. But as Fred Brooks explains in his famous book [4], the concept of "man-month" is a myth. One cannot trade months for programmers. One hundred programmers cannot finish the task in one month. In fact, 10 programmers probably couldn't finish it in 10 months. First of all, the 10 programmers need to learn about the project before they can get productive. Whenever there is a problem with a particular method, both the author and its users need to meet and discuss it, taking time away from all of them. A bug in one method may have other programmers twiddling their thumbs until it is fixed.

It is difficult to estimate these inevitable delays. They are one reason why software is often released later than originally promised. What is a manager to do when the delays mount? As Brooks points out, adding more personnel will make a late project even later, because the productive people have to stop working and train the newcomers.

You will experience these problems when you work on your first team project with other students. Be prepared for a major drop in productivity, and be sure to set ample time aside for team communications.

There is, however, no alternative to teamwork. Most important and worthwhile projects transcend the ability of one single individual. Learning to function well in a team is just as important as becoming a competent programmer.

17.2 Discovering Classes

In the design phase of software development, your task is to discover structures that make it possible to implement a set of tasks on a computer. When you use the object-oriented design process, you carry out the following tasks:

> In object-oriented design, you discover classes, determine the responsibilities of classes, and describe the relationships between classes.

1. Discover classes.

2. Determine the responsibilities of each class.

3. Describe the relationships between the classes.

A class represents some useful concept. You have seen classes for concrete entities, such as bank accounts, ellipses, and products. Other classes represent abstract concepts, such as streams and windows.

A simple rule for finding classes is to look for *nouns* in the task description. For example, suppose your job is to print an invoice such as the one in Figure 4. Obvious classes that come to mind are Invoice, LineItem, and Customer. It is a good idea to keep a list of *candidate classes* on a whiteboard or a sheet of paper. As you brainstorm, simply put all ideas for classes onto the list. You can always cross out the ones that weren't useful after all.

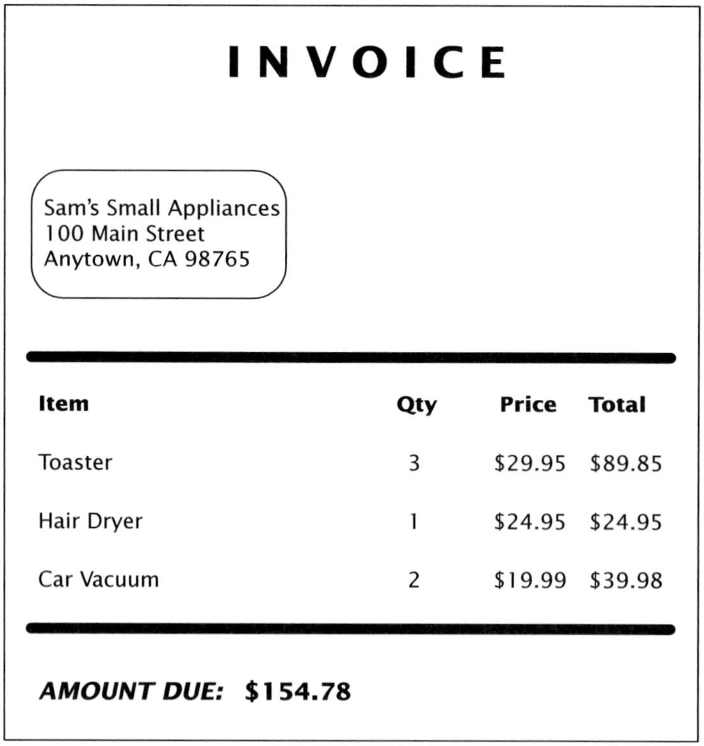

INVOICE

Sam's Small Appliances
100 Main Street
Anytown, CA 98765

Item	Qty	Price	Total
Toaster	3	$29.95	$89.85
Hair Dryer	1	$24.95	$24.95
Car Vacuum	2	$19.99	$39.98

AMOUNT DUE: **$154.78**

Figure 4 An Invoice

When finding classes, keep the following points in mind:

- A class represents a set of objects with the same behavior. Entities with multiple occurrences in your problem description, such as customers or products, are good candidates for objects. Find out what they have in common, and design classes to capture those commonalities.

- Some entities should be represented as objects, others as primitive types. For example, should an address be an object of an Address class, or should it simply be a string? There is no perfect answer—it depends on the task that you want to solve. If your software needs to analyze addresses (for example, to determine shipping costs), then an Address class is an appropriate design. However, if your software will never need such a capability, you should not waste time on an overly complex design. It is your job to find a balanced design; one that is not too limiting or excessively general.

- Not all classes can be discovered in the analysis phase. Most complex programs need classes for tactical purposes, such as file or database access, user interfaces, control mechanisms, and so on.

- Some of the classes that you need may already exist, either in the standard library or in a program that you developed previously. You also may be able to use inheritance to extend existing classes into classes that match your needs.

Once a set of classes has been identified, you need to define the behavior for each class. That is, you need to find out what methods each object needs to carry out to solve the programming problem. A simple rule for finding these methods is to look for *verbs* in the task description, and then match the verbs to the appropriate objects. For example, in the invoice program, a class needs to compute the amount due. Now you need to figure out *which class* is responsible for this method. Do customers compute what they owe? Do invoices total up the amount due? Do the items total themselves up? The best choice is to make "compute amount due" the responsibility of the Invoice class.

> A CRC card describes a class, its responsibilities, and its collaborating classes.

An excellent way to carry out this task is the "CRC card method." *CRC* stands for "classes", "responsibilities", "collaborators", and in its simplest form, the method works as follows. Use an index card for each *class* (see Figure 5). As you think about verbs in the task description that indicate methods, you pick the card of the class that you think should be responsible, and write that *responsibility* on the card. For each responsibility, you record which other classes are needed to fulfill it. Those classes are the *collaborators*.

For example, suppose you decide that an invoice should compute the amount due. Then you write "compute amount due" on the left-hand side of an index card with the title Invoice.

If a class can carry out that responsibility by itself, do nothing further. But if the class needs the help of other classes, write the names of these collaborators on the right-hand side of the card.

To compute the total, the invoice needs to ask each line item about its total price. Therefore, the LineItem class is a collaborator.

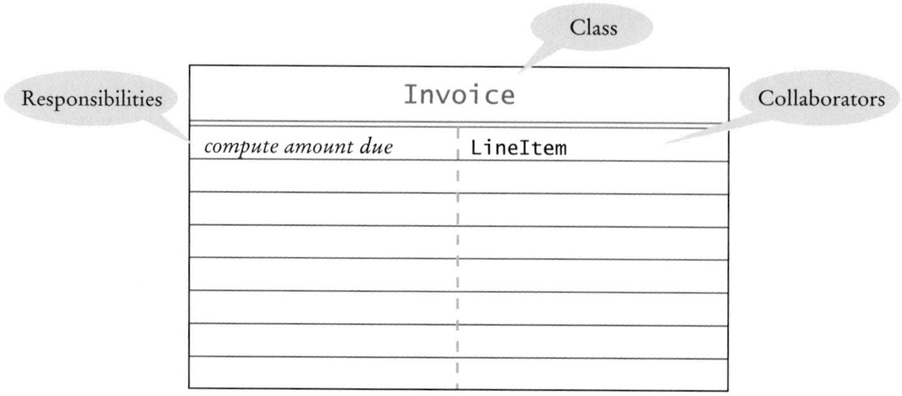

Figure 5 A CRC Card

This is a good time to look up the index card for the LineItem class. Does it have a "get total price" method? If not, add one.

How do you know that you are on the right track? For each responsibility, ask yourself how it can actually be done, using the responsibilities written on the various cards. Many people find it helpful to group the cards on a table so that the collaborators are close to each other, and to simulate tasks by moving a token (such as a coin) from one card to the next to indicate which object is currently active.

Keep in mind that the responsibilities that you list on the CRC card are on a *high level*. Sometimes a single responsibility may need two or more Java methods for carrying it out. Some researchers say that a CRC card should have no more than three distinct responsibilities.

The CRC card method is informal on purpose, so that you can be creative and discover classes and their properties. Once you find that you have settled on a good set of classes, you will want to know how they are related to each other. Can you find classes with common properties, so that some responsibilities can be taken care of by a common superclass? Can you organize classes into clusters that are independent of each other? Finding class relationships and documenting them with diagrams is the topic of the next section.

SELF CHECK

4. Suppose the invoice is to be saved to a file. Name a likely collaborator.

5. Looking at the invoice in Figure 4, what is a likely responsibility of the Customer class?

6. What do you do if a CRC card has ten responsibilities?

17.3 Relationships Between Classes

When designing a program, it is useful to document the relationships between classes. This helps you in a number of ways. For example, if you find classes with common behavior, you can save effort by placing the common behavior into a superclass. If you know that some classes are *not* related to each other, you can assign different programmers to implement each of them, without worrying that one of them has to wait for the other.

You have seen the inheritance relationship between classes many times in this book. Inheritance is a very important relationship, but, as it turns out, it is not the only useful relationship, and it can be overused.

Inheritance is a relationship between a more general class (the superclass) and a more specialized class (the subclass). This relationship is often described as the *is-a* relationship. Every truck is a vehicle. Every savings account is a bank account. Every circle is an ellipse (with equal width and height).

> Inheritance (the *is-a* relationship) is sometimes inappropriately used when the *has-a* relationship would be more appropriate.

Inheritance is sometimes abused, however. For example, consider a `Tire` class that describes a car tire. Should the class `Tire` be a subclass of a class `Circle`? It sounds convenient. There are quite a few useful methods in the `Circle` class—for example, the `Tire` class may inherit methods that compute the radius, perimeter, and center point, which should come in handy when drawing tire shapes. Though it may be convenient for the programmer, this arrangement makes no sense conceptually. It isn't true that every tire is a circle. Tires are car parts, whereas circles are geometric objects. There is a relationship between tires and circles, though. A tire *has a* circle as its boundary. Java lets us model that relationship, too. Use an instance variable:

```
class Tire
{
   . . .
   private String rating;
   private Circle boundary;
}
```

The technical term for this relationship is *aggregation*. Each `Tire` aggregates a `Circle` object. In general, a class aggregates another class if its objects have objects of the other class.

> Aggregation (the *has-a* relationship) denotes that objects of one class contain references to objects of another class.

Here is another example. Every car *is a* vehicle. Every car *has a* tire (in fact, it has four or, if you count the spare, five). Thus, you would use inheritance from `Vehicle` and use aggregation of `Tire` objects:

```
class Car extends Vehicle
{
   . . .
   private Tire[] tires;
}
```

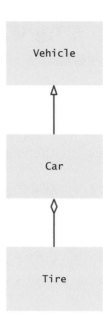

Figure 6
UML Notation for
Inheritance and Aggregation

In this book, we use the UML notation for class diagrams. You have already seen many examples of the UML notation for inheritance—an arrow with an open triangle pointing to the superclass. In the UML notation, aggregation is denoted by a solid line with a diamond-shaped symbol next to the aggregating class. Figure 6 shows a class diagram with an inheritance and an aggregation relationship.

> Dependency is another name for the "uses" relationship.

The aggregation relationship is related to the *dependency* relationship, which you saw in Chapter 9. Recall that a class depends on another if one of its methods *uses* an object of the other class in some way.

For example, many of our applications depend on the Scanner class, because they use a Scanner object to read input.

Aggregation is a stronger form of dependency. If a class has objects of another class, it certainly uses the other class. However, the converse is not true. For example, a class may use the Scanner class without ever defining an instance field of class Scanner. The class may simply construct a local variable of type Scanner, or its methods may receive Scanner objects as parameters. This use is not aggregation because the objects of the class don't contain Scanner objects—they just create or receive them for the duration of a single method.

> You need to be able to distinguish the UML notations for inheritance, interface implementation, aggregation, and dependency.

Generally, you need aggregation when an object needs to remember another object *between method calls.*

As you saw in Chapter 9, the UML notation for dependency is a dashed line with an open arrow that points to the dependent class.

The arrows in the UML notation can get confusing. Table 1 shows a summary of the four UML relationship symbols that we use in this book.

Table 1 UML Relationship Symbols

Relationship	Symbol	Line Style	Arrow Tip
Inheritance	——————▷	Solid	Triangle
Interface Implementation	- - - - - -▷	Dotted	Triangle
Aggregation	◇—————	Solid	Diamond
Dependency	- - - - - ->	Dotted	Open

SELF CHECK

7. Consider the Bank and BankAccount classes of Chapter 7. How are they related?

8. Consider the BankAccount and SavingsAccount objects of Chapter 12. How are they related?

9. Consider the BankAccountTester class of Chapter 3. Which classes does it depend on?

HOW TO 17.1

CRC Cards and UML Diagrams

Before writing code for a complex problem, you need to design a solution. The methodology introduced in this chapter suggests that you follow a design process that is composed of the following tasks:

1. Discover classes.
2. Determine the responsibilities of each class.
3. Describe the relationships between the classes.

CRC cards and UML diagrams help you discover and record this information.

Step 1 Discover classes.

Highlight the nouns in the problem description. Make a list of the nouns. Cross out those that don't seem reasonable candidates for classes.

Step 2 Discover responsibilities.

Make a list of the major tasks that your system needs to fulfill. From those tasks, pick one that is not trivial and that is intuitive to you. Find a class that is responsible for carrying out that task. Make an index card and write the name and the task on it. Now ask yourself how an object of the class can carry out the task. It probably needs help from other objects. Then make CRC cards for the classes to which those objects belong and write the responsibilities on them.

Don't be afraid to cross out, move, split, or merge responsibilities. Rip up cards if they become too messy. This is an informal process.

You are done when you have walked through all major tasks and are satisfied that they can all be solved with the classes and responsibilities that you discovered.

Step 3   Describe relationships.

Make a class diagram that shows the relationships between all the classes that you discovered.

Start with inheritance—the *is-a* relationship between classes. Is any class a specialization of another? If so, draw inheritance arrows. Keep in mind that many designs, especially for simple programs, don't use inheritance extensively.

The "collaborators" column of the CRC cards tell you which classes use others. Draw usage arrows for the collaborators on the CRC cards.

Some dependency relationships give rise to aggregations. For each of the dependency relationships, ask yourself: How does the object locate its collaborator? Does it navigate to it directly because it stores a reference? In that case, draw an aggregation arrow. Or is the collaborator a method parameter or return value? Then simply draw a dependency arrow.

ADVANCED TOPIC 17.1

Attributes and Methods in UML Diagrams

Sometimes it is useful to indicate class *attributes* and *methods* in a class diagram. An *attribute* is an externally observable property that objects of a class have. For example, name and price would be attributes of the Product class. Usually, attributes correspond to instance variables. But they don't have to—a class may have a different way of organizing its data. For example, a GregorianCalendar object from the Java library has attributes day, month, and year, and it would be appropriate to draw a UML diagram that shows these attributes. However, the class doesn't actually have instance fields that store these quantities. Instead, it internally represents all dates by counting the milliseconds from January 1, 1970—an implementation detail that a class user certainly doesn't need to know about.

You can indicate attributes and methods in a class diagram by dividing a class rectangle into three compartments, with the class name in the top, attributes in the middle, and methods in the bottom (see Figure 7). You need not list *all* attributes and methods in a particular diagram. Just list the ones that are helpful to understand whatever point you are making with a particular diagram.

Also, don't list as an attribute what you also draw as an aggregation. If you denote by aggregation the fact that a Car has Tire objects, don't add an attribute tires.

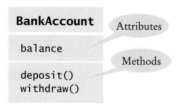

Figure 7   Attributes and Methods in a Class Diagram

ADVANCED TOPIC 17.2

Multiplicities

Some designers like to write *multiplicities* at the end(s) of an aggregation relationship to denote how many objects are aggregated. The notations for the most common multiplicities are:

- any number (zero or more): *
- one or more: 1..*
- zero or one: 0..1
- exactly one: 1

Figure 8 shows that a customer has one or more bank accounts.

Figure 8   An Aggregation Relationship with Multiplicities

ADVANCED TOPIC 17.3

Aggregation and Association

Some designers find the aggregation or *has-a* terminology unsatisfactory. For example, consider customers of a bank. Does the bank "have" customers? Do the customers "have" bank accounts, or does the bank "have" them? Which of these "has" relationships should be modeled by aggregation? This line of thinking can lead us to premature implementation decisions.

Early in the design phase, it makes sense to use a more general relationship between classes called *association*. A class is associated with another if you can *navigate* from objects of one class to objects of the other class. For example, given a Bank object, you can navigate to Customer objects, perhaps by accessing an instance field, or by making a database lookup.

The UML notation for an association relationship is a solid line, with optional arrows that show in which directions you can navigate the relationship. You can also add words to the line ends to further explain the nature of the relationship. Figure 9 shows that you can navigate from Bank objects to Customer objects, but you cannot navigate the other way around. That is, in this particular design, the Customer class has no mechanism to determine in which banks it keeps its money.

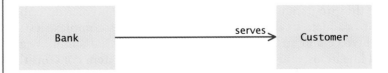

Figure 9   An Association Relationship

> Frankly, the differences between aggregation and association are confusing, even to experienced designers. If you find the distinction helpful, by all means use the relationship that you find most appropriate. But don't spend time pondering subtle differences between these concepts. From the practical point of view of a Java programmer, it is useful to know when objects of one class manage objects of another class. The aggregation or *has-a* relationship accurately describes this phenomenon.

17.4 Case Study: Printing an Invoice

In this chapter, we discuss a five-part development process that is particularly well suited for beginning programmers:

1. Gather requirements.
2. Use CRC cards to find classes, responsibilities, and collaborators.
3. Use UML diagrams to record class relationships.
4. Use javadoc to document method behavior.
5. Implement your program.

There isn't a lot of notation to learn. The class diagrams are simple to draw. The deliverables of the design phase are obviously useful for the implementation phase—you simply take the source files and start adding the method code. Of course, as your projects get more complex, you will want to learn more about formal design methods. There are many techniques to describe object scenarios, call sequencing, the large-scale structure of programs, and so on, that are very beneficial even for relatively simple projects. *The Unified Modeling Language User Guide* [1] gives a good overview of these techniques.

In this section, we will walk through the object-oriented design technique with a very simple example. In this case, the methodology may feel overblown, but it is a good introduction to the mechanics of each step. You will then be better prepared for the more complex example that follows.

17.4.1 Requirements

The task of this program is to print out an invoice. An invoice describes the charges for a set of products in certain quantities. (We omit complexities such as dates, taxes, and invoice and customer numbers.) The program simply prints the billing address, all line items, and the amount due. Each line item contains the description and unit price of a product, the quantity ordered, and the total price.

```
            I N V O I C E

Sam's Small Appliances
100 Main Street
Anytown, CA 98765

Description             Price  Qty  Total
Toaster                 29.95   3   89.85
Hair dryer              24.95   1   24.95
Car vacuum              19.99   2   39.98

AMOUNT DUE: $154.78
```

Also, in the interest of simplicity, we do not provide a user interface. We just supply a test program that adds line items to the invoice and then prints it.

17.4.2 CRC Cards

First, you need to discover classes. Classes correspond to nouns in the requirements description. In this problem, it is pretty obvious what the nouns are:

```
Invoice
Address
LineItem
Product
Description
Price
Quantity
Total
Amount Due
```

(Of course, Toaster doesn't count—it is the description of a LineItem object and therefore a data value, not the name of a class.)

Description and price are fields of the Product class. What about the quantity? The quantity is not an attribute of a Product. Just as in the printed invoice, let's have a class LineItem that records the product and the quantity (such as "3 toasters").

The total and amount due are computed—not stored anywhere. Thus, they don't lead to classes.

After this process of elimination, we are left with four candidates for classes:

```
Invoice
Address
LineItem
Product
```

Each of them represents a useful concept, so let's make them all into classes.

The purpose of the program is to print an invoice. However, the Invoice class won't necessarily know whether to display the output in System.out, in a text area, or in a file. Therefore, let's relax the task slightly and make the invoice responsible for *formatting* the invoice. The result is a string (containing multiple lines) that can be printed out or displayed. Record that responsibility on a CRC card:

```
┌─────────────────────────────────────────────┐
│                  Invoice                    │
├─────────────────────────────────────────────┤
│ format the invoice                          │
├─────────────────────────────────────────────┤
│                                             │
├─────────────────────────────────────────────┤
│                                             │
├─────────────────────────────────────────────┤
│                                             │
├─────────────────────────────────────────────┤
│                                             │
├─────────────────────────────────────────────┤
│                                             │
└─────────────────────────────────────────────┘
```

How does an invoice format itself? It must format the billing address, format all line items, and then add the amount due. How can the invoice format an address? It can't—that really is the responsibility of the Address class. This leads to a second CRC card:

```
┌─────────────────────────────────────────────┐
│                  Address                    │
├─────────────────────────────────────────────┤
│ format the address                          │
├─────────────────────────────────────────────┤
│                                             │
├─────────────────────────────────────────────┤
│                                             │
├─────────────────────────────────────────────┤
│                                             │
├─────────────────────────────────────────────┤
│                                             │
├─────────────────────────────────────────────┤
│                                             │
└─────────────────────────────────────────────┘
```

Similarly, formatting of a line item is the responsibility of the LineItem class.

The format method of the Invoice class calls the format methods of the Address and LineItem classes. Whenever a method uses another class, you list that other class as a collaborator. In other words, Address and LineItem are collaborators of Invoice:

```
┌─────────────────────────────────────────────┐
│                  Invoice                    │
├─────────────────────────────────────────────┤
│ format the invoice          Address         │
│                             LineItem        │
├─────────────────────────────────────────────┤
│                                             │
├─────────────────────────────────────────────┤
│                                             │
├─────────────────────────────────────────────┤
│                                             │
├─────────────────────────────────────────────┤
│                                             │
└─────────────────────────────────────────────┘
```

When formatting the invoice, the invoice also needs to compute the total amount due. To obtain that amount, it must ask each line item about the total price of the item.

How does a line item obtain that total? It must ask the product for the unit price, and then multiply it by the quantity. That is, the Product class must reveal the unit price, and it is a collaborator of the LineItem class.

Finally, the invoice must be populated with products and quantities, so that it makes sense to format the result. That too is a responsibility of the Invoice class.

We now have a set of CRC cards that completes the CRC card process.

Product	
get description	
get unit price	

LineItem	
format the item	Product
get total price	

Invoice	
format the invoice	Address
add a product and quantity	LineItem
	Product

17.4.3 UML Diagrams

The dependency relationships come from the collaboration column on the CRC cards. Each class depends on the classes with which it collaborates. In our example, the Invoice class collaborates with the Address, LineItem, and Product classes. The LineItem class collaborates with the Product class.

Now ask yourself which of these dependencies are actually aggregations. How does an invoice know about the address, line item, and product objects with which it collaborates? An invoice object must hold references to the address and the line items when it formats the invoice. But an invoice object need not hold a reference to a product object when adding a product. The product is turned into a line item, and then it is the item's responsibility to hold a reference to it.

Therefore, the Invoice class aggregates the Address and LineItem classes. The LineItem class aggregates the Product class. However, there is no *has-a* relationship between an invoice and a product. An invoice doesn't store products directly—they are stored in the LineItem objects.

There is no inheritance in this example.

Figure 10 shows the class relationships that we discovered.

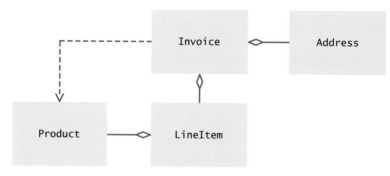

Figure 10 The Relationships Between the Invoice Classes

17.4.4 Method Documentation

> Use javadoc comments (with the method bodies left blank) to record the behavior of classes.

The final step of the design phase is to write the documentation of the discovered classes and methods. Simply write a Java source file for each class, write the method comments for those methods that you have discovered, and leave the bodies of the methods blank.

```
/**
    Describes an invoice for a set of purchased products.
*/
public class Invoice
{
```

```java
   /**
      Adds a charge for a product to this invoice.
      @param aProduct the product that the customer ordered
      @param quantity the quantity of the product
   */
   public void add(Product aProduct, int quantity)
   {
   }

   /**
      Formats the invoice.
      @return the formatted invoice
   */
   public String format()
   {
   }
}

/**
   Describes a quantity of an article to purchase and its price.
*/
public class LineItem
{
   /**
      Computes the total cost of this line item.
      @return the total price
   */
   public double getTotalPrice()
   {
   }

   /**
      Formats this item.
      @return a formatted string of this line item
   */
   public String format()
   {
   }
}

/**
   Describes a product with a description and a price.
*/
public class Product
{
   /**
      Gets the product description.
      @return the description
   */
   public String getDescription()
   {
   }
```

```
    /**
        Gets the product price.
        @return the unit price
    */
    public double getPrice()
    {
    }
}


/**
    Describes a mailing address.
*/
public class Address
{
    /**
        Formats the address.
        @return the address as a string with three lines
    */
    public String format()
    {
    }
}
```

Then run the javadoc program to obtain a prettily formatted version of your documentation in HTML format (see Figure 11).

This approach for documenting your classes has a number of advantages. You can share the HTML documentation with others if you work in a team. You use a format that is immediately useful—Java source files that you can carry into the implementation phase. And, most importantly, you supply the comments of the key methods—a task that less prepared programmers leave for later, and then often neglect for lack of time.

17.4.5 Implementation

Finally, you are ready to implement the classes.

You already have the method signatures and comments from the previous step. Now look at the UML diagram to add instance fields. Aggregated classes yield instance fields. Start with the Invoice class. An invoice aggregates Address and LineItem. Every invoice has one billing address, but it can have many line items. To store multiple LineItem objects, you can use an array list. Now you have the instance fields of the Invoice class:

```
public class Invoice
{
    . . .
    private Address billingAddress;
    private ArrayList<LineItem> items;
}
```

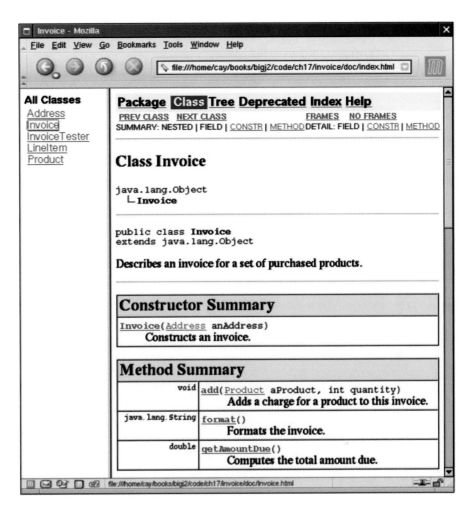

Figure 11   The Class Documentation in HTML Format

A line item needs to store a `Product` object and the product quantity. That leads to the following instance fields:

```
public class LineItem
{
   . . .
   private int quantity;
   private Product theProduct;
}
```

The methods themselves are now very easy. Here is a typical example. You already know what the `getTotalPrice` method of the `LineItem` class needs to do—get the unit price of the product and multiply it with the quantity.

```
/**
    Computes the total cost of this line item.
    @return the total price
*/
public double getTotalPrice()
{
    return theProduct.getPrice() * quantity;
}
```

We will not discuss the other methods in detail—they are equally straightforward.

Finally, you need to supply constructors, another routine task.

Here is the entire program. It is a good practice to go through it in detail and match up the classes and methods against the CRC cards and UML diagram.

File InvoiceTester.java

```
1  /**
2      This program tests the invoice classes by printing
3      a sample invoice.
4  */
5  public class InvoiceTester
6  {
7      public static void main(String[] args)
8      {
9          Address samsAddress
10             = new Address("Sam's Small Appliances",
11             "100 Main Street", "Anytown", "CA", "98765");
12
13         Invoice samsInvoice = new Invoice(samsAddress);
14         samsInvoice.add(new Product("Toaster", 29.95), 3);
15         samsInvoice.add(new Product("Hair dryer", 24.95), 1);
16         samsInvoice.add(new Product("Car vacuum", 19.99), 2);
17
18         System.out.println(samsInvoice.format());
19     }
20 }
```

File Invoice.java

```
1  import java.util.ArrayList;
2
3  /**
4      Describes an invoice for a set of purchased products.
5  */
6  public class Invoice
7  {
8      /**
9          Constructs an invoice.
10         @param anAddress the billing address
11     */
12     public Invoice(Address anAddress)
13     {
```

```java
14          items = new ArrayList<LineItem>();
15          billingAddress = anAddress;
16       }
17
18       /**
19          Adds a charge for a product to this invoice.
20          @param aProduct the product that the customer ordered
21          @param quantity the quantity of the product
22       */
23       public void add(Product aProduct, int quantity)
24       {
25          LineItem anItem = new LineItem(aProduct, quantity);
26          items.add(anItem);
27       }
28
29       /**
30          Formats the invoice.
31          @return the formatted invoice
32       */
33       public String format()
34       {
35          String r = "                    I N V O I C E\n\n"
36             + billingAddress.format()
37             + String.format("\n\n%-30s%8s%5s%8s\n",
38             "Description", "Price", "Qty", "Total");
39
40          for (LineItem i : items)
41          {
42             r = r + i.format() + "\n";
43          }
44
45          r = r + String.format("\nAMOUNT DUE: $%8.2f", getAmountDue());
46
47          return r;
48       }
49
50       /**
51          Computes the total amount due.
52          @return the amount due
53       */
54       public double getAmountDue()
55       {
56          double amountDue = 0;
57          for (LineItem i : items)
58          {
59             amountDue = amountDue + i.getTotalPrice();
60          }
61          return amountDue;
62       }
63
64       private Address billingAddress;
65       private ArrayList<LineItem> items;
66    }
```

File LineItem.java

```java
1  /**
2       Describes a quantity of an article to purchase.
3  */
4  public class LineItem
5  {
6      /**
7           Constructs an item from the product and quantity.
8           @param aProduct  the product
9           @param aQuantity  the item quantity
10     */
11     public LineItem(Product aProduct, int aQuantity)
12     {
13         theProduct = aProduct;
14         quantity = aQuantity;
15     }
16
17     /**
18          Computes the total cost of this line item.
19          @return  the total price
20     */
21     public double getTotalPrice()
22     {
23         return theProduct.getPrice() * quantity;
24     }
25
26     /**
27          Formats this item.
28          @return  a formatted string of this line item
29     */
30     public String format()
31     {
32         return String.format("%-30s%8.2f%5d%8.2f",
33             theProduct.getDescription(), theProduct.getPrice(),
34             quantity, getTotalPrice());
35     }
36
37     private int quantity;
38     private Product theProduct;
39 }
```

File Product.java

```java
1  /**
2       Describes a product with a description and a price.
3  */
4  public class Product
5  {
6      /**
7           Constructs a product from a description and a price.
8           @param aDescription  the product description
9           @param aPrice  the product price
10     */
11     public Product(String aDescription, double aPrice)
```

```
12      {
13          description = aDescription;
14          price = aPrice;
15      }
16
17      /**
18          Gets the product description.
19          @return the description
20      */
21      public String getDescription()
22      {
23          return description;
24      }
25
26      /**
27          Gets the product price.
28          @return the unit price
29      */
30      public double getPrice()
31      {
32          return price;
33      }
34
35      private String description;
36      private double price;
37  }
```

File Address.java

```
1   /**
2       Describes a mailing address.
3   */
4   public class Address
5   {
6       /**
7           Constructs a mailing address.
8           @param aName the recipient name
9           @param aStreet the street
10          @param aCity the city
11          @param aState the two-letter state code
12          @param aZip the ZIP postal code
13      */
14      public Address(String aName, String aStreet,
15              String aCity, String aState, String aZip)
16      {
17          name = aName;
18          street = aStreet;
19          city = aCity;
20          state = aState;
21          zip = aZip;
22      }
23
```

```
24    /**
25        Formats the address.
26        @return  the address as a string with three lines
27    */
28    public String format()
29    {
30        return name + "\n" + street + "\n"
31                + city + ", " + state + " " + zip;
32    }
33
34    private String name;
35    private String street;
36    private String city;
37    private String state;
38    private String zip;
39 }
```

SELF CHECK

10. Which class is responsible for computing the amount due? What are its collaborators for this task?

11. Why do the format methods return String objects instead of directly printing to System.out?

17.5 Case Study: An Automatic Teller Machine

17.5.1 Requirements

The purpose of this project is to design a simulation of an automatic teller machine (ATM). The ATM is used by the customers of a bank. Each customer has two accounts: a checking account and a savings account. Each customer also has a customer number and a personal identification number (PIN); both are required to gain access to the accounts. (In a real ATM, the customer number would be recorded on the magnetic strip of the ATM card. In this simulation, the customer will need to type it in.) With the ATM, customers can select an account (checking or savings). The balance of the selected account is displayed. Then the customer can deposit and withdraw money. This process is repeated until the customer chooses to exit.

The details of the user interaction depend on the user interface that we choose for the simulation. We will develop two separate interfaces: a graphical interface that closely mimics an actual ATM (see Figure 12), and a text-based interface that allows you to test the ATM and bank classes without being distracted by GUI programming.

In the GUI interface, the ATM has a keypad to enter numbers, a display to show messages, and a set of buttons, labeled A, B, and C, whose function depends on the state of the machine.

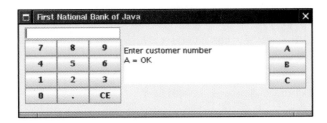

Figure 12   User Interface of the Automatic Teller Machine

Specifically, the user interaction is as follows. When the ATM starts up, it expects a user to enter a customer number. The display shows the following message:

```
Enter customer number
A = OK
```

The user enters the customer number on the keypad and presses the A button. The display message changes to

```
Enter PIN
A = OK
```

Next, the user enters the PIN and presses the A button again. If the customer number and ID match those of one of the customers in the bank, then the customer can proceed. If not, the user is again prompted to enter the customer number.

If the customer has been authorized to use the system, then the display message changes to

```
Select Account
A = Checking
B = Savings
C = Exit
```

If the user presses the C button, the ATM reverts to its original state and asks the next user to enter a customer number.

If the user presses the A or B buttons, the ATM remembers the selected account, and the display message changes to

```
Balance = balance of selected account
Enter amount and select transaction
A = Withdraw
B = Deposit
C = Cancel
```

If the user presses the A or B buttons, the value entered in the keypad is withdrawn from or deposited into the selected account. (This is just a simulation, so no money is dispensed and no deposit is accepted.) Afterwards, the ATM reverts to the preceding state, allowing the user to select another account or to exit.

If the user presses the C button, the ATM reverts to the preceding state without executing any transaction.

In the text-based interaction, we read input from System.in instead of the buttons. Here is a typical dialog:

```
Enter account number: 1
Enter PIN: 1234
A=Checking, B=Savings, C=Quit: A
Balance=0.0
A=Deposit, B=Withdrawal, C=Cancel: A
Amount: 1000
A=Checking, B=Savings, C=Quit: C
```

In our solution, only the user interface classes are affected by the choice of user interface. The remainder of the classes can be used for both solutions—they are decoupled from the user interface.

Because this is a simulation, the ATM does not actually communicate with a bank. It simply loads a set of customer numbers and PINs from a file. All accounts are initialized with a zero balance.

17.5.2 CRC Cards

We will again follow the recipe of Section 17.2 and show how to discover classes, responsibilities, and relationships and how to obtain a detailed design for the ATM program.

Recall that the first rule for finding classes is "Look for nouns in the problem description". Here is a list of the nouns:

```
ATM
User
Keypad
Display
Display message
Button
State
Bank account
Checking account
Savings account
Customer
Customer number
PIN
Bank
```

Of course, not all of these nouns will become names of classes, and we may yet discover the need for classes that aren't in this list, but it is a good start.

Users and customers represent the same concept in this program. Let's use a class Customer. A customer has two bank accounts, and we will require that a Customer object should be able to locate these accounts. (Another possible design would make the Bank class responsible for locating the accounts of a given customer—see Exercise P17.13.)

A customer also has a customer number and a PIN. We can, of course, require that a customer object give us the customer number and the PIN. But perhaps that isn't so secure. Instead, simply require that a customer object, when given a customer number and a PIN, will tell us whether it matches its own information or not.

Customer
get accounts
match number and PIN

A bank contains a collection of customers. When a user walks up to the ATM and enters a customer number and PIN, it is the job of the bank to find the matching customer. How can the bank do this? It needs to check for each customer whether its customer number and PIN match. Thus, it needs to call the *match number and PIN* method of the Customer class that we just discovered. Because the *find customer* method calls a Customer method, it collaborates with the Customer class. We record that fact in the right-hand column of the CRC card.

When the simulation starts up, the bank must also be able to read account information from a file.

Bank	
find customer	Customer
read customers	

The BankAccount class is our familiar class with methods to get the balance and to deposit and withdraw money.

In this program there is nothing that distinguishes checking accounts from savings accounts. The ATM does not add interest or deduct fees. Therefore, we decide not to implement separate subclasses for checking and savings accounts.

Finally, we are left with the ATM class itself. An important notion of the ATM is the *state*. The current machine state determines the text of the prompts and the function of the buttons. For example, when you first log in, you use the A and B buttons to select an account. Next, you use the same buttons to choose between deposit and withdrawal. The ATM must remember the current state so that it can correctly interpret the buttons.

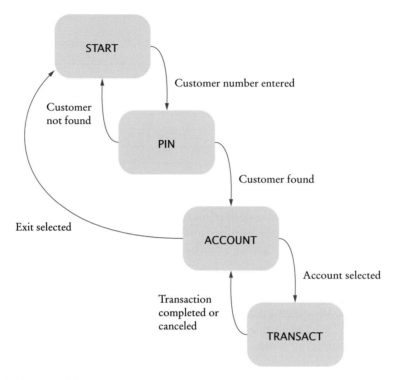

Figure 13 State Diagram for the ATM Class

There are four states:

1. START: Enter customer ID
2. PIN: Enter PIN
3. ACCOUNT: Select account
4. TRANSACT: Select transaction

To understand how to move from one state to the next, it is useful to draw a *state diagram* (Figure 13). The UML notation has standardized shapes for state diagrams. Draw states as rectangles with rounded corners. Draw state changes as arrows, with labels that indicate the reason for the change.

The user must type a valid customer number and PIN. Then the ATM can ask the bank to find the customer. This calls for a *select customer* method. It collaborates with the bank, asking the bank for the customer that matches the customer number and PIN. Next, there must be a *select account* method that asks the current customer for the checking or savings account. Finally, the ATM must carry out the selected transaction on the current account.

ATM	
manage state	Customer
select customer	Bank
select account	BankAccount
execute transaction	

Of course, discovering these classes and methods was not as neat and orderly as it appears from this discussion. When I designed these classes for this book, it took me several trials and many torn cards to come up with a satisfactory design. It is also important to remember that there is seldom one best design.

This design has several advantages. The classes describe clear concepts. The methods are sufficient to implement all necessary tasks. (I mentally walked through every ATM usage scenario to verify that.) There are not too many collaboration dependencies between the classes. Thus, I was satisfied with this design and proceeded to the next step.

17.5.3 UML Diagrams

Figure 14 shows the relationship between these classes, using the graphical user interface. (The console user interface uses a single class ATMTester instead of the ATMFrame and Keypad classes.)

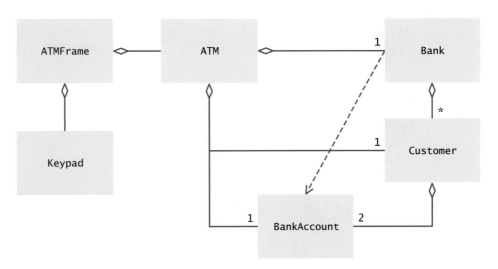

Figure 14 Relationships Between the ATM Classes

To draw the dependencies, use the "collaborator" columns from the CRC cards. Looking at those columns, you find that the dependencies are as follows:

- ATM uses Bank, Customer, and BankAccount.
- Bank uses Customer.
- Customer uses BankAccount.

It is easy to see some of the aggregation relationships. A bank has customers, and each customer has two bank accounts.

Does the ATM class aggregate Bank? To answer this question, ask yourself whether an ATM object needs to store a reference to a bank object. Does it need to locate the same bank object across multiple method calls? Indeed it does. Therefore, aggregation is the appropriate relationship.

Does an ATM aggregate customers? Clearly, the ATM is not responsible for storing all of the bank's customers. That's the bank's job. But in our design, the ATM remembers the *current* customer. If a customer has logged in, subsequent commands refer to the same customer. The ATM needs to either store a reference to the customer, or ask the bank to look up the object whenever it needs the current customer. It is a design decision: either store the object, or look it up when needed. We will decide to store the current customer object. That is, we will use aggregation. Note that the choice of aggregation is not an automatic consequence of the problem description—it is a design decision.

Similarly, we will decide to store the current bank account (checking or savings) that the user selects. Therefore, we have an aggregation relationship between ATM and BankAccount.

The class diagram is a good tool to visualize dependencies. Look at the GUI classes. They are completely independent from the rest of the ATM system. You can replace the GUI with a console interface, and you can take out the Keypad class and use it in another application. Also, the Bank, BankAccount, and Customer classes, although dependent on each other, don't know anything about the ATM class. That makes sense—you can have banks without ATMs. As you can see, when you analyze relationships, you look for both the absence and presence of relationships

17.5.4 Method Documentation

Now you are ready for the final step of the design phase: to document the classes and methods that you discovered. Here is a part of the documentation for the ATM class:

```
/**
    An ATM that accesses a bank.
*/
public class ATM
{
    /**
        Constructs an ATM for a given bank.
        @param aBank  the bank to which this ATM connects
    */
    public ATM(Bank aBank) { }
```

```
/**
    Sets the current customer number
    and sets state to PIN.
    (Precondition: state is START)
    @param number the customer number
*/
public void setCustomerNumber(int number) { }

/**
    Finds customer in bank.
    If found sets state to ACCOUNT, else to START.
    (Precondition: state is PIN)
    @param pin the PIN of the current customer
*/
public void selectCustomer(int pin) { }

/**
    Sets current account to checking or savings. Sets
    state to TRANSACT.
    (Precondition: state is ACCOUNT or TRANSACT)
    @param account one of CHECKING or SAVINGS
*/
public void selectAccount(int account) { }

/**
    Withdraws amount from current account.
    (Precondition: state is TRANSACT)
    @param value the amount to withdraw
*/
public void withdraw(double value) { }
    . . .
}
```

Then run the `javadoc` utility to turn this documentation into HTML format.

For conciseness, we omit the documentation of the other classes.

17.5.5 Implementation

Finally, the time has come to implement the ATM simulator. The implementation phase is very straightforward and should take *much less time than the design phase*.

A good strategy for implementing the classes is to go "bottom-up". Start with the classes that don't depend on others, such as `Keypad` and `BankAccount`. Then implement a class such as `Customer` that depends only on the `BankAccount` class. This "bottom-up" approach allows you to test your classes individually. You will find the implementations of these classes at the end of this section.

The most complex class is the `ATM` class. In order to implement the methods, you need to define the necessary instance variables. From the class diagram, you can tell that the ATM has a bank object. It becomes an instance variable of the class:

```
public class ATM
{
```

```
      . . .
   private Bank theBank;
}
```

From the description of the ATM states, it is clear that we require additional instance variables to store the current state, customer, and bank account.

```
class ATM
{  . . .
   private int state;
   private Customer currentCustomer;
   private BankAccount currentAccount;
   . . .
}
```

Most methods are very straightforward to implement. Consider the `selectCustomer` method. From the design documentation, we have the description

```
/**
    Finds customer in bank.
    If found sets state to ACCOUNT, else to START.
    (Precondition: state is PIN)
    @param pin the PIN of the current customer
*/
```

This description can be almost literally translated to Java instructions:

```
public void selectCustomer(int pin)
{
   assert state == PIN;
   currentCustomer = theBank.findCustomer(customerNumber, pin);
   if (currentCustomer == null)
      state = START;
   else
      state = ACCOUNT;
}
```

We won't go through a method-by-method description of the ATM program. You should take some time and compare the actual implementation against the CRC cards and the UML diagram.

File ATM.java

```
 1  /**
 2      An ATM that accesses a bank.
 3  */
 4  public class ATM
 5  {
 6     /**
 7         Constructs an ATM for a given bank.
 8         @param aBank the bank to which this ATM connects
 9     */
10     public ATM(Bank aBank)
11     {
12        theBank = aBank;
13        reset();
```

```
14      }
15
16      /**
17         Resets the ATM to the initial state.
18      */
19      public void reset()
20      {
21         customerNumber = -1;
22         currentAccount = null;
23         state = START;
24      }
25
26      /**
27         Sets the current customer number
28         and sets state to PIN.
29         (Precondition: state is START)
30         @param number the customer number
31      */
32      public void setCustomerNumber(int number)
33      {
34         assert state == START;
35         customerNumber = number;
36         state = PIN;
37      }
38
39      /**
40         Finds customer in bank.
41         If found, sets state to ACCOUNT, else to START.
42         (Precondition: state is PIN)
43         @param pin the PIN of the current customer
44      */
45      public void selectCustomer(int pin)
46      {
47         assert state == PIN;
48         currentCustomer = theBank.findCustomer(customerNumber, pin);
49         if (currentCustomer == null)
50            state = START;
51         else
52            state = ACCOUNT;
53      }
54
55      /**
56         Sets current account to checking or savings. Sets
57         state to TRANSACT.
58         (Precondition: state is ACCOUNT or TRANSACT)
59         @param account one of CHECKING or SAVINGS
60      */
61      public void selectAccount(int account)
62      {
63         assert state == ACCOUNT || state == TRANSACT;
64         if (account == CHECKING)
65            currentAccount = currentCustomer.getCheckingAccount();
66         else
67            currentAccount = currentCustomer.getSavingsAccount();
```

```
68       state = TRANSACT;
69    }
70
71    /**
72       Withdraws amount from current account.
73       (Precondition: state is TRANSACT)
74       @param value the amount to withdraw
75    */
76    public void withdraw(double value)
77    {
78       assert state == TRANSACT;
79       currentAccount.withdraw(value);
80    }
81
82    /**
83       Deposits amount to current account.
84       (Precondition: state is TRANSACT)
85       @param value the amount to deposit
86    */
87    public void deposit(double value)
88    {
89       assert state == TRANSACT;
90       currentAccount.deposit(value);
91    }
92
93    /**
94       Gets the balance of the current account.
95       (Precondition: state is TRANSACT)
96       @return the balance
97    */
98    public double getBalance()
99    {
100      assert state == TRANSACT;
101      return currentAccount.getBalance();
102   }
103
104   /**
105      Moves back to the previous state.
106   */
107   public void back()
108   {
109      if (state == TRANSACT)
110         state = ACCOUNT;
111      else if (state == ACCOUNT)
112         state = PIN;
113      else if (state == PIN)
114         state = START;
115   }
116
117   /**
118      Gets the current state of this ATM.
119      @return the current state
120   */
121   public int getState()
```

```
122     {
123         return state;
124     }
125
126     private int state;
127     private int customerNumber;
128     private Customer currentCustomer;
129     private BankAccount currentAccount;
130     private Bank theBank;
131
132     public static final int START = 1;
133     public static final int PIN = 2;
134     public static final int ACCOUNT = 3;
135     public static final int TRANSACT = 4;
136
137     public static final int CHECKING = 1;
138     public static final int SAVINGS = 2;
139 }
```

File Bank.java

```
1   import java.io.FileReader;
2   import java.io.IOException;
3   import java.util.ArrayList;
4   import java.util.Scanner;
5
6   /**
7       A bank contains customers with bank accounts.
8   */
9   public class Bank
10  {
11      /**
12          Constructs a bank with no customers.
13      */
14      public Bank()
15      {
16          customers = new ArrayList<Customer>();
17      }
18
19      /**
20          Reads the customer numbers and pins
21          and initializes the bank accounts.
22          @param filename the name of the customer file
23      */
24      public void readCustomers(String filename)
25              throws IOException
26      {
27          Scanner in = new Scanner(new FileReader(filename));
28          while (in.hasNext())
29          {
```

```
30              int number = in.nextInt();
31              int pin = in.nextInt();
32              Customer c = new Customer(number, pin);
33              addCustomer(c);
34          }
35          in.close();
36      }
37
38      /**
39          Adds a customer to the bank.
40          @param c the customer to add
41      */
42      public void addCustomer(Customer c)
43      {
44          customers.add(c);
45      }
46
47      /**
48          Finds a customer in the bank.
49          @param aNumber a customer number
50          @param aPin a personal identification number
51          @return the matching customer, or null if no customer
52          matches
53      */
54      public Customer findCustomer(int aNumber, int aPin)
55      {
56          for (Customer c : customers)
57          {
58              if (c.match(aNumber, aPin))
59                  return c;
60          }
61          return null;
62      }
63
64      private ArrayList<Customer> customers;
65  }
```

File Customer.java

```
1   /**
2       A bank customer with a checking and a savings account.
3   */
4   public class Customer
5   {
6       /**
7           Constructs a customer with a given number and PIN.
8           @param aNumber the customer number
9           @param aPin the personal identification number
10      */
11      public Customer(int aNumber, int aPin)
12      {
```

```java
13          customerNumber = aNumber;
14          pin = aPin;
15          checkingAccount = new BankAccount();
16          savingsAccount = new BankAccount();
17       }
18
19       /**
20          Tests if this customer matches a customer number
21          and PIN.
22          @param aNumber a customer number
23          @param aPin a personal identification number
24          @return true if the customer number and PIN match
25       */
26       public boolean match(int aNumber, int aPin)
27       {
28          return customerNumber == aNumber && pin == aPin;
29       }
30
31       /**
32          Gets the checking account of this customer.
33          @return the checking account
34       */
35       public BankAccount getCheckingAccount()
36       {
37          return checkingAccount;
38       }
39
40       /**
41          Gets the savings account of this customer.
42          @return the checking account
43       */
44       public BankAccount getSavingsAccount()
45       {
46          return savingsAccount;
47       }
48
49       private int customerNumber;
50       private int pin;
51       private BankAccount checkingAccount;
52       private BankAccount savingsAccount;
53   }
```

Here are the user interface classes for the GUI version of the user interface.

File ATMViewer.java

```java
1   import java.io.IOException;
2   import javax.swing.JFrame;
3   import javax.swing.JOptionPane;
4
5   /**
6       A graphical simulation of an automatic teller machine.
7   */
8   public class ATMViewer
```

```
 9   {
10       public static void main(String[] args)
11       {
12           ATM theATM;
13
14           try
15           {
16               Bank theBank = new Bank();
17               theBank.readCustomers("customers.txt");
18               theATM = new ATM(theBank);
19           }
20           catch(IOException e)
21           {
22               JOptionPane.showMessageDialog(null,
23                       "Error opening accounts file.");
24               return;
25           }
26
27           JFrame frame = new ATMFrame(theATM);
28           frame.setTitle("First National Bank of Java");
29           frame.setDefaultCloseOperation(JFrame.EXIT_ON_CLOSE);
30           frame.setVisible(true);
31       }
32   }
```

File ATMFrame.java

```
 1   import java.awt.FlowLayout;
 2   import java.awt.GridLayout;
 3   import java.awt.event.ActionEvent;
 4   import java.awt.event.ActionListener;
 5   import javax.swing.JButton;
 6   import javax.swing.JFrame;
 7   import javax.swing.JPanel;
 8   import javax.swing.JTextArea;
 9
10   /**
11       A frame displaying the components of an ATM.
12   */
13   public class ATMFrame extends JFrame
14   {
15       /**
16           Constructs the user interface of the ATM frame.
17       */
18       public ATMFrame(ATM anATM)
19       {
20           theATM = anATM;
21
22           // Construct components
23           pad = new KeyPad();
24
25           display = new JTextArea(4, 20);
26
27           aButton = new JButton("  A  ");
28           aButton.addActionListener(new AButtonListener());
```

```
29
30        bButton = new JButton("  B  ");
31        bButton.addActionListener(new BButtonListener());
32
33        cButton = new JButton("  C  ");
34        cButton.addActionListener(new CButtonListener());
35
36        // Add components
37
38        JPanel buttonPanel = new JPanel();
39        buttonPanel.setLayout(new GridLayout(3, 1));
40        buttonPanel.add(aButton);
41        buttonPanel.add(bButton);
42        buttonPanel.add(cButton);
43
44        setLayout(new FlowLayout());
45        add(pad);
46        add(display);
47        add(buttonPanel);
48        showState();
49
50        setSize(FRAME_WIDTH, FRAME_HEIGHT);
51     }
52
53     /**
54        Updates display message.
55     */
56     public void showState()
57     {
58        int state = theATM.getState();
59        pad.clear();
60        if (state == ATM.START)
61           display.setText("Enter customer number\nA = OK");
62        else if (state == ATM.PIN)
63           display.setText("Enter PIN\nA = OK");
64        else if (state == ATM.ACCOUNT)
65           display.setText("Select Account\n"
66                 + "A = Checking\nB = Savings\nC = Exit");
67        else if (state == ATM.TRANSACT)
68           display.setText("Balance = "
69                 + theATM.getBalance()
70                 + "\nEnter amount and select transaction\n"
71                 + "A = Withdraw\nB = Deposit\nC = Cancel");
72     }
73
74     private class AButtonListener implements ActionListener
75     {
76        public void actionPerformed(ActionEvent event)
77        {
78           int state = theATM.getState();
79           if (state == ATM.START)
80              theATM.setCustomerNumber((int) pad.getValue());
81           else if (state == ATM.PIN)
82              theATM.selectCustomer((int) pad.getValue());
```

```
 83             else if (state == ATM.ACCOUNT)
 84                theATM.selectAccount(ATM.CHECKING);
 85             else if (state == ATM.TRANSACT)
 86             {
 87                theATM.withdraw(pad.getValue());
 88                theATM.back();
 89             }
 90             showState();
 91          }
 92       }
 93
 94       private class BButtonListener implements ActionListener
 95       {
 96          public void actionPerformed(ActionEvent event)
 97          {
 98             int state = theATM.getState();
 99             if (state == ATM.ACCOUNT)
100                theATM.selectAccount(ATM.SAVINGS);
101             else if (state == ATM.TRANSACT)
102             {
103                theATM.deposit(pad.getValue());
104                theATM.back();
105             }
106             showState();
107          }
108       }
109
110       private class CButtonListener implements ActionListener
111       {
112          public void actionPerformed(ActionEvent event)
113          {
114             int state = theATM.getState();
115             if (state == ATM.ACCOUNT)
116                theATM.reset();
117             else if (state == ATM.TRANSACT)
118                theATM.back();
119             showState();
120          }
121       }
122
123       private JButton aButton;
124       private JButton bButton;
125       private JButton cButton;
126
127       private KeyPad pad;
128       private JTextArea display;
129
130       private ATM theATM;
131
132       private static final int FRAME_WIDTH = 300;
133       private static final int FRAME_HEIGHT = 400;
134    }
```

File KeyPad.java

```
1  import java.awt.BorderLayout;
2  import java.awt.GridLayout;
3  import java.awt.event.ActionEvent;
4  import java.awt.event.ActionListener;
5  import javax.swing.JButton;
6  import javax.swing.JPanel;
7  import javax.swing.JTextField;
8
9  /**
10     A component that lets the user enter a number, using
11     a keypad labeled with digits.
12  */
13  public class KeyPad extends JPanel
14  {
15     /**
16        Constructs the keypad panel.
17     */
18     public KeyPad()
19     {
20        setLayout(new BorderLayout());
21
22        // Add display field
23
24        display = new JTextField();
25        add(display, "North");
26
27        // Make button panel
28
29        buttonPanel = new JPanel();
30        buttonPanel.setLayout(new GridLayout(4, 3));
31
32        // Add digit buttons
33
34        addButton("7");
35        addButton("8");
36        addButton("9");
37        addButton("4");
38        addButton("5");
39        addButton("6");
40        addButton("1");
41        addButton("2");
42        addButton("3");
43        addButton("0");
44        addButton(".");
45
46        // Add clear entry button
47
48        clearButton = new JButton("CE");
49        buttonPanel.add(clearButton);
50
51        class ClearButtonListener implements ActionListener
52        {
```

```
53              public void actionPerformed(ActionEvent event)
54              {
55                  display.setText("");
56              }
57          }
58          ActionListener listener = new ClearButtonListener();
59
60          clearButton.addActionListener(new
61              ClearButtonListener());
62
63          add(buttonPanel, "Center");
64      }
65
66      /**
67          Adds a button to the button panel.
68          @param label the button label
69      */
70      private void addButton(final String label)
71      {
72          class DigitButtonListener implements ActionListener
73          {
74              public void actionPerformed(ActionEvent event)
75              {
76
77                  // Don't add two decimal points
78                  if (label.equals(".")
79                      && display.getText().indexOf(".") != -1)
80                      return;
81
82                  // Append label text to button
83                  display.setText(display.getText() + label);
84              }
85          }
86
87          JButton button = new JButton(label);
88          buttonPanel.add(button);
89          ActionListener listener = new DigitButtonListener();
90          button.addActionListener(listener);
91      }
92
93      /**
94          Gets the value that the user entered.
95          @return the value in the text field of the keypad
96      */
97      public double getValue()
98      {
99          return Double.parseDouble(display.getText());
100     }
101
102     /**
103         Clears the display.
104     */
105     public void clear()
106     {
107         display.setText("");
```

```
108      }
109
110      private JPanel buttonPanel;
111      private JButton clearButton;
112      private JTextField display;
113  }
```

The following class implements a console user interface for the ATM.

File ATMTester.java

```
1   import java.io.IOException;
2   import java.util.Scanner;
3
4   /**
5       A text-based simulation of an automatic teller machine.
6   */
7   public class ATMTester
8   {
9       public static void main(String[] args)
10      {
11          ATM theATM;
12          try
13          {
14              Bank theBank = new Bank();
15              theBank.readCustomers("customers.txt");
16              theATM = new ATM(theBank);
17          }
18          catch(IOException e)
19          {
20              System.out.println("Error opening accounts file.");
21              return;
22          }
23
24          Scanner in = new Scanner(System.in);
25
26          while (true)
27          {
28              int state = theATM.getState();
29              if (state == ATM.START)
30              {
31                  System.out.print("Enter account number: ");
32                  int number = in.nextInt();
33                  theATM.setCustomerNumber(number);
34              }
35              else if (state == ATM.PIN)
36              {
37                  System.out.print("Enter PIN: ");
38                  int pin = in.nextInt();
39                  theATM.selectCustomer(pin);
40              }
41              else if (state == ATM.ACCOUNT)
42              {
43                  System.out.print("A=Checking, B=Savings, C=Quit: ");
```

```
44              String command = in.next();
45              if (command.equalsIgnoreCase("A"))
46                 theATM.selectAccount(ATM.CHECKING);
47              else if (command.equalsIgnoreCase("B"))
48                 theATM.selectAccount(ATM.SAVINGS);
49              else if (command.equalsIgnoreCase("C"))
50                 theATM.reset();
51              else
52                 System.out.println("Illegal input!");
53           }
54           else if (state == ATM.TRANSACT)
55           {
56              System.out.println("Balance=" + theATM.getBalance());
57              System.out.print("A=Deposit, B=Withdrawal, C=Cancel: ");
58              String command = in.next();
59              if (command.equalsIgnoreCase("A"))
60              {
61                 System.out.print("Amount: ");
62                 double amount = in.nextDouble();
63                 theATM.deposit(amount);
64                 theATM.back();
65              }
66              else if (command.equalsIgnoreCase("B"))
67              {
68                 System.out.print("Amount: ");
69                 double amount = in.nextDouble();
70                 theATM.withdraw(amount);
71                 theATM.back();
72              }
73              else if (command.equalsIgnoreCase("C"))
74                 theATM.back();
75              else
76                 System.out.println("Illegal input!");
77           }
78        }
79     }
80  }
```

Output

```
Enter account number: 1
Enter PIN: 1234
A=Checking, B=Savings, C=Quit: A
Balance=0.0
A=Deposit, B=Withdrawal, C=Cancel: A
Amount: 1000
A=Checking, B=Savings, C=Quit: C
. . .
```

In this chapter, you learned a systematic approach for building a relatively complex program. However, object-oriented design is definitely not a spectator sport. To really learn how to design and implement programs, you have to gain experience by repeating this process with your own projects. It is quite possible that you don't immediately home in on a good solution and that you need to go back and reorganize your classes and responsibilities. That is normal and only to be expected. The purpose of the object-oriented design process is to spot these problems in the design phase, when they are still easy to rectify, instead of in the implementation phase, when massive reorganization is more difficult and time consuming.

SELF CHECK

12. Why does the Bank class in this example not store an array list of bank accounts?

13. Suppose the requirements change—you need to save the current account balances to a file after every transaction and reload them when the program starts. What is the impact of this change on the design?

RANDOM FACT 17.2

Software Development—Art or Science?

There has been a long discussion whether the discipline of computing is a science or not. We call the field "computer science", but that doesn't mean much. Except possibly for librarians and sociologists, few people believe that library science and social science are scientific endeavors.

A scientific discipline aims to discover certain fundamental principles dictated by the laws of nature. It operates on the *scientific method:* by posing hypotheses and testing them with experiments that are repeatable by other workers in the field. For example, a physicist may have a theory on the makeup of nuclear particles and attempt to confirm or refute that theory by running experiments in a particle collider. If an experiment cannot be confirmed, such as the "cold fusion" research in the early 1990s, then the theory dies a quick death.

Some software developers indeed run experiments. They try out various methods of computing certain results or of configuring computer systems, and measure the differences in performance. However, their aim is not to discover laws of nature.

Some computer scientists discover fundamental principles. One class of fundamental results, for instance, states that it is impossible to write certain kinds of computer programs, no matter how powerful the computing equipment is. For example, it is impossible to write a program that takes as its input any two Java program files and as its output prints whether or not these two programs always compute the same results. Such a program would be very handy for grading student homework, but nobody, no matter how clever, will ever be able to write one that works for all input files. However, the majority of computer scientists are not researching the limits of computation.

Some people view software development as an *art* or *craft*. A programmer who writes elegant code that is easy to understand and runs with optimum efficiency can indeed be considered a good craftsman. Calling it an art is perhaps far-fetched, because an art object requires an audience to appreciate it, whereas the program code is generally hidden from the program user.

Others call software development an *engineering discipline*. Just as mechanical engineering is based on the fundamental mathematical principles of statics, computing has certain mathematical foundations. There is more to mechanical engineering than mathematics, such as knowledge of materials and of project planning. The same is true for computing. A *software engineer* needs to know about planning, budgeting, design, test automation, documentation, and source code control, in addition to computer science subjects, such as programming, algorithm design, and database technologies.

In one somewhat worrisome aspect, software development does not have the same standing as other engineering disciplines. There is little agreement as to what constitutes professional conduct in the computer field. Unlike the scientist, whose main responsibility is the search for truth, the software developer must strive to satisfy the conflicting demands of quality, safety, and economy. Engineering disciplines have professional organizations that hold their members to standards of conduct. The computer field is so new that in many cases we simply don't know the correct method for achieving certain tasks. That makes it difficult to set professional standards.

What do you think? From your limited experience, do you consider software development an art, a craft, a science, or an engineering activity?

CHAPTER SUMMARY

1. The life cycle of software encompasses all activities from initial analysis until obsolescence.

2. A formal process for software development describes phases of the development process and gives guidelines for how to carry out the phases.

3. The waterfall model of software development describes a sequential process of analysis, design, implementation, testing, and deployment.

4. The spiral model of software development describes an iterative process in which design and implementation are repeated.

5. Extreme Programming is a development methodology that strives for simplicity by removing formal structure and focusing on best practices.

6. In object-oriented design, you discover classes, determine the responsibilities of classes, and describe the relationships between classes.

7. A CRC card describes a class, its responsibilities, and its collaborating classes.

8. Inheritance (the *is-a* relationship) is sometimes inappropriately used when the *has-a* relationship would be more appropriate.

9. Aggregation (the *has-a* relationship) denotes that objects of one class contain references to objects of another class.

10. Dependency is another name for the "uses" relationship.

11. You need to be able to distinguish the UML notations for inheritance, interface implementation, aggregation, and dependency.

12. Use `javadoc` comments (with the method bodies left blank) to record the behavior of classes.

FURTHER READING

1. Grady Booch, James Rumbaugh, and Ivar Jacobson, *The Unified Modeling Language User Guide*, Addison-Wesley, 1999.

2. Kent Beck, *Extreme Programming Explained*, Addison-Wesley, 1999.

3. W. H. Sackmann, W. J. Erikson, and E. E. Grant, "Exploratory Experimental Studies Comparing Online and Offline Programming Performance", *Communications of the ACM, vol. 11, no. 1* (January 1968), pp. 3–11.

4. F. Brooks, *The Mythical Man-Month*, Addison-Wesley, 1975.

REVIEW EXERCISES

Exercise R17.1. What is the software life cycle?

Exercise R17.2. Explain the process of object-oriented design that this chapter recommends for student use.

Exercise R17.3. Give a rule of thumb for how to find classes when designing a program.

Exercise R17.4. Give a rule of thumb for how to find methods when designing a program.

Exercise R17.5. After discovering a method, why is it important to identify the object that is *responsible* for carrying out the action?

Exercise R17.6. What relationship is appropriate between the following classes: aggregation, inheritance, or neither?

- a. University–Student
- b. Student–TeachingAssistant
- c. Student–Freshman
- d. Student–Professor
- e. Car–Door
- f. Truck–Vehicle
- g. Traffic–TrafficSign
- h. TrafficSign–Color

Exercise R17.7. Every BMW is a car. Should a class BMW inherit from the class Car? BMW is a car manufacturer. Does that mean that the class BMW should inherit from the class CarManufacturer?

Exercise R17.8. Some books on object-oriented programming recommend using inheritance so that the class Circle extends the class Point. Then the Circle class inherits the setLocation method from the Point superclass. Explain why the setLocation method need not be redefined in the subclass. Why is it nevertheless not a good idea to have Circle inherit from Point? Conversely, would inheriting Point from Circle fulfill the *is-a* rule? Would it be a good idea?

Exercise R17.9. Write CRC cards for the Coin and CashRegister classes described in Section 9.1.

Exercise R17.10. Write CRC cards for the Bank and BankAccount classes in Section 8.2.

Exercise R17.11. Draw a UML diagram for the Coin and CashRegister classes described in Section 9.1.

Exercise R17.12. Draw a UML diagram for the classes in the ChoiceTest program in Chapter 14. Use aggregations when appropriate.

Exercise R17.13. A file contains a set of records describing countries. Each record consists of the name of the country, its population, and its area. Suppose your task is to write a program that reads in such a file and prints

- The country with the largest area
- The country with the largest population
- The country with the largest population density (people per square kilometer)

Think through the problems that you need to solve. What classes and methods will you need? Produce a set of CRC cards, a UML diagram, and a set of javadoc comments.

Exercise R17.14. Discover classes and methods for generating a student report card that lists all classes, grades, and the grade point average for a semester. Produce a set of CRC cards, a UML diagram, and a set of javadoc comments.

PROGRAMMING EXERCISES

Exercise P17.1. Enhance the invoice-printing program by providing for two kinds of line items: One kind describes products that are purchased in certain numerical quantities (such as "3 toasters"), another describes a fixed charge (such as "shipping: $5.00"). *Hint:* Use inheritance. Produce a UML diagram of your modified implementation.

Exercise P17.2. The invoice-printing program is somewhat unrealistic because the formatting of the LineItem objects won't lead to good visual results when the prices and quantities have varying numbers of digits. Enhance the format method in two ways: Accept an int[] array of column widths as a parameter. Use the NumberFormat class to format the currency values.

Exercise P17.3. The invoice-printing program has an unfortunate flaw—it mixes "business logic", the computation of total charges, and "presentation", the visual appearance of the invoice. To appreciate this flaw, imagine the changes that would be necessary to draw the invoice in HTML for presentation on the Web.

Reimplement the program, using a separate `InvoiceFormatter` class to format the invoice. That is, the `Invoice` and `LineItem` methods are no longer responsible for formatting. However, they will acquire other responsibilities, because the `Invoice-Formatter` class needs to query them for the values that it requires.

Exercise P17.4. Implement a program to teach your baby sister to read the clock. In the game, present an analog clock, such as the one in Figure 15. Generate random times and display the clock. Accept guesses from the player. Reward the player for correct guesses. After two incorrect guesses, display the correct answer and make a new random time. Implement several levels of play. In level 1, only show full hours. In level 2, show quarter hours. In level 3, show five-minute multiples, and in level 4, show any number of minutes. After a player has achieved five correct guesses at one level, advance to the next level.

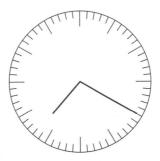

Figure 15 An Analog Clock

Exercise P17.5. Write a program that implements a different game, to teach arithmetic to your younger brother. The program tests addition and subtraction. In level 1 it tests only addition of numbers less than 10 whose sum is less than 10. In level 2 it tests addition of arbitrary one-digit numbers. In level 3 it tests subtraction of one-digit numbers with a nonnegative difference. Generate random problems and get the player input. The player gets up to two tries per problem. Advance from one level to the next when the player has achieved a score of five points. Your user interface can be text-based or graphical.

Exercise P17.6. Write a bumper car game with the following rules. A bumper car starts moving in a random direction, either left, right, up, or down. If it reaches a boundary, then it reverses direction. If it is about to bump into another bumper car, it reverses direction. Supply a user interface to add bumper cars, and to run the simulation. Use at least four classes in your program.

Exercise P17.7. Write a program that can be used to design a suburban scene, with houses, streets, and cars. Users can add houses and cars of various colors to a street. Write more specific requirements that include a detailed description of the user interface. Then, discover classes and methods, provide UML diagrams, and implement your program.

Exercise P17.8. Design a simple e-mail messaging system. A message has a recipient, a sender, and a message text. A mailbox can store messages. Supply a number of mailboxes for different users and a user interface for users to log in, send messages to other users, read their own messages, and log out. Your user interface can be text-based or graphical. Follow the design process that was described in this chapter.

Exercise P17.9. Write a program that simulates a vending machine. Products can be purchased by inserting the correct number of coins into the machine. A user selects a product from a list of available products, adds coins, and either gets the product or gets the coins returned if insufficient money was supplied or if the product is sold out. Products can be restocked and money removed by an operator. Follow the design process that was described in this chapter.

Exercise P17.10. Write a program to design an appointment calendar. An appointment includes the date, starting time, ending time, and a description; for example,

```
Dentist 2001/10/1 17:30 18:30
CS1 class 2001/10/2 08:30 10:00
```

Supply a user interface to add appointments, remove canceled appointments, and print out a list of appointments for a particular day. Your user interface can be text-based or graphical. Follow the design process that was described in this chapter.

Exercise P17.11. *Airline seating.* Write a program that assigns seats on an airplane. Assume the airplane has 20 seats in first class (5 rows of 4 seats each, separated by an aisle) and 180 seats in economy class (30 rows of 6 seats each, separated by an aisle). Your program should take three commands: add passengers, show seating, and quit. When passengers are added, ask for the class (first or economy), the number of passengers traveling together (1 or 2 in first class; 1 to 3 in economy), and the seating preference (aisle or window in first class; aisle, center, or window in economy). Then try to find a match and assign the seats. If no match exists, print a message. Your user interface can be text-based or graphical. Follow the design process that was described in this chapter.

Exercise P17.12. Write a simple graphics editor that allows users to add a mixture of shapes (ellipses, rectangles, lines, and text in different colors) to a panel. Supply commands to load and save the picture. For simplicity, you may use a single text size, and you don't have to fill any shapes. Design a user interface, discover classes, supply a UML diagram, and implement your program.

Exercise P17.13. Modify the implementations of the class in the ATM example so that the bank manages a collection of bank accounts and a separate collection of customers. Allow joint accounts in which some accounts can have more than one customer. You should design an appropriate mechanism by which all accounts that belong to a customer can be determined.

PROGRAMMING PROJECTS

Project 17.1. Produce a requirements document for a program that allows a company to send out personalized mailings, either by e-mail or through the postal service. Template files contain the message text, together with variable fields (such as Dear [Title] [Last Name] . . .). A database (stored as a text file) contains the field values for each recipient. Use HTML as the output file format. Then design and implement the program.

Project 17.2. Write a tic-tac-toe game that allows a human player to play against the computer. Your program will play many turns against a human opponent, and it will learn. When it is the computer's turn, the computer randomly selects an empty field, except that it won't ever choose a losing combination. For that purpose, your program must keep an array of losing combinations. Whenever the human wins, the immediately preceding combination is stored as losing. For example, suppose that x = computer and o = human. Suppose the current combination is

```
 O │ X │ X
───┼───┼───
   │ O │
───┼───┼───
   │   │
```

Now it is the human's turn, who will of course choose

```
 O │ X │ X
───┼───┼───
   │ O │
───┼───┼───
   │ O │
```

The computer should then remember the preceding combination

```
 O │ X │ X
───┼───┼───
   │ O │
───┼───┼───
   │   │
```

as a losing combination. As a result, the computer will never again choose that combination from

```
 O │ X │
───┼───┼───
   │ O │
───┼───┼───
   │   │
```

or

Discover classes and supply a UML diagram before you begin to program.

ANSWERS TO SELF-CHECK QUESTIONS

1. It is unlikely that the customer did a perfect job with the requirements document. If you don't accommodate changes, your customer may not like the outcome. If you charge for the changes, your customer may not like the cost.

2. An "extreme" spiral model, with lots of iterations.

3. To give frequent feedback as to whether the current iteration of the product fits customer needs.

4. FileWriter

5. To produce the shipping address of the customer.

6. Reword the responsibilities so that they are at a higher level, or come up with more classes to handle the responsibilities.

7. Through aggregation. The bank manages bank account objects.

8. Through inheritance.

9. The BankAccount, System, and PrintStream classes.

10. The Invoice class is responsible for computing the amount due. It collaborates with the LineItem class.

11. This design decision reduces coupling. It enables us to reuse the classes when we want to show the invoice in a dialog box or on a web page.

12. The bank needs to store the list of customers so that customers can log in. We need to locate all bank accounts of a customer, and we chose to simply store them in the customer class. In this program, there is no further need to access bank accounts.

13. The Bank class needs to have an additional responsibility: to load and save the accounts. The bank can carry out this responsibility because it has access to the customer objects and, through them, to the bank accounts.

Recursion

CHAPTER GOALS

- To learn about the method of recursion
- To understand the relationship between recursion and iteration
- To analyze problems that are much easier to solve by recursion than by iteration
- To learn to "think recursively"
- To be able to use recursive helper methods
- To understand when the use of recursion affects the efficiency of an algorithm

The method of recursion is a powerful technique to break up complex computational problems into simpler ones. The term "recursion" refers to the fact that the same computation recurs, or occurs repeatedly, as the problem is solved. Recursion is often the most natural way of thinking about a problem, and there are some computations that are very difficult to perform without recursion. This chapter shows you simple and complex examples of recursion and teaches you how to "think recursively".

CHAPTER CONTENTS

18.1 Triangle Numbers

We begin this chapter with a very simple example that demonstrates the power of thinking recursively. In this example, we will look at triangle shapes such as the ones from Section 7.3. We'd like to compute the area of a triangle of width n, assuming that each [] square has area 1. This value is sometimes called the nth *triangle number*. For example, as you can tell from looking at

```
[]
[][]
[][][]
```

the third triangle number is 6.

You may know that there is a very simple formula to compute these numbers, but you should pretend for now that you don't know about it. The ultimate purpose of this section is not to compute triangle numbers, but to learn about the concept of recursion in a simple situation.

Here is the outline of the class that we will develop:

```java
public class Triangle
{
    public Triangle(int aWidth)
    {
        width = aWidth;
    }

    public int getArea()
    {
        . . .
    }

    private int width;
}
```

If the width of the triangle is 1, then the triangle consists of a single square, and its area is 1. Let's take care of this case first.

```
public int getArea()
{
    if (width == 1) return 1;
    . . .
}
```

To deal with the general case, consider this picture.

```
[]
[] []
[] [] []
[] [] [] []
```

Suppose we knew the area of the smaller, colored triangle. Then we could easily compute the area of the larger triangle as

```
smallerArea + width
```

How can we get the smaller area? Let's make a smaller triangle and ask it!

```
Triangle smallerTriangle = new Triangle(width - 1);
int smallerArea = smallerTriangle.getArea();
```

Now we can complete the getArea method:

```
public int getArea()
{
    if (width == 1) return 1;
    Triangle smallerTriangle = new Triangle(width - 1);
    int smallerArea = smallerTriangle.getArea();
    return smallerArea + width;
}
```

> A recursive computation solves a problem by using the solution of the same problem with simpler values.

Here is an illustration of what happens when we compute the area of a triangle of width 4.

- The getArea method makes a smaller triangle of width 3.
  - It calls getArea on that triangle.
    - That method makes a smaller triangle of width 2.
      - It calls getArea on that triangle.
        - That method makes a smaller triangle of width 1.
          - It calls getArea on that triangle.
        - That method returns 1.
      - The method returns smallerArea + width = 1 + 2 = 3.
    - The method returns smallerArea + width = 3 + 3 = 6.
  - The method returns smallerArea + width = 6 + 4 = 10.

This solution has one remarkable aspect. To solve the area problem for a triangle of a given width, we use the fact that we can solve the same problem for a lesser width. This is called a *recursive* solution.

The call pattern of a recursive method looks complicated, and the key to the successful design of a recursive method is *not to think about it*. Instead, look at the getArea method one more time and notice how utterly reasonable it is. If the width is 1, then, of course, the area is 1. The next part is just as reasonable. Compute the area of the smaller triangle *and don't think about why that works.* Then the area of the larger triangle is clearly the sum of the smaller area and the width.

There are two key requirements to make sure that the recursion is successful:

- Every recursive call must simplify the computation in some way.
- There must be special cases to handle the simplest computations directly.

> For a recursion to terminate, there must be special cases for the simplest values.

The getArea method calls itself again with smaller and smaller width values. Eventually the width must reach 1, and there is a special case for computing the area of a triangle with width 1. Thus, the getArea method always succeeds.

Actually, you have to be careful. What happens when you call the area of a triangle with width –1? It computes the area of a triangle with width –2, which computes the area of a triangle with width –3, and so on. To avoid this, the getArea method should return 0 if the width is ≤ 0.

Recursion is not really necessary to compute the triangle numbers. The area of a triangle equals the sum

```
1 + 2 + 3 + . . . + width
```

Of course, we can program a simple loop:

```
double area = 0;
for (int i = 1; i <= width; i++)
   area = area + i;
```

Many simple recursions can be computed as loops. However, loop equivalents for more complex recursions—such as the one in our next example—can be complex.

Actually, in this case, you don't even need a loop to compute the answer. The sum of the first *n* integers can be computed as

$$1 + 2 + \cdots + n = n \times (n + 1)/2$$

Thus, the area equals

```
width * (width + 1) / 2
```

Therefore, neither recursion nor a loop is required to solve this problem. The recursive solution is intended as a "warm-up" to introduce you to the concept of recursion.

File Triangle.java

```
1   /**
2      A triangular shape composed of stacked unit squares like this:
3      []
4      [][]
5      [][][]
6      . . .
7   */
8   public class Triangle
9   {
```

```
10       /**
11           Constructs a triangular shape.
12           @param aWidth  the width (and height) of the triangle
13       */
14       public Triangle(int aWidth)
15       {
16           width = aWidth;
17       }
18
19       /**
20           Computes the area of the triangle.
21           @return  the area
22       */
23       public int getArea()
24       {
25           if (width <= 0) return 0;
26           if (width == 1) return 1;
27           Triangle smallerTriangle = new Triangle(width - 1);
28           int smallerArea = smallerTriangle.getArea();
29           return smallerArea + width;
30       }
31
32       private int width;
33  }
```

File TriangleTester.java

```
1   import java.util.Scanner;
2
3   public class TriangleTester
4   {
5       public static void main(String[] args)
6       {
7           Scanner in = new Scanner(System.in);
8           System.out.print("Enter width: ");
9           int width = in.nextInt();
10          Triangle t = new Triangle(width);
11          int area = t.getArea();
12          System.out.println("Area = " + area);
13      }
14  }
```

Output

```
Enter width: 10
Area = 55
```

SELF CHECK

1. Why is the statement if (width == 1) return 1; in the getArea method unnecessary?
2. How would you modify the program to recursively compute the area of a square?

COMMON ERROR 18.1

Infinite Recursion

A common programming error is an infinite recursion: a method calling itself over and over with no end in sight. The computer needs some amount of memory for bookkeeping for each call. After some number of calls, all memory that is available for this purpose is exhausted. Your program shuts down and reports a "stack fault".

Infinite recursion happens either because the parameter values don't get simpler or because a special terminating case is missing. For example, suppose the getArea method computes the area of a triangle with width 0. If it wasn't for the special test, the method would have constructed triangles with width –1, –2, –3, and so on.

18.2 Permutations

We will now turn to a more complex example of recursion that would be difficult to program with a simple loop. We will design a class that lists all permutations of a string. A *permutation* is simply a rearrangement of the letters. For example, the string "eat" has six permutations (including the original string itself):

```
"eat"
"eta"
"aet"
"ate"
"tea"
"tae"
```

As in the preceding section, we will define a class that is in charge of computing the answer. In this case, the answer is not a single number but a collection of permuted strings. Here is our class:

```
public class PermutationGenerator
{
    public PermutationGenerator(String aWord) { . . . }
    ArrayList<String> getPermutations() { . . . }
}
```

Here is the test program that prints out all permutations of the string "eat":

File PermutationGeneratorTester.java

```
1  import java.util.ArrayList;
2
3  /**
4     This program tests the permutation generator.
5  */
```

```
 6  public class PermutationGeneratorTester
 7  {
 8     public static void main(String[] args)
 9     {
10        PermutationGenerator generator
11              = new PermutationGenerator("eat");
12        ArrayList<String> permutations = generator.getPermutations();
13        for (String s : permutations)
14        {
15           System.out.println(s);
16        }
17     }
18  }
```

Output

```
eat
eta
aet
ate
tea
tae
```

Now we need a way to generate the permutations recursively. Consider the string
"eat". Let's simplify the problem. First, we'll generate all permutations that start
with the letter 'e', then those that start with 'a', and finally those that start with
't'. How do we generate the permutations that start with 'e'? We need to know
the permutations of the substring "at". But that's the same problem—to generate all
permutations—with a simpler input, namely the shorter string "at". Thus, we can
use recursion. Generate the permutations of the substring "at". They are

```
"at"
"ta"
```

For each permutation of that substring, prepend the letter 'e' to get the permutations of "eat" that start with 'e', namely

```
"eat"
"eta"
```

Now let's turn our attention to the permutations of "eat" that start with 'a'. We
need to produce the permutations of the remaining letters, "et". They are:

```
"et"
"te"
```

We add the letter 'a' to the front of the strings and obtain

```
"aet"
"ate"
```

We generate the permutations that start with 't' in the same way.

That's the idea. The implementation is fairly straightforward. In the get-
Permutations method, we loop through all positions in the word to be permuted.

For each of them, we compute the shorter word that is obtained by removing the ith letter:

```
String shorterWord = word.substring(0, i) + word.substring(i + 1);
```

We construct a permutation generator to get the permutations of the shorter word, and ask it to give us all permutations of the shorter word.

```
PermutationGenerator shorterPermutationGenerator
    = new PermutationGenerator(shorterWord);
ArrayList<String> shorterWordPermutations
    = shorterPermutationGenerator.getPermutations();
```

Finally, we add the removed letter to the front of all permutations of the shorter word.

```
for (String s : shorterWordPermutations)
{
    result.add(word.charAt(i) + s);
}
```

As always, we have to provide a special case for the simplest strings. The simplest possible string is the empty string, which has a single permutation—itself.

Here is the complete `PermutationGenerator` class.

File PermutationGenerator.java

```
1  import java.util.ArrayList;
2
3  /**
4      This class generates permutations of a word.
5  */
6  public class PermutationGenerator
7  {
8      /**
9          Constructs a permutation generator.
10         @param aWord  the word to permute
11     */
12     public PermutationGenerator(String aWord)
13     {
14         word = aWord;
15     }
16
17     /**
18         Gets all permutations of a given word.
19     */
20     public ArrayList<String> getPermutations()
21     {
22         ArrayList<String> result = new ArrayList<String>();
23
24         // The empty string has a single permutation: itself
25         if (word.length() == 0)
26         {
27             result.add(word);
28             return result;
29         }
```

```
30
31          // Loop through all character positions
32          for (int i = 0; i < word.length(); i++)
33          {
34             // Form a simpler word by removing the ith character
35             String shorterWord = word.substring(0, i)
36                   + word.substring(i + 1);
37
38             // Generate all permutations of the simpler word
39             PermutationGenerator shorterPermutationGenerator
40                   = new PermutationGenerator(shorterWord);
41             ArrayList<String> shorterWordPermutations
42                   = shorterPermutationGenerator.getPermutations();
43
44             // Add the removed character to the front of
45             // each permutation of the simpler word
46             for (String s : shorterWordPermutations)
47             {
48                result.add(word.charAt(i) + s);
49             }
50          }
51          // Return all permutations
52          return result;
53       }
54
55       private String word;
56    }
```

Compare the `PermutationGenerator` and `Triangle` classes. Both of them work on the same principle. When they work on a more complex input, they first solve the problem for a simpler input. Then they combine the result for the simpler input with additional work to deliver the results for the more complex input. There really is no particular complexity behind that process as long as you think about the solution on that level only. However, behind the scenes, the simpler input creates even simpler input, which creates yet another simplification, and so on, until one input is so simple that the result can be obtained without further help. It is interesting to think about this process, but it can also be confusing. What's important is that you can focus on the one level that matters—putting a solution together from the slightly simpler problem, ignoring the fact that it also uses recursion to get its results.

SELF CHECK

3. What are all permutations of the four-letter word `beat`?
4. Our recursion for the permutation generator stops at the empty string. What simple modification would make the recursion stop at strings of length 0 or 1?

COMMON ERROR 18.2

Tracing Through Recursive Methods

Debugging a recursive method can be somewhat challenging. When you set a breakpoint in a recursive method, the program stops as soon as that program line is encountered in *any call to the recursive method*. Suppose you want to debug the recursive getArea method of the Triangle class. Debug the TriangleTester program with an input of 4. Run until the beginning of the getArea method. Inspect the width instance variable. It is 4.

Remove the breakpoint and now run until the statement return smallerArea + width; (see Figure 1). When you inspect width again, its value is 2! That makes no sense. There was no instruction that changed the value of width. Is that a bug with the debugger?

No. The program stopped in the first recursive call to getArea that reached the return statement. If you are confused, look at the *call stack*. You will see that four calls to getArea are pending.

You can debug recursive methods with the debugger. You just need to be particularly careful, and watch the call stack to understand which nested call you currently are in.

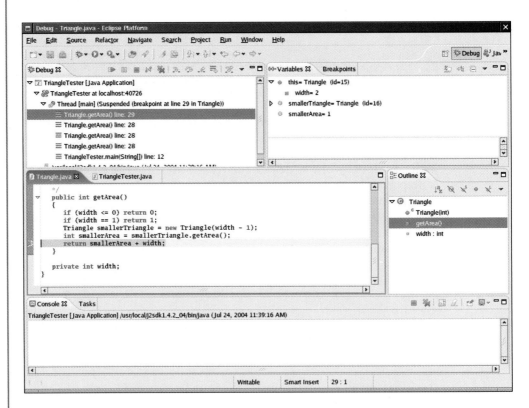

Figure 1 Debugging a Recursive Method

How To 18.1

Thinking Recursively

To solve a problem recursively requires a different mindset than to solve it by programming loops. In fact, it helps if you are, or pretend to be, a bit lazy and like others to do most of the work for you. If you need to solve a complex problem, pretend that "someone else" will do most of the heavy lifting and solve the problem for all simpler inputs. Then you only need to figure out how you can turn the solutions with simpler inputs into a solution for the whole problem.

To illustrate the method of recursion, let us consider the following problem. We want to test whether a sentence is a *palindrome*—a string that is equal to itself when you reverse all characters. Typical examples of palindromes are

- A man, a plan, a canal—Panama!

- Go hang a salami, I'm a lasagna hog

and, of course, the oldest palindrome of all:

- Madam, I'm Adam

When testing for a palindrome, we match upper- and lowercase letters, and ignore all spaces and punctuation marks.

We want to implement the isPalindrome method in the following class:

```java
public class Sentence
{
   /**
      Constructs a sentence.
      @param aText a string containing all characters of the sentence
   */
   public Sentence(String aText)
   {
      text = aText;
   }

   /**
      Tests whether this sentence is a palindrome.
      @return true if this sentence is a palindrome, false otherwise
   */
   public boolean isPalindrome()
   {
      . . .
   }

   private String text;
}
```

Step 1 Consider various ways to simplify inputs.

In your mind, fix a particular input or set of inputs for the problem that you want to solve.

Think how you can simplify the inputs in such a way that the same problem can be applied to the simpler input.

When you consider simpler inputs, you may want to remove just a little bit from the original input—maybe remove one or two characters from a string, or remove a small portion of a geometric shape. But sometimes it is more useful to cut the input in half and then see what it means to solve the problem for both halves.

In the palindrome test problem, the input is the string that we need to test. How can you simplify the input? Here are several possibilities:

- Remove the first character.
- Remove the last character.
- Remove both the first and last characters.
- Remove a character from the middle.
- Cut the string into two halves.

These simpler inputs are all potential inputs for the palindrome test.

Step 2 Combine solutions with simpler inputs into a solution of the original problem.

In your mind, consider the solutions of your problem for the simpler inputs that you discovered in Step 1. Don't worry *how* those solutions are obtained. Simply have faith that the solutions are readily available. Just say to yourself: These are simpler inputs, so someone else will solve the problem for me.

Now think how you can turn the solution for the simpler inputs into a solution for the input that you are currently thinking about. Maybe you need to add a small quantity, related to the quantity that you lopped off to arrive at the simpler input. Maybe you cut the original input in half and have solutions for each half. Then you may need to add both solutions to arrive at a solution for the whole.

Consider the methods for simplifying the inputs for the palindrome test. Cutting the string in half doesn't seem a good idea. If you cut

```
"Madam, I'm Adam"
```

in half, you get two strings:

```
"Madam, I"
```

and

```
"'m Adam"
```

Neither of them is a palindrome. Cutting the input in half and testing whether the halves are palindromes seems a dead end.

The most promising simplification is to remove the first *and* last characters.

Removing the M at the front and the m at the back yields

```
"adam, I'm Ada"
```

Suppose you can verify that the shorter string is a palindrome. Then *of course* the original string is a palindrome—we put the same letter in the front and the back. That's extremely promising. A word is a palindrome if

- The first and last letters match (ignoring letter case)

and

- The word obtained by removing the first and last letters is a palindrome.

Again, don't worry how the test works for the shorter string. It just works.

There is one other case to consider. What if the first or last letter of the word is not a letter? For example, the string

```
"A man, a plan, a canal, Panama!"
```

ends in a ! character, which does not match the A in the front. But we should ignore non-letters when testing for palindromes. Thus, when the last character is not a letter but the first character is a letter, it doesn't make sense to remove both the first and the last characters. That's not a problem. Remove only the last character. If the shorter string is a palindrome, then it stays a palindrome when you attach a nonletter.

The same argument applies if the first character is not a letter. Now we have a complete set of cases.

- If the first and last characters are both letters, then check whether they match. If so, remove both and test the shorter string.
- Otherwise, if the last character isn't a letter, remove it and test the shorter string.
- Otherwise, the first character isn't a letter. Remove it and test the shorter string.

In all three cases, you can use the solution to the simpler problem to arrive at a solution to your problem.

Step 3   Find solutions to the simplest inputs.

A recursive computation keeps simplifying its inputs. Eventually it arrives at very simple inputs. To make sure that the recursion comes to a stop, you must deal with the simplest inputs separately. Come up with special solutions for them, which is usually very easy.

However, sometimes you get into philosophical questions dealing with *degenerate* inputs: empty strings, shapes with no area, and so on. Then you may want to investigate a slightly larger input that gets reduced to such a trivial input and see what value you should attach to the degenerate inputs so that the simpler value, when used according to the rules you discovered in Step 2, yields the correct answer.

Let's look at the simplest strings for the palindrome test:

- Strings with two characters
- Strings with a single character
- The empty string

We don't have to come up with a special solution for strings with two characters. Step 2 still applies to those strings—either or both of the characters are removed. But we do need to worry about strings of length 0 and 1. In those cases, Step 2 can't apply. There aren't two characters to remove.

The empty string is a palindrome—it's the same string when you read it backwards. If you find that too artificial, consider a string "mm". According to the rule discovered in Step 2, this string is a palindrome if the first and last characters of that string match and the remainder—that is, the empty string—is also a palindrome. Therefore, it makes sense to consider the empty string a palindrome.

A string with a single letter, such as "I", is a palindrome. How about the case in which the character is not a letter, such as "!"? Removing the ! yields the empty string, which is a palindrome. Thus, we conclude that all strings of length 0 or 1 are palindromes.

Step 4   Implement the solution by combining the simple cases and the reduction step.

Now you are ready to implement the solution. Make separate cases for the simple inputs that you considered in Step 3. If the input isn't one of the simplest cases, then implement the logic you discovered in Step 2.

Here is the isPalindrome method.

```
public boolean isPalindrome()
{
```

```
int length = text.length();

// Separate case for shortest strings.
if (length <= 1) return true;

// Get first and last characters, converted to lowercase.
char first = Character.toLowerCase(text.charAt(0));
char last = Character.toLowerCase(text.charAt(length - 1));

if (Character.isLetter(first) && Character.isLetter(last))
{
    // Both are letters.
    if (first == last)
    {
        // Remove both first and last character.
        Sentence shorter = new Sentence(text.substring(1, length - 1));
        return shorter.isPalindrome();
    }
    else
        return false;
}
else if (!Character.isLetter(last))
{
    // Remove last character.
    Sentence shorter = new Sentence(text.substring(0, length - 1));
    return shorter.isPalindrome();
}
else
{
    // Remove first character.
    Sentence shorter = new Sentence(text.substring(1));
    return shorter.isPalindrome();
}
}
```

18.3 Recursive Helper Methods

Sometimes it is easier to find a recursive solution if you make a slight change to the original problem.

Sometimes it is easier to find a recursive solution if you change the original problem slightly. Then the original problem can be solved by calling a recursive helper method.

Here is a typical example. Consider the palindrome test of How To 18.1. It is a bit inefficient to construct new Sentence objects in every step. Now consider the following change in the problem. Rather than testing whether the entire sentence is a palindrome, let's check whether a substring is a palindrome:

```
/**
    Tests whether a substring of the sentence is a palindrome.
    @param start the index of the first character of the substring
    @param end the index of the last character of the substring
    @return true if the substring is a palindrome
*/
public boolean isPalindrome(int start, int end)
```

This method turns out to be even easier to implement than the original test. In the recursive calls, simply adjust the start and end parameters to skip over matching letter pairs and characters that are not letters. There is no need to construct new Sentence objects to represent the shorter strings.

```
public boolean isPalindrome(int start, int end)
{
    // Separate case for substrings of length 0 and 1.
    if (start >= end) return true;

    // Get first and last characters, converted to lowercase.
    char first = Character.toLowerCase(text.charAt(start));
    char last = Character.toLowerCase(text.charAt(end));

    if (Character.isLetter(first) && Character.isLetter(last))
    {
        if (first == last)
        {
            // Test substring that doesn't contain the matching letters.
            return isPalindrome(start + 1, end - 1);
        }
        else
            return false;
    }
    else if (!Character.isLetter(last))
    {
        // Test substring that doesn't contain the last character.
        return isPalindrome(start, end - 1);
    }
    else
    {
        // Test substring that doesn't contain the first character.
        return isPalindrome(start + 1, end);
    }
}
```

You should still supply a method to solve the whole problem—the user of your method shouldn't have to know about the trick with the substring positions. Simply call the helper method with positions that test the entire string:

```
public boolean isPalindrome()
{
    return isPalindrome(0, text.length() - 1);
}
```

Note that this call is *not* a recursive method. The isPalindrome() method calls the helper method isPalindrome(int, int). In this example, we use overloading to define two methods with the same name. The isPalindrome method without parameters is the method that we expect the public to use. The second method, with two int parameters, is the recursive helper method. If you prefer, you can avoid overloaded methods by choosing a different name for the helper method, such as substringIsPalindrome.

Use the technique of recursive helper methods whenever it is easier to solve a recursive problem that is slightly different from the original problem.

SELF CHECK

5. Do we have to give the same name to both isPalindrome methods?
6. When does the recursive isPalindrome method stop calling itself?

18.4 The Efficiency of Recursion

As you have seen in this chapter, recursion can be a powerful tool to implement complex algorithms. On the other hand, recursion can lead to algorithms that perform poorly. In this section, we will analyze the question of when recursion is beneficial and when it is inefficient.

Consider the Fibonacci sequence introduced in Exercise P7.5: a sequence of numbers defined by the equation

$$f_1 = 1$$
$$f_2 = 1$$
$$f_n = f_{n-1} + f_{n-2}$$

That is, each value of the sequence is the sum of the two preceding values. The first ten terms of the sequence are

$$1, 1, 2, 3, 5, 8, 13, 21, 34, 55$$

It is easy to extend this sequence indefinitely. Just keep appending the sum of the last two values of the sequence. For example, the next entry is $34 + 55 = 89$.

We would like to write a function that computes f_n for any value of n. Let us translate the definition directly into a recursive method:

File FibTester.java

```
1   import java.util.Scanner;
2
3   /**
4      This program computes Fibonacci numbers using a recursive
5      method.
6   */
7   public class FibTester
8   {
```

```
9      public static void main(String[] args)
10     {
11        Scanner in = new Scanner(System.in);
12        System.out.print("Enter n: ");
13        int n = in.nextInt();
14
15        for (int i = 1; i <= n; i++)
16        {
17           long f = fib(i);
18           System.out.println("fib(" + i + ") = " + f);
19        }
20     }
21
22     /**
23        Computes a Fibonacci number.
24        @param n  an integer
25        @return  the nth Fibonacci number
26     */
27     public static long fib(int n)
28     {
29        if (n <= 2) return 1;
30        else return fib(n - 1) + fib(n - 2);
31     }
32  }
```

Output

```
Enter n: 50
fib(1) = 1
fib(2) = 1
fib(3) = 2
fib(4) = 3
fib(5) = 5
fib(6) = 8
fib(7) = 13
. . .
fib(50) = 12586269025
```

That is certainly simple, and the method will work correctly. But watch the output closely as you run the test program. The first few calls to the fib method are quite fast. For larger values, though, the program pauses an amazingly long time between outputs.

That makes no sense. Armed with pencil, paper, and a pocket calculator you could calculate these numbers pretty quickly, so it shouldn't take the computer anywhere near that long.

To find out the problem, let us insert trace messages into the method:

File FibTrace.java

```
1   import java.util.Scanner;
2
3   /**
4       This program prints trace messages that show how often the
5       recursive method for computing Fibonacci numbers calls itself.
6   */
7   public class FibTrace
8   {
9       public static void main(String[] args)
10      {
11          Scanner in = new Scanner(System.in);
12          System.out.print("Enter n: ");
13          int n = in.nextInt();
14
15          long f = fib(n);
16
17          System.out.println("fib(" + n + ") = " + f);
18      }
19
20      /**
21          Computes a Fibonacci number.
22          @param n an integer
23          @return the nth Fibonacci number
24      */
25      public static long fib(int n)
26      {
27          System.out.println("Entering fib: n = " + n);
28          long f;
29          if (n <= 2) f = 1;
30          else f = fib(n - 1) + fib(n - 2);
31          System.out.println("Exiting fib: n = " + n
32                  + " return value = " + f);
33          return f;
34      }
35  }
```

Output

```
Enter n: 6

Entering fib: n = 6
Entering fib: n = 5
Entering fib: n = 4
Entering fib: n = 3
Entering fib: n = 2
Exiting fib: n = 2 return value = 1
Entering fib: n = 1
Exiting fib: n = 1 return value = 1
Exiting fib: n = 3 return value = 2
Entering fib: n = 2
Exiting fib: n = 2 return value = 1
Exiting fib: n = 4 return value = 3
```

```
Entering fib: n = 3
Entering fib: n = 2
Exiting fib: n = 2 return value = 1
Entering fib: n = 1
Exiting fib: n = 1 return value = 1
Exiting fib: n = 3 return value = 2
Exiting fib: n = 5 return value = 5
Entering fib: n = 4
Entering fib: n = 3
Entering fib: n = 2
Exiting fib: n = 2 return value = 1
Entering fib: n = 1
Exiting fib: n = 1 return value = 1
Exiting fib: n = 3 return value = 2
Entering fib: n = 2
Exiting fib: n = 2 return value = 1
Exiting fib: n = 4 return value = 3
Exiting fib: n = 6 return value = 8
fib(6) = 8
```

Figure 2 shows the call tree for computing fib(6). Now it is becoming apparent why the method takes so long. It is computing the same values over and over. For example, the computation of fib(6) calls fib(4) twice and fib(3) three times. That is very different from the computation we would do with pencil and paper. There we would just write down the values as they were computed and add up the last two to get the next one until we reached the desired entry; no sequence value would ever be computed twice.

If we imitate the pencil-and-paper process, then we get the following program.

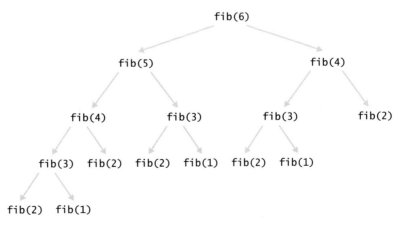

Figure 2 Call Pattern of the Recursive fib Method

File FibLoop.java

```java
 1  import java.util.Scanner;
 2
 3  /**
 4     This program computes Fibonacci numbers using an iterative method.
 5  */
 6  public class FibLoop
 7  {
 8     public static void main(String[] args)
 9     {
10        Scanner in = new Scanner(System.in);
11        System.out.print("Enter n: ");
12        int n = in.nextInt();
13
14        for (int i = 1; i <= n; i++)
15        {
16           long f = fib(i);
17           System.out.println("fib(" + i + ") = " + f);
18        }
19     }
20
21     /**
22        Computes a Fibonacci number.
23        @param n an integer
24        @return the nth Fibonacci number
25     */
26     public static long fib(int n)
27     {
28        if (n <= 2) return 1;
29        long fold = 1;
30        long fold2 = 1;
31        long fnew = 1;
32        for (int i = 3; i <= n; i++)
33        {
34           fnew = fold + fold2;
35           fold2 = fold;
36           fold = fnew;
37        }
38        return fnew;
39     }
40  }
```

Output

```
Enter n: 50
fib(1) = 1
fib(2) = 1
fib(3) = 2
fib(4) = 3
fib(5) = 5
fib(6) = 8
fib(7) = 13
. . .
fib(50) = 12586269025
```

This method runs *much* faster than the recursive version.

In this example of the fib method, the recursive solution was easy to program because it exactly followed the mathematical definition, but it ran far more slowly than the iterative solution, because it computed many intermediate results multiple times.

Can you always speed up a recursive solution by changing it into a loop? Frequently, the iterative and recursive solution have essentially the same performance. For example, here is an iterative solution for the palindrome test.

```java
public boolean isPalindrome()
{
    int start = 0;
    int end = text.length() - 1;
    while (start < end)
    {
        char first = Character.toLowerCase(text.charAt(start));
        char last = Character.toLowerCase(text.charAt(end);

        if (Character.isLetter(first) && Character.isLetter(last))
        {
            // Both are letters.
            if (first == last)
            {
                start++;
                end--;
            }
            else
                return false;
        }
        if (!Character.isLetter(last))
            end--;
        if (!Character.isLetter(first))
            start++;
    }
    return true;
}
```

This solution keeps two index variables: start and end. The first index starts at the beginning of the string and is advanced whenever a letter has been matched or a nonletter has been ignored. The second index starts at the end of the string and moves toward the beginning. When the two index variables meet, the iteration stops.

> Occasionally, a recursive solution runs much slower than its iterative counterpart. However, in most cases, the recursive solution is only slightly slower.

Both the iteration and the recursion run at about the same speed. If a palindrome has n characters, the iteration executes the loop between $n/2$ and n times, depending on how many of the characters are letters, since one or both index variables are moved in each step. Similarly, the recursive solution calls itself between $n/2$ and n times, because one or two characters are removed in each step.

In such a situation, the iterative solution tends to be a bit faster, because each recursive method call takes a certain amount of processor time. In principle, it is possible for a smart compiler to avoid recursive method calls if they follow simple patterns, but most compilers don't do that. From that point of view, an iterative solution is preferable.

There are quite a few problems that are dramatically easier to solve recursively than iteratively. For example, it is not at all obvious how you can come up with a nonrecursive solution for the permutation generator. As Exercise P18.11 shows, it is possible to avoid the recursion, but the resulting solution is quite complex (and no faster).

> In many cases, a recursive solution is easier to understand and implement correctly than an iterative solution.

Often, recursive solutions are easier to understand and implement correctly than their iterative counterparts. There is a certain elegance and economy of thought to recursive solutions that makes them more appealing. As the computer scientist (and creator of the Ghost-Script interpreter for the PostScript graphics description language) L. Peter Deutsch put it: "To iterate is human, to recurse divine."

SELF CHECK

7. You can compute the factorial function either with a loop, using the definition that $n! = 1 \times 2 \times \ldots \times n$, or recursively, using the definition that $0! = 1$ and $n! = (n-1)! \times n$. Is the recursive approach inefficient in this case?

8. Why isn't it easy to develop an iterative solution for the permutation generator?

RANDOM FACT 18.1

The Limits of Computation

Have you ever wondered how your instructor or grader makes sure your programming homework is correct? In all likelihood, they look at your solution and perhaps run it with some test inputs. But usually they have a correct solution available. That suggests that there might be an easier way. Perhaps they could feed your program and their correct program into a "program comparator", a computer program that analyzes both programs and determines whether they both compute the same results. Of course, your solution and the program that is known to be correct need not be identical—what matters is that they produce the same output when given the same input.

How could such a program comparator work? Well, the Java compiler knows how to read a program and make sense of the classes, methods, and statements. So it seems plausible that someone could, with some effort, write a program that reads two Java programs, analyzes what they do, and determines whether they solve the same task. Of course, such a program would be very attractive to instructors, because it could automate the grading process. Thus, even though no such program exists today, it might be tempting to try to develop one and sell it to universities around the world.

However, before you start raising venture capital for such an effort, you should know that theoretical computer scientists have proven that it is impossible to develop such a program, *no matter how hard you try.*

There are quite a few of these unsolvable problems. The first one, called the *halting problem,* was discovered by the British researcher Alan Turing in 1936 (see Figure 3). Because his research occurred before the first actual computer was constructed, Turing had to devise a theoretical device, the *Turing machine,* to explain how computers could work. The Turing machine consists of a long magnetic tape, a read/write head, and a program that has

Figure 3
Alan Turing

numbered instructions of the form: "If the current symbol under the head is x, then replace it with y, move the head one unit left or right, and continue with instruction n" (see Figure 4). Interestingly enough, with only these instructions, you can program just as much as with Java, even though it is incredibly tedious to do so. Theoretical computer scientists like Turing machines because they can be described using nothing more than the laws of mathematics.

Program

Instruction number	If tape symbol is	Replace with	Then move head	Then go to instruction
1	0	2	right	2
1	1	1	left	4
2	0	0	right	2
2	1	1	right	2
2	2	0	left	3
3	0	0	left	3
3	1	1	left	3
3	2	2	right	1
4	1	1	right	5
4	2	0	left	4

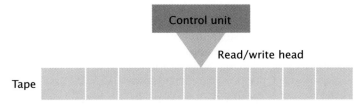

Figure 4 A Turing Machine

Expressed in terms of Java, the halting problem states: "It is impossible to write a program with two inputs, namely the source code of an arbitrary Java program *P* and a string *I*, and that decides whether the program *P*, when executed with the input *I*, will halt without getting into an infinite loop". Of course, for some kinds of programs and inputs, it is possible to decide whether the program halts with the given input. The halting problem asserts that it is impossible to come up with a single decision-making algorithm that works with all programs and inputs. Note that you can't simply run the program *P* on the input *I* to settle this question. If the program runs for 1,000 days, you don't know that the program is in an infinite loop. Maybe you just have to wait another day for it to stop.

Such a "halt checker", if it could be written, might also be useful for grading homework. An instructor could use it to screen student submissions to see if they get into an infinite loop with a particular input, and then stop checking them. However, as Turing demonstrated, such a program cannot be written. His argument is ingenious and quite simple.

Suppose a "halt checker" program existed. Let's call it *H*. From *H*, we will develop another program, the "killer" program *K*. *K* does the following computation. Its input is a string containing the source code for a program *R*. It then applies the halt checker on the input program *R* and the input string *R*. That is, it checks whether the program *R* halts if its input is its own source code. It sounds bizarre to feed a program to itself, but it isn't impossible. For example, the Java compiler is written in Java, and you can use it to compile itself. Or, as a simpler example, a word counting program can count the words in its own source code.

When *K* gets the answer from *H* that *R* halts when applied to itself, it is programmed to enter an infinite loop. Otherwise *K* exits. In Java, the program might look like this:

```
public class Killer
{
    public static void main(String[] args)
    {
        String r = read program input;
        HaltChecker checker = new HaltChecker();
        if (checker.check(r, r))
            while (true) { } // Infinite loop
        else
            return;
    }
}
```

Now ask yourself: What does the halt checker answer when asked whether *K* halts when given *K* as the input? Maybe it finds out that *K* gets into an infinite loop with such an input. But wait, that can't be right. That would mean that checker.check(r, r) returns false when r is the program code of *K*. As you can plainly see, in that case, the killer method returns, so *K* didn't get into an infinite loop. That shows that *K* must halt when analyzing itself, so checker.check(r, r) should return true. But then the killer method doesn't terminate—it goes into an infinite loop. That shows that it is logically impossible to implement a program that can check whether *every* program halts on a particular input.

It is sobering to know that there are *limits* to computing. There are problems that no computer program, no matter how ingenious, can answer.

Theoretical computer scientists are working on other research involving the nature of computation. One important question that remains unsettled to this day deals with problems that in practice are very time-consuming to solve. It may be that these problems are intrinsically hard, in which case it would be pointless to try to look for better algorithms. Such theoretical research can have important practical applications. For example, right now, nobody knows whether the most common encryption schemes used today could be broken by discovering a new algorithm (see Random Fact 16.1 for more information on encryption algorithms). Knowing that no fast algorithms exist for breaking a particular code could make us feel more comfortable about the security of encryption.

18.5 Mutual Recursions

> In a mutual recursion, a set of cooperating methods calls each other repeatedly.

In the preceding examples, a method called itself to solve a simpler problem. Sometimes, a set of cooperating methods calls each other in a recursive fashion. In this section, we will explore a typical situation of such a mutual recursion. This technique is significantly more advanced than the simple recursion that we discussed in the preceding sections. Feel free to skip this section if this is your first exposure to recursion.

We will develop a program that can compute the values of arithmetic expressions such as

```
3+4*5
(3+4)*5
1-(2-(3-(4-5)))
```

Computing such an expression is complicated by the fact that * and / bind more strongly than + and -, and that parentheses can be used to group subexpressions.

Figure 5 shows a set of *syntax diagrams* that describes the syntax of these expressions. To see how the syntax diagrams work, consider the expression 3+4*5. When

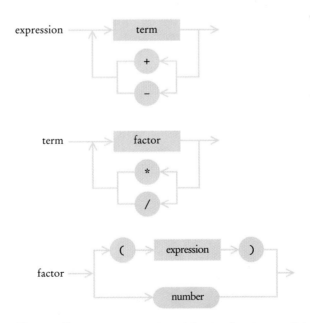

Figure 5   Syntax Diagrams for Evaluating an Expression

you enter the *expression* syntax diagram, the arrow points directly to *term*, giving you no alternative but to enter the *term* syntax diagram. The arrow points to *factor*, again giving you no choice. You enter the *factor* diagram, and now you have two choices: to follow the top branch or the bottom branch. Because the first input token is the number 3 and not a (, you must follow the bottom branch. You accept the input token because it matches the *number*. Follow the arrow out of *number* to the end of *factor*. Just like in a method call, you now back up, returning to the end of the *factor* element of the *term* diagram. Now you have another choice—to loop back in the *term* diagram, or to exit. The next input token is a +, and it matches neither the * or the / that would be required to loop back. So you exit, returning to *expression*. Again, you have a choice, to loop back or to exit. Now the + matches one of the choices in the loop. Accept the + in the input and move back to the *term* element.

In this fashion, an expression is broken down into a sequence of terms, separated by + or -, each term is broken down into a sequence of factors, each separated by * or /, and each factor is either a parenthesized expression or a number. You can draw this breakdown as a tree. Figure 6 shows how the expressions 3+4*5 and (3+4)*5 are derived from the syntax diagram.

Why do the syntax diagrams help us compute the value of the tree? If you look at the syntax trees, you will see that they accurately represent which operations should be carried out first. In the first tree, 4 and 5 should be multiplied, and then the result should be added to 3. In the second tree, 3 and 4 should be added, and the result should be multiplied by 5.

At the end of this section, you will find the implementation of the Evaluator class, which evaluates these expressions. The Evaluator makes use of an Expression-Tokenizer class, which breaks up an input string into tokens—numbers, operators, and parentheses. (For simplicity, we only accept positive integers as numbers, and we don't allow spaces in the input.)

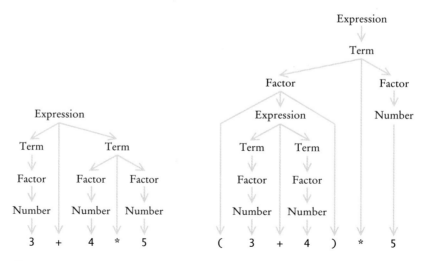

Figure 6   Syntax Trees for Two Expressions

When you call nextToken, the next input token is returned as a string. We also supply another method, peekToken, which allows you to see the next token without consuming it. To see why the peekToken method is necessary, consider the syntax diagram of the factor type. If the next token is a "*" or "/", you want to continue adding and subtracting terms. But if the next token is another character, such as a "+" or "-", you want to stop without actually consuming it, so that the token can be considered later.

To compute the value of an expression, we implement three methods: getExpressionValue, getTermValue, and getFactorValue. The getExpressionValue method first calls getTermValue to get the value of the first term of the expression. Then it checks whether the next input token is one of + or -. If so, it calls getTermValue again and adds or subtracts it.

```java
public int getExpressionValue()
{
   int value = getTermValue();
   boolean done = false;
   while (!done)
   {
      String next = tokenizer.peekToken();
      if ("+".equals(next) || "-".equals(next))
      {
         tokenizer.nextToken(); // Discard "+" or "-"
         int value2 = getTermValue();
         if ("+".equals(next)) value = value + value2;
         else value = value - value2;
      }
      else done = true;
   }
   return value;
}
```

The getTermValue method calls getFactorValue in the same way, multiplying or dividing the factor values.

Finally, the getFactorValue method checks whether the next input is a number, or whether it begins with a (token. In the first case, the value is simply the value of the number. However, in the second case, the getFactorValue method makes a recursive call to getExpressionValue. Thus, the three methods are mutually recursive.

```java
public int getFactorValue()
{
   int value;
   String next = tokenizer.peekToken();
   if ("(".equals(next))
   {
      tokenizer.nextToken(); // Discard "("
      value = getExpressionValue();
      tokenizer.nextToken(); // Discard ")"
   }
   else
      value = Integer.parseInt(tokenizer.nextToken());
   return value;
}
```

To see the mutual recursion clearly, trace through the expression (3+4)*5:

- `getExpressionValue` calls `getTermValue`
  - `getTermValue` calls `getFactorValue`
    - `getFactorValue` consumes the (input
    - `getFactorValue` calls `getExpressionValue`
      - `getExpressionValue` returns eventually with the value of 7, having consumed 3 + 4. This is the recursive call.
    - `getFactorValue` consumes the) input
    - `getFactorValue` returns 7
  - `getTermValue` consumes the inputs * and 5 and returns 35
- `getExpressionValue` returns 35

As always with a recursive solution, you need to ensure that the recursion terminates. In this situation, that is easy to see. If `getExpressionValue` calls itself, the second call works on a shorter subexpression than the original expression. At each recursive call, at least some of the tokens of the input string are consumed, so eventually the recursion must come to an end.

File Evaluator.java

```
1   /**
2       A class that can compute the value of an arithmetic expression.
3   */
4   public class Evaluator
5   {
6       /**
7           Constructs an evaluator.
8           @param anExpression a string containing the expression
9           to be evaluated
10      */
11      public Evaluator(String anExpression)
12      {
13          tokenizer = new ExpressionTokenizer(anExpression);
14      }
15
16      /**
17          Evaluates the expression.
18          @return the value of the expression
19      */
20      public int getExpressionValue()
21      {
22          int value = getTermValue();
23          boolean done = false;
24          while (!done)
25          {
26              String next = tokenizer.peekToken();
27              if ("+".equals(next) || "-".equals(next))
28              {
```

```java
29          tokenizer.nextToken(); // Discard "+" or "-"
30          int value2 = getTermValue();
31          if ("+".equals(next)) value = value + value2;
32          else value = value - value2;
33       }
34       else done = true;
35    }
36    return value;
37 }
38
39 /**
40    Evaluates the next term found in the expression.
41    @return the value of the term
42 */
43 public int getTermValue()
44 {
45    int value = getFactorValue();
46    boolean done = false;
47    while (!done)
48    {
49       String next = tokenizer.peekToken();
50       if ("*".equals(next) || "/".equals(next))
51       {
52          tokenizer.nextToken();
53          int value2 = getFactorValue();
54          if ("*".equals(next)) value = value * value2;
55          else value = value / value2;
56       }
57       else done = true;
58    }
59    return value;
60 }
61
62 /**
63    Evaluates the next factor found in the expression.
64    @return the value of the factor
65 */
66 public int getFactorValue()
67 {
68    int value;
69    String next = tokenizer.peekToken();
70    if ("(".equals(next))
71    {
72       tokenizer.nextToken(); // Discard "("
73       value = getExpressionValue();
74       tokenizer.nextToken(); // Discard ")"
75    }
76    else
77       value = Integer.parseInt(tokenizer.nextToken());
78    return value;
79 }
80
81    private ExpressionTokenizer tokenizer;
82 }
```

File ExpressionTokenizer.java

```java
1  /**
2      This class breaks up a string describing an expression
3      into tokens: numbers, parentheses, and operators.
4  */
5  public class ExpressionTokenizer
6  {
7     /**
8         Constructs a tokenizer.
9         @param anInput the string to tokenize
10    */
11    public ExpressionTokenizer(String anInput)
12    {
13       input = anInput;
14       start = 0;
15       end = 0;
16       nextToken();
17    }
18
19    /**
20        Peeks at the next token without consuming it.
21        @return the next token or null if there are no more tokens
22    */
23    public String peekToken()
24    {
25       if (start >= input.length()) return null;
26       else return input.substring(start, end);
27    }
28
29    /**
30        Gets the next token and moves the tokenizer to the following token.
31        @return the next token or null if there are no more tokens
32    */
33    public String nextToken()
34    {
35       String r = peekToken();
36       start = end;
37       if (start >= input.length()) return r;
38       if (Character.isDigit(input.charAt(start)))
39       {
40          end = start + 1;
41          while (end < input.length()
42                && Character.isDigit(input.charAt(end)))
43             end++;
44       }
45       else
46          end = start + 1;
47       return r;
48    }
49
50    private String input;
51    private int start;
52    private int end;
53 }
```

File EvaluatorTester.java

```java
1  import java.util.Scanner;
2
3  /**
4     This program tests the expression evaluator.
5  */
6  public class EvaluatorTester
7  {
8     public static void main(String[] args)
9     {
10        Scanner in = new Scanner(System.in);
11        System.out.print("Enter an expression: ");
12        String input = in.nextLine();
13        Evaluator e = new Evaluator(input);
14        int value = e.getExpressionValue();
15        System.out.println(input + "=" + value);
16     }
17  }
```

Output

```
Enter an expression: 3+4*5
3+4*5=23
```

SELF CHECK

9. What is the difference between a term and a factor? Why do we need both concepts?

10. Why does the expression parser use mutual recursion?

11. What happens if you try to parse the illegal expression 3+4*)5? Specifically, which method throws an exception?

CHAPTER SUMMARY

1. A recursive computation solves a problem by using the solution of the same problem with simpler values.

2. For a recursion to terminate, there must be special cases for the simplest values.

3. Sometimes it is easier to find a recursive solution if you make a slight change to the original problem.

4. Occasionally, a recursive solution runs much slower than its iterative counterpart. However, in most cases, the recursive solution is only slightly slower.

5. In many cases, a recursive solution is easier to understand and implement correctly than an iterative solution.

6. In a mutual recursion, a set of cooperating methods calls each other repeatedly.

REVIEW EXERCISES

Exercise R18.1. Define the terms

a. Recursion

b. Iteration

c. Infinite recursion

d. Indirect recursion

Exercise R18.2. Outline, but do not implement, a recursive solution for finding the smallest value in an array.

Exercise R18.3. Outline, but do not implement, a recursive solution for sorting an array of numbers. *Hint:* First find the smallest value in the array.

Exercise R18.4. Outline, but do not implement, a recursive solution for generating all subsets of the set $\{1, 2, \ldots, n\}$.

Exercise R18.5. Exercise P18.12 shows an iterative way of generating all permutations of the sequence $(0, 1, \ldots, n - 1)$. Explain why the algorithm produces the correct result.

Exercise R18.6. Write a recursive definition of x^n, where $n \geq 0$, similar to the recursive definition of the Fibonacci numbers. *Hint:* How do you compute x^n from x^{n-1}? How does the recursion terminate?

Exercise R18.7. Write a recursive definition of $n! = 1 \times 2 \times \ldots \times n$, similar to the recursive definition of the Fibonacci numbers.

Exercise R18.8. Find out how often the recursive version of `fib` calls itself. Keep a static variable `fibCount` and increment it once in every call of `fib`. What is the relationship between `fib(n)` and `fibCount`?

Exercise R18.9. How many moves are required in the "Towers of Hanoi" problem of Exercise P18.13 to move n disks? *Hint:* As explained in the exercises,

$$\text{moves}(1) = 1$$
$$\text{moves}(n) = 2 \cdot \text{moves}(n - 1) + 1$$

Exercise R18.10. Improve upon Exercise R18.6 by computing x^n as $(x^{n/2})^2$ if n is even. Why is this approach significantly faster? (*Hint:* Compute x^{1023} and x^{1024} both ways.)

PROGRAMMING EXERCISES

Exercise P18.1. Write a recursive method void reverse() that reverses a sentence. For example:

```
Sentence greeting = new Sentence("Hello!");
greeting.reverse();
System.out.println(greeting.getText());
```

prints the string "!olleH". Implement a recursive solution by removing the first character, reversing a sentence consisting of the remaining text, and combining the two.

Exercise P18.2. Redo Exercise P18.1 with a recursive helper method that reverses a substring of the message text.

Exercise P18.3. Implement the reverse method of Exercise P18.1 as an iteration.

Exercise P18.4. Use recursion to implement a method boolean find(String t) that tests whether a string is contained in a sentence:

```
Sentence s = new Sentence("Mississippi!");
boolean b = s.find("sip"); // Returns true
```

Hint: If the text starts with the string you want to match, then you are done. If not, consider the sentence that you obtain by removing the first character.

Exercise P18.5. Use recursion to implement a method int indexOf(String t) that returns the starting position of the first substring of the text that matches t. Return –1 if t is not a substring of s. For example,

```
Sentence s = new Sentence("Mississippi!");
int n = s.indexOf("sip"); // Returns 6
```

Hint: This is a bit trickier than the preceding problem, because you must keep track of how far the match is from the beginning of the sentence. Make that value a parameter of a helper method.

Exercise P18.6. Using recursion, find the largest element in an array.

```
public class DataSet
{
    public DataSet(int[] anArray) { . . . }
    public int getMaximum() { . . . }
    . . .
}
```

Hint: Find the largest element in the subset containing all but the last element. Then compare that maximum to the value of the last element.

Exercise P18.7. Using recursion, compute the sum of all values in an array.

```
public class DataSet
{
   public DataSet(int[] anArray) { . . . }
   public int getSum() { . . . }
   . . .
}
```

Exercise P18.8. Using recursion, compute the area of a polygon. Cut off a triangle and use the fact that a triangle with corners (x_1, y_1), (x_2, y_2), (x_3, y_3) has area

$$\frac{\left| x_1 y_2 + x_2 y_3 + x_3 y_1 - y_1 x_2 - y_2 x_3 - y_3 x_1 \right|}{2}$$

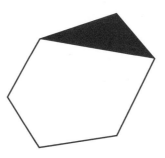

Exercise P18.9. Implement a `SubstringGenerator` that generates all substrings of a string. For example, the substrings of the string `"rum"` are the seven strings

`"r"`, `"ru"`, `"rum"`, `"u"`, `"um"`, `"m"`, `""`

Hint: First enumerate all substrings that start with the first character. There are *n* of them if the string has length *n*. Then enumerate the substrings of the string that you obtain by removing the first character.

Exercise P18.10. Implement a `SubsetGenerator` that generates all subsets of characters of a string. For example, the subsets of characters of the string `"rum"` are the eight strings

`"rum"`, `"ru"`, `"rm"`, `"r"`, `"um"`, `"u"`, `"m"`, `""`

Note that the subsets don't have to be substrings—for example, `"rm"` isn't a substring of `"rum"`.

Exercise P18.11. In this exercise, you will change the `PermutationGenerator` of Section 18.2 (which computed all permutations at once) to a `PermutationIterator` (which computes them one at a time.)

```
public class PermutationIterator
{
   public PermutationIterator(String s) { . . . }
   public String nextPermutation() { . . . }
   public boolean hasMorePermutations() { . . . }
}
```

Here is how you would print out all permutations of the string "eat":

```
PermutationIterator iter = new PermutationIterator("eat");
while (iter.hasMorePermutations())
   System.out.println(iter.nextPermutation());
```

Now we need a way to iterate through the permutations recursively. Consider the string "eat". As before, we'll generate all permutations that start with the letter 'e', then those that start with 'a', and finally those that start with 't'. How do we generate the permutations that start with 'e'? Make another PermutationIterator object (called tailIterator) that iterates through the permutations of the substring "at". In the nextPermutation method, simply ask tailIterator what *its* next permutation is, and then add the 'e' at the front. However, there is one special case. When the tail generator runs out of permutations, all permutations that start with the current letter have been enumerated. Then

- Increment the current position.
- Compute the tail string that contains all letters except for the current one.
- Make a new permutation generator for the tail string.

You are done when the current position has reached the end of the string.

Exercise P18.12. The following class generates all permutations of the numbers $0, 1, 2, \ldots, n-1$, without using recursion.

```
public class NumberPermutationIterator
{
   public NumberPermutationIterator(int n)
   {
      a = new int[n];
      done = false;
      for (int i = 0; i < n; i++) a[i] = i;
   }

   public int[] nextPermutation()
   {
      if (a.length <= 1) return a;

      for (int i = a.length - 1; i > 0; i--)
      {
         if (a[i - 1] < a[i])
         {
            int j = a.length - 1;
            while (a[i - 1] > a[j]) j--;
            swap(i - 1, j);
            reverse(i, a.length - 1);
            return a;
         }
      }
      return a;
   }

   public boolean hasMorePermutations()
   {
```

```
           if (a.length <= 1) return false;
           for (int i = a.length - 1; i > 0; i--)
           {
              if (a[i - 1] < a[i]) return true;
           }
           return false;
       }

       public void swap(int i, int j)
       {
           int temp = a[i];
           a[i] = a[j];
           a[j] = temp;
       }

       public void reverse(int i, int j)
       {
           while (i < j) { swap(i, j); i++; j--; }
       }
       private int[] a;
   }
```

The algorithm uses the fact that the set to be permuted consists of distinct numbers. Thus, you cannot use the same algorithm to compute the permutations of the characters in a string. You can, however, use this class to get all permutations of the character positions and then compute a string whose ith character is word.charAt(a[i]). Use this approach to reimplement the PermutationGenerator without recursion.

Exercise P18.13. *Towers of Hanoi.* This is a well-known puzzle. A stack of disks of decreasing size is to be transported from the leftmost peg to the rightmost peg. The middle peg can be used as temporary storage (see Figure 7). One disk can be moved at one time, from any peg to any other peg. You can place smaller disks only on top of larger ones, not the other way around.

Write a program that prints the moves necessary to solve the puzzle for *n* disks. (Ask the user for *n* at the beginning of the program.) Print moves in the form

```
   Move disk from peg 1 to peg 3
```

Hint: Implement a class DiskMover. The constructor takes

- The source peg from which to move the disks (1, 2, or 3)
- The target peg to which to move the disks (1, 2, or 3)
- The number of disks to move

A disk mover that moves a single disk from one peg to another simply has a nextMove method that returns a string

```
   Move disk from peg source to peg target
```

A disk mover with more than one disk to move must work harder. It needs another DiskMover to help it. In the constructor, construct a DiskMover(source, other, disks - 1) where other is the peg other than from and target.

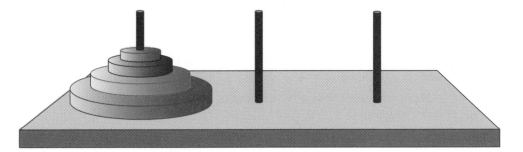

Figure 7 Towers of Hanoi

The nextMove asks that disk mover for its next move until it is done. The effect is to move the first disks - 1 disks to the other peg. Then the nextMove method issues a command to move a disk from the from peg to the to peg. Finally, it constructs another disk mover DiskMover(other, target, disks - 1) that generates the moves that move the disks from the other peg to the target peg.

Hint: It helps to keep track of the state of the disk mover:

- BEFORE_LARGEST: The helper mover moves the smaller pile to the other peg.
- LARGEST: Move the largest disk from the source to the destination.
- AFTER_LARGEST: The helper mover moves the smaller pile from the other peg to the target.
- DONE: All moves are done.

Test your program as follows:

```
DiskMover mover = new DiskMover(1, 3, n);
while (mover.hasMoreMoves())
    System.out.println(mover.nextMove());
```

Exercise P18.14. *Escaping a Maze.* You are currently located inside a maze, at the position marked with a period (.). The walls of the maze are indicated by asterisks (*).

```
*  *******
*     *  *
*  ***** *
*  *  *  *
*  * *** *
*   *  *  *
*** * * *
*     * *
******* *
```

Use the following recursive approach to escape from the maze: Try moving in each of the four possible directions. If you found an exit, return true. If you found a wall or a position that you have previously visited, return false. If you found an empty spot, mark it with a period, and recursively call the escape method again. This method merely tests whether there is a path out of the maze. Extra credit if you can print out the path that leads to an exit.

Exercise P18.15. *The Koch Snowflake.* A snowflake-like shape is recursively defined as follows. Start with an equilateral triangle:

Next, increase the size by a factor of three and replace each straight line with four line segments.

Repeat the process.

Write a program that draws the fifth iteration of this curve. Extra credit if you add a button that, when clicked, produces the next iteration.

Exercise P18.16. The recursive computation of Fibonacci numbers can be speeded up significantly by keeping track of the values that have already been computed. Provide an implementation of the `fib` method that uses this strategy. Whenever you return a new value, also store it in an auxiliary array. However, before embarking on a computation, consult the array to find whether the result has already been computed. Compare the running time of your improved implementation with that of the original recursive implementation and the loop implementation.

PROGRAMMING PROJECTS

Project 18.1. Enhance the expression parser of Section 18.5 to handle more sophisticated expressions, such as exponents, and mathematical functions, such as `sqrt` or `sin`.

Project 18.2. Implement a graphical version of the Towers of Hanoi program (see Exercise P18.13). Every time the user clicks on a button labeled "Next", draw the next move.

ANSWERS TO SELF-CHECK QUESTIONS

1. Suppose we omit the statement. When computing the area of a triangle with width 1, we compute the area of the triangle with width 0 as 0, and then add 1, to arrive at the correct area.

2. You would compute the smaller area recursively, then return `smallerArea + width + width - 1`.

   ```
   [] [] [] []
   [] [] [] []
   [] [] [] []
   [] [] [] []
   ```

   Of course, it would be simpler to compute the area simply as `width * width`. The results are identical because

   $$1 + 0 + 2 + 1 + 3 + 2 + \cdots + n + n - 1 = \frac{n(n+1)}{2} + \frac{(n-1)n}{2} = n^2.$$

3. They are b followed by the six permutations of eat, e followed by the six permutations of bat, a followed by the six permutations of bet, and t followed by the six permutations of bea.

4. Simply change `if (word.length() == 0)` to `if (word.length() <= 1)`, because a word with a single letter is also its sole permutation.

5. No—the first one could be given a different name such as `substringIsPalindrome`.

6. When `start >= end`, that is, when the investigated string is either empty or has length 1.

7. No, the recursive solution is about as efficient as the iterative approach. Both require $n - 1$ multiplications to compute $n!$.

8. An iterative solution would have a loop whose body computes the next permutation from the previous ones. But there is no obvious mechanism for getting the next permutation. For example, if you already found permutations eat, eta, and aet, it is not clear how you use that information to get the next permutation. Actually, there is an ingenious mechanism for doing just that, but it is far from obvious—see Exercise P18.12.

9. Factors are combined by multiplicative operators (* and /), terms are combined by additive operators (+, -). We need both so that multiplication can bind more strongly than addition.

10. To handle parenthesized expressions, such as 2+3*(4+5). The subexpression 4+5 is handled by a recursive call to getExpressionValue.

11. The `Integer.parseInt` call in `getFactorValue` throws an exception when it is given the string ")".

Sorting and Searching

CHAPTER GOALS

- To study several sorting and searching algorithms

- To appreciate that algorithms for the same task can differ widely in performance

- To understand the big-Oh notation

- To learn how to estimate and compare the performance of algorithms

- To learn how to measure the running time of a program

One of the most common tasks in data processing is sorting. For example, a collection of employees may need to be printed out in alphabetical order or sorted by salary. We will study several sorting methods in this chapter and compare their performance. This is by no means an exhaustive treatment of the subject of sorting. You will likely revisit this topic at a later time in your computer science studies. A good overview of the many sorting methods available can be found in [1].

Once a sequence of objects is sorted, one can locate individual objects rapidly. We will study the *binary search* algorithm, which carries out this fast lookup.

CHAPTER CONTENTS

19.1 Selection Sort

In this section, we show you the first of several sorting algorithms. A *sorting algorithm* rearranges the elements of a collection so that they are stored in sorted order. To keep the examples simple, we will discuss how to sort an array of integers before going on to sorting strings or more complex data. Consider the following array a:

| 11 | 9 | 17 | 5 | 12 |

> The selection sort algorithm sorts an array by repeatedly finding the smallest element of the unsorted tail region and moving it to the front.

An obvious first step is to find the smallest element. In this case the smallest element is 5, stored in a[3]. We should move the 5 to the beginning of the array. Of course, there is already an element stored in a[0], namely 11. Therefore we cannot simply move a[3] into a[0] without moving the 11 somewhere else. We don't yet know where the 11 should end up, but we know for certain that it should not be in a[0]. We simply get it out of the way by *swapping* it with a[3].

Now the first element is in the correct place. In the foregoing figure, the darker color indicates the portion of the array that is already sorted.

Next we take the minimum of the remaining entries a[1] . . . a[4]. That minimum value, 9, is already in the correct place. We don't need to do anything in this case and can simply extend the sorted area by one to the right:

| 5 | 9 | 17 | 11 | 12 |

Repeat the process. The minimum value of the unsorted region is 11, which needs to be swapped with the first value of the unsorted region, 17:

Now the unsorted region is only two elements long, but we keep to the same successful strategy. The minimum value is 12, and we swap it with the first value, 17.

That leaves us with an unprocessed region of length 1, but of course a region of length 1 is always sorted. We are done.

Let us program this algorithm. For this program, as well as the other programs in this chapter, we will use two utility methods—one to generate an array with random entries and the other to print the values of an array—which we pack up in a class ArrayUtil so that we don't have to repeat them for every code example.

This algorithm will sort any array of integers. If speed were not an issue, or if there simply were no better sorting method available, we could stop the discussion of sorting right here. As the next section shows, however, this algorithm, while entirely correct, shows disappointing performance when run on a large data set.

Advanced Topic 19.1 discusses insertion sort, another simple (and similarly inefficient) sorting algorithm.

File SelectionSorter.java

```
1  /**
2      This class sorts an array, using the selection sort
3      algorithm.
4  */
5  public class SelectionSorter
6  {
7      /**
8          Constructs a selection sorter.
9          @param anArray  the array to sort
10     */
11     public SelectionSorter(int[] anArray)
12     {
13         a = anArray;
14     }
15
16     /**
17         Sorts the array managed by this selection sorter.
18     */
19     public void sort()
20     {
21         for (int i = 0; i < a.length - 1; i++)
22         {
```

```
23              int minPos = minimumPosition(i);
24              swap(minPos, i);
25           }
26        }
27
28        /**
29           Finds the smallest element in a tail range of the array.
30           @param from  the first position in a to compare
31           @return  the position of the smallest element in the
32           range a[from] . . . a[a.length - 1]
33        */
34        private int minimumPosition(int from)
35        {
36           int minPos = from;
37           for (int i = from + 1; i < a.length; i++)
38              if (a[i] < a[minPos]) minPos = i;
39           return minPos;
40        }
41
42        /**
43           Swaps two entries of the array.
44           @param i  the first position to swap
45           @param j  the second position to swap
46        */
47        private void swap(int i, int j)
48        {
49           int temp = a[i];
50           a[i] = a[j];
51           a[j] = temp;
52        }
53
54        private int[] a;
55     }
```

File SelectionSortTester.java

```
1     /**
2        This program tests the selection sort algorithm by
3        sorting an array that is filled with random numbers.
4     */
5     public class SelectionSortTester
6     {
7        public static void main(String[] args)
8        {
9           int[] a = ArrayUtil.randomIntArray(20, 100);
10          ArrayUtil.print(a);
11
12          SelectionSorter sorter = new SelectionSorter(a);
13          sorter.sort();
14
15          ArrayUtil.print(a);
16       }
17    }
```

File ArrayUtil.java

```java
1   import java.util.Random;
2
3   /**
4      This class contains utility methods for array
5      manipulation.
6   */
7   public class ArrayUtil
8   {
9      /**
10        Creates an array filled with random values.
11        @param length the length of the array
12        @param n the number of possible random values
13        @return an array filled with length numbers between
14        0 and n - 1
15     */
16     public static int[] randomIntArray(int length, int n)
17     {
18        int[] a = new int[length];
19        for (int i = 0; i < a.length; i++)
20           a[i] = generator.nextInt(n);
21
22        return a;
23     }
24
25     /**
26        Prints all elements in an array.
27        @param a the array to print
28     */
29     public static void print(int[] a)
30     {
31        for (int e : a)
32           System.out.print(e + " ");
33        System.out.println();
34     }
35
36     private static Random generator = new Random();
37  }
```

Output

```
65 46 14 52 38 2 96 39 14 33 13 4 24 99 89 77 73 87 36 81
2 4 13 14 14 24 33 36 38 39 46 52 65 73 77 81 87 89 96 99
```

SELF CHECK

1. Why do we need the temp variable in the swap method? What would happen if you simply assigned a[i] to a[j] and a[j] to a[i]?

2. What steps does the selection sort algorithm go through to sort the sequence 6 5 4 3 2 1?

19.2 Profiling the Selection Sort Algorithm

To measure the performance of a program, you could simply run it and measure how long it takes by using a stopwatch. However, most of our programs run very quickly, and it is not easy to time them accurately in this way. Furthermore, when a program takes a noticeable time to run, a certain amount of that time may simply be used for loading the program from disk into memory (for which we should not penalize it) or for screen output (whose speed depends on the computer model, even for computers with identical CPUs). We will instead create a `StopWatch` class. This class works like a real stopwatch. You can start it, stop it, and read out the elapsed time. The class uses the `System.currentTimeMillis` method, which returns the milliseconds that have elapsed since midnight at the start of January 1, 1970. Of course, you don't care about the absolute number of seconds since this historical moment, but the *difference* of two such counts gives us the number of milliseconds of a time interval. Here is the code for the `StopWatch` class:

File StopWatch.java

```
1   /**
2       A stopwatch accumulates time when it is running. You can
3       repeatedly start and stop the stopwatch. You can use a
4       stopwatch to measure the running time of a program.
5   */
6   public class StopWatch
7   {
8       /**
9           Constructs a stopwatch that is in the stopped state
10          and has no time accumulated.
11      */
12      public StopWatch()
13      {
14          reset();
15      }
16
17      /**
18          Starts the stopwatch. Time starts accumulating now.
19      */
20      public void start()
21      {
22          if (isRunning) return;
23          isRunning = true;
24          startTime = System.currentTimeMillis();
25      }
26
27      /**
28          Stops the stopwatch. Time stops accumulating and is
29          is added to the elapsed time.
30      */
31      public void stop()
32      {
33          if (!isRunning) return;
```

```
34              isRunning = false;
35              long endTime = System.currentTimeMillis();
36              elapsedTime = elapsedTime + endTime - startTime;
37          }
38
39      /**
40          Returns the total elapsed time.
41          @return the total elapsed time
42      */
43      public long getElapsedTime()
44      {
45          if (isRunning)
46          {
47              long endTime = System.currentTimeMillis();
48              return elapsedTime + endTime - startTime;
49          }
50          else
51              return elapsedTime;
52      }
53
54      /**
55          Stops the watch and resets the elapsed time to 0.
56      */
57      public void reset()
58      {
59          elapsedTime = 0;
60          isRunning = false;
61      }
62
63      private long elapsedTime;
64      private long startTime;
65      private boolean isRunning;
66  }
```

Here is how we will use the stopwatch to measure the performance of the sorting algorithm:

File SelectionSortTimer.java

```
 1  import java.util.Scanner;
 2
 3  /**
 4      This program measures how long it takes to sort an
 5      array of a user-specified size with the selection
 6      sort algorithm.
 7  */
 8  public class SelectionSortTimer
 9  {
10      public static void main(String[] args)
11      {
12          Scanner in = new Scanner(System.in);
13          System.out.print("Enter array size: ");
14          int n = in.nextInt();
```

```
15
16          // Construct random array
17
18          int[] a = ArrayUtil.randomIntArray(n, 100);
19          SelectionSorter sorter = new SelectionSorter(a);
20
21          // Use stopwatch to time selection sort
22
23          StopWatch timer = new StopWatch();
24
25          timer.start();
26          sorter.sort();
27          timer.stop();
28
29          System.out.println("Elapsed time: "
30                + timer.getElapsedTime() + " milliseconds");
31      }
32 }
```

Output

```
Enter array size: 100000
Elapsed time: 27880 milliseconds
```

By starting to measure the time just before sorting, and stopping the stopwatch just after, you don't count the time it takes to initialize the array or the time during which the program waits for the user to type in n.

Here are the results of some sample runs:

n	Milliseconds
10,000	772
20,000	3,051
30,000	6,846
40,000	12,188
50,000	19,015
60,000	27,359

These measurements were obtained with a Pentium processor with a clock speed of 1.2 GHz, running Java 5.0 on the Linux operating system. On another computer the actual numbers will look different, but the relationship between the numbers will be the same. Figure 1 shows a plot of the measurements. As you can see, doubling the size of the data set more than doubles the time needed to sort it.

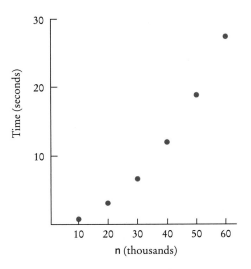

Figure 1   Time Taken by Selection Sort

3. Approximately how many seconds would it take to sort a data set of 80,000 values?

4. Look at the graph in Figure 1. What mathematical shape does it resemble?

19.3 Analyzing the Performance of the Selection Sort Algorithm

Let us count the number of operations that the program must carry out to sort an array with the selection sort algorithm. We don't actually know how many machine operations are generated for each Java instruction or which of those instructions are more time-consuming than others, but we can make a simplification. We will simply count how often an array element is *visited*. Each visit requires about the same amount of work by other operations, such as incrementing subscripts and comparing values.

Let n be the size of the array. First, we must find the smallest of n numbers. To achieve that, we must visit n array elements. Then we swap the elements, which takes two visits. (You may argue that there is a certain probability that we don't need to swap the values. That is true, and one can refine the computation to reflect that observation. As we will soon see, doing so would not affect the overall conclusion.) In the next step, we need to visit only $n - 1$ elements to find the minimum. In the following step, $n - 2$ elements are visited to find the minimum. The last step visits two elements to find the minimum. Each step requires two visits to swap the elements. Therefore, the total number of visits is

$$n + 2 + (n - 1) + 2 + \cdots + 2 + 2 = n + (n - 1) + \cdots + 2 + (n - 1) \cdot 2$$
$$= 2 + \cdots + (n - 1) + n + (n - 1) \cdot 2$$
$$= \frac{n(n + 1)}{2} - 1 + (n - 1) \cdot 2$$

because

$$1 + 2 + \cdots + (n - 1) + n = \frac{n(n + 1)}{2}$$

After multiplying out and collecting terms of n, we find that the number of visits is

$$\tfrac{1}{2}n^2 + \tfrac{5}{2}n - 3$$

We obtain a quadratic equation in n. That explains why the graph of Figure 1 looks approximately like a parabola.

Now let us simplify the analysis further. When you plug in a large value for n (for example, 1,000 or 2,000), then $\frac{1}{2}n^2$ is 500,000 or 2,000,000. The lower term, $\frac{5}{2}n - 3$, doesn't contribute much at all; it is only 2,497 or 4,997, a drop in the bucket compared to the hundreds of thousands or even millions of comparisons specified by the $\frac{1}{2}n^2$ term. We will just ignore these lower-level terms. Next, we will ignore the constant factor $\frac{1}{2}$. We are not interested in the actual count of visits for a single n. We want to compare the ratios of counts for different values of n. For example, we can say that sorting an array of 2,000 numbers requires four times as many visits as sorting an array of 1,000 numbers:

$$\frac{\left(\frac{1}{2} \cdot 2000^2\right)}{\left(\frac{1}{2} \cdot 1000^2\right)} = 4$$

The factor $\frac{1}{2}$ cancels out in comparisons of this kind. We will simply say, "The number of visits is of order n^2". That way, we can easily see that the number of comparisons increases fourfold when the size of the array doubles: $(2n^2) = 4n^2$.

To indicate that the number of visits is of order n^2, computer scientists often use *big-Oh notation*: The number of visits is $O(n^2)$. This is a convenient shorthand.

> Computer scientists use the big-Oh notation $f(n) = O(g(n))$ to express that the function *f* grows no faster than the function *g*.

In general, the expression $f(n) = O(g(n))$ means that f grows no faster than g, or, more formally, that for all n larger than some threshold, the ratio $f(n)/g(n) \leq C$ for some constant value C. The function g is usually chosen to be very simple, such as n^2 in our example.

To turn an exact expression such as

$$\tfrac{1}{2}n^2 + \tfrac{5}{2}n - 3$$

into big-Oh notation, simply locate the fastest-growing term, n^2, and ignore its constant coefficient, no matter how large or small it may be.

We observed before that the actual number of machine operations, and the actual number of microseconds that the computer spends on them, is approximately proportional to the number of element visits. Maybe there are about 10 machine operations (increments, comparisons, memory loads, and stores) for every element visit. The number of machine operations is then approximately $10 \times \frac{1}{2}n^2$. Again, we aren't interested in the coefficient, so we can say that the number of machine operations, and hence the time spent on the sorting, is of the order of n^2 or $O(n^2)$.

> Selection sort is an $O(n^2)$ algorithm. Doubling the data set means a fourfold increase in processing time.

The sad fact remains that doubling the size of the array causes a fourfold increase in the time required for sorting it with selection sort. When the size of the array increases by a factor of 100, the sorting time increases by a factor of 10,000. To sort an array of a million entries, (for example, to create a telephone directory) takes 10,000 times as long as sorting 10,000 entries. If 10,000 entries can be sorted in about 3/4 of a second (as in our example), then sorting one million entries requires more than 2 hours. That is a problem. We will see in the next section how one can dramatically improve the performance of the sorting process by choosing a more sophisticated algorithm.

SELF CHECK

5. If you increase the size of a data set tenfold, how much longer does it take to sort it with the selection sort algorithm?
6. How large does n need to be so that $\frac{1}{2}n^2$ is bigger than $\frac{5}{2}n - 3$?

ADVANCED TOPIC 19.1

Insertion Sort

Insertion sort is another simple sorting algorithm. In this algorithm, we assume that the initial sequence

```
a[0] a[1] . . . a[k]
```

of an array is already sorted. (When the algorithm starts, we set k to 0.) We enlarge the initial sequence by inserting the next array element, a[k + 1], at the proper location. When we reach the end of the array, the sorting process is complete.

For example, suppose we start with the array

11	9	16	5	7

Of course, the initial sequence of length 1 is already sorted. We now add a[1], which has the value 9. The element needs to be inserted before the element 11. The result is

9	11	16	5	7

Next, we add a[2], which has the value 16. As it happens, the element does not have to be moved.

9 11 16 5 7

We repeat the process, inserting a[3] or 5 at the very beginning of the initial sequence.

5 9 11 16 7

Finally, a[4] or 7 is inserted in its correct position, and the sorting is completed.

The following class implements the insertion sort algorithm:

```java
public class InsertionSorter
{
    /**
        Constructs an insertion sorter.
        @param anArray the array to sort
    */
    public InsertionSorter(int[] anArray)
    {
        a = anArray;
    }


    /**
        Sorts the array managed by this insertion sorter.
    */
    public void sort()
    {
        for (int i = 1; i < a.length; i++)
        {
            int next = a[i];
            // Find the insertion location
            // Move all larger elements up
            int j = i;
            while (j > 0 && a[j - 1] > next)
            {
                a[j] = a[j - 1];
                j--;
            }
            // Insert the element
            a[j] = next;
        }
    }

    private int[] a;
}
```

How efficient is this algorithm? Let n denote the size of the array. We carry out $n - 1$ iterations. In the kth iteration, we have a sequence of k elements that is already sorted, and we need to insert a new element into the sequence. For each insertion, we need to visit the elements of the initial sequence until we have found the location in which the new element can be inserted. Then we need to move up the remaining elements of the sequence. Thus, $k + 1$ array elements are visited. Therefore, the total number of visits is

$$2 + 3 + \cdots + n = \frac{n(n + 1)}{2} - 1$$

> Insertion sort is an $O(n^2)$ algorithm.

We conclude that insertion sort is an $O(n^2)$ algorithm, on the same order of efficiency as selection sort.

Insertion sort has one desirable property: Its performance is $O(n)$ if the array is already sorted—see Exercise R19.3. This is a useful property in practical applications, in which data sets are often partially sorted.

ADVANCED TOPIC 19.2

Oh, Omega, and Theta

We have used the big-Oh notation somewhat casually in this chapter, to describe the growth behavior of a function. Strictly speaking, $f(n) = O(g(n))$ means that f grows *no faster* than g. But it is permissible for f to grow much slower. Thus, it is technically correct to state that $f(n) = n^2 + 5n - 3$ is $O(n^3)$ or even $O(n^{10})$.

Computer scientists have invented additional notation to describe the growth behavior of functions more accurately. The expression

$$f(n) = \Omega(g(n))$$

means that f grows at least as fast as g, or, formally, that for all n larger than some threshold, the ratio $f(n)/g(n) \geq C$ for some constant value C. (The Ω symbol is the capital Greek letter omega.) For example, $f(n) = n^2 + 5n - 3$ is $\Omega(n^2)$ or even $\Omega(n)$.

The expression

$$f(n) = \Theta(g(n))$$

means that f and g grow at the same rate—that is, both $f(n) = O(g(n))$ and $f(n) = \Omega(g(n))$ hold. (The Θ symbol is the capital Greek letter theta.)

The Θ notation gives the most precise description of growth behavior. For example, $f(n) = n^2 + 5n - 3$ is $\Theta(n^2)$ but not $\Theta(n)$ or $\Theta(n^3)$.

The Ω and Θ notation is very important for the precise analysis of algorithms. However, in casual conversation it is common to stick with big-Oh, while still giving as good an estimate as one can.

19.4 Merge Sort

In this section, you will learn about the merge sort algorithm, a much more efficient algorithm than selection sort. The basic idea behind merge sort is very simple.

Suppose we have an array of 10 integers. Let us engage in a bit of wishful thinking and hope that the first half of the array is already perfectly sorted, and the second half is too, like this:

| 5 | 9 | 10 | 12 | 17 | 1 | 8 | 11 | 20 | 32 |

Now it is simple to *merge* the two sorted arrays into one sorted array, by taking a new element from either the first or the second subarray, and choosing the smaller of the elements each time:

5	9	10	12	17		1	8	11	20	32		1									

In fact, you probably performed this merging before when you and a friend had to sort a pile of papers. You and the friend split the pile in half, each of you sorted your half, and then you merged the results together.

> The merge sort algorithm sorts an array by cutting the array in half, recursively sorting each half, and then merging the sorted halves.

That is all well and good, but it doesn't seem to solve the problem for the computer. It still must sort the first and second halves of the array, because it can't very well ask a few buddies to pitch in. As it turns out, though, if the computer keeps dividing the array into smaller and smaller subarrays, sorting each half and merging them back together, it carries out dramatically fewer steps than the selection sort requires.

Let us write a `MergeSorter` class that implements this idea. When the `MergeSorter` sorts an array, it makes two arrays, each half the size of the original, and sorts them recursively. Then it merges the two sorted arrays together:

```java
public void sort()
{
   if (a.length <= 1) return;
   int[] first = new int[a.length / 2];
   int[] second = new int[a.length - first.length];
   System.arraycopy(a, 0, first, 0, first.length);
   System.arraycopy(a,
      first.length, second, 0, second.length);
   MergeSorter firstSorter = new MergeSorter(first);
   MergeSorter secondSorter = new MergeSorter(second);
   firstSorter.sort();
   secondSorter.sort();
   merge(first, second);
}
```

The `merge` method is tedious but quite straightforward. You will find it in the code that follows.

File MergeSorter.java

```
1   /**
2      This class sorts an array, using the merge sort algorithm.
3   */
4   public class MergeSorter
5   {
6      /**
7         Constructs a merge sorter.
8         @param anArray the array to sort
9      */
10     public MergeSorter(int[] anArray)
11     {
12        a = anArray;
13     }
14
15     /**
16        Sorts the array managed by this merge sorter.
17     */
18     public void sort()
19     {
20        if (a.length <= 1) return;
21        int[] first = new int[a.length / 2];
22        int[] second = new int[a.length - first.length];
23        System.arraycopy(a, 0, first, 0, first.length);
24        System.arraycopy(a, first.length, second, 0, second.length);
25        MergeSorter firstSorter = new MergeSorter(first);
26        MergeSorter secondSorter = new MergeSorter(second);
27        firstSorter.sort();
28        secondSorter.sort();
29        merge(first, second);
30     }
31
32     /**
33        Merges two sorted arrays into the array managed by this
34        merge sorter.
35        @param first the first sorted array
36        @param second the second sorted array
37     */
38     private void merge(int[] first, int[] second)
39     {
40        // Merge both halves into the temporary array
41
42        int iFirst = 0;
43           // Next element to consider in the first array
44        int iSecond = 0;
45           // Next element to consider in the second array
46        int j = 0;
47           // Next open position in a
48
49        // As long as neither iFirst nor iSecond past the end, move
50        // the smaller element into a
51        while (iFirst < first.length && iSecond < second.length)
52        {
53           if (first[iFirst] < second[iSecond])
```

```
54              {
55                  a[j] = first[iFirst];
56                  iFirst++;
57              }
58              else
59              {
60                  a[j] = second[iSecond];
61                  iSecond++;
62              }
63              j++;
64          }
65
66          // Note that only one of the two calls to arraycopy below
67          // copies entries
68
69          // Copy any remaining entries of the first array
70          System.arraycopy(first, iFirst, a, j, first.length - iFirst);
71
72          // Copy any remaining entries of the second half
73          System.arraycopy(second, iSecond, a, j, second.length - iSecond);
74      }
75
76      private int[] a;
77  }
```

File MergeSortTester.java

```
1   /**
2       This program tests the merge sort algorithm by
3       sorting an array that is filled with random numbers.
4   */
5   public class MergeSortTester
6   {
7       public static void main(String[] args)
8       {
9           int[] a = ArrayUtil.randomIntArray(20, 100);
10          ArrayUtil.print(a);
11          MergeSorter sorter = new MergeSorter(a);
12          sorter.sort();
13          ArrayUtil.print(a);
14      }
15  }
```

Output

```
8 81 48 53 46 70 98 42 27 76 33 24 2 76 62 89 90 5 13 21
2 5 8 13 21 24 27 33 42 46 48 53 62 70 76 76 81 89 90 98
```

SELF CHECK

7. Why does only one of the two arraycopy calls at the end of the merge method do any work?

8. Manually run the merge sort algorithm on the array 8 7 6 5 4 3 2 1.

19.5 Analyzing the Merge Sort Algorithm

The merge sort algorithm looks a lot more complicated than the selection sort algorithm, and it appears that it may well take much longer to carry out these repeated subdivisions. However, the timing results for merge sort look much better than those for selection sort:

n	Merge Sort (milliseconds)	Selection Sort (milliseconds)
10,000	31	772
20,000	47	3,051
30,000	62	6,846
40,000	80	12,188
50,000	97	19,015
60,000	113	27,359

Figure 2 shows a graph comparing both sets of performance data. That is a tremendous improvement. To understand why, let us estimate the number of array element visits that are required to sort an array with the merge sort algorithm. First, let us tackle the merge process that happens after the first and second halves have been sorted.

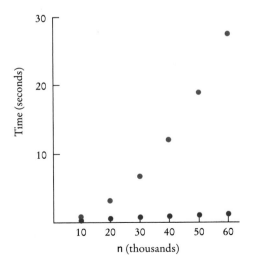

Figure 2
Merge Sort Timing (blue) versus Selection Sort (red)

Each step in the merge process adds one more element to a. That element may come from first or second, and in most cases the elements from the two halves must be compared to see which one to take. Let us count that as 3 visits (one for a and one each for first and second) per element, or $3n$ visits total, where n denotes the length of a. Moreover, at the beginning, we had to copy from a to first and second, yielding another $2n$ visits, for a total of $5n$.

If we let $T(n)$ denote the number of visits required to sort a range of n elements through the merge sort process, then we obtain

$$T(n) = T\left(\frac{n}{2}\right) + T\left(\frac{n}{2}\right) + 5n$$

because sorting each half takes $T(n/2)$ visits. Actually, if n is not even, then we have one subarray of size $(n-1)/2$ and one of size $(n+1)/2$. Although it turns out that this detail does not affect the outcome of the computation, we will nevertheless assume for now that n is a power of 2, say $n = 2^m$. That way, all subarrays can be evenly divided into two parts.

Unfortunately, the formula

$$T(n) = 2T\left(\frac{n}{2}\right) + 5n$$

does not clearly tell us the relationship between n and $T(n)$. To understand the relationship, let us evaluate $T(n/2)$, using the same formula:

$$T\left(\frac{n}{2}\right) = 2T\left(\frac{n}{4}\right) + 5\frac{n}{2}$$

Therefore

$$T(n) = 2 \times 2T\left(\frac{n}{4}\right) + 5n + 5n$$

Let us do that again:

$$T\left(\frac{n}{4}\right) = 2T\left(\frac{n}{8}\right) + 5\frac{n}{4}$$

hence

$$T(n) = 2 \times 2 \times 2T\left(\frac{n}{8}\right) + 5n + 5n + 5n$$

This generalizes from 2, 4, 8, to arbitrary powers of 2:

$$T(n) = 2^k T\left(\frac{n}{2^k}\right) + 5nk$$

Recall that we assume that $n = 2^m$; hence, for $k = m$,

$$T(n) = 2^m T\left(\frac{n}{2^m}\right) + 5nm$$

$$= nT(1) + 5nm$$

$$= n + 5n \log_2(n)$$

Because $n = 2^m$, we have $m = \log_2(n)$.

To establish the growth order, we drop the lower-order term n and are left with $5n \log_2(n)$. We drop the constant factor 5. It is also customary to drop the base of the logarithm, because all logarithms are related by a constant factor. For example,

$$\log_2(x) = \log_{10}(x)/\log_{10}(2) \approx \log_{10}(x) \times 3.32193$$

Hence we say that merge sort is an $O(n \log(n))$ algorithm.

> **Merge sort is an $O(n \log(n))$ algorithm. The $n \log(n)$ function grows much more slowly than n^2.**

Is the $O(n \log(n))$ merge sort algorithm better than the $O(n^2)$ selection sort algorithm? You bet it is. Recall that it took $100^2 = 10,000$ times as long to sort a million records as it took to sort 10,000 records with the $O(n^2)$ algorithm. With the $O(n \log(n))$ algorithm, the ratio is

$$\frac{1,000,000 \log(1,000,000)}{10,000 \log(10,000)} = 100\left(\frac{6}{4}\right) = 150$$

Suppose for the moment that merge sort takes the same time as selection sort to sort an array of 10,000 integers, that is, 3/4 of a second on the test machine. (Actually, it is much faster than that.) Then it would take about 0.75×150 seconds, or under 2 minutes, to sort a million integers. Contrast that with selection sort, which would take over 2 hours for the same task. As you can see, even if it takes you several hours to learn about a better algorithm, that can be time well spent.

In this chapter we have barely begun to scratch the surface of this interesting topic. There are many sorting algorithms, some with even better performance than the merge sort algorithm, and the analysis of these algorithms can be quite challenging. If you are a computer science major, you may revisit these important issues in a later computer science class.

> **The Arrays class implements a sorting method that you should use for your Java programs.**

However, when you write Java programs, you don't have to implement your own sorting algorithm. The Arrays class contains static sort methods to sort arrays of integers and floating-point numbers. For example, you can sort an array of integers simply as

```
int[] a = . . .;
Arrays.sort(a);
```

That sort method uses the Quicksort algorithm—see Advanced Topic 19.3 for more information about that algorithm.

9. Given the timing data for the merge sort algorithm in the table at the beginning of this section, how long would it take to sort an array of 100,000 values?

10. Suppose you have an array `double[] values` in a Java program. How would you sort it?

ADVANCED TOPIC 19.3

The Quicksort Algorithm

Quicksort is a commonly used algorithm that has the advantage over merge sort that no temporary arrays are required to sort and merge the partial results.

The quicksort algorithm, like merge sort, is based on the strategy of divide and conquer. To sort a range a[from] . . . a[to] of the array a, first rearrange the elements in the range so that no element in the range a[from] . . . a[p] is larger than any element in the range a[p + 1] . . . a[to]. This step is called *partitioning* the range.

For example, suppose we start with a range

| 5 | 3 | 2 | 6 | 4 | 1 | 3 | 7 |

Here is a partitioning of the range. Note that the partitions aren't yet sorted.

| 3 | 3 | 2 | 1 | 4 | | 6 | 5 | 7 |

You'll see later how to obtain such a partition. In the next step, sort each partition, by recursively applying the same algorithm on the two partitions. That sorts the entire range, because the largest element in the first partition is at most as large as the smallest element in the second partition.

| 1 | 2 | 3 | 3 | 4 | | 5 | 6 | 7 |

Quicksort is implemented recursively as follows:

```
public void sort(int from, int to)
{
   if (from >= to) return;
   int p = partition(from, to);
   sort(from, p);
   sort(p + 1, to);
}
```

Let us return to the problem of partitioning a range. Pick an element from the range and call it the *pivot*. There are several variations of the quicksort algorithm. In the simplest one, we'll pick the first element of the range, a[from], as the pivot.

Now form two regions a[from] . . . a[i], consisting of values at most as large as the pivot and a[j] . . . a[to], consisting of values at least as large as the pivot. The region a[i + 1] . . . a[j - 1] consists of values that haven't been analyzed yet. (See Figure 3.) At the beginning, both the left and right areas are empty; that is, i = from - 1 and j = to + 1.

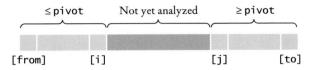

Figure 3   Partitioning a Range

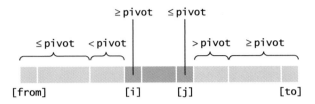

Figure 4   Extending the Partitions

Then keep incrementing i while a[i] < pivot and keep decrementing j while a[j] > pivot. Figure 4 shows i and j when that process stops.

Now swap the values in positions i and j, increasing both areas once more. Keep going while i < j. Here is the code for the partition method:

```
private int partition(int from, int to)
{
    int pivot = a[from];
    int i = from - 1;
    int j = to + 1;
    while (i < j)
    {
        i++; while (a[i] < pivot) i++;
        j--; while (a[j] > pivot) j--;
        if (i < j) swap(i, j);
    }
    return j;
}
```

On average, the quicksort algorithm is an $O(n \log(n))$ algorithm. Because it is simpler, it runs faster than merge sort in most cases. There is just one unfortunate aspect to the quicksort algorithm. Its *worst-case* runtime behavior is $O(n^2)$. Moreover, if the pivot element is chosen as the first element of the region, that worst-case behavior occurs when the input set is already sorted—a common situation in practice. By selecting the pivot element more cleverly, we can make it extremely unlikely for the worst-case behavior to occur. Such "tuned" quicksort algorithms are commonly used, because their performance is generally excellent. For example, as was mentioned, the sort method in the Arrays class uses a quicksort algorithm.

Another improvement that is commonly made in practice is to switch to insertion sort when the array is short, because the total number of operations of insertion sort is lower for short arrays. The Java library makes that switch if the array length is less than 7.

RANDOM FACT 19.1

The First Programmer

Before pocket calculators and personal computers existed, navigators and engineers used mechanical adding machines, slide rules, and tables of logarithms and trigonometric functions to speed up computations. Unfortunately, the tables—for which values had to be computed by hand—were notoriously inaccurate. The mathematician Charles Babbage (1791–1871) had the insight that if a machine could be constructed that produced printed tables automatically, both calculation and typesetting errors could be avoided. Babbage set out to develop a machine for this purpose, which he called a *Difference Engine* because it used successive differences to compute polynomials. For example, consider the function $f(x) = x^3$. Write down the values for $f(1)$, $f(2)$, $f(3)$, and so on. Then take the *differences* between successive values:

```
  1
        7
  8
       19
 27
       37
 64
       61
125
       91
216
```

Repeat the process, taking the difference of successive values in the second column, and then repeat once again:

```
  1
        7
  8          12
       19           6
 27          18
       37           6
 64          24
       61           6
125          30
       91
216
```

Now the differences are all the same. You can retrieve the function values by a pattern of additions—you need to know the values at the fringe of the pattern and the constant difference. This method was very attractive, because mechanical addition machines had been known for some time. They consisted of cog wheels, with 10 cogs per wheel, to represent digits, and mechanisms to handle the carry from one digit to the next. Mechanical multiplication machines, on the other hand, were fragile and unreliable. Babbage built a successful prototype of the Difference Engine (see Figure 5) and, with his own money and government grants, proceeded to build the table-printing machine. However, because of funding problems and the difficulty of building the machine to the required precision, it was never completed.

While working on the Difference Engine, Babbage conceived of a much grander vision that he called the *Analytical Engine*. The Difference Engine was designed to carry out a limited set of computations—it was no smarter than a pocket calculator is today. But Babbage realized that such a machine could be made *programmable* by storing programs as well

Figure 5 Babbage's Difference Engine

as data. The internal storage of the Analytical Engine was to consist of 1,000 registers of 50 decimal digits each. Programs and constants were to be stored on punched cards—a technique that was, at that time, commonly used on looms for weaving patterned fabrics.

Ada Augusta, Countess of Lovelace (1815–1852), the only child of Lord Byron, was a friend and sponsor of Charles Babbage. Ada Lovelace was one of the first people to realize the potential of such a machine, not just for computing mathematical tables but for processing data that were not numbers. She is considered by many the world's first programmer. The Ada programming language, a language developed for use in U.S. Department of Defense projects (see Random Fact 12.1), was named in her honor.

19.6 Searching

Suppose you need to find the telephone number of your friend. You look up his name in the telephone book, and naturally you can find it quickly, because the telephone book is sorted alphabetically. Quite possibly, you may never have thought how important it is that the telephone book is sorted. To see that, think of the following problem: Suppose you have a telephone number and you must know to what party it belongs. You could of course call that number, but suppose nobody picks up on the other end. You could look through the telephone book, a number at a time, until you find the number. That would obviously be a tremendous amount of work, and you would have to be desperate to attempt that.

This thought experiment shows the difference between a search through an unsorted data set and a search through a sorted data set. The following two sections will analyze the difference formally.

If you want to find a number in a sequence of values that occur in arbitrary order, there is nothing you can do to speed up the search. You must simply look through all elements until you have found a match or until you reach the end. This is called a *linear* or *sequential search*.

> A linear search examines all values in an array until it finds a match or reaches the end.

How long does a linear search take? If we assume that the element v is present in the array a, then the average search visits $n/2$ elements, where n is the length of the array. If it is not present, then all n elements must be inspected to verify the absence. Either way, a linear search is an $O(n)$ algorithm.

> A linear search locates a value in an array in $O(n)$ steps.

Here is a class that performs linear searches through an array a of integers. When searching for the value v, the search method returns the first index of the match, or -1 if v does not occur in a.

File LinearSearcher.java

```
1   /**
2        A class for executing linear searches through an array.
3   */
4   public class LinearSearcher
5   {
6      /**
7            Constructs the LinearSearcher.
8            @param anArray an array of integers
9      */
10     public LinearSearcher(int[] anArray)
11     {
12        a = anArray;
13     }
14
15     /**
16           Finds a value in an array, using the linear search
17           algorithm.
18           @param v the value to search
19           @return the index at which the value occurs, or -1
20           if it does not occur in the array
21     */
22     public int search(int v)
23     {
24        for (int i = 0; i < a.length; i++)
25        {
26           if (a[i] == v)
27              return i;
28        }
29        return -1;
30     }
31
32     private int[] a;
33  }
```

File LinearSearchTester.java

```java
1  import java.util.Scanner;
2
3  /**
4      This program tests the linear search algorithm.
5  */
6  public class LinearSearchTester
7  {
8     public static void main(String[] args)
9     {
10        // Construct random array
11
12        int[] a = ArrayUtil.randomIntArray(20, 100);
13        ArrayUtil.print(a);
14        LinearSearcher searcher = new LinearSearcher(a);
15
16        Scanner in = new Scanner(System.in);
17
18        boolean done = false;
19        while (!done)
20        {
21           System.out.print("Enter number to search for, -1 to quit: ");
22           int n = in.nextInt();
23           if (n == -1)
24              done = true;
25           else
26           {
27              int pos = searcher.search(n);
28              System.out.println("Found in position " + pos);
29           }
30        }
31     }
32  }
```

Output

```
46 99 45 57 64 95 81 69 11 97 6 85 61 88 29 65 83 88 45 88
Enter number to search for, -1 to quit: 11
Found in position 8
```

SELF CHECK

11. Suppose you need to look through 1,000,000 records to find a telephone number. How many records do you expect to search before finding the number?

12. Why can't you use a "for each" loop for (int element : a) in the search method?

19.7 Binary Search

Now let us search for an item in a data sequence that had been previously sorted. Of course, we could still do a linear search, but it turns out we can do much better than that.

Consider the following sorted array a. The data set is:

```
[0][1][2][3][4][5][6][7]
 1  5  8  9 12 17 20 32
```

We would like to see whether the value 15 is in the data set. Let's narrow our search by finding whether the value is in the first or second half of the array. The last point in the first half of the data set, a[3], is 9, which is smaller than the value we are looking for. Hence, we should look in the second half of the array for a match, that is, in the sequence:

```
[0][1][2][3][4][5][6][7]
 1  5  8  9 12 17 20 32
```

Now the last value of the first half of this sequence is 17; hence, the value must be located in the sequence:

```
[0][1][2][3][4][5][6][7]
 1  5  8  9 12 17 20 32
```

The last value of the first half of this very short sequence is 12, which is smaller than the value that we are searching, so we must look in the second half:

```
[0][1][2][3][4][5][6][7]
 1  5  8  9 12 17 20 32
```

> A binary search locates a value in a sorted array by determining whether the value occurs in the first or second half, then repeating the search in one of the halves.

It is trivial to see that we don't have a match, because 15 ≠ 17. If we wanted to insert 15 into the sequence, we would need to insert it just before a[5].

This search process is called a *binary search*, because we cut the size of the search in half in each step. That cutting in half works only because we know that the sequence of values is sorted.

The following class implements binary searches in a sorted array of integers. The search method returns the position of the match if the search succeeds, or –1 if v is not found in a.

File BinarySearcher.java

```
1  /**
2      A class for executing binary searches through an array.
3  */
4  public class BinarySearcher
5  {
```

```
 6      /**
 7         Constructs a BinarySearcher.
 8         @param anArray a sorted array of integers
 9      */
10      public BinarySearcher(int[] anArray)
11      {
12         a = anArray;
13      }
14
15      /**
16         Finds a value in a sorted array, using the binary
17         search algorithm.
18         @param v the value to search
19         @return the index at which the value occurs, or -1
20         if it does not occur in the array
21      */
22      public int search(int v)
23      {
24         int low = 0;
25         int high = a.length - 1;
26         while (low <= high)
27         {
28            int mid = (low + high) / 2;
29            int diff = a[mid] - v;
30
31            if (diff == 0) // a[mid] == v
32               return mid;
33            else if (diff < 0) // a[mid] < v
34               low = mid + 1;
35            else
36               high = mid - 1;
37         }
38         return -1;
39      }
40
41      private int[] a;
42   }
```

Let us determine the number of visits of array elements required to carry out a search. We can use the same technique as in the analysis of merge sort. Because we look at the middle element, which counts as one comparison, and then search either the left or the right subarray, we have

$$T(n) = T\left(\frac{n}{2}\right) + 1$$

Using the same equation,

$$T\left(\frac{n}{2}\right) = T\left(\frac{n}{4}\right) + 1$$

By plugging this result into the original equation, we get

$$T(n) = T\left(\frac{n}{4}\right) + 2$$

That generalizes to

$$T(n) = T\left(\frac{n}{2^k}\right) + k$$

As in the analysis of merge sort, we make the simplifying assumption that n is a power of 2, $n = 2^m$, where $m = \log_2(n)$. Then we obtain

$$T(n) = 1 + \log_2(n)$$

Therefore, binary search is an $O(\log(n))$ algorithm.

> A binary search locates a value in an array in $O(\log(n))$ steps.

That result makes intuitive sense. Suppose that n is 100. Then after each search, the size of the search range is cut in half, to 50, 25, 12, 6, 3, and 1. After seven comparisons we are done. This agrees with our formula, because $\log_2(100) \approx 6.64386$, and indeed the next larger power of 2 is $2^7 = 128$.

Because a binary search is so much faster than a linear search, is it worthwhile to sort an array first and then use a binary search? It depends. If you search the array only once, then it is more efficient to pay for an $O(n)$ linear search than for an $O(n \log(n))$ sort and an $O(\log(n))$ binary search. But if you will be making many searches in the same array, then sorting it is definitely worthwhile.

The `Arrays` class contains a static `binarySearch` method that implements the binary search algorithm, but with a useful enhancement. If a value is not found in the array, then the returned value is not –1, but $-k - 1$, where k is the position before which the element should be inserted. For example,

```
int[] a = { 1, 4, 9 };
int v = 7;
int pos = Arrays.binarySearch(a, v);
    // Returns -3; v should be inserted before position 2
```

SELF CHECK

13. Suppose you need to look through a sorted array with 1,000,000 elements to find a value. Using the binary search algorithm, how many records do you expect to search before finding the value?

14. Why is it useful that the `Arrays.binarySearch` method indicates the position where a missing element should be inserted?

15. Why does `Arrays.binarySearch` return $-k - 1$ and not $-k$ to indicate that a value is not present and should be inserted before position k?

19.8 Sorting Real Data

In this chapter we have studied how to search and sort arrays of integers. Of course, in application programs, there is rarely a need to search through a collection of integers. However, it is easy to modify these techniques to search through real data.

> The sort method of the Arrays class sorts objects of classes that implement the Comparable interface.

The Arrays class supplies a static sort method for sorting arrays of objects. However, the Arrays class cannot know how to compare arbitrary objects. Suppose, for example, that you have an array of Coin objects. It is not obvious how the coins should be sorted. You could sort them by their names, or by their values. The Arrays.sort method cannot make that decision for you. Instead, it requires that the objects belong to classes that implement the Comparable interface. That interface has a single method:

```
public interface Comparable
{
    int compareTo(Object otherObject);
}
```

The call

```
a.compareTo(b)
```

must return a negative number if a should come before b, 0 if a and b are the same, and a positive number otherwise.

Several classes in the standard Java library, such as the String and Date classes, implement the Comparable interface.

You can implement the Comparable interface for your own classes as well. For example, to sort a collection of coins, the Coin class would need to implement this interface and define a compareTo method:

```
public class Coin implements Comparable
{
    . . .
    public int compareTo(Object otherObject)
    {
        Coin other = (Coin) otherObject;
        if (value < other.value) return -1;
        if (value == other.value) return 0;
        return 1;
    }
    . . .
}
```

When you implement the compareTo method of the Comparable interface, you must make sure that the method defines a *total ordering relationship,* with the following three properties:

- *Antisymmetric:* If a.compareTo(b) ≤ 0, then b.compareTo(a) ≥ 0

- *Reflexive:* a.compareTo(a) = 0

- *Transitive:* If a.compareTo(b) ≤ 0 and b.compareTo(c) ≤ 0, then a.compareTo(c) ≤ 0

Once your `Coin` class implements the `Comparable` interface, you can simply pass an array of coins to the `Arrays.sort` method:

```
Coin[] coins = new Coin[n];
// Add coins
. . .
Arrays.sort(coins);
```

> The `Collections` class contains a sort method that can sort array lists.

If the coins are stored in an `ArrayList`, use the `Collections.sort` method instead; it uses the merge sort algorithm:

```
ArrayList<Coin> coins = new ArrayList<Coin>();
// Add coins
. . .
Collections.sort(coins);
```

As a practical matter, you should use the sorting and searching methods in the `Arrays` and `Collections` classes and not those that you write yourself. The library algorithms have been fully debugged and optimized. Thus, the primary purpose of this chapter was not to teach you how to implement practical sorting and searching algorithms. Instead, you have learned something more important, namely that different algorithms can vary widely in performance, and that it is worthwhile to learn more about the design and analysis of algorithms.

SELF CHECK

16. Why can't the `Arrays.sort` method sort an array of `Rectangle` objects?

17. What steps would you need to take to sort an array of `BankAccount` objects by increasing balance?

COMMON ERROR 19.1

The compareTo Method Can Return Any Integer, Not Just –1, 0, and 1

The call `a.compareTo(b)` is allowed to return *any* negative integer to denote that a should come before b, not necessarily the value –1. That is, the test

```
if (a.compareTo(b) == -1) // ERROR!
```

is generally wrong. Instead, you should test

```
if (a.compareTo(b) < 0) // OK
```

Why would a `compareTo` method ever want to return a number other than –1, 0, or 1? Sometimes, it is convenient to just return the difference of two integers. For example, the `compareTo` method of the `String` class compares characters in matching positions:

```
char c1 = charAt(i);
char c2 = other.charAt(i);
```

If the characters are different, then the method simply returns their difference:

```
if (c1 != c2) return c1 - c2;
```

This difference is a negative number if c1 is less than c2, but it is not necessarily the number –1.

ADVANCED TOPIC 19.4

The Parameterized Comparable Interface

As of Java version 5.0, the Comparable interface is a parameterized type, similar to the Array-List type:

```
public interface Comparable<T>
{
    int compareTo(T other)
}
```

The type parameter specifies the type of the objects that this class is willing to accept for comparison. Usually, this type is the same as the class type itself. For example, the Coin class would implement Comparable<Coin>, like this:

```
public class Coin implements Comparable<Coin>
{
    . . .
    public int compareTo(Coin other)
    {
        if (value < other.value) return -1;
        if (value == other.value) return 0;
        return 1;
    }
    . . .
}
```

The type parameter has a significant advantage: You need not use a cast to convert an Object parameter into the desired type.

ADVANCED TOPIC 19.5

The Comparator Interface

Sometimes, you want so sort an array or array list of objects, but the objects don't belong to a class that implements the Comparable interface. Or, perhaps, you want to sort the array in a different order. For example, you may want to sort coins by name rather than by value.

You wouldn't want to change the implementation of a class just in order to call Arrays.sort. Fortunately, there is an alternative. One version of the Arrays.sort method does not require that the objects belong to classes that implement the Comparable interface. Instead, you can supply arbitrary objects. However, you must also provide a *comparator* object whose job is to compare objects. The comparator object must belong to a class that implements the Comparator interface. That interface has a single method, compare, which compares two objects.

As of Java version 5.0, the Comparator interface is a parameterized type. The type parameter specifies the type of the compare parameters. For example, Comparator<Coin> looks like this:

```
public interface Comparator<Coin>
{
    int compare(Coin a, Coin b);
}
```

The call

```
comp.compare(a, b)
```

must return a negative number if a should come before b, 0 if a and b are the same, and a positive number otherwise. (Here, comp is an object of a class that implements Comparator<Coin>.)

For example, here is a Comparator class for coins:

```
public class CoinComparator implements Comparator<Coin>
{
   public int compare(Coin a, Coin b)
   {
      if (a.getValue() < b.getValue()) return -1;
      if (a.getValue() == b.getValue()) return 0;
      return 1;
   }
}
```

To sort an array of coins by value, call

```
Arrays.sort(coins, new CoinComparator());
```

CHAPTER SUMMARY

1. The selection sort algorithm sorts an array by repeatedly finding the smallest element of the unsorted tail region and moving it to the front.

2. Computer scientists use the big-Oh notation $f(n) = O(g(n))$ to express that the function f grows no faster than the function g.

3. Selection sort is an $O(n^2)$ algorithm. Doubling the data set means a fourfold increase in processing time.

4. Insertion sort is an $O(n^2)$ algorithm.

5. The merge sort algorithm sorts an array by cutting the array in half, recursively sorting each half, and then merging the sorted halves.

6. Merge sort is an $O(n \log(n))$ algorithm. The $n \log(n)$ function grows much more slowly than n^2.

7. The Arrays class implements a sorting method that you should use for your Java programs.

8. A linear search examines all values in an array until it finds a match or reaches the end.

9. A linear search locates a value in an array in $O(n)$ steps.

10. A binary search locates a value in a sorted array by determining whether the value occurs in the first or second half, then repeating the search in one of the halves.

11. A binary search locates a value in an array in $O(\log(n))$ steps.

12. The sort method of the Arrays class sorts objects of classes that implement the Comparable interface.

13. The Collections class contains a sort method that can sort array lists.

FURTHER READING

1. Michael T. Goodrich and Roberto Tamassia, *Data Structures and Algorithms in Java, 3rd edition,* John Wiley & Sons, 2003.

CLASSES, OBJECTS, AND METHODS INTRODUCED IN THIS CHAPTER

```
java.lang.Comparable<T>
    compareTo
java.lang.System
    currentTimeMillis
java.util.Arrays
    binarySearch
    sort
java.util.Collections
    binarySearch
    sort
java.util.Comparator<T>
    compare
```

REVIEW EXERCISES

Exercise R19.1. *Checking against off-by-one errors.* When writing the selection sort algorithm of Section 19.1, a programmer must make the usual choices of < against <=, a.length against a.length - 1, and from against from + 1. This is a fertile ground for off-by-one errors. Conduct code walkthroughs of the algorithm with arrays of length 0, 1, 2, and 3 and check carefully that all index values are correct.

Exercise R19.2. What is the difference between searching and sorting?

Exercise R19.3. For the following expressions, what is the order of the growth of each?

    a. $n^2 + 2n + 1$
    b. $n^{10} + 9n^9 + 20n^8 + 145n^7$
    c. $(n + 1)^4$
    d. $(n^2 + n)^2$
    e. $n + 0.001n^3$

f. $n^3 - 1000n^2 + 10^9$

g. $n + \log(n)$

h. $n^2 + n \log(n)$

i. $2^n + n^2$

j. $\dfrac{n^3 + 2n}{n^2 + 0.75}$

Exercise R19.4. We determined that the actual number of visits in the selection sort algorithm is

$$T(n) = \tfrac{1}{2}n^2 + \tfrac{5}{2}n - 3$$

We characterized this method as having $O(n^2)$ growth. Compute the actual ratios

$$T(2{,}000)/T(1{,}000)$$
$$T(4{,}000)/T(1{,}000)$$
$$T(10{,}000)/T(1{,}000)$$

and compare them with

$$f(2{,}000)/f(1{,}000)$$
$$f(4{,}000)/f(1{,}000)$$
$$f(10{,}000)/f(1{,}000)$$

where $f(n) = n^2$.

Exercise R19.5. Suppose algorithm A takes 5 seconds to handle a data set of 1,000 records. If the algorithm A is an $O(n)$ algorithm, how long will it take to handle a data set of 2,000 records? Of 10,000 records?

Exercise R19.6. Suppose an algorithm takes 5 seconds to handle a data set of 1,000 records. Fill in the following table, which shows the approximate growth of the execution times depending on the complexity of the algorithm.

	$O(n)$	$O(n^2)$	$O(n^3)$	$O(n \log(n))$	$O(2^n)$
1,000	5	5	5	5	5
2,000					
3,000		45			
10,000					

For example, because $3{,}000^2/1{,}000^2 = 9$, the algorithm would take 9 times as long, or 45 seconds, to handle a data set of 3,000 records.

Exercise R19.7. Sort the following growth rates from slowest to fastest growth.

$$O(n)$$

$$O(n^3)$$

$$O(n^n)$$

$$O(\log(n))$$

$$O(n^2 \log(n))$$

$$O(n \log(n))$$

$$O(2^n)$$

$$O(\sqrt{n})$$

$$O(n\sqrt{n})$$

$$O(n^{\log(n)})$$

Exercise R19.8. What is the growth rate of the standard algorithm to find the minimum value of an array? Of finding both the minimum and the maximum?

Exercise R19.9. What is the growth rate of the following method?

```java
public static int count(int[] a, int c)
{
   int count = 0;

   for (int i = 0; i < a.length; i++)
   {
      if (a[i] == c) count++;
   }
   return count;
}
```

Exercise R19.10. Your task is to remove all duplicates from an array. For example, if the array has the values

4 7 11 4 9 5 11 7 3 5

then the array should be changed to

4 7 11 9 5 3

Here is a simple algorithm. Look at a[i]. Count how many times it occurs in a. If the count is larger than 1, remove it. What is the growth rate of the time required for this algorithm?

Exercise R19.11. Consider the following algorithm to remove all duplicates from an array. Sort the array. For each element in the array, look at its next neighbor to decide whether it is present more than once. If so, remove it. Is this a faster algorithm than the one in Exercise R19.10?

Exercise R19.12. Develop a fast algorithm for removing duplicates from an array if the resulting array must have the same ordering as the original array.

Exercise R19.13. Why does insertion sort perform significantly better than selection sort if an array is already sorted?

Exercise R19.14. Consider the following speedup of the insertion sort algorithm of Advanced Topic 19.1. For each element, call `Arrays.binarySearch` to determine where it needs to be inserted. Does this speedup have a significant impact on the efficiency of the algorithm?

PROGRAMMING EXERCISES

Exercise P19.1. Modify the selection sort algorithm to sort an array of integers in descending order.

Exercise P19.2. Modify the selection sort algorithm to sort an array of coins by their value.

Exercise P19.3. Write a program that generates the table of sample runs of the selection sort times automatically. The program should ask for the smallest and largest value of n and the number of measurements and then make all sample runs.

Exercise P19.4. Modify the merge sort algorithm to sort an array of strings in lexicographic order.

Exercise P19.5. Write a telephone lookup program. Read a data set of 1,000 names and telephone numbers from a file that contains the numbers in random order. Handle lookups by name and also reverse lookups by phone number. Use a binary search for both lookups.

Exercise P19.6. Implement a program that measures the performance of the insertion sort algorithm described in Advanced Topic 19.1.

Exercise P19.7. Write a program that sorts an `ArrayList<Coin>` in decreasing order so that the most valuable coin is at the beginning of the array.

Exercise P19.8. Consider the binary search algorithm in Section 19.7. If no match is found, the search method returns −1. Modify the method so that if a is not found, the method returns $-k - 1$, where k is the position before which the element should be inserted. (This is the same behavior as `Arrays.binarySearch`.)

Exercise P19.9. Implement the sort method of the merge sort algorithm without recursion, where the length of the array is a power of 2. First merge adjacent regions of size 1, then adjacent regions of size 2, then adjacent regions of size 4, and so on.

Exercise P19.10. Implement the sort method of the merge sort algorithm without recursion, where the length of the array is an arbitrary number. Keep merging adjacent regions whose size is a power of 2, and pay special attention to the last area whose size is less.

Exercise P19.11. Use insertion sort and `Arrays.binarySearch` to sort an array as described in Exercise R19.14. Implement this algorithm and measure its performance.

Exercise P19.12. Supply a class `Person` that implements the `Comparable` interface. Compare persons by their names. Ask the user to input 10 names and generate 10 `Person` objects. Using the `compareTo` method, determine the first and last person among them and print them.

Exercise P19.13. Sort an array list of strings by increasing *length*. *Hint:* Supply a `Comparator`.

Exercise P19.14. Sort an array list of strings by increasing length, and so that strings of the same length are sorted lexicographically. *Hint:* Supply a `Comparator`.

PROGRAMMING PROJECTS

Project 19.1. Write a program that keeps an appointment book. Make a class `Appointment` that stores a description of the appointment, the appointment day, the starting time, and the ending time. Your program should keep the appointments in a sorted array list. Users can add appointments and print out all appointments for a given day. When a new appointment is added, use binary search to find where it should be inserted in the array list. Do not add it if it conflicts with another appointment.

Project 19.2. Implement a *graphical animation* of sorting and searching algorithms. Fill an array with a set of random numbers between 1 and 100. Draw each array element as a bar, as in Figure 6. Whenever the algorithm changes the array, wait for the user to click a button, then call the `repaint` method.

Animate selection sort, merge sort, and binary search. In the binary search animation, highlight the currently inspected element and the current values of `from` and `to`.

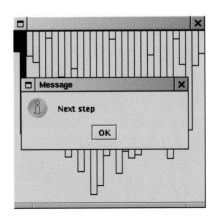

Figure 6
Graphical Animation

ANSWERS TO SELF-CHECK QUESTIONS

1. Dropping the `temp` variable would not work. Then `a[i]` and `a[j]` would end up being the same value.

2. 1 | 5 4 3 2 6, 1 2 | 4 3 5 6, 1 2 3 4 5 6

3. Four times as long as 40,000 values, or about 50 seconds.

4. A parabola.

5. It takes about 100 times longer.

6. If n is 4, then $\frac{1}{2}n^2$ is 8 and $\frac{5}{2}n - 3$ is 7.

7. When the preceding `while` loop ends, the loop condition must be false, that is, `iFirst >= first.length` or `iSecond >= second.length` (De Morgan's Law). Then `first.length - iFirst <= 0` or `iSecond.length - iSecond <= 0`.

8. First sort 8 7 6 5. Recursively, first sort 8 7. Recursively, first sort 8. It's sorted. Sort 7. It's sorted. Merge them: 7 8. Do the same with 6 5 to get 5 6. Merge them to 5 6 7 8. Do the same with 4 3 2 1: Sort 4 3 by sorting 4 and 3 and merging them to 3 4. Sort 2 1 by sorting 2 and 1 and merging them to 1 2. Merge 3 4 and 1 2 to 1 2 3 4. Finally, merge 5 6 7 8 and 1 2 3 4 to 1 2 3 4 5 6 7 8.

9. Approximately 100,000 · log(100,000) / 50,000 · log(50,000) = 2 · 5 / 4.7 = 2.13 times the time required for 50,000 values. That's 2.13 · 97 milliseconds or approximately 207 milliseconds.

10. By calling `Arrays.sort(values)`.

11. On average, you'd make 500,000 comparisons.

12. The `search` method returns the index at which the match occurs, not the data stored at that location.

13. You would search about 20. (The binary log of 1,024 is 10.)

14. Then you know where to insert it so that the array stays sorted, and you can keep using binary search.

15. Otherwise, you would not know whether a value is present when the method returns 0.

16. The `Rectangle` class does not implement the `Comparable` interface.

17. The `BankAccount` class needs to implement the `Comparable` interface. Its `compareTo` method must compare the bank balances.

Chapter **20**

An Introduction to Data Structures

CHAPTER GOALS

- To learn how to use the linked lists provided in the standard library
- To be able to use iterators to traverse linked lists
- To understand the implementation of linked lists
- To distinguish between abstract and concrete data types
- To know the efficiency of fundamental operations of lists and arrays
- To become familiar with the stack and queue types

Up to this point, we used arrays as a one-size-fits-all mechanism for collecting objects. However, computer scientists have developed many different data structures that have varying performance tradeoffs. In this chapter, you will learn about the *linked list*, a data structure that allows you to add and remove elements efficiently, without moving any existing elements. You will also learn about the distinction between concrete and abstract data types. An abstract type spells out what fundamental operations should be supported efficiently, but it leaves the implementation unspecified. The stack and queue types, introduced at the end of this chapter, are examples of abstract types.

CHAPTER CONTENTS

20.1 Using Linked Lists

A *linked list* is a data structure used for collecting a sequence of objects, which allows efficient addition and removal of elements in the middle of the sequence.

To understand the need for such a data structure, imagine a program that maintains a sequence of employee objects, sorted by the last names of the employees. When a new employee is hired, an object needs to be inserted into the sequence. Unless the company happened to hire employees in dictionary order, the new object probably needs to be inserted somewhere near the middle of the sequence. If we use an array to store the objects, then all objects following the new hire must be moved toward the end.

Conversely, if an employee leaves the company, the object must be removed, and the hole in the sequence needs to be closed up by moving all objects that come after it. Moving a large number of values can involve a substantial amount of processing time. We would like to structure the data in a way that minimizes this cost.

> A linked list consists of a number of nodes, each of which has a reference to the next node.

Rather than storing the values in an array, a linked list uses a sequence of *nodes*. Each node stores a value and a reference to the next node in the sequence (see Figure 1). When you insert a new node into a linked list, only the neighboring node references need to be updated. The same is true when you remove a node. What's the catch? Linked lists allow speedy insertion and removal, but element access can be slow.

> Adding and removing elements in the middle of a linked list is efficient.

For example, suppose you want to locate the fifth element. You must first traverse the first four. This is a problem if you need to access the elements in arbitrary order. The term "random access" is used in computer science to describe an access pattern in which elements are accessed in arbitrary (not necessarily random) order. In contrast, sequential access visits the elements in sequence. For example, a binary search requires random access, whereas a linear search requires sequential access.

> Visiting the elements of a linked list in sequential order is efficient, but random access is not.

Of course, if you mostly visit all elements in sequence (for example, to display or print the elements), the inefficiency of random access is not a problem. You use linked lists when you are concerned about the efficiency of inserting or removing elements and you rarely need element access in random order.

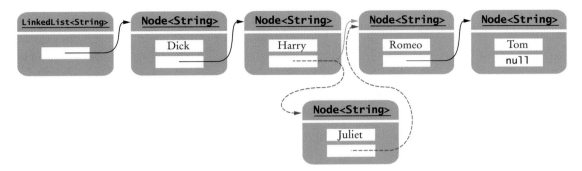

Figure 1 Inserting an Element into a Linked List

The Java library provides a linked list class. In this section you will learn how to use the library class. In the next section you will peek under the hood and see how some of its key methods are implemented.

The LinkedList class in the java.util package is a generic class, just like the ArrayList class. That is, you specify the type of the list elements in angle brackets, such as LinkedList<String> or LinkedList<Product>.

The following methods give you direct access to the first and the last element in the list. Here, E is the element type of LinkedList<E>.

```
void addFirst(E obj)
void addLast(E obj)
E getFirst()
E getLast()
E removeFirst()
E removeLast()
```

How do you add and remove elements in the middle of the list? The list will not give you references to the nodes. If you had direct access to them and somehow messed them up, you would break the linked list. As you will see in the next section, where you implement some of the linked list operations yourself, keeping all links between nodes intact is not trivial.

> You use a list iterator to access elements inside a linked list.

Instead, the Java library supplies a ListIterator type. A list iterator encapsulates a position anywhere inside the linked list (see Figure 2).

Figure 2 A List Iterator

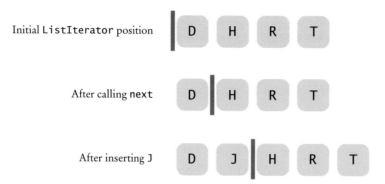

Figure 3   A Conceptual View of the List Iterator

Conceptually, you should think of the iterator as pointing between two elements, just as the cursor in a word processor points between two characters (see Figure 3). In the conceptual view, think of each element as being like a letter in a word processor, and think of the iterator as being like the blinking cursor between letters.

You obtain a list iterator with the listIterator method of the LinkedList class:

```
LinkedList<String> employeeNames = . . .;
ListIterator<String> iterator = employeeNames.listIterator();
```

Note that the iterator class is also a generic type. A ListIterator<String> iterates through a list of strings; a ListIterator<Product> visits the elements in a LinkedList<Product>.

Initially, the iterator points before the first element. You can move the iterator position with the next method:

```
iterator.next();
```

The next method throws a NoSuchElementException if you are already past the end of the list. You should always call the method hasNext before calling next—it returns true if there is a next element.

```
if (iterator.hasNext())
    iterator.next();
```

The next method returns the element that the iterator is passing. When you use a ListIterator<String>, the return type of the next method is String. In general, the return type of the next method matches the type parameter.

You traverse all elements in a linked list of strings with the following loop:

```
while (iterator.hasNext())
{
    String name = iterator.next();
    Do something with name
}
```

As a shorthand, if your loop simply visits all elements of the linked list, you can use the "for each" loop:

```
for (String name : employeeNames)
{
    Do something with name
}
```

Then you don't have to worry about iterators at all. Behind the scenes, the `for` loop uses an iterator to visit all list elements (see Advanced Topic 20.1).

The nodes of the `LinkedList` class store two links: one to the next element and one to the previous one. Such a list is called a *doubly linked list*. You can use the `previous` and `hasPrevious` methods of the `ListIterator` interface to move the iterator position backwards.

The `add` method adds an object after the iterator, then moves the iterator position past the new element.

```
iterator.add("Juliet");
```

You can visualize insertion to be like typing text in a word processor. Each character is inserted after the cursor, and then the cursor moves past the inserted character (see Figure 3). Most people never pay much attention to this—you may want to try it out and watch carefully how your word processor inserts characters.

The `remove` method removes the object that was returned by the last call to `next` or `previous`. For example, the following loop removes all names that fulfill a certain condition:

```
while (iterator.hasNext())
{
    String name = iterator.next();
    if (name fulfills condition)
        iterator.remove();
}
```

You have to be careful when calling `remove`. It can be called only once after calling `next` or `previous`, and you cannot call it immediately after a call to `add`. If you call the method improperly, it throws an `IllegalStateException`.

Here is a sample program that inserts strings into a list and then iterates through the list, adding and removing elements. Finally, the entire list is printed. The comments indicate the iterator position.

File ListTester.java

```
 1  import java.util.LinkedList;
 2  import java.util.ListIterator;
 3
 4  /**
 5      A program that demonstrates the LinkedList class.
 6  */
 7  public class ListTester
 8  {
 9      public static void main(String[] args)
10      {
11          LinkedList<String> staff = new LinkedList<String>();
12          staff.addLast("Dick");
13          staff.addLast("Harry");
```

```
14        staff.addLast("Romeo");
15        staff.addLast("Tom");
16
17        // | in the comments indicates the iterator position
18
19        ListIterator<String> iterator
20            = staff.listIterator(); // |DHRT
21        iterator.next(); // D|HRT
22        iterator.next(); // DH|RT
23
24        // Add more elements after second element
25
26        iterator.add("Juliet"); // DHJ|RT
27        iterator.add("Nina"); // DHJN|RT
28
29        iterator.next(); // DHJNR|T
30
31        // Remove last traversed element
32
33        iterator.remove(); // DHJN|T
34
35        // Print all elements
36
37        for (String name : staff)
38            System.out.println(name);
39     }
40 }
```

Output

```
Dick
Harry
Juliet
Nina
Tom
```

SELF CHECK

1. Do linked lists take more storage space than arrays of the same size?
2. Why don't we need iterators with arrays?

ADVANCED TOPIC 20.1

The **Iterable** Interface and the "For Each" Loop

You can use the "for each" loop

for (*Type variable* : *collection*)

with any of the collection classes in the standard Java library. This includes the ArrayList and LinkedList classes as well as the library classes which will be discussed in Chapter 21. In fact, the "for each" loop can be used with any class that implements the Iterable interface:

```
public interface Iterable<E>
{
    Iterator<E> iterator();
}
```

The interface has a type parameter E, denoting the element type of the collection. The single method, iterator, yields an object that implements the Iterator interface.

```
public interface Iterator<E>
{
    boolean hasNext();
    E next();
    void remove();
}
```

The ListIterator interface that you saw in the preceding section is a subinterface of Iterator with additional methods (such as add and previous).

The compiler translates a "for each" loop into an equivalent loop that uses an iterator. The loop

```
for (Type variable : collection)
    body
```

is equivalent to

```
Iterator<Type> iter = collection.iterator();
while (iter.hasNext())
{
    Type variable = iter.next();
    body
}
```

The ArrayList and LinkedList classes implement the Iterable interface. If your own classes implement the Iterable interface, you can use them with the "for each" loop as well—see Exercise P20.16.

20.2 Implementing Linked Lists

In the last section you saw how to use the linked list class supplied by the Java library. In this section, we will look at the implementation of a simplified version of this class. This shows you how the list operations manipulate the links as the list is modified.

To keep this sample code simple, we will not implement all methods of the linked list class. We will implement only a singly linked list, and the list class will supply direct access only to the first list element, not the last one. Our list will not use a type parameter. We will simply store raw Object values and insert casts when retrieving them. The result will be a fully functional list class that shows how the links are updated in the add and remove operations and how the iterator traverses the list.

A Node object stores an object and a reference to the next node. Because the methods of both the linked list class and the iterator class have frequent access to the Node instance variables, we do not make the instance variables private. Instead, we make Node a private inner class of the LinkedList class. Because none of the list methods returns a Node object, it is safe to leave the instance variables public.

```
public class LinkedList
{
    . . .
    private class Node
    {
        public Object data;
        public Node next;
    }
}
```

The LinkedList class holds a reference first to the first node (or null, if the list is completely empty).

```
public class LinkedList
{
    public LinkedList()
    {
        first = null;
    }

    public Object getFirst()
    {
        if (first == null)
            throw new NoSuchElementException();
        return first.data;
    }

    . . .
    private Node first;
}
```

Now let us turn to the addFirst method (see Figure 4). When a new node is added to the list, it becomes the head of the list, and the node that was the old list head becomes its next node:

```
public class LinkedList
{
    . . .
    public void addFirst(Object obj)
    {
        Node newNode = new Node();    ❶
        newNode.data = obj;
        newNode.next = first;    ❷
        first = newNode;    ❸
    }
    . . .
}
```

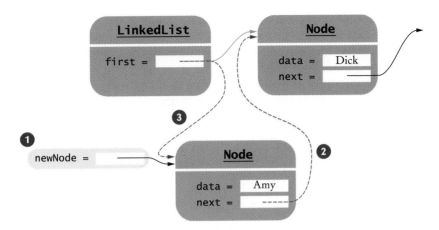

Figure 4 Adding a Node to the Head of a Linked List

Removing the first element of the list works as follows. The data of the first node are saved and later returned as the method result. The successor of the first node becomes the first node of the shorter list (see Figure 5). Then there are no further references to the old node, and the garbage collector will eventually recycle it.

```
public class LinkedList
{
   . . .
   public Object removeFirst()
   {
      if (first == null)
         throw new NoSuchElementException();
      Object obj = first.data;
      first = first.next; ①
      return obj;
   }
   . . .
}
```

Next, let us turn to the iterator class. The ListIterator interface in the standard library defines nine methods. We omit four of them (the methods that move the iterator backwards and the methods that report an integer index of the iterator).

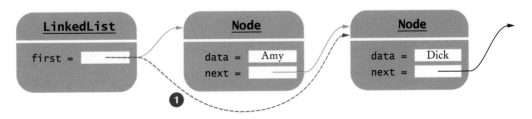

Figure 5 Removing the First Node from a Linked List

Our `LinkedList` class defines a private inner class `LinkedListIterator`, which implements the simplified `ListIterator` interface. Because `LinkedListIterator` is an inner class, it has access to the private features of the `LinkedList` class—in particular, the `first` field and the private `Node` class.

Note that clients of the `LinkedList` class don't actually know the name of the iterator class. They only know it is a class that implements the `ListIterator` interface.

```
public class LinkedList
{
   . . .
   public ListIterator listIterator()
   {
      return new LinkedListIterator();
   }

   private class LinkedListIterator
      implements ListIterator
   {
      public LinkedListIterator()
      {
         position = null;
         previous = null;
      }

      . . .
      private Node position;
      private Node previous;
   }
   . . .
}
```

Each iterator object has a reference `position` to the last visited node. We also store a reference to the last node before that. We will need that reference to adjust the links properly in the `remove` method.

The `next` method is simple. The `position` reference is advanced to `position.next`, and the old position is remembered in `previous`. There is a special case, however—if the iterator points before the first element of the list, then the old `position` is `null`, and `position` must be set to `first`.

```
private class LinkedListIterator
   implements ListIterator
{
   . . .
   public Object next()
   {
      if (!hasNext())
         throw new NoSuchElementException();
      previous = position; // Remember for remove

      if (position == null)
         position = first;
      else
         position = position.next;

      return position.data;
```

```
        }
        . . .
    }
```

The next method is supposed to be called only when the iterator is not yet at the end of the list. The iterator is at the end if the list is empty (that is, first == null) or if there is no element after the current position (position.next == null).

```
private class LinkedListIterator
    implements ListIterator
{
    . . .
    public boolean hasNext()
    {
        if (position == null)
            return first != null;
        else
            return position.next != null;
    }
    . . .
}
```

Implementing operations that modify a linked list is challenging—you need to make sure that you update all node references correctly.

Removing the last visited node is more involved. If the element to be removed is the first element, we just call removeFirst. Otherwise, an element in the middle of the list must be removed, and the node preceding it needs to have its next reference updated to skip the removed element (see Figure 6). If the previous reference equals position, then this call to remove does not immediately follow a call to next, and we throw an IllegalStateException.

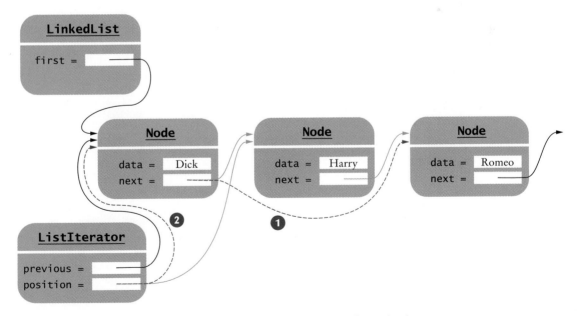

Figure 6   Removing a Node from the Middle of a Linked List

According to the definition of the remove method, it is illegal to call remove twice in a row. Therefore, the remove method sets the previous reference to position.

```
private class LinkedListIterator
    implements ListIterator
{
    . . .
    public void remove()
    {
        if (previous == position)
            throw new IllegalStateException();
        if (position == first)
        {
            removeFirst();
        }
        else
        {
            previous.next = position.next;   ❶
        }
        position = previous;   ❷
    }
    . . .
}
```

The set method changes the data stored in the previously visited element. Its implementation is straightforward because our linked lists can be traversed in only one direction. The linked-list implementation of the standard library must keep track of

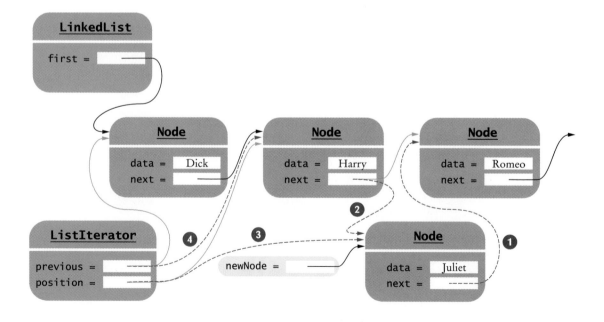

Figure 7   Adding a Node to the Middle of a Linked List

whether the last iterator movement was forward or backward. For that reason, the standard library forbids a call to the set method following an add or remove method. We do not enforce that restriction.

```java
public void set(Object obj)
{
   if (position == null)
      throw new NoSuchElementException();
   position.data = obj;
}
```

Finally, the most complex operation is the addition of a node. You insert the new node after the current position, and set the successor of the new node to the successor of the current position (see Figure 7).

```java
private class LinkedListIterator
   implements ListIterator
{
   . . .
   public void add(Object obj)
   {
      if (position == null)
      {
         addFirst(obj);
         position = first;
      }
      else
      {
         Node newNode = new Node();
         newNode.data = obj;
         newNode.next = position.next;    ❶
         position.next = newNode;         ❷
         position = newNode;              ❸
      }
      previous = position;               ❹
   }
   . . .
}
```

At the end of this section is the complete implementation of our LinkedList class.

You now know how to use the LinkedList class in the Java library, and you have had a peek "under the hood" to see how linked lists are implemented.

File LinkedList.java

```java
1  import java.util.NoSuchElementException;
2
3  /**
4     A linked list is a sequence of nodes with efficient
5     element insertion and removal. This class
6     contains a subset of the methods of the standard
7     java.util.LinkedList class.
8  */
9  public class LinkedList
10 {
```

```
11    /**
12        Constructs an empty linked list.
13    */
14    public LinkedList()
15    {
16        first = null;
17    }
18
19    /**
20        Returns the first element in the linked list.
21        @return the first element in the linked list
22    */
23    public Object getFirst()
24    {
25        if (first == null)
26            throw new NoSuchElementException();
27        return first.data;
28    }
29
30    /**
31        Removes the first element in the linked list.
32        @return the removed element
33    */
34    public Object removeFirst()
35    {
36        if (first == null)
37            throw new NoSuchElementException();
38        Object element = first.data;
39        first = first.next;
40        return element;
41    }
42
43    /**
44        Adds an element to the front of the linked list.
45        @param element the element to add
46    */
47    public void addFirst(Object element)
48    {
49        Node newNode = new Node();
50        newNode.data = element;
51        newNode.next = first;
52        first = newNode;
53    }
54
55    /**
56        Returns an iterator for iterating through this list.
57        @return an iterator for iterating through this list
58    */
59    public ListIterator listIterator()
60    {
61        return new LinkedListIterator();
62    }
63
```

```
64      private Node first;
65
66      private class Node
67      {
68          public Object data;
69          public Node next;
70      }
71
72      private class LinkedListIterator implements ListIterator
73      {
74          /**
75              Constructs an iterator that points to the front
76              of the linked list.
77          */
78          public LinkedListIterator()
79          {
80              position = null;
81              previous = null;
82          }
83
84          /**
85              Moves the iterator past the next element.
86              @return the traversed element
87          */
88          public Object next()
89          {
90              if (!hasNext())
91                  throw new NoSuchElementException();
92              previous = position; // Remember for remove
93
94              if (position == null)
95                  position = first;
96              else
97                  position = position.next;
98
99              return position.data;
100         }
101
102         /**
103             Tests if there is an element after the iterator
104             position.
105             @return true if there is an element after the iterator
106             position
107         */
108         public boolean hasNext()
109         {
110             if (position == null)
111                 return first != null;
112             else
113                 return position.next != null;
114         }
115
```

```
116    /**
117        Adds an element before the iterator position
118        and moves the iterator past the inserted element.
119        @param element the element to add
120    */
121    public void add(Object element)
122    {
123        if (position == null)
124        {
125            addFirst(element);
126            position = first;
127        }
128        else
129        {
130            Node newNode = new Node();
131            newNode.data = element;
132            newNode.next = position.next;
133            position.next = newNode;
134            position = newNode;
135        }
136        previous = position;
137    }
138
139    /**
140        Removes the last traversed element. This method may
141        only be called after a call to the next() method.
142    */
143    public void remove()
144    {
145        if (previous == position)
146            throw new IllegalStateException();
147
148        if (position == first)
149        {
150            removeFirst();
151        }
152        else
153        {
154            previous.next = position.next;
155        }
156        position = previous;
157    }
158
159    /**
160        Sets the last traversed element to a different
161        value.
162        @param element the element to set
163    */
164    public void set(Object element)
165    {
166        if (position == null)
167            throw new NoSuchElementException();
168        position.data = element;
169    }
```

```
170
171          private Node position;
172          private Node previous;
173       }
174    }
```

File ListIterator.java

```
1    /**
2        A list iterator allows access to a position in a linked list.
3        This interface contains a subset of the methods of the
4        standard java.util.ListIterator interface. The methods for
5        backward traversal are not included.
6    */
7    public interface ListIterator
8    {
9        /**
10           Moves the iterator past the next element.
11           @return the traversed element
12       */
13       Object next();
14
15       /**
16           Tests if there is an element after the iterator
17           position.
18           @return true if there is an element after the iterator
19           position
20       */
21       boolean hasNext();
22
23       /**
24           Adds an element before the iterator position
25           and moves the iterator past the inserted element.
26           @param element the element to add
27       */
28       void add(Object element);
29
30       /**
31           Removes the last traversed element. This method may
32           only be called after a call to the next() method.
33       */
34       void remove();
35
36       /**
37           Sets the last traversed element to a different
38           value.
39           @param element the element to set
40       */
41       void set(Object element);
42    }
```

3. Trace through the addFirst method when adding an element to an empty list.
4. Conceptually, an iterator points between elements (see Figure 3). Does the position reference point to the element to the left or to the element to the right?
5. Why does the add method have two separate cases?

ADVANCED TOPIC 20.2

Static Inner Classes

You first saw the use of inner classes for event handlers. Inner classes are useful in that context, because their methods have the privilege of accessing private data members of outer-class objects. The same is true for the LinkedListIterator inner class in the sample code for this section. The iterator needs to access the first instance variable of its linked list.

However, the Node inner class has no need to access the outer class. In fact, it has no methods. Thus, there is no need to store a reference to the outer list class with each Node object. To suppress the outer-class reference, you can declare the inner class as static:

```
public class LinkedList
{
   . . .
   private static class Node
   {
      . . .
   }
}
```

The purpose of the keyword static in this context is to indicate that the inner-class objects do not depend on the outer-class objects that generate them. In particular, the methods of a static inner class cannot access the outer-class instance variables. Declaring the inner class static is efficient, because its objects do not store an outer-class reference.

However, the LinkedListIterator class cannot be a static inner class. It frequently references the first element of the enclosing LinkedList.

20.3 Abstract and Concrete Data Types

There are two ways of looking at a linked list. One way is to think of the concrete implementation of such a list as a sequence of node objects with links between them (see Figure 8).

On the other hand, you can think of the *abstract* concept of the linked list. In the abstract, a linked list is an ordered sequence of data items that can be traversed with an iterator (see Figure 9).

> An abstract data type defines the fundamental operations on the data but does not specify an implementation.

Similarly, there are two ways of looking at an array list. Of course, an array list has a concrete implementation: a partially filled array of object references (see Figure 10). But you don't usually think about

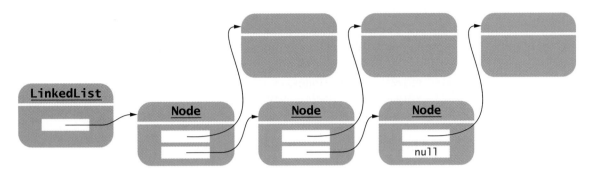

Figure 8   A Concrete View of a Linked List

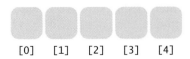

Figure 9   An Abstract View of a Linked List

the concrete implementation when using an array list. You take the abstract point of view. An array list is an ordered sequence of data items, each of which can be accessed by an integer index (see Figure 11).

The concrete implementations of a linked list and an array list are quite different. The abstractions, on the other hand, seem to be similar at first glance. To see the difference, consider the public interfaces stripped down to their minimal essentials.

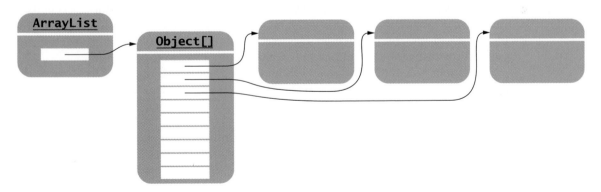

Figure 10   A Concrete View of an Array List

Figure 11   An Abstract View of an Array List

An array list allows *random access* to all elements. You specify an integer index, and you can get or set the corresponding element.

```
public class ArrayList
{
    public Object get(int index) { . . . }
    public void set(int index, Object value) { . . . }
    . . .
}
```

With a linked list, on the other hand, element access is a bit more complex. A linked list allows sequential access. You need to ask the linked list for an iterator. Using that iterator, you can easily traverse the list elements one at a time. But if you want to go to a particular element, say the 100th one, you first have to skip all elements before it.

```
public class LinkedList
{
    public ListIterator listIterator() { . . . }
    . . .
}

public interface ListIterator
{
    Object next();
    boolean hasNext();
    void add(Object value);
    void remove();
    void set(Object value);
    . . .
}
```

Here we show only the *fundamental* operations on array lists and linked lists. Other operations can be composed from these fundamental operations. For example, you can add or remove an element in an array list by moving all elements beyond the insertion or removal index, calling get and set multiple times.

Of course, the ArrayList class has methods to add and remove elements in the middle, even if they are slow. Conversely, the LinkedList class has get and set methods that let you access any element in the linked list, albeit very inefficiently, by performing repeated sequential accesses.

In fact, the term ArrayList signifies that its implementors wanted to combine the interfaces of an array and a list. Somewhat confusingly, both the ArrayList and the LinkedList class implement an interface called List that defines operations both for random access and for sequential access.

That terminology is not in common use outside the Java library. Instead, let us adopt a more traditional terminology. We will call the abstract types *array* and *list*. The Java library provides concrete implementations ArrayList and LinkedList for these abstract types. Other concrete implementations are possible in other libraries. In fact, Java arrays are another implementation of the abstract array type.

To understand an abstract data type completely, you need to know not just its fundamental operations but also their relative efficiency.

Table 1 Efficiency of Operations for Arrays and Lists

Table 1   Efficiency of Operations for Arrays and Lists

Operation	Array	List
Random access	$O(1)$	$O(n)$
Linear traversal step	$O(1)$	$O(1)$
Add/remove an element	$O(n)$	$O(1)$

> An abstract list is an ordered sequence of items that can be traversed sequentially and that allows for insertion and removal of elements at any position.

In a linked list, an element can be added or removed in constant time (assuming that the iterator is already in the right position). A fixed number of node references need to be modified to add or remove a node, regardless of the size of the list. Using the big-Oh notation, an operation that requires a bounded amount of time, regardless of the total number of elements in the structure, is denoted as $O(1)$. Random access in an array list also takes $O(1)$ time.

> An abstract array is an ordered sequence of items with random access via an integer index.

Adding or removing an arbitrary element in an array takes $O(n)$ time, where n is the size of the array list, because on average $n/2$ elements need to be moved. Random access in a linked list takes $O(n)$ time because on average $n/2$ elements need to be skipped.

Table 1 shows this information for arrays and lists.

Why consider abstract types at all? If you implement a particular algorithm, you can tell what operations you need to carry out on the data structures that your algorithm manipulates. You can then determine the abstract type that supports those operations efficiently, without being distracted by implementation details.

For example, suppose you have a sorted collection of items and you want to locate items using the binary search algorithm (see Section 19.7). That algorithm makes a random access to the middle of the collection, followed by other random accesses. Thus, fast random access is essential for the algorithm to work correctly. Once you know that an array supports fast random access and a linked list does not, you then look for concrete implementations of the abstract array type. You won't be fooled into using a LinkedList, even though the LinkedList class actually provides get and set methods.

In the next section, you will see additional examples of abstract data types.

SELF CHECK

6. What is the advantage of viewing a type abstractly?
7. How would you sketch an abstract view of a doubly linked list? A concrete view?
8. How much slower is the binary search algorithm for a linked list compared to the linear search algorithm?

20.4 Stacks and Queues

In this section we will consider two common abstract data types that allow insertion and removal of items at the ends only, not in the middle. A *stack* lets you insert and remove elements at only one end, traditionally called the *top* of the stack. To visualize a stack, think of a stack of books (see Figure 12).

> A stack is a collection of items with "last in first out" retrieval.

New items can be added to the top of the stack. Items are removed at the top of the stack as well. Therefore, they are removed in the order that is opposite from the order in which they have been added, called *last in, first out* or *LIFO* order. For example, if you add items A, B, and C and then remove them, you obtain C, B, and A. Traditionally, the addition and removal operations are called push and pop.

> A queue is a collection of items with "first in first out" retrieval.

A *queue* is similar to a stack, except that you add items to one end of the queue (the *tail*) and remove them from the other end of the queue (the *head*). To visualize a queue, simply think of people lining up (see Figure 13). People join the tail of the queue and wait until they have reached the head of the queue. Queues store items in a *first in, first out* or *FIFO* fashion. Items are removed in the same order in which they have been added.

There are many uses of queues and stacks in computer science. The Java graphical user interface system keeps an event queue of all events, such as mouse and keyboard events. The events are inserted into the queue whenever the operating system notifies the application of the event. Another thread of control removes them from the queue and passes them to the appropriate event listeners. Another example is a print queue. A printer may be accessed by several applications, perhaps running on different computers. If each of the applications tried to access the printer at the same time, the printout would be garbled. Instead, each application places all bytes that need to be sent to the printer into a file and inserts that file into the print queue. When the printer is done printing one file, it retrieves the next one from the queue. Therefore, print jobs are printed using the "first in, first out" rule, which is a fair arrangement for users of the shared printer.

Figure 12   A Stack of Books

Figure 13 A Queue

Stacks are used when a "last in, first out" rule is required. For example, consider an algorithm that attempts to find a path through a maze. When the algorithm encounters an intersection, it pushes the location on the stack, and then it explores the first branch. If that branch is a dead end, it returns to the location at the top of the stack. If all branches are dead ends, it pops the location off the stack, revealing a previously encountered intersection. Another important example is the *run-time stack* that a processor or virtual machine keeps to organize the variables of nested methods. Whenever a new method is called, its parameters and local variables are pushed onto a stack. When the method exits, they are popped off again. This stack makes recursive method calls possible.

There is a Stack class in the Java library that implements the abstract stack type and the push and pop operations. The following sample code shows how to use that class.

```
Stack<String> s = new Stack<String>();
s.push("A");
s.push("B");
s.push("C");
// The following loop prints C, B, and A
while (s.size() > 0)
    System.out.println(s.pop());
```

The Stack class in the Java library uses an array to implement a stack. Exercise P20.12 shows how to use a linked list instead.

The implementations of a queue in the standard library are designed for use with multithreaded programs. However, it is simple to implement a basic queue yourself:

```java
public class LinkedListQueue
{
    /**
        Constructs an empty queue that uses a linked list.
    */
    public LinkedListQueue()
    {
        list = new LinkedList();
    }

    /**
        Adds an item to the tail of the queue.
        @param x the item to add
    */
    public void add(Object x)
    {
        list.addLast(x);
    }

    /**
        Removes an item from the head of the queue.
        @return the removed item
    */
    public Object remove()
    {
        return list.removeFirst();
    }

    /**
        Gets the number of items in the queue.
        @return the size
    */
    int size()
    {
        return list.size();
    }

    private LinkedList list;
}
```

You would definitely not want to use an ArrayList to implement a queue. Removing the first element of an array list is inefficient—all other elements must be moved towards the beginning. However, Exercise P20.13 shows you how to implement a queue efficiently as a "circular" array, in which all elements stay at the position at which they were inserted, but the index values that denote the head and tail of the queue change when elements are added and removed.

In this chapter, you have seen the two most fundamental abstract data types, arrays and lists, and their concrete implementations. You also learned about the stack and queue types. In the next chapter, you will see additional data types that require more sophisticated implementation techniques.

9. Draw a sketch of the abstract queue type, similar to Figures 9 and 11.
10. Why wouldn't you want to use a stack to manage print jobs?

RANDOM FACT 20.1

Standardization

You encounter the benefits of standardization every day. When you buy a light bulb, you can be assured that it fits the socket without having to measure the socket at home and the light bulb in the store. In fact, you may have experienced how painful the lack of standards can be if you have ever purchased a flashlight with nonstandard bulbs. Replacement bulbs for such a flashlight can be difficult and expensive to obtain.

Programmers have a similar desire for standardization. Consider the important goal of platform independence for Java programs. After you compile a Java program into class files, you can execute the class files on any computer that has a Java virtual machine. For this to work, the behavior of the virtual machine has to be strictly defined. If virtual machines don't all behave exactly the same way, then the slogan of "write once, run anywhere" turns into "write once, debug everywhere". In order for multiple implementors to create compatible virtual machines, the virtual machine needed to be *standardized*. That is, someone needed to create a definition of the virtual machine and its expected behavior.

Who creates standards? Some of the most successful standards have been created by volunteer groups such as the Internet Engineering Task Force (IETF) and the World Wide Web Consortium (W3C). You can find the Requests for Comment (RFC) that standardize many of the Internet protocols at the IETF site, `http://www.ietf.org/rfc.html`. For example, RFC 822 standardizes the format of e-mail, and RFC 2616 defines the Hypertext Transmission Protocol (HTTP) that is used to serve web pages to browsers. The W3C standardizes the Hypertext Markup Language (HTML), the format for web pages—see `http://www.w3c.org`. These standards have been instrumental in the creation of the World Wide Web as an open platform that is not controlled by any one company.

Many programming languages, such as C++ and Scheme, have been standardized by independent standards organizations, such as the American National Standards Institute (ANSI) and the International Organization for Standardization—called ISO for short (not an acronym; see `http://www.iso.ch/iso/en/aboutiso/introduction/whatisISO.html`). ANSI and ISO are associations of industry professionals who develop standards for everything from car tires and credit card shapes to programming languages.

The process of standardizing the C++ language turned out to be very painstaking and time-consuming, and the standards organization followed a rigorous process to ensure fairness and to avoid being influenced by companies with vested interests.

When a company invents a new technology, it has an interest in its invention becoming a standard, so that other vendors produce tools that work with the invention and thus increase its likelihood of success. On the other hand, by handing over the invention to a standards committee, especially one that insists on a fair process, the company may lose control over the standard. For that reason, Sun Microsystems, the inventor of Java, never agreed to have a third-party organization standardize the Java language. They run their own standardization process, involving other companies but refusing to relinquish control. Another unfortunate but common tactic is to create a weak standard. For example, Netscape and Microsoft chose the European Computer Manufacturers Association (ECMA) to standardize the JavaScript language (see Random Fact 13.1). ECMA was willing to settle for something less than truly useful, standardizing the behavior of the core language and just a few of its libraries. Because most useful JavaScript programs need to use more libraries than those defined in the standard, programmers still go through a lot of tedious trial and error to write JavaScript code that runs identically on different browsers.

Often, competing standards are developed by different coalitions of vendors. For example, at the time of this writing, hardware vendors are in disagreement whether to use the IEEE 1394 (also called "FireWire" or iLink) or High-Speed USB for connecting external devices to computers. As Grace Hopper, the famous computer science pioneer, observed: "The great thing about standards is that there are so many to choose from".

Of course, many important pieces of technology aren't standardized at all. Consider the Windows operating system. Although Windows is often called a de-facto standard, it really is no standard at all. Nobody has ever attempted to define formally what the Windows operating system should do. The behavior changes at the whim of its vendor. That suits Microsoft just fine, because it makes it impossible for a third party to create its own version of Windows.

As a computer professional, there will be many times in your career when you need to make a decision whether to support a particular standard. Consider a simple example. In this chapter, we use the LinkedList class from the standard Java library. However, many computer scientists dislike this class because the interface muddies the distinction between abstract lists and arrays, and the iterators are clumsy to use. Should you use the LinkedList class in your own code, or should you implement a better list? If you do the former, you have to deal with a design that is less than optimal. If you do the latter, other programmers may have a hard time understanding your code because they aren't familiar with your list class.

CHAPTER SUMMARY

1. A linked list consists of a number of nodes, each of which has a reference to the next node.

2. Adding and removing elements in the middle of a linked list is efficient.

3. Visiting the elements of a linked list in sequential order is efficient, but random access is not.

4. You use a list iterator to access elements inside a linked list.

5. Implementing operations that modify a linked list is challenging—you need to make sure that you update all node references correctly.

6. An abstract data type defines the fundamental operations on the data but does not specify an implementation.

7. An abstract list is an ordered sequence of items that can be traversed sequentially and that allows for insertion and removal of elements at any position.

8. An abstract array is an ordered sequence of items with random access via an integer index.

9. A stack is a collection of items with "last in first out" retrieval.

10. A queue is a collection of items with "first in first out" retrieval.

CLASSES, OBJECTS, AND METHODS INTRODUCED IN THIS CHAPTER

java.util.Collection<E>
  iterator
java.util.Iterator<E>
  hasNext
  next
  remove
java.util.LinkedList<E>
  addFirst
  addLast
  getFirst
  getLast
  removeFirst
  removeLast

java.util.List<E>
  listIterator
java.util.ListIterator<E>
  add
  hasPrevious
  previous
  set

REVIEW EXERCISES

Exercise R20.1. Explain what the following code prints. Draw pictures of the linked list after each step. Just draw the forward links, as in Figure 1.

```
LinkedList<String> staff = new LinkedList<String>();
staff.addFirst("Harry");
staff.addFirst("Dick");
staff.addFirst("Tom");
System.out.println(staff.removeFirst());
System.out.println(staff.removeFirst());
System.out.println(staff.removeFirst());
```

Exercise R20.2. Explain what the following code prints. Draw pictures of the linked list after each step. Just draw the forward links, as in Figure 1.

```
LinkedList<String> staff = new LinkedList<String>();
staff.addFirst("Harry");
staff.addFirst("Dick");
staff.addFirst("Tom");
System.out.println(staff.removeLast());
System.out.println(staff.removeFirst());
System.out.println(staff.removeLast());
```

Exercise R20.3. Explain what the following code prints. Draw pictures of the linked list after each step. Just draw the forward links, as in Figure 1.

```
LinkedList<String> staff = new LinkedList<String>();
staff.addFirst("Harry");
staff.addLast("Dick");
staff.addFirst("Tom");
System.out.println(staff.removeLast());
System.out.println(staff.removeFirst());
System.out.println(staff.removeLast());
```

Exercise R20.4. Explain what the following code prints. Draw pictures of the linked list and the iterator position after each step.

```
LinkedList<String> staff = new LinkedList<String>();
ListIterator<String> iterator = staff.listIterator();
iterator.add("Tom");
iterator.add("Dick");
iterator.add("Harry");
iterator = staff.listIterator();
if (iterator.next().equals("Tom"))
    iterator.remove();
while (iterator.hasNext())
    System.out.println(iterator.next());
```

Exercise R20.5. Explain what the following code prints. Draw pictures of the linked list and the iterator position after each step.

```
LinkedList<String> staff = new LinkedList<String>();
ListIterator<String> iterator = staff.listIterator();
iterator.add("Tom");
iterator.add("Dick");
iterator.add("Harry");
iterator = staff.listIterator();
iterator.next();
iterator.next();
iterator.add("Romeo");
iterator.next();
iterator.add("Juliet");
iterator = staff.listIterator();
iterator.next();
iterator.remove();
while (iterator.hasNext())
    System.out.println(iterator.next());
```

Exercise R20.6. The linked list class in the Java library supports operations addLast and removeLast. To carry out these operations efficiently, the LinkedList class has an added reference last to the last node in the linked list. Draw a "before/after" diagram of the changes of the links in a linked list under the addLast and removeLast methods.

Exercise R20.7. The linked list class in the Java library supports bidirectional iterators. To go backward efficiently, each Node has an added reference, previous, to the predecessor node in the linked list. Draw a "before/after" diagram of the changes of the links in a linked list under the addFirst and removeFirst methods that shows how the previous links need to be updated.

Exercise R20.8. What advantages do lists have over arrays? What disadvantages do they have?

Exercise R20.9. Suppose you needed to organize a collection of telephone numbers for a company division. There are currently about 6,000 employees, and you know that the phone switch can handle at most 10,000 phone numbers. You expect several hundred lookups against the collection every day. Would you use an array or a list to store the information?

Exercise R20.10. Suppose you needed to keep a collection of appointments. Would you use a list or an array of Appointment objects?

Exercise R20.11. Suppose you write a program that models a card deck. Cards are taken from the top of the deck and given out to players. As cards are returned to the deck, they are placed on the bottom of the deck. Would you store the cards in a stack or a queue?

Exercise R20.12. Suppose the strings "A" . . . "Z" are pushed onto a stack. Then they are popped off the stack and pushed onto a second stack. Finally, they are all popped off the second stack and printed. In which order are the strings printed?

PROGRAMMING EXERCISES

Exercise P20.1. Using only the public interface of the linked list class, write a method

```
public static void downsize(LinkedList<String> staff)
```

that removes every other employee from a linked list.

Exercise P20.2. Using only the public interface of the linked list class, write a method

```
public static void reverse(LinkedList<String> staff)
```

that reverses the entries in a linked list.

Exercise P20.3. Add a method reverse to our implementation of the LinkedList class that reverses the links in a list. Implement this method by directly rerouting the links, not by using an iterator.

Exercise P20.4. Write a method draw to display a linked list graphically. Draw each element of the list as a box, and indicate the links with arrows.

Exercise P20.5. Add a method size to our implementation of the LinkedList class that computes the number of elements in the list, by following links and counting the elements until the end of the list is reached.

Exercise P20.6. Add a currentSize field to our implementation of the LinkedList class. Modify the add and remove methods of both the linked list and the list iterator to update the currentSize field so that it always contains the correct size. Change the size method of the preceding exercise so that it simply returns the value of this instance variable.

Exercise P20.7. The linked list class of the standard library has addLast and remove-Last methods that allow efficient insertion and removal at the end of the list. Implement these methods for the LinkedList class in Section 20.2. Add an instance field to the linked list class that points to the last node in the list.

Exercise P20.8. Repeat Exercise P20.7, but use a different implementation strategy. Remove the reference to the first node in the LinkedList class, and make the next reference of the last node point to the first node, so that all nodes form a cycle. Such an implementation is called a *circular linked list*.

Exercise P20.9. Reimplement the LinkedList class of Section 20.2 so that the Node and ListIterator classes are not inner classes.

Exercise P20.10. Add a previous field to the Node class in Section 20.2, and supply previous and hasPrevious methods in the iterator.

Exercise P20.11. The standard Java library implements a Stack class, but in this exercise you are asked to provide your own implementation. Do not implement type parameters. Use an Object[] array to hold the stack elements. When the array fills up, allocate a larger array and copy the values to the larger array.

Exercise P20.12. Implement a Stack class by using a linked list to store the elements. Do not implement type parameters.

Exercise P20.13. Implement a queue as a *circular array* as follows: Use two index variables head and tail that contain the index of the next element to be removed and the next element to be added. After an element is removed or added, the index is incremented (see Figure 14).

After a while, the tail element will reach the top of the array. Then it "wraps around" and starts again at 0—see Figure 15. For that reason, the array is called "circular".

```
public class CircularArrayQueue
{
   public CircularArrayQueue(int capacity) { . . . }
   public void add(Object x) { . . . }
   public Object remove() { . . . }
   public int size() { . . . }
   private int head;
   private int tail;
   private int theSize;
   private Object[] elements;
}
```

This implementation supplies a *bounded* queue—it can eventually fill up. See the next exercise on how to remove that limitation.

Exercise P20.14. The queue in Exercise P20.13 can fill up if more elements are added than the array can hold. Improve the implementation as follows. When the array fills up, allocate a larger array, copy the values to the larger array, and assign it to the elements instance variable. *Hint:* You can't just copy the elements into the same position of the new array. Move the head element to position 0 instead.

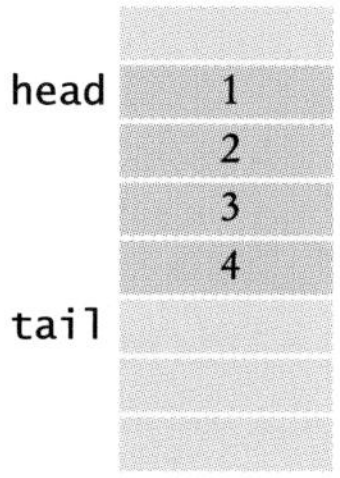

Figure 14
Adding and Removing
Queue Elements

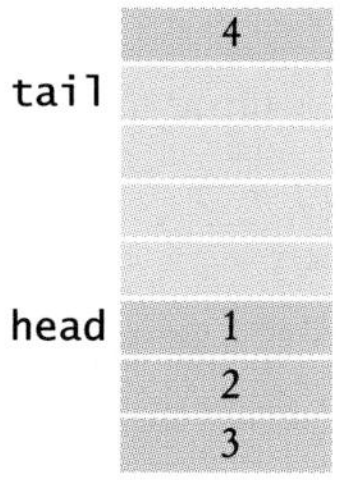

Figure 15
A Queue That Wraps Around
the End of the Array

Exercise P20.15. Modify the insertion sort algorithm of Advanced Topic 19.1 to sort a linked list.

Exercise P20.16. Modify the Invoice class of Chapter 17 so that it implements the Iterable<LineItem> interface. Then demonstrate how an Invoice object can be used in a "for each" loop.

PROGRAMMING PROJECTS

Project 20.1. Implement a class Polynomial that describes a polynomial such as

$$p(x) = 5x^{10} + 9x^7 - x - 10$$

Store a polynomial as a linked list of terms. A term contains the coefficient and the power of x. For example, you would store $p(x)$ as

$$(5, 10), (9, 7), (-1, 1), (-10, 0)$$

Supply methods to add, multiply, and print polynomials, and to compute the derivative of a polynomial.

Project 20.2. Make the list implementation of this chapter as powerful as the implementation of the Java library. (Do not implement type parameters, though.)

- Provide bidirectional iteration.
- Make Node a static inner class.
- Implement the standard List and ListIterator interfaces and provide the missing methods. (*Tip:* You may find it easier to extend AbstractList instead of implementing all List methods from scratch.)

Project 20.3. Implement the following algorithm for the evaluation of arithmetic expressions.

Each operator has a *precedence*. The + and - operators have the lowest precedence, * and / have a higher (and equal) precedence, and ∧ (which denotes "raising to a power" in this exercise) has the highest. For example,

3 * 4 ∧ 2 + 5

should mean the same as

(3 * (4 ∧ 2)) + 5

with a value of 53.

In your algorithm, use two stacks. One stack holds numbers, the other holds operators. When you encounter a number, push it on the number stack. When you encounter an operator, push it on the operator stack if it has higher precedence than the operator on the top of the stack. Otherwise, pop an operator off the operator stack, pop two numbers off the number stack, and push the result of the computation on the number stack. Repeat until the top of the operator stack has lower precedence. At the end of the expression, clear the stack in the same way. For example, here is how the expression 3 * 4 ∧ 2 + 5 is evaluated:

		Expression: 3 * 4 ∧ 2 + 5		
❶	Remaining expression:	* 4 ∧ 2 + 5	Number stack 3	Operator stack
❷	Remaining expression:	4 ∧ 2 + 5	Number stack 3	Operator stack *
❸	Remaining expression:	∧ 2 + 5	Number stack 4 3	Operator stack *
❹	Remaining expression:	2 + 5	Number stack 4 3	Operator stack ∧ *
❺	Remaining expression:	+ 5	Number stack 2 4 3	Operator stack ∧ *
❻	Remaining expression:	+ 5	Number stack 16 3	Operator stack *
❼	Remaining expression:	5	Number stack 48	Operator stack +
❽	Remaining expression:		Number stack 5 48	Operator stack +
❾	Remaining expression:		Number stack 53	Operator stack

You should enhance this algorithm to deal with parentheses. Also, make sure that subtractions and divisions are carried out in the correct order. For example, 12 - 5 - 3 should yield 4.

ANSWERS TO SELF-CHECK QUESTIONS

1. Yes, for two reasons. You need to store the node references, and each node is a separate object. (There is a fixed overhead to store each object in the virtual machine.)

2. An integer index can be used to access any array location.

3. When the list is empty, first is null. A new Node is allocated. It's data field is set to the newly inserted object. It's next field is set to null because first is null. The first field is set to the new node. The result is a linked list of length 1.

4. It points to the element to the left. You can see that by tracing out the first call to next. It leaves position to point to the first node.

5. If position is null, we must be at the head of the list, and inserting an element requires updating the first reference. If we are in the middle of the list, the first reference should not be changed.

6. You can focus on the essential characteristics of the data type without being distracted by implementation details.

7. The abstract view would be like Figure 9, but with arrows in both directions. The concrete view would be like Figure 8, but with references to the previous node added to each node.

8. To locate the midde element takes $n / 2$ steps. To locate the middle of the sub-interval to the left or right takes another $n / 4$ steps. The next lookup takes $n / 8$ steps. Thus, we expect almost n steps to locate an element. At this point, you are better off just making a linear search that, on average, takes $n / 2$ steps.

9.

10. Stacks use a "last in, first out" discipline. If you are the first one to submit a print job and lots of people add print jobs before the printer has a chance to deal with your job, they get their printouts first, and you have to wait until all other jobs are completed.

Chapter **21**

Advanced Data Structures

CHAPTER GOALS

- To learn about the set and map data types
- To understand the implementation of hash tables
- To be able to program hash functions
- To learn about binary trees
- To be able to use tree sets and tree maps
- To become familiar with the heap data structure
- To learn how to implement the priority queue data type
- To understand how to use heaps for sorting

In this chapter we study data structures that are more complex than arrays or lists. These data structures take control of organizing their elements, rather than keeping them in a fixed position. In return, they can offer better performance for adding, removing, and finding elements.

You will learn about the abstract set and map data types and the implementations that the standard library offers for these abstract types. You will see how two completely different implementations—hash tables and trees—can be used to implement these abstract types efficiently.

CHAPTER CONTENTS

21.1 Sets

In the preceding chapter you encountered two important data structures: arrays and lists. Both have one characteristic in common: These data structures keep the elements in the same order in which you inserted them. However, in many applications, you don't really care about the order of the elements in a collection. For example, a server may keep a collection of objects representing available printers (see Figure 1). The order of the objects doesn't really matter.

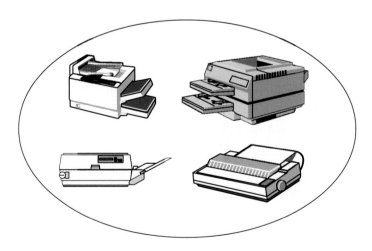

Figure 1   A Set of Printers

A set is an unordered collection of distinct elements. Elements can be added, located, and removed.

In mathematics, such an unordered collection is called a *set*. You have probably learned some set theory in a course in mathematics, and you may know that sets are a fundamental mathematical notion.

But what does that mean for data structures? If the data structure is no longer responsible for remembering the order of element insertion, can it give us better performance for some of its operations? It turns out that it can indeed, as you will see later in this chapter.

Let's list the fundamental operations on a set:

- Adding an element
- Removing an element
- Containment testing (does the set contain a given object?)
- Listing all elements (in arbitrary order)

Sets don't have duplicates. Adding a duplicate of an element that is already present is silently ignored.

In mathematics, a set rejects duplicates. If an object is already in the set, an attempt to add it again is ignored. That's useful in many programming situations as well. For example, if we keep a set of available printers, each printer should occur at most once in the set. Thus, we will interpret the add and remove operations of sets just as we do in mathematics: Adding an element has no effect if the element is already in the set, and attempting to remove an element that isn't in the set is silently ignored.

Of course, we could use a linked list to implement a set. But adding, removing, and containment testing would be relatively slow, because they all have to do a linear search through the list. (Adding requires a search through the list to make sure that we don't add a duplicate.) As you will see later in this chapter, there are data structures that can handle these operations much more quickly.

The HashSet and TreeSet classes both implement the Set interface.

In fact, there are two different data structures for this purpose, called *hash tables* and *trees*. The standard Java library provides set implementations based on both data structures, called HashSet and TreeSet. Both of these data structures implement the Set interface (see Figure 2).

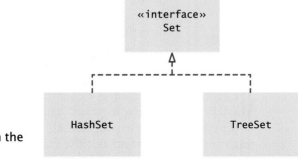

Figure 2
Set Classes and Interfaces in the Standard Library

You will see later in this chapter when it is better to choose a hash set over a tree set. For now, let's look at an example where we choose a hash set. To keep the example simple, we'll store only strings, not `Printer` objects.

```
Set<String> names = new HashSet<String>();
```

Note that we store the reference to the `HashSet<String>` object in a `Set<String>` variable. After you construct the collection object, the implementation no longer matters; only the interface is important.

Adding and removing set elements is straightforward:

```
names.add("Romeo");
names.remove("Juliet");
```

The contains method tests whether an element is contained in the set:

```
if (names.contains("Juliet")) . . .
```

> An iterator visits all elements in a set.

Finally, to list all elements in the set, get an iterator. As with list iterators, you use the next and hasNext methods to step through the set.

```
Iterator<String> iter = names.iterator();
while (iter.hasNext())
{
    String name = iter.next();
    Do something with name
}
```

Or, as with arrays and lists, you can use the "for each" loop instead of explicitly using an iterator:

```
for (String name : names)
{
    Do something with name
}
```

> A set iterator does not visit the elements in the order in which you inserted them. The set implementation rearranges the elements so that it can locate them quickly.

Note that the elements are *not* visited in the order in which you inserted them. Instead, they are visited in the order in which the `HashSet` keeps them for rapid execution of its methods.

There is an important difference between the `Iterator` that you obtain from a set and the `ListIterator` that a list yields. The `ListIterator` has an add method to add an element at the list iterator position. The `Iterator` interface has no such method. It makes no sense to add an element at a particular position in a set, because the set can order the elements any way it likes. Thus, you always add elements directly to a set, never to an iterator of the set.

> You cannot add an element to a set at an iterator position.

However, you can remove a set element at an iterator position, just as you do with list iterators.

Also, the `Iterator` interface has no previous method to go backwards through the elements. Because the elements are not ordered, it is not meaningful to distinguish between "going forward" and "going backward".

The following test program allows you to add and remove set elements. After each command, it prints out the current contents of the set. When you run this program, try adding strings that are already contained in the set and removing strings that aren't present in the set.

File SetTester.java

```java
1   import java.util.HashSet;
2   import java.util.Scanner;
3   import java.util.Set;
4
5   /**
6      This program demonstrates a set of strings. The user
7      can add and remove strings.
8   */
9   public class SetTester
10  {
11     public static void main(String[] args)
12     {
13        Set<String> names = new HashSet<String>();
14        Scanner in = new Scanner(System.in);
15
16        boolean done = false;
17        while (!done)
18        {
19           System.out.print("Add name, Q when done: ");
20           String input = in.next();
21           if (input.equalsIgnoreCase("Q"))
22              done = true;
23           else
24           {
25              names.add(input);
26              print(names);
27           }
28        }
29
30        done = false;
31        while (!done)
32        {
33           System.out.println("Remove name, Q when done");
34           String input = in.next();
35           if (input.equalsIgnoreCase("Q"))
36              done = true;
37           else
38           {
39              names.remove(input);
40              print(names);
41           }
42        }
43     }
44
45     /**
46        Prints the contents of a set of strings.
47        @param s a set of strings
48     */
49     private static void print(Set<String> s)
50     {
51        System.out.print("{ ");
52        for (String element : s)
53        {
```

```
54              System.out.print(element);
55              System.out.print(" ");
56         }
57         System.out.println("}");
58      }
59   }
```

Output

```
Add name, Q when done: Dick
{ Dick }
Add name, Q when done: Tom
{ Tom Dick }
Add name, Q when done: Harry
{ Harry Tom Dick }
Add name, Q when done: Tom
{ Harry Tom Dick }
Add name, Q when done: Q
Remove name, Q when done: Tom
{ Harry Dick }
Remove name, Q when done: Jerry
{ Harry Dick }
Remove name, Q when done: Q
```

SELF CHECK

1. Arrays and lists remember the order in which you added elements; sets do not. Why would you want to use a set instead of an array or list?
2. Why are set iterators different from list iterators?

QUALITY TIP 21.1

Use Interface References to Manipulate Data Structures

It is considered good style to store a reference to a HashSet or TreeSet in a variable of type Set.

```
Set<String> names = new HashSet<String>();
```

This way, you have to change only one line if you decide to use a TreeSet instead.

Also, methods that operate on sets should specify parameters of type Set:

```
public static void print(Set<String> s)
```

Then the method can be used for all set implementations.

In theory, we should make the same recommendation for linked lists, namely to save LinkedList references in variables of type List. However, in the Java library, the List interface is common to both the ArrayList and the LinkedList class. In particular, it has get and set methods for random access, even though these methods are very inefficient for linked lists. You can't write efficient code if you don't know whether random access is efficient or not. This is plainly a serious design error in the standard library, and I cannot recommend using the List interface for that reason. (To see just how embarrassing that error is, have a look at the source code for the binarySearch method of the Collections class. That method takes a List parameter, but binary search makes no sense for a linked list. The code then clumsily tries to discover whether the list is a linked list, and then switches to a linear search!)

The Set interface and the Map interface, which you will see in the next section, are well-designed, and you should use them.

21.2 Maps

A map keeps associations between key and value objects.

A map is a data type that keeps associations between *keys* and *values*. Figure 3 gives a typical example: a map that associates names with colors. This map might describe the favorite colors of various people.

Mathematically speaking, a map is a function from one set, the *key set*, to another set, the *value set*. Every key in the map has a unique value, but a value may be associated with several keys.

The HashMap and TreeMap classes both implement the Map interface.

Just as there are two kinds of set implementations, the Java library has two implementations for maps: HashMap and TreeMap. Both of them implement the Map interface (see Figure 4).

After constructing a HashMap or TreeMap, you should store the reference to the map object in a Map reference:

```
Map<String, Color> favoriteColors = new HashMap<String, Color>();
```

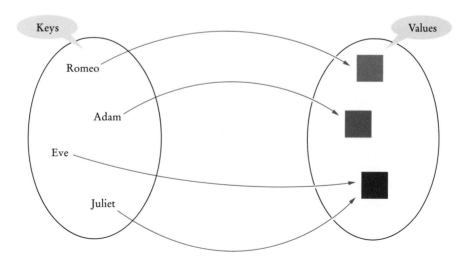

Figure 3 A Map

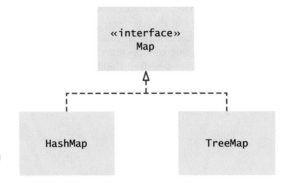

Figure 4
Map Classes and Interfaces in the Standard Library

Use the put method to add an association:

```
favoriteColors.put("Juliet", Color.PINK);
```

You can change the value of an existing association, simply by calling put again:

```
favoriteColors.put("Juliet", Color.RED);
```

The get method returns the value associated with a key.

```
Color julietsFavoriteColor = favoriteColors.get("Juliet");
```

If you ask for a key that isn't associated with any values, then the get method returns null.

To remove a key and its associated value, use the remove method:

```
favoriteColors.remove("Juliet");
```

To find all keys and values in a map, iterate through the key set and find the values that correspond to the keys.

Sometimes you want to enumerate all keys in a map. The keySet method yields the set of keys. You can then ask the key set for an iterator and get all keys. From each key, you can find the associated value with the get method. Thus, the following instructions print all key/value pairs in a map m:

```
Set<String> keySet = m.keySet();
for (String key : keySet)
{
   Color value = m.get(key);
   System.out.println(key + "->" + value);
}
```

The following sample program shows a map in action.

File MapTester.java

```
1   import java.awt.Color;
2   import java.util.HashMap;
3   import java.util.Iterator;
4   import java.util.Map;
5   import java.util.Set;
6
```

```
 7  /**
 8       This program tests a map that maps names to colors.
 9  */
10  public class MapTester
11  {
12     public static void main(String[] args)
13     {
14        Map<String, Color> favoriteColors
15              = new HashMap<String, Color>();
16        favoriteColors.put("Juliet", Color.PINK);
17        favoriteColors.put("Romeo", Color.GREEN);
18        favoriteColors.put("Adam", Color.BLUE);
19        favoriteColors.put("Eve", Color.PINK);
20
21        Set<String> keySet = favoriteColors.keySet();
22        for (String key : keySet)
23        {
24           Color value = favoriteColors.get(key);
25           System.out.println(key + "->" + value);
26        }
27     }
28  }
```

Output

```
Romeo->java.awt.Color[r=0,g=255,b=0]
Eve->java.awt.Color[r=255,g=175,b=175]
Adam->java.awt.Color[r=0,g=0,b=255]
Juliet->java.awt.Color[r=255,g=175,b=175]
```

SELF CHECK

3. What is the difference between a set and a map?

4. Why is the collection of the keys of a map a set?

21.3 Hash Tables

In this section, you will see how the technique of *hashing* can be used to find elements in a data structure quickly, without making a linear search through all elements. Hashing gives rise to the *hash table*, which can be used to implement sets and maps.

A *hash function* is a function that computes an integer value, the *hash code*, from an object, in such a way that different objects are likely to yield different hash codes. The Object class has a hashCode method that other classes need to redefine. The call

> A hash function computes an integer value from an object.

```
int h = x.hashCode();
```

computes the hash code of the object x.

Table 1 Sample Strings and Their Hash Codes

String	Hash Code
"Adam"	2035631
"Eve"	70068
"Harry"	69496448
"Jim"	74478
"Joe"	74656
"Juliet"	−2065036585
"Katherine"	2079199209
"Sue"	83491

> A good hash function minimizes *collisions*— identical hash codes for different objects.

It is possible for two or more distinct objects to have the same hash code; this is called a *collision*. A good hash function minimizes collisions. For example, the String class defines a hash function for strings that does a good job of producing different integer values for different strings. Table 1 shows some examples of strings and their hash codes. You will see in Section 21.4 how these values are obtained.

Section 21.4 explains how you should redefine the hashCode method for other classes.

A hash code is used as an array index into a hash table. In the simplest implementation of a hash table, you could make an array and insert each object at the location of its hash code (see Figure 5).

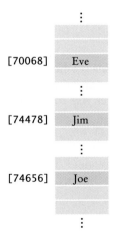

Figure 5
A Simplistic Implementation of a Hash Table

Then it is a very simple matter to find out whether an object is already present in the set or not. Compute its hash code and check whether the array position with that hash code is already occupied. This doesn't require a search through the entire array!

However, there are two problems with this simplistic approach. First, it is not possible to allocate an array that is large enough to hold all possible integer index positions. Therefore, we must pick an array of some reasonable size and then reduce the hash code to fall inside the array:

```
int h = x.hashCode();
if (h < 0) h = -h;
h = h % size;
```

Furthermore, it is possible that two different objects have the same hash code. After reducing the hash code modulo a smaller array size, it becomes even more likely that several objects will collide and need to share a position in the array.

> A hash table can be implemented as an array of *buckets*—sequences of nodes that hold elements with the same hash code.

To store multiple objects in the same array position, use short node sequences for the elements with the same hash code (see Figure 6). These node sequences are called *buckets*.

Now the algorithm for finding an object x in a hash table is quite simple.

1. Compute the hash code and reduce it modulo the table size. This gives an index h into the hash table.

2. Iterate through the elements of the bucket at position h. For each element of the bucket, check whether it is equal to x.

3. If a match is found among the elements of that bucket, then x is in the set. Otherwise, it is not.

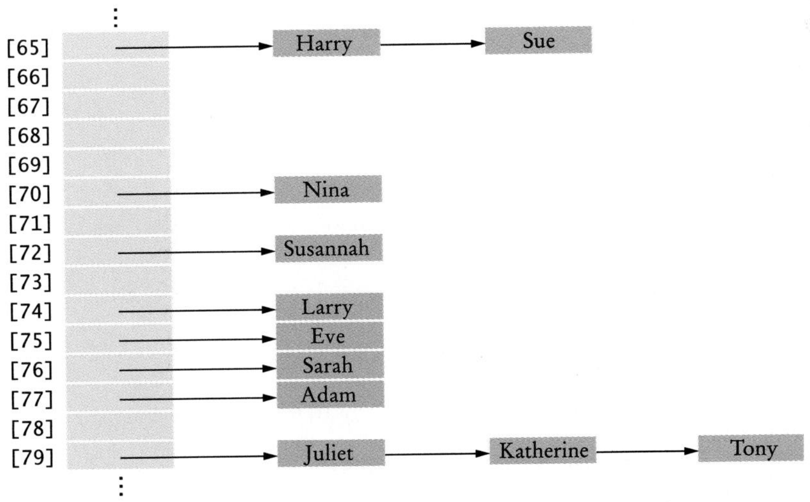

Figure 6 A Hash Table with Buckets to Store Elements with the Same Hash Code

> If there are no or only a few collisions, then adding, locating, and removing hash table elements takes constant or $O(1)$ time.

In the best case, in which there are no collisions, all buckets either are empty or have a single element. Then checking for containment takes constant or $O(1)$ time.

More generally, for this algorithm to be effective, the bucket sizes must be small. If the table length is small, then collisions are unavoidable, and each bucket will get quite full. Then the linear search through a bucket is time-consuming. In the worst case, where all elements end up in the same bucket, a hash table degenerates into a linked list!

> The table size should be a prime number, larger than the expected number of elements.

In order to reduce the chance for collisions, you should make a hash table somewhat larger than the number of elements that you expect to insert. An excess capacity of about 30 percent is typically recommended. According to some researchers, the hash table size should be chosen to be a prime number to minimize the number of collisions.

Adding an element is a simple extension of the algorithm for finding an object. First compute the hash code to locate the bucket in which the element should be inserted. Try finding the object in that bucket. If it is already present, do nothing. Otherwise, insert it.

Removing an element is equally simple. First compute the hash code to locate the bucket in which the element should be inserted. Try finding the object in that bucket. If it is present, remove it. Otherwise, do nothing.

As long as there are few collisions, an element can also be added or removed in constant or $O(1)$ time.

At the end of this section you will find the code for a simple implementation of a hash set. That implementation takes advantage of the `AbstractSet` class, which already implements most of the methods of the `Set` interface.

In this implementation you must specify the size of the hash table. In the standard library, you don't need to supply a table size. If the hash table gets too full, a new table of twice the size is created, and all elements are inserted into the new table.

File HashSet.java

```java
1  import java.util.AbstractSet;
2  import java.util.Iterator;
3  import java.util.NoSuchElementException;
4
5  /**
6     A hash set stores an unordered collection of objects, using
7     a hash table.
8  */
9  public class HashSet extends AbstractSet
10 {
11    /**
12       Constructs a hash table.
13       @param bucketsLength the length of the buckets array
14    */
15    public HashSet(int bucketsLength)
16    {
17       buckets = new Node[bucketsLength];
18       size = 0;
```

```
19      }
20
21      /**
22          Tests for set membership.
23          @param x  an object
24          @return  true if x is an element of this set
25      */
26      public boolean contains(Object x)
27      {
28          int h = x.hashCode();
29          if (h < 0) h = -h;
30          h = h % buckets.length;
31
32          Node current = buckets[h];
33          while (current != null)
34          {
35              if (current.data.equals(x)) return true;
36              current = current.next;
37          }
38          return false;
39      }
40
41      /**
42          Adds an element to this set.
43          @param x  an object
44          @return  true if x is a new object, false if x was
45          already in the set
46      */
47      public boolean add(Object x)
48      {
49          int h = x.hashCode();
50          if (h < 0) h = -h;
51          h = h % buckets.length;
52
53          Node current = buckets[h];
54          while (current != null)
55          {
56              if (current.data.equals(x))
57                  return false; // Already in the set
58              current = current.next;
59          }
60          Node newNode = new Node();
61          newNode.data = x;
62          newNode.next = buckets[h];
63          buckets[h] = newNode;
64          size++;
65          return true;
66      }
67
68      /**
69          Removes an object from this set.
70          @param x  an object
71          @return  true if x was removed from this set, false
72          if x was not an element of this set
73      */
```

```
74    public boolean remove(Object x)
75    {
76       int h = x.hashCode();
77       if (h < 0) h = -h;
78       h = h % buckets.length;
79
80       Node current = buckets[h];
81       Node previous = null;
82       while (current != null)
83       {
84          if (current.data.equals(x))
85          {
86             if (previous == null) buckets[h] = current.next;
87             else previous.next = current.next;
88             size--;
89             return true;
90          }
91          previous = current;
92          current = current.next;
93       }
94       return false;
95    }
96
97    /**
98       Returns an iterator that traverses the elements of this set.
99       @return a hash set iterator
100   */
101   public Iterator iterator()
102   {
103      return new HashSetIterator();
104   }
105
106   /**
107      Gets the number of elements in this set.
108      @return the number of elements
109   */
110   public int size()
111   {
112      return size;
113   }
114
115   private Node[] buckets;
116   private int size;
117
118   private class Node
119   {
120      public Object data;
121      public Node next;
122   }
123
124   private class HashSetIterator implements Iterator
125   {
126      /**
127         Constructs a hash set iterator that points to the
128         first element of the hash set.
```

```
129          */
130          public HashSetIterator()
131          {
132             current = null;
133             bucket = -1;
134             previous = null;
135             previousBucket = -1;
136          }
137
138          public boolean hasNext()
139          {
140             if (current != null && current.next != null)
141                return true;
142             for (int b = bucket + 1; b < buckets.length; b++)
143                if (buckets[b] != null) return true;
144             return false;
145          }
146
147          public Object next()
148          {
149             previous = current;
150             previousBucket = bucket;
151             if (current == null || current.next == null)
152             {
153                // Move to next bucket
154                bucket++;
155
156                while (bucket < buckets.length
157                      && buckets[bucket] == null)
158                   bucket++;
159                if (bucket < buckets.length)
160                   current = buckets[bucket];
161                else
162                   throw new NoSuchElementException();
163             }
164             else // Move to next element in bucket
165                current = current.next;
166             return current.data;
167          }
168
169          public void remove()
170          {
171             if (previous != null && previous.next == current)
172                previous.next = current.next;
173             else if (previousBucket < bucket)
174                buckets[bucket] = current.next;
175             else
176                throw new IllegalStateException();
177             current = previous;
178             bucket = previousBucket;
179          }
180
181       private int bucket;
182       private Node current;
```

```
183         private int previousBucket;
184         private Node previous;
185      }
186  }
```

File SetTester.java

```
1   import java.util.Iterator;
2   import java.util.Set;
3
4   /**
5       This program tests the hash set class.
6   */
7   public class SetTester
8   {
9      public static void main(String[] args)
10     {
11        HashSet names = new HashSet(101); // 101 is a prime
12
13        names.add("Sue");
14        names.add("Harry");
15        names.add("Nina");
16        names.add("Susannah");
17        names.add("Larry");
18        names.add("Eve");
19        names.add("Sarah");
20        names.add("Adam");
21        names.add("Tony");
22        names.add("Katherine");
23        names.add("Juliet");
24        names.add("Romeo");
25        names.remove("Romeo");
26        names.remove("George");
27
28        Iterator iter = names.iterator();
29        while (iter.hasNext())
30           System.out.println(iter.next());
31     }
32  }
```

Output

```
Harry
Sue
Nina
Susannah
Larry
Eve
Sarah
Adam
Juliet
Katherine
Tony
```

5. If a hash function returns 0 for all values, will the HashSet work correctly?
6. What does the hasNext method of the HashSetIterator do when it has reached the end of a bucket?

21.4 Computing Hash Codes

A hash function computes an integer hash code from an object, so that different objects are likely to have different hash codes. Let us first look at how you can compute a hash code from a string. Clearly, you need to combine the character values of the string to yield some integer. You could, for example, add up the character values:

```
int h = 0;
for (int i = 0; i < s.length(); i++)
    h = h + s.charAt(i);
```

However, that would not be a good idea. It doesn't scramble the character values enough. Strings that are permutations of another (such as "eat" and "tea") all have the same hash code.

Here is the method the standard library uses to compute the hash code for a string.

```
final int HASH_MULTIPLIER = 31;
int h = 0;
for (int i = 0; i < s.length(); i++)
    h = HASH_MULTIPLIER * h + s.charAt(i);
```

For example, the hash code of "eat" is

```
31 * (31 * 'e' + 'a') + 't' = 100184
```

The hash code of "tea" is quite different, namely

```
31 * (31 * 't' + 'e') + 'a' = 114704
```

(Use the Unicode table from Appendix B to look up the character values: 'a' is 97, 'e' is 101, and 't' is 116.)

Define hashCode methods for your own classes by combining the hash codes for the instance variables.

For your own classes, you should make up a hash code that combines the hash codes of the instance fields in a similar way. For example, let us define a hashCode method for the Coin class. There are two instance fields: the coin name and the coin value. First, compute their hash code. You know how to compute the hash code of a string. To compute the hash code of a floating-point number, first wrap the floating-point number into a Double object, and then compute its hash code.

```
class Coin
{
    public int hashCode()
    {
        int h1 = name.hashCode();
        int h2 = new Double(value).hashCode();
        . . .
```

```
        }
    }
```

Then combine the two hash codes.

```
final int HASH_MULTIPLIER = 29;
int h = HASH_MULTIPLIER * h1 + h2;
return h;
```

Use a prime number as the hash multiplier—it scrambles the values better.

If you have more than two instance fields, then combine their hash codes as follows:

```
int h = HASH_MULTIPLIER * h1 + h2;
h = HASH_MULTIPLIER * h + h3;
h = HASH_MULTIPLIER * h + h4;
. . .
return h;
```

If one of the instance fields is an integer, just use the field value as its hash code.

> Your hashCode method must be compatible with the equals method.

When you add objects of your class into a hash table, you need to double-check that the hashCode method is *compatible* with the equals method of your class. Two objects that are equal must yield the same hash code:

- If x.equals(y), then x.hashCode() == y.hashCode()

After all, if x and y are equal to each other, then you don't want to insert both of them into a set—sets don't store duplicates. But if their hash codes are different, x and y may end up in different buckets, and the add method would never notice that they are actually duplicates.

Of course, the converse of the compatibility condition is generally not true. It is possible for two objects to have the same hash code without being equal.

For the Coin class, the compatibility condition holds. We define two coins to be equal to each other if their names and values are equal. In that case, their hash codes will also be equal, because the hash code is computed from the hash codes of the name and value fields.

You get into trouble if your class defines an equals method but not a hashCode method. Suppose we forget to define a hashCode method for the Coin class. Then it inherits the hash code method from the Object superclass. That method computes a hash code from the *memory location* of the object. The effect is that any two objects are very likely to have a different hash code.

```
Coin coin1 = new Coin(0.25, "quarter");
Coin coin2 = new Coin(0.25, "quarter");
```

Now coin1.hashCode() is derived from the memory location of coin1, and coin2.hashCode() is derived from the memory location of coin2. Even though coin1.equals(coin2) is true, their hash codes differ.

However, if you define *neither* equals *nor* hashCode, then there is no problem. The equals method of the Object class considers two objects equal only if their memory location is the same. That is, the Object class has compatible equals and hashCode methods. Of course, then the notion of equality is very restricted: Only identical objects are considered equal. That is not necessarily a bad notion of equality: If you want to collect a set of coins in a purse, you may not want to lump coins of equal value together.

Whenever you use a hash set, you need to make sure that an appropriate hash function exists for the type of the objects that you add to the set. Check the equals method of your class. It tells you when two objects are considered equal. There are two possibilities. Either equals has been defined or it has not been defined. If equals has not been defined, only identical objects are considered equal. In that case, don't define hashCode either. However, if the equals method has been defined, look at its implementation. Typically, two objects are considered equal if some or all of the instance fields are equal. Sometimes, not all instance fields are used in the comparison. Two Student objects may be considered equal if their studentID fields are equal. Define the hashCode method to combine the hash codes of the fields that are compared in the equals method.

> In a hash map, only the keys are hashed.

When you use a HashMap, only the keys are hashed. They need compatible hashCode and equals methods. The values are never hashed or compared. The reason is simple—the map only needs to find, add, and remove keys quickly.

What can you do if the objects of your class have equals and hashCode methods defined that don't work for your situation, or if you don't want to define an appropriate hashCode method? Maybe you can use a TreeSet or TreeMap instead. Trees are the subject of the next section.

File Coin.java

```
1   /**
2      A coin with a monetary value.
3   */
4   public class Coin
5   {
6      /**
7         Constructs a coin.
8         @param aValue the monetary value of the coin
9         @param aName the name of the coin
10     */
11     public Coin(double aValue, String aName)
12     {
13        value = aValue;
14        name = aName;
15     }
16
17     /**
18        Gets the coin value.
19        @return the value
20     */
21     public double getValue()
22     {
23        return value;
24     }
25
```

```
26      /**
27          Gets the coin name.
28          @return the name
29      */
30      public String getName()
31      {
32          return name;
33      }
34
35      public boolean equals(Object otherObject)
36      {
37          if (otherObject == null) return false;
38          if (getClass() != otherObject.getClass()) return false;
39          Coin other = (Coin) otherObject;
40          return value == other.value && name.equals(other.name);
41      }
42
43      public int hashCode()
44      {
45          int h1 = name.hashCode();
46          int h2 = new Double(value).hashCode();
47          final int HASH_MULTIPLIER = 29;
48          int h = HASH_MULTIPLIER * h1 + h2;
49          return h;
50      }
51
52      public String toString()
53      {
54          return "Coin[value=" + value + ",name=" + name + "]";
55      }
56
57      private double value;
58      private String name;
59  }
```

File HashCodeTester.java

```
1   import java.util.HashSet;
2   import java.util.Set;
3
4   /**
5       A program to test hash codes of coins.
6   */
7   public class HashCodeTester
8   {
9       public static void main(String[] args)
10      {
11          Coin coin1 = new Coin(0.25, "quarter");
12          Coin coin2 = new Coin(0.25, "quarter");
13          Coin coin3 = new Coin(0.05, "nickel");
14
15          System.out.println("hash code of coin1="
16                  + coin1.hashCode());
```

```
17          System.out.println("hash code of coin2="
18                + coin2.hashCode());
19          System.out.println("hash code of coin3="
20                + coin3.hashCode());
21
22          Set<Coin> coins = new HashSet<Coin>();
23          coins.add(coin1);
24          coins.add(coin2);
25          coins.add(coin3);
26
27          for (Coin c : coins)
28                System.out.println(c);
29       }
30 }
```

Output

```
hash code of coin1=-1513525892
hash code of coin2=-1513525892
hash code of coin3=-1768365211
Coin[value=0.25,name=quarter]
Coin[value=0.05,name=nickel]
```

SELF CHECK

7. What is the hash code of the string "to"?
8. What is the hash code of new Integer(13)?

COMMON ERROR 21.1

Forgetting to Define hashCode

When putting elements into a hash table, make sure that the hashCode method is defined. (The only exception is that you don't need to define hashCode if equals isn't defined. In that case, distinct objects of your class are considered different, even if they have matching contents.)

If you forget to implement the hashCode method, then you inherit the hashCode method of the Object class. That method computes a hash code of the memory location of the object. For example, suppose that you do *not* define the hashCode method of the Coin class. Then the following code is likely to fail:

```
Set<Coin> coins = new HashSet<Coin>();
coins.add(new Coin(0.25, "quarter"));
// The following comparison will probably fail if hashCode not defined
if (coins.contains(new Coin(0.25, "quarter"))
   System.out.println("The set contains a quarter.");
```

The two Coin objects are constructed at different memory locations, so the hashCode method of the Object class will probably compute different hash codes for them. (As always with hash codes, there is a small chance that the hash codes happen to collide.) Then the contains method will inspect the wrong bucket and never find the matching coin.

The remedy is to define a hashCode method in the Coin class.

21.5 Binary Search Trees

A set implementation is allowed to rearrange its elements in any way it chooses so that it can find elements quickly. Suppose a set implementation *sorts* its entries. Then it can use *binary search* to locate elements quickly. Binary search takes $O(\log(n))$ steps, where n is the size of the set. For example, binary search in an array of 1,000 elements is able to locate an element in about 10 steps by cutting the size of the search interval in half in each step.

There is just one wrinkle with this idea. We can't use an array to store the elements of a set, because insertion and removal in an array is slow; an $O(n)$ operation.

In this section we will introduce the simplest of many *treelike* data structures that computer scientists have invented to overcome that problem. Binary search trees allow fast insertion and removal of elements, and they are specially designed for fast searching.

> A binary tree consists of nodes, each of which has at most two child nodes.

A linked list is a one-dimensional data structure. Every node has a reference to the next node. You can imagine that all nodes are arranged in line. In contrast, a *binary tree* is made of nodes with *two* references, called the *left* and *right children*. You should visualize it as a tree, except that it is traditional to draw the tree upside down, like a family tree or hierarchy chart (see Figure 7). In a binary tree, every node has at most two children; hence the name *binary*.

Finally, a *binary search tree* is carefully constructed to have the following important property:

> All nodes in a binary search tree fulfill the property that the descendants to the left have smaller data values than the node data value, and the descendants to the right have larger data values.

- The data values of *all* descendants to the left of *any* node are less than the data value stored in that node, and *all* descendants to the right have greater data values.

The tree in Figure 7 has this property. To verify the binary search property, you must check each node. Consider the node "Juliet". All descendants to the left have data before "Juliet". All descendants on the right have data after "Juliet". Move on to "Eve". There is a single descendant to the left, with data "Adam" before "Eve", and a single descendant to the right, with data "Harry" after "Eve". Check the remaining nodes in the same way.

Figure 8 shows a binary tree that is not a binary search tree. Look carefully—the root node passes the test, but its two children do not.

Let us implement these tree classes. Just as you needed classes for lists and their nodes, you need one class for the tree, containing a reference to the *root node,* and a separate class for the nodes. Each node contains two references (to the left and right child nodes) and a data field. At the fringes of the tree, one or two of the child references are null. The data field has type Comparable, not Object, because you must be able to compare the values in a binary search tree in order to place them into the correct position.

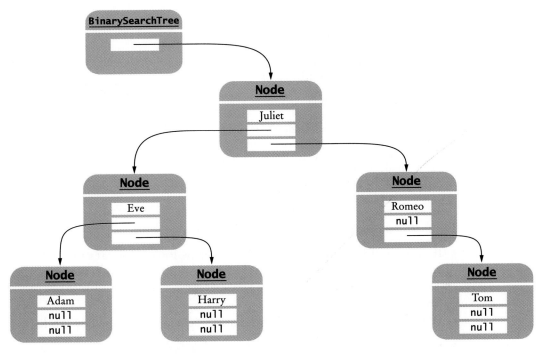

Figure 7 A Binary Search Tree

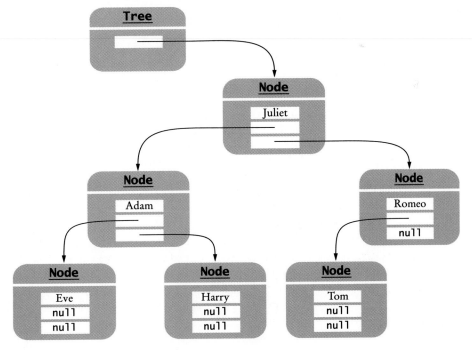

Figure 8 A Binary Tree That Is Not a Binary Search Tree

```
public class BinarySearchTree
{
   public BinarySearchTree() { . . . }
   public void add(Comparable obj) { . . . }
   . . .
   private Node root;

   private class Node
   {
      public void addNode(Node newNode) { . . . }
      . . .
      public Comparable data;
      public Node left;
      public Node right;
   }
}
```

To insert data into the tree, use the following algorithm:

- If you encounter a non-null node reference, look at its data value. If the data value of that node is larger than the one you want to insert, continue the process with the left child. If the existing data value is smaller, continue the process with the right child.

- If you encounter a null node reference, replace it with the new node.

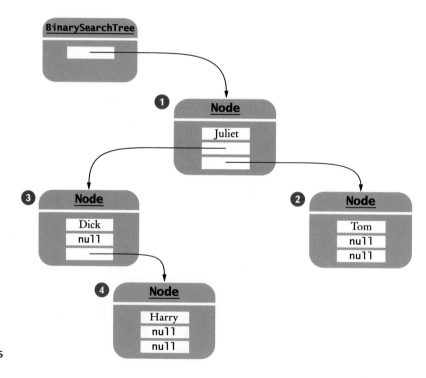

Figure 9
Binary Search Tree
After Four Insertions

For example, consider the tree in Figure 9. It is the result of the following statements:

```
BinarySearchTree tree = new BinarySearchTree();
tree.add("Juliet"); ❶
tree.add("Tom");        ❷
tree.add("Dick");   ❸
tree.add("Harry");      ❹
```

We want to insert a new element Romeo into it.

```
tree.add("Romeo");  ❺
```

Start with the root, Juliet. Romeo comes after Juliet, so you move to the right subtree. You encounter the node Tom. Romeo comes before Tom, so you move to the left subtree. But there is no left subtree. Hence, you insert a new Romeo node as the left child of Tom (see Figure 10).

You should convince yourself that the resulting tree is still a binary search tree. When Romeo is inserted, it must end up as a right descendant of Juliet—that is what the binary search tree condition means for the root node Juliet. The root node doesn't care where in the right subtree the new node ends up. Moving along to Tom, the right child of Juliet, all it cares about is that the new node Romeo ends up somewhere on its left. There is nothing to its left, so Romeo becomes the new left child, and the resulting tree is again a binary search tree.

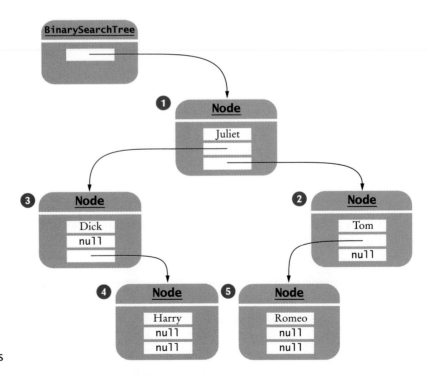

Figure 10
Binary Search Tree
After Five Insertions

Here is the code for the add method of the BinarySearchTree class:

```
public class BinarySearchTree
{
   . . .
   public void add(Comparable obj)
   {
      Node newNode = new Node();
      newNode.data = obj;
      newNode.left = null;
      newNode.right = null;
      if (root == null) root = newNode;
      else root.addNode(newNode);
   }
   . . .
}
```

If the tree is empty, simply set its root to the new node. Otherwise, you know that the new node must be inserted somewhere within the nodes, and you can ask the root node to perform the insertion. That node object calls the addNode method of the Node class, which checks whether the new object is less than the object stored in the node. If so, the element is inserted in the left subtree; if not, it is inserted in the right subtree:

```
   private class Node
   {
      . . .
      public void addNode(Node newNode)
      {
         int comp = newNode.data.compareTo(data);
         if (comp < 0)
         {
            if (left == null) left = newNode;
            else left.addNode(newNode);
         }
         else if (comp > 0)
         {
            if (right == null) right = newNode;
            else right.addNode(newNode);
         }
      }
      . . .
   }
```

Let us trace the calls to addNode when inserting Romeo into the tree in Figure 9. The first call to addNode is

```
root.addNode(newNode)
```

Because root points to Juliet, you compare Juliet with Romeo and find that you must call

```
root.right.addNode(newNode)
```

The node root.right is Tom. Compare the data values again (Tom vs. Romeo) and find that you must now move to the left. Since root.right.left is null, set root.right.left to newNode, and the insertion is complete (see Figure 10).

Unlike a linked list or an array, and like a hash table, a binary tree has no *insert positions.* You cannot select the position where you would like to insert an element into a binary search tree. The data structure is *self-organizing;* that is, each element finds its own place.

We will now discuss the removal algorithm. Our task is to remove a node from the tree. Of course, we must first *find* the node to be removed. That is a simple matter, due to the characteristic property of a binary search tree. Compare the data value to be removed with the data value that is stored in the root node. If it is smaller, keep looking in the left subtree. Otherwise, keep looking in the right subtree.

Let us now assume that we have located the node that needs to be removed. First, let us consider an easy case, when that node has only one child (see Figure 11).

To remove the node, simply modify the parent link that points to the node so that it points to the child instead.

If the node to be removed has no children at all, then the parent link is simply set to null.

The case in which the node to be removed has two children is more challenging. Rather than removing the node, it is easier to replace its data value with the next larger value in the tree. That replacement preserves the binary search tree property. (Alternatively, you could use the largest element of the left subtree—see Exercise P21.16).

To locate the next larger value, go to the right subtree and find its smallest data value. Keep following the left child links. Once you reach a node that has no left child, you have found the node containing the smallest data value of the subtree. Now remove that node—it is easily removed because it has at most one child to the right. Then store its data value in the original node that was slated for removal. Figure 12 shows the details. You will find the complete code at the end of this section.

> When removing a node with only one child from a binary search tree, the child replaces the node to be removed.

> When removing a node with two children from a binary search tree, replace it with the smallest node of the right subtree.

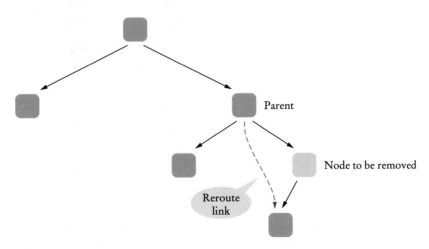

Figure 11   Removing a Node with One Child

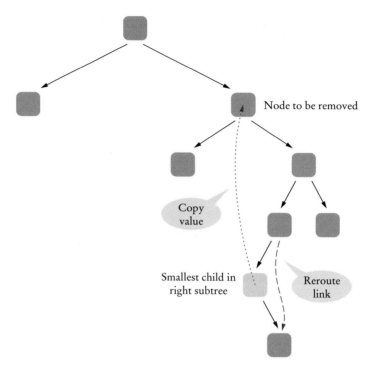

Figure 12 Removing a Node with Two Children

At the end of this section, you will find the source code for the BinarySearchTree class. It contains the add and remove methods that we just described, as well as a find method that tests whether a value is present in a binary search tree, and a print method that we will analyze in the following section.

> If a binary search tree is balanced, then adding an element takes $O(\log(n))$ time.

Now that you have seen the implementation of this complex data structure, you may well wonder whether it is any good. Like nodes in a list, nodes are allocated one at a time. No existing elements need to be moved when a new element is inserted in the tree; that is an advantage. How fast insertion is, however, depends on the shape of the tree. If the tree is *balanced*—that is, if each node has approximately as many descendants on the left as on the right—then insertion is very fast, because about half of the nodes are eliminated in each step. On the other hand, if the tree happens to be *unbalanced,* then insertion can be slow—perhaps as slow as insertion into a linked list. (See Figure 13.)

If new elements are fairly random, the resulting tree is likely to be well balanced. However, if the incoming elements happen to be in sorted order already, then the resulting tree is completely unbalanced. Each new element is inserted at the end, and the entire tree must be traversed every time to find that end!

Binary search trees work well for random data, but if you suspect that the data in your application might be sorted or have long runs of sorted data, you should not use a binary search tree. There are more sophisticated tree structures whose methods

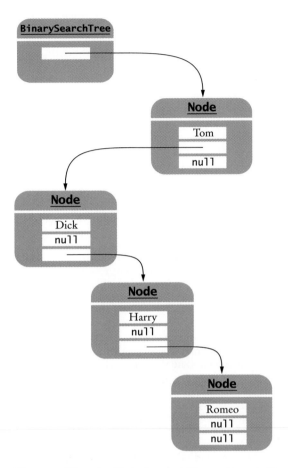

Figure 13   An Unbalanced Binary Search Tree

keep trees balanced at all times. In these tree structures, one can guarantee that finding, adding, and removing elements takes $O(\log(n))$ time. To learn more about those advanced data structures, you may want to enroll in a course about data structures.

The standard Java library uses *red-black trees*, a special form of balanced binary trees, to implement sets and maps. You will see in Section 21.7 what you need to do to use the TreeSet and TreeMap classes. For information on how to implement a red-black tree yourself, see [1].

File BinarySearchTree.java

```
1   /**
2       This class implements a binary search tree whose
3       nodes hold objects that implement the Comparable
4       interface.
5   */
6   public class BinarySearchTree
7   {
```

```java
8      /**
9         Constructs an empty tree.
10     */
11     public BinarySearchTree()
12     {
13        root = null;
14     }
15
16     /**
17        Inserts a new node into the tree.
18        @param obj the object to insert
19     */
20     public void add(Comparable obj)
21     {
22        Node newNode = new Node();
23        newNode.data = obj;
24        newNode.left = null;
25        newNode.right = null;
26        if (root == null) root = newNode;
27        else root.addNode(newNode);
28     }
29
30     /**
31        Tries to find an object in the tree.
32        @param obj the object to find
33        @return true if the object is contained in the tree
34     */
35     public boolean find(Comparable obj)
36     {
37        Node current = root;
38        while (current != null)
39        {
40           int d = current.data.compareTo(obj);
41           if (d == 0) return true;
42           else if (d > 0) current = current.left;
43           else current = current.right;
44        }
45        return false;
46     }
47
48     /**
49        Tries to remove an object from the tree. Does nothing
50        if the object is not contained in the tree.
51        @param obj the object to remove
52     */
53     public void remove(Comparable obj)
54     {
55        // Find node to be removed
56
57        Node toBeRemoved = root;
58        Node parent = null;
59        boolean found = false;
```

```
60          while (!found && toBeRemoved != null)
61          {
62             int d = toBeRemoved.data.compareTo(obj);
63             if (d == 0) found = true;
64             else
65             {
66                parent = toBeRemoved;
67                if (d > 0) toBeRemoved = toBeRemoved.left;
68                else toBeRemoved = toBeRemoved.right;
69             }
70          }
71
72          if (!found) return;
73
74          // toBeRemoved contains obj
75
76          // If one of the children is empty, use the other
77
78          if (toBeRemoved.left == null || toBeRemoved.right == null)
79          {
80             Node newChild;
81             if (toBeRemoved.left == null)
82                newChild = toBeRemoved.right;
83             else
84                newChild = toBeRemoved.left;
85
86             if (parent == null) // Found in root
87                root = newChild;
88             else if (parent.left == toBeRemoved)
89                parent.left = newChild;
90             else
91                parent.right = newChild;
92             return;
93          }
94
95          // Neither subtree is empty
96
97          // Find smallest element of the right subtree
98
99          Node smallestParent = toBeRemoved;
100         Node smallest = toBeRemoved.right;
101         while (smallest.left != null)
102         {
103            smallestParent = smallest;
104            smallest = smallest.left;
105         }
106
107         // smallest contains smallest child in right subtree
108
109         // Move contents, unlink child
110
111         toBeRemoved.data = smallest.data;
112         smallestParent.left = smallest.right;
113      }
```

```
114
115        /**
116            Prints the contents of the tree in sorted order.
117        */
118        public void print()
119        {
120            if (root != null)
121                root.printNodes();
122        }
123
124        private Node root;
125
126        /**
127            A node of a tree stores a data item and references
128            to the child nodes to the left and to the right.
129        */
130        private class Node
131        {
132            /**
133                Inserts a new node as a descendant of this node.
134                @param newNode  the node to insert
135            */
136            public void addNode(Node newNode)
137            {
138                int comp = newNode.data.compareTo(data);
139                if (comp < 0)
140                {
141                    if (left == null) left = newNode;
142                    else left.addNode(newNode);
143                }
144                if (comp > 0)
145                {
146                    if (right == null) right = newNode;
147                    else right.addNode(newNode);
148                }
149            }
150
151            /**
152                Prints this node and all of its descendants
153                in sorted order.
154            */
155            public void printNodes()
156            {
157                if (left != null)
158                    left.printNodes();
159                System.out.println(data);
160                if (right != null)
161                    right.printNodes();
162            }
163
164            public Comparable data;
165            public Node left;
166            public Node right;
167        }
168    }
```

9. What is the difference between a tree, a binary tree, and a balanced binary tree?
10. Give an example of a string that, when inserted into the tree of Figure 10, becomes a right child of Romeo.

21.6 Tree Traversal

Now that the data are inserted in the tree, what can you do with them? It turns out to be surprisingly simple to print all elements in sorted order. You *know* that all data in the left subtree of any node must come before the node and before all data in the right subtree. That is, the following algorithm will print the elements in sorted order:

1. Print the left subtree.
2. Print the data.
3. Print the right subtree.

Let's try this out with the tree in Figure 10. The algorithm tells us to

1. Print the left subtree of Juliet; that is, Dick and descendants.
2. Print Juliet.
3. Print the right subtree of Juliet; that is, Tom and descendants.

How do you print the subtree starting at Dick?

1. Print the left subtree of Dick. There is nothing to print.
2. Print Dick.
3. Print the right subtree of Dick, that is, Harry.

That is, the left subtree of Juliet is printed as

```
Dick
Harry
```

The right subtree of Juliet is the subtree starting at Tom. How is it printed? Again, using the same algorithm:

1. Print the left subtree of Tom, that is, Romeo.
2. Print Tom.
3. Print the right subtree of Tom. There is nothing to print.

Thus, the right subtree of Juliet is printed as

```
Romeo
Tom
```

Now put it all together: the left subtree, `Juliet`, and the right subtree:

```
Dick
Harry
Juliet
Romeo
Tom
```

The tree is printed in sorted order.

Let us implement the `print` method. You need a worker method `printNodes` of the `Node` class:

```java
private class Node
{
   . . .
   public void printNodes()
   {
      if (left != null)
         left.printNodes();
      System.out.println(data);

      if (right != null)
         right.printNodes();
   }
   . . .
}
```

To print the entire tree, start this recursive printing process at the root, with the following method of the `BinarySearchTree` class.

```java
public class BinarySearchTree
{
   . . .
   public void print()
   {
      if (root != null)
         root.printNodes();
   }
   . . .
}
```

> Tree traversal schemes include preorder traversal, inorder traversal, and postorder traversal.

This visitation scheme is called *inorder traversal*. There are two other traversal schemes, called *preorder traversal* and *postorder traversal*.

In preorder traversal,

- Visit the root
- Visit the left subtree
- Visit the right subtree

In postorder traversal,

- Visit the left subtree
- Visit the right subtree
- Visit the root

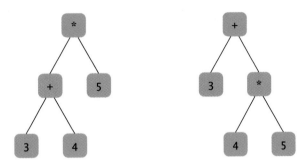

Figure 14 Expression Trees

These two visitation schemes will not print the tree in sorted order. However, they are important in other applications of binary trees. Here is an example.

In Chapter 18, we presented an algorithm for parsing arithmetic expressions such as

```
(3 + 4) * 5
3 + 4 * 5
```

It is customary to draw these expressions in tree form—see Figure 14. If all operators have two arguments, then the resulting tree is a binary tree. Its leaves store numbers, and its interior nodes store operators.

Note that the expression trees describe the order in which the operators are applied.

This order becomes visible when applying the postorder traversal of the expression tree. The first tree yields

```
3 4 + 5 *
```

whereas the second tree yields

```
3 4 5 * +
```

> Postorder traversal of an expression tree yields the instructions for evaluating the expression on a stack-based calculator.

You can interpret these sequences as instructions for a stack-based calculator. A number means:

- Push the number on the stack.

An operator means:

- Pop the top two numbers off the stack.
- Apply the operator to these two numbers.
- Push the result back on the stack.

Figure 15 shows the computation sequences for the two expressions.

This observation yields an algorithm for evaluating arithmetic expressions. First, turn the expression into a tree. Then carry out a postorder traversal of the

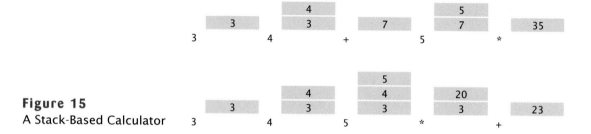

Figure 15
A Stack-Based Calculator

expression tree and apply the operations in the given order. The result is the value of the expression.

SELF CHECK

11. What are the inorder traversals of the two trees in Figure 14?
12. Are the trees in Figure 14 binary search trees?

RANDOM FACT 21.1

Reverse Polish Notation

In the 1920s, the Polish mathematician Jan Łukasiewicz realized that it is possible to dispense with parentheses in arithmetic expressions, provided that you write the operators *before* their arguments. For example,

Standard Notation	Łukasiewicz Notation
3 + 4	+ 3 4
3 + 4 * 5	+ 3 * 4 5
3 * (4 + 5)	* 3 + 4 5
(3 + 4) * 5	* + 3 4 5
3 + 4 + 5	+ + 3 4 5

The Łukasiewicz notation might look strange to you, but that is just an accident of history. Had earlier mathematicians realized its advantages, schoolchildren today would not learn an inferior notation with arbitrary precedence rules and parentheses.

Of course, an entrenched notation is not easily displaced, even when it has distinct disadvantages, and Łukasiewicz's discovery did not cause much of a stir for about 50 years.

However, in 1972, Hewlett-Packard introduced the HP 35 calculator that used *reverse Polish notation* or RPN. RPN is simply Łukasiewicz's notation in reverse, with the operators after their arguments. For example, to compute 3 + 4 * 5, you enter 3 4 5 * +. RPN calculators have no keys labeled with parentheses or an equals symbol. There is just a key labeled ENTER to push a number onto a stack. For that reason, Hewlett-Packard's marketing department used to refer to their product as "the calculators that have no equal". Indeed, the Hewlett-Packard calculators were a great advance over competing models that were unable to handle algebraic notation, leaving users with no other choice but to write intermediate results on paper.

Over time, developers of high-quality calculators have adapted to the standard algebraic notation rather than forcing its users to learn a new notation. However, those users who have made the effort to learn RPN tend to be fanatic proponents, and to this day, some Hewlett-Packard calculator models still support it.

21.7 Using Tree Sets and Tree Maps

Both the HashSet and the TreeSet classes implement the Set interface. Thus, if you need a set of objects, you have a choice.

> The TreeSet class uses a form of balanced binary tree that guarantees that adding and removing an element takes $O(\log(n))$ time.

If you have a good hash function for your objects, then hashing is usually faster than tree-based algorithms. But the balanced trees used in the TreeSet class can *guarantee* reasonable performance, whereas the HashSet is entirely at the mercy of the hash function.

If you don't want to define a hash function, then a tree set is an attractive option. Tree sets have another advantage: The iterators visit elements in *sorted order* rather than the completely random order given by the hash codes.

> To use a tree set, the elements must be comparable.

To use a TreeSet, your objects must belong to a class that implements the Comparable interface or you must supply a Comparator object. That is the same requirement that you saw in Section 19.8 for using the sort and binarySearch methods in the standard library.

To use a TreeMap, the same requirement holds for the *keys*. There is no requirement for the values.

For example, the String class implements the Comparable interface. The compareTo method compares strings in dictionary order. Thus, you can form tree sets of strings, and use strings as keys for tree maps.

If the class of the tree set elements doesn't implement the Comparable interface, or the sort order of the compareTo method isn't the one you want, then you can define your own comparison by supplying a Comparator object to the TreeSet or TreeMap constructor. For example,

```
Comparator comp = new CoinComparator();
Set s = new TreeSet(comp);
```

As described in Advanced Topic 19.5, a Comparator object compares two elements and returns a negative integer if the first is less than the second, zero if they are identical, and a positive value otherwise. The example program at the end of this section constructs a TreeSet of Coin objects, using the coin comparator of Advanced Topic 19.5.

File TreeSetTester.java

```
1   import java.util.Comparator;
2   import java.util.Set;
3   import java.util.TreeSet;
4
5   /**
6       A program to a test a comparator for coins.
7   */
8   public class TreeSetTester
9   {
10      public static void main(String[] args)
11      {
12         Coin coin1 = new Coin(0.25, "quarter");
13         Coin coin2 = new Coin(0.25, "quarter");
14         Coin coin3 = new Coin(0.01, "penny");
15         Coin coin4 = new Coin(0.05, "nickel");
16
17         class CoinComparator implements Comparator<Coin>
18         {
19            public int compare(Coin first, Coin second)
20            {
21               if (first.getValue() < second.getValue()) return -1;
22               if (first.getValue() == second.getValue()) return 0;
23               return 1;
24            }
25         }
26
27         Comparator<Coin> comp = new CoinComparator();
28         Set<Coin> coins = new TreeSet<Coin>(comp);
29         coins.add(coin1);
30         coins.add(coin2);
31         coins.add(coin3);
32         coins.add(coin4);
33
34         for (Coin c : coins)
35            System.out.println(c);
36      }
37   }
```

Output

```
Coin[value=0.01,name=penny]
Coin[value=0.05,name=nickel]
Coin[value=0.25,name=quarter]
```

SELF CHECK

13. When would you choose a tree set over a hash set?

14. Suppose we define a coin comparator whose compare method always returns 0. Would the TreeSet function correctly?

HOW TO 21.1

Choosing a Container

Suppose you need to store objects in a container. You have now seen a number of different data structures. This How To reviews how to pick an appropriate container for your application.

Step 1 Determine how you access the elements.

You store elements in a container so that you can later retrieve them. How do you want to access individual elements? You have several choices.

- It doesn't matter. Elements are always accessed "in bulk", by visiting all elements and doing something with them.
- Access by key. Elements are accessed by a special key. *Example:* Retrieve a bank account by the account number.
- Access by integer index. Elements have a position that is naturally an integer or a pair of integers. *Example:* A piece on a chess board is accessed by a row and column index.

If you need keyed access, use a map. If you need access by integer index, use an array list or array. For an index pair, use a two-dimensional array.

Step 2 Determine whether element order matters.

When you retrieve elements from a container, do you care about the order in which they are retrieved? You have several choices.

- It doesn't matter. As long as you get to visit all elements, you don't care in which order.
- Elements must be sorted.
- Elements must be in the same order in which they were inserted.

To keep elements sorted, use a TreeSet. To keep elements in the order in which you inserted them, use a LinkedList, ArrayList, or array.

Step 3 Determine which operations must be fast.

You have several choices.

- It doesn't matter. You collect so few elements that you aren't concerned about speed.
- Adding and removing elements must be fast.
- Finding elements must be fast.

Linked lists allow you to add and remove elements efficiently, provided you are already near the location of the change. Changing either end of the linked list is always fast.

If you need to find an element quickly, use a set.

At this point, you should have narrowed down your selection to a particular container. If you answered "It doesn't matter" for each of the choices, then just use an `ArrayList`. It's a simple container that you already know well.

Step 4   For sets and maps, choose between hash tables and trees.

If you decided that you need a set or map, you need to pick a particular implementation, either a hash table or a tree.

If your elements (or keys, in case of a map) are strings, use a hash table. It's more efficient.

If your elements or keys belong to a type that someone else defined, check whether the class implements its own `hashCode` and `equals` methods. The inherited `hashCode` method of the `Object` class takes only the object's memory address into account, not its contents. If there is no satisfactory `hashCode` method, then you must use a tree.

If your elements or keys belong to your own class, you usually want to use hashing. Define a `hashCode` and compatible `equals` method.

Step 5   If you use a tree, decide whether to supply a comparator.

Look at the class of the elements or keys that the tree manages. Does that class implement the `Comparable` interface? If so, is the sort order given by the `compareTo` method the one you want? If yes, then you don't need to do anything further. If no, then you must define a class that implements the `Comparator` interface and define the `compare` method. Supply an object of the comparator class to the `TreeSet` or `TreeMap` constructor.

RANDOM FACT 21.2

Software Piracy

As you read this, you have written a few computer programs, and you have experienced firsthand how much effort it takes to write even the humblest of programs. Writing a real software product, such as a financial application or a computer game, takes a lot of time and money. Few people, and fewer companies, are going to spend that kind of time and money if they don't have a reasonable chance to make more money from their effort. (Actually, some companies give away their software in the hope that users will upgrade to more elaborate paid versions. Other companies give away the software that enables users to read and use files but sell the software needed to create those files. Finally, there are individuals who donate their time, out of enthusiasm, and produce programs that you can copy freely.)

When selling software, a company must rely on the honesty of its customers. It is an easy matter for an unscrupulous person to make copies of computer programs without paying for them. In most countries that is illegal. Most governments provide legal protection, such as copyright laws and patents, to encourage the development of new products. Countries that tolerate widespread piracy have found that they have an ample cheap supply of foreign software, but no local manufacturers willing to design good software for their own citizens, such as word processors in the local script or financial programs adapted to the local tax laws.

When a mass market for software first appeared, vendors were enraged by the money they lost through piracy. They tried to fight back by various schemes to ensure that only the legitimate owner could use the software. Some manufacturers used *key disks:* disks with special patterns of holes burned in by a laser, which couldn't be copied. Others used *dongles:*

devices that are attached to a printer port. Legitimate users hated these measures. They paid for the software, but they had to suffer through the inconvenience of inserting a key disk every time they started the software or having multiple dongles stick out from their computer. In the United States, market pressures forced most vendors to give up on these copy protection schemes, but they are still commonplace in other parts of the world.

Because it is so easy and inexpensive to pirate software, and the chance of being found out is minimal, you have to make a moral choice for yourself. If a package that you would really like to have is too expensive for your budget, do you steal it, or do you stay honest and get by with a more affordable product?

Of course, piracy is not limited to software. The same issues arise for other digital products as well. You may have had the opportunity to obtain copies of songs or movies without payment. Or you may have been frustrated by a copy protection device on your music player that made it difficult for you to listen to songs that you paid for. Admittedly, it can be difficult to have a lot of sympathy for a musical ensemble whose publisher charges a lot of money for what seems to have been very little effort on their part, at least when compared to the effort that goes into designing and implementing a software package. Nevertheless, it seems only fair that artists and authors receive some compensation for their efforts. How to pay artists, authors, and programmers fairly, without burdening honest customers, is an unsolved problem at the time of this writing, and many computer scientists are engaged in research in this area.

21.8 Priority Queues

In Section 20.4, you encountered two common abstract data types: stacks and queues. Another important abstract data type, the *priority queue*, collects elements, each of which has a *priority*. A typical example of a priority queue is a collection of work requests, some of which may be more urgent than others.

> When removing an element from a priority queue, the element with the highest priority is retrieved.

Unlike a regular queue, the priority queue does not maintain a first-in, first-out discipline. Instead, elements are retrieved according to their priority. In other words, new items can be inserted in any order. But whenever an item is removed, that item has highest priority.

It is customary to give low values to high priorities, with priority 1 denoting the highest priority. The priority queue extracts the *minimum* element from the queue.

For example, consider this sample code:

```
PriorityQueue<WorkOrder> q = new PriorityQueue<WorkOrder>;
q.add(new WorkOrder(3, "Shampoo carpets"));
q.add(new WorkOrder(1, "Fix overflowing sink"));
q.add(new WorkOrder(2, "Order cleaning supplies"));
```

When calling `q.remove()` for the first time, the work order with priority 1 is removed. The next call to `q.remove()` removes the work order whose priority is highest among those remaining in the queue—in our example, the work order with priority 2.

The standard Java library supplies a `PriorityQueue` class that is ready for you to use. Later in this chapter, you will learn how to supply your own implementation.

Keep in mind that the priority queue is an *abstract* data type. You do not know how a priority queue organizes its elements. There are several concrete data structures that can be used to implement priority queues.

Of course, one implementation comes to mind immediately. Just store the elements in a linked list, adding new elements to the head of the list. The `remove` method then traverses the linked list and removes the element with the highest priority. In this implementation, adding elements is quick, but removing them is slow.

Another implementation strategy is to keep the elements in sorted order, for example in a binary search tree. Then it is an easy matter to locate and remove the largest element. However, another data structure, called a heap, is even more suitable for implementing priority queues.

21.9 Heaps

> A heap is an almost complete tree in which the values of all nodes are at most as large as those of their descendants.

A *heap* (or, for greater clarity, *min-heap*) is a binary tree with two special properties.

1. A heap is *almost complete:* all nodes are filled in, except the last level may have some nodes missing toward the right (see Figure 16).

2. The tree fulfills the *heap property:* all nodes store values that are at most as large as the values stored in their descendants (see Figure 17).

It is easy to see that the heap property ensures that the smallest element is stored in the root.

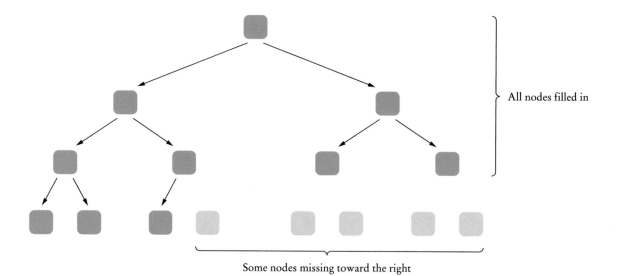

All nodes filled in

Some nodes missing toward the right

Figure 16 An Almost Complete Tree

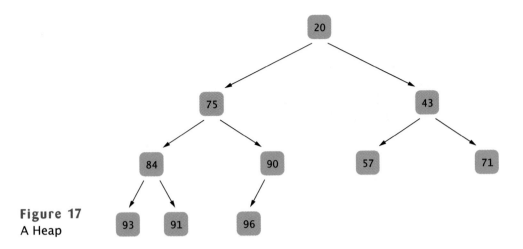

Figure 17
A Heap

A heap is superficially similar to a binary search tree, but there are two important differences.

1. The shape of a heap is very regular. Binary search trees can have arbitrary shapes.
2. In a heap, the left and right subtrees both store elements that are larger than the root element. In contrast, in a binary search tree, smaller elements are stored in the left subtree and larger elements are stored in the right subtree.

Suppose we have a heap and want to insert a new element. Afterwards, the heap property should again be fulfilled. The following algorithm carries out the insertion (see Figure 18).

1. First, add a vacant slot to the end of the tree.

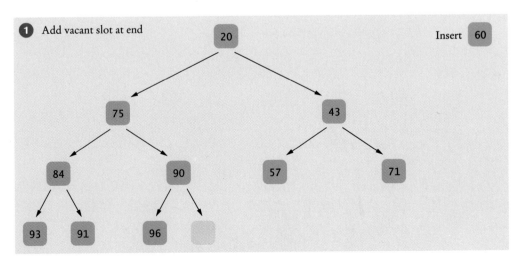

Figure 18   Inserting an Element into a Heap

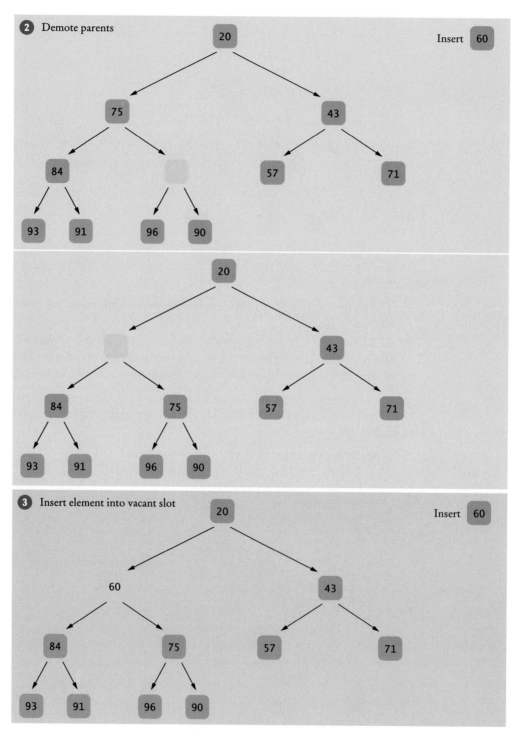

Figure 18 (continued)   Inserting an Element into a Heap

2. Next, demote the parent of the empty slot if it is larger than the element to be inserted. That is, move the parent value into the vacant slot, and move the vacant slot up. Repeat this demotion as long as the parent of the vacant slot is larger than the element to be inserted. (See Figure 18 continued.)

3. At this point, either the vacant slot is at the root, or the parent of the vacant slot is smaller than the element to be inserted. Insert the element into the vacant slot.

We will not consider an algorithm for removing an arbitrary node from a heap. The only node that we will remove is the root node, which contains the minimum of all of the values in the heap. Figure 19 shows the algorithm in action.

1. Extract the root node value.

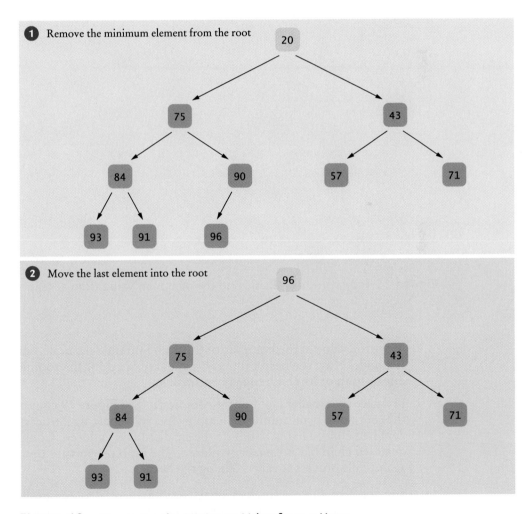

Figure 19   Removing the Minimum Value from a Heap

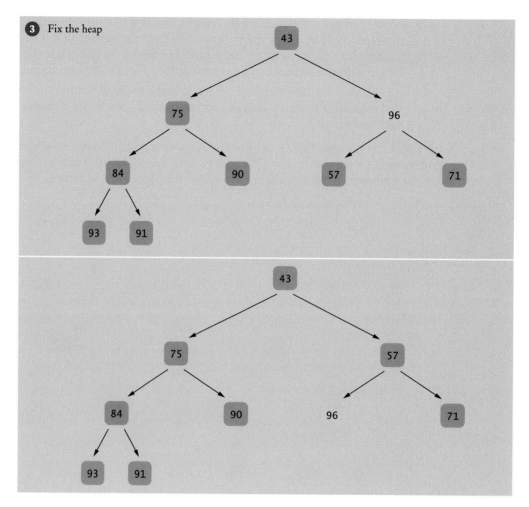

Figure 19 (continued) Removing the Minimum Value from a Heap

2. Move the value of the last node of the heap into the root node, and remove the last node. Now the heap property may be violated for the root node, because one or both of its children may be smaller.

3. Promote the smaller child of the root node. (See Figure 19 continued.) Now the root node again fulfills the heap property. Repeat this process with the demoted child. That is, promote the smaller of its children. Continue until the demoted child has no smaller children. The heap property is now fulfilled again. This process is called "fixing the heap".

Inserting and removing heap elements is very efficient. The reason lies in the balanced shape of a heap. The insertion and removal operations visit at most h nodes, where h is the height of the tree. A heap of height h contains at least 2^{h-1} elements, but less than 2^h elements. In other words, if n is the number of elements, then

$$2^{h-1} \leq n < 2^h$$

or

$$h - 1 \leq \log_2(n) < h$$

Inserting or removing a heap element is an $O(\log(n))$ operation.

This argument shows that the insertion and removal operations in a heap with n elements take $O(\log(n))$ steps.

Contrast this finding with the situation of binary search trees. When a binary search tree is unbalanced, it can degenerate into a linked list, so that in the worst case insertion and removal are $O(n)$ operations.

The regular layout of a heap makes it possible to store heap nodes efficiently in an array.

Heaps have another major advantage. Because of the regular layout of the heap nodes, it is easy to store the node values in an array. First store the first layer, then the second, and so on (see Figure 20). For convenience, we leave the 0 element of the array empty. Then the child nodes of the node with index i have index $2 \cdot i$ and $2 \cdot i + 1$, and the parent node of the node with index i has index $i/2$. For example, as you can see in Figure 20, the children of node 4 are nodes 8 and 9, and the parent is node 2.

Storing the heap values in an array may not be intuitive, but it is very efficient. There is no need to allocate individual nodes or to store the links to the child nodes. Instead, child and parent positions can be determined by very simple computations.

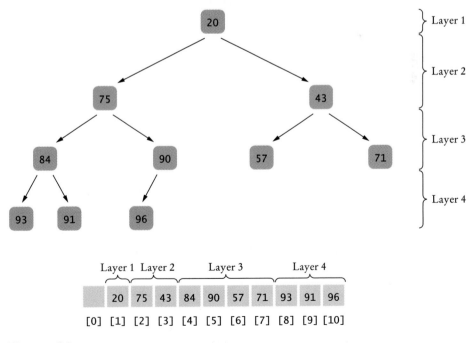

Figure 20   Storing a Heap in an Array

The program at the end of this section contains an implementation of a heap. For greater clarity, the computation of the parent and child index positions is carried out in methods `getParentIndex`, `getLeftChildIndex`, and `getRightChildIndex`. For greater efficiency, the method calls could be avoided by using expressions `index / 2`, `2 * index`, and `2 * index + 1` directly.

In this section, we have organized our heaps such that the smallest element is stored in the root. It is also possible to store the largest element in the root, simply by reversing all comparisons in the heap-building algorithm. If there is a possibility of misunderstanding, it is best to refer to the data structures as min-heap or max-heap.

The test program demonstrates how to use a min-heap as a priority queue.

File MinHeap.java

```
 1  import java.util.*;
 2
 3  /**
 4      This class implements a heap.
 5  */
 6  public class MinHeap
 7  {
 8      /**
 9          Constructs an empty heap.
10      */
11      public MinHeap()
12      {
13          elements = new ArrayList<Comparable>();
14          elements.add(null);
15      }
16
17      /**
18          Adds a new element to this heap.
19          @param newElement the element to add
20      */
21      public void add(Comparable newElement)
22      {
23          // Add a new leaf
24          elements.add(null);
25          int index = elements.size() - 1;
26
27          // Demote parents that are larger than the new element
28          while (index > 1
29                  && getParent(index).compareTo(newElement) > 0)
30          {
31              elements.set(index, getParent(index));
32              index = getParentIndex(index);
33          }
34
35          // Store the new element in the vacant slot
36          elements.set(index, newElement);
37      }
38
```

```
39      /**
40          Gets the minimum element stored in this heap.
41          @return the minimum element
42      */
43      public Comparable peek()
44      {
45          return elements.get(1);
46      }
47
48      /**
49          Removes the minimum element from this heap.
50          @return the minimum element
51      */
52      public Comparable remove()
53      {
54          Comparable minimum = elements.get(1);
55
56          // Remove last element
57          int lastIndex = elements.size() - 1;
58          Comparable last = elements.remove(lastIndex);
59
60          if (lastIndex > 1)
61          {
62              elements.set(1, last);
63              fixHeap();
64          }
65
66          return minimum;
67      }
68
69      /**
70          Turns the tree back into a heap, provided only the root
71          node violates the heap condition.
72      */
73      private void fixHeap()
74      {
75          Comparable root = elements.get(1);
76
77          int lastIndex = elements.size() - 1;
78          // Promote children of removed root while they are larger than last
79
80          int index = 1;
81          boolean more = true;
82          while (more)
83          {
84              int childIndex = getLeftChildIndex(index);
85              if (childIndex <= lastIndex)
86              {
87                  // Get smaller child
88
89                  // Get left child first
90                  Comparable child = getLeftChild(index);
91
```

```
92              // Use right child instead if it is smaller
93              if (getRightChildIndex(index) <= lastIndex
94                  && getRightChild(index).compareTo(child) < 0)
95              {
96                  childIndex = getRightChildIndex(index);
97                  child = getRightChild(index);
98              }
99
100             // Check if larger child is smaller than root
101             if (child.compareTo(root) < 0)
102             {
103                 // Promote child
104                 elements.set(index, child);
105                 index = childIndex;
106             }
107             else
108             {
109                 // root  is smaller than both children
110                 more = false;
111             }
112         }
113         else
114         {
115             // No children
116             more = false;
117         }
118     }
119
120     // Store root element in vacant slot
121     elements.set(index, root);
122 }
123
124 /**
125     Returns the number of elements in this heap.
126 */
127 public int size()
128 {
129     return elements.size() - 1;
130 }
131
132 /**
133     Returns the index of the left child.
134     @param index  the index of a node in this heap
135     @return  the index of the left child of the given node
136 */
137 private static int getLeftChildIndex(int index)
138 {
139     return 2 * index;
140 }
141
142 /**
143     Returns the index of the right child.
144     @param index  the index of a node in this heap
145     @return  the index of the right child of the given node
146 */
```

```
147        private static int getRightChildIndex(int index)
148        {
149            return 2 * index + 1;
150        }
151
152        /**
153            Returns the index of the parent.
154            @param index the index of a node in this heap
155            @return the index of the parent of the given node
156        */
157        private static int getParentIndex(int index)
158        {
159            return index / 2;
160        }
161
162        /**
163            Returns the value of the left child.
164            @param index the index of a node in this heap
165            @return the value of the left child of the given node
166        */
167        private Comparable getLeftChild(int index)
168        {
169            return elements.get(2 * index);
170        }
171
172        /**
173            Returns the value of the right child.
174            @param index the index of a node in this heap
175            @return the value of the right child of the given node
176        */
177        private Comparable getRightChild(int index)
178        {
179            return elements.get(2 * index + 1);
180        }
181
182        /**
183            Returns the value of the parent.
184            @param index the index of a node in this heap
185            @return the value of the parent of the given node
186        */
187        private Comparable getParent(int index)
188        {
189            return elements.get(index / 2);
190        }
191
192        private ArrayList<Comparable> elements;
193    }
```

File HeapTester.java

```
1    /**
2        This program demonstrates the use of a heap as a priority queue.
3    */
4    public class HeapTester
```

```
 5  {
 6      public static void main(String[] args)
 7      {
 8          MinHeap q = new MinHeap();
 9          q.add(new WorkOrder(3, "Shampoo carpets"));
10          q.add(new WorkOrder(7, "Empty trash"));
11          q.add(new WorkOrder(8, "Water plants"));
12          q.add(new WorkOrder(10, "Remove pencil sharpener shavings"));
13          q.add(new WorkOrder(6, "Replace light bulb"));
14          q.add(new WorkOrder(1, "Fix broken sink"));
15          q.add(new WorkOrder(9, "Clean coffee maker"));
16          q.add(new WorkOrder(2, "Order cleaning supplies"));
17
18          while (q.size() > 0)
19              System.out.println(q.remove());
20      }
21  }
```

File WorkOrder.java

```
 1  /**
 2      This class encapsulates a work order with a priority.
 3  */
 4  public class WorkOrder implements Comparable
 5  {
 6      /**
 7          Constructs a work order with a given priority and description.
 8          @param aPriority the priority of this work order
 9          @param aDescription the description of this work order
10      */
11      public WorkOrder(int aPriority, String aDescription)
12      {
13          priority = aPriority;
14          description = aDescription;
15      }
16
17      public String toString()
18      {
19          return "priority=" + priority + ", description=" + description;
20      }
21
22      public int compareTo(Object otherObject)
23      {
24          WorkOrder other = (WorkOrder) otherObject;
25          if (priority < other.priority) return -1;
26          if (priority > other.priority) return 1;
27          return 0;
28      }
29
30      private int priority;
31      private String description;
32  }
```

Output

```
priority=1, description=Fix broken sink
priority=2, description=Order cleaning supplies
priority=3, description=Shampoo carpets
priority=6, description=Replace light bulb
priority=7, description=Empty trash
priority=8, description=Water plants
priority=9, description=Clean coffee maker
priority=10, description=Remove pencil sharpener shavings
```

SELF CHECK

15. The software that controls the events in a user interface keeps the events in a data structure. Whenever an event such as a mouse move or repaint request occurs, the event is added. Events are retrieved according to their importance. What abstract data type is appropriate for this application?

16. Could we store a binary search tree in an array so that we can quickly locate the children by looking at array locations 2 * index and 2 * index + 1?

21.10 The Heapsort Algorithm

> The heapsort algorithm is based on inserting elements into a heap and removing them in sorted order.

Heaps are not only useful for implementing priority queues, they also give rise to an efficient sorting algorithm, heapsort. In its simplest form, the algorithm works as follows. First insert all elements to be sorted into the heap, then keep extracting the minimum.

This algorithm is an $O(n \log(n))$ algorithm: each insertion and removal is $O(\log(n))$, and these steps are repeated n times, once for each element in the sequence that is to be sorted.

> Heapsort is an $O(n \log(n))$ algorithm.

The algorithm can be made a bit more efficient. Rather than inserting the elements one at a time, we will start with a sequence of values in an array. Of course, that array does not represent a heap. We will use the procedure of "fixing the heap" that you encountered in the preceding section as part of the element removal algorithm. "Fixing the heap" operates on a binary tree whose child trees are heaps but whose root value may not be smaller than the descendants. The procedure turns the tree into a heap, by repeatedly promoting the smallest child value, moving the root value to its proper location.

Of course, we cannot simply apply this procedure to the initial sequence of unsorted values—the child trees of the root are not likely to be heaps. But we can first fix small subtrees into heaps, then fix larger trees. Because trees of size 1 are automatically heaps, we can begin the fixing procedure with the subtrees whose roots are located in the next-to-lowest level of the tree.

The sorting algorithm uses a generalized fixHeap method that fixes a subtree with a given root index:

```
void fixHeap(int rootIndex, int lastIndex)
```

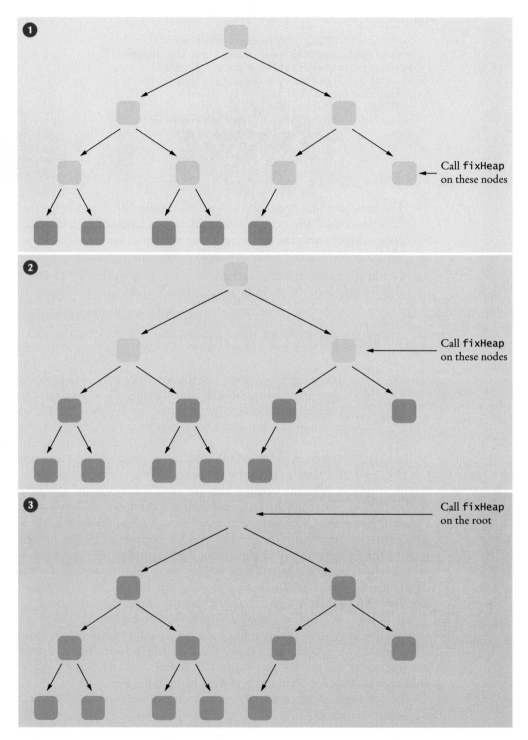

Figure 21   Turning a Tree into a Heap

Here, lastIndex is the index of the last node in the full tree. The fixHeap method needs to be invoked on all subtrees whose roots are in the next-to-last level. Then the subtrees whose roots are in the next level above are fixed, and so on. Finally, the fixup is applied to the root node, and the tree is turned into a heap (see Figure 21).

That repetition can be programmed easily. Start with the *last* node on the next-to-lowest level and work toward the left. Then go to the next higher level. The node index values then simply run backwards from the index of the last node to the index of the root.

```
int n = a.length - 1;
for (int i = (n - 1) / 2; i >= 0; i--)
   fixHeap(i, n);
```

Note that the loop ends with index 0. When working with a given array, we don't have the luxury of skipping the 0 entry. We consider the 0 entry the root and adjust the formulas for computing the child and parent index values.

After the array has been turned into a heap, we repeatedly remove the root element. Recall from the preceding section that removing the root element is achieved by placing the last element of the tree in the root and calling the fixHeap method.

Rather than moving the root element into a separate array, we will *swap* the root element with the last element of the tree and then reduce the tree length. Thus, the removed root ends up in the last position of the array, which is no longer needed by the heap. In this way, we can use the same array both to hold the heap (which gets shorter with each step) and the sorted sequence (which gets longer with each step).

There is just a minor inconvenience. When we use a min-heap, the sorted sequence is accumulated in reverse order, with the smallest element at the end of the array. We could reverse the sequence after sorting is complete. However, it is easier to use a max-heap rather than a min-heap in the heapsort algorithm. With this modification, the largest value is placed at the end of the array after the first step. After the next step, the next-largest value is swapped from the heap root to the second position from the end, and so on (see Figure 22).

The following class implements the heapsort algorithm.

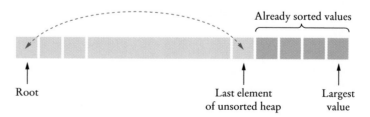

Figure 22 Using Heapsort to Sort an Array

File HeapSorter.java

```java
1  /**
2     This class applies the heapsort algorithm to sort an array.
3  */
4  public class HeapSorter
5  {
6     /**
7        Constructs a heap sorter that sorts a given array.
8        @param anArray an array of integers
9     */
10    public HeapSorter(int[] anArray)
11    {
12       a = anArray;
13    }
14
15    /**
16       Sorts the array managed by this heap sorter.
17    */
18    public void sort()
19    {
20       int n = a.length - 1;
21       for (int i = (n - 1) / 2; i >= 0; i--)
22          fixHeap(i, n);
23       while (n > 0)
24       {
25          swap(0, n);
26          n--;
27          fixHeap(0, n);
28       }
29    }
30
31    /**
32       Ensures the heap property for a subtree, provided its
33       children already fulfill the heap property.
34       @param rootIndex the index of the subtree to be fixed
35       @param lastIndex the last valid index of the tree that
36       contains the subtree to be fixed
37    */
38    private void fixHeap(int rootIndex, int lastIndex)
39    {
40       // Remove root
41       int rootValue = a[rootIndex];
42
43       // Promote children while they are larger than the root
44
45       int index = rootIndex;
46       boolean more = true;
47       while (more)
48       {
49          int childIndex = getLeftChildIndex(index);
50          if (childIndex <= lastIndex)
51          {
52             // Use right child instead if it is larger
53             int rightChildIndex = getRightChildIndex(index);
```

```
54          if (rightChildIndex <= lastIndex
55                  && a[rightChildIndex] > a[childIndex])
56          {
57              childIndex = rightChildIndex;
58          }
59
60          if (a[childIndex] > rootValue)
61          {
62              // Promote child
63              a[index] = a[childIndex];
64              index = childIndex;
65          }
66          else
67          {
68              // Root value is larger than both children
69              more = false;
70          }
71      }
72      else
73      {
74          // No children
75          more = false;
76      }
77   }
78
79   // Store root value in vacant slot
80   a[index] = rootValue;
81 }
82
83 /**
84    Swaps two entries of the array.
85    @param i the first position to swap
86    @param j the second position to swap
87 */
88 private void swap(int i, int j)
89 {
90    int temp = a[i];
91    a[i] = a[j];
92    a[j] = temp;
93 }
94
95 /**
96    Returns the index of the left child.
97    @param index the index of a node in this heap
98    @return the index of the left child of the given node
99 */
100 private static int getLeftChildIndex(int index)
101 {
102    return 2 * index + 1;
103 }
104
```

```
105        /**
106            Returns the index of the right child.
107            @param index  the index of a node in this heap
108            @return  the index of the right child of the given node
109        */
110        private static int getRightChildIndex(int index)
111        {
112            return 2 * index + 2;
113        }
114
115        private int[] a;
116    }
```

SELF CHECK

17. Which algorithm requires less storage, heapsort or mergesort?
18. Why are the computations of the left child index and the right child index in the HeapSorter different than in MinHeap?

CHAPTER SUMMARY

1. A set is an unordered collection of distinct elements. Elements can be added, located, and removed.

2. Sets don't have duplicates. Adding a duplicate of an element that is already present is silently ignored.

3. The HashSet and TreeSet classes both implement the Set interface.

4. An iterator visits all elements in a set.

5. A set iterator does not visit the elements in the order in which you inserted them. The set implementation rearranges the elements so that it can locate them quickly.

6. You cannot add an element to a set at an iterator position.

7. A map keeps associations between key and value objects.

8. The HashMap and TreeMap classes both implement the Map interface.

9. To find all keys and values in a map, iterate through the key set and find the values that correspond to the keys.

10. A hash function computes an integer value from an object.

11. A good hash function minimizes *collisions*—identical hash codes for different objects.

12. A hash table can be implemented as an array of *buckets*—sequences of nodes that hold elements with the same hash code.

13. If there are no or only a few collisions, then adding, locating, and removing hash table elements takes constant or $O(1)$ time.

14. The table size should be a prime number, larger than the expected number of elements.

15. Define `hashCode` methods for your own classes by combining the hash codes for the instance variables.

16. Your `hashCode` method must be compatible with the `equals` method.

17. In a hash map, only the keys are hashed.

18. A binary tree consists of nodes, each of which has at most two child nodes.

19. All nodes in a binary search tree fulfill the property that the descendants to the left have smaller data values than the node data value, and the descendants to the right have larger data values.

20. When removing a node with only one child from a binary search tree, the child replaces the node to be removed.

21. When removing a node with two children from a binary search tree, replace it with the smallest node of the right subtree.

22. If a binary search tree is balanced, then adding an element takes $O(\log(n))$ time.

23. Tree traversal schemes include preorder traversal, inorder traversal, and post-order traversal.

24. Postorder traversal of an expression tree yields the instructions for evaluating the expression on a stack-based calculator.

25. The `TreeSet` class uses a form of balanced binary trees that guarantees that adding and removing an element takes $O(\log(n))$ time.

26. To use a tree set, the elements must be comparable.

27. When removing an element from a priority queue, the element with the highest priority is retrieved.

28. A heap is an almost complete tree in which the values of all nodes are at most as large as those of their descendants.

29. Inserting or removing a heap element is an $O(\log(n))$ operation.

30. The regular layout of a heap makes it possible to store heap nodes efficiently in an array.

31. The heapsort algorithm is based on inserting elements into a heap and removing them in sorted order.

32. Heapsort is an $O(n \log(n))$ algorithm.

CLASSES, OBJECTS, AND METHODS INTRODUCED IN THIS CHAPTER

```
java.util.Collection<E>
    contains
    remove
    size
java.util.HashMap<K, V>
java.util.HashSet<K, V>
java.util.Map<K, V>
    get
    keySet
    put
    remove
java.util.PriorityQueue<E>
    remove
java.util.Set<E>
java.util.TreeMap<K, V>
java.util.TreeSet<K, V>
```

FURTHER READING

1. Thomas H. Cormen, Charles E. Leiserson, Ronald L. Rivest, and Clifford Stein, *Introduction to Algorithms,* 2nd edition, MIT Press, 2001.

REVIEW EXERCISES

Exercise R21.1. What is the difference between a set and a map?

Exercise R21.2. What implementations does the Java library provide for the abstract set type?

Exercise R21.3. What are the fundamental operations on the abstract set type? What additional methods does the Set interface provide? (Look up the interface in the API documentation.)

Exercise R21.4. The union of two sets *A* and *B* is the set of all elements that are contained in *A*, *B*, or both. The intersection is the set of all elements that are contained in *A* and *B*. How can you compute the union and intersection of two sets, using the fundamental set operations?

Exercise R21.5. How can you compute the union and intersection of two sets, using some of the methods that the Set interface provides? (Look up the interface in the API documentation.)

Exercise R21.6. Can a map have two keys with the same value? Two values with the same key?

Exercise R21.7. A map can be implemented as a set of (*key, value*) pairs. Explain.

Exercise R21.8. When implementing a hash map as a set of (*key, value*) pairs, what hash function should be used?

Exercise R21.9. Verify the hash codes of the strings "Jim" and "Joe" in Table 1.

Exercise R21.10. From the hash codes in Table 1, show that Figure 6 accurately shows the locations of the strings if the hash table size is 101.

Exercise R21.11. What is the difference between a binary tree and a binary search tree? Give examples of each.

Exercise R21.12. What is the difference between a balanced tree and an unbalanced tree? Give examples of each.

Exercise R21.13. The following elements are inserted into a binary search tree. Make a drawing that shows the resulting tree after each insertion.

    Adam
    Eve
    Romeo
    Juliet
    Tom
    Dick
    Harry

Exercise R21.14. Insert the elements of Exercise R21.13 in opposite order. Then determine how the BinarySearchTree.print method prints out both the tree from Exercise R21.13 and this tree. Explain how the printouts are related.

Exercise R21.15. Consider the following tree. In which order are the nodes printed by the BinarySearchTree.print method?

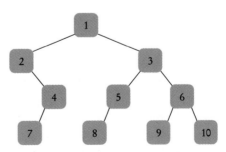

Exercise R21.16. Could a priority queue be implemented efficiently as a binary search tree? Give a detailed argument for your answer.

Exercise R21.17. Will preorder, inorder, or postorder traversal print a heap in sorted order? Why or why not?

Exercise R21.18. Prove that a heap of height h contains at least 2^{h-1} elements but less than 2^h elements.

Exercise R21.19. Suppose the heap nodes are stored in an array, starting with index 1. Prove that the child nodes of the heap node with index i have index $2 \cdot i$ and $2 \cdot i + 1$, and the parent heap node of the node with index i has index $i/2$.

Exercise R21.20. Simulate the heapsort algorithm manually to sort the array

    11 27 8 14 45 6 24 81 29 33

Show all steps.

PROGRAMMING EXERCISES

Exercise P21.1. Write a program that reads text from `System.in` and breaks it up into individual words. Insert the words into a tree set. At the end of the input file, print all words, followed by the size of the resulting set. This program determines how many unique words a text file has.

Exercise P21.2. Insert the 13 standard colors that the `Color` class predefines (that is, `Color.PINK`, `Color.GREEN`, and so on) into a set. Prompt the user to enter a color by specifying red, green, and blue floating-point values between 0 and 1. Then tell the user whether the resulting color is in the set.

Exercise P21.3. Add a `debug` method to the `HashSet` implementation in Section 21.3 that prints the nonempty buckets of the hash table. Run the test program at the end of Section 21.3. Call the `debug` method after all additions and removals and verify that Figure 6 accurately represents the state of the hash table.

Exercise P21.4. Write a program that keeps a map in which both keys and values are strings—the names of students and their course grades. Prompt the user of the program to add or remove students, to modify grades, or to print all grades. The printout should be sorted by name and formatted like this:

    Carl: B+
    Joe: C
    Sarah: A

Exercise P21.5. Reimplement Exercise P21.4 so that the keys of the map are objects of class `Student`. A student should have a first name, a last name, and an integer ID. The printout should be sorted by last name. If two students have the same last name, then use the first name as tie breaker. If the first names are also identical, then use the integer ID.

Exercise P21.6. Supply compatible `hashCode` and `equals` methods to the `Student` class described in Exercise P21.5. Test the hash code by adding `Student` objects to a hash set.

Exercise P21.7. Supply compatible hashCode and equals methods to the BankAccount class. Test the hashCode method by printing out hash codes and by adding Bank-Account objects to a hash set.

Exercise P21.8. Design an IntTree class that stores only integers, not objects. Support the same methods as the BinarySearchTree class in the book.

Exercise P21.9. Design a data structure IntSet that can hold a set of integers. Hide the private implementation: a tree set of Integer objects. Provide the following methods:

- A constructor to make an empty set
- add(int x) to add x if it is not present
- remove(int x) to remove x if it is present
- print() to print all elements currently in the set

Exercise P21.10. Enhance the set class from Exercise P21.9 by supplying an iterator object that supports *only* the hasNext/next methods.

```
IntSetIterator iterator = mySet.iterator();
while (iterator.hasNext())
    System.out.println(iterator.next());
```

Note that the next method returns an int, not an object. For that reason, you cannot simply return the iterator of the tree set.

Exercise P21.11. Implement the *sieve of Eratosthenes:* a method for computing prime numbers, known to the ancient Greeks. Choose an n. This method will compute all prime numbers up to n. First insert all numbers from 2 to n into a set. Then erase all multiples of 2 (except 2); that is, 4, 6, 8, 10, 12, ... Erase all multiples of 3; that is, 6, 9, 12, 15, ... Go up to $\sqrt{n}$. The remaining numbers are all primes. Of course, you should use only the public interface of the IntSet data structure.

Exercise P21.12. Enhance the set class from Exercises 21.9 and 21.10 by supplying methods

```
IntSet union(IntSet other)
IntSet intersection(IntSet other)
```

that compute the union and intersection of two sets.

Exercise P21.13. Write a method of the BinarySearchTree class

```
Comparable smallest()
```

that returns the smallest element of a tree. You will also need to add a method to the Node class.

Exercise P21.14. Change the BinarySearchTree.print method to print the tree as a tree shape. You can print the tree sideways. Extra credit if you instead display the tree graphically, with the root node centered on the top.

Exercise P21.15. Implement methods that use preorder and postorder traversal to print the elements in a binary search tree.

Exercise P21.16. In the `BinarySearchTree` class, modify the `remove` method so that a node with two children is replaced by the largest child of the left subtree.

Exercise P21.17. Suppose an interface `Visitor` has a single method

```
void visit(Object obj)
```

Supply methods

```
void inOrder(Visitor v)
void preOrder(Visitor v)
void postOrder(Visitor v)
```

to the `BinarySearchTree` class. These methods should visit the tree nodes in the specified traversal order and apply the `visit` method to the data of the visited node.

Exercise P21.18. Apply Exercise P21.17 to compute the average value of the elements in a binary search tree filled with `Integer` objects. That is, supply an object of an appropriate class that implements the `Visitor` interface.

Exercise P21.19. Modify the implementation of the `MinHeap` class so that the parent and child index positions are computed directly, without calling helper methods.

Exercise P21.20. Modify the implementation of the `MinHeap` class so that the 0 element of the array is not wasted.

Exercise P21.21. Time the results of heapsort and merge sort. Which algorithm behaves better in practice? For best timing results, you should eliminate the helper methods that compute parent and child index values.

PROGRAMMING PROJECTS

Project 21.1. Implement a `BinaryTreeSet` class that uses a `TreeSet` to store its elements. You will need to implement an iterator that iterates through the nodes in sorted order. This iterator is somewhat complex, because sometimes you need to backtrack. You can either add a reference to the parent node in each `Node` object, or have your iterator object store a stack of the visited nodes.

Project 21.2. Implement an expression evaluator that uses a parser to build an expression tree, such as in Section 21.6. (Note that the resulting tree is a binary tree but not a binary search tree.) Then use postorder traversal to evaluate the expression, using a stack for the intermediate results.

Project 21.3. Program an animation of the heapsort algorithm, displaying the tree graphically and stopping after each call to `fixHeap`.

ANSWERS TO SELF-CHECK QUESTIONS

1. Efficient set implementations can quickly test whether a given element is a member of the set.

2. Sets do not have an ordering, so it doesn't make sense to add an element at a particular iterator position, or to traverse a set backwards.

3. A set stores elements. A map stores associations between keys and values.

4. The ordering does not matter, and you cannot have duplicates.

5. Yes, the hash set will work correctly. All elements will be inserted into a single bucket.

6. It locates the next bucket in the bucket array and points to its first element.

7. $31 \times 116 + 111 = 3707$.

8. 13.

9. In a tree, each node can have any number of children. In a binary tree, a node has at most two children. In a balanced binary tree, all nodes have approximately as many descendants to the left as to the right.

10. For example, Sarah. Any string between Romeo and Tom will do.

11. For both trees, the inorder traversal is 3 + 4 * 5.

12. No—for example, consider the children of +. Even without looking up the Unicode codes for 3, 4, and +, it is obvious that + isn't between 3 and 4.

13. When it is desirable to visit the set elements in sorted order.

14. No—it would never be able to tell two coins apart. Thus, it would think that all coins are duplicates of the first.

15. A priority queue is appropriate because we want to get the important events first, even if they have been inserted later.

16. Yes, but a binary search tree isn't almost filled, so there may be holes in the array. We could indicate the missing nodes with null elements.

17. Heapsort requires less storage because it doesn't need an auxiliary array.

18. The MinHeap wastes the 0 entry to make the formulas more intuitive. When sorting an array, we don't want to waste the 0 entry, so we adjust the formulas instead.

Generic Programming

CHAPTER GOALS

- To understand the objective of generic programming
- To be able to implement generic classes and methods
- To understand the execution of generic methods in the virtual machine
- To know the limitations of generic programming in Java
- To understand the relationship between generic types and inheritance
- To learn how to constrain type variables

Generic programming involves the design and implementation of data structures and algorithms that work for multiple types. You are already familiar with the generic ArrayList class that can be used to produce array lists of arbitrary types. In this chapter, you will learn how to implement your own generic classes.

Chapter Contents

22.1 Type Variables

Generic programming is the creation of programming constructs that can be used with many different types. For example, the Java library programmers who implemented the ArrayList class engaged in generic programming. As a result, you can form array lists that collect different types, such as ArrayList<String>, ArrayList<BankAccount>, and so on.

The LinkedList class that we implemented in Section 20.2 is also an example of generic programming—you can store objects of any class inside a LinkedList. However, that LinkedList class achieves genericity with a different mechanism. It is a single LinkedList class that stores values of type Object. You can, if you like, store a String and a BankAccount object into the same LinkedList.

> In Java, generic programming can be achieved with inheritance or with type variables.

Our LinkedList class implements genericity by using *inheritance*. It stores objects of any class that inherits from Object. In contrast, the ArrayList class uses *type variables* to achieve genericity—you need to specify the type of the objects that you want to store.

Note that only our LinkedList class of Chapter 20 uses inheritance. The standard Java library has a LinkedList class that uses type variables. In the next section, we will add type variables to our LinkedList class as well.

> A generic class has one or more type variables.

The ArrayList class is a *generic class:* it has been declared with a *type variable* E. The type variable denotes the element type:

```
public class ArrayList<E>
{
    public ArrayList() { . . . }
    public void add(E element) { . . . }
    . . .
}
```

Here, E is the name of a type variable, not a Java keyword. You could use another name, such as ElementType, instead of E. However, it is customary to use short, uppercase names for type parameters.

Type variables can be instantiated with class or interface types.

In order to use a generic class, you need to *instantiate* the type variable, that is, supply an actual type. You can supply any class or interface type, for example

```
ArrayList<BankAccount>
ArrayList<Measurable>
```

However, you cannot substitute any of the eight primitive types for a type variable. It would be an error to declare an ArrayList<double>. Use the corresponding wrapper class instead, such as ArrayList<Double>.

The type that you supply replaces the type variable in the interface of the class. For example, the add method for ArrayList<BankAccount> has the type variable E replaced with the type BankAccount:

```
public void add(BankAccount element)
```

Contrast that with the add method of our LinkedList class:

```
public void add(Object element)
```

The ArrayList methods are safer. It is impossible to add a String object into an ArrayList<BankAccount>, but you can add a String into a LinkedList that is intended to hold bank accounts.

```
ArrayList<BankAccount> accounts1 = new ArrayList<BankAccount>();
LinkedList accounts2 = new LinkedList(); // Should hold BankAccount objects
accounts1.add("my savings"); // Compile-time error
accounts2.add("my savings"); // Not detected at compile time
```

The latter will give you grief when some other part of the code retrieves the string, believing it to be a bank account:

```
BankAccount account = (BankAccount) accounts2.getFirst(); // Run-time error
```

Type variables make generic code safer and easier to read.

Code that uses the generic ArrayList class is also easier to read. When you spot an ArrayList<BankAccount>, you know right away that it must contain bank accounts. When you see a LinkedList, you have to study the code to find out what it contains.

In Chapters 20 and 21, we used inheritance to implement generic linked lists, hash tables, and binary trees, because you were already familiar with the concept of inheritance. Using type variables requires new syntax and additional techniques—those are the topic of this chapter.

SYNTAX 22.1 **Instantiating a Generic Class**

GenericClassName<*Type*$_1$, *Type*$_2$, . . .>

Example:

```
ArrayList<BankAccount>
HashMap<String, Integer>
```

Purpose:

To supply specific types for the type variables of a generic class

1. The standard library provides a class HashMap<K, V> with key type K and value type V. Declare a hash map that maps strings to integers.
2. The binary search tree class in Chapter 21 is an example of generic programming because you can use it with any classes that implement the Comparable interface. Does it achieve genericity through inheritance or type variables?

22.2 Implementing Generic Classes

In this section, you will learn how to implement your own generic classes. We will first start out with a very simple generic class that stores pairs of objects. Then we will turn the LinkedList class of Chapter 20 into a generic class.

Our first example for writing a generic class stores *pairs* of objects, each of which can have an arbitrary type. For example,

```
Pair<String, BankAccount> result
        = new Pair<String, BankAccount>("Harry Hacker", harrysChecking);
```

The getFirst and getSecond methods retrieve the first and second values of the pair.

```
String name = result.getFirst();
BankAccount account = result.getSecond();
```

This class can be useful when you implement a method that computes two values at the same time. A method cannot simultaneously return a String and a BankAccount, but it can return a single object of type Pair<String, BankAccount>.

The generic Pair class requires two type variables, one for the type of the first element and one for the type of the second element.

We need to give names to the type variables. It is considered good form to give short uppercase names for type variables, such as the following:

Type Variable Name	Meaning
E	Element type in a collection
K	Key type in a map
V	Value type in a map
T	General type
S, U	Additional general types

Type variables of a generic class follow the class name and are enclosed in angle brackets.

You place the type variables for a generic class after the class name, enclosed in angle brackets (< and >):

```
public class Pair<T, S>
```

When you define the fields and methods of the class, use the type variable T for the first element type and S for the second element type:

```
public class Pair<T, S>
{
   public Pair(T firstElement, S secondElement)
   {
      first = firstElement;
      second = secondElement;
   }
   public T getFirst() { return first; }
   public S getSecond() { return second; }

   private T first;
   private S second;
}
```

Use type variables for the types of generic fields, method parameters, and return values.

This completes the definition of the generic Pair class. It is now ready to use whenever you need to form a pair of two objects of arbitrary types.

As a second example, let us turn our linked list class into a generic class. This class only requires one type variable for the element type, which we will call E.

```
public class LinkedList<E>
```

In the case of the linked list, there is a slight complication. Unlike the Pair class, the LinkedList class does not store the elements in its instance fields. Instead, a linked list manages a sequence of nodes, and the nodes store the data. Our LinkedList class uses an inner class Node for the nodes. The Node class must be modified to express the fact that each node stores an element of type E.

```
public class LinkedList<E>
{
   . . .
   private Node first;

   private class Node
   {
      public E data;
      public Node next;
   }
}
```

The implementation of some of the methods requires local variables whose type is variable, for example:

```
public E removeFirst()
{
   if (first == null)
      throw new NoSuchElementException();
   E element = first.data;
   first = first.next;
   return element;
}
```

Overall, the process is straightforward. Use the type E whenever you receive, return, or store an element object. Complexities arise only when your data structure uses helper classes, such as the nodes and iterators in a linked list. If the helpers are inner classes, you need not do anything special. However, helper types that are defined *outside* the generic class need to become generic classes as well.

Following is the complete reimplementation of our LinkedList class, as a generic class with a type variable.

SYNTAX 22.2 Defining a Generic Class

accessSpecifier class *GenericClassName*<*TypeVariable*$_1$, *TypeVariable*$_2$, . . .>
{
    constructors
    methods
    fields
}

Example:

```
public class Pair<T, S>
{
    . . .
}
```

Purpose:

To define a generic class with methods and fields that depend on type variables

---

LinkedList.java

```
1   import java.util.NoSuchElementException;
2
3   /**
4       A linked list is a sequence of nodes with efficient
5       element insertion and removal. This class
6       contains a subset of the methods of the standard
7       java.util.LinkedList class.
8   */
9   public class LinkedList<E>
10  {
11      /**
12          Constructs an empty linked list.
13      */
14      public LinkedList()
15      {
16          first = null;
17      }
18
```

```
19    /**
20        Returns the first element in the linked list.
21        @return the first element in the linked list
22    */
23    public E getFirst()
24    {
25        if (first == null)
26            throw new NoSuchElementException();
27        return first.data;
28    }
29
30    /**
31        Removes the first element in the linked list.
32        @return the removed element
33    */
34    public E removeFirst()
35    {
36        if (first == null)
37            throw new NoSuchElementException();
38        E element = first.data;
39        first = first.next;
40        return element;
41    }
42
43    /**
44        Adds an element to the front of the linked list.
45        @param element the element to add
46    */
47    public void addFirst(E element)
48    {
49        Node newNode = new Node();
50        newNode.data = element;
51        newNode.next = first;
52        first = newNode;
53    }
54
55    /**
56        Returns an iterator for iterating through this list.
57        @return an iterator for iterating through this list
58    */
59    public ListIterator<E> listIterator()
60    {
61        return new LinkedListIterator();
62    }
63
64    private Node first;
65
66    private class Node
67    {
68        public E data;
69        public Node next;
70    }
71
```

```
72      private class LinkedListIterator implements ListIterator<E>
73      {
74         /**
75            Constructs an iterator that points to the front
76            of the linked list.
77         */
78         public LinkedListIterator()
79         {
80            position = null;
81            previous = null;
82         }
83
84         /**
85            Moves the iterator past the next element.
86            @return the traversed element
87         */
88         public E next()
89         {
90            if (!hasNext())
91               throw new NoSuchElementException();
92            previous = position; // Remember for remove
93
94            if (position == null)
95               position = first;
96            else
97               position = position.next;
98
99            return position.data;
100        }
101
102        /**
103           Tests if there is an element after the iterator
104           position.
105           @return true if there is an element after the iterator
106           position
107        */
108        public boolean hasNext()
109        {
110           if (position == null)
111              return first != null;
112           else
113              return position.next != null;
114        }
115
116        /**
117           Adds an element before the iterator position
118           and moves the iterator past the inserted element.
119           @param element the element to add
120        */
121        public void add(E element)
122        {
123           if (position == null)
124           {
```

```
125                    addFirst(element);
126                    position = first;
127                }
128                else
129                {
130                    Node newNode = new Node();
131                    newNode.data = element;
132                    newNode.next = position.next;
133                    position.next = newNode;
134                    position = newNode;
135                }
136                previous = position;
137            }
138
139            /**
140                Removes the last traversed element. This method may
141                only be called after a call to the next method.
142            */
143            public void remove()
144            {
145                if (previous == position)
146                    throw new IllegalStateException();
147
148                if (position == first)
149                {
150                    removeFirst();
151                }
152                else
153                {
154                    previous.next = position.next;
155                }
156                position = previous;
157            }
158
159            /**
160                Sets the last traversed element to a different
161                value.
162                @param element the element to set
163            */
164            public void set(E element)
165            {
166                if (position == null)
167                    throw new NoSuchElementException();
168                position.data = element;
169            }
170
171            private Node position;
172            private Node previous;
173        }
174    }
```

ListIterator.java

```java
1   /**
2       A list iterator allows access to a position in a linked list.
3       This interface contains a subset of the methods of the
4       standard java.util.ListIterator interface. The methods for
5       backward traversal are not included.
6   */
7   public interface ListIterator<E>
8   {
9       /**
10          Moves the iterator past the next element.
11          @return the traversed element
12      */
13      E next();
14
15      /**
16          Tests if there is an element after the iterator
17          position.
18          @return true if there is an element after the iterator
19          position
20      */
21      boolean hasNext();
22
23      /**
24          Adds an element before the iterator position
25          and moves the iterator past the inserted element.
26          @param element the element to add
27      */
28      void add(E element);
29
30      /**
31          Removes the last traversed element. This method may
32          only be called after a call to the next method.
33      */
34      void remove();
35
36      /**
37          Sets the last traversed element to a different
38          value.
39          @param element the element to set
40      */
41      void set(E element);
42  }
```

ListTester.java

```java
1   /**
2       A program that demonstrates the LinkedList class.
3   */
4   public class ListTester
5   {
```

```
 6      public static void main(String[] args)
 7      {
 8         LinkedList<String> staff = new LinkedList<String>();
 9         staff.addFirst("Tom");
10         staff.addFirst("Romeo");
11         staff.addFirst("Harry");
12         staff.addFirst("Dick");
13
14         // | in the comments indicates the iterator position
15
16         ListIterator<String> iterator = staff.listIterator(); // |DHRT
17         iterator.next(); // D|HRT
18         iterator.next(); // DH|RT
19
20         // Add more elements after second element
21
22         iterator.add("Juliet"); // DHJ|RT
23         iterator.add("Nina"); // DHJN|RT
24
25         iterator.next(); // DHJNR|T
26
27         // Remove last traversed element
28
29         iterator.remove(); // DHJN|T
30
31         // Print all elements
32
33         iterator = staff.listIterator();
34         while (iterator.hasNext())
35         {
36            String element = iterator.next();
37            System.out.println(element);
38         }
39      }
40   }
```

Output

```
Dick
Harry
Juliet
Nina
Tom
```

SELF CHECK

3. How would you use the generic Pair class to construct a pair of strings "Hello" and "World"?

4. What change was made to the ListIterator interface, and why was that change necessary?

22.3 Generic Methods

Generic methods can be defined inside ordinary and generic classes.

A generic method is a method with a type variable. You can think of it as a template for a set of methods that differ only by one or more types. One way of defining a generic method is by starting with a method that operates on a specific type. As an example, consider the following print method:

```
public class ArrayUtil
{
    /**
        Prints all elements in an array of strings.
        @param a the array to print
    */
    public static void print(String[] a)
    {
        for (String e : a)
            System.out.print(e + " ");
        System.out.println();
    }
    . . .
}
```

This method prints the elements in an array of *strings*. However, we may want to print an array of Rectangle objects instead. Of course, the same algorithm works for an array of any type.

Supply the type variables of a generic method between the modifiers and the method return type.

In order to make the method into a generic method, replace String with a type variable, say E, to denote the element type of the array. Add a type variable list, enclosed in angle brackets, between the modifiers (public static) and the return type (void):

```
public static <E> void print(E[] a)
{
    for (E e : a)
        System.out.print(e + " ");
    System.out.println();
}
```

When calling a generic method, you need not instantiate the type variables.

When you call the generic method, you need not specify which type to use for the type variable. (In this regard, generic methods differ from generic classes.) Simply call the method with appropriate parameters, and the compiler will match up the type variables with the parameter types. For example, consider this method call:

```
Rectangle[] rectangles = . . .;
ArrayUtil.print(rectangles);
```

The type of the rectangles parameter is Rectangle[], and the type of the parameter variable is E[]. The compiler deduces that E is Rectangle.

This particular generic method is a static method in an ordinary class. You can also define generic methods that are not static. You can even have generic methods in generic classes.

SYNTAX 22.3 Defining a Generic Method

modifiers <*TypeVariable₁*, *TypeVariable₂*, . . .> *returnType methodName(parameters)*
{
   body
}

Example:

```
public static <E> void print(E[] a)
{
    . . .
}
```

Purpose:

To define a generic method that depends on type variables

As with generic classes, you cannot replace type variables with primitive types. The generic `print` method can print arrays of any type *except* the eight primitive types. For example, you cannot use the generic `print` method to print an array of type `int[]`. That is not a major problem. Simply implement a `print(int[] a)` method in addition to the generic `print` method.

SELF CHECK

5. Exactly what does the generic `print` method print when you pass an array of `BankAccount` objects containing two bank accounts with zero balances?

6. Is the `getFirst` method of the `Pair` class a generic method?

22.4 Constraining Type Variables

Type variables can be constrained with bounds.

It is often necessary to specify what types can be used in a generic class or method. Consider a generic `min` method that finds the smallest element in an array list of objects. How can you find the smallest element when you know nothing about the element type? You need to have a mechanism for comparing array elements. One solution is to require that the elements belong to a type that implements the `Comparable` interface. In this situation, we need to *constrain* the type variable.

```
public static <E extends Comparable> E min(E[] a)
{
    E smallest = a[0];
    for (int i = 1; i < a.length; i++)
        if (a[i].compareTo(smallest) < 0) smallest = a[i];
    return smallest;
}
```

You can call min with a String[] array but not with a Rectangle[] array—the String class implements Comparable, but Rectangle does not.

The Comparable bound is necessary for calling the compareTo method. Had it been omitted, then the min method would not have compiled. It would have been illegal to call compareTo on a[i] if nothing is known about its type. (Actually, the Comparable interface is itself a generic type, but for simplicity we do not supply a type parameter. See Advanced Topic 22.1 for more information.)

Very occasionally, you need to supply two or more type bounds. Then you separate them with the & character, for example

```
<E extends Comparable & Cloneable>
```

The extends keyword, when applied to type variables, actually means "extends or implements". The bounds can be either classes or interfaces, and the type variable can be replaced with a class or interface type.

SELF CHECK

7. Declare a generic BinarySearchTree class with an appropriate type variable.

8. Modify the min method to compute the minimum of an array of elements that implements the Measurable interface of Chapter 11.

COMMON ERROR 22.1

Genericity and Inheritance

If SavingsAccount is a subclass of BankAccount, is ArrayList<SavingsAccount> a subclass of ArrayList<BankAccount>? Perhaps surprisingly, it is not. Inheritance of type parameters does not lead to inheritance of generic classes. There is no relationship between Array-List<SavingsAccount> and ArrayList<BankAccount>.

This restriction is necessary for type checking. Suppose it was possible to assign an Array-List<SavingsAccount> object to a variable of type ArrayList<BankAccount>:

```
ArrayList<SavingsAccount> savingsAccounts
    = new ArrayList<SavingsAccount>();
ArrayList<BankAccount> bankAccounts = savingsAccounts;
    // Not legal, but suppose it was
BankAccount harrysChecking = new CheckingAccount();
bankAccounts.add(harrysChecking); // OK—can add BankAccount object
```

But bankAccounts and savingsAccounts refer to the same array list! If the assignment was legal, we would be able to add a CheckingAccount into an ArrayList<SavingsAccount>.

In many situations, this limitation can be overcome by using wildcards—see Advanced Topic 22.1.

ADVANCED TOPIC 22.1

Wildcard Types

It is often necessary to formulate subtle constraints of type variables. Wildcard types were invented for this purpose. There are three kinds of wildcard types:

Name	Syntax	Meaning
Wildcard with lower bound	`? extends B`	Any subtype of B
Wildcard with upper bound	`? super B`	Any supertype of B
Unbounded wildcard	`?`	Any type

A wildcard type is a type that can remain unknown. For example, we can define the following method in the `LinkedList<E>` class:

```
public void addAll(LinkedList<? extends E> other)
{
   ListIterator<E> iter = other.listIterator();
   while (iter.hasNext()) add(iter.next());
}
```

The method adds all elements of `other` to the end of the linked list.

The `addAll` method doesn't require a specific type for the element type of `other`. Instead, it allows you to use any type that is a subtype of `E`. For example, you can use `addAll` to add a `LinkedList<SavingsAccount>` to a `LinkedList<BankAccount>`.

To see a wildcard with a `super` bound, have another look at the `min` method of the preceding section. Recall that `Comparable` is a generic interface; the type parameter of the `Comparable` interface specifies the parameter type of the `compareTo` method.

```
public interface Comparable<T>
{
   int compareTo(T other)
}
```

Therefore, we might want to specify a type bound:

```
public static <E extends Comparable<E>> E min(E[] a)
```

However, this bound is too restrictive. Suppose the `BankAccount` class implements `Comparable<BankAccount>`. Then the subclass `SavingsAccount` also implements `Comparable<BankAccount>` and *not* `Comparable<SavingsAccount>`. If you want to use the `min` method with a `SavingsAccount` array, then the type parameter of the `Comparable` interface should be *any supertype* of the array element type:

```
public static <E extends Comparable<? super E>> E min(E[] a)
```

Here is an example of an unbounded wildcard. The `Collections` class defines a method

```
static void reverse(List<?> list)
```

You can think of that declaration as a shorthand for

```
static void <T> reverse(List<T> list)
```

22.5 Raw Types

The virtual machine works with raw types, not with generic classes.

The raw type of a generic type is obtained by erasing the type variables.

The virtual machine that executes Java programs does not work with generic classes or methods. Instead, it uses *raw* types, in which the type variables are replaced with ordinary Java types. Each type variable is replaced with its bound, or with Object if it is not bounded.

The compiler *erases* the type variables when it compiles generic classes and methods. For example, the generic class Pair<T, S> turns into the following raw class:

```java
public class Pair
{
   public Pair(Object firstElement, Object secondElement)
   {
      first = firstElement;
      second = secondElement;
   }
   public Object getFirst() { return first; }
   public Object getSecond() { return second; }

   private Object first;
   private Object second;
}
```

As you can see, the type variables T and S have been replaced by Object. The result is an ordinary class.

The same process is applied to generic methods. After erasing the type parameter, the min method of the preceding section turns into an ordinary method:

```java
public static Comparable min(Comparable[] a)
{
   Comparable smallest = a[0];
   for (int i = 1; i < a.length; i++)
      if (a[i].compareTo(smallest) < 0) smallest = a[i];
   return smallest;
}
```

Knowing about raw types helps you understand limitations of Java generics. For example, you cannot replace type variables with primitive types. Erasure turns type variables into the bounds type, such as Object or Comparable. The resulting types can never hold values of primitive types.

To interface with legacy code, you can convert between generic and raw types.

Raw types are necessary when you interface with *legacy code* that was written before generics were added to the Java language. For example, if a legacy method has a parameter ArrayList (without a type variable), you can pass an ArrayList<String> or Array-List<BankAccount>. This is not completely safe—after all, the legacy method might insert an object of the wrong type. The compiler will issue a warning, but your program will compile and run.

9. What is the erasure of the print method in Section 22.3?
10. What is the raw type of the LinkedList<E> class in Section 22.2?

COMMON ERROR 22.2

Writing Code That Does Not Work After Types Are Erased

Generic classes and methods were added to Java several years after the language became successful. The language designers decided to use the type erasure mechanism because it makes it easy to interface generic code with legacy programs. As a result, you may run into some programming restrictions when you write generic code.

For example, you cannot construct new objects of a generic type. For example, the following method, which tries to fill an array with copies of default objects, would be wrong:

```
public static <E> void fillWithDefaults(E[] a)
{
    for (int i = 0; i < a.length; i++)
        a[i] = new E(); // ERROR
}
```

To see why this is a problem, carry out the type erasure process, as if you were the compiler:

```
public static void fillWithDefaults(Object[] a)
{
    for (int i = 0; i < a.length; i++)
        a[i] = new Object(); // Not useful
}
```

Of course, if you start out with a Rectangle[] array, you don't want it to be filled with Object instances. But that's what the code would do after erasing types.

In situations such as this one, the compiler will report an error. You then need to come up with another mechanism for solving your problem. In this particular example, you can supply a default object:

```
public static <E> void fillWithDefaults(E[] a, E defaultValue)
{
    for (int i = 0; i < a.length; i++)
        a[i] = defaultValue;
}
```

Similarly, you cannot construct an array of a generic type. Because an array construction expression new E[] would be erased to new Object[], the compiler disallows it.

Using Generic Types in a Static Context

You cannot use type variables to define static fields, static methods, or static inner classes. For example, the following would be illegal:

```
public class LinkedList<E>
{
   . . .
   private static E defaultValue; // ERROR
   public static List<E> replicate(E value, int n) { . . . } // ERROR
   private static class Node { public E data; public Node next; } // ERROR
}
```

In the case of static fields, this restriction is very sensible. After the generic types are erased, there is only a single field LinkedList.defaultValue, whereas the static field declaration gives the false impression that there is a separate field for each LinkedList<E>.

For static methods and inner classes, there is an easy workaround; simply add a type parameter:

```
public class LinkedList<E>
{
   . . .
   public static <T> List<T> replicate(T value, int n) { . . . } // OK
   private static class Node<T> { public T data; public Node<T> next; } // OK
}
```

CHAPTER SUMMARY

1. In Java, generic programming can be achieved with inheritance or with type variables.

2. A generic class has one or more type variables.

3. Type variables can be instantiated with class or interface types.

4. Type variables make generic code safer and easier to read.

5. Type variables of a generic class follow the class name and are enclosed in angle brackets.

6. Use type variables for the types of generic fields, method parameters, and return values.

7. Generic methods can be defined inside ordinary and generic classes.

8. Supply the type variables of a generic method between the modifiers and the method return type.

9. When calling a generic method, you need not instantiate the type variables.

10. Type variables can be constrained with bounds.

11. The virtual machine works with raw types, not with generic classes.

12. The raw type of a generic type is obtained by erasing the type variables.

13. To interface with legacy code, you can convert between generic and raw types.

REVIEW EXERCISES

Exercise R22.1. What is a type variable?

Exercise R22.2. What is the difference between a generic class and an ordinary class?

Exercise R22.3. What is the difference between a generic class and a generic method?

Exercise R22.4. Find an example of a non-static generic method in the standard Java library.

Exercise R22.5. Find four examples of a generic class with two type parameters in the standard Java library.

Exercise R22.6. Find an example of a generic class in the standard library that is not a collection class.

Exercise R22.7. Why is a bound required for the type variable T in the following method?

```
<T extends Comparable> int binarySearch(T[] a, T key)
```

Exercise R22.8. Why is a bound not required for the type variable E in the HashSet<E> class?

Exercise R22.9. What is an ArrayList<Pair<T, T>>?

Exercise R22.10. Explain the type bounds of the following method of the Collections class:

```
public static <T extends Comparable<? super T>> void sort(List<T> a)
```

Why doesn't T extends Comparable or T extends Comparable<T> suffice?

Exercise R22.11. What happens when you pass an ArrayList<String> to a method with parameter ArrayList? Try it out and explain.

Exercise R22.12. What happens when you pass an ArrayList<String> to a method with parameter ArrayList, and the method stores an object of type BankAccount into the array list? Try it out and explain.

Exercise R22.13. What is the result of the following test?

```
ArrayList<BankAccount> accounts = new ArrayList<BankAccount>();
if (accounts instanceof ArrayList<String>) . . .
```

Try it out and explain.

Exercise R22.14. If a class implements the generic Iterable interface, then you can use its objects in the "for each" loop—see Advanced Topic 20.1. Describe the needed modifications to the LinkedList<E> class of Section 22.2.

PROGRAMMING EXERCISES

Exercise P22.1. Modify the generic Pair class so that both values have the same type.

Exercise P22.2. Add a method swap to the Pair class of Exercise P22.1 that swaps the first and second elements of the pair.

Exercise P22.3. Implement a static generic method PairUtil.swap whose parameter is a Pair object, using the generic class defined in Section 22.2. The method should return a new pair, with the first and second element swapped.

Exercise P22.4. Write a static generic method PairUtil.minmax that computes the minimum and maximum elements of an array of type T and returns a pair containing the minimum and maximum value. Require that the array elements implement the Measurable interface of Chapter 11.

Exercise P22.5. Repeat the problem of Exercise P22.4, but require that the array elements implement the Comparable interface.

Exercise P22.6. Repeat the problem of Exercise P22.5, but refine the bound of the type variable to extend the generic Comparable type.

Exercise P22.7. Implement a generic version of the binary search algorithm.

Exercise P22.8. Implement a generic version of the merge sort algorithm.

Exercise P22.9. Implement a generic version of the BinarySearchTree class of Chapter 21.

Exercise P22.10. Turn the HashSet implementation of Chapter 21 into a generic class.

Exercise P22.11. Define a suitable hashCode method for the Pair class of Section 22.2 and implement a HashMap class, using a HashSet<Pair<K, V>>.

Exercise P22.12. Implement a generic version of the permutation generator in Section 18.2. Generate all permutations of a List<E>.

Exercise P22.13. Write a generic static method print that can print the elements of any object that implements the Iterable<E> interface. Place your method into an appropriate utility class.

PROGRAMMING PROJECTS

Project 22.1. Design and implement a generic version of the DataSet class of Chapter 11 that can be used to analyze data of any class that implements the Measurable interface. Make the Measurable interface generic as well. Supply an addAll method that lets you add all values from another data set with a compatible type. Supply a generic Measurer<T> interface to allow the analysis of data whose classes don't implement the Measurable type.

Project 22.2. Turn the PriorityQueue class of Chapter 21 into a generic class. As with the TreeSet class of the standard library, allow a Comparator to compare queue elements. If no comparator is supplied, assume that the element type implements the Comparable interface.

ANSWERS TO SELF-CHECK QUESTIONS

1. HashMap<String, Integer>
2. It uses inheritance.
3. new Pair<String, String>("Hello", "World")
4. ListIterator<E> is now a generic type. Its interface depends on the element type of the linked list.
5. The output depends on the definition of the toString method in the Bank-Account class.
6. No—the method has no type parameters. It is an ordinary method in a generic class.
7. public class BinarySearchTree<E extends Comparable>
8. ```
public static <E extends Measurable> E min(E[] a)
{
    E smallest = a[0];
    for (int i = 1; i < a.length; i++)
        if (a[i].getMeasure() < smallest.getMeasure())
            smallest = a[i];
    return smallest;
}
```
9. ```
public static void print(Object[] a)
{
    for (Object e : a)
        System.out.print(e + " ");
    System.out.println();
}
```
10. The LinkedList class of Chapter 20.

Multithreading

CHAPTER GOALS

- To understand how multiple threads can execute in parallel
- To learn how to implement threads
- To understand race conditions and deadlocks
- To be able to avoid corruption of shared objects by using locks and conditions
- To be able to use threads for programming animations

It is often useful for a program to carry out two or more tasks at the same time. For example, a web browser can load multiple images of a web page at the same time. Or an animation program can show moving figures, with separate tasks computing the positions of each separate figure.

In this chapter, you will see how you can implement this behavior by running tasks in multiple threads, and how you can ensure that the tasks access shared data in a controlled fashion.

CHAPTER CONTENTS

23.1 Running Threads

> A thread is a program unit that is executed independently of other parts of the program.

A thread is a program unit that is executed independently of other parts of the program. The Java virtual machine executes each thread for a short amount of time and then switches to another thread. This gives the illusion of executing the threads in parallel to each other. Actually, if a computer has multiple central processing units (CPUs), then some of the threads *can* run in parallel, one on each processor.

Running a thread is simple in Java—follow these steps:

1. Implement a class that implements the Runnable interface. That interface has a single method called run:

```
public interface Runnable
{
    void run();
}
```

2. Place the code for your task into the run method of your class.

```
public class MyRunnable implements Runnable
{
    public void run()
    {
        // Task statements go here
        . . .
    }
}
```

3. Create an object of your subclass.

```
Runnable r = new MyRunnable();
```

4. Construct a Thread object from the runnable object.

```
Thread t = new Thread(r);
```

5. Call the start method to start the thread.

```
t.start();
```

The start method of the Thread class starts a new thread that executes the run method of the associated Runnable object.

Let us look at a concrete example. We want to print ten greetings of "Hello, World!", one greeting every second. We will add a time stamp to each greeting to see when it is printed.

```
Thu Dec 28 23:12:03 PST 2004 Hello, World!
Thu Dec 28 23:12:04 PST 2004 Hello, World!
Thu Dec 28 23:12:05 PST 2004 Hello, World!
Thu Dec 28 23:12:06 PST 2004 Hello, World!
Thu Dec 28 23:12:07 PST 2004 Hello, World!
Thu Dec 28 23:12:08 PST 2004 Hello, World!
Thu Dec 28 23:12:09 PST 2004 Hello, World!
Thu Dec 28 23:12:10 PST 2004 Hello, World!
Thu Dec 28 23:12:11 PST 2004 Hello, World!
Thu Dec 28 23:12:12 PST 2004 Hello, World!
```

Using the instructions for creating a thread, define a class that implements the Runnable interface:

```
public class GreetingRunnable implements Runnable
{
   public GreetingRunnable(String aGreeting)
   {
      greeting = aGreeting;
   }

   public void run()
   {
      // Task statements go here
      . . .
   }
   // Fields used by the task statements
   private String greeting;
}
```

The run method should loop ten times through the following task actions:

- Print a time stamp.
- Print the greeting.
- Wait a second.

Get the time stamp by constructing an object of the java.util.Date class. Its default constructor produces a date that is set to the current date and time.

```
Date now = new Date();
System.out.println(now + " " + greeting);
```

The sleep method puts the current thread to sleep for a given number of milliseconds.

To wait a second, we use the static sleep method of the Thread class. The call

```
Thread.sleep(milliseconds)
```

puts the current thread to sleep for a given number of milliseconds. In our case, it should sleep for 1,000 milliseconds, or one second.

When a thread is interrupted, the most common response is to terminate the run method.

There is, however, one technical problem. Putting a thread to sleep is potentially risky—a thread might sleep for so long that it is no longer useful and should be terminated. As you will see in Section 23.2, to terminate a thread, you interrupt it. When a sleeping thread is interrupted, an InterruptedException is generated. You need to catch that exception in your run method and terminate the thread.

The simplest way to handle thread interruptions is to give your run method the following form:

```
public void run()
{
    try
    {
        Task statements
    }
    catch (InterruptedException exception)
    {
    }
    Clean up, if necessary
}
```

We follow that structure in our example. Here is the complete code for the runnable class:

File GreetingRunnable.java

```
1   import java.util.Date;
2
3   /**
4       A runnable that repeatedly prints a greeting.
5   */
6   public class GreetingRunnable implements Runnable
7   {
8       /**
9           Constructs the runnable object.
10          @param aGreeting the greeting to display
11      */
12      public GreetingRunnable(String aGreeting)
13      {
14          greeting = aGreeting;
15      }
16
17      public void run()
18      {
19          try
20          {
```

```
21              for (int i = 1; i <= REPETITIONS; i++)
22              {
23                  Date now = new Date();
24                  System.out.println(now + " " + greeting);
25                  Thread.sleep(DELAY);
26              }
27          }
28          catch (InterruptedException exception)
29          {
30          }
31      }
32
33      private String greeting;
34
35      private static final int REPETITIONS = 10;
36      private static final int DELAY = 1000;
37  }
```

To start a thread, first construct an object of the runnable class.

```
Runnable r = new GreetingRunnable("Hello, World!");
```

Then construct a thread and call the start method.

```
Thread t = new Thread(r);
t.start();
```

Now a new thread is started, executing the code in the run method of your runnable in parallel with any other threads in your program.

In the GreetingThreadTester program, we start two threads: one that prints "Hello, World!" and one that prints "Goodbye, World!"

File GreetingThreadTester.java

```
1  import java.util.Date;
2
3  /**
4      This program tests the greeting thread by running two
5      threads in parallel.
6  */
7  public class GreetingThreadTester
8  {
9      public static void main(String[] args)
10     {
11         GreetingRunnable r1 = new GreetingRunnable("Hello, World!");
12         GreetingRunnable r2 = new GreetingRunnable("Goodbye, World!");
13         Thread t1 = new Thread(r1);
14         Thread t2 = new Thread(r2);
15         t1.start();
16         t2.start();
17     }
18 }
```

```
Thu Dec 28 23:12:03 PST 2004 Hello, World!
Thu Dec 28 23:12:03 PST 2004 Goodbye, World!
Thu Dec 28 23:12:04 PST 2004 Hello, World!
Thu Dec 28 23:12:05 PST 2004 Hello, World!
Thu Dec 28 23:12:04 PST 2004 Goodbye, World!
Thu Dec 28 23:12:05 PST 2004 Goodbye, World!
Thu Dec 28 23:12:06 PST 2004 Hello, World!
Thu Dec 28 23:12:06 PST 2004 Goodbye, World!
Thu Dec 28 23:12:07 PST 2004 Hello, World!
Thu Dec 28 23:12:07 PST 2004 Goodbye, World!
Thu Dec 28 23:12:08 PST 2004 Hello, World!
Thu Dec 28 23:12:08 PST 2004 Goodbye, World!
Thu Dec 28 23:12:09 PST 2004 Hello, World!
Thu Dec 28 23:12:09 PST 2004 Goodbye, World!
Thu Dec 28 23:12:10 PST 2004 Hello, World!
Thu Dec 28 23:12:10 PST 2004 Goodbye, World!
Thu Dec 28 23:12:11 PST 2004 Goodbye, World!
Thu Dec 28 23:12:11 PST 2004 Hello, World!
Thu Dec 28 23:12:12 PST 2004 Goodbye, World!
Thu Dec 28 23:12:12 PST 2004 Hello, World!
```

> The thread scheduler runs each thread for a short amount of time, called a time slice.

Because both threads are running in parallel, the two message sets are interleaved. However, if you look closely, you will find that the two threads aren't *exactly* interleaved. Sometimes, the second thread seems to jump ahead of the first thread. This shows an important characteristic of threads. The thread scheduler gives no guarantee about the order in which threads are executed. Each thread runs for a short amount of time, called a *time slice*. Then the scheduler activates another thread. However, there will always be slight variations in running times, especially when calling operating system services (such as input and output). Thus, you should expect that the order in which each thread gains control is somewhat random.

SELF CHECK

1. What happens if you change the call to the sleep method in the run method to Thread.sleep(1)?

2. What would be the result of the program if the main method called

   ```
   r1.run();
   r2.run();
   ```

   instead of starting threads?

QUALITY TIP 23.1

Use the Runnable Interface

In Java, you can define the task statements of a thread in two ways. As you have seen already, you can place the statements into the run method of a class that implements the Runnable interface. Then you use an object of that class to construct a Thread object. You can also form a subclass of the Thread class, and place the task statements into the run method of your subclass:

```java
public class MyThread extends Thread
{
   public void run()
   {
      // Task statements go here
      . . .
   }
}
```

Then you construct an object of the subclass and call the start method:

```java
Thread t = new MyThread();
t.start();
```

This approach is marginally easier than using a Runnable, and it also seems quite intuitive. However, if a program needs a large number of threads, or if a program executes in a resource-constrained device, such as a cell phone, it can be quite expensive to construct a separate thread for each task. Advanced Topic 23.1 shows how to use a *thread pool* to overcome this problem. A thread pool uses a small number of threads to execute a larger number of runnables.

The Runnable interface is designed to encapsulate the concept of a sequence of statements that can run in parallel with other tasks, without equating it with the concept of a thread, a potentially expensive resource that is managed by the operating system.

ADVANCED TOPIC 23.1

Thread Pools

A program that creates a huge number of short-lived threads can be inefficient. Threads are managed by the operating system, and there is a space and run-time cost for each thread that is created. This cost can be reduced by using a *thread pool*. A thread pool creates a number of threads and keeps them alive. When you add a Runnable object to the thread pool, the next idle thread executes its run method.

For example, the following statements submit two runnables to a thread pool:

```java
Runnable r1 = new GreetingRunnable("Hello, World!");
Runnable r2 = new GreetingRunnable("Goodbye, World!");
ExecutorService pool = Executors.newFixedThreadPool(MAX_THREADS);
pool.execute(r1);
pool.execute(r2);
```

If many runnables are submitted for execution, then the pool may not have enough threads available. In that case, some runnables are placed in a queue until a thread is idle. As a result, the cost of creating threads is minimized. However, the runnables that are run by a particular thread are executed sequentially, not in parallel.

Thread pools are particularly important for server programs, such as database and web servers, that repeatedly execute requests from multiple clients. Rather than spawning a new thread for each request, the requests are implemented as runnable objects and submitted to a thread pool.

23.2 Terminating Threads

> A thread terminates when its run method terminates.

A thread terminates when the run method of the associated runnable object returns. This is the normal way of terminating a thread—implement the run method so that it returns when it determines that no more work needs to be done.

However, sometimes you need to terminate a running thread. For example, you may have several threads try to find a solution to a problem. As soon as the first one has succeeded, you may want to terminate the other ones. In the initial release of the Java library, the Thread class had a stop method to terminate a thread. However, that method is now *deprecated*—computer scientists have found that stopping a thread can lead to dangerous situations when multiple threads share objects. (We will discuss access to shared objects in Section 23.3.) Instead of simply stopping a thread, you should notify the thread that it should be terminated. The thread needs to cooperate, by releasing any resources that it is currently using and doing any other required cleanup. In other words, a thread should be in charge of terminating itself.

To notify a thread that it should clean up and terminate, you use the interrupt method.

```
t.interrupt();
```

> The run method can check whether its thread has been interrupted by calling the interrupted method.

This method does not actually cause the thread to terminate—it merely sets a boolean field in the thread data structure.

The run method can check whether that flag has been set, by calling the static interrupted method. In that case, it should do any necessary cleanup and exit. For example, the run method of the Greeting-Runnable could check for interruptions at the beginning of each loop iteration:

```
public void run()
{
   for (int i = 1;
        i <= REPETITIONS && !Thread.interrupted();
        i++)
   {
      Do work
   }
   Clean up
}
```

However, if a thread is sleeping, it can't execute code that checks for interruptions. Therefore, the sleep method is terminated with an InterruptedException whenever a sleeping thread is interrupted. The sleep method also throws an InterruptedException when it is called in a thread that is already interrupted. If your run method calls sleep in each loop iteration, simply use the InterruptedException to find out whether the thread is terminated. The easiest way to do that is to surround the entire work portion of the run method with a try block, like this:

```java
public void run()
{
   try
   {
      for (int i = 1; i <= REPETITIONS; i++)
      {
         Do work
      }
   }
   catch (InterruptedException exception)
   {
   }
   Clean up
}
```

Strictly speaking, there is nothing in the Java language specification that says that a thread must terminate when it is interrupted. It is entirely up to the thread what it does when it is interrupted. Interrupting is a general mechanism for getting the thread's attention, even when it is sleeping. However, in this chapter, we will always terminate a thread that is being interrupted.

SELF CHECK

3. Suppose a web browser uses multiple threads to load the images on a web page. Why should these threads be terminated when the user hits the "Back" button?

4. Consider the following runnable.

```java
public class MyRunnable implements Runnable
{
   public void run()
   {
      try
      {
         System.out.println(1);
         Thread.sleep(1000);
         System.out.println(2);
      }
      catch (InterruptedException exception)
      {
         System.out.println(3);
      }
      System.out.println(4);
   }
}
```

Suppose a thread with this runnable is started and immediately interrupted.

```
Thread t = new Thread(new MyRunnable());
t.start();
t.interrupt();
```

What output is produced?

QUALITY TIP 23.2

Check for Thread Interruptions in the run Method of a Thread

By convention, a thread should terminate itself (or at least act in some other well-defined way) when it is interrupted. You should implement your threads to follow this convention.

Simply put the thread action inside a try block that catches the InterruptedException. That exception occurs when your thread is interrupted while it is not running, for example inside a call to sleep. When you catch the exception, do any required cleanup and exit the run method.

Some programmers don't understand the purpose of the InterruptedException and, out of ignorance and desperation, muzzle it by surrounding only the call to sleep inside a try block.

```
public void run()
{
   while (. . .)
   {
      . . .
      try
      {
         Thread.sleep(delay);
      }
      catch (InterruptedException exception) {} // DON'T
      . . .
   }
}
```

Don't do that. If you do, users of your thread class can't get your thread's attention by interrupting it. It is just as easy to place the entire thread action inside a single try block. Then interrupting the thread terminates the thread action.

```
public void run()
{
   try
   {
      while (. . .)
      {
         . . .
         Thread.sleep(delay);
         . . .
      }
   }
   catch (InterruptedException exception) {} // OK
}
```

23.3 Race Conditions

When threads share access to a common object, they can conflict with each other. To demonstrate the problems that can arise, we will investigate a sample program in which multiple threads manipulate a bank account. Each thread repeatedly deposits or withdraws an amount of money, and then sleeps for a short amount of time. Here is the run method of the DepositRunnable class:

```java
public void run()
{
   try
   {
      for (int i = 1; i <= count; i++)
      {
         account.deposit(amount);
         Thread.sleep(DELAY);
      }
   }
   catch (InterruptedException exception)
   {
   }
}
```

The WithdrawRunnable class is similar—it withdraws money instead.

In our sample program, we construct a bank account that starts out with a zero balance. We create two threads:

- t1 deposits $100 into the bank account for 10 iterations.
- t2 withdraws $100 from the bank account for 10 iterations.

The deposit and withdraw methods of the BankAccount class have been modified to print messages that show what is happening. For example, here is the code for the deposit method:

```java
public void deposit(double amount)
{
   System.out.print("Depositing " + amount);
   double newBalance = balance + amount;
   System.out.println(", new balance is " + newBalance);
   balance = newBalance;
}
```

You can find the complete source code at the end of this section.

Normally, the program output looks somewhat like this:

```
Depositing 100.0, new balance is 100.0
Withdrawing 100.0, new balance is 0.0
Depositing 100.0, new balance is 100.0
Depositing 100.0, new balance is 200.0
Withdrawing 100.0, new balance is 100.0
. . .
Withdrawing 100.0, new balance is 0.0
```

In the end, the balance should be zero. However, when you run this program repeatedly, you may sometimes notice messed-up output, like this:

```
Depositing 100.0Withdrawing 100.0, new balance is 100.0
, new balance is -100.0
```

And if you look at the last line of the output, you will notice that the final balance is not always zero. Clearly, something problematic is happening.

You may have to try the program several times to see this effect.

Here is a scenario that explains how a problem can occur.

1. The first thread executes the lines

   ```
   System.out.print("Depositing " + amount);
   double newBalance = balance + amount;
   ```

   in the deposit method of the BankAccount class. The value of the balance field is still 0, and the value of the newBalance local variable is 100.

2. Immediately afterwards, the first thread reaches the end of its time slice, and the second thread gains control.

3. The second thread calls the withdraw method, which prints a message and withdraws $100 from the balance variable. It is now −100.

4. The second thread goes to sleep.

5. The original thread regains control and picks up where it was interrupted. It now executes the lines

   ```
   System.out.println(", new balance is " + newBalance);
   balance = newBalance;
   ```

   The value of balance is now 100 (see Figure 1).

Thus, not only are the messages interleaved, but the balance is wrong. The balance after a withdrawal and deposit should again be 0, not 100. Because the deposit method was interrupted, it used the *old* balance (before the withdrawal) to compute the value of its local newBalance variable. Later, when it was activated again, it used that newBalance value to overwrite the changed balance field.

> A race condition occurs if the effect of multiple threads on shared data depends on the order in which the threads are scheduled.

As you can see, each thread has its own local variables, but both threads share access to the balance instance field. That shared access creates a problem. This problem is often called a *race condition*. Both threads, in their race to complete their respective tasks, manipulate a shared field, and the end result depends on which of them happens to win the race.

You might argue that the reason for this problem is that we made it too easy to interrupt the balance computation. Suppose the code for the deposit method is reorganized like this:

```
public void deposit(double amount)
{
   balance = balance + amount;
   System.out.print("Depositing " + amount
         + ", new balance is " + balance);
}
```

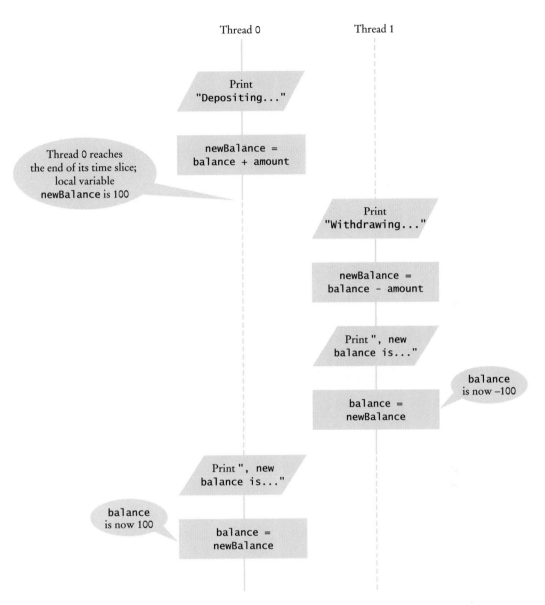

Figure 1 Corrupting the Contents of the balance Field

Suppose further that you make the same change in the withdraw method. If you run the resulting program, everything seems to be fine.

However, that is a *dangerous illusion*. The problem hasn't gone away; it has become much less frequent, and, therefore, more difficult to observe. It is still possible for the deposit method to reach the end of its time slice after it has computed the right-hand-side value

```
balance + amount
```

but before it performs the assignment

balance = *the right-hand-side value*

When the method regains control, it finally carries out the assignment, putting the wrong value into the balance field.

File BankAccountThreadTester.java

```
1   /**
2       This program runs two threads that deposit and withdraw
3       money from the same bank account.
4   */
5   public class BankAccountThreadTester
6   {
7      public static void main(String[] args)
8      {
9         BankAccount account = new BankAccount();
10        final double AMOUNT = 100;
11        final int REPETITIONS = 1000;
12
13        DepositRunnable d = new DepositRunnable(
14              account, AMOUNT, REPETITIONS);
15        WithdrawRunnable w = new WithdrawRunnable(
16              account, AMOUNT, REPETITIONS);
17
18        Thread t1 = new Thread(d);
19        Thread t2 = new Thread(w);
20
21        t1.start();
22        t2.start();
23     }
24  }
```

File DepositRunnable.java

```
1   /**
2       A deposit runnable makes periodic deposits to a bank account.
3   */
4   public class DepositRunnable implements Runnable
5   {
6      /**
7          Constructs a deposit runnable.
8          @param anAccount the account into which to deposit money
9          @param anAmount the amount to deposit in each repetition
10         @param aCount the number of repetitions
11      */
12     public DepositRunnable(BankAccount anAccount, double anAmount,
13           int aCount)
14     {
15        account = anAccount;
16        amount = anAmount;
17        count = aCount;
18     }
19
```

```
20      public void run()
21      {
22         try
23         {
24            for (int i = 1; i <= count; i++)
25            {
26               account.deposit(amount);
27               Thread.sleep(DELAY);
28            }
29         }
30         catch (InterruptedException exception) {}
31      }
32
33      private static final int DELAY = 1;
34      private BankAccount account;
35      private double amount;
36      private int count;
37 }
```

File WithdrawRunnable.java

```
1  /**
2      A withdraw runnable makes periodic withdrawals from a bank account.
3  */
4  public class WithdrawRunnable implements Runnable
5  {
6     /**
7         Constructs a withdraw runnable.
8         @param anAccount the account from which to withdraw money
9         @param anAmount the amount to deposit in each repetition
10        @param aCount the number of repetitions
11     */
12     public WithdrawRunnable(BankAccount anAccount, double anAmount,
13           int aCount)
14     {
15        account = anAccount;
16        amount = anAmount;
17        count = aCount;
18     }
19
20     public void run()
21     {
22        try
23        {
24           for (int i = 1; i <= count; i++)
25           {
26              account.withdraw(amount);
27              Thread.sleep(DELAY);
28           }
29        }
30        catch (InterruptedException exception) {}
31     }
32
```

```
33      private static final int DELAY = 1;
34      private BankAccount account;
35      private double amount;
36      private int count;
37  }
```

File BankAccount.java

```
1  /**
2      A bank account has a balance that can be changed by
3      deposits and withdrawals.
4  */
5  public class BankAccount
6  {
7      /**
8          Constructs a bank account with a zero balance.
9      */
10     public BankAccount()
11     {
12         balance = 0;
13     }
14
15     /**
16         Deposits money into the bank account.
17         @param amount the amount to deposit
18     */
19     public void deposit(double amount)
20     {
21         System.out.print("Depositing " + amount);
22         double newBalance = balance + amount;
23         System.out.println(", new balance is " + newBalance);
24         balance = newBalance;
25     }
26
27     /**
28         Withdraws money from the bank account.
29         @param amount the amount to withdraw
30     */
31     public void withdraw(double amount)
32     {
33         System.out.print("Withdrawing " + amount);
34         double newBalance = balance - amount;
35         System.out.println(", new balance is " + newBalance);
36         balance = newBalance;
37     }
38
39     /**
40         Gets the current balance of the bank account.
41         @return the current balance
42     */
43     public double getBalance()
44     {
45         return balance;
46     }
```

```
47
48     private double balance;
49 }
```

Output

```
Depositing 100.0, new balance is 100.0
Withdrawing 100.0, new balance is 0.0
Depositing 100.0, new balance is 100.0
Withdrawing 100.0, new balance is 0.0
  . . .
Withdrawing 100.0, new balance is 400.0
Depositing 100.0, new balance is 500.0
Withdrawing 100.0, new balance is 400.0
Withdrawing 100.0, new balance is 300.0
```

SELF CHECK

5. Give a scenario in which a race condition causes the bank balance to be −100 after one iteration of a deposit thread and a withdraw thread.

6. Suppose two threads simultaneously insert objects into a linked list. Using the implementation in Chapter 20, explain how the list can be damaged in the process.

23.4 Synchronizing Object Access

To solve problems such as the one that you observed in the preceding section, use a *lock object*. The lock object is used to control the threads that want to manipulate a shared resource.

The Java library defines a Lock interface and several classes that implement this interface. The ReentrantLock class is the most commonly used lock class, and the only one that we cover in this book. (Locks are a feature of Java version 5.0. Earlier versions of Java have a lower-level facility for thread synchronization—see Advanced Topic 23.2)

Typically, a lock object is added to a class whose methods access shared resources, like this:

```
public class BankAccount
{
   public BankAccount()
   {
      balanceChangeLock = new ReentrantLock();
      . . .
   }
   . . .
   private Lock balanceChangeLock;
}
```

All code that manipulates the shared resource is surrounded by calls to lock and unlock the lock object:

```
balanceChangeLock.lock();
Code that manipulates the shared resource
balanceChangeLock.unlock();
```

However, this sequence of statements has a potential flaw. If the code between the calls to lock and unlock throws an exception, the call to unlock never happens. This is a serious problem. After an exception, the current thread continues to hold the lock, and no other thread can acquire it. To overcome this problem, place the call to unlock into a finally clause:

```
balanceChangeLock.lock();
try
{
    Code that manipulates the shared resource
}
finally
{
    balanceChangeLock.unlock();
}
```

For example, here is the code for the deposit method:

```
public void deposit(double amount)
{
    balanceChangeLock.lock();
    try
    {
        System.out.print("Depositing " + amount);
        double newBalance = balance + amount;
        System.out.println(", new balance is " + newBalance);
        balance = newBalance;
    }
    finally
    {
        balanceChangeLock.unlock();
    }
}
```

By calling the lock method, a thread acquires a Lock object. Then no other thread can acquire the lock until the first thread releases the lock.

When a thread calls the lock method, it *owns the lock* until it calls the unlock method. If a thread calls lock while another thread owns the lock, it is temporarily deactivated. The thread scheduler periodically reactivates such a thread so that it can again try to acquire the lock. If the lock is still unavailable, the thread is again deactivated. Eventually, when the lock is available because the original thread unlocked it, the waiting thread can acquire the lock.

One way to visualize this behavior is to imagine that the lock object is the lock of an old-fashioned telephone booth and the threads are people wanting to make telephone calls (see Figure 2). The telephone booth can accommodate only one person at one time. If the booth is empty, then the first person wanting to make a call goes inside and closes the door. If another person wants to make a call and finds the booth occupied, then the second person needs to wait until the first person leaves

Figure 2   Visualizing Object Locks

the booth. If multiple people want to gain access to the telephone booth, they all wait outside. They don't necessarily form an orderly queue; a randomly chosen person may gain access when the telephone booth becomes available again. (Some computer programmers think of a rest-room stall instead of a telephone booth in order to visualize object locks. However, in the interest of good taste, we will not develop that analogy any further.)

With the ReentrantLock class, a thread can call the lock method on a lock object that it already owns. This can happen if one method calls another, and both start by locking the same object. The thread gives up ownership if the unlock method has been called as often as the lock method.

By surrounding the code in both the deposit and withdraw methods with lock and unlock calls, we ensure that our program will always run correctly. Only one thread at a time can execute either method on a given object. Whenever a thread acquires the lock, it is guaranteed to execute the method to completion before the other thread gets a chance to modify the balance of the same bank account object.

SELF CHECK

7. If you construct two BankAccount objects, how many lock objects are created?
8. What happens if we omit the call unlock at the end of the deposit method?

23.5 Avoiding Deadlocks

A deadlock occurs if no thread can proceed because each thread is waiting for another to do some work first.

You can use lock objects to ensure that shared data are in a consistent state when several threads access them. However, locks can lead to another problem. It can happen that one thread acquires a lock and then waits for another thread to do some essential work. If that other thread is currently waiting to acquire the same lock, then neither of the two threads can proceed. Such a situation is called a *deadlock* or *deadly embrace*. Let's look at an example.

Suppose we want to disallow negative bank balances in our program. Here's a naive way of doing that. In the run method of the WithdrawRunnable class, we can check the balance before withdrawing money:

```
if (account.getBalance() >= amount)
   account.withdraw(amount);
```

This works if there is only a single thread running that withdraws money. But suppose we have multiple threads that withdraw money. Then the time slice of the current thread may expire after the check account.getBalance() >= amount passes, but before the withdraw method is called. If in the interim another thread withdraws more money, then the test was useless, and we still have a negative balance.

Clearly, the test should be moved inside the withdraw method. That ensures that the test for sufficient funds and the actual withdrawal cannot be separated. Thus, the withdraw method could look like this:

```
public void withdraw(double amount)
{
   balanceChangeLock.lock();
   try
   {
      while (balance < amount)
         Wait for the balance to grow
      . . .
   }
   finally
   {
      balanceChangeLock.unlock();
   }
}
```

But how can we wait for the balance to grow? We can't simply call sleep inside the withdraw method. If a thread sleeps after acquiring a lock, it blocks all other threads that want to use the same lock. In particular, no other thread can successfully execute the deposit method. Other threads will call deposit, but they will simply be blocked until the withdraw method exits. But the withdraw method doesn't exit until it has funds available. This is the deadlock situation that we mentioned earlier.

To overcome this problem, we use a *condition object*. Condition objects allow a thread to temporarily release a lock, so that another thread can proceed, and to regain the lock at a later time.

In the telephone booth analogy, suppose that the coin reservoir of the telephone is completely filled, so that no further calls can be made until a service technician removes the coins. You don't want the person in the booth to go to sleep with the door closed. Instead, think of the person leaving the booth temporarily. That gives another person (hopefully a service technician) a chance to enter the booth.

Each condition object belongs to a specific lock object. You obtain a condition object with the newCondition method of the Lock interface. For example,

```
public class BankAccount
{
   public BankAccount()
   {
      balanceChangeLock = new ReentrantLock();
      sufficientFundsCondition = balanceChangeLock.newCondition();
      . . .
   }
   . . .
   private Lock balanceChangeLock;
   private Condition sufficientFundsCondition;
}
```

It is customary to give the condition object a name that describes the condition that you want to test (such as "sufficient funds"). You need to implement an appropriate test. As long as the test is not fulfilled, call the await method on the condition object:

```
public void withdraw(double amount)
{
   balanceChangeLock.lock();
   try
   {
      while (balance < amount)
         sufficientFundsCondition.await();
      . . .
   }
   finally
   {
      balanceChangeLock.unlock();
   }
}
```

> Calling await on a condition object makes the current thread wait and allows another thread to acquire the lock object.

When a thread calls await, it is not simply deactivated in the same way as a thread that reaches the end of its time slice. Instead, it is in a blocked state, and it will not be activated by the thread scheduler until it is unblocked. To unblock, another thread must execute the signalAll method *on the same condition object*. The signalAll method unblocks all threads waiting on the condition. They can then compete with all other threads that are waiting for the lock object. Eventually, one of them will gain access to the lock, and it will exit from the await method.

In our situation, the deposit method calls signalAll:

```
public void deposit(double amount)
{
```

```
balanceChangeLock.lock();
try
{
    . . .
    sufficientFundsCondition.signalAll();
}
finally
{
    balanceChangeLock.unlock();
}
}
```

A waiting thread is blocked until another thread calls `signalAll` or `signal` on the condition object for which the thread is waiting.

The call to `signalAll` notifies the waiting threads that sufficient funds *may be* available, and that it is worth testing the loop condition again.

In the telephone booth analogy, the thread calling `await` corresponds to the person who enters the booth and finds that the phone doesn't work. That person then leaves the booth and waits outside, depressed, doing absolutely nothing, even as other people enter and leave the booth. The person knows it is pointless to try again. At some point, a service technician enters the booth, empties the coin reservoir, and shouts a signal. Now all the waiting people stop being depressed and again compete for the telephone booth.

There is also a `signal` method, which randomly picks just one thread that is waiting on the object and unblocks it. The `signal` method can be more efficient, but it is useful only if you know that *every* waiting thread can actually proceed. In general, you don't know that, and `signal` can lead to deadlocks. For that reason, we recommend that you always call `signalAll`.

The `await` method can throw an `InterruptedException`. The `withdraw` method propagates that exception, because it has no way of knowing what the thread that calls the `withdraw` method wants to do if it is interrupted.

With the calls to `await` and `signalAll` in the `withdraw` and `deposit` methods, we can launch any number of withdrawal and deposit threads without a deadlock. If you run the sample program, you will note that all transactions are carried out without ever reaching a negative balance. Here is a sample program with four threads: two for withdrawals and two for deposits.

File BankAccountThreadTester.java

```
1  /**
2      This program runs four threads that deposit and withdraw
3      money from the same bank account.
4  */
5  public class BankAccountThreadTester
6  {
7     public static void main(String[] args)
8     {
9        BankAccount account = new BankAccount();
10       final double AMOUNT = 100;
11       final int REPETITIONS = 1000;
12
```

```
13        DepositRunnable d1 = new DepositRunnable(
14              account, AMOUNT, REPETITIONS);
15        WithdrawRunnable w1 = new WithdrawRunnable(
16              account, AMOUNT, REPETITIONS);
17        DepositRunnable d2 = new DepositRunnable(
18              account, AMOUNT, REPETITIONS);
19        WithdrawRunnable w2 = new WithdrawRunnable(account,
20              AMOUNT, REPETITIONS);
21
22        Thread t1 = new Thread(d1);
23        Thread t2 = new Thread(w1);
24        Thread t3 = new Thread(d2);
25        Thread t4 = new Thread(w2);
26
27        t1.start();
28        t2.start();
29        t3.start();
30        t4.start();
31     }
32  }
```

File BankAccount.java

```
1   import java.util.concurrent.locks.Condition;
2   import java.util.concurrent.locks.Lock;
3   import java.util.concurrent.locks.ReentrantLock;
4
5   /**
6       A bank account has a balance that can be changed by
7       deposits and withdrawals.
8   */
9   public class BankAccount
10  {
11     /**
12         Constructs a bank account with a zero balance.
13     */
14     public BankAccount()
15     {
16        balance = 0;
17        balanceChangeLock = new ReentrantLock();
18        sufficientFundsCondition = balanceChangeLock.newCondition();
19     }
20
21     /**
22         Deposits money into the bank account.
23         @param amount the amount to deposit
24     */
25     public void deposit(double amount)
26     {
27        balanceChangeLock.lock();
28        try
29        {
30           System.out.print("Depositing " + amount);
31           double newBalance = balance + amount;
```

```
32          System.out.println(", new balance is " + newBalance);
33          balance = newBalance;
34          sufficientFundsCondition.signalAll();
35       }
36       finally
37       {
38          balanceChangeLock.unlock();
39       }
40    }
41
42    /**
43       Withdraws money from the bank account.
44       @param amount the amount to withdraw
45    */
46    public void withdraw(double amount)
47          throws InterruptedException
48    {
49       balanceChangeLock.lock();
50       try
51       {
52          while (balance < amount)
53             sufficientFundsCondition.await();
54          System.out.print("Withdrawing " + amount);
55          double newBalance = balance - amount;
56          System.out.println(", new balance is " + newBalance);
57          balance = newBalance;
58       }
59       finally
60       {
61          balanceChangeLock.unlock();
62       }
63    }
64
65    /**
66       Gets the current balance of the bank account.
67       @return the current balance
68    */
69    public double getBalance()
70    {
71       return balance;
72    }
73
74    private double balance;
75    private Lock balanceChangeLock;
76    private Condition sufficientFundsCondition;
77 }
```

Output

```
Depositing 100.0, new balance is 100.0
Withdrawing 100.0, new balance is 0.0
Depositing 100.0, new balance is 100.0
Depositing 100.0, new balance is 200.0
. . .
Withdrawing 100.0, new balance is 100.0
Depositing 100.0, new balance is 200.0
Withdrawing 100.0, new balance is 100.0
Withdrawing 100.0, new balance is 0.0
```

SELF CHECK

9. What is the essential difference between calling `sleep` and `await`?

10. Why is the `sufficientFundsCondition` object a field of the `BankAccount` class and not a local variable of the `withdraw` and `deposit` methods?

COMMON ERROR 23.1

Calling `await` Without Calling `signalAll`

It is intuitively clear when to call `await`. If a thread finds out that it can't do its job, it has to wait. But once a thread has called `await`, it temporarily gives up all hope and doesn't try again until some other thread calls `signalAll` on the condition object for which the thread is waiting. In the telephone booth analogy, if the service technician who empties the coin reservoir doesn't notify the waiting people, they'll wait forever.

A common error is to have threads call `await` without matching calls to `signalAll` by other threads. Whenever you call `await`, ask yourself which call to `signalAll` will signal your waiting thread.

COMMON ERROR 23.2

Calling `signalAll` Without Locking the Object

The thread that calls `signalAll` must own the lock that belongs to the condition object on which `signalAll` is called. Otherwise, an `IllegalMonitorStateException` is thrown.

In the telephone booth analogy, the service technician must shout the signal while *inside* the telephone booth after emptying the coin reservoir.

In practice, this should not be a problem. Remember that `signalAll` is called by a thread that has just changed the state of some shared data in a way that may benefit waiting threads. That change should be protected by a lock in any case. As long as you use a lock to protect all access to shared data, and you are in the habit of calling `signalAll` after every beneficial change, you won't run into problems. But if you use `signalAll` in a haphazard way, you may encounter the `IllegalMonitorStateException`.

ADVANCED TOPIC 23.2

Object Locks and Synchronized Methods

The Lock and Condition classes were added in Java version 5.0. They overcome limitations of the thread synchronization mechanism in earlier Java versions. In this note, we discuss that classic mechanism.

Every Java object has one built-in lock and one built-in condition variable. The lock works in the same way as a ReentrantLock object. However, to acquire the lock, you call a *synchronized method*.

You simply tag all methods that contain thread-sensitive code (such as the deposit and withdraw methods of the BankAccount class) with the synchronized keyword.

```java
public class BankAccount
{
   public synchronized void deposit(double amount)
   {
      System.out.print("Depositing " + amount);
      double newBalance = balance + amount;
      System.out.println(", new balance is " + newBalance);
      balance = newBalance;
   }

   public synchronized void withdraw(double amount)
   {
      . . .
   }

   . . .
}
```

When a thread calls a synchronized method on a BankAccount object, it owns the lock of that object until it returns from the method and thereby unlocks the object. When an object is locked by one thread, no other thread can enter a synchronized method for that object. When another thread makes a call to a synchronized method for that object, the other thread is automatically deactivated, and it needs to wait until the first thread has unlocked the object again.

In other words, the synchronized keyword automatically implements the lock/try/finally/unlock idiom for the built-in lock.

The object lock has a single condition variable that you manipulate with the wait, notifyAll, and notify methods of the Object class. If you call x.wait(), the current thread is added to the set of threads that is waiting for the condition of the object x. Most commonly, you will call wait(), which makes the current thread wait on this. For example,

```java
public synchronized void withdraw(double amount)
      throws InterruptedException
{
   while (balance < amount)
      wait();
   . . .
}
```

The call notifyAll() unblocks all threads that are waiting for this:

```
public synchronized void deposit(double amount)
{
    . . .
    notifyAll();
}
```

This classic mechanism is undeniably simpler than using explicit locks and condition variables. However, there are limitations. Each object lock has one condition variable, and you can't test whether another thread holds the lock. If these limitations are not a problem, by all means, go ahead and use the synchronized keyword. If you need more control over threads, the Lock and Condition interfaces give you additional flexibility.

ADVANCED TOPIC 23.3

The Java Memory Model

In a computer with multiple CPUs, you have to be particularly careful when multiple threads access shared data. Since modern processors are quite a bit faster than RAM memory, each CPU has its own *memory cache* that stores copies of frequently used memory locations. If a thread changes shared data, another thread may not see the change until both processor caches are synchronized. The same effect can happen even on a computer with a single CPU—occasionally, memory values are cached in CPU registers.

The Java language specification contains a set of rules, called the *memory model*, that describes under which circumstances the virtual machine must ensure that changes to shared data are visible in other threads. One of the rules states the following:

- If a thread changes shared data and then releases a lock, and another thread acquires the same lock and reads the same data, then it is guaranteed to see the changed data.

However, if the first thread does not release a lock, then the virtual machine is not required to write cached data back to memory. Similarly, if the second thread does not acquire the lock, the virtual machine is not required to refresh its cache from memory.

Thus, you should always use locks or synchronized methods when you access data that is shared among multiple threads, even if you are not concerned about race conditions.

23.6 Case Study: Algorithm Animation

One popular use for thread programming is animation. A program that displays an animation shows different objects moving or changing in some way as time progresses. This is often achieved by launching one or more threads that compute how parts of the animation change.

You can use the Swing Timer class for simple animations without having to do any thread programming—see Exercise P23.8 for an example. However, more advanced animations are best implemented with threads.

In this section, you will see a particular kind of animation, namely the visualization of the steps of an algorithm. Algorithm animation is an excellent technique for gaining a better understanding of how an algorithm works. Many algorithms can be animated—type "Java algorithm animation" into your favorite web search engine, and you'll find lots of links to web pages with animations of various algorithms.

All algorithm animations have a similar structure. The algorithm runs in a separate thread that periodically updates an image of the current state of the algorithm and then pauses so that the user can view the image. After a short amount of time, the algorithm thread wakes up again and runs to the next point of interest in the algorithm. It then updates the image and pauses again. This sequence is repeated until the algorithm has finished.

Let's take the selection sort algorithm of Chapter 19 as an example. That algorithm sorts an array of values. It first finds the smallest element, by inspecting all elements in the array, and bringing the smallest element to the leftmost position. It then finds the smallest element among the remaining elements and brings it into the second position. It keeps going in that way. As the algorithm progresses, the sorted part of the array grows.

How can you visualize this algorithm? It is useful to show the part of the array that is already sorted in a different color. Also, we want to show how each step of the algorithm inspects another element in the unsorted part. That demonstrates why the selection sort algorithm is so slow—it first inspects all elements of the array, then all but one, and so on. If the array has n elements, the algorithm inspects $n + (n-1) + (n-2) + \cdots = n(n-1)/2 = O(n^2)$ elements. To demonstrate that, we mark the currently visited element in red.

Thus, the algorithm state is described by three items:

- The array of values
- The size of the already sorted area
- The currently marked element

This state is accessed by two threads: the thread that sorts the array and the thread that repaints the frame. We use a lock to synchronize access to the shared state.

Finally, we add a component instance field to the algorithm class and augment the constructor to set it. That instance field is needed for repainting the component and finding out the dimensions of the component when drawing the algorithm state.

```
public class SelectionSorter
{
   public SelectionSorter(int[] anArray, JComponent aComponent)
   {
      a = anArray;
      sortStateLock = new ReentrantLock();
      component = aComponent;
   }
   . . .
   private JComponent component;
}
```

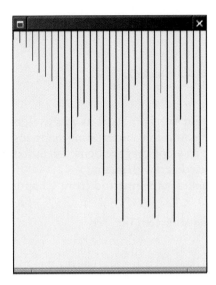

Figure 3
A Step in the Animation of
the Selection Sort Algorithm

At each point of interest, the algorithm needs to pause so that the user can admire
the graphical output. Supply the pause method shown below, and call it at various
places in the algorithm. The pause method repaints the component and sleeps for a
small delay that is proportional to the number of steps involved.

```
public void pause(int steps)
      throws InterruptedException
{
   component.repaint();
   Thread.sleep(steps * DELAY);
}
```

We add a draw method to the algorithm class that can draw the current state of the
data structure, with the items of special interest highlighted. The draw method is
specific to the particular algorithm. This draw method draws the array elements as a
sequence of sticks in different colors. The already sorted portion is blue, the marked
position is red, and the remainder is black (see Figure 3).

```
public void draw(Graphics2D g2)
{
   sortStateLock.lock();
   try
   {
      int deltaX = component.getWidth() / a.length;
      for (int i = 0; i < a.length; i++)
      {
         if (i == markedPosition)
            g2.setColor(Color.RED);
         else if (i <= alreadySorted)
            g2.setColor(Color.BLUE);
         else
            g2.setColor(Color.BLACK);
         g2.draw(new Line2D.Double(i * deltaX, 0,
               i * deltaX, a[i]));
```

```
        }
    }
    finally
    {
        sortStateLock.unlock();
    }
}
```

You need to update the special positions as the algorithm progresses and pause the animation whenever something interesting happens. The pause should be proportional to the number of steps that are being executed. For a sorting algorithm, pause one unit for each visited array element.

Here is the `minimumPosition` method from Chapter 19, before the animation code is inserted.

```
public int minimumPosition(int from)
{
    int minPos = from;
    for (int i = from + 1; i < a.length; i++)
        if (a[i] < a[minPos]) minPos = i;
    return minPos;
}
```

After each iteration of the `for` loop, update the marked position of the algorithm state; then pause the program. To measure the cost of each step fairly, pause for two units of time, because two array elements were inspected.

```
public int minimumPosition(int from)
    throws InterruptedException
{
    int minPos = from;
    for (int i = from + 1; i < a.length; i++)
    {
        sortStateLock.lock();
        try
        {
            if (a[i] < a[minPos]) minPos = i;
            markedPosition = i;
        }
        finally
        {
            sortStateLock.unlock();
        }
        pause(2);
    }
    return minPos;
}
```

The sort method is augmented in the same way. You will find the code at the end of this section. This concludes the modification of the algorithm class. Let us now turn to the component class.

The component's `paintComponent` method calls the `draw` method of the algorithm object.

```
public class SelectionSortComponent extends JComponent
{
   public void paintComponent(Graphics g)
   {
      if (sorter == null) return;
      Graphics2D g2 = (Graphics2D) g;
      sorter.draw(g2);
   }

   . . .
   private SelectionSorter sorter;
}
```

The `startAnimation` method constructs a `SelectionSorter` object, which supplies a new array and the `this` reference to the component that displays the sorted values. Then the method constructs a thread that calls the sorter's sort method.

```
public void startAnimation()
{
   int[] values = ArrayUtil.randomIntArray(30, 300);
   sorter = new SelectionSorter(values, this);

   class AnimationRunnable implements Runnable
   {
      public void run()
      {
         try
         {
            sorter.sort();
         }
         catch (InterruptedException exception)
         {
         }
      }
   }

   Runnable r = new AnimationRunnable();
   Thread t = new Thread(r);
   t.start();
}
```

The class for the program that displays the animation is at the end of this section. Run the program and the animation starts.

Exercise P23.10 asks you to animate the merge sort algorithm of Chapter 19. If you do that exercise, then start both programs and run them in parallel to see which algorithm is faster. Actually, you may find the result surprising. If you build fair delays into the merge sort animation to account for the copying from and to the temporary array, you will find that it doesn't perform all that well for small arrays. But if you increase the array size, then the advantage of the merge sort algorithm becomes clear.

File SelectionSortViewer.java

```java
1   import java.awt.BorderLayout;
2   import javax.swing.JButton;
3   import javax.swing.JFrame;
4
5   public class SelectionSortViewer
6   {
7      public static void main(String[] args)
8      {
9         JFrame frame = new JFrame();
10
11        final int FRAME_WIDTH = 300;
12        final int FRAME_HEIGHT = 400;
13
14        frame.setSize(FRAME_WIDTH, FRAME_HEIGHT);
15        frame.setDefaultCloseOperation(JFrame.EXIT_ON_CLOSE);
16
17        final SelectionSortComponent component
18              = new SelectionSortComponent();
19        frame.add(component, BorderLayout.CENTER);
20
21        frame.setVisible(true);
22        component.startAnimation();
23     }
24  }
```

File SelectionSortComponent.java

```java
1   import java.awt.Graphics;
2   import java.awt.Graphics2D;
3   import javax.swing.JComponent;
4
5   /**
6      A component that displays the current state of the selection sort algorithm.
7   */
8   public class SelectionSortComponent extends JComponent
9   {
10     /**
11        Constructs the component.
12     */
13     public SelectionSortComponent()
14     {
15        int[] values = ArrayUtil.randomIntArray(30, 300);
16        sorter = new SelectionSorter(values, this);
17     }
18
19     public void paintComponent(Graphics g)
20     {
21        Graphics2D g2 = (Graphics2D)g;
22        sorter.draw(g2);
23     }
24
```

```
25    /**
26       Starts a new animation thread.
27    */
28    public void startAnimation()
29    {
30       class AnimationRunnable implements Runnable
31       {
32          public void run()
33          {
34             try
35             {
36                sorter.sort();
37             }
38             catch (InterruptedException exception)
39             {
40             }
41          }
42       }
43
44       Runnable r = new AnimationRunnable();
45       Thread t = new Thread(r);
46       t.start();
47    }
48
49    private SelectionSorter sorter;
50 }
```

File SelectionSorter.java

```
1  import java.awt.Color;
2  import java.awt.Graphics2D;
3  import java.awt.geom.Line2D;
4  import java.util.concurrent.locks.Lock;
5  import java.util.concurrent.locks.ReentrantLock;
6  import javax.swing.JComponent;
7
8  /**
9     This class sorts an array, using the selection sort
10    algorithm.
11 */
12 public class SelectionSorter
13 {
14    /**
15       Constructs a selection sorter.
16       @param anArray the array to sort
17       @param aComponent the component to be repainted when the animation
18       pauses
19    */
20    public SelectionSorter(int[] anArray, JComponent aComponent)
21    {
22       a = anArray;
23       sortStateLock = new ReentrantLock();
24       component = aComponent;
25    }
```

```
26
27      /**
28         Sorts the array managed by this selection sorter.
29      */
30      public void sort()
31         throws InterruptedException
32      {
33         for (int i = 0; i < a.length - 1; i++)
34         {
35            int minPos = minimumPosition(i);
36            sortStateLock.lock();
37            try
38            {
39               swap(minPos, i);
40               // For animation
41               alreadySorted = i;
42            }
43            finally
44            {
45               sortStateLock.unlock();
46            }
47            pause(2);
48         }
49      }
50
51      /**
52         Finds the smallest element in a tail range of the array.
53         @param from the first position in a to compare
54         @return the position of the smallest element in the
55         range a[from] . . . a[a.length - 1]
56      */
57      private int minimumPosition(int from)
58         throws InterruptedException
59      {
60         int minPos = from;
61         for (int i = from + 1; i < a.length; i++)
62         {
63            sortStateLock.lock();
64            try
65            {
66               if (a[i] < a[minPos]) minPos = i;
67               // For animation
68               markedPosition = i;
69            }
70            finally
71            {
72               sortStateLock.unlock();
73            }
74            pause(2);
75         }
76         return minPos;
77      }
78
```

```
79      /**
80          Swaps two entries of the array.
81          @param i  the first position to swap
82          @param j  the second position to swap
83      */
84      private void swap(int i, int j)
85      {
86          int temp = a[i];
87          a[i] = a[j];
88          a[j] = temp;
89      }
90
91      /**
92          Draws the current state of the sorting algorithm.
93          @param g2  the graphics context
94      */
95      public void draw(Graphics2D g2)
96      {
97          sortStateLock.lock();
98          try
99          {
100             int deltaX = component.getWidth() / a.length;
101             for (int i = 0; i < a.length; i++)
102             {
103                 if (i == markedPosition)
104                     g2.setColor(Color.RED);
105                 else if (i <= alreadySorted)
106                     g2.setColor(Color.BLUE);
107                 else
108                     g2.setColor(Color.BLACK);
109                 g2.draw(new Line2D.Double(i * deltaX, 0,
110                     i * deltaX, a[i]));
111             }
112         }
113         finally
114         {
115             sortStateLock.unlock();
116         }
117     }
118
119     /**
120         Pauses the animation.
121         @param steps  the number of steps to pause
122     */
123     public void pause(int steps)
124         throws InterruptedException
125     {
126         component.repaint();
127         Thread.sleep(steps * DELAY);
128     }
129
130     private int[] a;
131     private Lock sortStateLock;
```

```
132
133        // The component is repainted when the animation is paused
134        private JComponent component;
135
136        // These fields are needed for drawing
137        private int markedPosition = -1;
138        private int alreadySorted = -1;
139
140        private static final int DELAY = 100;
141    }
```

SELF CHECK

11. Why is the `draw` method added to the `SelectionSorter` class and not the `SelectionSortComponent` class?

12. Would the animation still work if the `startAnimation` method simply called `sorter.sort()` instead of spawning a thread that calls that method?

RANDOM FACT 23.1

Embedded Systems

An *embedded system* is a computer system that controls a device. The device contains a processor and other hardware and is controlled by a computer program. Unlike a personal computer, which has been designed to be flexible and run many different computer programs, the hardware and software of an embedded system are tailored to a specific device. Computer-controlled devices are becoming increasingly common, ranging from washing machines to medical equipment, automobile engines, and spacecraft.

Several challenges are specific to programming embedded systems. Most importantly, a much higher standard of quality control applies. Vendors are often unconcerned about bugs in personal computer software, because they can always make you install a patch or upgrade to the next version. But in an embedded system, that is not an option. Few consumers would feel comfortable upgrading the software in their washing machines or automobile engines. If you ever handed in a programming assignment that you believed to be correct, only to have the instructor or grader find bugs in it, then you know how hard it is to write software that can reliably do its task for many years without a chance of changing it.

Quality standards are especially important in devices whose failure would destroy property or human life—see Random Facts 10.2 and 15.1.

Many personal computer purchasers buy computers that are fast and have a lot of storage, because the investment is paid back over time when many programs are run on the same equipment. But the hardware for an embedded device is not shared—it is dedicated to one device. A separate processor, memory, and so on, are built for every copy of the device (see Figure 4). If it is possible to shave a few pennies off the manufacturing cost of every unit, the savings can add up quickly for devices that are produced in large volumes. Thus, the embedded-system programmer has a much larger economic incentive to conserve resources than the programmer of desktop software. Unfortunately, trying to conserve resources usually makes it harder to write programs that work correctly.

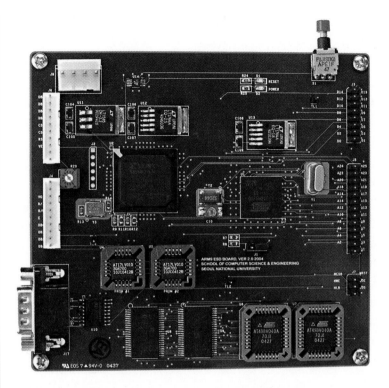

Figure 4   The Controller of an Embedded System

Generally, embedded systems are written in lower-level programming languages to avoid the overhead of a complex run-time system. The Java run-time system, with its safety mechanisms, garbage collector, support for multithreading, and so on, would be too costly to add to every washing machine. However, some devices are now being built with a scaled-down version of Java: the Java 2 Micro Edition. Examples are smart cell phones and onboard computers for automobiles. The Java 2 Micro Edition is a good candidate for devices that are connected to a network and that need to be able to run new applications safely. For example, you can download a program into a Java-enabled cell phone and be assured that it cannot corrupt other parts of the cell phone software.

CHAPTER SUMMARY

1. A thread is a program unit that is executed independently of other parts of the program.

2. The start method of the Thread class starts a new thread that executes the run method of the associated Runnable object.

3. The sleep method puts the current thread to sleep for a given number of milliseconds.

4. When a thread is interrupted, the most common response is to terminate the run method.

5. The thread scheduler runs each thread for a short amount of time, called a time slice.

6. A thread terminates when its run method terminates.

7. The run method can check whether its thread has been interrupted by calling the interrupted method.

8. A race condition occurs if the effect of multiple threads on shared data depends on the order in which the threads are scheduled.

9. By calling the lock method, a thread acquires a Lock object. Then no other thread can acquire the lock until the first thread releases the lock.

10. A deadlock occurs if no thread can proceed because each thread is waiting for another to do some work first.

11. Calling await on a condition object makes the current thread wait and allows another thread to acquire the lock object.

12. A waiting thread is blocked until another thread calls signalAll or signal on the condition object for which the thread is waiting.

CLASSES, OBJECTS, AND METHODS INTRODUCED IN THIS CHAPTER

```
java.lang.InterruptedException        java.util.concurrent.locks.Condition
java.lang.Object                         await
   notify                                signal
   notifyAll                             signalAll
   wait                               java.util.concurrent.locks.Lock
java.lang.Runnable                       lock
   run                                   newCondition
java.lang.Thread                         unlock
   interrupted                        java.util.concurrent.locks.ReentrantLock
   sleep
   start
```

REVIEW EXERCISES

Exercise R23.1. Run a program with the following instructions:

```
GreetingRunnable r1 = new GreetingRunnable("Hello, World!");
GreetingRunnable r2 = new GreetingRunnable("Goodbye, World!");
r1.run();
r2.run();
```

Note that the threads don't run in parallel. Explain.

Exercise R23.2. In the program of Section 23.1, is it possible that both threads are sleeping at the same time? Is it possible that neither of the two threads is sleeping at a particular time? Explain.

Exercise R23.3. In Java, a graphical user interface program has more than one thread. Explain how you can prove that.

Exercise R23.4. Why is the stop method for stopping a thread deprecated? How do you terminate a thread?

Exercise R23.5. Give an example of why you would want to terminate a thread.

Exercise R23.6. Suppose you surround each call to the sleep method with a try/ catch block to catch an InterruptedException and ignore it. What problem do you create?

Exercise R23.7. What is a race condition? How can you avoid it?

Exercise R23.8. What is a deadlock? How can you avoid it?

Exercise R23.9. What is the difference between a thread that sleeps by calling sleep and a thread that waits by calling await?

Exercise R23.10. What happens when a thread calls await and no other thread calls signalAll or signal?

Exercise R23.11. In the algorithm animation program of Section 23.6, we do not use any conditions. Why not?

PROGRAMMING EXERCISES

Exercise P23.1. Implement a Queue class whose add and remove methods are synchronized. Supply one thread, called the producer, which keeps inserting strings into the queue as long as there are fewer than 10 elements in it. When the queue gets too full, the thread waits. As sample strings, simply use time stamps new Date().toString(). Supply a second thread, called the consumer, that keeps removing and printing strings from the queue as long as the queue is not empty. When the queue is empty, the thread waits. Both the consumer and producer threads should run for 1,000 iterations.

Exercise P23.2. Enhance Exercise P23.1 by supplying a variable number of producer and consumer threads. Prompt the program user for the numbers.

Exercise P23.3. Reimplement Exercise P23.2 by using the ArrayBlockingQueue class from the standard library.

Exercise P23.4. Modify the car viewer of Chapter 5 so that the cars are moving. Use a separate thread for each car.

Exercise P23.5. Modify Exercise P23.4 so that the cars change direction when they hit an edge of the window.

Exercise P23.6. Write a program WordCount that counts the words in one or more files. Start a new thread for each file. For example, if you call

```
java WordCount report.txt address.txt Homework.java
```

then the program might print

```
address.txt: 1052
Homework.java: 445
report.txt: 2099
```

Exercise P23.7. Write a program Find that searches all files specified on the command line and prints out all lines containing a keyword. Start a new thread for each file. For example, if you call

```
java Find Buff report.txt address.txt Homework.java
```

then the program might print

```
report.txt: Buffet style lunch will be available at the
address.txt: Buffet, Warren|11801 Trenton Court|Dallas|TX
Homework.java: BufferedReader in;
address.txt: Walters, Winnie|59 Timothy Circle|Buffalo|MI
```

Exercise P23.8. Instead of using a thread and a pause method, use the Timer class of Chapter 12 to animate an algorithm. Whenever the timer sends out an action event, run the algorithm to the next step and display the state. That requires a more extensive recoding of the algorithm. You need to implement a runToNextStep method that is capable of running the algorithm one step at a time. Add sufficient instance fields to the algorithm to remember where the last step left off. For example, in the case of the selection sort algorithm, if you know the values of alreadySorted and markedPosition, you can determine the next step.

Exercise P23.9. Add a condition to the deposit method of the BankAccount class, restricting deposits to $100,000 (the insurance limit of the U.S. government). The method should block until sufficient money has been withdrawn by another thread. Test your program with a large number of deposit threads.

Exercise P23.10. Implement the merge sort algorithm of Chapter 19 by spawning a new thread for each smaller MergeSorter.

Exercise P23.11. Implement an animation of the merge sort algorithm of Chapter 19. Reimplement the algorithm so that the recursive calls sort the elements inside a sub-range of the the original array, rather than in their own arrays:

```
public void mergeSort(int from, int to)
{
   if (from == to) return;
   int mid = (from + to) / 2;
   mergeSort(from, mid);
   mergeSort(mid + 1, to);
   merge(from, mid, to);
}
```

The merge method merges the sorted ranges a[from] . . . a[mid] and a[mid + 1] . . . a[to].

Pause in the merge method whenever you inspect an array element. Color the range a[from] . . . a[to] in blue and the currently inspected element in red.

Exercise P23.12. Enhance the SelectionSorter of Section 23.6 so that the current minimum is painted in yellow.

Exercise P23.13. Enhance Exercise P23.11 so that it shows two frames, one for a merge sorter and one for a selection sorter. They should both sort arrays with the same values.

Exercise P23.14. Enhance the SelectionSortViewer of Section 23.6 so that the sorting only starts when the user clicks a "Start" button.

PROGRAMMING PROJECTS

Project 23.1. Implement a program that animates multiple sorting algorithms running in parallel. For each algorithm, provide buttons to pause and resume the animation, and to execute a single step. Provide sliders to control the animation speed.

Project 23.2. Implement a program that animates multiple robots moving through a maze. Each robot should be animated by its own thread, moving to an adjacent unoccupied maze position and then sleeping. Use locking to ensure that no two robots occupy the same cell of the maze.

ANSWERS TO SELF-CHECK QUESTIONS

1. The messages are printed about one millisecond apart.
2. The first call to run would print ten "Hello" messages, and then the second call to run would print ten "Goodbye" messages.
3. If the user hits the "Back" button, the current web page is no longer displayed, and it makes no sense to expend network resources for fetching additional image data.
4. The run method prints the values 1, 3, and 4. The call to interrupt merely sets the interruption flag, but the sleep method immediately throws an InterruptedException.
5. There are many possible scenarios. Here is one:
   - The first thread loses control after the first print statement.
   - The second thread loses control just before the assignment balance = newBalance.
   - The first thread completes the deposit method.
   - The second thread completes the withdraw method.

6. One thread calls addFirst and is preempted just before executing the assignment first = newLink. Then the next thread calls addFirst, using the old value of first. Then the first thread completes the process, setting first to its new link. As a result, the links are not in sequence.

7. Two, one for each bank account object. Each lock protects a separate balance field.

8. When a thread calls deposit, it continues to own the lock, and any other thread trying to deposit or withdraw money in the same bank account is blocked forever.

9. A sleeping thread is reactivated when the sleep delay has passed. A waiting thread is only reactivated if another thread has called signalAll or signal.

10. The calls to await and signal/signalAll must be made *to the same object.*

11. The draw method uses the array values and the values that keep track of the algorithm's progress. These values are available only in the SelectionSorter class.

12. Yes, provided you only show a single frame. If you modify the SelectionSortViewer program to show two frames, you want the sorters to run in parallel.

Internet
Networking

CHAPTER GOALS

- To understand the concept of sockets
- To learn how to send and receive data through sockets
- To implement network clients and servers
- To communicate with web servers and server-side applications through the Hypertext Transfer Protocol (HTTP)

You probably have quite a bit of experience with the *Internet:* the global network that links together millions of computers. In particular, you use the Internet whenever you browse the World Wide Web. Note that the Internet is not the same as the "Web". The World Wide Web is only one of many services offered over the Internet. E-mail, another popular service, also uses the Internet, but its implementation differs from that of the Web. In this chapter, you will see what goes on "under the hood" when you send an e-mail message or when you retrieve a web page from a remote server. You will also learn how to write your own programs that fetch data from sites across the Internet and how to write server programs that can serve information to other programs.

CHAPTER CONTENTS

24.1 The Internet Protocol

> The *Internet* is a worldwide collection of networks, routing equipment, and computers using a common set of protocols to define how each party will interact with each other.

Computers can be connected with each other through a variety of physical media. In a computer lab, for example, computers are connected by network cabling. Electrical impulses representing information flow across the cables. If you use a DSL modem to connect your own computer to the Internet, the signals travel across a regular telephone wire, encoded as tones. On a wireless network, signals are sent by transmitting a modulated radio frequency. The physical characteristics of these transmissions differ widely, but they ultimately consist of sending and receiving streams of zeroes and ones along the network connection.

These zeroes and ones represent two kinds of information: *application data*, the data that one computer actually wants to send to another, and *network protocol data*, the data that describe how to reach the intended recipient and how to check for errors and data loss in the transmission. The protocol data follow certain rules set forth by a particular *network protocol*. Various network protocols are in common use, such as Microsoft Networking, Novell NetWare, or AppleTalk; these are protocols for local area networks (see Random Fact 4.1). The *Internet Protocol (IP)*, on the other hand, was developed to enable different local area networks to communicate with each other and has become the basis for connecting computers around the world together over the Internet. We will discuss IP in this chapter.

Suppose that a computer A wants to send data to a computer B, both on the Internet. The computers aren't connected directly with a cable, as they could be if both were on the same local area network. Instead, A may be someone's home computer and connected to an *Internet service provider (ISP)*, which is in turn connected to an *Internet access point;* B might be a computer on a local area network belonging to a large firm that has an Internet access point of its own, which may be half a world away from A. The Internet itself, finally, is a complex collection of pathways on which a message can travel from one Internet access point to, eventually, any other Internet access point (see Figure 1). Those connections carry millions of messages, not just the data that A is sending to B.

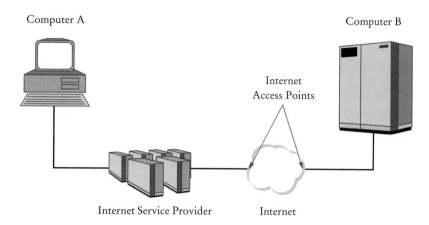

Figure 1 Two Computers Communicating Across the Internet

For the data to arrive at its destination, it must be marked with a *destination address*. In IP, addresses are denoted by sequences of four numbers, each one byte (that is, between 0 and 255); for example, 130.65.86.66. (Because there aren't enough four-byte addresses for all devices that would like to connect to the Internet, these addresses will be extended to sixteen bytes in the near future.) In order to send data, A needs to know the Internet address of B and include it in the protocol portion when sending the data across the Internet. The routing software that is distributed across the Internet can then deliver the data to B.

Of course, addresses such as 130.65.86.66 are not easy to remember. You would not be happy if you had to use number sequences every time you sent e-mail or requested information from a web server. On the Internet, computers can have so-called *domain names* that are easier to remember, such as cs.sjsu.edu or java.sun.com. A special service called the *Domain Naming Service (DNS)* translates between domain names and Internet addresses. Thus, if computer A wants to have information from java.sun.com, it first asks the DNS to translate this domain name into a numeric Internet address; then it includes the numeric address with the request.

One interesting aspect of IP is that it breaks large chunks of data up into more manageable *packets*. Each packet is delivered separately, and different packets that are part of the same transmission can take different routes through the Internet. Packets are numbered, and the recipient reassembles them in the correct order.

TCP/IP is the abbreviation for *Transmission Control Protocol over Internet Protocol*, the pair of communication protocols that is used to establish reliable transmission of data between two computers on the Internet.

The Internet Protocol has just one function—to attempt to deliver data from one computer to another across the Internet. If some data get lost or garbled in the process, IP has safeguards built in to make sure that the recipient is aware of that unfortunate fact and doesn't rely on incomplete data. However, IP has no provisions for retrying an incomplete transmission. That is the job of a higher-level protocol, the *Transmission Control Protocol (TCP)*. This protocol attempts reliable delivery of data, with retries if there are failures, and it notifies the sender whether or not the attempt succeeded. Most, but not all,

Internet programs use TCP for reliable delivery. (Exceptions are "streaming media" services, which bypass the slower TCP for the highest possible throughput and tolerate occasional information loss. However, the most popular Internet services — the World Wide Web and e-mail—use TCP.) TCP is independent of the Internet Protocol; it could in principle be used with another lower-level network protocol. However, in practice, TCP over IP (often called TCP/IP) is the most commonly used combination. We will focus on TCP/IP networking in this chapter.

A computer that is connected to the Internet may have programs for many different purposes. For example, a computer may run both a web server program and a mail server program. When data are sent to that computer, they need to be marked so that they can be forwarded to the appropriate program. TCP uses *port numbers* for this purpose. A port number is an integer between 0 and 65,535. The sending computer must know the port number of the receiving program and include it with the transmitted data. Some applications use "well-known" port numbers. For example, by convention, web servers use port 80, whereas mail servers running the Post Office Protocol (POP) use port 110. TCP packets, therefore, must contain

> A TCP connection requires the Internet addresses and port numbers of both end points.

- The Internet address of the recipient
- The port number of the recipient
- The Internet address of the sender
- The port number of the sender

You can think of a TCP connection as a "pipe" between two computers that links the two ports together. Data flow in either direction through the pipe. In practical programming situations, you simply establish a connection and send data across it without worrying about the details of the TCP/IP mechanism. You will see how to establish such a connection in Section 24.3.

SELF CHECK

1. What is the difference between an IP address and a domain name?
2. Why do some streaming media services not use TCP?

RANDOM FACT 24.1

The OSI Model

In 1984, the International Organization for Standardization (ISO) released a theoretical description of network protocols called the Open Systems Interconnection (OSI) reference model. The OSI model describes the various layers of abstraction for network software and hardware, and it sets rules for how the layers can communicate with each other. As Figure 2 shows, the layers form a stack. Each layer calls on services only from the layer immediately below it. This design shields the upper layers from implementation details of the lower layers.

Here is a brief description of the layers.

- The *physical layer* is concerned with transmitting bits over a physical medium, such as a copper cable, optical fiber, or wireless link.

- The *data link layer* groups bits of data into larger packets that are transmitted as a unit, and ensures that packets are delivered without transmission errors.

- The *network layer* manages connections across the network, such as routing packets and avoiding congestion.

- The *transport layer* ensures that packets are delivered from one computer to the other, requests retransmission of lost packets, and rearranges packets that arrived out of order.

- The *session layer* establishes connection sessions between two computers and regulates which side transmits data, and for how long.

- The *presentation layer* implements standardized data presentation services, such as data encryption, compression, and format conversion.

- The *application layer* is concerned with network applications, such as web browsing and electronic mail.

The OSI model is a theoretical model to which actual network implementations conform to various degrees. In the case of the Internet, IP lies at level 3, and TCP lies at level 4. That is, IP is responsible for delivering packets across the network. The job of IP is to make sure that packets are either delivered in their entirety to their intended recipient, or not delivered at all. TCP is responsible for guaranteed delivery of a stream of packets. If the TCP layer at the receiver finds that a packet is missing, it uses the IP layer (but not a lower layer) to ask the sender to retransmit the missing packet.

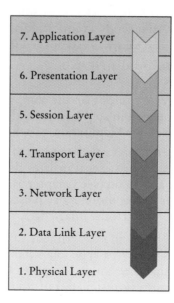

Figure 2
The OSI Reference Model

24.2 Application Level Protocols

HTTP, or *Hypertext Transfer Protocol*, is the protocol that defines communication between web browsers and web servers.

An URL, or *Uniform Resource Locator*, is a pointer to an information resource (such as a web page or an image) on the World Wide Web.

In the preceding section you saw how the TCP/IP mechanism can establish an Internet connection between two ports on two computers so that the two computers can exchange data. Each Internet application has a different *application protocol*, which describes how the data for that particular application are transmitted.

Consider, for example, HTTP: the *Hypertext Transfer Protocol*, which is used for the World Wide Web. Suppose you type a web address, called a *Uniform Resource Locator* (URL, often pronounced like "Earl"), such as http://java.sun.com/index.html, into the address window of your browser and ask the browser to load the page.

The browser now takes the following steps:

1. It examines the part of the URL between the double slash and the first single slash ("java.sun.com"), which identifies the computer to which you want to connect. Because this part of the URL contains letters, it must be a domain name rather than an Internet address, so the browser sends a request to a DNS server to obtain the Internet address of the computer with domain name java.sun.com.

2. From the http: prefix of the URL, the browser deduces that the protocol you want to use is HTTP, which by default uses port 80.

3. It establishes a TCP/IP connection to port 80 at the Internet address it obtained in step 1.

4. It deduces from the /index.html suffix that you want to see the file /index.html, so it sends a request, formatted as an HTTP command, through the connection that was established in step 3. The request looks like this:

   ```
   GET /index.html HTTP/1.0
   blank line
   ```

5. The web server running on the computer whose Internet address is the one the browser obtained in step 1 receives the request and decodes it. It then fetches the file /index.html and sends it back to the browser on your computer.

6. The browser displays the contents of the file. Because it happens to be an HTML file, the browser translates the HTML codes into fonts, bullets, separator lines, and so on (see Chapter 5). If the HTML file contains images, then the browser makes more GET requests, one for each image, through the same connection, to fetch the image data.

You can try the following experiment to see this process in action. The "Telnet" program enables a user to type characters for sending to a remote computer and view characters that the remote computer sends back. On Windows, the Telnet program is usually already installed, but you probably won't see it on your desktop; try clicking on the Start button, selecting "Run . . . ", and typing telnet at the "Open" window. UNIX, Linux, and Mac OS X systems normally have Telnet

Figure 3 Using Telnet to Connect to a Web Server

preinstalled. For this experiment, you want to start Telnet with a host of java.sun.com and port 80. The details depend on your Telnet program. If you start the program from the command line, simply type

```
telnet java.sun.com 80
```

(With some versions of Telnet, you need to enter the host and port into a dialog box instead of supplying the values on the command line.)

Once the program starts, type very carefully, without making any typing errors and without hitting the backspace key,

```
GET / HTTP/1.0
```

Then hit the Enter key twice.

The first / denotes the root page of the web server. Note that there are spaces before and after the first /, but there are no spaces in HTTP/1.0.

> The Telnet program is a useful tool to establish test connections with servers.

You may not see what you type, because the Telnet program sends your keystrokes directly to the server. (Some versions of Telnet have a "local echo" option that show you what you typed. If yours does, it is a good idea to turn it on for this experiment.)

The server now sends a response to the request—see Figure 3. The response, of course, consists of the root web page that you requested.

The Telnet program is not a browser and does not understand HTML tags, so it simply displays the HTML file—text, tags, and all.

Table 1   HTTP Commands

Command	Meaning
GET	Return the requested item
HEAD	Request only the header information of an item
OPTIONS	Request communications options of an item
POST	Supply input to a server-side command and return the result
PUT	Store an item on the server
DELETE	Delete an item on the server
TRACE	Trace server communication

The GET command is one of the commands of HTTP. Table 1 shows the other commands of the protocol. As you can see, the protocol is pretty simple.

The HTTP GET command requests information from a web server. The web server returns the requested item, which may be a web page, an image, or other data.

By the way, be sure not to confuse HTML with HTTP. HTML is a *document format* (with commands such as <h1> or <ul>) that describes the structure of a document, including headings, bulleted lists, images, hyperlinks, and so on. HTTP is a *protocol* (with commands such as GET and POST) that describes the command set for web server requests. Web *browsers* know how to display HTML documents and how to issue HTTP commands. Web *servers* know nothing about HTML. They merely understand HTTP and know how to fetch the requested items. Those items may be HTML documents, GIF or JPEG images, or any other data that a web browser can display.

```
+OK San Quentin State POP server
USER harryh
+OK Password required for harryh
PASS secret
+OK harryh has 2 messages (320 octets)
STAT
+OK 2 320
RETR 1
+OK 120 octets
the message is included here
DELE 1
+OK message 1 deleted
QUIT
+OK POP server signing off
```

Figure 4
A Sample POP Session

Black = mail client requests
Color = mail server responses

HTTP is just one of many application protocols in use on the Internet. Another commonly used protocol is the Post Office Protocol (POP), which is used to download received messages from e-mail servers. To *send* messages, you use yet another protocol called the Simple Mail Transfer Protocol (SMTP). We don't want to go into the details of these protocols, but Figure 4 gives you a flavor of the commands used by the Post Office Protocol.

Both HTTP and POP use plain text, which makes it particularly easy to test and debug client and server programs (see How To 24.1).

SELF CHECK

3. Why don't you need to know about HTTP when you use a web browser?
4. Why is it important that you don't make typing errors when you type HTTP commands in Telnet?

24.3 A Client Program

In this section you will see how to write a Java program that establishes a TCP connection to a server, sends a request to the server, and prints the response.

> A socket is an object that encapsulates a TCP connection. To communicate with the other end point of the connection, use the input and output streams attached to the socket.

In the terminology of TCP/IP, there is a *socket* on each side of the connection (see Figure 5). In Java, a client establishes a socket with a call

```
Socket s = new Socket(hostname, portnumber);
```

For example, to connect to the HTTP port of the server java.sun.com, you use

```
final int HTTP_PORT = 80;
Socket s = new Socket("java.sun.com", HTTP_PORT);
```

The socket constructor throws an `UnknownHostException` if it can't find the host.

Once you have a socket, you obtain its input and output streams:

```
InputStream instream = s.getInputStream();
OutputStream outstream = s.getOutputStream();
```

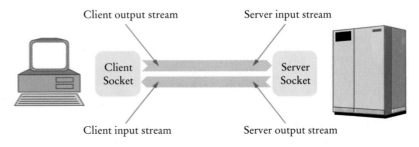

Figure 5 Client and Server Sockets

When you send data to outstream, the socket automatically forwards it to the server. The socket catches the server's response, and you can read the response through instream (see Figure 5).

When transmission over a socket is complete, remember to close the socket.

When you are done communicating with the server, you should close the socket:

```
s.close();
```

In Chapter 15, you saw that the InputStream and OutputStream classes are used for reading and writing bytes. If you want to communicate with the server by sending and receiving text, you should turn the streams into scanners and writers, as follows:

For text protocols, turn the socket streams into scanners and writers.

```
Scanner in = new Scanner(instream);
PrintWriter out = new PrintWriter(outstream);
```

A print writer *buffers* the characters that you send to it. That is, characters are not immediately sent to their destination. Instead, they are placed into an array. When the array is full, then the print writer sends all characters in the array to its destination. The advantage of buffering is increased performance—it takes some amount of time to contact the destination and send it data, and it is expensive to pay for that contact time for every character. However, when communicating with a server that responds to requests, you want to make sure that the server gets a complete request at a time. Therefore, you need to *flush* the buffer manually whenever you send a command:

```
out.print(command);
out.flush();
```

Flush the writer attached to a socket at the end of every command. Then the command is sent to the server, even if the writer's buffer isn't completely filled.

The flush method empties the buffer and forwards all waiting characters to the destination.

The WebGet program at the end of this section lets you retrieve any item from a web server. You need to specify the host and the item from the command line. For example,

```
java WebGet java.sun.com /
```

The / item denotes the root page of the web server that listens to port 80 of the host java.sun.com. Note that there is a space before the /.

The program simply establishes a connection to the host, sends a GET command to the host, and then receives input from the server until the server closes its connection.

File WebGet.java

```
1  import java.io.InputStream;
2  import java.io.IOException;
3  import java.io.OutputStream;
4  import java.io.PrintWriter;
5  import java.net.Socket;
6  import java.util.Scanner;
7
```

```
8   /**
9       This program demonstrates how to use a socket to communicate
10      with a web server. Supply the name of the host and the
11      resource on the command-line, for example,
12      java WebGet java.sun.com index.html.
13  */
14  public class WebGet
15  {
16      public static void main(String[] args) throws IOException
17      {
18          // Get command-line arguments
19
20          String host;
21          String resource;
22
23          if (args.length == 2)
24          {
25              host = args[0];
26              resource = args[1];
27          }
28          else
29          {
30              System.out.println("Getting / from java.sun.com");
31              host = "java.sun.com";
32              resource = "/";
33          }
34
35          // Open socket
36
37          final int HTTP_PORT = 80;
38          Socket s = new Socket(host, HTTP_PORT);
39
40          // Get streams
41
42          InputStream instream = s.getInputStream();
43          OutputStream outstream = s.getOutputStream();
44
45          // Turn streams into scanners and writers
46
47          Scanner in = new Scanner(instream);
48          PrintWriter out = new PrintWriter(outstream);
49
50          // Send command
51
52          String command = "GET " + resource + " HTTP/1.0\n\n";
53          out.print(command);
54          out.flush();
55
56          // Read server response
57
58          while (in.hasNextLine())
59          {
60              String input = in.nextLine();
61              System.out.println(input);
```

```
62        }
63
64        // Always close the socket at the end
65
66        s.close();
67    }
68 }
```

Output

```
Getting / from java.sun.com
HTTP/1.1 200 OK
Server: Netscape-Enterprise/6.0
Date: Wed, 21 Jul 2004 23:47:27 GMT
Content-type: text/html;charset=ISO-8859-1
Connection: close

<!DOCTYPE HTML PUBLIC "-//W3C//DTD HTML 4.01 Transitional//EN">
<html>
<head>
<title>Java Technology</title>
. . .
</body>
</html>
```

SELF CHECK

5. What happens if you call WebGet with a nonexistent resource, such as wombat.html at java.sun.com?

6. How do you open a socket to read e-mail from the POP server at e-mail.sjsu.edu?

24.4 A Server Program

Now that you have seen how to write a network client, we will turn to the server side. In this section we will develop a server program that enables clients to manage a set of bank accounts in a bank.

Whenever you develop a server application, you need to specify some application-level protocol that clients can use to interact with the server. For the purpose of this example, we will create a "Simple Bank Access Protocol". Table 2 shows the protocol format. Of course, this is just a toy protocol to show you how to implement a server.

The server program waits for clients to connect to a particular port. We choose port 8888 for this service. This number has not been preassigned to another service, so it is unlikely to be used by another server program. To listen to incoming connections, you use a *server socket*. To construct a server socket, you need to supply the port number.

Table 2 A Simple Bank Access Protocol

Client Request	Server Response	Meaning
BALANCE n	n and the balance	Get the balance of account n
DEPOSIT n a	n and the new balance	Deposit amount a into account n
WITHDRAW n a	n and the new balance	Withdraw amount a from account n
QUIT	None	Quit the connection

```
ServerSocket server = new ServerSocket(8888);
```

The accept method of the ServerSocket class waits for a client connection. When a client connects, then the server program obtains a socket through which it communicates with the client.

```
Socket s = server.accept();
BankService service = new BankService(s, bank);
```

> The ServerSocket class is used by server applications to listen for client connections.

The BankService class carries out the service. This class implements the Runnable interface, and its run method will be executed in each thread that serves a client connection. The run method gets a scanner and writer from the socket in the same way as we discussed in the preceding section. Then it executes the following method:

```
public void doService() throws IOException
{
   while (true)
   {
      if (!in.hasNext()) return;
      String command = in.next();
      if (command.equals("QUIT")) return;
      executeCommand(command);
   }
}
```

The executeCommand method processes a single command. If the command is DEPOSIT, then it carries out the deposit.

```
int account = in.nextInt();
double amount = in.nextDouble();
bank.deposit(account, amount);
```

The WITHDRAW command is handled in the same way. After each command, the account number and new balance are sent to the client:

```
out.println(account + " " + bank.getBalance(account));
```

The doService method returns to the run method if the client closed the connection or the command equals "QUIT". Then the run method closes the socket and exits.

Let us go back to the point where the server socket accepts a connection and constructs the BankService object. At this point, we could simply call the run method.

But then our server program would have a serious limitation: only one client could connect to it at any point in time. To overcome that limitation, server programs spawn a new thread whenever a client connects. Each thread is responsible for serving one client.

Our `BankService` class implements the `Runnable` interface. Therefore, the server program simply starts a thread with the following instructions:

```
Thread t = new Thread(service);
t.start();
```

The thread dies when the client quits or disconnects and the `run` method exits. In the meantime, the `BankServer` loops back to accept the next connection.

```
while (true)
{
   Socket s = server.accept();
   BankService service = new BankService(s, bank);
   Thread t = new Thread(service);
   t.start();
}
```

The server program never stops. When you are done running the server, you need to kill it. For example, if you started the server in a shell window, hit Ctrl+C.

To try out the program, run the server. Then use Telnet to connect to `localhost`, port number 8888. Start typing commands. Here is a typical dialog (see Figure 6):

```
DEPOSIT 3 1000
3 1000.0
WITHDRAW 3 500
3 500.0
QUIT
```

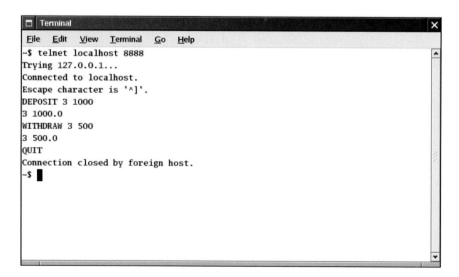

Figure 6   Using the Telnet Program to Connect to the Bank Server

Alternatively, you can use a client program that connects to the server. You will find a sample client program at the end of this section.

File BankServer.java

```java
1  import java.io.IOException;
2  import java.net.ServerSocket;
3  import java.net.Socket;
4
5  /**
6     A server that executes the Simple Bank Access Protocol.
7  */
8  public class BankServer
9  {
10    public static void main(String[] args) throws IOException
11    {
12       final int ACCOUNTS_LENGTH = 10;
13       Bank bank = new Bank(ACCOUNTS_LENGTH);
14       final int SBAP_PORT = 8888;
15       ServerSocket server = new ServerSocket(SBAP_PORT);
16       System.out.println("Waiting for clients to connect . . . ");
17
18       while (true)
19       {
20          Socket s = server.accept();
21          System.out.println("Client connected.");
22          BankService service = new BankService(s, bank);
23          Thread t = new Thread(service);
24          t.start();
25       }
26    }
27  }
```

File BankService.java

```java
1  import java.io.InputStream;
2  import java.io.IOException;
3  import java.io.OutputStream;
4  import java.io.PrintWriter;
5  import java.net.Socket;
6  import java.util.Scanner;
7
8  /**
9     Executes Simple Bank Access Protocol commands
10    from a socket.
11  */
12  public class BankService implements Runnable
13  {
14    /**
15       Constructs a service object that processes commands
16       from a socket for a bank.
17       @param aSocket the socket
18       @param aBank the bank
19    */
```

```
20    public BankService(Socket aSocket, Bank aBank)
21    {
22       s = aSocket;
23       bank = aBank;
24    }
25
26    public void run()
27    {
28       try
29       {
30          try
31          {
32             in = new Scanner(s.getInputStream());
33             out = new PrintWriter(s.getOutputStream());
34             doService();
35          }
36          finally
37          {
38             s.close();
39          }
40       }
41       catch (IOException exception)
42       {
43          exception.printStackTrace();
44       }
45    }
46
47    /**
48       Executes all commands until the QUIT command or the
49       end of input.
50    */
51    public void doService() throws IOException
52    {
53       while (true)
54       {
55          if (!in.hasNext()) return;
56          String command = in.next();
57          if (command.equals("QUIT")) return;
58          else executeCommand(command);
59       }
60    }
61
62    /**
63       Executes a single command.
64       @param command the command to execute
65    */
66    public void executeCommand(String command)
67    {
68       int account = in.nextInt();
69       if (command.equals("DEPOSIT"))
70       {
71          double amount = in.nextDouble();
72          bank.deposit(account, amount);
73       }
```

```
74              else if (command.equals("WITHDRAW"))
75              {
76                  double amount = in.nextDouble();
77                  bank.withdraw(account, amount);
78              }
79              else if (!command.equals("BALANCE"))
80              {
81                  out.println("Invalid command");
82                  out.flush();
83                  return;
84              }
85              out.println(account + " " + bank.getBalance(account));
86              out.flush();
87          }
88
89      private Socket s;
90      private Scanner in;
91      private PrintWriter out;
92      private Bank bank;
93  }
```

File Bank.java

```
1   /**
2       A bank consisting of multiple bank accounts.
3   */
4   public class Bank
5   {
6       /**
7           Constructs a bank account with a given number of accounts.
8           @param size the number of accounts
9       */
10      public Bank(int size)
11      {
12          accounts = new BankAccount[size];
13          for (int i = 0; i < accounts.length; i++)
14              accounts[i] = new BankAccount();
15      }
16
17      /**
18          Deposits money into a bank account.
19          @param accountNumber the account number
20          @param amount the amount to deposit
21      */
22      public void deposit(int accountNumber, double amount)
23      {
24          BankAccount account = accounts[accountNumber];
25          account.deposit(amount);
26      }
27
28      /**
29          Withdraws money from a bank account.
30          @param accountNumber the account number
31          @param amount the amount to withdraw
32      */
```

```
33      public void withdraw(int accountNumber, double amount)
34      {
35         BankAccount account = accounts[accountNumber];
36         account.withdraw(amount);
37      }
38
39      /**
40         Gets the balance of a bank account.
41         @param accountNumber the account number
42         @return the account balance
43      */
44      public double getBalance(int accountNumber)
45      {
46         BankAccount account = accounts[accountNumber];
47         return account.getBalance();
48      }
49
50      private BankAccount[] accounts;
51   }
```

File BankClient.java

```
1   import java.io.InputStream;
2   import java.io.IOException;
3   import java.io.OutputStream;
4   import java.io.PrintWriter;
5   import java.net.Socket;
6   import java.util.Scanner;
7
8   /**
9      This program tests the bank server.
10  */
11  public class BankClient
12  {
13     public static void main(String[] args) throws IOException
14     {
15        final int SBAP_PORT = 8888;
16        Socket s = new Socket("localhost", SBAP_PORT);
17        InputStream instream = s.getInputStream();
18        OutputStream outstream = s.getOutputStream();
19        Scanner in = new Scanner(instream);
20        PrintWriter out = new PrintWriter(outstream);
21
22        String command = "DEPOSIT 3 1000\n";
23        System.out.print("Sending: " + command);
24        out.print(command);
25        out.flush();
26        String response = in.nextLine();
27        System.out.println("Receiving: " + response);
28
29        command = "WITHDRAW 3 500\n";
30        System.out.print("Sending: " + command);
31        out.print(command);
32        out.flush();
```

```
33          response = in.nextLine();
34          System.out.println("Receiving: " + response);
35
36          command = "QUIT\n";
37          System.out.print("Sending: " + command);
38          out.print(command);
39          out.flush();
40
41          s.close();
42       }
43  }
```

Output

```
Sending: DEPOSIT 3 1000
Receiving: 3 1000.0
Sending: WITHDRAW 3 500
Receiving: 3 500.0
Sending: QUIT
```

SELF CHECK

7. Why didn't we choose port 80 for the bank server?
8. Can you read data from a server socket?

HOW TO 24.1

Designing Client/Server Programs

The bank server of this section is a typical example of a client/server program. A web browser/web server is another example. Follow these steps when designing a client/server application.

Step 1 Determine whether it really makes sense to implement a stand-alone server and a matching client.

Many times it makes more sense to build a web application instead. Chapter 27 discusses the construction of web applications in detail. For example, the bank application of this section could easily be turned into a web application, using an HTML form with Withdraw and Deposit buttons. However, programs for chat or peer-to-peer file sharing cannot easily be implemented as web applications.

Step 2 Design a communication protocol.

Figure out exactly what messages the client and server send to each other and what the success and error responses are.

With each request and response, ask yourself how the *end of data* is indicated.

- Do the data fit on a single line? Then the end of the line serves as the data terminator.
- Can the data be terminated by a special line (such as a blank line after the HTTP header or a line containing a period in SMTP)?
- Does the sender of the data close the socket? That's what a web server does at the end of a GET request.
- Can the sender indicate how many bytes are contained in the request? Web browsers do that in POST requests.

Use text, not binary data, for the communication between client and server. A text-based protocol is easier to debug.

Step 3   Implement the server program.

The server listens for socket connections and accepts them. It starts a new thread for each connection. Supply a class that implements the Runnable interface. The run method receives commands, interprets them, and sends responses back to the client.

Step 4   Test the server with the Telnet program.

Try out all commands in the communication protocol.

Step 5   Once the server works, write a client program.

The client program interacts with the program user, turns user requests into protocol commands, sends the commands to the server, receives the response, and displays the response for the program user.

24.5 URL Connections

> The URLConnection class makes it easy to communicate with a web server without having to issue HTTP commands.

In Section 24.3, you saw how to use sockets to connect to a web server and how to retrieve information from the server by sending HTTP commands. However, because HTTP is such an important protocol, the Java library contains an URLConnection class, which provides convenient support for the HTTP. The URLConnection class takes care of the socket connection, so you don't have to fuss with sockets when you want to retrieve from a web server. As an additional benefit, the URLConnection class can also handle FTP, the *file transfer protocol*.

The URLConnection class makes it very easy to fetch a file from a web server given the file's URL as a string. First, you construct an URL object from the URL in the familiar format, starting with the http or ftp prefix. Then you use the URL object's openConnection() method to get the URLConnection object itself.

```
URL u = new URL("http://java.sun.com/index.html");
URLConnection connection = u.openConnection();
```

Then you call the getInputStream method to obtain an input stream:

```
InputStream instream = connection.getInputStream();
```

You can turn the stream into a scanner in the usual way, and read input from the scanner.

The URLConnection and HttpURLConnection classes can give you additional information about HTTP requests and responses.

The URLConnection class can give you additional useful information. To understand those capabilities, we need to have a closer look at HTTP requests and responses. You saw in Section 24.2 that the command for getting an item from the server is

```
GET item HTTP/1.0
blank line
```

You may have wondered why you need to provide a blank line. This blank line is a part of the general request format. The first line of the request is a command, such as GET or POST. The command may be followed by *request properties,* and some commands—in particular, the POST command—send input data to the server. The reason for the blank line is to denote the boundary between the request property section and the input data section.

A typical request property is If-Modified-Since. If you request an item with

```
GET item HTTP/1.0
If-Modified-Since: date
blank line
```

the server sends the item only if it is newer than the date. Browsers use this feature to speed up redisplay of previously loaded web pages. When a web page is loaded, the browser stores it in a *cache* directory. When the user wants to see the same web page again, the browser asks the server to get a new page only if it has been modified since the date of the cached copy. If it isn't, the browser simply redisplays the cached copy without spending time on downloading another identical copy.

The URLConnection class has methods to set request properties. For example, you can set the If-Modified-Since property with the setIfModifiedSince method:

```
connection.setIfModifiedSince(date);
```

You need to set request properties before calling the getInputStream method. The URLConnection class then sends to the web server all the request properties that you set.

Similarly, the response from the server starts with a status line followed by a set of response parameters. The response parameters are terminated by a blank line and followed by the requested data (for example, an HTML page). Here is a typical response:

```
HTTP/1.1 200 OK
Date: Sun, 28 Aug 2005 00:15:48 GMT
Server: Apache/1.3.3 (Unix)
Last-Modified: Thu, 23 Jun 2005 20:53:38 GMT
Content-Length: 4813
Content-Type: text/html
blank line
requested data
```

Normally, you don't see the response code. However, you may have run across bad links and seen a page that contained a response code 404 Not Found. (A successful response has status 200 OK.)

To retrieve the response code, you need to cast the `URLConnection` object to the `HttpURLConnection` subclass. You can retrieve the response code (such as the number 200 in this example, or the code 404 if a page was not found) and response message with the `getResponseCode` and `getResponseMessage` methods:

```
HttpURLConnection httpConnection = (HttpURLConnection) connection;
int code = httpConnection.getResponseCode(); // e.g., 404
String message = httpConnection.getResponseMessage(); // e.g., "Not found"
```

As you can see from the response example, the server sends some information about the requested data, such as the content length and the content type. You can request this information with methods from the `URLConnection` class:

```
int length = connection.getContentLength();
String type = connection.getContentType();
```

You need to call these methods after calling the `getInputStream` method.

To summarize: You don't need to use sockets to communicate with a web server, and you need not master the details of the HTTP protocol. Simply use the `URLConnection` and `HttpURLConnection` classes to obtain data from a web server, to set request parameters, or to obtain response information.

The program at the end of this section puts the `URLConnection` class to work. The program fulfills the same purpose as that of Section 24.3—to retrieve a web page from a server—but it works at a higher level of abstraction. There is no longer a need to issue an explicit GET command. The `URLConnection` class takes care of that. Similarly, the parsing of the HTTP request and response headers is handled transparently to the programmer. Our sample program takes advantage of that fact. It checks whether the server response code is 200. If not, it exits. You can try that out by testing the program with a bad URL, like `http://java.sun.com/wombat.html`. Then the program prints a server response, such as 404 Not Found.

This program completes our introduction into Internet programming with Java. You have seen how to use sockets to connect client and server programs. You also saw how to use the higher-level `URLConnection` class to obtain information from web servers.

File URLGet.java

```
 1   import java.io.InputStream;
 2   import java.io.IOException;
 3   import java.io.OutputStream;
 4   import java.io.PrintWriter;
 5   import java.net.HttpURLConnection;
 6   import java.net.URL;
 7   import java.net.URLConnection;
 8   import java.util.Scanner;
 9
10   /**
11      This program demonstrates how to use an URL connection
12      to communicate with a web server. Supply the URL on
13      the command-line, for example
14      java URLGet http://java.sun.com/index.html.
15   */
```

```
16  public class URLGet
17  {
18     public static void main(String[] args) throws IOException
19     {
20        // Get command-line arguments
21
22        String urlString;
23        if (args.length == 1)
24           urlString = args[0];
25        else
26        {
27           urlString = "http://java.sun.com/";
28           System.out.println("Using " + urlString);
29        }
30
31        // Open connection
32
33        URL u = new URL(urlString);
34        URLConnection connection = u.openConnection();
35
36        // Check if response code is HTTP_OK (200)
37
38        HttpURLConnection httpConnection
39              = (HttpURLConnection) connection;
40        int code = httpConnection.getResponseCode();
41        String message = httpConnection.getResponseMessage();
42        System.out.println(code + " " + message);
43        if (code != HttpURLConnection.HTTP_OK)
44           return;
45
46        // Read server response
47
48        InputStream instream = connection.getInputStream();
49        Scanner in = new Scanner(instream);
50
51        while (in.hasNextLine())
52        {
53           String input = in.nextLine();
54           System.out.println(input);
55        }
56     }
57  }
```

Output

```
Using http://java.sun.com/
200 OK
<!DOCTYPE HTML PUBLIC "-//W3C//DTD HTML 4.01 Transitional//EN">
<html>
<head>
<title>Java Technology</title>
. . .
</body>
</html>
```

SELF CHECK

9. Why is it better to use an URLConnection instead of a socket when reading data from a web server?

10. What happens if you use the URLGet program to request an image (such as http://java.sun.com/im/logo_java.gif)?

PRODUCTIVITY HINT 24.1

Use High-Level Libraries

When you communicate with a web server to obtain data, you have two choices. You can make a socket connection and send GET and POST commands to the server over the socket. Or you can use the URLConnection class and have it issue the commands on your behalf.

Similarly, to communicate with a mail server, you can write programs that send SMTP and POP commands, or you can learn how to use the Java mail extensions. (See [1] for more information on the Java Mail API.)

In such a situation, you may be tempted to use the low-level approach and send commands over a socket connection. It seems simpler than learning a complex set of classes. However, that simplicity is often deceptive. Once you go beyond the simplest cases, the low-level approach usually requires hard work. For example, to send binary mail attachments, you may need to master complex data encodings. The high-level libraries have all that knowledge built in, so you don't have to reinvent the wheel.

For that reason, you should not actually use sockets to connect to web servers. Always use the URLConnection class instead. Why did this book teach you about sockets if you aren't expected to use them? There are two reasons. Some client programs don't communicate with web or mail servers, and you may need to use sockets when a high-level library is not available. And, just as importantly, knowing what the high-level library does under the hood helps you understand it better. For the same reason, you saw in Chapter 20 how to implement linked lists, even though you probably will never program your own lists and will just use the LinkedList class.

CHAPTER SUMMARY

1. The *Internet* is a worldwide collection of networks, routing equipment, and computers using a common set of protocols to define how each party will interact with each other.

2. TCP/IP is the abbreviation for *Transmission Control Protocol over Internet Protocol*, the pair of communication protocols that is used to establish reliable transmission of data between two computers on the Internet.

3. A TCP connection requires the Internet addresses and port numbers of both end points.

4. HTTP, or *Hypertext Transfer Protocol*, is the protocol that defines communication between web browsers and web servers.

5. An URL, or *Uniform Resource Locator*, is a pointer to an information resource (such as a web page or an image) on the World Wide Web.

6. The Telnet program is a useful tool to establish test connections with servers.

7. The HTTP GET command requests information from a web server. The web server returns the requested item, which may be a web page, an image, or other data.

8. A socket is an object that encapsulates a TCP connection. To communicate with the other end point of the connection, use the input and output streams attached to the socket.

9. When transmission over a socket is complete, remember to close the socket.

10. For text protocols, turn the socket streams into scanners and writers.

11. Flush the writer attached to a socket at the end of every command. Then the command is sent to the server, even if the writer's buffer isn't completely filled.

12. The ServerSocket class is used by server applications to listen for client connections.

13. The URLConnection class makes it easy to communicate with a web server without having to issue HTTP commands.

14. The URLConnection and HttpURLConnection classes can give you additional information about HTTP requests and responses.

FURTHER READING

1. http://java.sun.com/products/javamail/index.html   JavaMail API information.

2. http://www.rgpfaq.com/basic-rules.html   The basic rules of poker.

3. http://www.cia.gov/cia/publications/factbook   The CIA World Fact Book.

CLASSES, OBJECTS, AND METHODS INTRODUCED IN THIS CHAPTER

```
java.net.HttpURLConnection
   getResponseCode
   getResponseMessage
java.net.ServerSocket
   accept
   close
java.net.Socket
   close
   getInputStream
   getOutputStream
java.net.URL
   openConnection
java.net.URLConnection
   getContentLength
   getContentType
   getInputStream
   setIfModifiedSince
```

REVIEW EXERCISES

Exercise R24.1. What is a server? What is a client? How many clients can connect to a server at one time?

Exercise R24.2. What is a socket? What is the difference between a Socket object and a ServerSocket object?

Exercise R24.3. Under what circumstances would an UnknownHostException be thrown?

Exercise R24.4. What happens if the Socket constructor's second parameter is not the same as the port number at which the server waits for connections?

Exercise R24.5. When a socket is created, which Internet address is used?
   a. The address of the computer to which you want to connect
   b. The address of your computer
   c. The address of your ISP

Exercise R24.6. What is the purpose of the accept method of the ServerSocket class?

Exercise R24.7. After a socket establishes a connection, what mechanism will your client program use to read data from the server computer?
   a. The Socket will fill a buffer with bytes.
   b. You will use a Reader obtained from the Socket.
   c. You will use an InputStream obtained from the Socket.

Exercise R24.8. Why is it not common to work directly with the InputStream and OutputStream objects obtained from a Socket object?

Exercise R24.9. When a client program communicates with a server, it sometimes needs to flush the output stream. Explain why.

Exercise R24.10. What is the difference between HTTP and HTML?

Exercise R24.11. How can you communicate with a web server without using sockets?

Exercise R24.12. What is the difference between an URL instance and an URLConnection instance?

Exercise R24.13. What is an URL? How do you create an URL? How do you connect to an URL?

PROGRAMMING EXERCISES

Exercise P24.1. Modify the WebGet program to print only the HTTP header of the returned HTML page. The HTTP header is the beginning of the response data. It consists of several lines, such as

```
HTTP/1.1 200 OK
Date: Sun, 12 Jun 2005 16:10:34 GMT
Server: Apache/1.3.19 (Unix)
Cache-Control: max-age=86400
Expires: Mon, 13 Jun 2005 16:10:34 GMT
Connection: close
Content-Type: text/html
```

followed by a blank line.

Exercise P24.2. Modify the WebGet program to print only the *title* of the returned HTML page. An HTML page has the structure

```
<html><head><title> . . . </title></head><body> . . . </body></html>
```

For example, if you run the program by typing at the command line java WebGet java.sun.com /, the output should be the title of the root web page at java.sun.com, such as The Source for Java(TM) Technology.

Exercise P24.3. Modify the BankServer program so that it can be terminated more elegantly. Provide another socket on port 8889 through which an administrator can log in. Support the commands LOGIN *password*, STATUS, PASSWORD *newPassword*, LOGOUT, and SHUTDOWN. The STATUS command should display the total number of clients that have logged in since the server started.

Exercise P24.4. Modify the BankServer program to provide complete error checking. For example, checking to make sure that there is enough money in the account when withdrawing. Send appropriate error reports back to the client. Enhance the protocol to be similar to HTTP, in which each server response starts with a number indicating the success or failure condition, followed by a string with response data or an error description.

Exercise P24.5. Write a client application that executes an infinite loop that does the following: (*a*) prompts the user for a number, (*b*) sends that value to the server, (*c*) receives the number, and (*d*) displays the new number. Also write a server that executes an infinite loop to read a number from a client, compute the square root of the value, and write the result to the client.

Exercise P24.6. Implement a client-server program in which the client will print the date and time given by the server. Two classes should be implemented: `DateClient` and `DateServer`. The `DateServer` simply prints `new Date().toString()` whenever it accepts a connection and then closes the socket.

Exercise P24.7. Write a program to display the protocol, host, port, and file components of an URL. *Hint:* Look at the API documentation of the URL class.

Exercise P24.8. Write a simple web server that recognizes only the `GET` request. When a client connects to your server and sends a command, such as `GET` *filename* `HTTP/1.0`, then return a header

```
HTTP/1.1 200 OK
```

followed by a blank line and all lines in the file. If the file doesn't exist, return 404 Not Found instead.

Your server should listen to port 8080. Test your web server by starting up your web browser and loading a page, such as `localhost:8080/c:\cs1\myfile.html`.

Exercise P24.9. Write a chat server and client program. The chat server accepts connections from clients. Whenever one of the clients sends a chat message, it is displayed for all other clients to see. Use a protocol with three commands: `LOGIN` *name*, `CHAT` *message*, and `LOGOUT`.

Exercise P24.10. A query such as

```
http://mach.usno.navy.mil/cgi-bin/aa_moonphases?year=2005
```

returns a page containing the moon phases in a given year. Write a program that asks the user for a year, month, and day and then prints the phase of the moon on that day.

PROGRAMMING PROJECTS

Project 24.1. Write a program that allows several people to play a networked game. Each player connects to a game server. Each player's move is transmitted to the game server. The game server checks that the move is valid and informs all client programs of the updated game status.

You can either implement your favorite multiplayer game, or simply use Poker (see [2] for the rules). Extra credit if your code is structured to separate the generic mechanism that is required for all games and the specific rules of a particular game.

Project 24.2. Write a program that allows a user to query the *CIA World Fact Book* [3] for facts about a country, such as the size, average income, capital city, and so on. To get the answers for user queries, connect to the web site, retrieve the web page, and extract the requested information. You will find that task simpler if you access the text version of the fact book.

ANSWERS TO SELF-CHECK QUESTIONS

1. An IP address is a numerical address, consisting of four or sixteen bytes. A domain name is an alphanumeric string that is associated with an IP address.
2. TCP is reliable but somewhat slow. When sending sounds or images in real time, it is acceptable if a small amount of the data is lost. But there is no point in transmitting data that is late.
3. The browser software translates your requests (typed URLs and mouse clicks on links) into HTTP commands that it sends to the appropriate web servers.
4. All keystrokes that you type, including the backspace key, are sent to the server. The server does not recognize a character sequence such as G W Backspace E T as a valid command.
5. The program makes a connection to the server, sends the GET request, and prints the error message that the server returns.
6. `Socket s = new Socket("e-mail.sjsu.edu", 110);`
7. Port 80 is the standard port for HTTP. If a web server is running on the same computer, then one can't open a server socket on an open port.
8. No, a server socket just waits for a connection and yields a regular `Socket` object when a client has connected. You use that socket object to read the data that the client sends.
9. The `URLConnection` class understands the HTTP protocol, freeing you from assembling requests and analyzing response headers.
10. The bytes that encode the images are displayed on the console, but they will appear to be random gibberish.

Relational Databases

- To understand how relational databases store information

- To learn how to query a database with the Structured Query Language (SQL)

- To connect to databases with Java Database Connectivity (JDBC)

- To write database programs that insert, update, and query data in a relational database

In Chapter 16 you saw how to store data in a file. When you store data, you will want to be able to add more data items, remove data, change data items, and find items that match certain criteria. However, if you have a lot of data, it can be difficult to carry out these operations quickly and efficiently. Because data storage is such a common task, special *database management systems (DBMS)* have been invented that let the programmer think in terms of the data rather than file storage. In this chapter you will learn how to use SQL, the Structured Query Language, to query and update information in a relational database, and how to access database information from Java programs.

25.1 Organizing Database Information

25.1.1 Database Tables

A relational database stores information in tables. Each table column has a name and a data type.

A relational database stores information in *tables*. Figure 1 shows a typical table. As you can see, each *row* in this table corresponds to a product. The *column headers* correspond to attributes of the product: the product code, description, and unit price. Note that all items in a particular column have the same type: product codes and descriptions are strings, unit prices are floating-point numbers. The allowable column types differ somewhat from one database to another. Table 1 shows types that are commonly available in relational databases that follow the SQL (for Structured Query Language; often pronounced "sequel") standard. (See *A Guide to the SQL Standard* [1] for more information.)

Product

Product_Code	Description	Price
116-064	Toaster	24.95
257-535	Hair dryer	29.95
643-119	Car vacuum	19.99

Figure 1   A Product Table in a Relational Database

Table 1 Some Standard SQL Types and Their Corresponding Java Types

SQL Data Type	Java Data Type
INTEGER or INT	int
REAL	float
DOUBLE	double
DECIMAL (m, n)	Fixed-point decimal numbers with m total digits and n digits after the decimal point; similar to BigDecimal.
BOOLEAN	boolean
CHARACTER (n) or CHAR (n)	Fixed-length string of length n; similar to String.

SQL (Structured Query Language) is a command language for interacting with a database.

Most relational databases follow the SQL standard. There is no relationship between SQL and Java—they are different languages. However, as you will see later in this chapter, you can use Java to send SQL commands to a database. You will see in the next section how to use SQL commands to carry out queries, but there are other SQL commands.

For example, here is the SQL command to create a product table:

Use the SQL commands CREATE TABLE and INSERT INTO to add data to a database.

```
CREATE TABLE Product
(
    Product_Code CHAR(11),
    Description CHAR(40),
    Price DECIMAL(10, 2)
)
```

Unlike Java, SQL is not case sensitive. For example, you could spell the command create table instead of CREATE TABLE. However, as a matter of convention, we will use uppercase letters for SQL keywords and mixed case for table and column names.

To insert rows into the table, use the INSERT INTO command. Issue one command for each row, such as

```
INSERT INTO Product
    VALUES ('257-535', 'Hair dryer', 29.95)
```

SQL uses single quotes ('), not double quotes, to delimit strings. What if you have a string that contains a single quote? Rather than using an escape sequence (such as \') as in Java, you just write the single quote twice, such as

```
'Sam''s Small Appliances'
```

If you create a table and subsequently want to remove it, use the DROP TABLE command. For example,

```
DROP TABLE Test
```

Stick with the Standard

The Java language is highly standardized. You will rarely find compilers that allow you to specify Java code that differs from the standard, and if they do, it is always a compiler bug. However, SQL implementations are often much more forgiving. For example, many SQL vendors allow you to use a Java-style escape sequence such as

```
'Sam\'s Small Appliances'
```

in a SQL string. The vendor probably thought that this would be "helpful" to programmers who are familiar with Java or C. (The C language uses the same escape mechanism for denoting special characters.)

However, this is an illusion. Deviating from the standard limits portability. Suppose you later want to move your database code to another vendor, perhaps to improve performance or to lower the cost of the database software. If the other vendor hasn't implemented a particular deviation, then your code will no longer work and you need to spend time fixing it.

To avoid these problems, you should stick with the standard. With SQL, you cannot rely on your database to flag all errors—some of them may be considered "helpful" extensions. That means that you need to *know* the standard and have the discipline to follow it.

25.1.2 Linking Tables

If you have objects whose instance fields are strings, numbers, dates, or other types that are permissible as table column types, then you can easily store them as rows in a database table. For example, consider a Java class `Customer`:

```
public class Customer
{
   . . .
   private String name;
   private String address;
   private String city;
   private String state;
   private String zip;
}
```

It is simple to come up with a database table structure that allows you to store customers—see Figure 2.

Customer

Name	Address	City	State	Zip
CHAR (40)	CHAR (40)	CHAR (30)	CHAR (2)	CHAR (10)
Sam's Small Appliances	100 Main Street	Anytown	CA	98765

Figure 2 A Customer Table

Invoice

Invoice_ Number	Customer_ Name	Customer_ Address	Customer_ City	Customer_ State	Customer_ Zip	. . .
INTEGER	CHAR (40)	CHAR (40)	CHAR (30)	CHAR (2)	CHAR (10)	. . .
11731	Sam's Small Appliances	100 Main Street	Anytown	CA	98765	. . .
11732	Electronics Unlimited	1175 Liberty Ave	Pleasantville	MI	45066	. . .
11733	Sam's Small Appliances	100 Main Street	Anytown	CA	98765	. . .

Figure 3 A Poor Design for an Invoice Table with Replicated Customer Data

For other objects, it is not so easy. Consider an invoice. Each invoice object contains a reference to a customer object.

```
public class Invoice
{
   . . .
   private int invoiceNumber;
   private Customer theCustomer;
   . . .
}
```

Because Customer isn't a standard SQL type, you might consider simply entering all the customer data into the invoice tables—see Figure 3. However, this is not a good idea. If you look at the sample data in Figure 3, you will notice that Sam's Small Appliances had two invoices, number 11731 and 11733. Yet all information for the customer was *replicated* in two rows.

This replication has two problems. First, it is wasteful to store the same information multiple times. If the same customer places many orders, then the replicated information can take up a lot of space. More importantly, the replication is *dangerous*. Suppose the customer moves to a new address. Then it would be an easy mistake to update the customer information in some of the invoice records and leave the old address in place in others.

In a Java program, neither of these problems occurs. Multiple Invoice objects can contain references to a single shared Customer object.

The first step in achieving the same effect in a database is to organize your data into multiple tables as in Figure 4. Dividing the columns into two tables solves the replication problem. The customer data are no longer replicated—the Invoice table contains no customer information, and the Customer table contains a single record for each customer. But how can we refer to the customer to which an invoice is issued? Notice in Figure 4 that there is now a Customer_Number column in *both*

> You should avoid rows with replicated data. Instead, distribute the data over multiple tables.

Invoice

Invoice_ Number	Customer_ Number	Payment
INTEGER	INTEGER	DECIMAL (10, 2)
11731	3175	0
11732	3176	249.95
11733	3175	0

Customer

Customer_ Number	Name	Address	City	State	Zip
INTEGER	CHAR (40)	CHAR (40)	CHAR (30)	CHAR (2)	CHAR (10)
3175	Sam's Small Appliances	100 Main Street	Anytown	CA	98765
3176	Electronics Unlimited	1175 Liberty Ave	Pleasantville	MI	45066

Figure 4   Two Tables for Invoice and Customer Data

the Customer table and the Invoice table. Now all invoices for Sam's Small Appliances share only the customer number. The two tables are *linked* by the Customer_Number field. To find out more details about this customer, you need to use the customer number to look up the customer in the Customer table.

Note that the customer number is a *unique identifier*. We introduced the customer number because the customer name by itself may not be unique. For example, there may well be multiple Electronics Unlimited stores in various locations. Thus, the customer name alone does not uniquely identify a record, so we cannot use the name as a link between the two tables.

> A primary key is a column (or set of columns) whose value uniquely specifies a table record.

In database terminology, a column (or combination of columns) that uniquely identifies a row in a table is called a *primary key*. In our Customer table, the Customer_Number column is a primary key. Not all database tables need a primary key. You need a primary key if you want to establish a link from another table. For example, the Customer table needs a primary key so that you can link customers to invoices.

> A foreign key is a reference to a primary key in a linked table.

When a primary key is linked to another table, the matching column (or combination of columns) in that table is called a *foreign key*. For example, the Customer_Number in the Invoice table is a foreign key, linked to the primary key in the Customer table. Unlike primary keys, foreign keys need not be unique. For example, in our Invoice table we have several records that have the same value for the Customer_Number foreign key.

PRODUCTIVITY HINT 25.2

Avoid Unnecessary Data Replication

It is very common for beginning database designers to replicate data. When replicating data in a table, ask yourself if you can move the replicated data into a separate table and use a key, such as a code or ID number, to link the tables.

Consider this example in an Invoice table:

Invoice

...	Product_Code	Description	Price	...
...	CHAR (10)	CHAR (40)	DECIMAL (10, 2)	...
...	116-064	Toaster	24.95	...
...	116-064	Toaster	24.95	...
...	...	...	...	...

As you can see, some product information is replicated. Is this replication an error? It depends. The product description for the product with code 116-064 is always going to be "Toaster". Therefore, that correspondence should be stored in an external Product table.

The product price, however, can change over time. When it does, the old invoices don't automatically use the new price. Thus, it makes sense to store the price that the customer was actually charged in an Invoice table. The current list price, however, is best stored in an external Product table.

ADVANCED TOPIC 25.1

Primary Keys and Indexes

Recall that a *primary key* is a column (or combination of columns) that uniquely identifies a row in a table. When a table has a primary key, then the database can build an *index file:* a file that stores information on how to access a row quickly when the primary key is known. Indexing can greatly increase the speed of database queries.

If the primary key is contained in a single column, then you can tag the column with the PRIMARY KEY attribute, like this:

```
CREATE TABLE Product
(
    Product_Code CHAR(10) PRIMARY KEY,
    Description CHAR(40),
    Price DECIMAL(10, 2)
)
```

If the primary key is contained in multiple columns, then add a PRIMARY KEY clause to the end of the CREATE TABLE command, like this:

```
CREATE TABLE Item
(
    Invoice_Number INTEGER,
    Product_Code CHAR(10),
    Quantity INTEGER,
    PRIMARY KEY (Invoice_Number, Product_Code)
)
```

Occasionally, one can speed queries up by building *secondary indexes:* index files that index other column sets, which are not necessarily unique. That is an advanced technique that we will not discuss here.

25.1.3 Implementing One-to-Many Relationships

Each invoice is linked to exactly one customer. That is called a *one-to-one* relationship. On the other hand, each invoice has many items. (As in Chapter 17, an *item* identifies the product, quantity, and unit price.) Thus, there is a *one-to-many* relationship between invoices and items. In the Java class, the Item objects are stored in an array list:

```
public class Invoice
{
    . . .
    private int invoiceNumber;
    private Customer theCustomer;
    private ArrayList items; // Contains Item objects
    private double payment;
}
```

However, in a relational database, you need to store the information in tables. Surprisingly many programmers, when faced with this situation, commit a major faux pas and replicate columns, one for each item, as in Figure 5.

Clearly, this design is not satisfactory. What should we do if there are more than three items on an invoice? Perhaps we should have 10 items instead? But that is

Invoice

Invoice_Number	Customer_Number	Product_Code1	Quantity1	Product_Code2	Quantity2	Product_Code3	Quantity3	Payment
INTEGER	INTEGER	CHAR (10)	INTEGER	CHAR (10)	INTEGER	CHAR (10)	INTEGER	DECIMAL (10, 2)
11731	3175	116-064	3	257-535	1	643-119	2	0

Figure 5 A Poor Design for an Invoice Table with Replicated Columns

wasteful if the majority of invoices have only a couple of items, and it still does not solve our problem for the occasional invoice with lots of items.

Instead, distribute the information into two tables: one for invoices and another for items. Link each item back to its invoice with an Invoice_Number foreign key in the Item table — see Figure 6.

Our database now consists of four tables:

- Invoice
- Customer
- Item
- Product

Figure 7 shows the links between these tables. In the next section you will see how to query this database for information about invoices, customers, and products. The queries will take advantage of the links between the tables.

Invoice

Invoice_Number	Customer_Number	Payment
INTEGER	INTEGER	DECIMAL (10, 2)
11731	3175	0
11732	3176	249.50
11733	3175	0

Item

Invoice_Number	Product_Code	Quantity
INTEGER	CHAR (10)	INTEGER
11731	116-064	3
11731	257-535	1
11731	643-119	2
11732	116-064	10
11733	116-064	2
11733	643-119	1

Figure 6 Linked Invoice and Item Tables Implement a One-to-Many Relationship

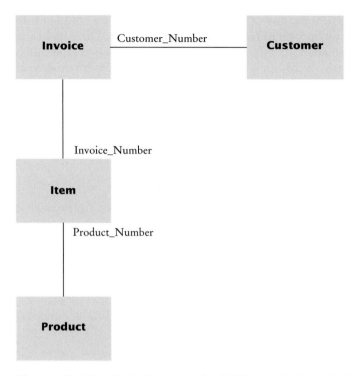

Figure 7   The Links Between the Tables in the Sample Database

SELF CHECK

1. Would a telephone number be a good primary key for a customer table?
2. In the database of Section 25.1.3, what are all the products that customer 3176 ordered?

PRODUCTIVITY HINT 25.3

Don't Replicate Columns in a Table

If you find yourself numbering columns in a table with suffixes 1, 2, and so forth (such as Quantity1, Quantity2, Quantity3 in the preceding example), then you are probably on the wrong track. How do you know there are exactly three quantities? In that case, it's time for another table.

Add a table to hold the information for which you replicated the columns. In that table, add a column that links back to a key in the first table, such as the invoice number in our example. By using an additional table, you can implement a one-to-many relationship.

25.2 Queries

Let us assume that the tables in our database have been created and that records have been inserted. Once a database is filled with data, you will want to *query* the database for information, such as

- What are the names and addresses of all customers?
- What are the names and addresses of all customers in California?
- What are the names and addresses of all customers who buy toasters?
- What are the names and addresses of all customers with unpaid invoices?

In this section you will learn how to formulate simple and complex queries in SQL. We will use the data shown in Figure 8 for our examples.

Invoice

Invoice_ Number	Customer_ Number	Payment
INTEGER	INTEGER	DECIMAL (10, 2)
11731	3175	0
11732	3176	249.50
11733	3175	0

Product

Product_Code	Description	Price
CHAR (10)	CHAR (40)	DECIMAL (10, 2)
116-064	Toaster	24.95
257-535	Hair dryer	29.95
643-119	Car vacuum	19.99

Item

Invoice_ Number	Product_ Code	Quantity
INTEGER	CHAR (10)	INTEGER
11731	116-064	3
11731	257-535	1
11731	643-119	2
11732	116-064	10
11733	116-064	2
11733	643-119	1

Customer

Customer_ Number	Name	Address	City	State	Zip
INTEGER	CHAR (40)	CHAR (40)	CHAR (30)	CHAR (2)	CHAR (10)
3175	Sam's Small Appliances	100 Main Street	Anytown	CA	98765
3176	Electronics Unlimited	1175 Liberty Ave	Pleasantville	MI	45066

Figure 8   A Sample Database

25.2.1 Simple Queries

Use the SQL SELECT command to query a database.

In SQL, you use the SELECT command to issue queries. For example, the command to select all data from the Customer table is

```
SELECT * FROM Customer
```

The result is

Customer_Number	Name	Address	City	State	Zip
3175	Sam's Small Appliances	100 Main Street	Anytown	CA	98765
3176	Electronics Unlimited	1175 Liberty Ave	Pleasantville	MI	45066

The outcome of the query is a *view*—a set of rows and columns that provides a "window" through which you can see some of the database data. If you select all rows and columns from a single table, of course you get a view into just that table.

Many database systems have tools that let you issue interactive SQL commands—Figure 9 shows a typical example. When you issue a SELECT command, the tool displays the resulting view. You may want to skip ahead to Section 25.3 and install a database. Or perhaps your computer lab has a database installed already. Then you can run the interactive SQL tool of your database and try out some queries.

25.2.2 Selecting Columns

Often, you don't care about all columns in a table. Suppose your traveling salesperson is planning a trip to all customers. To plan the route, the salesperson wants to know the cities and states of all customers. Here is the query:

```
SELECT City, State FROM Customer
```

The result is

City	State
Anytown	CA
Pleasantville	MI

As you can see, the syntax for selecting columns is straightforward. Simply specify the names of the columns you want, separated by commas.

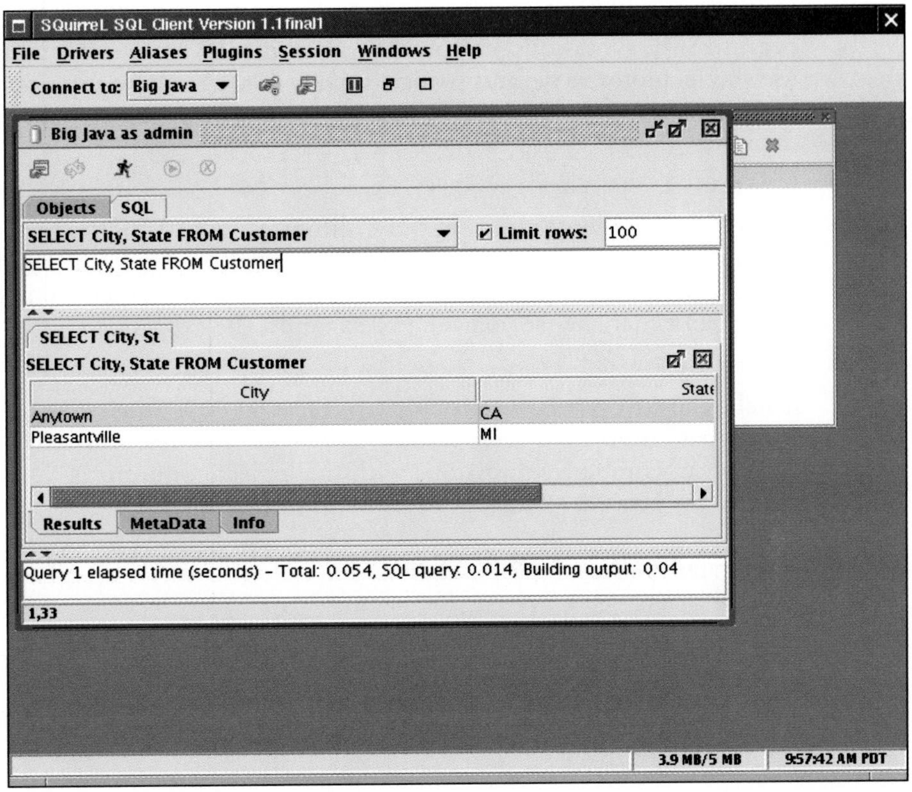

Figure 9 An Interactive SQL Tool

25.2.3 Selecting Subsets

You just saw how you can restrict a view to show selected columns. Sometimes you want to select certain rows that fit a particular criterion. For example, you may want to find all customers in California. Whenever you want to select a subset, you use the WHERE clause, followed by the condition that describes the subset. Here is an example.

```
SELECT * FROM Customer WHERE State = 'CA'
```

The result is

Customer_ Number	Name	Address	City	State	Zip
3175	Sam's Small Appliances	100 Main Street	Anytown	CA	98765

You have to be a bit careful with expressing the condition in the WHERE clause, because SQL syntax differs from the Java syntax. As you already know, in SQL you use single quotes to delimit strings, such as 'CA'. You also use a single =, not a double ==, to test for equality. To test for inequality, you use the <> operator. For example

```
SELECT * FROM Customer WHERE State <> 'CA'
```

selects all customers that are not in California.

You can match patterns with the LIKE operator. The right-hand side must be a string that can contain the special symbols _ (match exactly one character) and % (match any character sequence). For example, the expression

```
Name LIKE '_o%'
```

matches all strings whose second character is an "o". Thus, "Toaster" is a match but "Crowbar" is not.

You can combine expressions with the logical connectives AND, OR, and NOT. (Do not use the Java &&, ||, and ! operators.) For example,

```
SELECT *
   FROM Product
   WHERE Price < 100
      AND Description <> 'Toaster'
```

selects all products whose price is less than 100 that are not toasters.

Of course, you can select both row and column subsets, such as

```
SELECT Name, City FROM Customer WHERE State = 'CA'
```

25.2.4 Calculations

Suppose you want to find out *how many* customers there are in California. Use the COUNT function:

```
SELECT COUNT(*) FROM Customer WHERE State = 'CA'
```

In addition to the COUNT function, there are four other functions: SUM, AVG (average), MAX, and MIN.

The * means that you want to calculate entire records. That is appropriate only for the COUNT function. For other functions, you have to access a specific column. Put the column name inside the parentheses:

```
SELECT AVG(Price) FROM Product
```

25.2.5 Joins

The queries that you have seen so far all involve a single table. However, usually, the information that you want is distributed over multiple tables. For example, suppose you are asked to find all invoices that include an item for a car vacuum. From the Product table, you can issue a query to find the product code:

```
SELECT Product_Code
    FROM Product
    WHERE Description = 'Car vacuum'
```

You will find out that the car vacuum has product code 643-119. Then you can issue a second query

```
SELECT Invoice_Number
    FROM Item
    WHERE Product_Code = '643-119'
```

But it makes sense to combine these two queries so that you don't have to keep track of the intermediate result. When combining queries, note that the two tables are linked by the Product_Code field. We want to look at matching rows in both tables. In other words, we want to restrict the search to rows where

```
Product.Product_Code = Item.Product_Code
```

Here, the syntax

TableName.ColumnName

denotes the column in a particular table. Whenever a query involves multiple tables, you should specify both the table name and the column name. Thus, the combined query is

```
SELECT Item.Invoice_Number
    FROM Product, Item
    WHERE Product.Description = 'Car vacuum'
        AND Product.Product_Code = Item.Product_Code
```

The result is

Invoice_Number
11731
11733

A join is a query that involves multiple tables.

In this query, the FROM clause contains the names of multiple tables, separated by commas. (It doesn't matter in which order you list the tables.) Such a query is often called a *join* because it involves joining multiple tables.

You may want to know in what cities hair dryers are popular. Now you need to add the Customer table to the query—it contains the customer addresses. The customers are referenced by invoices, so you need that table as well. Here is the complete query:

```
SELECT Customer.City, Customer.State, Customer.Zip
    FROM Product, Item, Invoice, Customer
    WHERE Product.Description = 'Hair dryer'
        AND Product.Product_Code = Item.Product_Code
        AND Item.Invoice_Number = Invoice.Invoice_Number
        AND Invoice.Customer_Number = Customer.Customer_Number
```

The result is

City	State	Zip
Anytown	CA	98765

Whenever you formulate a query that involves multiple tables, remember to:

- List all tables that are involved in the query in the FROM clause.
- Use the *TableName.ColumnName* syntax to refer to column names.
- List all join conditions (*TableName1.ColumnName1 =
  TableName2.ColumnName2*) in the WHERE clause.

As you can see, these queries can get a bit complex. However, databases are very good at answering these queries (see Productivity Hint 25.4). One remarkable aspect of SQL is that you tell the database *what* you want, not *how* it should find the answer. It is entirely up to the database to come up with a plan for how to find the answer to your query in the shortest number of steps. Commercial database manufacturers take great pride in coming up with clever ways to speed up queries: query optimization strategies, caching of prior results, and so on. In this regard, SQL is a very different language from Java. SQL statements are descriptive and leave it to the database to determine how to execute them. Java statements are prescriptive—you spell out exactly the steps you want your program to carry out.

COMMON ERROR 25.1

Joining Tables Without Specifying a Link Condition

If you select data from multiple tables without a restriction, the result is somewhat surprising—you get a result set containing *all combinations* of the values, whether or not one of the combinations exists with actual data. For example, the query

```
SELECT Invoice.Invoice_Number, Customer.Name
    FROM Invoice, Customer
```

returns the result set

Invoice.Invoice_Number	Customer.Name
11731	Sam's Small Appliances
11732	Sam's Small Appliances
11733	Sam's Small Appliances
11731	Electronics Unlimited
11732	Electronics Unlimited
11733	Electronics Unlimited

As you can see, the result set contains all six combinations of invoice numbers (11731, 11732, 11733) and customer names (Sam's Small Appliances and Electronics Unlimited), even though three of those combinations don't occur with real invoices. You need to supply a WHERE clause to restrict the set of combinations. For example,

```
SELECT Invoice.Invoice_Number, Customer.Name
    FROM Invoice, Customer
    WHERE Invoice.Customer_Number = Customer.Customer_Number
```

yields

Invoice.Invoice_Number	Customer.Name
11731	Sam's Small Appliances
11732	Electronics Unlimited
11733	Sam's Small Appliances

25.2.6 Updating and Deleting Data

The UPDATE and DELETE SQL commands modify the data in a database.

Up to now, you have been shown how to formulate increasingly complex SELECT queries. The outcome of a SELECT query is a *result set* that you can view and analyze. Two related statement types, UPDATE and DELETE, don't produce a result set. Instead, they modify the database. The DELETE statement is the easier of the two. It simply deletes the rows that you specify. For example, to delete all customers in California, you issue the statement

```
DELETE FROM Customer WHERE State = 'CA'
```

The UPDATE query allows you to update columns of all records that fulfill a certain condition. For example, here is how you can add another unit to the quantity of every item in invoice number 11731.

```
UPDATE Item
    SET Quantity = Quantity + 1
    WHERE Invoice_Number = '11731'
```

You can update multiple column values by specifying multiple update expressions in the SET clause, separated by commas.

Both the DELETE and the UPDATE statements return a value, namely the number of rows that are deleted or updated.

SELF CHECK

3. How do you query the names of all customers that are not from Alaska or Hawaii?

4. How do you query all invoice numbers of all customers in Hawaii?

RANDOM FACT 25.1

Databases and Privacy

Most companies use computers to keep huge data files of customer records and other business information. Databases not only lower the cost of doing business; they improve the quality of service that companies can offer. Nowadays it is almost unimaginable how time-consuming it used to be to withdraw money from a bank branch or to make travel reservations.

Many companies collect large amounts of data on their customers and often share the data with other companies. The data are used not just for good customer service but for other commercial purposes—for example, to select targets for advertising. A company may have a file of addresses of car owners and a file of people with good payment history. It can then send special offers to all of its customers who placed an order in the last month, drive an expensive car, and pay their bills on time.

This kind of query is, of course, much faster if all customer files use the *same* key, which is why so many organizations in the United States try to collect the Social Security numbers of their customers.

The Social Security Act of 1935 provided that each contributor be assigned a Social Security number to track contributions into the Social Security Fund. These numbers have a distinctive format, such as 078-05-1120. (This particular number was printed on sample cards that were inserted in wallets. It actually was the Social Security number of the secretary of a vice president at the wallet manufacturer. When thousands of people used it as their own, the number was voided, and the secretary received a new number. For more information, see http://www.ssa.gov/history/ssn/misused.html.) Figure 10 shows a Social Security card.

Although they were not intended for use as a universal identification number, Social Security numbers have become just that in the last 60 years. The tax authorities and many other government agencies are required to collect the numbers, as are banks (for the reporting of interest income) and, of course, employers. Many other organizations find it convenient to use the number as well.

From a technical standpoint, Social Security numbers are a lousy method for indexing a database. There is a risk of having two records with the same number, because many illegal immigrants use fake numbers. Not everyone has a number—in particular, foreign customers. Because there is no checksum, a clerical error (such as transposing two digits) cannot be detected. (Credit card numbers have a checksum.) For the same reason, it is easy for anyone to make up a number.

Figure 10   A Social Security Card

Some people are very concerned about the fact that just about every organization wants to store their Social Security number. Unless there is a legal requirement, such as for banks, one can usually fight it or take one's business elsewhere. Even when an organization is required to collect the number, such as an employer, one can insist that the number be used only on tax and Social Security paperwork, not on the face of an ID card. Unfortunately, it usually takes near-superhuman effort to climb the organizational ladder to find someone with the authority to process paperwork with no Social Security number or to assign another identification number.

As the Internet becomes a more pervasive part of our lives, you can witness firsthand the voracious appetite for personal information by marketers of products and services. There are many opportunities to obtain free services (such as free e-mail), if you are willing to divulge some personal information, and if you agree to the monitoring of your browsing and purchasing habits.

The discomfort that many people have about the computerization of their personal information is understandable. There is the possibility that companies and the government can merge multiple databases and derive information about us that we may wish they did not have or that simply may be untrue. An insurance company may deny coverage, or charge a higher premium, if it finds that you have too many relatives with a certain disease. You may be denied a job because of an inaccurate credit or medical report, and you may not even know the reason. These are very disturbing developments that have had a very negative impact for a small but growing number of people. See [3] and [4] for more information.

25.3 Installing a Database

A wide variety of database systems are available. Among them are

- High-performance commercial databases, such as Oracle, IBM DB2, or Microsoft SQL Server
- Open-source databases, such as PostgreSQL or MySQL
- Lightweight Java databases, such as McKoi and HSQLDB
- Desktop databases, such as Microsoft Access

Which one should you choose for learning database programming? That depends greatly on your available budget, computing resources, and experience with installing complex software. In a laboratory environment with a trained administrator, it makes a lot of sense to install a commercial database, such as Oracle, but the products themselves, the hardware to run them, and the staff to administer them are expensive. Open-source alternatives are available free of charge, and their quality has greatly increased in recent years. Although they may not be suited for large-scale applications, they work fine for learning purposes. However, installation is generally not for the faint of heart. Lightweight Java databases are much easier to install and work on a variety of platforms. This makes them a good choice for the beginner. Desktop databases have limited SQL support and can be difficult to configure for Java programming.

If you work in a computing laboratory, someone will have installed a database for you, and you should be able to find instructions on how to use it. If you install your own database, we recommend that you start out with a lightweight Java database.

Detailed instructions for installing a database vary widely. Here we give you a general sequence of steps on how to install a database and test your installation.

1. Obtain the database program, either on CD-ROM or by downloading it from the Web.

2. Read the installation instructions.

3. Install the program. This may be as simple as running an installation program, or you may need to recompile the program from its source code.

4. Start the database. With most database systems (but not some of the lightweight Java database systems), you need to start the database server before you can carry out any database operations. Read the installation instructions for details.

5. Set up user accounts. This typically involves running an administration program, logging in as administrator with a default administration account, and adding user names and passwords. If you are the only user of the database, you may simply be able to use a default account. Again, details vary greatly among databases, and you should consult the documentation.

6. Run a test. Most databases come with a program that allows you to execute interactive SQL instructions. Locate that program and find out how to log on as a database user. Then run the following SQL instructions:

```
CREATE TABLE Test (Name CHAR(20))
INSERT INTO Test VALUES ('Romeo')
SELECT * FROM Test
DROP TABLE Test
```

At this point, you should get a display that shows a single row and column of the Test database, containing the string "Romeo". If not, carefully read the documentation of your SQL tool to see how you need to enter SQL statements. For example, with some SQL tools, you need a special terminator for each SQL statement.

> You need a JDBC (Java Database Connectivity) driver to access a database from a Java program.

Once your database is set up and functioning correctly, you need to install a *JDBC driver*. The acronym JDBC stands for Java Database Connectivity, the name of the technology that enables Java programs to interact with databases. Different databases require different drivers, which may be supplied by either the database manufacturer or a third party. You need to locate and install the driver that matches your database. When your Java program issues SQL commands, the driver forwards them to the database and lets your program analyze the results (see Figure 11).

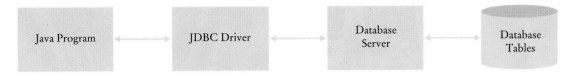

Figure 11 JDBC Architecture

> Make sure the JDBC driver is on the class path when you launch the Java program.

After you install the JDBC driver, you should run a test program to verify that the installation was successful. For this test program, we assume that you already created a Test table in your database, as described in the database test instructions. Here are the steps for testing the JDBC driver.

1. Every JDBC driver contains some Java code that your Java programs require to connect to the database. From the JDBC driver documentation, find the *class path* for the driver. Here is a typical example—the class path for the McKoi JDBC driver, installed on the C drive of a computer running the Windows operating system.

   ```
   c:\mckoi\mkjdbc.jar
   ```

   One version of the Oracle database uses a class path

   ```
   /usr/local/oracle/jdbc/classes111b.zip
   ```

   You will find this information in the documentation of the JDBC driver.

2. Find the name of the driver class that you need to load. Here is a typical driver class, also from the McKoi database:

   ```
   com.mckoi.JDBCDriver
   ```

   The Oracle database uses a driver

   ```
   oracle.jdbc.driver.OracleDriver
   ```

   In general, you should expect the class name to be in a package that matches the vendor name (such as `com.mckoi` or `oracle`), followed by some vendor-specific class name. Your JDBC driver documentation will have this documentation.

3. Find the name of the *database URL* that your driver expects. All database URLs have the format

   jdbc:*subprotocol*:*driver-specific data*

   The subprotocol is a code that identifies the driver manufacturer, such as `mckoi` or `oracle`. The driver-specific data encode the database name and the location of the database. Here are typical examples:

   ```
   jdbc:mckoi://localhost/
   jdbc:oracle:thin:@larry.mathcs.sjsu.edu:1521:InvoiceDB
   ```

   Again, consult your JDBC driver information for details on the format of the database URL and how to specify the database that you use.

4. In order to run the `TestDB.java` program at the end of this section, edit the file `database.properties` and supply

- The driver class name
- The database URL
- Your database user name
- Your database password

5. Compile the program as

```
javac TestDB.java
```

6. Run the program as

```
java -classpath driver_class_path;. TestDB database.properties
```

In UNIX/Linux, use a : separator in the class path:

```
java -classpath driver_class_path:. TestDB database.properties
```

If everything works correctly, you will get an output that lists all data in the Test table. If you followed the test instructions precisely, you will see one line of output with the name "Romeo".

If your program doesn't work, there are several possible causes.

- If you get an error message about a missing driver, then the program cannot load the JDBC driver. Check the class path and the driver name.
- If you get an error message that the driver cannot connect to the database, then the database may not be started, or, if the database is located on another computer, then the database may not be reachable. Check that the database is working by connecting with a SQL tool.
- If you get an error message about failed login, check the database name in the database URL, the user name, and the password.
- If you get an error message about a missing Test table, make sure you create and populate the table as described in the database test.

Here is the test program. We will explain the Java instructions of this program in the following section.

File TestDB.java

```
 1  import java.sql.Connection;
 2  import java.sql.ResultSet;
 3  import java.sql.Statement;
 4
 5  /**
 6      Tests a database installation by creating and querying
 7      a sample table. Call this program as
 8      java -classpath driver_class_path;. TestDB database.properties
 9  */
10  public class TestDB
11  {
12     public static void main(String[] args) throws Exception
13     {
```

```
14          if (args.length == 0)
15          {
16              System.out.println(
17                      "Usage: java -classpath driver_class_path;."
18                      + " TestDB propertiesFile");
19              return;
20          }
21          else
22              SimpleDataSource.init(args[0]);
23
24          Connection conn = SimpleDataSource.getConnection();
25          try
26          {
27              Statement stat = conn.createStatement();
28
29              stat.execute("CREATE TABLE Test (Name CHAR(20))");
30              stat.execute("INSERT INTO Test VALUES ('Romeo')");
31
32              ResultSet result = stat.executeQuery("SELECT * FROM Test");
33              result.next();
34              System.out.println(result.getString("Name"));
35
36              stat.execute("DROP TABLE Test");
37          }
38          finally
39          {
40              conn.close();
41          }
42      }
43 }
```

File SimpleDataSource.java

```
1  import java.sql.Connection;
2  import java.sql.DriverManager;
3  import java.sql.SQLException;
4  import java.io.FileInputStream;
5  import java.io.IOException;
6  import java.util.Properties;
7
8  /**
9      A simple data source for getting database connections.
10 */
11 public class SimpleDataSource
12 {
13     /**
14         Initializes the data source.
15         @param fileName the name of the property file that
16         contains the database driver, URL, username, and password
17     */
18     public static void init(String fileName)
19             throws IOException, ClassNotFoundException
20     {
```

```
21          Properties props = new Properties();
22          FileInputStream in = new FileInputStream(fileName);
23          props.load(in);
24
25          String driver = props.getProperty("jdbc.driver");
26          url = props.getProperty("jdbc.url");
27          username = props.getProperty("jdbc.username");
28          password = props.getProperty("jdbc.password");
29
30          Class.forName(driver);
31       }
32
33       /**
34          Gets a connection to the database.
35          @return the database connection
36       */
37       public static Connection getConnection() throws SQLException
38       {
39          return DriverManager.getConnection(url, username, password);
40       }
41
42       private static String url;
43       private static String username;
44       private static String password;
45    }
```

Sample File database.properties

```
1   jdbc.driver=com.mckoi.JDBCDriver
2   jdbc.url=jdbc:mckoi://localhost/
3   jdbc.username=admin
4   jdbc.password=secret
```

SELF CHECK

5. After installing a database system, how can you test that it is properly installed?

6. You are starting a Java database program to connect to the McKoi database and get the following error message:

   ```
   Exception in thread "main" java.lang.ClassNotFoundException:
   com.mckoi.JDBCDriver
   ```

   What is the most likely cause of this error?

25.4 Database Programming in Java

25.4.1 Connecting to the Database

Use a Connection object to access a database from a Java program.

To connect to a database, you need an object of the class Connection. The following code fragment shows you how to obtain such a connection. First, load the database driver; then ask the DriverManager for a connection. You need to initialize the driver, url, username, and password strings with the values that apply to your database.

```
String driver = . . .;
String url = . . .;
String username = . . .;
String password = . . .;

Class.forName(driver); // Load driver
Connection conn = DriverManager.getConnection(url,
    username, password);
```

When you are done issuing your database commands, close the database connection by calling the close method:

```
conn.close();
```

This is actually a somewhat simplistic view of connection management. Two problems occur in practice. Larger programs (such as the bank example in Section 25.5) need to connect to the database from many classes. You don't want to propagate the database login information to a large number of classes. Also, it is usually not feasible to use a single connection for all database requests. In particular, as you will see in Chapter 27, a container for Java server pages can run many simultaneous web page requests from different browsers. Each page request needs its own database connection. But because opening a database connection is quite slow and page requests come so frequently, database connections need to be pooled rather than closed and reopened. The details can be complex, and there is currently no standard implementation available.

It is always a good idea to decouple connection management from the other database code. We supply a SimpleDataSource class for this purpose. You can find the implementation at the end of the preceding section. This class is a very simple tool for connection management. At the beginning of your program, call the static init method with the name of the database configuration file, for example

```
SimpleDataSource.init("database.properties");
```

The configuration file is a text file containing four lines

```
jdbc.driver= . . .
jdbc.url= . . .
jdbc.username= . . .
jdbc.password= . . .
```

The init method uses the Properties class, which is designed to make it easy to read such a file.

The Properties class has a load method to read a file of key/value pairs from a stream:

```
Properties props = new Properties();
FileInputStream in = new FileInputStream(fileName);
props.load(in);
```

The getProperty method returns the value of a given key:

```
String driver = props.getProperty("jdbc.driver");
```

You don't actually have to think about this—the init method takes care of the details.

Whenever you need a connection, call

```
Connection conn = SimpleDataSource.getConnection();
```

You need to close the connection by calling

```
conn.close();
```

when you are done using it.

Real-world connection managers have slightly different methods, but the basic principle is the same.

QUALITY TIP 25.1

Don't Hardwire Database Connection Parameters into Your Program

It is considered inelegant to hardwire the database parameters into a program.

```
public class MyProg
{
    public static void main(String[] args)
    {
        // Don't do this:
        String driver = "com.mckoi.JDBCDriver";
        String url = "jdbc:mckoi://localhost/";
        String username = "admin";
        String password = "secret";
        . . .
    }
}
```

If you want to change to a different database, you must locate these strings, update them, and recompile.

Instead, place the strings into a separate configuration file. The SimpleDataSource.java file reads in a configuration file with the database connection parameters. To connect to a different database, you simply supply a different configuration file name on the command line.

25.4.2 Executing SQL Statements

Once you have a connection, you can use it to create Statement objects. You need Statement objects to execute SQL statements.

> A Connection object can create Statement objects that are used to execute SQL commands.

```
Statement stat = conn.createStatement();
```

The execute method of the Statement class executes a SQL statement. For example,

```
stat.execute("CREATE TABLE Test (Name CHAR(20))");
stat.execute("INSERT INTO Test VALUES ('Romeo')");
```

> The result of a SQL query is returned in a ResultSet object.

To issue a query, use the executeQuery method of the Statement class. The query result is returned as a ResultSet object. For example,

```
String query = "SELECT * FROM Test";
ResultSet result = stat.executeQuery(query);
```

You will see in the next section how to use the ResultSet object to analyze the result of the query.

For UPDATE statements, you can use the executeUpdate method. It returns the number of rows affected by the statement:

```
String command = "UPDATE Item"
    + " SET Quantity = Quantity + 1"
    + " WHERE Invoice_Number = '11731'";
int count = stat.executeUpdate(command);
```

If your statement has variable parts, then you should use a PreparedStatement instead.

```
String query = "SELECT * WHERE Account_Number = ?";
PreparedStatement stat = conn.prepareStatement(query);
```

The ? symbols in the query string denote variables that you fill in when you make an actual query. You call a set method for that purpose, for example

```
stat.setString(1, accountNumber);
```

The first parameter of the set methods denotes the variable position: 1 is the first ?, 2 the second, and so on. There are also methods setInt and setDouble for setting numerical variables. After you set all variables, you call executeQuery or executeUpdate.

Finally, you can use the generic execute method to execute arbitrary SQL statements. It returns a boolean value to indicate whether the SQL command yields a result set. If so, you can obtain it with the getResultSet method. Otherwise, you can get the update count with the getUpdateCount method.

```
String command = . . .;
boolean hasResultSet = stat.execute(command);
if (hasResultSet)
{
    ResultSet result = stat.getResultSet();
    . . .
}
else
{
```

```
        int count = stat.getUpdateCount();
        . . .
    }
```

You can reuse a `Statement` or `PreparedStatement` object to execute as many SQL commands as you like. However, for each statement, you should only have one active `ResultSet`. If your program needs to look at several result sets at the same time, then you need to create multiple `Statement` objects.

When you are done using a `ResultSet`, you should close it before issuing a new query on the same statement.

```
    result.close();
```

When you are done with a `Statement` object, you should close it. That automatically closes the associated result set.

```
    stat.close();
```

When you close a connection, it automatically closes all statements and result sets.

COMMON ERROR 25.2

Delimiters in Manually Constructed Queries

Suppose you need to issue the following query with different names.

```
    SELECT * FROM Customer WHERE Name = customerName
```

Many students try to construct a `SELECT` statement manually, like this:

```
    String customerName = . . . ;
    String query
        = "SELECT * FROM Customer WHERE Name = '" + customerName + "'";
    ResultSet result = stat.executeQuery(query);
```

However, this code will fail if the name contains single quotes, such as `"Sam's Small Appliances"`. The query string has a syntax error: a mismatched quote.

The remedy is to use a `PreparedStatement` instead:

```
    String query = "SELECT * FROM Customer WHERE Name = ?";
    PreparedStatement stat = conn.prepareStatement(query);
    stat.setString(1, aName);
    ResultSet result = stat.executeQuery(query);
```

25.4.3 Analyzing Query Results

A `ResultSet` lets you fetch the query result, one row at a time. You iterate through the rows, and for each row, you can inspect the column values. Like the collection iterators that you saw in Chapter 20, the `ResultSet` class has a `next` method to visit the next row. However, the behavior of the `next` method is somewhat different. The `next` method does not return any data but a `boolean` value that indicates whether more data are available. Moreover, when you first get a result set from the `executeQuery` method, no row data are available. You need to call next to move to the first row. This appears curious, but it makes the iteration loop simple:

```
while (result.next())
{
    Inspect column data from the current row
}
```

If the result set is completely empty, then the first call to result.next() returns false, and the loop is never entered. Otherwise, the first call to result.next() fetches the data for the first row from the database. As you can see, the loop ends when the next method returns false, which indicates that all rows have been fetched.

Once the result set object has fetched a particular row, you can inspect its columns. Various get methods return the column value formatted as a number, string, date, and so on. In fact, for each data type, there are two get methods. One of them has an integer parameter that indicates the column position. The other has a string parameter for the column name. For example, you can fetch the product code as

```
String productCode = result.getString(1);
```

or

```
String productCode = result.getString("Product_Code");
```

Note that the integer index starts at one, not at zero; that is, getString(1) inspects the first column. Database column indexes are different from array subscripts.

Accessing a column by an integer index is marginally faster and perfectly acceptable if you explicitly named the desired columns in the SELECT statement, such as

```
SELECT Invoice_Number FROM Invoice WHERE Payment = 0
```

However, if you make a SELECT * query, it is a good idea to use a column name instead of a column index. It makes your code easier to read, and you don't have to update the code when the column layout changes.

In the preceding example, you saw the getString method in action. To fetch a number, use the getInt and getDouble methods instead, for example

```
int quantity = result.getInt("Quantity");
double unitPrice = result.getDouble("Price");
```

PRODUCTIVITY HINT 25.4

Let the Database Do the Work

You now know how to issue a SQL query from a Java program and iterate through the result set. A common error that students make is to iterate through one table at a time to find a result. For example, suppose you want to find all invoices that contain car vacuums. You could use the following plan:

1. Issue the query SELECT * FROM Product and iterate through the result set to find the product code for a car vacuum.

2. Issue the query SELECT * FROM Item and iterate through the result set to find the items with that product code.

However, that plan is *extremely inefficient.* Such a program does in very slow motion what a database has been designed to do quickly.

Instead, you should let the database do all the work. Give the complete query to the database:

```
SELECT Item.Invoice_Number
   FROM Product, Item
   WHERE Product.Description = 'Car vacuum'
      AND Product.Product_Code = Item.Product_Code
```

Then iterate through the result set to read off all invoice numbers.

Beginners are often afraid of issuing complex SQL queries. However, you are throwing away a major benefit of a relational database if you don't take advantage of SQL.

25.4.4 Result Set Meta Data

Meta data are data about an object. Result set meta data describe the properties of a result set.

When you have a result set from an unknown table, you may want to know the names of the columns. You can use the ResultSetMetaData class to find out about properties of a result set. Start by requesting the meta data object from the result set:

```
ResultSetMetaData metaData = result.getMetaData();
```

Then you can get the number of columns with the getColumnCount method. The getColumnLabel method gives you the column name for each column. Finally, the getColumnDisplaySize method returns the column width, which is useful if you want to print table rows and have the columns line up. Note that the indexes for these methods start with 1. For example,

```
for (int i = 1; i <= metaData.getColumnCount(); i++)
{
   String columnName = metaData.getColumnLabel(i);
   int columnSize = metaData.getColumnDisplaySize(i);
   . . .
}
```

At the end of this section, you will find a useful program that puts these concepts to work. The program reads a file containing SQL statements and executes them all. When a statement has a result set, the result set is printed, using the result set meta data to determine the column count and column labels.

For example, suppose you have the following file:

File Product.sql

```
1  CREATE TABLE Product
2       (Product_Code CHAR(10), Description CHAR(40), Price DECIMAL(10, 2))
3  INSERT INTO Product VALUES ('116-064', 'Toaster', 24.95)
4  INSERT INTO Product VALUES ('257-535', 'Hair dryer', 29.95)
5  INSERT INTO Product VALUES ('643-119', 'Car vacuum', 19.95)
6  SELECT * FROM Product
```

Then run the program as

```
java ExecSQL database.properties product.sql
```

The program executes the statements in the file and prints out the result of the SELECT query.

You can also use the program as an interactive testing tool. Run

```
java ExecSQL database.properties
```

Type in SQL commands at the command line. Every time you hit the Enter key, the command is executed.

File ExecSQL.java

```
1  import java.sql.Connection;
2  import java.sql.ResultSet;
3  import java.sql.ResultSetMetaData;
4  import java.sql.Statement;
5  import java.sql.SQLException;
6  import java.io.FileReader;
7  import java.io.IOException;
8  import java.util.Scanner;
9
10 /**
11    Executes all SQL statements in a file.
12    Call this program as
13    java -classpath driver_class_path;. ExecSQL
14       database.properties commands.sql
15 */
16 public class ExecSQL
17 {
18    public static void main (String args[])
19          throws SQLException, IOException, ClassNotFoundException
20    {
21       if (args.length == 0)
22       {
23          System.out.println(
24                "Usage: java ExecSQL propertiesFile [statementFile]");
25          return;
26       }
27
28       SimpleDataSource.init(args[0]);
29
30       Scanner in;
31       if (args.length > 1)
32          in = new Scanner(new FileReader(args[1]));
```

```
33        else
34            in = new Scanner(System.in);
35
36        Connection conn = SimpleDataSource.getConnection();
37        try
38        {
39            Statement stat = conn.createStatement();
40            while (in.hasNextLine())
41            {
42                String line = in.nextLine();
43                boolean hasResultSet = stat.execute(line);
44                if (hasResultSet)
45                {
46                    ResultSet result = stat.getResultSet();
47                    showResultSet(result);
48                    result.close();
49                }
50            }
51        }
52        finally
53        {
54            conn.close();
55        }
56    }
57
58    /**
59        Prints a result set.
60        @param result the result set
61    */
62    public static void showResultSet(ResultSet result)
63            throws SQLException
64    {
65        ResultSetMetaData metaData = result.getMetaData();
66        int columnCount = metaData.getColumnCount();
67
68        for (int i = 1; i <= columnCount; i++)
69        {
70            if (i > 1) System.out.print(", ");
71            System.out.print(metaData.getColumnLabel(i));
72        }
73        System.out.println();
74
75        while (result.next())
76        {
77            for (int i = 1; i <= columnCount; i++)
78            {
79                if (i > 1) System.out.print(", ");
80                System.out.print(result.getString(i));
81            }
82            System.out.println();
83        }
84    }
85 }
```

SELF CHECK

7. Suppose you want to test whether there are any customers in Hawaii. Issue the statement

```
ResultSet result = stat.executeQuery(
    "SELECT * FROM Customer WHERE State = 'HI'");
```

Which Boolean expression answers your question?

8. Suppose you want to know how many customers are in Hawaii. What is an efficient way to get this answer?

25.5 Case Study: A Bank Database

In this section, we will develop a complete database program. We will reimplement the ATM simulation of Chapter 17, storing the customer and account data in a database. Recall that in the simulation, every customer has a customer number, a PIN, and two bank accounts: a checking account and a savings account. We'll store the information in two tables:

BankCustomer

Customer_Number	PIN	Checking_Account_Number	Savings_Account_Number
INTEGER	INTEGER	INTEGER	INTEGER

Account

Account_Number	Balance
INTEGER	DECIMAL (10, 2)

The Bank class now needs to connect to the database whenever it is asked to find a customer. Here is the implementation of the method that finds a customer. The method makes a query

```
SELECT * FROM BankCustomer WHERE Customer_Number = . . .
```

It then checks that the PIN matches, and it constructs a Customer object. This method turns the row-and-column information of the database into object-oriented data.

```
public Customer findCustomer(int customerNumber, int pin)
    throws SQLException
{
```

```
Connection conn = SimpleDataSource.getConnection();
try
{
   Customer c = null;
   PreparedStatement stat = conn.prepareStatement(
         "SELECT * FROM BankCustomer WHERE Customer_Number = ?");
   stat.setInt(1, customerNumber);

   ResultSet result = stat.executeQuery();
   if (result.next() && pin == result.getInt("PIN"))
      c = new Customer(customerNumber,
            result.getInt("Checking_Account_Number"),
            result.getInt("Savings_Account_Number"));
   return c;
}
finally
{
   conn.close();
}
}
```

Note that the method throws a SQLException. Why don't we catch that exception and return null if an exception occurs? There are many potential reasons for a SQL exception, and the Bank class doesn't want to hide the exception details. But the Bank class also doesn't know anything about the user interface of the application, so it can't display information about the exception to the user. By throwing the exception to the caller, the information can reach the part of the program that interacts with the user.

The BankAccount class in this program is quite different from the implementation you have seen throughout the book. Now we do not store the balance of the bank account in the object; instead, we look it up from the database:

```
public double getBalance()
      throws SQLException
{
   Connection conn = SimpleDataSource.getConnection();
   try
   {
      double balance = 0;
      PreparedStatement stat = conn.prepareStatement(
            "SELECT Balance FROM Account WHERE Account_Number = ?");
      stat.setInt(1, accountNumber);
      ResultSet result = stat.executeQuery();
      if (result.next())
         balance = result.getDouble(1);
      return balance;
   }
   finally
   {
      conn.close();
   }
}
```

The deposit and withdraw operations immediately update the database as well:

```java
public void deposit(double amount)
      throws SQLException
{
   Connection conn = SimpleDataSource.getConnection();
   try
   {
      PreparedStatement stat = conn.prepareStatement(
            "UPDATE Account"
            + " SET Balance = Balance + ?"
            + " WHERE Account_Number = ?");
      stat.setDouble(1, amount);
      stat.setInt(2, accountNumber);
      stat.executeUpdate();
   }
   finally
   {
      conn.close();
   }
}
```

It seems somewhat inefficient to connect to the database whenever the bank balance is accessed, but it is much safer than storing it in an object. Suppose you have two instances of the ATM program running at the same time. Then it is possible that both programs modify the same bank account. If each of them copied the bank balances from the database into objects, then the modifications made by one user would not be seen by the other.

You can try out this simultaneous access yourself, simply by running two instances of the ATM simulation. Alternatively, you can modify the main method of the ATMViewer class to pop up two ATM frames.

Clearly, access by multiple users is very important in practice. Most real database applications have many simultaneous users. Therefore, you must design the translation from the database data to program objects with some care. You can't just copy data into objects that other users might modify. On the other hand, database lookups are pretty slow compared to object lookups, so you want to hold immutable data in objects. Programming real-world database applications that run quickly and correctly can get quite complex. In recent years, *application servers* have become available that manage some of this burden for developers. An application server monitors the objects that mirror database information and makes sure that the object and database data are always synchronized. The Java 2 Enterprise Edition defines a technology standard for Java-based application servers.

The source code for the modified ATM application follows. The source code for the ATM and ATMTester/ATMFrame classes is only changed minimally, by adding code to deal with the SQLException. The Customer class is unchanged. We do not list those classes.

This example completes our chapter on Java database programming. You have seen how you can use SQL to query and update data in a database and how the JDBC library makes it easy for you to issue SQL commands in a Java program.

File Bank.java

```java
1   import java.sql.Connection;
2   import java.sql.ResultSet;
3   import java.sql.PreparedStatement;
4   import java.sql.SQLException;
5
6   /**
7       A bank consisting of multiple bank accounts.
8   */
9   public class Bank
10  {
11      /**
12          Finds a customer with a given number and PIN.
13          @param customerNumber the customer number
14          @param pin the personal identification number
15          @return the matching customer, or null if none found
16      */
17      public Customer findCustomer(int customerNumber, int pin)
18              throws SQLException
19      {
20          Connection conn = SimpleDataSource.getConnection();
21          try
22          {
23              Customer c = null;
24              PreparedStatement stat = conn.prepareStatement(
25                  "SELECT * FROM BankCustomer WHERE Customer_Number = ?");
26              stat.setInt(1, customerNumber);
27
28              ResultSet result = stat.executeQuery();
29              if (result.next() && pin == result.getInt("PIN"))
30                  c = new Customer(customerNumber,
31                      result.getInt("Checking_Account_Number"),
32                      result.getInt("Savings_Account_Number"));
33              return c;
34          }
35          finally
36          {
37              conn.close();
38          }
39      }
40  }
```

File BankAccount.java

```java
1   import java.sql.Connection;
2   import java.sql.ResultSet;
3   import java.sql.PreparedStatement;
4   import java.sql.SQLException;
5
6   /**
7       A bank account has a balance that can be changed by
8       deposits and withdrawals.
9   */
```

```
10   public class BankAccount
11   {
12      /**
13         Constructs a bank account with a given balance.
14         @param anAccountNumber the account number
15      */
16      public BankAccount(int anAccountNumber)
17      {
18         accountNumber = anAccountNumber;
19      }
20
21      /**
22         Deposits money into a bank account.
23         @param amount the amount to deposit
24      */
25      public void deposit(double amount)
26            throws SQLException
27      {
28         Connection conn = SimpleDataSource.getConnection();
29         try
30         {
31            PreparedStatement stat = conn.prepareStatement(
32                  "UPDATE Account"
33                  + " SET Balance = Balance + ?"
34                  + " WHERE Account_Number = ?");
35            stat.setDouble(1, amount);
36            stat.setInt(2, accountNumber);
37            stat.executeUpdate();
38         }
39         finally
40         {
41            conn.close();
42         }
43      }
44
45      /**
46         Withdraws money from a bank account.
47         @param amount the amount to withdraw
48      */
49      public void withdraw(double amount)
50            throws SQLException
51      {
52         Connection conn = SimpleDataSource.getConnection();
53         try
54         {
55            PreparedStatement stat = conn.prepareStatement(
56                  "UPDATE Account"
57                  + " SET Balance = Balance - ?"
58                  + " WHERE Account_Number = ?");
59            stat.setDouble(1, amount);
60            stat.setInt(2, accountNumber);
61            stat.executeUpdate();
62         }
```

```
63        finally
64        {
65            conn.close();
66        }
67    }
68
69    /**
70        Gets the balance of a bank account.
71        @return the account balance
72    */
73    public double getBalance()
74            throws SQLException
75    {
76        Connection conn = SimpleDataSource.getConnection();
77        try
78        {
79            double balance = 0;
80            PreparedStatement stat = conn.prepareStatement(
81                    "SELECT Balance FROM Account WHERE Account_Number = ?");
82            stat.setInt(1, accountNumber);
83            ResultSet result = stat.executeQuery();
84            if (result.next())
85                balance = result.getDouble(1);
86            return balance;
87        }
88        finally
89        {
90            conn.close();
91        }
92    }
93
94    private int accountNumber;
95 }
```

SELF CHECK

9. Why doesn't the Bank class store an array of Customer objects?

10. Why do the BankAccount methods throw an SQLException instead of catching it?

ADVANCED TOPIC 25.2

Transactions

An important part of database processing is *transaction handling*. A *transaction* is a set of database updates that should either succeed in their entirety or not happen at all. For example, consider a banking application that transfers money from one account to another. This operation involves two steps: reducing the balance of one account and increasing the balance of another account. No software system is perfect, and there is always the possibility of an error. The banking application, the database program, or the network connection between them could exhibit an error right after the first part—then the money would be withdrawn from the first account but never deposited to the second account. Clearly, this would be very bad. There are many other similar situations. For example, if you change an airline reservation, you don't want to give up your old seat until the new one is confirmed.

What all these situations have in common is that there is a set of database operations that are grouped together to carry out the transaction. All operations in the group must be carried out together—a partial completion cannot be tolerated. In SQL, you use the COMMIT and ROLLBACK commands to manage transactions. For example, to transfer money from one account to another, you issue the commands

```
UPDATE Account SET Balance = Balance - 1000
    WHERE Account_Number = '95667-2574'
UPDATE Account SET Balance = Balance + 1000
    WHERE Account_Number = '82041-1196'
COMMIT
```

The COMMIT command makes the updates permanent. Conversely, the ROLLBACK command undoes all changes up to the last COMMIT.

When you program with JDBC, by default the JDBC library automatically commits all database updates. That is convenient for simple programs, but it is not what you want for transaction processing. Thus, you should first turn the autocommit mode off:

```
Connection conn = . . .;
conn.setAutoCommit(false);
Statement stat = conn.createStatement();
```

Then issue the updates that form the transaction and call the commit method of the Statement class.

```
stat.executeUpdate(
    "UPDATE Account SET Balance = Balance - "
    + amount + " WHERE Account_Number = " + fromAccount);
stat.executeUpdate(
    "UPDATE Account SET Balance = Balance + "
    + amount + " WHERE Account_Number = " + toAccount);
conn.commit();
```

Conversely, if you encounter an error, then call the rollback method. This typically happens in an exception handler:

```
try
{
    . . .
}
catch(SQLException exception)
{
    conn.rollback();
}
```

You may wonder how a database can undo updates when a transaction is rolled back. The database actually stores your changes in a set of temporary tables. If you make queries within a transaction, the information in the temporary tables is merged with the permanent data for the purpose of computing the query result, giving you the illusion that the updates have already taken place. When you commit the transaction, the temporary data are made permanent. When you execute a rollback, the temporary tables are simply discarded.

CHAPTER SUMMARY

1. A relational database stores information in tables. Each table column has a name and a data type.

2. SQL (Structured Query Language) is a command language for interacting with a database.

3. Use the SQL commands CREATE TABLE and INSERT INTO to add data to a database.

4. You should avoid rows with replicated data. Instead, distribute the data over multiple tables.

5. A primary key is a column (or set of columns) whose value uniquely specifies a table record.

6. A foreign key is a reference to a primary key in a linked table.

7. Use the SQL SELECT command to query a database.

8. A join is a query that involves multiple tables.

9. The UPDATE and DELETE SQL commands modify the data in a database.

10. You need a JDBC (Java Database Connectivity) driver to access a database from a Java program.

11. Make sure the JDBC driver is on the class path when you launch the Java program.

12. Use a Connection object to access a database from a Java program.

13. A Connection object can create Statement objects that are used to execute SQL commands.

14. The result of a SQL query is returned in a ResultSet object.

15. Meta data are data about an object. Result set meta data describe the properties of a result set.

FURTHER READING

1. Chris J. Date and Hugh Darwen, *A Guide to the SQL Standard: A User's Guide to the Standard Database Language SQL,* 4th edition, Addison-Wesley, 1997.

2. Maydene Fisher, Jon Ellis, and Jonathan Bruce, *JDBC API Tutorial and Reference,* 3rd edition, Addison-Wesley, 2003.

3. http://www.cpsr.org/cpsr/privacy/ssn/ssn.faq.html   A list of frequently asked questions about Social Security numbers, by Computer Professionals for Social Responsibility.

4. http://www.ftc.gov/privacy/   A web site on information privacy by the Federal Trade Commission.

CLASSES, OBJECTS, AND METHODS INTRODUCED IN THIS CHAPTER

```
java.lang.Class                    java.sql.ResultSet
   forName                            close
java.sql.Connection                   getDouble
   close                              getInt
   commit                             getMetaData
   createStatement                    getString
   prepareCall                        next
   prepareStatement                java.sql.ResultSetMetaData
   rollback                           getColumnCount
   setAutoCommit                      getColumnDisplaySize
java.sql.DriverManager                getColumnLabel
   getConnection                   java.sql.SQLException
java.sql.PreparedStatement         java.sql.Statement
   execute                            close
   executeQuery                       execute
   executeUpdate                      executeQuery
   setDouble                          executeUpdate
   setInt                             getResultSet
   setString                          getUpdateCount
                                   java.util.Properties
                                      getProperty
                                      load
```

REVIEW EXERCISES

Exercise R25.1. Design a set of database tables to store people and cars. A person has a name, a unique driver license number, and an address. Every car has a unique vehicle identification number, manufacturer, type, and year. Every car has one owner, but one person can own multiple cars.

Exercise R25.2. Design a set of database tables to store library books and patrons. A book has an ISBN (International Standard Book Number), an author, and a title. The library may have multiple copies of each book, each with a different book ID. A patron has a name, a unique ID, and an address. A book may be checked out by at most one patron, but one patron can check out multiple books.

Exercise R25.3. Design a set of database tables to store sets of coins in purses. Each purse has an owner name and a unique ID. Each coin type has a unique name and a value. Each purse contains some quantity of coins of a given type.

Exercise R25.4. Design a set of database tables to store students, classes, professors, and classrooms. Each student takes zero or more classes. Each class has one professor, but a professor can teach multiple classes. Each class has one classroom.

Exercise R25.5. Give SQL commands to create a Book table, with columns for the ISBN, author, and title, and to insert all textbooks that you are using this semester.

Exercise R25.6. Give SQL commands to create a Car table, with columns for the vehicle identification number, manufacturer, type, and year of cars, and to insert all cars that your family members own.

Exercise R25.7. Give a SQL query that lists all products in the invoice database of Section 25.2.

Exercise R25.8. Give a SQL query that lists all customers in California.

Exercise R25.9. Give a SQL query that lists all customers in California or Nevada.

Exercise R25.10. Give a SQL query that lists all customers not in Hawaii.

Exercise R25.11. Give a SQL query that lists all customers who have an unpaid invoice.

Exercise R25.12. Give a SQL query that lists all products that have been purchased by a customer in California.

Exercise R25.13. Give a SQL query that lists all items that are part of invoice number 11731.

Exercise R25.14. Give a SQL query that computes the sum of all quantities that are part of invoice number 11731.

Exercise R25.15. Give a SQL query that computes the total cost. SUM(Product.Price * Item.Quantity) of all items in invoice number 11731.

Exercise R25.16. Give a SQL update statement that raises all prices by 10%.

Exercise R25.17. Give a SQL statement that deletes all customers in California.

Exercise R25.18. Pick a database system (such as DB2, Oracle, Postgres, or SQL Server) and determine from the web documentation:
- What JDBC driver do you need?
- What is the database URL?

Exercise R25.19. What is the difference between a Connection and a Statement?

Exercise R25.20. Of the SQL commands introduced in this chapter, which yield result sets, which yield an update count, and which yield neither?

Exercise R25.21. How is a ResultSet different from an Iterator?

PROGRAMMING EXERCISES

Exercise P25.1. Write a Java program that creates a Coin table with coin names and values; inserts coin types penny, nickel, dime, quarter, half dollar, and dollar; and prints out the sum of the coin values. Use CREATE TABLE, INSERT, and SELECT SUM SQL commands.

Exercise P25.2. Write a Java program that creates a Car table with car manufacturers, types, model years, and fuel efficiency ratings. Insert several cars. Print out the average fuel efficiency. Use CREATE TABLE, INSERT, and SELECT AVG SQL commands.

Exercise P25.3. Reimplement the bank data program from Section 16.4 using a database table for the bank accounts.

Exercise P25.4. Improve the ExecSQL program and make the columns of the output line up. *Hint:* Use the getColumnDisplaySize method of the ResultSetMetaData class.

Exercise P25.5. Write a Java program that uses the database tables from the invoice database in Section 25.2. Prompt the user for an invoice number and print out the invoice, formatted as in Chapter 17.

Exercise P25.6. Write a Java program that uses the database tables from the invoice database in Section 25.2. Produce a report that lists all customers, their invoices, the amounts paid, and the unpaid balances.

Exercise P25.7. Write a Java program that uses a library database of books and patron data, as described in Exercise R25.2. Patrons should be able to check out and return books. Supply commands to print the books that a patron has checked out and to find who has checked out a particular book. You may create and populate Patron and Book tables before running the program.

Exercise P25.8. Write a Java program that creates a grade book for a class. You may create and populate a Student table and other tables that you need before running the program. The program should be able to display all grades for a given student. It should allow the instructor to add a new grade (such as "Homework 4: 100") or modify an existing grade.

Exercise P25.9. Write a program that assigns seats on an airplane as described in Exercise P17.11. Keep the passenger and seating information in a database.

Exercise P25.10. Write a program that keeps an appointment calendar in a database. An appointment includes a description, a date, the starting time, and the ending time; for example,

```
Dentist 2005/10/1 17:30 18:30
CS1 class 2005/10/2 08:30 10:00
```

Supply a user interface to add appointments, remove canceled appointments, and print out a list of appointments for a particular day. Your user interface can be text-based or graphical.

Exercise P25.11. Modify the ATM simulation program of Section 25.5 so that the program pops up two ATM frames. Verify that the database can be accessed simultaneously by two users.

PROGRAMMING PROJECTS

Project 25.1. Implement a message board application that stores users and messages in a database. Users can post messages, reply to messages, and view posted messages. Provide views that list the messages by topic, by user, and by posting date. Allow the user to view all replies to a given message.

Project 25.2. Implement a group calendar application that stores users, groups, and event dates in a database. Users can join groups. Meetings and other events can be scheduled, and individuals and groups can be added as participants. Users can accept or reject invitations to events. Provide views that show all events of a user in a given time interval, and all users for an event, showing whether they have accepted or rejected the invitation.

ANSWERS TO SELF-CHECK QUESTIONS

1. The telephone number for each customer is unique—a necessary requirement for the primary key. However, if a customer moves and the telephone number changes, both the primary and all foreign keys would need to be updated. Therefore, a customer ID is a better choice.

2. Customer 3176 ordered ten toasters.

3. `SELECT Name FROM Customer WHERE State <> 'AK' AND State <> 'HI'`

4. ```
   SELECT Invoice.Invoice_Number FROM Invoice, Customer
       WHERE Invoice.Invoice_Number = Customer.Customer_Number
       AND Customer.State = 'HI'
   ```

5. Connect to the database with a program that lets you execute SQL instructions. Try creating a small database table, adding a record, and selecting all records. Then drop the table again.

6. You didn't set the class path correctly. The JAR file containing the JDBC driver must be on the class path.

7. `result.hasNext()`. If there is at least one result, then `hasNext` returns `true`.

8. ```
   ResultSet result = stat.executeQuery(
           "SELECT COUNT(*) FROM Customer WHERE State = 'HI'");
   result.next();
   int count = result.getInt(1);
   ```
   Note that the following alternative is significantly slower if there are many such customers.
   ```
   ResultSet result = stat.executeQuery(
           "SELECT * FROM Customer WHERE State = 'HI'");
   while (result.next()) count++; // Inefficient
   ```

9. The customer data are stored in the database. The `Bank` class is now merely a conduit to the data.

10. The methods are not equipped to handle the exception. What could they do? Print an error report? To the console or a GUI window? In which language?

XML

CHAPTER GOALS

- Understanding XML elements and attributes
- Understanding the concept of an XML parser
- Being able to read and write XML documents
- Being able to design Document Type Definitions for XML documents

In this chapter, you will learn about the Extensible Markup Language (XML), a mechanism for encoding data that is independent of any programming language. XML allows you to encode complex data in a form that the recipient can easily parse. XML is becoming very popular for data exchange. It is simple enough that a wide variety of programs can easily generate XML data. XML data has a nested structure, so you can use it to describe hierarchical data sets—for example, an invoice that contains many items, each of which consists of a product and a quantity. Because the XML format is standardized, libraries for parsing the data are widely available and—as you will see in this chapter—easy to use for a programmer.

It is particularly easy to read and write XML documents in Java. In fact, it is generally easier to use XML than it is to use an "ad hoc" file format. Thus, using XML makes your programs easier to write and more professional.

CHAPTER CONTENTS

26.1 XML Tags and Documents

26.1.1 Advantages of XML

> XML allows you to encode complex data, independent from any programming language, in a form that the recipient can easily parse.

To understand the advantages of using XML for encoding data, let's look at a typical example. We will encode product descriptions, so that they can be transferred to another computer. Your first attempt might be a naïve encoding like this:

```
Toaster
29.95
```

In contrast, here is an XML encoding of the same data:

```
<product>
    <description>Toaster</description>
    <price>29.95</price>
</product>
```

> XML files are readable by computer programs and by humans.

The advantage of the XML version is clear: You can look at the data and understand what they mean. Of course, this is a benefit for the programmer, not for a computer program. A computer program has no understanding of what a "price" is. As a programmer, you still need to write code to extract the price as the contents of the price element. Nevertheless, the fact that an XML document is comprehensible by humans is a huge advantage for program development.

A second advantage of the XML version is that it is *resilient to change*. Suppose the product data change, and an additional data item is introduced, to denote the manufacturer. In the naïve format, the manufacturer might be added after the price, like this:

XML-formatted data files are resilient to change.

```
Toaster
29.95
General Appliances
```

A program that can process the old format might get confused when reading a sequence of products in the new format. The program would think that the price is followed by the name of the next product. Thus, the program needs to be updated to work with both the old and new data formats. As data get more complex, programming for multiple versions of a data format can be difficult and time-consuming.

When using XML, on the other hand, it is easy to add new elements:

```
<product>
    <description>Toaster</description>
    <price>29.95</price>
    <manufacturer>General Appliances</manufacturer>
</product>
```

Now a program that processes the new data can still extract the old information in the same way—as the contents of the description and price elements. The program need not be updated, and it can tolerate different versions of the data format.

26.1.2 Differences Between XML and HTML

If you know HTML, you may have noticed that the XML format of the product data looked somewhat like HTML code. However, there are some differences that we will discuss in this section.

Let us start with the similarities. The XML tag pairs, such as <price> and </price> look just like HTML tag pairs, for example <li> and </li>. Both in XML and in HTML, tags are enclosed in angle brackets < >, and a start-tag is paired with an end-tag that starts with a slash / character.

However, web browsers are quite permissive about HTML. For example, you can omit an end-tag </li> and the browser will try to figure out what you mean. In XML, this is not permissible. When writing XML, pay attention to the following rules:

- In XML, you *must* pay attention to the letter case of the tags; for example, <li> and <LI> are different tags that bear no relation to each other.

- Every start-tag *must* have a matching end-tag. You cannot omit tags, such as </li>. However, if a tag has no end-tag, it must end in />, for example

```
<img src="hamster.jpeg"/>
```

When the parser sees the `/>`, it knows not to look for a matching end-tag.

- Finally, attribute values must be enclosed in quotes. For example,

```
<img src="hamster.jpeg" width=400 height=300/>
```

is not acceptable. You must use

```
<img src="hamster.jpeg" width="400" height="300"/>
```

Moreover, there is an important conceptual difference between HTML and XML. HTML has one specific purpose: to describe web documents. In contrast, XML is an *extensible* syntax that can be used to specify many different kinds of data. For example, the VRML language uses the XML syntax to describe virtual reality scenes. The MathML language uses the XML syntax to describe mathematical formulas. You can use the XML syntax to describe your own data, such as product records or invoices.

> XML describes the meaning of data, not how to display them.

Most people who first see XML wonder how an XML document looks inside a browser. However, that is *not* generally a useful question to ask. Most data that are encoded in XML have nothing to do with browsers. For example, it would probably not be exciting to display an XML document with nothing but product records (such as the ones in the previous section) in a browser. Instead, you will learn in this chapter how to write programs that analyze XML data. XML does not tell you how to display data; it is merely a convenient format for representing data.

RANDOM FACT 26.1

Word Processing and Typesetting Systems

You have almost certainly used a *word processor* for writing letters or reports. A word processor is a program to write and edit documents made up of text and images. The text can contain characters in various fonts. It can be arranged in paragraphs, tables, and footnotes. Paragraphs can be formatted in various ways, such as ragged right (that is, the left ends of the lines of text are aligned under each other, but the right ends aren't), centered, and fully justified (that is, both the left and right ends of the lines are aligned). What is characteristic of modern word processors is their "what you see is what you get" operation. You enter text and commands, using the keyboard and the mouse. The computer screen instantly shows what the printed document will look like (see Figure 1).

However, there are disadvantages to the "what you see is what you get" (WYSIWYG, pronounced *wis-ee-wig*) nature of a word processor. You may labor to arrange various related images and tables on the same page. Later, you find that you need to add a couple of paragraphs on the preceding page. Now half of the material moves to the next page, and you have do the arranging all over again. It would have been more useful if you could have told the word processor your intention, namely: "Always keep these images and tables together on the same page". In general, "what you see is what you get" programs are very good in letting you arrange material, but they don't know *why* you arranged the material in a certain way. Thus, they can't keep the arrangement when your document changes. Some people call these programs "what you see is all you've got".

More fundamentally, "what you see is what you get" programs break down when you need to publish the same material in multiple ways. You may want to format product information

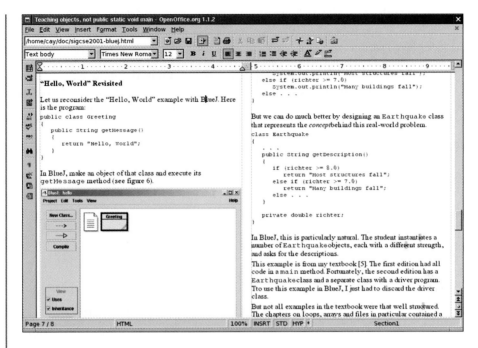

Figure 1   A "What You See Is What You Get" Word Processor

as a product parts list and an advertising brochure. Or you may want to publish the information in printed form, on the Web, and in spoken form for telephone retrieval. Now you no longer want to "get" a single result, so it isn't as helpful to see what you get. Instead, it becomes much more important to visualize the *structure* of the information.

A program for editing structured text needs to capture three pieces of information:

- The text itself
- The structural element (paragraph, bulleted list, heading, and so on) to which each part of the text belongs
- The rules for formatting the structural elements

To make it easy to interchange structured documents between computer systems, the structural information is often encoded in *markup tags*. For example, XML and HTML use tags that are enclosed in angle brackets, such as the familiar <p>, <ul>, and <h1> tags.

In the 1970s, when publishers began to move away from traditional manual typesetting to computer-based typesetting, the result at first was inferior quality, particularly for mathematical formulas. Arranging the symbols in complex formulas in a way that makes mathematical sense is an art that requires practice and good judgment, and the first typesetting programs were definitely not up to the job. Frustrated by this situation, the famous computer scientist Donald Knuth of Stanford University decided to do something about it and invented a typesetting program that he called T$_E$X (pronounced "tek" because the "X" is a capital Greek chi). Input to that program consists of text with markup tags that start with a backslash; curly braces {} for grouping; and other special markup symbols, such as _ and ^ to indicate subscript and superscript. For example, to specify a summation, you type

```
\sum_{i=1}^n i^2
```

The T_EX program typesets the summation as shown in Figure 2. Note that the expression is formatted one way when it occurs inside text and another way when it appears as part of a displayed formula.

A markup tag such as `<h1>` in HTML or `\sum` in T_EX is mainly beneficial for exchanging documents among different computer systems. Only the most hardened HTML or T_EX authors produce the markup by hand. For HTML in particular, many programs are available that display the structure of an HTML document and allow authors to edit both text and structure in a convenient way that combines the benefits of visual feedback and structure editing.

A sum inside text: $\sum_{i=1}^{n} i^2$

The same sum as a displayed formula:

$$\sum_{i=1}^{n} i^2$$

Figure 2   A Formula Typeset in the T_EX Typesetting System

26.1.3 The Structure of an XML Document

> An XML document starts out with an XML declaration and contains elements and text.

In this section, you will see the rules for properly formatted XML. In XML, text and tags are combined into a *document*. The XML standard recommends that every XML document start with a declaration

```
<?xml version="1.0"?>
```

Next, the XML document contains the actual data. The data are contained in a root element. For example,

```
<?xml version="1.0"?>
<invoice>
   more data
</invoice>
```

The root element is an example of an XML element. An element has one of two forms:

<elementName> content *</elementName>*

or

<elementName/>

In the first case, the element has content—elements, text, or a mixture of both. A good example is a paragraph in an HTML document:

```
<p>Use XML for <strong>robust</strong> data formats.</p>
```

The p element contains

1. The text: "Use XML for "
2. A strong child element
3. More text: " data formats."

An element can contain text, child elements, or both (mixed content). For data descriptions, avoid mixed content.

For XML files that contain documents in the traditional sense of the term, the mixture of text and elements is useful. The XML specification calls this type of content *mixed content*. But for files that describe data sets—such as our product data—it is better to stick with elements that contain *either* other elements or text. Content that consists only of elements is called *element content*.

An element can have *attributes*. For example, the a element of HTML has an href attribute that specifies the URL of a hyperlink:

```
<a href="http://java.sun.com"> . . . </a>
```

Elements can have attributes. Use attributes to describe how to interpret the element content.

An attribute has a name (such as href) and a value. In XML, the value must be enclosed in single or double quotes.

An element can have multiple attributes, for example

```
<img src="hamster.jpeg" width="400" height="300"/>
```

And, as you have already seen, an element can have both attributes and content.

```
<a href="http://java.sun.com">Sun's Java web site</a>
```

Programmers often wonder whether it is better to use attributes or child elements. For example, should a product be described as

```
<product description="Toaster" price="29.95"/>
```

or

```
<product>
  <description>Toaster</description>
  <price>29.95</price>
</product>
```

The former is shorter. However, it violates the spirit of attributes. Attributes are intended to provide information *about* the element content. For example, the price element might have an attribute currency that helps interpret the element content. The content 29.95 has a different interpretation in the element

```
<price currency="USD">29.95</price>
```

than it does in the element

```
<price currency="EUR">29.95</price>
```

You have now seen the components of an XML document that are needed to use XML for encoding data. There are other XML constructs for more specialized situations—see [1] for more information. In the next section, you will see how to use Java to parse XML documents.

SELF CHECK

1. Write XML code with a student element and child elements name and id that describe you.
2. What does your browser do when you load an XML file, such as the items.xml file that is contained in the companion code for this book?
3. Why does HTML use the src attribute to specify the source of an image instead of `<img>hamster.jpeg</img>`?

HOW TO 26.1

Designing an XML Document Format

This How To walks you through the process of designing an XML document format. You will see in Section 26.4 how to formally describe the format with a document type definition. Right now, we focus on an informal definition of the document content. The "output" of this activity is a sample document.

Step 1 Gather the data that you must include in the XML document.

Write them on a sheet of paper. If at all possible, work from some real-life examples. For example, suppose you need to design an XML document for an invoice. An invoice has

- An invoice number
- A shipping address
- A billing address
- A list of items ordered

If possible, gather some actual invoices. Decide which features of the actual invoices you need to include in your XML document.

Step 2 Analyze which data elements need to be refined.

Continue refinement until you reach data values that can be described by single strings or numbers. Make a note of all data items that you discovered during the refinement process. When done, you should have a list of data elements, some of which can be broken down further and some of which are simple enough to be described by a single string or number.

For example, the "shipping address" actually contains the customer name, street, city, state, and ZIP code.

The "list of items ordered" contains items. Each item contains a product and the quantity ordered. Each product contains the product name and price.

Thus, our list now contains

- Invoice number
- Address
- Name
- Street
- City
- State

- ZIP code
- List of items ordered
- Item
- Product
- Description
- Price
- Quantity

Keep breaking the data items down until each of them can be described by a single *string* or *number*. For example, an address cannot be described by a single string, but a city can be described by a single string.

Step 3 Come up with a suitable element name that describes the entire XML document.

This element becomes the root element. For example, the invoice data would be contained in an element named `invoice`.

Step 4 Come up with suitable element names for the top-level decomposition that you found in Step 1.

These become the children of the root element. For example, the `invoice` element has children

- `number`
- `address`
- `items`

Step 5 Repeat this process to give names to the other elements that you discovered in Step 2.

As you do this, make a comprehensive example that shows all elements at work. For the invoice problem, here is an example.

```
<invoice>
   <number>11365</number>
   <address>
      <name>John Meyers</name>
      <company>ACME Computer Supplies Inc.</company>
      <street>1195 W. Fairfield Rd.</street>
      <city>Sunnyvale</city>
      <state>CA</state>
      <zip>94085</zip>
   </address>
   <items>
      <item>
         <product>
            <description>Ink Jet Refill Kit</description>
            <price>29.95</price>
         </product>
         <quantity>8</quantity>
      </item>
      <item>
         <product>
            <description>4-port Mini Hub</description>
            <price>19.95</price>
```

```
        </product>
        <quantity>4</quantity>
      </item>
    </items>
  </invoice>
```

Step 6   Check that the document doesn't have mixed content.

That is, make sure each element has as its children either additional elements or text, but not both. If necessary, add more child elements to wrap any text.

For example, suppose the product element looked like this:

```
<product>
    <description>Ink Jet Refill Kit</description>
    29.95
</product>
```

Perhaps someone thought it was "obvious" that the last entry was the price. However, following Quality Tip 26.2, it is best to wrap the price inside a price element, like this:

```
<product>
    <description>Ink Jet Refill Kit</description>
    <price>29.95</price>
</product>
```

QUALITY TIP 26.1

Prefer XML Elements over Attributes

Attributes are shorter than elements. For example,

```
<product description="Toaster" price="29.95"/>
```

seems simpler than

```
<product>
    <description>Toaster</description>
    <price>29.95</price>
</product>
```

There is the temptation to use attributes because they are "easier to type". But of course, you don't type XML documents, except for testing purposes. In real-world situations, XML documents are generated by programs.

Attributes are less flexible than elements. Suppose we want to add a currency indication to the value. With elements, that's easy to do:

```
<price currency="USD">29.95</price>
```

or even

```
<price>
    <currency>USD</currency>
    <amount>29.95</amount>
</price>
```

With attributes, you are stuck—you can't refine the structure. Of course, you could use

```
<product description="Toaster" price="USD 29.95"/>
```

But then your program has to parse the string USD 29.95 and manually take it apart. That's just the kind of tedious and error-prone coding that XML is designed to avoid.

In HTML, there is a simple rule when using attributes. All strings that are not part of the displayed text are attributes. For example, consider a link.

```
<a href="http://java.sun.com">The Java web page</a>
```

The text inside the a element, The Java web page, is part of what the user sees on the web page, but the href attribute value http://java.sun.com is not displayed on the page.

Of course, HTML is a little different from the XML documents that you construct to describe data, such as product lists, but the same basic rule applies. Anything that's a part of your data should not be an attribute. An attribute is appropriate only if it tells something *about* the data but isn't a part of the data itself. If you find yourself engaged in metaphysical discussions to determine whether an item is part of the data or tells something about the data, make the item an element, not an attribute.

QUALITY TIP 26.2

Avoid Children with Mixed Elements and Text

The children of an element can be

1. Elements
2. Text
3. A mixture of both

In HTML, it is common to mix elements and text, for example

```
<p>Use XML for <strong>robust</strong> data formats.</p>
```

But when describing data sets, you should not mix elements and text. For example, you should not do the following:

```
<price>
   <currency>USD</currency>
   29.95
</price>
```

Instead, the children of an element should be either text

```
<price>29.95</price>
```

or elements

```
<price>
   <currency>USD</currency>
   <amount>29.95</amount>
</price>
```

There is an important reason for this design rule. As you will see later in this chapter, you can specify much stricter rules for elements that have only child elements than for elements whose children can contain text.

26.2 Parsing XML Documents

A parser is a program that reads a document, checks whether it is syntactically correct, and takes some action as it processes the document.

To read and analyze the contents of an XML document, you need an XML *parser*. A parser is a program that reads a document, checks whether it is syntactically correct, and takes some action as it processes the document.

Two kinds of XML parsers are in common use. One of them follows a specification called SAX (Simple API for XML), and the other follows a specification called DOM (Document Object Model). A SAX parser is *event-driven*. Whenever the parser encounters a particular construct (for example, a start-tag, such as <price>), it calls a method that you must provide. In contrast, a DOM parser builds a tree that represents the parsed document. Once the parser is done, you can analyze the tree. SAX parsers are more efficient for handling large XML documents whose tree structure would require large amounts of memory. DOM parsers, however, are easier to use for most applications—the parse tree gives you a complete overview of the data, whereas a SAX parser gives you the information in bits and pieces. In this section, you will learn how to use a DOM parser.

A SAX parser fires events as it analyzes a document. A DOM parser builds a document tree.

The DOM standard defines interfaces and methods to analyze and modify the tree structure that represents an XML document. In addition, Sun Microsystems defined a specification called JAXP (Java API for XML Processing; recall that API stands for Application Programming Interface) for creating, reading, and writing XML documents.

The Document interface describes the tree structure of an XML document. To generate an object of a class that implements the Document interface, you need a DocumentBuilder. To get a DocumentBuilder object, first call the static newInstance method of the DocumentBuilderFactory class, then call the newDocumentBuilder method on the factory object.

```
DocumentBuilderFactory factory = DocumentBuilderFactory.newInstance();
DocumentBuilder builder = factory.newDocumentBuilder();
```

A DocumentBuilder can read an XML document from a file, URL, or input stream. The result is a Document object, which contains a tree.

Once you have a DocumentBuilder, you can read a document. To read a document from a file, first construct a File object from the file name, then call the parse method of the DocumentBuilder class.

```
String fileName = . . .;
File f = new File(fileName);
Document doc = builder.parse(f);
```

If the document is located on the Internet, use an URL:

```
String urlName = . . .;
URL u = new URL(urlName);
Document doc = builder.parse(u);
```

You can also read a document from an arbitrary input stream:

```
InputStream in = . . .;
Document doc = builder.parse(in);
```

```
<?xml version="1.0"?>
<items>
   <item>
      <product>
         <description>Ink Jet Refill Kit</description>
         <price>29.95</price>
      </product>
      <quantity>8</quantity>
   </item>
   <item>
      <product>
         <description>4-port Mini Hub</description>
         <price>19.95</price>
      </product>
      <quantity>4</quantity>
   </item>
</items>
```

Figure 3   An XML Document

Once you have created a new document or read a document from a file, you can inspect and modify it.

The easiest method for inspecting a document is the *XPath* syntax. An XPath describes a node or set of nodes, using a syntax that is similar to directory paths. For example, consider the following XPath, applied to the document in Figure 4:

```
/items/item[1]/quantity
```

This XPath selects the quantity of the first item, that is, the value 8. (In XPath, array positions start with 1. Accessing /items/item[0] would be an error.)

Similarly, you can get the price of the second product as

```
/items/item[2]/product/price
```

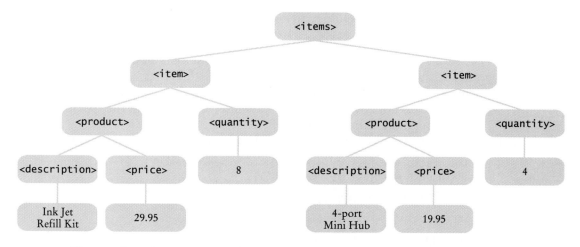

Figure 4   The Tree View of the Document

Table 1   XPath Syntax Summary

Syntax Element	Purpose	Example
name	Matches an element	`item`
/	Separates elements	`/items/item`
[*n*]	Selects a value from a set	`/items/item[1]`
@*name*	Matches an attribute	`price/@currency`
*	Matches anything	`/items/*[1]`
count	Counts matches	`count(/items/item)`
name	The name of a match	`name(/items/*[1])`

To get the number of items, use the XPath expression

```
count(/items/item)
```

In our example, the result is 2.

The total number of children can be obtained as

```
count(/items/*)
```

In our example, the result is again 2 because the items element has exactly two children.

To select attributes, use an @ followed by the name of the attribute. For example,

```
/items/item[2]/product/price/@currency
```

would select the currency price attribute if it had one.

Finally, if you have a document with variable or unknown structure, you can find out the name of a child with an expression such as the following:

```
name(/items/item[1]/*[1])
```

The result is the name of the first child of the first item, or product.

That is all you need to know about the XPath syntax to analyze simple documents. (See Table 1 for a summary.) There are many more options in the XPath syntax that we do not cover here. If you are interested, look up the specification [2] or work through the online tutorial [3].

To evaluate an XPath expression in Java, first create an XPath object:

```
XPathFactory xpfactory = XPathFactory.newInstance();
XPath path = xpfactory.newXPath();
```

Then call the evaluate method, like this:

```
String result = path.evaluate(expression, doc)
```

Here, expression is an XPath expression and doc is the Document object that represents the XML document. For example, the statement

```
String result = path.evaluate("/items/item[2]/product/price", doc)
```

sets result to the string "19.95".

Now you have all the tools that you need to read and analyze an XML document. The example program at the end of this section puts these techniques to work. (The program uses the LineItem and Product classes from Chapter 17.) The class Item-ListParser can parse an XML document that contains a list of product descriptions. Its parse method takes the file name and returns an array list of LineItem objects:

```
ItemListParser parser = new ItemListParser();
ArrayList<LineItem> items = parser.parse("items.xml");
```

The ItemListParser class translates each XML element into an object of the corresponding Java class. We first get the number of items:

```
int itemCount = Integer.parseInt(path.evaluate(
    "count(/items/item)", doc));
```

For each item element, we gather the product data and construct a Product object:

```
String description = path.evaluate(
    "/items/item[" + i + "]/product/description", doc);
double price = Double.parseDouble(path.evaluate(
    "/items/item[" + i + "]/product/price", doc));
Product pr = new Product(description, price);
```

Then we construct a LineItem object in the same way, and add it to the items array list. Here is the complete source code.

File ItemListParser.java

```java
1   import java.io.File;
2   import java.io.IOException;
3   import java.util.ArrayList;
4   import javax.xml.parsers.DocumentBuilder;
5   import javax.xml.parsers.DocumentBuilderFactory;
6   import javax.xml.parsers.ParserConfigurationException;
7   import javax.xml.xpath.XPath;
8   import javax.xml.xpath.XPathExpressionException;
9   import javax.xml.xpath.XPathFactory;
10  import org.w3c.dom.Document;
11  import org.xml.sax.SAXException;
12
13  /**
14      An XML parser for item lists.
15  */
16  public class ItemListParser
17  {
18      /**
19          Constructs a parser that can parse item lists.
20      */
21      public ItemListParser()
22              throws ParserConfigurationException
23      {
24          DocumentBuilderFactory dbfactory
25                  = DocumentBuilderFactory.newInstance();
26          builder = dbfactory.newDocumentBuilder();
```

```
27          XPathFactory xpfactory = XPathFactory.newInstance();
28          path = xpfactory.newXPath();
29       }
30
31       /**
32          Parses an XML file containing an item list.
33          @param fileName the name of the file
34          @return an array list containing all items in the XML file
35       */
36       public ArrayList<LineItem> parse(String fileName)
37             throws SAXException, IOException, XPathExpressionException
38       {
39          File f = new File(fileName);
40          Document doc = builder.parse(f);
41
42          ArrayList<LineItem> items = new ArrayList<LineItem>();
43          int itemCount = Integer.parseInt(path.evaluate(
44             "count(/items/item)", doc));
45          for (int i = 1; i <= itemCount; i++)
46          {
47             String description = path.evaluate(
48                "/items/item[" + i + "]/product/description", doc);
49             double price = Double.parseDouble(path.evaluate(
50                "/items/item[" + i + "]/product/price", doc));
51             Product pr = new Product(description, price);
52             int quantity = Integer.parseInt(path.evaluate(
53                "/items/item[" + i + "]/quantity", doc));
54             LineItem it = new LineItem(pr, quantity);
55             items.add(it);
56          }
57          return items;
58       }
59
60       private DocumentBuilder builder;
61       private XPath path;
62    }
```

File ItemListParserTester.java

```
1    import java.util.ArrayList;
2
3    /**
4       This program parses an XML file containing an item list.
5       It prints out the items that are described in the XML file.
6    */
7    public class ItemListParserTester
8    {
9       public static void main(String[] args) throws Exception
10      {
11         ItemListParser parser = new ItemListParser();
12         ArrayList<LineItem> items = parser.parse("items.xml");
13         for (LineItem anItem : items)
14            System.out.println(anItem.format());
15      }
16   }
```

Output

```
Ink Jet Refill Kit        29.95   8    239.6
4-port Mini Hub           19.95   4    79.8
```

SELF CHECK

4. What is the result of evaluating the XPath statement /items/item[1]/quantity in the XML document of Figure 4?
5. Which XPath statement yields the name of the root element of any XML document?

COMMON ERROR 26.1

XML Elements Describe Instance Fields, Not Classes

When you convert XML documents to Java classes, you need to determine a class for each element type. A common mistake is to make a separate class for each XML element. For example, consider a slightly different invoice description, with separate shipping and billing addresses:

```
<invoice>
    <number>11365</number>
    <shipto>
        <name>John Meyers</name>
        <company>ACME Computer Supplies Inc.</company>
        <street>1195 W. Fairfield Rd.</street>
        <city>Sunnyvale</city>
        <state>CA</state>
        <zip>94085</state>
    </shipto>
    <billto>
        <name>Accounts Payable</name>
        <company>ACME Computer Supplies Inc.</company>
        <street>P.O. Box 11098</street>
        <city>Sunnyvale</city>
        <state>CA</state>
        <zip>94080-1098</zip>
    </billto>
    <items>
    . . .
    </items>
</invoice>
```

Should you have a class Shipto to match the shipto element and another class Billto to match the billto element? That makes no sense, because both of them have the same contents: elements that describe an address.

Instead, you should think of the XML element as the equivalent of an instance field and then determine an appropriate class. For example, an invoice object has instance fields

- `billto`, of type `Address`
- `shipto`, also of type `Address`

Note that you don't see the classes in the XML document. There is no notion of a class `Address` in the XML document describing an invoice. To make element classes explicit, you use an XML schema—see Advanced Topic 26.1 for more information.

RANDOM FACT 26.2

Grammars, Parsers, and Compilers

Grammars are very important in many areas of computer science to describe the structure of computer programs or data formats. To introduce the concept of a grammar, consider this set of rules for a set of simple English language sentences:

1. A sentence has a noun phrase followed by a verb and another noun phrase.
2. A noun phrase consists of an article followed by an adjective list followed by a noun.
3. An adjective list consists of an adjective or an adjective followed by an adjective list.
4. Articles are "a" and "the".
5. Adjectives are "quick", "brown", "lazy", and "hungry".
6. Nouns are "fox", "dog", and "hamster".
7. Verbs are "jumps over" and "eats".

Here are two sentences that follow these rules:

- The quick brown fox jumps over the lazy dog.
- The hungry hamster eats a quick brown fox.

Symbolically, these rules can be expressed by a formal grammar:

```
<sentence> ::= <noun-phrase> <verb> <noun-phrase>
<noun-phrase> ::= <article> <adjective-list> <noun>
<adjective-list> ::= <adjective> | <adjective> <adjective-list>
<article> ::= a | the
<adjective> ::= quick | brown | lazy | hungry
<noun> ::= fox | dog | hamster
<verb> ::= jumps over | eats
```

Here the symbol `::=` means "can be replaced with" and | separates alternate choices. For example, `<article>` can be replaced with "a" or "the".

The grammar symbols, such as `<noun>`, happen to be enclosed in angle brackets just like XML tags, but they are different from tags. One purpose of a grammar is to produce strings that are valid according to the grammar, by starting with the start symbol (`<sentence>` in this example) and applying replacement rules until the resulting string is free from symbols. See the table on the facing page for an example of the replacement process.

If you have a grammar and a string, such as "the hungry hamster eats a quick brown fox" or "a brown jumps over hamster quick lazy", you can parse the sentence: that is, check whether the sentence is described by the grammar rules and, if it is, show how it can be

String	Rule
<sentence>	Start
<noun-phrase> <verb> <noun-phrase>	1
<noun-phrase> eats <noun-phrase>	7
<article> <adjective-list> <noun> eats <noun-phrase>	2
the <adjective-list> <noun> eats <noun-phrase>	4
the <adjective> <noun> eats <noun-phrase>	3
the hungry <noun> eats <noun-phrase>	5
the hungry hamster eats <noun-phrase>	6
the hungry hamster eats <article> <adjective-list> <noun>	2
the hungry hamster eats a <adjective-list> <noun>	4
the hungry hamster eats a <adjective> <adjective-list> <noun>	3
the hungry hamster eats a quick <adjective-list> <noun>	5
the hungry hamster eats a quick <adjective> <noun>	3
the hungry hamster eats a quick brown <noun>	5
the hungry hamster eats a quick brown fox	6

derived from the start symbol. One way to show the derivation is to construct a *parse tree* (see Figure 5).

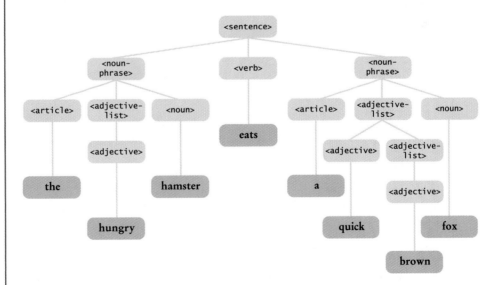

Figure 5 A Parse Tree for a Simple Sentence

A *parser* is a program that reads strings and decides whether the input conforms to the rules of a certain grammar. Some parsers—such as the DOM XML parser—build a parse tree in the process or report an error message when a parse tree cannot be constructed. Other parsers—such as the SAX XML parser—call user-specified methods whenever a part of the input was successfully parsed.

The most important use for parsers is inside compilers for programming languages. Just as our grammar can describe (some) simple English language sentences, the valid "sentences"

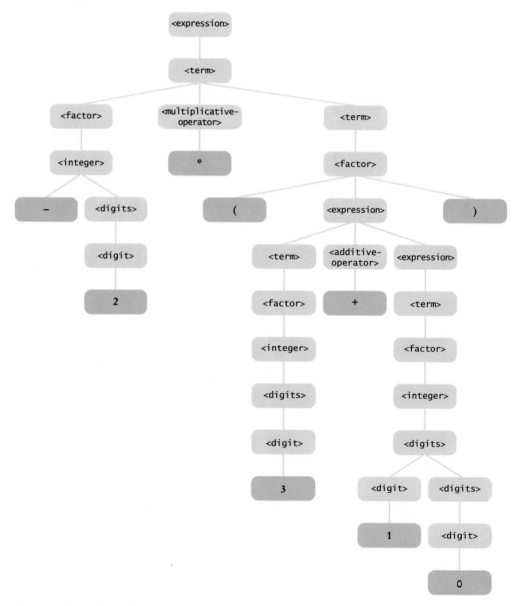

Figure 6   A Parse Tree for an Expression

in a programming language can be described by a grammar. The actual grammar for the Java programming language occupies about 15 pages in *The Java Language Specification* [4]. To give a flavor of a small subset of such a grammar, here is a grammar that describes arithmetic expressions.

```
<expression> ::= <term> | <term> <additive-operator> <expression>
<additive-operator> ::= + | -
<term> ::= <factor> | <factor> <multiplicative-operator> <term>
<multiplicative-operator> ::= * | /
<factor> ::= <integer> | ( <expression> )
<integer> ::= <digits> | - <digits>
<digits> ::= <digit> | <digit> <digits>
<digit> ::= 0 | 1 | 2 | 3 | 4 | 5 | 6 | 7 | 8 | 9
```

An example of a valid expression in this grammar is

```
-2 * (3 + 10)
```

Figure 6 shows the parse tree for this expression.

In a compiler, parsing the program source is the first step toward generating code that the target processor (the Java virtual machine in the case of Java) can execute. Writing a parser is a challenging and interesting task. You may at one point in your studies take a course in compiler construction, in which you learn how to write a parser and how to generate code from the parsed input. Fortunately, to use XML you don't have to know how the parser does its job. You simply ask the XML parser to read the XML input and then process the resulting Document tree.

26.3 Creating XML Documents

In the preceding section, you saw how to read an XML file into a Document object and how to analyze the contents of that object. In this section, you will see how to do the opposite—build up a Document object and then save it as an XML file. Of course, you can also generate an XML file simply as a sequence of print statements. However, that is not a good idea—it is easy to build an illegal XML document in this way, as when data contain special characters such as < or &.

Recall that you needed a DocumentBuilder object to read in an XML document. You also need such an object to create a new, empty document. Thus, to create a new document, first make a document builder factory, then a document builder, and finally the empty document:

```
DocumentBuilderFactory factory =
        DocumentBuilderFactory.newInstance();
DocumentBuilder builder = factory.newDocumentBuilder();
Document doc = builder.newDocument();
// An empty document
```

> The Document class has methods to create elements and text nodes.

Now you are ready to insert nodes into the document. You use the createElement method of the Document interface to create the elements that you need.

```
Element priceElement = doc.createElement("price");
```

You set element attributes with the `setAttribute` method. For example,

```
priceElement.setAttribute("currency", "USD");
```

You have to work a bit harder for inserting text. First create a text node:

```
Text textNode = doc.createTextNode("29.95");
```

Then add the text node to the element:

```
priceElement.appendChild(textNode);
```

Figure 7 shows the DOM interfaces for XML document nodes. To construct the tree structure of a document, it is a good idea to use a set of helper methods. We start out with a helper method that creates an element with text:

```
private Element createTextElement(String name, String text)
{
   Text t = doc.createTextNode(text);
   Element e = doc.createElement(name);
   e.appendChild(t);
   return e;
}
```

Using this helper method, we can construct a `price` element like this:

```
Element priceElement = createTextElement("price", "29.95");
```

Next, we write a helper method to create a `product` element from a `Product` object:

```
private Element createProduct(Product p)
{
   Element e = doc.createElement("product");
   e.appendChild(createTextElement("description", p.getDescription()));
   e.appendChild(createTextElement("price", "" + p.getPrice()));
   return e;
}
```

This helper method is called from the `createItem` helper method:

```
private Element createItem(LineItem anItem)
{
   Element e = doc.createElement("item");
   e.appendChild(createProduct(anItem.getProduct()));
   e.appendChild(createTextElement(
         "quantity", "" + anItem.getQuantity()));
   return e;
}
```

A helper method

```
private Element createItems(ArrayList<LineItem> items)
```

for the `items` element is implemented in the same way—see the program listing at the end of this section.

Now you build the document as follows:

```
ArrayList<LineItem> items = . . .;
doc = builder.newDocument();
Element root = createItems(items);
doc.appendChild(root);
```

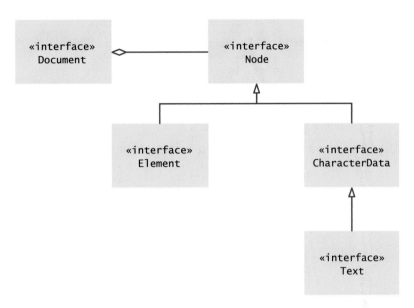

Figure 7 UML Diagram of DOM Interfaces Used in This Chapter

Once you have built the document, you will want to write it to a file. There are several ways of writing an XML document. Here, we use the LSSerializer interface. You obtain an LSSerializer with the following magic incantation:

```
DOMImplementation impl = doc.getImplementation();
DOMImplementationLS implLS
    = (DOMImplementationLS) impl.getFeature("LS", "3.0");
LSSerializer ser = implLS.createLSSerializer();
```

Then you simply use the writeToString method:

```
String str = ser.writeToString(doc);
```

The LSSerializer produces an XML document without spaces or line breaks. As a result, the output looks less pretty, but it is actually more suitable for parsing by another program because it is free from unnecessary white space.

Here is an example program that shows how to build an XML document and print it.

File ItemListBuilder.java

```
1   import java.util.ArrayList;
2   import javax.xml.parsers.DocumentBuilder;
3   import javax.xml.parsers.DocumentBuilderFactory;
4   import javax.xml.parsers.ParserConfigurationException;
5   import org.w3c.dom.Document;
6   import org.w3c.dom.Element;
7   import org.w3c.dom.Text;
8
```

```
 9    /**
10        Builds a DOM document for an array list of items.
11    */
12    public class ItemListBuilder
13    {
14        /**
15            Constructs an item list builder.
16        */
17        public ItemListBuilder()
18                throws ParserConfigurationException
19        {
20            DocumentBuilderFactory factory
21                    = DocumentBuilderFactory.newInstance();
22            builder = factory.newDocumentBuilder();
23        }
24
25        /**
26            Builds a DOM document for an array list of items.
27            @param items the items
28            @return a DOM document describing the items
29        */
30        public Document build(ArrayList<LineItem> items)
31        {
32            doc = builder.newDocument();
33            doc.appendChild(createItems(items));
34            return doc;
35        }
36
37        /**
38            Builds a DOM element for an array list of items.
39            @param items the items
40            @return a DOM element describing the items
41        */
42        private Element createItems(ArrayList<LineItem> items)
43        {
44            Element e = doc.createElement("items");
45
46            for (LineItem anItem : items)
47                e.appendChild(createItem(anItem));
48
49            return e;
50        }
51
52        /**
53            Builds a DOM element for an item.
54            @param anItem the item
55            @return a DOM element describing the item
56        */
57        private Element createItem(LineItem anItem)
58        {
59            Element e = doc.createElement("item");
60
61            e.appendChild(createProduct(anItem.getProduct()));
```

```
62          e.appendChild(createTextElement(
63              "quantity", "" + anItem.getQuantity()));
64
65          return e;
66      }
67
68      /**
69          Builds a DOM element for a product.
70          @param p the product
71          @return a DOM element describing the product
72      */
73      private Element createProduct(Product p)
74      {
75          Element e = doc.createElement("product");
76
77          e.appendChild(createTextElement(
78              "description", p.getDescription()));
79          e.appendChild(createTextElement(
80              "price", "" + p.getPrice()));
81
82          return e;
83      }
84
85      private Element createTextElement(String name, String text)
86      {
87          Text t = doc.createTextNode(text);
88          Element e = doc.createElement(name);
89          e.appendChild(t);
90          return e;
91      }
92
93      private DocumentBuilder builder;
94      private Document doc;
95  }
```

File ItemListBuilderTester.java

```
1   import java.util.ArrayList;
2   import org.w3c.dom.DOMImplementation;
3   import org.w3c.dom.Document;
4   import org.w3c.dom.ls.DOMImplementationLS;
5   import org.w3c.dom.ls.LSSerializer;
6
7   /**
8       This program tests the item list builder. It prints the XML file
9       corresponding to a DOM document containing a list of items.
10  */
11  public class ItemListBuilderTester
12  {
13      public static void main(String[] args) throws Exception
14      {
15          ArrayList<LineItem> items = new ArrayList<LineItem>();
16          items.add(new LineItem(new Product("Toaster", 29.95), 3));
17          items.add(new LineItem(new Product("Hair dryer", 24.95), 1));
```

```
18
19          ItemListBuilder builder = new ItemListBuilder();
20          Document doc = builder.build(items);
21          DOMImplementation impl = doc.getImplementation();
22          DOMImplementationLS implLS
23                  = (DOMImplementationLS) impl.getFeature("LS", "3.0");
24          LSSerializer ser = implLS.createLSSerializer();
25          String out = ser.writeToString(doc);
26
27          System.out.println(out);
28      }
29 }
```

This program uses the `Product` and `LineItem` classes from Chapter 17. The `LineItem` class has been modified by adding `getProduct` and `getQuantity` methods.

Output

```
<?xml version="1.0" encoding="UTF-8"?><items><item><product>
<description>Toaster</description><price>29.95</price></product>
<quantity>3</quantity></item><item><product><description>Hair dryer
</description><price>24.95</price></product><quantity>1</quantity>
</item></items>
```

SELF CHECK

6. Suppose you need to construct a `Document` object that represents an XML document other than an item list. Which methods from the `ItemListBuilder` class can you reuse?

7. How would you write a document to the file `output.xml`?

HOW TO 26.2

Writing an XML Document

What is the best way to write an XML document? This How To shows you how to produce a `Document` object and how to generate an XML document from it.

Step 1   Provide the outline of a document builder class.

To construct the `Document` object from an object of some class, you should implement a class such as this one:

```
public class MyBuilder
{
    public Document build(SomeClass x) { . . . }
    . . .
    private Element createTextElement(String name, String text)
    {
```

```
            Text t = doc.createTextNode(text);
            Element e = doc.createElement(name);
            e.appendChild(t);
            return e;
        }

        private DocumentBuilder builder;
        private Document doc;
    }
```

Step 2   Look at the format of the XML document that you want to create.

Consider all elements, except for those that only have text content. Find the matching Java classes. In the `ItemListBuilder` example, we ignore `quantity`, `description`, and `price` because they have text content. The remaining elements and their Java classes are

- `product` - `Product`
- `item` - `LineItem`
- `items` - `ArrayList<LineItem>`

Step 3   For each element in Step 2, add a helper method to your builder class.

Each helper method has the form

```
    private Element createElementName(ClassForElement x)
```

For example,

```
    public class MyBuilder
    {
        public Document build(ArrayList<LineItem> x) { . . . }
        private Element createProduct(Product x)  { . . . }
        private Element createItem(LineItem x)  { . . . }
        private Element createItems(ArrayList<LineItem> x)  { . . . }
        . . .
    }
```

Step 4   Implement the helper methods.

For each element, call the helper methods of its children. However, if a child has text content, call `createTextElement` instead.

For example, the `item` element has two children: `product` and `quantity`. The former has a helper method, and the latter has text content. Therefore, the `createItem` method calls `createProduct` and `createTextElement`:

```
    private Element createItem(LineItem anItem)
    {
        Element e = doc.createElement("item");
        e.appendChild(createProduct(anItem.getProduct()));
        e.appendChild(createTextElement("quantity", "" + anItem.getQuantity()));
        return e;
    }
```

You may find it helpful to implement the helper methods "bottom up", starting with the simplest method (such as `createProduct`) and finishing with the method for the root element (`createItems`).

Step 5 Finish off your builder by writing a constructor and the `build` method.

```
public class MyBuilder
{
    public MyBuilder()
          throws ParserConfigurationException
    {
        DocumentBuilderFactory factory
            = DocumentBuilderFactory.newInstance();
        builder = factory.newDocumentBuilder();
    }
    public Document build(ClassForRootElement x)
    {
        doc = builder.newDocument();
        doc.appendChild(createRootElementName(x));
        return doc;
    }
    . . .
}
```

Step 6 Use a class, such as the `LSSerializer`, to convert the `Document` to a string.

For example,

```
Invoice x = . . .;
InvoiceBuilder builder = new InvoiceBuilder();
Document doc = builder.build(x);
LSSerializer ser = . . .;
String str = ser.writeToString(doc);
```

26.4 Validating XML Documents

In this section you will learn how to specify rules for XML documents of a particular type. There are several mechanisms for this purpose. The oldest and simplest mechanism is a Document Type Definition (DTD), the topic of this section. We discuss other mechanisms in Advanced Topic 26.1.

26.4.1 Document Type Definitions

> A DTD is a sequence of rules that describes the valid child elements and attributes for each element type.

Consider a document of type `items`. Intuitively, `items` denotes a sequence of `item` elements. Each `item` element contains a `product` and a `quantity`. A `product` contains a `description` and a `price`. Each of these elements contains text describing the product's description, price, and quantity. The purpose of a DTD is to formalize this description.

A DTD is a sequence of rules that describes

- The valid attributes for each element type
- The valid child elements for each element type

Table 2	Replacements for Special Characters	
Character	**Encoding**	**Name**
<	&lt;	Less than (left angle bracket)
>	&gt;	Greater than (right angle bracket)
&	&amp;	Ampersand
'	&apos;	Apostrophe
"	&quot;	Quotation mark

Let us first turn to child elements. The valid child elements of an element are described by an ELEMENT rule:

```
<!ELEMENT items (item*)>
```

This means that an item list must contain a sequence of 0 or more item elements.

As you can see, the rule is delimited by <!...>, and it contains the name of the element whose children are to be constrained (items), followed by a description of what children are allowed.

Next, let us turn to the definition of an item node:

```
<!ELEMENT item (product, quantity)>
```

This means that the children of an item node must be a product node, followed by a quantity node.

The definition for a product is similar:

```
<!ELEMENT product (description, price)>
```

Finally, here are the definitions of the three remaining node types:

```
<!ELEMENT quantity (#PCDATA)>
<!ELEMENT description (#PCDATA)>
<!ELEMENT price (#PCDATA)>
```

The symbol #PCDATA refers to text, called "parsed character data" in XML terminology. The character data can contain any characters. However, certain characters, such as < and &, have special meaning in XML and need to be replaced if they occur in character data. Table 2 shows the replacements for special characters.

The complete DTD for an item list has six rules, one for each element type:

```
<!ELEMENT items (item*)>
<!ELEMENT item (product, quantity)>
<!ELEMENT product (description, price)>
<!ELEMENT quantity (#PCDATA)>
<!ELEMENT description (#PCDATA)>
<!ELEMENT price (#PCDATA)>
```

Let us have a closer look at the descriptions of the allowed children. Table 3 shows the expressions used to describe the children of an element. The EMPTY keyword is self-explanatory: an element that is declared as EMPTY may not have any children.

Table 3 Regular Expressions for Element Content

Rule Description	Element Content
EMPTY	No children allowed
$(E*)$	Any sequence of 0 or more elements E
$(E+)$	Any sequence of 1 or more elements E
$(E?)$	Optional element E (0 or 1 occurrences allowed)
$(E_1, E_2, \ldots)$	Element E_1, followed by $E_2, \ldots$
$(E_1 \mid E_2 \mid \ldots)$	Element E_1 or E_2 or $\ldots$
(#PCDATA)	Text only
$(\text{\#PCDATA} \mid E_1 \mid E_2 \ldots)*$	Any sequence of text and elements $E_1, E_2, \ldots$, in any order
ANY	Any children allowed

For example, the HTML DTD defines the img element to be EMPTY—an image has only attributes, specifying the image source, size, and placement, and no children.

More interesting child rules can be formed with the *regular expression* operations (* + ? , |). (See Table 3 and Figure 8. Also see Productivity Hint 9.2 for more information on regular expressions.) You have already seen the * ("0 or more") and , (sequence) operations. The children of an items element are 0 or more item elements, and the children of an item are a sequence of product and description elements.

You can also combine these operations to form more complex expressions. For example,

```
<!ELEMENT section (title, (paragraph | (image, title?)))+)
```

defines an element section whose children are:

1. A title element
2. A sequence of one or more of the following:
   - paragraph elements
   - image elements followed by optional title elements

Thus,

```
<section>
   <title/>
   <paragraph/>
   <image/>
   <title/>
   <paragraph/>
</section>
```

is valid, but

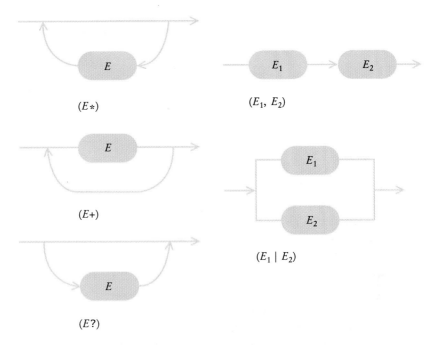

Figure 8 DTD Regular Expression Operations

```
<section>
  <paragraph/>
  <paragraph/>
  <title/>
</section>
```

is not—there is no starting title, and the title at the end doesn't follow an image.

You already saw the (#PCDATA) rule. It means that the children can consist of any character data. For example, in our product list DTD, the description element can have any character data inside.

You can also allow *mixed content*—any sequence of character data and specified elements. However, in mixed content, you have no control over the order in which the elements appear. As explained in Quality Tip 26.2, you should avoid mixed content for DTDs that describe data sets. This feature is intended for documents that contain both text and markup instructions, such as HTML pages.

Finally, you can allow a node to have children of any type—you should avoid that for DTDs that describe data sets.

You now know how to specify what children a node may have. A DTD also gives you control over the allowed attributes of an element. An attribute description looks like this:

<!ATTLIST *Element Attribute Type Default*>

The most useful attribute type descriptions are listed in Table 4. The CDATA type describes any sequence of character data. As with #PCDATA, certain characters, such

Table 4 **Common Attribute Types**	
Type Description	**Attribute Type**
CDATA	Any character data
$(V_1 \mid V_2 \mid \ldots)$	One of $V_1, V_2, \ldots$

as < and &, need to be encoded (as <, & and so on). There is no practical difference between the CDATA and #PCDATA types. Simply use CDATA in attribute declarations and #PCDATA in element declarations.

Rather than allowing arbitrary attribute values, you can specify a finite number of choices. For example, you may want to restrict a currency attribute to U.S. dollar, euro, and Japanese yen. Then use the following declaration:

```
<!ATTLIST price currency (USD | EUR | JPY) #REQUIRED>
```

You can use letters, numbers, and the characters - _ for the attribute values.

There are other type descriptions that are less common in practice. You can find them in the XML reference [1].

The attribute type description is followed by a "default" declaration. The keywords that can appear in a "default" declaration are listed in Table 5.

For example, this attribute declaration describes that each price element must have a currency attribute whose value is any character data:

```
<!ATTLIST price currency CDATA #REQUIRED>
```

To fulfill this declaration, each price element must have a currency attribute, such as <price currency="USD">. A price without a currency would not be valid.

For an optional attribute, you use the #IMPLIED keyword instead.

```
<!ATTLIST price currency CDATA #IMPLIED>
```

That means that you can supply a currency attribute in a price element, or you can omit it. If you omit it, then the application that processes the XML data implicitly assumes some default currency.

Table 5 **Attribute Defaults**	
Default Declaration	**Explanation**
#REQUIRED	Attribute is required
#IMPLIED	Attribute is optional
V	Default attribute, to be used if attribute is not specified
#FIXED V	Attribute must either be unspecified or contain this value

A better choice would be to supply the default value explicitly:

```
<!ATTLIST price currency CDATA "USD">
```

That means that the currency attribute is understood to mean USD if the attribute is not specified. An XML parser will then report the value of currency as USD if the attribute was not specified.

Finally, you can state that an attribute can only be identical to a particular value. For example, the rule

```
<!ATTLIST price currency CDATA #FIXED "USD">
```

means that a price element must either not have a currency attribute at all (in which case the XML parser will report its value as USD), or specify the currency attribute as USD. Naturally, this kind of rule is not very common.

You have now seen the most common constructs for DTDs. Using these constructs, you can define your own DTDs for XML documents that describe data sets. In the next section, you will see how to specify which DTD an XML document should use, and how to have the XML parser check that a document conforms to its DTD.

26.4.2 Specifying a DTD in an XML Document

When you reference a DTD with an XML document, you can instruct the parser to check that the document follows the rules of the DTD. That way, the parser can check errors in the document.

> An XML document can contain its DTD or refer to a DTD that is stored elsewhere.

In the preceding section you saw how to develop a DTD for a class of XML documents. The DTD specifies the permitted elements and attributes in the document. An XML document has two ways of referencing a DTD:

1. The document may contain the DTD.
2. The document may refer to a DTD that is stored elsewhere.

A DTD is introduced with the DOCTYPE declaration. If the document contains its DTD, then the declaration looks like this:

```
<!DOCTYPE rootElement [ rules ]>
```

For example, an item list can include its DTD like this:

```
<?xml version="1.0"?>
<!DOCTYPE items [

<!ELEMENT items (item*)>
<!ELEMENT item (product, quantity)>
<!ELEMENT product (description, price)>
<!ELEMENT quantity (#PCDATA)>
<!ELEMENT description (#PCDATA)>
<!ELEMENT price (#PCDATA)>

]>
<items>
```

```
<item>
   <product>
      <description>Ink Jet Refill Kit</description>
      <price>29.95</price>
   </product>
   <quantity>8</quantity>
</item>
<item>
   <product>
      <description>4-port Mini Hub</description>
      <price>19.95</price>
   </product>
   <quantity>4</quantity>
</item>
</items>
```

> When referencing an external DTD, you must supply an URL for locating the DTD.

However, if the DTD is more complex, then it is better to store it outside the XML document. In that case, you use the SYSTEM keyword inside the DOCTYPE declaration to indicate that the system that hosts the XML processor must locate the DTD. The SYSTEM keyword is followed by the location of the DTD. For example, a DOCTYPE declaration might point to a local file

```
<!DOCTYPE items SYSTEM "items.dtd">
```

Alternatively, the resource might be an URL anywhere on the Web:

```
<!DOCTYPE items SYSTEM "http://www.mycompany.com/dtds/items.dtd">
```

For commonly used DTDs, the DOCTYPE declaration can contain a PUBLIC keyword. For example,

```
<!DOCTYPE faces-config PUBLIC
   "-//Sun Microsystems, Inc.//DTD JavaServer Faces Config 1.0//EN"
   "http://java.sun.com/dtd/web-facesconfig_1_0.dtd">
```

A program parsing the DTD can look at the public identifier. If it is a familiar identifier, then it need not spend time retrieving the DTD from the URL.

26.4.3 Parsing and Validation

> When your XML document has a DTD, you can request validation when parsing.

When you include a DTD with an XML document, then you can tell the parser to *validate* the document. That means that the parser will check that all child elements and attributes of an element conform to the ELEMENT and ATTLIST rules in the DTD. If a document is invalid, then the parser reports an error. To turn on validation, you use the setValidating method of the DocumentBuilderFactory class before calling the newDocumentBuilder method:

```
DocumentBuilderFactory factory = DocumentBuilderFactory.newInstance();
factory.setValidating(true);
DocumentBuilder builder = factory.newDocumentBuilder();
Document doc = builder.parse(. . .);
```

Validation can simplify your code for processing XML documents. For example, if the DTD specifies that the child elements of each `item` element are `product` and `quantity` elements in that order, then you can rely on that fact and don't need to put tedious checks in your code.

> When you parse an XML file with a DTD, tell the parser to ignore white space.

If the parser has access to the DTD, it can make another useful improvement. By default, the parser converts all spaces in the input document to text, even if the spaces are only used to logically line up elements. As a result, the document contains text nodes that are wasteful and can be confusing when you analyze the document tree.

To make the parser ignore white space, call the `setIgnoringElementContent-Whitespace` method of the `DocumentBuilderFactory` class.

```
factory.setValidating(true);
factory.setIgnoringElementContentWhitespace(true);
```

Finally, if the parser has access to the DTD, it can fill in default values for attributes. For example, suppose a DTD defines a `currency` attribute for a `price` element:

```
<!ATTLIST price currency CDATA "USD">
```

If a document contains a `price` element without a `currency` attribute, then the parser can supply the default:

```
String attributeValue = priceElement.getAttribute("currency");
   // Gets "USD" if no currency specified
```

This concludes our discussion of XML. You now know enough XML to put it to work for describing data formats. Whenever you are tempted to use a "quick and dirty" file format, you should consider using XML instead. By using XML for data interchange, your programs become more professional, robust, and flexible. This chapter covers the most important aspects of XML for everyday programming. For more advanced features that can be useful in specialized situations, please see [1]. Furthermore, XML technology is still undergoing rapid change at the time of this writing. Therefore, it is a good idea to check out the latest developments. Good web sites are [5] and [7].

SELF CHECK

8. How can a DTD specify that the `quantity` element in an `item` is optional?

9. How can a DTD specify that a `product` element can contain a `description` and a `price` element, in any order?

10. How can a DTD specify that the `description` element has an optional attribute `language`?

How To 26.3

Writing a DTD

You write a DTD to describe a set of XML documents of the same type. The DTD specifies which elements contain child elements (and the order in which they may appear) and which elements contain text. It also specifies which elements may have attributes, which attributes are required, and which defaults are used for missing attributes.

These rules are for DTDs that describe program data. DTDs that describe documents generally have a much more complex structure.

Step 1   Get or write a couple of sample XML documents.

For example, if you wanted to make a DTD for XML documents that describe an invoice, you could study samples such as the one in How To 26.1.

Step 2   Make a list of all elements that can occur in the XML document.

In the invoice example, they are
- invoice
- number
- address
- name
- company
- street
- city
- state
- zip
- items
- item
- product
- description
- quantity

Step 3   For each of the elements, decide whether its children are elements or text.

Following Quality Tip 26.2, it is best to avoid elements whose children are a mixture of both. In the invoice example, the following elements have element content:
- invoice
- address
- items
- item
- product

The remainder contain text.

Step 4   For elements that contain text, the DTD rule is

```
<!ELEMENT elementName (#PCDATA)>
```

Thus, we have the following simple rules for the invoice elements that contain text:

```
<!ELEMENT number (#PCDATA)>
<!ELEMENT name (#PCDATA)>
<!ELEMENT company (#PCDATA)>
<!ELEMENT street (#PCDATA)>
<!ELEMENT city (#PCDATA)>
<!ELEMENT state (#PCDATA)>
<!ELEMENT zip (#PCDATA)>
<!ELEMENT quantity (#PCDATA)>
<!ELEMENT description (#PCDATA)>
```

Step 5 For each element that contains other elements, make a list of the possible child elements.

Here are the lists in the invoice example:

invoice
- number
- address
- items

address
- name
- company
- street
- city
- state
- zip

items
- item

item
- product
- quantity

product
- description
- price

Step 6 For each of those elements, decide in which order the child elements should occur and how often they should occur.

Then form the rule

```
<!ELEMENT elementName child₁ count₁, child₂ count₂, . . .>
```

where each *count* is one of the following:

Quantity	Count
0 or 1	?
1	omit
0 or more	*
1 or more	+

In the invoice example, the items element can contain any number of items, so the rule is

```
<!ELEMENT items (item*)>
```

In the remaining cases, each child element occurs exactly once. That leads to the rules

```
<!ELEMENT invoice (number, address, items)>
<!ELEMENT address (name, company, street, city, state, zip)>
<!ELEMENT item (product, quantity)>
<!ELEMENT product (descripton, price)>
```

Step 7   Decide whether any elements should have attributes.

Following Quality Tip 26.1, it is best to avoid attributes altogether or to minimize the use of attributes. Because we have no good reason to add attributes in the invoice example, our invoice is complete without attributes.

ADVANCED TOPIC 26.1

Schema Languages

Several mechanisms have been developed to deal with the limitations of DTDs. DTDs cannot express certain details about the structure of an XML document. For example, you can't force an element to contain just a number or a date—any text string is allowed for a (#PCDATA) element.

The XML Schema specification is one mechanism for overcoming these limitations. An XML schema is like a DTD in that it is a set of rules that documents of a particular type need to follow, but a schema can contain far more precise rule descriptions.

Here is just a hint of how an XML schema is specified. For each element, you specify the element name and the type. For example, this definition restricts the contents of quantity to an integer.

```
<xsd:element name="quantity" type="xsd:integer"/>
```

Note that an XML schema is itself written in XML—unlike a DTD, which uses a completely different syntax. (The xsd: prefix is a *name space* prefix to denote that xsd:element and xsd:integer are part of the XML Schema Definition name space. See Advanced Topic 26.2 for more information about name spaces.)

In XML Schema, you can define complex types, much as you define classes in Java. Here is the definition of an Address type:

```
<xsd:complexType name="Address">
  <xsd:sequence>
    <xsd:element name="name" type="xsd:string"/>
    <xsd:element name="company" type="xsd:string"/>
    <xsd:element name="street" type="xsd:string"/>
    <xsd:element name="city" type="xsd:string"/>
    <xsd:element name="state" type="xsd:string"/>
    <xsd:element name="zip" type="xsd:string"/>
  </xsd:sequence>
</xsd:complexType>
```

Then you can specify that an invoice should have shipto and billto fields that are both of type Address:

```
<xsd:element name="shipto" type="Address"/>
<xsd:element name="billto" type="Address"/>
```

These examples show that an XML schema can be more precise than a DTD.

The XML Schema specification has many advanced features—see the W3C web site [5] for details. However, some programmers find that specification overly complex and instead use a competing standard called Relax NG—see [6]. Relax NG is simpler than XML Schema, and it shares a feature with DTDs: a compact notation that is not XML. For example, in Relax NG, you simply write

```
element quantity { xsd:integer }
```

to denote that `quantity` is an element containing an integer. The designers of Relax NG realized that XML, despite its many advantages, is not always the best notation for humans.

ADVANCED TOPIC 26.2

Other XML Technologies

This chapter covers the subset of the XML 1.0 specification that is most useful for common programming situations. Since version 1.0 of the XML specification was released, there has been a huge amount of interest in advanced XML technologies. A number of useful technologies have recently been standardized. Among them are:

- Schema Definitions
- Name Spaces
- XHTML
- XSL and Transformations

Advanced Topic 26.1 contains more information about schema definitions.

Name spaces were invented to ensure that many different people and organizations can develop XML documents without running into conflicts with element names. For example, if you look inside Advanced Topic 26.1, you will see that XML Schema definitions have element names that are prefixed with a tag `xsd:`, such as

```
<xsd:element name="city" type="xsd:string"/>
```

That way, the tag and attribute names, such as `element` and `string`, don't conflict with other names. In that regard, name spaces are similar to Java packages. However, a name space prefix such as `xsd:` is just a shortcut for the actual name space identifier, which is a much longer, unique string. For example, the full name space for XML Schema definitions is `http://www.w3.org/2000/08/XMLSchema`. Each schema definition starts out with the statement

```
<xsd:schema xmlns:xsd="http://www.w3.org/2000/08/XMLSchema">
```

which binds the `xsd` prefix to the full name space.

XHTML is the most recent recommendation of the W3C for formatting web pages. Unlike HTML, XHTML is fully XML-compliant. Once web-editing tools switch to XHTML, it will become much easier to write programs that parse web pages. The XHTML standard has been carefully designed to be backwards compatible with existing browsers.

While XHTML documents are intended to be viewed by browsers, general XML documents are not designed to be viewed at all. Nevertheless, it is often desirable to *transform* an XML document into a viewable form. XSL (Extensible Stylesheet Language) was created for this purpose. A style sheet indicates how to change an XML document into an HTML document, or even a completely different format, such as PDF.

For more information on these and other emerging technologies, see the W3C web site [5].

CHAPTER SUMMARY

1. XML allows you to encode complex data, independent from any programming language, in a form that the recipient can easily parse.

2. XML files are readable by computer programs and by humans.

3. XML-formatted data files are resilient to change.

4. XML describes the meaning of data, not how to display them.

5. An XML document starts out with an XML declaration and contains elements and text.

6. An element can contain text, child elements, or both (mixed content). For data descriptions, avoid mixed content.

7. Elements can have attributes. Use attributes to describe how to interpret the element content.

8. A parser is a program that reads a document, checks whether it is syntactically correct, and takes some action as it processes the document.

9. A SAX parser fires events as it analyzes a document. A DOM parser builds a document tree.

10. A `DocumentBuilder` can read an XML document from a file, URL, or input stream. The result is a `Document` object, which contains a tree.

11. The `Document` class has methods to create elements and text nodes.

12. A DTD is a sequence of rules that describes the valid child elements and attributes for each element type.

13. An XML document can contain its DTD or refer to a DTD that is stored elsewhere.

14. When referencing an external DTD, you must supply an URL for locating the DTD.

15. When your XML document has a DTD, you can request validation when parsing.

16. When you parse an XML file with a DTD, tell the parser to ignore white space.

FURTHER READING

1. `http://www.xml.com/axml/axml.html`   Annotated XML specification.

2. `http://www.w3.org/TR/xpath`   The XPath specification.

3. `http://www.zvon.org/xxl/XPathTutorial/General/examples.html`   An interactive XPath tutorial.

4. `http://java.sun.com/docs/books/jls`   James Gosling et al., *The Java Language Specification*, 2nd ed., Addison-Wesley, 2000.

5. `http://www.w3c.org/xml`   The W3C XML web site.

6. `http://www.relaxng.org/`   The web site for the Relax NG schema language.

7. `http://java.sun.com/xml`   The Sun Microsystems XML web site.

CLASSES, OBJECTS, AND METHODS INTRODUCED IN THIS CHAPTER

```
javax.xml.parsers.DocumentBuilder
   newDocument
   parse
javax.xml.parsers.DocumentBuilderFactory
   newDocumentBuilder
   newInstance
   setIgnoringElementContentWhitespace
   setValidating
javax.xml.xpath.XPath
   evaluate
javax.xml.xpath.XPathExpressionException
javax.xml.xpath.XPathFactory
   newInstance
   newXPath
org.w3c.dom.Document
   createElement
   createTextNode
   getImplementation
org.w3c.dom.DOMImplementation
   getFeature
org.w3c.dom.Element
   getAttribute
   setAttribute
org.w3c.dom.ls.DOMImplementationLS
   createLSSerializer
org.w3c.dom.ls.LSSerializer
   writeToString
```

REVIEW EXERCISES

Exercise R26.1. Give some examples to show the differences between XML and HTML.

Exercise R26.2. Design an XML document that describes a bank account.

Exercise R26.3. Draw a tree view for the XML document you created in Exercise R26.2.

Exercise R26.4. Write the XML document that corresponds to the parse tree in Figure 5.

Exercise R26.5. Write the XML document that corresponds to the parse tree in Figure 6.

Exercise R26.6. Make an XML document describing a book, with child elements for the author name, the title, and the publication year.

Exercise R26.7. Add a description of the book's language to the document of the preceding exercise. Should you use an element or an attribute?

Exercise R26.8. What is mixed content? What problems does it cause?

Exercise R26.9. Design an XML document that describes a purse containing three quarters, a dime, and two nickels.

Exercise R26.10. Explain why a paint program, such as Microsoft Paint, is a WYSIWYG program that is also "what you see is all you've got".

Exercise R26.11. Consider the XML file

```
<purse>
   <coin>
      <value>0.5</value>
      <name lang="en">half dollar</name>
   </coin>
   <coin>
      <value>0.25</value>
      <name lang="en">quarter</name>
   </coin>
</purse>
```

What are the values of the following XPath expressions?

a. /purse/coin[1]/value

b. /purse/coin[2]/name

c. /purse/coin[2]/name/@lang

d. name(/purse/coin[2]/*[1])

e. count(/purse/coin)

f. count(/purse/coin[2]/name)

Exercise R26.12. With the XML file of Exercise R26.11, give XPath expressions that yield the following:

a. the value of the first coin

b. the number of coins

c. the name of the first child element of the first coin element

d. the name of the first attribute element of the first name element

e. the value of the en attribute of the second name element

Exercise R26.13. Design a DTD that describes a bank with bank accounts.

Exercise R26.14. Design a DTD that describes a library patron who has checked out a set of books. Each book has an ID number, an author, and a title. The patron has a name and telephone number.

Exercise R26.15. Write the DTD file for the following XML document

```
<?xml version="1.0"?>
<productlist>
   <product>
      <name>Comtrade Tornado</name>
      <price currency="USD">2495</price>
      <score>60</score>
   </product>
   <product>
      <name>AMAX Powerstation 75</name>
      <price>2999</price>
      <score>62</score>
   </product>
</productlist>
```

Exercise R26.16. Design a DTD for invoices, as described in How To 26.3.

Exercise R26.17. Design a DTD for simple English sentences, as described in Random Fact 26.2.

Exercise R26.18. Design a DTD for arithmetic expressions, as described in Random Fact 26.2.

PROGRAMMING EXERCISES

Exercise P26.1. Write a program that can read XML files, such as

```
<purse>
   <coin>
      <value>0.5</value>
      <name>half dollar</name>
   </coin>
   . . .
</purse>
```

Your program should construct a `Purse` object and print the total value of the coins in the purse.

Exercise P26.2. Building on Exercise P26.1, make the program read an XML file as described in that exercise. Then print an XML file of the form

```
<purse>
   <coins>
      <coin>
         <value>0.5</value>
         <name>half dollar</name>
      </coin>
      <quantity>3</quantity>
   </coins>
   <coins>
      <coin>
         <value>0.25</value>
         <name>quarter</name>
      </coin>
      <quantity>2</quantity>
   </coins>
</purse>
```

Exercise P26.3. Repeat Exercise P26.1, using a DTD for validation.

Exercise P26.4. Write a program that can read XML files, such as

```
<bank>
   <account>
      <number>3</number>
      <balance>1295.32</balance>
   </account>
   . . .
</bank>
```

Your program should construct a `Bank` object and print the total value of the balances in the accounts.

Exercise P26.5. Repeat Exercise P26.4, using a DTD for validation.

Exercise P26.6. Enhance Exercise P26.4 as follows: First read the XML file in, then add 10% interest to all accounts, and write an XML file that contains the increased account balances.

Exercise P26.7. Write a program that can read an XML document of the form

```
<rectangle>
   <x>5</x>
   <y>10</y>
   <width>20</width>
   <height>30</height>
</rectangle>
```
Draw the shape in a window.

Exercise P26.8. Write a program that can read an XML document of the form

```
<ellipse>
    <x>5</x>
    <y>10</y>
    <width>20</width>
    <height>30</height>
</ellipse>
```

Draw the shape in a window.

Exercise P26.9. Write a program that can read an XML document of the form

```
<rectangularshape shape="ellipse">
    <x>5</x>
    <y>10</y>
    <width>20</width>
    <height>30</height>
</rectangularshape>
```

Support shape attributes "rectangle", "diamond", and "ellipse".

Draw the shape in a window.

Exercise P26.10. Write a program that can read an XML document of the form

```
<drawing>
    <rectangle>
        <x>5</x>
        <y>10</y>
        <width>20</width>
        <height>30</height>
    </rectangle>
    <line>
        <x1>5</x1>
        <y1>10</y1>
        <x2>25</x2>
        <y2>40</y2>
    </line>
    <message>
        <text>Hello, World!</text>
        <x>20</x>
        <y>30</y>
    </message>
</drawing>
```

Show the drawing in a window.

Exercise P26.11. Repeat Exercise P26.10, using a DTD for validation.

Exercise P26.12. Write a program that can read an XML document of the form

```
<polygon>
    <point>
        <x>5</x>
        <y>10</y>
    </point>
    . . .
</polygon>
```

Draw the shape in a window.

Exercise P26.13. Write a DTD file that describes documents that contain information about countries: name of the country, its population, and its area. Create an XML file that has five different countries. The DTD and XML should be in different files. Write a program that uses the XML file you wrote and prints:

- The country with the largest area
- The country with the largest population
- The country with the largest population density (people per square kilometer)

Exercise P26.14. Write a parser to parse invoices using the invoice structure described in How To 26.1. The parser should create a tree structure of the invoice first, then print it out in the format used in Chapter 17.

Exercise P26.15. Modify Exercise P26.14 to support separate shipping and billing addresses.

Exercise P26.16. Write a document builder that turns an invoice object, as defined in Chapter 17, into an XML file of the format described in How To 26.1.

Exercise P26.17. Modify Exercise P26.16 to support separate shipping and billing addresses.

PROGRAMMING PROJECTS

Project 26.1. Following Exercise P17.10, design an XML format for the appointments in an appointment calendar. Write a program that first reads in a file with appointments, then another file of the format

```
<commands>
   <add>
      <appointment>
         . . .
      </appointment>
   </add>
   . . .
   <remove>
      <appointment>
         . . .
      </appointment>
   </remove>
</commands>
```

Your program should process the commands and then produce an XML file that consists of the updated appointments.

Project 26.2. Write a program to simulate an airline seat reservation system, using XML documents. Reference Exercise P17.11 for the airplane seat information. The program reads a seating chart, in an XML format of your choice, and a command file, in an XML format of your choice, similar to the command file of the preceding exercise. Then the program processes the commands and produces an updated seating chart.

ANSWERS TO SELF-CHECK QUESTIONS

1. Your answer should look similar to this:

```
<student>
    <name>James Bond</name>
    <id>007</id>
</student>
```

2. Most browsers display a tree structure that indicates the nesting of the tags. Some browsers display nothing at all because they can't find any HTML tags.

3. The text `hamster.jpg` is never displayed, so it should not be a part of the document. Instead, the `src` attribute tells the browser where to find the image that should be displayed.

4. 8.

5. `name(/*[1])`.

6. The `createTextElement` method is useful for creating other documents.

7. First construct a string, as described, and then use a `PrintWriter` to save the string to a file.

8. `<!ELEMENT item (product, quantity?)>`

9. `<!ELEMENT product ((description, price) | (price, description))>`

10. `<!ATTLIST description language CDATA #IMPLIED>`

JavaServer Faces

Web applications are a new type of software that has become very important in recent years. Applications for a wide variety of purposes, such as e-mail, banking, shopping, and playing games, run on servers and interact with users through a web browser. Developing web-based user interfaces is more complex and challenging than writing graphical user interfaces. Until recently, only primitive technologies (such as Java servlets) were available for this purpose. Fortunately, more capable frameworks for web programming have emerged that are roughly analogous to the Swing framework for client-side user interface programming. In this chapter, you will learn how to write web applications using the JavaServer Faces (JSF) framework.

CHAPTER CONTENTS

27.1 A Simple JSF Program

In this section, you will learn how to set up the tools that are required for Java-Server Faces™(JSF) programming, and you will see a very simple JSF application.

To develop a JSF application, you need a web server that is integrated with a *JSF container*. One excellent and freely available server is Apache Tomcat [1]. As this chapter is written, Apache does not yet have JSF built in. Instead, it supports an earlier technology called JavaServer Pages (JSP). Sun Microsystems has developed a JSF implementation that is based upon JSP—see [2]. You should install both Tomcat and the "reference implementation" from Sun Microsystems to try out the examples in this chapter. You will find detailed installation instructions in the companion web site for this book.

The user interface of a JSF application is described by a set of *JSF pages*. Each JSF page has the following structure:

```
<html>
   <%@ taglib uri="http://java.sun.com/jsf/core" prefix="f" %>
   <%@ taglib uri="http://java.sun.com/jsf/html" prefix="h" %>
   <f:view>
      <head>
         <title>Page title</title>
      </head>
      <body>
         <h:form>
            Page contents
         </h:form>
      </body>
   </f:view>
</html>
```

A JavaServer Faces (JSF) page contains HTML and JSF tags.

You can think of this as the required "plumbing", similar to the `public static void main` incantation that is required for every Java program. As you can see, the plumbing consists of three parts:

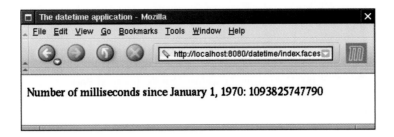

Figure 1 Executing the datetime Web Application

- The `taglib` directives are required by Tomcat to locate two JSF libraries. Tags from the core library have the prefix `f:` (such as `f:view`). Tags from the HTML library have the prefix `h:` (such as `h:form`)

- All JSF tags (from the core and HTML libraries) must be contained inside an `f:view` tag.

- The `h:form` tag encloses all user interface elements.

Here is a concrete example.

File datetime/index.jsp

```
1   <html>
2      <%@ taglib uri="http://java.sun.com/jsf/core" prefix="f" %>
3      <%@ taglib uri="http://java.sun.com/jsf/html" prefix="h" %>
4
5      <f:view>
6         <head>
7            <title>The datetime application</title>
8         </head>
9         <body>
10           <h:form>
11              <p>Number of milliseconds since January 1, 1970:
12                 <h:outputText value="#{dateTime.time}"/>
13              </p>
14           </h:form>
15        </body>
16     </f:view>
17  </html>
```

Figure 1 shows the result of executing the program.

The purpose of a JSF page is to *generate* an HTML page. The basic process is as follows:

- The HTML tags that are present in the JSF page (such as `title` and `p`) are retained. These are the *static* part of the page: the formatting instructions that do not change.

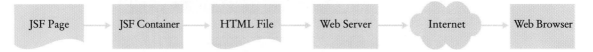

Figure 2 The JSF Container Rewrites the Requested Page

- The JSF tags are translated into HTML. This translation is *dynamic:* it depends on the state of Java objects. (Technically, only the h: tags generate HTML. The f: tags from the core library describe structural information that the h: tags use in the translation process.)

- The taglib directives are stripped out.

Figure 2 shows the basic process. The browser requests a JSF page. The JSF container (in our case, Tomcat) processes the page. The JSF tags generate text and HTML markup instructions. The resulting document contains only text and HTML tags. The web server (another part of Tomcat) sends that document to the browser. The browser displays the page.

> The JSF container converts a JSF page to an HTML page, replacing all JSF tags with text and HTML tags.

Figure 3 shows the HTML code that the JSF page generated. It is similar to the JSF page; however, the h:outputText tag has been replaced by dynamically generated text: the number of milliseconds since January 1, 1970. You can use the "View Source" option of your browser to see the HTML code.

> The Java objects of a JSF application are defined in a configuration file.

If you look closely at the h:outputText tag in the index.jsp file of the sample application, you will notice a *value binding* #{dateTime.time}. Value bindings link JSF pages with Java objects. The Java objects are defined in a configuration file, named faces-config.xml. The configuration file must be placed in the WEB-INF subdirectory of the web application's base directory. Here is the configuration file for our application:

File datetime/WEB-INF/faces-config.xml

```
1   <?xml version="1.0"?>
2
3   <!DOCTYPE faces-config PUBLIC
4      "-//Sun Microsystems, Inc.//DTD JavaServer Faces Config 1.0//EN"
5      "http://java.sun.com/dtd/web-facesconfig_1_0.dtd">
6
7   <faces-config>
8      <managed-bean>
9         <managed-bean-name>dateTime</managed-bean-name>
10        <managed-bean-class>java.util.Date</managed-bean-class>
11        <managed-bean-scope>request</managed-bean-scope>
12     </managed-bean>
13  </faces-config>
```

Figure 3 The HTML Code That Is Generated by a JSF Page

> A value binding links a JSF component with a bean property.

As you can see, this file defines an object with name dateTime and type java.util.Date. A new object is constructed with each "request". That means, whenever a browser requests the page, a new Date object is constructed and attached to the dateTime variable. Because the Date constructor constructs an object with the current time, the application always shows the millisecond count that was current when the page was requested.

The value binding expression #{dateTime.time} calls the getTime method on the Java object dateTime. (You will see in the next section why the called method is getTime and not time.) The getTime method of the Date class returns the number of milliseconds between January 1, 1970 and the time at which the Date object was created. The h:outputText tag uses the result of that method call and converts it to text.

> The JSF technology enables the separation of presentation and business logic.

Value bindings support a very important design principle of the JSF technology: the separation of presentation and business logic.

Here, the *presentation logic* refers to the user interface of the web application: the arrangement of the text, images, buttons, and so on. The *business logic* is the part of the application that is independent of the visual presentation. In commercial applications, it contains the rules that are used for business decisions: what products to offer, how much to charge, to whom to extend credit, and so on. In our example, we simulated the business logic with a Date object.

JSF pages define the presentation logic. Java objects define the business logic. The value bindings tie the two together.

The separation of presentation logic and business logic is very important when designing web applications. Some web technologies place the code for the business logic right into the web page. However, this quickly turned into a serious problem. Programmers are rarely skilled in web design (as you can see from the boring web pages in this chapter). Graphic designers don't usually know much about programming and find it very challenging to improve web pages that contain a lot of code. JSF solves this problem. In JSF, the graphic designer only sees the elements that make up the presentation logic. It is easy to take a boring JSF page and make it pretty by adding banners, icons, and so on.

To deploy a JSF application, follow these steps:

1. Make a subdirectory with the name of your web application in the `webapps` directory of your Tomcat installation. For example, for the `datetime` application, you would make a subdirectory

   ```
   /usr/local/jakarta-tomcat/webapps/datetime
   ```
   or
   ```
   c:\Tomcat\webapps\datetime
   ```

2. Place the `index.jsp` file into that directory.

3. Create a subdirectory `WEB-INF` in your application directory, such as

   ```
   /usr/local/jakarta-tomcat/webapps/datetime/WEB-INF
   ```
   or
   ```
   c:\Tomcat\webapps\datetime\WEB-INF
   ```

4. Place the `faces-config.xml` file into the `WEB-INF` subdirectory.

5. If your web application contains Java classes, place them inside a subdirectory `classes` of the `WEB-INF` directory. Most web applications require Java classes, but in our first sample application, we skip this step and make do with the `Date` class from the standard library.

6. Place the file `web.xml` (which is shown below) inside the `WEB-INF` subdirectory. Tomcat needs this file to load the JSF library.

7. Start the web server.

8. Point your browser to `http://localhost:8080/datetime/index.faces`. Note that the URL has a suffix `.faces`. That suffix tells Tomcat to interpret the file as a JSF page. (Unlike the URL, the file has the extension `.jsp`. When future versions of Tomcat have built-in JSF support, this anomaly should go away.)

Figure 4 shows the directory structure for the application.

It is a bit painful to write all these files by hand, and to put them in the right places. There are development tools available that do much of the routine work for you—see Figure 5 for an example. For simple applications—such as the ones in this

Figure 4 The Directory Structure of the datetime Application

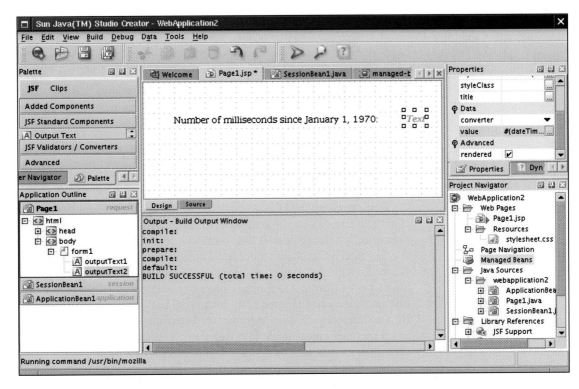

Figure 5 The Java Studio Creator Tool

chapter—the manual process is certainly feasible. For large applications, you will want to use a professional JSF development tool.

File datetime/WEB-INF/web.xml

```
1   <?xml version="1.0"?>
2
3   <!DOCTYPE web-app PUBLIC
4       "-//Sun Microsystems, Inc.//DTD Web Application 2.3//EN"
5       "http://java.sun.com/dtd/web-app_2_3.dtd">
6
7   <web-app>
8       <servlet>
9           <servlet-name>Faces Servlet</servlet-name>
10          <servlet-class>javax.faces.webapp.FacesServlet</servlet-class>
11          <load-on-startup>1</load-on-startup>
12      </servlet>
13
14      <servlet-mapping>
15          <servlet-name>Faces Servlet</servlet-name>
16          <url-pattern>*.faces</url-pattern>
17      </servlet-mapping>
18  </web-app>
```

1. What steps are required to add the image of a clock to the datetime application? (The clock doesn't have to show the correct time.)
2. Does a Swing program automatically separate presentation and business logic?

27.2 JavaBeans Components

> Properties of a software component can be accessed without having to write Java code.

A *software component* is an entity that encapsulates functionality and can be plugged into a software system without programming. For example, when we added the dateTime object to the web application, we did not write code to construct the object or to call its methods. Instead, we specified the object's behavior in configuration files. Some programming languages have explicit support for components, but Java does not. Instead, in Java, you use a programming convention to implement components. A *JavaBean* is a Java class that follows this convention. A JavaBean exposes *properties*—values of the component that can be accessed without programming.

> A JavaBean is a class with a default constructor that exposes properties through its get and set methods.

Just about any Java class can be a JavaBean—there are only two requirements.

- A JavaBean must have a public constructor with no parameters.
- A JavaBean must have methods for accessing the component properties that follow the get/set naming convention. For example, to get or set the time property of a Date object, the methods must be called getTime and setTime.

In general, if the name of the property is *propertyName*, and its type is *Type*, then the associated methods must be of the form

```
public Type getPropertyName()
public void setPropertyName(Type newValue)
```

This is, of course, a convention that we have used for most accessor and mutator methods. There is one exception—the accessor of a boolean property can use an is prefix, for example

```
public boolean isShopping()
```

Note that the name of a property starts with a lowercase letter (such as shopping), but the corresponding methods have an uppercase letter (isShopping). The only exception is that property names can be all capitals, such as ID or URL, with corresponding methods getID or setURL.

If a property has only a get method, then it is a *read-only* property. If it has only a set method, then it is a write-only property.

A JavaBean can have additional methods, but they are not connected with properties.

Finally, many programmers follow the additional convention that the name of a bean class should end in Bean, but this is not a requirement.

Here is a simple example of a bean class:

```
public class UserBean
{
    // Required default constructor
    public UserBean() { . . . }

    // creditCard property
    public String getCreditCard() { . . . }
    public void setCreditCard(String newValue) { . . . }

    // shopping property
    public boolean isShopping() { . . . }
    public void setShopping(boolean newValue) { . . . }

    // Other methods
    . . .
    // Instance fields
    . . .
}
```

This bean has two properties: creditCard and shopping.

You should *not* make any assumptions about the internal representation of properties in the bean class. The bean class *may* simply have an instance field for every property:

```
private String creditCard;
private boolean shopping;
```

On the other hand, perhaps the bean class stores the credit card state in a database, so that the get and set methods actually contain database operations. Alternatively, the isShopping method might compute the property value:

```
public boolean isShopping() { return shoppingCart != null; }
```

To use a bean in a JSF page, define it in the faces-config.xml file. For example, you can define a bean with the following directive:

```
<managed-bean>
    <managed-bean-name>user</managed-bean-name>
    <managed-bean-class>bigjava.UserBean</managed-bean-class>
    <managed-bean-scope>session</managed-bean-scope>
</managed-bean>
```

This directive invokes the default constructor of the UserBean class in the bigjava package to make an object with the name user. Recall that every bean must have a default constructor.

The bean is called a *managed bean* because the JSF container manages its lifetime. If the scope has been set to session, then the bean stays alive during multiple requests from the same browser. This is the behavior that you want in most web applications. However, in the example of the preceding section, we specified request scope because we wanted a new Date object for each connection.

A bean with session scope is available for multiple requests by the same browser.

There is also an `application` scope for a bean that stays alive for the entire web application and that is shared among different users. In contrast, if multiple users are simultaneously accessing a JSF application, each of them has a separate set of beans with session scope.

Once the bean has been defined, you can access its properties in value bindings, such as

```
<h:outputText value="#{user.creditCard}"/>
```

You specify the name of the property, not the name of the `get` or `set` methods, which is convenient for input tags. For example, the tag

```
<h:inputText value="#{user.creditCard}"/>
```

first calls `getCreditCard` to display the current value of the property to the user. The user can then make changes to the number. When the user submits the form, the `setCreditCard` method is called to store the edited property value in the bean.

Let's put these concepts to work in an actual JSF page. Suppose we want to display the current time, not the number of milliseconds since January 1, 1970. Because the default time computation uses the time zone *at the server location*, it is not very useful if the user is in another time zone. We will prompt for the city in which the user is located, and then display the time in the user's time zone (see Figure 6).

The Java library contains a convenient `TimeZone` class that knows about time zones across the world. A time zone is identified by a string such as `"America/Los_Angeles"` or `"Asia/Tokyo"`. The static method `getAvailableIDs` returns a string array containing all IDs:

```
String[] ids = TimeZone.getAvailableIDs();
```

There are several hundred time zone IDs. (We are using time zones in this example because the `TimeZone` class gives us an interesting data source with lots of data. Later in this chapter, you will see how to access data from a database, but of course that's more complex.)

The static `getTimeZone` method returns a `TimeZone` object for a given ID string:

```
String id = "America/Los_Angeles";
TimeZone zone = TimeZone.getTimeZone(id);
```

Once you have a `TimeZone` object, you can use it in conjunction with a `DateFormat` object to get a time string in that time zone.

```
DateFormat timeFormatter = DateFormat.getTimeInstance();
timeFormatter.setTimeZone(zone);
Date now = new Date();
// Suppose the server is in New York, and it's noon there
System.out.println(timeFormatter.format(now));
// Prints 9:00:00 AM
```

Of course, we don't expect the user to know about time zone ID strings, such as `"America/Los_Angeles"`. Instead, we assume that the user will simply enter the city name. The time zone bean will check whether that string, with spaces replaced by underscores, appears at the end of one of the valid time zone IDs.

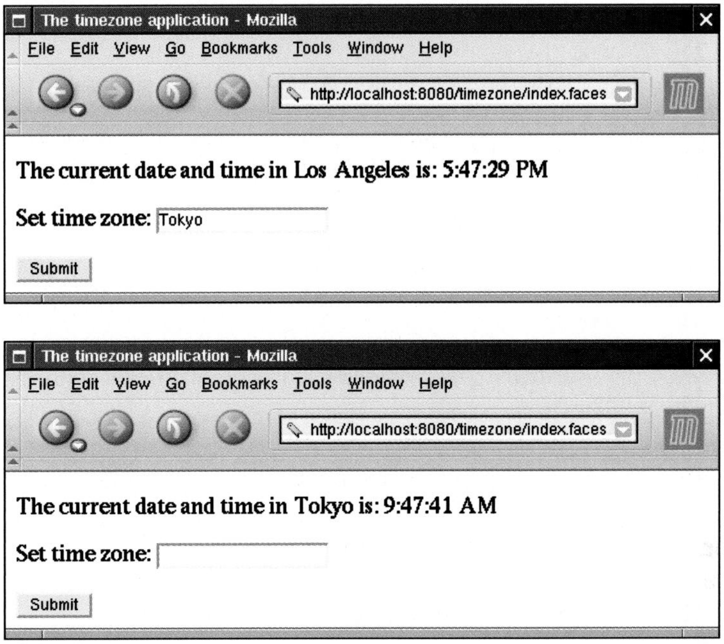

Figure 6 The timezone Application

Here is the code for the bean class. The class must be placed inside the WEB-INF/ classes directory. Tomcat requires that all classes are contained in a package. We place the classes of our sample examples inside the bigjava package. Therefore, the class is actually contained in the WEB-INF/classes/bigjava directory.

File timezone/WEB-INF/classes/bigjava/TimeZoneBean.java

```java
1   package bigjava;
2
3   import java.text.DateFormat;
4   import java.util.Date;
5   import java.util.TimeZone;
6
7   /**
8      This bean formats the local time of day for a given date
9      and city.
10  */
11  public class TimeZoneBean
12  {
13     /**
14        Initializes the formatter.
15     */
16     public TimeZoneBean()
17     {
18        timeFormatter = DateFormat.getTimeInstance();
19     }
```

```
20
21      /**
22         Setter for city property.
23         @param aCity the city for which to report the local time
24      */
25      public void setCity(String aCity)
26      {
27         city = aCity;
28         zone = getTimeZone(city);
29      }
30
31      /**
32         Getter for city property.
33         @return the city for which to report the local time
34      */
35      public String getCity()
36      {
37         return city;
38      }
39
40      /**
41         Read-only time property.
42         @return the formatted time
43      */
44      public String getTime()
45      {
46         if (zone == null) return "not available";
47         timeFormatter.setTimeZone(zone);
48         Date time = new Date();
49         String timeString = timeFormatter.format(time);
50         return timeString;
51      }
52
53      /**
54         Looks up the time zone for a city.
55         @param city the city for which to find the time zone
56         @return the time zone or null if no match is found
57      */
58      private static TimeZone getTimeZone(String city)
59      {
60         String[] ids = TimeZone.getAvailableIDs();
61         for (int i = 0; i < ids.length; i++)
62            if (timeZoneIDmatch(ids[i], city))
63               return TimeZone.getTimeZone(ids[i]);
64         return null;
65      }
66
67      /**
68         Checks whether a time zone ID matches a city.
69         @param id the time zone ID (e.g., "America/Los_Angeles")
70         @param city the city to match (e.g., "Los Angeles")
71         @return true if the ID and city match
72      */
```

```
73      private static boolean timeZoneIDmatch(String id, String city)
74      {
75         String idCity = id.substring(id.indexOf('/') + 1);
76         return idCity.replace('_', ' ').equals(city);
77      }
78
79      private DateFormat timeFormatter;
80      private String city;
81      private TimeZone zone;
82   }
```

The bean is defined in the `faces-config.xml` file. Note the `managed-property` tag that sets the `city` property to an initial value `"Los Angeles"`.

File timezone/WEB-INF/faces-config.xml

```
1    <?xml version="1.0"?>
2
3    <!DOCTYPE faces-config PUBLIC
4       "-//Sun Microsystems, Inc.//DTD JavaServer Faces Config 1.0//EN"
5       "http://java.sun.com/dtd/web-facesconfig_1_0.dtd">
6
7    <faces-config>
8       <managed-bean>
9          <managed-bean-name>zone</managed-bean-name>
10         <managed-bean-class>bigjava.TimeZoneBean</managed-bean-class>
11         <managed-bean-scope>session</managed-bean-scope>
12         <managed-property>
13            <property-name>city</property-name>
14            <value>Los Angeles</value>
15         </managed-property>
16      </managed-bean>
17   </faces-config>
```

Here is the JSF page that invokes the time zone bean. There are two `h:outputText` tags that display the `city` and `time` properties. These tags invoke the `getCity` and `getTime` methods of the bean class. The `h:inputText` tag produces an input field. Finally, the `h:commandButton` tag produces a button. When the user clicks the button, the browser sends the form values (that is, the contents of the input field) back to the web application. The web application calls the `setCity` method on the bean because the input field has a `#{zone.city}` value binding. Then the web application redisplays the form.

File timezone/index.jsp

```
1    <html>
2       <%@ taglib uri="http://java.sun.com/jsf/core" prefix="f" %>
3       <%@ taglib uri="http://java.sun.com/jsf/html" prefix="h" %>
4
5       <f:view>
6          <head>
7             <title>The timezone application</title>
```

```
 8          </head>
 9          <body>
10             <h:form>
11                <p>
12                   The current date and time in
13                   <h:outputText value="#{zone.city}"/>
14                   is:
15                   <h:outputText value="#{zone.time}"/>
16                </p>
17                <p>
18                   Set time zone:
19                   <h:inputText value="#{zone.city}"/>
20                </p>
21                <p>
22                   <h:commandButton value="Submit"/>
23                </p>
24             </h:form>
25          </body>
26       </f:view>
27    </html>
```

Figure 7 shows the directory structure of the timezone application. The web.xml file is unchanged from the datetime application.

This example demonstrates the separation of the presentation from the Java code. The user interface (that is, the text, input field, and button) are specified in the JSF page. The Java code is contained in the bean class. A graphic designer can improve the look of the page by editing the HTML document to change the layout, add images, and so on, without having to do any programming. Conversely, a programmer can modify the code of the bean class without doing any web design.

Figure 7   The Directory Structure of the timezone Application

SELF CHECK

3. Is the Random class a Java bean?

4. What work does the setCity method of the TimeZoneBean do besides setting the city instance field?

5. When you start the timezone application for the first time, why does the input field contain the string "Los Angeles"?

COMMON ERROR 27.1

Fussy JSF Syntax

It is very easy to make errors in the JSF syntax, because it is a mixture of HTML and JSF-specific tags. Also, because the JSF processing step is hidden from the programmer, you don't get good error messages. Here are some of the most common errors:

- Forgetting the / before a closing angle bracket, such as <h:outputText . . . />. The JSF tags use the XML syntax, and a closing / is required (unless you supply a separate closing tag </h:outputText>).
- Letter case errors, such as h:outputtext instead of h:outputText. HTML is not case-sensitive, but the JSF tags are.
- Forgetting the h: or f: prefixes. A tag such as <outputText . . . /> is simply passed on to the browser. The browser has no idea how to display it and ignores it.
- Forgetting quotation marks for attribute values. In HTML it is OK to omit these quotation marks, but the JSF tags follow the stricter XML syntax. For example, <h:outputText value=#{dateTime.time}/> is an error.
- Forgetting the #{. . .} delimiters around value bindings. For example, <h:outputText value="dateTime.time"/> simply produces a string dateTime.time in the output.

HOW TO 27.1

Designing a Bean

A bean is just a regular Java class, with two special characteristics.
- The bean must have a default constructor.
- Methods of the form

    Type get*PropertyName*()
    void set*PropertyName*(*Type* x)

    define properties that can be accessed from JSF pages.

Here are step-by-step instructions for designing a bean class.

Step 1 Decide on the responsibility of the bean.

When designing a JSF application, it is tempting to stuff all code into a single bean class. Some development environments even encourage this approach. However, from a software engineering perspective, it is best to come up with different beans for different responsibilities. For example, a shopping application might have a UserBean to describe the current user, a SiteBean to describe how the user visits the shopping site, and a ShoppingCartBean that holds the items that the user is purchasing.

Step 2 Discover the properties that the bean should expose.

A property is an entity that you want to access or modify from your JSF pages. For example, a UserBean might have properties firstName, lastName, and password.

Sometimes, you have to resort to a bit of trickery. For example, consider adding an item to the shopping cart. You could use a property items, but it would be cumbersome to access all items in a JSF page and then set items to a new collection that contains one additional element. Instead, you can design a property addedItem. When that property is set, the setAddedItem method of your bean adds its value to the collection of items.

Step 3   Settle on the type and access permissions for each property.

Properties that are used in h:outputText tags can be read-only. Properties that are used in h:inputText and other input tags must have read-write access.

Step 4   Implement the default constructor.

It initializes any fields that are reused whenever the bean's computation is executed. Examples are formatters, random number generators, and so on.

Step 5   Implement the get and set methods for all properties.

Most get and set methods simply get or set an instance field. However, you can carry out arbitrary computations in these methods if it is convenient. For example, a get method may retrieve information from a database instead of an instance field.

Step 6   Supply any needed helper methods.

Your bean can have methods that are not property getters and setters. For example, the TimeZoneBean has helper methods to look up the time zone for a city.

ADVANCED TOPIC 27.1

Session State and Cookies

You may recall from Chapter 24 that HTTP is a *stateless* protocol. A browser sends a request to a web server. The web server sends the reply and then disconnects. This is different from other protocols, such as POP, where the mail client logs into the mail server and stays connected until it has retrieved all e-mail messages. In contrast, a browser makes a new connection to the web server for each web page, and the web server has no way of knowing that those connections originate from the same browser. This makes it difficult to implement web applications. For example, in a shopping application, it is essential to track which requests came from a particular shopper.

Cookies were invented to overcome this restriction. A cookie consists of a small string that the web server sends to a browser, and that the browser sends back to the same server with all further requests. That way, the server can tie the stream of requests together. The JSF container matches up the cookies with the beans that have session scope. When a browser request contains a cookie, the value bindings in the JSF page refer to the matching beans.

You may have heard some privacy advocates complaining about cookies. Cookies are not inherently evil. When used to establish a session or to remember login information, they can make web applications more user-friendly. But when cookies are used to track your identity while you surf the Web, there can be privacy concerns. For example, Figure 8 shows some of the cookies that my browser held on a particular day. I have no recollection of visiting the advertising and shopping sites, so it is a bit disconcerting to see that my browser communicated with them.

Some people turn off cookies, and then web applications need to use another scheme to establish a session, typically by embedding a session identifier in the request URL or a hidden field of a form. The JSF session mechanism automatically switches to URLs with session identifiers if the client browser doesn't support cookies.

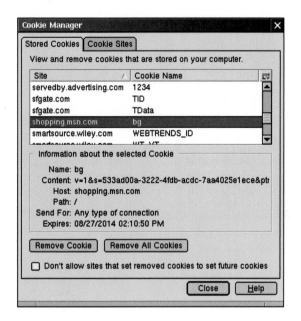

Figure 8
Viewing the Cookies
in a Browser

27.3 JSF Components

In this section, you will see the most useful user interface components that you can place on a JSF form. Table 1 shows a summary. For a comprehensive discussion of all JSF components, see [3].

> The value attribute of an input component denotes the value that the user supplies.

Each component has a `value` attribute that allows you to connect the component value with a bean property, for example

```
<h:inputSecret value="#{user.password}"/>
```

The `h:inputTextArea` component has attributes to specify the rows and columns, such as

```
<h:inputTextArea value="#{user.comment}" rows="10" cols="40"/>
```

The radio button and checkbox groups allow you to specify horizontal or vertical layout:

```
<h:selectOneRadio value="#{burger.topping}" layout="lineDirection">
```

In European languages, `lineDirection` means horizontal and `pageDirection` means vertical. However, in some languages, lines are written top-to-bottom, and the meanings are reversed.

Component	JSF Tag	Common Attributes	Example
Text Field	h:inputText	value	`12345678901234567890`
Password Field	h:inputSecret	value	`**********`
Text Area	h:inputTextArea	value rows cols	line one line two line three
Radio Button Group	h:selectOneRadio h:selectManyRadio	value layout	◌ Cheese ◉ Pickle ◌ Mustard ◌ Lettuce ◌ Onions
Checkbox	h:selectOneCheckbox	value	Receive email: ☑
Checkbox Group	h:selectManyCheckbox	value layout	☑ Cheese ☐ Pickle ☑ Mustard ☐ Lettuce ☐ Onions
Menu	h:selectOneMenu h:selectManyMenu	value	Cheese Pickle Mustard Lettuce
Image	h:graphicImage	value	
Submit Button	h:commandButton	value action	press me

Table 1   **Common JSF Components**

Button groups and menus are more complex than the other user interface components. They require you to specify two properties:

- the collection of possible choices
- the actual choice

> Use an f:selectItems tag to specify all choices for a component that allows selection from a list of choices.

The value attribute of the component specifies the actual choice to be displayed. The collection of possible choices is defined by a nested f:selectItems tag, like this:

```
<h:selectOneRadio value="#{creditCard.expirationMonth}"
      layout="pageDirection">
   <f:selectItems value="#{creditCard.monthChoices}"/>
</h:selectOneRadio>
```

Here, the monthChoices property must have a type that can describe a list of choices. There are several types that you can use, but the easiest—and the only one that we will discuss—is a Map. The keys of the map are the *labels*—the strings that are displayed next to each choice. The corresponding map values are the *label values*—the values that correspond to the selection. For example, a choice map for months would map January to 1, February to 2, and so on:

```java
public class CreditCardBean
{
   . . .
   public Map<String, Integer> getMonthChoices()
   {
      Map<String, Integer> choices = new LinkedHashMap<String, Integer>();
      choices.put("January", 1);
      choices.put("February", 2);
      . . .
      return choices;
   }
}
```

Here, we use a LinkedHashMap because we want to visit entries in the order in which they are inserted. This is more useful than a HashMap, which would visit the labels in random order or a TreeMap, which would visit them in alphabetical order (starting with April!).

The type of the value property of the component must match the type of the map value. For example, creditCard.expirationMonth must be an integer, not a string. If multiple selections are allowed, the type of the value property must be a list or array of matching types. For example, if one could choose multiple months, a selectManyRadio component would have a value property with a type such as int[] or ArrayList<Integer>.

We will discuss submit buttons in detail in the following section.

SELF CHECK

6. Which JSF components can be used to give a user a choice between "AM/PM" and "military" time?

7. How would you supply a set of choices for a credit card expiration year to a h:selectOneMenu component?

27.4 Navigation Between Pages

In most web applications, users will want to move between different pages. For example, a shopping application might have a login page, a page to show products for sale, and a checkout page that shows the shopping cart. In this section, you will learn how to enable users to navigate from one page to another.

Consider an enhancement of our timezone program. We start with a page that prompts the user to enter the name of a city. When the user clicks the "Submit" button, a new page appears. The next page is either the page with the time display or an error page if no time zone is available for the city (see Figure 9).

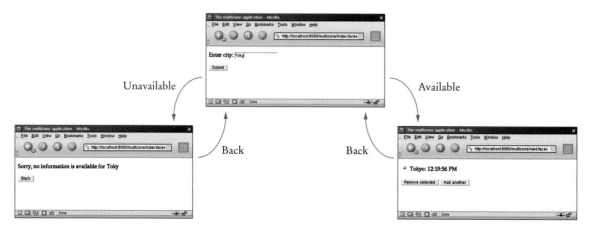

Figure 9   Navigating Between Pages

The JSF container needs to determine which page to show next.

> The outcome string of an action determines the next page that the JSF container sends to the browser.

Each button has an *outcome,* a string that is used to look up the next page. In many situations, the next page depends on the result of some computation. In our example, we need different outcomes depending on the city that the user entered. To achieve this flexibility, you specify a *method binding* as the action attribute:

```
<h:commandButton value="Submit" action="#{zone.addCity}"/>
```

> A method binding specifies a bean and a method that should be invoked on the bean.

A method binding consists of the name of a bean and the name of a method. When the form is submitted, the JSF engine calls zone.addCity(). The addCity method returns a string:

```
public class TimeZoneBean
{
    . . .
    public String addCity()
    {
        if (zone == null) return "unavailable";
        // Add the city
        . . .
        return "available";
    }
}
```

If the next page does not depend on a computation, then you set the action attribute of the button to a fixed outcome string, like this:

```
<h:commandButton value="Back" action="back"/>
```

> A navigation rule maps outcome strings to JSF pages.

The faces-config.xml file contains a *navigation rule* that maps outcome strings to pages:

```
<faces-config>
    <navigation-rule>
        <navigation-case>
```

```
            <from-outcome>available</from-outcome>
            <to-view-id>/next.jsp</to-view-id>
         </navigation-case>
         <navigation-case>
            <from-outcome>unavailable</from-outcome>
            <to-view-id>/error.jsp</to-view-id>
         </navigation-case>
         <navigation-case>
            <from-outcome>back</from-outcome>
            <to-view-id>/index.jsp</to-view-id>
         </navigation-case>
      </navigation-rule>
      . . .
   </faces-config>
```

For example, if the addCity method returns the string "unavailable", then the page error.jsp is displayed.

If a button has no action attribute, or if the action outcome is not listed in the navigation rules, then the current page is redisplayed.

SELF CHECK

8. What tag would you need to add to error.jsp so that the user can click on a button labeled "Help" and see help.jsp? What other changes do you need to make to the web application?

9. Which page would be displayed if the addCity method returned null?

HOW TO 27.2

Building a Web Application

Step 1 On separate sheets of paper, sketch a screen for each web page of the application.

Start out with the initial screen, often a login screen. On each screen will be one or more buttons that post data to the server and switch to another page (or maybe the same page with more information added). Be sure to include error screens for invalid inputs.

Step 2 Draw a navigation diagram similar to the one in Figure 9.

For each page, draw an arrow to its successor page and label it with an outcome string.

Step 3 On each web page, mark the static and dynamic parts.

The static parts always stay the same (such as titles, logos, instructions, and so on). The dynamic parts change according to user input.

Step 4 Design beans to supply the dynamically generated output and to hold the user input.

See How To 27.1 for more information on designing beans.

Step 5   Analyze the navigation behavior and supply action methods.

In JSF, navigation between pages is defined by navigation rules that are triggered by outcome strings. If a button always selects a fixed successor page, use a fixed action string. Otherwise, implement an action method that determines the successor page.

Step 6   Code the JSF pages.

You can use a text editor, a JSF-aware HTML editor, or a JSF development tool.

Step 7   Implement the Java code for the beans and compile it.

You need get and set methods for the bean properties as well as action methods for the command buttons that require dynamic navigation.

Step 8   Define beans and navigation rules in the configuration file.

Add navigation-case and managed-bean tags to the faces-config.xml file.

Step 9   Deploy your application.

Place the JSF files and any necessary images into the web application directory, the web.xml and faces-config.xml files into the WEB-INF subdirectory, and the class files into the WEB-INF/classes subdirectory.

27.5 A Three-Tier Application

> A three-tier application has separate tiers for presentation, business logic, and data storage.

In the final JSF example, you will see a web application with a very common structure. In this example, we will use a database for information storage. We will enhance the time zone example by storing additional cities that are not known to the TimeZone class in a database. Such an application is called a *three-tier application* because it consists of three separate layers or tiers (see Figure 10):

- The presentation tier: the web browser
- The "business logic" tier: the JSF container, the JSF pages, and the JavaBeans
- The storage tier: the database

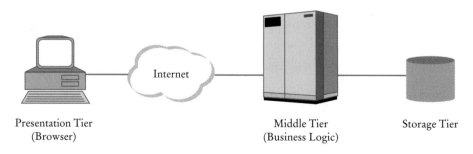

Figure 10   Three-Tier Architecture

Figure 11   Two-Tier Client-Server Architecture

Contrast the three-tier architecture with the more traditional *client-server* or *two-tier architecture* that you saw in the database programs of Chapter 25. In that architecture, one of the tiers is the database server, which is accessed by multiple client programs on desktops. Each client program has a presentation layer—usually with a specially programmed graphical user interface—and business logic code. (See Figure 11.) When the business logic changes, a new client program must be distributed over all desktops. In contrast, in a three-tier application, the business logic resides on a server. When the logic changes, the server code is updated, while the presentation tier—the browser—remains unchanged. That is much simpler to manage than updating multiple desktops.

In our example, we will have a single database table, CityZone, with city and time zone names (see Figure 12).

File multizone/misc/CityZone.sql

```
1   CREATE TABLE CityZone (City TEXT, Zone TEXT)
2   INSERT INTO CityZone VALUES ('San Francisco', 'America/Los_Angeles')
3   INSERT INTO CityZone VALUES ('Kaoshiung', 'Asia/Taipei')
4   . . .
```

If the TimeZoneBean can't find the city among the standard time zone IDs, it makes a database query:

```
SELECT Zone FROM CityZone WHERE City = the requested city
```

If there is a matching entry in the database, that time zone is returned.

CityZone

City	Zone
San Francisco	America/Los_Angeles
Kaoshiung	Asia/Taipei
. . .	. . .

Figure 12   The CityZone Table

Database connections
are configured in the
JSF container.
To query the database, the bean needs a Connection object. In Chapter 25, we used the static getConnection method of the DriverManager class to obtain a database connection. However, JSF containers usually have a better mechanism for configuring a database in one central location so that multiple web applications can access it. With Tomcat, you specify the database configuration in the server.xml file in the conf directory. Locate the element

```
<Host name="localhost" . . . >
```

Immediately after that element, add the following configuration information:

```
<DefaultContext>
   <Resource name="jdbc/mydb" auth="Container"
       type="javax.sql.DataSource"/>
   <ResourceParams name="jdbc/mydb">
      <parameter>
         <name>factory</name>
         <value>org.apache.commons.dbcp.BasicDataSourceFactory</value>
      </parameter>
      <parameter>
         <name>driverClassName</name>
         <value>driver class</value>
      </parameter>
      <parameter>
         <name>url</name>
         <value>database URL</value>
      </parameter>
      <parameter>
        <name>username</name>
        <value>database user name</value>
      </parameter>
      <parameter>
        <name>password</name>
        <value>database user password</value>
      </parameter>
   </ResourceParams>
</DefaultContext>
```

You need to place the JDBC driver file into the common/lib directory of your Tomcat directory. Remember to restart the server after you have made the changes to the configuration file.

In your bean code, you get a database connection with the following code:

```
InitialContext ctx = new InitialContext();
DataSource source = (DataSource) ctx.lookup("java:comp/env/jdbc/mydb");
Connection conn = source.getConnection();
try
{
    Use the connection
}
finally
{
    conn.close();
}
```

To obtain a database connection, first look up the data source that was configured in the JSF container.

The `lookup` method locates the environment resource with name `jdbc/mydb` that was defined in the Tomcat configuration file.

Tomcat provides an additional service: it *pools* database connections. When a pooled connection is closed, it is not physically terminated but instead returned to a queue and given out again to another caller of the `getConnection` method. Pooling avoids the overhead of creating new database connections. In a web application, it would be particularly inefficient to connect to the database with every web request. Connection pooling is completely automatic.

JSF containers such as Tomcat manage a pool of database connections.

In order to make the application more interesting, we enhanced the `TimeZoneBean` so that it manages a list of cities. You can add cities to the list and remove a selected city (see Figure 13). You will find the complete code for this web application at the end of this section. Figure 14 shows the directory structure of the application.

You have now seen how to use the JavaServer Faces technology to build web applications. JSF takes care of low-level details so that you don't have to think about HTML forms and the HTTP protocol. Instead, you can focus on the presentation and business logic of your application.

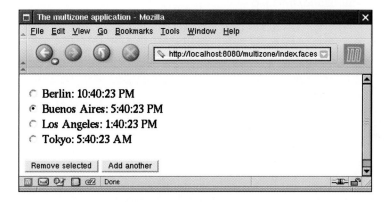

Figure 13 The `multizone` Application Shows a List of Cities

Figure 14 The Directory Structure of the `multizone` Application

File multizone/index.jsp

```
1  <html>
2     <%@ taglib uri="http://java.sun.com/jsf/core" prefix="f" %>
3     <%@ taglib uri="http://java.sun.com/jsf/html" prefix="h" %>
4
5     <f:view>
6        <head>
7           <title>The multizone application</title>
8        </head>
9        <body>
10          <h:form>
11             <p>
12                Enter city:
13                <h:inputText value="#{zone.city}"/>
14             </p>
15             <p>
16                <h:commandButton value="Submit" action="#{zone.addCity}"/>
17             </p>
18          </h:form>
19       </body>
20    </f:view>
21 </html>
```

File multizone/next.jsp

```
1  <html>
2     <%@ taglib uri="http://java.sun.com/jsf/core" prefix="f" %>
3     <%@ taglib uri="http://java.sun.com/jsf/html" prefix="h" %>
4
5     <f:view>
6        <head>
7           <title>The multizone application</title>
8        </head>
9        <body>
10          <h:form>
11             <p>
12                <h:selectOneRadio value="#{zone.cityToRemove}"
13                      layout="pageDirection">
14                   <f:selectItems value="#{zone.citiesAndTimes}"/>
15                </h:selectOneRadio>
16             </p>
17             <p>
18                <h:commandButton value="Remove selected"
19                      action="#{zone.removeCity}"/>
20                <h:commandButton value="Add another" action="back"/>
21             </p>
22          </h:form>
23       </body>
24    </f:view>
25 </html>
```

File multizone/error.jsp

```
1   <html>
2     <%@ taglib uri="http://java.sun.com/jsf/core" prefix="f" %>
3     <%@ taglib uri="http://java.sun.com/jsf/html" prefix="h" %>
4
5     <f:view>
6        <head>
7           <title>The multizone application</title>
8        </head>
9        <body>
10          <h:form>
11             <p>
12                Sorry, no information is available for
13                <h:outputText value="#{zone.city}"/>
14             </p>
15             <p>
16                <h:commandButton value="Back" action="back"/>
17             </p>
18          </h:form>
19       </body>
20    </f:view>
21 </html>
```

File multizone/WEB-INF/classes/bigjava/TimeZoneBean.java

```
1    package bigjava;
2
3    import java.sql.Connection;
4    import java.sql.PreparedStatement;
5    import java.sql.ResultSet;
6    import java.sql.SQLException;
7    import java.text.DateFormat;
8    import java.util.ArrayList;
9    import java.util.Date;
10   import java.util.Map;
11   import java.util.TimeZone;
12   import java.util.TreeMap;
13   import java.util.logging.Logger;
14   import javax.naming.InitialContext;
15   import javax.naming.NamingException;
16   import javax.sql.DataSource;
17
18   /**
19      This bean formats the local time of day for a given date
20      and city.
21   */
22   public class TimeZoneBean
23   {
24      /**
25         Initializes the formatter.
26      */
27      public TimeZoneBean()
28      {
```

```
29          timeFormatter = DateFormat.getTimeInstance();
30          cities = new ArrayList<String>();
31       }
32
33       /**
34          Setter for city property.
35          @param aCity the city to add to the list of cities
36       */
37       public void setCity(String aCity)
38       {
39          city = aCity;
40          zone = getTimeZone(city);
41       }
42
43       /**
44          Getter for city property.
45          @return the city to add to the list of cities
46       */
47       public String getCity()
48       {
49          return city;
50       }
51
52       /**
53          Setter for the cityToRemove property.
54          @param aCity the city to remove
55       */
56       public void setCityToRemove(String aCity)
57       {
58          cityToRemove = aCity;
59       }
60
61       /**
62          Getter for the cityToRemove property.
63          @return the empty string
64       */
65       public String getCityToRemove()
66       {
67          return cityToRemove;
68       }
69
70       /**
71          Read-only citiesAndTime property.
72          @return a map containing the cities and formatted times
73       */
74       public Map<String, String> getCitiesAndTimes()
75       {
76          Date time = new Date();
77          Map<String, String> result = new TreeMap<String, String>();
78          for (int i = 0; i < cities.size(); i++)
79          {
80             String city = cities.get(i);
81             String label = city + ": ";
82             TimeZone zone = getTimeZone(city);
```

```
 83               if (zone != null)
 84               {
 85                  timeFormatter.setTimeZone(zone);
 86                  String timeString = timeFormatter.format(time);
 87                  label = label + timeString;
 88               }
 89               else
 90                  label = label + "unavailable";
 91               result.put(label, city);
 92            }
 93
 94            return result;
 95         }
 96
 97         /**
 98            Action for adding a city.
 99            @return "available" if time zone information is available for the city,
100            "unavailable" otherwise
101         */
102         public String addCity()
103         {
104            if (zone == null) return "unavailable";
105            cities.add(city);
106            cityToRemove = city;
107            city = "";
108            return "available";
109         }
110
111         /**
112            Action for removing a city.
113            @return null if there are more cities to remove, "back" otherwise
114         */
115         public String removeCity()
116         {
117            cities.remove(cityToRemove);
118            if (cities.size() > 0) return null;
119            else return "back";
120         }
121
122         /**
123            Looks up the time zone for a city.
124            @param city the city for which to find the time zone
125            @return the time zone or null if no match is found
126         */
127         private static TimeZone getTimeZone(String city)
128         {
129            String[] ids = TimeZone.getAvailableIDs();
130            for (int i = 0; i < ids.length; i++)
131               if (timeZoneIDmatch(ids[i], city))
132                  return TimeZone.getTimeZone(ids[i]);
133            try
134            {
```

```
135              String id = getZoneNameFromDB(city);
136              if (id != null)
137                 return TimeZone.getTimeZone(id);
138           }
139           catch (Exception exception)
140           {
141              Logger.global.info("Caught in TimeZone.getTimeZone: "
142                    + exception);
143           }
144           return null;
145        }
146
147        private static String getZoneNameFromDB(String city)
148              throws NamingException, SQLException
149        {
150           InitialContext ctx = new InitialContext();
151           DataSource source
152                 = (DataSource) ctx.lookup("java:comp/env/jdbc/mydb");
153           Connection conn = source.getConnection();
154           try
155           {
156              PreparedStatement stat = conn.prepareStatement(
157                    "SELECT Zone FROM CityZone WHERE City=?");
158              stat.setString(1, city);
159              ResultSet result = stat.executeQuery();
160              if (result.next())
161                 return result.getString(1);
162              else
163                 return null;
164           }
165           finally
166           {
167              conn.close();
168           }
169        }
170
171        /**
172           Checks whether a time zone ID matches a city.
173           @param id  the time zone ID (e.g., "America/Los_Angeles")
174           @param city  the city to match (e.g., "Los Angeles")
175           @return  true if the ID and city match
176        */
177        private static boolean timeZoneIDmatch(String id, String city)
178        {
179           String idCity = id.substring(id.indexOf('/') + 1);
180           return idCity.replace('_', ' ').equals(city);
181        }
182
183        private DateFormat timeFormatter;
184        private ArrayList<String> cities;
185        private String city;
186        private TimeZone zone;
187        private String cityToRemove;
188     }
```

File multizone/WEB-INF/faces-config.xml

```
1   <?xml version="1.0"?>
2
3   <!DOCTYPE faces-config PUBLIC
4      "-//Sun Microsystems, Inc.//DTD JavaServer Faces Config 1.0//EN"
5      "http://java.sun.com/dtd/web-facesconfig_1_0.dtd">
6
7   <faces-config>
8      <navigation-rule>
9         <navigation-case>
10           <from-outcome>available</from-outcome>
11           <to-view-id>/next.jsp</to-view-id>
12        </navigation-case>
13        <navigation-case>
14           <from-outcome>unavailable</from-outcome>
15           <to-view-id>/error.jsp</to-view-id>
16        </navigation-case>
17        <navigation-case>
18           <from-outcome>back</from-outcome>
19           <to-view-id>/index.jsp</to-view-id>
20        </navigation-case>
21     </navigation-rule>
22     <managed-bean>
23        <managed-bean-name>zone</managed-bean-name>
24        <managed-bean-class>bigjava.TimeZoneBean</managed-bean-class>
25        <managed-bean-scope>session</managed-bean-scope>
26     </managed-bean>
27  </faces-config>
```

SELF CHECK

10. Why don't we just keep a database connection as an instance field in the `TimeZoneBean`?

11. Why does the `removeCity` method of the `TimeZoneBean` return `null` or `"back"`, depending on the size of the `cities` field?

RANDOM FACT 27.1

Cataloging Your Necktie Collection

People and companies use computers to organize just about every aspect of daily life. On the whole, computers are tremendously good for collecting and analyzing data. In fact, the power offered by computers and their software makes them seductive solutions for just about any organizational problem. It is easy to lose sight of the fact that using a computer is not always the best solution to a problem.

In 1983, the author John Bear wrote about a person who had come up with a novel use for the personal computers that had recently become available. That person cataloged his necktie collection, putting descriptions of the ties into a database and generating reports that listed them by color, price, or style. We can hope he had another use to justify the purchase of a piece of equipment worth several thousand dollars, but that particular application was so dear to his heart that he wanted the world to know about it. Perhaps not surprisingly, few other computer users shared that excitement, and you don't find the shelves of your local software store lined with necktie-cataloging software.

The phenomenon of using technology for its own sake is quite widespread. In the "Internet bubble" of 2000, hundreds of companies were founded on the premise that the Internet made it technologically possible to order items such as groceries and pet food from a home computer, and therefore the traditional stores would be replaced by web stores. However, technological feasibility did not ensure economic success. Trucking groceries and pet food to households was expensive, and few customers were willing to pay a premium for the added convenience.

At the same time, many elementary schools spent tremendous resources to bring computers and the Internet into the classroom. Indeed, it is easy to understand why teachers, school administrators, parents, politicians and equipment vendors are in favor of computers in classrooms. Isn't computer literacy absolutely essential for youngsters in the new millennium? Isn't it particularly important to give low-income kids, whose parents may not be able to afford a home computer, the opportunity to master computer skills? However, schools have found that the total cost of running computers far exceeds the initial cost of the equipment. As schools purchased more equipment than could be maintained by occasional volunteers, they had to make hard choices—should they lay off librarians and art instructors to hire more computer technicians, or should they let the equipment become useless? Unfortunately, many schools were so caught up in the technology hype that they never asked themselves whether the educational benefits justified the expense. See [4] for more information.

As computer programmers, we like to computerize everything. As computer professionals, though, we owe it to our employers and clients to understand which problems they want to solve and to deploy computers and software only where they add more value than cost.

CHAPTER SUMMARY

1. A JavaServer Faces (JSF) page contains HTML and JSF tags.

2. The JSF container converts a JSF page to an HTML page, replacing all JSF tags with text and HTML tags.

3. The Java objects of a JSF application are defined in a configuration file.

4. A value binding links a JSF component with a bean property.

5. The JSF technology enables the separation of presentation and business logic.

6. Properties of a software component can be accessed without having to write Java code.

7. A JavaBean is a class with a default constructor that exposes properties through its get and set methods.

8. A bean with session scope is available for multiple requests by the same browser.

9. The value attribute of an input component denotes the value that the user supplies.

10. Use an `f:selectItems` tag to specify all choices for a component that allows selection from a list of choices.

11. The outcome string of an action determines the next page that the JSF container sends to the browser.

12. A method binding specifies a bean and a method that should be invoked on the bean.

13. A navigation rule maps outcome strings to JSF pages.

14. A three-tier application has separate tiers for presentation, business logic, and data storage.

15. Database connections are configured in the JSF container.

16. To obtain a database connection, first look up the data source that was configured in the JSF container.

17. JSF containers such as Tomcat manage a pool of database connections.

FURTHER READING

1. `http://jakarta.apache.org/tomcat/index.html` The web page for the Apache Tomcat server.

2. `http://javaserverfaces.dev.java.net/` The Sun Microsystems JSF reference implementation.

3. David Geary and Cay Horstmann, *Core JavaServer Faces*, Sun Microsystems Press/ Prentice Hall, 2004.

4. Oppenheimer, Todd. "The Computer Delusion," *The Atlantic Monthly* 280, no. 1 (July 1997): 45–62, available online at `http://www.catholiceducation.org/articles/education/ed0026.html`.

CLASSES, OBJECTS, AND METHODS INTRODUCED IN THIS CHAPTER

```
java.text.DateFormat
   format
   setTimeZone
java.util.TimeZone
   getAvailableIDs
   getTimeZone
```

REVIEW EXERCISES

Exercise R27.1. What is the difference between a JSF page and a JSF container?

Exercise R27.2. What is a bean?

Exercise R27.3. What is a bean property?

Exercise R27.4. Is a JButton a bean? Why or why not?

Exercise R27.5. What is the software engineering purpose of using beans in conjunction with JSF pages?

Exercise R27.6. How are JSF variables (that is, the variables that are defined in faces-config.xml and referenced in value binding expressions) different from variables in Java programs?

Exercise R27.7. What are the choices for the scope of a bean? What is the default? When should you choose which scope?

Exercise R27.8. How can you implement error checking in a JSF application? Explain, using a login dialog as an example.

Exercise R27.9. What input elements can you place on a JSF form? What are their Swing equivalents?

Exercise R27.10. What is the difference between a client-server application and a three-tier application?

PROGRAMMING EXERCISES

Exercise P27.1. Write a JSF application that reports the values of the following system properties of the web server:
- The Java version (java.version)
- The operating system name (os.name)
- The operating system version (os.version)

Supply a bean that uses the getProperties method of the System class.

Exercise P27.2. Write a JSF application that simulates two rolls of a die, producing an output such as "Rolled a 4 and a 6". When the user reloads the page, a new pair of values should be displayed. Supply a bean that encapsulates a Random object.

Exercise P27.3. Enhance Exercise P27.2 by producing a web page that shows images of the rolled dice. Find GIF images of dice with numbers 1 through 6 on the front, and generate an HTML page that references the appropriate images. *Hint:* Use the tag <h:graphicImage value=*imageURL*/> and take advantage of the fact that you can embed a value binding expression into regular text, such as "/image#{*expression*}.gif"

Exercise P27.4. Write a web application that allows a user to specify six lottery numbers. Generate your own combination on the server, and then print out both combinations together with a count of matches.

Exercise P27.5. Add error checking to Exercise P27.4. If the lottery numbers are not within the correct range, or if there are duplicates, show an appropriate message and allow the user to fix the error.

Exercise P27.6. Personalize the time zone application of Section 27.1. Prompt the user to log in and specify a city to be stored in a profile. The next time the user logs in, the time of their favorite city is displayed automatically. Store users, passwords, and favorite cities in a database. You need a logout button to switch users.

Exercise P27.7. Extend Exercise P27.6 so that a user can choose multiple cities and all cities chosen by the user are remembered on the next login.

Exercise P27.8. Write a web version of the ExecSQL utility of Chapter 25. Allow users to type arbitrary SQL queries into a text area. Then submit the query to the database and display the result.

Exercise P27.9. Produce a web front end for the ATM program in Chapter 17.

Exercise P27.10. Produce a web front end for the appointment book application of Exercise P17.10.

Exercise P27.11. Produce a web front end for the airline reservation program of Exercise P17.11.

PROGRAMMING PROJECTS

Project 27.1. Write a shopping cart application. A database contains items that can be purchased and their prices, descriptions, and available quantities. If the user wants to check out, ask for the user account. If the user does not yet have an account, create one. The user name and address should be stored with the account in the database. Display an invoice as the last process in the checkout step. When the user has confirmed the purchase, update the quantities in the warehouse.

Project 27.2. Write a web-based grade book application that your instructor might use to manage student grades in this course. Your application should have one account for the instructor, and one account for each student. Instructors can enter and view grades for all students. Students can only see their own grades and their ranking within the course. Implement the features that your instructor uses for determining the course grade (such as dropping the lowest quiz score, counting homework as 30% of the total grade, and so on.) All information should be stored in a database.

ANSWERS TO SELF-CHECK QUESTIONS

1. Place an image file, say `clock.gif`, into the `datetime` directory, and add a tag `<img src="clock.gif"/>` to the `index.jsp` file.

2. No—it is possible (and sadly common) for programmers to place the business logic into the frame and component classes of the user interface.

3. Technically, yes. It has a default constructor. However, it has no methods whose name start with `get` or `set`, so it exposes no properties.

4. It sets the zone instance field to match the time zone of the city.

5. When the zone bean was constructed, its `city` property was set to "Los Angeles". When the input field is rendered, its default value is the current value of the `city` property.

6. `h:selectOneRadio`, `h:selectOneMenu`, or `h:selectOneCheckbox`

7. You would need a bean with a property such as the following:

```
public Map<String, Integer> getYearChoices()
{
    Map<String, Integer> choices = new TreeMap<String, Integer>();
    choices.put("2003", 2003);
    choices.put("2004", 2004);
    . . .
    return choices;
}
```

Then supply a tag `<f:selectItems value="#{creditCard.yearChoices}"/>`.

8. Add the tag `<h:commandButton value="Help" action="help"/>` to `error.jsp`, and add a navigation rule to `faces-config.xml`:

```
<navigation-case>
    <from-outcome>help</from-outcome>
    <to-view-id>/help.jsp</to-view-id>
</navigation-case>
```

9. The current page would be redisplayed.

10. Then the database connection would be kept open for the entire session.

11. As long as there are cities, the `next.jsp` page is redisplayed. If all cities are removed, it is pointless to display the `next.jsp` page, so the application navigates to the `index.jsp` page.

Java Language Coding Guidelines

Introduction

This coding style guide is a simplified version of one that has been used with good success both in industrial practice and for college courses.

A style guide is a set of mandatory requirements for layout and formatting. Uniform style makes it easier for you to read code from your instructor and classmates. You will really appreciate that if you do a team project. It is also easier for your instructor and your grader to grasp the essence of your programs quickly.

A style guide makes you a more productive programmer because it *reduces gratuitous choice*. If you don't have to make choices about trivial matters, you can spend your energy on the solution of real problems.

In these guidelines, several constructs are plainly outlawed. That doesn't mean that programmers using them are evil or incompetent. It does mean that the constructs are not essential and can be expressed just as well or even better with other language constructs.

If you already have programming experience, in Java or another language, you may be initially uncomfortable at giving up some fond habits. However, it is a sign of professionalism to set aside personal preferences in minor matters and to compromise for the benefit of your group.

These guidelines are necessarily somewhat dull. They also mention features that you may not yet have seen in class. Here are the most important highlights:

- Tabs are set every three spaces.
- Variable and method names are lowercase, with occasional upperCase characters in the middle.
- Class names start with an Uppercase letter.
- Constant names are UPPERCASE, with an occasional UNDER_SCORE.
- There are spaces after keywords and surrounding binary operators.
- Braces must line up horizontally or vertically.
- No magic numbers may be used.
- Every method, except for `main` and overridden library methods, must have a comment.
- At most 30 lines of code may be used per method.
- No `continue` or `break` is allowed.
- All non-`final` variables must be private.

Note to the instructor: Of course, many programmers and organizations have strong feelings about coding style. If this style guide is incompatible with your own preferences or with local custom, please feel free to modify it. For that purpose, this coding style guide is available in electronic form from the Companion Web Site for this book at `http://www.wiley.com/college/horstmann`.

Source Files

Each Java program is a collection of one or more source files. The executable program is obtained by compiling these files. Organize the material in each file as follows:

- `package` statement, if appropriate
- `import` statements
- A comment explaining the purpose of this file
- A `public` class
- Other classes, if appropriate

The comment explaining the purpose of this file should be in the format recognized by the `javadoc` utility. Start with a `/**`, and use the `@author` and `@version` tags:

```
/**
   COPYRIGHT (C) 2005 Harry Hacker. All Rights Reserved.
   Classes to manipulate widgets.
   Solves CS101 homework assignment #3
   @author  Harry Hacker
   @version 1.01 2005-02-15
*/
```

Classes

Each class should be preceded by a class comment explaining the purpose of the class.

First list all public features, then all private features.

Within the public and private sections, use the following order:

1. Constructors
2. Instance methods
3. Static methods
4. Instance fields
5. Static fields
6. Inner classes

Leave a blank line after every method.

All non-`final` variables must be private. (However, instance variables of a private inner class may be public.) Methods and final variables can be either public or private, as appropriate.

All features must be tagged `public` or `private`. Do not use the default visibility (that is, package visibility) or the `protected` attribute.

Avoid static variables (except `final` ones) whenever possible. In the rare instance that you need static variables, you are permitted one static variable per class.

Methods

Every method (except for `main`) starts with a comment in `javadoc` format.

```
/**
    Convert calendar date into Julian day.
    Note: This algorithm is from Press et al., Numerical Recipes
    in C, 2nd ed., Cambridge University Press, 1992.
    @param day  day of the date to be converted
    @param month  month of the date to be converted
    @param year  year of the date to be converted
    @return the Julian day number that begins at noon of the
    given calendar date.
*/
public static int getJulianDayNumber(int day, int month, int year)
{
   . . .
}
```

Parameter names must be explicit, especially if they are integers or Boolean:

```
public Employee remove(int d, double s)
    // Huh?
public Employee remove(int department, double severancePay)
    // OK
```

Methods must have at most 30 lines of code. The method signature, comments, blank lines, and lines containing only braces are not included in this count. This rule forces you to break up complex computations into separate methods.

Variables and Constants

Do not define all variables at the beginning of a block:

```
{
    double xold; // Don't
    double xnew;
    boolean more;
    . . .
}
```

Define each variable just before it is used for the first time:

```
{
    . . .
    double xold = Integer.parseInt(input);
    boolean more = false;
    while (more)
    {
        double xnew = (xold + a / xold) / 2;
        . . .
    }
    . . .
}
```

Do not define two variables on the same line:

```
int dimes = 0, nickels = 0; // Don't
```

Instead, use two separate definitions:

```
int dimes = 0; // OK
int nickels = 0;
```

In Java, constants must be defined with the keyword `final`. If the constant is used by multiple methods, declare it as `static final`. It is a good idea to define static final variables as `private` if no other class has an interest in them.

Do not use *magic numbers!* A magic number is a numeric constant embedded in code, without a constant definition. Any number except −1, 0, 1, and 2 is considered magic:

```
if (p.getX() < 300) // Don't
```

Use `final` variables instead:

```
final double WINDOW_WIDTH = 300;
. . .
if (p.getX() < WINDOW_WIDTH) // OK
```

Even the most reasonable cosmic constant is going to change one day. You think there are 365 days per year? Your customers on Mars are going to be pretty unhappy about your silly prejudice. Make a constant

```
public static final int DAYS_PER_YEAR = 365;
```

so that you can easily produce a Martian version without trying to find all the 365s, 364s, 366s, 367s, and so on, in your code.

When declaring array variables, group the [ ] with the type, not the variable.

```
int[] values; // OK
int values[]; // Ugh—this is an ugly holdover from C
```

When using collections, use type parameters and not "raw" types.

```
ArrayList<String> names = new ArrayList<String>(); // OK
ArrayList names = new ArrayList(); // Not OK
```

Control Flow

The if Statement

Avoid the "if . . . if . . . else" trap. The code

```
if ( . . . )
    if ( . . . ) . . .;
else . . .;
```

will not do what the indentation level suggests, and it can take hours to find such a bug. Always use an extra pair of { . . . } when dealing with "if . . . if . . . else":

```
if ( . . . )
{
    if ( . . . ) . . .;
} // { . . . } are necessary
else . . .;

if ( . . . )
{
    if ( . . . ) . . .;
    else . . .;
} // { . . . } not necessary, but they keep you out of trouble
```

The for Statement

Use for loops only when a variable runs from somewhere to somewhere with some constant increment/decrement:

```
for (int i = 0; i < a.length; i++)
    System.out.println(a[i]);
```

Or, even better, use the "for each" loop:

```
for (int e : a)
    System.out.println(e);
```

Do not use the for loop for weird constructs such as

```
for (a = a / 2; count < ITERATIONS; System.out.println(xnew))
    // Don't
```

Make such a loop into a `while` loop. That way, the sequence of instructions is much clearer.

```
a = a / 2;
while (count < ITERATIONS) // OK
{
   . . .
   System.out.println(xnew);
}
```

Nonlinear Control Flow

Avoid the `switch` statement, because it is easy to fall through accidentally to an unwanted case. Use `if`/`else` instead.

Avoid the `break` or `continue` statements. Use another `boolean` variable to control the execution flow.

Exceptions

Do not tag a method with an overly general exception specification:

```
Widget readWidget(Reader in) throws Exception // Bad
```

Instead, specifically declare any checked exceptions that your method may throw:

```
Widget readWidget(Reader in)
      throws IOException, MalformedWidgetException // Good
```

Do not "squelch" exceptions:

```
try
{
   double price = in.readDouble();
}
catch (Exception e)
{ } // Bad
```

Beginners often make this mistake "to keep the compiler happy". If the current method is not appropriate for handling the exception, simply use a `throws` specification and let one of its callers handle it.

Lexical Issues

Naming Conventions

The following rules specify when to use upper- and lowercase letters in identifier names.

- All variable and method names and all data fields of classes are in lowercase (maybe with an occasional upperCase in the middle); for example, `firstPlayer`.
- All constants are in uppercase (maybe with an occasional UNDER_SCORE); for example, `CLOCK_RADIUS`.

- All class and interface names start with uppercase and are followed by lowercase letters (maybe with an occasional UpperCase letter); for example, `BankTeller`.
- Generic type variables are in uppercase, usually a single letter.

Names must be reasonably long and descriptive. Use `firstPlayer` instead of `fp`. No drppng f vwls. Local variables that are fairly routine can be short (`ch`, `i`) as long as they are really just boring holders for an input character, a loop counter, and so on. Also, do not use `ctr`, `c`, `cntr`, `cnt`, `c2` for variables in your method. Surely these variables all have specific purposes and can be named to remind the reader of them (for example, `current`, `next`, `previous`, `result`, ...). However, it is customary to use single-letter names, such as `T` or `E` for generic types.

Indentation and White Space

Use tab stops every three columns. That means you will need to change the tab stop setting in your editor!

Use blank lines freely to separate parts of a method that are logically distinct.

Use a blank space around every binary operator:

```
x1 = (-b - Math.sqrt(b * b - 4 * a * c)) / (2 * a);
// Good

x1=(-b-Math.sqrt(b*b-4*a*c))/(2*a);
// Bad
```

Leave a blank space after (and not before) each comma or semicolon. Do not leave a space before or after a parenthesis or bracket in an expression. Leave spaces around the (. . .) part of an `if`, `while`, `for`, or `catch` statement.

```
if (x == 0) y = 0;

f(a, b[i]);
```

Every line must fit in 80 columns. If you must break a statement, add an indentation level for the continuation:

```
a[n] = .............................................
     + .................;
```

Start the indented line with an operator (if possible).

If the condition in an `if` or `while` statement must be broken, be sure to brace the body in, even if it consists of only one statement:

```
if ( ...........................................
     && .................
     || .......... )
{
   . . .
}
```

If it weren't for the braces, it would be hard to separate the continuation of the condition visually from the statement to be executed.

Braces

Opening and closing braces must line up, either horizontally or vertically:

```
while (i < n) { System.out.println(a[i]); i++; }

while (i < n)
{
   System.out.println(a[i]);
   i++;
}
```

Some programmers don't line up vertical braces but place the { behind the keyword:

```
while (i < n) { // DON'T
   System.out.println(a[i]);
   i++;
}
```

Doing so makes it hard to check that the braces match.

Unstable Layout

Some programmers take great pride in lining up certain columns in their code:

```
firstRecord = other.firstRecord;
lastRecord  = other.lastRecord;
cutoff      = other.cutoff;
```

This is undeniably neat, but the layout is not stable under change. A new variable name that is longer than the preallotted number of columns requires that you move all entries around:

```
firstRecord = other.firstRecord;
lastRecord  = other.lastRecord;
cutoff      = other.cutoff;
marginalFudgeFactor = other.marginalFudgeFactor;
```

This is just the kind of trap that makes you decide to use a short variable name like mff instead. Use a simple layout that is easy to maintain as your programs change.

The Basic Latin and Latin-1 Subsets of Unicode

This appendix lists the Unicode characters that are most commonly used for processing Western European languages. A complete listing of Unicode characters can be found at http://unicode.org.

Table 1 Selected Control Characters

Character	Code	Decimal	Escape Sequence
Tab	'\u0009'	9	'\t'
Newline	'\u000A'	10	'\n'
Return	'\u000D'	13	'\r'
Space	'\u0020'	32	

Table 2 The Basic Latin (ASCII) Subset of Unicode

Char.	Code	Dec.	Char.	Code	Dec.	Char.	Code	Dec.
			@	'\u0040'	64	`	'\u0060'	96
!	'\u0021'	33	A	'\u0041'	65	a	'\u0061'	97
"	'\u0022'	34	B	'\u0042'	66	b	'\u0062'	98
#	'\u0023'	35	C	'\u0043'	67	c	'\u0063'	99
$	'\u0024'	36	D	'\u0044'	68	d	'\u0064'	100
%	'\u0025'	37	E	'\u0045'	69	e	'\u0065'	101
&	'\u0026'	38	F	'\u0046'	70	f	'\u0066'	102
'	'\u0027'	39	G	'\u0047'	71	g	'\u0067'	103
(	'\u0028'	40	H	'\u0048'	72	h	'\u0068'	104
)	'\u0029'	41	I	'\u0049'	73	i	'\u0069'	105
*	'\u002A'	42	J	'\u004A'	74	j	'\u006A'	106
+	'\u002B'	43	K	'\u004B'	75	k	'\u006B'	107
,	'\u002C'	44	L	'\u004C'	76	l	'\u006C'	108
-	'\u002D'	45	M	'\u004D'	77	m	'\u006D'	109
.	'\u002E'	46	N	'\u004E'	78	n	'\u006E'	110
/	'\u002F'	47	O	'\u004F'	79	o	'\u006F'	111
0	'\u0030'	48	P	'\u0050'	80	p	'\u0070'	112
1	'\u0031'	49	Q	'\u0051'	81	q	'\u0071'	113
2	'\u0032'	50	R	'\u0052'	82	r	'\u0072'	114
3	'\u0033'	51	S	'\u0053'	83	s	'\u0073'	115
4	'\u0034'	52	T	'\u0054'	84	t	'\u0074'	116
5	'\u0035'	53	U	'\u0055'	85	u	'\u0075'	117
6	'\u0036'	54	V	'\u0056'	86	v	'\u0076'	118
7	'\u0037'	55	W	'\u0057'	87	w	'\u0077'	119
8	'\u0038'	56	X	'\u0058'	88	x	'\u0078'	120
9	'\u0039'	57	Y	'\u0059'	89	y	'\u0079'	121
:	'\u003A'	58	Z	'\u005A'	90	z	'\u007A'	122
;	'\u003B'	59	[	'\u005B'	91	{	'\u007B'	123
<	'\u003C'	60	\	'\u005C'	92	|	'\u007C'	124
=	'\u003D'	61	]	'\u005D'	93	}	'\u007D'	125
>	'\u003E'	62	^	'\u005E'	94	~	'\u007E'	126
?	'\u003F'	63	_	'\u005F'	95			

Table 3 The Latin-1 Subset of Unicode

Char.	Code	Dec.	Char.	Code	Dec.	Char.	Code	Dec.
			À	'\u00C0'	192	à	'\u00E0'	224
¡	'\u00A1'	161	Á	'\u00C1'	193	á	'\u00E1'	225
¢	'\u00A2'	162	Â	'\u00C2'	194	â	'\u00E2'	226
£	'\u00A3'	163	Ã	'\u00C3'	195	ã	'\u00E3'	227
¤	'\u00A4'	164	Ä	'\u00C4'	196	ä	'\u00E4'	228
¥	'\u00A5'	165	Å	'\u00C5'	197	å	'\u00E5'	229
¦	'\u00A6'	166	Æ	'\u00C6'	198	æ	'\u00E6'	230
§	'\u00A7'	167	Ç	'\u00C7'	199	ç	'\u00E7'	231
¨	'\u00A8'	168	È	'\u00C8'	200	è	'\u00E8'	232
©	'\u00A9'	169	É	'\u00C9'	201	é	'\u00E9'	233
ª	'\u00AA'	170	Ê	'\u00CA'	202	ê	'\u00EA'	234
«	'\u00AB'	171	Ë	'\u00CB'	203	ë	'\u00EB'	235
¬	'\u00AC'	172	Ì	'\u00CC'	204	ì	'\u00EC'	236
	'\u00AD'	173	Í	'\u00CD'	205	í	'\u00ED'	237
®	'\u00AE'	174	Î	'\u00CE'	206	î	'\u00EE'	238
¯	'\u00AF'	175	Ï	'\u00CF'	207	ï	'\u00EF'	239
°	'\u00B0'	176	Ð	'\u00D0'	208	ð	'\u00F0'	240
±	'\u00B1'	177	Ñ	'\u00D1'	209	ñ	'\u00F1'	241
²	'\u00B2'	178	Ò	'\u00D2'	210	ò	'\u00F2'	242
³	'\u00B3'	179	Ó	'\u00D3'	211	ó	'\u00F3'	243
´	'\u00B4'	180	Ô	'\u00D4'	212	ô	'\u00F4'	244
µ	'\u00B5'	181	Õ	'\u00D5'	213	õ	'\u00F5'	245
¶	'\u00B6'	182	Ö	'\u00D6'	214	ö	'\u00F6'	246
·	'\u00B7'	183	×	'\u00D7'	215	÷	'\u00F7'	247
¸	'\u00B8'	184	Ø	'\u00D8'	216	ø	'\u00F8'	248
¹	'\u00B9'	185	Ù	'\u00D9'	217	ù	'\u00F9'	249
º	'\u00BA'	186	Ú	'\u00DA'	218	ú	'\u00FA'	250
»	'\u00BB'	187	Û	'\u00DB'	219	û	'\u00FB'	251
¼	'\u00BC'	188	Ü	'\u00DC'	220	ü	'\u00FC'	252
½	'\u00BD'	189	Ý	'\u00DD'	221	ý	'\u00FD'	253
¾	'\u00BE'	190	Þ	'\u00DE'	222	þ	'\u00FE'	254
¿	'\u00BF'	191	ß	'\u00DF'	223	ÿ	'\u00FF'	255

The Java Library

This appendix lists all classes and methods from the standard Java library that are used in this book.

In the following inheritance hierarchy, superclasses that are not used in this book are shown in parentheses. Some classes implement interfaces not covered in this book; they are omitted. Classes are sorted first by package, then alphabetically within a package.

```
java.awt.Shape
java.io.Serializable
java.lang.Cloneable
java.lang.Object
    java.awt.Color implements Serializable
    java.awt.Component implements Serializable
        java.awt.Container
            javax.swing.JComponent
                javax.swing.AbstractButton
                    javax.swing.JButton
                    javax.swing.JMenuItem
                        javax.swing.JMenu
                    (javax.swing.JToggleButton)
                        javax.swing.JCheckBox
                        javax.swing.JRadioButton
                javax.swing.JComboBox
                javax.swing.JFileChooser
                javax.swing.JMenuBar
                javax.swing.JPanel
                javax.swing.JOptionPane
                javax.swing.JScrollPane
                javax.swing.JSlider
                javax.swing.text.JTextComponent
                    javax.swing.JTextArea
                    javax.swing.JTextField
```

```
      (java.awt.Panel)
          java.applet.Applet
          javax.swing.JApplet
    java.awt.Window
      java.awt.Frame
          javax.swing.JFrame
  java.awt.FlowLayout implements Serializable
  java.awt.Font implements Serializable
  java.awt.Graphics
    java.awt.Graphics2D;
  java.awt.GridLayout implements Serializable
  java.awt.event.MouseAdapter implements MouseListener
  java.awt.geom.Line2D implements Cloneable, Shape
    java.awt.geom.Line2D.Double
  java.awt.geom.Point2D implements Cloneable
    java.awt.geom.Point2D.Double
  java.awt.geom.RectangularShape implements Cloneable, Shape
    (java.awt.geom.Rectangle2D)
        java.awt.Rectangle implements Serializable
    java.awt.geom.Ellipse2D
        java.awt.geom.Ellipse2D.Double
  java.io.File implements Comparable, Serializable
  java.io.InputStream
    java.io.FileInputStream
    java.io.ObjectInputStream
  java.io.OutputStream
    java.io.FileOutputStream
    java.io.ObjectOutputStream
  java.io.RandomAccessFile
  java.io.Reader
    java.io.BufferedReader
    java.io.InputStreamReader
      java.io.FileReader
  java.io.Writer
    java.io.PrintWriter
    (java.io.OutputStreamWriter)
        java.io.FileWriter
  java.lang.Boolean implements Serializable
  java.lang.Character implements Comparable, Serializable
  java.lang.Class implements Serializable
  java.lang.Math
(java.lang.Number implements Serializable)
    java.math.BigDecimal implements Comparable
    java.math.BigInteger implements Comparable
    java.lang.Double implements Comparable
    java.lang.Integer implements Comparable
  java.lang.String implements Comparable, Serializable
  java.lang.System
  java.lang.Thread implements Runnable
  java.lang.Throwable
    java.lang.Error
    java.lang.Exception
        java.lang.CloneNotSupportedException
        java.lang.InterruptedException
        java.io.IOException
          java.io.EOFException
          java.io.FileNotFoundException
        java.lang.RuntimeException
```

```
                     java.lang.IllegalArgumentException
                        java.lang.NumberFormatException
                     java.lang.IllegalStateException
                     java.util.NoSuchElementException
                         java.util.InputMismatchException
                     java.lang.NullPointerException
              java.sql.SQLException
               (javax.xml.xpath.XPathException)
                     javax.xml.xpath.XPathExpressionException
      (java.text.Format implements Cloneable, Serializable)
              java.text.DateFormat
      (java.util.AbstractCollection<E>)
          java.util.AbstractList<E>
            (java.util.AbstractSequentialList<E>)
                 java.util.LinkedList<E>
            (java.util.AbstractSet<E>)
                 java.util.HashSet<E> implements Cloneable, Serializable, Set<E>
                 java.util.TreeSet<E> implements Cloneable, Serializable,
                     SortedSet<E>
             java.util.ArrayList<E> implements Cloneable, List<E>, Serializable
      (java.util.AbstractMap<K, V>)
          java.util.HashMap<K, V> implements Cloneable, Map<K, V>, Serializable
            java.util.LinkedHashMap<K, V>
          java.util.TreeMap<K, V> implements Cloneable, Serializable,
                SortedMap<K, V>
      java.util.Arrays
      java.util.Collections
      java.util.Calendar
          java.util.GregorianCalendar
      java.util.Scanner
      java.util.logging.Level implements Serializable
      java.util.logging.Logger
      java.net.ServerSocket
      java.net.Socket
      java.net.URL implements Serializable
      java.net.URLConnection
          java.net.HttpURLConnection
      java.sql.DriverManager
      java.util.Arrays
      java.util.EventObject implements Serializable
        (java.awt.AWTEvent)
            java.awt.event.ActionEvent
           (java.awt.event.ComponentEvent)
               java.awt.event.InputEvent
                   java.awt.event.MouseEvent
        javax.swing.event.ChangeEvent
      java.util.Random implements Serializable
      java.util.StringTokenizer
      java.util.TimeZone implements Cloneable, Serializable
      java.util.concurrent.locks.ReentrantLock implements Lock, Serializable
      javax.swing.ButtonGroup implements Serializable
      javax.swing.ImageIcon implements Serializable
      javax.swing.Timer implements Serializable
      (javax.swing.border.AbstractBorder implements Serializable)
          javax.swing.border.EtchedBorder
          javax.swing.border.TitledBorder
      javax.xml.parsers.DocumentBuilder
      javax.xml.parsers.DocumentBuilderFactory
```

```
    javax.xml.xpath.XPathFactory
java.lang.Comparable<T>
java.lang.Runnable
java.sql.Connection
java.sql.ResultSet
java.sql.ResultSetMetaData
java.sql.Statement
    java.sql.PreparedStatement
java.util.Collection<E>
    java.util.List<E>
    java.util.Set<E>
        java.util.SortedSet<E>
java.util.Comparator<T>
(java.util.EventListener)
    java.awt.event.ActionListener
    java.awt.event.MouseListener
    javax.swing.event.ChangeListener
java.util.Iterator<E>
    java.util.ListIterator<E>
java.util.Map<K, V>
    java.util.SortedMap<K, V>
java.util.concurrent.locks.Condition
java.util.concurrent.locks.Lock
javax.xml.xpath.XPath
org.w3c.dom.DOMImplementaton
(org.w3c.dom.Node)
  (org.w3c.dom.CharacterData)
        org.w3c.dom.Text
    org.w3c.dom.Document
    org.w3c.dom.Element
    org.w3c.dom.ls.DOMImplementationLS
    org.w3c.dom.ls.LSSerializer
```

In the following descriptions, the phrase "this object" ("this component", "this container", and so forth) means the object (component, container, and so forth) on which the method is invoked (the implicit parameter, `this`).

Package `java.applet`

Class `java.applet.Applet`

- `void destroy()`
  This method is called when the applet is about to be terminated, after the last call to `stop`.
- `void init()`
  This method is called when the applet has been loaded, before the first call to `start`. Applets override this method to carry out applet-specific initialization and to read applet parameters.
- `void start()`
  This method is called after the `init` method and each time the applet is revisited.
- `void stop()`
  This method is called whenever the user has stopped watching this applet.

Package `java.awt`

Class `java.awt.BorderLayout`

- `BorderLayout()`
  This constructs a border layout. A border layout has five regions for adding components, called `"North"`, `"East"`, `"South"`, `"West"`, and `"Center"`.
- `static final int CENTER`
  This value identifies the center position of a border layout.
- `static final int EAST`
  This value identifies the east position of a border layout.
- `static final int NORTH`
  This value identifies the north position of a border layout.
- `static final int SOUTH`
  This value identifies the south position of a border layout.
- `static final int WEST`
  This value identifies the west position of a border layout.

Class `java.awt.Color`

- `Color(float red, float green, float blue)`
  This creates a color with the specified red, green, and blue values between `0.0F` and `1.0F`.
  Parameters: `red` The red component
  `green` The green component
  `blue` The blue component

Class java.awt.Component

- void **addMouseListener**(MouseListener listener)
  This method adds a mouse listener to the component.
  Parameters: listener The mouse listener to be added
- int **getHeight**()
  This method gets the height of this component.
  Returns: The height in pixels.
- int **getWidth**()
  This method gets the width of this component.
  Returns: The width in pixels.
- void **repaint**()
  This method repaints this component by scheduling a call to the paint method.
- void **setSize**(int width, int height)
  This method sets the size of this component.
  Parameters: width the component width
  height the component height
- void **setVisible**(boolean visible)
  This method shows or hides the component.
  Parameters: visible true to show the component, or false to hide it

Class java.awt.Container

- void **add**(Component c)
- void **add**(Component c, Object position)
  These methods add a component to the end of this container. If a position is given, the layout manager is called to position the component.
  Parameters: c The component to be added
  position An object expressing position information for the layout manager
- void **setLayout**(LayoutManager manager)
  This method sets the layout manager for this container.
  Parameters: manager A layout manager

Class java.awt.FlowLayout

- **FlowLayout**()
  This constructs a new flow layout. A flow layout places as many components as possible in a row, without changing their size, and starts new rows when necessary.

Class java.awt.Font

- Font(String name, int style, int size)

  This constructs a font object from the specified name, style, and point size.

  Parameters: name   The font name, either a font face name or a logical font name, which must be one of "Dialog", "DialogInput", "Monospaced", "Serif", or "SansSerif"

  style   One of Font.PLAIN, Font.ITALIC, Font.BOLD, or Font.ITALIC+Font.BOLD

  size   The point size of the font

Class java.awt.Frame

- void setTitle(String title)

  This method sets the frame title.

  Parameters: title   The title to be displayed in the border of the frame

Class java.awt.Graphics

- void setColor(Color c)

  This method sets the current color. From now on, all graphics operations use this color.

  Parameters: c   The new drawing color

Class java.awt.Graphics2D

- void draw(Shape s)

  This method draws the outline of the given shape. Many classes—among them Rectangle and Line2D.Double—implement the Shape interface.

  Parameters: s   The shape to be drawn

- void drawString(String s, int x, int y)
- void drawString(String s, float x, float y)

  These methods draw a string in the current font.

  Parameters: s   The string to draw

  x,y   The basepoint of the first character in the string

- void fill(Shape s)

  This method draws the given shape and fills it with the current color.

  Parameters: s   The shape to be filled

Class java.awt.GridLayout

- GridLayout(int rows, int cols)

  This constructor creates a grid layout with the specified number of rows and columns. The components in a grid layout are arranged in a grid with equal widths and heights. One, but not both, of rows and cols can be zero, in which case any number of objects can be placed in a row or in a column, respectively.

  Parameters: rows   The number of rows in the grid

  cols   The number of columns in the grid

Class java.awt.Rectangle

- **Rectangle**()
  This constructs a rectangle whose top left corner is at (0, 0) and whose width and height are both zero.

- **Rectangle**(int x, int y, int width, int height)
  This constructs a rectangle with given top-left corner and size.

  Parameters: x,y The top-left corner
  width The width
  height The height

- double **getHeight**()
- double **getWidth**()
  These methods get the height and width of the rectangle.

- double **getX**()
- double **getY**()
  These methods get the *x*- and *y*-coordinates of the top-left corner of the rectangle.

- Rectangle **intersection**(Rectangle other)
  This method computes the intersection of this rectangle with the specified rectangle.

  Parameters: other A rectangle
  Returns: The largest rectangle contained in both this and other

- void **setLocation**(int x, int y)
  This method moves this rectangle to a new location.

  Parameters: x,y The new top-left corner

- void **translate**(int dx, int dy)
  This method moves this rectangle.

  Parameters: dx The distance to move along the *x*-axis
  dy The distance to move along the *y*-axis

- Rectangle **union**(Rectangle other)
  This method computes the union of this rectangle with the specified rectangle. This is not the set-theoretic union but the smallest rectangle that contains both this and other.

  Parameters: other A rectangle
  Returns: The smallest rectangle containing both this and other

Interface java.awt.Shape

The Shape interface describes shapes that can be drawn and filled by a Graphics2D object.

Package java.awt.event

Interface java.awt.event.ActionListener

- void **actionPerformed**(ActionEvent e)
  The event source calls this method when an action occurs.

Class java.awt.event.MouseEvent

- int **getX**()
  This method returns the horizontal position of the mouse as of the time the event occurred.
  Returns: The *x*-position of the mouse
- int **getY**()
  This method returns the vertical position of the mouse as of the time the event occurred.
  Returns: The *y*-position of the mouse

Interface java.awt.event.MouseListener

- void **mouseClicked**(MouseEvent e)
  This method is called when the mouse has been clicked (that is, pressed and released in quick succession).
- void **mouseEntered**(MouseEvent e)
  This method is called when the mouse has entered the component to which this listener was added.
- void **mouseExited**(MouseEvent e)
  This method is called when the mouse has exited the component to which this listener was added.
- void **mousePressed**(MouseEvent e)
  This method is called when a mouse button has been pressed.
- void **mouseReleased**(MouseEvent e)
  This method is called when a mouse button has been released.

Package java.awt.geom

Class java.awt.geom.Ellipse2D.Double

- **Ellipse2D.Double**(double x, double y, double w, double h)
  This constructs an ellipse from the specified coordinates.
  Parameters: x, y The top-left corner of the bounding rectangle
              w The width of the bounding rectangle
              h The height of the bounding rectangle

Class java.awt.geom.Line2D

- double **getX1**()
- double **getX2**()
- double **getY1**()
- double **getY2**()
  These methods get the requested coordinate of an endpoint of this line.
  Returns: The *x*- or *y*-coordinate of the first or second endpoint

- void **setLine**(double x1, double y1, double x2, double y2)
  This methods sets the endpoints of this line.
  Parameters: x1, y1   A new endpoint of this line
  x2, y2   The other new endpoint

Class java.awt.geom.Line2D.Double

- **Line2D.Double**(double x1, double y1, double x2, double y2)
  This constructs a line from the specified coordinates.
  Parameters: x1, y1   One endpoint of the line
  x2, y2   The other endpoint
- **Line2D.Double**(Point2D p1, Point2D p2)
  This constructs a line from the two endpoints.
  Parameters: p1, p2   The endpoints of the line

Class java.awt.geom.Point2D

- double **getX**()
- double **getY**()
  These methods get the requested coordinates of this point.
  Returns: The x- or y-coordinate of this point
- void **setLocation**(double x, double y)
  This method sets the x- and y-coordinates of this point.
  Parameters: x, y   The new location of this point

Class java.awt.geom.Point2D.Double

- **Point2D.Double**(double x, double y)
  This constructs a point with the specified coordinates.
  Parameters: x, y   The coordinates of the point

Class java.awt.geom.RectangularShape

- int **getHeight**()
- int **getWidth**()
  These methods get the height or width of the bounding rectangle of this rectangular shape.
  Returns: The height or width, respectively
- double **getCenterX**()
- double **getCenterY**()
- double **getMaxX**()
- double **getMaxY**()
- double **getMinX**()
- double **getMinY**()
  These methods get the requested coordinate value of the corners or center of the bounding rectangle of this shape.
  Returns: The center, maximum, or minimum x- and y-coordinates

Package java.io

Class java.io.BufferedReader

- **BufferedReader**(Reader in)

  This constructs a buffered reader, an object that stores characters in a buffer for more efficient reading.

  Parameters: in A reader

- String **readLine**()

  This method reads a line of input from this buffered reader.

  Returns: The input line, or null if the end of input has been reached

Class java.io.EOFException

- **EOFException**(String message)

  This constructs an "end of file" exception object.

  Parameters: message The detail message

Class java.io.File

- **File**(String name)

  This constructs a File object that describes a file (which may or may not exist) with the given name.

  Parameters: name The name of the file

- boolean **exists**()

  This method checks whether there is a file in the local file system that matches this File object.

  Returns: true if there is a matching file, false otherwise

Class java.io.FileInputStream

- **FileInputStream**(File f)

  This constructs a file input stream and opens the chosen file. If the file cannot be opened for reading, a FileNotFoundException is thrown.

  Parameters: f The file to be opened for reading

- **FileInputStream**(String name)

  This constructs a file input stream and opens the named file. If the file cannot be opened for reading, a FileNotFoundException is thrown.

  Parameters: name The name of the file to be opened for reading

Class java.io.FileNotFoundException

This exception is thrown when a file could not be opened.

Class java.io.FileOutputStream

- FileOutputStream(File f)

  This constructs a file output stream and opens the chosen file. If the file cannot be opened for writing, a FileNotFoundException is thrown.

  Parameters: f The file to be opened for writing

- FileOutputStream(String name)

  This constructs a file output stream and opens the named file. If the file cannot be opened for writing, a FileNotFoundException is thrown.

  Parameters: name The name of the file to be opened for writing

Class java.io.FileReader

- FileReader(File f)

  This constructs a file reader and opens the chosen file. If the file cannot be opened for reading, a FileNotFoundException is thrown.

  Parameters: f The file to be opened for reading

- FileReader(String name)

  This constructs a file reader and opens the named file. If the file cannot be opened for reading, a FileNotFoundException is thrown.

  Parameters: name The name of the file to be opened for reading

Class java.io.FileWriter

- FileWriter(File f)

  This constructs a file writer and opens the chosen file. If the file cannot be opened for writing, a FileNotFoundException is thrown.

  Parameters: f The file to be opened for writing

- FileWriter(String name)

  This constructs a file writer and opens the named file. If the file cannot be opened for writing, a FileNotFoundException is thrown.

  Parameters: name The name of the file to be opened for writing

Class java.io.InputStream

- void close()

  This method closes this input stream (such as a FileInputStream) and releases any system resources associated with the stream.

- int read()

  This method reads the next byte of data from this input stream.

  Returns: The next byte of data, or -1 if the end of the stream is reached.

Class java.io.InputStreamReader

- InputStreamReader(InputStream in)

  This constructs a reader from a specified input stream.

  Parameters: in The stream to read from

Class java.io.IOException

This type of exception is thrown when an input/output error is encountered.

Class java.io.ObjectInputStream

- ObjectInputStream(InputStream in)
  This constructs an object input stream.
  Parameters: in   The stream to read from
- Object readObject()
  This method reads the next object from this object input stream.
  Returns: The next object

Class java.io.ObjectOutputStream

- ObjectOutputStream(OutputStream out)
  This constructs an object output stream.
  Parameters: out   The stream to write to
- Object writeObject(Object obj)
  This method writes the next object to this object output stream.
  Parameters: obj   The object to write

Class java.io.OutputStream

- void close()
  This method closes this output stream (such as a FileOutputStream) and releases any system resources associated with this stream. A closed stream cannot perform output operations and cannot be reopened.
- void write(int b)
  This method writes the lowest byte of b to this output stream.
  Parameters: b   The integer whose lowest byte is written

Class java.io.PrintStream

- void print(int x)
- void print(double x)
- void print(Object x)
- void print(String x)
- void println()
- void println(int x)
- void println(double x)
- void println(Object x)
- void println(String x)
  These methods print a value to this print stream. The println methods print a newline after the value. Objects are printed by converting them to strings with their toString methods.
  Parameters: x   The value to be printed

- PrintStream **printf**(Sting format, Object... values)
  This method prints the format string, substituting the given values for placeholders that start with %.
  Parameters: format   The format string
                    values   The values to be printed. You can supply any number of values
  Returns: The implicit parameter

Class java.io.PrintWriter

- **PrintWriter**(String name)
  This constructs a print writer and opens the named file. If the file cannot be opened for writing, a FileNotFoundException is thrown.
  Parameters: name   The name of the file to be opened for writing
- **PrintWriter**(Writer out)
  This constructs a print writer from a specified writer (such as a FileWriter).
  Parameters: out   The writer to write output to
- void **print**(int x)
- void **print**(double x)
- void **print**(Object x)
- void **print**(String x)
- void **println**()
- void **println**(int x)
- void **println**(double x)
- void **println**(Object x)
- void **println**(String x)
  These methods print a value to this print writer. The println methods print a newline after the value. Objects are printed by converting them to strings with their toString methods.
  Parameters: x   The value to be printed

Class java.io.RandomAccessFile

- **RandomAccessFile**(String name, String mode)
  This method opens a named random access file for reading or read/write access.
  Parameters: name   The file name
                    mode   "r" for reading or "rw" for read/write access
- long **getFilePointer**()
  This method gets the current position in this file.
  Returns: The current position for reading and writing
- long **length**()
  This method gets the length of this file.
  Returns: The file length

- char **readChar**()
- double **readDouble**()
- int **readInt**()

  These methods read a value from the current position in this file.

  Returns: The value that was read from the file

- void **seek**(long position)

  This method sets the position for reading and writing in this file.

  Parameters: position The new position

- void **writeChar**(int x)
- void **writeChars**(String x)
- void **writeDouble**(double x)
- void **writeInt**(int x)

  These methods write a value to the current position in this file.

  Parameters: x The value to be written

Class java.io.Reader

- void **close**()

  This method closes this reader and releases any associated system resources.

- int **read**()

  This method reads the next character from this reader (such as a FileReader).

  Returns: The next character, or −1 if the end of the input is reached

Interface java.io.Serializable

A class must implement this interface to enable its objects to be written to object streams.

Class java.io.Writer

- void **close**()

  This method closes this writer and releases any associated system resources.

- void **write**(int b)

  This method writes the lowest two bytes of b to this writer (such as a FileWriter).

  Parameters: b The integer whose lowest two bytes are written

Package java.lang

Class java.lang.Boolean

- **Boolean**(boolean value)

  This constructs a wrapper object for a boolean value.

  Parameters: value The value to store in this object

- boolean **booleanValue**()

  This method returns the boolean value stored in this Boolean object.

  Returns: The Boolean value of this object

Class java.lang.Character

- static boolean **isDigit**(ch)
  This method tests whether a given character is a Unicode digit.
  Parameters: ch The character to test
  Returns: true if the character is a digit

- static boolean **isLetter**(ch)
  This method tests whether a given character is a Unicode letter.
  Parameters: ch The character to test
  Returns: true if the character is a letter

- static boolean **isLowerCase**(ch)
  This method tests whether a given character is a lowercase Unicode letter.
  Parameters: ch The character to test
  Returns: true if the character is a lowercase letter

- static boolean **isUpperCase**(ch)
  This method tests whether a given character is an uppercase Unicode letter.
  Parameters: ch The character to test
  Returns: true if the character is an uppercase letter

Class java.lang.Class

- static Class **forName**(String className)
  This method loads a class with a given name. Loading a class initializes its static fields.
  Parameters: className The name of the class to load
  Returns: The type descriptor of the class

Interface java.lang.Cloneable

A class implements this interface to indicate that the Object.clone method is allowed to make a shallow copy of its instance variables.

Class java.lang.CloneNotSupportedException

This exception is thrown when a program tries to use Object.clone to make a shallow copy of an object of a class that does not implement the Cloneable interface.

Interface java.lang.Comparable<T>

- int **compareTo**(T other)
  This method compares this object with the other object.
  Parameters: other The object to be compared
  Returns: A negative integer if this object is less than the other, zero if they are equal, or a positive integer otherwise

Class java.lang.Double

- **Double**(double value)
  This constructs a wrapper object for a double-precision floating-point number.
  Parameters: value   The value to store in this object

- double **doubleValue**()
  This method returns the floating-point value stored in this Double wrapper object.
  Returns: The value stored in the object

- static double **parseDouble**(String s)
  This method returns the floating-point number that the string represents. If the string cannot be interpreted as a number, a NumberFormatException is thrown.
  Parameters: s   The string to be parsed
  Returns: The value represented by the string parameter

Class java.lang.Error

This is the superclass for all unchecked system errors.

Class java.lang.IllegalArgumentException

- **IllegalArgumentException**()
  This constructs an IllegalArgumentException with no detail message.

Class java.lang.IllegalStateException

This exception is thrown if the state of an object indicates that a method cannot currently be applied.

Class java.lang.Integer

- **Integer**(int value)
  This constructs a wrapper object for an integer.
  Parameters: value   The value to store in this object

- int **intValue**()
  This method returns the integer value stored in this wrapper object.
  Returns: The value stored in the object

- static int **parseInt**(String s)
  This method returns the integer that the string represents. If the string cannot be interpreted as an integer, a NumberFormatException is thrown.
  Parameters: s   The string to be parsed
  Returns: The value represented by the string parameter

- static Integer **parseInt**(String s, int base)
  This method returns the integer value that the string represents in a given number system. If the string cannot be interpreted as an integer, a NumberFormatException is thrown.
  Parameters: s   The string to be parsed
                   base   The base of the number system (such as 2 or 16)
  Returns: The value represented by the string parameter

- static String **toString**(int i)
- static String **toString**(int i, int base)

  This method creates a string representation of an integer in a given number system. If no base is given, a decimal representation is created.

  Parameters: i An integer number

  base The base of the number system (such as 2 or 16)

  Returns: A string representation of the number parameter in the specified number system

- static final int MAX_VALUE

  This constant is the largest value of type int.

- static final int MIN_VALUE

  This constant is the smallest (negative) value of type int.

Class java.lang.InterruptedException

This exception is thrown to interrupt a thread, usually with the intent of terminating it.

Class java.lang.Math

- static double **abs**(double x)

  This method returns the absolute value $|x|$.

  Parameters: x A floating-point value

  Returns: The absolute value of the parameter

- static double **acos**(double x)

  This method returns the angle with the given cosine, $\cos^{-1} x \in [0, \pi]$.

  Parameters: x A floating-point value between -1 and 1

  Returns: The arc cosine of the parameter, in radians

- static double **asin**(double x)

  This method returns the angle with the given sine, $\sin^{-1} x \in [-\pi/2, \pi/2]$.

  Parameters: x A floating-point value between -1 and 1

  Returns: The arc sine of the parameter, in radians

- static double **atan**(double x)

  This method returns the angle with the given tangent, $\tan^{-1} x\ (-\pi/2, \pi/2)$.

  Parameters: x A floating-point value

  Returns: The arc tangent of the parameter, in radians

- static double **atan2**(double y, double x)

  This method returns the arc tangent, $\tan^{-1} (y/x) \in (-\pi, \pi)$. If x can equal zero, or if it is necessary to distinguish "northwest" from "southeast" and "northeast" from "southwest", use this method instead of atan(y/x).

  Parameters: y,x Two floating-point values

  Returns: The angle, in radians, between the points $(0,0)$ and (x,y)

- static double **ceil**(double x)

  This method returns the smallest integer $\geq x$ (as a double).

  Parameters: x A floating-point value

  Returns: The "ceiling integer" of the parameter

- `static double` **cos**`(double radians)`
  This method returns the cosine of an angle given in radians.
  Parameters: radians   An angle, in radians
  Returns: The cosine of the parameter
- `static double` **exp**`(double x)`
  This method returns the value e^x, where e is the base of the natural logarithms.
  Parameters: x   A floating-point value
  Returns: e^x
- `static double` **floor**`(double x)`
  This method returns the largest integer $\leq x$ (as a `double`).
  Parameters: x   A floating-point value
  Returns: The "floor integer" of the parameter
- `static double` **log**`(double x)`
  This method returns the natural (base e) logarithm of x, ln x.
  Parameters: x   A number greater than 0.0
  Returns: The natural logarithm of the parameter
- `static int` **max**`(int x, int y)`
- `static double` **max**`(double x, double y)`
  These methods return the larger of the given parameter values.
  Parameters: x, y   Two integers or floating-point values
  Returns: The maximum of the parameter values
- `static int` **min**`(int x, int y)`
- `static double` **min**`(double x, double y)`
  These methods return the smaller of the given parameter values.
  Parameters: x, y   Two integers or floating-point values
  Returns: The minimum of the parameter values
- `static double` **pow**`(double x, double y)`
  This method returns the value x^y ($x > 0$, or $x = 0$ and $y > 0$, or $x < 0$ and y is an integer).
  Parameters: x, y   Two floating-point values
  Returns: The value of the first parameter raised to the power of the second parameter
- `static long` **round**`(double x)`
  This method returns the closest `long` integer to the parameter.
  Parameters: x   A floating-point value
  Returns: The value of the parameter rounded to the nearest `long` value
- `static double` **sin**`(double radians)`
  This method returns the sine of an angle given in radians.
  Parameters: radians   An angle, in radians
  Returns: The sine of the parameter
- `static double` **sqrt**`(double x)`
  This method returns the square root of x, $\sqrt{x}$.
  Parameters: x   A nonnegative floating-point value
  Returns: The square root of the parameter

- static double **tan**(double radians)

  This method returns the tangent of an angle given in radians.

  Parameters: radians An angle, in radians

  Returns: The tangent of the parameter

- static double **toDegrees**(double radian)

  This method converts radians to degrees.

  Parameters: radians An angle, in radians

  Returns: The angle in degrees

- static double **toRadians**(double degrees)

  This methods converts degrees to radians.

  Parameters: degrees An angle, in degrees

  Returns: The angle in radians

- static final double E

  This constant is the value of *e*, the base of the natural logarithms.

- static final double PI

  This constant is the value of π.

Class java.lang.NullPointerException

This exception is thrown when a program tries to use an object through a null reference.

Class java.lang.NumberFormatException

This exception is thrown when a program tries to parse the numerical value of a string that is not a number.

Class java.lang.Object

- protected Object **clone**()

  This constructs and returns a shallow copy of this object whose instance variables are copies of the instance variables of this object. If an instance variable of the object is an object reference itself, only the reference is copied, not the object itself. However, if the class does not implement the Cloneable interface, a CloneNotSupportedException is thrown. Subclasses should redefine this method to make a deep copy.

  Returns: A copy of this object

- boolean **equals**(Object other)

  This method tests whether this and the other object are equal. This method tests only whether the object references are to the same object. Subclasses should redefine this method to compare the instance variables.

  Parameters: other The object with which to compare

  Returns: true if the objects are equal, false otherwise

- void **notify**()

  This method notifies one of the threads that is currently on the wait list for the lock of this object.

- void **notifyAll**()
  This method notifies all of the threads that are currently on the wait list for the lock of this object.

- String **toString**()
  This method returns a string representation of this object. This method produces only the class name and locations of the objects. Subclasses should redefine this method to print the instance variables.
  Returns: A string describing this object

- void **wait**()
  This method blocks the currently executing thread and puts it on the wait list for the lock of this object.

Interface java.lang.Runnable

- void **run**()
  This method should be overridden to define the tasks to be carried out when this runnable is executed.

Class java.lang.RuntimeException

This is the superclass for all unchecked exceptions.

Class java.lang.String

- int **compareTo**(String other)
  This method compares this string and the other string lexicographically.
  Parameters: other The other string to be compared
  Returns: A value less than 0 if this string is lexicographically less than the other, 0 if the strings are equal, and a value greater than 0 otherwise.

- boolean **equals**(String other)
- boolean **equalsIgnoreCase**(String other)
  These methods test whether two strings are equal, or whether they are equal when letter case is ignored.
  Parameters: other The other string to be compared
  Returns: true if the strings are equal

- static String **format**(String format, Object... values)
  This method formats the given string by substituting placeholders that start with % with the given values.
  Parameters: format The string with the placeholders
  values The values to be substituted for the placeholders
  Returns: The formatted string, with the placeholders replaced by the given values

- int **length**()
  This method returns the length of this string.
  Returns: The count of characters in this string

- String **replace**(String match, String replacement)

  This method replaces matching substrings with a given replacement.

  Parameters: match   The string whose matches are to be replaced

  replacement   The string with which matching substrings are replaced

  Returns: A string that is identical to this string, with all matching substrings replaced by the given replacement

- String **substring**(int begin)

- String **substring**(int begin, int pastEnd)

  These methods return a new string that is a substring of this string, made up of all characters starting at position begin and up to either position pastEnd - 1, if it is given, or the end of the string.

  Parameters: begin   The beginning index, inclusive

  pastEnd   The ending index, exclusive

  Returns: The specified substring

- String **toLowerCase**()

  This method returns a new string that consists of all characters in this string converted to lowercase.

  Returns: A string with all characters in this string converted to lowercase

- String **toUpperCase**()

  This method returns a new string that consists of all characters in this string converted to uppercase.

  Returns: A string with all characters in this string converted to uppercase

Class java.lang.System

- static void **arraycopy**(

     Object from, int fromStart, Object to, int toStart, int count)

  This method copies values from one array to the other. (The array parameters are of type Object because you can convert an array of numbers to an Object but not to an Object[].)

  Parameters: from   The source array

  fromStart   Start position in the source array

  to   The destination array

  toStart   Start position in the destination data

  count   The number of array elements to be copied

- static long **currentTimeMillis**()

  This method returns the difference, measured in milliseconds, between the current time and midnight, Universal Time, January 1, 1970.

  Returns: The current time in milliseconds

- static void **exit**(int status)

  This method terminates the program.

  Parameters: status   Exit status. A nonzero status code indicates abnormal termination

- static final InputStream **in**

  This object is the "standard input" stream. Reading from this stream typically reads keyboard input.

- `static final PrintStream out`
  This object is the "standard output" stream. Printing to this stream typically sends output to the console window.

Class `java.lang.Thread`

- `boolean interrupted()`
  This method tests whether another thread has called the `interrupt` method on the current thread.
  Returns: true if the thread has been interrupted

- `static void sleep(int millis)`
  This method puts the calling thread to sleep.
  Parameters: `millis` the number of millseconds to sleep

- `void start()`
  This method starts the thread and executes its `run` method.

Class `java.lang.Throwable`

This is the superclass of exceptions and errors.

- `Throwable()`
  This constructs a `Throwable` with no detail message.

- `String getMessage()`
  This method gets the message that describes the exception or error.
  Returns: The message

- `void printStackTrace()`
  This method prints a stack trace to the "standard error" stream. The stack trace contains a printout of this object and of all calls that were pending at the time it was created.

Package java.math

Class `java.math.BigDecimal`

- `BigDecimal(String value)`
  This constructs an arbitrary-precision floating-point number from the digits in the given string.
  Parameters: `value` A string representing the floating-point number

- `BigDecimal add(BigDecimal other)`
- `BigDecimal multiply(BigDecimal other)`
- `BigDecimal subtract(BigDecimal other)`
  These methods return a `BigDecimal` whose value is the sum, difference, product, or quotient of this number and the other.
  Parameters: `other` The other number
  Returns: The result of the arithmetic operation

Class `java.math.BigInteger`

- **BigInteger**(String value)

  This constructs an arbitrary-precision integer from the digits in the given string.

  Parameters: value   A string representing an arbitrary-precision integer

- BigInteger **add**(BigInteger other)
- BigInteger **divide**(BigInteger other)
- BigInteger **mod**(BigInteger other)
- BigInteger **multiply**(BigInteger other)
- BigInteger **subtract**(BigInteger other)

  These methods return a `BigInteger` whose value is the sum, difference, product, quotient, or remainder of this number and the other.

  Parameters: other   The other number

  Returns: The result of the arithmetic operation

Package `java.net`

Class `java.net.HttpURLConnection`

- int **getResponseCode**()

  This method gets the response status code from this connection. A value of `HTTP_OK` indicates success.

  Returns: The HTTP response code

- String **getResponseMessage**()

  This method gets the response message of this connection's HTTP request.

  Returns: The message, such as `"OK"` or `"File not found"`

- static int **HTTP_OK**

  This response code indicates a successful fulfillment of the request.

Class `java.net.ServerSocket`

- **ServerSocket**(int port)

  This constructs a server socket that listens to the given port.

  Parameters: port   The port number to listen to

- Socket **accept**()

  This method waits for a client to connect to the port to which this server socket listens. When a connection occurs, the method returns a socket through which the server can communicate with the client.

  Returns: The socket through which the server can communicate with the client

- void **close**()

  This method closes the server socket. Clients can no longer connect.

Class java.net.Socket

- **Socket**(String host, int port)

  This constructs a socket that connects to a server.

  Parameters: host   The host name

  port   The port number to connect to

- void **close**()

  This method closes the connection with the server.

- InputStream **getInputStream**()

  This method gets the input stream through which the client can read the information that the server sends.

  Returns: The input stream associated with this socket

- OutputStream **getOutputStream**()

  This method gets the output stream through which the client can send information to the server.

  Returns: The output stream associated with this socket

Class java.net.URL

- **URL**(String s)

  This constructs an URL object from a string containing the URL.

  Parameters: s   The URL string, such as "http://java.sun.com/index.html"

- InputStream **openConnection**()

  This method gets the input stream through which the client can read the information that the server sends.

  Returns: The input stream associated with this URL

Class java.net.URLConnection

- **URLConnection**(URL u)

  This constructs an URLConnection object from an URL object.

  Parameters: u   The resource to which you intend to connect

- int **getContentLength**()

  This method gets the value of the content-length header of this URL connection.

  Returns: The number of bytes in the content that the server is sending

- String **getContentType**()

  This method gets the value of the content-type header of this URL connection.

  Returns: The MIME type of the content that the server is sending, such as "text/plain" or "image/gif"

- InputStream **getInputStream**()

  This method gets the input stream through which the client can read the information that the server sends.

  Returns: The input stream associated with this URL

- void **setIfModifiedSince**(Date d)

  This method instructs the connection to request that the server send data only if the content has been modified since a given date.

  Parameters: d The modification date

Package java.sql

Interface java.sql.Connection

- void **close**()

  This method closes the connection with the database.

- void **commit**()

  This method commits all database changes since the last call to commit or rollback.

- Statement **createStatement**()

  This method creates a statement object, which can be used to issue database commands.

  Returns: A statement object

- CallableStatement **prepareCall**(String command)

  This method creates a callable SQL statement for a stored procedure call.

  Parameters: command The command to call the procedure

  Returns: The SQL statement object for setting parameters and executing the call

- PreparedStatement **prepareStatement**(String command)

  This method creates a prepared statement for a SQL command that is issued repeatedly.

  Parameters: command The SQL command

  Returns: The statement object for setting parameters and executing the call

- void **rollback**()

  This method abandons all database changes since the last call to commit or rollback.

- void **setAutoCommit**(boolean b)

  This method sets the auto commit mode. By default, it is true. If it is set to false, then transactions are indicated with calls to commit or rollback. Creates a prepared statement for a SQL command that is issued repeatedly.

  Parameters: command The SQL command

  b The desired auto commit mode

Class java.sql.DriverManager

- static Connection **getConnection**(String url, String username, String password)

  This method obtains a connection to the database specified in the database URL.

  Parameters: url The database URL

  username The database user name

  password The password for the database user

  Returns: A connection to the database

Interface `java.sql.PreparedStatement`

- `boolean` **`execute()`**
  This method executes this prepared statement.
  Returns: `true` if the execution yielded a result set

- `ResultSet` **`executeQuery()`**
  This method executes this prepared query.
  Returns: The query result

- `int` **`executeUpdate()`**
  This method executes this prepared update command.
  Returns: The number of records affected by the update

- `void` **`setDouble`**`(int index, double value)`
  This method sets a floating-point parameter for a call of this prepared statement.
  Parameters: `index` The parameter index (starting with 1)
  `value` The parameter value

- `void` **`setInt`**`(int index, int value)`
  This method sets an integer parameter for a call of this prepared statement.
  Parameters: `index` The parameter index (starting with 1)
  `value` The parameter value

- `void` **`setString`**`(int index, String value)`
  This method sets a string parameter for a call of this prepared statement.
  Parameters: `index` The parameter index (starting with 1)
  `value` The parameter value

Interface `java.sql.ResultSet`

- `void` **`close()`**
  This method closes the result set.

- `double` **`getDouble`**`(int column)`
  This method returns the floating-point value at the cursor row and the given column.
  Parameters: `column` The column index (starting with 1)
  Returns: The data value

- `double` **`getDouble`**`(String columnName)`
  This method returns the floating-point value at the cursor row and the given column.
  Parameters: `columnName` The column name
  Returns: The data value

- `int` **`getInt`**`(int column)`
  This method returns the integer value at the cursor row and the given column.
  Parameters: `column` The column index (starting with 1)
  Returns: The data value

- `int` **`getInt`**`(String columnName)`
  This method returns the integer value at the cursor row and the given column.
  Parameters: `columnName` The column name
  Returns: The data value

- ResultSetMetaData **getMetaData**()
  This method returns the meta data associated with this result set.
  Returns: The meta data

- String **getString**(int column)
  This method returns the value at the cursor row and the given column.
  Parameters: column The column index (starting with 1)
  Returns: The data value, as a string

- String **getString**(String columnName)
  This method returns the value at the cursor row and the given column.
  Parameters: columnName The column name
  Returns: The data value, as a string

- boolean **next**()
  This method positions the cursor to the next row. You must call next once before calling any of the get methods to move the cursor to the first row.
  Returns: true if the cursor has been positioned on a row, false at the end of the result set

Interface java.sql.ResultSetMetaData

- int **getColumnCount**()
  This method returns the number of columns of this result set.
  Returns: The number of columns

- int **getColumnDisplaySize**(int column)
  This method returns the number of characters that should be used to display the specified column in this result set.
  Parameters: column The column index (starting with 1)
  Returns: The number of characters that should be used to display this column

- String **getColumnLabel**(int column)
  This method returns the label for a column in this result set.
  Parameters: column The column index (starting with 1)
  Returns: The column label

Class java.sql.SQLException

This exception is thrown when a database error occurs.

Interface java.sql.Statement

- void **close**()
  This method closes this statement.

- boolean **execute**(String command)
  This method executes a SQL command.
  Parameters: command The command to execute
  Returns: true if the execution yielded a result set

- ResultSet **executeQuery**(String command)
  This method executes a SQL query.
  Parameters: command The query command to execute
  Returns: The query result
- int **executeUpdate**(String command)
  This method executes a SQL update command.
  Parameters: command The update command to execute
  Returns: The number of records affected by the update
- ResultSet **getResultSet**()
  This method gets the result of the last command.
  Returns: The query result from the last command
- int **getUpdateCount**()
  This method gets the update count of the last command.
  Returns: The number of records affected by the last command

Package java.text

Class java.text.DateFormat

- String **format**(Date aDate)
  This method formats a date.
  Parameters: aDate The date to format
  Returns: A string containing the formatted date
- static DateFormat **getTimeInstance**()
  This method returns a formatter that formats only the time portion of a date.
  Returns: The formatter object
- void **setTimeZone**(TimeZone zone)
  This method sets the time zone to be used when formatting dates.
  Parameters: zone The time zone to use

Package java.util

Class java.util.ArrayList<E>

- ArrayList()
  This constructs an empty array list.
- boolean **add**(E element)
  This method appends an element to the end of this array list.
  Parameters: element The element to add
  Returns: true (This method returns a value because it overrides a method in the List interface.)

- void **add**(int index, E element)
  This method inserts an element into this array list.
  Parameters: index Insert position
  element The element to insert
- E **get**(int index)
  This method gets the element at the specified position in this array list.
  Parameters: index Position of the element to return
  Returns: The requested element
- E **remove**(int index)
  This method removes the element at the specified position in this array list and returns it.
  Parameters: index Position of the element to remove
  Returns: The removed element
- E **set**(int index, E element)
  This method replaces the element at a specified position in this array list.
  Parameters: index Position of element to replace
  element Element to be stored at the specified position
  Returns: The element previously at the specified position
- int **size**()
  This method returns the number of elements in this array list.
  Returns: The number of elements in this array list

Class java.util.Arrays

- static int **binarySearch**(Object[] a, Object key)
  This method searches the specified array for the specified object using the binary search algorithm. The array elements must implement the Comparable interface. The array must be sorted in ascending order.
  Parameters: a The array to be searched
  key The value to be searched for
  Returns: The position of the search key, if it is contained in the array; otherwise, −*index* − 1, where *index* is the position where the element may be inserted
- static void **sort**(Object[] a)
  This method sorts the specified array of objects into ascending order. Its elements must implement the Comparable interface.
  Parameters: a The array to be sorted

Class java.util.Calendar

- int **get**(int field)
  This method returns the value of the given field.
  Parameters: One of Calendar.YEAR, Calendar.MONTH, Calendar.DAY_OF_MONTH,
  Calendar.HOUR, Calendar.MINUTE, Calendar.SECOND, or
  Calendar.MILLISECOND

Interface `java.util.Collection<E>`

- `boolean` **`add`**`(E element)`

  This method adds an element to this collection.

  Parameters: `element` The element to add

  Returns: `true` if adding the element changes the collection

- `boolean` **`contains`**`(E element)`

  This method tests whether an element is present in this collection.

  Parameters: `element` The element to find

  Returns: `true` if the element is contained in the collection

- `Iterator` **`iterator`**`()`

  This method returns an iterator that can be used to traverse the elements of this collection.

  Returns: An object of a class implementing the `Iterator` interface

- `boolean` **`remove`**`(E element)`

  This method removes an element from this collection.

  Parameters: `element` The element to remove

  Returns: `true` if removing the element changes the collection

- `int` **`size`**`()`

  This method returns the number of elements in this collection.

  Returns: The number of elements in this collection

Class `java.util.Collections`

- `static <T> int` **`binarySearch`**`(List<T> a, T key)`

  This method searches the specified list for the specified object using the binary search algorithm. The list elements must implement the `Comparable` interface. The list must be sorted in ascending order.

  Parameters: `a`   The list to be searched

  `key`   The value to be searched for

  Returns: The position of the search key, if it is contained in the list; otherwise, −*index* − 1, where *index* is the position where the element may be inserted

- `static <T> void` **`sort`**`(T[] a)`

  This method sorts the specified list of objects into ascending order. Its elements must implement the `Comparable` interface.

  Parameters: `a`   The list to be sorted

Class `java.util.Comparator<T>`

- `int` **`compare`**`(T first, T second)`

  This method compares the given objects.

  Parameters: `first, second`   The objects to be compared

  Returns: A negative integer if the first object is less than the second, zero if they are equal, or a positive integer otherwise

Class java.util.EventObject

- Object **getSource**()
  This method returns a reference to the object on which this event initially occurred.
  Returns: The source of this event

Class java.util.GregorianCalendar

- **GregorianCalendar**()
  This constructs a calendar object that represents the current date and time.
- **GregorianCalendar**(int year, int month, int day)
  This constructs a calendar object that represents the start of the given date.
  Parameters: year, month, day The given date

Class java.util.HashMap<K, V>

- HashMap<K, V>()
  This constructs an empty hash map.

Class java.util.HashSet<K, V>

- HashSet<K, V>()
  This constructs an empty hash set.

Class java.util.InputMismatchException

This exception is thrown if the next available input item does not match the type of the requested item.

Interface java.util.Iterator<E>

- boolean **hasNext**()
  This method checks whether the iterator is past the end of the list.
  Returns: true if the iterator is not yet past the end of the list
- E **next**()
  This method moves the iterator over the next element in the linked list. This method throws an exception if the iterator is past the end of the list.
  Returns: The object that was just skipped over
- void **remove**()
  This method removes the element that was returned by the last call to next or previous. This method throws an exception if there was an add or remove operation after the last call to next or previous.

Class java.util.LinkedHashMap<K, V>

- LinkedHashMap<K, V>()
  This constructs an empty linked hash map. The key set iterator of a linked hash map traverses elements in the order in which they were added to the map.

Class `java.util.LinkedList<E>`

* `void addFirst(E element)`
* `void addLast(E element)`

  These methods add an element before the first or after the last element in this list.

  Parameters: `element` The element to be added

* `E getFirst()`
* `E getLast()`

  These methods return a reference to the specified element from this list.

  Returns: The first or last element

* `E removeFirst()`
* `E removeLast()`

  These methods remove the specified element from this list.

  Returns: A reference to the removed element

Interface `java.util.List<E>`

* `ListIterator<E> listIterator()`

  This method gets an iterator to visit the elements in this list.

  Returns: An iterator that points before the first element in this list

Interface `java.util.ListIterator<E>`

  Objects implementing this interface are created by the `listIterator` methods of list classes.

* `void add(E element)`

  This method adds an element after the iterator position and moves the iterator after the new element.

  Parameters: `element` The element to be added

* `boolean hasPrevious()`

  This method checks whether the iterator is before the first element of the list.

  Returns: `true` if the iterator is not before the first element of the list

* `E previous()`

  This method moves the iterator over the previous element in the linked list. This method throws an exception if the iterator is before the first element of the list.

  Returns: The object that was just skipped over

* `void set(E element)`

  This method replaces the element that was returned by the last call to `next` or `previous`. This method throws an exception if there was an add or remove operation after the last call to `next` or `previous`.

  Parameters: `element` The element that replaces the old list element

Interface java.util.Map<K, V>

- V **get**(K key)

  Gets the value associated with a key in this map.

  Parameters: key The key for which to find the associated value

  Returns: The value associated with the key, or null if the key is not present in the table

- Set<K> **keySet**()

  This method returns all keys in the table of this map.

  Returns: A set of all keys in the table of this map

- V **put**(K key, V value)

  This method associates a value with a key in this map.

  Parameters: key The lookup key

  value The value to associate with the key

  Returns: The value previously associated with the key, or null if the key was not present in the table

- V **remove**(K key)

  This method removes a key and its associated value from this map.

  Parameters: key The lookup key

  Returns: The value previously associated with the key, or null if the key was not present in the table

Class java.util.NoSuchElementException

This exception is thrown if an attempt is made to retrieve a value that does not exist.

Class java.util.PriorityQueue<E>

- **PriorityQueue**<E>()

  This constructs an empty priority queue. The element type E must implement the Comparable interface.

- E **remove**()

  This method removes the smallest element in the priority queue.

  Returns: The removed value

Class java.util.Properties

- String **getProperty**(String key)

  This method gets the value associated with a key in this properties map.

  Parameters: key The key for which to find the associated value

  Returns: The value, or null if the key is not present in the table

- void **load**(InputStream in)

  This method loads a set of key/value pairs into this properties map from a stream.

  Parameters: in The stream from which to read the key/value pairs (it must be a sequence of lines of the form key=value)

Class `java.util.Random`

- `Random()`

  This constructs a new random number generator.

- `double nextDouble()`

  This method returns the next pseudorandom, uniformly distributed floating-point number between 0.0 (inclusive) and 1.0 (exclusive) from this random number generator's sequence.

  Returns: The next pseudorandom floating-point number

- `int nextInt(int n)`

  This method returns the next pseudorandom, uniformly distributed integer between 0 (inclusive) and the specified value (exclusive) drawn from this random number generator's sequence.

  Parameters: n Number of values to draw from

  Returns: The next pseudorandom integer

Class `java.util.Scanner`

- `Scanner(InputStream in)`
- `Scanner(Reader in)`

  These construct a scanner that reads from the given input stream or reader.

  Parameters: in The input stream or reader from which to read

- `boolean hasNext()`
- `boolean hasNextDouble()`
- `boolean hasNextInt()`
- `boolean hasNextLine()`

  These methods test whether it is possible to read any non-empty string, a floating-point value, an integer, or a line, as the next item.

  Returns: `true` if it is possible to read an item of the requested type, `false` otherwise (either because the end of the file has been reached, or because a number type was tested and the next item is not a number)

- `String next()`
- `double nextDouble()`
- `int nextInt()`
- `String nextLine()`

  These methods read the next whitespace-delimited string, floating-point value, integer, or line.

  Returns: The value that was read

Interface `java.util.Set<E>`

This interface describes a collection that contains no duplicate elements.

Class java.util.StringTokenizer

- **StringTokenizer**(String s)

  This constructs a string tokenizer that breaks the specified string into tokens. Tokens are delimited by white space.

  Parameters: s The string to break up into tokens

- int **countTokens**()

  This method counts the number of tokens in the string being processed by this tokenizer.

  Returns: The token count

- boolean **hasMoreTokens**()

  This method checks whether all tokens in the string being processed by this tokenizer have been skipped over by nextToken().

  Returns: true if more tokens are available

- String **nextToken**()

  This method skips over and returns the next token in the string being processed by this tokenizer.

  Returns: A string containing the token that was just skipped over

Class java.util.TimeZone

- static String[] **getAvailableIDs**()

  This method gets the supported time zone IDs.

  Returns: An array of ID strings

- static TimeZone **getTimeZone**(String id)

  This method gets the time zone for a time zone ID.

  Parameters: id The time zone ID, such as "America/Los_Angeles"

  Returns: The time zone object associated with the ID, or null if the ID is not supported

Class java.util.TreeMap<K, V>

- **TreeMap**<K, V>()

  This constructs an empty tree map.

Class java.util.TreeSet<K, V>

- **TreeSet**<K, V>()

  This constructs an empty tree set.

Package java.util.concurrent.locks

Interface java.util.concurrent.locks.Condition

*   void **await**()
    This method blocks the current thread until it is signalled or interrupted.
*   void **signal**()
    This method unblocks one thread that is waiting on this condition.
*   void **signalAll**()
    This method unblocks all threads that are waiting on this condition.

Interface java.util.concurrent.locks.Lock

*   void **lock**()
    This method causes the current thread to acquire this lock. The thread blocks if the lock is not available.
*   Condition **newCondition**()
    This method creates a new condition object for this lock.
    Returns: The condition object
*   void **unlock**()
    This method causes the current thread to relinquish this lock.

Class java.util.concurrent.locks.ReentrantLock

*   **ReentrantLock**()
    This constructs a new reentrant lock.

Package java.util.logging

Class java.util.logging.Level

*   static final int ALL
    This value indicates logging of all messages.
*   static final int INFO
    This value indicates informational logging.
*   static final int NONE
    This value indicates logging of no messages.

Class java.util.logging.Logger

*   static Logger **getLogger**(String id)
    This method gets the logger for a given ID. Use the ID "global" to get the default global logger.
    Parameters: id   the logger ID such as "global" or "com.mycompany.mymodule"
    Returns: The logger with the given ID

APPENDIX C ■ The Java Library

- void **info**(String message)
  This method logs an informational message.
  Parameters: message   The message to log
- void **setLevel**(Level aLevel)
  This method sets the logging level. Logging messages with a lesser severity than the current level are ignored.
  Parameters: aLevel   The minimum level for logging messages

Package javax.swing

Class javax.swing.AbstractButton

- void **addActionListener**(ActionListener listener)
  This method adds an action listener to the button.
  Parameters: listener   The action listener to be added
- boolean **isSelected**()
  This method returns the selection state of the button.
  Returns: true if the button is selected
- void **setSelected**(boolean state)
  This method sets the selection state of the button. This method updates the button but does not trigger an action event.
  Parameters: state   true to select, false to deselect

Class javax.swing.ButtonGroup

- void **add**(AbstractButton button)
  This method adds the button to the group.
  Parameters: button   The button to add

Class javax.swing.ImageIcon

- **ImageIcon**(String filename)
  This constructs an image icon from the specified graphics file.
  Parameters: filename   A string specifying a file name

Class javax.swing.JButton

- **JButton**(String label)
  This constructs a button with the given label.
  Parameters: label   The button label

Class javax.swing.JCheckBox

- **JCheckBox**(String text)
  This constructs a check box, having the given text, initially deselected. (Use the setSelected() method to make the box selected; see the javax.swing.AbstractButton class.)
  Parameters: text   The text displayed next to the check box

Class javax.swing.JComboBox

- JComboBox()
  This constructs a combo box with no items.
- void **addItem**(Object item)
  This method adds an item to the item list of this combo box.
  Parameters: item The item to add
- Object **getSelectedItem**()
  This method gets the currently selected item of this combo box.
  Returns: The currently selected item
- boolean **isEditable**()
  This method checks whether the combo box is editable. An editable combo box allows the user to type into the text field of the combo box.
  Returns: true if the combo box is editable
- void **setEditable**(boolean state)
  This method is used to make the combo box editable or not.
  Parameters: state true to make editable, false to disable editing

Class javax.swing.JComponent

- protected void **paintComponent**(Graphics g)
  Override this method to paint the surface of a component. Your method needs to call super.paintComponent(g).
  Parameters: g The graphics context used for drawing
- void **setBorder**(Border b)
  This method sets the border of this component.
  Parameters: b The border to surround this component
- void **setFont**(Font f)
  Sets the font used for the text in this component.
  Parameters: f A font

Class javax.swing.JFileChooser

- JFileChooser()
  This constructs a file chooser.
- File **getSelectedFile**()
  This method gets the selected file from this file chooser.
  Returns: The selected file
- int **showOpenDialog**(Component parent)
  This method displays an "Open File" file chooser dialog box.
  Parameters: parent The parent component or null
  Returns: The return state of this file chooser after it has been closed by the user: either APPROVE_OPTION or CANCEL_OPTION. If APPROVE_OPTION is returned, call getSelectedFile() on this file chooser to get the file

- int **showSaveDialog**(Component parent)
  This method displays a "Save File" file chooser dialog box.
  Parameters: parent The parent component or null
  Returns: The return state of the file chooser after it has been closed by the user: either APPROVE_OPTION or CANCEL_OPTION

Class javax.swing.JFrame

- void **setDefaultCloseOperation**(int operation)
  This method sets the default action for closing the frame.
  Parameters: operation The desired close operation. Choose among
  DO_NOTHING_ON_CLOSE, HIDE_ON_CLOSE (the default), DISPOSE_ON_CLOSE, or EXIT_ON_CLOSE
- void **setJMenuBar**(JMenuBar mb)
  This method sets the menu bar for this frame.
  Parameters: mb The menu bar. If mb is null, then the current menu bar is removed
- static final int EXIT_ON_CLOSE
  This value indicates that when the user closes this frame, the application is to exit.

Class javax.swing.JLabel

- **JLabel**(String text)
- **JLabel**(String text, int alignment)
  These containers create a JLabel instance with the specified text and horizontal alignment.
  Parameters: text The label text to be displayed by the label
  alignment One of SwingConstants.LEFT, SwingConstants.CENTER, or SwingConstants.RIGHT

Class javax.swing.JMenu

- **JMenu**()
  This constructs a menu with no items.
- JMenuItem **add**(JMenuItem menuItem)
  This method appends a menu item to the end of this menu.
  Parameters: menuItem The menu item to be added
  Returns: The menu item that was added

Class javax.swing.JMenuBar

- **JMenuBar**()
  This constructs a menu bar with no menus.
- JMenu **add**(JMenu menu)
  This method appends a menu to the end of this menu bar.
  Parameters: menu The menu to be added
  Returns: The menu that was added

Class `javax.swing.JMenuItem`

- `JMenuItem(String text)`
  This constructs a menu item.
  Parameters: `text` The text to appear in the menu item

Class `javax.swing.JOptionPane`

- `static String showInputDialog(Object prompt)`
  This method brings up a modal input dialog box, which displays a prompt and waits for the user to enter an input in a text field, preventing the user from doing anything else in this program.
  Parameters: `prompt` The prompt to display
  Returns: The string that the user typed

- `static void showMessageDialog(Component parent, Object message)`
  This method brings up a confirmation dialog box that displays a message and waits for the user to confirm it.
  Parameters: `parent` The parent component or `null`
              `message` The message to display

Class `javax.swing.JPanel`

This class is a component without decorations. It can be used as an invisible container for other components.

Class `javax.swing.JRadioButton`

- `JRadioButton(String text)`
  This constructs a radio button having the given text that is initially deselected. (Use the `setSelected()` method to select it; see the `javax.swing.AbstractButton` class.)
  Parameters: `text` The string displayed next to the radio button

Class `javax.swing.JScrollPane`

- `JScrollPane(Component c)`
  This constructs a scroll pane around the given component.
  Parameters: `c` The component that is decorated with scroll bars

Class `javax.swing.JSlider`

- `JSlider(int min, int max, int value)`
  This constructor creates a horizontal slider using the specified minimum, maximum, and value.
  Parameters: `min` The smallest possible slider value
              `max` The largest possible slider value
              `value` The initial value of the slider

- `void addChangeListener(ChangeListener listener)`
  This method adds a change listener to the slider.
  Parameters: `listener` The change listener to add

- int **getValue**()
  This method returns the slider's value.
  Returns: The current value of the slider

Class javax.swing.JTextArea

- **JTextArea**()
  This constructs an empty text area.
- **JTextArea**(int rows, int columns)
  This constructs an empty text area with the specified number of rows and columns.
  Parameters: rows The number of rows
                  columns The number of columns
- void **append**(String text)
  This method appends text to this text area.
  Parameters: text The text to append

Class javax.swing.JTextField

- **JTextField**()
  This constructs an empty text field.
- **JTextField**(int columns)
  This constructs an empty text field with the specified number of columns.
  Parameters: columns The number of columns

Class javax.swing.Timer

- **Timer**(int millis, ActionListener listener)
  This constructs a timer that notifies an action listener whenever a time interval has elapsed.
  Parameters: millis The number of milliseconds between timer notifications
                  listener The object to be notified when the time interval has elapsed
- void **start**()
  This method starts the timer. Once the timer has started, it begins notifying its listener.
- void **stop**()
  This method stops the timer. Once the timer has stopped, it no longer notifies its listener.

Package javax.swing.border

Class javax.swing.border.EtchedBorder

- EtchedBorder()
  This constructor creates a lowered etched border.

Class javax.swing.border.TitledBorder

- TitledBorder(Border b, String title)
  This constructor creates a titled border that adds a title to a given border.
  Parameters: b The border to which the title is added
  title The title the border should display

Package javax.swing.event

Class javax.swing.event.ChangeEvent

Components such as sliders emit change events when they are manipulated by the user.

Interface javax.swing.event.ChangeListener

- void stateChanged(ChangeEvent e)
  This event is called when the event source has changed its state.
  Parameters: e A change event

Package javax.swing.text

Class javax.swing.text.JTextComponent

- String getText()
  This method returns the text contained in this text component.
  Returns: The text
- boolean isEditable()
  This method checks whether this text component is editable.
  Returns: true if the component is editable
- void setEditable(boolean state)
  This method is used to make this text component editable or not.
  Parameters: state true to make editable, false to disable editing
- void setText(String text)
  This method sets the text of this text component to the specified text. If the text is empty, the old text is deleted.
  Parameters: text The new text to be set

Package javax.xml.parsers

Class javax.xml.parsers.DocumentBuilder

- Document **newDocument**()
  This constructs a new document object.
  Returns: An empty document
- Document **parse**(File in)
  This method parses an XML document in a file.
  Parameters: in The file containing the document
  Returns: The parsed document
- Document **parse**(InputStream in)
  This method parses an XML document in a stream.
  Parameters: in The stream containing the document
  Returns: The parsed document

Class javax.xml.parsers.DocumentBuilderFactory

- DocumentBuilder **newDocumentBuilder**()
  This method creates a new document builder object.
  Returns: The document builder
- static DocumentBuilderFactory **newInstance**()
  This method creates a new document builder factory object.
  Returns: The document builder factory object
- void **setIgnoringElementContentWhitespace**(boolean b)
  This method sets the parsing mode for ignoring white space in element content for all
  document builders that are generated from this factory.
  Parameters: b true if white space should be ignored
- void **setValidating**(boolean b)
  This method sets the validation mode for all document builders that are generated from
  this factory.
  Parameters: b true if documents should be validated during parsing

Package javax.xml.xpath

Interface javax.xml.xpath.XPath

- String **evaluate**(String path, Object context)
  This method evaluates the given path expression in the given context.
  Parameters: path An XPath expression
  context The starting context for the evaluation, such as a document,
  node, or node list
  Returns: The result of the evaluation

Class `javax.xml.xpath.XPathExpressionException`

This exception is thrown when an XPath expression cannot be evaluated.

Class `javax.xml.xpath.XPathFactory`

- `static XPathFactory newInstance()`
  This method returns a factory instance that can be used to construct XPath objects.
  Returns: An XPathFactory instance

- `XPath newXPath()`
  This method returns an XPath object that can be used to evaluate XPath expressions.
  Returns: An XPath object

Package org.w3c.dom

Interface `org.w3c.dom.Document`

- `Element createElement(String tagName)`
  This method creates a new document element with a given tag.
  Parameters: tagName The name of the XML tag
  Returns: The created element

- `Text createTextNode(String text)`
  This method creates a text node with the given text.
  Parameters: text The text for the text node
  Returns: The created text node

- `DOMImplementation getImplementation()`
  This method returns the DOMImplementation object associated with this document.

Interface `org.w3c.dom.DOMImplementation`

- `Object getFeature(String feature, String version)`
  This method gets an object that implements a specialized API (such as loading and saving of DOM trees).
  Parameters: feature The feature version (such as "LS")
              version The version number (such as "3.0")
  Returns: The feature object

Interface org.w3c.dom.Element

- String **getAttribute**(String attributeName)
  This method returns the value of a given attribute.
  Parameters: attributeName The name of the XML attribute
  Returns: The attribute value, or the empty string "" if that attribute does not exist for this element
- void **setAttribute**(String name, String value)
  This method sets the value of a given attribute.
  Parameters: name The name of the XML attribute
  value The desired value of the XML attribute

Interface org.w3c.dom.Text

This interface describes a node that contains the textual content of an XML element.

Package org.w3c.dom.ls

Interface org.w3c.dom.ls.DOMImplementationLS

- LSSerializer **createLSSerializer**()
  This method creates a serializer object that can be used to convert a DOM tree to a string or stream.
  Returns: The serializer object

Interface org.w3c.dom.ls.LSSerializer

- String **writeToString**(Node root)
  This method converts the DOM tree starting at the given node to a string.
  Parameters: node The root node of the tree
  Returns: The string representation of the tree

Adapting Java 5 Programs to Older Compilers

Many sample programs in this book use features that are specific to Java version 5.0. This appendix summarizes the changes that you need to make to the sample programs so that they compile and run with an older compiler.

"For each" Loops

Turn the "for each" loop into a traditional loop.

Java 5	Older Compiler

`for (type variable : array)`
`{`
   `body`
`}`
	`for (int i = 0; i < array.length; i++)`
	`{`
	     `type variable = array[i];`
	     `body`
	`}`

`for (type variable : arrayList)`
`{`
   `body`
`}`
	`for (int i = 0; i < arrayList.size(); i++)`
	`{`
	     `type variable = (type) arrayList.get(i);`
	     `body`
	`}`

Array Lists

Remove the type parameter and add a cast to every get operation.

Java 5	Older Compiler
ArrayList<*type*> *arrayList* = new ArrayList<*type*>()	ArrayList *arrayList* = new ArrayList();
arrayList.get(i)	(*type*) *arrayList*.get(i)

Console Input

Use JOptionPane instead of Scanner.

Java 5	Older Compiler

`Scanner in = new Scanner(System.in);`
`System.out.print(prompt);`
`int n = in.nextInt();`
`System.out.print(prompt2);`
`double x = in.nextDouble();`
	`String input = JOptionPane.showInputDialog(prompt);`
	`int n = Integer.parseInt(input);`
	`input = JOptionPane.showInputDialog(prompt2);`
	`double x = Double.parseDouble(input);`

Formatted Output

Use NumberFormat instead of printf.

Java 5	Older Compiler

`System.out.printf("$%.2f", balance);`	`NumberFormat formatter`
	`        = NumberFormat.getNumberInstance();`
	`System.out.print(formatter.format(balance));`

`System.out.printf("%8.2f", balance);`	`NumberFormat formatter`
	`        = NumberFormat.getNumberInstance();`
	`formatter.setMinimumFractionDigits(2);`
	`formatter.setMaximumFractionDigits(2);`
	`String formatted`
	`        = formatter.format(balance);`
	`for (int i = formatted.length(); i < 8; i++)`
	`    System.out.print(" ");`
	`System.out.print(formatted);`

Reading Text Files

Use BufferedReader instead of Scanner.

Java 5	Older Compiler
`Scanner in = new Scanner(`*filename*`);`	`BufferedReader in = new BufferedReader(` `    new FileReader(`*filename*`));`

`while (in.hasNextLine())`
`{`
`    String line = in.nextLine();`
`    `*process* `line`
`}`
	`String line;`
	`while ((line = in.readLine()) != null)`
	`{`
	`    `*process* `line`
	`}`

Writing Text Files

You must construct a PrintWriter from a FileWriter:

Java 5	Older Compiler
`PrintWriter out = new PrintWriter(`*filename*`);`	`PrintWriter out = new PrintWriter(` `    new FileWriter(`*filename*`));`

Adding Components to Frames

A JFrame stores child components in its *content pane*. Starting with Java version 5.0, you can add components directly to the frame, and it adds them to the content pane. In older versions, you had to explicitly add components to the content pane. If you tried to add components to the frame, the program compiled, but an error message was issued at run time.

Java 5	Older Compiler
`add(`*component*`)`	`getContentPane().add(`*component*`)`
`setLayout(`*manager*`)`	`getContentPane().setLayout(`*manager*`)`

Java Syntax Summary

In this syntax summary, we use a monospaced font for actual Java keywords and tokens such as `while`. An italic font denotes language constructs such as *condition* or *variable*. Items enclosed in brackets [ ] are optional. Items separated by vertical bars | are alternatives. Do not include the brackets or vertical bars in your code!

The summary reflects the parts of the Java language that were covered in this book. For a full overview of the Java syntax, see [1].

As always, please be careful to distinguish an ellipsis . . . from the ... token. The latter appears twice in this appendix in the "variable parameters" discussion in the "Methods" section.

Types

A type is a primitive type or a reference type. The primitive types are

- The numeric types `int`, `long`, `short`, `char`, `byte`, `float`, `double`
- The `boolean` type

The reference types are

- Classes such as `String` or `Employee`
- Enumerated types such as `enum Sex { FEMALE, MALE }`
- Interfaces such as `Comparable`
- Array types such as `Employee[]` or `int[][]`

Variables

Local variable declarations have the form

[final] *Type variableName* [= *initializer*];

Examples:

```
int n;
double x = 0;
String harry = "Harry Handsome";
Rectangle box = new Rectangle(5, 10, 20, 30);
int[] a = { 1, 4, 9, 16, 25 };
```

The variable name consists only of letters, numbers, and underscores. It must begin with a letter or underscore. Names are case-sensitive: totalscore, TOTALSCORE, and totalScore are three different variables.

The scope of a local variable extends from the point of its definition to the end of the enclosing block.

A variable that is declared as final can have its value set only once.

Instance variables will be discussed under "Classes".

Expressions

An *expression* is a variable, a method call, or a combination of subexpressions joined by operators. Examples are:

```
x
Math.sin(x)
x + Math.sin(x)
x * (1 + Math.sin(x))
x++
x == y
x == y && (z > 0 || w > 0)
p.x
e.getSalary()
v[i]
```

Operators can be *unary*, *binary*, or *ternary*. A unary operator acts on a single expression, such as x++. A binary operator combines two expressions, such as x + y. A ternary operator combines three expressions. Java has one ternary operator, ? : (see Advanced Topic 6.1).

Unary operators can be *prefix* or *postfix*. A prefix operator is written before the expression on which it operates, as in -x. A postfix operator is written after the expression on which it operates, such as x++.

Operators are ranked by *precedence* levels. Operators with a higher precedence bind more strongly than operators with a lower precedence. For example, * has a higher precedence than +, so x + y * z is the same as x + (y * z), even though the + comes first.

Most operators are *left-associative*. That is, operators of the same precedence are evaluated from the left to the right. For example, x - y + z is interpreted as (x - y) + z, not x - (y + z). The exceptions are the unary prefix operators and the assignment operator which are right-associative. For example, z = y = Math.sin(x) means the same as z = (y = Math.sin(x)).

Appendix F has a list of all Java operators.

Classes

The syntax for a *class* is

```
[public] [abstract|final] class ClassName
        [extends SuperClassName]
        [implements InterfaceName₁, InterfaceName₂, . . .]
{
    feature₁
    feature₂
    . . .
}
```

Each *feature* is either a declaration of the form

modifiers   constructor|method|field|class

or an initialization block

```
[static] { body }
```

See the section "Constructors" for more information about initialization blocks.

Potential *modifiers* include public, private, protected, static, and final.

A *constructor* has the form

```
ClassName(parameter₁, parameter₂, . . .)
        [throws ExceptionType₁, ExceptionType₂, . . .]
{
    body
}
```

A *method* has the form

```
Type methodName(parameter₁, parameter₂, . . .)
        [throws ExceptionType₁, ExceptionType₂, . . .]
{
    body
}
```

An *abstract method* has the form

```
abstract Type methodName(parameter₁, parameter₂, . . .);
```

A *field* declaration has the form

```
Type variableName [= initializer];
```

Here is an example:

```
public class Point
{
```

```
    public Point()
    {
        x = 0; y = 0;
    }

    public Point(double xx, double yy)
    {
        x = xx; y = yy;
    }

    public double getX()
    {
        return x;
    }

    public double getY()
    {
        return y;
    }

    private double x;
    private double y;
}
```

A class can have both instance fields and `static` fields. Each object of the class has a separate copy of the instance fields. There is only one per-class copy of the `static` fields.

A class that is declared as `abstract` cannot be instantiated. That is, you cannot construct objects of that class.

A class that is declared as `final` cannot be extended.

Interfaces

The syntax for an interface is

```
[public] interface InterfaceName
        [extends InterfaceName₁, InterfaceName₂, . . .]
{
    feature₁
    feature₂
        . . .
}
```

Each feature has the form

modifiers method|field

Potential modifiers are `public`, `static`, `final`. However, modifiers are never necessary because methods are automatically `public` and fields are automatically `public static final`.

A method declaration has the form

Type methodName(parameter₁, parameter₂, . . .);

A field declaration has the form

Type variableName = initializer;

Here is an example:

```
public interface Measurable
{
    int getMeasure();
    int CM_PER_INCH = 2.54;
}
```

Enumerated Types

The syntax for an enumerated type is

```
[public] enum EnumeratedTypeName
{
    constant₁, constant₂, . . .;
    feature₁
    feature₂
    . . .
}
```

where the subscript forms are: $constant_1$, $constant_2$, . . .; $feature_1$, $feature_2$.

Each constant is a constant name, followed by optional construction parameters.

$$constantName[(parameter_1, \ parameter_2, \ . \ . \ .)]$$

The semicolon after the constants is only required if the enumeration defines additional features. An enumeration can have the same features as a class. Each feature has the form

modifiers method|field

Potential modifiers are `public`, `static`, `final`.

Here are two examples:

```
public enum Suit { HEARTS, DIAMONDS, SPADES, CLUBS };
public enum Card
{
    TWO(2), THREE(3), FOUR(4), FIVE(5), SIX(6),
        SEVEN(7), EIGHT(8), NINE(9), TEN(10),
        JACK(10), QUEEN(10), KING(10), ACE(11);
    public void Card(int aValue) { value = aValue; }
    public int getValue() { return value; }
    private int value;
}
```

Methods

A method definition has the form

$$modifiers \ Type \ methodName(parameter_1, \ parameter_2, \ . \ . \ ., \ parameter_n)$$
$$[\text{throws} \ ExceptionType_1, \ ExceptionType_2, \ . \ . \ .]$$

```
{
    body
}
```

The return type *Type* is any Java type, or the special type void to indicate that the method returns no value.

Each *parameter* has the form

[final] *Type parameterName*

A method has *variable parameters* if the last parameter has the special form

Type... *parameterName*

Such a method can be called with a sequence of values of the given type of any length. The parameter variable with the given name is an array of the given type that holds the parameter values. For example, the method

```java
public static double sum(double... values)
{
    double s = 0;
    for (double v : values) s = s + v;
    return s;
}
```

can be called as

```java
double result = sum(1, -2.5, 3.14);
```

In Java, all parameters are passed by *value*. Each parameter is a local variable whose scope extends to the end of the method body. It is initialized with a copy of the value supplied in the call. That value may be a primitive type or a reference type. If it is a reference type, invoking a mutator on the reference will modify the object whose reference has been passed to the method.

Changing the value of the parameter variable has no effect outside the method. Tagging the parameter as final disallows such a change altogether. This is commonly done to allow access of the parameter from an inner class defined in the method.

Java distinguishes between *instance* methods and *static* methods. Instance methods have a special parameter, the *implicit* parameter, supplied in the method call with the syntax

implicitParameterValue.*methodName*(*parameterValue*$_1$, *parameterValue*$_2$, . . .)

Example:

```java
harry.setSalary(30000)
```

The type of the implicit parameter must be the same as the type of the class containing the method definition. A static method does not have an implicit parameter.

In the method body, the this variable is initialized with a copy of the implicit parameter value. Using a field name without qualification means to access the field of the implicit parameter. For example,

```java
public void setSalary(double s)
{
    salary = s; // i.e., this.salary = s
}
```

By default, methods are *dynamically bound*. The virtual machine determines the class to which the implicit parameter object belongs and invokes the method defined in that class. However, if a method is invoked on the special variable super, then the method defined in the superclass is invoked on this. For example,

```java
public class MyPanel extends JPanel
{
    public void paintComponent(Graphics g)
    {
        super.paintComponent(g);
        // Calls JPanel.paintComponent
        . . .
    }
    . . .
}
```

The return statement causes a method to exit immediately. If the method type is not void, you must return a value. The syntax is

```java
return [value];
```

For example,

```java
public double getSalary()
{
    return salary;
}
```

A method can call itself. Such a method is called *recursive*:

```java
public static int factorial(int n)
{
    if (n <= 1) return 1;
        return n * factorial(n - 1);
}
```

Constructors

A constructor definition has the form

```
modifiers ClassName(parameter₁, parameter₂, . . .)
        [throws ExceptionType₁, ExceptionType₂, . . .]
{
    body
}
```

You invoke a constructor to allocate and construct a new object with a new expression

```
new ClassName(parameterValue₁, parameterValue₂, . . .)
```

A constructor can call the body of another constructor of the same class with the syntax

```
this(parameterValue₁, parameterValue₂, . . .)
```

For example,

```
public Employee()
{
    this("", 0);
}
```

It can call a constructor of its superclass with the syntax

super($parameterValue_1$, $parameterValue_2$, . . .)

The call to this or super must be the first statement in the constructor.
Arrays are constructed with the syntax

new *ArrayType* [= { $initializer_1$, $initializer_2$, . . . }]

For example,

new int[] = { 1, 4, 9, 16, 25 }

When an object is constructed, the following actions take place:

- All fields are initialized with 0, false, or null.
- The initializers and initialization blocks are executed in the order in which they are declared.
- The body of the constructor is invoked.

When a class is loaded, the following actions take place:

- All static fields are initialized with 0, false, or null.
- The initializers of static fields and static initialization blocks are executed in the order in which they are declared.

Statements

A *statement* is one of the following:

- An expression followed by a semicolon
- A branch or loop statement
- A return statement
- A throw statement
- A block, that is, a group of variable declarations and statements enclosed in braces {. . .}
- A try block

Java has two branch statements (if and switch), three loop statements (while, for, and do), and two mechanisms for nonlinear control flow (break and continue).
The if statement has the form

if (*condition*) $statement_1$ [else $statement_2$]

If the *condition* is true, then the first *statement* is executed. Otherwise, the second *statement* is executed.

The switch statement has the form

```
switch (expression)
{
    group1:
    group2:
    . . .
      [default:
        statement1
        statement2
        . . .]
}
```

Where each group has the form

```
case constant1
case constant2
. . .
    statement1
    statement2
    . . .
```

The *expression* must be an integer or an enumerated type. Depending on its value, control is transferred to the first statement following the matching case label, or to the first statement following the default label if none of the case labels match. Execution continues with the next statement until a break or return statement is encountered, an exception is thrown, or the end of the switch is reached. Execution skips over any case labels.

The while loop has the form

```
while (condition) statement
```

The *statement* is executed while the *condition* is true.

The for loop has the form

```
for (initExpression|variableDeclaration;
     condition;
     updateExpression1, updateExpression2, . . .)
    statement
```

The initialization expression or the variable declaration are executed once. While the *condition* remains true, the loop *statement* and the *updateExpressions* are executed. Examples:

```
for (i = 0; i < 10; i++)
    sum = sum + i;
for (int i = 0, j = 9; i < 10; i++, j--)
    a[j] = b[i];
```

The enhanced for loop or "for each" loop has the form

```
for (Type variable : array|iterableObject)
    statement
```

When this loop traverses an array, it is equivalent to

```
for (int i = 0; i < array.length; i++)
{
    Type variable = array[i];
    statement
}
```

Otherwise, the *iterableObject* must belong to a class that implements the Iterable interface. Then the loop is equivalent to

```
Iterator i = iterableObject.iterator();
while (i.hasNext())
{
    Type variable = i.next();
    statement
}
```

The do loop has the form

```
do statement while (condition);
```

The *statement* is repeatedly executed until the *condition* is no longer true. In contrast to a while loop, the statement of a do loop is executed at least once.

The break statement exits the innermost enclosing while, do, for, or switch statement (not counting if or block statements).

Any statement (including if and block statements) can be tagged with a label:

```
label: statement
```

The labeled break statement

```
break label;
```

exits the labeled statement.

The continue statement skips past the end of the *statement* part of a while, do, or for loop. In the case of the while or do loop, the loop *condition* is executed next. In the case of the for loop, the *updateExpressions* are executed next.

The labeled continue statement

```
continue label;
```

skips past the end of the *statement* part of a while, do, or for loop with the matching label.

Exceptions

The throw statement

```
throw expression;
```

abruptly terminates the current method and resumes control inside the innermost matching catch clause of a surrounding try block. The *expression* must evaluate to a reference to an object of a subclass of Throwable.

The `try` statement has the form

```
try tryBlock
[catch (ExceptionType₁ exceptionVariable₁) catchBlock₁
catch (ExceptionType₂ exceptionVariable₂) catchBlock₂
 . . .]
[finally finallyBlock]
```

- The `try` statement must have at least one `catch` or `finally` clause.
- All blocks are block statements in the usual sense, that is, { . . . }-delimited statement sequences.

The statements in the *tryBlock* are executed. If one of them throws an exception object whose type is a subtype of one of the types in the `catch` clauses, then its *catchBlock* is executed. As soon as the catch block is entered, that exception is handled.

If the *tryBlock* exits for any reason at all (because all of its statements executed completely; because one of its statements was a `break`, `continue`, or `return` statement; or because an exception was thrown), then the *finallyBlock* is executed.

If the *finallyBlock* was entered because an exception was thrown and it itself throws another exception, then that exception masks the prior exception.

Packages

A class can be placed in a package by putting the package declaration

```
package packageName;
```

as the first non-`import` declaration of the source file.

A package name has the form

identifier₁.*identifier₂*. . . .

For example,

```
java.util
com.horstmann.bigjava
```

A fully qualified name of a class is

packageName.*ClassName*

Classes can always be referenced by their fully qualified class names. However, this can be inconvenient. For that reason, you can reference imported classes by just their *ClassName*. All classes in the package `java.lang` and in the package of the current source file are alway imported. To import additional classes, use an import directive

```
import packageName.ClassName;
```

or

```
import packageName.*;
```

The second version imports all classes in the package.

Generic Types and Methods

A generic type is declared with one or more *type parameters*, placed after the type name:

modifiers class|interface *TypeName*<*typeParameter*$_1$, *typeParameter*$_2$, . . .>

Similarly, a generic method is declared with one or more type parameters, placed *before* the method's return type:

modifiers <*typeParameter*$_1$, *typeParameter*$_2$, . . .> *returnType methodName*

Each type parameter has the form

typeParameterName [extends *bound*$_1$ & *bound*$_2$ & . . .]

For example,

```
public class BinarySearchTree<T extends Comparable>
public interface Comparator<T>
public <T extends Comparable & Cloneable> T cloneMin(T[] values)
```

Type parameters can be used in the definition of the generic type or method as if they were regular types. They can be replaced with any types that match the bounds. For example, the BinarySearchTree<String> type substitutes the String type for the type parameter T.

Type parameters can also be replaced with *wildcard types*. A wildcard type has the form

? [super|extends *Type*]

It denotes a specific type that is unknown at the time that is defined. For example, Comparable<? super Rectangle> is a type Comparable<S> for a specific type S, which can be Rectangle or a supertype such as RectangularShape or Shape.

Comments

There are three kinds of comments:

```
/* comment */
// one-line-comment
/** documentationComment */
```

The one-line comment extends to the end of the line. The other comments can span multiple lines and extend to the */ delimiter.

Documentation comments are further explained in Appendix K.

FURTHER READING

1. http://java.sun.com/docs/books/jls/   The Java Language Specification.

Java Operator Summary

The operators are listed in groups of decreasing precedence in the table below. The horizontal lines in the table indicate a change in operator precedence. For example, z = x - y; means z = (x - y); because = has lower precedence than -.

The prefix unary operators and the assignment operators associate right-to-left. All other operators associate left-to-right.

Operator	Description	Associativity
.	Access class feature	
[]	Array subscript	Left to right
()	Function call	
++	Increment	
--	Decrement	
!	Boolean not	
~	Bitwise not	
+ (unary)	(Has no effect)	Right to left
- (unary)	Negative	
(*TypeName*)	Cast	
new	Object allocation	

Operator	Description	Associativity
*	Multiplication	
/	Division or integer division	Left to right
%	Integer remainder	
+	Addition, string concatenation	Left to right
-	Subtraction	
<<	Shift left	
>>	Arithmetic shift right	Left to right
>>>	Bitwise shift right	
<	Less than	
<=	Less than or equal	
>	Greater than	
>=	Greater than or equal	Left to right
==	Equal	
!=	Not equal	
instanceof	Tests whether an object's type is a given type or a subtype thereof	
&	Bitwise and	Left to right
^	Bitwise exclusive or	Left to right
|	Bitwise or	Left to right
&&	Boolean "short circuit" and	Left to right
||	Boolean "short circuit" or	Left to right
=	Assignment	
op=	Assignment with binary operator (*op* is one of +, -, *, /, &, |, ^, <<, >>, >>>)	Right to left

Java Keyword Summary

Keyword	Description
abstract	An abstract class or method
assert	An assertion that a condition is fulfilled
boolean	The Boolean type
break	Breaks out of the current loop or labeled statement
byte	The 8-bit signed integer type
case	A label in a switch statement
catch	The handler for an exception in a try block
char	The 16-bit Unicode character type
class	Defines a class
const	Not used
continue	Skip the remainder of a loop body
default	The default label in a switch statement
do	A loop whose body is executed at least once
double	The 64-bit double-precision floating-point type

Keyword	Description
else	The alternative clause in an if statement
enum	An enumerated type
extends	Indicates that a class is a subclass of another class
final	A value that cannot be changed after it has been initialized, a method that can't be overridden, or a class that can't be executed
finally	A clause of a try block that is always executed
float	The 32-bit single-precision floating-point type
for	A loop with initialization, condition, and update expressions
goto	Not used
if	A conditional branch statement
implements	Indicates that a class realizes an interface
import	Allows the use of class names without the package name
instanceof	Tests whether an object's type is a given type or a subtype thereof
int	The 32-bit integer type
interface	An abstract type with only abstract methods and constants
long	The 64-bit integer type
native	A method implemented in non-Java code
new	Allocates an object
package	A collection of related classes
private	A feature that is accessible only by methods of the same class
protected	A feature that is accessible only by methods of the same class, a subclass, or another class in the same package
public	A feature that is accessible by all methods
return	Returns from a method
short	The 16-bit integer type
static	A feature that is defined for a class, not for individual instances
strictfp	Use strict rules for floating-point computations

Keyword	Description
`super`	Invoke the superclass constructor or a superclass method
`switch`	A selection statement
`synchronized`	A block of code that is accessible to only one thread at a time
`this`	The implicit parameter of a method; or invocation of another constructor of the same class
`throw`	Throws an exception
`throws`	The exceptions that a method may throw
`transient`	Fields that should not be serialized
`try`	A block of code with exception handlers or a `finally` handler
`void`	Tags a method that doesn't return a value
`volatile`	A field that may be accessed by multiple threads without synchronization
`while`	A loop statement

Metric Conversion Factors

Table 1 Metric Measurements

Measure	Name	Type
m	meter	Distance
L	liter	Volume ($= 1000 \text{ cm}^3$)
g	gram	Weight
°C	degree Celsius	Temperature

Table 2 Metric Unit Factors

Unit	Name	Factor
μ	micro	10^{-6}
m	milli	10^{-3}
c	centi	10^{-2}
k	kilo	10^{3}

Table 3 Conversions from Nonmetric Units to Metric Units

To convert from	To	Perform this operation
Fluid ounce (fl. oz.)	mL	Multiply by 29.586
Gallon	L	Multiply by 3.785
Ounce (oz.)	g	Multiply by 28.3495
Pound (lb.)	kg	Multiply by 0.4536
Inch (in.)	cm	Multiply by 2.54
Foot (ft.)	cm	Multiply by 30.5
Mile	km	Multiply by 1.609
Degrees Fahrenheit (°F)	°C	Subtract 32, then multiply by 5 and divide by 9

HTML
Summary

A Brief Introduction to HTML

A web page is written in a language called HTML (Hypertext Markup Language). Like Java code, HTML code is made up of text that follows certain strict rules. When a browser reads a web page, the browser *interprets* the code and *renders* the page, displaying characters, fonts, paragraphs, tables, and images.

HTML files are made up of text and *tags* that tell the browser how to render the text. Nowadays, there are dozens of HTML tags—see Table 1 for a summary of the most important tags. Fortunately, you need only a few to get started. Most HTML tags come in pairs consisting of an opening tag and a closing tag, and each pair applies to the text between the two tags. Here is a typical example of a tag pair:

```
Java is an <i>object-oriented</i> programming language.
```

The tag pair `<i>` `</i>` directs the browser to display the text inside the tags in *italics*:

Java is an *object-oriented* programming language.

The closing tag is just like the opening tag, but it is prefixed by a slash (/). For example, bold-faced text is delimited by `<b>` `</b>`, and a paragraph is delimited by the tag pair `<p>` `</p>`.

```
<p><b>Java</b> is an <i>object-oriented</i> programming language.</p>
```

The result is the paragraph

Java is an *object-oriented* programming language.

Another common construct is a bulleted list. For example:

Java is

- object-oriented
- safe
- platform-independent

Here is the HTML code to display it:

```
<p>Java is</p>
<ul><li>object-oriented</li>
<li>safe</li>
<li>platform-independent</li></ul>
```

Each item in the list is delimited by `<li> </li>` (for "list item"), and the whole list is surrounded by `<ul> </ul>` (for "unnumbered list").

As in Java code, you can freely use white space (spaces and line breaks) in HTML code to make it easier to read. For example, you can lay out the code for a list as follows:

```
<p>Java is</p>
<ul>
<li>object-oriented</li>
<li>safe</li>
<li>platform-independent</li>
</ul>
```

The browser ignores the white space.

If you omit a tag (such as a `</li>`), most browsers will try to guess the missing tags—sometimes with differing results. It is always best to include all tags.

You can include images in your web pages with the `img` tag. In its simplest form, an image tag has the form

```
<img src="hamster.jpeg"/>
```

This code tells the browser to load and display the image that is stored in the file `hamster.jpeg`. This is a slightly different type of tag. Rather than text inside a tag pair `<img> </img>`, the `img` tag uses an attribute to specify a file name. Attributes have names and values. For example, the `src` attribute has the value `"hamster.jpeg"`. Table 2 contains commonly used attributes.

It is considered polite to use several additional attributes with the `img` tag, namely the *image size* and an *alternate description*:

```
<img src="hamster.jpeg" width="640" height="480"
alt="A photo of Harry, the Horrible Hamster"/>
```

These additional attributes help the browser lay out the page and display a temporary description while gathering the data for the image (or if the browser cannot display images, such as a voice browser for blind users). Users with slow network connections really appreciate this extra effort.

Because there is no closing `</img>` tag, we put a slash / before the closing >. This is not a requirement of HTML, but it is a requirement of the emerging XHTML standard, the XML-based successor to HTML. See [1] for more information on XHTML.

Table 1 Selected HTML Tags

Tag	Meaning	Children	Commonly Used Attributes
html	HTML document	head, body	
head	Head of an HTML document	title	
title	Title of an HTML document		
body	Body of an HTML document		
h1 . . . h6	Heading level 1 . . . 6		
p	Paragraph		
ul	Unnumbered list	li	
ol	Ordered list	li	
dl	Definition list	dt, dd	
li	List item		
dt	Term to be defined		
dd	Definition data		
table	Table	tr	
tr	Table row	th, td	
th	Table header cell		
td	Table cell data		
a	Anchor		href, name
img	Image		src, width, height
applet	Applet		code, width, height
pre	Preformatted text		
hr	Horizontal rule		
br	Line break		
i or em	Italic		
b or strong	Bold		
tt or code	Typewriter or code font		
s or strike	Strike through		
u	Underline		
super	Superscript		
sub	Subscript		
form	Form		action, method
input	Input field		type, name, value, size, checked
select	Combo box style selector	option	name
option	Option for selection		
textarea	Multiline text area		name, rows, cols

Table 2   Selected HTML Attributes

Attribute	Description	Commonly Contained in Element
name	Name of form element or anchor	`input`, `select`, `textarea`, `a`
href	Hyperlink reference	`a`
src	Source (as of an image)	`img`
code	Applet code	`applet`
width, height	Width, height of image or applet	`img`, `applet`
rows, cols	Rows, columns of text area	`textarea`
type	Type of input field, such as `text`, `password`, `checkbox`, `radio`, `submit`, `hidden`	`input`
value	Value of input field, or label of submit button	`input`
size	Size of text field	`input`
checked	Check radio button or checkbox	`input`
action	URL of form action	`form`
method	GET or POST	`form`

The most important tag in web pages is the `<a>` `</a>` tag pair, which makes the enclosed text into a *link* to another file. The links between web pages are what makes the Web into, well, a web. The browser displays a link in a special way (for example, underlined text in blue color). Here is the code for a typical link:

```
<a href="http://java.sun.com">Java</a> is an object-oriented
programming language.
```

When the viewer of the web page clicks on the word Java, the browser loads the web page located at `java.sun.com`. (The value of the `href` attribute is a *Universal Resource Locator* (URL), which tells the browser where to go. The prefix `http:`, for *Hypertext Transfer Protocol*, tells the browser to fetch the file as a web page. Other protocols allow different actions, such as `ftp:` to download a file, `mailto:` to send e-mail to a user, and `file:` to view a local HTML file.)

Finally, the `applet` tag includes an applet in a web page. To display an applet, you need first to write and compile a Java file to generate the applet code—see Advanced Topic 5.1. Then you tell the browser how to find the code for the applet and how much screen space to reserve for the applet. Here is an example:

```
<applet code="HamsterApplet.class" width="400" height="300">An
animation of Harry, the Horrible Hamster</applet>
```

The text between the `<applet>` and `</applet>` tags is only displayed in lieu of the actual applet by browsers that can't run Java applets.

You have noticed that tags are enclosed in angle brackets (less-than and greater-than signs). What if you want to show an angle bracket on a web page? HTML provides the notations `&lt;` and `&gt;` to produce the < and > symbols, respectively. Other codes of this kind produce symbols such as accented letters. The `&` (ampersand)

Table 3 Selected HTML Entities

Entity	Description	Appearance
<	Less than	<
>	Greater than	>
&	Ampersand	&
"	Quotation mark	"
	Nonbreaking space	
©	Copyright symbol	©

symbol introduces these codes; to get that symbol itself, use &. See Table 3 for a summary.

You may already have created web pages with a web editor that works like a word processor, giving you a WYSIWYG (what you see is what you get) view of your web page. But the tags are still there, and you can see them when you load the HTML file into a text editor. If you are comfortable using a WYSIWYG web editor, and if your editor can insert applet tags, you don't need to memorize HTML tags at all. But many programmers and professional web designers prefer to work directly with the tags at least some of the time, because it gives them more control over their pages.

FURTHER READING

1. www.w3c.org/TR/xhtml1 The official web site for the XHTML 1.0 specification.

Tool Summary

In this summary, we use a monospaced font for actual commands such as javac. An italic font denotes descriptions of tool command components such as *options*. Items enclosed in brackets [. . .] are optional. Items separated by vertical bars | are alternatives. Do not include the brackets or vertical bars when typing in the commands.

The Java Compiler

> javac [*options*] *sourceFile₁*|*@fileList₁* *sourceFile₂*|*@fileList₂* . . .

A file list is a text file that contains one file name per line. For example,

File Greeting.list

```
1  Greeting.java
2  GreetingTest.java
```

Then you can compile all files with the command

> javac @Greeting.list

The Java compiler options are summarized in Table 1.

Table 1 Common Compiler Options

Option	Description
-classpath *locations* or -cp *locations*	The compiler is to look for classes on this path, overriding the CLASSPATH environment variable. If neither is specified, the current directory is used. Each *location* is a directory, JAR file, or ZIP file. Locations are separated by a platform-dependent separator (: on Unix, ; on Windows).
-sourcepath *locations*	The compiler is to look for source files on this path. If not specified, source files are searched in the class path.
-g	Generate debugging information.
-verbose	Include information about all classes that are being compiled (useful for troubleshooting).
-deprecation	Give detailed information about the usage of deprecated messages.
-Xlint:*errorType*	Carry out additional error checking. If you get warnings about unchecked conversions, compile with the -Xlint:unchecked option.

The Java Virtual Machine Launcher

The following command loads the given class and starts its main method, passing it an array containing the provided command line arguments.

java [*options*] *ClassName* [*argument₁ argument₂* . . .]

The following command loads the main class of the given JAR file and starts its main method, passing it an array containing the provided command line arguments.

java [*options*] -jar *jarFileName* [*argument₁ argument₂* . . .]

The Java virtual machine options are summarized in Table 2.

Table 2 Common Virtual Machine Launcher Options

Option	Description
-classpath *locations* or -cp *locations*	Look for classes on this path, overriding the CLASSPATH environment variable. If neither is specified, the current directory is used. Each *location* is a directory, JAR file, or ZIP file. Locations are separated by a platform-dependent separator (: on Unix, ; on Windows).
-verbose	Trace class loading
-D*property*=*value*	Set a system property that you can retrieve with the System.getProperties method.

The Applet Viewer

appletviewer *url*$_1$ *url*$_2$ . . .

The *urls* are searched for applets, and each applet is displayed in a separate window. An applet should be specified as an HTML tag of the form

```
<applet
    code=appletClassFile
    width=pixels
    height=pixels
    [codebase=relativeURL]>
    <param name=parameterName1 value=parameterValue1>
    <param name=parameterName2 value=parameterValue2>
    . . .
</applet>
```

The codebase parameter is an URL that is relative to the URL of the HTML file containing the applet or object tag.

The JAR Tool

To combine one or more files into a JAR (Java Archive) file, use the command

jar cvf *jarFile* *file*$_1$ *file*$_2$ . . .

The resulting JAR file can be included in a class path.

To build a program that can be launched with java -jar, you must create a *manifest file,* such as

File myprog.mf

```
1  Main-Class: com/horstmann/MyProg
```

The manifest must specify the path name of the class file that launches the application, but with the .class extension removed. Then build the JAR file as

jar cvfm *jarFile* *manifestFile* *file*$_1$ *file*$_2$ . . .

You can also use JAR as a replacement for a ZIP utility, simply to compress and bundle a set of files for any purpose. Then you may want to suppress the generation of the JAR manifest, with the command

jar cvfM *jarFile* *file*$_1$ *file*$_2$ . . .

To extract the contents of a JAR file into the current directory, use

jar xvf *jarFile*

To see the files contained in a JAR file without extracting the files, use

jar tvf *jarFile*

javadoc Summary

Setting Documentation Comments in Source

A documentation comment is delimited by /** and */. You can comment

- Classes
- Methods
- Fields

Each comment is placed *immediately above* the feature it documents.

Each /** . . . */ documentation comment contains introductory text followed by tagged documentation. A tag starts with an @ character, such as @author or @param. Tags are summarized in Table 1. The *first sentence* of the introductory text should be a summary statement. The javadoc utility automatically generates summary pages that extract these sentences.

You can use HTML tags such as em for emphasis, code for a monospaced font, img for images, ul for bulleted lists, and so on.

Table 1 Common javadoc Tags

Tag	Description
@param *parameter explanation*	A parameter of a method. Use a separate tag for each parameter.
@return *explanation*	The return value of a method.
@throws *exceptionType explanation*	An exception that a method may throw. Use a separate tag for each exception.
@deprecated	A feature that remains for compatibility but that should not be used for new code.
@see *packageName.ClassName* @see *packageName.ClassName* *#methodName(Type$_1$, Type$_2$, . . .)* @see *packageName.ClassName#fieldName*	A reference to a related documentation entry.
@author	The author of a class or interface. Use a separate tag for each author.
@version	The version of a class or interface.

Here is a typical example. The summary sentence (in color) will be included with the method summary.

```
/**
    Withdraws money from the bank account. Increments the
    transaction count.
    @param amount  the amount to withdraw
    @return the balance after the withdrawal
    @throws IllegalArgumentException  if the balance is not sufficient
*/
public double withdraw(double amount)
{
    if (balance - amount < minimumBalance)
        throw new IllegalArgumentException();
    balance = balance - amount;
    transactions++;
    return balance;
}
```

Generating Documentation from Commented Source

To extract the comments, run the javadoc program:

javadoc [*options*] *sourceFile₁*| *packageName₁*| *@fileList₁*
    sourceFile₂| *packageName₂*| *@fileList₂* . . .

See the documentation of the javac command in Appendix J for an explanation of file lists. Commonly used options are summarized in Table 2.

To document all files in the current directory, use (all on one line)

```
javadoc -link http://java.sun.com/j2se/1.5.0/docs/api
    -d docdir *.java
```

Table 2 Common javadoc Command Line Options

Option	Description
-link *URL*	Link to another set of Javadoc files. You should include a link to the standard library documentation, either locally or at the Sun web site, http://java.sun.com/j2se/1.5.0/docs/api.
-d *directory*	Store the output in *directory*. This is a useful option, because it keeps your current directory from being cluttered up with javadoc files.
-classpath *locations*	Look for classes on the specified paths, overriding the CLASSPATH environment variable. If neither is specified, the current directory is used. Each *location* is a directory, JAR file, or ZIP file. Locations are separated by a platform-dependent separator (: on Unix, ; on Windows).
-sourcepath *locations*	Look for source files on the specified paths. If not specified, source files are searched in the class path.
-author, -version	Include author, version information in the documentation. This information is omitted by default.

Number Systems

Binary Numbers

Decimal notation represents numbers as powers of 10, for example

$$1729_{\text{decimal}} = 1 \times 10^3 + 7 \times 10^2 + 2 \times 10^1 + 9 \times 10^0$$

There is no particular reason for the choice of 10, except that several historical number systems were derived from people's counting with their fingers. Other number systems, using a base of 12, 20, or 60, have been used by various cultures throughout human history. However, computers use a number system with base 2 because it is far easier to build electronic components that work with two values, which can be represented by a current being either off or on, than it would be to represent 10 different values of electrical signals. A number written in base 2 is also called a *binary* number.

For example,

$$1101_{\text{binary}} = 1 \times 2^3 + 1 \times 2^2 + 0 \times 2^1 + 1 \times 2^0 = 8 + 4 + 1 = 13$$

For digits after the "decimal" point, use negative powers of 2.

$$1.101_{\text{binary}} = 1 \times 2^0 + 1 \times 2^{-1} + 0 \times 2^{-2} + 1 \times 2^{-3}$$
$$= 1 + \frac{1}{2} + \frac{1}{8}$$
$$= 1 + 0.5 + 0.125 = 1.625$$

In general, to convert a binary number into its decimal equivalent, simply evaluate the powers of 2 corresponding to digits with value 1, and add them up. Table 1 shows the first powers of 2.

Table 1 Powers of Two	
Power	**Decimal Value**
2^0	1
2^1	2
2^2	4
2^3	8
2^4	16
2^5	32
2^6	64
2^7	128
2^8	256
2^9	512
2^{10}	1,024
2^{11}	2,048
2^{12}	4,096
2^{13}	8,192
2^{14}	16,384
2^{15}	32,768
2^{16}	65,536

To convert a decimal integer into its binary equivalent, keep dividing the integer by 2, keeping track of the remainders. Stop when the number is 0. Then write the remainders as a binary number, starting with the *last* one. For example,

$$100 \div 2 = 50 \text{ remainder } 0$$
$$50 \div 2 = 25 \text{ remainder } 0$$
$$25 \div 2 = 12 \text{ remainder } 1$$
$$12 \div 2 = 6 \text{ remainder } 0$$
$$6 \div 2 = 3 \text{ remainder } 0$$
$$3 \div 2 = 1 \text{ remainder } 1$$
$$1 \div 2 = 0 \text{ remainder } 1$$

Therefore, $100_{\text{decimal}} = 1100100_{\text{binary}}$.

Conversely, to convert a fractional number less than 1 to its binary format, keep multiplying by 2. If the result is greater than 1, subtract 1. Stop when the number is 0. Then use the digits before the decimal points as the binary digits of the fractional part, starting with the *first* one. For example,

$$0.35 \cdot 2 = 0.7$$
$$0.7 \cdot 2 = 1.4$$
$$0.4 \cdot 2 = 0.8$$
$$0.8 \cdot 2 = 1.6$$
$$0.6 \cdot 2 = 1.2$$
$$0.2 \cdot 2 = 0.4$$

Here the pattern repeats. That is, the binary representation of 0.35 is 0.01 0110 0110 0110 . . .

To convert any floating-point number into binary, convert the whole part and the fractional part separately.

Two's Complement Integers

To represent negative integers, there are two common representations, called "signed magnitude" and "two's complement". Signed magnitude notation is simple: use the leftmost bit for the sign (0 = positive, 1 = negative). For example, when using 8-bit numbers,

$$-13 = 10001101_{\text{signed magnitude}}$$

However, building circuitry for adding numbers gets a bit more complicated when one has to take a sign bit into account. The two's complement representation solves this problem. To form the two's complement of a number,

- Flip all bits.
- Then add 1.

For example, to compute −13 as an 8-bit value, first flip all bits of 00001101 to get 11110010. Then add 1:

$$-13 = 11110011_{\text{two's complement}}$$

Now no special circuitry is required for adding two numbers. Simply follow the normal rule for addition, with a carry to the next position if the sum of the digits and the prior carry is 2 or 3. For example,

```
        1 1111 111
+13       0000 1101
-13       1111 0011
        1 0000 0000
```

But only the last 8 bits count, so +13 and −13 add up to 0, as they should.

In particular, −1 has two's complement representation 1111 . . . 1111, with all bits set.

The leftmost bit of a two's complement number is 0 if the number is positive or zero, 1 if it is negative.

Two's complement notation with a given number of bits can represent one more negative number than positive numbers. For example, the 8-bit two's complement numbers range from −128 to +127.

This phenomenon is an occasional cause for a programming error. For example, consider the following code:

```
byte b = . . .;
if (b < 0) b = -b;
```

This code does not guarantee that b is nonnegative afterwards. If b happens to be −128, then computing its negative again yields −128. (Try it out—take 10000000, flip all bits, and add 1.)

IEEE Floating-Point Numbers

The Institute for Electrical and Electronics Engineering (IEEE) defines standards for floating-point representations in the IEEE-754 standard. Figure 1 shows how single-precision (float) and double-precision (double) values are decomposed into

- A sign bit
- An exponent
- A mantissa

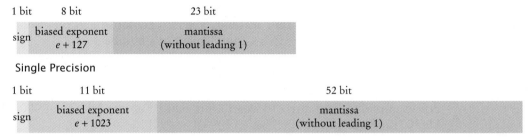

Figure 1   IEEE Floating-Point Representation

Floating-point numbers use scientific notation, in which a number is represented as

$$b_0.b_1b_2b_3\ldots \times 2^e$$

In this representation, e is the exponent, and the digits $b_0.b_1b_2b_3\ldots$ form the mantissa. The *normalized* representation is the one where $b_0 \neq 0$. For example,

$$100_{\text{decimal}} = 1100100_{\text{binary}} = 1.100100_{\text{binary}} \times 2^6$$

Because in the binary number system the first bit of a normalized representation must be 1, it is not actually stored in the mantissa. Therefore, you always need to add it on to represent the actual value. For example, the mantissa 1.100100 is stored as 100100.

The exponent part of the IEEE representation uses neither signed magnitude nor two's complement representation. Instead, a bias is added to the actual exponent. The bias is 127 for single-precision numbers, 1023 for double-precision numbers. For example, the exponent $e = 6$ would be stored as 133 in a single-precision number.

Thus,

$$100_{\text{decimal}} = \boxed{0\ 10000110\ 10010000000000000000000}\ \text{single-precision IEEE}$$

In addition, there are several special values. Among them are:

- *Zero:* biased exponent = 0, mantissa = 0.
- *Infinity:* biased exponent = 11...1, mantissa = 0.
- *NaN (not a number):* biased exponent = 11...1, mantissa ≠ 10...0.

Hexadecimal Numbers

Because binary numbers can be hard to read for humans, programmers often use the hexadecimal number system, with base 16. The digits are denoted as 0, 1, . . . , 9, A, B, C, D, E, F (see Table 2).

Four binary digits correspond to one hexadecimal digit. That makes it easy to convert between binary and hexadecimal values. For example,

$$11 \mid 1011 \mid 0001_{\text{binary}} = 3B1_{\text{hexadecimal}}$$

In Java, hexadecimal numbers are used for Unicode character values, such as \u03B1 (the Greek lowercase letter alpha). Hexadecimal integers are denoted with a 0x prefix, such as 0x3B1.

Table 2 Hexadecimal Digits		
Hexadecimal	**Decimal**	**Binary**
0	0	0000
1	1	0001
2	2	0010
3	3	0011
4	4	0100
5	5	0101
6	6	0110
7	7	0111
8	8	1000
9	9	1001
A	10	1010
B	11	1011
C	12	1100
D	13	1101
E	14	1110
F	15	1111

Bit and Shift Operations

There are four bit operations in Java: the unary negation (~) and the binary and (&), or (|), and exclusive or (^), often called xor.

Tables 1 and 2 show the truth tables for the bit operations in Java. When a bit operation is applied to integer values, the operation is carried out on corresponding bits.

Table 1 The Unary Negation Operation

a	~a
0	1
1	0

Table 2 The Binary And, Or, and Xor Operations

a	b	a & b	a | b	a ^ b
0	0	0	0	0
0	1	0	1	1
1	0	0	1	1
1	1	1	1	0

For example, suppose we want to compute 46 & 13. First convert both values to binary. $46_{\text{decimal}} = 101110_{\text{binary}}$ (actually 00000000000000000000000000101110 as a 32-bit integer), and $13_{\text{decimal}} = 1101_{\text{binary}}$. Now combine corresponding bits:

$$
\begin{array}{r}
0.....0101110 \\
\&\ 0.....0001101 \\
\hline
0.....0001100
\end{array}
$$

The answer is $1100_{\text{binary}} = 12_{\text{decimal}}$.

You sometimes see the | operator being used to combine two bit patterns. For example, Font.BOLD is the value 1, Font.ITALIC is 2. The binary or combination Font.BOLD | Font.ITALIC has both the bold and the italic bit set:

$$
\begin{array}{r}
0.....0000001 \\
|\ 0.....0000010 \\
\hline
0.....0000011
\end{array}
$$

Don't confuse the & and | bit operators with the && and || operators. The latter work only on boolean values, not on bits of numbers.

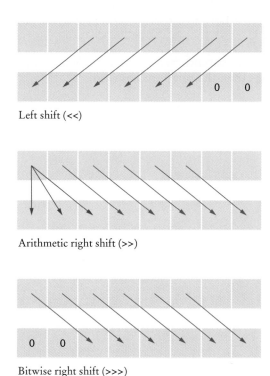

Left shift (<<)

Arithmetic right shift (>>)

Bitwise right shift (>>>)

Figure 1 The Shift Operations

Besides the operations that work on individual bits, there are three *shift* operations that take the bit pattern of a number and shift it to the left or right by a given number of positions. There are three shift operations: shift left (<<), arithmetic shift right (>>), and bitwise shift right (>>>).

The left shift moves all bits to the left, filling in zeroes in the least significant bits. Shifting to the left by n bits yields the same result as multiplication by 2^n. The arithmetic right shift moves all bits to the right, propagating the sign bit. Therefore, the result is the same as integer division by 2^n, both for positive and negative values. Finally, the bitwise right shift moves all bits to the right, filling in zeroes in the most significant bits. (See Figure 1.)

Note that the right-hand-side value of the shift operators is reduced modulo 32 (for int values) or 64 (for long values) to determine the actual number of bits to shift. For example, 1 << 35 is the same as 1 << 3. Actually shifting 1 by 35 bits to the left would make no sense—the result would be 0.

The expression

    1 << n

yields a bit pattern in which the nth bit is set (where the 0 bit is the least significant bit).

To set the nth bit of a number, carry out the operation

    x = x | 1 << n

To check whether the nth bit is set, execute the test

    if ((x & 1 << n) != 0) . . .

Note that the parentheses around the & are required—the & operator has a lower precedence than the relational operators.

UML Summary

In this book, we use a very restricted subset of the UML notation. This appendix lists the components of the subset. For a complete discussion of the UML notation, see [1].

Figures 1 and 2 show the notation for classes and interfaces. Table 1 shows the arrows that indicate relationships between them.

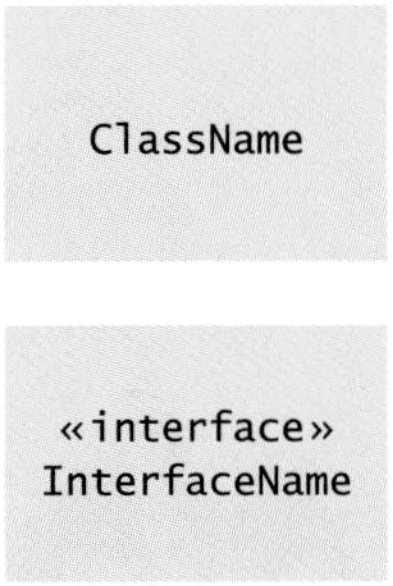

ClassName

«interface»
InterfaceName

Figure 1
UML Symbols for Classes and Interfaces

BankAccount   Attributes

balance

deposit()   Methods
withdraw()

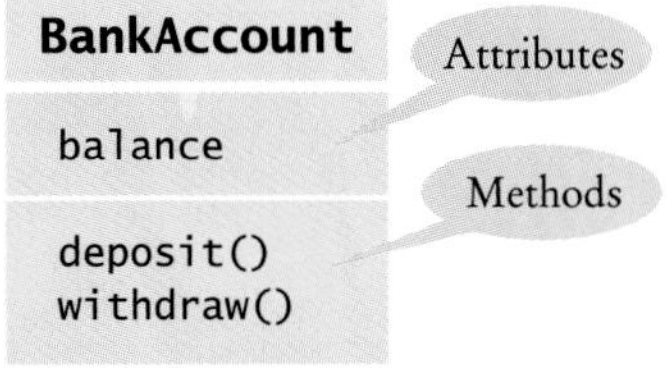

Figure 2
Attributes and Methods in a Class Diagram

Table 1 UML Symbols for Relationships Between Classes

Relationship	Symbol	Line Style	Arrow Tip
Inheritance	——————▷	Solid	Triangle
Interface Implementation	--------▷	Dotted	Triangle
Aggregation	◇——————	Solid	Diamond
Dependency	--------▷	Dotted	Open

FURTHER READING

1. Grady Booch, James Rumbaugh, and Ivar Jacobson, *The Unified Modeling Language User Guide*, Addison-Wesley, 1999.

Glossary

Abstract array   An ordered sequence of items that can be efficiently accessed at random through an integer index.

Abstract class   A class that cannot be instantiated.

Abstract list   An ordered sequence of items that can be traversed sequentially and that allows for efficient insertion and removal of elements at any position.

Abstract method   A method with a name, parameter types, and return type but without an implementation.

Abstraction   The process of finding the essential feature set for a building block of a program such as a class.

Access specifier   A keyword that indicates the accessibility of a feature, such as `private` or `public`.

Accessor method   A method that accesses an object but does not change it.

Actual parameter   The expression supplied for a formal parameter of a method by the caller.

ADT (Abstract Data Type)   A specification of the fundamental operations that characterize a data type, without supplying an implementation.

Aggregation   The *has-a* relationship between classes.

Algorithm   An unambiguous, executable, and terminating specification of a way to solve a problem.

Anonymous class   A class that does not have a name.

Anonymous object   An object that is not stored in a named variable.

API (Application Programming Interface)   A code library for building programs.

Applet   A graphical Java program that executes inside a web browser or applet viewer.

Argument   An actual parameter in a method call, or one of the values combined by an operator.

Array   A collection of values of the same type stored in contiguous memory locations, each of which can be accessed by an integer index.

Array list   A Java class that implements a dynamically growable array of objects.

Assertion   A claim that a certain condition holds in a particular program location.

Assignment   Placing a new value into a variable.

Association   A relationship between classes in which one can navigate from objects of one class to objects of the other class, usually by following object references.

Asymmetric bounds   Bounds that include the starting index but not the ending index.

Attribute   A named property that an object is responsible for maintaining.

Auto-boxing   Automatically converting a primitive type value into a wrapper type object.

Balanced tree   A tree in which each subtree has the property that the number of descendants to the left is approximately the same as the number of descendants to the right.

Big-Oh notation   The notation $g(n) = O(f(n))$, which denotes that the function g grows at a rate that is bounded by the growth rate of the function f with respect to n. For example, $10n^2 + 100n - 1000 = O(n^2)$.

Binary file   A file in which values are stored in their binary representation and cannot be read as text.

Binary operator   An operator that takes two arguments, for example $+$ in $x + y$.

Binary search   A fast algorithm to find a value in a sorted array. It narrows the search down to half of the array in every step.

Binary search tree   A binary tree in which *each* subtree has the property that all left descendants are smaller than the value stored in the root, and all right descendants are larger.

Binary tree   A tree in which each node has at most two child nodes.

Bit   Binary digit; the smallest unit of information, having two possible values: 0 and 1. A data element consisting of n bits has 2^n possible values.

Black-box testing   Testing a method without knowing its implementation.

Block   A group of statements bracketed by {}.

Blocked thread   A thread that cannot proceed because it is waiting for some external event.

Boolean operator   See **Logical operator**

Boolean type   A type with two possible values: true and false.

Border layout   A layout management scheme in which components are placed into the center or one of the four borders of their container.

Boundary test case   A test case involving values that are at the outer boundary of the set of legal values. For example, if a function is expected to work for all nonnegative integers, then 0 is a boundary test case.

Bounds error   Trying to access an array element that is outside the legal range.

Breakpoint   A point in a program, specified in a debugger, at which the debugger stops executing the program and lets the user inspect the program state.

break statement   A statement that terminates a loop or switch statement.

Bucket   In a hash table, a set of values with the same hash code.

Buffer A temporary storage location for holding values that have been produced (for example, characters typed by the user) and are waiting to be consumed (for example, read a line at a time).

Buffered input Input that is gathered in batches, for example, a line at a time.

Bug A programming error.

Byte A number made up of eight bits. Essentially all currently manufactured computers use a byte as the smallest unit of storage in memory.

Bytecode Instructions for the Java virtual machine.

Call by reference A method call mechanism in which the method receives the location in memory of a variable supplied as an actual parameter. Call by reference enables a method to change the contents of the original variable so that the change remains in effect after the method returns.

Call by value A method call mechanism in which the method receives a copy of the contents of a variable supplied as an actual parameter. Java uses only call by value. If a parameter variable's type is a class, its value is an object reference, so the method can alter that object but cannot make the parameter variable refer to a different object.

Call stack The ordered set of all methods that currently have been called but not yet terminated, starting with the current method and ending with `main`.

Case-sensitive Distinguishing upper- and lowercase characters.

Cast Explicitly converting a value from one type to a different type. For example, the cast from a floating-point number x to an integer is expressed in Java by the cast notation `(int) x`.

catch clause A part of a `try` block that is executed when a matching exception is thrown by any statement in the `try` block.

Character A single letter, digit, or symbol.

Check box A user interface component that can be used for a binary selection.

Checked exception An exception that the compiler checks. All checked exceptions must be declared or caught.

Class A programmer-defined data type.

Class method See **Static method**

Class path The set of directories and archives that the virtual machine searches for class files.

Client A computer program or system that issues requests to a server and processes the server responses.

Cloning Making a copy of an object whose state can be modified independently of the original object.

Cohesion A class is cohesive if its features support a single abstraction.

Collaborator A class on which another class depends.

Combo box A user interface component that combines a text field with a drop-down list of selections.

Command line   The line the user types to start a program in DOS or UNIX or a command window in Windows. It consists of the program name followed by any necessary arguments.

Comment   An explanation to help the human reader understand a section of a program; ignored by the compiler.

Compiler   A program that translates code in a high-level language (such as Java) to machine instructions (such as bytecode for the Java virtual machine).

Compile-time error   An error that is detected when a program is compiled.

Component   See **User interface component**

Compound statement   A statement such as if or while that is made up of several parts such as a condition and a body.

Concatenation   Placing one string after another to form a new string.

Concrete class   A class that can be instantiated.

Condition   See **Condition object**

Condition object   An object that manages threads that currently cannot proceed.

Console program   A Java program that does not have a graphical window. A console program reads input from the keyboard and writes output to the terminal screen.

Constant   A value that cannot be changed by a program. In Java, constants are defined with the keyword final.

Construction   Setting a newly allocated object to an initial state.

Constructor   A method that initializes a newly instantiated object.

Container   A user interface component that can hold other components and present them together to the user. Also, a data structure, such as a list, that can hold a collection of objects and present them individually to a program.

Content pane   The part of a Swing frame that holds the user interface components of the frame.

Coupling   The degree to which classes are related to each other by dependency.

CPU (Central Processing Unit)   The part of a computer that executes the machine instructions.

CRC card   An index card representing a class that lists its responsibilities and collaborating classes.

De Morgan's Law   A law about logical operations that describes how to negate expressions formed with *and* and *or* operations.

Deadlock   A state in which no thread can proceed because each thread is waiting for another to do some work first.

Deadly embrace   A set of blocked threads, each of which could only be unblocked by the action of other threads in the set.

Debugger   A program that lets a user run another program one or a few steps at a time, stop execution, and inspect the variables in order to analyze it for bugs.

Default constructor   A constructor that is invoked with no parameters.

Dependency The *uses* relationship between classes, in which one class needs services provided by another class.

Dictionary ordering See **Lexicographic ordering**

Directory A structure on a disk that can hold files or other directories; also called a folder.

Documentation comment A comment in a source file that can be automatically extracted into the program documentation by a program such as javadoc.

Dot notation The notation *object.method(parameters)* or *object.field* used to invoke a method or access a field.

Doubly linked list A linked list in which each link has a reference to both its predecessor and successor links.

DTD (Document Type Definition) A sequence of rules that describes the legal child elements and attributes for each element type in an SGML or XML document.

Early binding Choosing at compile time among several methods with the same name but different parameter types.

Editor A program for writing and modifying text files.

Embedded system A processor, software, and supporting circuitry that is included in a device other than a computer.

Encapsulation The hiding of implementation details.

End of file The condition that is true when all characters of a file have been read. Note that there is no special "end of file character". When composing a file on the keyboard, you may need to type a special character to tell the operating system to end the file, but that character is not part of the file.

Enumerated type A type with a finite number of values, each of which has its own symbolic name.

Escape character A character in text that is not taken literally but has a special meaning when combined with the character or characters that follow it. The \ character is an escape character in Java strings.

Event class A class that contains information about an event, such as its source.

Event adapter A class that implements an event listener interface by defining all methods to do nothing.

Event handler A method that is executed when an event occurs.

Event listener An object that is notified by an event source when an event occurs.

Event source An object that can notify other classes of events.

Exception A class that signals a condition that prevents the program from continuing normally. When such a condition occurs, an object of the exception class is thrown.

Exception handler A sequence of statements that is given control when an exception of a particular type has been thrown and caught.

Explicit parameter A parameter of a method other than the object on which the method is invoked.

Expression A syntactical construct that is made up of constants, variables, method calls, and operators combining them.

Extension The last part of a file name, which specifies the file type. For example, the extension `.java` denotes a Java file.

Extreme Programming A development methodology that strives for simplicity, by removing formal structure and focusing on best practices.

Fibonacci numbers The sequence of numbers 1, 1, 2, 3, 5, 8, 13, ..., in which every term is the sum of its two predecessors.

File A sequence of bytes that is stored on disk.

File pointer The position within a random-access file of the next byte to be read or written. It can be moved so as to access any byte in the file.

`finally` clause A part of a `try` block that is executed no matter how the `try` block is exited.

Flag See **Boolean type**

Floating-point number A number that can have a fractional part.

Flow layout A layout management scheme in which components are laid out left to right.

Flushing a stream Sending all characters that are still held in a buffer to its destination.

Folder See **Directory**

Font A set of character shapes in a particular style and size.

Foreign key A reference to a primary key in a linked table.

Formal parameter A variable in a method definition; it is initialized with an actual parameter value when the method is called.

Frame A window with a border and a title bar.

Garbage collection Automatic reclamation of memory occupied by objects that are no longer referenced.

Generic class A class with one or more type parameters.

Generic method A method with one or more type parameters.

Generic programming Providing program components that can be reused in a wide variety of situations.

`goto` statement A statement that transfers control to some other statement, which is tagged with a label. Java does not have a `goto` statement.

Grammar A set of rules that specifies which sequences of tokens are legal for a particular document set.

Graphics context A class through which a programmer can cause shapes to appear on a window or off-screen bitmap.

`grep` The "global regular expression print" search program, useful for finding all strings matching a pattern in a set of files.

Grid layout A layout management scheme in which components are placed into a two-dimensional grid.

GUI (Graphical User Interface)   A user interface in which the user supplies inputs through graphical components such as buttons, menus, and text fields.

Hash code   A value that is computed by a hash function.

Hash collision   Two different objects for which a hash function computes identical values.

Hash function   A function that computes an integer value from an object in such a way that different objects are likely to yield different values.

Hash table   A data structure in which elements are mapped to array positions according to their hash function values.

Hashing   Applying a hash function to a set of objects.

Heap   A balanced binary tree that is used for implementing sorting algorithms and priority queues.

Heapsort algorithm   A sorting algorithm that inserts the values to be sorted into a heap.

HTML (Hypertext Markup Language)   The language in which web pages are described.

HTTP (Hypertext Transfer Protocol)   The protocol that defines communication between web browsers and web servers.

IDE (Integrated Development Environment)   A programming environment that includes an editor, compiler, and debugger.

Immutable class   A class without a mutator method.

Implementing an interface   See **Realizing an interface**

Implicit parameter   The object on which a method is invoked. For example, in the call x.f(y), the object x is the implicit parameter of the method f.

Importing a class or package   Indicating the intention of referring to a class, or all classes in a package, by the simple name rather than the qualified name.

Inheritance   The *is-a* relationship between a more general superclass and a more specialized subclass.

Initialization   Setting a variable to a well-defined value when it is created.

Inner class   A class that is defined inside another class.

Instance method   A method with an implicit parameter; that is, a method that is invoked on an instance of a class.

Instance of a class   An object whose type is that class.

Instance field   A variable defined in a class for which every object of the class has its own value.

Instantiation of a class   Construction of an object of that class.

Integer   A number that cannot have a fractional part.

Integer division   Taking the quotient of two integers and discarding the remainder. In Java the / symbol denotes integer division if both arguments are integers. For example, 11/4 is 2, not 2.75.

Interface   A type with no instance variables, only abstract methods and constants.

Internet   A worldwide collection of networks, routing equipment, and computers using a common set of protocols that define how participants interact with each other.

Interpreter   A program that reads a set of codes and carries out the commands specified by them.

Iterator   An object that can inspect all elements in a container such as a linked list.

JavaBean   A class with a default constructor that exposes properties through its `get` and `set` methods.

javadoc   The documentation generator in the Java SDK. It extracts documentation comments from Java source files and produces a set of linked HTML files.

JavaServer Faces (JSF)   A framework for developing web applications that aids in the separation of user interface and program logic.

JDBC (Java Database Connectivity)   The technology that enables a Java program to interact with relational databases.

JDK   The Java software development kit that contains the Java compiler and related development tools.

Join   A database query that involves multiple tables.

JSF container   A program that executes JSF applications.

JVM   The Java Virtual Machine

Late binding   Choosing at run time among several methods with the same name invoked on objects belonging to subclasses of the same superclass.

Layout manager   A class that arranges user interface components inside a container.

Lazy evaluation   Deferring the computation of a value until it is needed, thereby avoiding the computation if the value is never needed.

Legacy code   Software that has existed for a long time and that continues to operate.

Lexicographic ordering   Ordering strings in the same order as in a dictionary, by skipping all matching characters and comparing the first nonmatching characters of both strings. For example, "orbit" comes before "orchid" in lexicographic ordering. Note that in Java, unlike a dictionary, the ordering is case-sensitive: Z comes before a.

Library   A set of precompiled classes that can be included in programs.

Linear search   Searching a container (such as an array or list) for an object by inspecting each element in turn.

Linked list   A data structure that can hold an arbitrary number of objects, each of which is stored in a link object, which contains a pointer to the next link.

Local variable   A variable whose scope is a block.

Lock   A data structure to regulate the scheduling of multiple threads. Once a thread has acquired a lock, other threads that also wish to acquire it must wait until the first thread relinquishes it.

Lock object   An object that allows a single thread to execute a section of a program.

Logging   Sending messages that trace the progress of a program to a file or window.

Logical operator An operator that can be applied to Boolean values. Java has three logical operators: &&, ||, and !.

Logic error An error in a syntactically correct program that causes it to act differently from its specification.

Loop A sequence of instructions that is executed repeatedly.

Loop and a half A loop whose termination decision is neither at the beginning nor at the end.

Loop invariant A statement about the program state that is preserved when the statements in the loop are executed once.

Machine code Instructions that can be executed directly by the CPU.

Magic number A number that appears in a program without explanation.

main method The method that is first called when a Java application executes.

Managed bean A JavaBean that is managed by a JSF container.

Map A data structure that keeps associations between key and value objects.

Markup Information about data that is added as humanly readable instructions. An example is the tagging of HTML documents with elements such as <h1> or <b>.

Member A method, field, or type defined inside a class.

Memory location A value that specifies the location of data in computer memory.

Merge sort A sorting algorithm that first sorts two halves of a data structure and then merges the sorted subarrays together.

Meta data Data that describe properties of a data set.

Method A sequence of statements that has a name, may have formal parameters, and may return a value. A method can be invoked any number of times, with different values for its parameters.

Method binding In JSF, an expression describing a bean and a method that is to be applied to the bean at a later time.

Method signature The name of a method and the types of its parameters.

Mixed content In XML, a markup element that contains both text and other elements.

Mutator method A method that changes the state of an object.

Mutual recursion Cooperating methods that call each other.

Name clash Accidentally using the same name to denote two program features in a way that cannot be resolved by the compiler.

Navigation rule In JSF, a rule that describes when to move from one web page to another.

Negative test case A test case that is expected to fail. For example, when testing a root-finding program, an attempt to compute the square root of −1 is a negative test case.

Nested block A block that is contained inside another block.

Nested loop A loop that is contained in another loop.

Network protocol   A set of rules that must be followed by programs that communicate over a network.

new operator   An operator that allocates new objects.

Newline   The '\n' character, which indicates the end of a line.

Null reference   A reference that does not refer to any object.

Object   A value of a class type.

Object-oriented design   Designing a program by discovering objects, their properties, and their relationships.

Object reference   A value that denotes the location of an object in memory. In Java, a variable whose type is a class contains a reference to an object of that class.

Off-by-one error   A common programming error in which a value is one larger or smaller than it should be.

Opening a file   Preparing a file for reading or writing.

Operating system   The software that launches application programs and provides services (such as a file system) for those programs.

Operator   A symbol denoting a mathematical or logical operation, such as + or &&.

Operator associativity   The rule that governs in which order operators of the same precedence are executed. For example, in Java the - operator is left-associative because a - b - c is interpreted as (a - b) - c, and = is right-associative because a = b = c is interpreted as a = (b = c).

Operator precedence   The rule that governs which operator is evaluated first. For example, in Java the && operator has a higher precedence than the || operator. Hence a || b && c is interpreted as a || (b && c).

Oracle   A program that predicts how another program should behave.

Overloading   Giving more than one meaning to a method name.

Overriding   Redefining a method in a subclass.

Package   A collection of related classes. The import statement is used to access one or more classes in a package.

Package access   Accessibility by methods of classes in the same package.

Panel   A user interface component with no visual appearance. It can be used to group other components.

Parallel arrays   Arrays of the same length, in which corresponding elements are logically related.

Parameter   An item of information that is specified to a method when the method is called. For example, in the call System.out.println("Hello, World!"), the parameters are the implicit parameter System.out and the explicit parameter "Hello, World!".

Parameter passing   Specifying expressions to be actual parameter values for a method when it is called.

Parse tree   A tree structure that shows how a string conforms to rules of a grammar.

Parser A program that reads a document, checks whether it is syntactically correct, and takes some action as it processes the document.

Partially-filled array An array that is not filled to capacity, together with a companion variable that indicates the number of elements actually stored.

Permutation A rearrangement of a set of values.

Polymorphism Selecting a method among several methods that have the same name on the basis of the actual types of the implicit parameters.

Positive test case A test case that a method is expected to handle correctly.

Postcondition A condition that is true after a method has been called.

Postfix operator A unary operator that is written after its argument.

Precondition A condition that must be true when a method is called if the method is to work correctly.

Predicate method A method that returns a Boolean value.

Prefix operator A unary operator that is written before its argument.

Prepared statement A SQL statement with a precomputed query strategy.

Primary key A column (or combination of columns) whose value uniquely specifies a table record.

Primitive type In Java, a number type or `boolean`.

Priority queue An abstract data type that enables efficient insertion of elements and efficient removal of the smallest element.

Private feature A feature that is accessible only by methods of the same class or an inner class.

Project A collection of source files and their dependencies.

Prompt A string that tells the user to provide input.

Property A named value that is managed by a component.

Protected feature A feature that is accessible by a class, its inner classes, its subclasses, and the other classes in the same package.

Pseudo-random number A number that appears to be random but is generated by a mathematical formula.

Public feature A feature that is accessible by all classes.

Qualified name A name that is made unambiguous because it starts with the package name.

Queue A collection of items with "first in, first out" retrieval.

Quicksort A generally fast sorting algorithm that picks an element, called the pivot, partitions the sequence into the elements smaller than the pivot and those larger than the pivot, and then recursively sorts the subsequences.

Race condition A condition in which the effect of multiple threads on shared data depends on the order in which the threads are scheduled.

Radio button   A user interface component that can be used for selecting one of several options.

RAM (Random-Access Memory)   Electronic circuits in a computer that can store code and data of running programs.

Random access   The ability to access any value directly without having to read the values preceding it.

Reader   In the Java input/output library, a class from which to read characters.

Realizing an interface   Implementing a class that defines all methods specified in the interface.

Recursion   A method for computing a result by decomposing the inputs into simpler values and applying the same method to them.

Recursive method   A method that can call itself with simpler values. It must handle the simplest values without calling itself.

Redirection   Linking the input or output of a program to a file instead of the keyboard or display.

Reference   See **Object reference**

Regression testing   Keeping old test cases and testing every revision of a program against them.

Regular expression   A string that defines a set of matching strings according to their content. Each part of a regular expression can be a specific required character; one of a set of permitted characters such as [abc], which can be a range such as [a-z]; any character not in a set of forbidden characters, such as [^0-9]; a repetition of one or more matches, such as [0-9]+, or zero or more, such as [ACGT]*; one of a set of alternatives, such as and|et|und; or various other possibilities. For example, "[A-Za-z]*[0-9]+" matches "Cloud9" or "007" but not "Jack".

Relational database   A data repository that stores information in tables and retrieves data as the result of queries that are formulated in terms of table relationships.

Relational operator   An operator that compares two values, yielding a Boolean result.

Reserved word   A word that has a special meaning in a programming language and therefore cannot be used as a name by the programmer.

Return value   The value returned by a method through a `return` statement.

Reverse Polish notation   A style of writing expressions in which the operators are written following the operands, such as 2 3 4 * + for 2 + 3 * 4.

Roundoff error   An error introduced by the fact that the computer can store only a finite number of digits of a floating-point number.

Runnable thread   A thread that can proceed provided it is given a time slice to do work.

Run-time error   See **Logic error**

Run-time stack   The data structure that stores the local variables of all called methods as a program runs.

Scope   The part of a program in which a variable is defined.

Scripting language A programming language that favors rapid development over execution speed and code maintainability.

Selection sort A sorting algorithm in which the smallest element is repeatedly found and removed until no elements remain.

Sentinel A value in input that is not to be used as an actual input value but to signal the end of input.

Sequential access Accessing values one after another without skipping over any of them.

Sequential search See **Linear search**

Serialization The process of saving an object, and all the objects that it references, to a stream.

Server A computer program or system that receives requests from a client, obtains or computes the requested information, and sends it to the client.

Session A sequence of page requests from the same browser to the same web server.

Set An unordered collection that allows efficient addition, location, and removal of elements.

Shadowing Hiding a variable by defining another one with the same name.

Shallow copy Copying only the reference to an object.

Shell A part of an operating system in which the user types command lines to execute programs and manipulate files.

Shell script A file that contains commands for running programs and manipulating files. Typing the name of the shell script file on the command line causes those commands to be executed.

Shell window A window for interacting with an operating system through textual commands.

Short circuit evaluation Evaluating only a part of an expression if the remainder cannot change the result.

Side effect An effect of a method other than returning a value.

Sign bit The bit of a binary number that indicates whether the number is positive or negative.

Signature See **Method signature**

Simple statement A statement consisting only of an expression.

Single-stepping Executing a program in the debugger one statement at a time.

Socket An object that encapsulates a TCP/IP connection. To communicate with the other endpoint of the connection, you use the input and output streams attached to the socket.

Software life cycle All activities related to the creation and maintenance of the software from initial analysis until obsolescence.

Source code Instructions in a programming language that need to be translated before execution on a computer.

Source file A file containing instructions in a programming language such as Java.

Spaghetti code Tangled control flow that is difficult to understand.

Spiral model   An iterative process model of software development in which design and implementation are repeated.

SQL (Structured Query Language)   A command language for interacting with a database.

Stack   A data structure with "last in, first out" retrieval. Elements can be added and removed only at one position, called the top of the stack.

Stack trace   A printout of the call stack, listing all currently pending method calls.

State   The current value of an object, which is determined by the cumulative action of all methods that were invoked on it.

State diagram   A diagram that depicts state transitions and their causes.

Statement   A syntactical unit in a program. In Java a statement is either a simple statement, a compound statement, or a block.

Static method   A method with no implicit parameter.

Static field   A variable defined in a class that has only one value for the whole class, which can be accessed and changed by any method of that class.

Stored procedures   A database procedure that is executed in the database kernel.

Stream   An abstraction for a sequence of bytes from which data can be read or to which data can be written.

String   A sequence of characters.

Stub   A method with no or minimal functionality.

Subclass   A class that inherits variables and methods from a superclass but adds instance variables, adds methods, or redefines methods.

Superclass   A general class from which a more specialized class (a subclass) inherits.

Swing   A Java toolkit for implementing graphical user interfaces.

Symmetric bounds   Bounds that include the starting index and the ending index.

Synchronized method   A method that is controlled by a lock. In order to execute the method, the calling thread must acquire the lock.

Syntax   Rules that define how to form instructions in a particular programming language.

Syntax diagram   A graphical representation of grammar rules.

Syntax error   An instruction that does not follow the programming language rules and is rejected by the compiler.

Synchronized block   A block of code that is controlled by a lock. To start execution, a thread must acquire the lock. Upon completion, it relinquishes the lock.

Tab character   The '\t' character, which advances the next character on the line to the next one of a set of fixed positions known as tab stops.

TCP/IP (Transmission Control Protocol/Internet Protocol)   The pair of communication protocols that is used to establish reliable transmission of data between two computers on the Internet.

Ternary operator   An operator with three arguments. Java has one ternary operator, a ? b : c.

Test coverage   The instructions of a program that are executed in a set of test cases.

Test harness   A program that calls a function that needs to be tested, supplying parameters and analyzing the function's return value.

Test suite   A set of test cases for a program.

Text field   A user interface component that allows a user to provide text input.

Text file   A file in which values are stored in their text representation.

Thread   A program unit that is executed independently of other parts of the program.

Three-tier application   An application that is composed of separate tiers for presentation logic, business logic, and data storage.

Throwing an exception   Indicating an abnormal condition by terminating the normal control flow of a program and transferring control to a matching `catch` clause.

throws specifier   Indicates the types of the checked exceptions that a method may throw.

Time slicing   Scheduling threads by giving each thread a small amount of time in which to do its work, then giving control to another thread.

Token   A sequence of consecutive characters from an input source that belongs together for the purpose of analyzing the input. For example, a token can be a sequence of characters other than whitespace.

Total ordering   An ordering relationship in which all elements can be compared to each other.

Trace message   A message that is printed during a program run for debugging purposes.

Transaction   A set of database operations that should either succeed in their entirety, or not happen at all.

try block   A block of statements that contains exception processing clauses. A `try` block contains at least one `catch` or `finally` clause.

Turing machine   A very simple model of computation that is used in theoretical computer science to explore computability of problems.

Two-dimensional array   A tabular arrangement of elements in which an element is specified by a row and a column index.

Type   A named set of values and the operations that can be carried out with them.

Type parameter   A parameter in a generic class or method that can be replaced with an actual type.

Unary operator   An operator with one argument.

Unchecked exception   An exception that the compiler doesn't check.

Unicode   A standard code that assigns code values consisting of two bytes to characters used in scripts around the world. Java stores all characters as their Unicode values.

Unified Modeling Language (UML)   A notation for specifying, visualizing, constructing, and documenting the artifacts of software systems.

Uninitialized variable   A variable that has not been set to a particular value. In Java, using an uninitialized local variable is a syntax error.

Unit test   A test of a method by itself, isolated from the remainder of the program.

URL (Uniform Resource Locator)   A pointer to an information resource (such as a web page or an image) on the World Wide Web.

User interface component   A building block for a graphical user interface, such as a button or a text field. User interface components are used to present information to the user and allow the user to enter information to the program.

Value binding   In JSF, an expression describing a bean and a property that is to be accessed at a later time.

Variable   A symbol in a program that identifies a storage location that can hold different values.

Virtual machine   A program that simulates a CPU that can be implemented efficiently on a variety of actual machines. A given program in Java bytecode can be executed by any Java virtual machine, regardless of which CPU is used to run the virtual machine itself.

Visual programming   Programming by arranging graphical elements on a form, setting program behavior by selecting properties for these elements, and writing only a small amount of "glue" code linking them.

void keyword   A keyword indicating no type or an unknown type.

Watch window   A window in a debugger that shows the current values of selected variables.

Waterfall model   A sequential process model of software development, consisting of analysis, design, implementation, testing, and deployment.

White-box testing   Testing functions taking their implementations into account, in contrast to black-box testing; for example, by selecting boundary test cases and ensuring that all branches of the code are covered by some test case.

Whitespace   Any sequence of only space, tab, and newline characters.

Wrapper class   A class that contains a primitive type value, such as `Integer`.

Writer   In the Java input/output library, a class to which characters are to be sent.

XML (Extensible Markup Language)   A simple format for structured data in which the structure is indicated by markup instructions.

Index

Page references followed by *t* indicate material in tables. Java library classes are indexed under java, as for example "java.util.Scanner class."

Illustration Credits

Chapter 1

Page 4: Copyright © 2004, Intel Corporation.
Page 5 (top): PhotoDisc, Inc./Getty Images.
Page 5 (bottom): PhotoDisc, Inc./Getty Images.
Page 6: Copyright © 2004, Intel Corporation.
Page 8: Courtesy of Sperry Univac, Division of Sperry Corporation.

Chapter 2

Page 56: Corbis Digital Stock.

Chapter 3

Page 94: David Young-Wolff/PhotoEdit.
Page 95: Bob Daemmrich/The Image Works.

Chapter 5

Page 170: Punchstock.
Page 174: Copyright © 2001-2004 Lev Givon. All rights reserved.
Page 175 (top): Keith Kapple/SUPERSTOCK.
Page 175 (bottom): Daniel Biggs/SUPERSTOCK.

Chapter 6

Page 214: © 2004 Sidney Harris.

Chapter 9

Page 359: Screen captures or other materials © 2004 IBM Corporation. Used with permission of IBM Corporation.

Chapter 10

Page 400: Naval Surface Weapons Center, Dahlgren, VA.

Chapter 11

Page 434: Image courtesy of Mad Penguin™.

Chapter 15

Page 569 (left), page 569 (center), and page 569 (right): © AP/Wide World Photos.

Chapter 17

Page 611: *Unified Modeling Language Users Guide (AW Object Tech Series)*, © 1999 Pearson Education, Inc. Reprinted by permission of Pearson Education Inc. Publishing as Pearson Addison Wesley.

Chapter 18

Page 685: Science Photo Library/Photo Researchers.

Chapter 19

Page 725: Topham/The Image Works.

Chapter 20

Page 763: Photodisc/Punchstock.

Chapter 21

Page 811: Courtesy of Nigel Tout.

Chapter 23

Page 881: Creatas/Punchstock.
Page 899: Courtesy of Professor Naeyuck Chang, Computer Systems Lab, Department of Computer Engineering, Seoul National University.